Directions

To run the program, type **IA** at the prompt and press the [ENTER] key.
When the IA/PC logo appears, press [ENTER] to see the IA/PC main menu.

One of two things will occur when you choose a routine from the main menu: (1) a submenu will appear from which you will make another choice, or (2) an IA/PC work screen will appear.

The typical work screen is divided into four distinct areas:

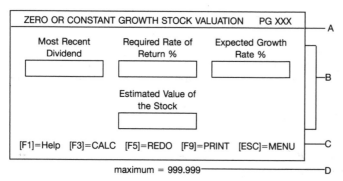

A   The title area identifies the routine with which you are working and also gives a page reference from the text.

B   The data entry section is where you will enter the inputs needed to solve a problem. The answer will also be given in this section. You enter your inputs (usually numbers) into IA/PC by typing them and pressing [ENTER]. Note that some routines (e.g., financial statement analysis) have multiple data entry and answer screens. You move between them by using the [PgDn] and [PgUp] keys.

C   The function key prompt area tells you which function keys are operable for a screen and provides a brief description of the action invoked when the key is pressed.

D   The message line provides special instructions for entering data and displays error messages if you make a mistake while using IA/PC.

A Word of Caution

The primary purpose of IA/PC is to save you time. While using IA/PC, you must remember that final decisions are up to you. IA/PC provides answers to numerical problems, but you must evaluate the output to determine a logical course of action. Thus, IA/PC is not a substitute for your ability to think; instead, it is a tool that helps you evaluate various problems encountered by investors.

INVESTMENTS

AN INTRODUCTION

FOURTH EDITION

INVESTMENTS

AN INTRODUCTION

HERBERT B. MAYO

TRENTON STATE COLLEGE

THE DRYDEN PRESS
HARCOURT BRACE COLLEGE PUBLISHERS

Fort Worth   Philadelphia   San Diego   New York   Orlando   Austin   San Antonio
Toronto   Montreal   London   Sydney   Tokyo

Publisher	Liz Widdicombe
Acquisitions Editor	Rick Hammonds
Project Editor	Joan Harlan
Production Manager	Marilyn Williams
Book Designer	Melinda Huff
Copy Editor	Judi McClellan
Compositor	GTS Graphics, Inc.
Text Type	10/12 New Caledonia

Requests for permission to make copies of any part of the work should be mailed to: Permissions Department, Harcourt Brace & Company, Orlando, FL 32887.

Address for Editorial Correspondence
The Dryden Press, 301 Commerce Street, Suite 3700, Fort Worth, TX 76102

Address for Orders
The Dryden Press, 6277 Sea Harbor Drive, Orlando, FL 32887
1-800-782-4479, or 1-800-433-0001 (in Florida)

ISBN: 0-03-097647-2

Library of Congress Catalog Card Number: 92-76104

Printed in the United States of America
4 5 6 7 8 9 0 1 2   069   9 8 7 6 5 4 3 2

The Dryden Press
Harcourt Brace College Publishers

While many individuals have contributed to my education, four stand out: Estelle Tankard, my sophomore high school teacher, who taught me the importance of correct grammar; Clarence Philbrook, my micro-economics professor, who taught me the importance of competitive markets and fluctuating prices; Paul Davidson, my thesis advisor, who taught me the importance of structure; and Ernest Mayo, my father, who taught me the importance of perseverance and a strong balance sheet.

The Dryden Press Series in Finance

PREFACE

Virtually everyone makes investments. Even if the individual does not select specific assets such as the stock of AT&T or the federal government series EE bonds, investments are still made through participation in pension plans and employee savings programs or through the purchase of life insurance or a home. Each of these investments has common characteristics such as the potential return they offer and the risk that the individual must bear, and over time the investor earns a return consummate with the risk taken.

Two major tenets affect my perception of investing, and both have a major impact on this text. First, I believe that investment decisions are made in exceedingly competitive financial markets. This means that information is disseminated rapidly so that few individual investors are able to take advantage of new information. This theme of efficient financial markets reappears throughout the text. You could conclude that the reality of efficient financial markets ends your chances of making good investments, but that is the wrong conclusion. The presence of efficient markets ensures that you can make investment decisions on a level playing field. In other words, the return you earn does not have to be inferior to the returns generated by more seasoned or professional investors.

This leads to my second belief. It is easy to fool yourself or to let yourself be fooled, which may result in inferior investment results. But you don't have to be fooled if you are reasonably well-informed and you use common sense.

You may find investing daunting because of specialized jargon and terms, sophisticated professionals, and an almost unlimited number of possible alternatives. A primary aim of this textbook is to make investing a little less difficult by explaining the terms, by elucidating the possible alternatives, and by discussing many of the techniques used by professionals to value an asset and to construct a portfolio. While this textbook cannot show you a shortcut to financial wealth, it can reduce your chances of making uninformed investment decisions.

This textbook uses a substantial number of examples and illustrations employing data that are generally available to the investing public. This information is believed to be accurate; however, you should not assume that mention of a specific firm and its securities is a recommendation to buy or sell those securities. The examples have been chosen to illustrate specific points, not to pass judgment on individual investments.

Many textbooks on investments are written for students with considerable background in accounting, finance, and economics. Not every student, however, who takes an investment course has such background, and these students cannot cope with (or be expected to cope with) the material in well-written, but advanced, textbooks on investments. *Investments: An Introduction* is aimed at these students and covers the basics of investing ranging from descriptive material to the theory of portfolio construction and efficient markets. Some of the concepts (for example, portfolio theory) and some of the alternative investments (such as puts and calls) are difficult to understand. There are no shortcuts to learning this material just as there are no shortcuts to wealth. The textbook does assume that the student has a desire to tackle a fascinating subject and to devote real energy to the material.

Changes from the Previous Edition

The revisions in the fourth edition of *Investments: An Introduction* range from minor rewording and updating to a complete rethinking of the presentation. The number of chapters and their order have not been changed, and while material has been added, some has been deleted so that the length of the text is not significantly expanded. Chapter-by-chapter alterations include the following:

Chapter 1, which introduces the text, includes material on reinvestment risk. The large decline in interest rates has resulted in investors experiencing declines in income when they rollover investments. Emphasis on this source of risk is now placed throughout the textbook and introduced in this chapter. Material has been added to clarify the distinction between the academic and the professional use of the term *liquidity*.

Obtaining information on investing in socially responsible firms has been added to Chapter 4.

Chapter 5 has new material on netting short-term and long-term losses and the carryforward of capital losses. Employee stock option plans have been added as an illustration of a tax shelter.

Chapter 7 has been substantially revised to encompass a more complete coverage of portfolio theory, especially the Markowitz model, portfolio betas, and graphical presentations of the efficient frontier, the capital market line, and the security market line. Arbitrage pricing theory is also introduced.

Stock valuation, covered in Chapter 8, has been expanded to include coverage of the efficient market hypothesis, especially material on the anomalies.

Chapter 9 on the returns earned by stocks has a more extensive discussion of the computation of geometric averages and the difference between dollar-weighted returns and time-weighted returns.

Material on book entry bonds has been added to Chapter 14.

In Chapter 15, the material on duration has been expanded to illustrate how duration is used to reduce the risk associated with fluctuations in interest rates.

Chapter 16 now includes material on the large returns earned in junk bonds during 1991 and 1992.

Chapter 17 has been expanded to include material on collateralized mortgage obligations (CMOs) and certificates of participation (COPs).

Chapter 18 covers a new security, preferred equity redemption cumulative stock (PERCS), which is a variation on the traditional convertible preferred stock.

An extensive new appendix has been added to Chapter 19 that covers a variety of strategies using options (for example, covered puts, straddles, bull and bear spreads, and the butterfly spread).

Chapter 24 has expanded coverage of the risks and advantages associated with foreign investments.

Chapter 25 includes increased coverage of performance evaluation, especially the Jensen, Sharpe, and Treynor measures of performance.

PEDAGOGICAL FEATURES

This textbook has a variety of features designed to assist the student in the learning process. Each chapter starts with a set of **learning objectives.** These point out topics to look for as the chapter develops. **Terms to remember** are defined in the **marginal glossary** that appears when each term is introduced in the text. The terms are repeated in order of presentation at the end of the chapter. A **Security Summary,** which outlines the features of various securities (for example, their liquidity, sources of return, and risk), is provided at the end of the appropriate chapter to help review individual assets. Chapters also include **questions** and, where appropriate, **problems.** The questions and problems are straightforward and designed primarily to review the material. Answers to selected problems are provided in Appendix B.

The chapters end with **suggested readings** intended to give the student a brief description of selected sources of further information. These are drawn from a cross section of the literature on finance and investments. They include academic publications (such as *Financial Management*), the professional literaure (such as *Financial Analysts Journal*), and general business publications (such as *Forbes*). This literature and the books cited should be readily available in many libraries. The suggested readings are generally not technical, and while they may require serious reading, they should be accessible to the student using this book.

While teaching this course over the years, I have asked my students to try their hands at building their own "paper" portfolio of securities as they progress through the course. This **Investment Project** has proven to be popular with students because it allows them to experience "hands-on" investing. Starting with Chapter 1, the student is asked to begin a weekly tracking of eight stocks (four preselected stocks and four of the student's own choosing) as well as the S&P 500 index. *The Wall Street Journal* is suggested as a good source for information, and the student is encouraged to buy the paper weekly. In subsequent chapters (7, 10, 12, 14, 19, and 25), the student's portfolio takes on a different dimension as debt securities and option contracts are added. As various techniques for evaluating individual securities as well as the portfolio as a whole are learned, the student is asked to evaluate the success or failure of the "paper" portfolio.

There are many investing sidelight points that may not fit neatly into a particular chapter. To include these, I have added boxed **Points of Interest** to many of the chapters. These boxes may amplify the text material or present new material to supplement the coverage in the text. The tone of the points of interest is somewhat lighter than the text and is designed to increase reader interest in the chapter as a whole.

This textbook ends with a collection of **case studies** that cover the material presented in several chapters. These cases serve both as a review and a means to tie various chapters together. They may be used as a basis for class discussions or homework assignments.

ANCILLARY MATERIALS

A number of supplements are included in the *Investments* package and are avaialble free of charge to instructors who adopt the textbook.

Instructor's Manual and Test Bank. The *Instructor's Manual* includes points to consider when answering the questions as well as complete solutions for the problems. The *Test Bank* section of the manual includes approximately 1,000 true/false and multiple-choice questions. In addition, suggestions are given for using the **Investment Project** feature in the classroom; teaching notes are provided for the cases; and instructions are provided for the new software that accompanies the book, *Investment Analysis on the Personal Computer (IA/PC)*.

Investment Analysis on the Personal Computer (IA/PC). *IA/PC* by James P. Pettijohn is designed to accompany the book and is free to adopters of the text. This IBM computer software includes numerous routines that may be used to help solve the end-of-chapter problems. The software is menu driven and assumes that the user has no previous computer experience. The software is a useful tool for solving complex problems, but it should be noted that it is not designed as a substitute for understanding the mechanics of problem analysis and solution. Thus, while the software may help determine a stock's value, it cannot answer the question of whether or not the stock should be bought or sold; such a judgment must come from the user of the software.

POSSIBLE ORGANIZATIONS OF INVESTMENT COURSES

The textbook has 25 chapters, but few instructors are able to complete the entire book in a semester course. Many of the chapters are self-contained units, so individual chapters may be omitted (or transposed) without loss of continuity. There are, however, exceptions. For example, the valuation of preferred stock uses the same model as the valuation of bonds, and that model uses the material on the time value of money. The valuation of common stock employs much of the material covered in the chapter on risk.

Part I covers investment fundamentals. It includes how securities come into existence and the role of financial intermediaries (Chapter 2); how securities are traded (Chapters 3); and risk, its measurement, and portfolo theory (Chapter 7).

This is essential material on investments, which most students have not had. These chapters are not easily omitted. Other chapters in Part I could be omitted if the students have covered the material in other courses (for example, taxation in Chapter 5 and the time value of money in Chapter 6).

The bread and butter of investing in financial assets is the analysis and selection of common stocks (Part II) and fixed income securities (Part III). Virtually all of this material should be covered in class with the possible exceptions of the material on technical analysis, high-yield securities, and convertibles.

The remaining parts of this text leave the individual instructor considerable choice. Since each instructor has personal preferences, any of the remaining seven chapters is easily omitted or included depending on the availability of time. My personal preference is to include the material on options (Chapter 19), which many students find both difficult and exciting, and the material on financial planning (Chapter 25), as the latter serves as a means to tie the course together.

Acknowledgments

A textbook requires the input and assistance of many individuals in addition to the author. Over the years, The Dryden Press has provided thoughtful reviews from individuals who sincerely offer suggestions for improvement. Unfortunately suggestions sometimes are contradictory. Since an author cannot please all of the reviewers at the same time, I trust that individuals who offered advice that was not taken will not be offended.

The following individuals provided valuable suggestions for improving the fourth edition: Avram Kahn, Prudential Securities; Jim Kuttner, College for Financial Planning; David Louton, Bryant College; Debbie Shillingburg, College for Financial Planning; Siamack Shojai, Manhattan College; and Elizabeth Yelland, Northhampton Community College.

In addition, Christian Guvernator III from Legg Mason provided specific information that clarified many of the illustrations.

At this point in the preface, it is traditional for the author to thank members of the editorial and production staff for their help in bringing the book to fruition. Over the years I have been spoiled by the staff at The Dryden Press, and the crew who worked on this text is no exception. I wish to thank Rick Hammonds, acquisitions editor; Melinda Huff, designer; Marilyn Williams, production manager; and Sheryl Nelson, ancillary project editor, for their efforts. Joan Harlan, the project editor, deserves a special thanks for efficiently taking the manuscript through production to the final book.

I encourage readers to contact me with suggestions and comments. Please feel free to write me at 85 Linvale Road, Ringoes, New Jersey 08551.

Herbert B. Mayo

CONTENTS

The Environment of Investing

TO ENHANCE THE LEARNING PROCESS, THIS

I

TEXTBOOK HAS BEEN DIVIDED INTO DISTINCT SECTIONS. THE FIRST CONSIDERS THE ENVIRONMENT IN WHICH INVESTMENT DECISIONS ARE MADE SINCE THIS BACKGROUND CAN HAVE CONSIDERABLE IMPACT ON WHICH INVESTMENTS THE INVESTOR CHOOSES TO INCLUDE IN HIS OR HER PORTFOLIO. ◆ THE INDIVIDUAL SHOULD START BY SPECIFYING INVESTMENT GOALS. INVESTING IS A means to an end, such as financial security or the ability to make the down payment on a house. These ends should be specified before the individual acquires a portfolio, because not all assets will serve to meet a particular financial goal.

Once these goals are established, the individual should be aware of the mechanics of investing and the environment in which investment decisions are made. These include the process by which securities are issued and subsequently bought and sold, the regulations and tax laws that have been enacted by the various levels of government, and the sources of information concerning investments that are available to the individual.

An understanding of this financial background leads to three important general financial concepts that apply to investing. The first is the time value of money, which stresses that a dollar received today and a dollar received tomorrow do not have the same value. Linking the future and the present is an extremely important concept in the valuation of assets for possible inclusion in a portfolio.

The second crucial financial concept is the construction of a diversified portfolio. Since virtually all investments involve risk, the management of this risk through diversification may be important to the individual's financial health. The last general financial concept is the efficiency of financial markets. Rapid dissemination of information and competition among investors produce efficient financial markets. Such markets imply that the individual cannot expect to earn abnormally high returns over an extended period of time. Instead the investor should earn a return that compensates for the risk taken. While an individual investment may do exceptionally well, such performance on a consistent basis over an extended period is exceedingly rare.

1

An Introduction to Investments

*I*n 1986, Microsoft Corporation first offered its stock to the public. Six years later, the stock's value had increased over 3,000 percent—a $10,000 investment was worth over $300,000. In the same year, Worlds of Wonder also offered its stock to the public. Six years later, the company was defunct—a $10,000 investment was worth nothing. These are two examples of emerging firms that could do exceedingly well or fail. Would investing in large, well-established firms generate more consistent returns? The answer depends, of course, on which firms were invested in. In 1972, the common stock of Xerox reached an all-time high of $171⅞ per share. Twenty years later, Xerox's common stock was trading in the $80 range—53 percent below its historic high. Limiting investments to large firms does not ensure a positive return. Over the years, some investments have generated extraordinary gains, while others have produced only mediocre returns, and still others have generated substantial losses.

Today the field of investments is even more dynamic than it was only a decade ago. World events occur rapidly—events that alter the value of specific assets. The individual has so many assets to choose from, and the amount of information available to the investor is staggering and continually growing. The development of personal computers and their use at home has increased individuals' ability to track investments and to perform investment analysis. Furthermore, the inflation of the early 1980s and the recession of the early 1990s have served to increase awareness of the importance of financial planning and wise investing.

✦ ✦ ✦

LEARNING OBJECTIVES

After completing this chapter you should be able to

1. Explain why individuals should specify investment goals.

2. Differentiate between liquidity and marketability.

3. Distinguish between primary and secondary markets.

4. Identify the sources of risk.

5. Understand why financial markets are considered efficient.

PORTFOLIO CONSTRUCTION

Once an individual receives income, there are two choices: to spend it or to save it. If the individual chooses to save, an additional decision must be made: What is to be done with the savings? This is an extremely important question because in 1991,

3

Americans' personal income was \$4,834.4 billion and they saved \$219.3 billion.[1] The saver must decide where to invest this command over goods and services that is currently not being used. This is an important decision for the individual because these assets are the means by which today's purchasing power is transferred to the future. In effect, the saver must decide on a **portfolio** of assets to own. A portfolio is a combination of assets designed to serve as a store of value. Poor management of these assets may destroy the portfolio's value, and the individual will not achieve his or her investment goals.

portfolio
An accumulation of assets owned by the investor and designed to transfer purchasing power to the future.

There are many assets that the investor may include in the portfolio, and this textbook will discuss many of them. The stress, however, will be on long-term financial assets. While the saver may hold a portion of the portfolio in short-term assets, such as savings accounts, these assets do not seem to present the problem of valuation and choice that accompanies the decision to purchase a stock or a bond. Understanding the nature of long-term assets (i.e., how they are bought and sold, how they are valued, and how they may be used in portfolio construction) is the primary thrust of this text.

Several factors affect the construction of a portfolio. These include the goals of the investor, the risks involved, the taxes that will be imposed on any gain, and a knowledge of the available opportunities and alternative investments. This text will cover the range of these alternative investments, their use in a portfolio, the risks associated with owning them, and their valuation.

The investor's goals should largely determine the construction and management of the portfolio. Investing must have a purpose, for without a goal a portfolio is like a boat without a rudder. There must be some objective that offers a guide to the composition of the portfolio.

There are many reasons for saving and accumulating assets. Individuals may postpone current consumption to accumulate funds to make the down payment on a house, finance a child's education, start a business, meet financial emergencies, finance retirement, leave a sizable estate, or even accumulate for the sake of accumulating. For any or all of these reasons, people acquire a portfolio of assets rather than spend all of their current income.

The motives for saving should dictate, or at least affect, the composition of the portfolio. Not all assets are appropriate to meet the investor's financial goals. For example, savings that are held to meet emergencies, such as an extended illness or being unemployed, should not be invested in assets whose return and safety of principal are uncertain. Instead emphasis should be placed on safety of principal and assets that may be readily converted into cash, such as savings accounts or shares in money market mutual funds. The emphasis should not be on growth and high returns. However, the funds should not sit idle, but should be invested in relatively safe assets that offer a modest return.

Other goals such as financing a child's education or retirement have a longer and more certain time horizon. The investor knows approximately when the funds will be needed and so can construct a portfolio with a long-term horizon. Bonds that mature when the funds will be needed or common stocks that offer the potential for growth would be more appropriate than savings accounts or certificates of

---

[1] *Survey of Current Business.* (May 1992): S-1.

deposit. The longer time horizon means the individual can seek to acquire long-term assets that may offer a higher yield.

Most investors have several financial goals that must be met simultaneously. Thus, it is not surprising to learn that their portfolios contain a variety of assets. Of course, priorities and needs differ. The individual in a cyclical industry who may be laid off during a recession may place more stress on funds to cover unemployment than the tenured professor. An individual with a poor medical history may seek to have more short-term investments than the person with good health. Medical coverage or disability insurance will also affect the individual's need for funds to cover a short-term emergency. If the investor has this coverage, more of the portfolio may be directed toward other financial goals. If the investor lacks such coverage, a greater proportion of the portfolio may have to be devoted to meeting this financial goal, and correspondingly fewer resources may be devoted to meeting alternative financial goals.

In addition to the individual's goals, his or her capacity or willingness to bear risk plays an important role in constructing the portfolio. Some individuals are more willing and able to bear risk, and these persons will tend to select assets on which the return involves greater risk to obtain the specified investment goals. For example, if the saver wants to build a retirement fund, he or she can choose from a variety of possible investments. However, not all investments are equal with regard to risk and potential return. Those investors who are more willing to accept risk may construct portfolios with assets involving greater risk that may earn higher returns. Although conservative investors may select securities issued by the more financially stable firms, investors who are less averse to taking risk may select stocks issued by younger, less seasoned firms that may offer better opportunities for growth over a period of years.

Taxes also help to decide the composition of an individual's portfolio. Investments are subject to a variety of different taxes. The income that is generated is taxed, as is the capital appreciation that is realized. Some states levy personal property taxes on one's securities. When a person dies, the federal government taxes the value of the estate, which includes the portfolio. In addition to the federal estate tax, several states tax the distribution of the wealth (i.e., they levy a tax on an individual's inheritance). Such taxes and the desire to reduce them affect the composition of each person's portfolio.

Although decisions regarding the portfolio's construction and management as a whole are certainly important, the investor's primary decisions center around the acquisition of one asset at a time. The selection of a specific asset is the domain of security analysis. Security analysis considers the merits of the specific asset, while portfolio management determines the effect that the individual asset has on the whole portfolio.

A large portion of this text is devoted to descriptions and analysis of securities because it is impossible to know an asset's effect on the portfolio as a whole without first knowing its characteristics. Stock and bonds differ greatly with regard to risk, potential return, and valuation. Even within a single type of asset such as bonds, there can be considerable variation. For example, a corporate bond is different from a municipal bond, and a convertible bond differs from a straight bond that lacks the conversion feature. The investor needs to know and to understand these differences as well as the relative merits and risks associated with each of the assets. After understanding how individual assets are valued, the investor may then construct a portfolio that will aid in the realization of his or her financial goals.

SOME PRELIMINARY DEFINITIONS

investment (in economics)
The purchase of plant, equipment, or inventory.

investment (in lay terms)
Acquisition of an asset such as a stock or a bond.

The term **investment** can have more than one meaning. In economics it refers to the purchase of a physical asset, such as a firm's acquisition of a plant, equipment, or inventory, or an individual's purchase of a new home. To the layperson the word denotes buying stocks or bonds (or maybe even a house), but it probably does not mean purchasing a plant, equipment, or inventory.

In either case, the firm or the individual wants a productive asset. The difference in definition rests upon the aggregate change in productive assets that results from the investment. When firms invest in plant and equipment, there is a net increase in productive assets. This increase generally does not occur when individuals purchase stock and bonds. Instead, for every investment by the buyer there is an equal *dis*investment by the seller. These buyers and sellers are trading one asset for another: The seller trades the security for cash, and the buyer trades cash for the security. These transactions occur in secondhand markets, and for that reason security markets are often referred to as **secondary markets.** Only when the securities are initially issued and sold in the **primary market** is there an investment in an economic sense. Then and only then does the firm receive the money that it, in turn, may use to purchase a plant, equipment, or inventory.

secondary market
A market for buying and selling previously issued securities.

primary market
The initial sale of securities.

In this text, the word *investment* is used in the layperson's sense. Purchases of an asset for the purpose of storing value (and, hopefully, increasing that value over time) will be called an investment, even if in the aggregate there is only a transfer of ownership from a seller to a buyer. The purchases of stocks, bonds, speculative options, commodity contracts, and even antiques, stamps, and real estate are all considered to be investments if the individual's intent is to transfer purchasing power to the future. If these assets are acting as stores of value, they are investments for that individual.

value
What something is worth; the present value of future benefits.

valuation
The process of determining the current worth of an asset.

Assets have **value** because of the future benefits they offer. The process of determining what an asset is worth today is called **valuation.** An investor appraises the asset and assigns a current value to it based on the belief that the asset will generate income or a flow of services or will appreciate in price. After computing this value, the individual compares it with the current market price to determine if the asset is currently overpriced or underpriced.

In some cases this valuation is relatively easy. For example, the bonds of the federal government pay a fixed amount of interest each year and mature at a specified date. Thus, the future benefits are known. However, the future benefits of other assets are not so readily identified. For example, while the investor may anticipate future dividends, neither their payment nor their amount can be known with certainty. Forecasting future benefits may be very difficult, but they are still crucial to the process of valuation. Without forecasts and an evaluation of the asset, the investor cannot know if the asset should be purchased or sold.

The valuation of some assets is complicated, and two people may have different estimates of the future benefits. It is therefore easy to understand why two people may have completely divergent views on the worth of a particular asset. One person may believe that an asset is overvalued and hence seek to sell it, while another may seek to buy it in the belief that it is undervalued. Valuation may be very subjective, which leads to such inconsistencies as one person's buying while the other is selling. That does not mean that one person is necessarily irrational or incompetent. People's goals and perceptions (or estimates) of an asset's potential may change, affecting their valuation of the specific asset.

An investment is made because the investor anticipates a **return.** The return on an investment is what the investor earns. This may be in the form of **income,** such as dividends and interest, or in the form of **capital gains** or appreciation if the asset's price rises. Not all assets offer both income and capital appreciation. Some stocks pay no current dividends but may appreciate in value. Other assets, including savings accounts, do not appreciate in value, and the return is solely the interest income.

Return is frequently expressed in percentages such as the **rate of return,** which is the annual return that is earned by the investment relative to its cost. Before purchasing an asset, the investor anticipates that the return will be greater than that of other assets of similar risk. Without this anticipation, the purchase would not be made. The realized return may, of course, be quite different from the anticipated rate of return. That is the element of risk.

Risk is the uncertainty that the anticipated return will be achieved. As is discussed in the next section, there are many sources of risk. The investor must be willing to bear this risk to achieve the expected return. Even relatively safe investments involve some risk; there is no completely safe investment. For example, savings accounts that are insured still involve some element of risk of loss. If the rate of inflation exceeds the rate of interest that is earned on these insured accounts, the investor suffers a loss of purchasing power.

The term *risk* has a negative connotation, but uncertainty works both ways. For example, events may occur that cause the value of an asset to rise more than anticipated. Certainly the stockholders of Signal Corp., SCM, or Richardson-Vicks reaped returns that were larger than had been anticipated. All three firms were taken over, and the prices paid for their stock were considerably higher than the prices these securities commanded before the announcements of the takeovers.

A term that is frequently used in conjunction with risk is **speculation.** Many years ago virtually all investments were called speculations. Today the word implies only a high degree of risk. However, risk is not synonymous with speculation. Speculation has the connotation of gambling in which the odds are against the player. Many securities are risky, but over a period of years the investor will reap a positive return. The odds are not really against the investor, and such investments are not speculations.

The term *speculation* is rarely used in this text, and when it is employed, the implication is that the investor runs a good chance of losing the funds invested in the speculative asset. Although a particular speculation may pay off handsomely, the investor should not expect that many such gambles will reap large returns. After the investor adjusts for the larger amount of risk that must be borne to own such speculative investments, the anticipated return may not justify the risk involved.

Besides involving risk and offering an expected return, stores of value have marketability or liquidity or both. **Marketability** means that the asset can readily be bought and sold. Frequently this is confused with **liquidity,** which is ease of converting the asset into cash *without significant loss.* An asset, such as stock that is traded on the New York Stock Exchange, may be very marketable but not very liquid, since its price could decline. Other assets may be very liquid but not marketable. A savings account in a commercial bank is liquid because it may be readily converted into cash, but it is not a marketable asset. Instead the saver withdraws the funds from the account.

Recognizing the difference between liquidity and marketability is important when selecting assets to meet specific investment goals. If the goal is safety of principal or the need for funds to meet financial emergencies, then the investor should

return
The sum of income plus capital gains earned on an investment in an asset.

income
The flow of money or its equivalent produced by an asset; dividends and interest.

capital gain
An increase in the value of a capital asset, such as a stock.

rate of return
The annual percentage return realized on an investment.

risk
The possibility of loss; the uncertainty of future returns.

speculation
An investment that offers a potentially large return but is also very risky; a reasonable probability that the investment will produce a loss.

marketability
The ease with which an asset may be bought and sold.

liquidity
Moneyness; the ease with which assets can be converted into cash with little risk of loss of principal.

POINTS OF INTEREST

DEFINITIONS OF LIQUIDITY

Liquidity is defined in the text as "the ease of converting an asset into cash *without loss*." This definition differentiates between the terms *liquidity* and *marketability*, since the latter refers to the ease of selling an asset but makes no reference to the possibility of loss.

While this distinction between liquidity and marketability is often made in academic writings on investments, this is not the case in the popular press or in the financial community. Liquidity may be used to refer to the ease of converting an asset into cash at the current price. For instance, if the individual is able to

sell 300 shares of AT&T at the current price, the asset is considered to be liquid. Real estate, on the other hand, would not be considered liquid, since it may take months to sell and possibly only if the asking price is lowered.

The distinction between the two definitions of liquidity is subtle. If the investor can sell 300 shares of AT&T at the current price, what is the risk of loss? The answer, of course, is that the investor does not know what that price will be when the shares are acquired. If the stock is purchased for $40 and subsequently sold for $35, the investor sustains a loss even though the shares are easily sold at the then current market price.

Such a loss could not occur if the asset were liquid in the academic sense of the term, and the stock of AT&T would not be considered a liquid asset.

Since both definitions of liquidity are used, the student of investments should be aware of each. The context in which the term is used generally indicates the definition being employed. In this text, the academic definition is consistently employed since it implies something about the riskiness of the asset. Liquidity, then, will only be applied to an asset that is readily convertible into cash without the investor sustaining a loss.

acquire liquid assets. Liquidity implies safety of principal and applies to assets that may be readily converted into cash with little risk of loss of the funds invested. It is the safety and accessibility of the funds and not the marketability of the asset that is the important consideration. Of course, the investor may acquire a liquid asset that is also marketable (e.g., a U.S. Treasury bill), but the emphasis is placed on the asset's liquidity.

In other cases marketability may be more important than liquidity. Suppose an investor seeks to accumulate funds to finance a child's college education. This goal does not require that the asset be immediately convertible into cash with little risk of loss. Instead the investor wants an asset that offers safety of principal and the potential for growth over time through the compounding of interest or through price appreciation. However, the asset must ultimately be converted into cash at the specified time in the future. For most assets to meet this requirement, there must exist a market in which the asset may be sold. Without such a market, the investor may be unable to convert the asset back into cash when the funds are needed.

All assets that serve as potential stores of value possess some combination of marketability, liquidity, and the potential to generate income and/or appreciate in price.[2] These features, along with the risk associated with each asset, are considered when including the asset in the individual's portfolio. Since assets differ with regard to their features, it is important for the investor to know the characteristics of each

---

[2]The investor must realize that investments are made to transfer purchasing power to the future (i.e., to store value). However, some investments may not be successful and thus do not transfer purchasing power to the future.

asset. Much of the balance of this text considers each asset's features as well as the sources of its risk and return. In Chapter 25, Exhibit 25.1 gives a summary of the various assets' characteristics—their liquidity, marketability, sources of return, and risk exposure.

SOURCES OF RISK

As was mentioned previously, risk refers to the uncertainty that the actual return the investor realizes will differ from the expected return. As is illustrated in Exhibit 1.1, this variability in returns is often differentiated into two types of risk: systematic and unsystematic risk. **Systematic risk** refers to those factors that affect the returns on all comparable investments. For example, when the market as a whole rises, the prices of most individual securities also rise. There is a systematic relationship between the return on a specific asset and the return on all other assets in its class (i.e., all other comparable assets). Since this systematic relationship exists, diversifying the portfolio by acquiring other comparable assets does not reduce this source of risk; thus, systematic risk is often referred to as *nondiversifiable risk*. The individual investor must ultimately decide on how much systematic risk he or she is willing to bear. (How systematic risk is measured and how such measurement helps the individual determine the amount of systematic risk being borne is discussed in Chapter 7.)

Unsystematic risk, which is also referred to as *diversifiable risk*, depends on factors that are unique to the specific asset. For example, a firm's earnings may decline because of a strike. Other firms in the industry may not experience the same labor problem, and thus their earnings may not be hurt or may even rise as customers divert purchases from the firm whose operations are temporarily halted. In either case, the change in the firm's earnings is independent of factors that affect the industry, the market, or the economy in general. Since this source of risk applies only to the specific firm, it may be reduced through the construction of a diversified portfolio.

The total risk the investor bears therefore consists of unsystematic and systematic risk. The sources of unsystematic risk may be subdivided into two general classifications—business risk and financial risk. The sources of systematic risk may be

systematic risk
Associated with fluctuation in security prices; market risk.

unsystematic risk
The risk associated with individual events that affect a particular security.

Exhibit 1.1   THE SOURCES OF RISK

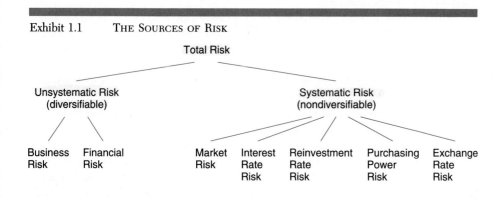

subdivided into market risk, interest rate risk, reinvestment rate risk, purchasing power risk, and exchange rate risk.

business risk
The risk associated with the nature of business.

Business risk is the risk associated with the nature of the enterprise itself. Not all businesses are equally risky. Drilling for new oil deposits is considerably more risky than running a commercial bank. The chances of finding oil may be slim, and only one of many new wells may actually produce oil and earn a positive return. Commercial banks, however, can make loans that are secured by particular assets, such as residences or inventories. While these loans are not risk-free, they may be relatively safe because even if the debtor defaults, the creditor (the bank) can seize the security to meet its claims. Some businesses are by their very nature riskier than others, and, therefore, investing in them is inherently riskier.

All assets must be financed. Either creditors or owners or both provide the funds to start and to sustain the business. Firms use debt financing for two primary reasons. First, under current tax laws interest is a tax deductible expense while dividends paid to stockholders from earnings are not. Second, debt financing is a source of financial leverage that may increase the return on equity (i.e., the return to the owners). If the firm earns more on the borrowed funds than it must pay in interest, the return to the equity is increased.

For many firms the use of debt financing is a major source of funds. Leveraged buyouts and corporate restructuring often involve the issuing of a substantial amount of debt and have led to the development of so-called *junk bonds*. Even conservatively managed firms use debt financing. Virtually every firm has some debt outstanding even if the debt is limited to accrued wages and accounts payable generated by the normal course of business.

financial risk
The risk associated with a firm's sources of financing.

This use of financial leverage is the source of **financial risk.** Borrowing funds to finance a business may increase risk, because creditors require that the borrower meet certain terms to obtain the funds. The most common of these requirements is the paying of interest and the repayment of principal. The creditor can (and usually does) demand other terms, such as collateral or restrictions on dividend payments, that the borrower must meet. These restrictions mean that the firm that uses debt financing bears more risk because it must meet these obligations in addition to its other obligations. When sales and earnings are rising, these constraints may not be burdensome, but during periods of financial stress the firm must meet the obligations required by its debt financing. Failure of the firm to meet these terms may result in financial ruin and bankruptcy. A firm that does not use borrowed funds to acquire its assets does not have these additional responsibilities and does not have the element of financial risk.

market risk
Systematic risk; the risk associated with the tendency of a stock's price to fluctuate with the market.

Market risk refers to the tendency of security prices to move together. While it may be frustrating to invest in a firm that appears to have a minimum amount of business risk and financial risk and then to watch the price of its securities fall as the market as a whole declines, that is the nature of market risk. Security prices do fluctuate, and the investor must either accept the risk associated with those fluctuations or not participate in the market.

While market risk is generally applied to stocks, the concept also applies to other assets, such as stamps, art objects, and real estate. The prices of each of these assets fluctuate. If the value of houses were to rise in general, then the value of a particular house would also tend to increase. But the converse is also true because the prices of houses could decline, causing the value of a specific house to fall. Market risk cannot be avoided if the individual acquires assets whose prices may fluctuate.

Interest rate risk refers to the tendency of security prices, especially fixed-income securities, to move inversely with changes in the rate of interest. As is explained in detail in Chapters 15 and 16, the prices of bonds and preferred stock depend in part on the current rate of interest. Rising interest rates decrease the current price of fixed-income securities because current purchasers require a competitive yield. The investor who acquires these securities must face the fact that interest rates can and do fluctuate, thus causing the price of these fixed-income securities to fluctuate. The source of this risk depends on the demand and supply of credit. Thus, diversification cannot affect interest rate risk because it applies to all securities. Instead the investor may alter the term (i.e., length of time to maturity) of the securities acquired to reduce the impact of interest rate fluctuations.

interest rate risk
The uncertainty associated with changes in interest rates; the possibility of loss resulting from increases in interest rates.

Reinvestment rate risk refers to the risk associated with reinvesting funds generated by an investment. If an individual receives interest or dividends, these funds could be spent on goods and services. For example, individuals who live on a pension consume a substantial portion, and perhaps all, of the income generated by their assets. Other investors, however, will reinvest their investment earnings in order to accumulate wealth.

reinvestment rate risk
The risk associated with reinvesting earnings on principal at a lower rate than was initially earned.

Consider an individual who wants to accumulate a sum of money and purchases a $1,000 bond that pays $100 a year and matures after ten years. The anticipated annual return based on the annual interest and the amount invested is 10 percent ($100/$1,000). The investor wants to reinvest the annual interest, and the question then becomes what rate will be earned on these reinvested funds: Will the return be more or less than the 10 percent initially earned? The essence of reinvestment rate risk is, will the investor earn more or less than the return anticipated when the investment was initially made?

In addition to the previously mentioned risks, the investor must also bear the risk associated with inflation. Inflation is the loss of purchasing power through a general rise in prices. If prices of goods and services increase, the real purchasing power of the investor's assets and the income generated by them is reduced. Thus, **purchasing power risk** is the risk that inflation will erode the buying power of the investor's assets and income.[3]

purchasing power risk
The uncertainty that future inflation will erode the purchasing power of assets and income.

Investors will naturally seek to protect themselves from loss of purchasing power by constructing a portfolio of assets with an anticipated return that is higher than the anticipated rate of inflation. It is important to note the word *anticipated,* because it influences the selection of particular assets. If inflation is expected to be 4 percent, a savings account offering 6 percent will produce a gain and thereby "beat" inflation. In this illustration the real rate of return is 2 percent (at least before taxes). However, if the inflation rate were to increase unexpectedly to 7 percent, the savings account would result in a loss of purchasing power. The real rate of return is negative. If the higher rate of inflation had been expected, the investor might not have chosen the savings account but might have purchased some other asset with a higher potential return.

The last source of systematic risk is **exchange rate risk,** which occurs when one currency is converted into another. This source of risk applies only if the

exchange rate risk
The uncertainty associated with changes in the value of foreign currencies.

---

[3]The opposite of inflation is deflation, which is a general decline in prices. During a period of deflation, the real purchasing power of the investor's assets and income is increased (unless the value of the assets or the total amount of income is also declining).

investor acquires foreign assets denominated in a foreign currency. Avoiding such assets means the investor avoids this source of risk. However, since the individual may acquire shares in domestic firms with foreign operations or shares in mutual funds that make foreign investments, the individual still may indirectly bear exchange rate risk.

If the investor bears more risk, he or she may earn a higher return. This is the essential trade-off that all investors must face. Federally insured savings accounts offer lower yields but are less risky than bonds issued by AT&T, and AT&T bonds are less risky than the stock of a small, emerging firm whose securities are traded over-the-counter.

The investor may select riskier assets in anticipation of a higher return, but this higher return is not necessarily superior to a lower return. The investor must decide if the anticipated additional return is worth the additional risk that he or she must bear. The aim, then, is for the investor to optimize the risk/return trade-off and to construct a portfolio that offers the highest expected return for the individual's willingness to bear risk.

By now it should be obvious that all investors bear risk. Even an investor who does nothing cannot avoid risk. By "doing nothing" and holding cash or placing the funds in a savings account, the investor is still making an investment and is bearing some element of risk. The very nature of transferring purchasing power from today to tomorrow requires accepting some risk, because the future is uncertain. Risk simply cannot be avoided, as any choice will involve at least one of the sources of risk: business risk, financial risk, market risk, interest rate risk, reinvestment rate risk, purchasing power risk, and interest rate risk.

EFFICIENT AND COMPETITIVE MARKETS

In addition to bearing risk, investors participate in very efficient and competitive financial markets. Economics teaches that markets with many participants (i.e., buyers and sellers) who may enter and exit freely will be competitive. That certainly describes financial markets. Investors may participate freely in the purchase and sale of stocks and bonds. Virtually anyone, from a child to a grandmother, may own a financial asset, even if it is just a savings account. Many firms, including banks, insurance companies, and mutual funds, compete for the funds of investors. The financial markets are among the most (and perhaps *the* most) competitive of all markets.

Financial markets tend to be very efficient. As is explained throughout this text, security prices depend on future cash flows such as interest or dividend payments. If new information suggests that these flows will be altered, the market rapidly adjusts the asset's price. Thus, an efficient financial market implies that a security's current price embodies all the known information concerning the potential return and risk associated with the particular asset. If an asset such as a stock were undervalued and offered an excessive return, investors would seek to buy it, which would drive the price up and reduce the return that subsequent investors would earn. Conversely, if the asset were overvalued and offered an inferior return, investors would seek to sell it, which would drive down its price and increase the return to subsequent investors. The fact that there are sufficient investors who are informed means that a security's price will reflect the investment community's consensus regarding the asset's true value and also that the expected return will be consistent with the amount of risk the investor must bear to earn the return.

The concept of an efficient financial market has an important and sobering corollary. Efficient markets imply that investors (or at least the vast majority of investors) cannot expect on the average to beat the market *consistently*. Of course, that does not mean an individual will never select an asset that does exceedingly well. Individuals can earn large returns on particular assets, as the stockholders of many firms know. Certainly the investor who bought UAL (United Airlines) in January 1989 for about $115 and sold it in August for $250 made a large return on that investment. What the concept of efficient markets implies is that this investor will not consistently select those individual securities that earn abnormally large returns.

If investors cannot expect to outperform the market consistently, they also should not consistently underperform the market. Of course, some securities may decline in price and inflict large losses on their owners, but efficient markets imply that the individual will not always select the stocks and bonds of firms that fail. If such individuals do exist, they will soon lose their resources and will no longer be able to participate in the financial markets.

Thus, efficient financial markets imply that investors should, over an extended period of time, earn neither excessively positive nor excessively negative returns. Instead their returns should mirror the returns earned by the financial markets as a whole and the risk the investor bears. While security prices and returns are ultimately determined by the interactions of buyers and sellers, there is little that the typical investor can do to affect a security's price. Instead, the individual investor selects among the various alternatives to build a portfolio that is consistent with that individual's financial goals and willingness to bear risk.

THE PLAN AND PURPOSE OF THIS TEXT

Since the individual participates in efficient financial markets and competes with informed investors, including professional security analysts and financial managers, each individual investor needs fundamental information concerning investments. This text seeks to help those investors, especially individuals with little knowledge and understanding of investments, to increase their knowledge of the risks and returns from various investment alternatives. Perhaps because investing deals with individuals' money and the potential for large gains or losses, it has a mystery about it that is not justified. By introducing the various investments and the methods of their acquisition, analysis, and valuation, this text seeks to remove the mystery associated with investing.

The number of possible investment alternatives is virtually unlimited. Shares in several thousand corporations are actively traded, and if an investor does not want to select individual stocks, that investor still has over two thousand mutual funds to choose from. Corporations, the federal government, and state and local governments issue a variety of debt instruments that range in maturity from a few days to 30 or 40 years. More than 10,000 commercial banks and thrift institutions (i.e., savings banks) offer a variety of savings accounts and certificates of deposit. Real estate, futures, options, and collectibles further increase the available alternatives, and as if there were insufficient choice among domestic investments, the investor may purchase foreign securities. The problem is not one of availability but of choice. The investor cannot own every asset but must choose among the alternatives.

Frequently investment alternatives are classified as short-term or long-term or as variable income, fixed income, or speculative. Short-term assets, such as certificates of deposits and shares in money market mutual funds, are readily converted into cash and offer investors modest returns. Bonds and stocks have a longer time horizon and may be referred to as long-term investments. Common stock is also referred to as variable income security because the dividends and capital gains may fluctuate from year to year. Bonds are illustrative of a fixed income security. While the investor's return from such investment can vary, the flow of income generated by bonds and preferred stock is fixed, so these securities are referred to as fixed income securities. Options, convertible bonds, and futures may be considered speculative investments since they may offer high returns but require the investor to bear substantial risk. Other possible investments include nonfinancial assets (tangible or real assets) such as real estate, gold, and collectibles.

The subject of investments is sometimes viewed as complex, but the approach in this text is to isolate each type of asset. The sources of return, the risks, and the features that differentiate each are described. Techniques for analyzing and valuing the assets are explained. Most of the material is essential information for all investors, whether they have large or small portfolios.

The text is divided into several parts. The first lays the foundation on which security selection is based. This encompasses how securities come into existence (Chapter 2), the mechanics of buying and selling securities (Chapter 3), sources of information (Chapter 4), the tax environment (Chapter 5), the process of compounding and discounting (Chapter 6), and the analysis of risk and its measurement (Chapter 7).

Part II is devoted to investments in common stock. Chapter 8 discusses the valuation of common stock. This is followed by measures of the market and historical returns (Chapter 9), dividends (Chapter 10), and the economic and industrial environment (Chapter 11). The last two chapters of Part Two consider techniques used to analyze a specific stock—the analysis of financial statements (Chapter 12), and technical analysis (Chapter 13).

Part III covers fixed income securities. Chapter 14 describes the features common to all debt instruments, and Chapter 15 discusses the pricing of bonds and the impact of changing interest rates. Chapter 16 is devoted to hybrid types of securities: preferred stock and high-yield securities (i.e., the so-called junk bonds). Next follows the various types of federal, state, and local government bonds (Chapter 17). The last chapter of Part Three (Chapter 18) discusses convertible bonds and convertible preferred stock, which may be exchanged for the issuing firm's common stock.

Part IV considers the alternatives to the traditional financial securities that many investors now include in their portfolios. Chapter 19 serves as a general introduction to options (warrants, puts, and calls). This is followed in Chapter 20 by a discussion of futures, which are perhaps the riskiest of all investments covered in the text. Chapters 21 and 22 cover nonfinancial assets: precious metals such as gold and collectibles (Chapter 21) and real estate (Chapter 22).

The last part of the text (Part V) is devoted to the construction and management of a well-diversified portfolio. While the individual investor may acquire a variety of assets and construct a diversified portfolio, the easiest means for many is to buy shares in an investment company, especially a mutual fund (Chapter 23). As this chapter stresses, the instant diversification achieved through an investment in a mutual fund is one of the prime advantages offered by these funds.

The globalization of investments has led to increased interest in foreign securities. The possible advantages and risks associated with foreign investments are considered in Chapter 24. The text concludes in Chapter 25 with a discussion of financial planning: the establishment of goals, the enumeration of the investor's resources, and the management and evaluation of the portfolio.

Terms to Remember

portfolio	marketability
investment	liquidity
primary and secondary markets	systematic risk
value	unsystematic risk
valuation	business risk
return	financial risk
income	market risk
capital gains	interest rate risk
rate of return	reinvestment rate risk
risk	purchasing power risk
speculation	exchange rate risk

Questions

1. What is the distinction between liquidity and marketability?
2. What is risk and what are the sources of risk that every investor must face?
3. A significant part of this text is devoted to valuation. What causes an asset to have value today?
4. What is the relationship between risk and expected return?
5. What is the implication of an efficient security market for the return an investor will earn over a period of time?

Annotated Bibliography and Readings

The subsequent chapters have lists of annotated readings. The criteria for selection included accessibility and readability. The lists are not exhaustive and do not include many references to academic journals; such readings may be found in more advanced texts. The suggested readings in this text are more pragmatic and develop the basic material covered in each chapter.

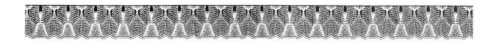

INVESTMENT PROJECT

Investments is one subject in which you, the student, can participate actively, at least on paper, in the content of the course. Constructing a paper portfolio is not the same as actually investing your own money, but a paper portfolio can illustrate several of the important points developed throughout the text. The following investment project runs for the duration of this text and requires that you collect weekly data on stock prices and interest rates. As the text progresses, the project is expanded so that it becomes more applicable to the various investments being discussed.

The data needed to complete this project are readily available in *The Wall Street Journal.* Each Monday during the course term, you should buy *The Wall Street Journal* or use a library copy. Since additional information will be added as the project progresses, it is wise to save the papers so that you can go back and look up different security prices.

The project requires you to complete the following data sheet during the semester. The first section is devoted to stocks; other securities will be added in later sections. I have selected four stocks for you to watch, and you should add four more. My choices are firms whose shares are traded on the New York Stock Exchange. You should also choose common stocks traded on the NYSE or over-the-counter (the NASDAQ).

My choices are Chesapeake Corporation (CSK), GTE (GTE), International Business Machines (IBM), and Microsoft (MSFT). I selected these because they appear in illustrations in the text. The capital letters that appear after each firm's name are the ticker symbols that are used to identify each firm whose shares are traded on the New York or American stock exchanges or through the National Security Dealers Automated Quotation System (NASDAQ). If you follow specific securities for an extended period of time, you may start to remember them in terms of the symbol instead of the company's name.

THE DATA SHEET

Stock	Week 1	2	3	4	5	6	7	8	9	10	11	12	13	14	15
1 S&P 500															
2 CSK															
3 GTE															
4 IBM															
5 MSFT															
6															
7															
8															
9															

On the first row, record the value of the Standard and Poor's 500 stock index, which is an aggregate measure of the stock market. If the market rises during the semester, the value of the index will rise. Conversely, if the market declines, the value of the index will fall. The Standard and Poor 500 stock index is readily available in *The Wall Street Journal* and is usually found in the last section on the second page, which gives the summary of market activity for the previous day.

On the next four lines, record the prices of the stocks I have chosen. On lines 6 through 9, add your four selections and record their prices. Trading activity in a stock is presented in the following way:

Hi	Low	Firm	Sym.	Div.	P/E	Div. Yield	Vol.	High	Low	Close	Change
24	19	Ches	CSK	.72	18	3.6	130	20¼	19¾	20	+¼

The Hi and Low are the highest and lowest prices of the stock during the preceding twelve months. Next follows the name of the firm (usually abbreviated for Chesapeake Corp.) and the ticker symbol (CSK). Other entries include the annual dividend ($0.72), the price/earnings ratio (18, which is explained in Chapter 3), the dividend yield (3.6 percent, which is the dividend divided by the closing price of the stock), the number of shares trades in hundreds (so 130 is 13,000 shares), the high, low, and closing prices (20¼, 19¾, and 20 respectively), and the net change for the day (+¼). Record the last price (i.e., the closing price) under the column for Week 1. If you are using an alternative source of information, the layout may be different and may not be as complete as the information presented in *The Wall Street Journal;* however, the last price should be the closing price. As the project starts, you should have nine entries: the Standard and Poor 500 stock index and the eight individual stock prices. Continue to record the prices each Monday as the term progresses.

2

THE CREATION OF
FINANCIAL ASSETS

There are many diverse types of businesses in many industries, but they all have at least two things in common: Somebody had to provide the funds to start them, and someone must supply the funds to sustain them. From the modest corner store to the large corporate giant, each must have a source of capital. This capital comes from owners who have equity in the firm and from creditors who have lent funds to the firm.

It is through the financing of business that securities come into existence. Firms issue securities, such as stocks or bonds, which are bought by the general public and by financial institutions such as pension funds or mutual funds. Once in existence, many of these securities may be traded in the secondary markets, such as the New York Stock Exchange. These secondary markets make securities more attractive to individuals, because investors know there is a place to sell the securities should the need arise.

This chapter is concerned with the financing of business needs, the role of financial intermediaries, and the advantages offered to individuals by short-term investments in various financial intermediaries. It begins with a general discussion of transferring funds from savers to business. This transfer occurs either directly, when firms issue new securities, or indirectly through financial intermediaries. The second section describes the process of issuing new securities and the role of the investment banker. The last sections of the chapter are devoted to the role of financial intermediaries. Increased competition and the deregulation of banking has led to a blurring of distinctions among the various intermediaries; however, all offer individuals modest yields and safe short-term investments. The chapter concludes with a discussion of money market mutual funds that directly compete with the traditional financial intermediaries (e.g., commercial banks).

✦ ✦ ✦

THE TRANSFER OF FUNDS TO BUSINESS

Securities and other financial assets are created to facilitate the transfer of savings from those with funds to those who need funds. Savers may include individuals, firms, or governments. Savings represent a command of resources that is currently not being used. Thus a government that has collected tax receipts but has not spent the funds has, in effect, savings. So has a firm that has earned profits from the sale of goods but has not distributed the earnings. Until the earnings are distributed, the firm has savings.

Those in need of funds may include individuals, firms, and governments. For example, an individual may need funds to purchase a house. The local school board may need funds to build a school, or AT&T may require funds to purchase new equipment. The individual cannot obtain a mortgage to purchase a house, the school board cannot build the school, or AT&T cannot purchase the equipment if some individual, firm, or government does not put up the funds.

All financial assets (e.g., stocks, bonds, bank deposits, and government bonds) are created to facilitate this transfer. The creation of financial assets and the transfer of funds are crucial for the well-being of every economy. The individual could not obtain the resources to acquire the house, the local government could not build the school, and AT&T could not obtain the new equipment without the transfer of resources. And this transfer could not occur without the creation of financial assets.

All financial assets represent claims, and these claims may be divided into two types: debt obligations and equity obligations. Debt obligations, such as bonds or certificates of deposit with a commercial bank, are loans. The borrower pays interest for the use of the funds and agrees to repay the principal after some specified period of time. These debt obligations represent legal obligations on the part of the borrower that are enforceable in a court of law.

An equity claim represents ownership. Owners of common stock are the owners of the corporation that issued the stock. The individual who owns a home has equity in the home. Equity claims are paid after all debt obligations are met. This residual status means that owners reap the rewards when a business is successful but may sustain substantial losses when the operation is unsuccessful. This does not mean that lenders (creditors) may not sustain losses. It means that the owner has the riskier position than the creditor. Correspondingly the owner may earn a greater return for bearing more risk.

While all financial assets represent a debt or an equity claim, the individual assets come in a variety of forms with differing features. One of the purposes of this text is to explain this variety and to clarify the advantages and risks associated with each financial asset. Nor are all financial assets clearly debt or equity instruments. Some have elements of both such as the convertible bond, which is a debt instrument that may be converted into equity. Such bonds have to be analyzed from both perspectives: as a debt instrument and as an equity instrument.

The Direct and Indirect Transfers of Funds

There are basically two methods for transferring funds to business. One is the direct investment of funds into businesses by the general public. This occurs when firms issue new securities that are purchased by investors or when individuals invest in partnerships or sole proprietorships. The second method is the indirect transfer through a **financial intermediary,** which transfers funds to firms and other borrowers from individuals such as savers or from firms that currently are not using the funds. The financial intermediary stands between the ultimate supplier and the ultimate user of the funds and facilitates the flow of money and credit between the suppliers and the users.

financial intermediary
A financial institution such as a commercial bank that borrows from one group and lends to another.

When a corporation issues a new security such as a bond and sells it to the general public, the following transaction occurs:

The saver purchases the security with money, thereby trading one asset for another. The firm acquires the funds by issuing the security; thus there is a direct transfer of money from the saver to the firm.

The indirect transfer is a little more complicated because an intermediary operates between the saver and the firm. The intermediary acquires funds from savers by issuing a claim on itself, such as a savings account at a commercial bank. The intermediary then lends the funds or buys new securities issued by an entity that is in need of money.

The flow of funds to the financial intermediary is illustrated by the following chart:

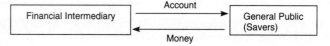

The saver trades one asset (the money) for another (the claim on the financial intermediary), and the financial intermediary acquires the funds by issuing a claim on itself.

The financial intermediary then lends the funds to an entity such as a firm, government, or household in need of the funds. That is, the financial intermediary buys a security such as a bond or makes a new loan, at which time the following transaction occurs:

The financial intermediary gives up one asset, the money, to acquire another asset, the claim on the borrower. The borrower acquires the funds by promising to return them in the future and to pay interest while the loan is outstanding.

The preceding charts may be combined to illustrate the process of transferring funds from the ultimate lender (the saver) to the ultimate borrower.

The saver's funds are transferred to the borrower through the financial intermediary. Through this process the borrower is able to acquire the funds because the financial intermediary was able to issue a *claim on itself* (i.e., the account) that the saver would accept.

private placement
The nonpublic sale of securities to a financial institution.

The direct sale of an entire issue of bonds or stock to a financial institution, such as a pension fund or a life insurance company, is called a **private placement.** The primary advantages of a private placement to the firm are the elimination of the cost of selling securities to the general public and the ready availability of large amounts of cash. In addition, the firm does not have to meet the disclosure requirements that are necessary to sell securities to the general public. This disclosure of information is for the protection of the investing public; it is presumed that the financial institution can protect itself by requiring information as a precondition for granting a loan.[1] The disclosure requirements are both a cost to the firm when securities are issued to the public and a possible source of information to its competitors that the firm may wish to avoid divulging. An additional advantage to both the firm and the financial institution is that the terms of securities may be tailored to meet both parties' needs.

The advantages of private placement are similar for the financial institution and for the firm that is obtaining the funds. A substantial amount of money may be invested at one time, and the maturity date can be set to meet the lender's needs. In addition, brokerage fees associated with purchasing securities on an organized exchange are avoided. The financial intermediary can gain more control over the firm that receives the funds by building restrictive covenants into the agreement. These covenants may restrict the firm from issuing additional securities without the prior permission of the lender and may limit the firm's dividends, its merger activity, and the types of investments that it may make. All of these restrictive covenants are designed to protect the lender from risk of loss and are part of any private sale of securities from a firm to a financial institution. Because each sale is separately negotiated, the individual terms vary with the bargaining powers of the parties and the economic conditions at the time of the agreement.

THE ISSUING AND SELLING OF NEW SECURITIES

Firms, in addition to acquiring funds through private placements, may issue new securities and sell them to the general public, usually through **investment bankers.** If this sale is the first sale of common stock to the general public, it is referred to as an **initial public offering (IPO).** Firms sell securities when internally generated funds are insufficient to finance the desired level of investment spending and when the firm believes it to be advantageous to obtain outside funding from the general public instead of from a financial intermediary. Such outside funding may increase public interest in the firm and its securities and may also bypass some of the restrictive covenants that are required by financial institutions.

investment banker
An underwriter: a firm that sells new issues of securities to the general public.

initial public offering (IPO)
The first sale of common stock to the general public.

The following section deals with the sale of new securities to the general public through an investment banker.[2] It covers the role played by the investment banker, the mechanics of selling new securities, and the potential volatility of the new issue market.

The Role of Investment Bankers

A firm can market securities directly to the public in several ways: by contacting its current stockholders and creditors and asking them to purchase the new securities;

---

[1] Private lenders frequently negotiate for and receive a seat on the borrowing firm's board of directors.

[2] While the discussion is limited to the sale of stock, the mechanics of selling new stock also apply to new bonds.

by advertising the securities; or even by peddling them from door to door.[3] Although this last scenario is exaggerated, it illustrates that there is a cost to selling new securities, which may be considerable if the firm itself undertakes the task. For this reason, firms employ help in marketing new securities; they use the services of investment bankers, who sell new securities to the general public. In effect, an investment banker serves as a middleman to channel money from investors to the firm that needs the capital.

Investment banking is an important financial practice, but confusion exists concerning it, part of which may be attributable to the misnomer *investment banker.* An investment banker is rarely a banker and does not generally invest. Instead, the investment banker is usually a brokerage firm, like Merrill Lynch Pierce Fenner and Smith or First Boston Corporation. Although these brokerage firms may own securities, they do not necessarily buy and hold the newly issued securities on their own account for investment purposes.

Investment bankers perform a middleman function that brings together individuals who have money to invest and firms that need financing.[4] Since brokerage firms have many customers, they are able to sell new securities without the costly search that the individual firm may have to make to sell its own securities. Thus, although the firm in need of financing must pay for the services, it is able to raise external capital at less expense through the investment banker than it could by selling the securities itself.

The Mechanics of Underwriting

If a firm needs funds from an external source, it can approach an investment banker to discuss an underwriting. The term *underwriting* refers to the process of selling new securities. In an underwriting the firm that is selling the securities, and not the firm that is issuing the shares, bears the risk associated with the sale. When an investment banker agrees to underwrite a sale of securities, it is agreeing to supply the firm with a specified amount of money. The investment banker buys the securities with the intention to resell them. If it fails to sell the securities, the investment banker must still pay the agreed-upon sum to the firm at the time of the offering (i.e., the sale) of the securities. Failure to sell the securities imposes significant losses on the underwriter, who must remit funds for securities that have not been sold.

The firm in need of financing and the investment banker discuss the amount of funds needed, the type of security to be issued, the price and any special features of the security, and the cost to the firm of issuing the securities. All of these factors are negotiated by the firm seeking capital and the investment banker. If mutually acceptable terms are reached, the investment banker will be the middleman through which the securities are sold by the firm to the general public.

originating house
An investment banker that makes an agreement with a firm to sell a new issue of securities and forms the syndicate to market them.

Because an underwriting starts with a particular brokerage firm, which manages the underwriting, that firm is called the **originating house.** The originating house need not be a single firm if the negotiation involves several investment bankers. In

---

[3] As is explained later, the formal offer to sell the securities must be made by a prospectus, and the securities must be registered with the SEC.

[4] Investment bankers are not financial intermediaries because they do not create claims on themselves.

GREEN SHOES

When a firm and an investment banker agree to an underwriting, only the approximate number of shares and their approximate price can be established. Obviously conditions can change, and underwriters need flexibility when selling the securities. If market conditions worsen, the underwriters may seek to sell a smaller issue at a lower price. If conditions improve, the issue may be increased. Firms often grant the underwriters an option to increase the size of the issue. This option is sometimes referred to as a "green shoe" after the first company that gave the option to its underwriters.

How the option works is very simple. Suppose the initial agreement calls for the sale of 1,000,000 shares at approximately $10 a share. The issuing firm grants the underwriter an option to purchase up to 10 percent additional shares.

If the issue is well received, the underwriter can sell up to an additional 100,000 shares. Of course, the underwriters do not have to sell any additional shares, nor do they have to sell all 100,000 shares if they do exercise the option. They may only accept, for example, an additional 45,600 shares if that number is needed to balance the market's initial demand for the stock.

---

this case, several firms can join together to manage the underwriting and the sale of securities to the general public.

The originating house does not usually try to sell all of the securities by itself but forms a **syndicate** to market them. The syndicate is a group of brokerage houses that join together to underwrite a specific sale of securities. The firm that manages the sale is frequently referred to as the *lead underwriter*. It is the lead underwriter that allocates the specific number of securities each individual member of the syndicate is responsible for selling.

syndicate
A selling group assembled to market an issue of securities.

The use of a syndicate has several advantages. First, the syndicate may have access to more potential buyers for the securities. Second, by using a syndicate the number of securities that each brokerage firm must sell is reduced. The increase in the number of potential customers and the decrease in the amount that each broker must sell increases the probability that the entire issue of securities will be sold. Thus, syndication makes possible both the sale of a large offering of securities and a reduction in the risk borne by each member of the selling group.

In some cases, the firm seeking funds may not choose to negotiate the terms of the securities with an underwriter. Instead, the firm designs the issue and auctions the securities to the investment banker making the highest bid. In preparation for bidding, the investment banker will form a syndicate as well as determine the price it is willing to pay. The underwriter, and its syndicate that wins the auction and purchases the securities, marks up the price of the securities and sells them to the general public. Obviously, if the investment banker bids too high, it will be unable to sell the securities for a profit. Then the underwriter may sustain a loss when it lowers the securities' price in order to sell them.

Types of Agreements

The agreement between the investment bankers and the firm may be one of two types. The investment bankers may make a **best efforts agreement** in which they agree to make their best effort to sell the securities but do not guarantee that a specified amount of money will be raised. The risk of selling the securities rests with the firm issuing the securities. If the investment bankers are unable to find buyers, the firm does not receive the desired amount of money.

best efforts agreement
Agreement with an investment banker who does not guarantee the sale of a security but who agrees to make the best effort to sell it.

underwriting
Agreement with an investment banker who guarantees a sale of securities by agreeing to purchase the entire issue.

The alternative is an **underwriting** in which the investment bankers purchase (i.e., underwrite) the entire issue of securities and subsequently sell them to the general public. Most sales of new securities are made through an underwriting, and best effort sales are generally limited to small security issues by less well-known firms. In an underwriting the investment bankers pay the expenses with the anticipation of recouping these costs through the sale. Since the underwriters have agreed to purchase the entire issue, they must pay the firm for all the securities even if the syndicate is unable to sell them. Thus the risk of the sale rests with the underwriters.

It is for this reason that the pricing of the securities being underwritten is crucial. If the initial offer price is too high, the syndicate will be unable to sell the securities. When this occurs, the investment bankers have two choices: (1) to maintain the offer price and hold the securities in inventory until they are sold or (2) to let the market find a lower price level that will induce investors to purchase the securities. Neither choice benefits the investment bankers. If the underwriters purchase the securities and hold them in inventory, they either must tie up their own funds, which could be earning a return elsewhere, or must borrow funds to pay for the securities. Like any other firm, the investment bankers must pay interest on these borrowed funds. Thus, the decision to support the offer price of the securities requires the investment bankers to invest their own capital or (and this case is the more likely) requires that they borrow substantial amounts of capital. In either case, the profit margins on the underwriting are substantially decreased, and the investment bankers may even experience a loss on the underwriting.

Instead of supporting the price, the underwriters may choose to let the price of the securities fall. The inventory of unsold securities can then be sold, and the underwriters will not tie up capital or have to borrow money from their sources of credit. If the underwriters make this choice, they take losses when the securities are sold at less than cost. But they also cause the customers who bought the securities at the initial offer price to have a higher cost basis. The underwriters certainly do not want to inflict losses on these customers, because if they experience losses continually, the underwriters' market for future security issues will vanish. Therefore, the investment bankers do not try to overprice a new issue of securities, for overpricing will ultimately result in their suffering losses.

There is also an incentive to avoid underpricing new securities. If the issue is underpriced, all of the securities will be readily sold and their price will rise because demand will have exceeded supply. The buyers of the securities will be satisfied, for the price of the securities will have increased as a result of the underpricing. The initial purchasers of the securities reap windfall profits, but these gains are really at the expense of the company whose securities were underpriced. If the underwriters had assigned a higher price to the securities, the company would have raised more capital. Underwriting is a very competitive business, and each security issue is negotiated individually; hence, if one investment banker consistently underprices securities, firms will employ competitors to underwrite their securities.

preliminary prospectus (red herring)
Initial document detailing the financial condition of a firm that must be filed with the SEC to register a new issue of securities.

Marketing Securities

Once the terms of the sale have been agreed upon, the managing house may issue a **preliminary prospectus.** This is often referred to as a **red herring** because of the red lettering on the title page. This lettering informs the prospective buyer that

---

POINTS OF INTEREST

TAPPING YOUR CUSTOMERS

While firms generally acquire funds from the general public through investment bankers, a selected few also raise funds from their customers. Schwegmann Giant Supermarkets in New Orleans sells its bonds as well as groceries. These bonds have been very popular with its customers because Schwegmann will raise the interest rate it pays on outstanding bonds in response to general increases in interest rates. In addition, Schwegmann will redeem the bonds at par at the option of the holder. The bonds have been so popular that when a holder does redeem them, Schwegmann is able to sell more bonds to other customers.

Dominion Resources, parent company of Virginia Electric and Power, permits its customers to subscribe to its common stock. Customers may pledge annually a specified amount that is paid in monthly installments. After the year has elapsed, the accumulated funds are applied to buy common stock at the average of the high and low sale prices on the twentieth day of each month during the twelve-month period. Like Schwegmann Giant Supermarkets, Virginia Electric and Power has found its customers to be a good source of funds. In 1991, customers subscribed for over $31.7 million of the common stock.

---

the securities are being registered with the **Securities and Exchange Commission (SEC)** and may subsequently be offered for sale. **Registration** refers to the disclosure of information concerning the firm, the securities being offered for sale, and the use of the proceeds from the sale.[5]

The cost of printing the red herring is borne by the underwriters, who recoup this cost through the underwriting fees. This preliminary prospectus describes the company and the securities to be issued; it includes the firm's income statement and balance sheets, its current activities (such as a pending merger or labor negotiation), the regulatory bodies to which it is subject, and the nature of its competition. The preliminary prospectus is thus a detailed document concerning the company and is, unfortunately, usually tedious reading.

The preliminary prospectus does not include the price of the securities. That will be determined on the day that the securities are issued. If security prices decline or rise, the price of the new securities may be adjusted for the change in market conditions. In fact, if prices decline sufficiently, the firm has the option of postponing or even canceling the underwriting.

After the shares have been approved for issue by the SEC, a final prospectus is published. The SEC does not approve the issue as to its investment worth but rather sees that all information has been provided and the prospectus is complete in format and content. Except for changes that are required by the SEC, it is virtually identical to the preliminary prospectus. The red lettering is removed, and information regarding the price of the security, the underwriting discount, and the proceeds to the company, along with any more recent financial data, is added. Exhibit 2.1 illustrates the title pages for the final prospectus for an issue of 2,500,000 shares of Chesapeake Corporation. The name of the managing underwriter is in large print at the bottom of the page. This managing underwriter formed the

Securities and Exchange Commission (SEC)
Federal government agency that enforces the federal security laws.

registration
Process of filing information with the SEC concerning a proposed sale of securities to the general public.

---

[5]While unregistered corporate securities may not be sold to the general public, the debt of governments (e.g., state and municipal bonds) is *not* registered with the SEC and may be sold to the general public.

Exhibit 2.1 ✦ TITLE PAGE FOR THE PROSPECTUS OF AN ISSUE OF COMMON STOCK OF CHESAPEAKE CORPORATION

2,500,000 Shares

Chesapeake
CORPORATION

Type of Security ────────────────▶ **Common Stock**
(par value $1.00 per share)

Of the 2,500,000 shares of Common Stock offered, 2,000,000 shares are being offered hereby in the United States and 500,000 shares are being offered in a concurrent international offering outside the United States. The initial public offering price and the aggregate underwriting discount per share will be identical for both offerings. See "Underwriting".

The Common Stock is traded on the New York Stock Exchange under the symbol "CSK". On March 25, 1992, the last reported sale price of the Common Stock on the New York Stock Exchange was $25.00 per share. See "Price Range of Common Stock and Dividend Policy"

THESE SECURITIES HAVE NOT BEEN APPROVED OR DISAPPROVED BY THE SECURITIES AND EXCHANGE COMMISSION OR BY ANY STATE SECURITIES COMMISSION NOR HAS THE SECURITIES AND EXCHANGE COMMISSION OR ANY STATE SECURITIES COMMISSION PASSED UPON THE ACCURACY OR ADEQUACY OF THIS PROSPECTUS. ANY REPRESENTATION TO THE CONTRARY IS A CRIMINAL OFFENSE.

Flotation Cost of the Sale ──────────

	Initial Public Offering Price	Underwriting Discount(1)	Proceeds to Company(2)
Per Share	$25.00	$1.12	$23.88
Total(3)	$62,500,000	$2,800,000	$59,700,000

Proceeds Received ──────────

(1) The Company has agreed to indemnify the Underwriters against certain liabilities, including liabilities under the Securities Act of 1933.
(2) Before deducting estimated expenses of $170,000 payable by the Company.
(3) The Company has granted the U.S. Underwriters an option for 30 days to purchase up to an additional 300,000 shares at the initial public offering price per share, less the underwriting discount, solely to cover over-allotments. Additionally, the Company has granted the International Underwriters an option for 30 days to purchase up to an additional 75,000 shares at the initial public offering price per share, less the underwriting discount, solely to cover over-allotments. If such options are exercised in full, the total initial public offering price, underwriting discount and proceeds to the Company will be $71,875,000, $3,220,000 and $68,655,000, respectively. See "Underwriting".

The shares are offered severally by the U.S. Underwriters, as specified herein, subject to receipt and acceptance by them and subject to their right to reject any order in whole or in part. It is expected that the certificates for the shares will be ready for delivery at the offices of Goldman, Sachs & Co., New York, New York, on or about April 1, 1992.

Managing Underwriter ────────────▶ **Goldman, Sachs & Co.**

The date of this Prospectus is March 25, 1992.

Source: Reproduced with the permission of Chesapeake Corporation.

syndicate that sold the shares to the general public. In this example, more than 40 firms participated in the selling group.

The cost of the underwriting (also called *flotation costs* or *underwriting discount*) is the difference between the price of the securities to the public and the proceeds to the firm. In this example, the cost is $1.12 per share, which is 2.13 percent of the proceeds received by the firm for each share. The total cost is $2,800,000 for the sale of these shares. Underwriting fees tend to vary with the dollar value of the securities being underwritten and the type of securities being sold. Since some of the expenses are fixed (e.g., preparation of the prospectus), the unit cost for a large underwriting is smaller. Also, since it may be more difficult to sell speculative bonds than high-quality bonds, underwriting fees for speculative issues tend to be higher.

In addition to the fee, the underwriter may receive indirect compensation, which may be in the form of the right (or option) to buy additional securities or to have a membership on the firm's board of directors. Such indirect compensation may be as important as the monetary fee because it unites the underwriter and the firm. After the initial sale, the underwriter often becomes a market maker for the securities, which is particularly important to the investing public.[6] Without a secondary market in which to sell the security, investors would be less interested in buying the securities initially. By maintaining a market in the security, the brokerage firm eases the task of selling the securities originally.

Volatility of Initial Public Offerings

The new issue market (especially for common stock) is extremely volatile. There have been periods when the investing public seemed willing to purchase virtually any new security that was being sold on the market. There have also been periods during which new companies were simply unable to raise money, and large, well-known companies did so only under onerous terms.

The market for initial public offerings is not only volatile regarding the number of securities that are offered but also regarding the price changes of new issues. When the new issue market is "hot," it is not unusual for the prices to rise dramatically. In many cases, however, prices subsequently decline even more remarkably. The dramatic price behavior of Four Seasons Nursing Homes is illustrated in Figure 2.1, which shows the annual price range of the stock and the firm's earnings per share. The firm went public on May 10, 1968. The price rose dramatically from the initial price of $11 to $102. Only two years later the firm was bankrupt, and the price of the stock declined to $0.16 (i.e., $\frac{3}{16}$ in the fractional prices that are used in the security markets).

A price of $102 for a share of Four Seasons Nursing Homes was indeed excessive. The company had 3.4 million shares outstanding, and, at a price of $102, the firm was worth $346.8 million ($102 × 3.4 million) according to the market. Since the firm had revenues of only $19.3 million and earnings of less than $2 million, it made no sense in terms of the firm's earning capacity to value the company in excess of $300 million. Subsequently Four Seasons Nursing Homes was reorganized as

---

[6] For a detailed discussion of making a market, see "Market Makers" in Chapter 3.

Figure 2.1 ✦ ANNUAL PRICE RANGE AND EARNINGS PER SHARE OF STOCK OF FOUR SEASONS NURSING HOMES (ANTA CORPORATION)

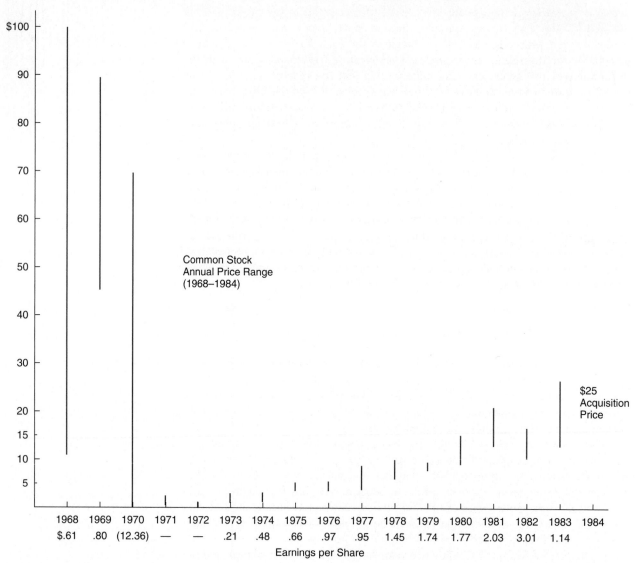

Source: Standard and Poor's *Stock Guide*, various issues.

Anta Corporation and was acquired by Manor Care for $25 a share. While this acquisition price was a small fraction of the stock's price during the late 1960s, it was considerably higher than the valuation placed on the company during the period of bankruptcy.

Not all new issues perform like that of Four Seasons Nursing Homes. Despite the fact that some firms do not fulfill their development potential and fail, others succeed and grow steadily. For example, Microsoft went public in 1987 and has grown rapidly. This exceptional performance is illustrated in Figure 2.2, which plots

Figure 2.2 ✦ ANNUAL PRICE RANGE AND EARNINGS PER SHARE FOR MICROSOFT CORPORATION (1987–1992)

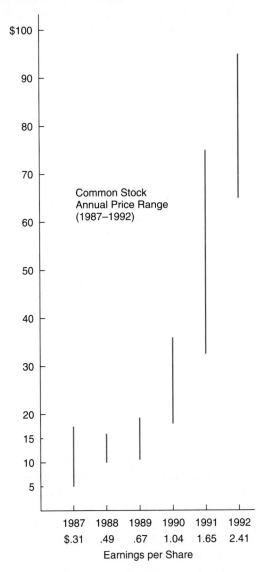

Source: Microsoft Corporation annual reports, various issues.

the annual range of the stock's price and the firm's earnings per share. As may be seen from the figure, there has been a substantial increase in the firm's earnings and in the price of the stock.

The potential for large gains is, of course, the lure that attracts speculative investors. All firms were small at one time, and each one had to go public to have a market for its shares. Someone bought the shares of IBM, Xerox, and Johnson & Johnson when these firms went public. The ability to spot the companies that promise the greatest growth for the future is rare. However, the new issue market has offered and continues to offer the opportunity to invest in emerging firms, some of which may achieve substantial returns for those investors or speculators who are willing to accept the risk. It is the possibility of such large rewards that makes the new issue market so exciting. However, if the past is an indicator of the future, many firms that go public will fail and will inflict significant losses on those investors who have accepted this risk by purchasing securities issued by the small, emerging firms.

THE ROLE OF FINANCIAL INTERMEDIARIES

While the securities of publicly held firms had to be sold to the public initially, these same firms acquire a substantial proportion of their financing from financial intermediaries. This is particularly true of short-term funds that are borrowed from commercial banks or are obtained by issuing short-term debt obligations that are purchased by a variety of financial intermediaries. Of course, for the intermediaries to make these loans, they too must have funds. These funds are acquired from savers and other economic units who do not currently need them and who thus invest the money in obligations issued by the financial intermediary. In effect, the savers are ultimately supplying the funds to the firms (or to any economic unit) in need of the funds. However, this transfer of money occurs indirectly through the financial intermediary instead of directly.

In advanced economies, a variety of financial intermediaries have developed to facilitate the indirect transfer of savers' funds to borrowers. These intermediaries include commercial banks, savings and loan associations, mutual savings banks, credit unions, life insurance companies, pension plans, and money market mutual funds. Whenever these firms borrow from one group and lend to another, they are acting as financial intermediaries. However, it should be noted that if they purchase existing financial assets, such as stock traded on the New York Stock Exchange or existing mortgages, they are not acting as financial intermediaries. Instead they are investing in assets traded in secondary markets, in which case funds flow from buyer to seller and not to the economic unit that initially issued the security.[7]

Historically, a clear differentiation existed among the various financial intermediaries. For example, the differences between commercial banks and "thrift institutions" such as savings banks and savings and loan associations (S & Ls) encompassed both the types of assets they acquired and the types of liabilities (accounts) they offered. Savings and loan associations were depository organizations that issued savings accounts and used the savers' funds to originate home mortgage loans. Such thrift institutions were clearly differentiated from commercial banks, which issued a variety of accounts, especially checking accounts, and made various loans including personal loans (such as car loans) and short-term financing for businesses and governments.

Today it is probably safe to assert that many savers and potential borrowers are no longer aware of differences among financial intermediaries. Commercial banks, savings and loan associations, savings banks, and credit unions offer similar services (e.g., checking accounts and savings accounts) and pay virtually the same rates of

---

[7] Secondary markets such as the New York Stock Exchange are discussed in the next chapter.

interest on deposits. In addition, the portfolio of assets acquired by each depository institution is more similar than in the past. For example, previously S & Ls made primarily mortgage loans, but now their portfolios have been broadened to include a more varied mix of assets.

This blurring of the distinctions among the various financial intermediaries is the result of changes in the regulatory environment. Under the Depository Institutions Deregulation and Monetary Control Act of 1980, all depository institutions became subject to the regulation of the Federal Reserve. These regulations extended to the types of accounts these institutions may offer and the amount they must hold in reserve against deposits. In return for this change in the regulatory environment, the depository institutions were permitted to offer more accounts to depositors, such as checking accounts, which previously could be offered only by commercial banks. The intermediaries were also permitted to broaden the services offered to depositors, such as brokerage services that link the accounts in the bank to brokerage accounts. Deregulation also led to the end of controls on maximum interest rates. Now the depository institutions may pay whatever rate of interest on deposits they deem necessary to compete with other financial intermediaries, such as the money market mutual funds.[8]

Advantages Offered by Financial Intermediaries

Investors will not deposit funds with a financial intermediary unless some benefit is offered. The advantages provided by the intermediaries include convenience, interest income, and safety of principal. Various accounts offer several features that make them convenient. Checking accounts and **NOW accounts** (NOW is an acronym that stands for "negotiable order of withdrawal" and is a checking account that pays interest) are a convenient means by which to make payments. Savings and checking accounts accommodate small deposits and small withdrawals. Other assets, such as stocks and bonds, may not be divisible into such small units or the commission costs associated with small units may make them impractical.

NOW account
A bank account that earns interest and against which negotiable orders of withdrawal may be written.

Interest is paid on savings accounts, NOW accounts, and time deposits that are called **certificates of deposit** or **CDs.** Funds deposited in savings accounts and NOW accounts may be withdrawn at will, making them among the most liquid assets available to investors. Certificates of deposit are time deposits that have a specified maturity date but that may be redeemed prior to maturity. Such early redemptions result in a penalty, such as the loss of interest for a quarter. The yields offered by these accounts depend on the term of the instrument. Exhibit 2.2 gives the term and yields provided by the savings accounts and certificates of deposit offered by a savings bank. Notice that as the term increases, the interest rate paid on the certificate also increases.

certificate of deposit (CD)
A time deposit with a specified maturity date.

Exhibit 2.2 also illustrates that interest rates change over time. The yields on CDs offered in 1989 were considerably greater than those available to savers in 1992. For example, the yield on the two-year CD fell from 8.79 percent in 1989 to 5.25 percent in 1992. This decline in yields illustrates reinvestment rate risk. Individuals who owned certificates that matured in 1991 and 1992 were unable to

---

[8] Money market mutual funds are discussed later in this chapter.

Exhibit 2.2 ✦ SAVINGS AND TIME DEPOSITS OFFERED BY A SAVINGS BANK

Type of Deposit	Minimum Amount Required	Term	Annual Rate of Interest 1989	Annual Rate of Interest 1992
Money market account	$1,000	None	7.15%	4.14%
Savings account	250	None	5.25	4.14
Certificate of deposit	500	6 months	7.86	4.75
Certificate of deposit	500	1 year	8.33	4.95
Certificate of deposit	500	2 years	8.79	5.25
Certificate of deposit	500	3 years	9.11	5.40
Certificate of deposit	500	4 years	9.20	5.40
Certificate of deposit	500	5 years	9.29	5.40

reinvest the funds at old rates, since comparable certificates of deposit offered lower yields. If these investors want to earn higher rates, they would have to invest elsewhere and probably bear additional risk in order to earn the higher returns that were previously available on investments in certificates of deposit.

If the investor has $100,000 or more to invest, depository institutions may sell **negotiable certificates of deposit** or **jumbo CDs** directly to the investor in which case the yield and term of these certificates is agreed upon by the investor and the depository institution. In other cases the depository institutions establish the terms and yields they are willing to pay and offer the CDs for sale. Maturities are generally one to three months, and the yields are comparable to those earned on other money market instruments, such as commercial paper. While the CDs may not be redeemed prior to maturity, they are negotiable; that is, the holder may sell them because there is a secondary market in jumbo CDs.

The large amount required to purchase a jumbo CD (i.e., the $100,000 minimum investment, with $1 million being the usual unit of trading) precludes most investors. However, as is explained later, many investors do indirectly invest in negotiable certificates of deposit when they acquire shares in money market mutual funds, since these funds invest in negotiable certificates of deposit.

Perhaps one of the most appealing features of an account with a depository institution is its safety. While there is the possibility of loss of purchasing power through the inflation rate exceeding the rate earned on the account, there is no risk of loss from default since the majority of these accounts are insured by the federal government. If an individual places $1,000 in a federally insured savings account, the $1,000 is safe. If the investor had invested $1,000 in a corporate bond, the market value of the bond could decline or the firm could default on the interest payment or principal repayment.

Federal government deposit insurance was one of the positive results of the Great Depression in the 1930s. The large losses sustained by commercial banks' depositors led to the establishment of the **Federal Deposit Insurance Corporation (FDIC).** As of this writing, FDIC insures depositors with accounts in commercial banks and savings banks up to $100,000. If a commercial bank were to fail, FDIC would reimburse each depositor up to the $100,000 limit. As most individuals do not have more than $100,000 on deposit, these investors know that their principal

negotiable certificate of deposit

A certificate of deposit in which the rate and the term are individually negotiated by the bank and the lender and which may be bought and sold.

Federal Deposit Insurance Corporation (FDIC)

Federal government agency that supervises commercial banks and insures commercial bank deposits.

EURODOLLAR CERTIFICATES OF
DEPOSIT

In addition to the traditional CDs discussed in the text, there are Eurodollar
CDs. Eurodollar CDs are time deposits
with fixed rates and specified maturity
dates that are generally issued in units of
$1 million by branches of major U.S.
banks. These CDs are sold in Europe
(primarily in London) and pay yields that
are usually higher than those available on
domestic CDs. While the majority of investors who acquire Eurodollar CDs are
foreign, some U.S. portfolio managers
acquire them when their yields rise sufficiently above the yields offered by domestic negotiable CDs.

is completely safe. However, the investor should note that the insurance is *not* automatic but must be purchased from FDIC by the bank. A few banks have chosen
not to purchase the insurance. Thus, if safety of principal is a major concern, it is
best for the funds to be deposited only in an account insured by the federal
government.

MONEY MARKET MUTUAL FUNDS

One of the most important innovations in the realm of financial intermediaries has
been the development and growth of **money market mutual funds.** While the
discussion of mutual funds will be deferred to Chapter 23, money market mutual
funds differ from regular mutual funds. The money market funds directly compete
with commercial banks and other depository institutions for the deposits of savers,
while regular mutual funds offer investors an alternate means to own stocks and
bonds. It was probably the development and rapid growth in the assets of money
market mutual funds that forced banks to support deregulation.

money market mutual funds
*Mutual funds that specialize in
short-term securities.*

Until the deregulation of the banking system, money market mutual funds
offered investors an asset that was unique. Under regulation, the maximum rate of
interest that banks could pay was constrained. Thus, when the rates paid by short-
term securities (i.e., **money market instruments**) rose, the banks could not raise
the interest rate they paid to be competitive with other money market yields. Investors sought means to acquire these short-term securities, which included treasury
bills, negotiable certificates of deposit, commercial paper, and repurchase
agreements.

money market instruments
*Short-term securities, such as
treasury bills, negotiable
certificates of deposit, or
commercial paper.*

The money market mutual funds were not subject to the same regulations as
banks and thus could offer the higher yields. The money funds thus gave individuals
the opportunity to invest indirectly in short-term securities and earn the higher
yields available to the holders of these instruments. As a result, deposits flowed out
of the financial intermediaries into the money funds.

Of course, individual investors may purchase money market instruments directly
instead of acquiring the shares of the money funds who in turn acquire the securities. However, the large denominations (e.g., $100,000 minimum for negotiable
CDs) exclude most investors. By pooling the resources of many savers, these funds
are able to offer high money market yields to investors who otherwise would be

limited in their choices. Those investors with $10,000 could acquire a treasury bill or purchase a non-negotiable certificate of deposit offered by a commercial bank. However, the money market mutual fund permits investors to broaden their portfolios of short-term securities and simultaneously to reduce risk as the portfolios of the funds are diversified. (The creation in 1983 of money market accounts with banks further expanded investors' choices.)

Since the portfolios are entirely invested in short-term obligations, the shares of money market funds are very liquid. The shares may be converted to cash with little risk of loss. This lack of risk emanates from the very nature of money market instruments. **U.S. Treasury bills** are short-term debt instruments issued by the federal government, and there is no question that the federal government has the capacity to retire the principal and pay the interest on its debt obligations. In addition, since the term of treasury bills is short, there is only a modest amount of interest rate risk. If interest rates were to rise and thus the prices of debt instruments were to fall, the quick maturity of T-bills means that any price decrease would be small and for a brief duration, because as the bills approach maturity, their value approaches the face amount (i.e., the principal).

As was discussed earlier in this chapter, negotiable certificates of deposit are issued by large commercial banks. While there is some risk of default, the possibility of several large banks failing seems remote. In general, the term of negotiable certificates of deposit is relatively short (one to three months), meaning that there is little interest rate risk associated with these CDs. Even if interest rates were to rise, the short term to maturity implies that the investor will soon recover the face amount of the debt.

Commercial paper is an unsecured promissory note issued by a corporation as an alternative to borrowing funds from commercial banks. Since the paper is unsecured, only firms with excellent credit ratings are able to sell it; hence, the risk of default is small, and the repayment of principal is virtually assured. Once again the term is short, so there is little risk from an investment in commercial paper.

In addition to T-bills, negotiable CDs, and commercial paper, money market funds may acquire other short-term debt instruments, such as those issued by agencies of the federal government. These securities are virtually as safe as treasury bills, but since they are obligations of a federal agency and not the federal government, their yields are slightly higher than the yields on T-bills.

Money market mutual funds also participate in **repurchase agreements.** In these agreements, which are often called "repos," the seller of a security agrees to buy back (i.e., repurchase) the security at a set price at a specified date. This repurchase price is higher than the initial sale price. The difference between the sale price and the repurchase price is the source of return to the holder of the security. Money market funds often participate in the market for repurchase agreements since they permit the money market funds to invest for short periods of time. The money market funds buy the securities knowing exactly when and for how much they can sell the securities in the future. Thus repurchase agreements offer the money market funds an attractive combination of return and liquidity.

While there are similarities among the portfolios of money market mutual funds, there can be many differences. For example, First Variable Rate Fund invests only in U.S. government securities or securities that are collateralized by obligations of the federal government. Other funds invest in a wider spectrum of short-term debt obligations and thus have a larger proportion of their portfolios in negotiable CDs and commercial paper. For example, Merrill Lynch's Ready Assets Trust Money

---

U.S. Treasury bills
Short-term debt of the federal government.

commercial paper
Unsecured short-term promissory notes issued by the most creditworthy corporations.

repurchase agreement
A security sale and agreement to buy back the security at a specified price at a specified future date.

Fund had 37.6 percent of its assets in treasury obligations, 20 percent in negotiable CDs, and 35.5 percent in commercial paper.[9]

Funds invested in a money market fund may be readily withdrawn by the investor. The individual who redeems the shares receives the amount invested plus any dividends that have been credited to the account.[10] Unless all investors sought to redeem their shares at the same time and thus forced the fund to liquidate its portfolio rapidly and perhaps at a loss, there is little risk that the investor would not receive the full value of the shares. It is this safety of principal plus the money market yields that were not available through other means (such as a savings account with a commercial bank) that made these funds so attractive to investors.[11]

The yields earned on investments in money market funds closely mirror the yields on short-term securities. For example, Alliance Government Reserves invests solely in government or government-backed securities. Thus the yield it offers investors should mirror the return on these government securities. This relationship must occur because when the short-term debt held by the fund matures, the proceeds can be reinvested only at the going rate of interest paid by short-term government securities. Hence changes in short-term interest rates are quickly felt by the individual money market mutual fund.

In addition to offering safety and money market yields, many money market funds offer a service that is similar to a checking account. The investor is permitted to write drafts against his or her shares. The drafts are technically not checks, but they do permit the transfer of funds from the money market mutual fund to whomever the draft is payable. While there is a limit as to the minimum amount of the draft (e.g., $250), these instruments are an excellent means for increased money management. The investor can accumulate shares in the funds and, when disbursements become necessary, pay by the draft drawn on the fund. The funds invested in the money market fund continue to earn interest until the draft clears, at which time shares are redeemed to cover the amount of the draft. The existence of this service permits the investor to earn interest while waiting for the disbursement of funds. Money that may previously have been sitting in a noninterest-bearing checking account is now put to work for the investor.

Many brokerage firms have arrangements with money market funds that facilitate transfers of money between the two. Once a security is sold and the funds received by the broker on the settlement date, the broker transfers the funds to the money market fund. Later, when the investor buys a new security and must make payment, the funds are transferred back to the broker from the money market fund. All these transactions can occur without processing checks, as the money is transferred electronically from one account to another. This service permits the investor to earn interest on funds between investments even if the amount of time is only a few days. The amount of interest that the investor can earn by such transfers can be substantial. For example, at 4 percent, an investor earns about $11 per day on an investment of $100,000. Thus the transfer of $100,000 to a money market mutual fund for just a week will earn over $76.71 (i.e., $100,000 \times 7/365 \times 0.04$).

---

[9] The remaining 6.9 percent was a variety of short-term assets (as of December 31, 1990).

[10] Dividends are credited daily to the investor's account.

[11] In January 1983, commercial banks and other depository institutions were permitted to offer accounts that pay money market rates. These new accounts compete directly with the money market mutual fund shares for the funds of savers.

Figure 2.3 ✦ MONEY MARKET MUTUAL FUNDS ASSETS, 1975–1990 (IN BILLIONS)

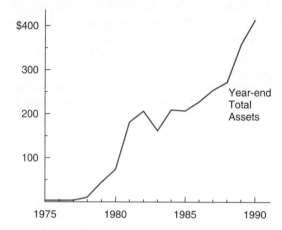

Source: Derived from *1991 Mutual Fund Fact Book,* p. 20.

Given the advantages offered by money market mutual funds, their initial popularity was not surprising. However, the growth in the assets of the money funds was nothing short of phenomenal. This is documented in Figure 2.3, which shows the huge increase in funds invested in money market mutual funds as the value of their assets rose from $3.6 billion in 1976 to more than $400 billion in 1990.

Figure 2.3 also illustrates the sudden change in the rate of growth that occurred with the deregulation of the banking system. Once the various types of banks were better able to compete with the money market mutual funds, the rate of growth in the funds' assets stopped as dramatically as it had risen. Their total assets actually fell in 1983. After a period of adjustment to the new regulatory environment, the assets of the money market mutual funds resumed their growth in 1984 but not at the rate of growth in total assets achieved during 1978–1982.

TRENDS IN COMPETITION AMONG FINANCIAL INTERMEDIARIES

A commercial bank or any other financial intermediary can only lend what has been lent to it. Unless the individual bank is able to induce individuals, firms, and governments to make deposits, that bank will be unable to grant loans and make investments. That general statement, of course, holds for all other financial intermediaries. None can make investments without a source of funds, whether these funds come through issuing certificates of deposit or selling life insurance or selling shares in money market mutual funds.

As this implies, financial intermediaries compete among each other for funds. This competition occurs through yields and services offered. With the deregulation of the interest rates that commercial banks and savings banks may pay, virtually all depository institutions offer competitive and comparable yields for comparable accounts. If a particular bank did not offer competitive yields, funds would be removed from that institution and deposited with a competitor.

Historically, investors could differentiate one financial intermediary from another by the services it offered. Savers bought life insurance from insurance companies. The life insurance companies then used the funds to make investments. Banks offered checking accounts and other banking services to depositors, and stockbrokers bought and sold stocks and bonds for their customers. Those days of specialization are over. Bankers, stockbrokers, and insurance salespeople offer a wide spectrum of financial services and products. Commercial banks not only offer savers the traditional services of savings and checking accounts but other financial products such as discount brokerage (to compete with stockbrokers), money market accounts (to compete with money market mutual funds), and pension plans (to compete with insurance companies).

Brokerage firms have also encroached on the domain of the banks through the creation of cash management accounts. For example, Merrill Lynch's pioneering Cash Management Account, which is known by a registered trademark CMA, combines the traditional brokerage custodial services with checking privileges, a credit card (VISA), and money market yields on funds in the account. Other brokerage firms either have instituted similar accounts or have correspondent relationships with money market mutual funds that offer checking privileges, credit cards, and rates comparable to other money market yields.

While the distinctions among financial institutions have become blurred, the Glass-Steagle Act of 1933 forbids banks from underwriting corporate securities. Commercial banks are permitted to serve as investment bankers for government securities, but they cannot serve in this capacity for corporate clients. Thus, the distinction still exists between brokerage firms that have investment banking divisions for the underwriting of corporate securities and commercial banks that do not. Whether this distinction will continue to exist is questionable. In many European countries commercial banks are permitted to serve as investment bankers for corporate clients. Legislation has been proposed that would permit U.S. banks to do the same. As might be expected, the large commercial banks support repeal of the Glass-Steagle Act, but brokerage firms do not want the additional competition that would result. It is impossible to tell what changes, if any, will occur.

If commercial banks are permitted to underwrite corporate securities, the distinctions between brokerage firms and commercial banks will be blurred further. However, some distinctions will still remain. Commercial banks will continue to be the primary depository for checking accounts as well as a major source of short-term financing for corporations. Savings and loan associations will remain a major source of mortgage loans. Insurance companies will still provide their primary products— life, health, and casualty insurance.

Summary

All firms must have a source of funds with which to acquire assets and retire outstanding liabilities as they come due. Besides retaining earnings, the firm may obtain these funds from savers who are not currently using all of their income to buy goods and services. The transfer of these savings may occur directly when firms issue new securities or indirectly through a financial intermediary.

When a firm issues new stocks or bonds, it usually employs the services of an investment banker to facilitate the sale of the securities by acting as a middleman between the firm and the savers. In many cases investment bankers underwrite the issue of new securities, which means that they guarantee a specified amount of money to the issuing firm and then sell the securities to the public. Since the under-writers are obligated to remit the specified amount for the securities, they bear the risk of the sale.

Firms may also obtain funds by borrowing from financial intermediaries, who raise funds by creating liabilities on themselves (e.g., a savings account), then lend the funds to the ultimate users. Prior to the deregulation of the banking system, the various types of financial intermediaries were clearly distinguished from one another. However, now that regulation is centralized with the Federal Reserve and depository institutions may offer whatever interest rates they deem necessary to raise funds, the differences among the intermediaries is disappearing, as they tend to offer comparable yields and services.

One of the newest and most important financial intermediaries is the money market mutual fund, which offers savers an important alternative to the traditional depository institution. These funds offer services similar to banks (e.g., checking privileges) and pay yields that are comparable to those available on money market instruments such as negotiable certificates of deposit, commercial paper, treasury bills, and repurchase agreements. Since the minimum denominations of these money market instruments are sufficiently large so that most individuals are excluded from participating in the market for them, the money market mutual funds offer savers a means to indirectly acquire these money market securities.

Security Summary

Money Market Securities

Source of return: Interest income

Liquidity and marketability: Active secondary market in some money market instruments (e.g., treasury bills). Short maturities imply these instruments are very liquid.

Sources of risk: Among the safest of all investment alternatives. Unsystematic risk from events that affect the issuer's capacity to service its debt (i.e., pay the interest and timely retire the bonds) is virtually nonexistent for high-quality short-term money market instruments. Systematic risk is also minimal since short maturities and frequent rollovers of securities produce changes in yields that minimize interest rate risk and purchasing power risk.

Taxation: Interest is subject to federal and state income taxation.

Security Summary

Treasury Bills

Source of return: Interest income

Liquidity and marketability: Active secondary market and short maturities imply investor may readily convert treasury bills into cash.

Sources of risk: No default risk and only modest risk of loss from inflation. Short maturities permit reinvestment of proceeds so that interest rate risk is virtually nonexistent.

Taxation: Interest is subject to federal income taxation but exempt from state and local government taxation.

Security Summary

Certificates of Deposit

Source of return: Interest income

Liquidity and marketability: Active secondary market in negotiable CDs but non-negotiable CDs may be redeemed prior to maturity by the issuing bank.

Sources of risk: For federally insured CDs, there is no unsystematic risk (i.e., risk of default of interest and principal repayment). Negotiable CDs in excess of $100,000 do have some unsystematic risk since there is no deposit insurance that guarantees repayment of the principal. Systematic risk is related to the term of the CD. Negotiable CDs have virtually no interest rate risk since their term to maturity is so short. Since there is no market for non-negotiable CDs, there is no market and no interest rate risk. Systematic risk may result from penalties for early withdrawal and from the risk of loss of purchasing power if the interest rate is less than the rate of inflation. These sources of risk increase as the term of the certificate increases.

Taxation: Interest is subject to federal and state income taxation.

Security Summary

Eurodollar CDs

Source of income: Interest income

Liquidity and marketability: Generally Eurodollar CDs are considered to be liquid investments, but the secondary market is not as active as that for domestic CDs.

Sources of risk: Small risk of default, but since their maturities can exceed a year there is market risk from changes in interest rates and the possibility of loss of purchasing power from inflation. FDIC insurance does not apply if the Eurodollar CDs are issued by foreign banks.

Taxation: Interest is subject to federal and state income taxation.

Security Summary

Commercial Paper

Source of return: Interest income

Liquidity and marketability: No active secondary market; commercial paper is usually held to its maturity.

Sources of risk: As long as the investor acquires quality paper, there is minimal risk of default. Possible loss may occur from loss of purchasing power from inflation. Lack of a secondary market suggests investor may sustain a loss if the individual seeks to sell the paper prior to maturity, since such sales will require price concessions to obtain a buyer.

Taxation: Interest is subject to federal and state income taxation.

Security Summary

Repurchase Agreements

Source of return: Interest income

Liquidity and marketability: Issuer agrees to buy back (i.e., repurchase) the security, so there is no secondary market. Extremely short maturities (e.g., as short as overnight) imply liquidity.

Sources of risk: Extremely short maturities suggest no risk from loss of purchasing power, market risk, or interest rate risk. There is, however, the possibility of default (i.e., the issuer fails to repurchase the security).

Taxation: Interest is subject to federal and state income taxation.

Security Summary

Money Market Mutual Funds

Source of return: Interest income

Liquidity and marketability: Shares are redeemed on demand by the issuing fund, so they are liquid.

Sources of risk: As long as the securities acquired by the fund do not default, the fund should not default. There is the possibility of loss from inflation or from higher interest rates. However, the yield earned by the fund's portfolio should rapidly adjust to changes in short-term rates so that higher inflation or higher interest rates should produce increased yields.

Taxation: Interest is subject to federal income taxation unless the fund solely invests in tax-exempt, short-term securities.

Terms to Remember

financial intermediary
private placement
investment bankers
initial public offering (IPO)
originating house
syndicate
best efforts agreement
underwriting
preliminary prospectus (red herring)

Securities and Exchange Commission (SEC)
registration
NOW account
certificate of deposit (CD)
negotiable certificate of deposit (jumbo CD)
Federal Deposit Insurance Corporation (FDIC)
money market mutual fund

money market instruments   commercial paper
U.S. Treasury bills   repurchase agreements

Questions

1. In an underwriting, what role does each of the following play? (a) the investment banker, (b) the syndicate, (c) the red herring, (d) the SEC, and (e) the saver.
2. Why is it important that in an underwriting the investment banker does not overvalue (that is, overprice) the securities? If the securities are overpriced, who suffers the loss?
3. What differentiates an underwriting from a best efforts agreement? Who bears the risk in each of these agreements?
4. Why do investors buy new issues of securities? Besides the risk associated with fluctuations in the market as a whole and the loss of purchasing power through inflation, what is the source of risk associated with initial public offerings?
5. What is a financial intermediary? What role does it play? What differentiates a financial intermediary from an investment banker?
6. What features differentiate savings accounts, certificates of deposit, and negotiable certificates of deposit?
7. What are the trends that are directly related to the deregulation of the banking system that affect brokerage firms?
8. If a saver had $12,540 to invest for a short period of time, what alternatives would be available?
9. What assets do money market mutual funds acquire? Could an individual saver acquire these assets?
10. Explain the initial rapid growth and subsequent decline in the rate of growth of money market mutual funds.

Suggested Readings

There are many excellent textbooks on money, banking, and other financial institutions. In general these texts discuss banking and financial intermediation in a macroeconomic context and include the impact of monetary and fiscal policy on the banking system and on the level of income and employment. See, for instance:

Cooper, S. Kerry, and Donald R. Fraser. *The Financial Marketplace*, 4th ed. Reading, Mass.: Addison-Wesley Publishing Company, 1993.

Kaufman, George G. *The U.S. Financial System: Money, Markets & Institutions*, 4th ed. Englewood Cliffs, N.J.: Prentice-Hall, 1988.

Kidwell, David S., and Richard L. Peterson. *Financial Institutions, Markets, and Money.* 4th ed. Hinsdale, Ill.: The Dryden Press, 1990.

Meyer, Paul A. *Money, Financial Institutions and the Economy.* Homewood, Ill.: Richard D. Irwin, 1986.

Ritter, Lawrence S., and William L. Silber. *Principles of Money, Banking and Financial Markets.* 6th ed. New York: Basic Books, 1988.

For a general reference consult:

Gart, Alan. *Handbook of the Money and Capital Markets.* Westport, Ct.: Quorum Books, 1988.

Other readings concerning financial intermediaries, investment banking, and the flow of resources from savers to business include:

Dougall, Herbert E., and Jack E. Gaumnitz. *Capital Markets and Institutions.* 5th ed. Englewood Cliffs, N.J.: Prentice-Hall, 1986.
This concise text covers various financial intermediaries, their sources of funds, and portfolios.

For material on initial public offerings that includes the pricing (and *mis*pricing) of new shares, selecting new issues for possible investments, and the returns from investing in initial public offerings consult:

Aggarwal, Reena, and Pietra Rivoli. "Fads in the Initial Public Market?" *Financial Management* (Winter 1990): 45–52.
Chalk, A. J., and J. W. Peavey. "Initial Public Offerings: Daily Returns, Offering Types and the Price Effect." *Financial Analysts Journal* (September–October 1987): 65–69.
Hulbert, Mark, "Getting Taken." *Forbes* (June 24, 1991): 216–220.
Miller, Robert E., and Frank K. Reilly. "An Examination of Mispricing, Returns, and Uncertainty for Initial Public Offerings." *Financial Management* (Summer 1987): 33–38.
Pare, Terrence P. "Picking the Stars of Tomorrow From Today's New Stocks." *Fortune* (November 4, 1991): 27–32.
Ritter, Jay R. "The Long-Run Performance of Initial Public Offerings." *Journal of Finance* (March 1991): 3–27.

3

Security Markets

On January 4, 1993, 3,357,000 shares of IBM traded on the New York Stock Exchange. In all 199,680,000 shares of stock traded that day on the New York Stock Exchange. Not one penny of the proceeds of those sales went to the firms whose stocks were exchanged. Instead all of these transactions were among investors. Obviously, many individuals were altering their portfolios either through buying or selling these existing securities.

This buying and selling of securities has a certain mystique or fascination for both the novice and the seasoned investor. Investors may be drawn to securities by the jargon used in the stock market or the excitement generated by trading securities. Perhaps the investor's fascination is the result of the fact that many dollars can be earned or lost through investments in stocks and bonds. For whatever reason, investors who are drawn to Wall Street must understand both how security markets work and the mechanics of buying and selling securities.

It is the purpose of this chapter to explain the machinations of the market and the mechanics of buying and selling securities. The first section discusses security dealers and the role of security exchanges. The bulk of the chapter describes how the individual buys securities. The role of the broker, the types of orders and accounts, the delivery of the securities, and the brokerage cost of buying and selling are explained. The chapter ends with a brief discussion of the regulation of the securities industry and the Securities Investor Protection Corporation (SIPC), which insures investors against losses incurred from the failure of a brokerage firm.

✦ ✦ ✦

Market Makers

Securities are bought and sold every day by investors who never meet each other. The market impersonally transfers securities from individuals who are selling to those who are buying. This transfer may occur on an **organized exchange,** such as the New York Stock Exchange, or on an unorganized, informal market that is called the **over-the-counter (OTC) market.** In either case there exist professional

LEARNING OBJECTIVES

After completing this chapter you should be able to

1. Explain the role of market makers, and distinguish between security exchanges and over-the-counter markets.
2. List the services provided by brokers and brokerage firms.
3. Differentiate between the types of security orders, and identify the costs of investing in securities.
4. Contrast cash and margin accounts.
5. Contrast long and short positions and explain the source of profit from each.
6. Define American depository receipts (ADRs) and explain their advantages.
7. State the purpose of the Securities and Exchange Commission (SEC) and the Securities Investor Protection Corporation (SIPC) and the role of regulation in security markets.

organized exchange
A formal market for buying and selling securities or commodities.

over-the-counter (OTC) market
The informal secondary market for unlisted securities.

43

specialist

A market maker on the New York Stock Exchange who maintains an orderly market in the security.

dealers

Over-the-counter market makers who buy and sell securities for their own accounts.

round lot

The general unit of trading in a security, such as 100 shares.

odd lot

A unit of trading, such as 22 shares, that is smaller than the general unit of sale.

bid and ask

Prices at which a security dealer offers to buy and sell stock.

security dealers who make markets in securities and facilitate their transfer from sellers to buyers. Market makers for securities that are listed on the New York and American stock exchanges are called **specialists.** Market makers for over-the-counter securities are called **dealers.** These market makers offer to buy the securities from any seller to sell the securities to any purchaser.[1]

Transactions are made in either round lots or odd lots. A **round lot** is the basic unit for trading. For stock, it is usually 100 shares. Smaller transactions (for example, 37 shares), are called **odd lots.** The round lot does not have to be 100 shares for all stocks. For example, for very cheap stocks (sometimes called cats and dogs), a round lot may be 500 or 1,000 shares. For bonds, a round lot may be five $1,000 bonds (i.e., $5,000) or bonds totaling $10,000 or even $100,000 in face value. Odd lots are less profitable for brokerage firms and market makers because the paperwork and the time involved in executing a trade are the same for 10 shares or 100 shares, but the dollar volume of the trade is smaller for the odd lot. Thus, the price per share that the buyer is charged for an odd lot is usually higher than the price per share for a round lot. This additional fee may be hidden in a higher asking price for the security rather than being explicitly stated.[2]

Both specialists and dealers quote prices on a **bid and ask** basis; they buy at one price and sell at the other. For example, a market maker may be willing to purchase a specific stock for $20 per share and sell it for $21. The security is then quoted "20–21," which are the bid and ask prices. Selected quotes are illustrated in Exhibit 3.1. As can be seen in the exhibit, the market makers in DeBeers are willing to purchase (bid for) the stock at $14¼ and to sell (ask) the stock for $14⅜.

The Spread

spread

The difference between the bid and the ask prices.

The difference between the bid and ask is the **spread** (i.e., the $0.125 difference between $14¼ and 14⅜ for DeBeers). Although the value of the security is the bid price, the investor pays the asking price. The spread, like brokerage commissions, is part of the cost of investing. These two costs should not be confused. The spread is one source of compensation for maintaining a market in the security. The broker's commission is compensation for executing the investor's purchase or sale order.

The spread may be quite large (at least as a percentage of the bid price). In Exhibit 3.1, for example, the spread is 2 points for American Filtrona stock, which is 7.8 percent of the bid price. The spread for DeBeers Consolidated Mines is only ⅛ point, which is 0.9 percent of the bid. Since the spread is larger, the investor's effective cost of buying and selling the stock of American Filtrona is greater than the cost of buying and selling the stock of DeBeers.

The size of the differential between the bid and the ask is affected by various factors. If there are several market makers in a particular security, the spread tends to be smaller because of competition. The difference is also affected by the volume

---

[1] As of December 31, 1991, 416 individuals operated as specialists. New York Stock Exchange, *1991 Annual Report*, 2.

[2] There is no odd lot differential for a market order on the New York Stock Exchange. For a limit order, the odd lot fee is ⅛ of a point (i.e., $0.125 per share) for stock prices up to $50 and ¼ of a point for prices above $50. Thus if a stock cost $25, the price of an odd lot would be $25.125 to buy and $24.875 to sell through a limit order. (See "Types of Orders" later in this chapter for an explanation of market and limit orders.)

Exhibit 3.1 ◆ SELECTED BID AND ASK QUOTES AND NUMBER OF SHARES
OUTSTANDING AS OF JANUARY 15, 1993

| | Price | | Number of Shares |
Company	Bid	Ask	Outstanding
American Filtrona	$25½	$27½	3,717,000
General Cinema	37⅜	37⅝	75,106,000
DeBeers Consolidated Mines	14¼	14⅜	380,054,000
American Telephone & Telegraph	53¼	53⅜	1,306,187,000

Source: Courtesy of Legg Mason.

of transactions in the security and the number of shares that the firm has outstanding. If the volume of transactions or the number of outstanding securities is large, then the spread between the bid and the ask is small. DeBeers has over 380 million shares outstanding, and thousands of shares are traded daily. When the number of outstanding securities is small (i.e., it is a **thin issue**), the spread is usually larger. In the case of American Filtrona in Exhibit 3.1, the firm has 3.7 million shares outstanding, and only a few hundred may be traded on a given day.

thin issue
An issue of securities with either a small number of securities in the hands of the general public or a small volume of transactions.

The spread is one source of profit for dealers as they turn over the securities in their portfolios. The market makers also earn income when they receive dividends and interest from the securities they own. Another source of profit is an increase in security prices, for the value of the dealers' portfolios rises. These profits are a necessary element of security markets because they induce the market makers to serve the crucial functions of buying and selling securities and of bearing the risk of loss from unforeseen price declines. These market makers guarantee to buy and sell at the prices they announce. Thus, an investor knows what the securities are worth at any given time and is assured that there is a place to sell current security holdings or to purchase additional securities. For this service, the market makers must be compensated, and this compensation is generated through the spread between the bid and ask prices, dividends and interest earned, and profits on the inventory of securities should their prices rise. (Of course, the market makers must bear any losses on securities that they hold when prices fall.)

Determination of Prices

Although the bid and ask prices are quoted by market makers, the security prices are set by the demand from all buyers and the supply from all sellers of securities. Market makers try to quote an **equilibrium price** that equates the supply with the demand. If market makers bid too low a price, too few shares will be offered to satisfy the demand. If they ask too high a price, too few shares will be purchased, which will result in a glut, or excess shares, in their portfolios.

equilibrium price
A price that equates supply and demand.

Could market makers set a security's equilibrium price? For large companies the answer is probably no. If the market makers tried to establish a price above the equilibrium price that is set by supply and demand, they would have to absorb all of the excess supply of securities that would be offered at the artificially higher price. Conversely, if the market makers attempted to establish a price below the equilibrium price, they would have to sell a sufficient number of securities to meet the excess demand that would exist at the artificially lower price. The buying of securities requires the delivery of the securities sold. Market makers do not have an infinite well of money with which to purchase the securities nor an unlimited supply of securities to deliver. They may increase or decrease their inventory, but they cannot support the price indefinitely by buying securities, nor can they prevent a price increase by selling them.

Although market makers cannot set the market price, they perform an extremely important role: They maintain an orderly market in securities so that buyers and sellers will have an established market in which to trade securities. To establish this orderly market, the market makers offer to buy and sell at the quoted bid and ask prices but guarantee only one round lot transaction at these prices. If a market maker sets too low a price for a certain stock, a large quantity will be demanded by investors. The market maker is required to sell only one round lot at this price and then may increase the bid and ask prices. The increase in the price of the stock will (1) induce some holders of the stock to sell their shares and (2) induce some investors who wanted to purchase the stock to drop out of the market.

If the market maker sets too high a price for the stock, a large quantity of shares will be offered for sale, but these shares will remain unsold. If the market maker is unable to or does not want to absorb all of these shares, the security dealer may purchase a round lot and then lower the bid and ask prices. The decline in the price of the stock will (1) induce some potential sellers to hold their stock and (2) induce some investors to enter the market by purchasing the shares, thereby reducing any of the market maker's surplus inventory.

SECURITY EXCHANGES

listed security
A security that is traded on an organized exchange.

When a company first sells its securities to the public, the securities are traded in the over-the-counter market. However, the firm may subsequently desire to have its securities **listed** on one of the major organized exchanges—the New York Stock Exchange (NYSE, or "the big board") or the American Stock Exchange (AMEX, or "the curb"). (Although the inclusion of the word *stock* in the names implies a market that deals solely in stock, some bond issues and options are also traded on these exchanges.) The listing of a firm's securities on a major exchange has an element of prestige, for it indicates that the company has grown above local importance and has attained a specified level of size and profitability.[3] Listing may also facilitate selling securities in the future, for investors may be more willing to purchase the securities of companies whose stocks or bonds are publicly traded on an exchange.

In addition to these national exchanges, there are several regional stock exchanges, including the Philadelphia Exchange, the Midwest Exchange, and the Pacific Exchange. These regional exchanges list companies of particular interest to their geographic areas. For example, Alaska Gold is primarily a regional company

---

[3] Many corporations (e.g., Microsoft, MCI Communications, and U.S. Healthcare) choose *not* to be listed.

Exhibit 3.2 ✦ LISTING REQUIREMENTS

Requirements	New York Stock Exchange	American Stock Exchange
Number of shares held by the general public	1,100,000	400,000
Number of stockholders owning 100 or more shares	2,000	1,200, of which 500 must own 100 to 500 shares
Pretax income for latest fiscal year	$2,500,000	$750,000
Pretax income for preceding two years	$2,000,000	
Minimum aggregate value of shares publicly held	$18,000,000	$300,000
Tangible assets	$16,000,000	$4,000,000

and is listed on the Pacific Exchange. Other firms in the region, like Georgia Pacific, are listed on several exchanges. This company has a national market for its stock but is also of particular interest to investors living on the West Coast, since it has large timber holdings there. Its securities are actively traded on both the New York and the Pacific stock exchanges.

The NYSE is the largest exchange and lists the securities of companies of national interest. The AMEX is smaller than the NYSE but, unlike the regional exchanges, lists smaller firms with national followings. Many of the firms listed on the NYSE were originally listed on the AMEX. After achieving larger earnings and size, these firms transferred their listing from the AMEX to the NYSE.

The listing requirements for both exchanges are presented in Exhibit 3.2. As may be seen in the exhibit, the criteria that must be fulfilled in order to be listed are essentially the same for both exchanges, but the required sums are larger for the NYSE. In addition to the conditions stated in Exhibit 3.2, listing requires the firm to conform to certain procedures, including publishing quarterly reports, soliciting proxies, and publicly announcing any developments that may affect the value of the securities.

Once the securities are accepted for trading on an exchange, the firm must continue to meet the listing requirements. The exchange may delist the securities if the firm is unable to continue to meet the criteria for listing. Such delistings do occur, but over a period of years the number of listed securities has increased. Whereas 1,253 stocks were traded on the NYSE in 1965, the number had grown to 2,284 issues of 1,774 companies in 1990.[4]

---

[4] New York Stock Exchange, *1991 Fact Book,* 8.

Reporting of Transactions

Daily transactions on the listed exchanges are reported by the financial press (e.g., *The Wall Street Journal*). Weekly summaries are also reported in several publications (e.g., *The New York Times* and *Barron's*). Although there is variation in this reporting, the typical entry appears as follows:

| 52 Weeks | | Stock | | Yield | | Sales | | | | Net |
High	Low	(Company)	Dividend	(%)	P/E	in 100s	High	Low	Close	Change
100⅜	45⅞	IBM	2.16	4.2	30	20046	53⅛	50½	51⅝	−1⅞

P/E ratio
The ratio of the price of a stock to the firm's per-share earnings.

"High" and "low" at the far left indicate the high and low prices (100⅜ and 45⅞, respectively, for IBM) of the security during the preceding fifty-two weeks. Then the name of the company is given, usually in an abbreviated form, followed by the amount of the dividend ($2.16), which is generally the annual rate that the firm is paying. If the amount is not the annual rate, a symbol is placed after the dividend that refers the reader to a key explaining the particular exceptions. After the dividend the current yield is given, which is the amount of the dividend divided by the price of the stock (4.2 percent for IBM). This dividend yield is a measure of the flow of income that is produced by an investment in that particular stock. (Dividends are discussed in more detail in Chapter 10.) The **P/E ratio** (30 for IBM) is the ratio of the price of the stock to the earnings per share of the firm. The P/E ratio may be interpreted as a measure of what the market is willing to pay for the stock.

The last five entries of the typical listing pertain to the trading in that particular security on the preceding trading day. The first is the volume of transactions, which, for stocks, is expressed in hundreds of shares (i.e., 20046 means 2,004,600). (For bonds the volume is expressed in terms of the face value in denominations of $1,000 of the bonds traded; for example, 7 means that the face value of the bonds that changed hands was $7,000.) After volume of trading are the price statistics, which include the high, low, and closing prices. If the stock is traded for a new high for the preceding 12 months, a "u" is placed next to the value. If it is traded at a new low, a "d" is placed next to the price. The last entry is the change in price from the closing price of the previous day of trading.

Many daily newspapers report trading in stocks listed on the New York Stock Exchange in the general form illustrated above. *The Wall Street Journal* provides this data and some additional information that the investor may find useful. Exhibit 3.3 is an excerpt from the stock pages for trading on January 4, 1993. The reporting for each common stock includes the ticker symbol, the hi, low, and closing prices, the dividend and dividend yield, the P/E ratio, and volume of transactions.

In addition to this information, the reporting indicates significant changes in prices and volume. If the price of the stock changed by more than 5 percent from the previous day, the entries are in boldface (e.g., Ahmanson). If there is a large change in the volume of transactions from the average daily trading, the entries are underlined (e.g., Alcan). If the stock is a new issue within the past 52 weeks, the symbol *n* is given at the far left (e.g., Acordia). If the stock has been split during the last 12 months, that is indicated by the symbol *s* (e.g., Abbot Labs). If the stock traded at a new 52-week high or low price, an arrow indicates the direction of this trade (e.g., the up arrow for Acme Electric and the down arrow for BancoCentral).

Exhibit 3.3 ✦ Reporting of Security Transactions

NEW YORK STOCK EXCHANGE COMPOSITE TRANSACTIONS

Quotations as of 5 p.m. Eastern Time
Monday, January 4, 1993

Stock split within last 52 weeks

New 52-week high price

New issue within last 52 weeks

Price declined by more than 5 percent

New 52-week low price

Large change in volume of trading

	52 Weeks Hi	Lo	Stock	Sym	Div	Yld %	PE	Vol 100s	Hi	Lo	Close	Net Chg
			-A-A-A-									
	15⅞	10¾	AAR	AIR	48	4.0	22	497	12	11¾	11⅞	+ ⅛
	11⅝	10⅛	ACM Gvt Fd	ACG	.96e	8.8	...	791	11	10¾	10⅞	– ⅛
	10⅜	9	ACM OppFd	AOF	.80	8.6	...	119	9½	9¼	9¼	– ⅛
	11⅞	9⅞	ACM SecFd	GSF		...	...	943	10¾	10½	10⅝	...
	9¾	8⅜	ACM SpctmFd	SI		...	...	313	9	8¾	9	...
	10⅝	8⅝	ACM MgdIncFd	AMF	1.15e	11.4	...	236	10⅛	10	10⅛	...
	12⅞	8⅝	ACM MgdMultFd	MMF	.99e	11.3	...	151	8⅞	8⅝	8¾	...
	9½	6	ADT	ADT	a	...	...	853	7¾	7⅝	7⅝	– ⅛
▲	34⅞	24	AFLAC	AFL	.44	1.2	16	2007	35¾	34¾	35¼	+ ¾
	28½	18	AL Labs A	BMD	.18	.7	63	622	26⅛	25½	25¾	– ⅛
	45¼	30	Ambac	ABK	.44f	1.0	12	821	43	42	42⅝	– ⅜
	2⅛	3/16	AM Int	AM		...	dd	478	11/32	5/16	11/32	+ 1/16
	8¾	11/16	AM Int pf		1.50j	...	...	92	1⅛	1	1⅛	+ ¼
	80¼	54⅜	AMR	AMR		...	dd	6197	67¼	66⅜	67	– ½
	28	25	ANR pf		2.68	9.9	...	5	27	27	27	+ ⅜
	2⅜	**1⅜**	**ARX**	**ARX**		**...**	**12**	**40**	**1⅞**	**1¾**	**1¾**	**– ¼**
	53½	30½	ASA	ASA	2.00	6.5	...	547	31⅜	31	31	– ⅞
s	34⅛	26⅛	AbbotLab	ABT	.60	2.0	21	15123	30⅞	30⅛	30⅜	...
n	**9⅞**	**4⅜**	**Abex**	**ABE**		**...**	**...**	**202**	**5½**	**5⅜**	**5⅜**	**– ⅜**
	13⅞	10⅜	Abitibi g	ABY	.50	...	...	7	11¼	11¼	11¼	– ⅛
s	15	6	AcceptIns	AIF		...	dd	35	9½	9½	9½	– ⅛
n	2¾	2⅛	AcceptIns rt			...	...	52	2¾	2¾	2¾	...
	11¾	4¾	AcmeCleve	AMT	.40	4.9	15	55	8¼	8⅛	8⅛	– ⅛
▲	7⅛	3¾	AcmeElec	ACE	.32j	...	...	232	7¼	6⅞	6⅞	– ¼
n	22¼	15⅛	Acordia	ACO	.09p	.4	...	57	21½	21⅛	21⅛	– ⅜
	33⅜	14⅜	Acuson	ACN		...	12	1855	16	15½	15½	– ¼
	21⅛	18⅛	AdamsExp	ADX	1.62e	8.1	...	263	20	19¾	20	...
n	2½	15/16	ADT wt			...	...	48	1⅛	1	1⅛	...
	21½	7⅜	AdvMicro	AMD		...	6	6227	18⅛	17⅝	17⅝	– ½
	49⅛	29½	AdvMicro pf		3.00	6.5	...	95	46¾	46¼	46½	– ½
	9⅛	4⅞	Advest	ADV	.16j	...	...	210	5¾	5½	5¾	– ⅛
s	42¾	33	Aegon	AEG	.67e	1.6	...	21	41⅝	41½	41½	– ⅛
	48⅞	37¼	AetnaLife	AET	2.76	5.9	10	1811	46⅞	46½	46⅝	+ ⅛
	12⅞	8⅜	AffilPub	AFP	.24	2.0	dd	800	12⅛	11¾	12	...
	25¾	20⅝	AgriMinl	AMC	2.42	11.3	...	117	21¾	21½	21½	+ ⅛
	19½	**13**	**Ahmanson**	**AHM**	**.88**	**4.8**	**11**	**7111**	**18⅞**	**18**	**18¼**	**–1**
	27⅝	25⅛	Ahmanson pf		2.40	9.2	...	68	26	25⅞	26	+ ⅛
	22½	4	Aileen	AEE		...	39	485	7⅝	7⅜	7½	+ ¼
s	49½	36⅜	AirProduct	APD	.86	1.8	19	3421	47½	46¼	47⅜	+ ⅝
	29¾	12½	AirbornFrght	ABF	.30	1.6	cc	1190	18⅞	18⅜	18½	– ⅛
s	23	11⅛	Airgas	ARG		...	33	217	21⅜	20⅞	21⅜	– ⅜
	12⅜	8⅛	Airlease	FLY	1.60	15.2	8	51	10⅞	10⅜	10½	– ⅛
n	25¾	23⅝	AlaPwr pfA		1.90	7.6	...	66	25	24⅞	24⅞	– ⅛
	11¼	10½	AlaPwr pfS		.87	8.0	...	7	11	10⅞	10⅞	– ⅛
	23⅞	14¾	AlaskaAir	ALK	.20	1.2	dd	946	17⅛	16¾	16¾	+ ¼
	21¼	11¼	AlbanyInt	AIN	.35	2.3	64	399	15½	15¼	15¼	– ⅜
	32	21¼	AlbertoCl	ACV	.24a	.9	19	251	25⅞	25½	25¾	+ ¼
	25¾	19⅝	AlbertoCl A	ACVA	.24a	1.0	18	160	23⅞	23⅝	23⅞	...
	53⅜	36¾	Albertsons	ABS	.64	1.3	23	1656	50½	49½	50¼	– ¼
	22¾	15¼	Alcan	AL	.30	1.7	dd	9771	18⅛	17½	18⅛	+ ½
n	27⅛	22⅝	AlcatelAsthom	ALA	.62e	2.5	...	823	24⅝	24½	24½	– ¼
	42⅝	33⅛	AlcoStd	ASN	.96f	2.6	18	1073	36⅝	35¾	36⅝	+ ¼
	27¾	14½	AlexBrown	AB	.50f	2.5	6	321	20⅜	20	20⅛	+ ⅛
	27⅝	18	Alex&Alex	AAL	1.00	3.8	94	1102	26⅝	26¼	26⅜	– ⅛
	50⅝	**8⅜**	**vjAlexanders**	**ALX**		**...**	**...**	**260**	**47⅝**	**44⅝**	**44⅝**	**–3⅛**
	135	105⅝	AlleghanyCp	Y	2.42t	1.8	11	32	133¾	132⅞	133¾	...
	36⅝	27½	AllegLud	ALS	.88	2.5	21	423	35⅛	35	35⅛	+ ⅜
	48¾	41½	AllegPwr	AYP	3.24f	6.8	13	990	47⅝	47¼	47⅝	– ¼
	30	18⅞	AllenGp	ALN	.24f	.9	16	665	27	26¾	26⅞	– ⅛

NYSE EXTENDED TRADING

January 4, 1993

	Total Volume	Market Value
First crossing session	45,600	b-$1,305,112
Second session (baskets)	1,451,300	$57,310,301

MOST ACTIVE ISSUES

(First session)

Issue	Sym.	a-Volume 100s	NYSE Close	Comp. Close
LatinAmDiscv	LDF	250	14	14
FundAmEnt	FFC	84	72	72
BunkerHill	BHL	43	15⅜	15⅜
NoStPwr	NSP	17	43⅜	43⅜
VanKampMun	VMT	17	11⅞	11⅞
CPCInt	CPC	15	50	49⅞
CocaCola	KO	9	42	42
Mobil Cp	MOB	3	63¼	63¼
ACM Gvt Fd	ACG	3	10⅞	10⅞
JohnsJohns	JNJ	2	49½	49½

a-From 4:15 p.m. to 5:00 p.m. Eastern time, NYSE only. b-WSJ calculation, estimate.

	52 Weeks Hi	Lo	Stock	Sym	Div	Yld %	PE	Vol 100s	Hi	Lo	Close	Net Chg
	18	10	BJ Svc	BJS		...	dd	197	16⅛	15¾	15¾	– ½
	12⅛	**6½**	**BMC**	**BMC**		**...**	**9**	**310**	**10⅝**	**9⅞**	**10**	**–1**
	32¼	27⅞	BP Prudhoe	BPT	3.03e	9.7	...	230	31⅛	31	31⅛	...
	32⅝	28⅜	BRE Prop	BRE	2.40	7.4	13	37	32½	32⅛	32½	+ ⅛
	4	**1⅞**	**BRT RltyTr**	**BRT**		**...**	**dd**	**227**	**3¾**	**3½**	**3⅝**	**+ ¼**
	8¼	5⅝	Bairnco	BZ	.20	2.9	13	202	7⅛	6¾	7	+ ¼
	25⅜	15⅞	BakrHughs	BHI	.46	2.4	...	3747	19⅞	19⅜	19½	– ⅛
	19⅛	16⅝	BakrFentrs	BKF	1.81e	10.4	...	233	17⅜	17	17⅜	+ ⅜
s	**22½**	**14¾**	**BaldorElec**	**BEZ**	**.38**	**1.8**	**23**	**133**	**21¾**	**20⅞**	**20⅞**	**–1⅛**
	39½	28	Ball Cp	BLL	1.24	3.5	15	230	35¾	34⅞	35	– ⅜
	8¼	4⅛	BallyMfg	BLY	.30j	...	...	4032	8	7¼	7½	– ⅜
	9⅜	4½	BaltimrBcp	BBB		...	dd	627	7⅛	6⅞	7	+ ⅛
s	24⅜	19¾	BaltimrGE	BGE	1.44	6.2	17	2677	23⅜	23⅛	23⅛	– ¼
s	53½	42⅛	BancOne	ONE	1.28	2.4	16	5747	53½	53¼	53⅜	+ ¼
	15	2¾	BancFla	BFL	.33j	...	...	431	12⅝	12	12⅛	+ ⅛
	30	18⅞	BancoBilV	BBV	1.26e	6.1	...	71	20⅝	20⅜	20⅝	– ⅛
	28½	24⅜	BancoBilV pf		1.83e	7.0	...	241	26¼	26	26⅛	– ⅛
n	25	24½	BancoBilV pfB			...	...	500	24⅞	24¾	24¾	...
▼	20⅛	12⅝	BancoCentrl	BCM	.94e	7.4	...	99	12¾	12½	12⅝	– ⅝
n	17⅛	12⅝	BanComercial	BPC		...	...	200	14⅜	14¼	14¼	– ⅛
	49½	33	BancoSantdr	STD	2.32e	6.1	...	42	38	37½	37¾	– ⅝
n	30¾	20⅛	BancoLatin	BLX		...	...	148	29⅞	29¼	29¼	– ¾
	52	40¼	BcpHawii	BOH	1.29	2.9	10	1024	44	43⅞	44	...
	3¾	⅜	BancTexas	BTX		...	cc	177	1⅞	1¾	1⅞	+ ⅛
s	73¼	56	Bandag	BDG	.65f	1.1	19	504	59¼	58	58⅞	+ ¾
n	71	55	Bandag A		.65f	1.2	...	105	56½	55⅞	56⅛	– ⅛
	20¼	16¾	BangorHyd	BGR	1.32	6.8	12	98	19⅞	19½	19½	– ½
	26⅜	11¼	BankBost	BKB	.10e	.4	9	3563	26	25⅛	25⅜	– ⅛
	44⅜	31	BankBost pfA		3.13e	7.6	...	12	41⅜	41⅛	41⅛	– ½
n	25½	23⅞	BankBost pfE			...	...	123	24⅝	24¼	24⅝	+ ⅜
	54⅝	30	BankNY	BK	1.52	2.8	13	2949	53¾	53⅛	53⅜	– ½
	48	40	BankNY pfA		3.28e	7.3	...	17	45⅛	44¾	45⅛	– ⅛
n	25⅞	25¼	BankNY pfB			...	...	71	25⅞	25¾	25¾	– ⅛
	49¾	35⅜	BankAmer	BAC	1.30	2.8	11	5173	46⅝	46¼	46½	...

Source: The Wall Street Journal, January 5, 1993, p. C3.

THE P/E RATIO

One term often used by investors is the P/E ratio, which is the ratio of a stock's price to the firm's per-share earnings. By expressing each firm's stock price relative to its earnings, this ratio facilitates the comparison of firms. The P/E ratio indicates the amount that the market is willing to pay for each dollar of earnings. A P/E of 12 means that the stock is selling for 12 times the firm's earnings and that the market believes that $1 of earnings is currently worth $12. There is also the im-plication that if earnings increase by $1, the price of the stock will rise by $12.

Firms in the same industry tend to have similar P/E ratios. This is illustrated in the accompanying exhibit, which gives the earnings, the price of the stock, and the P/E ratio for eight chemical companies. The average P/E ratio for the industry (i.e., 20.6) may be indicative of the appropriate P/E ratio for an individual firm's stock. If the company's ratio is higher than the industry's average, the stock may be overpriced. Conversely, if the P/E ratio is lower than the industry's average, it may indicate that the stock is undervalued.

Unfortunately, security analysis and selection are not that simple. If a firm has an excellent record of earnings growth and the security market anticipates that this growth will continue, the P/E ratio tends to be higher than the industry's average. This higher growth has value. These earnings may achieve a higher price, in which case the stock sells for a higher P/E ratio. If a firm is considered to be riskier than is typical of firms in its industry, the P/E ratio tends to be lower. The earnings of a firm involving greater risk are worth less. Thus, the stock's price and the P/E ratio are lower than the industry's average.

While the P/E ratio is frequently used, it does not tell the investor much about the firm. Of course, it does permit easy comparison of firms, but it considers only the earnings and the price of the stock. It tells nothing of how the earnings were achieved or why the market may view one firm's earnings as inferior or superior to the earnings of another firm.

Company	Per-Share Earnings for the Preceding Twelve Months	Price of the Stock	P/E Ratio
Allied-Signal	$4.00	$52	13.0
ARCO Chemical	1.89	44⅝	23.6
Dow Chemical	1.77	56⅛	31.7
DuPont	1.75	47⅛	26.9
Ethyl	1.86	27⅞	15.0
Monsanto	3.64	54⅞	15.1
Rohm and Haas	3.08	54¾	17.8
Union Carbide	0.60	13⅛	21.9

Source: Standard & Poor's *Stock Guide*, October 1992.

If the stock is trading exclusive of the dividend, which means that the owners of the stock on the previous day are entitled to receive the dividend, that is indicated by the symbol *x*.

Securities of companies with shares issued to the general public that are not traded on an exchange are traded over-the-counter. The prices of many of these securities are also reported daily in the financial sections of newspapers. In *The Wall Street Journal* these entries are subdivided into the NASDAQ over-the-counter national market, NASDAQ bid and asked quotations, and additional OTC quotes.

NASDAQ
National Association of Security Dealers Automatic Quotation system; quotation system for over-the-counter securities.

NASDAQ is an acronym for National Association of Security Dealers Automated Quotation system, which is the impressive system of communication for over-the-counter price quotations. All major unlisted stocks are included in this system. A broker may thereby readily obtain the bid and ask prices for many stocks and bonds by simply entering the firm's code into the NASDAQ system.

The reporting of the NASDAQ national market issues is virtually the same as the reporting of listed securities. The information given includes the 52-week high and low prices, the firm's dividend, the volume of transactions, the high, low, and closing prices, and the net change from the previous day. Some papers even include the yield and the P/E ratio.

In addition to the NASDAQ national market issues, *The Wall Street Journal* and other papers that give thorough coverage of security prices report smaller, less actively traded NASDAQ stocks, called NASDAQ Small Cap Issues. This reporting is limited to the company, the dividend (if any), the volume of transactions, the closing price, and the net change price from the previous day.

Some papers also report additional OTC quotes. These are generally limited to the bid and ask prices, and, in many cases, these quotations are limited to small firms traded in the geographical area served by the paper.

Composite Transactions

With the development of NASDAQ, the distinction between the various exchanges and the over-the-counter market is being erased. Since New York Stock Exchange securities trade on other exchanges, the actual reporting of New York Stock Exchange listings includes all the trades and is reported as the NYSE-Composite transactions. The bulk of the transactions in listed securities, however, still occurs on the NYSE.

In addition to listed securities and stocks traded over-the-counter through security dealers, there are also large block transactions executed through the exchange by brokers and not through specialists. This over-the-counter trading in listed securities is often referred to as the **third market.** Large institutional investors such as pension plans, mutual funds, or insurance companies may seek to purchase or sell large amounts of stocks in listed securities, such as the stock of IBM, which usually trades on the NYSE. Such large transactions (i.e., 10,000 shares or more) are called "blocks" of stocks, and the brokers who organize and execute the trades are referred to as "block positioners."

In the third market the financial institution works through a large brokerage firm that serves to complete the transaction. If the financial institution desires to buy a large position, the brokerage firm seeks potential sellers. If the institution desires to sell a large position, the brokerage firm seeks potential buyers. After the brokerage firm finds the required sellers (or buyers), the block of securities is traded off the floor of the exchange.

In the *fourth market,* the financial institutions do not use a brokerage firm but trade securities through a computerized system called "Instinet," which provides bid and ask price quotations and executes orders. This system is limited to those financial institutions that subscribe to the service. Transactions through Instinet are reported in the financial press through the composite transactions just as trades on the various exchanges are reported.

Block trades, the third market, and the fourth market offer financial institutions two advantages: lower commissions and quicker executions. Competition among brokerage firms for this business has reduced the commissions charged the financial institutions. In addition, the effort and time required to put together a block to purchase or to find buyers for a sale is significantly reduced through the development of block trading and over-the-counter trading of listed securities. The effect of this trading and the change in the regulatory environment for financial institutions

third market
Over-the-counter market for securities listed on an exchange.

is leading to a national market system for the execution of security orders, since these orders need not go through an exchange in a particular geographical area.[5]

THE MECHANICS OF INVESTING IN SECURITIES

broker
An agent who handles buy and sell orders for an investor.

Individual investors usually purchase securities through **brokers,** who buy and sell securities for their customers' accounts. Whereas some securities may be purchased directly from firms, the majority of purchases are made through brokerage firms, such as Merrill Lynch Pierce Fenner and Smith or A. G. Edwards. The firms have salespersons who service the individual's account. These brokers are the investor's agents, who execute the investor's buy and sell orders. In order to be permitted to buy and sell, these salespersons must pass a proficiency examination that is administered by the National Association of Security Dealers. Once the individual has passed the test, he or she is referred to as a **registered representative** and can buy or sell securities for customers.

registered representative
A person who buys and sells securities for customers; a broker.

Although registered representatives must pass this proficiency examination, the investor should not assume that the broker is an expert. There are many aspects of investing, and even an individual who spends a considerable portion of the working day servicing accounts cannot be an expert on all of the aspects of investing. Thus, many recommendations are based on research that is done by analysts employed by the brokerage firm rather than by individual salespersons.

The investor should also realize that brokers make their living through transactions (i.e., buying and selling for their customers' accounts). There are essentially two types of working relationships between the brokerage firm and the salesperson. In one case the firm pays a basic salary, but the salesperson must bring in a specified amount in commissions, which go to the firm. After the minimum amount of sales has been met, the registered representative's salary is increased in proportion to the amount of additional commissions generated. In the second type of relationship, the salesperson's income is entirely related to the commissions generated. In either case the investor should realize that the broker's livelihood depends on the sale of securities. Thus, the broker's advice on investing may be colored by the desire to secure commissions. However, the investor is ultimately responsible for the investment decisions. Although advice may be requested from the broker, and it is sometimes offered even though unsolicited, the investor must weigh the impact of a specific investment decision in terms of fulfilling his or her personal goals.

Selecting a brokerage firm can be a difficult task. Various firms offer different services; for example, some may specialize in bonds and others may deal solely in the securities of corporations located in a particular geographic region. The best source of information on stocks of local interest (e.g., local commercial banks) is often the small regional brokerage firm. Other brokerage firms offer a variety of services, including estate planning and life insurance, as well as the trading of stocks

---

[5] For a detailed discussion of the development of a national market system, see Morris Mendelson and Junius W. Peake, "The ABCs of Trading on a National Market System," *Financial Analysts Journal* (September–October 1979): 31–42.

and bonds. Still other firms offer virtually no services other than executing orders at discount (i.e., lower commissions). Each investor therefore needs to identify his or her personal investment goals and decide on the strategies to attain those goals in order to select the firm that is best suited to that individual's needs.

Choosing a registered representative is perhaps a more difficult task than selecting a brokerage firm. This individual will need to know specific information, including the investor's income, other assets and outstanding debt, and financial goals, in order to give the best service to the account. Since people are reluctant to discuss some of this information, trust and confidence in the registered representative are probably the most important considerations in selecting a broker. Good rapport between the broker and the investor is particularly important if the relationship is going to be mutually successful.

The Long and Short Positions

Essentially, an investor has only two courses of action, which involve opposite positions. They are frequently referred to as the bull and bear positions and are symbolized by a statue, which is located outside the NYSE, of a bull and a bear locked in mortal combat.[6]

If an investor expects a security's price to rise, the security may be purchased. The investor takes a **long position** in the security in anticipation of the price increase. The investor is **bullish** because he or she believes that the price will rise. The long position earns profits for the investor if the price rises after the security has been purchased. For example, if an investor buys 100 shares of AB&C for $55 (i.e., $5,500 plus brokerage fees) and the price rises to $60, the profit on the long position is $5 per share (i.e., $500 on 100 shares before commissions).

Opposite the long position is the **short position** (**bearish**), in which the investor anticipates that the security's price will fall. The investor may sell the security and hold cash or place the funds in interest-bearing short-term securities, such as treasury bills or a savings account. Some investors who are particularly bearish or who are willing to speculate on the decline in prices may even "sell short," which is a sale for future delivery. (The process of selling short is discussed later in this section.)

long position
Owning assets for their income and possible price appreciation.

bullish
Expecting that prices will rise.

short position
Owing assets for possible price deterioration; being short in a security or a commodity.

bearish
Expecting prices will decline.

Types of Orders

After an investor decides to purchase a security, a buy order is placed with the broker. The investor may ask the broker to buy the security at the best price currently available, which is the asking price set by the market maker. Such a request is a **market order.** The investor is not assured of receiving the security at the currently quoted price, since that price may change by the time the order is executed. However, the order is generally executed at or very near the asking price.

market order
An order to buy or sell at the current market price or quote.

---

[6]The derivations of "bull" and "bear" are lost in time. "Bearish" may originate from trading in pelts when bearskins were sold before the bears were caught. Bullbaiting and bearbaiting were also sports in the eighteenth century. See Steele Commager, "Watch Your Language," *Forbes* (October 27, 1980): 113–116.

POINTS OF INTEREST

STOP ORDERS AND LIMIT ORDERS

Investors often use the terms *limit order* and *stop order*, which are easily confused, since both specify prices at which stocks are to be bought or sold. A limit order instructs the broker to buy (or sell) a stock at the specified price or better. If a stock price is $10.50 and the investor enters a good-till-canceled limit order to buy at $10, the order will not be executed until the price declines to $10 (a $10 "ask" price in the case of an OTC stock) and may be executed for less than $10. Limit orders, however, are filled in order of receipt. Thus, it is possible for the stock's price to decline to $10 and the order not executed, if other investors have previously entered purchase orders at that price.*

A stop order also specifies a price. Once the price is reached, the order becomes a market order and is executed. Since the stop becomes a market order, the actual price at which it is executed may not necessarily be the specified price. For example, an investor buys a stock for $25 and enters a "stop–loss order" to sell at $20 to limit the possible loss on the stock. If the price declines to $20, the stop loss becomes a market order and the stock is sold. While the investor may anticipate receiving $20, there is no assurance that the stock will be sold at that price. If, for example, the firm reported lower earnings and immediately the price dropped from, say, $22 to $19, the stop–loss order may be executed at $19 instead of the specified $20.

If the individual is unwilling to bear the risk of not receiving $20, that investor could enter the sale order as a "stop–limit" order which combines a stop loss with a limit order. However, the stock would not be sold if the price declined through the specified price before the limit order was executed. If, after the earnings announcement, the price immediately declined from $22 to $19, the stop–limit order at $20 would not be executed unless the price subsequently rose to $20. With any limit order, there is no assurance that the order will be executed. In other words, investors cannot have their cake and eat it too. Once the specific price is reached, the stop order guarantees an execution but not the price, whereas a limit order guarantees the price but not an execution.

---

* Since individuals tend to think in terms of simpler numbers such as $10 or $10½, it may be a good strategy to place the purchase order at $10⅛, so that it will be executed prior to all orders placed at $10. The same applies to sell orders. A limit order to sell at $13 is executed once the stock price rises to $13 and prior sell orders are executed. A sell order at $12⅞ stands before all sell orders at $13.

---

limit order
An order placed with a broker to buy or sell at a specified price.

day order
An order placed with a broker that is canceled at the end of the day if it is not executed.

good-till-canceled order
An order placed with a broker that remains in effect until it is executed by the broker or canceled by the investor.

stop order
A purchase or sell order designed to limit an investor's loss or to assure a profit on a position in a security.

The investor may enter a **limit order** and specify a price below the current asking price and wait until the price declines to the specified level. Such an order may be placed for one day (i.e., a **day order**), or the order may remain in effect indefinitely (i.e., a **good-till-canceled order**). Such an order remains on the books of the broker until it is either executed or canceled. If the price of the security does not decline to the specified level, the purchase is never made. Such an order may then become a nuisance for the broker, who must periodically inform the customer that the order is still in effect.

After purchasing the security an investor may place a **stop order** to sell, which may be at a higher or lower price.[7] Once the stock reaches that price, the stop order becomes a market order. An investor who desires to limit potential losses may place a stop–loss order, which specifies the price below the cost of the security at which the broker is authorized to sell. For example, if an investor buys a stock for $50 a share, a stop–loss order at $45 limits the loss to $5 a share, plus the commission fees for the purchase and the sale. If the price of the stock should fall to $45, the stop–loss order becomes a market order, and the stock is sold.[8] Such a sale protects

---

[7] For a description of the 21 possible orders recognized by NYSE Rule 13, see Morris Mendelson and Junius W. Peake, "The ABCs of Trading on a National Market System," *Financial Analyst Journal* (September–October 1979): 39–40.

[8] Since the order is now a market order, there is no guarantee the investor will get $45. If there is an influx of sell orders, the sale may occur at less than $45.

Exhibit 3.4 ✦ CONFIRMATION STATEMENT FOR THE PURCHASE OF 100 SHARES OF CLEVEPAK CORPORATION

Scott & Stringfellow Inc.
909 EAST MAIN STREET
RICHMOND, VIRGINIA 23219
(804) 643-1811
SIPC

OFFICE ACCOUNT NO.	TYPE	A E	TRADE DATE	SETTLEMENT DATE	TRANS. NO.	CUSIP NO.	EXCH	ORIG
45078	1		4/12/9x	4/19/9x	112	1667661		

YOU BOUGHT	YOU SOLD	SECURITY DESCRIPTION
100		CLEVEPAK CORP

PRICE: 12 1/8

GROSS AMOUNT	1212 50
INTEREST	
COMMISSION	51 76
STATE TAX	
SERVICE CHG	
SEC/POST	
AMOUNT DUE	1264 26

SYMBOL: CLV

PLEASE RETURN THIS COPY WITH SECURITIES SOLD OR PAYMENT IN THE AMOUNT DUE BY SETTLEMENT DATE IN THE ENCLOSED ENVELOPE

IN ACCORDANCE WITH YOUR INSTRUCTIONS WE ARE PLEASED TO CONFIRM THE ABOVE TRANSACTION FOR YOUR ACCOUNT AND RISK SUBJECT TO TERMS LISTED ON REVERSE SIDE

BRANCH COPY

Source: Reprinted with permission from Scott & Stringfellow, Inc.

the investor from riding the price of the stock down to $40 or lower. Of course, if the stock rebounds from $45 to $50, the investor has sold out at the bottom price.

The investor may also place a stop–sell order above the purchase price. For example, the investor who purchases a stock at $50 may place a sell order at $60. Should the price of the stock reach $60, the order becomes a market order, and the stock is sold. Such an order limits the potential profit, for if the stock's price continues to rise, the investor who has already sold the stock does not continue to gain. However, the investor has protected the profit that resulted as the price increased from $50 to $60. In many cases the investor watches the stock's price rise, decides not to sell, and then watches the price subsequently decline. Stop–sell orders are designed to reduce the possibility of this occurring.

The placing of sell orders can be an important part of an investor's strategy. For example, in the previous case the investor who purchased a stock at $50 may place sell orders at $45 and $60. If the price of the stock subsequently rises, this investor may change these sell orders. For example, if the price rises to $56 per share, the investor may change the sell orders to $52 and $64. This will preserve the capital invested, for the price of the stock cannot fall below $52 without triggering the sell order, but the price can now rise above $60, which was the previous upper limit for the sell order. By continuously raising the prices for the sell orders as the stock's price rises, the investor can continue to profit from any price increase and at the same time protect the funds invested in the security against price declines.

Once the purchase has been made, the broker sends the investor a **confirmation statement,** an example of which is shown in Exhibit 3.4. This confirmation statement gives the number of shares and name of the security purchased (100 shares of Clevepak Corporation), the unit price ($12⅛), and the total amount that is due ($1,264.26). The amount that is due includes both the price of the securities and the transaction fees. The major transaction fee is the brokerage firm's

confirmation statement
A statement received from a brokerage firm detailing the sale or purchase of a security and specifying a settlement date.

settlement date

Date on which an investor must pay for a security purchase or receive payment for a security sale.

commission, but there may also be state transfer fees and other miscellaneous fees. The investor has five business days after the date of purchase (April 12, 199x) to pay the amount that is due; the date by which payment must be made (April 19, 199x) is called the **settlement date.**

Cash and Margin Accounts

margin

The amount that an investor must put down to buy securities on credit.

The investor must pay for the securities as they are purchased. This can be done either with cash or with a combination of cash and borrowed funds. The latter is called buying on **margin.** The investor then has either a cash account or a margin account. A cash account is what the name implies: The investor pays the entire cost of the securities (i.e., $1,264.26 in Exhibit 3.4) in cash.

When an investor uses margin, that is, purchases the security partially with cash and partially with credit supplied by the brokers, he or she makes an initial payment that is similar to a down payment on a house and borrows the remaining funds necessary to make the purchase. To open a margin account, the investor signs an agreement with the broker that gives use of the securities and some control over the account to the broker. The securities serve as collateral for the loan. Should the amount of collateral on the account fall below a specified level, the broker can require that the investor put more assets in the account. This is called a "margin call," and it may be satisfied by cash or additional securities. If the investor fails to meet a margin call, the broker will sell some securities in the account to raise the cash needed to protect the loan.

margin requirement

The minimum percentage, established by the Federal Reserve, that the investor must put up in cash to buy securities.

The **margin requirement** is the minimum percentage of the total price that the investor must pay and is set by the Federal Reserve Board. Individual brokers, however, may require more margin. The minimum payment required of the investor is the value of the securities times the margin requirement. Thus, if the margin requirement is 60 percent and the price plus the commission on 100 shares of Clevepak Corporation is $1,264.26, the investor must supply $758.56 in cash and borrow $505.70 from the broker, who in turn borrows the funds from a commercial bank. The investor pays interest to the broker on $505.70. The interest rate will depend on the rate that the broker must pay to the lending institution. The investor, of course, may avoid the interest charges by paying the entire $1,264.26 and not using borrowed funds.

Investors use margin to increase the potential return on the investment. When they expect the price of the security to rise, some investors pay for part of their purchases with borrowed funds. How the use of borrowed funds increases the potential return is illustrated in Exhibit 3.5. If the price of shares of Clevepak Corporation rises from 12⅛ to 15, the profit is $235.74 (excluding commissions on the sale). If the investor pays the entire $1,264.26, the percentage return is 18.7 percent. However, if the investor uses margin and pays for the stock with $758.56 in equity and $505.70 in borrowed funds, the investor's percentage return is increased (before the interest expense)[9] to 31.1 percent. In this case, the use of margin is favorable because it increases the investor's return on the invested funds.[10]

---

[9] For ease and clarity, dividends received and interest paid are omitted. For a complete illustration, see Problem 3 at the end of this chapter.

[10] Firms also use financial leverage when they finance their assets with debt instead of equity.

Exhibit 3.5 ✦ Potential Return Earned on Cash and Margin Purchases

	Cash Purchase	Margin Purchase
Purchase price	$1,264.26	$1,264.26 cash—$758.56 debt—$505.70
Sale price	$1,500.00	$1,500.00
Profit on sale	$ 235.74	$ 235.74
Percent earned	$\dfrac{\$235.74}{\$1,264.26} \times 100\% = 18.7\%$	$\dfrac{\$235.74}{\$758.56} \times 100\% = 31.1\%$

Of course, if *the price of the stock falls*, the reverse occurs—that is, *the percentage loss is greater*, as is illustrated in Exhibit 3.6. If the price falls to $10, the investor loses $264.26 before commissions on the sale. The percentage loss is 20.9 percent. However, if the investor uses margin, the percentage loss is increased to 34.8 percent. Since the investor has borrowed money and thus reduced the amount of funds that he or she has committed to the investment, the percentage loss is greater. The use of margin magnifies not only the potential gain but also the potential loss. Because the potential loss is increased, buying securities on credit increases the element of risk that must be borne by the investor.

Delivery of Securities

Once the shares have been purchased and paid for, the investor must decide whether to leave the securities with the broker or to take delivery. (In the case of a margin account, the investor *must* leave the securities with the broker.) If the shares are left with the broker, they will be registered in the broker's name (i.e., in the **street name**). The broker then becomes custodian of the securities, is responsible for them, and sends a monthly statement of the securities that are being held in the street name to the investor. The monthly statement also includes any transactions that have taken place during the month and any dividends and interest that

street name
The registration of securities in a broker's name instead of in the buyer's name.

Exhibit 3.6 ✦ Potential Loss from Cash and Margin Purchases

	Cash Purchase	Margin Purchase
Purchase price	$1,264.26	$1,264.26 cash—$758.56 debt—$505.70
Sale price	$1,000.00	$1,000.00
Loss on sale	$ 264.26	$ 264.26
Percent lost	$\dfrac{\$264.26}{\$1,264.26} \times 100\% = 20.9\%$	$\dfrac{\$264.26}{\$758.56} \times 100\% = 34.8\%$

have been received. The investor may either leave the dividends and interest payments to accumulate with the broker or receive payment from the broker.

An example of the general form used for monthly statements is given in Exhibit 3.7. The statement has three parts. The first gives summary data such as the beginning and closing cash balances and interest and dividends received to date. The summary of dividend and interest income received so far during the year may help the investor plan for income tax purposes. The statement may also include the value of securities for which prices are available. If, for example, a stock is inactively traded (e.g., CFW Communications), price data may not be available.

The second part of the statement gives the activity during the month. In this case, 100 shares of Chesapeake Corp. were purchased and 58 shares of IBM were sold. The investor deposited 220 shares on Conquest Exploration in the account, and no securities were delivered. Dividends were received from three companies, and the NJ Housing Authority bond paid $150 in interest. Also during the month, the investor deposited $2,000 in the account but later withdrew $6,070.10.

The last part of the statement enumerates the various securities (i.e., positions) held in street name by the brokerage firm for the investor. This information may include the number of shares or principal amount of debt, the ticker symbol (if available), prices of the securities on the statement's closing day, and the value of each holding. In this case the investor owns stock in seven companies and $5,000 face amount of bonds.

The main advantage of leaving the securities with the broker is convenience. The investor does not have to worry about storing the securities and can readily sell them, since they are in the broker's possession. The accrued interest and dividends may be viewed as a kind of forced savings program, for they may be immediately reinvested before the investor has an opportunity to spend the money elsewhere. The monthly statements are a readily accessible source of information for tax purposes.

There are, however, several important disadvantages in leaving the securities in the broker's name. If the brokerage firm fails or becomes insolvent, the investor may encounter difficulty in transferring the securities into his or her name and even greater difficulty in collecting any accrued dividends and interest.[11] In addition, since the securities are registered in the brokerage firm's name, interim financial statements, annual reports, and other announcements that are sent by the firm to its stockholders are mailed to the brokerage firm and not to the investor. The brokerage firm should forward this material to the investor but may not, or the material may arrive late. To circumvent this problem, an investor may write to the firm and ask to be placed on its mailing list. The firm may choose not to do so, for it sends the material to the brokerage firm and may view the additional mailing as an unnecessary expense.

trader
An investor who frequently buys and sells.

Whether the investor ultimately decides to leave the securities with the broker or to take delivery depends on the individual. However, if the investor frequently buys and sells securities (i.e., is a **trader**), the securities ought to be left with the broker to facilitate the transactions. If the investor is satisfied with the services of the broker and is convinced that the firm is financially secure, leaving the securities registered in the street name may be justified for reasons of convenience.

---

[11] The Securities Investor Protection Corporation (SIPC) has reduced the investor's risk of loss from the failure of a brokerage firm. SIPC is discussed later in this chapter.

Exhibit 3.7 ✦ ADAPTED BROKERAGE FIRM MONTHLY STATEMENT

Statement of Security Account

Account #876 55352
SS# or ID #223 54 4321
Account Executive A. B. Broker, III

Statement Period	Financial Summary	
Beginning 06-29-XX	Opening Money Balance	$.00
Ending 07-30-XX	Closing Money Balance	$120.00
	Price Portfolio Balance	$54,075.88

Year-to-Date

Dividends	$1200.00
Interest	.00
Municipal Bond Interest	150.00

Activity for This Period

Date	Bought/ Received	Sold/ Delivered	Description	Price	Amount Charged	Amount Credited
06-30			CFW Communications	Div		100.00
07-01			GT&E	Div		60.00
07-01			NJ Housing Auth.	Int		150.00
07-03			Funds received			2000.00
07-04	100		Chesapeake Corp.	19	1950.00	
07-10		58	IBM	100		5710.10
07-13			Check balance		6070.10	
07-25	220		Conquest Exp.	Rec		
07-25			James River	Div		120.00

Positions

Long	Short		Ticker Symbol	Price	Value
200		CFW Communications	NA°	NA°	NA
250		Chesapeake Corp.	CSK	20	5000.00
220		Conquest Exp.	CQX	2	440.00
300		GT&E	GTE	58⅜	17512.50
400		James River	JR	27½	11000.00
259		Kerr-McGee Corp.	KMG	49⅛	12723.38
100		Salomon Incorp.	SB	24	2400.00
5000		NJ Housing Auth. 6.00% 07-01-99	NA†	100	5000.00

° The symbols and prices of inactively traded OTC stocks may not be reported.
† Ticker symbols do not apply to municipal bonds.

If the investor chooses to take delivery of the securities, that individual receives the stock certificates or bonds. Since the certificates may become negotiable, the investor may suffer a loss if they are stolen. Therefore, care should be taken to store them in a safe place (e.g., a lockbox or safe-deposit box in a bank). If the certificates are lost or destroyed, they can be replaced, but only at considerable expense in terms of money and time.

The Cost of Investing

Investing, like everything else, is not free. The individual must pay certain costs, the most obvious of which are **commission** fees. There may also be transfer fees, and some states tax the transfer of securities. These last expenses tend to be small, but they do add up as the dollar value or the number of trades increases.

commissions
Fees charged by brokers for executing orders.

Commission costs are not insignificant, and for small investors they may constitute a substantial portion of the total amount spent on the investment. Commission rates are supposed to be set by supply and demand, but in reality only large investors (e.g., financial institutions such as insurance companies or mutual funds) are able to negotiate commissions with brokerage firms. These institutions do such a large dollar volume that they are able to negotiate lower rates. For these institutions, the commission rates (as a percentage of the dollar amount of the transaction) may be quite small.

Individuals, however, do not have this influence and generally have to accept the rate that is offered by the brokerage firm. Although the fee schedule may not be made public by the brokerage firm, the registered representative will generally tell the investor what the fee will be before executing the transaction.

In general, commission rates are quoted in terms of round lots of 100 shares. Most firms also set a minimum commission fee (e.g., $50) that may cover all transactions involving $1,000 or less. Then, as the value of the 100 shares increases to greater than $1,000, the fee also increases. However, this commission fee as a percentage of the dollar value of the transaction will usually fall.

There are some brokerage firms that offer lower commission rates. However, these firms may not offer some of the services that are provided by the nondiscount houses. Research facilities and advisory services cost money and therefore may not be available through **discount brokers.** If the individual does not need these services, the discount brokers may be a means to reduce the cost of investing by decreasing the commission fees.[12]

discount broker
A broker who charges lower commissions on security purchases and sales.

The commissions for a purchase (or sale) of 100 shares and 300 shares charged by a discount and a full-service broker are presented in Exhibit 3.8. The fees of both brokers rise as the amount invested rises. For example, the commissions on a purchase of 300 shares at $20 ($6,000) is $82.00 at the discount broker, but the commission rises to $103.00 when the price of the stock rises to $30 ($9,000). The exhibit shows that the commissions as a percent of the amount invested decline as the cost of the investment rises. The commissions on 300 shares at $30 is only 1.14

---

[12] Full service brokers may offer discounts, but the investor must ask for them. Receiving the requested discount will depend on such factors as the volume of trades generated by the investor.

Exhibit 3.8 ◆ COMMISSIONS CHARGED BY DISCOUNT AND FULL-SERVICE BROKERS

Price of Stock	Discount Broker Commission	Commission as a Percent of Cost of Stock	Full-Service Broker Commission	Commission as a Percent of Cost of Stock
	(100 shares)		(100 shares)	
$10	$ 53.00	5.30%	$ 52.32	5.23%
20	61.00	3.05	75.09	3.75
30	69.00	2.30	89.45	2.98
40	77.00	1.93	99.00	2.48
50	85.00	1.70	99.00	1.96
75	92.50	1.23	99.00	1.32
100	115.00	1.15	99.00	0.99
	(300 shares)		(300 shares)	
$10	$ 69.00	2.30%	$119.15	3.97%
20	82.00	1.37	168.00	2.80
30	103.00	1.14	206.99	2.30
40	124.00	1.03	241.60	2.01
50	145.00	0.97	274.03	1.82
75	147.50	0.66	297.00	1.32
100	185.00	0.62	297.00	0.99

Source: Two anonymous brokerage firms.

percent of the purchase price, whereas the commission would be 1.37 percent on a purchase of 300 shares at $20.

The exhibit also illustrates the potential savings from using a discount broker. The difference on a purchase of 300 shares at $100 (an investment of $30,000) is $112. However, the difference in commission costs for small purchases is modest ($89.45 versus $69.00 for the purchase of 100 shares at $30). Investors with modest sums may find the services offered by the full service brokers to be worth the additional costs in commissions.

Whereas commissions and other fees are explicit costs, there is also an important implicit cost of investing. This cost is the spread between the bid and the ask price of the security. As was explained earlier in this chapter, the investor pays the ask price but receives only the bid price when the securities are sold. This spread should be viewed as a cost of investing. Thus, if an investor wants to buy 100 shares of a stock quoted 20–21, he or she will have to pay $2,100 plus commissions to buy stock that is currently worth (if it were to be sold) only $2,000. If the commission rate is 2.5 percent on purchases and sales, the cost of a round trip in the security (i.e., a purchase and a subsequent sale) is substantial, as is illustrated in Exhibit 3.9. First, the investor pays $61.80 to buy the stock, for a total cost of $2,161.80 ($2,100 + $61.80). If the stock is then sold, the investor will receive $1,939. Although the investor paid $2,161.80, only $1,939 will be received in the event that the stock must be liquidated at the bid price.

The cost of this purchase and the subsequent sale exceeded $220. This loss through the spread is regarded as a capital loss for income tax purposes. It is not

---

Exhibit 3.9 ✦ Effect of the Spread on the Cost of Investing

Purchase price $2,100.00	Discount brokerage commission $61.80	Total cost $2,161.80
Sale price $2,000.00	Commission $61.00	Total received $1,939.00

Net Loss
Total cost minus total received = net loss
$2,161.80 − $1,939.00 = $222.80

---

considered to be part of the actual cost of investing. However, the individual investor should view this spread as an implicit cost of investing and should consider its impact on the total cost. As the previous example illustrates, the investor loses the difference in value between the bid and ask prices (the spread) upon purchasing the security. Thus, the bid price of the security must rise sufficiently to cover both the commission fees and the spread before the investor realizes any capital appreciation.

The Short Sale

short sale

The sale of borrowed securities in anticipation of a price decline; a contract for future delivery.

How does an investor make money in the security markets? The obvious answer is to buy at low prices and to sell at high prices. For most people this implies that the investor first buys the security and then sells it at some later date. Can the investor sell the security first and buy it back later at a lower price? The answer is yes, for a **short sale** reverses the order. The investor sells the security first with the intention of purchasing it in the future at a lower price.

Since the sale precedes the purchase, the investor does not own the securities that are being sold short. Selling something that a person does not own may sound illegal, but there are many examples of such short selling in normal business relationships. A magazine publisher who sells a subscription, a professional such as a lawyer, engineer, or teacher who signs a contract for future services, and a manufacturer who signs a contract for future delivery are all making short sales.[13] If the cost of fulfilling the contract increases, the short seller loses. If the cost declines, the short seller profits. Selling securities short is essentially no different: It is a current sale with a contract for future delivery. If the securities are subsequently purchased at a lower price, the short seller will profit. However, if the cost of the securities rises in the future, the short seller will suffer a loss.

The mechanics of the short sale can be illustrated by a simple example employing the stock of XYZ, Inc. If the current price of the stock is $50 per share, the investor may buy 100 shares at $50 per share for a total cost of $5,000. Such a purchase represents taking a long position in the stock. If the price subsequently rises to $75 per share and the stock is sold, the investor will earn a profit of $2,500 ($7,500 − $5,000).

---

[13] See Mark Weaver, *The Technique of Short Selling* (Palisades Park, N.J.: Investors' Press, 1963), 2. When your school collected the semester's tuition, it established a short position. It contracted for the future delivery of educational services.

Figure 3.1 ✦ The Flow of Money and Certificates in a Short Sale

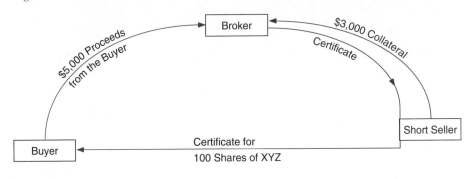

The short position reverses this procedure: The investor sells the stock first and buys it back at some time in the future. For example, an investor sells 100 shares of XYZ short at $50 ($5,000). Such a sale is made because the investor believes that the stock is *overpriced* and that the price of the stock will *fall*. In a short sale the investor does not own the 100 shares sold. The buyer of the shares, however, certainly expects delivery of the stock certificate. (Actually, the buyer does not know if the shares come from an investor who is selling short or an investor who is liquidating a position in the security.) The short seller has to *borrow* 100 shares to deliver to the buyer. The shares are usually borrowed from a broker, who in turn probably borrows them from clients who have left their securities with him or her. (Shares held in a margin account may be used by the broker, and one such possible use is to lend the shares to a short seller. However, shares left with the broker in a cash account cannot be lent to a short seller.)

Although the investor has sold the securities, the proceeds of the sale are not delivered to the seller but are held by the broker. These proceeds will be subsequently used to repurchase the shares. (In the jargon of security markets such repurchases are referred to as **covering the short sale.**) In addition, the short seller must deposit with the broker an amount of money equal to the margin requirement for the purchase of the stock. Thus, if the margin requirement is 60 percent, the short seller in the above illustration must deposit $3,000 ($5,000 × 0.6) with the broker. This money protects the broker (i.e., it is the short seller's collateral) and is returned to the short seller plus any profits or minus any losses when he or she buys the shares and returns them to the broker. This flow of certificates and money is illustrated in Figure 3.1. The broker receives the money from the short seller (the $3,000 collateral) and from the buyer of the stock (the $5,000 in proceeds from the sale). The investor who sells the stock short receives nothing, but the borrowed securities flow through this investor's account en route to the buyer. The buyer then receives the securities and remits the funds to pay for them.

If the price of a share declines to $40, the short seller can buy the stock for $4,000. This purchase is no different from any purchase made on an exchange or in the over-the-counter market. The stock is then returned to the broker, and the loan of the stock is repaid. The short seller will have made a profit of $1,000 because the shares were purchased for $4,000 and sold for $5,000. The investor's collateral is then returned by the broker plus the $1,000 profit. These events are illustrated in Figure 3.2. The 100 shares of XYZ stock are purchased for $4,000 by the short

covering the short sale
The purchase of securities or commodities to close a short position.

Figure 3.2 ✦ THE FLOW OF MONEY AND CERTIFICATES WHEN COVERING A PROFITABLE SHORT SALE

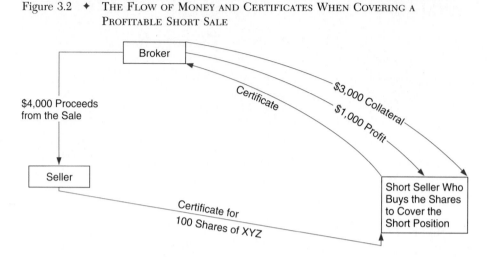

seller. When the certificate for the 100 shares is received, it is returned by the short seller to the broker (who, in turn, returns the shares to whomever they were borrowed from). The broker returns the investor's $3,000 that was put up for collateral. Since the investor uses only $4,000 of the $5,000 in proceeds from the short sale to purchase the stock, the broker sends the investor the remainder of the proceeds (the $1,000 profit).

If the price of the stock had risen to $60 per share and the short seller had purchased the shares and returned them to the broker, the short position would have resulted in a $1,000 loss. The proceeds from the short sale would have been insufficient to purchase the shares. One thousand dollars of the collateral would have had to be used in addition to the proceeds to buy the stock and cover the short position. The broker would owe the short seller only what was left of the collateral ($2,000) after the transactions had been completed.

Although the previous transactions may sound complicated, they really are not. All that has occurred is that an investor has bought and sold a security. Instead of the investor's first purchasing the security and then selling it, the investor initially sold the security and subsequently purchased the shares to cover the short position. Because the sale occurred first, there is additional bookkeeping to account for the borrowed securities, but the transaction itself is not complicated.

Unfortunately, there is a belief among many investors that short selling is gambling. They believe that if investors sell short and the price of the stock rises substantially, the losses could result in financial ruin. However, short sellers can protect themselves by placing stop–loss purchase orders to cover the short position if the stock's price rises to a particular level. Furthermore, if these investors fail to place stop–loss orders, the brokers will cover the position for them once their collateral has shrunk and can no longer support the short position. Thus the amount that an investor can lose is limited to the collateral. Short selling really involves no greater risk than purchasing securities, for when investors buy securities, they can lose all of their invested funds.

POINTS OF INTEREST

The Uptick Rule

When bulls stampede to buy stock, the result can be a dramatic price increase. For example, on October 19, 1989, the Dow Jones industrial average rose 39.6 points in one day. Correspondingly, when bears dump their securities, there can be equally dramatic price declines, such as the 47.3 point drop in the Dow Jones industrial average on November 6, 1989. Can bears also magnify these price declines by selling borrowed securities, that is, by selling short? The answer is "no" because of the "uptick rule."

Securities trade daily. If the price of a stock moves up from the previous trade, that is an uptick. If the price of the stock declines from the previous trade, that is a downtick. Short sales can be executed only when the previous change in the price of the stock was an uptick. Thus if the stock moves from 10 to 9⅞, a short sale cannot be executed. If, however, the stock moves back to 10 from 9⅞, that is an uptick and a short sale may be made.

The purpose of this regulation is to reduce the ability of investors and speculators to manipulate the market. Without this rule, short sellers could borrow large quantities of a stock which, when sold, would drive down the stock's price. By such manipulation, the short sellers could guarantee themselves profits. By instituting the uptick rule, the SEC has reduced the ability of short sellers to manipulate the market for their own benefit.

Actually, short selling is consistent with a rational approach to the selection of securities. If an investor analyzes a company and finds that its securities are overpriced, he or she will certainly not buy the securities. Instead, any that are currently owned should be sold. In addition, if the individual has confidence in the analysis and believes that the price will decline, the investor may sell short. The short sale, then, is the logical strategy given the basic analysis. Securities that are overpriced should be considered for short sales, just as securities that the investor believes are undervalued are the logical choice for purchase.

Short selling is not limited to individual investors, as market makers may also sell short. If there is an influx of orders to buy, the market makers may partially satisfy this demand by selling short. They will then repurchase the shares in the future to cover the short position after the influx of orders has subsided. Frequently this transaction can be profitable. After the speculative increase in price that results from the increased demand, the price of the security may decline. When this occurs, the market makers profit because they sell short when the price rises but cover their positions after the price subsequently falls.

Foreign Securities

Foreign companies, like U.S. companies, issue a variety of securities as a means to acquire funds. These securities subsequently trade on foreign exchanges or foreign over-the-counter markets. For example, there are stock exchanges in London, Paris, Tokyo, and other foreign financial centers. Unless Americans and other foreigners are forbidden to acquire these securities, Americans can buy and sell stocks through these exchanges in much the same way that they purchase domestic U.S. stocks and bonds. Thus, foreign securities may be purchased through the use of U.S. brokers who have access to trading on these exchanges. In many cases this access is obtained through a correspondent relationship with foreign security brokers.

Foreign securities may differ significantly from U.S. securities. For example, terminology differs. In Britain a debenture is secured by the firm's assets, while in the United States a debenture is an unsecured, general obligation of the firm. Foreign dividends are usually paid semiannually or annually, and the amount is expressed as a percent of par and not as an amount, as is done in the United States (e.g., 10% of $2 par instead of $0.20). Foreign investors such as Americans may be limited to acquiring only nonvoting shares, and the unit of trading may be greater than the 100 share round lot used in the United States. This is especially true in Japan, where frequent stock splits and stock dividends are used to reduce the security's price.

There are also differences in business practices. For example, Japanese firms use more financial leverage than is customary in the United States. It is not unusual for more than three-fourths of a Japanese firm's assets to be financed with debt. Accounting practices such as the consolidation of subsidiaries' balance sheets or the depreciation of assets differ from generally accepted U.S. accounting practices. Such differences make comparisons of foreign and U.S. accounting data exceedingly difficult.

By far the easiest way to buy foreign stocks is to purchase the shares of firms that are traded on U.S. exchanges or through U.S. over-the-counter markets (i.e., through NASDAQ). To be eligible for such trading, the foreign securities must be registered with the SEC. About 100 foreign stocks are listed on the New York and American stock exchanges and more than 250 trade through NASDAQ.

Exhibit 3.10 enumerates several foreign firms whose shares are traded in the United States. The exhibit gives the company, its country of origin, its primary industry, and where the shares are traded. As may be seen in the exhibit, many foreign stocks, such as SONY and Royal Dutch Airlines, are traded on the New York Stock Exchange. Others, such as BAT Industries (British Tobacco), trade on the American Stock Exchange, and many others trade through NASDAQ.[14] The majority of the firms whose securities are actively traded in the United States are either Japanese or Canadian.

American Depository Receipts (ADRs)

Receipts issued for foreign securities held by a trustee.

These domestic markets do not actually trade the foreign shares but trade receipts for the stock called **American Depository Receipts** or **ADRs.**[15] Such receipts are created by large financial institutions such as commercial banks. The ADRs are sold to the public and continue to trade in the United States.

There are two types of ADRs. "Sponsored" ADRs are created when the firm wants the securities to trade in the United States. The firm employs a bank to perform the paperwork to create the ADRs and to act as transfer agent. In this case the costs are absorbed by the firm. All ADRs listed on the NYSE and AMEX are sponsored ADRs. "Unsponsored" ADRs come into existence when a brokerage firm believes there will be sufficient interest in a stock or bond to make a market in the security. The brokerage firm buys a block of securities and hires a commercial bank to create the ADRs and to act as transfer agent. However, fees for this service and

---

[14] Foreign stock exchanges may also list U.S. securities. The London Stock Exchange is the most liberal and actually encourages foreign listings.

[15] Foreign stocks traded on listed exchange are also referred to as American Depository Shares.

Exhibit 3.10 ✦ SELECTED FOREIGN SECURITIES TRADED ON THE NEW YORK STOCK EXCHANGE, ON THE AMERICAN STOCK EXCHANGE, AND THROUGH NASDAQ

Firm	Country of Origin	Primary Industry	Where Traded in the United States
Alcan Aluminum	Canada	Aluminum	NYSE
BAT Industries	Great Britain	Tobacco products	AMEX
Campbell Resources	Canada	Gold mining	NYSE
Hitachi	Japan	Electronics	NYSE
Imperial Group	Britain	Tobacco, food	AMEX
Japan Airlines	Japan	Airline	NASDAQ
KLM Royal Dutch Airlines	Netherlands	Airline	NYSE
Kloof Gold Mines	South Africa	Gold mining	NASDAQ
SONY	Japan	Electronics	NYSE
TDK	Japan	Electronics	NYSE
Volkswagenwerk	Germany	Automobiles	NASDAQ

for converting dividend payments from the foreign currency into U.S. dollars will be paid by the stockholders, not the issuing firm.

The creation of ADRs greatly facilitates trading in foreign securities. First, ADRs reduce the risk of fraud. If the investor purchased a foreign stock issued by a Japanese firm, the stock certificate would be written in Japanese. It is highly unlikely that the U.S. investor could read the language, and thus he or she could become prey to bogus certificates. ADRs erase that risk, since the certificates are in English and their authenticity is certified by the issuing agent. The investor is assured that the receipt is genuine even though it is an obligation of the issuing agent. The ADR represents only the underlying securities held by the agent and is not an obligation of the firm that issued the stock.

Besides reducing the risk of fraud, ADRs are convenient. Securities do not have to be delivered through international mail; prices are quoted in dollars; and dividend payments are received in dollars. The ADR can represent any number of foreign shares. For example, one ADR of Telefonos de Mexico, which is traded on the NYSE, represents twenty regular shares.

If there are no ADRs issued for the stock the investor seeks to purchase, then the actual foreign securities will have to be acquired. The individual instructs his or her broker to purchase the foreign stock in the appropriate foreign market. As with any other security purchase, the shares or bonds are acquired through exchanges or over-the-counter from dealers who make a market in the security. The trading practices followed by foreign exchanges need not coincide with U.S. practices. For example, after a stock is purchased, a settlement date is established at which time payment is due. This settlement date may not coincide with the U.S. practice of payment due after five business days. However, such differences are more a matter of detail than substance and are diminishing with increased global investing. After the purchases are completed, the investor may choose to leave the securities registered with the broker or may take delivery.

Exhibit 3.11 ✦ SELECTED CLOSING PRICES FOR FOREIGN SECURITIES

FOREIGN MARKETS

Monday, January 4, 1993

TOKYO
(in yen)

	Close	Prev. Close
ANA	988	960
Aiwa	1090	1060
Ajinomoto	1250	1270
Alps Elec	832	830
Amada Co	1000	1020
Ando Elec	710	720
Anritsu	745	770
Asahi Chem	593	595
Asahi Glass	986	981
Bank of Tokyo	1340	1370
Bk of Yokohama	1000	1030
Banyu Pharm	822	822
Bridgestone	1170	1150
CSK	2260	2260
Canon Inc	1370	1370
Canon Sales	2030	2070
Casio Computer	1040	1060
Chubu Pwr	2390	2360
Chugai Pharm	1220	1230
Citizen Watch	925	926
Dai Nippon Print	1290	1260
Dai-ichi Kangyo	1680	1670
Daiei	810	805
Daiichi Seiyaku	1610	1590
Dainippon Ink	408	406
Dainippon Pharm	1140	1120
Daiwa House	1390	1400
Daiwa Securities	865	890
Eisai	1440	1440
Ezaki Glico	1150	1160
Fanuc	3420	3500
Fuji Bank	1780	1800
Fuji Hi	359	347
Fuji Photo Film	2640	2640
Fujisawa Pharm	830	844
Fujitsu	552	550
Furukawa Elec	390	380
Green Cross	1290	1300
Haseko	576	565
Hirose Elec	3750	3750
Hitachi Cable	549	561
Hitachi Credit	1270	1270
Hitachi Ltd	757	752
Hitachi Maxell	1660	1670
Hitachi Metals	785	785
Hitachi Sales	415	411
Honda Motor	1320	1300
Hosiden Elec	1610	1610
Hoya	-	0
IHI	443	450
Ind Bank Japan	2430	2470
Intec	1220	1240
Isetan	2460	2510
Isuzu	344	332
Ito-yokado	3730	3680
Itochu Corp	412	415
Iwatsu Elec	315	320
JAL	585	595
JEOL	517	523
JUSCO	1400	1420
Japan Aviat El	510	510

	Close	Prev. Close
Mitsubishi Hi	529	530
Mitsubishi Kasei	397	390
Mitsubishi Matl	413	410
Mitsubishi Trust	949	945
Mitsubishi Whse	1280	1280
Mitsui Fudosan	991	980
Mitsui Mar&Fire	887	882
Mitsui Trust	770	740
Mitsui & Co	600	598
Mitsukoshi	722	728
Mochida Pharm	2920	2960
NCR Japan	761	760
NEC	680	681
NGK Spark	915	910
NIFCO	1170	1160
NKK	252	255
NSK	482	489
NTN	462	465
NTT	574000	571000
Nikko Kyodo	458	444
Nikko Securities	645	636
Nikon Corp	706	707
Nintendo	10700	10600
Nippon Chemi-con	530	531
Nippon Columbia	465	483
Nippon El Glass	1050	1040
Nippon Express	750	742
Nippon Hodo	2270	2220
Nippon Meat	1690	1720
Nippon Oil	597	591
Nippon Sanso	399	414
Nippon Shinpan	622	610
Nippon Steel	293	292
Nissan Motor	564	560
Nissin Food	2210	2230
Nitsuko	530	520
Nomura Securities	1480	1490
OKK	508	518
Obayashi Corp	510	510
Odakyu Railway	682	681
Oji Paper	863	849
Oki Elec Ind	346	338
Okuma Corp	809	802
Olympus Optical	1070	1070
Omron	1030	1050
Ono Pharm	5370	5370
Onoda Cement	569	556
Onward	1080	1100
Orient Corp	654	645
Pioneer Electron	2680	2670
Renown	456	464
Ricoh Co	602	607
Royal Co	1030	1020
Ryobi	455	440
SMK	403	403
Sakura Bank	1180	1200
Sankyo Co	2530	2500
Sanrio	1050	1050
Sanwa Bank	1630	1630
Sanyo Elec	368	367
Sapporo Brewery	871	890
Secom	5570	5570
Sekisui House	1060	1060
Seven-eleven	6860	6860

	Close	Prev. Close
Toyobo	341	348
Toyoda Mach	583	584
Toyota Motor	1460	1480
Tsugami	397	401
Uny	1150	1110
Ushio	586	585
Wacoal	875	865
Yamaha	918	900
Yamaichi Sec	542	557
Yamanouchi Phm	2550	2550
Yamatake-Hnywl	1330	1320
Yamato Transport	970	975
Yamazaki Baking	1770	1790
Yasuda Fire	795	808
Yokogawa Elec	700	710

LONDON
(in pence)

	Close	Prev. Close
Abbey National	392	389.5
Albert Fisher	58	55
Allied-Lyons	645	643
Argyll Group	393	393
Arjo Wiggins	154	151.5
Assoc Brit Fds	509	509
BAA PLC	785	787
Barclays	389	381.5
Bass	645	635
BAT Indus	981	983
Blue Circle	211	199
BOC Group	761	766
Body Shop	194	192
Boots	559	561
Borland	1550	1500
Bowater Indus	481	484
BPB Indus	199	195
British Aero	175	165
British Airwys	308	308.5
British Gas	292.5	291.5
British Pete	246	248.5
British Steel	55.5	57.5
British Telcom	403.5	403.5
BTR	553	550
Burmah Castrol	739	737
Cable&Wireless	714	699
Cadbury Schwp	452	444
Charter Cons	613	611
Coats Viyella	224	225
Commercial Un	632	621
Courtaulds	599	595
Dixons	264	259
Eng Ch Clay	453	457
Euro Tunnel	337	339
Fisons	245	245
Forte	195	188
GEC	282.5	283.5
Genrl Accidnt	591	578
GKN	464	448
Glaxo Hldgs	799	793
Granada	365	376
Grand Metrop	459	465

	Close	Prev. Close
RTZ Corp	685	683.5
Stchi&Stchi	155	152
J Sainsbury	574	564
Sears	99.5	101
Sedgwick Grp	177	168
Shell Trnspt	558	562.5
Siebe PLC	445	440
Smithkln Bchm	506	496
Smith&Nephew	163.5	163
Std Chartrd	588	576
Storehouse	196.5	202
Sun Alliance	347	342
Tarmac	106	103
Tate & Lyle	405	403
Tesco	256	249
Thorn EMI	881	881
Trafalgar Hse	80	79
TSB Group	155	152.5
Utd Biscuits	362	355
Unilever	1117	1115
Vodafone	430	427
Warburg	567	563
Wellcome	979	967
WPP Group	52	47

South African Mines
(in U.S. dollars)

	Close	Prev. Close
Bracken	0.33	0.33
Deelkraal	0.58	0.63
Doornfontein	0.16	0.18
Durban Deep	1.88	1.88
E. Rand Gold	0.73	0.78
E. Rand Prop	1.00	1.00
Elandsrand	2.12	2.00
Grootvlei	0.80	0.80
Harmony	1.30	1.30
Hartebstftn	1.45	1.40
Impala Pltm	8.12	8.12
Kinross	5.25	5.12
Leslie	0.38	0.38
Loraine	0.20	0.20
Randfontein	2.44	2.62
Rustenburg	14.12	14.25
Southvaal	7.25	7.75
Stilfontein	0.28	0.28
Unisel	0.90	0.90
West Areas	0.45	0.47
Winkelhaak	5.12	5.12

HONG KONG
(in Hong Kong dollars)

	Close	Prev. Close
Bank E Asia	33.50	34
Cathay Pacific	9.20	9.45
Cheung Kong	18.60	18.80
China L & P	32.25	33
Dairy Farm	11.50	11.60
Hang Seng Bk	52.50	53
HK Electric	15	15.60
HK Land	11.80	11.90
HK Telecom	9.55	9.65
HSBC Hldgs	54.50	55.50

PARIS
(in French francs)

	Close	Prev. Close
Accor	610	615
Air Liquide	788	799
Alcatel Alstm	692	692
BSN-Gervais	945	954
Carrefour	2345	2364
Club Med	386.5	381.8
Dassault Avitn	375	368
Elf Aquitaine	356	362.2
Elf Sanofi	1116	1125
Euro Disneyld	62.5	63.8
Generale Eaux	2155	2170
Hachette	78.5	81.5
Havas	431.9	432.7
Imetal	349	350
Lafarge Coppe	335.3	339.9
LVMH	3580	3688
Machines Bull	20	21
Matra	187.5	191
Michelin	183.1	181.5
L'Oreal	1055	1067
Paribas	340.7	345.5
Pernod Ricard	370.8	366.5
Peugeot	578	591
Saint Gobain	510	510
Schneider	593	599
Soc Generale	613	618
Suez	247.1	249.5
Thomson CSF	144	145
Total Francals	234.3	232.7

AMSTERDAM
(in guilders)

	Close	Prev. Close
ABN Amro	51.40	50.80
Aegon	76.50	75.20
Ahold	89.90	87.80
Akzo	139.20	140.10
AMEV	60.30	60
Buhrmn-Tett	27.90	28.40
DSM	75.30	75.40
Elsevier	120.80	120.60
Fokker	14.60	15.50
Gist-Brocades	33.30	33.50
Heineken	171.60	172
Hoogovens	21.90	23
Hunter Douglas	43.50	42.70
Intl Ndrlndn Gr	55.80	54.60
KLM	24.90	24.10
KNP	28	28.60
Nedlloyd	32	31.70
Oce-van Grntn	40.60	41
Pakhoed Hldg	35.80	35.80
Philips	20.20	19.60
Robeco	99.30	98.50
Rodamco	46.90	47.30
Rolinco	98.50	97.50
Rorento	80.30	80
Royal Dutch	148.50	147.80
Unilever	190.40	190.10
VOC	33.80	34.70
VNU	88	87.70

FRANKFURT
(in Marks)

	Close	Prev. Close
AEG	158	162.8
Allianz	1965	1984
Asko	600	605
BASF	207	210.4
Bayer	267	268
Byr Vereinsbk	418	422
BMW	482	488
Commerzbank	244	246
Continental	197	198
Daimler Benz	535	537
Degussa	335	347.5
Deutsche Bank	638	647
Dresdner Bank	351.8	353.9
Henkel	549	555
Hochtief	924	919
Hoechst	248	249.4
Karstadt	482	500
Kaufhof	412	417
Linde	694.5	694
Lufthansa	104	104.5
Mannesmann	234.8	235.4
MAN	276.2	282
Metallges	334.9	334.8
Munchen Ruck	2215	2230
Porsche	450	449
RWE	399.5	402.9
Schering	736.2	745
Siemens	589.5	594.4
Thyssen	158.5	161.5
Veba	360	361.5
VEW	215	214.2
Volkswagen	242.5	243

SYDNEY
(in Australian dollars)

	Close	Prev. Close
Amcor	7.80	7.73
ANZ Group	3.06	3
Ashton	1.33	1.33
Boral	2.92	2.90
Bougainville	0.45	0.44
Brambles Inds	16.86	16.80
Brokn Hill Prp	13.56	13.28
Burns Philp	3.96	3.94
Coles Myer	4.83	4.84
Comalco	3.18	3.16
Centrl Norsemn	0.34	0.35
CRA	13.40	13.14
CSR	4.32	4.27
Fletcher Chl	a	2.45
Foster's	1.36	1.36
Gld Mns Kalgo	0.89	0.88
Goodman	1.76	1.74
Leighton	1.32	1.32
Mayne Nickless	6.40	6.20
MIM Holdings	2.49	2.47
Nat Aust Bnk	7.69	7.60
News Corp	29.90	29.94

Source: The Wall Street Journal, January 5, 1993, p. C11.

The prices of a number of foreign stocks are given daily in the U.S. financial press. For example, *The Wall Street Journal* gives prices for selected securities traded on several exchanges. Exhibit 3.11 reproduces a sample of the prices reported in *The Wall Street Journal.* As may be seen in the exhibit, the information is limited to prices—there is no reporting of volume of transactions, dividends, or P/E ratios. In addition, the number of foreign stock prices reported in the U.S. press is small. If the investor seeks to track the prices of many foreign stocks, that will require access to a foreign publication such as the *Financial Times,* a British newspaper that is comparable to *The Wall Street Journal.*

REGULATION

Like many industries, the securities industry is subject to a substantial degree of regulation from both the federal and state governments. Since the majority of securities are traded across state lines, most regulation is at the federal level.

The purpose of these laws is to protect the investor by ensuring honest and fair practices. The laws require that the investor be provided with information upon which to base decisions. Hence, these acts are frequently referred to as the **full disclosure laws,** because publicly owned companies must inform the public of certain facts relating to the firm. The regulations also attempt to prevent fraud and the manipulation of stock prices. However, they do not try to protect investors from their own folly and greed. The purpose of legislation governing the securities industry is not to ensure that investors will profit from their investments; instead the laws try to provide fair market practices while allowing investors to make their own mistakes.

full disclosure laws
The federal and state laws requiring publicly held firms to disclose financial and other information that may affect the value of their securities.

Although current federal regulation developed during the 1930s as a direct result of the debacle in the security markets during the early part of that decade, state regulation started in 1911 with the pioneering legislation in the state of Kansas. These state laws are frequently called blue sky laws because fraudulent securities were referred to as pieces of blue sky. Although there are differences among the state laws, they generally require that (1) security firms and brokers be licensed, (2) financial information concerning issues of new securities be filed with state regulatory bodies, (3) new securities meet specific standards before they may be sold, and (4) regulatory bodies be established to enforce the laws.

The Federal Security Laws

The first modern federal legislation governing the securities industry was the Security Act of 1933. This act is primarily concerned with the issuing of new securities. It requires that new securities be "registered" with the Security and Exchange Commission (SEC). Registration consists of supplying the SEC with information concerning the firm, the nature of its business and competition, and its financial position. This information is then summarized in the prospectus (refer to Exhibit 2.1), which makes the formal offer to sell the securities to the public.

Once the SEC has determined that all material facts that may affect the value of the firm have been disclosed, the securities are released for sale. When the securities are sold, the buyer must be given a copy of the prospectus. If the investor incurs a loss on an investment in a new issue of securities, a suit may be filed to recover the loss if the prospectus or the registration statement that was filed with the SEC contained false or misleading information. Liability for this loss may rest on the firm, its executives and directors, the brokerage firm selling the securities, and any experts (e.g., accountants, appraisers) who were employed in preparing the documents. Owing to this legal accountability, those involved exercise caution and diligence in the preparation of the prospectus and the registration statement.

Although the Security Act of 1933 applies only to new issues, the Security Exchange Act of 1934 (and subsequent amendments) extends the regulation to existing securities. This act forbids market manipulation, deception and misrepresentation

ILLEGAL USE OF INSIDE INFORMATION

The use of inside (privileged) information for personal gain is illegal. Management cannot buy a stock, make an announcement that causes the value of the stock to rise, and then sell the stock for a profit. If insiders do this, the corporation or its stockholders may sue, and if the defendants are found guilty, any profits must be returned to the corporation.

The law does not forbid insiders from buying and subsequently selling the stock. However, the Securities Exchange Act of 1934 requires that each officer, director, and major stockholder (i.e., any individual who owns more than 5 percent of the stock) of a publicly held corporation must file a report with the SEC disclosing the amount of stock held. These individuals must also file a monthly report if there are any changes in the holdings. This information is subsequently published by the SEC. If these insiders make a profit on a transaction that is completed (i.e., the stock is bought and sold) within six months, it is assumed the profit is the result of illegally using confidential corporate information.

Individuals who may be considered insiders are not limited to the corporation's officers and directors. An insider is any individual with "material information" not yet disclosed to the public. Material information implies information that could reasonably be expected to affect the value of the firm's securities. The individual need not necessarily be employed by the firm but could have access to inside information through business relationships, family ties, or being informed (tipped off) by insiders. Use of such privileged information even by nonemployees is also illegal. In one of the most famous cases concerning the illegal use of inside information, several officers and directors of Texas Gulf Sulfur became aware of new mineral discoveries. Not only were their purchases ruled illegal, but purchases made by individuals they had informed were also ruled illegal. Thus, an insider who may not directly profit through the use of inside information cannot pass that information to another party who profits from using that knowledge.

of facts, and fraudulent practices. The SEC was also created by this act to enforce the laws pertaining to the securities industry.

Under the Security Exchange Act of 1934, publicly held companies are required to keep current the information on file with the SEC. This is achieved by having the firm file an annual report (called the 10-K report) with the SEC. The 10-K report contains a substantial amount of factual information concerning the firm, and this information is usually sent in summary form to the stockholders in the company's annual report. (Companies must upon request and without charge send a copy of the 10-K report to stockholders.)

Firms are also required to release any information during the year that may materially affect the value of their securities. Information concerning new discoveries, lawsuits, or merger discussions must be disseminated to the general public. The SEC has the power to suspend trading in a company's securities for up to ten days if, in its opinion, the public interest and the protection of investors necessitate such a ban on trading. If a firm fails to keep investors informed, the SEC can suspend trading pending the release of the required information. Such a suspension is a drastic act and is seldom used, for most companies frequently issue news releases that inform the investing public of significant changes affecting the firm. Sometimes the company itself asks to have trading in its securities halted until a news release can be prepared and disseminated.

The disclosure laws do not require that the company tell everything about its operations. All firms have trade secrets that they do not want known by their competitors. The purpose of the full disclosure laws is not to restrict the corporation but (1) to inform the investors so that they can make intelligent decisions and (2) to prevent a firm's employees from using privileged information for personal gain.

It should be obvious that employees ranging from president of the company to those of lesser positions may have access to information before it reaches the general public. Such information (called inside information) may significantly enhance the employees' ability to make profits by buying or selling the company's securities before the announcement is made. Such profiteering from inside information is illegal. Officers and directors of the company must report their holdings and any changes in their holdings of the firm's securities to the SEC. Thus, it is possible for the SEC to determine if transactions have been made prior to any public announcement that affected the value of the securities. If insiders do profit illegally from the use of such information, they may be prosecuted under criminal law and their gains may have to be surrendered to the firm.

Other Regulations

Although the Security Act of 1933 and the Security Exchange Act of 1934 are the backbone of such regulations, subsequent laws have been passed. These include the Public Holding Company Act of 1935, which reorganized the utility industry by requiring better methods of financial accounting and more thorough reporting and by constraining the use of debt financing. The Investment Company Act of 1940 extended the regulations to include mutual funds and other investment companies. The most recent act of importance is the Securities Investors Protection Act of 1970, which is designed to protect investors from brokerage firm bankruptcies and is explained below.

In addition to the laws affecting the issuing of securities and their subsequent trading, there are also laws requiring disclosure by investment advisors. Investment advisory services and individuals who "engage for compensation in the business of advising others about securities shall register" with the SEC.[16] Investment advisors must disclose their backgrounds, business affiliations, and the compensation charged for their services. Failure to register with the SEC can lead to an injunction against supplying the service or to prosecution for violating the security laws.

Besides the state and federal securities laws, the industry itself regulates its members. The stock exchanges and the trade association, the National Association of Security Dealers, have established codes of behavior for their members. These include the relationships between brokers and customers, the auditing of members' accounts, and proficiency tests for brokers. While such rules may not have the force of law, they can have a significant impact on the quality and credibility of the industry and its representatives.

SECURITIES INVESTOR PROTECTION CORPORATION

Most investors are aware that accounts in virtually all commercial banks are insured by the Federal Deposit Insurance Corporation (FDIC). Should an insured commercial bank fail, the FDIC reimburses the depositor for any losses up to

---

[16] Securities and Exchange Commission, *The Work of the Securities and Exchange Commission* (Washington, D.C.: Government Printing Office, 1978), 17.

$100,000.[17] If a depositor has more than $100,000 on account at the time of the commercial bank's failure, the depositor becomes a general creditor for the additional funds.

This insurance has greatly increased the stability of the commercial banking system. Small depositors know that their funds are safe and therefore do not panic if a commercial bank fails (as one occasionally does). This stability simply did not exist prior to the formation of the FDIC. When panicky depositors tried to make withdrawals, some commercial banks could not meet the sudden requests for cash. Many had to close, which only increased the panic that caused the initial withdrawals. Since the advent of the FDIC, however, such panic withdrawals should not occur because the FDIC reimburses depositors (up to the limit) for any losses they sustain.

Security Investors Protection Corporation (SIPC)

The agency that insures investors against failures by brokerage firms.

Like commercial banks, brokerage firms are also insured by an agency that was created by the federal government—the **Securities Investor Protection Corporation (SIPC).** The SIPC is managed by a seven-member board of directors. Five members are appointed by the president of the United States, and their appointments must be confirmed by the Senate. Two of the five represent the general public, and three represent the securities industry. The remaining two members are selected by the secretary of the treasury and the Federal Reserve board of governors.

The SIPC performs a role similar to that of the FDIC. Its objective is to preserve public confidence in the securities markets and industry. Although the SIPC does not protect investors from losses resulting from fluctuations in security prices, it does insure investors against losses arising from the failure of a brokerage firm. The insurance provided by the SIPC protects a customer's cash and securities up to $500,000.[18] If a brokerage firm fails, the SIPC reimburses the firm's customers up to this specified limit. If a customer's claims exceed the $500,000 limit, that customer becomes a general creditor for the remainder of the funds.

The cost of this insurance is paid for by the brokerage firms that are members of the SIPC. All brokers and dealers that are registered with the Securities and Exchange Commission (SEC) and all members of national security exchanges must be members of the SIPC. Most security dealers are thus covered by the SIPC insurance. Some firms have even chosen to supplement this coverage by purchasing additional insurance from private insurance firms.

Summary

This chapter has covered security markets and the mechanics of buying securities. Securities are traded on organized exchanges, such as the NYSE, or in the informal over-the-counter markets. Securities are primarily bought through brokers, who buy and sell for their customers' accounts. The brokers obtain the securities from dealers, who make markets in them. These dealers offer to buy and sell at specified

---

[17] As of January 1993.

[18] Only $100,000 of the $500,000 insurance applies to cash balances on an account.

prices (quotes), which are called the bid and the ask. Brokers and investors obtain these prices through a sophisticated electronic system that transmits the quotes from the various dealers.

After securities are purchased, the investor must pay for them with either cash or a combination of cash and borrowed funds. When the investor uses borrowed funds, that individual is buying on margin. Buying on margin increases both the potential return and the potential risk of loss for the investor.

Investors may take delivery of their securities or leave them with the broker. Leaving securities registered in the street name offers the advantage of convenience because the broker becomes the custodian of the certificates. Since the advent of the SIPC and its insurance protection, there is little risk of loss to the investor from leaving securities with the broker.

Investors establish long or short positions. With a long position, the investor purchases stock in anticipation of its price rising. If the price of the stock rises, the individual may sell it for a profit. With a short position, the individual sells borrowed stock in anticipation of its price declining. If the price of the stock falls, the individual may repurchase it at the lower price and return it to the lender. The position generates a profit because the selling price exceeds the purchase price.

Both the long and short positions are the logical outcomes of security analysis. If the investor thinks a stock is underpriced, a long position (i.e., purchase of the stock) should be established. If the investor thinks a stock is overvalued, a short position should be established. In either case if the investor is correct, the position will generate a profit. Either position may, however, generate a loss if prices move against the investor's prediction.

Investors living in the United States may take a global view of investing and acquire stocks and bonds issued in foreign countries. These securities may be bought and sold through U.S. brokers in much the same way that investors acquire domestic securities. American depository receipts (ADRs) representing foreign securities have been created to facilitate trading in foreign stocks. These ADRs are

Summary of the Objectives of the SEC

1. To ensure that individuals have sufficient information to make informed investment decisions.
2. To provide the public with information by the registration of corporate securities prior to their sale to the general public, and to require timely and regular disclosure of corporate information and financial statements.
3. To prevent manipulation of security prices by regulating trading in the securities markets; by requiring insiders to register the buying and selling of securities; and by regulating the activities of corporate officers and directors.
4. To regulate investment companies (e.g., mutual funds) and investment advisors.
5. To work in conjunction with the Federal Reserve to limit the use of credit to acquire securities.
6. To supervise the regulation of member firms, brokers, and security dealers by working with the National Association of Security Dealers, which is the self-regulatory association of brokers and dealers.

denominated in dollars. Their prices are quoted in dollars, and their units of trading are consistent with the units of trading used in the United States.

The federal laws governing the securities industry are enforced by the Securities and Exchange Commission (SEC). The purpose of these laws is to ensure that individual investors have access to information upon which to base investment decisions. Publicly owned firms must supply investors with financial statements and make timely disclosure of information that may affect the value of the firms' securities.

Investors' accounts with brokerage firms are insured by the Securities Investor Protection Corporation (SIPC). This insurance covers up to $500,000 worth of securities held by the broker for the investor. The intent of SIPC is to increase public confidence in the securities industry by reducing the risk of loss to investors from failure by brokerage firms.

Terms to Remember

organized exchange	market order
over-the-counter (OTC) market	limit order
specialist	day order
dealer	good-till-canceled order
round lot	stop order
odd lot	confirmation statement
bid and ask	settlement date
spread	margin
thin issue	margin requirement
equilibrium price	street name
listed security	trader
P/E ratio	commissions
NASDAQ	discount broker
third market	short sale
broker	covering the short sale
registered representative	American Depository Receipts
long position	(ADRs)
bullish	full disclosure laws
short position	Securities Investor Protection
bearish	Corporation (SIPC)

Questions

1. What is the role of market makers, and how do they earn profits?
2. What is the difference between listed securities and securities traded in over-the-counter markets?
3. How is the market price of a security determined?
4. What is the difference between a market order, a good-till-canceled order, and a stop–loss order?
5. In addition to commission fees, are there any costs of investing?
6. What are the advantages of leaving securities registered in the street name?
7. Why is it riskier to buy stocks on margin?

8. When should an investor sell short? How can an investor sell something that he or she does not own? How is the short position closed? What is the source of profit in a short position?

9. Why do U.S. investors purchase ADRs in preference to the actual securities? How do ADRs come into existence?

10. How is the SIPC similar to the FDIC?

11. Why are the laws governing the securities industry frequently referred to as "full disclosure laws"?

12. What are the roles of the SIPC and the SEC? Can trading in a security be suspended?

Problems

1. A stock sells for $10 per share. You purchase one hundred shares for $10 a share (i.e., $1,000), and after a year the price rises to $17½. What will be the percentage return on your investment if you bought the stock on margin and the margin requirement was (a) 25 percent, (b) 50 percent, and (c) 75 percent? (Ignore commissions, dividends, and interest expense.)

2. Repeat Problem 1 to determine the percentage return on your investment but in this case suppose the price of the stock falls to $7½ per share. What generalization can be inferred from your answers to Problems 1 and 2?

3. Investor A makes a cash purchase of 100 shares of AB&C common stock for $55 a share. Investor B also buys 100 shares of AB&C but uses margin. Each holds the stock for one year, during which dividends of $5.00 a share are distributed. Commissions are 2 percent of the value of a purchase or sale; the margin requirement is 60 percent, and the interest rate is 10 percent annually on borrowed funds. What is the percentage earned by each investor if he or she sells the stock after one year for (a) $40, (b) $55, (c) $60, or (d) $70? If the margin requirement had been 40 percent, what would have been the annual percentage returns? What conclusion do these percentage returns imply?

4. An investor sells a stock short for $36 a share. A year later, the investor covers the position at $30 a share. If the margin requirement is 60 percent, what is the percentage return earned on the investment? Redo the calculations, assuming the price of the stock is $42 when the investor closes the position.

Suggested Readings

For histories of the New York and American Stock Exchanges, see:
Sobel, Robert. *The Big Board: A History of the New York Stock Market.* New York: The Free Press, 1965.
Sobel, Robert. *The Curbstone Brokers: The Origins of the American Stock Exchange.* New York: Macmillan, 1970.

For a discussion of the nature, origin, and workings of the SEC, see:
Skousen, K. Fred. *An Introduction to the SEC.* 5th ed. Cincinnati: South-Western Publishing, 1990.

For a reference book on the NASDAQ market system that provides information on trading procedures, acquire:

Loll, Leo M. Jr., and Julian G. Buckley. *The Over-the-Counter Security Markets.* Englewood Cliffs, N.J.: Prentice-Hall, 1986.

National Association of Securities Dealers. *The NASDAQ Handbook,* rev. ed. Chicago: Probus Publishing, 1992.

For a history of financial disasters on Wall Street including the sharp decline in October 1987, read:

Sobel, Robert. *Panic on Wall Street.* New York: E. P. Dutton, 1988.

The sharp decline in securities prices that occurred in October 1987 is chronicled in:

Barro, Robert J. *Black Monday and the Future of Financial Markets.* Homewood, Ill.: Dow Jones-Irwin, 1989.

Stewart, James B., and Daniel Hertzberg. "How the Stock Market Almost Disintegrated a Day after the Crash." *The Wall Street Journal,* November 20, 1987, 1.

Stewart, James B., and Daniel Hertzberg. "Speculative Fever Ran High in the 10 Months Prior to Black Monday." *The Wall Street Journal,* December 11, 1987, 1.

Other possible readings include:

Hayes, Samuel L. III, ed. *Wall Street and Regulation.* Boston: Harvard Business School Press, 1987.

Stoll, Hans. *The Stock Exchange Specialist System: An Economic Analysis.* New York: New York University Graduate School of Business Administration, 1985.

Stoll, Hans, and Robert E. Whaley. *Stock Market Structure, Volatility, and Volume.* Charlottesville, VA: Institute of Chartered Financial Analysts Research Foundation, 1990.

4

SOURCES OF INFORMATION

*I*nvesting requires knowledge. Savers who want to buy securities have a vast supply of information available to them. Their problems lie not in obtaining information but in determining which information is useful and then interpreting it. This chapter will describe and illustrate the variety of sources that are available to investors who are interested in purchasing stocks and bonds. Other types of investments, such as art, require specialized knowledge and specialized sources of information, which are not discussed in this chapter.

The major sources of information available to potential investors include corporate publications, brokerage firms' research reports, and investment advisory services. Some of this information, such as a firm's annual report, may be obtained at very little cost. Other information, such as the Value Line Investment Survey, can be purchased only at considerable expense. The costly sources of information, however, may be available in the public library or in a local college library.

◆ ◆ ◆

LEARNING OBJECTIVES

After completing this chapter you should be able to

1. Name four categories of financial information that are generally available to investors.

2. List several publications concerning investments that are available in many libraries.

3. Distinguish between the contents of an annual report, a brokerage firm's research report, and an investment advisory report.

4. Define inside information.

5. Identify several government publications concerning economic conditions.

WHY INFORMATION?

Unless individuals follow a very simple investment strategy (e.g., investing all funds in savings accounts and certificates of deposit at the local bank) or a very naive strategy (e.g., randomly selecting securities and holding them indefinitely), they need to be informed. The regulatory environment (e.g., the SEC) encourages access to information, and corporations, advisory services, brokerage firms, and the popular press provide voluminous amounts of information that are readily available.

Much of the analysis explained and illustrated in this text requires such readily available information. This is particularly true for the examination of financial statements, which is the foundation of the fundamental analysis discussed in detail in Chapters 11 and 12. The investor can measure such things as a firm's profitability, its sources of funds, the return it earns for its stockholders, and its capacity to meet debt obligations.

Exhibit 4.1 ✦ CONTENTS OF THE ALLIED-SIGNAL 1991 ANNUAL REPORT

Letter to shareholders
Allied-Signal's vision/values
The Hennessy years
1991: A review
Allied-Signal at a glance
Management's discussion and analysis
Consolidated statement of income
Consolidated statement of retained earnings
Consolidated balance sheet
Consolidated statement of cash flows

Many investors, of course, do not perform the analysis themselves. Instead they may consult publications such as Standard & Poor's *The Outlook*, the *Value Line Investment Survey*, and brokerage firm reports on specific firms or specific industries. These publications report the results of fundamental analysis and apply them to recommendations for specific securities or investment strategies. The existence of these publications means that the individual investor does not have to redo what has already been done. However, the investor still needs to know where the results of the analysis may be obtained and how to understand and interpret the material.

CORPORATE SOURCES OF INFORMATION

Publicly held firms are required by both federal and state laws, including the full disclosure laws, to publish annual and quarterly reports, which are sent to stockholders. Furthermore, the SEC requires publicly held firms to publish news bulletins giving any pertinent changes in the firm's financial position and any other information that may alter the value of its securities.

Although this information is sent free of charge to all stockholders in whose name the securities are registered, other investors and potential investors may request that the firm place their names on its mailing list. Firms are not required to do this, but many will honor such requests.

The Annual Report

annual report
A financial report sent yearly to a publicly held firm's shareholders.

Perhaps the most important publication of the firm is its **annual report.** This covers a wide variety of topics, as may be seen in Exhibit 4.1, which presents the contents of the Allied-Signal 1991 Annual Report.

Although the annual report includes a substantial amount of factual and financial information, it should be viewed as a public relations document. It is frequently printed on expensive paper and filled with colorful pictures of products and of smiling employees. One notable exception was the 1991 Bell Atlantic Annual Report,

---

POINTS OF INTEREST

READING AN ANNUAL REPORT

While there is no correct way to read an annual report, the fact that the report includes both factual financial information and public relations material suggests that the prudent investor should read the annual report with caution. The tone of most annual reports, especially the message from management or the descriptions of the firm's products, markets, and potential for success and growth, is upbeat and positive. Even a year in which the firm experienced serious problems such as declining sales and earnings, labor unrest, or internal strife may be described with optimistic rhetoric.

With this in mind, the investor approaching an annual report should probably stress reading the numbers and how they were computed (i.e., the financial statements and the footnotes). Immediately after the financial statements, the firm must state the general accounting principles used in the construction of the financial statements. These principles, along with the subsequent footnotes, may offer a better clue to the firm's true financial condition than the blurbs describing sales, earnings, and dividends. Legal problems, nonrecurring sources of income, unfunded pension liabilities, lease obligations not on the balance sheet, current and deferred tax obligations, and the calculation of fully diluted earnings will be discussed (if applicable) in the various footnotes. Since any of these factors could affect the future value of the firm's securities, the prudent investor should take the time and effort to be aware of them.

---

which was brief, contained no pictures, and was printed on recycled paper to demonstrate the company's concern for the environment. Prior to 1991, the company had published the colorful, public-relations type of annual report favored by most firms.

Firms use the annual report to explain, at least superficially, their achievements of the past year. These discussions are in general terms, but the firm's careful selection of words may allow the investor to read between the lines. Generally, the more substantive material is presented in the financial statements, particularly in the explanatory footnotes.

The typical annual report begins with a letter from the president of the company to the stockholders. The chairman of the board of directors also frequently signs this letter. The letter reviews the highlights of the year and points out certain noteworthy events, such as a dividend increase or a merger. It may also forecast events in the immediate future, such as next year's sales growth and earnings.

After the letter to the stockholders, the annual report may describe the various components of the business. For example, it may illustrate with words and pictures the various products that the firm makes, the type of research and development in which the company is engaged, the particular application of the firm's goods and services in different industries, and the outlook for the firm's products in the various industries in which it operates.

After the descriptive material, there follows a set of financial statements. These statements include the balance sheet as of the end of the firm's fiscal year, its income statement for the fiscal year, and the statement of cash flows. A summary of financial information for the past several years may also be given. This summary permits the investor to view the firm's growth in sales, earnings, and dividends as well as the book value of the stock. Some of this information is frequently illustrated by graphs. Since the financial data have been audited, the investors may assume that the information is accurate and that the appropriate accounting principles have been applied consistently. Without this audit, year-by-year comparisons may be meaningless.

THE PRESIDENT'S LETTER

Every annual report includes a letter from the president or chairman of the board. Generally these are carefully worded documents that summarize the firm's achievements during the fiscal year. In addition, a discussion of the firm's prospects for the future may also be included. Does this forecast have useful information for investors? Does it "signal" how the firm's stock will perform in the near future?

These questions were addressed in a recent study that analyzed letters by corporate presidents or chairmen of the board of firms whose stocks subsequently performed very well or very poorly.* The letters of firms whose stocks subsequently did well tended to forecast gains and indicated confidence in the firm's potential. The letters of firms whose stock did poorly discussed the potential for losses and made references to forthcom-

ing problems. Few of these letters forecasted gains.

The results of this research clearly suggest that the president's letter to stockholders offers more than public relations material. Instead, the investor may associate discussions of imminent losses, lack of confidence, or poor growth potential with poor future performance by the stock.

*See Dennis McConnell, John Haslem, and Virginia Gibson, "The President's Letter to Stockholders," *Financial Analysts Journal* (September–October 1986): 66–70.

Quarterly Reports and News Bulletins

quarterly report
A financial report sent every three months to a firm's stockholders.

During the year, the firm publishes **quarterly reports** that summarize its performance during the preceding three months. They usually include a brief account of pertinent events as well as various financial statements. Although these statements are rarely as complete as the financial statements in the annual report, they do permit the investor to see the changes in the firm's earnings and sales for the quarter and often for the last 12 months. Such quarterly statements are usually not audited and may subsequently be restated.

In addition to the annual report and quarterly reports, a firm typically issues news bulletins to the financial press concerning any major event that may alter the value of its shares. These reports include announcements of new products, merger activity, dividend payments, and new financing that the firm is in the process of obtaining. This information is readily accessible because the financial press efficiently disseminates it to the general public. In many cases the firm also sends copies of the news bulletins to its stockholders.

10-K report
A required annual report filed with the SEC by publicly held firms.

Firms must file several documents with the Securities and Exchange Commission (SEC). These also are available to investors. The **10-K report** is the firm's annual report to the SEC. Since it gives a much more detailed statement of the firm's fundamental financial position than is provided in the stockholders' annual report, the 10-K is the basic source of data for the professional financial analyst. Contents of the 10-K include audited financial statements, breakdowns of product lines including sales and expenses, investments in plant and equipment (and the depreciation of these assets), subsidiaries owned, foreign operations, and the variety and amounts of debt outstanding. Although the 10-K is not automatically sent to stockholders, a company must supply stockholders with this document upon written request.

10-Q report
A required quarterly report filed with the SEC by publicly held firms.

The **10-Q report** is the firm's quarterly report to the SEC. Like the 10-K, it is a detailed report of the firm's financial condition. The quarterly report the firm sends to its stockholders is basically a summary of the 10-Q. The **8-K report** must be filed with the SEC within 15 days after an event that may materially affect the value of the firm's securities. This document often details materials previously announced through a press release.[1]

The firm also must file a prospectus when it sells securities to the general public. While the firm prepares a 10-K report annually, a prospectus is required only when the securities are initially sold to the general public. In some cases a preliminary prospectus (called a *red herring*) also may be prepared. The final prospectus is published when the securities are sold, and the buyers receive a copy of the final prospectus along with their confirmation statements. (See Exhibit 2.1 for the cover page of a prospectus for an issue of Chesapeake Corporation common stock that was sold to the general public.)

Individuals as well as firms may have to file forms with the SEC. Any stockholder who acquires 5 percent of a publicly held corporation's stock must submit a **13-D report.** This document requires crucial information, such as the intentions of the stockholder acquiring the large stake. Many takeover attempts start with the acquiring stockholder accumulating a substantial stake in the corporation. The required filing of the 13-D means that once the position reaches 5 percent of the outstanding shares, the buyer's intentions can no longer be hidden.

8-K report
A document filed with the SEC that describes a change in a firm that may affect the value of its securities.

13-D report
Document filed with the SEC by an individual who acquires 5 percent of a publicly held firm's stock.

Inside Information

In addition to the sources that have been previously discussed, there is the possibility of an investor's obtaining **inside information.** Inside information is not available to the general public, and it may be of great value in guiding investments in a particular firm. For example, news of a dividend cut or increment may affect a stock's price. Such knowledge before it is made public should increase the individual's ability to make profitable investment decisions. However, the use of such information for personal gain by employees of the firm, by brokers or investment managers, or by anyone else is illegal.

This does not mean that employees cannot own securities issued by their firm; however, the SEC requires holdings by management to be made public and changes in these holdings to be disclosed. These changes are periodically reported in the financial press, and one publication, *The Insiders' Chronicle,* is devoted solely to reporting transactions by insiders.

The reasons for insiders buying or selling their shares are varied. For example, an individual may be using the proceeds of a sale to retire personal debt, or an executive may be exercising an option to buy the stock. Such transactions are legal and are done for reasonable, legitimate financial purposes. However, some financial analysts and investors believe that inside transactions offer a clue to management's perception of the future price performance of the stock. If many insiders sell their shares, this may be interpreted as a bearish sign, indicating that the market price of the stock will decline in the future. Conversely, a large number of purchases by insiders implies that management expects the price of the stock to rise. Such purchases by insiders are interpreted as being bullish. The reason for these interpretations is obvious: If managers believe that the firm's earnings are growing, they will buy the stock. Insiders' purchases and sales may mirror management's view of the

inside information
Privileged information concerning a firm.

---

[1] For a complete list of forms required by the SEC, see K. Fred Skousen, *An Introduction to the SEC,* 2d ed. (Cincinnati: South-Western Publishing, 1980), 58–60.

company's potential. This information may then be used by outside investors as a key to the direction of future stock prices.[2]

BROKERAGE FIRMS' RESEARCH REPORTS

One service that some brokers offer to their customers is research on specific securities. Many brokerage firms have research staffs who analyze firms and their securities; the purpose of such research is to identify undervalued securities that have the potential for price appreciation. In some cases these findings are published by the brokerage firm and are readily available to its customers.[3] The cost of such research is included in the commission fee.

buy, sell, or hold
A brokerage firm's investment strategy recommendations for a particular security.

Brokerage firms' recommendations take the form of **buy, sell, or hold.**[4] The word *buy* means that the investor should purchase the security or add to existing holdings. *Sell* indicates the opposite, and existing shares should be sold. *Hold* signifies that the investor should not purchase the security but should not sell shares that are already owned. A hold recommendation should not be considered to be neutral, because the investor still holds securities even though no additional shares are purchased.

In most cases, brokerage firms' research reports tend to recommend purchasing the security. Rarely do such reports recommend the outright sale of shares. For this reason, the individual investor should probably use such reports in conjunction with other information. It should be remembered that brokerage firms and their salespeople profit from commissions; hence, there is a natural bias to encourage purchasing securities as opposed to placing money in a savings account or money market mutual fund.

PURCHASED SOURCES OF INFORMATION

The investor may buy a variety of publications and services rendering information that is potentially useful in making investment decisions. This section will describe several of these sources of information.

Newspapers and Magazines

The foremost financial newspaper is *The Wall Street Journal*. This daily newspaper publishes not only daily stock prices and quotes but also bond prices and transac-

---

[2] See the material on insider trading in Chapters 8 and 13.

[3] One particularly useful source of information is the *Wall Street Transcript*, which compiles and publishes brokerage firm reports. This is a very detailed publication and may be obtained by writing the Wall Street Transcript, 99 Wall Street, New York, NY 10005.

[4] Some brokerage firms refine their buy and sell recommendations. For example, Merrill Lynch has five classes: buy, ok to buy, neutral, ok to sell, and sell.

Exhibit 4.2 ✦ DIVIDENDS REPORTED AND EARNINGS ANNOUNCEMENT

GENERAL CINEMA CORP. (N)

Quar Oct 31:	1992	1991
Revenues ..	$911,089,000	$797,854,000
Net income	19,861,000	a(283,090,000)
Avg shares	79,366,000	78,867,000
Shr earns (com & com equiv):		
Net income .	.25	(3.62)
Year:		
Revenues ..	3,716,918,000	3,587,777,000
Income	114,099,000	a(293,122,000)
Extrd cred	b419,557,000	....
Acct adj .	c(39,196,000)	....
Net income	494,460,000	(293,122,000)
Avg shares	79,139,000	78,876,000
Shr earns (com & com equiv):		
Income	1.44	(3.88)
Net income .	6.25	(3.88)

a-Includes a pretax charge of $72,-777,000 related to restructuring. b-From purchase of debt. c-Cumulative effect of an accounting change.
Figures in parentheses are losses.

Dividends Reported December 17

Company	Period	Amt.	Payable date	Record date
REGULAR				
Aloette Cosmetics	Q	.08	2 − 15 − 93	1 − 26
Analysts Intl	Q	.15	2 − 16 − 93	1 − 29
Bando McGlocklin	Q	.22	1 − 31 − 93	12 − 31
Bankers Corp	Q	.14½	1 − 30 − 93	1 − 15
Bell Atlantic	Q	.65	2 − 1 − 93	1 − 11
BergenBrunswig clA	Q	.10	3 − 1 − 93	2 − 1
Boston Ed 8.88%pf	Q	2.22	2 − 1 − 93	1 − 8
CmnwlthEd$1.425prf	Q	.35⅝	2 − 1 − 93	12 − 31
CmnwlthEd$1.90pref	Q	.47½	2 − 1 − 93	12 − 31
CmnwlthEd $2pref	Q	.50	2 − 1 − 93	12 − 31
CmnwlthE$2.375pref	Q	.59⅜	2 − 1 − 93	12 − 31
CmnwlthE$2.875pref	Q	.71⅞	2 − 1 − 93	12 − 31
CmnwlthEd$7.24pref	Q	1.81	2 − 1 − 93	12 − 31
CmnwlthEd$8.38pref ....,....	Q	2.09½	2 − 1 − 93	12 − 31
CmnwlthEd$8.40pref	Q	2.10	2 − 1 − 93	12 − 31
CmnwlthE$11.70pref	Q	2.92½	2 − 1 − 93	12 − 31
CmnwlthEd prefB	Q	2.10	2 − 1 − 93	12 − 31
Cmmnwlth Enrgy Sys	Q	.73	2 − 1 − 93	1 − 13
Country Credit	Q	.10	1 − 18 − 93	12 − 28
Excel Industries	Q	.06	1 − 18 − 93	1 − 4
1stColonialBkshs A	Q	.12½	1 − 8 − 93	12 − 31
Franklin Bank pf A	Q	.22½	1 − 15 − 93	12 − 31
General Cinema	Q	.14	1 − 29 − 93	1 − 11
Generl Cinema serA	Q	.14¾	1 − 29 − 93	1 − 11
Gillette Co	Q	.18	3 − 5 − 93	2 − 1
Great Southrn Bncp	Q	.09	1 − 19 − 93	1 − 8
Harper Group	S	.10	3 − 15 − 93	2 − 15
Independent Bk MI	Q	.13	1 − 29 − 93	1 − 5
Keystone Intl Inc	Q	.17	2 − 25 − 93	2 − 2
Knight-Ridder Inc	Q	.35	1 − 12 − 93	1 − 4
Lawson Products	Q	.10	1 − 18 − 93	1 − 4
Loewen Group	S	b.02	1 − 15 − 93	1 − 5
Natl Intrgrp $5pf	Q	1.25	1 − 15 − 93	1 − 6
Northbay Fncl	Q	.07	1 − 29 − 93	1 − 15

Source: The Wall Street Journal, December 18, 1992, C21.

tions, option transactions and prices, quotes on treasury securities, and prices of commodities and foreign currencies. In addition to financial news, *The Wall Street Journal* includes news bulletins that are issued by firms and editorial comments on national economic policy. Editorials tend to stress those policies that affect the investment community (e.g., the fiscal policy of the federal government, the monetary policy of the Federal Reserve Board, and proposed changes in federal tax laws).

The Wall Street Journal also publishes earnings reports and announcements of dividends that have been declared. These reports and dividends for General Cinema are illustrated in Exhibit 4.2. The left-hand side of the exhibit presents the earnings for General Cinema for the period ending October 31, 1992. These earnings are presented for both the last quarter and twelve months. The right-hand side of Exhibit 4.2 illustrates the announcement of a cash dividend. The entry indicates the per-share amount of the dividend ($0.14) (if it is a quarterly dividend, this will be indicated by Q), the date of record (1-11), and the payment date (1-29-93). The date of record is the day on which the firm closes its books. All stockholders owning shares at that time receive the dividend. The date of payment is the day on which the investor is to receive the dividend.

In addition to *The Wall Street Journal*, there are several newspapers of interest to the investment community. These include *Barron's, Media General Financial Weekly, The Journal of Commerce, Over-the-Counter Weekly Review,* and *The Wall Street Transcript.* Particularly noteworthy is *Barron's*, which, along with *The Wall Street Journal,* is published by Dow Jones. *Barron's* is a weekly newspaper that

---

Exhibit 4.3 ✦ Selected Magazines of Potential Value to the Investment Community

General Financial News
Business Week
Forbes
Fortune
Financial World
Fact
Personal Investor
Sylvia Porter's Personal Finance

Academic and Professional
AAII Journal
Financial Management
Journal of Finance
Harvard Business Review
Journal of Portfolio Management
Financial Analysts Journal

Specialized
Oil and Gas Journal
Realty Trust Review
Public Utilities Fortnightly

---

reports weekly security transactions and that includes various feature articles of interest to the financial community as well as investment advisory reports. One particularly important piece of information is *Barron's* confidence index, which will be described in Chapter 13.

A variety of magazines also report financial news. These range from *Money,* which is a popular press magazine related primarily to personal finance and financial planning, to more sophisticated publications. A selected list of these publications is given in Exhibit 4.3. The list is divided into three categories to designate the nature of the publications. General investors should be particularly interested in *Forbes, Business Week,* and *Fortune,* all of which publish analytical articles concerning the general financial community and specific companies.

These publications also cover specific topics on investment decisions and security selection. For example, *Forbes* periodically devotes specific issues to the reporting of financial information that facilitates comparisons of firms. There is the *Annual Report on American Industry* that ranks more than 1,000 firms with regard to sales and growth in earnings, stock price performance, and return on equity. The issue also classifies the firms by industry and reports such additional information as use of debt and profit margins for the individual firms and medians for the industry.

In addition to the *Annual Report on Industry, Forbes* also periodically presents other specialized information, such as an enumeration of the largest non-American firms and the annual performance of mutual funds. (*Barron's* also publishes quarterly the performance rating of mutual funds.) Perhaps one of the most awaited issues of *Forbes* is devoted to enumerating the 400 richest Americans. While that issue may not help the individual invest, it can illustrate the potential return for the successful management of investments and careers.

The academically and professionally oriented journals are more specialized, and their contents tend to be more difficult for the inexperienced or untrained investor to understand. *Financial Management* and the *Journal of Finance* are primarily designed for individuals doing research in financial topics, such as capital budgeting, cost of funds, or valuation theory. The *Harvard Business Review* is not limited to topics in finance but covers the gamut of business operations. The *Journal of Portfolio Management* and the *Financial Analysts Journal* are a cross between academic and professional publications, as they include articles by both practitioners and academicians. The *Financial Analysts Journal,* which is a professional magazine published six times a year by the Association for Investment Management and Research, is almost exclusively devoted to professional financial analysis.

One relatively new source that the individual should consider after obtaining some experience in investing is the *AAII Journal* published by the American Association of Individual Investors. This journal covers a variety of investment topics ranging from interviews with portfolio managers to taxation, insurance, computerized investing, and financial planning. The purpose of the association is educational, and the publication accepts no advertising. Its costs are covered through membership in the association (625 N. Michigan Ave., Chicago, IL 60611).

The recent interest in financial planning has spawned publications devoted to the professional financial planner such as *Financial Planning,* published by the International Association of Financial Planners. Publications stressing financial planning have a more aggregate or macro emphasis that encompasses such topics as portfolio management, tax shelters, and retirement and estate planning. The publications also tend to be more descriptive and less theoretical than the other academic and professional journals.

The individual who is interested in a particular area of investment may also read specialized trade journals. For example, those who are considering investments in the oil and gas industry may find the *Oil and Gas Journal* a good source of information concerning discoveries of new oil fields and the amounts of reserves that have been determined to exist in these fields. Such trade publications will help the investor keep abreast of events in a particular industry.[5]

Investment Advisory Services

For the investor who wants additional information or advice, a variety of sources may be purchased, some of which are illustrated in this chapter. These sources include the corporate records that are published by Standard & Poor and by Moody. In addition, Standard & Poor publishes each month a *Stock Guide* and a *Bond Guide.* Exhibit 4.4 reproduces a page from the *Stock Guide.* As may be seen in the exhibit, which highlights the stock of General Cinema, a considerable amount of information is given, including not only the price but also financial data such as

---

[5] A source of this material is the *Guide to Industry Publications for Security Analysts,* published by the New York Society for Securities Analysts.

POINTS OF INTEREST

STANDARD & POOR'S CORPORATION RECORDS AND MOODY'S MANUALS

Two of the most important sources of factual information concerning firms and their securities are the *Corporation Records* published by Standard & Poor and the various *Manuals* published by Moody. S&P's *Corporation Records* contains descriptions of companies listed on the major exchanges and many over-the-counter stocks. (Firms that are included must pay a fee for the service. As of 1992, Moody charged from $1,800 to $6,600 depending on the extent of the coverage.) These corporate records are updated quarterly and include the most recent fiscal year's financial statements. For larger firms, S&P's *Corporation Records* includes de-scriptions of the firm's various securities, its earnings, dividends, and the annual range of security prices for the previous decade.

Moody's manuals compile information similar to S&P's *Corporation Records*, but Moody publishes this material in specialized volumes. The titles include: *Moody's Industrial Manual, Moody's Bank and Finance Manual, Moody's Public Utility Manual, Moody's Municipal & Government Manual, Moody's Transportation Manual, Moody's International Manual, Moody's OTC Industrial Manual*. In addition to these annually published manuals, Moody also publishes *News Reports*, which continually updates the material in the manuals.

Like S&P's *Corporation Records*, Moody's manuals require that the firm or government pay an annual fee for inclusion. Material in these manuals includes descriptions of the firm, its securities, and recent financial statements. The manuals are an excellent reference for descriptions of the important features of a firm's securities, especially its bonds.

S&P's *Corporation Records* and Moody's *Manuals* include essentially the same information. However, occasionally a firm is listed in one and not the other. This is particularly true for small firms whose securities are traded over-the-counter. Corporations whose securities are traded on the major exchanges generally choose to be included in both S&P's *Manuals* and Moody's *Corporation Records*.

---

dividends, earnings per share, and certain balance sheet items (current assets, current liabilities, long-term debt, and number of shares outstanding). Since this publication packs so much information into such a small space and is updated monthly, it is a widely used reference.

In addition to the *Stock Guide, Bond Guide,* and *Corporation Records,* Standard & Poor publishes *The Outlook,* an investment advisory service that lists stocks appropriate for investors seeking income or growth. It also lists moderately speculative securities that may offer more potential for higher returns. Each issue describes several securities that the publisher believes are attractive investments. These lists and suggestions are continuously updated so that the subscriber may alter his or her portfolio as conditions and suggestions change. It should be noted that material is generally descriptive and does not report how the conclusions were determined.

One important investor advisory service is the *Value Line Investment Survey.* Each week this publication includes new information on selected industries and specific firms within these industries and updates previously published information. During a three-month period, *Value Line* evaluates most of the important firms that trade their securities on the major exchanges or in the over-the-counter markets. In addition to evaluating individual firms, this service analyzes the industry and makes a recommendation for the price performance of specific stocks relative to the price movements of the market for the immediate future. These recommendations consist of scores ranging from 5 (the lowest performance) to 1 (the highest performance). A score of 1 does not necessarily mean that the stock will earn a positive return;

Exhibit 4.4   ✦   PAGE FROM STANDARD & POOR'S *STOCK GUIDE*

86 FUL-GEN — Standard & Poor's Corporation

Index	Ticker Symbol	Name of Issue (Call Price of Pfd. Stocks)	Market	Com. Rank. & Pfd. Rating	Par Val.	Inst. Hold Cos	Inst. Hold Shs. (000)	Principal Business
#1	FULL	Fuller (HB)	NMS	B+	1	121	7903	Industrial adhesives
2	FFC	Fund Amer Enterpr Hldgs	NMS	NR	1			Mortgage/finl svcs
3	FQA	Fuqua Indus	NY,B,M,P,Ph	B	1	62	6808	Consumer prod,photo finish'g
4	FCBN	Furon Co	NMS	B+	No	39	4830	Mfr non-metallic ind'l pr
5	CHI	Furr's/Bishop's Inc'A'	NY	NR	1¢	9	120	Operates cafeterias
6	Pr	Series A cm Cv Pfd(**10)	NY	NR	1¢	7	296	
7	FGF	Future Germany Fund	NY	NR	.001	16	1217	Closed-end inv:cap apprec
8	FNOW	Future Now	NMS	NR	1¢	24	1553	Provides computer support svcs
9	GIII	G-III Apparel Group	NMS	NR	1¢	16	1753	Mfr men/women leather apparel
10	GKSRA	G & K Services Cl'A'	NMS	A-	50¢	72	6727	Rents & launders textile prod
11	GAB	Gabelli Equity Trust	NY,M,P	NR	No	27	1166	Closed-end investment co
12	GNA	Gainsco Inc	AS,M	B	10¢	46	5234	Property & casualty insur
13	GLC	Galactic Resources	AS,Mo,M	NR	1¢	16	4328	Acq/devel min'l resource prop
14	GTV	Galaxy Cablevision L.P.	AS	NR		9	83	Owns/operates CATV systems
15	GANL	Galey & Lord Inc	NMS	NR	1¢	14	5917	Mfr cotton apparel fabrics
16	AJG	Gallagher (Arthur J.)	NY,M,P	B+	1	56	6315	Ins brokerage,risk mgmt svc
17	GAL	Galoob (Lewis) Toys	NY,M,P	C	1¢	31	3555	Develops,mkts,dstr toy prod
18	Pr	$1.70 Cm Cv^d Dep^A ExPfd(**21.19)	NY	NR		5	691	
19	GHX	Galveston Houston	NY,B,M,Ph	B-	25¢	52	9666	Mfr valve actuator:min'g eq
20	GAMBY	Gambro AB Cl'B'ADR**	NSC	NR	5$		24	Devices/sys for medical indus
21	GBL	Gamma Biologicals	AS,M	C	10¢	14	663	Blood transfusion prod
22	GANDF	Gandalf Technologies	NMS,To	C	No	18	3847	Electr data communic prod
23	GNDR	Gander Mountain	NMS	NR	1¢	32	1155	Retails outdoor clothing,eqp
24	GCI	Gannett Co	NY,B,M,P,Ph	A	1	563	113586	Newspapers:TV/radio:adv
25	GTOS	Gantos Inc	NMS	C	1¢	31	2128	Woman's apparel stores
26	GPS	Gap Inc	NY,B,M,P,Ph	A-	5¢	402	53251	Apparel specialty stores
27	GAN	Garan Inc	AS	B	1	56	1102	Knitted/woven apparel
28	GARN	Garnet Resources	AS	NR	1¢	28	3169	Oil & gas exploration,devel'nt
29	GMT	GATX Corp	NY,B,M,P,Ph	B+	62½¢	123	14803	Railcar leas'g/equip financ'g
30	Pr	$2.50 cm Cv Pfd (63)vtg	NY,M	NR	1	1	8	tank terminals, shipping
31	Pr A	$3.875 cm Cv Pfd $2.7125)	NY,M	BBB-	1¢	12	2840	
32	QGCR	Gaylord Container'A'	AS,M	D	1¢	13	856	Mfr paper packaging prod
33	GET	Gaylord Entertainment 'A'	NY,Ph	NR	1¢	74	10393	Entert'nt,cable TV, broadc'stg
34	GEHL	Gehl Co	NMS	NR	10¢	19	799	Mfr farm,constr'n,indus equip
35	GEC	GEICO Corp	NY,B,M,P,Ph	A	1	124	59217	Property & casualty insurance
36	GSC	Gelman Sciences	AS	B-	10¢	8	493	Lab health devices: filters
37	GNL	Gemco Nat'l	AS	C	50¢	7	117	Assets sold seeking acquis
38	GNI	Gemini II	AS	NR	1¢	11	720	Dual purpose investment co
39	GNCR	Gencare Health Sys	NMS	NR	2¢	19	1049	Managed hlth care svcs IL,MO
#40	GY	GenCorp	NY,B,C,M,P,Ph	B	10¢	110	16682	Aerospace,auto,polymer prods
41	GNLB	Genelabs Technologies	NMS	NR	No	26	2701	Disease/cancer prevent'n prd
42	GNE	Genentech**Inc''	NY	NR	2¢	152	17373	Health care pr-gene-splic'g
43	GAM	Genl Amer Investors	NY,M,Ph	NR	1¢	36	728	Medium sized closed end
44	GA	Genl Automation	AS	NR	1¢	6	83	Multi-user microcomputers
45	GBND	Genl Binding	NMS	B+	12½¢	37	4839	Mfr business machines & sup
46	GCN	Genl Cinema	NY,B,M,P	A-	1	234	40513	Retail stores, publishing
47	Pr A	Ser''A cm Cv Stk(NC)	NY,M	NR	5	235		theatres,insurance

Uniform Footnote Explanations-See Page 1. Other: ¹CBOE:Cycle 3. ²Ph ³M ⁴P:Cycle 1. ⁵Ph:Cycle 3. ⁶CBOE:Cycle 1. ⁷CBOE:Cycle 2. ⁵¹Approve conclusion of liquid'n plan. ⁵²Liq divd.

Source: Standard & Poor's Stock Guide. Reprinted with permission.

rather, it indicates that *Value Line* believes the stock should outperform the market, which in declining markets may mean that the investor will still suffer losses but that the losses will be smaller.

A page from the *Value Line Investment Survey* is given in Exhibit 4.5. As may be seen from this exhibit, *Value Line* reports a considerable amount of information. Most of these data are factual, but there are some projections. In this example *Value Line* suggests that the stock of General Cinema will perform better than the market (i.e., the timeliness rating is 2) in the near term.

Value Line asserts that the securities it recommends have outperformed the market.[6] It also maintains that the stocks ranked 1 and 2 by its analysis consistently achieve higher returns than those ranked 4 and 5. There is some outside empirical support for *Value Line*'s claims, for one study found that stocks ranked 1 by *Value Line* consistently outperformed (even after adjusting for risk) a strategy of randomly selected stocks.[7]

For individual investors, *Value Line*'s performance is somewhat misleading because to achieve the same results, they would have to duplicate the recommendations. *Value Line* assigns a ranking of 1 to 100 stocks. Thus, if only $1,000 is invested in each, a total outlay of $100,000 would be required. Even if the investor could make the purchases as soon as the recommendations were made (which may be impossible), the large commission costs on so many small purchases would reduce the return. Generally investors must select among the recommendations, so the results could be very different from the return earned by all of *Value Line*'s recommendations, since some of the individual selections will outperform the market but others will not.[8]

Specialized Investment Advisory Services

In addition to the information published by publicly held firms, by Standard & Poor and Moody, and by advisory services such as *Value Line*, there is a host of specialized investment advice that the investor may purchase. A casual survey of the

---

[6] See, for instance, "The Value Line Ranking System," *The Value Line Investment Survey Selection & Opinion* (January 18, 1985): 960. How the system is constructed is discussed in Zvi Bodie, Alex Kane, and Alan J. Marcus, *Investments* (Homewood, Ill.: Irwin, 1989), 514–515.

[7] Fisher Black, "Yes, Virginia, There Is Hope: Tests of the Value Line Ranking System." Paper presented at the Center for Research in Security Prices, Graduate School of Business, University of Chicago, May 1971 and Thomas E. Copeland and David Mayers, "The Value Line Enigma (1965–1978): A Case Study of Performance Issues," *Journal of Financial Economics* (November 1982). However, there have been periods when the Value Line recommendations did poorly. For example, during the first eight months of 1992, the Value Line selections declined over 11 percent while the S&P 500 stock index rose 1 percent. See John Dorfman, "Value Line's Top Picks Flopped in 1st Half," *The Wall Street Journal* (September 14, 1992): C1–C2.

[8] Value Line also manages several mutual funds that permit the investor to obtain a diversified portfolio based on its analysts' recommendations. However, the investor should realize that while the ranking system for picking stocks has done well, the mutual funds managed by Value Line have not performed as well. See William Baldwin, "Paying the Piper," *Forbes* (October 19, 1987): 208–210.

Exhibit 4.5 ✦ PAGE FROM THE *VALUE LINE INVESTMENT SURVEY*

| GEN'L CINEMA NYSE-GCN | RECENT PRICE | 33 | P/E RATIO | 20.8 | (Trailing: 24.4 / Median: 21.0) | RELATIVE P/E RATIO | 1.26 | DIV'D YLD | 1.8% | VALUE LINE | 1761 |

TIMELINESS 2 Above Average (Relative Price Performance Next 12 Mos.)

SAFETY 3 Average (Scale: 1 Highest to 5 Lowest)

BETA .90 (1.00 = Market)

1995-97 PROJECTIONS

	Price	Gain	Ann'l Total Return
High	50	(+50%)	13%
Low	40	(+20%)	7%

Insider Decisions

	A	M	J	J	A	S	O	N	D
to Buy	0	0	0	0	0	1	0	0	0
Options	0	0	0	0	0	0	0	0	0
to Sell	1	0	0	0	0	0	0	0	0

Institutional Decisions

	1Q'92	2Q'92	3Q'92
to Buy	54	50	70
to Sell	68	54	48
Hld's(000)	38430	39022	39059

Percent shares traded: 6.0 / 4.0 / 2.0

High/Low bars: 5.1/3.1 7.6/3.7 11.4/6.8 14.0/8.4 21.1/12.1 29.5/18.3 31.8/13.8 25.8/15.8 28.5/23.1 27.0/16.5 24.8/16.5 36.6/18.0

Target Price Range 1995 1996 1997

9.0 x "Cash Flow" p sh — 2-for-1 split — 2-for-1 split — 2-for-1 split — Relative Price Strength — Shaded areas indicate recessions

Options: CBOE

1976	1977	1978	1979	1980	1981	1982	1983	1984	1985	1986	1987	1988	1989	1990	1991	1992	1993	© VALUE LINE PUB., INC.	95-97
4.14	5.25	6.79	7.47	8.64	9.36	11.93	12.39	12.18	13.29	13.68	14.22	31.69	26.02	29.18	45.41	46.94	51.00	Revenues per sh A	63.15
.36	.42	.54	.65	.74	.93	1.09	1.27	1.43	1.75	1.89	1.54	2.02	1.53	1.52	1.69	3.54	4.00	"Cash Flow" per sh	5.15
.19	.23	.28	.28	.34	.50	.60	.76	.95	1.17	1.23	.93	.85	.73	.67	d.66	1.35	1.65	Earnings per sh B	2.50
.04	.05	.06	.07	.09	.11	.12	.14	.17	.22	.27	.32	.37	.41	.45	.49	.53	.58	Div'd Decl'd per sh C ■	.80
.28	.38	.57	.65	.57	.54	.58	.73	.69	.95	1.19	1.17	1.68	1.47	1.44	2.17	2.55	3.05	Cap'l Spending per sh	3.75
1.13	1.27	1.47	1.67	1.92	2.32	2.28	3.46	4.73	5.31	6.78	7.41	8.25	21.06	22.11	5.98	11.67	12.90	Book Value per sh D	19.00
88.34	88.56	87.56	87.82	87.91	88.03	74.25	74.94	75.25	72.72	72.93	73.14	73.34	73.55	73.67	79.02	79.18	79.35	Capital Shs Outst'g E	80.00
6.7	6.7	7.8	8.9	7.8	7.8	8.8	11.6	11.6	13.7	18.6	27.1	22.4	34.2	33.5	--	16.7		Avg Ann'l P/E Ratio	18.0
.86	.88	1.06	1.29	1.04	.95	.97	.98	1.08	1.11	1.26	1.81	1.86	2.59	2.49	--	1.01		Relative P/E Ratio	1.40
2.8%	3.0%	2.7%	3.0%	3.3%	2.7%	2.3%	1.6%	1.5%	1.4%	1.2%	1.3%	1.9%	1.6%	2.0%	2.3%	2.4%		Avg Ann'l Div'd Yield	1.8%

CAPITAL STRUCTURE as of 10/31/92

Total Debt $1104.5 mill. Due in 5 Yrs $532.0 mill.
LT Debt $1086.1 mill. LT Interest $85.0 mill.

(Total interest coverage: 3.0x) (54% of Cap'l)

Leases, Uncapitalized Annual rentals $140 mill.
Pension Liability None

Capital Stock 79,182,007 shares (46% of Cap'l)
Incl. 2.9 mill. Series A limited vote shs.,
22.0 mill. Class B preferential vote shs.

						885.9	928.6	916.3	966.8	997.8	1039.7	2323.8	1913.8	2149.5	3587.8	3716.9	4050	Revenues ($mill) A	5050
						14.9%	14.4%	14.8%	15.2%	15.3%	12.8%	9.9%	7.9%	5.7%	8.8%	11.2%	11.5%	Operating Margin	11.0%
						38.3	38.0	36.6	39.1	47.6	44.6	85.4	58.6	62.5	185.4	173.6	185	Depreciation ($mill)	210
						42.9	57.1	71.4	88.2	90.0	68.3	63.0	54.1	49.3	d39.1	106.6	130	Net Profit ($mill)	200
						43.6%	39.3%	33.9%	29.0%	25.9%	27.9%	33.4%	39.8%	34.7%	--	39.2%	39.0%	Income Tax Rate	39.0%
						4.8%	6.2%	7.8%	9.1%	9.0%	6.6%	2.7%	2.8%	2.3%	NMF	2.9%	3.2%	Net Profit Margin	4.0%
						.1	d36.6	33.2	d75.0	d17.7	276.0	226.5	1126.4	1616.3	d.8	548.4	600	Working Cap'l ($mill)	800
						283.2	140.6	407.9	294.2	313.2	686.7	868.9	737.9	803.1	980.2	1086.1	1050	Long-Term Debt ($mill)	1100
						169.2	259.1	355.9	386.3	494.4	542.3	605.0	1548.9	1629.0	472.8	924.4	1025	Net Worth ($mill)	1515
						12.9%	17.2%	11.9%	15.2%	13.1%	8.0%	7.0%	4.2%	4.0%	.7%	7.4%	8.0%	% Earned Total Cap'l	9.5%
						25.4%	22.0%	20.1%	22.8%	18.2%	12.6%	10.4%	3.3%	3.0%	NMF	11.5%	13.0%	% Earned Net Worth	13.0%
						19.5%	17.7%	16.2%	18.7%	14.4%	8.5%	6.0%	1.6%	1.0%	NMF	7.1%	8.5%	% Retained to Comm Eq	9.0%
						23%	22%	20%	19%	18%	21%	33%	42%	54%	65%	38%	35%	% All Div'ds to Net Prof	32%

CURRENT POSITION ($MILL.)

	1990	1991	10/31/92
Cash Assets	1634.4	1619.0	430.7
Receivables	235.9	318.2	399.3
Inventory (FIFO)	276.9	417.6	411.1
Other	49.7	198.5	52.9
Current Assets	2196.9	2553.3	1294.0
Accts Payable	443.3	241.3	258.9
Debt Due	50.1	1821.2	18.4
Other	87.2	491.6	468.3
Current Liab.	580.6	2554.1	745.6

ANNUAL RATES

of change (per sh)	Past 10 Yrs.	Past 5 Yrs.	Est'd '90-'92 to '95-'97
Revenues	15.0%	24.0%	9.5%
"Cash Flow"	9.5%	5.5%	18.0%
Earnings	-.5%	-16.5%	NMF
Dividends	16.5%	13.0%	10.5%
Book Value	20.0%	15.5%	7.5%

QUARTERLY REVENUES ($ mill.) A

Fiscal Year Ends	Jan.31	Apr.30	Jul.31	Oct.31	Full Fiscal Year
1989	439.7	536.9	491.3	445.9	1913.8
1990	516.9	642.8	506.0	483.8	2149.5
1991	886.6	931.1	972.2	797.9	3587.8
1992	883.0	930.7	992.1	911.1	3716.9
1993	960	1015	1080	995	4050

EARNINGS PER SHARE A,B

Fiscal Year Ends	Jan.31	Apr.30	Jul.31	Oct.31	Full Fiscal Year
1989	.04	.24	.35	.10	.73
1990	.27	.40	.08	d.08	.45
1991	d.14	d.69	.57	d.40	d.66
1992	.25	d.03	.88	.25	1.35
1993	.33	.01	1.00	.31	1.65

QUARTERLY DIVIDENDS PAID C ■

Calendar	Mar.31	Jun.30	Sep.30	Dec.31	Full Year
1989	.10	.10	.10	.11	.41
1990	.11	.11	.11	.12	.45
1991	.12	.12	.12	.13	.49
1992	.13	.13	.13	.14	.53
1993	.14				

BUSINESS: General Cinema Corporation, which acquired Harcourt Brace Jovanovich in November 1991, is a leading publisher in educational, scientific, technical, medical, legal, and trade fields. Owns 65% interest in The Neiman Marcus Group, including Bergdorf Goodman and Contempo Casuals. Has an insurance operation that underwrites accident, health, life & credit policies. Operates a major theater chain with about 1,400 screens at 270 locations. '92 deprec. rate: 11.5%. Est'd plant age: 7 yrs. Has 34,000 employees, about 15,000 shareholders. Family of Chairman R.A. Smith owns 29% of stock, conditionally 80% of vote. Two institutions own 10%. Pres. & C.E.O.: R.J. Tarr, Jr. Incorp.: Delaware. Address: 27 Boylston St., Chestnut Hill, MA 02167. Tel.: 617-232-8200.

The lengthy stagnation at General Cinema ended last year. Record earnings for the year ended October, 1993 commend the persistence of management in pursuing the favorable 1991 buyout of Harcourt Brace despite impediments. Attention and capital are now all directed at improving operations. There remains significant opportunity to tap unrealized profit potential. And the effort will get an assist from Administration programs that stress education. The stock has a good chance of continuing to outperform the market in the year ahead. Although largely discounted by the recent price, earnings prospects 3 to 5 years out are well-defined.
Harcourt Brace is leading the way to higher profits in 1993. By far the chief contribution to fourth-quarter income came from the reviving publishing segment. Reforms were just getting started a year ago, so there is much more to be accomplished. This business is highly seasonal, so shareholders need not be alarmed at break-even or loss operations in the April quarter. The schoolbook-buying deluge regularly follows in the July period, which we estimate will bring record earnings again this year, reflecting a heavy textbook adoption schedule.
Major investments in Neiman Marcus are ready to start paying off. Higher consumer spending is starting to improve same-store sales trends. Atop that, recent expansions are lifting overall growth rates to double digits. In addition, the high-cost phase of modernization programs are mostly past, and new merchandising strategies are aiding profitability. Excellent bottom-line results so far this year reflect contributions from Neiman Marcus and Bergdorf Goodman that outweigh current adversity at Contempo Casuals.
The insurance divisions survived their probationary period well. There might have been some uncertainty about staying with insurance, which happened to come with Harcourt. These operations continue to provide a steady return, however, so only group medical insurance is slated to exit.
More than the corporate name secures tenure for the theaters. A costly modernization program is now complete, and the chain generates large cash.
Edmund B. Swort *March 5, 1993*

(A) Fiscal year ends Oct. 31st. (B) Fully diluted. Excludes nonrecurring income (loss): '82, 6¢; '83, 55¢; '84, 53¢; '86, 49¢; '87, 1¢; '88, 28¢; '89, $12.43; '90, 44¢; '91, ($3.22); '92, $5.40. Next earnings report due mid-March. (C) Next dividend meeting about March 12. Goes ex about April 8. Dividend payment dates: end of January, April, July, October. ■ Dividend reinvestment plan available. (D) Includes intangibles. In '92: $415 mill., $5.24/sh. (E) In millions, adjusted for stock splits.

Company's Financial Strength	B++
Stock's Price Stability	70
Price Growth Persistence	45
Earnings Predictability	15

Factual material is obtained from sources believed to be reliable, but the publisher is not responsible for any errors or omissions contained herein.
For the confidential use of subscribers. Reprinting, copying, and distribution by permission only. Copyright 1993 by Value Line Publishing, Inc. ® Reg. TM—Value Line, Inc.

Source: *Value Line Investment Survey*. Copyright © 1993 by Value Line, Inc.; used by permission.

advertisements in *The Wall Street Journal* or *Barron's* proves this. A representative list of this material is given in Exhibit 4.6. Since these publishers and authors earn their living by selling these services, the purchaser should be somewhat cautious when acting on any specific recommendations. Previous recommendations that proved successful do not guarantee future success.[9] Furthermore, if the service makes several recommendations, some, according to the laws of probability, should be correct. The service's true performance may be reflected in the number of successes relative to the number of recommendations or in the returns earned on all the recommendations relative to a measure of the market such as the Standard & Poor's 500 stock index.

One means to compare the performance of the various investment advisory services is to obtain *The Hulbert Financial Digest,* a monthly publication that rates the performance of the services. The address is 316 Commerce St., Alexandria, VA 22314. The editor, Mark Hulbert, also writes columns on the performance of the services for *Forbes* and the *AAII Journal* of the American Association of Individual Investors. In addition, Hulbert is the author of "The Second Hulbert Financial Digest Almanac," a guide to investment newsletters and available from the same address.

Socially Responsible Investing

Socially responsible investing refers to buying securities in firms that produce socially desirable goods and services or pursue socially desirable policies. Of course, what is considered socially desirable is determined by each individual. For one investor, manufacturers of military and defense products or electric utilities with nuclear facilities may be examples of firms that do not produce socially desirable products. The securities of these firms would be excluded from consideration for possible investments. Another investor, however, may believe that a strong defense is socially responsible or that nuclear power is less polluting than oil and cold-fired

---

[9]The SEC and state regulatory agencies forbid advisory services from providing single illustrations or examples of previously successful recommendations. All recommendations ever made must be presented.

Exhibit 4.6 ◆ SELECTED INVESTMENT ADVISORY SERVICES

Astute Investor
Diners Letter
Dow Theory Letters
Elliot Wave Theorist
Granville Market Letter
Indicator Digest
Lynn Elgert Report
Mutual Fund Strategist
Professional Tape Reader
Telephone Switch Newsletter
Value Line Investment Survey
Zweig Forecast

generators and would include the securities of defense contractors and nuclear utilities as possible investments.

Socially responsible investing may be applied not only to products but to other facets of business enterprise. Does the firm have a good record for promoting women and minorities? Does the firm perform research on live animals? Does the firm sponsor socially desirable programs such as research on cancer or AIDS? These are but a few of the possible social considerations individual investors may apply when selecting firms for possible investment.

If socially desirable investing appeals to an individual, he or she must determine which firms meet whatever social goals or criteria are deemed important. If the individual does not want to identify specific firms, then an alternative is to identify mutual funds such as the Fidelity Social Principles Fund with portfolios consistent with the investor's social aims. Possible sources of this information include Jack Brill and Alan Reder, *Investing from the Heart* (New York: Crown Publishers, 1992); Peter Kinder, Steven Lydenberg, and Amy Domini, *The Social Investment Almanac* (New York: Henry Holt & Co., Inc. 1992); Ritchie Lowry, *Good Money: Profitable Social Investing in the '90s* (New York: W. W. Norton & Co., 1991). These three books facilitate social investing by identifying firms and mutual funds that meet social criteria. The books also discuss the risks and returns earned from such investments. While social investing has been a recent concern of some investors, the initial results do suggest that realized returns are comparable to the returns generated by the Standard and Poors 500 stock index. If these results hold for an extended period of time, it suggests that the investor is not hurt (or helped) by making socially conscientious investments.

OTHER SOURCES OF INFORMATION

The U.S. federal government publishes a considerable amount of material that may be useful to investors. These publications include the *Survey of Current Business*, which presents business statistics, and the *Business Conditions Digest*, which

THE *ENCYCLOPEDIA OF INVESTMENTS*

The *Encyclopedia of Investments*, 2d ed. Warren Gorham & Lamont, 1991, is a standardized compilation of articles on over 50 possible investments. Each piece is individually written by an expert in that particular field. The length and form of each article are uniform (about 15 to 20 pages), and each piece includes a glos-sary and a bibliography. The entries ex-amine such practical considerations as how to buy and sell the asset, the primary factors that determine the asset's value, for whom the asset is suitable, the tax im-plications, and where professional advice may be obtained.

The *Encyclopedia of Investments* covers traditional investments such as stocks, bonds, and mutual funds, and less traditional investments such as folk art, gemstones, mortgage-backed securities, motion pictures, paintings, period furni-ture, and stamps. Approximately one-half of the book is devoted to these non-traditional investments. Since there is a dearth of conveniently compiled material on such investment alternatives, this en-cyclopedia is a convenient source of in-formation for investors interested in these assets.

---

provides information on business indicators. The *Economic Report of the President* and the *Annual Report of the Council of Economic Advisors* are published annually; they cover business conditions and provide economic forecasts. For statistics on interest rates, the money supply, national income, and unemployment rates, the investor may consult the *Federal Reserve Bulletin,* which is published monthly by the board of governors of the Federal Reserve.[10]

investment club
A club whose members make contributions for the purpose of investing.

The investor may also join an **investment club.** Such clubs pool the members' funds and invest them in securities. Most clubs invest only moderate sums. For example, members may pay $10 per month in dues, which are then invested in the club's name. Although such sums of money are trivial, the potential knowledge and experience that can be gained through membership in such clubs is not. Since mem-bers must agree on the club's investment goals, strategies, and choice of investments, the individual may learn a considerable amount concerning investments as the club formulates and executes policy. These clubs may have an additional advantage in that they may be able to obtain professional help at a fraction of the cost. For exam-ple, a salesperson from a brokerage firm may be willing to talk with members of the club and execute orders for them. The broker may do this for the potential commissions not only from the club but also from individual members of the club who may become clients. Unfortunately, the club may be dominated by one or a few outspoken individuals, and the club's goals may not coincide with the individual's goals or financial needs. Because of these factors, the individual should not rely solely on investment clubs to make personal investment decisions.[11]

Last, the individual investor should not exclude the possibility of taking courses in investments. Many adult education programs offer special courses in areas of investing such as portfolio planning and management. These classes usually have

---

[10] "The Individual Investor's Guide to Investment Information" is a convenient source of addresses and may be obtained from the American Association of Individual Investors, 625 N. Michigan Avenue, Chicago, IL, 60611.

[11] For a description of the procedures for establishing an investment club consult the *Investors Manual* published by the National Association of Investors Corporation, 1515 E. 11 Mile Road, Royal Oak, MI 48067.

nominal tuition fees and may offer the individual investor an excellent source of information.

There is no shortage of readily available information. The problem for the investor is separating "the wheat from the chaff" and processing it into a useful form from which to draw conclusions. Even if the investor relies solely on the advice of others, such as brokers or investment services, that individual must still select from the alternatives that are suggested. For example, each week the *Value Line Investment Survey* recommends 100 stocks that should, in its opinion, outperform the market. No investor is going to buy all of them. If an investor follows the advice of the publication and purchases several of its recommended stocks, he or she must still choose from the various recommended investment alternatives. Hence, the final investment decision rests with the individual investor, who earns the returns and bears the risk.

Data Bases and Computer Programs

With the spread of personal computers, computer programs, and peripheral equipment, there have developed data bases such as *The Source* and the *Dow Jones News/Retrieval Service*. *The Source* and *CompuServe* are general information services, while the *Dow Jones News/Retrieval Service* specializes in on-line financial information. Other on-line financial information services include *Telescan, FCI-Invest/Net, Nite-Line,* and *Warner Computer Systems*. Subscribers pay a connection fee and usage rates. Such services provide current price quotations, historical price information, financial news items, and filings with the SEC such as annual reports and quarterly filings.

Data is of little use if it cannot be processed. Since the advent of inexpensive personal computers, a large number of software programs have been developed that may help the investor process information. The availability, capability, and cost of these products change rapidly, so what is applicable in 1993 will probably be outdated by 1995. One means of staying reasonably up-to-date is to consult *The Individual Investor's Guide to Computerized Investing*. This publication of the American Association of Individual Investors provides a summary of software and the systems for which the software was created, the cost of the software, its most recent updates, and the addresses and phone numbers of software publishers.

The next step after the development of data bases and software to process the data may be the institution of on-line trading. For example, the discount broker Schwab offers on-line trading through Spear Securities. While the service is not widely used by the general investing public, the concept is being nurtured by some discount brokerage firms. As may be expected, full commission brokerage firms are not inclined to encourage this development, since on-line investing can circumvent the broker.

SUMMARY

This chapter has described some of the extensive literature that is available to investors. These publications range from the annual and quarterly reports of publicly held firms to specialized investment advisory services. Some of this information is readily available and may be obtained with little effort and at little cost. Other sources require that the investor pay a substantial sum for the material. Many brokerage firms carry some of the publications that have been described, and the investor may often find them at a local library.

Although none of the publications can consistently predict the future (and the investor should be skeptical of any publication claiming that the subscriber can make a fortune), investors do need to be well informed. Reading financial literature from diverse sources is an excellent means of keeping abreast of events in the financial markets. The investor should be aware of the many sources of potentially useful financial information. In addition to the material cited in this chapter, each chapter in this text ends with a list of readings on the material covered in the chapter.

Investment services, which are available from a professional counselor or a bank, are another source of financial information. Although such services may be costly for the small investor, the effective cost of professional counseling decreases as the value of the portfolio increases.

There is no shortage of information on financial markets and investing. Instead, the problems for the investor are processing this information and putting it into a usable form for making financial decisions. Ultimately it is the individual who reaps the returns earned by the investment and bears the risk of loss.

Terms to Remember

annual report	13-D report
quarterly report	inside information
10-K report	buy, sell, or hold
10-Q report	investment club
8-K report	

Questions

1. Describe the contents of an annual report.
2. What is a 10-K report? What is a prospectus?
3. Name several sources of information on investments that are available to individuals. In general, is there a shortage of available information?
4. Why may investment advisory research reports be self-serving?
5. The act of finding information is one of the best means to learn about the literature that is available to the investor. The student should try to locate the following and skim through each to become familiar with its contents. (a) *The Wall Street Journal* and *Barron's;* (b) *Value Line Investment Survey, The Outlook,* or some other advisory service publication; (c) *Forbes, Fortune,* or *Business Week;* and (d) *Moody's Industrial Manual* or *Standard & Poor's Corporation Records.*

Suggested Readings

For definitions of terms, historical background, illustrations, laws and regulations, statistical data, and a bibliography of 4,200 items concerning financing, banking, and investing see

Mann, Glenn G., F. L. Garcia, and Charles J. Woelfel. *Encyclopedia of Banking and Finance,* 9th ed. Rolling Meadows, IL: Bankers Publishers Company, 1991.

In addition to the material presented in this chapter, the reader may consult the following general source material.

Consolidated Capital Communications Group, Inc. *The Financial Desk Book.* Emeryville, Calif.: Consolidated Capital Communications Group, 1985.

Lehman, Michael B. *The Dow Jones-Irwin Guide to Using The Wall Street Journal.* 2d ed. Homewood, Ill.: Dow Jones-Irwin, 1986.

Levine, Sumner, ed. *Business One-Irwin Business and Investment Almanac.* Homewood, Ill.: Dow Jones-Irwin, 1991.

Pessin, Allan H. *Illustrated Encyclopedia of the Securities Industry.* New York: New York Institute of Finance, 1988.

Stock Market Encyclopedia. New York: Standard & Poor's Corp., published annually.

5

THE TAX ENVIRONMENT

liver Wendell Holmes, Jr., said that "taxes are what we pay for civilized society." If you judge by the variety and amount of taxes, we live in a very civilized society. Income from all sources is taxed. Sales taxes are levied on consumer purchases. Excise taxes are levied on imported goods and selected domestic goods, such as beer, wine, and gasoline. Property taxes are levied on real estate. Tolls are levied when you use some highways, bridges, and tunnels.

While there are many types of taxes, only two affect investment decision making: income taxes, which alter the return earned on an investment, and wealth taxes, which affect the value of an estate. Estate taxation is, of course, levied only once, but income taxation recurs throughout the investor's life. For this reason considerable time and effort are devoted to reducing taxes and sheltering income from taxation.

This chapter briefly covers the main sources of taxation and offers several illustrations of tax shelters. Tax laws change virtually every year. This is unfortunate because it means that investment decisions made under one set of laws may be taxed under a different set of laws. Changes in tax laws will also mean that some of the specific information in this chapter (e.g., tax rates) may become outdated. However, the basic tax principles tend to remain the same.

✦ ✦ ✦

LEARNING OBJECTIVES

After completing this chapter you should be able to

1. Identify the taxes that affect investment decision making.

2. Define progressive, proportionate, and regressive taxes.

3. Illustrate how capital losses are used to offset capital gains and ordinary income.

4. Explain how pension plans, IRAs, Keogh accounts, and 401(k) accounts are tax shelters.

5. Explain the tax advantages associated with municipal bonds, annuities, and life insurance.

6. Differentiate between estate and inheritance taxes.

7. Explain the impact of accelerated depreciation on taxes owed.

TAX BASES

Since one of the main purposes of taxes is to raise revenues, a tax base must be large in order to produce any sizable amount of revenue. In general, there are three bases that can be taxed: one's income, one's wealth, and one's consumption (i.e., spending). In the United States all three are used as tax bases at various levels of government. The federal government and many states tax income. Several states and virtually all local governments tax wealth (e.g., property taxes). The federal government also may tax an individual's wealth when that person dies (i.e., estate taxes).

Many state governments tax spending (i.e., sales taxes), and the federal government taxes specific spending when it levies import duties, taxes telephone usage, and levies excise taxes on gasoline.

All three major sources of taxation may affect investment decisions. The tax that has the most impact on investments is the federal income tax, which is levied on investment income (i.e., interest and dividends) and on capital gains. Hence, the material on taxes appearing throughout this text emphasizes the federal income tax. However, taxes on wealth, such as the federal estate tax or property taxes on real estate, can be very important considerations for individual investors in specific circumstances. The least important general tax from an investment viewpoint is the sales tax (i.e., taxes on consumption). The purchase of securities or the acquisition of a savings account or shares in a mutual fund are not subject to sales tax. There are, however, a few investments, such as the purchase of gold or collectibles such as antiques, that are subject to sales tax in some localities. These taxes, of course, reduce the potential return from the investments and may reduce their attractiveness in comparison to financial assets that are exempt from sales taxes.

INCOME TAXATION

Personal and corporate income is subject to taxation. These taxes are levied both by the federal government and by many state governments. Some states also permit the taxation of income by their municipalities. For example, the income of New York City residents is subject to federal, state, and city taxes.

In general, income taxes apply to all sources of income. Thus, dividend and interest income is subject to this taxation. However, the tax is not applied evenly to the returns from all investments. For example, dividend income is taxed by the federal government, while interest on municipal bonds is not.

Income taxes levied by the federal government and by many state governments are progressive. A tax is **progressive** if the tax rate increases as the tax base (income) rises. If the tax rate declines as the base increases, the tax is **regressive.** If the tax rate remains constant, the tax is **proportionate.**

The differences in progressive, regressive, and proportionate taxes are illustrated in Exhibit 5.1. The first column gives an individual's income. The second and third columns illustrate a progressive tax (the tax rate increases with the increases in income). The fourth and fifth columns illustrate a regressive tax (the tax rate declines as incomes rise). The last two columns illustrate a proportionate tax (the rate remains constant as income changes). As shown, the absolute amount of tax paid increases in each case. However, the effect of the higher tax rates on the total amount of tax is considerable as income rises from $10,000 to $50,000. With the regressive tax structure, the tax rises from $1,000 to $3,000. With the progressive tax, the amount paid in taxes rises to $15,000.

Many people believe that taxes should be progressive, so that individuals with higher incomes bear a larger proportion of the cost of government. Regressive taxes are criticized on this basis. Regressive taxes place a greater share of the cost of government on those individuals with the least ability to afford the burden. The argument for progressive taxes is based on ethical or normative beliefs. It is a moral judgment that some taxpayers should pay a proportionately higher amount of tax.

progressive tax
A tax whose rate increases as the tax base increases.

regressive tax
A tax whose rate declines as the tax base increases.

proportionate tax
A tax in which the tax rate remains constant as the tax base changes.

Exhibit 5.1 ✦ DIFFERENCES IN TAXES PAID UNDER HYPOTHETICAL PROGRESSIVE, REGRESSIVE, AND PROPORTIONATE

Income	Progressive Tax Rate	Total Tax Paid	Regressive Tax Rate	Total Tax Paid	Proportionate Tax Rate	Total Tax Paid
$10,000	10%	$ 1,000	10%	$1,000	20%	$ 2,000
20,000	15	3,000	9	1,800	20	4,000
30,000	20	6,000	8	2,400	20	6,000
40,000	25	10,000	7	2,800	20	8,000
50,000	30	15,000	6	3,000	20	10,000

The federal personal income tax is progressive because as the individual's income rises, the tax rate increases. For example, the federal income tax rates for a married couple filing a joint return in 1993 for income earned during 1992 follow:

Taxable Income	Marginal Tax Rate
$0–35,800	15%
35,801–86,500	28
above 86,500	31

Given this tax schedule, an individual with taxable income of $25,000 owes income taxes of $3,750 (.15 × $25,000). If taxable income were $40,000, the taxes owed are $6,546 ($35,800 × .15 + 4,200 × .28). This tax is 16.37 percent ($6,780/$40,000) of the couple's taxable income.

marginal tax rate
The tax rate paid on an additional last dollar of taxable income; an individual's tax bracket.

The right-hand column (i.e., the tax rate on additional income) is often referred to as the **marginal tax rate.** As may be seen from the schedule, the tax rate increases as income increases, which indicates that the federal income tax structure is progressive. The tax brackets (e.g., $0–35,800) change every year, because under tax reform the brackets will be adjusted for inflation (i.e., there is a cost-of-living adjustment or COLA). As prices increase, the tax brackets are raised so that individuals are not taxed at a higher marginal tax rate solely as the result of higher prices. Unless the tax law is changed, the tax rates will remain 15, 28, and 31 percent.

TAX SHELTERS

tax shelter
An asset or investment that defers, reduces, or avoids taxation.

Even though tax reform eliminated many tax shelters and reduced marginal tax rates, individuals are still concerned with sheltering income from taxation. A **tax shelter,** as the name implies, is anything that avoids, reduces, or defers taxes; it is a shelter or protection against taxes. An investor does not have to be wealthy to enjoy these benefits, and many investors of modest means use tax shelters. Unfortunately the term *tax shelter* may evoke a variety of emotions and misunderstandings. In the minds of some people, tax shelter means all those taxes that other people (especially the rich) are not paying. For some investors, the possibility of sheltering income from taxation may be sufficient to make irrational (and costly) investments. Still others may not realize the tax shelters that they themselves enjoy.

An example of a tax shelter that avoids taxation is the municipal bond. These bonds are generally referred to as **tax-exempt bonds,** since the interest earned on most state and municipal debt is exempt from federal income taxation. (Correspondingly, interest on federal debt is exempt from state and local government taxation). The interest is also exempt from state and local income taxes if the owner is a resident of the state of issue. Thus, for a resident of New York City, the interest on a New York state bond is exempt from federal income taxes, New York state income taxes, and New York City income taxes. This can be a significant tax shelter as one's income and marginal tax bracket rise. An individual living in New York City who has a combined federal, state, and local marginal tax rate near 40 percent will find that the after-tax yields on a 6.5 percent New York state bond are equivalent to a yield of 10.8 percent on a corporate bond.[1]

An example of a tax shelter that reduces taxes is the deductibility of interest on mortgages and property taxes. A home is, of course, an investment, and the deductibility of these expenses associated with home ownership reduces the individual's federal income taxes. In addition to being a major tax shelter, this makes home ownership less expensive and more attractive.

An example of a tax shelter that defers taxes is the tax-deferred retirement account. While the individual does not avoid paying the tax, the payment is postponed until some time in the future. In effect, the individual has the free use of the funds until the tax must be paid, which in this case will be during retirement. For a 30-year-old worker, this will be in the distant future.

tax-exempt bond
A bond whose interest is excluded from federal income taxation.

Capital Gains and Losses

Many investments are purchased and subsequently sold. If the sale results in a profit, that profit is considered a **capital gain;** if the sale results in a loss, that is a **capital loss.** If the gain or loss is realized within a year, it is a short-term capital gain or loss. If the sale occurs after a year from the date of purchase, it is a long-term gain or loss.

Short-term capital gains are taxed at the individual's marginal tax rate (i.e., 15, 28, or 31 percent). Thus, if an investor buys a stock for $10,000 and sells it for $13,000 after nine months, the $3,000 short-term capital gain is taxed as any other source of taxable income. If the stock had been held for fifteen months, the $3,000 long-term capital gain would be taxed at either 15 or 28 percent, depending on the individual's marginal tax rate. Taxpayers in the 15 and 28 percent brackets pay the same tax on long-term capital gains as they do on other sources of income. For taxpayers in the 31 percent marginal tax bracket, however, long-term capital gains are taxed at 28 percent. An individual in the 31 percent tax bracket would pay $930 on a $3,000 short-term capital gain while a $3,000 long-term capital gain generates $840 in taxes, a reduction of $90.

The investor may use capital losses to offset capital gains. If the above investor bought a second stock for $15,000 and sold it for $12,000, the $3,000 loss would

capital gain
The increase in the value of an asset such as a stock or a bond.

capital loss
A decrease in the value of an asset such as a stock or a bond.

---

[1] How the equivalence of taxable and nontaxable yields is calculated is explained in Chapter 17.

offset the $3,000 capital gain. This offsetting of capital gains by capital losses applies to both short- and long-term gains. However, there is a specified order in which losses offset gains.

Initially short-term losses are used to offset short-term gains, and long-term losses are used to offset long-term gains. If there is a net short-term loss (i.e., short-term losses exceed short-term gains), it is used to offset long-term gains. For example, if an investor has realized net short-term losses of $3,000, that short-term loss may be used to offset up to $3,000 in long-term capital gains. If net short-term losses are less than long-term gains, the resulting net capital gain is taxed as long term.

If there is a net long-term loss (i.e., long-term losses exceed long-term gains), the loss is used to offset short-term gains. For example, $3,000 in net long-term capital losses is used to offset up to $3,000 in short-term capital losses. If net long-term losses are less than short-term gains, the resulting net capital gain is taxed as short term.

If the investor has a net short- or long-term capital loss after subtracting short- or long-term capital gains, that net capital loss is used to offset income from other sources, such as dividends or interest. However, only $3,000 in capital losses may be used in a given year to offset income from other sources. If the individual has a larger loss (e.g., $5,000), only $3,000 may be used in the current year. The remainder ($2,000) is carried forward to offset capital gains or income received in future years. Under this system of carry-forward, a current capital loss of $10,000 offsets only $3,000 in current income and the remaining $7,000 is carried forward to offset capital gains and income in subsequent years. If the investor has no capital gains in the second year, only $3,000 of the remaining loss offsets income in the second year and the balance ($4,000) is carried forward to the third year. In the case of a large capital loss, this $3,000 limitation may be an incentive for the investor to take gains in the current year rather than carry forward the loss.

While capital gains are taxed at the same rate as ordinary income, they are still illustrative of a tax shelter. The taxes on capital gains may be deferred indefinitely, since investment profits are taxed only after they have been realized. Many profits on security positions are only **paper profits,** because some investors do not sell the securities and realize the gains. The tax laws encourage such retention of securities by taxing the gains only when they are realized.

paper profits
Price appreciation that has not been realized.

If the holder gives the securities to someone as a gift (for example, if a grandparent gives securities whose value has risen to a grandchild), the cost basis is transferred to the recipient, and the capital gains taxes continue to be deferred. If the recipient sells the securities and realizes the gain, then capital gains taxes will have to be paid by the owner of the securities (i.e., the recipient of the gift).

Capital gains taxes can be avoided entirely if the individual holds the securities until he or she dies. The value of securities are taxed as part of the deceased's estate. The securities are then transferred through the deceased's will to other individuals, such as children or grandchildren, and the cost basis becomes the security's value as of the date of death. For example, suppose an individual owns shares of IBM that were purchased in the 1950s. The current value of the shares is probably many times their costs. If the investor were to sell these shares, he or she would incur a large capital gain. However, if the shares are held until the investor dies, their new cost basis becomes the current value of the shares, and the capital gains tax on the appreciation is avoided.

Tax-Deferred Pension Plans

One tax shelter that may also ease the burden of retirement is the pension plan. Many firms contribute to these plans for their employees. The funds are invested in income-earning assets, such as stocks and bonds. In some cases the individual employee is required to make payments in addition to the employer's contributions. The amount of the employer's contribution is usually related to the employee's earnings. These contributions are not included in taxable income, so the worker does not have to pay taxes on the employer's payments to the pension plan. Instead, the funds are taxed when the worker retires and starts to use the money that has accumulated through the plan.

IRAs   One criticism of these pension plans was that they were not available to all workers. However, Congress passed legislation that enables all employees as well as the self-employed to set up their own pension plans; thus, the tax shelter that was previously provided only through employer-sponsored pension plans is now available to all. An employee who is not covered by a pension plan may set up an **individual retirement account (IRA).** In 1981 Congress passed additional legislation that extended IRAs to all employees, even if they were already participating in an employer-sponsored pension plan.

IRA
A retirement plan (individual retirement account) that is available to workers.

Under an IRA, an individual worker may open an account with a financial institution, such as a commercial bank, savings and loan association (S&L), insurance company, brokerage firm, or mutual fund and may deposit up to $2,000 per year. The funds must be earned, which means that any employee who earns $2,000 or more may place as much as $2,000 in an IRA account.[2] However, if the individual's source of income is dividends or interest, these funds cannot be placed in an IRA.

The amount invested in the IRA is deducted from the individual's taxable income. Income earned by the funds in the account is also not taxed. All taxes are deferred until the funds are withdrawn from the IRA, and then they are taxed as ordinary income. If the individual prematurely withdraws the funds (before age 59½), the money is taxed as ordinary income and a penalty tax is added.

IRA accounts soon became one of the most popular tax shelters, but in 1986 Congress placed important restrictions on the deductibility of the IRA contribution.

---

[2]The ability of part-time workers to establish IRAs creates interesting possibilities for tax savings for spouses that work part-time while the other spouse maintains a full-time job.

WHEN TO START AN IRA

While an individual worker's ability to start an IRA is constrained by the availability of funds, the earlier the account is started, the better. Since many young workers often have other priorities for which they are saving (e.g., down payment on a house) and are not contemplating retirement, they may not open an IRA. This is unfortunate, since the final amount in the account is greatly enhanced if the deposits are made at an early age.

This difference in the terminal value is illustrated by the following examples. An individual deposits $1,000 in an IRA starting at age 25 and continues the contribution for 40 years (i.e., until age 65). If the funds earn 8 percent annually, the account grows to $259,050. If the same individual started the account at age 45 and contributed $2,000 annually until age 65, the account would have $91,524. (How these amounts may be calculated is explained in the next chapter.) Even though total contributions in both cases are $40,000, the final amounts are considerably different. When the funds are deposited earlier, they earn more interest, which produces the larger terminal value. Thus it is to the individual's benefit to start IRA contributions as soon as possible, even if the amount of the contributions is modest.

For workers *covered by a pension plan,* full deductibility is applicable only for couples filing a joint return with adjusted gross income of *less than $40,000.* (For single workers covered by a pension plan the limit is $25,000.) Note that adjusted gross income is used and not earned income. If an individual earns a modest salary but has significant amounts of interest or dividend income, this additional income counts when determining the deductibility of IRA contributions. Once the cutoff level of income is reached, the deductibility of the contribution is reduced, so that it is completely phased out once the couple reaches adjusted gross income of $50,000 ($35,000 for individuals).

It is important to realize that the complete loss of deductibility of the IRA contribution applies only to workers filing a joint return who earn more than $50,000 ($35,000 filing a single return). For the majority of workers, the deductibility of the IRA contribution still applies. And the deductibility still applies to any individual, no matter what the level of income, if that individual is not covered by an employer-sponsored pension plan.

Even if the individual loses the deductibility of the IRA contributions, there is still reason to establish an IRA because the income earned by the funds invested in the account is tax-deferred. If a worker places $2,000 in the account for 20 years, it would earn a substantial return and that return would not have been taxed. For example, if $2,000 were placed in an IRA each year for 20 years and it earns 8 percent annually, the amount in the account would grow to $91,524.[3] Only $40,000 of the total represents the annual contributions. The remaining $51,524 is earnings that have not been taxed but will be taxed when the funds are withdrawn from the account. Thus while the change in the tax laws did reduce the attractiveness of the IRA for workers with substantial total income, it did not completely erase the tax shelter generated by IRA accounts.

Keogh Accounts   Self-employed persons may establish a pension plan called a **Keogh account** or **HR-10 plan.** The account is named after the congressman who

Koegh account (HR-10 plan)
A retirement plan that is available to self-employed individuals.

---

[3] How this amount is determined is shown in Chapter 6, which explains how the value of a future sum is calculated.

POINTS OF INTEREST

Whose Name for an IRA

Consider a married man whose wife is not employed. He earns $35,000 a year and knows that he can contribute up to $2,000 in an IRA for himself and $250 in a spousal IRA. Is such a distribution of IRA funds optimal? Many financial planners may suggest the opposite division of the $2,250: place $2,000 in the wife's name and only $250 in the husband's name. Under the law an individual may place any amount up to $2,000 in one ac-count, so the man could put $2,000 in his wife's name and $250 in his, or he could place $1,125 in either name. However, he cannot annually place more than $2,000 in an individual account, nor can he open a joint account. IRAs are *individual* retirement accounts.

What is the advantage of putting the larger amount in the wife's name? The answer really depends on the age of the wife. Women are frequently younger than their husbands. Withdrawals from IRA accounts do not have to start until the individual reaches 70½. If the wife is younger than the husband and the funds are in the wife's name, the potential tax shelter is greater, as the funds may remain tax-deferred for a longer period of time. In addition, the husband is better providing for his wife's old age, when the probability is greater that she will be a widow. Of course, once the funds are in the spouse's name, the spouse is the owner and controls the account.

---

sponsored the enabling legislation. A Keogh is similar to an IRA or a company-sponsored pension plan. The individual places funds in the account and deducts the amount from taxable income. The maximum annual contribution is the lesser of 25 percent of income or $30,000. The funds placed in the account earn a return that (like the initial contributions) will not be taxed until the funds are withdrawn. As in the case of the IRA, there is a penalty for premature withdrawals before age 59½, and withdrawals must start after reaching the age of 70½.

The determination of the amount an individual may contribute to a Keogh account is somewhat confusing. The individual may contribute up to 25 percent of net earned income, but the calculation of net earned income subtracts the pension contribution as a business expense. The effect is that the individual can contribute 20 percent of income before the contribution. Consider a self-employed individual who earns $100,000 before the pension contribution. If that individual contributes $20,000 (i.e., 20 percent of $100,000), he or she has contributed 25 percent of income after deducting the pension contribution:

Net income after contribution:
$100,000 − $20,000 = $80,000.
Contribution as percent of net earned income: $20,000/$80,000 = 25%.

It is probably easier to determine one's maximum possible contribution by taking 20 percent of income before the contribution than by determining 25 percent of net earned income.[4]

---

[4]The formula for determining the maximum contribution is

$$\frac{\text{Income} \times 0.25}{1 + 0.25}$$

If the individual's income is $100,000, the maximum contribution is

$$\frac{\$100,000 \times 0.25}{1 + 0.25} = \frac{\$100,000 \times 0.25}{1.25} = \$20,000.$$

POINTS OF INTEREST

THE USE OF PERSONAL COMPUTERS TO COMPLETE YOUR 1040

For many investors, record keeping, tax planning, and the completion of tax forms required for filing with the IRS can be complicated, time consuming, and expensive. However, by using a personal computer and a tax preparation package, the investor may significantly reduce the amount of work necessary for the completion of the required tax forms. There are many tax packages to choose among including Turbo Tax from ChipSoft, Sylvia Porter's Rapid Tax by DacEasy, Parson's Personal Tax Preparer, and J. K. Lasser's Your Income Tax. The following is a list of factors the investor should consider when acquiring such a program.

1. The investor needs to identify the use of the program. There are many tax packages available, offering a wide range of features. Modest tax packages will complete the most frequently used tax schedules (e.g., form 1040 and schedules A, B, C, D, E, and G). If, however, the investor needs to complete other schedules, a more elaborate (and more expensive) program may be necessary.

2. The investor must be certain the program is compatible with the computer to be used, as many programs can be used only on a specific computer. The investor may want to examine the tax packages before buying the personal computer.

3. Since tax laws change frequently, the investor should consider the adaptability of the program to changes in the tax laws. Otherwise he or she may have to purchase new programs to handle alterations in the tax laws.

4. Computer programs designed to complete tax papers are "cookbooks." They can only do what the investor tells them to perform. Their primary advantages are the reduction in mathematical errors and the simplification of both tax planning and the completion of the tax forms. For example, the investor may enter into the program charitable deductions, interest expenses, or business deductions throughout the year. Such running entries will simplify year-end tax planning. However, the investor must still know what to enter. The tax preparation package is not a substitute for knowledge of the tax laws.

A self-employed person may also open an IRA in addition to a Keogh account. For example, a doctor who earns $100,000 may place $20,000 in a Keogh account. That individual may also place $2,000 in an IRA, but the contribution may not be deducted from taxable income, since the doctor's income exceeds the IRA limits previously discussed. However, even though the contribution is not deductible, the income earned by the account is tax-deferred.

If a self-employed person does open a Keogh plan, it must also apply to other people employed by this individual. There are some exceptions, such as new and young employees; however, if a self-employed individual establishes a Keogh account for him- or herself, other regular employees cannot be excluded. By establishing the account, the self-employed individual takes on fiduciary responsibilities for the management of Keogh accounts for his or her employees. This individual can avoid these responsibilities by establishing a Simplified Employee Pension (SEP) plan. SEPs are a type of pension plan that was designed by Congress to encourage small employers to establish pension plans for their employees but that avoid the complexities of the pension laws.

SRAs   Many employers also offer supplementary retirement accounts (SRAs), which are often referred to as "401(k)" plans. These programs permit individuals to contribute a portion of their earned income, up to a specified limit, to a savings plan. The contribution is deducted from the individual's earnings before determining taxable income; thus, a 401(k) plan is similar in its effect on the employee's federal income taxes to IRAs and Keogh accounts. The funds may be invested in one of several plans offered by the company. These often include a stock fund, a bond fund, and a money market fund. The individual has the choice as to the distribution of the contributions among the plans and may be allowed to shift the funds at periodic intervals.

403(b) Plans   Nonprofit organizations such as hospitals, religious organizations, foundations, and public and private schools sometimes offer similar salary reduction plans referred to as "403(b)" plans. They work essentially in the same way as 401(k) plans for employees of profit organizations. In both cases, the employee's income is reduced by the contribution, so that federal income tax is deferred until the funds are withdrawn from the account. The contributions are invested, and the tax on the earnings is also deferred until the funds are withdrawn.

SEPs   In addition to regular pension plans, 401(k)s, and 403(b)s, pension plans include the "Simplified Employee Plan" (SEP). As mentioned previously, pension plans and the laws governing them are complex and may be costly for an employer to administer. For this reason many small employers do not set up pension plans. To overcome this criticism of pension laws, Congress enacted legislation that enables small firms to set up simplified plans (i.e., SEPs). In a SEP plan, employers make IRA contributions on behalf of employees and thus avoid the administrative costs associated with developing their own pension plans. The limitations on contributions to regular IRA accounts do not apply to SEP plans. In addition to employee contributions, the 1986 tax law permits employers to use salary reductions to make contributions to their SEP, so the SEP–IRA can also serve as a 401(k) plan.

Savings from Tax-Deferred Pension Plans

An example of the savings that are possible with these tax shelters is presented in Exhibit 5.2. For illustrative purposes, it is assumed that the individual earns $40,000. The individual's personal income tax rate is assumed to be 28 percent, so for each dollar of additional income, the individual must pay $0.28 in taxes. The example illustrates two cases. In case A, the individual pays the income tax and then saves $2,000, which is placed in a taxable investment (e.g., a certificate of deposit) that pays 10 percent annually. The interest income earned by the account is, of course, taxable. In case B, the individual places $2,000 in a tax-sheltered retirement account, which also pays 10 percent annually. However, the tax on this interest is deferred until the individual retires and withdraws the money.

In case A the saver starts with the $40,000 and pays the income tax ($11,200), which leaves a disposable income of $28,800. Of this, $2,000 is invested, leaving $26,800. In case B the saver initially contributes $2,000 to an IRA, which reduces taxable income by $2,000 to $38,000. Taxes of $10,640 are then paid, which leaves a spendable income of $27,360. By placing $2,000 in the IRA account and reducing taxable income, the saver reduces taxes by $560.

The initial tax saving, however, is only the first part of the potential savings. The $2,000 in case A now earns $200 in interest, but $56 of that is lost in taxes. Hence, the saver nets only $144 in interest. The 10 percent interest rate generates a return after taxes of only 7.2 percent. The $2,000 in the IRA earns $200 but none of that interest is currently subject to tax.

After the first year (i.e., the beginning of the second year), there is $2,144 in the account in case A, but in case B, in which the saver placed funds in the

Exhibit 5.2 ✦ POTENTIAL SAVINGS WITH A TAX-SHELTERED RETIREMENT ACCOUNT

	Case A	Case B
Present		
Taxable income	$40,000.00	$40,000.00
Contribution	0	2,000.00
Net taxable income	40,000.00	38,000.00
Taxes	11,200.00	10,640.00
Disposable income	28,800.00	27,360.00
Contribution to savings	2,000.00	0
Net disposable income	26,800.00	27,360.00
Tax savings	0	560.00
Year 1		
Amount invested	$ 2,000.00	$ 2,000.00
Interest earned	200.00	200.00
Taxes on interest	56.00	0
Net interest earned	144.00	200.00
Year 2		
Amount in account	$ 2,144.00	$ 2,200.00
Interest earned	214.40	220.00
Taxes on interest	60.03	0
Net interest earned	154.37	220.00
Year 3		
Amount in account	$ 2,298.37	$ 2,420.00
	·	·
	·	·
	·	·
Year 20		
Amount in account	$ 8,033.89	$13,455.00
Tax savings	0	5,421.00

retirement account, the amount in the account is $2,200.[5] The amounts in the accounts in case A and in case B grow to $2,298.37 and $2,420, respectively, at the beginning of the third year. After 20 years the initial $2,000 placed in the account in case A will have grown to $8,033.89 after taxes have been paid, but the proceeds in the tax-deferred account will have grown to $13,455. The tax savings over 20 years will amount to $5,421.[6]

This example assumes that the saver makes only one payment of $2,000. However, savings plans usually imply that the investor periodically places funds in the account. If the investor were to place at the beginning of each year $2,000 in the taxable investment or the tax-sheltered retirement account every year for 20 years,

---

[5] This example assumes that the tax on interest in case A is deducted from the interest and is not paid from other disposable income.

[6] How these figures are determined is explained in the next chapter. See in particular Problems 3 and 8 at the end of that chapter.

the tax savings would be even greater. In that case the tax-sheltered account would have $126,005 but the taxable alternative would have $89,838 after taxes. The difference then would be $36,167. This difference is the result of the tax savings on the interest alone and does not include the $560 tax savings generated each year by depositing the $2,000 in the account. In 20 years, $11,200 ($560 each year × 20) would be saved in taxes, for a total tax savings of more than $47,300.

These tax savings would be even greater if the investor were to place a larger sum each year in the retirement plan account (as is possible under the Keogh plan) or if income tax rates were higher. For the self-employed professional with a substantial amount of taxable income, such as a lawyer or a doctor, these retirement plans offer one of the best means available to shelter income from current taxation. However, the individual will still have to pay tax on this income when the funds are withdrawn from the plan, while the tax has already been paid on the funds in the taxable alternative.

Tax-Deferred Annuities

In addition to tax-deferred pension plans, an individual may acquire a **tax-deferred annuity,** which is a contract for a series of payments in the future whose earnings are not subject to current income taxation. Tax-deferred annuities are sold by life insurance companies, and they work like life insurance in reverse. Instead of periodically paying for the insurance, the insurance company makes regular payments to the individual who owns the annuity.[7] A tax-deferred annuity has two components: a period in which funds accumulate and a period in which payments are made by the insurance company to the owner of the annuity.

> **tax-deferred annuity**
> *A contract sold by an insurance company in which the company guarantees a series of payments and whose earnings are not taxed until they are distributed.*

The investor buys the annuity by making a payment to the insurance company (e.g., a lump-sum distribution from a pension plan may be used to buy an annuity). The insurance company then invests the funds and contractually agrees to a repayment schedule, which can start immediately or at some other time specified in the contract. While the funds are left with the insurance company, they earn a return for the annuity's owner. The individual's personal income tax obligation on these funds is deferred until the earnings are actually paid out by the insurance company.

Since the tax on the earnings is deferred, it is possible that the amount of tax actually paid will be less than would have been the case if the earnings were taxed as accumulated. Many individuals use these annuities to accumulate funds for retirement. If after reaching retirement their income has fallen, their tax bracket may be reduced. In this case the withdrawals from the annuity will be taxed at a lower rate. Of course, it is possible that if the individual has saved sufficiently through pension plans, IRA accounts, Keogh accounts, and personal savings, the tax bracket could be higher instead of lower when funds are withdrawn from any of the tax-sheltered accounts (including the tax-deferred annuity). But even if a higher tax rate were to occur in the future, the individual still has had the advantage of tax-free accumulation during the period when the tax obligation was deferred.

---

[7] For descriptions of various types of annuities, see Robert S. Rubinstein, "Life Insurance Investments—Annuities," in *The Encyclopedia of Investments*, eds. M.E. Blume and J.P. Friedman (Boston: Warrent, Gorham & Lamont, 1982), 355–382.

LIFE INSURANCE AS A TAX SHELTER

face value
An insurance policy's death benefit.

cash value
The amount that would be received if a life insurance policy were canceled.

term
The period during which the individual's life is insured.

While the primary focus of this text is on investing in stocks and bonds, an individual's portfolio may include life insurance. Such insurance offers both financial protection from premature death and a means to accumulate wealth. The death protection offered by the insurance policy is the amount or **face value** of the policy. It is this face value that is paid to the named beneficiary at the insured's death.

Life insurance may be classified into two types: policies with a savings program and policies without savings. Life insurance with a savings component accumulates funds, which are referred to as the policy's **cash value.** The owner of the policy may cancel it and receive the cash value. As long as the policy is in force, the cash value continues to grow as the invested funds earn interest.

Life insurance policies that lack the savings feature are called **term** insurance. The individual purchases insurance for a specified period of time (i.e., the term). The cost of the policy covers only the financial protection in the event of death. There is no savings component and no investment. Term life insurance is essentially no different from property or casualty insurance. In each case the buyer acquires protection against some peril for the term of the policy.

Since term insurance lacks a savings component, it is cheaper, but more costly insurance policies with savings programs offer important advantages. If the individual has difficulty saving, the periodic insurance payment (i.e., the policy's premium) is a means to force saving. Perhaps the most important advantage of this type of insurance is the tax shelter associated with the savings component.

Returns earned on many investments such as interest on a certificate of deposit or dividends earned on a common stock are taxed in the year earned. Even if the individual leaves the funds in the bank to earn interest or participates in a dividend reinvestment program that accumulates additional shares, that individual is subject to income tax on the funds as if they were received. Reinvesting funds does not result in tax deferral.

The taxation of the return earned on funds invested in the savings component of life insurance policies is perceptibly different from the taxation of interest earned on savings accounts or dividends of stock. The funds earned on the policy's cash value are subject to tax only when they are received. Current interest earned on the cash value is sheltered from current income taxation. Furthermore, if the insured should die before the policy is cashed in, the interest is *never* subject to federal income tax.

Under federal income laws, taxation of the policy's cash value only occurs if the policyholder cashes in the policy and removes the funds. In this case, the individual is subject to federal income taxation but only if the amount received exceeds the total premiums paid. For example, if the insured had made policy payments over the years of $2,000, cashed in the policy, and received $1,500, there would be no federal income tax. The amount received is less than the cost of the policy. If, however, the insured had made payments of $2,000 and received $3,200, then the individual would be subject to federal income taxes on the amount that exceeds the payments (i.e., $1,200 in this illustration).

This tax treatment of the receipts from an insurance policy is not truly taxation of earned interest. No attempt is made to differentiate what part of the cost of the policy covers the death benefit and what part is the savings component. The individual is able to recover the entire amount spent to maintain the policy before there are any tax implications. Only after the cash value has grown sufficiently that the amount the contributions have earned exceeds the total premiums does the policyholder become subject to federal income taxation.

While there is considerable variety in the types of policies that offer a savings component, most are purchased through periodic payments. These premium payments may be made annually, quarterly, or even monthly, and as long as the payments are made, the policy remains in force.

Insurance companies, however, also offer a single payment (i.e., single premium) policy in which the individual makes only one payment. If an individual were to receive a large payment (e.g., a distribution from a pension plan or an inheritance), the individual could use those funds to purchase a single premium life insurance policy. The policy offers the same general features associated with traditional life insurance. It protects the insured's beneficiaries against the financial impact of premature death, and the cash value of the policy generates a tax-deferred return with a guaranteed minimum return.

Single premium life insurance policies offer a major cost advantage over traditional policies. In the typical life insurance policy, a large percentage of the initial payments is used to cover the commissions associated with selling the policy. Only a modest amount is actually invested to increase the policy's cash value. With a single premium policy, sales commissions and other fees are paid from the earnings generated by the policy's cash value. Virtually all of the initial payment of the policy is invested and immediately contributes to increasing the policy's cash value.[8]

EMPLOYEE STOCK OPTION PLANS AS A TAX SHELTER

One tax shelter available to some corporate employees is the employee stock option plan, which permits individuals to buy their employer's stock at a specified price within a specified time period. These stock option plans are considered a tax shelter because they defer tax obligations until the employees realize gains from exercising their options. Taxes will be owed only after the employee sells the stock acquired through the stock option for a profit.

There are two types of corporate stock option plans: the *stock purchase plan* and *incentive stock options*. The stock purchase plan permits employees to buy their corporate employer's stock at a price which is generally set at a modest discount (up to 15 percent). This type of stock option plan must be offered to virtually all employees. Only new hires, part-time employees, highly compensated personnel, and employees owning more than 5 percent of the stock are excluded.

For tax purposes, employees receive no taxable income when they receive or when they exercise the option granted under a stock purchase plan. If the shares are held for at least a year after the option is exercised *and* for at least two years after the option was granted, any profits on the sale of the stock are considered to be long-term capital gains. Thus, if an employee is granted the option and exercises it after five months, that individual must hold the stock for nineteen months for a total of two years after the option is granted for any profit on the sale to be treated

---

[8] For descriptions of the various types of life and casualty insurance, see George E. Rejda, *Principles of Insurance*, 3rd ed. Glenview, Ill.: Scott, Foresman and Company, 1989.

as a long-term capital gain. If the stock is held for a shorter time period, the profit is treated as ordinary income for the year in which the gain is realized.

Unlike stock purchase options, which are explained in Chapter 19, incentive stock options are granted to selected employees. These plans, which require stockholder approval, specify the number of shares that may be purchased and the employees (or class of employees) eligible to receive the options. The price at which the option may be exercised must be equal to or exceed the market price of the stock when the option is granted. This option must be exercisable within ten years and may not be transferred by the recipient (except through an estate). For options granted after 1986, the value of the stock that may be purchased through the option cannot exceed $100,000 per employee.

The recipient of the incentive stock option experiences no taxable income when the option is granted or exercised. If the employee exercises the option and holds the stock for one year and for two years after the option was granted, any profit on exercising the option and subsequent sale of the stock is a long-term capital gain. If the time requirements are not met, the profit is considered ordinary income for the year in which the gain is realized.

The distinction between treating incentive stock option profits as ordinary income or as capital gains is obviously important if the income tax rate on long-term capital gains differs from the rate on ordinary income. Even the small difference in the 1992 tax laws which allow long-term capital gains to be taxed at 28 percent versus 31 percent for individuals in the 31 percent income tax bracket can result in substantial differences in taxes owed (i.e., $3,000 difference per $100,000 of long-term capital gains).

If tax rates on ordinary income and long-term capital gains are the same, the distinction between the two may still be important. First, there is always the possibility that the tax laws may be changed so that long-term capital gains receive more favorable tax treatment, in which case the distinction obviously becomes important. Even if there is not change in the income tax laws favoring capital gains or if the change in rates is only negligible, there is a second reason why the distinction is important. If an employee realizes a long-term capital gain through exercising the option and selling the stock, that gain may be offset by losses realized on the sale of other capital assets. (Correspondingly if the stockholder realizes a loss through the employee stock option plan, that loss may be used against capital gains from other transactions.) There is no limitation on the dollar amount of this offset. An individual who previously made a poor investment and has, for example, a $36,000 capital loss can offset that loss by realizing long-term capital gains generated by exercising the incentive stock option and selling the stock. By such judicious timing of gains and losses, the employee may be able to erase capital gains generated through exercising the incentive stock option and selling the stock.

If the gains from the incentive stock options are considered ordinary income, the taxpayer's ability to use capital losses from other sources to offset the gains from the incentive stock options is severely limited. As explained earlier in this chapter, only $3,000 ($1,500 for married individuals filing separately) of ordinary income may be offset by capital losses in a given year. Thus, the ability to use capital losses to offset capital gains from incentive stock option plans requires that the latter be treated as a capital gains and not as ordinary income. Thus, the classification of profits from employee stock option plans as capital gains instead of ordinary income can have a positive tax implication even if the tax rate on capital gains and ordinary income are equal.

TAXATION OF WEALTH

There are also taxes on wealth in the form of estate, gift, and property taxes. Two types of taxes are exacted when a person dies: estate taxes and inheritance taxes. Estate taxes are imposed on the corpus or body of the deceased's estate. That includes the value of investments such as stocks and bonds as well as the value of personal effects such as automobiles and other personal property. The inheritance tax is levied on the share of an estate received by another individual. Like the estate tax, it is imposed on the value of personal effects as well as on financial assets.

Estate taxes are primarily the domain of the federal government, while both estate and inheritance taxes are levied by state governments. Like the personal income tax, estate and inheritance taxes are usually progressive. Selected rates from the federal estate tax are given in Exhibit 5.3.[9] As may be seen from this exhibit, the tax rates increase with the value of the estate up to 55 percent on estates in excess of $3,000,000.

estate tax
A tax on the value of a deceased individual's assets.

Estate tax laws are extremely complex, and an investor who is planning the distribution of his or her estate should consult a lawyer or financial planner. However, the basic components of these taxes are as follows. First, a married individual may leave the entire estate to his or her spouse without the spouse's paying any tax. Thus, a married individual with a net worth of $1,000,000 may leave the entire estate to a spouse and avoid estate taxes. This is really only a deferment of the tax liability, because this wealth is added to the wealth of the surviving spouse and is thus subject to estate tax when the spouse dies. Unless there are perceptible differences in the net worth of the individuals, leaving the maximum amount possible to a spouse may only defer some of the tax.

Second, the estate receives a **tax credit,** which reduces the amount of taxes due. The maximum credit is $192,800. The effect of this credit is to exempt all estates valued at less than $600,000 from federal estate taxation. As a result of this tax credit and the ability to leave tax-free funds to one's spouse, most estates will avoid federal taxation. For example, an individual with a spouse and two children whose estate is $1,200,000 can leave $600,000 to the spouse and $600,000 to the children. The $600,000 bequest to the spouse reduces the taxable value of the estate to $600,000. Tax on $600,000 would be $192,800, which is reduced to nothing by the tax credit.[10] However, larger estates may be taxed heavily after the tax credit is applied, since the rates rise rapidly for sums over the sheltered amount.

tax credit
A credit against one's tax liabilities that reduces the amount of tax owed.

Inheritance taxes are levied by state governments on the distribution of the estates of individuals living in the state. Even though the recipient of the inheritance may live in another state, that individual's inheritance is subject to tax by the state in which the deceased resided.

inheritance tax
A tax on what an individual receives from an estate.

As with state income taxes, there are substantial differences in state inheritance taxes. There are also differences in the tax rates for recipients of an inheritance, depending on their relation to the deceased. The deceased's immediate family pays lower rates. Maximum rates apply to nonrelatives who receive a share of the estate.

---

[9]These rates also apply to gifts.
[10]The tax on $600,000 is $155,800 + (.37) ($100,000) − $192,800 = $0. (See Exhibit 5.3.)
   This example assumes no taxable gifts were made during the individual's life.

Exhibit 5.3 ✦ SELECTED FEDERAL ESTATE TAX RATES IN EFFECT AS OF JANUARY, 1993

Taxable Value of the Estate	Tax		
	On the Base°	Plus Percentage†	On Excess Over
$ 0–10,000	$ 0	18%	$ 0
10,000–20,000	1,800	20	10,000
20,000–40,000	3,800	22	20,000
.	.	.	.
.	.	.	.
.	.	.	.
10,000–150,000	23,800	30	100,000
150,000–250,000	38,800	32	150,000
250,000–500,000	70,800	34	250,000
500,000–750,000	155,800	37	500,000
.	.	.	.
.	.	.	.
.	.	.	.
2,500,000–3,000,000	1,025,800	53	2,500,000
above 3,000,000	1,290,000	55	3,000,000

°The base is the tax paid on the amount shown in the left-hand column under the heading "Taxable Value of the Estate."
†The percentage applies to any amount in excess of that shown in the left-hand column and up to the amount shown in the right-hand column under the heading "Taxable Value of the Estate."

property tax
A tax levied against the value of real or financial assets.

In addition to estate and inheritance taxes, the investor must also be concerned with **property taxes.** These are primarily levied by counties, municipalities, and townships. Since there are thousands of such local governments, there is great diversity in property taxes.

Personal property taxes may be levied on tangible or intangible personal property. Tangible property is physical property, such as a house or an automobile. Intangible personal property includes nonphysical assets and financial assets, such as stocks and bonds. Many localities tax only tangible property, with particular emphasis on real estate. However, some states, including Florida and Pennsylvania, permit the taxation of intangible personal property. In such states the individual's portfolio of stocks and bonds may be subject to property taxation. Since there is considerable variation in this type of taxation, the investor would be wise to learn the specific tax laws that apply in his or her own state.

CORPORATE TAXATION

Like individuals, firms are subject to taxation by the various levels of government. Income, capital gains, and property may all be subject to taxation. Although any of these taxes may affect the individual firm, this brief discussion is limited to the federal corporate income tax.

As with the individual federal income taxes, the tax reform law enacted in 1986 reduced both the number of brackets and the corporate income tax rates. As of January 1993, the federal corporate tax structure for income earned in 1990 was the following:

Corporate Income	Tax Rate
$0–$50,000	15%
$50,001–$75,000	25
over $75,000	34

Under this tax structure, the maximum rate applies to virtually all corporations of any significant size. Certainly for publicly held firms, the investor might as well view the amount of taxes owed as being about one-third of the firm's taxable income.[11] Although it is extremely difficult to isolate who ultimately bears the cost of the corporate income tax, it is at least partially borne by investors, since the tax reduces either cash dividends and/or the firm's capacity to reinvest its earnings and grow.

Like individual investors, corporate managements seek to reduce or at least to defer tax payments by taking advantage of certain deductions and making selected investments. For example, the cost of long-term assets, such as plant and equipment, is allocated (i.e., deducted from income) over a period of time; that is, the asset is depreciated. Under **straightline depreciation,** the amount of the deduction is the same each year, but under **accelerated depreciation** this expense is increased during the early years of the asset's life. The effect of accelerated depreciation is to increase expenses in the early years of the asset's life, which decreases current income and current taxes. The tax is deferred until after the period of accelerated depreciation has elapsed.

Prior to tax reform, another means to alter the amount of taxes owed was the **investment tax credit,** which, as the name implies, is a credit to be applied against taxes for making certain investments. In an effort to stimulate spending on plant and equipment, the federal government permitted corporations to reduce their taxes if they made certain investments in plant and equipment. By channeling a firm's funds into these investments, management was able to reduce the amount of income tax that the firm had to pay.

President Clinton's proposal to raise corporate income tax rates and reinstate the investment tax credit could have a major implication for investors if the new investment tax credit applies to firms in industries that require a substantial investment in plant and equipment. The future profitability of these firms may be increased while firms that provide services, such as retail operations, may experience reduced profitability. The investment tax credit offers service firms few tax benefits, but the higher tax rates should decrease their future net income.

Another way corporate financial managers can reduce income taxes is through investments in the stock of other corporations. Only 30 percent of any dividends received are subject to corporate income tax, and the remaining 70 percent are excluded from federal income taxation. If the stock's value rises and is subsequently

straightline depreciation
The allocation of the cost of plant and equipment by equal annual amounts over a period of time.

accelerated depreciation
The allocation of the cost of plant and equipment in unequal annual amounts such that most of the cost is recovered in the early years of an asset's life.

investment tax credit
A direct reduction in taxes owed resulting from investment in plant or equipment.

---

[11] For companies earning more than $100,000 the benefits of the 15 and 25 percent tax brackets are phased out. The tax rate on income between $100,000 and $335,000 is 39 percent. All income over $335,000 is taxed at 34 percent.

sold for a profit, this profit is a capital gain and is taxed, as any other source of income. However, as with individuals, corporate capital gains taxes are paid only after the profits are realized. Management may defer this tax indefinitely by not realizing the gains. Thus, the exclusion of 70 percent of dividend income and the tax deferral of capital gains help explain why some firms own stock in other firms instead of operating assets such as plant and equipment.[12]

Accelerated depreciation and investments in other corporations' stocks are two means available to corporate management to reduce the firm's income taxes. The potential impact of taxes influences management's decision making (just as it affects an individual investor's choice of assets). From the viewpoint of the individual investor, corporate income tax laws make analyzing and comparing companies more difficult. However, if a firm pays less than one-third of its earnings in taxes, that may be a clue to the investor to examine the firm more closely. Although management may be able to reduce taxes temporarily, this may also imply that current earnings are overstated and that taxes may be higher in the future.

SUMMARY

Tax laws have a significant impact on the environment of investing. These laws are issued by all levels of government, but the most important laws affecting investment decisions have been passed by the federal government.

The federal government taxes income from investments, capital gains, and the individual's estate. Tax rates are progressive, which means that as the tax base increases, the tax rate increases. This taxation—especially the progressivity of tax rates—induces individuals to find ways to reduce their tax liabilities. Investments that reduce, defer, or avoid taxes are called tax shelters. Important tax shelters include tax-exempt bonds and pension plans. The interest on tax-exempt bonds completely avoids federal income taxes, while pension plans (including IRAs, Keogh accounts, and 401(k) plans) defer taxes until the funds are withdrawn from the plans.

Capital gains occur when an investor buys an asset such as stock and subsequently sells it for a profit. A capital loss occurs when the asset is sold for a loss. If the investor has capital losses that exceed capital gains, the losses may be used to offset up to $3,000 annually in income from other sources.

Estate taxes are levied on the value of a decedent's estate, and some states also levy taxes on an individual's share of an estate (i.e., the inheritance). State and local governments also tax an individual's property, which may include the investor's financial assets.

Corporations also pay federal and state income taxes. The tax reform law enacted in 1986 reduced both corporate income tax rates and the ability of corporations to avoid paying income taxes. However, accelerated depreciation and the 70 percent exclusion of dividends earned on investments in the stock of other com-

---

[12] For additional discussion of the corporate dividend exclusion, see Chapter 16 on preferred stock.

panies permit corporations to reduce or defer the current amount of taxes they must pay.

Terms to Remember

progressive tax	tax-deferred annuity
regressive tax	face value
proportionate tax	cash value
marginal tax rate	term insurance
tax shelter	estate tax
tax-exempt bond	tax credit
capital gain	inheritance tax
capital loss	property tax
paper profits	straightline depreciation
individual retirement account (IRA)	accelerated depreciation
Keogh account or HR-10 plan	investment tax credit

Questions

1. What is a progressive tax? Why is the federal estate tax illustrative of a progressive tax?
2. Does a tax shelter necessarily imply that the investor avoids paying taxes?
3. What is a capital gain? When are capital gains taxes levied? May capital losses be used to offset capital gains and income from other sources?
4. Which of the following illustrate a tax shelter?
   a. dividend income
   b. interest earned on a savings account
   c. a stock purchased for $10 that is currently worth $25
   d. interest earned on a municipal bond
   e. interest earned on the cash value of an insurance policy
5. What are Keogh, 401(k), and IRA plans? What are their primary advantages to investors?
6. What is the difference between an estate tax and an inheritance tax?
7. What is depreciation? How does it reduce a firm's taxes? Should a firm use accelerated depreciation instead of straightline depreciation?
8. How can a corporation shelter income by purchasing stock in another company?

Problems

1. A corporation owns 10,000 shares of MNO Corp. The stock pays a dividend of $2.35 a share. If the corporation that owns the stock is in the 34 percent federal income tax bracket, how much tax does it owe on the dividend income?
2. a. An individual in the 28 percent federal income tax bracket bought and sold the following securities during the year:

	Cost Basis of Stock	Proceeds of Sale
ABC	$24,500	$28,600
DEF	35,400	31,000
GHI	31,000	36,000

What are the taxes owed on the short-term capital gains?

b. An individual in the 28 percent federal income tax bracket bought and sold the following securities during the year:

	Cost Basis of Stock	Proceeds of Sale
ABC	$34,600	$28,600
DEF	29,400	31,000
GHI	21,500	19,000

What are the taxes owed as a result of these sales?

3. A corporation in the 34 percent federal income tax bracket collects the following investment income:

Dividends on preferred stock owned	$12,000
Interest on municipal bonds	10,000
Interest on corporate bonds	7,000
Dividends on common stock owned	8,500
Interest on federal government bonds	5,000

How much federal income tax does this firm owe on its investment income?

4. An investor is in the 31 percent tax bracket and pays long-term capital gains taxes of 28 percent. What are the taxes owed (or saved in the cases of losses) in the current tax year for each of the following situations?
   a. net short-term capital gains of $3,000
      net long-term capital gains of $4,000
   b. net short-term capital gains of $3,000
      net long-term capital losses of $4,000
   c. net short-term capital losses of $3,000
      net long-term capital gains of $4,000
   d. net short-term capital gains of $3,000
      net long-term capital losses of $2,000
   e. net short-term capital losses of $4,000
      net long-term capital gains of $3,000
   f. net short-term capital losses of $1,000
      net long-term capital losses of $1,500
   g. net short-term capital losses of $3,000
      net long-term capital losses of $2,000

Suggested Readings

It is both difficult and time consuming to stay current on the tax laws, which partially explains why tax services such as H and R Block can be profitable. The individual should realize that tax reforms initiated in 1986 have rendered outdated much of the material previously published on federal income taxes.

Investors who do not use accountants to prepare their tax papers often do use the services of tax consultants. For the current federal tax laws, the investor may consult:
Federal Tax Course. Englewood Cliffs, N.J.: Prentice-Hall.
This book is published annually and is perhaps the most convenient means to keep current on the federal tax laws.

Lasser Institute. *J. K. Lasser's Your Income Tax.* New York: Simon & Schuster.
This annual publication is designed to help an individual file federal income tax forms; thus, it has current information on many of the tax laws pertaining to investments. It is also considerably easier to read than the *Federal Tax Course;* the latter, however, is both more comprehensive and more thorough.

Books that include material on taxation and tax shelters for the investor include:
Lasser, J. K. *All You Should Know About IRA, Keogh, and Other Retirement Plans.* New York: Prentice-Hall, updated annually.
Sheen, Brian J. *Nest Egg Investing.* New York: G. P. Putnam's Sons, 1987.

6

The Time Value of Money

*I*f $2,000 is invested annually in an IRA, how much will be in the account in the year 2000? If your salary grows by 10 percent annually, how much will you be earning after 20 years? If you expect an investment in real estate to earn $10,000 a year for 15 years, how much is that investment worth to you today? These questions illustrate a major concept in finance—the time value of money. A dollar in the future is not equivalent in value to a dollar in the present: That is the time value of money.

The time value of money is one of the most crucial concepts in finance. An investment decision is made at a given time. For example, an investor buys stock or a firm decides to establish a pension plan today. The returns on these investment decisions will be received in the future. There has to be a means to compare the future results of these investments with their present cost. Such comparisons require an understanding of the time value of money, which is the subject of this chapter.

This chapter considers four concepts: (1) the future value of a dollar, (2) the present value of a dollar, (3) the future sum of an annuity, and (4) the present value of an annuity. Several examples apply these concepts to investments. The chapter closes with a brief introduction to security valuation, employing the time value of money.

You may already have studied the time value of money in other courses such as accounting or corporate finance. If that is so, go straight to the problems at the end of this chapter and see if you can solve them. If you know the topic, you should be able to answer most of them. The answers are provided at the end of the text so that you can determine if your answers are correct.

You may use financial calculators or computer programs such as the software accompanying this text to solve these problems. However, every problem may not readily fit into a preprogrammed calculator or computer template. Computer programs may facilitate the calculations, but only if you can properly set up the problem. Even then the specific question being asked may not be answered. You may have to work with the numbers or interpret them.

In this text the purpose of understanding the time value of money is to facilitate understanding investments and to perform problems that pertain to valuation of assets and financial planning. If you already know the topic and can derive answers to the problems that employ the time value of money, you may go on to the next chapter. However, if you do not fully understand the time value of money, careful *attention to this chapter is critical since much of what follows in the remainder of this text depends upon it. Knowledge of the topic and the ability to work problems are essential for comprehending important concepts in investments.*

✦ ✦ ✦

THE FUTURE VALUE OF A DOLLAR

If $100 is deposited in a savings account that pays 5 percent annually, how much money will be in the account at the end of the year? The answer is easy to determine: $100 plus $5 interest, for a total of $105. This answer is derived by multiplying $100 by 5 percent, which gives the interest earned during the year, and then by adding this interest to the initial principal. That is,

Initial principal + (Interest rate × Initial principal) = Principal after one year.

This simple calculation is expressed in algebraic form in Equation 6.1, in which P represents the principal and i is the rate of interest. This equation employs subscripts to represent time. The subscript 0 indicates the present, and 1 means the end of the first year. (The second year, third year, and so on to any number of years will be represented by 2, 3, . . . n, respectively.)

$$P_0 + iP_0 = P_1 \qquad\qquad (6.1)$$

If P_0 is the initial principal ($100) and i is the interest rate (5%), the principal after one year (P_1) will be

$$\$100 + 0.05(\$100) = \$105.$$

How much will be in the account after two years? This answer is obtained in the same manner by adding the interest earned during the second year to the principal at the beginning of the second year, that is, $105 plus 0.05 times $105 equals $110.25, which may be expressed in algebraic terms:

$$P_1 + iP_1 = P_2. \qquad\qquad (6.2)$$

After two years the initial deposit of $100 will have grown to $110.25; the savings account will have earned $10.25 in interest. This total interest is composed of $10 representing interest on the initial principal and $0.25 representing interest that has accrued during the second year on the $5 in interest earned during the first year. This earning of interest on interest is called **compounding.** Money that is deposited in savings accounts is frequently referred to as being compounded, for interest is earned on both the principal and the previously earned interest.

The words *interest* and *compounded* are frequently used together. For example, banks may advertise that interest is compounded daily for savings accounts, or the cost of a loan may be expressed as 12 percent compounded annually. In the previous

compounding
The process by which interest is paid on interest that has been previously earned.

example, interest was earned only once during the year; thus it is an example of interest that is compounded annually. In many cases interest is not compounded annually but quarterly, semiannually, or even daily. The more frequently it is compounded (i.e., the more frequently the interest is added to the principal), the more rapidly the interest is put to work to earn even more interest.

How much will be in the account at the end of three years? This answer can be determined by the same general formula that was previously used. The amount in the account at the end of the second year ($110.25) is added to the interest that is earned during the third year (5% × $110.25); that is,

$$\$110.25 + \$5.5125 = \$115.76,$$

or the formula may be expressed algebraically as

$$P_2 + iP_2 = P_3. \tag{6.3}$$

By continuing with this method, it is possible to determine the amount that will be in the account at the end of 20 or more years, but doing so is obviously a lot of work. Fortunately, there is a much easier way to ascertain how much will be in the account after any given number of years by using an interest table called the future value of a dollar table.

The first table in Appendix A gives the interest factors for the future value of a dollar. The interest rates at which a dollar is compounded periodically are read horizontally at the top of the table. The number of periods (e.g., years) is read vertically along the left-hand margin. To determine the amount to which $100 will grow in three years at 5 percent interest, find the interest factor (1.158) and multiply it by $100. That calculation yields $115.80, which is the answer that was derived previously by working out the equations (except for rounding). To ascertain the amount to which $100 will grow after 25 years at 5 percent interest compounded annually, multiply $100 by the interest factor, 3.386, to obtain the answer, $338.60. Thus, if $100 were placed in a savings account that paid 5 percent interest annually, there would be $338.60 in the account after 25 years.

Interest tables for the future value of a dollar are based on a general formulation of the simple equations used previously. To determine the amount in the savings account at the end of Year 1, the following equation was used:

$$P_0 + iP_0 = P_1, \tag{6.1}$$

which may be written as

$$P_0(1 + i) = P_1.$$

To calculate the amount after two years, the following equation was used:

$$P_1 + iP_1 = P_2, \tag{6.2}$$

which may be written as

$$P_1(1 + i) = P_2.$$

Since P_1 equals $P_0(1 + i)$, the amount in the account at the end of Year 2 may be expressed as

$$P_0(1 + i)(1 + i) = P_2.$$

This equation uses the term $1 + i$ twice, for P_0 is being multiplied by $1 + i$ twice. Thus, it is possible to write Equation 6.2 as

$$P_0(1 + i)^2 = P_2.$$

The amount to which a dollar will grow may always be expressed in terms of the initial dollar (i.e., P_0). The general formula for finding the amount to which a dollar will grow in n number of years, if it is compounded annually, is

$$P_0(1 + i)^n = P_n. \qquad (6.4)$$

Thus, the general formula for finding the future value of a dollar for any number of years consists of (1) the initial dollar (P_0), (2) the interest $(1 + i)$, and (3) the number of years (n). Taken together, $(1 + i)^n$, the interest rate and time are referred to as the *interest factor*. This interest factor for selected interest rates and time periods is given in the interest tables in Appendix A.

As may be seen in the first table in Appendix A, the value of a dollar grows with increases in the length of time and in the rate of interest. These relationships are illustrated in Figure 6.1. If \$1 is compounded at 5 percent interest (*AB* in the figure), it will grow to \$1.28 after five years and to \$1.63 after ten years. However, if \$1 is compounded at 10 percent interest (*AC* on the graph), it will grow to \$2.59 in ten years. These cases illustrate the basic nature of compounding: The longer the funds continue to grow and the higher the interest rate, the higher will be the ultimate value.

It also should be noted that doubling the interest rate more than doubles the amount of interest that is earned over a number of years. In the example just given, the interest rate doubled from 5 percent to 10 percent; however, the amount of interest that will have accumulated in ten years rises from \$0.63 at 5 percent to \$1.59 at 10 percent. This is the result of the fact that compounding involves a geometric progression. The interest factor $(1 + i)$ has been raised to some power (n).

THE PRESENT VALUE OF A DOLLAR

In the preceding section, a dollar grew or compounded over time. In this section the reverse situation is considered. How much is a dollar that will be received in the future worth today? For example, how much will a payment of \$1,000 twenty years hence be worth today if the funds earn 10 percent annually? This question incorporates the time value of money, but instead of asking how much a dollar will be worth at some future date, it asks how much that future dollar is worth today. This is a question of **present value.** The process by which this question is answered is called **discounting.** Discounting determines the worth of funds that are to be received in the future in terms of their present value.

present value
The current worth of an amount to be received in the future.

discounting
The process of determining present value.

Figure 6.1 ✦ FUTURE VALUE OF ONE DOLLAR

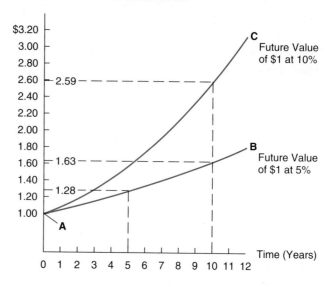

In the earlier section, the future value of a dollar was calculated by Equation 6.4.

$$P_0(1 + i)^n = P_n.$$ (6.4)

Discounting reverses this equation. The present value (P_0) is ascertained by dividing the future value (P_n) by the interest factor $(1 + i)^n$. This is expressed in Equation 6.5.

$$P_0 = \frac{P_n}{(1 + i)^n}.$$ (6.5)

The future amount is discounted by the appropriate interest factor to determine the present value. For example, if the interest rate is 10 percent, the present value of $100 to be received five years from today is

$$P_0 = \frac{\$100}{(1 + 0.1)^5}$$

$$= \frac{\$100}{1.611}$$

$$= \$62.07.$$

As with the future value of a dollar, interest tables have been developed that ease the calculation of present values. The second table in Appendix A gives the interest factors for the present value of a dollar for selected interest rates and time periods. The interest rates are read horizontally at the top, and time is read vertically along the left-hand side. To determine the present value of $1 that will be received

Figure 6.2   ✦   PRESENT VALUE OF ONE DOLLAR TO BE RECEIVED IN THE FUTURE

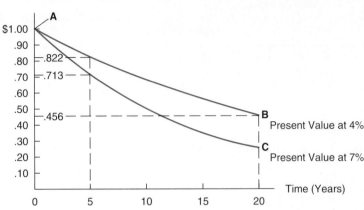

in five years if the current interest rate is 10 percent, multiply $1 by the interest factor, which is found in the table under the vertical column for 10 percent and in the horizontal column for five years. The present value of $1 is

$$\$1 \times 0.621 = \$0.621.$$

Thus, $100 that will be received after five years is currently worth only $62.10 if the interest rate is 10 percent. This is the same answer that was determined with Equation 6.5 (except for rounding off).

As may be seen in Equation 6.5, the present value of a dollar depends on (1) the length of time before it will be received and (2) the interest rate. The further into the future the dollar will be received and the higher the interest rate, the lower the present value of the dollar. This is illustrated by Figure 6.2, which gives the relationship between the present value of a dollar and the length of time at various interest rates. Lines *AB* and *AC* give the present value of a dollar at 4 percent and 7 percent, respectively. As may be seen in this graph, a dollar to be received after 20 years is worth considerably less than a dollar to be received after five years when both are discounted at the same percentage rate. At 4 percent (line *AB*) the current value of $1 to be received after 20 years is only $0.456, whereas $1 to be received after five years is worth $0.822. Also, the higher the interest rate (i.e., discount factor), the lower the present value of a dollar. For example, the present value of $1 to be received after five years is $0.822 at 4 percent, but it is only $0.713 at 7 percent.

THE FUTURE SUM OF AN ANNUITY

How much will be in a savings account after three years if $100 is deposited annually and the account pays 5 percent interest? This is similar to the future value of a dollar except that the payment is not received as one lump sum but as a series. If the

Exhibit 6.1 ✦ THE FLOW OF PAYMENTS FOR THE FUTURE VALUE OF AN ANNUITY DUE AND AN ORDINARY ANNUITY

Annuity Due

	1/1/x0	1/1/x1	1/1/x2	1/1/x3	Sum
	$100.00	5.00	5.25	5.51	$115.76
		100.00	5.00	5.25	110.25
			100.00	5.00	105.00
Amount in the account	$100.00	205.00	315.25	330.01	$330.01

Ordinary Annuity

	1/1/x0	1/1/x1	1/1/x2	1/1/x3	Sum
	—	$100.00	5.00	5.25	$110.25
			100.00	5.00	105.00
				100.00	100.00
Amount in the account	—	$100.00	205.00	315.25	$315.25

annuity
A series of equal annual payments.

future sum of an annuity
Compound value of a series of equal annual payments.

annuity due
A series of equal annual payments with the payments made at the beginning of the year.

ordinary annuity
A series of equal annual payments in which the payments are made at the end of each year.

payments are equal, the series is called an **annuity.** The above question is then an illustration of the **future sum of an annuity.**

To determine how much will be in the account we must consider not only the interest rate earned but also whether deposits are made at the beginning of the year or the end of the year. If each payment is made at the beginning of the year, the series is called an **annuity due.** If the payments are made at the end of the year, the series is an **ordinary annuity.** What is the future sum of an annuity if $100 is deposited in an account for three years starting right now? What is the future sum of an annuity if $100 is placed in an account for three years starting at the end of the first year? The first question concerns an annuity due, while the second question illustrates an ordinary annuity.

The flow of payments for these two types of annuities is illustrated in Exhibit 6.1. In both cases the $100 is deposited for three years in a savings account that pays 5 percent interest. The top half of the figure shows the annuity due, while the bottom half illustrates the ordinary annuity. In both cases, three years elapse from the present to when the final amount is determined and three payments are made. The difference in the timing of the payment results in a difference in the interest earned. Since in an annuity due the payments are made at the beginning of each year, the annuity due earns more interest ($30.01 versus $15.25) and thus has the higher terminal value ($330.01 versus $315.25). As will be illustrated later in the chapter, the greater the interest rate and the longer the time period, the greater will be this difference in terminal values.

The procedures for determining the future sum of an annuity due (FSAD) and the future sum of an ordinary annuity (FSOA) are stated formally in Equations 6.6 and 6.7, respectively. In each equation, I represents the equal, periodic payment, i represents the rate of interest, and n represents the number of years that elapse from the present until the end of the time period. For the annuity due, the equation is

$$\text{FSAD} = I(1 + i)^1 + I(1 + i)^2 + \cdots + I(1 + i)^n. \tag{6.6}$$

When this equation is applied to the previous example in which $i = 0.05$, $n = 3$, and the annual payment ($I = \$100$), the accumulated sum is

$$\text{FSAD} = \$100(1 + 0.05)^1 + 100(1 + 0.05)^2 + 100(1 + 0.05)^3$$

$$= \$105 + 110.25 + 115.76$$

$$= \$330.01.$$

For the ordinary annuity the equation is

$$\text{FSOA} = I(1 + i)^0 + I(1 + i)^1 \cdots + I(1 + i)^{n-1}. \tag{6.7}$$

When this equation is applied to the above example, the accumulated sum is

$$\text{FSOA} = \$100(1 + 0.05)^0 + 100(1 + 0.05)^1 + 100(1 + 0.05)^{3-1}$$

$$= \$100 + 105 + 110.25$$

$$= \$315.25.$$

Although it is possible to derive the sum of an annuity in this manner, it is very cumbersome. Fortunately, interest tables have been developed to facilitate these calculations. In the third table in Appendix A we find the interest factors for the future sum of an ordinary annuity for selected time periods and selected interest rates. (Interest tables are usually presented only for ordinary annuities. How these tables may be used for annuities due is discussed below.) The number of periods is read vertically at the left, and the interest rates are read horizontally at the top. To ascertain the future sum of the ordinary annuity in the previous example, this table is used as follows. The FSOA at 5 percent interest for three years (three annual $100 payments with interest being earned for two years) is $100 times the interest factor found in Table 3 of Appendix A for three periods at 5 percent. This interest factor is 3.153; therefore, the future value of this ordinary annuity is $100 times 3.153, which equals $315.30. This is the same answer that was derived by determining the future value of each $100 deposit and totaling them. (The slight difference in the two answers is the result of rounding off.)

The value of an ordinary annuity of a dollar compounded annually depends on the number of payments (i.e., the number of periods over which deposits are made) and the interest rate. The longer the time period and the higher the interest rate, the greater will be the sum that will have accumulated in the future. This is illustrated by Figure 6.3. Lines *AB* and *AC* show the value of the $1 annuity at 4 and 8 percent, respectively. After five years the value of the annuity will grow to $5.87 at 8 percent but to only $5.42 at 4 percent. If these annuities are continued for another five years, they will be worth $14.49 and $12.01, respectively. Thus, both the rate at which the annuity compounds and the length of time affect the annuity's value.

Figure 6.3 ✦ FUTURE SUM OF AN ORDINARY ANNUITY OF ONE DOLLAR

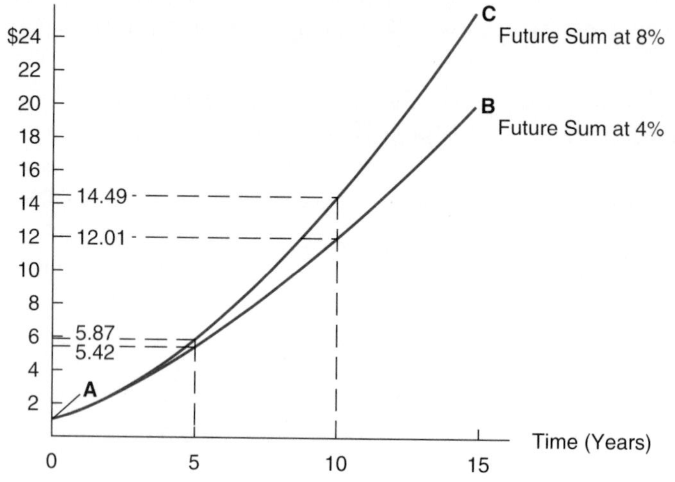

While this interest table is constructed for an ordinary annuity, it may be converted into a table for an annuity due by multiplying the interest factor given in the table by $(1 + i)$. For example, in the illustration of the $100 deposited annually in the savings account for three years, the interest factor for the ordinary annuity was 3.153. This interest factor may be converted for an annuity due at 5 percent for three years by multiplying 3.153 by $1 + 0.05$. That is,

$$3.153(1 + 0.05) = 3.3107.$$

When this interest factor is applied to the example of $100 deposited in the bank at 5 percent for three years with the deposits starting immediately, the resulting terminal value is

$$\$100(3.3107) = \$331.07.$$

This is the same answer as derived by making each calculation individually and summing them. (Once again the small difference in the two answers is the result of rounding off.)

The difference between the terminal value of the two kinds of annuity payments can be quite substantial as the number of years increases or the interest rate rises. Consider an IRA account in which the saver places $2,000 annually for 20 years. If the deposits are made at the end of the year (an ordinary annuity) and the rate of interest is 7 percent, the terminal amount will be

$$\$2,000(40.995) = \$81,990.$$

However, if the deposits had been made at the beginning of each year (an annuity due), the terminal amount would be

$$\$2,000(40.995)(1 + 0.07) = \$87,729.30.$$

The difference is $5,739.30! Almost $6,000 in additional interest is earned if the deposits are made at the beginning, not at the end, of each year.

The difference between the ordinary annuity and the annuity due becomes even more dramatic if the interest rate rises. Suppose the above IRA offered 12 percent instead of 7 percent. If the deposits are made at the end of each year, the terminal value is

$$\$2,000(72.052) = \$144,104.$$

If the payments are at the beginning of the year, the terminal value will be

$$\$2,000(72.052)(1 + 0.12) = \$161,396.48.$$

The difference is now $17,292.48.

THE PRESENT VALUE OF AN ANNUITY

In investment analysis, the investor is often not concerned with the future value but with the **present value of an annuity.** The investor who receives periodic payments often wishes to know the current (i.e., present) value. As with the future sum of an annuity, this value depends on whether the payments are made at the beginning of each period (an annuity due) or at the end of each period (an ordinary annuity).

present value of an annuity
The present worth of a series of equal payments.

If the annuity is an ordinary annuity, the present value of the future payments could be determined by obtaining the present value of each payment and summing these values. This approach is illustrated by the following simple example. The recipient expects to receive $100 at the end of each year for three years and wants to know how much this series of annual payments is currently worth if 12 percent can be earned on alternative investments. One method to determine current worth is to calculate the present value of each of the $100 payments (find the appropriate interest factors in the Present Value of One Dollar table in Appendix A and multiply them by $100) and to sum these individual present values, which in this case yields $240.20.

Payment	Year	Interest Factor	Present Value
$100	1	0.893	$ 89.30
100	2	0.797	79.70
100	3	0.712	71.20
			$240.20

This process is expressed in more general terms by Equation 6.8. The present value (PV) of the annual payments (I) is then found by discounting these payments at the appropriate interest rate (i) for n time periods.

$$PV = \frac{I}{(1+i)^1} + \ldots + \frac{I}{(1+i)^n},$$
$$PV = \sum_{t=1}^{n} \frac{I}{(1+i)^t}.$$

(6.8)

Figure 6.4 ✦ PRESENT VALUE OF AN ORDINARY ANNUITY OF ONE DOLLAR

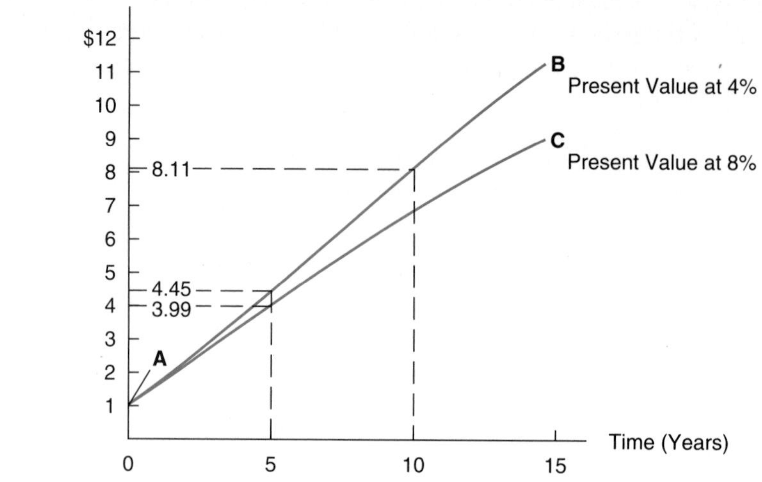

When the values from the previous example are inserted into the equation, it reads

$$PV = \frac{\$100}{(1 + 0.12)} + \frac{\$100}{(1 + 0.12)^2} + \frac{\$100}{(1 + 0.12)^3}$$

$$= \frac{\$100}{1.120} + \frac{\$100}{1.254} + \frac{\$100}{1.405}$$

$$= \$240.20.$$

The calculation of the present value of an annuity can be a long and tedious process. To simplify this task, interest tables have been developed for the interest factors for the present value of an annuity (see the fourth table in Appendix A). Selected interest rates are read horizontally along the top, and the number of periods is read vertically at the left. To determine the present value of an annuity of $100 that is to be received for three years when interest rates are 12 percent, find the interest factor for three years at 12 percent (2.402) and then multiply $100 by this interest factor. The present value of this annuity is $240.20, which is the same value that was derived by obtaining each of the individual present values and summing them. The price that one would be willing to pay at the present time in exchange for three future annual payments of $100 when the rate of return on alternative investments is 12 percent is $240.20.

As with the present value of a dollar, the present value of an annuity is related to the interest rate and the length of time over which the annuity payments are made. The lower the interest rate and the longer the duration of the annuity, the greater the present value of the annuity. Figure 6.4 illustrates these relationships. As may be seen by comparing Lines AB and AC, the lower the interest rate, the higher the present dollar value. For example, if payments are to be made over five years, the present value of an annuity of $1 is $4.45 at 4 percent but only $3.99 at 8 percent. The longer the duration of the annuity, the higher the present value;

Exhibit 6.2 ✦ Flow of Payments and Determination of the Present Value of an Ordinary Annuity and an Annuity Due at 10 Percent for Three Years

Ordinary Annuity			
1/1/x0	1/1/x1	1/1/x2	1/1/x3
$1,818 ◄——— (0.909) 2,000			
1,652 ◄————————————— (0.826) 2,000			
1,505 ◄—————————————————————————— (0.751) 2,000			
$4,972			

Annuity Due			
1/1/x0	1/1/x1	1/1/x2	1/1/x3
$2,000			
1,818 ◄——— (0.909) 2,000			
1,652 ◄————————————— (0.826) 2,000			
$5,470			

hence, the present value of an annuity of $1 at 4 percent is $4.45 for five years, whereas it is $8.11 for ten years.

Many payments to be received in investments occur at the end of a time period and not at the beginning and thus are illustrative of ordinary annuities. For example, the annual interest payment made by a bond occurs after the bond is held for a while, and distributions from earnings (e.g., dividends from stock or disbursements from a real estate tax shelter) are made after, not at the beginning of, a period of time. There are, however, payments that may occur at the beginning of the time period, such as the annual distribution from a retirement plan; these would be illustrative of annuities due.

The difference in the flow of payments and the determination of the present values of an ordinary annuity and an annuity due are illustrated in Exhibit 6.2. In each case the annuity is for $2,000 a year for three years and the interest rate is 10 percent. In the top half of the exhibit, the payments are made at the end of the year (an ordinary annuity), while in the bottom half of the exhibit, the payments are made at the beginning of the year (an annuity due). As may be seen by the totals, the present value of the annuity due is higher ($5,470 versus $4,972). This is because the payments are received sooner and, hence, are more valuable. As may also be seen in the illustration, since the first payment of the annuity due is made immediately, its present value is the actual amount received. Because the first payment of the ordinary annuity is made at the end of the first year, that amount is discounted, and, hence, its present value is less than the actual amount received.

The interest tables for the present value of an annuity presented in this text (and in other finance and investment texts) apply to ordinary annuities. These interest factors may be converted into annuity due factors by multiplying them by $(1 + i)$. Thus the interest factor for the present value of an ordinary annuity for $1 at 10 percent for three years (2.487) may be converted into the interest factor for an annuity due of $1 at 10 percent for five years as follows:

$$2.487(1 + i) = 2.487(1 + 0.1) = 2.736.$$

When this interest factor is used to determine the present value of an annuity due of $2,000 for three years at 10 percent, the present value is

$$\$2,000(2.736) = \$5,472.$$

The present value of an ordinary annuity of $2,000 at 10 percent for three years is

$$\$2,000(2.487) = \$4,974.$$

These are essentially the same answers given in Exhibit 6.2 with the small differences being the result of rounding.

APPLICATIONS OF COMPOUNDING AND DISCOUNTING

The previous sections have explained the various computations involving time value, and this section will illustrate them in a series of problems that the investor may encounter. These illustrations are similar to examples that are used throughout the text. If one understands these examples, comprehending the rest of the text material should be much easier, because the emphasis can then be placed on the analysis of the value of specific assets instead of on the mechanics of the valuation.

Answering the time value of money problems requires determining which of the four tables to use. The following decision tree may aid in this selection process. First, determine if the problem involves a lump sum payment or a set of equal payments (i.e., an annuity). Then determine if the problem concerns going from the present to the future (future value) or from the future to the present (present value).

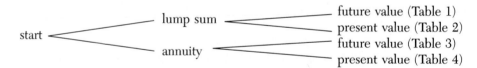

For example, if the current tuition cost of a four-year college education is $20,000, what will be the cost after ten years if prices rise annually by 6 percent? First, determine if the problem is concerned with an annuity or a lump sum. Since the question asks about total tuition costs, it is an illustration of a lump sum and not an annuity. Second, determine the time dimension. Since the problem is not concerned with the current cost of an education but with future costs, it is an example of future value and not present value. Thus, from the decision tree presented below, the appropriate table is determined to be the future value of a dollar table (Table 1, Appendix A).

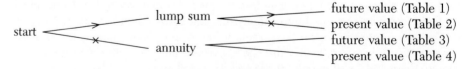

1. An investor buys a stock for $10 per share and expects to watch the value of the stock grow annually at 9 percent for ten years, at which time the

individual plans to sell it. What is the anticipated sale price? This is an example of the future value of a dollar growing at 9 percent for ten years. The future value is

$$P_n = P_0(1 + i)^n,$$

$$P_{10} = \$10(1 + 0.09)^{10},$$

$$P_{10} = \$10(2.367) = \$23.67,$$

where 2.367 is the interest factor for the future sum of a dollar at 9 percent for ten years. The investor anticipates selling the stock for $23.67.

2. An investor sells a stock for $23.67 that was purchased ten years ago. A return of 9 percent was earned. What was the original cost of the investment? This is an example of the present value of a dollar discounted back at 9 percent for ten years. The initial value ten years ago, or the former price, was

$$P_{-n} = \frac{P_0}{(1 + i)^n},$$

$$P_{-10} = \frac{\$23.67}{(1 + 0.09)^{10}},$$

$$P_{-10} = \$23.67(0.4224) = \$10,$$

where 0.4224 is the interest factor for the present value of a dollar discounted at 9 percent for ten years. The investment cost $10 when it was purchased ten years ago.

The student should know that Questions 1 and 2 are two views of the same investment. In Question 1 the $10 investment grew to $23.67. In Question 2 the value at the time the stock was sold was brought back to the value of the initial investment. Another variation of this question would be as follows. If an investor bought stock for $10, held it for ten years, and then sold it for $23.67, what was the return on the investment? In this case the values of the stock at the time it was bought and sold are known, but the rate of growth (the rate of return) is unknown. The answer can be found by using *either* the future value of a dollar table or the present value of a dollar table.

If the future value table is used, the question is at what rate (x) will $10 grow in ten years to equal $23.67. The answer is

$$P_0(1 + x)^n = P_n$$

$$\$10(1 + x)^{10} = \$23.67$$

$$(1 + x)^{10} = 2.367.$$

The interest factor is 2.367, which, according to the future value of a dollar table for ten years, makes the growth rate 9 percent. This interest factor is located under the vertical column for 9 percent and in the horizontal column for ten years.

If the present value table is used, the question asks what discount factor (x) at ten years will bring $23.67 back to $10. The answer is

$$P_0 = \frac{P_n}{(1 + x)^n}$$

$$\$10 = \frac{\$23.67}{(1 + x)^{10}}$$

$$0.4224 = \frac{1}{(1 + x)^{10}}.$$

The interest factor is 0.4224, which may be found in the present value of a dollar table for ten years in the 9 percent column (i.e., the growth rate is 9 percent). Thus, this problem may be solved by the proper application of either the future value or present value tables.

3. An employer offers to start a pension plan for a 45-year-old employee. The plan is to place $1,000 at the end of each year in a certificate of deposit that earns 8 percent annually. The employee wants to know how much will have accumulated by retirement at age 65.

This is an example of the future value of an ordinary annuity. The payment is $1,000 annually, and it will grow at 8 percent for 20 years. The fund will thus grow to

$$CS = I(1 + i)^0 + \cdots + I(1 + i)^{n-1}$$

$$= \$1,000(1 + 0.08)^0 + \cdots + \$1,000(1 + 0.08)^{19}$$

$$= \$1,000(45.762) = \$45,762,$$

where 45.762 is the interest factor for the future sum of an ordinary annuity of one dollar compounded annually at 8 percent for 20 years.

4. The same employer decides to place a lump sum in an investment that earns 8 percent and to draw on the funds to make the annual payments of $1,000. After 20 years all of the funds in the account will be depleted. How much must be deposited initially in the account?

This is an example of the present value of an ordinary annuity. The annuity is $1,000 per year at 8 percent for 20 years. Thus, the present value (i.e., the amount of the initial investment) is

$$PV = \sum_{i=1}^{n} \frac{I}{(1 + i)} + \cdots + \frac{I}{(1 + i)^n}$$

$$= \frac{\$1,000}{1 + 0.08} + \cdots + \frac{\$1,000}{(1 + 0.08)^{20}}$$

$$= \$1,000(9.818) = \$9,818,$$

where 9.818 is the interest factor for the present value of an ordinary annuity of one dollar at 8 percent for 20 years. Thus, the employer need invest only $9,818 in an account that earns 8 percent to meet the $1,000 annual pension payment for 20 years.

The student should notice the difference between the answers in the equations in Examples 3 and 4. In the equation in Example 3, a set of payments earns interest, and thus the future value is larger than just the sum of the 20 payments of $1,000. In the equation in Example 4, a future set of payments is valued in present terms. Since future payments are worth less today, the current value is less than the sum of the 20 payments of $1,000.

5. An investment pays $50 per year for ten years, after which $1,000 is returned to the investor. If the investor can earn 9 percent, how much should this investment cost? This question really contains two questions: What is the present value of an ordinary annuity of $50 at 9 percent for ten years, and what is the present value of $1,000 after ten years at 9 percent? The answer is

$$PV = \sum_{t=1}^{n} \frac{I_1}{(1 + i)^1} + \cdots + \frac{I_n}{(1 + i)^t} + \frac{P_n}{(1 + i)^t}$$

$$= \frac{\$50}{(1 + 0.09)} + \cdots + \frac{\$50}{(1 + 0.09)^{10}} + \frac{\$1,000}{(1 + 0.09)^{10}}$$

$$= \$50(6.418) + \$1,000(0.422) = \$742.9,$$

where 6.418 and 0.422 are the interest factors for the present value of an ordinary annuity of a dollar and the present value of a dollar, respectively, both at 9 percent for ten years.

This example illustrates that an investment may involve both a series of payments (the annuity component) and a lump sum payment. This particular investment is similar to a bond, the valuation of which is discussed in Chapter 15. Other examples of valuation and the computation of rates of return are given in Chapters 8 and 9, which consider investments in common stock.

6. A corporation's dividend has grown annually at the rate of 6 percent. If this rate is maintained and the current dividend is $5.40, what will the dividend be after ten years? This is a simple future value of a dollar problem. The dividend will grow to

$$P_n = P_0(1 + i)^n$$

$$= \$5.40(1 + 0.06)^{10}$$

$$= \$5.40(1.629) = \$8.80,$$

where 1.629 is the interest factor for the future value of $1 at 6 percent for ten years. Although such a growth rate in future dividends may not be achieved, this problem illustrates how modest annual increments can result in a substantial increase in an investor's dividend income over a number of years.

The previous examples illustrate the use of interest tables. These problems can also be done without the tables if the student has access to an electronic calculator programmed to perform the calculations or a calculator with a y^x key and/or logs.

Also, computer programs such as the Investment Analysis programs that accompany this text may be used as a substitute for interest tables or electronic calculators to solve the problems. (The use of electronic calculators to determine interest factors that are not in the tables is discussed later in this chapter.)

NONANNUAL COMPOUNDING

semiannual compounding
The payment of interest twice a year.

The student should have noticed that in the previous examples compounding occurred only once a year. Since compounding can and often does occur more frequently, for example, **semiannually**, the equations that were presented earlier must be adjusted. This section extends the discussion of the compound value of a dollar to include compounding for time periods other than a year.

This discussion, however, is limited to the future value of a dollar. Similar adjustments must be made in the present value of a dollar or present value of an annuity when the funds are compounded more frequently than annually. These adjustments are not explained here but may be found in specialized texts concerning the time value of money.[1]

Converting annual compounding to other time periods necessitates two adjustments in Equation 6.4. These adjustments are not particularly difficult. First, a year is divided into the same number of time periods that the funds are being compounded. For semiannual compounding a year consists of two time periods, whereas for quarterly compounding the year comprises four time periods.

After adjusting for the number of time periods, the individual adjusts the interest rate to find the rate per time period. This is done by dividing the stated interest rate by the number of time periods. If the interest rate is 8 percent compounded semiannually, then 8 percent is divided by 2, giving an interest rate of 4 percent earned in *each* time period. If the annual rate of interest is 8 percent compounded quarterly, the interest rate is 2 percent (8% ÷ 4) in each of the four time periods.

These adjustments may be expressed in more formal terms by modifying Equation 6.4 as follows:

$$P_0\left(1 + \frac{i}{c}\right)^{n \times c} = P_n. \tag{6.9}$$

The only new symbol is c, which represents the frequency of compounding. The interest rate (i) is divided by the frequency of compounding (c) to determine the interest rate in each period. The number of years (n) is multiplied by the frequency of compounding to determine the number of time periods.

The application of this equation may be illustrated in a simple example. An individual invests $100 in an asset that pays 8 percent compounded quarterly. What will the future value of this asset be after five years, that is, $100 will grow to what

---

[1] See, for instance, Gary Clayton and Christopher Spivey, *The Time Value of Money* (Philadelphia: W.B. Saunders, 1978).

POINTS OF INTEREST

THE RULE OF 72

Do you want a short-cut method that answers the question, "How long will it take to double my money if I earn a specified percent?" The rule of 72 does just that! Divide 72 by the rate earned, and the answer is an approximation of how long it takes for the initial amount to double.

For example, if the rate is 6 percent, funds double in 72/6 = 12 years. At 10 percent, funds double in 7.2 years.

How accurate is this short cut? As may be seen from this table, the rule of 72 gives a rather accurate approximation of the time necessary to double one's funds at a specified rate of growth.

Rate (%)	Years for Funds to Double Using the Rule of 72	Actual Years for Funds to Double
5	14.4	14.3
7	10.3	10.2
10	7.2	7.3
12	6.0	6.1
16	4.5	4.7
20	3.6	3.8

amount after five years if it is compounded quarterly at 8 percent? Algebraically, this is

$$P_5 = P_0\left(1 + \frac{i}{c}\right)^{n \times c}$$

$$= \$100\left(1 + \frac{0.08}{4}\right)^{5 \times 4}$$

$$= \$100(1 + 0.02)^{20}.$$

In this formulation the investor is earning 2 percent for 20 time periods. To solve this equation, the interest factor for the future value of a dollar at 2 percent for 20 years (1.486) is multiplied by $100. Thus, the future value is

$$P_5 = 100 \ (1.486) = \$148.60.$$

The difference between compounding annually and compounding more frequently can be seen by comparing this problem with a problem in which the values are identical except that the interest is compounded annually. The question is, then, to what amount will $100 grow after five years at 8 percent compounded annually? The answer is

$$P_5 = \$100 \ (1 + 0.08)^5$$

$$= \$100 \ (1.469)$$

$$= \$146.90.$$

This sum, $146.90, is less than the amount that was earned when the funds were compounded quarterly, which suggests the general conclusion that the more frequently interest is compounded, the greater will be the future amount.

The discussion throughout this text is generally limited to annual compounding. There is, however, one important exception: the valuation of bonds. Bonds pay interest semiannually, and this affects their value. Therefore, semiannual compounding is incorporated in the bond valuation model that is presented in Chapter 15.

PRESENT VALUE AND SECURITY VALUATION

The valuation of assets is a major theme of this text. Investors must be able to analyze securities to determine their value. This valuation requires forecasting future cash flows and discounting them back to the present. The present value of an investment, then, is related to future benefits, in the form of either future income or capital appreciation. For example, stocks are purchased for their *future* dividends and potential capital gains but *not* for their previous dividends and price performance. Bonds are purchased for *future* income. Real estate is bought for the *future* use of the property and for the potential price appreciation. The concept of discounting future cash flows back to the present applies to all investments: It is the future and not the past that matters. The past is relevant only to the extent that it may be used to predict the future.

Some types of analysis (including the technical approach to selecting investments that is discussed in Chapter 13) use the past in the belief that it forecasts the future. Technical analysts employ such information as the past price movements of a stock to determine the most profitable times to buy and sell a security. However, most of the analytical methods that are discussed in this text use some form of discounting in the process of valuing the assets. Prices are the present value of anticipated future cash flows, such as dividends.

Subsequent chapters will discuss a variety of assets and the means for analyzing and valuing them. For debt, the current price is related to the series of interest payments and the repayment of the principal, both of which are discounted at the current market interest rate. The current price of a stock is related to the firm's future earnings and its investment opportunities. Cash flows are discounted back to the present at the appropriate discount factor. For these reasons it is important that the reader start in this introductory chapter to view current prices as the present value of future cash flows. The various features of the different investments, including stocks and bonds, will be discussed, and their prices will be analyzed in terms of present value. If the reader does not understand the material on the time value of money presented in this chapter, the analytical sections of subsequent chapters may be incomprehensible.

Electronic Calculators

Once a student has mastered the concepts of future value and present value and understands how the amounts are determined, the tedium associated with the actual calculations may be reduced through the use of electronic calculators programmed to solve time value problems. Even if your electronic calculator is not preprogrammed to perform these types of problems, you may still be able to derive the interest factors for the future value of a dollar and the present value of a dollar. This derivation requires that the calculator have the exponent key (y^x).

The equation for the interest factor for the future value of a dollar (FVIF) is

$$\text{FVIF} = (1 + i)^n. \tag{6.10}$$

To find the interest factor for 6 percent for three years [i.e., $(1 + .06)^3$], first enter 1 plus the interest rate: 1.06. The display should read 1.06. Next, raise this amount to the third power, which is achieved by striking the y^x key and the number 3. Press "equal," and the display should read 1.1910, which is the interest factor that may be found in the first table of Appendix A under the column for 6 percent and three years.

The equation for the interest factor for the present value of a dollar (PVIF) is

$$\text{PVIF} = \frac{1}{(1 + i)^n}. \tag{6.11}$$

The interest factor for the present value is the reciprocal of the interest factor for the future value of \$1. To derive the interest factor for the present value of a dollar at 6 percent for three years, do the above steps used to determine the future value of a dollar and then take the reciprocal. If the calculator has the $1/x$ key, press this key, and the reciprocal is automatically determined. If the calculator lacks this key, the reciprocal is found by dividing 1 by the number derived above. In the above illustration, the reciprocal for 1.191 is .8396 (1/1.191), which is the interest factor for the present value of a dollar at 6 percent for three years. You may verify this number by looking under the column for the present value of a dollar at 6 percent for three years in the second table in Appendix A, which gives the interest factor as .840. The difference is, of course, the result of rounding.

The above discussion indicates that the interest factors for the future value of a dollar and the present value of a dollar may be derived using an electronic calculator. However, the derivation of the interest factors for the future value of an annuity and the present value of an annuity can be quite tedious. These calculations require adding individual interest factors for each year. For example, the interest factor for the present value of an ordinary annuity for 20 years requires summing 20 different interest factors for the present value of \$1. In such a case, even if the electronic calculator is used to derive the interest factors, adding the individual interest factors may be impractical.

Fortunately, there is a simpler method. The equation for the interest factor for the future sum of an annuity (FVAIF) is

$$\text{FVAIF} = \frac{(1 + i)^n - 1}{i}. \tag{6.12}$$

Thus if the interest rate is 5 percent and the number of years is four, then the interest factor is

$$\text{FVAIF} = \frac{(1 + 0.05)^4 - 1}{0.05} = \frac{1.2155 - 1}{0.05} = 4.310,$$

which is the same number found in the table for the future value of an annuity for four years at 5 percent.

The equation for the interest factor for the present value of an annuity (PVAIF) is

$$PVAIF = \frac{1 - \dfrac{1}{(1 + i)^n}}{i}. \tag{6.13}$$

If the interest rate is 6 percent and the number of years is three, then the interest factor is

$$PVAIF = \frac{1 - \dfrac{1}{(1 + 0.06)^3}}{0.06} = \frac{1 - .8396}{0.06} = 2.673,$$

which is the interest factor found in the table for the present value of an annuity at 6 percent for three years.

In addition to facilitating the calculation of interest factors, the electronic calculator also offers a major advantage over the use of interest tables. While more detailed tables may be available, most interest tables are limited to exact rates (e.g., 5 percent) and whole years (e.g., 6 years). Unless the individual interpolates between the given interest factors, the tables cannot provide the interest factor for 6.7 percent for 5 years and 3 months. However, this interest factor can be determined by using the electronic calculator. The interest factor for the future value of $1 at 6.7 percent for 5 years and 3 months may be found as follows:

1. Enter 1.067.
2. Raise 1.067 by 5.25 (i.e., $y^x = 1.076^{5.25}$).
3. Press "equal" to derive the interest factor: 1.4056.

Thus if $100 is invested at 6.7 percent, compounded annually for 5 years and 3 months, the future value is $140.56.

While electronic calculators may ease the burden of the arithmetic, they cannot set up the problems to be solved. You must still determine if the problem concerns future value or present value and whether the problem deals with a lump sum or an annuity. Since failure to set up the problem correctly will only lead to incorrect results, it is imperative that the student be able to determine what is being used and which of the various cases apply to the particular problem.

SUMMARY

Money has time value. A dollar to be received in the future is worth less than a dollar received today. People will forgo current consumption only if future growth in their funds is possible. Invested funds earn interest, and the interest in turn earns more interest—a process called compounding. The longer funds compound and the higher the rate at which they compound, the greater will be the final amount in the future.

Discounting, the opposite of compounding, determines the present value of funds to be received in the future. The present value of a future sum depends on how far into the future the funds are to be received and on the discount rate. The further into future or the higher the discount factor, the lower will be the present value of the sum.

Compounding and discounting may apply to a single payment (lump sum) or to a series of payments. If the payments are equal, the series is called an annuity. When the payments start at the beginning of each time period, it is called an annuity due; when the payments are made at the end of each time period, the series is called an ordinary annuity.

Although an investment is made in the present, returns are earned in the future. These returns (e.g., the future flows of interest and dividends) must be discounted by the appropriate discount factor to determine the investment's present value. It is this process of discounting by which an investment's value is determined. As is developed throughout this text, valuation of assets is a crucial step in the selection of assets to acquire and hold in an investor's portfolio.

Terms to Remember

compounding	annuity due
present value	ordinary annuity
discounting	present value of an annuity
annuity	semiannual compounding
future sum of an annuity	

Questions

1. What is the difference between a lump-sum payment and an annuity? Are all series of payments annuities?
2. What is the difference between compounding (the determination of future value) and discounting (the determination of present value)?
3. For a given interest rate, what happens to the numerical value of the interest factor as time increases for the
    a. future value of a dollar;
    b. future value of an annuity;
    c. present value of a dollar;
    d. present value of an annuity?
4. For a given time period, what happens to the numerical value of the interest factor as the interest rate increases for the
    a. future value of a dollar;
    b. future value of an annuity;
    c. present value of a dollar;
    d. present value of an annuity?
5. What does the phrase "discounting the future at a high rate" imply?
6. As is explained in subsequent chapters, increases in interest rates cause the value of assets to decline. Why would you expect this relationship?

Problems

1. A saver places $1,000 in a certificate of deposit that matures after twenty years and that each year pays 6 percent interest, which is compounded annually until the certificate matures.
   a. How much interest will the saver earn if the interest is left to accumulate?
   b. How much interest will the saver earn if the interest is withdrawn each year?

2. An investor bought a stock ten years ago for $20 and sold it today for $35. What is the annual rate of return on the investment?

3. At the end of each year a self-employed person deposits $1,500 in a Keogh retirement account that earns 10 percent annually.
   a. How much will be in the account when the individual retires at the age of 65 if the savings program starts when the person is age 45?
   b. How much additional money will be in the account if the saver defers retirement until age 70 and continues the annual contributions?
   c. How much additional money will be in the account if the saver discontinues the contributions but does not retire until the age of 70?

4. A saver wants $100,000 after ten years and believes that it is possible to earn an annual rate of 8 percent on invested funds.
   a. What amount must be invested each year to accumulate $100,000 if (1) the payments are made at the beginning of each year or (2) if they are made at the end of each year?
   b. How much must be invested annually if the expected yield is only 5 percent?

5. An investment offers $10,000 per year for 20 years. If an investor can earn 8 percent annually on other investments, what is the current value of this investment? If its current price is $120,000, should the investor buy it?

6. Today graduating seniors may earn $25,000 each year. If the annual rate of inflation is 4 percent, what must these graduates earn after 20 years to maintain their current purchasing power? If the rate of inflation rises to 12 percent, will they be maintaining their standard of living if they earn $250,000 after 20 years?

7. A person who is retiring at the age of 65 and who has $200,000 wants to leave an estate of at least $30,000. How much can the individual draw annually on the $200,000 (starting at the end of the year) if the funds earn 8 percent and the person's life expectancy is 85 years?

8. A 40-year-old individual establishes an IRA account with a commercial bank. The account is expected to pay 7 percent annually, and deposits will be $2,000 annually at the beginning of each year. Initially the saver expects to start drawing on the account at age 60.
   a. How much will be in the account when the saver is age 60?
   b. If this investor found a riskier investment that offered 10 percent, how much in additional funds would be earned?
   c. The investor selects the 10 percent investment and retires at the age of 60. How much can be drawn from the account at the beginning of each year if life expectancy is 85 and the funds continue to earn 10 percent?

9. You are offered $900 five years from now or $150 at the end of each year

for the next five years. If you can earn 6 percent on your funds, which offer will you accept? If you can earn 14 percent on your funds, which offer will you accept? Why are your answers different?

10. The following questions illustrate nonannual compounding.
    a. $100 is placed in an account that pays 12 percent. How much will be in the account after one year if interest is compounded annually, semi-annually, or monthly?
    b. $100 is to be received after one year. What is the present value of this amount if you can earn 12 percent compounded annually, semiannually, or monthly?

11. Annually, at the end of each year, Tom invests $2,000 in a retirement account. Joan also invests $2,000 in a retirement account but makes her deposits at the beginning of each year. They both earn 9 percent on their funds. How much will each have in their accounts at the end of 20 years?

12. You are 60 years old. Currently you have $10,000 invested in an IRA account and have just received a lump sum distribution of $50,000 from a pension plan, which you roll over into an IRA rollover account. You continue to make $2,000 annual payments to the regular IRA and expect to earn 8 percent on these funds until you start withdrawing the money at age 70 (i.e., after ten years). The IRA rollover account will earn 9 percent for the same duration.
    a. How much will you have when you start to make withdrawals at age 70?
    b. If your funds continue to earn 9 percent annually and you withdraw $17,000 annually, how long will it take to exhaust your funds?
    c. If your funds continue to earn 9 percent annually and your life expectancy is 18 years, what is the maximum you may withdraw each year?

13. You are offered an annuity of $12,000 a year for 15 years. The annuity payments start after five years have elapsed. If the annuity costs $75,000, is the annuity a good purchase if you can earn 9 percent on invested funds?

14. You purchase a $1,000 asset for $800. It pays $60 a year for seven years at which time you receive the $1,000 principal. Prove that the rate of return on this investment is not 9 percent.

15. You invest $1,000 a year for ten years at 10 percent and then invest $2,000 a year for an additional ten years at 10 percent. How much will you have accumulated at the end of the twenty years?

16. You are promised $10,000 a year for six years after which you will receive $5,000 a year for six years. If you can earn 8 percent annually, what is the present value of this stream of payments?

17. A township expects its 5,000 population to grow annually at the rate of 5 percent. The township currently spends $300 per inhabitant, but, as the result of inflation and wage increments, expects the per capita expenditure to grow annually by 7 percent. How much will be the township's budget after 10, 15, and 20 years?

18. Bob places $1,000 a year in his IRA for ten years and then invests $2,000 a year for the next ten years. Mary places $2,000 a year in her IRA for ten years and then invests $1,000 a year for the next ten years. They both have invested $30,000. If they earn 8 percent annually, how much more will Mary have earned than Bob at the end of twenty years?

19. Bob and Barbara are 55 and 50 years old. Bob, the breadwinner, annually

contributes $1,500 to Barbara's IRA. They plan to make contributions until Bob retires at age 65 and then to leave the funds in as long as possible (i.e., age 70 to ease calculations).

Mike and Mary are 55 and 50 years old. Mike, the breadwinner, annually contributes $2,000 to Mike's IRA. They plan to make contributions until Mike retires at age 65 and then leave the funds in as long as possible (i.e., age 70 to ease calculations).

Both Barbara's and Mike's IRAs yield 10 percent annually.

The combined life expectancy of both couples is to age 85 of the wife. What will be each couple's annual withdrawal from the IRA based on life expectancy?

(This problem is designed to illustrate an important point in financial planning for retirement. What is the point?)

20. You want $100,000 after eight years in order to start a business. Currently you have $26,000 which may be invested to earn 7 percent annually. How much additional money must you set aside each year if these funds also earn 7 percent in order to meet your goal of $100,000 at the end of eight years? By how much would your answer differ if you invested the additional funds at the beginning of each year instead of at the end of each year?

Supplemental Problems

All of the above problems can be solved using the interest tables supplied in the appendix. To test your ability to construct your own interest factors or to use the computer programs available with this text, do the following problems.

1. You place $1,300 in a savings account that pays 5.3 percent annually. How much will you have in the account at the end of six years and three months?
2. You invest $1,000 annually for seven years and earn 7.65 percent annually. How much interest will you have accumulated at the end of the seventh year?
3. An investment promises to pay you $10,000 each year for ten years. If you want to earn 8.42 percent on your investments, what is the maximum price you should pay for this asset?
4. You bought a stock for $10 a share and sold it for $25.60 after five and a half years. What was your annual return on the investment?
5. You can earn 7.2 percent annually; how much must you invest annually to accumulate $50,000 after five years?

Suggested Readings

Cissell, Robert, Helen Cissell, and David Flaspohler. *Mathematics of Finance.* 7th ed. Boston: Houghton Mifflin, 1986.
This is a basic text that explains many of the variations on the four essential cases presented in this chapter.

Clayton, Gary, and Christopher B. Spivey. *The Time Value of Money.* Philadelphia: W. B. Saunders, 1978.
This is a primer illustrating many problems that can be solved by the basic time value of money tables.

Charles J. Woelfel. *The Desktop Guide to Money, Time, Interest and Yields.* Chicago: Probus Publishing, 1986.
This is a reference book on time value of money calculations that includes loan amortization tables and mortgage balance tables.

7

RISK AND PORTFOLIO THEORY

LEARNING OBJECTIVES

After completing this chapter you should be able to

1. Identify the general sources of risk.

2. Identify the relationship between securities that is necessary to achieve diversification.

3. Contrast the sources of return and differentiate between expected and realized returns.

4. Explain how standard deviations and beta coefficients measure risk. Interpret the difference between beta coefficients of 1.5, 1.0, and 0.5.

5. Contrast efficient and inefficient portfolios and identify which portfolio the individual will select.

6. Compare the explanation of a stock's return according to the capital asset pricing model and arbitrage pricing theory.

I n War As I Knew It, George Patton said, "Take calculated risks; that is quite different from being rash." Because the future is uncertain, investors should realize that they too must take calculated risks. The reward for taking these risks is the possible return on the investment.

This chapter serves as an introduction to the sources and measurements of risk and how these measurements are used in portfolio theory. Risk may be measured by a standard deviation, which measures the dispersion (or variability) around a central tendency such as an average return. Risk also may be measured by a beta coefficient, which is an index of the volatility of a security's return relative to the return on the market. Much of this chapter is devoted to an exposition of these measures of risk and the reduction of risk through the construction of diversified portfolios.

The chapter ends with a discussion of portfolio theory and explanations of security returns. Portfolio theory is built around the investor seeking to construct an efficient portfolio that offers the highest return for a given level of risk or the least amount of risk for a given level of return. Of all the possible efficient portfolios, the individual investor selects the portfolio that offers the highest level of satisfaction or utility.

Models of security returns are built around the specification of what variables affect an asset's return. In the capital asset pricing model, a security's return primarily depends upon interest rates such as the rate of safe treasury securities, movements in security prices in general, and how the individual stock responds to changes in the market. In arbitrage pricing theory, security returns are related to more variables that may include unexpected changes in inflation or industrial production.

◆ ◆ ◆

SOURCES OF RISK

The word *risk* is used frequently in this text. As was explained in the first chapter, there are several sources of risk. These are frequently classified as diversifiable (unsystematic) risk or nondiversifiable (systematic) risk. As explained in Chapter 1, diversifiable risk refers to the risk associated with the individual firm, its operations, and methods of financing. Nondiversifiable risk refers to the risk associated with (1) fluctuating security prices in general, (2) fluctuating interest rates, (3) reinvestment rates, (4) the loss of purchasing power through inflation, and (5) loss from changes in the value of exchange rates.

Asset returns tend to move together. If security prices rise in general, the price of a specific security tends to rise in sympathy with the market. Conversely, if the market were to decline, the value of an individual security would also tend to fall. Thus there is a systematic relationship between the price of a specific asset, such as a common stock, and the market as a whole. As long as investors buy securities, they cannot avoid bearing this source of systematic risk.

Asset values are also affected by changes in interest rates. As is explained in Chapter 15, rising interest rates depress the prices of fixed income securities, such as long-term bonds and preferred stock. Conversely, if interest rates fall, the value of these assets rises. There is a systematic negative relationship between the prices of fixed income securities and changes in interest rates. As long as investors acquire fixed income securities, they must bear the risk associated with fluctuations in interest rates.

Investors receive payments such as dividends or interest, which may be reinvested. When yields change (e.g., when interest rates rise or decline), the amount received on these reinvested funds also changes. This, then, is the source of reinvestment risk. In the early 1980s, when interest rates were relatively high, investors benefited when their funds were reinvested. However, in 1992 and 1993, when yields were the lowest in twenty years, many investors' incomes declined as they earned less on reinvested funds. This was particularly true for savers such as retirees with conservative investments such as certificates of deposit. When these CDs came due in 1992, investors had to accept much lower interest yields when they renewed the certificates.

Investors must also endure a fourth source of systematic risk: the loss of purchasing power through inflation. It is obvious that rising prices of goods and services erode the purchasing power of both investors' income and assets. Like fluctuating security prices or changes in interest rates, there is nothing the individual can do to stop inflation; therefore, the goal should be to earn a return that exceeds the rate of inflation. If the investor cannot earn such a return, he or she may benefit more from spending the funds and consuming goods now.

The last source of systematic risk is the risk associated with changes in the value of currencies. If investors acquire foreign investments, the proceeds of the sale of the foreign asset must be converted from the foreign currency into the domestic currency before they may be spent. (The funds, of course, may be spent in the foreign country without the conversion.) Since the value of currencies changes, the value of the foreign investments will rise or decline with changes in the value of the currencies. If the value of the foreign currency rises, the value of the foreign investment increases and the domestic investor gains. The converse occurs when the price of the foreign currency declines.

Individuals can avoid this risk by not acquiring foreign assets and, of course, miss the opportunities such investments may offer. However, investors may still bear some of this risk since many firms are affected by changes in the value of foreign currencies. Many U.S. firms invest abroad, and even if they do not, they may compete with foreign firms in domestic markets. Hence investors who do not own foreign assets may still be affected, albeit indirectly, by changes in the value of foreign currencies relative to their own.

Besides systematic risk, the investor also faces the unsystematic risk associated with each asset. Since the investor buys specific assets, for example, the common stock of IBM or bonds issued by the township of Princeton, that individual must bear the risk associated with each specific investment.

For firms, the sources of unsystematic risk are the business and financial risks associated with the operation. Business risk refers to the nature of the firm's operations, and financial risk refers to how the firm finances its assets (i.e., whether the firm uses a substantial or modest amount of debt financing). For example, the business risk associated with United or Delta Airlines is affected by such factors as the cost of fuel, the legal and regulatory environment, the capacity of planes, and seasonal changes in demand. Financial risk for airlines depends on how the airline finances its planes and other assets—that is, whether the assets were acquired by issuing bonds, preferred stock, or common stock, by leasing, or by borrowing from other sources.

The investor may be unable to anticipate all the events that will affect a certain firm, such as a strike or natural disaster, but these events may affect the value of the firm's securities in positive or negative ways. In either case, the possibility of these events occurring increases the risk associated with investing in a specific asset.

portfolio risk
The total risk associated with owning a portfolio; the sum of systematic and unsystematic risk.

diversification
The process of accumulating different securities to reduce the risk of loss.

The combination of systematic and unsystematic risk is defined as the total risk (or **portfolio risk**) that the investor bears. While the investor can do little to reduce systematic risk, he or she can affect unsystematic risk. Unsystematic risk may be significantly reduced through **diversification,** which occurs when the investor purchases the securities of firms in different industries. Buying the stock of five telephone companies is not considered diversification, because the events that affect one company tend to affect the others. A diversified portfolio may consist of stocks and bonds issued by a telephone company, an electric utility, an insurance firm, a commercial bank, an oil refinery, a retail business, and a manufacturing firm. This is a diversified mixture of industries and types of assets. The impact of particular events on the earnings and growth of one firm need not apply to all of the firms; therefore, the risk of loss in owning the portfolio is reduced.[1]

How diversification reduces risk is illustrated in Figure 7.1, which shows the price performance of three stocks and their composite. Stock A's price initially falls, then rises, and starts to fall again. Stock B's price ultimately rises but tends to fluctuate. Stock C's price fluctuates the least of the three but ends with only a modest gain. Purchasing stock B and holding it would have produced a substantial profit while A would have generated a moderate loss.

The last quadrant illustrates what happens if the investor buys an equal dollar amount of each stock (i.e., buys a diversified portfolio).[2] First, the value of the port-

---

[1] Since stock and bond prices may move together, even a diversified mixture of securities is not a completely diversified portfolio. Further diversification may be achieved by including such assets as real estate, gold, savings accounts, and collectibles in the portfolio. It is through such diversification of type of asset and industry that unsystematic risk is eliminated.

[2] Later in this chapter, the statistical condition that must be met to achieve diversification is discussed and illustrated using returns from investments in the common stocks of Mobil and Public Service Enterprise Group.

Figure 7.1 ✦ PRICES OF THREE STOCKS

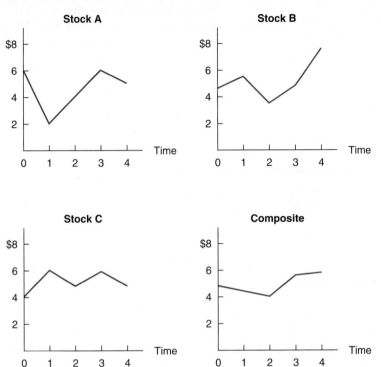

folio as a whole may rise even though the value of an individual security may not. Second, and most importantly, the fluctuation in the value of the portfolio is less than the fluctuations in individual security prices. By diversifying the portfolio, the investor is able to reduce the risk of loss. Of course, the investor also gives up the possibility of a large gain (as was achieved by stock B).

In effect, a diversified portfolio reduces the element of unsystematic risk. The risk associated with each individual investment is reduced by accumulating a diversified portfolio of assets. Even if one company fails (or does extremely well), the impact on the portfolio as a whole is reduced through diversification. Distributing investments among different industries, however, does not eliminate systematic or market risk. The value of a group of securities will tend to follow the market values in general. The price movements of securities will be mirrored by the diversified portfolio; hence, the investor cannot eliminate this source of systematic risk.

How many securities are necessary to achieve a diversified portfolio that reduces and almost eliminates unsystematic risk? The answer may be "surprisingly few." Several studies have found that risk has been significantly reduced in portfolios consisting of from 10 to 15 securities.[3]

---

[3] For further discussion, see the following: John Evans and Stephen Archer, "Diversification and the Reduction of Dispersion: An Empirical Analysis," *Journal of Finance* (December 1968): 761–767; Bruce D. Fielitz, "Indirect Versus Direct Diversification," *Financial*

Figure 7.2 ✦ PORTFOLIO RISK CONSISTING OF SYSTEMATIC AND UNSYSTEMATIC RISK

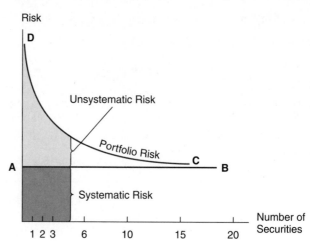

This reduction in unsystematic risk is illustrated in Figure 7.2. The vertical axis measures units of risk, and the horizontal axis gives the number of securities. Since market risk is independent of the number of securities in the portfolio, this element of risk is illustrated by a line, *AB*, that runs parallel to the horizontal axis. Regardless of the number of securities that an individual owns, the amount of market risk remains the same.

Portfolio risk (i.e., the sum of systematic and unsystematic risk) is indicated by line *CD*. The difference between line *AB* and line *CD* is the unsystematic risk associated with the specific securities in the portfolio. The amount of unsystematic risk depends on the number of securities held. As this number increases, unsystematic risk diminishes; this reduction in risk is illustrated in Figure 7.2 where line *CD* approaches line *AB*. For portfolios consisting of ten or more securities, the risk involved is primarily systematic.

Such diversified portfolios, as mentioned previously, do not consist of ten public utilities but of a cross section of U.S. businesses. Investing $20,000 in ten stocks (i.e., $2,000 for each) may achieve a reasonably well-diversified portfolio. While such a portfolio may cost somewhat more in commissions than two $10,000 purchases, the small investor achieves a diversified mixture of securities, which should reduce the risk of loss associated with investment in a specific security. Unfortunately, the investor must still bear the systematic risk associated with investing and the risk of loss in purchasing power that results from inflation.

Management (Winter 1974): 54–62; H. Latané and W. Young, "Tests of Portfolio Building Rules," *Journal of Finance* (September 1969): 595–612; and William Sharpe, "Risk, Market Sensitivity and Diversification," *Financial Analysts Journal* (January–February 1972): 74–79. However, George Frankfurter suggests that even well-diversified portfolios have a substantial amount of nonsystematic risk. See his "Efficient Portfolios and Non-Systematic Risk," *The Financial Review* (Fall 1981): 1–11.

THE EXPECTED RETURN ON AN INVESTMENT

Portfolio theory is primarily concerned with systematic risk and expected return. Its purpose is to determine that combination of return and risk that will allow the individual investor to achieve the highest return for a given level of risk. To do this, a means for measuring return and risk must be devised. Such measurement is the focus of the next section of this chapter.

The **expected return** is the anticipated flow of income and/or price appreciation. An investment may offer a return from either of two sources. The first source is the flow of income that may be generated by the investment. A savings account yields the holder a flow of interest income while the account is held. The second source of return is capital appreciation. If an investor buys stock and its price subsequently increases, the investor will receive a capital gain. All investments offer the investor either potential income and/or capital appreciation. Some investments, like the savings account, offer only income, whereas other investments, such as an investment in land, may offer only capital appreciation. In fact, some investments may require that expenditures (e.g., property tax on the land) be made by the investor.

This expected return is summarized in Equation 7.1:

$$r = \frac{D}{P} + g \qquad (7.1)$$

The symbols are

- r the return (as a percentage).
- D the dividend (or interest in the case of a debt instrument).
- P the price of the asset.
- g the growth in the value of the asset (i.e., the capital gain).

If an investor buys a stock for $10 and expects to earn a dividend of $0.60 and sells the stock for $12 so there is a capital gain of 20 percent, the expected return is

$$r = \frac{\$0.60}{\$10} + .2 = .26 = 26\%.$$

The investor is expecting to earn a return of 26 percent during the time period.[4]

It is important to realize that this return is anticipated. The yield that is achieved on the investment is not known until after the investment is sold and converted to cash. It is important to differentiate between *the expected return* and *the realized return*. The expected return is the incentive for accepting risk, and it must be compared with the investor's **required return,** which is the return necessary to induce

expected return
The sum of the anticipated dividend yield and capital gains.

required return
The expected return necessary to induce the investor to purchase an asset.

---

[4] Since the time period has not been specified, this return should not be confused with an *annual* rate of return. In Chapter 9, returns that do not specify the time period are referred to as *holding period returns*. The calculation of annual rates of return are also addressed in Chapter 9.

that investor to bear the risk associated with a particular investment. As is discussed later in this chapter, the required return includes (1) what the investor may earn on alternative investments, such as the risk-free return available on treasury bills, and (2) a premium for bearing risk that includes compensation for the expected inflation rate and for fluctuations in security prices. Since each individual's willingness to bear risk is different, the required return differs from one investor to another.[5]

Despite this difference, virtually all investors have the same attitude toward risk—they do not like to bear it. To induce them to bear additional risk, the expected return from the investment must be sufficient to compensate investors for assuming the risk inherent in the investment. Such a relationship between risk and expected return is consistent with investors' aversion to risk taking. A greater anticipated return is necessary to induce investors to bear an increased risk of loss; if the expected return is less than the required return, the investment will not be made.

THE MEASUREMENT OF RISK

Risk is concerned with the uncertainty that the realized return will not equal the expected return. Emphasis is placed on the extent to which the return may differ from the average return or on the volatility of the return relative to fluctuations in the market. The former may be measured by a statistical concept called the standard deviation, while the latter may be measured by what has been termed a beta coefficient. This section considers the standard deviation; beta coefficients are covered later in this chapter.

A measurement of risk is also implied when individuals refer to the annual range in an asset's price. One may encounter statements such as "The stock is trading near its low for the year," or "245 stocks reached new highs while only 41 fell to new lows." Some individuals plan their investment strategy as if a stock trades within a price range. If the stock is near the low for the year, it may be a good time to purchase. Correspondingly, if it is trading near the high for the year, it may be a good time to sell. The range in the stock's price, then, can be used as a guide to strategy, because the price tends to gravitate to a mean between these two extremes. In other words, there is a "central tendency" for the price of the stock. The range in a stock's price then becomes a measure of risk. Stocks with wider ranges are "riskier" because their prices tend to deviate further from the average (mean) price.

One problem with using the range as a measure of risk is that two securities of different prices can have the same range. For example, a stock whose price ranges from $10 to $30 has the same range as a stock whose price varies from $50 to $70. The range is $20 in both cases, but an increase from $10 to $30 is a 200 percent increment, whereas the increase from $50 to $70 is only a 40 percent increase. The price of the latter stock appears to be more stable; hence, less risk is associated with this security, even though both stocks involve equal risk according to the range.

---

[5]The discussion and calculation of rates of return that have been *realized* are covered in Chapter 9.

Dispersion around an Investment's Return

The problem that is inherent in using only two observations (e.g., a stock's high and low prices) to determine risk may be avoided by analyzing **dispersion** around an average value, such as an investment's return. This technique considers all possible outcomes. If there is not much difference among the possible returns (i.e., they are close together), then the dispersion will be small. If most of the returns are near the extremes and differ considerably from the average return, then the dispersion will be large. The larger this dispersion, the greater the risk associated with a particular stock.

dispersion
Deviation from the average.

This concept is perhaps best illustrated by a simple example. An investment in either of two stocks yields an average return of 15 percent, but stocks could have the following returns:

Stock A	Stock B
13½%	11 %
14	11½
14¼	12
14½	12½
15	15
15½	17½
15¾	18
16	18½
16½	19

Although the average return is the same for both stocks, there is considerable difference in the possible returns. Stock A's returns are very close to the average value, whereas stock B's returns are closer to the possible high and low values. The possible returns of stock A cluster around the average return. Since there is considerably less fluctuation in returns, it is the less risky of the two securities.

These differences in risk are illustrated in Figure 7.3, which plots the various returns on the horizontal axis and the frequency of their occurrence on the vertical axis. This is basically the same information that was previously given for stocks A and B, except that more observations would be necessary to construct such a graph.[6] Most of stock A's returns are close to the average return, so the frequency distribution is higher and narrower. The frequency distribution for stock B's return is lower and wider, which indicates a greater dispersion in that stock's returns.

The larger dispersion around the average return implies that the stock involves greater risk because the investor can be less certain of the stock's future return. The larger the dispersion, the greater is the chance of a large loss from the investment, and, correspondingly, the greater is the chance of a large gain. However, this potential for increased gain is concomitant with bearing more risk. Stock A involves less risk; it has the smaller dispersion. But it also has less potential for a large gain. A reduction in risk also means a reduction in possible return on the investment.

---

[6]While there are only nine observations in the illustration, the figure is drawn as if there were a large number of observations.

Standard Deviation as a Measure of Risk: One Asset

This dispersion around the mean value (i.e., the average return) is measured by the standard deviation. Since the standard deviation measures the tendency for the various returns to cluster around the average return (i.e., it is a measure of the variability of the returns), the standard deviation may be used as a measure of risk. The larger the dispersion, the greater the standard deviation and the larger the risk associated with the particular security.

The standard deviation is calculated as follows:

1. For the range of possible returns, subtract the individual observations from the average return.
2. Square this difference.
3. Add these squared differences.
4. Divide this sum by the number of observations less 1.
5. Take the square root.

For stock A the standard deviation is determined as follows:

Expected Return	Individual Return	Difference	Difference Squared
15%	13.50%	1.5	2.2500
15	14	1	1.0000
15	14.25	0.75	0.5625
15	14.50	0.5	0.25
15	15	0	0
15	15.50	−0.5	0.25
15	15.75	−0.75	0.5625
15	16	−1	1.000
15	16.50	−1.5	2.2500
	The sum of the squared differences:		8.1250

The sum of the squared differences divided by the number of observations less 1:

$$\frac{8.1250}{6} = 1.0156.$$

The square root: $\sqrt{1.0156} = \pm 1.01$

Thus, the standard deviation is ± 1.01.

The investor must then interpret this result. Plus and minus one standard deviation has been shown to encompass approximately 68 percent of all observations (in this case, that is 68 percent of the returns). The standard deviation for stock A is ± 1.01, which means that approximately two-thirds of the returns fall between 13.99 and 16.01 percent. These returns are simply the expected average return (15 percent) plus 1.01 and minus 1.01 percent (i.e., plus and minus the standard deviation).

For stock B the standard deviation is ± 3.30, which means that approximately 68 percent of the returns fall between 11.7 percent and 18.3 percent. Stock B's

Figure 7.3 ♦ Distribution of the Returns of Two Stocks

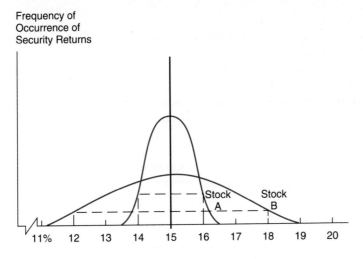

returns have a wider dispersion from the average return, and this fact is indicated by the greater standard deviation.

These differences in the standard deviations are illustrated in Figure 7.4, which reproduces Figure 7.3 but adds the standard deviations. The average return for both stocks is 15 percent, but the standard deviation is greater for stock B than for stock A (i.e., ± 3.30 for B versus ± 1.01 for A). By computing the standard deviation, the analyst quantifies risk. This will help in the selection of individual securities,

Figure 7.4 ♦ Distribution of the Returns of Two Stocks

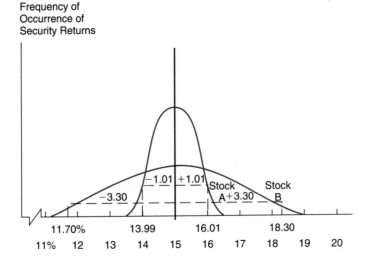

since the investor will prefer those assets with the least risk for a given expected return.

The Return and Standard Deviation of a Portfolio

While the above discussion was limited to the return on an individual security and the dispersion around that return, the concepts can be applied to an entire portfolio. A portfolio also has an average return and a dispersion around that return. The investor is concerned not only with the return and the risk associated with each investment, but also with the return and risk associated with the portfolio as a whole. This aggregate is, of course, the result of the individual investments and of each one's weight in the portfolio (i.e., the value of each asset, expressed in percentages, in proportion to the total value of the portfolio).

Consider two portfolios consisting of the following three stocks:

Stock	Return
1	8.3%
2	10.6
3	12.3

If 25 percent of the total value of the portfolio is invested in stocks 1 and 2 and 50 percent is invested in stock 3, the return is more heavily weighted in favor of stock 3. The return is a weighted average of each return times its proportion in the portfolio.

Return	×	Weight (percentage value of stock in proportion to total value of portfolio)	=	Weighted average
8.3%	×	0.25	=	2.075%
10.6	×	0.25	=	2.650
12.3	×	0.50	=	6.150.

The return is the sum of these weighted averages.

$$2.075\%$$
$$2.650$$
$$\underline{6.150}$$
$$10.875\%$$

The previous example is generalized in Equation 7.2, which states that the return on a portfolio R_p is a weighted average of the returns of the individual assets $[(R_1) \ldots (R_n)]$, each weighted by its proportion in the portfolio ($w_1 \ldots w_n$):

$$R_p = w_1(R_1) + w_2(R_2) + \ldots + w_n(R_n). \tag{7.2}$$

Thus, if a portfolio has 20 securities, each plays a role in the determination of the portfolio's return. The extent of that role depends on the weight that each asset has in the portfolio. Obviously those securities that compose the largest part of the individual's portfolio have the largest impact on the portfolio's return.[7]

Unfortunately, an aggregate measure of the portfolio's risk (i.e., the portfolio's standard deviation) is more difficult to construct than the weighted average of the returns. This is because security prices are not independent of each other. However, while security prices do move together, there can be considerable difference in these price movements. For example, prices of stocks of firms in homebuilding may be more sensitive to recession than stock prices of utilities, whose prices may decline only moderately. These relationships among the assets in the portfolio must be considered in the construction of a measure of risk associated with the entire portfolio. In more advanced texts, these inner relationships among stocks are called covariation. Covariation considers not only the volatility of the individual asset but also its relationship with the other assets in the portfolio.

Since the determination of a portfolio's standard deviation becomes very complicated for a portfolio of many assets, the following illustrations will be limited to portfolios of only two assets. Three cases are illustrated in Figure 7.5. In the first case, the two assets' returns move exactly together; in the second, the two assets' returns move exactly opposite; and in the third, the returns are independent of each other. While these examples are simple, they do illustrate how a portfolio's standard deviation is determined and the effect of the relationships among the assets in the portfolio on the risk associated with the portfolio as a whole.

The standard deviation of the returns on a portfolio (Sd) with two assets is given in Equation 7.3:

$$S_d = \sqrt{w_a^2\, S_a^2 + w_b^2\, S_b^2 + 2w_a w_b \mathrm{cov}_{ab}} \tag{7.3}$$

While this is formidable looking, it says that the standard deviation of the portfolio's return is the square root of the sum of (1) the squared standard deviation of the return of the first asset (S_a) times its squared weight in the portfolio (w_a) plus (2) the squared standard deviation of the return on the second asset (S_b) times its squared weight (w_b) in the portfolio plus (3) two times the weight of the first asset times the weight of the second asset times the covariance of the two assets.

The covariance of the returns on assets a and b (cov_{ab}) is

$$\mathrm{cov}_{ab} = S_a + S_b \times (\text{correlation coefficient of a and b}).$$

Thus, to determine the covariation the analyst needs the standard deviations of each asset's return and the correlation coefficient between the returns on the two securities. The numerical values of correlation coefficients range from $+1.0$ for a perfect positive correlation to -1.0 for a perfect negative correlation.[8]

---

[7] The same general equation may be applied to expected returns, in which case the expected return on a portfolio, $E(R_p)$, is a weighted average of the expected returns of the individual assets $[(E(R_1) \ldots E(R_n)]$ each weighted by its proportion in the portfolio $(w_1 \ldots w_n)$:

$$E(R_p) = w_1 E(R_1) + w_2 E(R_2) + \ldots + w_n E(R_n).$$

[8] How the correlation coefficient is determined may be found in an elementary text on statistics. See, for instance, George W. Summers, William S. Peters, and Charles P. Armstrong, *Basic Statistics in Business and Economics*, 4th ed. (Belmont, Calif.: Wadsworth, 1985), 307–308 and 534–537.

Figure 7.5 ✦ STOCK RETURNS, INDIVIDUALLY AND COMBINED

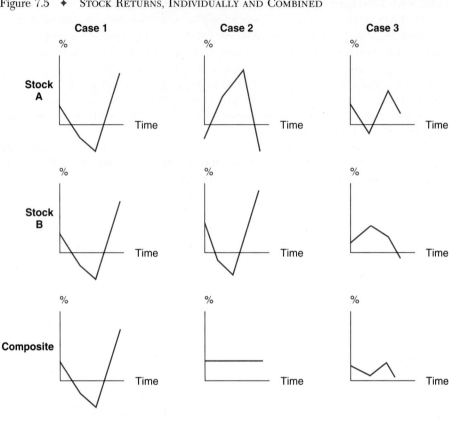

To illustrate the determination of the portfolio's standard deviation, consider the returns earned by securities A and B in the following three cases in which the portfolio is divided equally between the two securities. The three cases are also shown in Figure 7.5, which plots the returns on the assets and on the portfolio composed of equal amounts invested in each (i.e., 50 percent of the portfolio in each asset).

Case 1 ✦ PERFECT POSITIVE CORRELATION

Year	Return on Security A	Return on Security B	Return on Portfolio
1	10%	10%	10%
2	−12	−12	−12
3	−25	−25	−25
4	37	37	37
Average return	2.5%	2.5%	2.5%
Standard deviation of security returns	±.2716	±.2716	—

In this case the securities move exactly together (i.e., their correlation coefficient is 1.0). The standard deviation of the portfolio is computed as follows:

$$S_d = \sqrt{w_a^2 S_a^2 + w_b^2 S_b^2 + 2w_a w_b \text{cov}_{ab}}$$

$$= \sqrt{.5^2(.2716)^2 + .5^2(.2716)^2 + 2(.5)(.5)(.2716)(.2716)(1)}$$

$$= \pm.2716.$$

Case 2 ✦ PERFECT NEGATIVE CORRELATION

Year	Return on Security A	Return on Security B	Return on Portfolio
1	−15%	25%	10%
2	12	−2	10
3	25	−15	10
4	−37	47	10
Average return	−3.75%	13.75%	10%
Standard deviation of security returns	±.277293	±.277293	—

In this case the returns move exactly opposite (i.e., the correlation coefficient is −1.0), and the standard deviation of the portfolio is

$$S_d = \sqrt{w_a^2 S_a^2 + w_b^2 S_b^2 + 2w_a w_b \text{cov}_{ab}}$$

$$= \sqrt{.5^2(.277293)^2 + .5^2(.277293)^2 + 2(.5)(.5)(.277293)(.277293)(-1)}$$

$$= 0.$$

Case 3 ✦ PARTIAL NEGATIVE CORRELATION

Year	Return on Security A	Return on Security B	Return on Portfolio
1	10%	2%	6%
2	−8	12	2
3	14	6	10
4	4	−2	1
Average return	5%	4.5%	4.75%
Standard deviation of security returns	±.095917	±.0597	—

In this last case the returns do not move together. In the first and third years they both generated positive returns, but in the other two years one generated a loss while the other produced a positive return. In this illustration the correlation coefficient between the returns equals −0.524. Thus, the standard deviation of the portfolio is

$$S_d = \sqrt{w_a^2 S_a^2 + w_b^2 S_b^2 + 2 w_a w_b \text{cov}_{ab}}$$

$$= \sqrt{.5^2 (.095917)^2 + .5^2 (.0597)^2 + 2(.5)(.5)(.095917)(.0597)(-.524)}$$

$$= \pm.041.$$

Notice how, in the first case, the standard deviation of the portfolio is the same as the standard deviation of the two assets. Combining these assets in the portfolio has no impact on the risk associated with the portfolio. In Case 2, the portfolio's risk is reduced to zero (i.e., the portfolio's standard deviation is zero). This indicates that combining these assets whose returns fluctuate exactly in the opposite directions has the effect on the portfolio of completely erasing risk. The fluctuations associated with one asset are exactly offset by the fluctuations in the other asset.

In the third case, which is the most realistic of the three illustrations, the standard deviation of the portfolio is less than the standard deviations of the individual assets. The risk associated with the portfolio as a whole is less than the risk associated with either of the individual assets. Even though the assets' returns do fluctuate, the fluctuations partially offset each other, so that by combining these assets in the portfolio, the investor reduces his or her exposure to risk with almost no reduction in the return.

Diversification and the reduction in unsystematic risk require that assets' returns not be positively correlated. When there is a high positive correlation (as in Case 1), there is no risk reduction. When the returns are perfectly negatively correlated (as in Case 2), risk is erased (i.e., there is no variability in the combined returns). If one asset's return falls, the decline is exactly offset by the increase in the return earned by the other asset. The effect is to achieve a risk-free return. In the third case, which is the most likely of the three illustrations, there is neither a perfect positive nor a perfect negative correlation. However, there is risk reduction, because the returns are negatively correlated. The lower the positive correlation and the greater the negative correlation among the returns, the greater will be the risk reduction achieved by combining the various assets in the portfolio.

While the above illustration is extended, it points out a major consideration in the selection of assets to be included in a portfolio. The individual asset's expected return and risk are important, but the asset's impact on the portfolio as a whole is also important. The asset's return and the variability of that return should be considered in a portfolio context. It is quite possible that the inclusion of a volatile asset will reduce the risk exposure of the portfolio as a whole if the return is negatively correlated with the returns offered by the other assets in the portfolio. Failure to consider the relationships among the assets in the portfolio could prove to be counterproductive if including the asset reduces the portfolio's potential return without reducing the variability of the portfolio's return (i.e., without reducing the element of risk).

RISK REDUCTION THROUGH DIVERSIFICATION — AN ILLUSTRATION

The previous discussion has been in the abstract, but the concept of diversification through securities whose returns are not positively correlated may be illustrated by considering the returns earned on two specific stocks, Public Service Enterprise

Figure 7.6 ✦ ANNUAL RETURNS

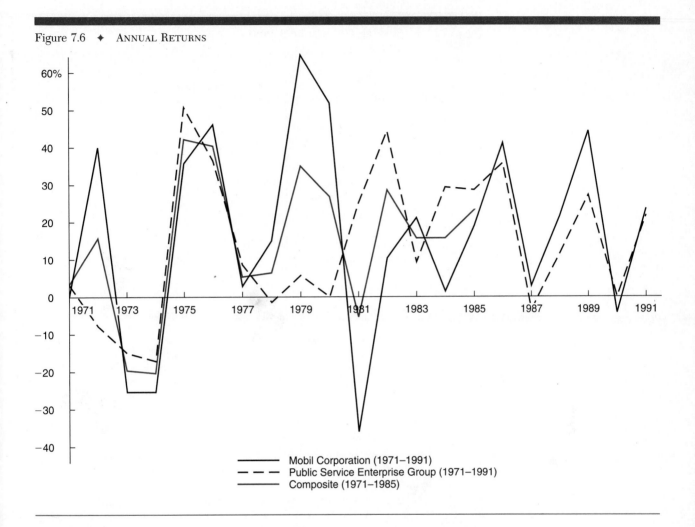

Mobil Corporation (1971–1991)
Public Service Enterprise Group (1971–1991)
Composite (1971–1985)

Group and Mobil Corporation. Public Service Enterprise Group is primarily an electric and gas utility whose stock price fell with higher interest rates and inflation. Mobil is a resource company whose stock price rose during inflation in response to higher oil prices but fell during the 1980s as oil prices weakened and inflation receded.

The annual returns (dividends plus price change) on investments in these two stocks are given in Figure 7.6 for the period 1971 through 1991. As may be seen in the graph, there were several periods when the returns on the two stocks moved in opposite directions. For example, during 1971 and 1978, an investment in Public Service Enterprise Group generated a loss while an investment in Mobil produced profits. However, the converse occurred during 1981 as the trend in Public Service Enterprise Group's stock price started to improve. From 1980 to 1985 the price of Public Service Enterprise Group doubled, but the price of Mobil's stock declined so that most of the return earned on Mobil's stock during the mid-1980s was its dividend.

Figure 7.7 presents a scatter diagram of the returns on these two stocks. The horizontal axis presents the average annual return on Public Service Enterprise

Figure 7.7 ✦ SCATTER DIAGRAM OF RETURNS

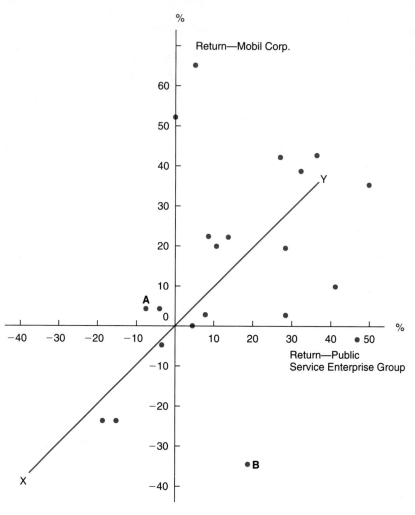

Group, while the vertical axis presents the average annual return on Mobil Corporation. As may be seen in the graph, the individual points lie throughout the plane representing the returns. For example, point A represents a positive return on Mobil but a negative return on Public Service Enterprise Group, and point B represents a positive return on Public Service Enterprise Group but a negative return on Mobil.

Combining these securities in a portfolio reduces the individual's risk exposure, as is also shown in Figures 7.6 and 7.7. The line representing the composite return in Figure 7.6 runs between the lines representing the returns on the individual securities. Over the entire time period, the average annual returns on Mobil and Public Service Enterprise Group were 16.6 and 13.0 percent, respectively. The average annual return on the composite was 14.8 percent. The risk reduction (i.e., the reduction in the dispersion of the returns) can be seen by comparing the standard deviations of the returns. For the individual stocks the standard deviations were ±26.5 percent and ±19.4 percent, respectively, for Mobil and Public Service Enterprise Group. However, the standard deviation for the composite return was ±18.9, so the dispersion of the returns associated with the portfolio is less than the dispersion of the returns on either stock by itself.

In this illustration the correlation coefficient between the two returns is only 0.34. This lack of correlation is visible in Figure 7.7. If there were a high positive correlation between the two returns, the points would lie close to the line XY. Instead the points are scattered throughout the figure. Thus, there is little correlation between the two returns, which is why combining the two securities reduces the individual's risk exposure.

It should be noted that combining these two stocks achieved diversification in the past because their returns were not highly correlated. Such diversification, however, may not be achieved in the future if the returns become positively correlated. This higher correlation appears to have occurred since 1985. The annual returns plotted in Figure 7.6 appear to have moved together from 1985 through 1991. This movement suggests that investing in these two stocks had little impact on diversification after 1985. This inference is confirmed because the correlation coefficient for years 1971 through 1985 is 0.231, but 0.884 for years 1986 through 1991.

While diversification is a prime goal because it reduces the investor's risk exposure without necessarily reducing the portfolio's return, the investor is faced with the problem of identifying those assets whose returns will not be positively correlated in the future. Unfortunately, the returns on many financial assets are positively correlated. In addition, as illustrated in Figure 7.6, returns that are negatively correlated under one set of economic conditions may not be negatively correlated in a different economic environment.

If investors include a broad spectrum of assets in their portfolios, a substantial level of diversification and risk reduction should be achieved. A portfolio that includes stocks, bonds, money market mutual funds, real estate, tangible assets, and foreign securities should be well diversified. In reality, the strongest argument for inclusion of foreign securities, real estate, and collectibles may be their potential impact on diversification and not their potential return.

PORTFOLIO THEORY

Harry Markowitz is credited with being the first individual to use the above material to develop a theory of portfolio construction employing returns and risk as measured by a portfolio's standard deviation.[9] This contribution was a major advance in finance and led to the development of the capital asset pricing model (CAPM) and subsequently to the arbitrage pricing model, generally referred to as arbitrage pricing theory (APT). Both the CAPM and the APT seek to explain portfolio and security return as a response to change in identifiable variables.

---

[9] Harry M. Markowitz, "Portfolio Selection," *The Journal of Finance* (March 1952); and Harry M. Markowitz, *Portfolio Selection Efficient Diversification of Investments* (New York: Wiley, 1959).

Figure 7.8 ✦ THE EFFICIENT FRONTIER

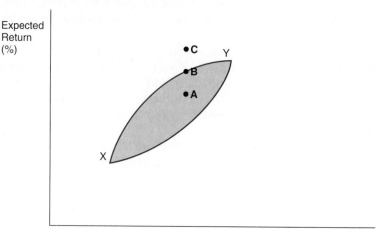

Risk: Portfolio Standard Deviation (σ_p)

The Markowitz Model

The Markowitz model is premised on a risk-averse individual constructing a diversified portfolio that maximizes the individual's satisfaction (i.e., generally referred to as *utility* by economists) my maximizing portfolio returns for a given level of risk. This process is depicted in Figures 7.8 through 7.10, which illustrate the optimal combinations of risk and return available to investors, the desire of investors to maximize their utility, and the determination of the optimal portfolio that integrates utility maximization within the constraint of the available portfolios.

Figure 7.8 illustrates the determination of the optimal portfolios available to investors. The vertical axis measures portfolio expected returns expressed as a percentage. The horizontal axis measures the risk associated with the portfolio, using the portfolio's standard deviation (σ_p).[10] In Figure 7.8, the shaded area represents all the possible portfolios composed of various combinations of risky securities. This area is generally referred to as the "attainable" or "feasible" set of portfolios. Some of these portfolios are **inefficient** because they offer an inferior return for a given amount of risk. For example, portfolio *A* is inefficient since portfolio *B* offers a higher return for the same amount of risk.

All portfolios that offer the highest return for a given amount of risk are referred to as **efficient.** The line that connects all of these portfolios (*XY* in Figure 7.8) defines the "efficient frontier" and is referred to as the "efficient set" of portfolios. Any portfolio that offers the highest return for a given amount of risk must lie on the efficient frontier. Any portfolio that offers a lower return is inefficient and lies

inefficient portfolio
A portfolio whose return is not maximized given the level of risk.

efficient portfolio
The portfolio that offers the highest expected return for a given amount of risk.

[10]Sometimes the portfolio's variance is used instead of the standard deviation. Since the standard deviation is the square root of the variance, the use of the standard deviation or the variance is essentially the same.

Figure 7.9 ♦ INDIFFERENCE MAP

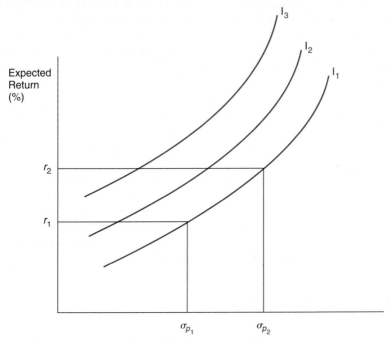

Risk: Portfolio Standard Deviation (σ_p)

below the efficient frontier in the shaded area. Since inefficient portfolios will not be selected, the efficient frontier establishes the best set of portfolios available to investors.

A portfolio such as *C* that lies above the efficient frontier offers a superior yield for the amount of risk. Investors would prefer that portfolio to portfolio *B* on the efficient frontier because *C* offers a higher return for the same level of risk. Unfortunately, combination *C* of risk and return does not exist. It is not a feasible solution. No combination of risk and expected return that lies above the efficient frontier is attainable.

While the efficient frontier gives all the best attainable combinations of risk and return, it does not tell *which* of the possible combinations an investor will select. That selection depends on the individual's willingness to bear risk. The combining of the efficient frontier and the willingness to bear risk determines the investor's optimal portfolio. Figure 7.8 gives only the efficient frontier; it says nothing about the investor's willingness to bear risk.

This willingness to bear risk may be shown by the use of indifference curves, which are often used in economic analysis to show trade-offs. A set of indifference curves is illustrated in Figure 7.9. On indifference curve I_1, the investor would be willing to accept a modest return such as r_1 and bear a modest amount of risk (σ_{p_1}); however, the same investor would be willing to bear more risk for a higher return (e.g., r_2 and σ_{p_2}). The additional return is enough to induce bearing the additional risk so the investor is *indifferent between the two alternatives*. Thus, all the points on the same indifference curve represent the same level of satisfaction.

The indifference curves in Figure 7.9 are for a risk-averse investor. The analysis assumes that investors do not like bearing risk; hence, additional risk requires more return. However, notice that these curves are concave from above; their slope increases as risk increases. This indicates that investors require ever-increasing amounts of additional return for equal increments of risk to maintain the same level of satisfaction.

Investors would like to earn a higher return without having to bear additional risk. A higher return without additional risk increases total satisfaction. Higher levels of satisfaction are indicated by indifference curves I_2 and I_3, which lie above indifference curve I_1. Once again the investor is *indifferent between any combination of risk and return* on I_2. All combinations of risk and return on indifference curve I_2 are preferred to all combinations on indifference curve I_1. Correspondingly, all points on indifference curve I_3 are preferred to all points on I_2. Since there is an indefinite number of levels of satisfaction, an indefinite number of indifference curves could be constructed for an individual. Each would represent a different level of satisfaction, and the higher the curves, the higher the level of satisfaction. (One of the advantages offered by this type of analysis is that indifference curves themselves do not measure satisfaction; they only indicate rankings; that is, I_2 is preferred to I_1.)

The investor seeks to reach the highest level of satisfaction but is, of course, constrained by what is available. The best combinations of risk and return available are given by the efficient frontier. Superimosing the indifference curves on the efficient frontier defines the investor's optimal portfolio. This is shown in Figure 7.10, which combines Figures 7.8 and 7.9. The optimal combination of risk and return represented by point O is the investor's optimal combination of risk and return.

If the investor selects any other portfolio with a different combination of risk and return on the efficient frontier (e.g., A), that portfolio would not be the individual's best choice. While portfolio A is an efficient combination of risk and return, it is not the optimal choice, as may be seen using the following logic. Portfolio B is equal to portfolio A (i.e., the investor is indifferent between A and B), but B is not efficient and is inferior to portfolio O, since O offers a higher level of return for the same amount of risk. Portfolio O must be preferred to B, and because A and B are equal, O must also be preferred to A. By similar reasoning, only one portfolio offers the highest level of satisfaction *and* lies on the efficient frontier. That unique combination of risk and return is represented by portfolio O, which occurs at the *tangency* of the efficient frontier and indifference curve I_2.

If an indifference curve cuts through the efficient frontier (e.g., I_1), it is attainable but inferior, and it can always be shown that the investor can reach a higher level of satisfaction by altering the portfolio. If an indifference curve lies above the efficient frontier (e.g., I_3), such a level of satisfaction is not obtainable. The investor would like to reach that level of satisfaction, but no combination of assets offers such a high expected return for that amount of risk.

Different investors may have varying indifferences curves. If the investor is very risk-averse, the curves tend to be steep, indicating a large amount of additional return is necessary to induce this individual to bear additional risk and maintain the same level of satisfaction. If the curves are relatively flat, the individual is less risk-averse. Only a modest amount of additional return is necessary to induce this indi-

Figure 7.10 ✦ DETERMINATION OF THE OPTIMAL PORTFOLIO

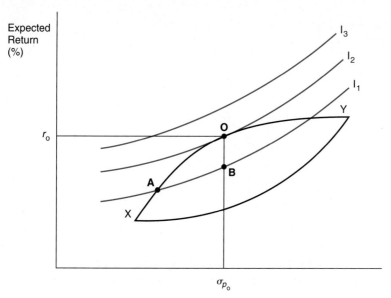

Risk: Portfolio Standard Deviation (σ_p)

vidual to bear additional risk and still maintain the same level of satisfaction. However, both investors are still averse to bearing risk. The difference is the degree of risk-aversion.

This difference in attitude toward risk is illustrated in Figure 7.11, which has two sets of indifference curves imposed on the efficient frontier. One investor is more risk-averse and selects the combination of risk and return represented by point A while the other investor is more willing to bear risk and selects the combination of risk and return represented by point B. Both investors, however, select a combination of risk and return that lies on the efficient frontier. Each selects that particular combination determined by the tangency of their highest obtainable indifference curve and the efficient frontier.

CAPITAL ASSET PRICING MODEL

Constructing an efficient frontier by the individual investor may be virtually impossible, since it requires estimates of return and dispersion for a large number of portfolios. The Markowitz model, however, does explain diversified portfolio construction in the utility-maximization framework generally used by economists. Moreover, this model subsequently led to the development of the capital asset pricing model

Figure 7.11 ◆ DIFFERENT OPTIMAL PORTFOLIOS FOR DIFFERENT INVESTORS

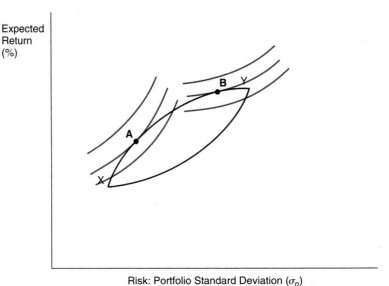

Risk: Portfolio Standard Deviation (σ_p)

(CAPM) by William F. Sharpe, John Lintner, and Jan Mossin.[11] The CAPM is among the most important theoretical concepts in finance; it advances the relationship between risk and return, adds the possibility of earning a risk-free return, and is easier to implement than the Markowitz model. The CAPM is an outgrowth of the Markowitz model and extends the concept of optimal diversified portfolios to the market in general and to the valuation of individual securities. That is, the concept is applied in both a macro-context that specifies the relationship between risk and the return on a portfolio and a micro-context that specifies the relationship between risk and the return on a specific asset.

The macro-aspect of the CAPM is the development of the *capital market line*. Figure 7.12 begins with all the possible portfolios of risky securities (i.e., the shaded area from Figure 7.8) and adds line *AB* which begins at r_f on the Y-axis and is tangent to the efficient frontier. *AB* is the capital market line specified by the capital asset pricing model. If investors bear no risk and invest their entire portfolios in risk-free assets, they should earn a return equal to r_f. As investors substitute risky securities for the risk-free assets, both risk and return increase (i.e., there is movement along the capital market line). Point Z, the point of tangency, represents a

[11] See William Sharpe, "Capital Asset Prices: A Theory of Market Equilibrium," *The Journal of Finance*, September 1964; John Lintner, "The Valuation of Risk Assets and the Selection of Risk Investments in Stock Portfolios and Capital Budgets," *Review of Economics and Statistics*, February 1965; and Jan Mossin, "Equilibrium in a Capital Asset Market," *Econometrica*, October 1966. The seminal contributions of Markowitz and Sharpe to the analysis of risk and the development of portfolio theory are so important that they, along with Merton Miller, were awarded the Nobel prize in economics in 1990.

Figure 7.12 ✦ CAPITAL MARKET LINE

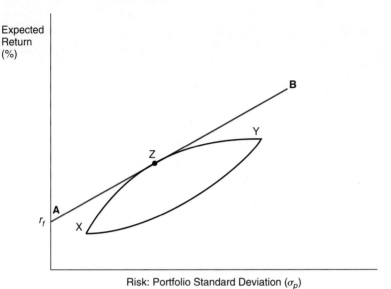

Risk: Portfolio Standard Deviation (σ_p)

portfolio consisting solely of risky securities. (To the right of Z, an investor is using margin to increase return further, but the use of margin continues to increase risk.) In effect, the capital market line, *AZB*, becomes the efficient frontier. Combinations of risk and return on this line represent the best attainable portfolios, and these combinations include the possibility of a portfolio with a risk-free return and portfolios in which securities are bought on margin.

The formula for the capital market line is based on the equation for a straight line:

$$Y = a + bX$$

in which Y becomes the return on the portfolio (r_p); *a*, the intercept, becomes the risk-free rate (r_f); X becomes the risk premium; and *b* is the slope of the line. The equation for the capital market line is

$$r_p = r_f + \left(\frac{r_m - r_f}{\sigma_m}\right)\sigma_p \tag{7.4}$$

This equation states that the expected return on a portfolio (r_p) is the sum of the expected return earned on a risk-free asset (risk-free return = r_f) such as a Treasury bill and a risk premium that depends on (1) the extent to which the expected return on the market exceeds the risk-free return (i.e., $r_m - r_f$) and (2) the dispersion of the portfolio (σ_p) relative to the dispersion of the market (σ_m). If the dispersion of the portfolio is equal to the dispersion of the market, these two considerations cancel; the return on such a portfolio depends solely on the risk-free rate and the risk premium associated with investing in securities. If, however, the dispersion of the

Figure 7.13 ✦ DIFFERENT PORTFOLIOS FOR DIFFERENT INVESTORS

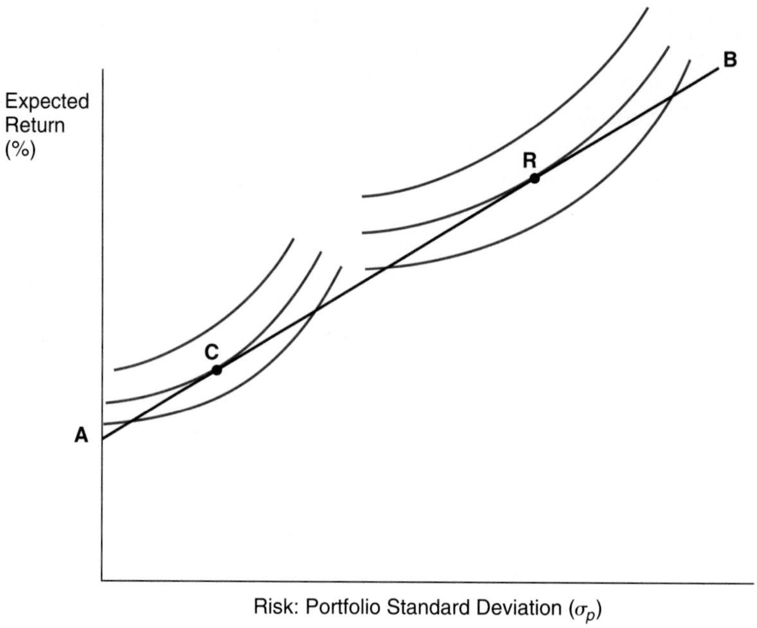

Risk: Portfolio Standard Deviation (σ_p)

portfolio is greater than the dispersion of the market, the return will have to exceed the return associated with the market. The risk premium is larger. Thus, the capital market line indicates that to earn larger returns, the investor is required to take greater risks.

The capital market line by itself does not determine which portfolio the individual will acquire. The actual portfolio the individual selects depends on the capital market line and the individual's willingness to bear risk, as indicated by indifference curves. Figure 7.13 represents the combination of risk and return selected by both a conservative and an aggressive investor. The conservative investor, who is represented by the steeper indifference curves, is very averse to bearing risk and selects a portfolio represented by point C, in which a large proportion of the portfolio consists of the risk-free asset. The more aggressive investor (i.e., the flatter indifference curves) selects a portfolio, represented by R, in which part of the securities are purchased on margin and the portfolio is leveraged.

The Capital Asset Pricing Model and Beta Coefficients

The second component of the capital asset pricing model is the specification of the relationship between risk and return for the individual asset. At the micro-level this relationship is referred to as the security market line (SML). Although this relationship is very similar to the capital market line, the difference is important. In the capital market line, risk is measured by the portfolio's standard deviation. In the security market line, the individual asset's risk is measured by a *beta coefficient*.

Understanding the security market line requires understanding beta coefficients. Thus, it is necessary to explain this measure of risk before discussing its use in the capital asset pricing model.

BETA COEFFICIENTS

When an individual constructs a well-diversified portfolio, the unsystematic sources of risk are diversified away. That leaves the systematic sources of risk as the relevant risks. A **beta coefficient** is a measure of systematic risk; it is an index of the volatility of the individual asset relative to the volatility of the market. The beta coefficient for a specific security (β_i) is defined as follows:

beta coefficient
An index of risk; a measure of the systematic risk associated with a particular stock.

$$\beta_i = \frac{\text{Standard deviation of the return on stock } i}{\text{Standard deviation of the return on the market}} \times \begin{array}{c}\text{Correlation coefficient between} \\ \text{the return on the stock and the} \\ \text{return on the market}\end{array} \quad (7.5)$$

Thus, beta depends on (1) the variability of the individual stock's return, (2) the variability of the market return (both measured by their respective standard deviations), and (3) the correlation between the return on the security and the return on the market.

The ratio of the standard deviations measures how variable the stock is relative to the variability of the market. The more variable a stock's return (i.e., the larger the standard deviation of the stock's return) relative to the variability of the market's return, the greater the risk associated with the individual stock. The correlation coefficient indicates whether this greater variability is important. If there is no relationship between the individual stock and the market (i.e., the correlation coefficient equals zero), the variability has no importance. The beta equals 0.0, and the security has no market risk.

A beta coefficient of 1 means that the stock's return moves exactly with an index of the market as a whole. A 10 percent return in the market could be expected to produce a 10 percent return on the specific stock. Correspondingly, a 10 percent decline in the market would result in a 10 percent decline in the return on the stock. A beta coefficient of less than 1 implies that the return on the stock would tend to fluctuate less than the market as a whole. A coefficient of 0.7 indicates that the stock's return would rise only 7 percent as a result of a 10 percent increase in the market but would fall by only 7 percent when the market declined by 10 percent. A coefficient of 1.2 means that the return on the stock could be expected to be 12 percent if the market return was 10 percent, but the return on the stock would decline by 12 percent when the market declined by 10 percent.

The greater the beta coefficient, the more the systematic risk associated with the individual stock. High beta coefficients may indicate exceptional profits during rising markets, but they also indicate greater losses during declining markets. Stocks with high beta coefficients are referred to as "aggressive." The converse is true for stocks with low beta coefficients, which should underperform the market during periods of rising stock prices but outperform the market as a whole during periods of declining prices. Such stocks are referred to as "defensive."

Figure 7.14 ✦ STOCK WITH A BETA COEFFICIENT OF GREATER THAN 1.0

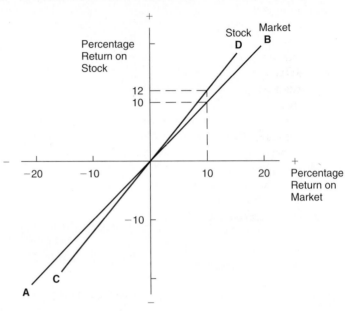

This relationship between the return on a specific security and the market index as a whole is illustrated in Figures 7.14 and 7.15. In each graph the horizontal axis represents the percentage return on the market index and the vertical axis represents the percentage return on the individual stock. The line *AB*, which represents the market, is the same in both graphs. It is a positive-sloped line that runs through the point of origin and is equidistant from both axes (i.e., it makes a 45° angle with each axis).

Figure 7.14 illustrates a stock with a beta coefficient greater than 1. Line *CD* represents a stock whose return rose and declined more than the market. In this case the beta coefficient is 1.2, so when the return on the market index is 10 percent, this stock's return is 12 percent.

Figure 7.15 illustrates a stock with a beta coefficient of less than 1. Line *EF* represents a stock whose return rose (and declined) more slowly than that of the market. In this case the beta coefficient is 0.8, so when the market's return is 10 percent, this stock's return is 8 percent.

Beta coefficients do vary among firms. This is illustrated in Exhibit 7.1, which presents the beta coefficients for selected firms as computed by Value Line. As may be seen in the table, some firms (e.g., AT&T and Exxon) have relatively low beta coefficients, while the coefficients for other firms (e.g., Kmart and Alcoa) are much higher. Investors who are willing to bear more risk may be attracted to these stocks with higher beta coefficients. Investors who are less inclined to bear risk may prefer the stocks with low beta coefficients. Although these investors forgo some potential return during rising market prices, they should suffer milder losses during periods of declining stock prices.

Figure 7.15 ✦ STOCK WITH A BETA COEFFICIENT OF LESS THAN 1.0

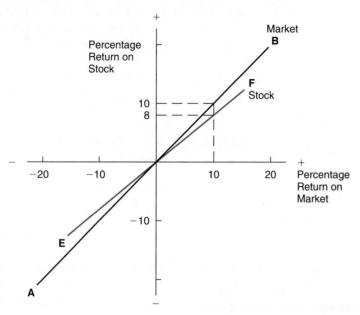

Exhibit 7.1 ✦ SELECTED BETA COEFFICIENTS AS COMPUTED BY VALUE LINE

| | Beta Coefficient | |
Company	1978	1992
AT&T	0.65	0.85
Exxon	0.90	0.75
Philip Morris, Inc.	0.90	1.05
Johnson & Johnson	0.95	1.05
IBM	0.95	0.95
GE	1.00	1.10
CBS, Inc.	1.00	1.00
E. I. DuPont	1.05	1.10
Kmart	1.05	1.20
McDonalds	1.05	0.95
Alcoa	1.15	1.25
Boeing	1.25	1.05

Computing beta coefficients for a significant number of securities over a reasonably long period is also an extremely time-consuming and tedious job. (How betas are estimated is illustrated in the appendix to this chapter.) Fortunately, the investor may obtain beta coefficients from several sources. (Standard deviations of portfolio returns are not available.) The *Value Line Investment Survey* supplies beta coefficients for all securities covered by the service.[12] The information may also be available through the investor's brokerage firm. Although not all brokers compute beta coefficients, the research departments of the larger brokerage firms determine beta coefficients, and these are available to the firms' customers.

To be useful, beta coefficients must be reliable predictors of future stock price behavior. For example, a conservative investor who desires stocks that will be stable will probably purchase stocks with low beta coefficients. An investor selecting a stock with a beta coefficient of 0.6 will certainly be upset if the market prices decline by 10 percent and this stock's price falls by 15 percent, since a beta coefficient of 0.6 indicates that the stock's expected return should decline by only 6 percent when the market declines by 10 percent.

Unfortunately, beta coefficients are constructed with historical price data. Although such data may be accumulated and tabulated for many years, it still does not mean that coefficients based on historical data will be accurate predictors of future movements in stock prices. Beta coefficients can and do change over time. Empirical studies have shown that beta coefficients for individual securities may be very unstable (e.g., the decrease in Boeing's beta or increase in AT&T's beta in Exhibit 7.1).[13] Therefore, the investor should not rely solely on these coefficients for selecting a particular security. However, beta coefficients do give the investor some indication of the systematic risk associated with specific stocks and thus can play an important role in the selection of a security.

Unlike the beta coefficient for individual securities, the beta coefficient for a portfolio composed of several securities is fairly stable over time. Changes in the different beta coefficients tend to average out; while one stock's beta coefficient is increasing, the beta coefficient of another stock is declining. A portfolio's historical beta coefficients, then, can be used as a tool to forecast its future beta coefficient, and this projection should be more accurate than forecasts of an individual security's beta coefficient. For example, in both 1978 and 1992 the average beta coefficient of the portfolio illustrated in Exhibit 7.1 is approximately 1.[14] If an equal dollar

---

[12]Betas are also available through the *Merrill Lynch Security Risk Evaluation Report*. Since Value Line and Merrill Lynch use different data, the numerical values of their respective betas may differ. For a discussion of these differences, see Frank K. Reilly and David J. Wright, "A Comparison of Published Betas," *Journal of Portfolio Management* (Spring 1988): 64–69.

[13]See, for instance, Robert A. Levy, "Stationarity of Beta Coefficients," *Financial Analysts Journal* (November–December 1971): 55–62. In general the evidence suggests that the numerical value of beta coefficients moves toward 1.0 (i.e., riskier securities become less volatile and vice versa). See Marshall E. Blume, "Portfolio Theory: A Step Toward Its Practical Application," *Journal of Business* (April 1970): 152–173 and Marshall Blume, "Beta and Their Regression Tendencies," *Journal of Finance* (June 1975): 785–796.

[14]The average for the twelve stocks in Exhibit 7.1 is 0.992 in 1978 and 1.025 in 1992. This suggests that the beta for a portfolio consisting of these stocks would have changed only marginally over the years even though the individual betas may have changed.

amount were invested in each security, the value of the portfolio should follow the market values fairly closely, even though individual beta coefficients are greater or less than 1. This tendency of the portfolio to mirror the performance of the market should occur even though selected securities may achieve a return that is superior (or inferior) to that of the market as a whole.

Beta coefficients may also be used if the investor believes that the market prices will move in a particular direction. For example, if the individual anticipates an increase in prices, he or she may construct an aggressive portfolio consisting solely of securities with high beta coefficients. However, if the anticipated price increases do not occur and the market prices decline, such a strategy may result in a considerable loss.

Beta and the Security Market Line

Beta's primary use in finance has been its incorporation into the capital asset pricing model as the key variable that explains individual security returns. The relationship between risk, as measured by beta, and an asset's return is specified in the security market line (SML). The security market line stipulates the return on a stock (r_s) as

$$r_s = r_f + (r_m - r_f)\beta. \tag{7.6}$$

The return on a stock depends on the risk-free rate of interest (r_f) and a risk premium composed of the extent to which the return on the market (r_m) exceeds the risk-free rate and the individual stock's beta coefficient. This relationship (i.e., the security market line) is shown in Figure 7.16.

The similarity of the capital market line and the security market line are immediately apparent if Figure 7.16 is compared to Figure 7.12. The Y-axis is the same, and the relationship between risk and return is represented as a straight line (i.e., $Y = a + bX$). The difference between the two figures is the measure of risk on the X-axis. The capital market line uses the portfolio's standard deviation while the security market line uses the individual security's beta coefficient.

Both the capital market line and the security market line play an important role in the selection of securities and the analysis of portfolio performance. For example, in the next chapter, the security market line component of the CAPM is used to determine the required return for an investment. This return is then used in the dividend-growth model in the next chapter to determine the value of a common stock. The model is also used in portfolio evaluation in Chapter 25, in which a realized return is compared to the required return specified by the model. Thus, the CAPM not only is an integral part of the theory of portfolio construction and security selection, but also establishes a criterion by which portfolio performance may be judged.

Portfolio Betas

The security market line relates a particular stock's beta to the security's return. However, beta coefficients may also be computed for an entire portfolio and related to the portfolio's return. If a portfolio is well-diversified, its beta is an appropriate

Figure 7.16 ✦ SECURITY MARKET LINE

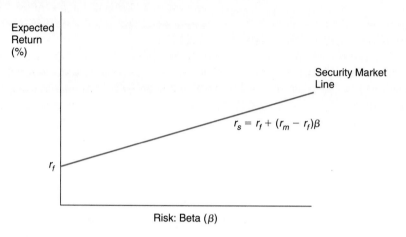

index of the portfolio's risk since diversification virtually eliminates the portfolio's unsystematic risk. The portfolio beta is a weighted average of each security in the portfolio and its beta. Thus, if a portfolio has the following stocks and their betas,

Stock	Amount Invested	Percent of Portfolio	Beta
A	$100	10%	0.9
B	200	20	1.2
C	300	30	1.6
D	400	40	1.7

the portfolio's beta is

$$(0.1)(0.9) + (0.2)(1.2) + (0.3)(1.6) + (.4)(1.7) = 1.49.$$

This portfolio's beta is greater than 1.0, which indicates that the portfolio is more volatile than the market. Of course, the portfolio beta would have been different if the weights were different. If the portfolio had been more heavily weighted in stock A instead of stock D, for example, the numerical value of the beta would have been lower.

Portfolio betas can play an important role in the evaluation of mutual fund performance, since the betas are a means to standardize for each fund's risk. Such standardization is necessary to compare performance of funds with differing amounts of risk. However, the discussion of assessing portfolio performance is deferred until the material is presented on investment companies in Chapter 23 and on portfolio assessment in Chapter 25.

ARBITRAGE PRICING THEORY

The previous material discussed beta coefficients and their use in the capital asset pricing model. While the CAPM is a major component in financial theory, it has been criticized as being too limited. The model reduces the explanation of a stock's return to two variables: (1) the market return and (2) the volatility of the stock in response to movements in the market (i.e., the beta). Of course in a well-diversified portfolio, systematic risk is *the* important source of risk. However, unsystematic risk may be important in the determination of an individual stock's return, if the stock's price is responsive to changes in some other variable. For example, an increase in the rate of inflation or a decrease in the rate of interest could have an important impact on an individual stock's return. Thus, other factors could play an important role in the explanation of security returns.

Arbitrage pricing theory (APT), initially developed by Stephen A. Ross, seeks to add additional variables to the explanation of security returns.[15] It is a multi-variable model in which security returns are dependent upon several variables in addition to the volatility of the market. APT derives its name from the economic premise that prices cannot differs in two markets. **Arbitrage** is the act of buying a good or security and simultaneously selling it in another market at a higher price.[16] If IBM stock were selling for $50 in New York and $60 in San Francisco, an opportunity for a riskless profit exists. Arbitrageurs would buy the stock in New York and simultaneously sell it in San Francisco, thus earning the $10 profit without bearing any risk. Of course, the act of buying in New York will drive up the stock's price and the act of selling in San Francisco will drive down the price until the prices in the two markets are equal and the opportunity for arbitrage is erased.

Arbitrage also implies that portfolios with the same risk generate the same returns. If portfolio *A* has the same risk as portfolio *B*, the two are substitutes for each other. Just as the stock of IBM must trade for the same price in New York and San Francisco, the returns on portfolios *A* and *B* must be the same or an opportunity for arbitrage would exist. Once again, the role of arbitrage is to erase differentials. Differences in returns then must be related to differences in how the portfolios respond to the changes in the sources of risk that the investor faces. These sources of risk may be a major determinant of the return the investor earns.

In arbitrage, the security's price movement and return are *not* explained by a relationship between risk and return. The CAPM is built upon an assumption concerning investors' willingness to bear risk (i.e., investors must expect to earn a higher return to be induced to bear more risk). While this assumption may be reasonable, APT explains movements in security prices without making an assumption concerning risk preferences. Security returns are the result of arbitrage as investors seek to take advantage of perceived differences in prices of risk exposure.

Arbitrage pricing theory states that the return on a security (r_s) depends on the

arbitrage
Simultaneous purchase and sale to take advantage of price differences in two markets.

---

[15] See Stephen A. Ross, "The Arbitrage Theory of Capital Asset Pricing," *Journal of Economic Theory* (December 1976), and "Return, Risk, and Arbitrage," in I. Friend and J. L. Bicksler, eds., *Risk and Return in Finance* (Cambridge, MA: Ballinger, 1977).

[16] Arbitrage is discussed further in the section on futures in Chapter 20.

expected return (r_e) and on a set of factors $(F_1 \ldots F_n)$. For example, if the number of factors were four, the general model would be

$$r_s = r_e + b_1F_1 + b_2F_2 + b_3F_3 + b_4F_4 + e. \qquad (7.7)$$

The individual parameters (i.e., the estimated coefficients $b_1 \ldots b_4$) measure the responsiveness or sensitivity of the return on the stock (or portfolio) to changes in the respective factors. The e represents an error term. If the model captures the important factors, the errors tend to cancel out (i.e., a positive error is canceled by a negative error), and the numerical value of the error term should be zero ($e = 0$). If there is a consistent error, the error term will not be equal to zero and the model is misspecified. That is, an important factor has been excluded.

The factors that could affect the return on a stock (or a portfolio) are numerous. Empirical work on APT generally classifies these variables into *sector* influences and *systematic* influences. An example of a sector variable is a firm's industry. What affects a bank stock may not affect a retailer or an airline. A systematic influence may be interest rates or the level of economic activity. For example, high-dividend-paying stocks may more readily respond to changes in interest rates, while cyclical stocks may more readily respond to changes in the level of economic activity.

While there could be a large number of possible variables, empirical results suggest that only a few seem to have a lasting or continuous impact on security returns. For example, a change in inflation may have an important impact on security returns. However, it is unanticipated (rather than anticipated) inflation that has the impact. In competitive financial markets, expected inflation is already incorporated into a security's price. If inflation is expected to rise from 4 percent to 8 percent, security prices would have been previously adjusted downward and yields would be higher. It is the unexpected change that arbitrage pricing theory is seeking to build into the return. The expected return plus the responsiveness to the unexpected change in inflation (and to other factors) determine the realized return.

Unexpected events will always occur, so realized returns usually deviate from expected returns. What the investor does not know is which unexpected events will occur and how the individual stock will respond to the change. In addition, not all securities or portfolios will respond in the same direction or by the same amount. Two portfolios may respond differently to a change in a particular factor; hence, the returns on two (or more) portfolios may also differ.

Consider the following three-variable multi-factor model:

$$r_s = .12 + b_1F_1 + b_2F_2 + b_3F_3 + e$$

in which the return on a stock will be 12 percent (the expected return) plus the impact of three risk factors. However, the estimated parameters for two stocks differ. Suppose the estimated equations for stocks A and B are

$$r_{sA} = .12 + .02F_1 - .01F_2 + .01F_3$$

and

$$r_{sB} = .12 + .05F_1 + .01F_2 + .02F_3.$$

The error terms wash out (i.e., $e = 0$), and the equations for the returns on the two stocks differ. The stocks have different responsiveness to changes in the risk factors, so the returns on each stock must differ. For example, the estimated coefficients for the second factor have different signs (minus versus plus), indicating this factor has an opposite impact on the returns of the two stocks.

Suppose the numerical values of the factors are 0, 1, and 2, respectively. The returns on the stocks will be

$$r_{sA} = .12 + .02(0) - .01(1) + .01(2) = .13 = 13\%$$

and

$$r_{sB} = .12 + .05(0) + .01(1) + .02(2) = .17 = 17\%.$$

Since the numerical value of factor 1 is zero during the time period, the expected value for this factor and the actual value were the same (i.e., $F_1 = 0$), so this factor had no impact on the returns. The actual values of factors 2 and 3 differed from the expected values; thus, these two variables affected each security's return. Factor 2 had a negative impact on stock A and a positive impact on stock B, while factor 3 had a positive influence on both stocks with a slightly larger effect (.02 versus .01) on stock B.

While there may be many possible factors, research suggests that four are pre-eminent. These are (1) unexpected inflation, (2) unexpected changes in the level of industrial production, (3) unanticipated shifts in risk premiums, and (4) unanticipated changes in the structure of yields (measured by the slope of the term structure of interest rates).[17]

Again, since expected changes are already incorporated into the expected return, APT stresses the importance of unanticipated change. If the actual values and expected values are equal, the factor washes out. If factor 1 in the model above is the difference between the actual rate of inflation and the expected rate of inflation, the equation would be

$$r_s = .12 + b_1 \text{ (actual rate of inflation } - \text{ expected rate of inflation)} + b_2F_2 + b_3F_3.$$

If the actual rate of inflation is 4 percent and the expected rate of inflation is also 4 percent, this factor has no impact on the stock's return, i.e., $b_1(.04 - .04) = 0$.

The factors will have an impact on the stock's return only when the actual values differ from the expected values. If the actual rate of inflation is 7 percent (an increase from the expected 4 percent), this risk factor becomes relevant and has an impact on the stock's return. The amount of impact and its direction depend on the estimated parameter (i.e., the estimated coefficient and its sign). An increase in the rate of inflation could cause the returns on some stocks (e.g., utilities) to fall and cause the returns to rise on others (e.g., resource companies).

---

[17] The term structure of interest rates is discussed in Chapter 14 in the section on yields and in the appendix.

How each stock and each portfolio responds to the differences between the realized and the expected variables is crucial to the return the stock or the portfolio earns. Even though two stocks have the same beta coefficients and have responded in a similar fashion to a change in the market, they may respond differently to changes in other factors. For this reason, a portfolio stressing fixed-income securities may experience a larger response to a change in inflation than a portfolio stressing economic growth. This difference in responsiveness may play a crucial role in security selection or portfolio management. It suggests that buying low beta stocks may not be a defensive strategy if the securities are responsive to another variable that is subject to change.

Unfortunately, one of the largest problems facing the investor or portfolio manager who seeks to apply APT is the measurement of unanticipated changes in the factors. If one of the factors changes (e.g., an unanticipated increase in the rate of inflation) and the financial portfolio manager seeks to analyze how the market (or particular stock) responds to the change, that individual cannot separate the movement in the price caused by changes in expected inflation and the movement caused by unanticipated inflation. The movement in the market or the stock's price would encompass both. This is, of course, a major hurdle in the implementation of the model.

APT is currently in the process of being further developed and may someday supplant the capital asset pricing model as the primary model relating risk and return. Intuitively, APT is appealing since it is less limiting than the capital asset pricing model. The CAPM is based on an assumption concerning risk preferences and explains returns solely in terms of movements in the market. In the CAPM, the impact of asset-specific variables is erased through the construction of a diversified portfolio, so the volatility of the stock relative to the volatility of the market is the prime variable that explains an asset's risk and return. APT, however, is less limiting. It suggests that differences in returns are driven by an arbitrage process and that two securities or portfolios with the same risk must generate the same return. APT permits the inclusion of more explanatory variables. The inclusion of these other factors, especially economic variables such as unexpected changes in industrial production, make APT an appealing alternative explanation of an asset's return. Additional econometric research obviously is necessary to make the model more usable by individuals and portfolio managers, but it is reasonable to anticipate that further research will occur and that arbitrage pricing theory will remain at the forefront of security valuation and portfolio management.

SUMMARY

Because the future is uncertain, all investment involves risk. The return the investor anticipates through income and/or capital appreciation may differ considerably from the realized return. This deviation of the realized return from the expected return is the risk associated with investing.

Risk emanates from several sources, which include fluctuations in market prices, fluctuations in interest rates, changes in reinvestment rates, fluctuations in exchange rates, and loss of purchasing power through inflation. These sources of risk are often referred to as *systematic risk* because the returns on assets tend to move together (i.e., there is a systematic relationship between security returns and market returns). Systematic risk is also referred to as "nondiversifiable risk" because it is not reduced by the construction of a diversified portfolio.

Diversification does, however, reduce *unsystematic risk,* which applies to the specific firm and encompasses the nature of the firm's operations and its financing. Since unsystematic risk applies only to the individual asset, there is no systematic relationship between the source of risk and the market as a whole. A portfolio composed of ten to fifteen unrelated assets—for example, stocks in companies in different industries or different types of assets such as common stock, bonds, mutual funds, and real estate—virtually eradicates the impact of unsystematic risk on the portfolio as a whole.

Risk may be measured by the standard deviation, which measures the dispersion around a central tendency, such as an asset's or portfolio's average return. If the individual returns differ considerably from the average returns, the dispersion is larger (i.e., the standard deviation is larger) and the risk associated with the asset is increased.

An alternative measure of risk, the beta coefficient, measures the responsiveness of an asset's return relative to the return on the market as a whole. If the beta coefficient exceeds 1.0, the stock's return is more volatile than the return on the market, but if the beta is less than 1.0, the return on the stock is less volatile. Since the beta coefficient relates the return on the stock to the market's return, it is an index of the systematic risk associated with the stock.

Portfolio theory is built around risk and return. Portfolios that offer the highest return for a given amount of risk are *efficient;* portfolios that do not offer the highest return for a given level of risk are *inefficient.* A major component of portfolio theory is the capital asset pricing model, which has a macro- (aggregate) and a micro-component. In the macro-component, the capital market line gives the return on each efficient portfolio associated with each level of risk, which is measured by the portfolio's standard deviation. The individual investor selects that efficient portfolio which generates the highest level of satisfaction or utility.

In the micro-component of the capital asset pricing model, beta coefficients are used to explain an individual security's return. Riskier securities with higher beta coefficients should have greater returns to justify bearing the additional risk. The security market line gives the return on a specific asset associated with each level of risk as measured by the asset's beta coefficient.

The use of beta as the primary explanatory variable of security returns has been criticized as too limiting. An alternate explanation of security returns is arbitrage pricing theory, which is a multi-variable model. In this model, variables such as unexpected inflation or unexpected changes in industrial production may also affect security returns in addition to the security's response to changes in the market.

Terms to Remember

systematic risk	dispersion
unsystematic risk	inefficient portfolio
portfolio risk	efficient portfolio
diversification	beta coefficient
expected return	arbitrage
required return	

Questions

1. What is the difference between nondiversifiable (systematic) risk and diversifiable (unsystematic) risk?
2. What is a diversified portfolio? What type of risk is reduced through diversification? How many securities are necessary to achieve this reduction in risk? What characteristics must these securities possess?
3. What are the sources of return on an investment? What are the differences among the expected return, the required return, and the realized return?
4. If the expected return of two stocks is the same but the standard deviation of the returns differs, which security is to be preferred?
5. If an investor desires diversification, should he or she seek investments that have a high positive correlation?
6. Indifference curves used in portfolio theory relate risk and return. How is the portfolio's risk measured? If one investor's indifference curves are steeper than another investor's, what does that indicate about their respective willingness to bear risk?
7. What is a beta coefficient? What do beta coefficients of 0.5, 1.0, and 1.5 mean?
8. If the correlation coefficient for a stock and the market equals 0.0, what is the market risk associated with the stock?
9. How are the capital market line and the security market line different? What does each represent?
10. How does arbitrage pricing theory advance our understanding of security returns?

Problems

1. You are considering three stocks with the following expected dividend yields and capital gains:

	Dividend Yield	Capital Gain
A	14%	0%
B	8	6
C	0	14

   a. What is the expected return on each stock?
   b. How many transactions costs and capital gains taxes affect your choices among the three securities?

2. A portfolio consists of assets with the following expected returns:

	Expected Return	Weight in Portfolio
Real estate	16%	20%
Low-quality bonds	15	10
AT&T stock	12	30
Savings account	5	40

a. What is the expected return on the portfolio?

b. What will be the expected return if the individual reduces the holdings of the AT&T stock to 15 percent and puts the funds into real estate investments?

3. You are given the following information concerning two stocks:

	A	B
Expected return	10%	14%
Standard deviation of the expected return	±3.0	±5.0
Correlation coefficient of the returns	−.1	

a. What is the expected return on a portfolio consisting of 40 percent in stock A and 60 percent in stock B?

b. What is the standard deviation of this portfolio?

c. Discuss the risk and return associated with investing (a) all of your funds in stock A, (b) all of your funds in stock B, and (c) 40 percent in A and 60 percent in B. (This answer *must* use the numerical information in your answers derived above.)

4. You are given the following information:

Expected return on stock A	12%
Expected return on stock B	20%
Standard deviation of returns	
stock A	±1.0
stock B	±6.0
Correlation coefficient of the returns on stocks A and B	+.2

a. What are the expected returns and standard deviations of a portfolio consisting of:
   1. 100 percent in stock A?
   2. 100 percent in stock B?
   3. 50 percent in each stock?
   4. 25 percent in stock A and 75 percent in stock B?
   5. 75 percent in stock A and 25 percent in stock B?

b. Compare the above returns and the risk associated with each portfolio.

c. Redo the calculations assuming that the correlation coefficient of the returns on the two stocks is −.6. What is the impact of this difference in the correlation coefficient?

5. What is the beta of a portfolio consisting of one share of each of the following stocks given their respective prices and beta coefficients?

Stock	Price	Beta
A	$10	1.4
B	24	0.8
C	41	1.3
D	19	1.8

How would the portfolio beta differ if (a) the investor purchased 200 shares of stocks B and C for every 100 shares of A and D and (b) equal dollar amounts were invested in each stock?

6. What is the return on a stock according to the security market line if the risk-free rate is 6 percent, the return on the market is 10 percent, and the stock's beta is 1.5? If the beta had been 2.0, what would be the return? Is this higher return consistent with the portfolio theory explained in this chapter? Why?

Suggested Readings

The following books include discussions of risk, security selection, and returns earned by investors:

Brealy, Richard A. *An Introduction to Risk and Return from Common Stocks.* 2d ed. Cambridge, MA.: The MIT Press, 1983.

Lorie, James H., et al. *The Stock Market: Theories and Evidence.* 2d ed. Homewood, Ill.: Richard D. Irwin, 1985.

Malkiel, Burton G. *A Random Walk Down Wall Street.* 4th ed. New York: W. W. Norton, 1985.

Articles that discuss beta include:

Levy, Robert A. "Stationarity of Beta Coefficients." *Financial Analysis Journal* (November–December 1971): 55–62.

Rosenberg, Barr, and James Guy. "Prediction of Beta from Investment Fundamentals." *Financial Analysts Journal* (May–June 1976): 60–73, and *Financial Analysts Journal* (July–August 1976): 62–71.

Sharpe, William. "Risk, Market Sensitivity, and Diversification." *Financial Analysts Journal* (January–February 1972): 74–79.

The Sharpe article discusses beta in general germs and explains how it is computed. The Levy article shows that betas for individual stocks may not be stable that the betas for a portfolio are stable and can be used as predictors. The Rosenberg and Guy article discusses the estimation of beta with historical data and explains why betas may change, thus reducing their usefulness as predictors for individual securities.

For a discussion and extensive bibliography of the determinants of beta and its estimation, see:

Callahan, Carolyn M., and Rosanne M. Mohr. "The Determinants of Systematic Risk: A Synthesis." *The Financial Review* (May 1989): 157–181.

More comprehensive discussions of portfolio theory and arbitrage pricing theory may be found in advanced textbooks on investments such as:

Radcliffe, Robert C. *Investments—Concepts, Analysis, Strategy.* 3d ed. Glenview, Ill.: Scott, Foresman/Little, Brown Higher Education, 1990.

Diversification is frequently referred to as "asset allocation." For a layman's guide to measuring risk, return, and the construction of efficient portfolios consult:

Givson, Roger C. *Asset Allocation—Balancing Financial Risk.* Homewood, Ill.: Business One Irwin, 1990.

INVESTMENT PROJECT

This chapter explains how beta coefficients are used as an index of systematic risk. Find the beta coefficients for the eight stocks that you are following and record the information on the data sheet. Beta coefficients are published in the *Value Line Investment Survey*. If *Value Line* is not available, ask your librarian or instructor how you may obtain beta coefficients at your school.

Stock	Beta
1 S&P 500	1.0
2 CSK	
3 GTE	
4 IBM	
5 MSFT	
6	
7	
8	
9	

Average Beta: ——

What is the average beta for the portfolio of eight stocks? (If you purchased an equal number of shares so that the dollar amounts invested in each corporation differed, your aggregate beta must be weighted by each stock's proportion in the total portfolio.) Remember that the beta for the market is 1.0, so if the beta of the portfolio is less than 1.0, the portfolio is less risky than the market if you invested an equal dollar amount in each stock. Of course, if the beta exceeds 1.0, the portfolio should tend to be more volatile than the market as a whole.

Appendix

THE ESTIMATION OF BETA COEFFICIENTS

As explained in the body of this chapter, investors must bear the systematic and unsystematic risks associated with an individual security. This appendix explains and illustrates how systematic risk may be estimated. The estimation technique uses linear regression analysis, and thus this appendix assumes that the student has had exposure to the use of regression to estimate equations.

The tendency for the returns on an investment in a stock to follow the market is shown in Figure 7.17, which is a scatter diagram of monthly returns earned by CBS stock and the Dow Jones Industrial average. The horizontal axis measures the monthly return earned by the Dow Jones Industrial average, while the vertical axis gives the monthly returns earned on the stock. For example, point A represents a return on the Dow Jones Industrials of 7.6 percent and a return on CBS stock of 7.8 percent.

As may be seen from Figure 7.17, the returns on the stock and the returns on the market move in the same direction. The individual points rise from the third quadrant to the first quadrant, which indicates the positive relationship between the return on the market and the return on the individual stock. This relationship is the systematic risk associated with the market. Even though individual observations (e.g., point B, which represents a positive return on the stock when the market fell) may not be consistent with the general pattern, most of the individual observations seem to indicate the positive relationship between movements in the market and the individual stock's price.

Simple linear regression analysis may be used to estimate an equation that summarizes these observations relating returns on CBS stock to changes in the Dow Jones Industrial average. The analysis estimates the linear equation:

$$r_s = a + br_m + e.$$

The r_s is the return on the stock, while the r_m is the return on the market. The a is the Y intercept, b is the slope of the line, and e is an error term. In statistics e is assumed to equal zero, since errors should be both $+$ and $-$ and tend to cancel out. This slope is the beta coefficient, which measures the systematic risk associated with the stock.

When linear regression analysis is applied to the data used to construct Figure 7.18, the following equation is estimated:

$$r_s = 0.0014 + 0.962 \ r_m.$$

The Y intercept (0.0014) is virtually zero, and the slope of the line (i.e., the beta coefficient) is 0.962. This equation is line AB in Figure 7.18, which reproduces Figure 7.17 and adds the estimated regression equation. As may be seen in Figure 7.18, the line AB runs through the points. Some of the observations are above the line while others are below it. Some of the individual points are close to the line while

Figure 7.17 ✦ RETURNS ON CBS STOCK AND THE DOW JONES INDUSTRIAL AVERAGE

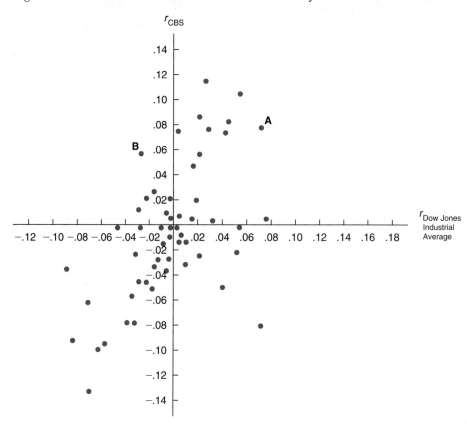

others appear further away. The closer the points are to the line, the stronger is the relationship between the two variables. This closeness may be measured by the correlation coefficient. A perfect positive correlation would yield a correlation coefficient of 1. No relationship would yield a correlation coefficient of 0. In this illustration the correlation coefficient is 0.6181.

The estimated regression equation may be used to forecast the expected return on the stock. If the analyst expects that the market will rise by 20 percent (i.e., $r_m = 0.2$), the stock should yield a return of

$$r_s = 0.0014 + 0.962(0.2)$$

$$= 0.0014 + 0.1924$$

$$= 19.38\%.$$

As with any forecast, the expected result may not be realized because factors other than a change in the market may affect the stock's price (i.e., the factors associated with nonsystematic risk). The proportion of the return on an investment in CBS stock explained by the movement in the market is measured by the coefficient

Figure 7.18 ✦ REGRESSION LINE RELATING RETURNS ON CBS STOCK AND THE DOW JONES INDUSTRIAL AVERAGE

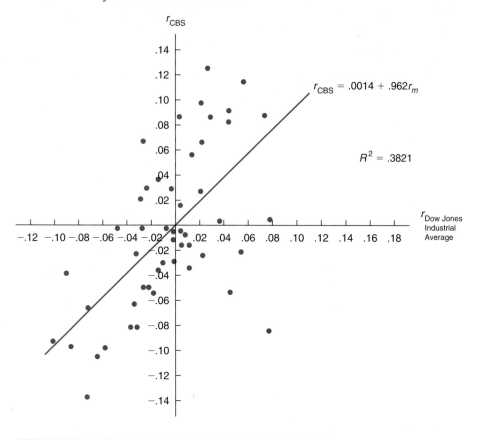

of determination. This coefficient is the square of the correlation coefficient and is commonly referred to as R^2. In this illustration the R^2 is 0.3821 (0.6181 × 0.6181), which indicates that about 38 percent of the variation in the return on CBS stock is explained by fluctuations in the market.[18] Obviously some other variables must cause the remaining 62 percent of the variability in the return on CBS stock. These factors are the sources of the unsystematic risk associated with the investment.

---

[18] Computation of the correlation coefficient and the coefficient of determination is part of statistics and computer programs that generate descriptive statistics or estimate regression equations that routinely give the numerical values of the correlation coefficient and the coefficient of determination. See, for instance, George W. Summers, William S. Peters, and Charles P. Armstrong, *Basic Statistics in Business and Economics,* 4th ed. Belmont, CA: Wadsworth, 1985, 307–308 and 534–537. For computer programs developed for financial analysis that include the computation of the correlation coefficient and the coefficient of determination, see James Pettijohn's *Profit +,* Forth Worth, Texas: The Dryden Press, 1988. They are also available in the software package that accompanies this book.

Since there is considerable unsystematic risk in this illustration, the estimated beta coefficient may be a poor predictor. That, however, need not mean the coefficient is useless. As was explained in the body of this chapter, the portfolio's beta, which is an aggregate of the individual stocks' betas, may be a good predictor of the return the investor can expect from movements in the market. Factors that adversely affect the return earned on one security may be offset by factors that enhance the return earned on other securities in the portfolio.

Since unsystematic risk can be significantly reduced, the investor needs to determine how much systematic risk he or she is willing to bear. Such determination is subjective and is affected by considerations such as age, family responsibilities, and stability of employment. Once each security's beta coefficients are known, the investor can construct a diversified portfolio with an aggregate beta that is consistent with that individual's willingness to bear systematic risk.

Problem

This problem illustrates how beta coefficients are estimated. It may be answered using any program that performs linear regression analysis, such as the beta calculation in the section on the capital asset pricing model in the *Investment Analysis* package that accompanies this text. The following information is given:

Period	Return on Market	Stock X	Stock Y
1	10%	−2%	13%
2	26	13	41
3	−2	3	3
4	−14	−7	−7
5	7	9	9
6	14	5	19
7	−5	2	−8
8	19	13	13
9	8	−3	17
10	−5	8	−14

a. Using regression analysis, compute the estimated equations relating the return on each stock to the return on the market. According to the equations, what is each stock's beta coefficient? What does each beta coefficient imply about the systematic risk associated with each stock?

b. What is the difference between the return on each stock given by the estimated equation for period 10 and the actual return? What may account for any differences in the estimated return and the actual return? (To answer this question use the estimated equation and compare the results with the actual results.)

c. What is the R square for each equation? Interpret the R square. How could you improve the results?

Investing in Common Stock

II

FOR MANY INDIVIDUALS THE WORD *INVESTING* IS SYNONYMOUS WITH BUYING AND SELLING COMMON STOCK. ALTHOUGH ALTERNATIVES ARE CERTAINLY AVAILABLE, COMMON STOCKS ARE THE PRIMARY INSTRUMENT OF INVESTING FOR MANY PEOPLE, PERHAPS BECAUSE OF THE CONSIDERABLE EXPOSURE INDIVIDUALS HAVE TO THEM. NEWSPAPERS REPORT STOCK TRANSACTIONS, MARKET AVERAGES ARE QUOTED ON THE NIGHTLY news, and brokerage firms advertise the attractiveness of such investments.

Unlike bonds, which pay a fixed amount of interest, common stocks offer a dividend with the potential to grow. As the economy prospers and corporate earnings rise, the dividends and the value of common stocks may also increase. For this reason, common stocks are a good investment for individuals who have less need for current income but desire capital appreciation.

This section discusses investing in common stocks. Various techniques are used to analyze a firm and its financial statements. The purpose is to identify the stocks that have the greatest potential or are the most undervalued. This section also considers how measures of the market are constructed and the returns that investors in the aggregate have earned over a period of years.

8

THE VALUATION
OF COMMON STOCK

*T*he valuation of common stock is one of the most elusive and perplexing topics covered in this text. But it is also one of the most crucial, because the investor must estimate the current value of a stock to determine if the security should be purchased. Without such valuation the selection of common stock is based on hunches, intuition, or tips. Conceptually the valuation of stock is the same as the valuation of a bond, as presented in Chapter 15. In both cases the payments that the investor receives in the future are discounted back to the present. For debt instruments this process is relatively easy, because a bond pays a fixed amount of interest and matures at a specified date. Common stock, however, does not pay a fixed dividend, nor does it mature. These two facts considerably increase the difficulty of valuing common stock.

Initially in this chapter the features of common stock are described. Then follows a simple model for the valuation of common stock. Next a means for adjusting this model for risk is suggested. This dividend-growth model is then related to P/E ratios.

The chapter ends with a discussion of the efficient market hypothesis and the empirical evidence that supports the hypothesis. This hypothesis asserts that financial markets are so efficient that security prices properly measure what a stock is worth and that the investor cannot expect to consistently outperform the market on a risk-adjusted basis. While empirical evidence generally supports the efficient market hypothesis, there are some anomalies that suggest some investors may be able to earn a return in excess of the return they should earn relative to the market as a whole.

❖ ❖ ❖

LEARNING OBJECTIVES

After completing this chapter you should be able to

1. Identify the components of an investor's required rate of return.

2. Differentiate required and expected returns.

3. Examine the determinants of a stock's price.

4. Calculate the value of a stock using a simple present value model.

5. Explain the use of P/E ratios to select stocks.

6. Differentiate the three forms of the efficient market hypothesis.

7. Describe several anomalies that are inconsistent with the efficient market hypothesis.

THE CORPORATE FORM OF BUSINESS

A corporation is an artificial legal economic unit established by a state. Since there is variation in the state laws that establish corporations, some states are more popular than others for the formation of corporations. Under state laws, the firm is

191

certificate of incorporation
A document creating a corporation.

stock
A security representing ownership in a corporation.

charter
A document specifying the relationship between a firm and the state in which it is incorporated.

bylaws
A document specifying the relationship between a corporation and its stockholders.

issued a **certificate of incorporation** that indicates the name of the corporation, the location of its principal office, its purpose, and the number of shares of stock that are authorized (i.e., the number of shares that the firm may issue). **Stock,** both preferred and common, represents ownership or equity in a corporation. In addition to a certificate of incorporation, the firm receives a **charter** that specifies the relationship between the corporation and the state. At the initial meeting of stockholders, **bylaws** are established that set the rules by which the firm is governed, including such issues as the voting rights of the stockholders.

The firm issues stock certificates to its owners as evidence of their ownership in the corporation. An example of a stock certificate is presented in Exhibit 8.1. The face of the certificate identifies the name of the owner, the number of shares, and the bank that serves as the transfer agent. The transfer agent keeps the firm's record of stockholders and transfers the certificates as they are bought and sold.

In the eyes of the law, a corporation is a legal entity that is separate from its owners. It may enter into contracts and is legally responsible for its obligations. Once a firm is incorporated, the owners are only liable for the amount of their investment in the company. Creditors may sue the corporation for payment if it defaults on its obligations, but the creditors cannot sue the stockholders. Therefore, an investor knows that if he or she purchases stock in a publicly held corporation such as General Motors, the maximum that can be lost is the amount of the investment.[1] Occasionally a large corporation (e.g., Columbia Gas, Macy's, or Texaco) does go bankrupt, but owing to limited liability, its stockholders cannot be sued by its creditors.

The Rights of Stockholders

voting rights
The rights of stockholders to vote their shares.

director
A person who is elected by stockholders to determine the goals and policies of the firm.

Since stock represents ownership in a corporation, investors who purchase it obtain all of the rights of ownership. These rights include the option to **vote** the shares. The stockholders elect a board of **directors** that selects the firm's management. Management is then responsible to the board of directors, which in turn is responsible to the firm's stockholders. If the stockholders do not think that the board is doing a competent job, they may elect another board to represent them.

For publicly held corporations, such democracy rarely works. Stockholders are usually widely dispersed, while the firm's management and board of directors generally form a cohesive unit. Rarely does the individual investor's vote mean much.[2] However, there is always the possibility that if the firm does poorly, another firm may offer to buy the outstanding stock held by the public. Once such purchases are made, the stock's new owners may remove the board of directors and establish new

---

[1] Stockholders in privately held corporations who pledge their personal assets to secure loans do not have limited liability. If the corporation defaults, the creditors may seize the assets that the stockholders have pledged. In this event, the liability of the shareholders is not limited to their investment in the firm.

[2] One notable exception occurred in 1981 when Penn Central stockholders voted down a merger with Colt Industries. Management supported the merger but lost the vote: 10,245,440 shares against versus 10,104,220 shares in favor. For evidence of the impact of proxy fights on stockholder returns see Lisa F. Borstadt and Thomas J. Zwirlein, "The Efficient Monitoring Role of Proxy Contests: An Empirical Analysis of Post-Contest Control Changes and Firm Performance," *Financial Management*, (Autumn 1992), 22–34.

Exhibit 8.1   ✦   THE NEIMAN MARCUS GROUP STOCK CERTIFICATE

NUMBER
FBU 21698

SHARES

Common Stock

PAR VALUE
$.01 PER SHARE

INCORPORATED UNDER THE LAWS
OF THE
STATE OF DELAWARE

The
Neiman
Marcus
Group

The Neiman-Marcus Group, Inc.

CUSIP 640204 10 3

THIS CERTIFICATE IS TRANSFERABLE IN BOSTON, MASS. AND NEW YORK, N.Y.

SEE REVERSE FOR KEY TO ABBREVIATIONS

This Certifies that

is the owner of

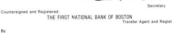

FULLY PAID AND NON-ASSESSABLE SHARES OF THE COMMON STOCK OF

The Neiman-Marcus Group, Inc. (herein called the "Corporation") transferable upon the books of the Corporation upon surrender of this certificate duly endorsed or assigned. This certificate and the shares represented hereby are subject to the laws of the State of Delaware and to the Certificate of Incorporation and the By-Laws of the Corporation, as amended from time to time (copies of which are on file with the Transfer Agent). This certificate is not valid until countersigned by a Transfer Agent and registered by a Registrar.

In Witness Whereof, The Neiman-Marcus Group, Inc. has caused its facsimile corporate seal and the facsimile signatures of its duly authorized officers to be hereunto affixed.

Dated:

Secretary

Chairman

Countersigned and Registered:
THE FIRST NATIONAL BANK OF BOSTON
Transfer Agent and Registrar

By

Authorized Officer

Source: Reprinted with permission of Harcourt General, Inc.

management. To some extent this encourages a corporation's board of directors and management to pursue the goal of increasing the value of the firm's stock.

A stockholder generally has one vote for each share owned, but there are two ways to distribute this vote. With the traditional method of voting, each share gives the stockholder the right to vote for one individual for *each* seat on the board of directors. Under this system, if a majority group voted as a block, a minority group could never elect a representative. The alternative system, **cumulative voting,** gives minority stockholders a means to obtain representation on the firm's board. While cumulative voting is voluntary in most states, it is mandatory in several, including California, Illinois, and Michigan.

How cumulative voting works is best explained by a brief example. Suppose a firm has a board of directors composed of five members. With traditional voting, a stockholder with 100 shares may vote 100 votes for a candidate for each seat. The total 500 votes are split among the seats. Under cumulative voting, the individual may cast the entire 500 votes for a candidate for one seat. Of course, then the stockholder cannot vote for anyone running for the remaining four seats.

cumulative voting
A voting scheme that encourages minority representation by permitting each stockholder to cast all of his or her votes for one candidate for the firm's board of directors.

A minority group of stockholders can use the cumulative method of voting to elect a representative to the firm's board of directors. By banding together and casting all of their votes for a specific candidate, the minority may be able to win a seat. Although this technique cannot be used to win a majority, it does offer the opportunity for representation that is not possible through the traditional method of distributing votes (i.e., one vote for each elected position). As would be expected, management rarely supports the cumulative voting system.

Since stockholders are owners, they are entitled to the firm's earnings. These earnings may be distributed in the form of cash dividends, or they may be retained by the corporation. If they are retained, the individual's investment in the firm is increased (i.e., the stockholder's equity increases). However, for every class of stock, the individual investor's relative position is not altered. Some owners of common stock cannot receive cash dividends, whereas others have their earnings reinvested. The distribution or retention of earnings applies equally to all stockholders.[3]

Although limited liability is one of the advantages of investing in publicly held corporations, stock ownership does involve risk. As long as the firm prospers, it may be able to pay dividends and grow. However, if earnings fluctuate, dividends and growth may also fluctuate. It is the owners—the stockholders—who bear the business risk associated with these fluctuations. If the firm should default on its debt, it can be taken to court by its creditors to enforce its obligations. If the firm should fail or become bankrupt, the stockholders have the last claim on its assets. Only after all of the creditors have been paid will the stockholders receive any funds. In many cases of bankruptcy, this amounts to nothing. Even if the corporation survives bankruptcy proceedings, the amount received by the stockholders is uncertain.

Preemptive Rights

preemptive rights
The right of current stockholders to maintain their proportionate ownership in the firm.

rights offering
Sale of new securities to stockholders.

Some stockholders have **preemptive rights,** which is their prerogative to maintain their proportionate ownership in the firm. If the firm wants to sell additional shares to the general public, these new shares must be offered initially to the existing stockholders in a sale called a **rights offering.** If the stockholders wish to maintain their proportionate ownership in the firm, they can exercise their rights by purchasing the new shares. However, if they do not want to take advantage of this offering, they may sell their privilege to whoever wants to purchase the new shares. (The formula for the value of a right is discussed in the appendix to Chapter 19.)

Preemptive rights may be illustrated by a simple example. If a firm has 1,000 shares outstanding and an individual has 100 shares, that individual owns 10 percent of the firm's stock. If the firm wants to sell 400 new shares and the stockholders have preemptive rights, these new shares must be offered to the existing stockholders before they are sold to the general public. The individual who owns 100 shares would have the right to purchase 40, or 10 percent, of the new shares. If the purchase is made, then that stockholder's relative position is maintained, for the

---

[3] Some corporations have different classes of stock. For example, Food Lion, Inc., has two classes of common stock, both of which are publicly traded. The class A stock does not have voting power while the class B does. However, if management chooses to pay dividends to the class B stock, it must pay a larger dividend to the class A stock.

stockholder owns 10 percent of the firm both before and after the sale of the new stock.

Although preemptive rights are required in some states for incorporation, their importance has diminished and the number of rights offerings has declined. In 1969 there were 118 public rights offerings, but the number declined to only 21 in 1991 involving NYSE and AMEX companies.[4] Some firms have tried to have their bylaws changed in order to eliminate preemptive rights. For example, AT&T asked its stockholders to relinquish these rights. The rationale for this request was that issuing new shares through rights offerings was more expensive than selling the shares to the general public through an underwriting. Investors who desired to maintain their relative position could still purchase the new shares, and all stockholders would benefit through the cost savings and the flexibility given to the firm's management. Most stockholders accepted management's request and voted to relinquish their preemptive rights. Now AT&T does not have to offer any new shares to its current stockholders before it offers them publicly.

Investors' Expected Return

Investors purchase stock with the anticipation of a **total return** consisting of a dividend yield and a capital gain. The dividend yield is the flow of dividend income paid by the stock. The capital gain is the increase in the value of the stock that is related to the growth in earnings. If the firm is able to achieve growth in earnings, then dividends can be increased, and over time the shares should grow in value.

total return
The sum of dividend yield and capital gains.

The return on an investment, which was discussed in Chapter 7 and expressed algebraically in Equation 7.1, is reproduced here:

$$r = \frac{D}{P} + g \qquad (7.1)$$

The return (r) is the sum of the dividend yield, which is the dividend (D) divided by the price of the stock (P) plus the growth rate (g). If a firm's $1 dividend is expected to grow at 7 percent and the price of the stock is $25, the anticipated return on an investment in the stock is

$$r = \frac{\$1}{\$25} + 0.07 = 0.11 = 11\%.$$

For an investment to be attractive, the expected return must be equal to or exceed the investor's required return. (Specification of the required return will be discussed later in this chapter.) If an individual requires an 11 percent return on investments in common stock of comparable risk, then this stock meets the investor's requirement. If, however, the investor's required rate of return is in excess of 11 percent, the anticipated yield on this stock is inferior, and the investor will not purchase the shares. Conversely, if the required rate of return on comparable

---

[4] *Moody's Dividend Record*, 1991, 263–265. The majority of NYSE and AMEX firms with rights offerings were foreign and not domestic corporations.

REAL RETURNS

As used in this text, the word *returns* implies nominal returns; no adjustment is made for the rate of inflation. If such an adjustment were made, the resulting returns would be expressed in "real" terms. Real returns measure the increase in purchasing power earned by the investor. If the nominal return was 15 percent when the rate of inflation was 10 percent, the investor is worse off than the investor who earns a nominal return of 10 percent during a period when prices increase by only 3 percent. In the latter case, the investor earns a higher real return.

The real return (i.e., the inflation-adjusted return) that the investor earns may be determined by the following equation:

$$\left(\frac{1 + \text{nominal return}}{1 + \text{rate of inflation}} - 1\right) \times 100\%$$

Thus, if the rate of nominal return is 15 percent when the rate of inflation is 10 percent, the real return is

$$\left(\frac{1 + .15}{1 + .10} - 1\right) \times 100\% = 4.545\%.$$

This rate is less than the real return when the nominal return is 10 percent and the rate of inflation is 3 percent. Under that circumstance the real return is

$$\left(\frac{1 + .10}{1 + .03} - 1\right) \times 100\% = 6.796\%.$$

There is no doubt that inflation has eroded the purchasing power of the dollar. Figure 9.5, in the next chapter, illustrates the real loss investors experienced after adjusting for inflation during the 1970s. However, during the 1980s, investors in common stock experienced a positive real return. Research on returns and inflation indicates that, over an extended period of time, the return on common stocks has exceeded the rate of inflation by about 6 percent.[*] This suggests that individuals who invested for the long haul earned a real return on their positions in common stock.

[*] See Roger Ibbotson and Rex Sinquefield, *Stocks, Bonds, Bills, and Inflation* (Charlottesville, VA: Financial Analyst Research Foundation, 1987).

investments in common stock is 10 percent, this particular stock is an excellent purchase because the anticipated return exceeds the required rate of return.

In a world of no commission fees and if the tax on dividends were the same as on capital gains, investors would be indifferent to the composition of their return. An investor seeking an 11 percent return should be willing to accept a dividend yield of zero if the capital gain is 11 percent. Conversely, a capital growth rate of zero should be acceptable if the dividend yield is 11 percent. Of course, any combination of growth rate and dividend yield with an 11 percent return should be acceptable.

However, because of commissions the investor may be concerned with the composition of the return. To realize the growth in the value of the shares, the investor must sell the security and pay commission fees. This cost suggests a preference for dividend yield. In addition, capital gains occur in the future and may be less certain than the flow of current dividends. The uncertainty of future capital gains (and the uncertainty of the capital gains tax rate) versus the likelihood of current dividends also favors dividends over capital appreciation.

Since each investor's situation and financial goals are different, it is not surprising that the composition of the required rate of return for various investors is different. Retired people may prefer a dividend yield for the income it provides. Investors with other sources of income may prefer growth and capital gains, since the capital gains tax is deferred until the shares are sold. And any investor who wishes to reduce risk may prefer dividends to capital growth.

Since the required rates of return differ among investors and since the individual's financial needs and goals change, it is not surprising to find investors making changes in their portfolios. It is the role of security markets to bring these buyers and sellers together so that their portfolio changes can be consummated.

VALUATION AS THE PRESENT VALUE OF DIVIDENDS AND THE GROWTH OF DIVIDENDS

As with the valuation of debt, the valuation of stock involves bringing future cash flows (e.g., dividends) back to the present at the appropriate discount factor. For the individual investor, that discount factor is the required return, which is the return the investor demands to justify purchasing the stock. This return includes what the investor may earn on a risk-free security (e.g., a treasury bill) plus a premium for bearing the risk associated with investments in common stock. The anticipated return must equal or exceed the investor's required rate of return. The process of valuation and security selection is similar to comparing expected and required returns, except the emphasis is placed on determining what the investor believes the security is worth. Future cash flows are discounted back to the present at the required rate of return. The resulting valuation is then compared with the stock's current price to determine if the stock is under- or overvalued.

The process of valuation and security selection is readily illustrated by the simple case in which the stock pays a fixed dividend of $1 that is not expected to change. That is, the anticipated flow of dividend payments is

Year	1	2	3	4	. . .
	$1	$1	$1	$1	. . .

The current value of this indefinite flow of payments (i.e., the dividend) depends on the discount rate (i.e., the investor's required rate of return). If this rate is 12 percent, the stock's value (V) is

$$V = \frac{\$1}{(1 + .12)} + \frac{1}{(1 + .12)^2} + \frac{1}{(1 + .12)^3} + \frac{1}{(1 + .12)^4} + \cdots$$

$$V = \$8.33.$$

This process is expressed in the following equation in which the new variables are the dividend (D) and the required rate of return (k):

$$V = \frac{D}{(1 + k)^1} + \frac{D}{(1 + k)^2} + \cdots + \frac{D}{(1 + k)^\infty} \tag{8.1}$$

which simplifies to

$$V = \frac{D}{k}. \tag{8.2}$$

Thus if a stock pays a dividend of $1 and the investor's required rate of return is 12 percent, then the valuation is

$$\frac{\$1}{0.12} = \$8.33.$$

Any price greater than $8.33 will result in a yield that is less than 12 percent. Therefore, for this investor to achieve the required rate of return of 12 percent, the price of the stock must not exceed $8.33.

There is, however, no reason to anticipate that common stock dividends will be fixed indefinitely into the future. Common stocks offer the potential for growth, both in value and in dividends. For example, if the investor expects the $1 dividend to grow annually at 6 percent, the anticipated flow of dividend payments is

Year	1	2	3	4	. . .
	$1	$1.06	$1.124	$1.191	. . .

The current value of this indefinite flow of growing payments (i.e., the growing dividend) also depends on the discount rate (i.e., the investor's required rate of return). If this rate is 12 percent, the stock's value is

$$V = \frac{\$1}{(1 + .12)} + \frac{1.06}{(1 + .12)^2} + \frac{1.124}{(1 + .12)^3} + \frac{1.191}{(1 + .12)^4} + \cdots$$

$$V = \$17.67.$$

Equation 8.2 may be modified for the growth in dividends. This is expressed in Equations 8.3 and 8.4. The only new variable is the rate of growth in the dividend (g), and it is assumed that this growth rate is fixed and will continue indefinitely into the future. Given this assumption, the **dividend-growth valuation model** is

dividend-growth valuation model
A valuation model that deals with dividends and their growth properly discounted back to the present.

$$V = \frac{D(1 + g)^1}{(1 + k)^1} + \frac{D(1 + g)^2}{(1 + k)^2} + \frac{D(1 + g)^3}{(1 + k)^3} + \cdots + \frac{D(1 + g)^\alpha}{(1 + k)^\alpha}, \tag{8.3}$$

which simplifies to

$$V = \frac{D_0(1 + g)}{k - g}. \tag{8.4}$$

The stock's intrinsic value is thus related to (1) the current dividend, (2) the growth in earnings and dividends, and (3) the required rate of return.[5] Notice the current dividend is D_0 with the subscript 0 representing the present. The application of this dividend-growth model may be illustrated by a simple example. If the investor's required rate of return is 12 percent and the stock is currently paying a $1 per share dividend and is growing at 6 percent annually, the stock's value is

$$V = \frac{\$1(1 + 0.06)}{0.12 - 0.06} = \$17.67.$$

---

[5] For a derivation of this equation, see Eugene F. Brigham and Louis G. Gapenski, *Financial Management Theory and Practice*, 6th ed. (Hinsdale, Ill.: The Dryden Press, 1991): 238. The model assumes that the required rate of return exceeds the rate of growth (i.e., $k > g$).

Any price greater than $17.67 will result in a total yield of less than 12 percent. Conversely, a price of less than $17.67 will produce a return in excess of 12 percent. For example, if the price is $20, according to Equation 7.1 the expected return is

$$\text{Expected return} = \frac{\$1(1 + 0.06)}{\$20} + 0.06$$

$$= 11.3\%.$$

Since this return is less than the 12 percent required by the investor, it is inferior.[6] Therefore, this investor would not buy the stock and would sell it if he or she owned it.

If the price is $15, the expected return is

$$\text{Expected return} = \frac{\$1(1 + 0.06)}{\$15} + 0.06$$

$$= 13.1\%.$$

This return is greater than the 12 percent required by the investor. Since the security offers a superior return, it is undervalued. This investor then would try to buy the security.

Only at a price of $17.67 does the stock offer a return of 12 percent. At that price it equals the rate of return available on alternative investments of the same risk. The investment will yield 12 percent because the dividend yield during the year is 6 percent and the earnings and dividends are growing annually at the rate of 6 percent. These relationships are illustrated in Figure 8.1, which shows the growth in dividends and prices of the stock that will produce a constant yield of 12 percent. After 12 years the dividend will have grown to $2.02, and the price of the stock will be $35.55. The total return on this investment will still be 12 percent. During that year the dividend will grow to $2.14, giving a 6 percent dividend yield, and the price will continue to appreciate annually at the 6 percent growth rate in earnings and dividends.

The student should note that in Figure 8.1 the lines representing the dividend and the price of the stock are curved. The earnings and the price of the stock are growing at the same rate, but they are not growing by the same amount each year. This is another illustration of the time value of money, as the earnings, dividends, and prices of the stock are all compounding annually at 6 percent.

A firm's earnings need not grow steadily at this rate. Figure 8.2 illustrates a case in which the firm's earnings grow annually at an average of 6 percent, but the year-to-year changes stray considerably from 6 percent. These fluctuations are not in themselves necessarily reason for concern. The firm does exist within the economic environment, which fluctuates over time. Exogenous factors, such as a strike or an energy curtailment, may also affect earnings during a particular year. If these factors continue to plague the firm, they will obviously play an important role in the valuation of the shares. However, the emphasis in valuation is on the flow of dividends and the growth in earnings over a period of years. This longer time dimension smoothes out temporary fluctuations in earnings and dividends.

---

[6] Notice the expected dividend is $1.06, which is the $1 current dividend plus the anticipated $0.06 (6 percent) increment in the dividend.

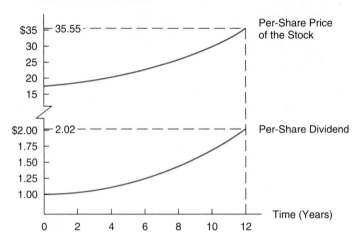

Figure 8.1 ✦ EARNINGS, DIVIDENDS, AND PRICE OF STOCK OVER TIME YIELDING 12 PERCENT ANNUALLY

Although the previous model assumes that the firm's earnings will grow indefinitely and that the dividend policy will be maintained, such need not be the case. The model may be modified to encompass a period of increasing or declining growth or one of stable earnings. Many possible variations in growth patterns can be built into the model. Although these variations change the equation and make it appear far more complex, the fundamentals of valuation remain unaltered. Valuation is still the process of discounting future dividends and growth in earnings and dividends back to the present at the appropriate discount rate.

To illustrate such a variation, consider the following pattern of expected earnings and dividends.

Year	Earnings	Yearly Dividends	Change in Earnings and Dividends from Previous Year
1	$1.00	$0.40	. . .
2	1.60	0.64	60%
3	1.94	0.77	21
4	2.20	0.87	12
5	2.29	0.91	4
6	2.38	0.95	4
7	2.47	0.98	4

After the initial period of rapid growth, the firm matures and is expected to grow annually at the rate of 4 percent. Each year the firm pays dividends, which contribute to its current value. However, the simple model summarized in Equation 8.4 cannot be used, because the earnings and dividends are not growing at a constant rate. Equation 8.3 can be used, and when these values, along with a required

Figure 8.2 ♦ EARNINGS GROWTH AVERAGING 6 PERCENT ANNUALLY

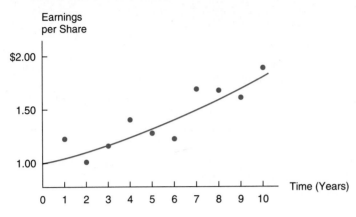

rate of return of 12 percent, are inserted into the equation, the stock's value is

$$V = \frac{\$0.40}{(1 + 0.12)^1} + \frac{\$0.64}{(1 + 0.12)^2} + \frac{\$0.77}{(1 + 0.12)^3} + \frac{\$0.87}{(1 + 0.12)^4}$$

$$+ \frac{\$0.91}{(1 + 0.12)^5} + \frac{\$0.95}{(1 + 0.12)^6} + \frac{\$0.98}{(1 + 0.12)^7} + \cdots$$

$$= \$9.16.$$

This answer is derived by dividing the flow of dividends into two periods: a period of super growth (years 1 through 4) and a period of normal growth (from year 5 on). The present value of the dividends in the first four years is

$$V_{1-4} = \frac{\$0.40}{(1 + 0.12)^1} + \frac{\$0.64}{(1 + 0.12)^2} + \frac{\$0.77}{(1 + 0.12)^3} + \frac{\$0.87}{(1 + 0.12)^4}$$

$$= \$0.36 + \$0.51 + \$0.55 + \$0.55$$

$$= \$1.97.$$

The dividend-growth model is applied to the dividends from year 5 on, so the value of the dividends during normal growth is

$$V_{5-\alpha} = \frac{\$0.87(1 + 0.04)}{0.12 - 0.04} = \$11.31.$$

This $11.31 is the value at the end of year 4, so it must be discounted back to the present to determine the current value of this stream of dividend payments. That is,

$$\frac{\$11.31}{(1 + 0.12)^4} = \$11.31(0.636) = \$7.19.$$

The value of the stock, then, is the sum of the two parts:[7]

$$V = V_{1-4} + V_{5-\alpha}$$

$$= \$1.97 + 7.19 = \$9.16.$$

As this example illustrates, modifications can be made in this valuation model to account for the different periods of growth and dividends. Adjustments can also be made for differences in risk. The student should realize that the model does not by itself adjust for different degrees of risk. If a security analyst applies the model to several firms to determine which stocks are underpriced, there is the implication that investing in all of the firms involves equal risk. If the analyst uses the same required rate of return for each firm, then no risk adjustment has been made. The element of risk is assumed to be equal for each company.

THE INVESTOR'S REQUIRED RETURN AND STOCK VALUATION

The generally accepted means to adjust for risk is to incorporate into the valuation model the beta coefficients presented earlier in Chapter 7. In that chapter beta coefficients, which are an index of the systematic risk associated with the security, were used as part of the capital asset pricing model to explain returns. In this context, beta coefficients and the capital asset pricing model are used to specify the risk-adjusted, required return on an investment.

The required return has two components: the risk-free rate that the investor can earn on a risk-free security (r_f) such as a U.S. Treasury bill, and a risk premium. The risk premium is also composed of two components: (1) the additional return that investing in securities offers above the risk-free rate, and (2) the volatility of the particular security relative to the market as a whole (i.e., the beta). The additional return is the extent to which the return on the market (r_m) exceeds the risk-free rate ($r_m - r_f$). Thus, the required return (k) is

$$k = r_f + (r_m - r_f)\,\beta. \tag{8.5}$$

---

[7] This valuation procedure may be summarized by the following general equation:

$$V = V_s + V_n.$$

V_s is the present value of the dividends during the period of super growth; that is,

$$V_s = \sum_{t=1}^{n} \frac{D_0(1 + g_s)^t}{(1 + k)^t}.$$

V_n is the present value of the dividends during the period of normal growth; that is,

$$V_n = \left[\frac{D_n(1 + g)}{k - g}\right]\left(\frac{1}{(1 + k)^n}\right).$$

The value of the stock is the sum of the individual present values; that is,

$$V = \sum_{t=1}^{n} \frac{D_0(1 + g_s)^t}{(1 + k)^t} + \left[\frac{D_n(1 + g)}{k - g}\right]\left(\frac{1}{(1 + k)^n}\right).$$

This is the same equation as the security market line in Chapter 7 which was used to explain a stock's return. In equilibrium, the required return and the expected return should be the same and so, the two equations are equal (i.e., $r = k$).

The following examples illustrate how the equation for the required return is used. The risk-free rate is 9 percent and it is anticipated that the market will rise by 12 percent. Stock A is relatively risky and has a beta coefficient of 1.8, while stock B is relatively safe and has a beta of 0.83. What return is necessary to justify purchasing either stock? Certainly it would not be correct to require a return of 12 percent for either, since that is the expected return on the market. Since stock A is riskier than the market, the required return for A should exceed 12 percent. However, the required return for B should be less than 12 percent because it is less risky than the market as a whole.

Given the above information concerning the risk-free rate and the anticipated return on the market, the required rates of return for stocks A and B are

$$k_A = 9\% + (12\% - 9\%)1.8 = 9\% + 5.4\% = 14.4\%$$

and

$$k_B = 9\% + (12\% - 9\%).83 = 9\% + 2.5\% = 11.5\%.$$

Thus the required rates of return for stocks A and B are 14.4 percent and 11.5 percent, respectively. These required returns are different from each other and from the expected return on the market, because the analysis now explicitly takes into consideration risk (i.e., the volatility of the individual stock relative to the market). Stock A's required rate of return is greater than the expected return on the market (14.4 percent versus 12 percent) because stock A is more volatile than the market. Stock B's required rate of return is less than the return expected for the market (11.5 percent versus 12 percent) because stock B is less volatile than the market as a whole.

The relationship between the required rate of return and risk expressed in Equation 8.5 is illustrated in Figure 8.3. The horizontal axis represents risk as measured by the beta coefficient, and the vertical axis measures the required rate of return. Line *AB* represents the required rates of return associated with each level of risk. Line *AB* uses the information given in the above example: the y intercept is the risk-free return (9 percent), and the slope of the line is the difference between the market return and the risk-free return (12 percent minus 9 percent). If the beta coefficient were 1.8, the figure indicates that the required return would be 14.4 percent; if the beta coefficient were 0.83, the required return would be 11.5 percent.

The security market line will change if the variables that are used to construct it change. For example, if the expected return on the market were to increase from 12 percent to 14 percent and there was no simultaneous change in the risk-free rate, then *AB* would pivot to *AC* in Figure 8.4. At each beta the required return is increased. For example, the required return for a stock with a beta of 1.8 now rises from 14.4 percent to 18 percent, and the required return for a stock with a beta of 0.83 increases from 11.5 percent to 13.2 percent.

How this risk-adjusted discount rate may be applied to the valuation of a specific stock is illustrated by the following example. Suppose a firm's dividend would grow at 5 percent, U.S. Treasury bills of six-month duration offered a risk-free return of

Figure 8.3 ◆ RELATIONSHIP BETWEEN RISK AND REQUIRED RATE OF RETURN

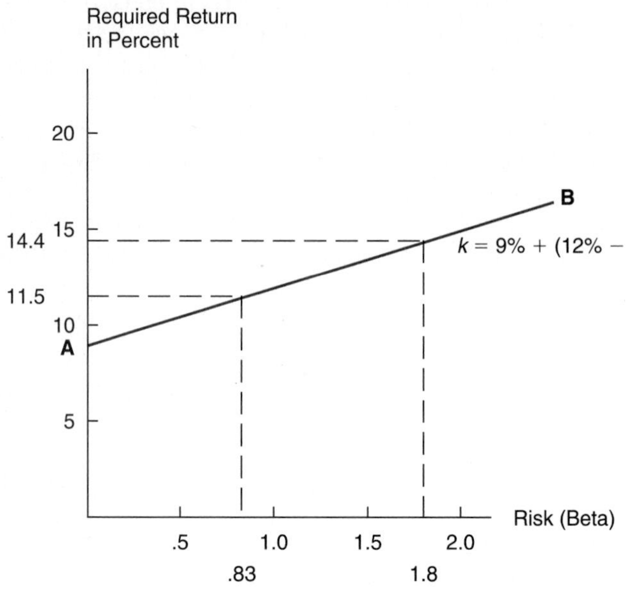

7.5 percent, and an investor anticipated that the market would rise annually at a compound rate of 13.5 percent (i.e., about 6 percentage points more than the risk-free rate),[8] what would be the maximum price this investor should pay for the stock?

The first step in answering the question is to determine the risk-adjusted required return:

$$k = r_f + (r_m - r_f)\beta$$

$$= 0.75 + (.135 - .075)0.75$$

$$= 0.12.$$

Next this risk-adjusted required return is used in the dividend-growth model presented above:

$$V = \frac{D_0(1 + g)}{k - g}$$

$$= \frac{\$2.20(1 + 0.05)}{.12 - .05}$$

$$= \$33.$$

---

[8] Ibbotson and Sinquefield found that over a period of years stocks have yielded a return of approximately 6 percent in excess of the return on U.S. Treasury bills. Thus if bills are yielding 13 percent, an expected return on the market of 18 percent is not excessive and may even be low. See Roger G. Ibbotson and Rex A. Sinquefield, *Stocks, Bonds, Bills,*

Figure 8.4 ✦ Relationship between Risk and Required Rate of Return

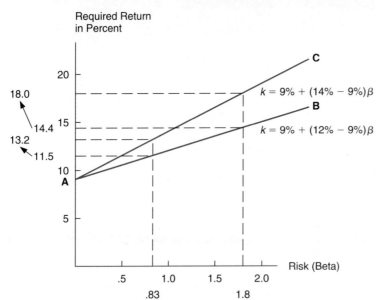

At a price of $33 (and only at $33), the expected and required returns are equated. If the market price is below $33, the stock would be considered undervalued and a good purchase. Correspondingly, if the price exceeds $33, the stock should not be purchased but should be sold short.

While this procedure does bring a risk adjustment into the valuation model, it should be remembered that the results or conclusions can only be as good as the data employed. While this model and others presented in this text may be theoretically sound, their accuracy depends on the data used. The possibility of inaccurate data should be obvious in the valuation model. Any of the estimates (i.e., the growth rate, the expected return on the market, the beta coefficient) may be incorrect, in which case the resulting valuation would be incorrect. For example, if the expected growth rate in the previous example were increased from 5 percent to 7 percent, the effect would be to raise the valuation from $33 to $47.08.

The problem of inaccurate data does not mean that the use of models in financial decision making is undesirable. Without such models there would be no means to value an asset. Hunches, intuition, or just plain guessing would then be used to value and select assets. By using theoretical models, the financial manager is forced to identify real economic forces (e.g., earnings and growth rates) and alternatives (e.g., the risk-free rate and the return earned by the market as a whole). Even if the analysis may sometimes be inaccurate, it is still fundamentally sound and should prove better than random guessing or intuitive feelings.

and Inflation: The Past (1926–1976) and the Future (1977–2000). This material is reprinted in J. C. Francis, C. Lee, and D. E. Farrar, eds., *Readings in Investments* (New York: McGraw-Hill, 1980).

POINTS OF INTEREST

INFLATION AND THE INVESTOR'S
REQUIRED RETURN

While inflation is not explicitly part of the equation for the required rate of return, it is implicitly included. Anticipation of inflation will increase the rate on treasury bills and the required return on the market. Higher rates of inflation will increase the T-bill rate as (1) the Federal Reserve takes steps to reduce inflation and (2) individuals seek to protect themselves by investing only if yields are sufficiently high to compensate them for the anticipated inflation.

A higher T-bill rate will result in an increase in the required return on the market. Investors certainly will not buy risky securities in general if their return declines relative to the T-bill rate. Increases in the T-bill rate must lead to corresponding increases in the required return on the market. The net effect will be to increase the required rate of return on an investment in common stock. For example, suppose the expected rate of inflation rises by 2 percent from 4 to 6 percent, which, in turn, causes the T-bill rate to rise from 6 to 8 percent and the required return on the market to increase from 12 to 14 percent. If a stock has a beta of 1.2, the required return rises from

$$k = 0.06 + (0.12 - 0.06)1.2 = 13.2\%$$

to

$$k = 0.08 + (0.14 - 0.08)1.2 = 15.2\%.$$

AN ALTERNATE VALUATION: USE OF P/E RATIOS

While the dividend-growth model can be employed for any firm that pays a dividend, a problem arises for the valuation of a common stock that pays no dividend. An alternative means to valuing common stock is to estimate future earnings and then to multiply the estimated earnings by a P/E ratio. For example, suppose the financial analyst determines that the firm will earn $4.50 next year. If the appropriate P/E ratio is 10, then the future price of the stock should be $45. Obviously, if the price of the stock is $35, it would appear to be a good purchase.

The use of a P/E approach to valuation and security selection is often found in the financial press (if not the academic press). The crux of the analysis is (1) the appropriate P/E ratio and (2) the determination of future earnings. Since many stocks tend to trade within a range of P/E ratios, it would seem appropriate to maintain this range. If the stock of Merck has had P/E ratios ranging from 18 to 10, it would be inappropriate to suggest the ratio should be 25 or 7. Unless there has been a fundamental change in the firm, the financial analyst can anticipate the P/E ratio to remain within its historic range.

The second problem is estimating earnings. As will be illustrated in the section on ratio analysis, the financial analyst may compute many ratios based on data found in a firm's financial statements that may help to identify trends and weaknesses within the firm. By combining analysis of the firm's financial statements, its position within its industry, and the direction of the economy, the financial analyst may be able to forecast future earnings. These forecasts are then combined with the P/E ratio to estimate the stock's future price. If, for example, the forecasted earnings are $4.00 and the firm's P/E ratio has ranged from 8 to 12, this suggests that the price of the stock could reach as high as $48 but would not fall below $32.

An alternative method using P/E ratios is to divide the forecasted earnings by the current price to express the P/E ratio in terms of future earnings. For example, suppose the stock was selling for $33 when the estimated earnings were $4.00. The

POINTS OF INTEREST

OBTAINING EARNINGS FORECASTS

To apply P/E ratio analysis, the individual needs forecasts of earnings. It is probably safe to assume that individual investors do not want to construct their own forecasts, so where can these estimates be obtained? There are several answers.

Many brokerage firms have estimates for specific companies. The *Value Line Investment Survey* gives estimates for the stocks it covers. *Forbes* periodically publishes earnings estimates that are averages of several earnings forecasts. *Forbes* also gives the number of and the variation in the original estimates from which

it compiles its averages. *Standard & Poor's* also publishes an *Earnings Guide* that includes investment analysts' estimates, the number of estimates, and the high, low, and average estimate for the next quarter and the next fiscal year.

P/E ratio using the estimated earnings is 8.25, which is at the low end of the 8 to 12 range. This suggests that the stock may be undervalued and there is little risk that its price will decline. If the appropriate P/E ratio is believed to be 10, the stock is underpriced in terms of future earnings. As those earnings are achieved, the price should rise from \$33 to \$40. From this analysis, the stock is undervalued and should be purchased.

While the use of forecasted earnings and P/E ratios seems considerably different from the dividend-growth model presented in the previous section, they are essentially very similar. The dividend-growth model was

$$V = \frac{D_0(1 + g)}{k - g}.$$

Since the firm's current dividend (D_0) is related to its current earnings (E_0) and the proportion of the earnings that are distributed (d), then

$$D_0 = dE_0.$$

When this is substituted back into the dividend-growth model, the model becomes

$$V = \frac{dE_0(1 + g)}{k - g}.$$

If both sides of the equation are divided by earnings (E_0), the stock's valuation is expressed as a P/E ratio:

$$\frac{V}{E_0} = \frac{d(1 + g)}{k - g}.$$

From this perspective, a P/E ratio depends on the same fundamental financial variables as the stock's valuation achieved through use of the dividend-growth model.

The use of P/E ratios instead of the dividend-growth model offers one major advantage and one major disadvantage. As previously stated, the advantage is that P/E ratios may be applied to common stocks that are not currently paying cash dividends. The dividend-growth model assumes that the firm will eventually pay cash dividends and that it is these future dividends that give the stock current value. The major weakness of the use of P/E ratios is that these ratios do not tell the analyst if the security is under- or overvalued. Instead the analysis indicates whether the firm's stock is selling near its historic high or low P/E ratio and then draws an inference from this information. The dividend-growth model establishes a value based on the investor's required rate of return, the firm's dividends, and the future growth in those dividends. This valuation is then compared to the actual price to answer the question of whether the stock is under- or overvalued.

THE EFFICIENT MARKET HYPOTHESIS

Perhaps it is conceit that makes some individuals think they can use the above valuation model, or P/E ratios, or some other technique to outperform the market on a risk-adjusted basis. Notice the use of the phrase "risk-adjusted basis." Bearing more risk implies the individual should earn a higher return than the market. To outperform the market and earn an excess return, the investor must do better than the return that would be expected given the amount of risk. This implies that the investor could earn a lower return than the market but still earn an excess return and outperform the market if the investor bears less risk.

efficient market hypothesis (EMH)

A theory that security prices correctly measure the firm's future earnings and dividends and that investors should not consistently outperform the market on a risk-adjusted basis.

The **efficient market hypothesis (EMH)** suggests that investors cannot expect to outperform the market consistently on a risk-adjusted basis. Notice that the hypothesis does not say an individual will not outperform the market since obviously some investors may do exceptionally well for a period of time. Being an occasional winner is not what is important, however, since most investors have a longer time horizon. The efficient market hypothesis suggests that investors will not outperform the market on a risk-adjusted basis over an extended period of time.

The efficient market hypothesis is based on the premise that security prices reflect all available information concerning a firm and that security prices change rapidly in response to new information. Because security prices fully incorporate known information and prices change rapidly, day-to-day price changes will follow in a "random walk" over time. A random walk essentially means that price changes are unpredictable and patterns formed are accidental. If prices do follow a random walk, trading rules are useless, and various techniques such as charting, moving averages, or odd lot purchases relative to sales cannot lead to superior security selection. (These techniques are discussed in Chapter 13.)

The conventional choice of the term "random walk" to describe the pattern of changes in security prices is perhaps unfortunate for two reasons. First, it is reasonable to expect that over a period of time, stock prices will rise. Unless the return is entirely the result of dividends, stock prices must rise to generate a positive return. In addition, stock prices will tend to rise over time as firms and the economy grow.

Second, the phase "random walk" is often misinterpreted as meaning that security prices are randomly determined, an interpretation that is completely backwards. It is *changes* in security prices that are random. Security prices themselves are rationally and efficiently determined by such fundamental considerations as earnings, interest rates, dividend policy, and the economic environment. Changes in these variables are quickly reflected in a security's price. All known information is

Figure 8.5 ✦ Adjustments in Expected Returns When Securities are Under- or Overvalued

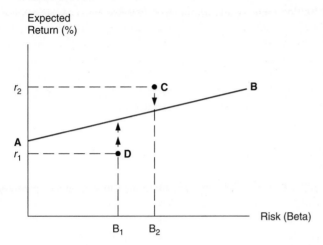

embodied in the current price, and only new information will alter that price. New information has to be unpredictable; if it were predictable, the information would be known and stock prices would have already adjusted for that information. Hence, new information *must be random,* and security prices should change randomly in response to that information. If changes in security prices were not random and could be predicted, then some investors could consistently outperform the market (i.e., earn a return in excess of the expected return given the amount of risk) and security markets would not be efficient.

Since security prices incorporate all known information concerning a firm, the efficient market hypothesis also asserts that the current price of a stock properly values the firm's future growth and dividends. Today's price, then, is a true measure of the security's worth. Security analysis that is designed to determine if the stock is over- or underpriced is futile, because the stock is neither. If prices were not true measures of the firm's worth, an opportunity to earn excess returns would exist. Investors who recognized these opportunities (e.g., that a particular stock is undervalued) and took advantage of the mispricing (e.g., bought the undervalued stock) would consistently outperform the market on a risk-adjusted basis.

This process by which security prices would adjust may be illustrated by using the figure relating risk and return presented earlier in the chapter. Figure 8.5 reproduces this relationship between risk and return. Suppose stock C offered an expected return of r_2 for bearing B_2 of risk. What would the investor do? The obvious answer is rush to purchase the stock, because it offers an exceptional return for the given amount of risk. If several investors had a similar perception of this risk/return relationship, they also would seek to purchase the stock, which would certainly increase its price and reduce the expected return. This price increase and reduction in expected return stops when point C in Figure 8.5 moves back to line AB, which represents all the optimal combinations of risk and expected returns that are available. Thus, the security that was initially undervalued becomes fairly priced and no longer offers an exceptional return.

The converse case (i.e., overvaluation) is illustrated by stock D in Figure 8.5, which offers an inferior expected return for the given amount of risk. In this case investors perceive the stock as being overvalued and will seek to sell it. This increased desire to sell will depress the stock's price and thus increase the expected return. The decline in the stock's price will cease only after the expected return has risen sufficiently to move point D in Figure 8.5 back to the line representing the optimal risk/return relationship. The efficient market hypothesis thus asserts that the price of any under- or overvalued stock is unstable and will change. The security's equilibrium price (when there is no incentive to change) is a true valuation of what the investment community believes the asset is worth.

The Speed of Price Adjustments

For security markets to be efficient, security prices must adjust rapidly. The efficient market hypothesis asserts that the market prices adjust extremely rapidly as new information is disseminated. In the modern world of advanced communication, information is rapidly disbursed in the investment community. The market then adjusts security prices in accordance with the impact of the news on the firm's future earnings and dividends. By the time that the individual investor has learned the information, security prices probably will have already changed. Thus, the investor will not be able to profit from acting on the information.

This adjustment process is illustrated in Figure 8.6, which plots the price of AMR (American Airlines) stock during October 1989. In early October, AMR received a buyout offer at $120, and the stock rose quickly and dramatically. However, the offer was terminated on October 16, and the price of the stock fell 22⅛ points from $98⅝ to $76½ in one day. Such price behavior is exactly what the efficient market hypothesis suggests: The market adjusts very rapidly to new information. By the time the announcement was reported in the financial press on October 17, it was too late for the individual investor to react, as the price change had already occurred.

If the market were not so efficient and prices did not adjust rapidly, some investors would be able to adjust their holdings and take advantage of differences in investors' knowledge. Consider the broken line in Figure 8.6. If some investors knew that the agreement had been terminated but others did not, the former could sell their holdings to those who were not informed. The price then may fall over a period of time as the knowledgeable sellers accepted progressively lower prices in order to unload their stock. Of course, if a sufficient number of investors had learned quickly of the termination, the price decline would be rapid as these investors adjusted their valuations of the stock in accordance with the new information. That is exactly what happened, because a sufficient number of investors were rapidly informed and the efficient market quickly adjusted the stock's price.

If an investor were able to anticipate the termination of the merger before it was announced, that individual could avoid the price decline. Obviously some investors did sell their shares just prior to the announcement, but it is also evident that some individuals bought those shares. Certainly one of the reasons for learning the material and performing the various types of analysis throughout this text is to increase one's ability to anticipate events before they occur. However, the investor should realize that considerable evidence supports the efficient market hypothesis and strongly suggests few investors will over a period of time outperform the market consistently.

Figure 8.6   ✦   DAILY CLOSING PRICES OF AMR (AMERICAN AIRLINES), OCTOBER 2, 1989–OCTOBER 20, 1989

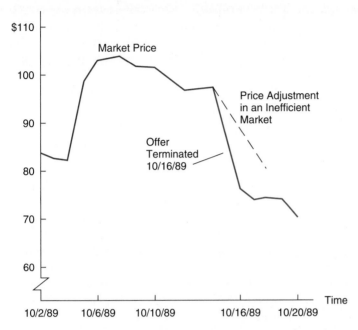

Forms of the Efficient Market Hypothesis

The previous discussion of the efficient market hypothesis suggested that financial markets are efficient. The competition among investors, the rapid dissemination of information, and the swiftness with which security prices adjust to this information produce efficient financial markets in which an individual cannot expect to consistently outperform the market. Instead the investor can expect to earn a return that is consistent with the amount of risk he or she bears.

While the investor may know that financial markets are efficient, he or she may not know *how* efficient. The degree of efficiency is important, because it determines the value the individual investor places on various types of analysis to select securities. If financial markets are inefficient, then many techniques may aid the investor in selecting securities, and these techniques will lead to superior results. However, as markets become more efficient and various tools of analysis become well known, their usefulness for security selection is reduced, since they will no longer produce superior results (i.e., beat the market on a risk-adjusted basis).

The investor may believe that the financial markets are weakly efficient, semistrongly efficient, or strongly efficient. The *weak form* of the efficient market hypothesis suggests that the fundamental analysis discussed in Chapters 11 and 12 may produce superior investment results but that the technical analysis discussed in Chapter 13 will not. Thus, studying past price behavior and other technical indicators of the market will not produce superior investment results. For example, if a stock's price rises, the next change cannot be forecasted by studying previous price behavior. According to the weak form of the efficient market hypothesis, technical indicators do not produce returns on securities that are in excess of the return consistent with the amount of risk borne by the investor.

The *semi-strong form* of the efficient market hypothesis asserts that the current price of a stock reflects all of the public's information concerning the company. This knowledge includes both the firm's past history and the information learned through studying a firm's financial statements, its industry, and the general economic environment. Analysis of this material cannot be expected to produce superior investment results. Notice that the hypothesis does not state that the analysis cannot produce superior results. It just asserts that superior results should not be expected. However, there is the implication that even if the analysis of information produces superior results in some cases, it will not produce superior results over many investment decisions.

This conclusion should not be surprising to anyone who thinks about the investment process. Many investors and analysts study the same information. Their thought processes and training are similar, and they are in competition with one another. Certainly, if one perceives a fundamental change in a particular firm, this information will be readily transferred to other investors, and the price of the security will change. The competition among the potential buyers and the potential sellers will result in the security's price reflecting the firm's intrinsic worth.

As may be expected, the investment community is not particularly elated with this conclusion. It implies that the fundamental analysis considered in Chapters 11 and 12 will not produce superior investment results. Thus, neither technical nor fundamental analysis will generate consistently superior investment performance. Of course, if the individual analyst is able to perceive fundamental changes before other analysts do, that individual can outperform the market as a whole. However, few, if any, individuals should be able to *consistently* perceive such changes. Thus, there is little reason to expect investors to achieve consistently superior investment results.

There is, however, one major exception to this general conclusion of the semi-strong form of the efficient market hypothesis. If the investor has access to *inside information,* that individual may consistently achieve superior results. In effect, this individual has information that is not known by the general investing public. Such privileged information as dividend cuts or increments, new discoveries, or potential takeovers may have a significant impact on the value of the firm and its securities. If the investor has advance knowledge of such events and has the time to act, he or she should be able to achieve superior investment returns.

Of course, most investors do not have access to inside information or at least do not have access to information concerning a number of firms. An individual may have access to privileged information concerning a firm for which he or she works. But as was previously pointed out, the use of such information for personal gain is illegal. To achieve continuous superior results, the individual would have to have a continuous supply of correct inside information and to use it illegally. Probably few, if any, investors have this continuous supply, which may explain why both fundamentalists and technical analysts watch sales and purchases by insiders as a means to glean a clue as to the true future potential of the firm as seen by its management.

The *strong form* of the efficient market hypothesis asserts that the current price of a stock reflects all known (i.e., public) information *and* all privileged or inside information concerning the firm. Thus, not even access to inside information can be expected to result in superior investment performance. Once again, this does not mean that an individual who acts on inside information cannot achieve superior results. It means that these results cannot be expected and that success in one case will tend to be offset by failure in other cases, so over time the investor will not achieve superior results.

This conclusion rests on a very important assumption: Inside information cannot be kept inside! Too many people know about the activities of a firm. This information is discerned by a sufficient number of investors, and the prices of the firm's securities adjust for the informational content of this inside knowledge. Notice that the conclusion that the price of the stock still reflects its intrinsic value does not require that all investors know this additional information. All that is necessary is for a sufficient number to know. Furthermore, the knowledge need not be acquired illegally. It is virtually impossible to keep some information secret, and there is a continual flow of rumors concerning a firm's activities. Denial by the firm is not sufficient to stop this spread of rumors, and when some are later confirmed, it only increases the credibility of future rumors as a possible means to gain inside information.

Although considerable empirical work has been designed to verify the forms of the efficient market hypothesis, these tests generally support only the weak and semi-strong forms. The use of privileged information may result in superior investment performance, but the use of publicly known information cannot be expected to produce superior investments. Thus, neither technical nor fundamental analysis may be of help to the individual investor, because the current price of a stock fully incorporates this information.

Empirical Evidence for the Efficient Market Hypothesis: The Anomalies

While it is generally believed that security markets are efficient, the question as to how efficient markets are remains to be answered. This raises a second question: If the financial markets are not completely efficient, what are the exceptions? The question of degree has led to three forms of the efficient market hypothesis referred to as the *weak form,* the *semi-strong form,* and the *strong form.* The second question has led to the identification of exceptions to market efficiency referred to as *anomalies.*

Empirical testing of various types of technical indicators strongly supports the weak form of the efficient market hypothesis, and the techniques explained in Chapter 13, generally referred to as "technical analysis," do not lead to superior investment results. The evidence suggests that successive price changes are random, and that the correlation between stock prices is virtually nil. Thus, past price behavior provides little useful information for predicting future stock prices.[9] However, there has been recent empirical evidence that suggests some inefficiency may exist with regard to using these techniques.[10] Whether the inefficiencies are sufficient that

---

[9] For a summary of this empirical work, see James H. Lorie et al., *The Stock Market: Theories and Evidence,* 2d ed. (Homewood, Ill.: Richard D. Irwin, 1985).

[10] See Andrew W. Lo and A. Craig MacKinlay, "Stock Market Prices Do Not Follow Random Walks: Evidence From a Simple Specification Test" NBER Working Paper No. 2168, February 1987, and Donald B. Keim and Robert F. Stambaugh, "Predicting Returns in the Stock and Bond Markets," *Journal of Financial Economics* (December 1986).

investors may develop trading strategies that generate excess returns has not been determined.

At the other extreme, the strong form of the efficient market hypothesis asserts that even access to inside information will not lead to excess returns. Initial empirical evidence does not support the strong form and suggests that insiders may be able to trade profitably in their own stocks.[11] Such evidence suggests that financial markets are not completely efficient.[12]

Knowledge of this inefficiency, however, may have led to its demise (in other words, the inefficiency corrected itself). Insiders must register their trading activity with the SEC. Since the SEC publishes an *Official Summary of Insider Trading*, non-insiders can track purchases and sales by insiders and act accordingly. Once individuals start to follow such a strategy, the inefficiency may disappear. One study found that a strategy of buying after insider purchases and selling after insider sales failed to produce a return that was large enough to overcome the commissions associated with the trading strategy.[13] Thus, unless the investor had minimal transaction costs (a few large mutual funds may have sufficiently small transaction costs), the strategy did not produce excess returns. This result supports the strong form of the efficient market hypothesis.

By far the most research and the most interest lies with the semi-strong form of the efficient market hypothesis. Studies of strategies that use publicly available information such as the data found in a firm's financial statements have generally concluded that this information does not produce superior results.[14] Prices change very rapidly once information becomes public, and thus the security's price embodies all known information. If an investor could anticipate the new information and act before the information became public, that individual might be able to outperform the market, but once the information becomes public, it rarely can be used to generate superior investment results.

While the evidence generally supports market efficiency, there are exceptions, the *anomalies*. A market anomaly is a situation or strategy that cannot be explained away but would not be expected to happen if the efficient market hypothesis were completely true. For example, if buying shares in companies that announced a stock split led to excess returns, such a strategy would imply that security markets are not completely efficient. (How such a test may be constructed is explained in the appendix to this chapter.)

Two of the most important anomalies are the "P/E effect" and the "small-firm effect." The P/E effect suggests that portfolios consisting of stocks with low price-

[11] See Joseph E. Finnerty, "Insiders and Market Efficiency," *Journal of Finance* (September 1976): 1141–1148 and the references given in this article.

[12] See, for instance, Dan Givoly and Dan Palmon, "Insider Trading and the Exploitation of Inside Information: Some Empirical Evidence," *Journal of Business* (January 1985): 69–87 and Stephen H. Penman, "Insider Trading and Dissemination of Firms' Forecast Information," *Journal of Business* (October 1982): 479–503.

[13] H. Nejat Seyhun, "Insiders' Profits, Costs of Trading, and Market Efficiency," *Journal of Financial Economics*, 1986, 189–212.

[14] For several studies that test the semi-strong form of the efficient market hypothesis, see the section on market efficiency in James Lorie and Richard Brealey, eds., *Modern Developments in Investment Management* (New York: Praeger Publishers, 1972).

earnings ratios have a higher average return than portfolios with higher P/E ratios. The "small-firm effect" (or *small cap* for small capitalization) suggests that returns diminish as the size of the firm rises. Size is generally measured by the market value of its stock. If all common stocks on the New York Stock Exchange are divided into five groups, the smallest quintile (the smallest 20 percent of the total firms) has tended to earn a return that exceeds the return on investments in the stocks that comprise the largest quintile, even after adjusting for risk.

Subsequent studies have found that the small-firm effect occurs primarily in January, especially the first five trading days. This anomaly is referred to as the "January effect." However, there is no negative mirror-image December effect (i.e., small stocks do not consistently underperform the market in December) that would be consistent with December selling and January buying. The January effect is often explained by the fact that investors buy stocks in January after selling for tax reasons in December. And there is some evidence that within a size class those stocks whose prices declined the most in the preceding year tended to rebound the most during January.

The "neglected-firm effect" suggests that small firms which are neglected by large financial institutions (e.g., mutual funds, insurance companies, trust departments, and pension plans) tend to generate higher returns than those firms covered by financial institutions. By dividing firms into the categories of highly researched stocks, moderately researched stocks, and neglected stocks (based on the number of institutions holding the stock), researchers have found that the last group outperformed the more well-researched firms. This anomaly is probably another variation of the small-firm effect, and both the neglected-firm effect and the small-firm effect suggest that the market gets less efficient as firms get smaller. Since large financial institutions may exclude these firms from consideration, their lack of participation reduces the market's efficiency.

Besides the January effect, there is also a "day-of-the-week effect." Presumably there is no reason to anticipate that day-to-day returns should differ except over the weekend when the return should exceed the return earned from one weekday to the next. However, research has suggested that the weekend does not generate a higher return but a *lower* return. If this anomaly is true, it implies that investors anticipating the purchase of stock should not buy on Friday but wait until Monday. Investors anticipating the sale of stock should reverse the procedure. If this anomaly does exist, it should be erased by investors selling short on Friday and covering their positions on Monday (i.e., an act of arbitrage should erase the anomaly). The existence of the anomaly is generally resolved by asserting that the excess return is too small to cover transaction costs.

The *Value Line Investment Survey* (see Exhibit 4.6 in Chapter 4) weekly ranks all the stocks that it covers into five groups ranging from those most likely to outperform the market during the next twelve months (i.e., stocks ranked "1") to those most likely to underperform the market during the next twelve months (stocks ranked "5"). Several studies have found that using the Value Line ranking system (i.e., selecting stocks ranked "1") generates an excess return, hence the "Value Line effect." Once again, the smaller firms tended to generate the largest excess return. While the amount of this excess return differed among the various studies, its existence is inconsistent with the efficient market hypothesis. However, it may be exceedingly difficult for the individual investor to take advantage of the anomaly since the Value Line rankings change weekly, which will require substantial transaction costs as the investor frequently adjusts his or her portfolio.

While most evidence supports the efficient market hypothesis, the above discussion indicates that there appear to be exceptions. Perhaps the observed exceptions are the result of flaws in the research methodology. Furthermore, any evidence supporting a particular inefficiency cannot be used to support other possible inefficiencies; it applies only to the specific anomaly under study.

Before any investor rushes out to take advantage of these alleged inefficiencies, that individual should remember several sobering considerations. First, the empirical results are only consistent with inefficiencies; they do not prove their existence. Second, for the investor to take advantage of the inefficiency, it must be ongoing. Once an inefficiency is discovered and investors seek to take advantage of it, the inefficiency will probably disappear. Third, transaction costs are important, and the investor must pay the transaction costs associated with the strategy. If a substantial amount of trading is required, any excess return may be consumed by transaction costs. Fourth, the investor still must select individual issues. Even if small firms outperform the market in the first week of January, the individual investor cannot purchase all of them. There is no assurance that the selected stocks will be those that outperform the market in that particular year. Fifth, for an anomaly to be useful for an active investment strategy, its signals must be transferable to the individual investor. Just because the Value Line rankings produce excess returns in an empirical study does not mean that the individual investor may be able to receive the information rapidly enough to act upon it. The anomaly may exist for those investors with the first access to the information, but not to all investors who receive the recommendations.

Implications of the Efficient Market Hypothesis

Ultimately, investors must decide for themselves the market's degree of efficiency and whether the anomalies are grounds for particular strategies. Any investor who has a proclivity toward active investment management may see the anomalies as an opportunity. Those investors who prefer more passive investment management may see them as nothing more than interesting curiosities.

Whether the investor tends to follow a more passive strategy or one that is designed to take advantage of an anomaly, the individual needs to understand the efficient market hypothesis. First, an efficient market implies that investors and financial analysts are using known information to value correctly what a security is worth. The individual may not be able to use public information to achieve superior investment results because the investment community is already using and acting on that information. If the investment community did not use this information and properly apply it to security valuation, the individual could achieve superior investment results. It is the very fact that investors as a whole are competent and are trying to beat each other that helps to produce efficient financial markets.

Secondly, while security markets are efficient, such efficiency may not apply to other markets. For example, the investor may not buy and sell nonfinancial assets in an efficient market. This means that the current prices of these assets need not reflect their intrinsic value, that is, the price may not reflect the asset's potential flow of future income or price appreciation. If the markets for assets other than financial assets are dispersed and all transactions are, in effect, over-the-counter, the dissemination of information and prices is limited. This tends to reduce the efficiency of

---

POINTS OF INTEREST

THE MONEY MASTERS

The efficient market hypothesis suggests that few, if any, investors will outperform the market for an extended period of time. Nine individuals who seem to have achieved that feat are highlighted in a fascinating book, *The Money Masters,* by John Train (Harper and Row, 1980). In this book, Train explores the ideas and strategies of these nine portfolio managers who achieved extraordinary records of capital appreciation for a period of at least ten years.

The strategies and characteristics of these nine individuals have common threads. They sought undervalued securities and tended to avoid stocks that were currently popular. They avoided new ventures, well-known firms (the so-called "blue chips"), and gimmicks such as options. They made realistic appraisals and favored stocks that tended to sell below book value. Each of these investors was patient and willing to wait until the prices of his stocks rose to reflect the securities' true value.

These nine men (there were no women) tended to be loners. While they were obviously very well informed concerning Wall Street, they were geographically dispersed and not necessarily located in New York City. While their success could be interpreted to refute the efficient market hypothesis, the opposite inference is more correct. The paucity of individuals who have achieved such success is strong support for the hypothesis that few individuals will achieve superior returns over an extended period of time.

---

markets and to result in prices that can be too high or too low. While such a situation may offer excellent opportunities for the astute and the knowledgeable, it can also spell disaster for the novice.

The third and perhaps most important implication of the efficient market hypothesis applies to an individual's portfolio. The efficient market hypothesis seems to suggest that the individual investor could randomly select a diversified portfolio of securities and earn a return consistent with the market as a whole. Furthermore, once the portfolio has been selected, there is no need to change it. The strategy, then, is to buy and hold. Such a policy offers the additional advantage of minimizing commissions.

The problem with this naive policy is that it fails to consider the reasons an investor saves and acquires securities and other assets. The goals behind the portfolio are disregarded, and different goals require different portfolio construction strategies. Furthermore, goals and conditions change, which in turn requires changes in an individual's portfolio. Altering the portfolio for the sake of change will probably result in additional commissions and not produce superior investment returns. However, when the investor's goals or financial situation change, the portfolio should be altered in a way that is consistent with the new goals and conditions.

The importance to the individual investor of the efficient market hypothesis is not the implication that investment decision making is useless. Instead, it brings to the foreground the environment in which the investor must make decisions. The hypothesis should make the investor realize that investments in securities may not produce superior returns. Rather, the investor should earn a return over a period of time that is consistent with the return earned by the market as a whole and the amount of risk borne by the investor. This means that individual investors should devote more time and effort to the specifications of their investment goals and the selection of securities to meet those goals than to the analysis of individual securities. Since such analysis cannot be expected to produce superior returns, it takes resources and time away from the important questions of why we save and invest.

SUMMARY

A corporation is an economic unit created by a state. Ownership in the corporation is represented by stock. Stock certificates may be readily transferred from one individual to another. In addition, investors in publicly held corporations have limited liability.

Investors in common stock anticipate a return in the form of cash dividends and/or capital appreciation. Capital gains taxation laws favor price appreciation over cash dividends: cash dividends are taxed as received, while capital gains receive favorable tax treatment. Such gains are taxed only when realized (i.e., when the stock is sold).

A simple model of stock valuation suggests that this value depends on the firm's earnings, its dividend policy, and investors' required rate of return. According to the model, future dividends should be discounted back to the present to determine a stock's value. The discount factor used depends on returns available on alternative investments and the risk associated with the particular stock. An alternate to the dividend-growth model is the use of P/E ratios and forecasted earnings to determine if the stock should be purchased. Both the dividend-growth model and the use of P/E ratios place emphasis on future earnings and dividends.

Risk is incorporated into the valuation of stock through the application of the capital asset pricing model. In the CAPM the risk adjustment uses a firm's beta coefficient, which is an index of the stock's systematic risk. These beta coefficients alter the investor's required return so that individual stocks with higher numerical betas have greater required returns.

Financial assets are bought and sold in competitive financial markets. This competition as well as the rapid dissemination of information among investors and the rapid changes in security prices results in efficient security markets. The efficient market hypothesis suggests that the individual investor cannot expect to outperform the market on a risk-adjusted basis over an extended period of time. Instead the investor should earn a return that is consistent with the market return and the amount of systematic risk the individual bears.

Empirical work tends to support the efficient market hypothesis, at least the weak and semi-strong forms. These studies give evidence that investors cannot use public information to earn a return in excess of what could be expected given the return on the market and the risk the investor bears. There are, however, several anomalies such as the January effect, the small-firm effect, or the analysis of P/E ratios that are inconsistent with the efficient market hypothesis. These anomalies suggest that the investor may be able to earn excess returns and that financial markets may have pockets of inefficiency.

Security Summary:

Common Stock

Source of return: Dividend income and possible capital gains

Liquidity and marketability: Common stocks listed on an organized exchange or actively traded over-the-counter are easily bought and sold. Investors may sustain a loss, so common stock may not be viewed as liquid.

Sources of risk: Unsystematic risk from events that happen to the specific firm that affect its earnings and hence alter its capacity to grow and pay dividends. Systematic risk from the tendency of the return on a stock to move in tandem with the return on the market as a whole.

Taxation: Dividends subject to personal income taxation. Capital gains subject to taxation only when realized.

Terms to Remember

certificate of incorporation
common stock
charter
bylaws
voting rights
directors
cumulative voting

preemptive rights
rights offering
total return
required rate of return
dividend-growth valuation model
capital asset pricing model (CAPM)
efficient market hypothesis

Questions

1. What does it mean for investors in the shares of IBM to have limited liability?
2. What role does each of the following play for the investor?
   a. preemptive rights
   b. cumulative voting
   c. Board of Directors
3. What is the difference between the expected return and the required return? When should the two returns be equal?
4. What is the difference between the value of a stock and its price? When should they be equal?
5. What variables affect the value of a stock according to the dividend-growth model? What role does earnings play in this model?
6. How do interest rates and risk affect a stock's price in the capital asset pricing model?
7. Does the efficient market hypothesis suggest that an investor cannot outperform the market? What role does the dissemination of information and the speed with which security prices change have on the efficient market hypothesis?
8. What are the three forms of the efficient market hypothesis?
9. While security markets are generally believed to be efficient, there appear to be some exceptions. For these exceptions (i.e., the anomalies) to be important for the individual investor, what must apply?
10. If investors had to limit themselves to one anomaly, which exception to the efficient market hypothesis seems to offer the most hope?

Problems

1. Given the following data, what should the price of the stock be?

Required return	10%
Present dividend	$1
Growth rate	5%

    a. If the growth rate increases to 6 percent and the dividend remains $1, what should the stock's price be?

    b. If the required return declines to 9 percent and the dividend remains $1, what should the price of the stock be? If the stock is selling for $20, what does that imply?

2. An investor requires a return of 12 percent. A stock sells for $25, it pays a dividend of $1, and the dividends compound annually at 7 percent. Will this investor find the stock attractive? What is the maximum amount that this investor should pay for the stock?

3. A firm's stock earns $2 per share, and the firm distributes 40 percent of its earnings as cash dividends. Its dividends grow annually at 7 percent.

    a. What is the stock's price if the required return is 10 percent?

    b. The aforementioned firm borrows funds and, as a result, its per-share earnings and dividends increase by 20 percent. What happens to the stock's price if the growth rate and the required return are unaffected? What will the stock's price be if after using financial leverage and increasing the dividend to $1, the required return rises to 12 percent? What may cause this required return to rise?

4. The annual risk-free rate of return is 9 percent and the investor believes that the market will rise annually at 15 percent. If a stock has a beta coefficient of 1.5 and its current dividend is $1, what should be the value of the stock if its earnings and dividends are growing annually at 6 percent?

5. You are considering two stocks. Both pay a dividend of $1, but the beta coefficient of A is 1.5 while the beta coefficient of B is 0.7. Your required return is

$$k = 8\% + (15\% - 8\%)\text{beta}.$$

    a. What is the required return for each stock?

    b. If A is selling for $10 a share, is it a good buy if you expect earnings and dividends to grow at 5 percent?

    c. The earnings and dividends of B are expected to grow annually at 10 percent. Would you buy the stock for $30?

    d. If the earnings and dividends of A were expected to grow annually at 10 percent, would it be a good buy at $30?

6. You are offered two stocks. The beta of A is 1.4 while the beta of B is 0.8. The growth rates of earnings and dividends are 10 percent and 5 percent, respectively. The dividend yields are 5 percent and 7 percent, respectively.

    a. Since A offers higher potential growth, should it be purchased?

    b. Since B offers a higher dividend yield, should it be purchased?

    c. If the risk-free rate of return were 7 percent and the return on the market is expected to be 14 percent, which of these stocks should be bought?

7. Your broker suggests that the stock of QED is a good purchase at $25. You do an analysis of the firm determining that the $1.40 dividend and earnings should continue to grow indefinitely at 8 percent annually. The firm's beta coefficient is 1.34, and the yield on treasury bills is 7.4 percent. If you expect the market to earn a return of 12 percent, should you follow your broker's suggestion?

8. The required return on an investment is 12 percent. You estimate that Firm X's dividends will grow as follows:

Year	Dividend
1	$1.20
2	2.00
3	3.00
4	4.50

For the subsequent years you expect the dividend to grow but at the more modest rate of 7 percent annually. What is the maximum price that you should pay for this stock?

9. Management has recently announced that expected dividends for the next three years will be as follows:

Year	Dividend
1	$2.50
2	3.25
3	4.00

For the subsequent years management expects the dividend to grow at 5 percent annually. If the risk-free rate is 4.3 percent, the return on the market is 10.3 percent, and the firm's beta is 1.4, what is the maximum price that you should pay for this stock?

10. Management has recently announced that expected dividends for the next three years will be as follows:

Year	Dividend
1	$3.00
2	2.25
3	1.50

The firm's assets will then be liquidated and the proceeds invested in the preferred stock of other firms so that the company will be able to pay an annual dividend of $1.25 indefinitely. If your required return on investments in common stock is 12 percent, what is the maximum you should pay for this stock?

Suggested Readings

For a layperson's explanation of the dividend-growth model and other techniques used to value securities, see:

Bajkowski, John. "From Theory to Reality: Applying the Valuation Models," *AAII Journal,* (January 1993), 34–37.

Markese, John. "A Fundamental Guide to Common Stock Valuation," *AAII Journal,* (January 1993), 30–33.

Valuation is a major topic covered in depth in more advanced texts. See, for instance:

Bodie, Zvi, Alex Kane, and Alan J. Marcus. *Investments.* 2d ed. Homewood, Ill.: Richard D. Irwin, 1992.

Radcliffe, Robert C. *Investment Concepts, Analysis, and Strategy.* 3d ed. Glenview, Ill.: Scott, Foresman, 1990, Chapter 13.

Schwartz, Robert A. *Reshaping the Equity Markets: A Guide for the 1990s.* New York: Harper Business, 1991.

For a discussion of the excessive use of financial theory and its inapplicability to financial and investment decisions consult:

Lowenstein, Louis. *Sense and Nonsense in Corporate Finance.* Reading, MA.: Addison-Wesley Publishing Company, Inc., 1991.

Appendix

TESTING THE EFFICIENT MARKET HYPOTHESIS: THE EVENT STUDY

One method employed to test the efficient market hypothesis is to study how a stock responds to the change in a variable, such as an unexpected increase in earnings or a decrease in the dividend. This technique is called an "event" study. If the market anticipated the event, the price should have already adjusted (i.e., the information is fully discounted), and the announcement of the event should have no impact. If the market did not anticipate the event, the price should immediately adjust for the new information so that few, if any, individuals are able to profit by acting upon the announcement of the event. If the market is not completely efficient, prior to the announcement, the price should move in the direction implied by the event but not fully discount the event.

These three scenarios are illustrated in Figure 8.7. Panel A illustrates the case in which the information is fully discounted and the price has already adjusted before the event which occurs at t_1. Even though some individuals may acquire the stock prior to the announcement, the time lapse between the price increase (from A to B in panel A) is sufficient that the time value of money consumes any possible excess return. For example, if individuals buy a stock in anticipation of a $1 dividend increment and bid up the stock's price, any excess return implied by the dividend increment is consumed by the cost of carrying the security until the announcement is made. This pattern is consistent with market efficiency.

Panel B illustrates the case in which there is no price change prior to the event at which time the price quickly adjusts for the new information. Since the price change (i.e., the vertical distance AB in panel B) is rapid and by an amount equal to the valuation of the event, there is no opportunity for an excess gain once the information is public. This price pattern also is consistent with efficient markets.

Panel C illustrates the case in which the market is not efficient; some price change (i.e., the movement from A to B in panel C) occurs prior to the event, but either the amount of the increment or its timing is insufficient to discount fully the impact of the announcement. Thus, investors who buy the stock prior to the announcement earn an excess return. If this pattern exists for several events (e.g., for all dividend increments), then the individual investor who perceives the pattern may earn consistent excess returns. For such inefficiency to exist, it is not necessary that every, or even many, investors perceive the pattern. If some investors, be they skilled or have some particular knowledge of the event, are able to outperform the market consistently, the market is not completely efficient.

Testing for the patterns illustrated in Figure 8.7 would appear to be easy, but two important observations need to be made. First, at any moment in time many factors (e.g., a movement in the market, a change in interest rates, a change in expected inflation, or a political event) may be affecting a stock's price, so the impact of one event must be isolated to determine if it has an impact on the stock's price and hence on the return. Second, returns must be adjusted for risk. One individual may acquire a very risky portfolio and achieve a higher return that the market. Another individual may acquire a portfolio consisting of certificates of deposit and

Figure 8.7 ✦ Stock Price Changes in Response to an Event

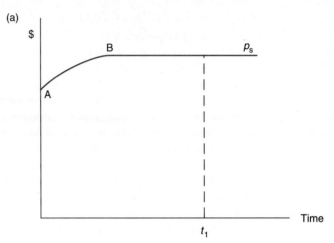

(a)

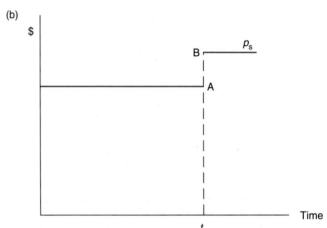

(b)

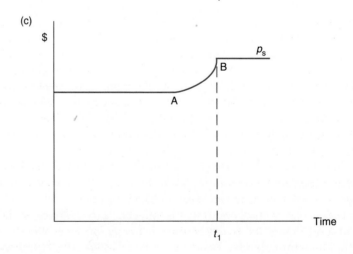

(c)

achieve a lower return. The different returns earned by these individuals are not sufficient evidence that the former outperformed the market while the latter under-performed the market. A higher (or lower) return may be the result of a different amount of risk. Thus, returns must be adjusted for risk. To demonstrate market inefficiency, the individual must consistently achieve a higher (or lower) return on a *risk-adjusted basis*. Thus, it is possible for a return to be less than the market return but still be considered superior after adjusting for risk, in which case the return indicates an inefficient market.

Testing of the efficient market hypothesis using event studies assumes that the stock's return (r_s) is a function of the return the security would earn in response to the return on the market $(a + br_m)$ and the impact of a firm-specific event repre-sented by the e in the following equation:

$$r_s = a + br_m + e.$$

The a measures the return the stock would earn if the market return equals zero. The r_m measures the market return during the period, while the b gives the response of the individual stock's return to the market return (i.e., it is the stock's beta). The e, or error term, picks up the impact of a firm-specific event such as a reduction in the dividend.

Rearranging the equation to solve for e gives an estimate of the firm-specific component of the return:

$$e = r_s - (a + br_m).$$

This equation states that if the return associated with changes in the market (i.e., $a + br_m$) is subtracted from the actual return (i.e., r_s), the residual is the firm-specific component of the return. The impact of this residual, of course, plays an important role in the rationale for the diversification of a portfolio. Since diversification erases the impact of firm-specific events, the value of e approaches zero as the number of securities increases, and the impact of firm-specific events is eliminated.

In an event study, however, the e is used to test for the impact of a firm-specific event such as a dividend cut. The value of e will not equal zero if the event has an impact on the stock's return. If, for example, a dividend cut has a negative impact on a stock's return, e will be negative after subtracting the return generated by the movements in the market. It is possible that e could be positive if the market approves of the dividend cut and causes the stock's return to exceed the return asso-ciated with movements in the market as a whole. If the firm-specific event has no impact, the value of e is zero, and the stock's return is completely explained by the movement in the market.

Even though an investor can earn an excess return or sustain an excess loss in a single event, that is not sufficient evidence to verify an inefficiency. To overcome this, researchers measure superior performance by computing the "cumulative excess return" the investor earns. If the individual consistently outperforms the mar-ket, these excess returns will grow over time. The three possible patterns (i.e., con-sistently superior excess returns, consistently inferior returns, and no excess returns) are illustrated in Figure 8.8. The efficient market hypothesis suggests that the pat-tern of cumulative excess returns should look like panel C, in which returns fluctuate around zero. If the investor consistently outperforms the market, the cumulative

Figure 8.8 ✦ CUMULATIVE RETURNS

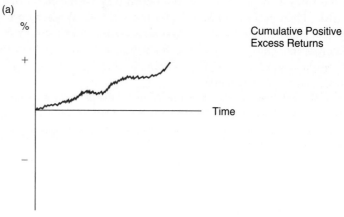

(a)

Cumulative Positive
Excess Returns

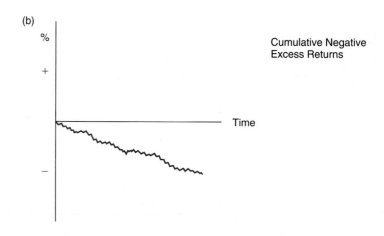

(b)

Cumulative Negative
Excess Returns

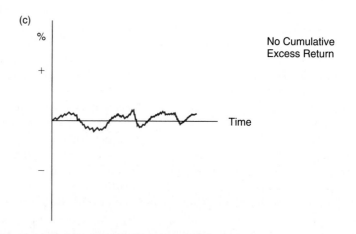

(c)

No Cumulative
Excess Return

excess returns will rise (i.e., panel A). Conversely, if the performance is consistently inferior, the cumulative excess returns will be negative and falling (i.e., panel B).

How cumulative excess returns may be used to test for an inefficiency can be illustrated by employing one of the so-called "technical" indicators such as the 200-day moving average. (Technical analysis is covered in Chapter 13.) The 200-day moving average suggests buying or selling a stock when the price of the stock goes through the 200-day moving average. For example, if the moving average has been declining, the daily price of the stock will have been less than the moving average. If the price of the stock rises sufficiently so that it is equal to the moving average and then moves above the average, the movement is interpreted to be a buy signal. Conversely, if the moving average has been rising, the daily price of the stock will have been greater than the moving average. If the price of the stock declines sufficiently to equal the moving average and subsequently moves below the average, that is interpreted as a sell signal.

Such buy and sell signals beg to be tested. The stock returns generated by strategies such as this should be compared to the returns generated by the market during each time period. That is, the residuals (i.e., the excess returns) are isolated and summed. If the strategy outperformed the market, then the cumulative excess return would rise over time. Such a pattern would indicate superior performance and suggest the market is not efficient, at least with regard to the particular buy-sell strategy being tested.

9

Rates of Return on Common Stock Investments

LEARNING OBJECTIVES

After completing this chapter you should be able to

1. Differentiate between a simple price average, a value-weighted average, and a geometric average.

2. Contrast the Dow Jones averages with other aggregate measures of the stock market.

3. Explain the differences among the holding period return, an average rate of return, and the true annual rate of return.

4. Compute the rate of return on an investment.

5. Compare the results of various studies concerning the rates of return earned on investments in common stock.

6. Identify the advantages associated with dollar cost averaging and averaging down.

he valuation model for common stock presented in the previous chapter had three components: the annual dividend, the growth in the dividend, and the required rate of return. The required rate of return depended upon the risk-free rate (i.e., the rate of treasury bills), the return on the market, and the firm's beta. Treasury bills were discussed in Chapter 2 in the section on money market mutual funds and money market instruments. Beta was considered in Chapter 7 on risk and its measurement. Dividends and growth are developed in the next chapter. This chapter considers the return on the market.

Those investors who own stock obviously expect security prices to rise over a period of time. But security prices fluctuate, and investors who acquire stock must endure the risk associated with those fluctuations. The investor could simply place funds in an insured bank account, earn a modest return, and bear none of the risk associated with fluctuating stock prices. By bearing the additional risk, the investor should be able to earn a higher return.

The measurement of performance and the historical returns earned by investments in stocks are the primary focus of this chapter. The first section discusses the construction of aggregate measures of the stock market. These include the Dow Jones averages, Standard & Poor's 500 stock index, the New York Stock Exchange index, and the Wilshire 5000 stock index.

The second section is devoted to the historical returns earned on investments in securities. It includes an explanation of the methods employed to compute rates of return, the various methods used to show the returns, and academic studies of the returns actually earned by investments in common stock. The chapter concludes with a discussion of buying stock systematically to smooth out price fluctuations and reduce the average cost of a position in a stock.

◆ ◆ ◆

Measures of Stock Performance: Averages and Indices

Constructing an aggregate measure of stock prices may appear to be easy, but there are several possible problems. The first concerns the choice of which securities to include and how many. Although the number to include certainly was a problem before the advent of computers, it is not a major concern today when a measure may include any number of securities (e.g., all stocks listed on the NYSE). However, the question of which specific companies remains. Unless all are included, choices must be made among the possible securities to include in the aggregate measure of the market.

A more important problem concerns the weight that should be given to each security. For example, suppose there are two stocks. Company A has 1 million shares outstanding and the stock sells for $10. Company B has 10 million shares outstanding, and its stock sells for $20. The total market value of A is $10 million while the total market value of B is $200 million. How should these two securities be weighted? There are basically two choices: to treat each stock's price equally or to adjust for B's larger number of shares.

A Simple Average

The first choice is a simple average of both stocks whereby the two prices are treated equally and the average price is

$$\text{Average price} = \frac{(\$10 + \$20)}{2} = \$15.$$

If the prices of the stocks rise to $18 and $22 respectively, the new average price is

$$\text{Average price} = \frac{(\$18 + \$22)}{2} = \$20.$$

In both calculations, the simple average gives equal weight to each stock and does not recognize the difference in the number of shares outstanding.

A Value-Weighted Average

An alternative means used to measure stock performance is to construct an average that allows for differences in the number of shares each company has outstanding. If the preceding numbers are used, the total value of A and B is

$$\text{Price} \times \text{Number of shares} = \text{Total value}$$

$$\$10 \times \quad 1,000,000 = \$ \ 10,000,000$$

$$\$20 \times 10,000,000 = \underline{\$200,000,000}$$

$$\$210,000,000.$$

The average value of a share of stock is

$$\text{Average price} = \frac{\$210,000,000}{(10,000,000 + 1,000,000)}$$

$$= \$19.09.$$

Average price = Total value of all shares ÷ Total number of shares

If the prices of the stocks rose to $18 and $22 respectively, the new total value of all shares is

Price × Number of shares = Total value

$$\$18 \times 1,000,000 = \quad \$ \ 18,000,000$$

$$\underline{\$22 \times 10,000,000 = \$220,000,000}$$

$$\$238,000,000.$$

The average value of a share of stock becomes

$$\text{Average price} = \frac{\$238,000,000}{(10,000,000 + 1,000,000)}$$

$$= \$21.64.$$

A Geometric Average

The third way to construct an aggregate measure of security prices is to construct a geometric average. Instead of adding the prices of the various stocks and dividing by the number of entries, a geometric average multiplies the various prices and then takes the nth root with n equal to the number of stocks. For example, if the prices of two stocks are $10 and $20, the geometric average is

$$\text{Average price} = \sqrt[2]{(\$10)(\$20)} = \$14.14.$$

If the prices of the stocks rise to $18 and $22, the new average price is

$$\text{Average price} = \sqrt[2]{(\$18)(\$22)} = \$19.90.$$

As this discussion indicates, there are several ways to view an aggregate market price. Each of these three methods produced a different average price, and when the stock prices were changed, the changes in the averages differed. In the above illustration, the simple average rose from $15 to $20 for a 33.3 percent increase, but the value-weighted average price rose from $19.09 to $21.64, which is only a 13.34 percent increase. The geometric average price rose from $14.14 to $19.90 for a 40.74 percent increase.

It is even possible for the average prices to move in opposite directions. This may be seen in the following example using three stocks whose prices and number of shares outstanding are as follows:

Stock	A	B	C
Number of shares outstanding	1,000	10,000	3,000
Price as of 1/1/x1	$10	$15	$25
Price as of 1/1/x2	18	13	25

The simple averages of their prices for the two years are

$$\frac{(\$10 + 15 + 25)}{3} = \$16.67,$$

$$\frac{(\$18 + 13 + 25)}{3} = \$18.66.$$

The value weighted averages are

$$\frac{(\$10 \times 1,000 + 15 \times 10,000 + 25 \times 3,000)}{14,000} = \$16.78,$$

$$\frac{(\$18 \times 1,000 + 13 \times 10,000 + 25 \times 3,000)}{14,000} = \$15.93.$$

The geometric averages are

$$\sqrt[3]{(\$10 \times 15 \times 25)} = \$15.54,$$

$$\sqrt[3]{(\$18 \times 13 \times 25)} = \$18.02.$$

These examples show that the average value of a share of stock differs in each case. The value of a share of stock rose from $16.67 to $18.66 according to the simple average, but when the weighted average was used, the price of a share decreased from $16.78 to $15.93. The value of a share according to the geometric average rose from $15.54 to $18.02.

The previous discussion covered the calculation of average price. Average price is generally converted into an index whose advantage is ease of comparison over time. In the example of simple average in which the initial price was $16.67, this amount could be used as the base year in which all subsequent years are compared. In the second year, the average price rose to $18.66. The new average price can then be expressed relative to the average in the initial year which is called the base year:

$$\frac{\$18.66}{\$16.67} = 1.1193.$$

1.1193 means that the current price is .1193 (1.1193 − 1) or 11.9 percent greater than the prior year's price. If the price rises to $19.56 in the next year, then the increase relative to the base year is

$$\frac{\$19.56}{\$16.67} = 1.1734.$$

Thus the price in the second year is 17.34 percent higher than in the initial year.

The Dow Jones Averages

One of the first measures of stock prices was the average developed by Charles Dow.[1] Initially the average consisted of the stock from only 11 companies, but it was later expanded to include more firms. Today this average is called the Dow Jones industrial average, and it is probably the best known and most widely quoted average of stock prices.

Dow Jones industrial average
An average of the stock prices of 30 industrial firms.

The **Dow Jones industrial average** is a simple average. It is computed by summing the prices of the stocks of 30 companies and then dividing that total by an adjusted value. The divisor is not the number of stocks (30) but a value that has been adjusted over the years so that the index is not affected by stock splits and stock dividends in excess of 10 percent. No adjustment is made for cash dividends; hence, the index declines when stocks like AT&T or Exxon go ex-div (pay a dividend) and their prices decline. (The reason a stock's price declines when the firm pays a dividend is explained in Chapter 10.)

The Dow Jones industrial average for the period from 1939 to 1992 is presented in Figure 9.1, which plots the high and low values of the average for each year. As may be seen in the graph, there was a pronounced increase in the average during the 1950s, when the annual high rose from less than 300 to almost 700. During the 1960s and 1970s, the Dow Jones industrial average (and the stock market) was erratic and certainly did not experience the steady growth achieved during the 1950s. In 1970 and in 1974 the Dow Jones industrial average even fell below the highs achieved during 1959. The 1980s, however, showed a different pattern, as stock prices soared and the Dow Jones industrial average reached new highs, only to suffer a major setback in 1987.

In addition to the industrial average, Dow Jones computes an average for transportation stocks, utility stocks, and a composite of all of the stocks included in the three separate averages. All three averages are composed of a relatively small number of companies. Thirty stocks are included in the industrial average, 20 stocks compose the transportation average, and 15 stocks make up the utilities average. The firms included are among the largest (in terms of sales and total assets) and best known in the nation, as may be seen in Exhibit 9.1. Many firms that have grown into prominence since World War II (e.g., Xerox and Johnson & Johnson), however, are excluded from these averages.

This small number of firms is one source of criticism of the Dow Jones averages. It is argued that the small sample is not indicative of the market as a whole. For this reason, other measures of stock prices that have broader bases, such as the NYSE index or Standard & Poor's 500 stock index, may be better indicators of the general market's performance.

Other Indices of Stock Prices

Standard & Poor's 500 stock index
A value-weighted index of 500 stocks.

Unlike the Dow Jones industrial average, **Standard & Poor's 500 stock index** is a value-weighted index. The base year, 1943, is the time at which the index was 10. Thus, if the index is currently 100, the value of these stocks is ten times their value

---

[1] In 1882 Edward Jones joined Charles Dow to form a partnership that grew into Dow, Jones and Company.

Figure 9.1   ✦   ANNUAL PRICE RANGE OF THE DOW JONES INDUSTRIAL AVERAGE, 1939–1992

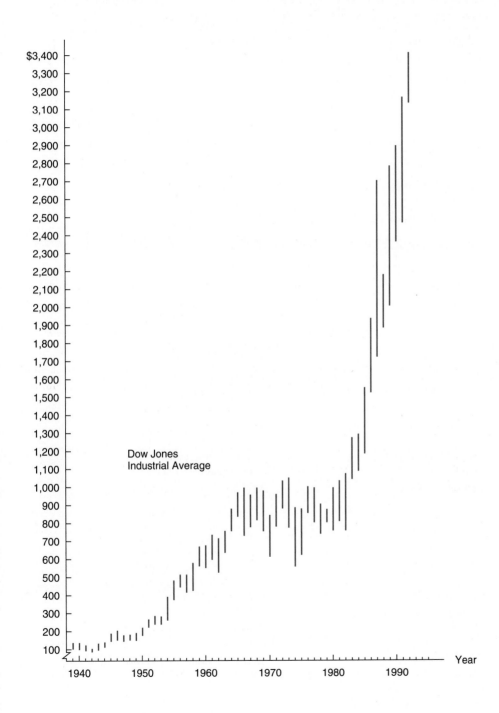

Exhibit 9.1 ✦ STOCKS INCLUDED IN THE DOW JONES AVERAGES

The Dow Jones Industrial Stocks

Allied-Signal	Goodyear
Aluminum Co. of America (Alcoa)	IBM
American Express	International Paper
AT&T	McDonalds
Bethlehem Steel	Merck
Boeing	Minnesota Mining and Manufacturing
Caterpillar	J. P. Morgan & Co.
Chevron Corp.	Philip Morris
Coca Cola	Procter & Gamble
Walt Disney	Sears, Roebuck & Co.
DuPont	Texaco
Eastman Kodak	Union Carbide
Exxon	United Technologies
General Electric	Westinghouse Electric
General Motors	Woolworth

The Dow Jones Transportation Stocks

Airborne Freight	Federal Express
Alaska Air	Norfolk Sourthern Corp.
AMR Corp. (American Airlines)	Roadway Services
American President	Ryder Systems
Burlington Northern	Santa Fe Southern Pacific
Carolina Freight Carriers	Southwest Air
Consolidated Freight	UAL Inc. (United Airlines)
Consolidated Rail	Union Pacific Corp.
CSX Corp.	USAir Group
Delta Air Lines	XTRA Corp.

The Dow Jones Public Utility Stocks

American Electric Power	Niagara Mohawk Power
Arkla	Pacific Gas & Electric
Centerior Energy	Panhandle Eastern
Commonwealth Edison	Peoples Energy
Consolidated Edison	Philadelphia Electric
Consolidated Natural Gas	Public Service Enterprise Group
Detroit Edison	Southern California Edison (SCE Corp.)
Houston Industries	

Source: The Wall Street Journal.

in 1943. Standard & Poor's also computes an index of 400 industrial stocks and indices of 20 transportation, 40 utility, and 40 financial companies.

There is also the **New York Stock Exchange composite index,** which includes all common stocks listed on the NYSE. Like Standard & Poor's averages, the NYSE index is a value-weighted index with a base of 50 as of December 31, 1965. Value Line computes another index of more than 1,700 stocks that includes stocks traded on the New York Stock Exchange, on the American Stock Exchange, and over the counter. Unlike the Dow Jones industrial average, which is a simple average, and the S&P 500, which is a value-weighted average, the Value Line index is a geometric average.

NYSE composite index
New York Stock Exchange index; an index of prices of all the stocks listed on the New York Stock Exchange.

The Wilshire 5000 stock index is the broadest-based aggregate measure of stock prices. It is constructed using all stocks traded on the New York and American stock exchanges plus the actively traded over-the-counter stocks. Other stock indices include those limited to AMEX and OTC stocks. The American Stock Exchange index is a value-weighted index that encompasses all of the common stocks on that exchange. The National Association of Security Dealers Automatic Quotation System (NASDAQ) index of over-the-counter stocks covers more than 2,000 issues. The National Association of Security Dealers also publishes nonindustrial OTC indices for banking and insurance.

Besides aggregate measures of U.S. stock markets, there are measures of foreign stock markets. The Nikkei 225 stock average, the Financial Times–Stock Exchange 100 index, and the TSE 300 composite index measure, respectively, aggregate performance of the Tokyo, London, and Toronto stock exchanges. (How these foreign markets have performed relative to the U.S. stock market is considered in Chapter 24.)

In addition to indices of stock prices, there are also aggregate measures of the bond market. These averages may be expressed in terms of yields, such as the yields used to construct Figures 14.3, 15.4, and 17.1. In addition there are the Dow Jones bond averages, one of which is the Dow Jones composite corporate bond average, consisting of ten public utility and ten industrial bonds. (See Exhibit 9.2 for the specific bonds included in the average.) The average is expressed as a percentage of the debt's face amount or principal. When the composite of the 20 bonds was 103.49 on January 16, 1993, the average price of the 20 bonds was $1034.90.

Price Fluctuations

The fluctuations in stock prices are illustrated in Figure 9.2, which plots the Dow Jones industrial average, Standard & Poor's 500 stock index, and the NYSE index from January 1973 to October 1992. All three aggregate measures document the decline in stock prices that started in January 1973. In two years, the Dow Jones industrial average fell from above 1000 to just above 600, which is a 40 percent decline. Standard & Poor's 500 stock index fell from 117 to under 70 (a 40 percent decline), and the NYSE index declined from 68 to 35, representing a 49 percent fall in prices.

All three measures also show the large increase in stock prices that occurred during the mid-1980s. From 1985 to the fall of 1987, the Dow Jones industrials, the Standard & Poor's 500, and the NYSE composite consistently rose. However, in October 1987, stock prices declined dramatically and by the end of 1987 were back

Exhibit 9.2 ✦ Bonds Included in the Dow Jones 20-Bond Average

Ten Public Utilities

Company	Coupon	Maturity Date
Alabama Power	9¾%	2004
AT&T	8.80	2005
Commonwealth Edison	8¾	2005
Consolidated Edison	7.9	2001
Consumers Power	9¾	2006
Detroit Edison	9.00	1999
Michigan Bell	7.00	2012
Pacific Gas & Electric	7¾	2005
Philadelphia Electric	7⅜	2001
Public Service of Indiana	9.60	2005

Ten Industrials

Company	Coupon	Maturity Date
Bank America	7⅞	2003
Bethlehem Steel	6⅞	1999
Eastman Kodak	8⅝	2016
Exxon	6.00	1997
General Electric	8½	2004
General Motors Acceptance Corp.	12	2005
IBM	9⅜	2004
Pfizer	9½	2000
Socony	4⅛	1993

Source: Sumner N. Levine, ed., *Business One Irwin Business and Investment Almanac,* 1992 ed., 412.

to approximately the same levels they were at the beginning of the year. By 1990, stock prices had climbed back to and even exceeded the highs reached prior to the debacle experienced during October 1987.

Figure 9.2 indicates, as would be expected, that all three measures of stock prices move together. The amount of movement, however, differs. For example, from 1973 to 1975, the percentage decline in the Dow Jones industrial average was about 40 percent, but the NYSE index declined by almost 50 percent. From January 1986 to January 1989, the Dow Jones industrials rose by 39 percent, but the S & P 500 and the NYSE composite rose only 34 and 31 percent, respectively. Such differences between the Dow Jones industrials and other measures of the market give some credibility to the argument that the Dow Jones industrial average is not typical of the market as a whole.

Figure 9.3 illustrates fluctuations in bond prices and presents the Dow Jones 20-bond composite average and the yields on Moody's Aaa-rated bonds from January 1978 through 1991. The figure vividly illustrates an inverse relationship between bond prices and yields. For example, the bond average fell from 85.4 to 55.4 between January 1979 and September 1981, when interest rates on the Aaa-rated bonds rose from 9.3 to over 15 percent. However, from May 1984 to early 1987,

Figure 9.2 ✦ AGGREGATE MEASURES OF STOCK PRICES, 1973–1992

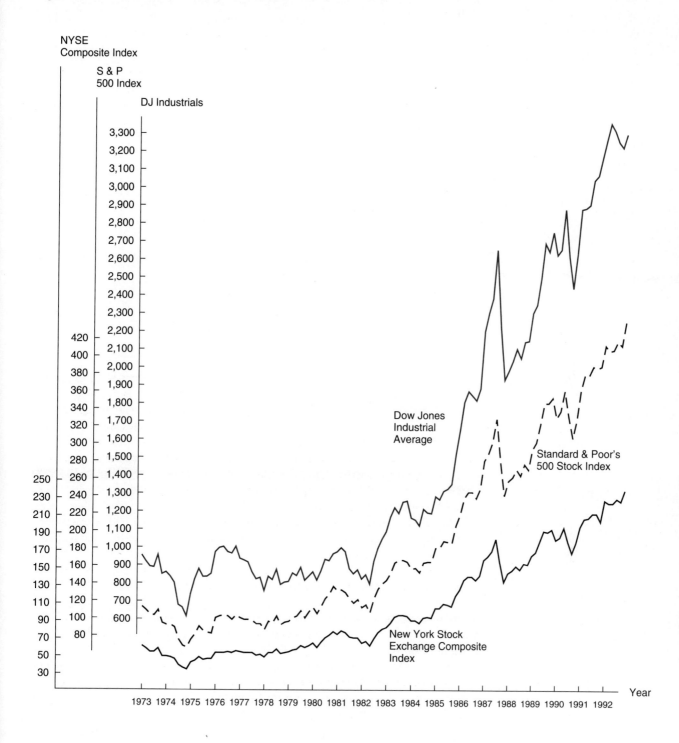

Figure 9.3 ✦ Dow Jones Bond Average and Yields on Moody's Aaa-Rated Bonds, 1977–1991

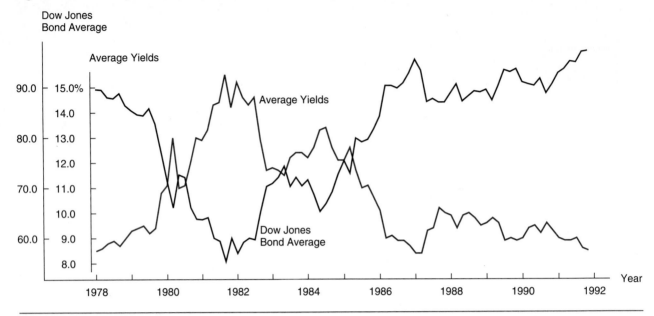

the prices of bonds rose as interest rates fell. (This negative relationship is explained in detail in Chapter 15.)

The relationship between bond and stock prices may be seen by comparing Figures 9.2 and 9.3. This is done in Figure 9.4, which combines the Dow Jones industrial average and the Dow Jones composite bond average. As shown by the graph, falling interest rates tend to coincide with rising stock prices (e.g., 1990–1991), and rising interest rates (falling bond prices) coincide with declining stock prices (e.g., mid-1987). Figure 9.4 also illustrates that over time stock values may grow, but bond prices are limited to fluctuations around their principal value. From 1978 to 1992, the Dow Jones industrial average rose from about 800 to over 3300, but the bond average stood at about 103, only slightly higher than the 89.6 in 1978.

Security Prices and Investors' Purchasing Power

Another means to measure security price performance is to compare one of the measures of the market with a general price index. This gives an indication of the losses inflicted on the investing public by inflation. If the general price index rises more rapidly than the index of security prices, the implication is that stock holders suffer a loss of purchasing power.[2] This loss occurs even if stock prices rise if the increase is at a slower rate than consumer prices.

---

[2] This loss is before considering dividend income that may offset the loss of purchasing power.

Figure 9.4 ◆ DOW JONES INDUSTRIAL AVERAGE AND DOW JONES BOND AVERAGE, 1978–1992

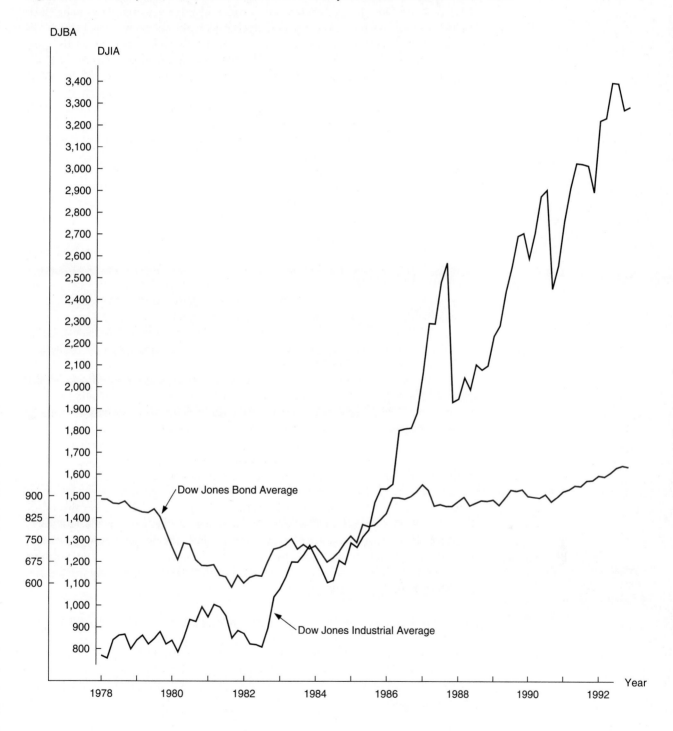

The loss of purchasing power is illustrated in Figure 9.5, which is divided into three panels. The first plots the Dow Jones industrial average from 1970 through 1991 and the Dow Jones deflated (i.e., expressed relative to the Consumer Price Index). As may be seen in this panel, stock prices did not grow during the 1970s but a different pattern emerged during the 1980s. The figure also shows the purchasing power of stocks declined from 1970 to 1981 and then started to rise. However, at the end of 1991, the purchasing power of the Dow Jones was approximately the same as at the beginning of the period, because from 1970 through 1991, the Consumer Price Index rose annually at 6.61 percent while the Dow rose at 6.54 percent. Of course, investors who purchased these stocks earned a higher return through the receipt of dividends, but the purchasing power of the value of the stocks was virtually unchanged at the end of 20 years.

The second panel presents the annual percentage change in the Dow and the Consumer Price Index. While the CPI fluctuates from year to year, the amount of fluctuation is perceptibly smaller than for stock prices. Furthermore, the CPI never declines (i.e., all the annual changes are positive) while stocks can, and do, suffer years of large, negative change.

The third panel presents the real change in annual stock prices. In some years stock prices rose more than the rate of inflation (e.g., 1991), so that investors experienced a positive real return. There were years in which stock prices fell while consumer prices continued to rise (e.g., 1984), and there were years in which stock prices increased, but not at the level that consumer prices increased. For example, during 1979 and 1980, stock prices rose but inflation exceeded the stocks' price increase, so that investors experienced negative real returns even though they earned positive returns on the securities.

Figure 9.5 also suggests that inflation is detrimental to stock prices. Once inflation started to diminish, common stock prices began to rise. While inflation did not cease in the 1980s, the rate was perceptibly smaller and stock prices rose dramatically after 1984, reaching new highs virtually every year.

Rates of Return on Investments in Common Stock

holding period return
Total return (income plus price appreciation during a specified time period) divided by the cost of the investment.

What returns have been earned on investments in securities? To answer this question, the investor should consider the purchase price of the security, the sale price, the flow of income such as dividends or interest, and how long the investor owned the asset. The easiest (and perhaps the most misleading) return is the **holding period return (HPR).** It is derived by dividing the profit (or loss) plus any income by the price paid for the asset. That is

$$\text{HPR} = \frac{P_1 + D - P_0}{P_0} \tag{9.1}$$

in which P_1 is the sale price, D is the income, and P_0 is the purchase price. If an investor buys a stock for $40, collects dividends of $2, and sells the stock for $50, the holding period return is

$$\text{HPR} = \frac{\$50 + 2 - 40}{\$40} = 30\%.$$

Figure 9.5 ✦ PURCHASING POWER OF DOW JONES INDUSTRIAL AVERAGE, 1970–1991

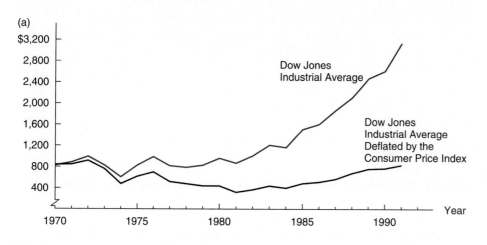

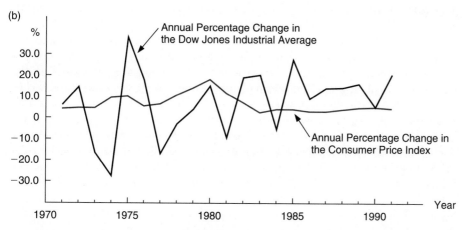

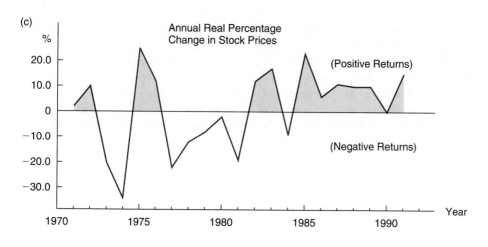

The holding period has a major weakness because it fails to consider how long it took to earn the return. This problem is immediately apparent if the information in the previous example had been a stock that cost $40, that paid annual dividends of $1, and that was sold at the end of the *second* year for $50. Given this information, what is the return? While the holding period return remains the same, 30 percent is obviously higher than the true annual return. If the time period is greater than a year, the holding period return overstates the true, annualized rate of return. (Conversely, for a period that is less than a year, the holding period return understates the true, annual rate of return.)

Since the holding period return is easy to compute, it is frequently used, producing misleading results. Consider the following example. An investor buys a stock for $10 per share and sells it after ten years for $20. What is the holding period return on the investment? This simple question can produce several misleading answers. The individual may respond by answering "I doubled my money!" or "I made 100 percent!" That certainly sounds impressive, but it completely disregards the *length of time* needed to double the individual's money. The investor may assert that he or she made 10 percent annually (100% ÷ 10 years). This figure is less impressive than the claim that the return is 100 percent, but it is also misleading because it fails to consider compounding. Some of the return earned during the first year in turn earned a return in subsequent years, which was not taken into consideration when the investor averaged the return over the ten years.

rate of return
The discount rate that equates the cost of an investment with the cash flows generated by the investment.

The correct way to determine what **rate of return** was earned is to phrase the question as follows: "At what rate does $10 grow to $20 after ten years?" The student should recognize this as another example of the time value of money. The equation used to answer this question is

$$P_0(1 + r)^n = P_n,$$

where P_0 is the cost of the security, r is the rate of return per period, n is the number of periods (e.g., years), and P_n is the price at which the security is sold. When the proper values are substituted, the equation becomes

$$\$10(1 + r)^{10} = \$20,$$

which asks at what rate $10 will grow for ten years to become $20. To answer this question, the student solves the equation to determine the interest factor.

$$(1 + r)^{10} = \$20 \div \$10 = 2.$$

Thus, 2 is the interest factor for the future value of $1 for ten years. If the student locates this factor in the compound value of a dollar table (Appendix A), he or she will find that the value of r is approximately 7 percent.

The use of the table for the compound value of a $1 leads only to an approximate answer. If the investor desires a more accurate answer, the appropriate root must be found. That is

$$\$10(1 + r)^{10} = \$20.00,$$
$$(1 + r)^{10} = 2,$$
$$r = \sqrt[10]{2} - 1 = 1.0708 - 1 = 7.08\%,$$

so the annual rate of return is 7.08 percent, which is a more accurate statement than "approximately 7 percent." However, either the use of the time-value table or the above procedure indicates that the correct rate of return on the investment (excluding any dividend income) is considerably less impressive than "I doubled my money!" or "I average 10 percent each year."

If the individual does not have access to interest tables or does not want to go through the procedure of taking the nth root, he or she may be tempted to determine the percentage return for each year. For example, if the price of the stock were to rise from $20 to $22, the annual return would be 10 percent ($2 ÷ $20). If the stock were to fall in price from $20 to $15, the annual rate of return would be −25 percent (−$5 ÷ $20).

There is nothing wrong with this technique until the investor averages the resulting annual percentage changes. Like the average of the ten-year total return, this procedure can be misleading. Consider the following example. An investor buys a stock for $20. At the end of the year it is selling for $25, but the investor holds the stock for a second year and then sells it at cost (i.e., $20). What is the rate of return? Obviously the investor earned nothing and the rate of return should indicate this fact.

If, however, the investor computes the annual rate of return each year, and then averages these annual rates, the investment will have a positive rate of return. In the first year the stock's price rose from $20 to $25, indicating a 25 percent gain ($5 ÷ $20). During the second year the stock declined from $25 to $20, for a 20 percent loss (−$5 ÷ $25). What is the average rate of return? The answer is

$$25\% - 20\% = 5\%$$
$$\frac{5\%}{2} = 2.5\% = \text{Average return.}$$

Owing to the magic of numbers, the investor has earned a 2.5 percent average return, even though the investment produced neither a gain nor a loss. This example illustrates how averaging positive and negative numbers can provide misleading results.

The correct method to determine the annual rate of return is to use a geometric average. In the first year, the stock rose from $20 to $25 (or $25 ÷ $20 = 1.25). In the second year, the stock declined from $25 to $20 (or $20 ÷ $25 = 0.8). The geometric average is

$$\sqrt[2]{(1.25)(0.80)} = 1.00,$$

so the average return is 1.00% − 1.00 = 0.0%.

Geometric averages are often used to obtain rates of return over a period of years. Suppose the annual rates of return are as follows:

Year	Rate of Return
1	25%
2	3
3	−18
4	−10
5	15

The geometric average return is

$$\sqrt[5]{(1.25)(1.03)(0.82)(0.90)(1.15)} - 1 = 0.0179\%.$$

This annual return is lower than the arithmetic return of 3 percent which would be obtained by adding each of the returns and dividing by 5. As in the previous example, the averaging of positive and negative annual return (i.e., the computation of an arithmetic average) overstates the true return.

The inclusion of income makes the calculation of a rate of return perceptibly more difficult. Consider the example that started this section in which the investor bought a stock for $40, collected $2 in dividends for two years, and then sold the stock for $50. What is the rate of return? The holding period return is overstated because it fails to consider the time value of money. If the investor computes the rate of growth and only considers the original cost and the terminal value, the rate of return is understated because the dividend payments are excluded.

internal rate of return

Percentage return that equates the present value of an investment's cash inflows with its cost.

These problems are avoided by computing an investment's **internal rate of return,** an approach that determines the rate that equates the present value of all a future investment's cash inflows with the present cost of the investment. An example of an internal rate of return is the yield to maturity on a bond discussed in Chapter 15. Since the yield to maturity equates the present value of the cash inflows (the interest and principal repayment) with the present cost of the investment, it is the true, annualized rate of return.

The general equation for the internal rate of return (r) for a stock is

$$P_0 = \frac{D_1}{(1+r)} + \cdots + \frac{D_n}{(1+r)^n} + \frac{P_n}{(1+r)^{n}}, \tag{9.2}$$

in which D is the annual dividend received in n years, and P is the price received for the stock in the nth year.[3]

---

[3] The same equation will be used to determine the yield to maturity in Chapter 15. The yield to maturity is, in effect, the internal rate of return on an investment in a bond that is purchased today and redeemed at maturity.

If the internal rate of return were computed for the previous illustration of a stock that cost $40, paid an annual dividend of $1, and was sold at the end of the second year for $50, the equation to be solved is

$$\$40 = \frac{\$1}{(1 + r)} + \frac{\$1}{(1 + r)^2} + \frac{\$50}{(1 + r)^2}.$$

Notice that there are three cash inflows: the dividend received each year and the sale price. The internal rate of return equates *all* cash inflows to the investor with the cost of the investment. These cash inflows include periodic payments as well as the sale price. (The calculation for the holding period return combined the dividend plus the capital gain on the investment and treated them as occurring at the end as a single cash inflow.)

Solving this equation is very tedious, especially if there is a large number of years. Select a rate (e.g., 12 percent) and substitute it into the equation. If the results equate both sides of the equation, the internal rate of return has been determined. If the sides are not equal, select another rate and repeat the process. For example if 12 percent is selected, then

$40 = $1 × (interest factor for the present value of an annuity at 12 percent for two years) + $50 × (interest factor for the present value of 12 percent for two years)

= $1(1.690) + $50(.797) = $41.54.

Since the two sides are not equal, 12 percent is not the internal rate of return. Since $41.54 exceeds $40, the rate is too small, so a greater rate would be selected and the process repeated. Obviously this is a tedious procedure that is made considerably easier with a preprogrammed electronic calculator or computer. When the data for this illustration are entered into such a program, the internal rate of return on the investment of 14.17 percent is readily determined. This 14.17 percent is the true, annualized rate of return on the investment.

The internal rate of return has two potential problems. The first concerns the reinvestment of cash inflows received by the investor. The internal rate of return assumes that cash inflows are reinvested at the investment's internal rate. In the above illustration that means the $1 received in the first year is reinvested at 14.17 percent. If the dividend payment is reinvested at a lower rate, the true return on the investment will be less than the rate determined by the equation. Conversely, if the investor earns more than 14.17 percent when the $1 is reinvested, the true return on the investment will exceed the internal rate of return determined by the equation.

The second problem occurs when the investor makes more than one purchase of the security. While the problem is not insurmountable, it makes the calculation more difficult. Suppose the investor buys one share for $40 at the beginning of the first year, buys a second share for $42 at the end of the first year, and sells both shares at the end of the second year for $50 each. The firm pays an annual dividend of $1, so $1 is collected at the end of year 1 and $2 at the end of year 2. What is the rate of return on the investment?

To answer this question using the internal rate of return, the investor must equate the present value of the cash inflows and the cash outflows. The cash flows are as follows:

Time	Year 0	End of Year 1	End of Year 2
Cash outflow	$40	$42	
Cash inflow		$ 1	$2 + $100

There are two cash outflows (the purchases of $40 and $42) that occur in the present (year 0) and at the end of year 1. There are two cash inflows, the $1 dividend received at the end of year 1 and the $2 dividend at the end of year 2 plus the receipts from the sale of the shares ($100) at the end of year 2. The equation for the internal rate of return is

$$\$40 + \frac{42}{(1 + r)} = \frac{\$1}{(1 + r)} + \frac{2 + 100}{(1 + r)^2}$$

and the rate of return is 16.46 percent.

In this example, the investor owns one share during the first year and two shares during the second year. The return in the second year has more impact on the overall return than the rate earned during the first year when the investor owned only one share. Since the number of shares and hence the amount invested differs each year, this approach to determining rates of return is sometimes referred to as a "dollar-weighted rate of return."

An alternative to the dollar-weighted rate of return or internal rate of return is the "time-weighted return," which ignores the amount of funds' invested during each time period. This technique computes the return for each period and averages the results. In the above illustration, the initial price was $40; the investor collected $1 in dividends, and had stock worth $42 at the end of the year. The return for the first year was

$$(\$42 + 1 - 40) \div \$40 = 7.5\%.$$

During the second year, a share rose from $42 to $50 and paid a $1 dividend. The return was

$$(\$50 + 1 - 42) \div 42 = 21.43\%.$$

The simple average return is

$$(7.5\% + 21.43) \div 2 = 14.47\%,$$

and the geometric average return is

$$\sqrt{(1.075)(1.2143)} - 1 = \sqrt{1.3054} - 1 = 1.1425 - 1 = 14.25\%.$$

As discussed above, the geometric average is the compound rate while the simple average is only a simple rate and tends to overstate the true, annual rate of return.

In this illustraton, the dollar-weighted return (i.e, the internal rate of return) is higher than the time-weighted return. This is the result of the stock performing better in the second year when the investor owned more shares. The results would have been reversed if the stock had performed better the first year than during the second year (i.e., 21.4 percent in year 1 and 7.5 percent in year 2). In that case, the larger amount invested would have earned the smaller return, so the dollar-weighted return would have been less than the time-weighted return.

Which of the two methods, the dollar-weighted return or the time-weighted return, is preferred? There is no absolute right answer. Since the investor is concerned with the return earned on *all* the dollars invested, the dollar-weighted return would appear to be superior. However, there is an argument for the use of a time-weighted return to evaluate the performance of a portfolio manager. For example, a firm may make periodic contributions to its employee pension plan. Because the timing and amount of the cash inflows are beyond the pension plan manager's control, the use of a dollar-weighted return is inappropriate. Thus, money managers often use a time-weighted return instead of a dollar-weighted return to evaluate portfolio performance.

Rates of Return and Graphic Illustrations

The investor who reads certain financial publications, such as the *Media General Financial Weekly* or the *Value Line Investment Survey,* will find charts constructed on semilogarithmic paper. This type of graph is used because it gives a truer picture of the *change* in the price of the stock.

This fact may be illustrated by the following monthly range of stock prices and percentage increases:

Month	Price of Stock	Percentage Change in Monthly Highs
January	$10–5	. . .
February	15–10	50
March	20–15	33
April	25–20	25

Even though the monthly price increases are equal ($5), the percentage increments decline. The investor who bought the stock at $10 and sold it for $15 made $5 and earned a return of 50 percent. The investor who bought it at $20 and sold for $25 also made $5, but the return was only 25 percent.

These monthly prices may be plotted on graph paper that uses absolute dollar units for the vertical axis. This is done on the left-hand side of Figure 9.6. Such a graph gives the appearance that equal price movements yield equal returns. However, this is not so, as the preceding illustration demonstrates.

To avoid this problem, **semilogarithmic paper** can be used (see Figure 9.6). The prices are plotted on the right-hand side, and equal units on the vertical axis are in terms of percentage change. Thus, a price movement from $10 to $15 appears to be a greater price movement than one from $20 to $25, because in percentage terms it *is* greater.

The impact of using semilog paper may be seen by comparing Figures 9.1 and 9.7. Both present the annual price range of the Dow Jones industrial average. Figure 9.1 uses an absolute scale while Figure 9.7 employs a semilogarithmic scale. The general shape is the same in both cases, but the large absolute increase in the Dow Jones industrial average from 1980 through 1992 is considerably less impressive in

semilogarithmic paper
Graph paper on which one axis is expressed in logarithms.

Figure 9.6 ✦ USE OF SEMILOGARITHMIC PAPER TO ILLUSTRATE STOCK PRICE
MOVEMENTS

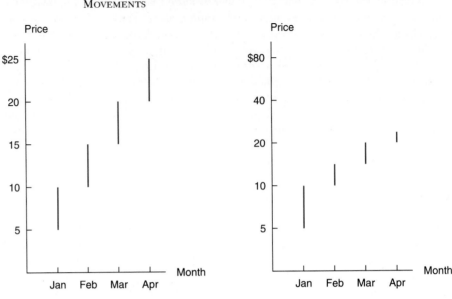

Figure 9.7, which expresses the increase in percentage of change instead of absolute numbers. Since absolute price changes are reduced to percentage price changes, graphs such as Figure 9.7 are better indicators of rates of return.

Studies of Investment Returns

Several studies have been conducted by academicians on the returns earned by investments in common stocks; hence, these reports should not contain any bias. Unfortunately, research done by brokerage firms, investment advisory services, or the trust departments of commercial banks may involve a conflict of interest. Although the results may seem valid, one may still be hesitant to accept them as honest appraisals of the returns earned by investors.

An early study on the rates of return earned by investments in common stocks was done by Fisher and Lorie. They studied the annual rates of return from investments in all common stocks listed on the NYSE from 1926 through 1965 and found that the annual rate of return was 9.3 percent.[4] (The student should remember that an annual return of 9.3 percent means $1,000 will grow to more than $2,000 in eight years.[5]) The rates of return were even higher during the 1950s and early 1960s when the country and the stock market experienced prosperity and rapid growth. During this time the annual rates of return on stocks averaged as high as 15 percent.

---

[4] Lawrence Fisher and James H. Lorie, "Rates of Return on Investments in Common Stock—The Year-by-Year Record, 1926–1965," *Journal of Business* 40 (July 1968): 1–26.

[5] $1,000 (1 + 0.093)^8 = $2,036.86.

Figure 9.7 ✦ ANNUAL PRICE RANGE OF THE DOW JONES INDUSTRIAL AVERAGE, 1939–1992

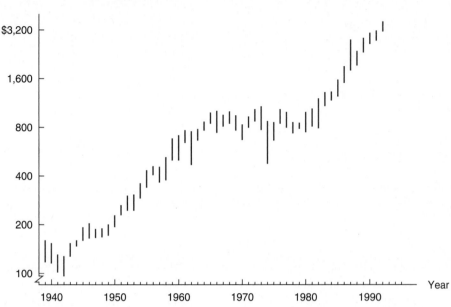

These results are impressive, but the student should remember that although this study encompassed all of the common stocks listed on the big board, no investor could have duplicated these results. The individual investor owns a portfolio of selected securities and not all stocks. Thus, an aggregate measure of the rate of return does not necessarily apply to a particular individual's portfolio. In fact, one study found that securities selected by individual investors (i.e., nonprofessional money managers) tended to outperform the market (before considering transaction costs).[6]

Studies of the stock market by Holmes and by Brigham and Pappas corroborated the results of Fisher and Lorie.[7] Holmes's study covered the period between 1871 and 1971. The annual rate of return earned for the 100-year period was 7.8 percent. For the years that overlapped with Fisher and Lorie's study, the rate of return was 9.7 percent. This small difference (9.7 versus 9.3 percent) could be attributed to commission costs. Fisher and Lorie included a commission cost for stock purchases, while Holmes's study did not. Hence, one would expect Fisher and Lorie's rates of return to be less.

---

[6] See Gary G. Schlarbaum, Wilbur G. Lewellen, and Ronald C. Lease, "Realized Returns on Common Stock Investments: The Experience of Individual Investors," *Journal of Business* 51 (April 1978): 299–325.

[7] See John Russell Holmes, "100 Years of Common Stock Investing," *Financial Analysts Journal* 30 (November–December 1974): 38–45, and Eugene F. Brigham and James L. Pappas, "Rates of Return on Common Stock," *Journal of Business* 42 (July 1969): 302–316.

Exhibit 9.3 ✦ ANNUAL RATES OF RETURN, 1926–1990, ESTIMATED BY IBBOTSON AND SINQUEFIELD

Security	Annual Rate of Return	Standard Deviation of Return
Common stocks	10.1%	±20.8%
Small stocks	11.6	35.4
Long-term corporate bonds	5.2	8.4
Long-term government bonds	4.5	8.5
Treasury bills	3.7	3.4
Rate of inflation	3.1	4.7

Source: Roger Ibbotson and Rex Sinquefield, *Stocks, Bonds, Bills, and Inflation* (Charlottesville, Va.: Financial Analysts Research Foundation). Updated annually in the SBBI Yearbook.

Brigham and Pappas's study covered the period from 1946 to 1965. They concluded that the annual rate of return was about 15 percent. Although this figure is considerably higher than the overall returns in Fisher and Lorie's and in Holmes's studies, it is similar to their returns for the comparable time period.

Ibbotson and Sinquefield initially extended the results of previous studies to 1981.[8] Their study was more comprehensive than the previous studies in that it considered not only stocks but also corporate bonds, federal government bonds and bills, and the rate of inflation. Since 1981, Ibbotson and Sinquefield annually update their results, and this work is generally considered to be the most definitive study of rates of return on alternative investments. A summary of their results is presented in Exhibit 9.3. As may be seen in the exhibit, the annual rate of return for common stocks as measured by the Standard & Poor's 500 common stock index was 10.1%. If only smaller stocks are considered, the annual rate of return rose to 11.6 percent. Ibbotson and Sinquefield defined small stocks as the lowest one-fifth of New York Stock Exchange firms with the lowest total value (i.e., price times number of shares outstanding).

Exhibit 9.3 includes the annual rates of return earned by long-term corporate debt, federal government bonds, and treasury bills. In addition, the exhibit includes the standard deviation of each rate of return, which indicates the associated risk. As would be expected, the risk is largest for the small stocks. While their annual return was 11.6 percent, the standard deviation was ±35.4 percent, which means that in 68 percent of the years the annual return ranged from +47.0 percent to −23.8 percent. This is a very large range in returns when compared to that of treasury bills, which had a standard deviation of ±3.4 percent. Obviously if the investor limited the portfolio to riskier securities and were forced to sell the stocks, the investor could sustain a large loss if the sale occurred during a declining market. Conversely, over a period of years, the riskier stocks produced a higher return.

---

[8] Roger Ibbotson and Rex Sinquefield, *Stocks, Bonds, Bills, and Inflation: The Past and the Future* (Charlottesville, Va.: Financial Analysts Research Foundation, 1982).

The higher return does not imply that investments in the small stocks outperformed the market. The material in Chapter 7 on the measurement of risk suggested that additional risk requires a higher return. If the actual return exceeds this higher required return, then the investment truly was superior and outperformed the market. However, a higher return by itself is not sufficient evidence to indicate superior performance.

Exhibit 9.3 also gives the annual rate of inflation, and it is interesting to note that the rate earned on treasury bills slightly exceeded the rate of inflation. This suggests that the investor who is concerned with maintaining purchasing power can meet this goal (at least before federal income taxes are considered) by acquiring treasury bills. The exhibit suggests that over time, the yield on stocks tends to be approximately 6 percent above the rate on treasury securities. This information may be important when trying to establish a return necessary to justify purchasing equities. For example, if the current yield on treasury bills is 4.5 percent, that suggests a return of 10.5 percent may be necessary to justify purchasing common stock.

The investor may ask whether securities traded in a particular market, such as the over-the-counter market or the American Stock Exchange, outperform the securities traded on the New York Stock Exchange. Such a conclusion seems to be indicated by Figure 9.8, which plots the NASDAQ index, the American Stock Exchange index, and the Standard & Poor's 500 stock index. Over the time period, both the NASDAQ and the AMEX indices rose more than the S & P 500 index. This conclusion, however, is not corroborated by a study by Jessup and Upson, who computed returns for OTC stocks. While their study covered an earlier time period (1946–1970), they found that over extended periods of time (five years) the returns were similar for listed and OTC stocks.[9]

These results suggest that OTC stocks may be inferior investments. Since the rates of return on listed stocks and OTC stocks are similar, these investments should involve equal risk. However, the study also found that the OTC stocks are more volatile, and because their prices tend to fluctuate more, these stocks are riskier. Presumably, if an investment involves greater risk, it should offer a higher return. If it does not, the investment is inferior, because, given a choice of two portfolios with the same rate of return, the investor will always prefer the portfolio with less risk. For this reason, Jessup and Upson concluded that investments in OTC stocks have resulted in inferior risk-adjusted returns.

The Reinvestment Assumption

Before jumping to conclusions as to what an investor in the stock market will earn, the student should realize that studies of investment returns are aggregates and that historical returns may not be indicators of future returns. In addition, studies of investment returns make a crucial assumption that dividends and interest are reinvested (i.e., the flow of income is compounded). For most individuals that assumption does not apply. Income taxes must be paid out of the interest and dividend income, and many individuals spend the income their securities generate. (One of the advantages offered by mutual funds and corporate dividend reinvestment plans

---

[9]Paul F. Jessup and Roger B. Upson, *Returns in Over-the-Counter Stock Markets* (Minneapolis, Minn.: University of Minnesota Press, 1973).

Figure 9.8 ✦ NASDAQ, AMEX, AND S & P 500 STOCK INDICES, 1975–1992

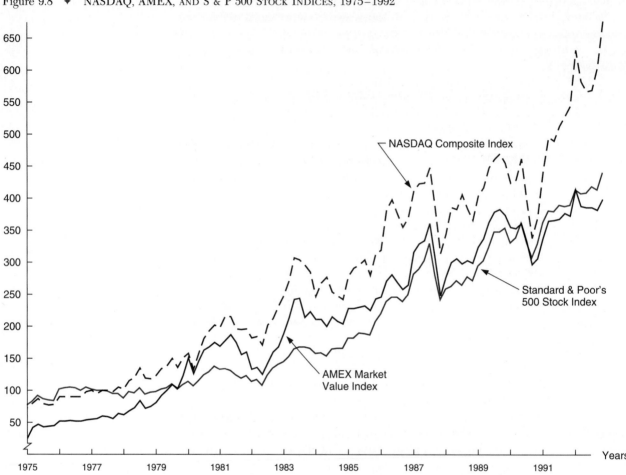

is that the income is reinvested so the individual obtains the benefits associated with compounding.) However, all is not lost. Suppose the individual consumes 5 percent of his or her wealth each year. In that case a portfolio averaging an annual return of 9 percent will more than cover the consumption, and the investor's wealth will grow. Of course, if the individual consumes more than the portfolio earns, the investor's wealth will decline.

At best historical returns may be taken as a starting point in the valuation of stock. They may help determine if an individual stock is over- or undervalued. However, the individual must remember that not all stocks meet specific investment goals. For example, individuals who are in need of income should select securities whose return consists primarily of dividends or interest. Other investors may desire capital appreciation and therefore should choose stocks whose price is expected to increase. A randomly selected portfolio would not meet either of these specific goals. Thus, investors with different needs would still have to make investment decisions in order to construct portfolios that meet their financial goals.

REDUCING THE IMPACT OF PRICE FLUCTUATIONS: AVERAGING

One strategy for accumulating shares and reducing the impact of security price fluctuations is to "average" the position. By buying shares at different times, the investor accumulates the shares at different prices. Such a policy may be achieved through the dividend reinvestment plans that are discussed in Chapter 10. An alternative is for the investor to systematically purchase shares of stock through a broker. There are two basic methods for achieving this averaging: the periodic purchase of shares and the purchase of additional shares if the stock's price falls.

Periodic Purchases

Under the periodic purchase plan, the investor decides to buy additional shares of a stock at regular intervals. For example, the investor may elect to buy $2,000 worth of a stock every quarter or every month. This purchase is made at the appropriate interval, no matter what the price of the stock is. Since the dollar amount is the same, this technique is referred to as **dollar cost averaging.**

The effect of such a program is illustrated in Exhibit 9.4, which shows the number of shares of EMEC stock purchased at various prices when $2,000 is invested each quarter. The first column gives the dates of purchase, and the second column presents the various prices of the stock; the third and fourth columns list the number of shares purchased and the total number of shares held in the position. The last column presents the average price of the stock held in the position. The student should notice that when the price of the stock rises, $2,000 buys fewer shares. For example, at $33 per share, $2,000 buys only 60 shares, but at $18 per share the investor receives 111 shares. Because more shares are acquired when the price of the stock falls, this has the effect of pulling down the average cost of a share. In this example, after two years the average cost of the stock had fallen to $23.85 and the investor had accumulated 671 shares. If the price of the stock subsequently rises, the investor will earn more profits on the lower-priced shares and thus will increase the return on the entire position.

dollar cost averaging
The purchase of securities at different intervals to reduce the impact of price fluctuations.

Averaging Down

Some investors find it difficult to purchase stock periodically, especially if the price of the stock has increased. Instead, they prefer to purchase additional shares of the stock only if the price declines. Such investors are following a policy of averaging down. Averaging down is a means by which the investor reduces the cost basis of an investment in a particular security by buying more shares as the price declines so that the average cost of the entire position in the security is reduced. This may be particularly rewarding if the price subsequently rises, because the investor has accumulated shares at decreased prices and earns a gain when the price increases. The investor may dollar cost average, which means that the same dollar amount is spent on shares each time a purchase is made. Or the investor may average down by purchasing the same number of shares (i.e., **share average**) every time a purchase is made.

share averaging
A system for the accumulation of shares in which the investor periodically buys the same number of shares.

Exhibit 9.4 ✦ Average Position in EMEC Stock When $2,000 Worth Is Purchased Each Quarter

Date	Price of Stock	Number of Shares Owned	Cumulative Number of Shares Owned	Average Cost of Position
1/1/x0	$25	80	80	$25.00
4/1/x0	28	71	151	26.50
7/1/x0	33	60	211	28.44
10/1/x0	27	74	285	28.07
1/1/x0	21	95	380	26.32
4/1/x0	18	111	491	24.44
7/1/x0	20	100	591	23.69
10/1/x1	25	80	671	23.85

Exhibit 9.5 illustrates these averaging down strategies. The price of the stock is given in column 1. Column 2 uses the dollar cost averaging method; the investor purchases $1,000 worth of stock every time the price declines by $5. As is readily seen in column 2, the number of shares in each successive purchase is larger. The last entries in the column give the total amount that the investor has spent ($5,000), the total number of shares that have been purchased (289), and the average cost of the shares ($17.30). The average cost of the total position has declined perceptibly below the $30 price of the initial commitment. However, if the price of the stock were to increase to $30, the entire position would be worth $8,670. The investor would have made a profit of $3,670 and earned a gain of 73 percent on the entire position.[10]

Column 3 illustrates the share averaging method, which means that the same number of shares are bought every time the investor makes a purchase. When the price declines by $5, the investor buys 100 shares. If the price of the stock were to fall to $10, the investor would have accumulated 500 shares under share averaging, for a total cost of $10,000. If the price of the stock were to return to $30, the entire position would be worth $15,000, and the investor's profit would be $5,000, for a gain of 50 percent.

There is a greater reduction in the average cost of the entire position with dollar cost averaging than with share averaging. When the investor dollar cost averages, the amount spent is held constant and the number of shares purchased varies. When the investor share averages, the number of shares purchased is held constant and the dollar amount varies. Because the investor purchases a fixed number of shares with share averaging regardless of how low their price falls, the average cost of a share in the position is not reduced to the extent that it is with dollar cost averaging.

The preceding discussion and examples explain the essentials of averaging. The investor may choose any number of variations on this basic concept. For example,

---

[10] Of course, the annual *rate* of return will be different if it takes more or less than a year for this profit to be made.

Exhibit 9.5 ◆ AVERAGING DOWN STRATEGIES

Price of the Stock	Number of Shares Purchased ($1,000 Each Purchase)	Cost of 100 Shares
$30	33	$ 3,000
25	40	2,500
20	50	2,000
15	66	1,500
10	100	1,000
	289 shares	$10,000
	(for a cost of $5,000 and an average cost of $17.30 per share)	(500 shares, for a cost of $10,000 and an average cost of $20 per share)

the investor may choose to average down on declines of any dollar amount in the price of the stock or may select any dollar amount to invest for periodic purchases or for averaging down. The effect is the same, that is, to reduce the average cost basis of the position in that particular security.

Averaging down obviously requires that the investor have the funds to acquire the additional shares once their price has declined. In addition, dollar cost averaging will involve purchasing odd lots (33 shares, for example) or combinations of odd and even lots (such as 133 shares, composed of one round lot of 100 shares and one odd lot of 33 shares). Such purchases may not be cost efficient when considering commissions. Dividend reinvestment plans that permit additional contributions may alleviate the problem of commission costs, but the purchases then cannot be made at a particular desired price.[11] Instead the investor must accept the price on the day the funds are invested.

The investor who follows a policy of dollar cost averaging should not assume that such a strategy will lead to a positive return on the investments. Stocks that have a downward price trend may not change course, or many years may pass before the price of the security rises to its previous level. The individual should view the funds spent on the initial investment as a fixed or sunk cost that should not influence the decision to buy additional shares. This type of reasoning is difficult to put into practice. Most individuals will not readily admit that they have made a poor investment. Unfortunately, they then follow a program of averaging down in the belief that it will vindicate their initial investment decision.

The investor should not automatically follow a policy of averaging down. Before additional purchases are made, the stock should be reanalyzed. If the potential of the company has deteriorated (which may be why the price of the stock has fallen),

---

[11] Corporate dividend reinvestment plans are discussed in Chapter 10. Mutual funds also permit the investor to reinvest dividends.

the investor would be wiser to discontinue the policy of averaging down, to sell the stock, and to take a tax loss. If the stock lacks potential, it makes no sense to throw good money (the money used to buy the additional shares) after bad (the money previously invested in the stock). Some questions that the investor should ask are "Does the firm still have potential?" or "Is there a substantive reason for maintaining the current position in the stock?" If the answer is yes, then averaging down and periodic purchase are two means of accumulating shares while reducing their cost basis. Such strategies reduce the impact of security price fluctuations and may produce greater profits if the price of the stock rises subsequently.

SUMMARY

Security prices fluctuate daily. Several measures have been developed to show these price movements. These include the Dow Jones averages, Standard & Poor's indices of stock prices, and the NYSE index. Although the composition of each measure differs, the indices show the same movements in security prices.

Studies have shown that during a certain period, investors in common stock have earned a return in excess of 10 percent annually. The returns earned during the 1970s were smaller, and the real rate of return was even less when the rate of inflation was considered. These poor results explain in part why investors sought alternative investments to common stocks during that time period. However, during the 1980s, stock prices once again achieved their historical returns.

Averaging is one strategy designed to reduce the impact of price fluctuations. The investor either makes periodic purchases or buys additional shares of stock after their price has declined. Such purchases reduce the average cost of the position in the stock and may result in larger gains if the price of the stock rises.

Terms to Remember

Dow Jones industrial average	internal rate of return
Standard & Poor's 500 stock index	semilogarithmic paper
NYSE composite index	dollar cost averaging
holding period return	share averaging
rate of return	

Questions

1. What is a value-weighted average? Why does such an average place more emphasis on firms such as General Motors or Exxon than on other companies?
2. How does the Dow Jones industrial average differ from Standard & Poor's 500 stock index, the NYSE composite index, and the Value Line Index?
3. What has happened to the real return (i.e., the return adjusted for price-level changes) earned by investors in common stock?
4. Why may averaging rates of return yield an inaccurate measure of the true rate of return?

5. Historically, what rates of return have investors earned on investments in common stocks?
6. What is the advantage of using semilogarithmic paper to construct graphs of security prices?
7. What is dollar cost averaging? What is averaging down? Why may averaging down result in poor investment decisions?

Problems

1. What is the holding period return and the annual rate of return on a stock that cost $32 and was sold for $99 after ten years?
2. An investor buys a stock for $35 and sells it for $56⅜ (i.e., $56.38) after five years.
   a. What is the holding period return?
   b. What is the true annual rate of return?
3. A stock costs $80 and pays a $4 dividend each year for three years.
   a. If an investor buys the stock for $80 and expects to sell it for $100 after three years, what is the anticipated rate of return?
   b. What would be the rate of return if the purchase price were $75?
   c. What would be the rate of return if the dividend was $1 annually and the purchase price was $79 and the sale price was $100?
4. You purchase a stock for $100 that pays an annual dividend of $5.50. At the beginning of the second year you purchase an additional share for $130. At the end of the second year you sell both shares for $140. Determine the dollar-weighted return and the time-weighted compounded (i.e., geometric) return on this investment. Repeat the process but assume that the second share was purchased for $110 instead of $130. Why do the rates of return differ?
5. You purchase a stock for $40 and sell it for $50 after holding it for five years. During this time period you collected an annual dividend of $2. Did you earn more than 12 percent on your investment?
6. You believe that QED stock may be a good investment and decide to buy 100 shares at $40. You subsequently buy an additional $4,000 worth of the stock every time the stock's price declines by an additional $5. If the stock's price declines to $28 and rebounds to $44, at which time you sell your holdings, what is your profit? (Assume that no fractional shares may be purchased.)
7. Given the following information concerning four stocks,

	Price	Number of Shares
Stock A	$10	100,000
Stock B	17	50,000
Stock C	13	150,000
Stock D	20	200,000

   a. Construct a simple price average, a value-weighted average, and a geometric average.

b. What is the percentage increase in each average if the stocks' prices become:
   (1) A: $10, B: $17, C: $13, D: $40,
   (2) A: $10, B: $34, C: $13, D: $20?
c. Why were the percentage changes different in (1) and (2)?

8. You are given the following information concerning four stocks:

Stock	A	B	C	D
Shares outstanding	1,000	300	2,000	400
Price 19X0	$50	30	20	60
19X1	50	30	40	60
19X2	50	60	20	60

a. Using 19X0 as the base year, construct three aggregate measures of the market that simulate the Dow Jones industrial average, the S & P 500 stock index, and the Value Line stock index (i.e., a simple average, a weighted average, and a geometric average).
b. What is the percentage change in each aggregate market measure from 19X0 to 19X1, and 19X0 to 19X2? Why are the results different even though only one stock's price changed and in each case the price that changed doubled?
c. If you were managing funds and wanted a source to compare your results, which market measure would you use in 19X2?

Suggested Readings

For material on the returns earned from investments in common stocks, consult:

Bernstein, Peter L. "Do You Know What Long-Run Rate of Return to Expect?" *Financial Analysts Journal* (July–August 1988) 4–6 and "A Correction," *Financial Analysts Journal*, (November–December 1988), 14–15.

Fisher, Lawrence, and James H. Lorie. *A Half Century of Returns on Stocks and Bonds.* Chicago: University of Chicago Press, 1977.

Ibbotson, Roger G., and Rex A. Sinquefield. *Stocks, Bonds, Bills, and Inflation* (SBBI). Annual Yearbook. Chicago: Ibbotson Associates.

Sharpe, William F., and H. B. Sosin. "Risk, Return and Yield on Common Stocks." *Financial Analysts Journal* 32 (March–April 1976): 33–43.

For material on indices, their construction, and use:

Bobie, Zvi, Alex Kane, and Alan J. Marcas. *Investments.* Homewood, Ill.: Irwin, 1989, 60–67.

Latane, Henry A., Donald L. Tuttle, and William E. Young. "Market Indexes and Their Implications for Portfolio Management." *Financial Analysts Journal* (September–October 1971): 75–85.

Radcliffe, Robert C. *Investment Concepts, Analysis, and Strategy.* 3d ed. Glenview, Ill.: Scott, Foresman, 1990, 109–138.

Stillman, Richard J. *Dow Jones Industrial Average: History and Role in an Investment Strategy.* Homewood, Ill.: Irwin, 1986.

10

DIVIDENDS:
PAST, PRESENT, AND FUTURE

R̶eal estate investment trusts distribute virtually all of their profits as div-idends. Many utilities such as Public Service Enterprise Group Inc. of New Jersey distribute more than half of their earnings. Other firms such as "Toys Я Us" pay no cash dividends. Obviously there can be great diversity in firms' dividend policies.

After a corporation has earned a profit, it must decide what to do with these earnings, which may be either retained or distributed as cash dividends. If the firm retains its earnings, it will put the funds to work by investing in income-earning assets or by retiring debt. The retention of earnings increases the stockholders' equity in the firm and should generate higher earnings and increased dividends in the future.

This chapter is concerned with the various forms of dividends, ranging from regular quarterly cash dividends to irregular and stock dividends. Stock splits, the retention of earnings, and their impact on stock prices are described. The chapter ends with a discussion of estimating future dividends, since an estimate of the firm's future dividend growth rate is one of the crucial components of the dividend-growth model.

◆ ◆ ◆

LEARNING OBJECTIVES

After completing this chapter you should be able to

1. List the important dates for dividend payments.
2. Explain why changes in dividends generally follow changes in earnings.
3. Determine the impact of stock dividends and stock splits on the earning capacity of the firm.
4. Explain the effect of stock splits and stock dividends on the price of a stock and on the stock-holder's wealth.
5. Identify the advantages of dividend reinvestment plans.
6. Analyze the tax implications of dividend reinvestment plans, stock repurchases, and liquidations.
7. Estimate the growth rate in a firm's cash dividend.

CASH DIVIDENDS

A **dividend** is a distribution from earnings. Many companies pay cash dividends and have a dividend policy that is known to the investment community. Even if the policy is not explicitly stated by management, the continuation of such practices as paying a quarterly cash dividend implies a specific policy.

Most American companies that distribute cash dividends pay a **regular dividend** on a quarterly basis. A few companies make monthly distributions (e.g., Winn-Dixie Stores and Wrigley), and some make the distribution semiannually or annually. Frequently in the case of semiannual and annual payments, the dollar amount is

dividend
A payment to stockholders that is usually in cash but may be in stock or property.

regular dividends
Steady dividend payments that are distributed at regular intervals.

259

POINTS OF INTEREST

THE LONGEVITY OF CASH DIVIDENDS

The dividend-growth model presented in Chapter 8 assumes that firms pay cash dividends indefinitely. Do firms in fact continue to pay cash dividends year after year? For many corporations the answer is "Yes!" Judging by Standard & Poor's *Stock Guide,* over sixty have paid a cash dividend every year for more than 100 years, and ten of these firms have paid a cash dividend for over 150 years.

Many of these firms are banks since banking was one of the first important industries to develop. Both the First National of Boston and the Bank of New York started paying dividends in the eighteenth century (1784 and 1785, respectively). Other banks with longevity records include Central Penn National (1828), Chemical New York (1827), Citicorp (1813), First Maryland Bancorporation (1806), First National Bancorporation (1812), Midlantic Banks (1805), and United Bank Corporation of New York (1804).

America's industrial giants developed after the banks, and while their dividend longevity records may not be as impressive as the banks', the accompanying list illustrates the extended period over which industrial firms have maintained cash dividends.

Do dividend payments ever end? Unfortunately the answer is "Yes." The financial difficulty Unisys experienced in 1990 caused the firm to cease paying cash dividends. Previously the firm had paid a cash dividend every year since 1895.

Firm	Cash Dividends Every Year Since
Amoco	1894
AT&T	1881
Borden, Inc.	1899
Boston Edison	1890
Carter Wallace	1883
Cincinnati Gas and Electric	1853
Coca-Cola	1893
Colgate-Palmolive	1895
Consolidated Edison	1885
Continental Corp.	1854
Corning Inc.	1881
Exxon	1882
General Electric	1899
General Mills	1898
Eli Lilly	1885
PPG Industries	1899
Procter & Gamble	1891
Stanley Works	1877
Travelers	1864
UGI	1885
Washington Gas & Light	1852
Westvaco Corp.	1892

---

small. Instead of paying $0.025 per share quarterly, the company pays $0.10 per share annually, which reduces the expense of distributing the dividend.

Although most companies with cash dividend policies pay regular quarterly dividends, there are other types of dividend policies. Some companies pay quarterly dividends plus an additional sum (**extra dividend**). In the past General Motors paid a quarterly dividend but distributed extras twice a year if the company had a profitable year. Such a policy is appropriate for a firm in a cyclical industry because earnings fluctuate over time and the firm may be hard pressed to maintain a higher level of regular quarterly dividends. By having a set cash payment that is supplemented with extras in good years, the firm is able not only to maintain a fixed payment that is relatively assured but also to supplement the cash dividend when the extra is warranted by the earnings.

Occasionally a firm distributes property as a supplement to or instead of cash dividends. For example, from 1985 through 1989, Freeport-McMoran distributed shares in two of its subsidiaries, Freeport-McMoran Energy Partners, Ltd. and Freeport-McMoran Gold Company. These property distributions were a supplement to the firm's usual quarterly cash dividend. Distributing property (i.e., stock

extra dividend
A dividend that is in addition to the firm's regular dividend.

in the subsidiaries) permits the stockholders to benefit directly from the market value of the subsidiaries, both of which are publicly traded, and from any of the subsidiaries' cash dividends.

Management may view the dividend policy as the distribution of a certain proportion of the firm's earnings. The ratio of dividends to earnings is the **payout ratio,** which is the proportion of the earnings that the firm is distributing. For some firms this ratio has remained rather stable for a period of time, indicating that management views the best dividend policy in terms of a particular payout ratio.

payout ratio
The ratio of dividends to earnings.

Other firms pay cash dividends that are **irregular:** There is no set dividend payment. For example, real estate investment trusts (frequently referred to as REITs) are required by law to distribute their earnings to maintain their favorable tax status.[1] These trusts pay no corporate income tax; instead, their earnings are distributed and the stockholders pay the tax. To ensure this favorable tax treatment, REITs must distribute at least 95 percent of their earnings. Since the earnings of such trusts fluctuate, the cash dividends also fluctuate. The special tax laws pertaining to REITs cause them to have irregular dividend payments.

irregular dividends
Dividend payments that either do not occur in regular intervals or vary in amount.

While American firms tend to follow a policy of quarterly dividend distributions, firms in other countries do not. Instead, dividend payments are irregular. Even when the cash payments occur at regular intervals, the dollar amount tends to vary. Of course, part of this variation is the result of fluctuations in the dollar value of each currency. Hence, if the value of the dollar falls relative to the German mark, any dividends that are distributed in marks translate into more dollars when the marks are converted. The converse is also true. If the dollar value of the mark should fall, the dividend buys fewer dollars when the currency is converted.[2] Americans seeking predictable flows of dividend income are usually advised to purchase American stocks and to avoid foreign securities.

Earnings, Growth, and Dividend Increments

As the earnings of a corporation grow, cash dividends may increase. Management, however, is usually reluctant to increase the cash dividend immediately when earnings increase because it wants to be certain that the higher level of earnings will be maintained. Therefore, dividend increments tend to lag behind increases in earnings. This pattern is illustrated in Figure 10.1, which presents the quarterly per share earnings and cash dividends that were paid by Chesapeake Corporation from 1986 through 1991. Initially earnings rose (1986–1988), and the large increases in earnings during the last quarters of 1987 and 1988 did not lead to immediate dividend increments.

During 1989 and 1990, earnings declined but did not result in a dividend cut. As management is reluctant to raise the cash dividend, it is also reluctant to cut the cash dividend as the reduction may be interpreted as a sign of financial weakness. In addition, a decrease in earnings may not imply that the firm's capacity to pay cash dividends is reduced. For example, an increase in the noncash expense will reduce

---

[1] For a discussion of REITs, see Chapter 22.
[2] For a discussion of fluctuations in exchange rates, see Chapter 24.

earnings but not cash. Since cash has not been reduced, the firm's capacity to pay the dividend is maintained.[3]

Most companies announce their dividend policy. Many areas of a firm's operation are unknown to investors and perhaps would not be understood even if they were known. The dividend policy is readily understood and may be a deciding factor in purchasing stock in the firm. Some stockholders need income from their investments and prefer stocks that pay generous cash dividends. These investors will purchase the stock of companies that distribute a large proportion of their earnings in dividends. Other investors prefer capital gains and purchase the stock of companies that retain their earnings to finance future growth. Because investors need to know the dividend policy, it is advisable that firms make this knowledge public, and most companies do.

The Distribution of Dividends

The process by which dividends are distributed is time-consuming. First, the firm's directors meet. If they declare a dividend, two important dates are established. The first date determines who is to receive the dividend. On the **date of record,** the ownership books of the corporation are closed, and everyone who owns stock in the company at the end of that day receives the dividend. (Exhibit 4.2 illustrated the record date for a General Cinema Co. dividend.)

date of record
The day on which an investor must own shares in order to receive the dividend payment.

If the stock is purchased after the date of record, the purchaser does not receive the dividend. The stock is traded **ex dividend,** for the price of the stock does not include the dividend payment. This **ex dividend date** is four trading days prior to the date of record, because the settlement date for a stock purchase is five working days after the transaction.

ex dividend
Stock that trades exclusive of any dividend payment.

ex dividend date
The day on which a stock trades exclusive of any dividends.

In the financial press, transactions in the stock on the ex dividend day are indicated by an *X* before the volume of transactions. The following entry, derived from *The Wall Street Journal,* indicates the stock of Xerox traded on a sample day exclusive of the dividend.

Firm	Dividend	Volume	High	Low	Close	Net Change
Xerox	3.00	x551	78½	77¾	78	—

The $0.75 (i.e., $3.00 ÷ 4) quarterly dividend will be paid to whoever bought the stock on the previous day and will not be paid to investors who purchased the stock on the ex dividend day.

The investor should realize that buying or selling stock on the ex dividend date may not result in a windfall gain or a substantial loss. If a stock that pays a $0.75 dividend is worth $78 on the day before it goes ex dividend, it cannot be worth $78 on the ex dividend date. If it were worth $78 on both days, investors would purchase the stock for $78 the day before the ex dividend day, sell it for $78 on the ex dividend day, and collect the $0.75 dividend. If investors could do this, the price would

---

[3] At least one empirical study has shown that dividends are more highly correlated with cash flow (i.e., earnings plus depreciation) than with earnings. See John A. Brittain, *Corporate Dividend Policy* (Washington, D.C.: The Brookings Institute, 1966): 10–12.

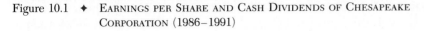

Figure 10.1 ✦ Earnings per Share and Cash Dividends of Chesapeake
Corporation (1986–1991)

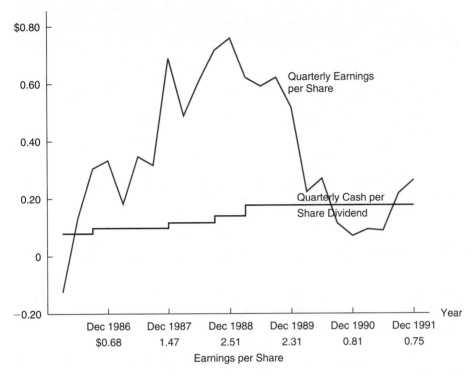

exceed $78 on the day preceding the ex dividend date and would be less than $78 on the ex dividend date. In effect, this price pattern does occur because this stock would sell for $78 and then be worth $78 minus $0.75 on the ex dividend date.[4]

This price change is illustrated in the previous example from *The Wall Street Journal.* There was no net change in the price of Xerox stock for the ex dividend day. This indicates that the closing price on the previous day was $78¾ and not $78, as might be expected. Since the current buyers will not receive the dividend, the net change in the price of the stock is reduced for the dividend. The net change is figured from the adjusted price (i.e., $78¾ minus the $0.75 dividend). If the stock had closed at 78½, the net change would have been +½, and if it had closed at 77¾, the net change would have been −¼.

---

[4] Since dividend payments are not necessarily the same amount as price changes (e.g., a dividend of $0.10 is not equal to ⅛ of a point), the opportunity for abnormal returns may exist. See David A. Dubofsky, "A Market Microstructure Explanation of Ex-Day Abnormal Returns," *Financial Management* (Winter 1992): 32–43. There is also some empirical work that suggests the prices of stocks with high dividend yields tend to fall *more* than the amount of the dividend. See John D. Finnerty, "The Behavior of Electric Utility Common Stock Prices Near the Ex-Dividend Date," *Financial Management* (Winter 1981): 59–69.

distribution date
The day on which a dividend is paid to stockholders.

The second important date established when a dividend is declared is the day on which the dividend is paid, or the **distribution date.** The distribution date may be several weeks after the date of record, as the company must determine who the owners were as of the date of record and process the dividend checks. The company may not perform this task itself; instead, it may use the services of its commercial bank, for which the bank charges a fee. The day that the dividend is received by the stockholder is thus likely to be many weeks after the board of directors announces the dividend payment. For example, the distribution date for the General Cinema dividend in Exhibit 4.2 was January 29, which was about three weeks after the date of record, January 11.

Many firms try to maintain consistency in their dividend payment dates. For example, Xerox makes payments on the first business day of January, April, July, and October. Public Service Electric & Gas pays its dividends on the last day of March, June, September, and December. Such consistency in payments is beneficial to investors and the firm, as both can plan for this receipt and disbursement.

STOCK DIVIDENDS

stock dividend
A dividend paid in stock.

recapitalization
An alteration in a firm's sources of finance, such as the substitution of long-term debt for equity.

Some firms make a practice of paying stock dividends in addition to or in lieu of cash dividends. **Stock dividends** are a form of **recapitalization** and do *not* affect the assets or liabilities of the firm. Since the assets and their management produce income for the firm, a stock dividend does not by itself increase the potential earning power of the company. Some investors, however, may believe that stock dividends will enhance the earning capacity of the firm and consequently the value of the stock. They mistakenly believe that the stock dividend increases the firm's assets.

The following balance sheet demonstrates the transactions that occur when a firm issues a stock dividend:

Assets		Liabilities and Equity	
Total assets	$10,000,000	Total liabilities	$2,500,000
		Equity: $2 par common stock (2,000,000 shares authorized; 1,000,000 outstanding)	2,000,000
		Additional paid-in capital	500,000
		Retained earnings	5,000,000

Since a stock dividend is only a recapitalization, the assets and the liabilities are not affected by the declaration and payment of the stock dividend. However, the entries in the equity section of the balance sheet are affected. The stock dividend transfers amounts from retained earnings to common stock and additional paid-in capital. The amount transferred depends on (1) the number of new shares issued through the stock dividend and (2) the market price of the stock.

If the company in the preceding example issued a 10 percent stock dividend when the price of the common stock was $20 per share, 100,000 shares would be issued with a market value of $2,000,000. This amount is subtracted from retained earnings and transferred to common stock and additional paid-in capital. The amount transferred to common stock will be 100,000 times the par value of the stock ($2 × 100,000 = $200,000). The remaining amount ($1,800,000) is transferred to additional paid-in capital. The balance sheet then becomes:

Assets		Liabilities and Equity	
Total assets	$10,000,000	Total liabilities	$2,500,000
		Equity: $2 par common stock (2,000,000 shares authorized; 1,100,000 outstanding)	2,200,000
		Additional paid-in capital	2,300,000
		Retained earnings	3,000,000

The student should note that no funds (or money) have been transferred. While there has been an increase in the number of shares outstanding, there has been no increase in cash and no increase in assets that may be used to earn profits. All that has happened is a recapitalization: The equity entries have been altered.

The major misconception concerning the stock dividend is that it increases the ability of the firm to grow. If the stock dividend is a substitute for a cash dividend, then this belief may be partially true, because the firm still has the asset cash that would have been paid to stockholders if a cash dividend had been declared. However, the firm will still have the cash even if it does not pay the stock dividend because a firm may retain its earnings. Hence, the decision to pay the stock dividend does not increase the amount of cash; it is the decision *not to pay* the cash dividend that conserves the money. When a stock dividend is paid in lieu of cash, it may even be interpreted as a screen: The stock dividend is hiding the firm's reluctance to pay cash dividends.

Although the stock dividend does not increase the wealth of the stockholder, it does increase the number of shares owned. In the previous example, a stockholder who owned 100 shares before the stock dividend had $2,000 worth of stock. After the stock dividend is distributed, this stockholder owns 110 shares that are also worth $2,000, for the price of the stock falls from $20 to $18.18. The price of the stock declines because there are 10 percent more shares outstanding, but there has been no increase in the firm's assets and earning power. The old shares have been diluted, and hence the price of the stock must decline to indicate this **dilution.**

dilution
A reduction in earnings per share due to the issuing of new securities.

If the price of the stock did not fall to adjust for the stock dividend, all companies could make their stockholders wealthier by declaring stock dividends. However, because the stock dividend does not increase the assets or earning power of the firm, investors are not willing to pay the former price for a larger number of shares; hence, the market price must fall to adjust for the dilution of the old shares.

There are some significant disadvantages associated with stock dividends. The primary disadvantage is the expense. The costs associated with these dividends include the expense of issuing new certificates, payments for any fractional shares, any taxes or listing fees on the new shares, and the revision of the firm's record of stockholders. These costs are indirectly borne by the stockholders. There are also costs that fall directly on the stockholders, including increased transfer fees and commissions (if the new securities are sold), additional odd lot differentials, and the cost of storage.

Perhaps the primary advantage of the stock dividend is that it brings to the current stockholders' attention the fact that the firm is retaining its cash in order to grow. The stockholders may subsequently be rewarded through the firm's retention of assets and its increased earning capacity. By retaining its assets, the firm may be able to earn more than the stockholders could if the funds were distributed. This should increase the price of the stock in the future. However, this same result may be achieved without the expenses associated with the stock dividend.

THE STOCK SPLIT

stock split
Recapitalization that affects the number of shares outstanding, their par value, the earnings per share, and the price of stock.

After the price of a stock has risen substantially, management may decide to split the stock. The rationale for the **stock split** is that it lowers the price of the stock and makes it more accessible to investors. For example, when Dominion Resources split its stock three for two, management stated that the split "will make our stock more attractive to individual investors."[5] Implicit in this reasoning are the beliefs that investors prefer lower priced shares and that reducing the price of the stock benefits the current stockholders by widening the market for their stock.

Like the stock dividend, the stock split is a recapitalization. It does not affect the assets or liabilities of the firm, nor does it increase its earning power. The wealth of the stockholder is increased only if investors prefer lower priced stocks, which will increase the demand for this stock.

The balance sheet used previously for illustrating the stock dividend may also be used to illustrate a two-for-one stock split. In a two-for-one stock split, one old share becomes two new shares, and the par value of the old stock is halved. There are no changes in the additional paid-in capital or retained earnings. The new balance sheet becomes:

Assets		Liabilities and Equity	
Total assets	$10,000,000	Total liabilities	$2,500,000
		Equity: $1 par common stock (2,000,000 shares authorized; 2,000,000 outstanding)	2,000,000
		Additional paid-in capital	500,000
		Retained earnings	5,000,000

There are now twice as many shares outstanding, and each new share is worth half as much as one old share. If the stock had sold for $80 before the split, each share becomes worth $40. The stockholder with 100 old shares worth $8,000 now owns 200 shares worth $8,000 (i.e., $40 × 200).

An easy way to find the price of the stock after the split is to multiply the stock's price before the split by the reciprocal of the terms of the split. For example, if a stock is selling for $54 per share and is split three for two, then the price of the

---

[5] Dominion Resources, Inc. December Interim Report 1991, p. 3.

Exhibit 10.1 ✦ SELECTED STOCK SPLITS DISTRIBUTED IN 1993

Progressive (Ohio)	3 for 1
Comerica Inc.	2 for 1
Wal-Mart Stores	2 for 1
Wachovia	2 for 1
Modine Mfg.	2 for 1
Piedmont Natural Gas	2 for 1
Motorola	2 for 1
Leucadia National	2 for 1
UNIFI	3 for 2
Provident Bancorp.	3 for 2
Public Service North Carolina	3 for 2
Wausau Paper	4 for 3
MedGroup	1 for 6

stock after the split will be $54 × ⅔ = $36. Such price adjustments must occur because the old shares are diluted and the earning capacity of the firm is not increased.

Stock splits may be any combination of terms. Exhibit 10.1 illustrates the terms of several stock splits in 1993. Although two-for-one splits are the most common, there can be unusual terms, such as the five-for-four split of ADVO Inc. in 1993. There is no obvious explanation for such terms except that management wanted to reduce the stock's price to a particular level and selected the terms that would achieve the desired price.

Occasionally there is a reverse split, such as the 1992 Reading & Bates one-for-five split. A reverse split reduces the number of shares and raises the price of the stock. The purpose of such a split is to add respectability to the stock (i.e., to raise the price above the level of the "cats and dogs"). Since some investors will not buy low-priced stock and since commissions on such purchases are higher (at least for full service brokers), it may be in the best interest of all stockholders to raise the stock's price through a reverse split.

Stock splits, like stock dividends, do not increase the assets or earning capacity of the firm. The split does decrease the price of the stock and thereby may increase its marketability. Thus, the split stock may be more widely distributed, which increases investor interest in the company. This wider distribution may increase the wealth of the current stockholders over time.

Academic studies, however, are inconclusive as to whether stock splits or stock dividends increase the value of stock.[6] These studies consistently show that other factors, such as increased earnings, increased cash dividends, or a rise in the general market, result in higher prices for individual stocks. In fact, stock splits generally

---

[6] See, for instance, Michael T. Maloney and J. Harold Mulherin, "The Effects of Splitting on the Ex: A Microstructure Reconciliation," *Financial Management* (Winter 1992): 44–59. This article has over fifty references on the impact of stock splits.

occur *after* the price of the stock has risen. Instead of being a harbinger of good news, they mirror an increase in the firm's earnings and growth.

From the investor's point of view, there is little difference between a stock split and a stock dividend. In both cases the stockholders receive additional shares, but their proportionate ownership in the firm is unaltered. In addition, the price of the stock adjusts for the dilution of per-share earnings caused by the new shares.

Accountants, however, do differentiate between stock splits and stock dividends. Stock dividends are generally less than 20 to 25 percent. A stock dividend of 50 percent would be treated as a three-for-two stock split. Only the par value and the number of shares that the firm has outstanding would be affected. There would be no change in the firm's retained earnings. A stock split of 11 for 10 would be treated as a 10 percent stock dividend. In this case, retained earnings would be reduced, and the amount would be transferred to the other accounts (i.e., common stock and paid-in capital accounts). Total equity, however, would not be affected.

DIVIDEND REINVESTMENT PLANS

dividend reinvestment plan
A plan that permits stockholders to have cash dividends reinvested in stock instead of received in cash.

Many corporations that pay cash dividends also have **dividend reinvestment plans** in which the cash dividends are used to purchase additional shares of stock. Dividend reinvestment programs started in the 1960s, but the expansion of the programs occurred in the early 1970s. By 1990, more than 1,000 companies offered some version of the dividend reinvestment plan.[7]

Types of Dividend Reinvestment Plans

There are two general types of dividend reinvestment programs. In most plans a bank acts on behalf of the corporation and its stockholders. The bank collects the cash dividends for the stockholders and in some plans offers the stockholders the option of making additional cash contributions. The bank pools all of the funds and purchases the stock on the open market. Since the bank is able to purchase a larger block of shares, it receives a substantial reduction in the per-share commission cost of the purchase. This reduced brokerage fee applies to all of the shares purchased by the bank. Thus, all investors, ranging from the smallest to the largest, receive this advantage. The bank does charge a fee for its service, but this fee is usually modest and does not offset the savings in brokerage fees.

In the second type of reinvestment plan, the company issues new shares of stock for the cash dividend, and the money is directly rechanneled to the company. The investor may also have the option of making additional cash contributions. This type of plan offers the investor an additional advantage in that the brokerage fees are completely circumvented. The entire amount of the cash dividend is used to purchase shares, with the cost of issuing the new shares being paid by the company.

---

[7]Moody's annual *Dividend Record* lists the firms traded on the NYSE and Amex that offer dividend reinvestment plans. See, for instance, the January 1, 1992, issue, pages 268–269.

This type of reinvestment plan is offered primarily by utilities, such as telephone, electric, and gas companies. Utilities need continual sources of new equity funds, and dividend reinvestment plans are one means of raising this capital.

Advantages of Dividend Reinvestment Plans

Dividend reinvestment plans offer advantages to both firms and investors. For stockholders the advantages include the purchase of shares at a substantial reduction in commissions. Even reinvestment plans in which the fees are paid by the stockholder offer this savings. Both types of plans are particularly attractive to the small investor, for few brokerage firms are interested or willing to buy $100 worth of stock, and substantial commissions are charged on such small transactions.

Perhaps the most important advantage to investors is the fact that the plans are automatic. The investor does not receive the dividends, for the proceeds are automatically reinvested. The plans are a means to force the individual to save. For any investor who lacks the discipline to save, such forced saving may be a means to systematically accumulate shares.

For the firm the primary advantages are the goodwill that is achieved by providing another service for its stockholders and some cost savings in the delivery of dividend checks. The plans that involve the issue of new shares also raise new equity capital. Firms that frequently must raise large amounts of externally generated funds may find the dividend reinvestment plan to be a major source of new capital. For example, GT&E stated in its 1991 annual report that its plan resulted in the issue of 3.9 million shares, which raised over $120 million in equity capital. This automatic flow of new equity reduced the need for the sale of shares through underwriters.

The Internal Revenue Service considers dividends that are reinvested to be no different from cash dividends that are received. Such dividends are subject to federal income taxation. The exclusion of dividend income that is reinvested from federal income taxation has been considered as one possible change in the tax code, but there is little chance of passage since Congress has been closing, rather than opening, loopholes.

EARNINGS RETENTION AND GROWTH

Since management seeks to maximize the wealth of the stockholders, the dividend decision should depend on who can put the funds to better use, the stockholders or the firm. Management, however, probably does not know the stockholders' alternative uses for the funds and thus pursues a policy that it believes is in the stockholders' best interests. Stockholders who do not like the dividend policy of the firm may sell their shares. If sellers exceed buyers, the price of the stock will be depressed, and management will be made aware of the investors' attitude toward the dividend policy.

Some managements may view dividends as a residual. Their rationale is simple and pragmatic: They do not know with certainty the stockholders' preference and the firm has investment opportunities that may be financed through the retention of earnings. After all attractive investments have been made, then any residual is left for distribution to stockholders. Such a policy places emphasis on growth, and if the firm does have excellent investment alternatives, may lead to higher stock prices over a period of time.

Earnings Retention and Security Prices

In the 1960s dividend policy was not a major concern of management. During this period the emphasis was on growth and the retention of earnings to finance that growth. Management retained as much of the earnings as it believed necessary to finance growth, and any residual was paid to stockholders. It was a period of spectacular growth by major firms, such as IBM, Xerox, and Johnson & Johnson. For example, during the years between 1964 and 1972, IBM's earnings and stock price increased at an annual rate of 14 percent. Investors in these growth-oriented companies were rewarded as the price of the stocks rose. Obviously, the best use of corporate funds was to finance growth, for few investors could have earned a comparable return through alternative uses of the money. These stockholders were well rewarded for forgoing current dividend income.

With the onset of inflation in the 1980s and the increase in interest rates, dividend policy became more important. Investors had several potential uses for funds, such as the purchase of material goods whose price investors anticipated would continue to rise. Bonds, which were yielding historically high interest rates, were an attractive investment. Since investors had more obvious alternative uses for the money earned by companies, the dividend policy of the firm became more important to them as they viewed the return on their investments to include not only growth in the value of the shares but also the dividend return.

During the 1980s earnings and dividend growth were rewarded by higher security prices. The companies that experienced growth tended to be smaller, and the growth in their earnings and stock prices were less well publicized than the success stories of the 1960s. Such a case is Teledyne, whose growth in earnings per share and stock price is illustrated in Exhibit 10.2. While Teledyne may not have achieved the publicity of IBM or Johnson & Johnson, its earnings per share grew from $15.24 in 1980 to $34.03 in 1988, and the price of the stock rose from a high of $58⅞ in 1978 to a high of $348½ in 1988.

Exhibit 10.2 ✦ TELEDYNE'S EARNINGS PER SHARE AND HIGH-LOW STOCK PRICES

Year	Percent Earned on Equity	Earnings per Share	High-Low Stock Prices
1988	18.3%	$34.03	$348.5–290.3
1987	18.8	31.68	390.0–242.0
1986	14.6	20.35	367.8–291.0
1985	34.6	46.66	338.0–227.0
1984	49.5	37.69	302.4–147.3
1983	11.5	14.87	173.5–123.0
1982	12.5	12.62	143.8– 69.5
1981	24.2	19.96	174.7–118.0
1980	24.5	15.24	153.0– 63.0

REPURCHASES OF STOCK AND LIQUIDATIONS

A firm with excess cash may choose to repurchase some of its outstanding shares of stock or to liquidate the corporation. This section briefly covers **stock repurchases** and **liquidations.** A repurchase is in effect a partial liquidation, as it decreases the number of shares outstanding. This reduction should increase the earnings per share because the earnings are spread over fewer shares.

While the repurchase of shares is a partial liquidation, it may also be viewed as an alternative to the payment of cash dividends. Instead of distributing the money as cash dividends, the firm offers to purchase shares from stockholders. If the stockholders believe that the firm's potential is sufficient to warrant the retention of the shares, they do not have to sell them. If the shares are sold back to the company, any resulting profits will be taxed as capital gains.

One company that followed a policy of retiring shares was Teledyne. Prior to 1987, Teledyne did not pay cash dividends but either offered stockholders the option to exchange their shares for debt issued by the company or repurchased stock.[8] The result of these recapitalizations was to reduce the number of shares outstanding from 59.6 million to 11.2 million. This reduced number of shares plus an excellent growth in earnings resulted in a substantial increase in Teledyne's per-share earnings. As may be seen in Exhibit 10.2, from 1980 through 1987, the price of the stock rose, which has certainly benefited the remaining stockholders. Even those stockholders who sold their shares cannot complain, because they were not forced to sell. These investors sold their shares presumably because they thought that selling was better than continuing to hold the shares.[9]

stock repurchases
The buying and retiring of stock by the issuing corporation.

liquidation
The process of converting assets into cash; dissolving a corporation.

---

[8] Teledyne's largest single purchase occurred in May 1984, when it repurchased 8.7 million shares at a cost of $1.74 billion.

[9] In 1987, Teledyne adopted a new policy and started to pay cash dividends. It is perhaps coincidental, but earnings started to decline, and the firm operated at a loss in 1991.

Occasionally a firm is liquidated. The final distribution of the firm's assets is called a liquidating dividend. The use of the term *dividend* is a bit misleading, because the distribution is not really a dividend. It is treated for tax purposes as a distribution of capital and is taxed at the appropriate capital gains tax rate. Thus, liquidating dividends are treated in the same manner as realized sales for federal income tax purposes.

A simple example may illustrate how such a dividend works. A firm decides to liquidate and sells all of its assets for cash. The stockholders then receive the cash. If the sales raise $25 in cash per share, a stockholder surrenders the stock certificate and receives $25 in cash. The capital gain is then determined by subtracting the stockholder's cost basis of the share from the $25. If the stockholder paid $10 for the share, the capital gain would be $15. The stockholder then pays the appropriate capital gains tax. If the cost basis were $40, the investor would suffer a capital loss of $15, which may be used for tax purposes to offset other capital gains or income. In either case, this is no different than if the stockholder had sold the shares. However, in a sale the stockholder does have the option to refuse to sell and thus may postpone any capital gains tax. In a liquidation the stockholder must realize the gain or loss. Once the firm has adopted a plan of liquidation, it must execute the plan or face penalties. When a firm liquidates, the stockholder cannot postpone the capital gains tax.

In the preceding example, the liquidating dividend was cash. However, the dividend need not be cash but may be property. For example, a real estate holding company could distribute the property it owns. Or a company that has accumulated stock in other companies could distribute the stock instead of selling it. Such distributions may be desirable if the stockholders want the particular assets being distributed. However, if the stockholders want or need cash (perhaps to pay the capital gains tax), then the burden of liquidating the assets is passed on to them.

An example of a firm that did liquidate is Tishman Realty. The stockholders adopted a plan of liquidation; the firm then sold most of its assets to Equitable Life Assurance for $200 million. The company paid an initial $11 per share liquidating dividend. After additional cash distributions were made, a partnership was established to hold the remaining assets, which consisted primarily of mortgages on properties sold. These partnership shares were then distributed to stockholders to complete the liquidation.

ESTIMATING DIVIDEND GROWTH RATES

To make the dividend-growth model operational, the analyst needs numerical values for three variables: (1) the current dividend (D_0), (2) the required rate of return (k), and (3) the growth rate of future dividends (g). The current dividend is known. The required return, which was discussed in the previous chapter, needs estimates of the risk-free rate and the risk premium applicable to the specific stock. The third variable, the growth rate, requires an estimate of future dividends. It may be the most difficult variable to calculate, and, as illustrated, a small change in this estimate can have a large impact on the stock's valuation.

The following example of estimating the growth rate uses the stock of Chesapeake Corporation (CSK). If you are recording stock prices from Chapter 1, you may remember that CSK was one of the author's selections. The company reappears in the chapter on the use of ratios (Chapter 12) to analyze a firm's financial statements. CSK is a particularly interesting illustration of some of the problems that the analyst may encounter when attempting to make the dividend-growth model operational.

Growth as the Product of the Return on Equity and the Retention Ratio

Retained earnings may be used to acquire additional assets. If these assets generate income, they will permit future growth in the firm's cash dividends. This points out that current dividends and internally financed growth are mutually exclusive. If the firm retains earnings, it cannot pay dividends, and if the firm distributes earnings, this source of funds cannot be used to finance expansion of plant and equipment. Of course, the firm could expand by issuing new stock, but then the old stock may be diluted. By not issuing new shares and by retaining earnings, all of the potential for growth accrues to the existing stockholders. Since earnings are either distributed or retained, the retention ratio is equal to

$$\text{Retention ratio} = 1 - \text{Payout ratio.}$$

The impact of different retention ratios may be seen by considering the following balance sheets:

Assets		Liabilities and Equity	
Assets	$200	Liabilities	$100
		Equity	100
	$200		$200

During the year the firm nets $20 after deducting all operating and finance expenses. The return on equity is $20/$100 = 20 percent. If it retains all of its earnings (retention ratio = 1.0 and the payout ratio = 0), the new balance sheet becomes:

Assets		Liabilities and Equity	
Assets	$220	Liabilities	$100
		Equity	120
	$220		$220

Suppose, however, the firm had retained only $12 (i.e., the retention ratio is 60 percent and the payout ratio is 40 percent), the new balance sheet becomes:

Assets		Liabilities and Equity	
Assets	$212	Liabilities	$100
		Equity	112
	$212		$212

The firm's assets and equity have not risen as much because the firm has retained less of its earnings. The future growth in earnings is now less, because management has made a small investment in assets.

This relationship between growth (g), the return on equity (ROE), and the retention ratio (b) is summarized in equation 10.1:

$$g = \text{ROE} \times b. \tag{10.1}$$

In the first illustration, growth is

$$g = .2 \times 1 = 20\%$$

while in the second illustration, growth is

$$g = .2 \times .6 = 12\%.$$

Unless the return on the equity can be increased, future earnings (and hence future dividends) can only grow at 12 percent.

If the firm were able to increase the return on equity, the dividend could be increased without a corresponding decrease in the growth rate. For example, if the return on equity had been 33.3 percent, the firm could distribute 40 percent of its earnings and retain 60 percent and still achieve a 20 percent growth rate (i.e., .333 $\times$ .6 = 20%). If, however, the return on equity is not increased and management increases the dividend, the higher payment must imply lower retention of earnings. If the firm distributes \$12 instead of \$8, the retention ratio falls to 40 percent, and the rate of growth is reduced to

$$g = .2 \times .4 = 8\%.$$

What impact will the increased dividend at the expense of growth have on the price of the stock? The answer is indeterminant. Examine the arrows placed in the dividend-growth model from Chapter 8:

$$V = \frac{D_0 \uparrow (1 + g \downarrow)}{k - g \downarrow}.$$

The increase in the dividend (i.e., a higher numerator) argues for a higher stock price, but the lower growth rate, which increases the denominator, argues for a lower stock price. The converse also applies. A lower dividend decreases the numerator and suggests a lower price while a higher growth rate means a smaller denominator and a higher stock price. A dividend increment at the expense of the retention of earnings could result in the price of the stock rising or falling.

The above discussion indicates that the future growth rate in dividends may be estimated by the product of the retention ratio and the return on equity. What is the estimated growth rate for Chesapeake Corporation? In 1991, the firm's return on equity was 4.8 percent and its retention ratio was 4 percent.[10] Thus the implied growth rate is

$$g = (4.8)(.04) = 0.2\%.$$

---

[10] How these and other ratios are used to analyze a firm's financial statements is discussed in Chapter 12.

However, 1991 was an exceptionally poor year for the firm. Its ten-year average return on equity and retention ratio were 10.4 percent and 49.3 percent. This suggests a growth rate of 10.4 × .493 = 5.1 percent. The difference between 0.2 percent and 5.1 percent is substantial, but the analyst must choose between them or derive an alternative estimate of growth.

Alternative Means to Estimate Growth Rates

An alternative means to estimate growth is to analyze past growth and use this information to project future growth. The per-share dividends and their annual percentage change for Chesapeake were as follows:

Year	Dividend	Percentage Change
1981	$0.33	—
1982	0.36	9.1%
1983	0.38	5.3
1984	0.39	2.6
1985	0.42	7.7
1986	0.43	2.4
1987	0.46	7.0
1988	0.52	11.5
1989	0.68	30.8
1990	0.72	5.9
1991	0.72	0.0

The individual annual percentage changes are averaged, and then this average is used as the projected growth rate. By this method, the annual rate of growth in Chesapeake's dividend is 8.2 percent.[11]

   The discussion in the previous chapter suggested that averaging percentage changes could overstate the growth rate. An alternative method uses the future value equation presented in Chapter 6. The question to be solved is: At what annual rate did Chesapeake's dividend grow from $0.33 during 1981 to $0.72 during 1991 (i.e., 10 completed years)? That is

$$\$.033(1 + g)^{10} = \$0.72$$

$$(1 + g)^{10} = 0.68/0.24 = 2.833.$$

The interest factor for the future value of $1 for ten years is 2.833, which according to Appendix A for the future value of $1, yields an annual growth rate of about 8 percent. The exact rate is

$$g = \sqrt[10]{2.182} - 1 = 1.081 - 1 = 8.1\%.$$

---

[11] This calculation is an arithmetic average. If a geometric average had been computed, the average rate of change would be 7.9 percent. Notice that the arithmetic average exceeds the geometric average and may overstate the compound rate of growth.

This calculation uses only two observations, the first and last years. A third way to use the above data estimates an equation that summarizes the observations relating dividends and time. Such an equation yields an estimate of the annual growth rate in the dividend. This estimation technique is least-squares regression analysis and is illustrated in the appendix to this chapter. Using this technique yields an annual growth rate of 8.6 percent.

Application: Chesapeake Corporation's Common Stock

Which growth rate should the individual use to value the stock? Currently there are five estimates ranging from 0.2 percent using the return on equity and the retention ratio for the last year to 8.6 percent using regression analysis. In between are 8.2 percent (the average percentage change in the dividend), 8.1 percent (the rate using the terminal values of the dividend), and 5.1 percent from the average return on equity and the retention ratio over ten years. The answer requires judgment on the part of the analyst because the valuation will differ depending on the choice. Obviously the lower the rate, the more conservative choice, may be appropriate if the analyst anticipates that the pace of economic activity will decline. However, if the analyst believes that the firm's financial condition is improving, the use of a lower growth rate will argue against acquiring the stock. (Chapter 12 will consider the analysis of financial statements to help determine if the firm's performance is improving or deteriorating and thus help answer the question of which growth rate to use.)

Since 8.6 percent and 0.2 percent are the highest and lowest estimated growth rates, the analyst may decide to disregard these two extremes. The remaining estimates (8.2, 8.1, and 5.1) seem more reasonable for extended periods of time. Since the 8.2 percent is an arithmetic average, the analyst may prefer the 8.1 percent because it was determined using a geometric function and thus includes compounding. The geometric average of 7.9 percent (from footnote 11) also lends support to the selection of 8.1 percent.

Next the analyst must determine the required rate of return. As was explained in the previous chapter, the required rate depends on the risk-free rate, the return on the market, and the firm's beta coefficient. As of 1992, the yield on six-month treasury bills was approximately 5 to 6 percent. If the Ibbotson-Sinquefield study is used, then the return on the market should be approximately 12 percent (i.e., a return on the market that is 5 to 7 percent greater than the treasury bill rate). According to the *Value Line Investment Survey*, Chesapeake Corporation's beta is 0.9. Thus the required rate of return is

$$k = r_f + (r_m - r_f)\beta$$

$$= 0.5 + (0.12 - 0.5)0.9$$

$$= 11.3\%.$$

Since the required rate of return has been determined and the annual dividend at the time of this valuation was $0.72, the valuation model may be applied. In this illustration the value of Chesapeake Corporation's stock is

$$V = \frac{D_0(1 + g)}{k - g}$$

$$= \frac{\$0.72(1 + .081)}{0.113 - 0.081}$$

$$= 24.32.$$

In June 1992, the stock was selling for \$23.50, which indicates that the stock was reasonably priced (i.e., neither under- nor over-valued).

If the valuation model generates a large divergence between the valuation and the market price (e.g., \$30 when the price is \$15), the investor should reconsider the estimates used in the model. A large divergence would indicate that the stock is either well undervalued or overvalued. Such mispricings should be rare because, as discussed in several places in this text, security markets are competitive and efficient. If a security were undervalued, investors would seek to buy it, which would drive up the price. If a security were overvalued, investors would seek to sell it, which would drive down the price. Thus if the dividend-growth model indicates a large divergence between the estimated value and the current market price, it would be advisable for the analyst to determine if the data used in the model are inaccurate.

If the analyst believes that the firm can sustain a 8.6 percent rate of growth (the highest of the estimates), the valuation model yields:

$$V = \frac{\$0.72(1 + 0.086)}{.113 - .086}$$

$$= \$28.96.$$

This valuation indicates that the firm's stock at \$23.50 is undervalued and should be purchased. The question then becomes: can 8.6 percent be sustained? At 8.1 percent, the valuation is \$24.32, which is reasonably close to the price of \$23.50. It appears that the market consensus of a sustainable growth rate is around 8.1 percent, for at 8.1 percent the valuation is about \$24.

By now it should be obvious that stock valuation is more an art than a science. However, the use of equations such as the dividend-growth model may give valuation an appearance of being more exact than in reality it can be. The model determines a unique value but that number obviously depends on the data used. Instead of determining a unique value, an analyst may employ data derived under varying assumptions and derive a range of values for a given stock. This may lead to investment advice that reads something like "We believe that Chesapeake's stock is fairly priced at \$23 to \$25 and would buy the stock on any weakness that drives the price below \$20." Prices do fluctuate and may briefly create buy or sell opportunities that may offer the individual the chance of opening or liquidating positions.

SUMMARY

After a firm has earned profits, it may either retain them or distribute them in the form of cash dividends. Many publicly held corporations follow a stated dividend policy and distribute quarterly cash dividends. A few firms supplement this dividend with extra dividends if earnings warrant the additional distribution. Some firms pay irregular dividends that vary in amount from quarter to quarter.

Dividends are related to the firm's capacity to pay them. As earnings rise, dividends also tend to increase, but there is usually a lag between higher earnings and increased dividends. Most managements are reluctant to cut dividends and thus do not raise the dividend until they believe that the higher level of earnings can be sustained.

In addition to cash dividends, some firms distribute stock dividends. These dividends and stock splits do not increase the earning capacity of the firm. Instead, they are recapitalizations that alter the number of shares the firm has outstanding. Since stock dividends and stock splits do not alter the firm's earning capacity, they do not increase the wealth of the stockholders. The price of the stock adjusts for the change in the number of shares that results from stock dividends and stock splits.

The retention or distribution of earnings should be a question of who can put the funds to better use—the firm or its stockholders. If a firm retains earnings, it should grow and the value of the shares should increase. When this occurs, the stockholders may be able to sell their shares for a profit.

Many firms offer their stockholders the option of having their dividends reinvested in the firm's stock. This is achieved either through the firm's issuing new shares or purchasing existing shares. Dividend reinvestment plans offer the stockholders the advantages of forced savings and a reduction in brokerage fees.

Instead of paying cash dividends, a firm may offer to repurchase some of its existing shares. Such repurchases reduce the number of shares outstanding and may enhance the growth in the firm's per-share earnings because there will be fewer shares outstanding. Any profits earned on such repurchases are taxed as capital gains, as are liquidating dividends that occur when a corporation is disbanded and its assets are distributed to the stockholders.

Estimating the growth rate of a firm's future dividends is necessary for the application of the dividend-growth model. One possible estimation of the dividend-growth rate is the product of the firm's return on equity and its retention ratio. Other possible estimates are based on the annual changes in the firm's dividend or the use of regression analysis that estimates the growth rate based on the past dividends over a period of years.

Terms to Remember

dividend	distribution date
regular dividend	stock dividend
extra dividend	recapitalization
payout ratio	dilution
irregular dividends	stock split
date of record	dividend reinvestment plan
ex dividend	stock repurchase
ex dividend date	liquidation

Questions

1. Why may a firm distribute dividends even though earnings decline?
2. Why may a dividend increment lag after an increase in earnings?

3. Define *ex dividend date, date of record,* and *distribution date.*
4. Explain the differences between the following dividend policies: (a) regular quarterly dividends; (b) regular quarterly dividends plus extras; and (c) irregular dividends.
5. How are stock dividends and stock splits similar?
6. What are the advantages to stockholders of dividend reinvestment plans?
7. What tax advantages apply to stock repurchases that do not apply to cash dividend distributions?
8. Why should dividend policy be a question of who can put the funds to better use, the firm or its stockholders?

Problems

1. A firm has the following items on its balance sheet:

Cash	$ 20,000,000
Inventory	134,000,000
Notes payable to bank	31,500,000
Common stock (1,000,000 shares, $10 par)	10,000,000
Retained earnings	98,500,000

How would each of these accounts appear after:
   a. a cash dividend of $1 per share;
   b. a 10 percent stock dividend (fair market value of stock is $13 per share);
   c. a three-for-one stock split;
   d. a one-for-two reverse stock split;
   e. a repurchase of 100,000 shares for $13 per share?
2. A company whose stock is selling for $60 has the following balance sheet:

Assets	$30,000,000	Liabilities	$14,000,000
		Preferred stock	1,000,000
		Common stock ($12 par;	1,200,000
		100,000 shares outstanding	
		Paid-in capital	1,800,000
		Retained earnings	12,000,000

   a. Construct a new balance sheet showing the effects of a three-for-one stock split. What is the new price of the stock?
   b. Construct a new balance sheet showing the effects of a 10 percent stock dividend. What will be the approximate new price of the stock?
3. An investor who buys 100 shares of a stock for $40 a share that pays a per-share dividend of $2.00 annually signs up for the dividend reinvestment plan. If neither the price of the stock nor the dividend is changed, how many shares will the investor have at the end of ten years?
4. A firm's dividend payments have been as follows:

Year	Dividend
1980	$1.00
1981	1.05
1982	1.12
1983	1.30
1984	1.30
1985	1.45
1986	1.50
1987	1.62
1988	1.70
1989	1.88
1990	2.00

Ten years have elapsed since the dividend rose from $1.00 at the *end* of 1980 to $2.00 at the *end* of 1990. You want to determine the annual rate of growth in the dividend.

a. What was the average percentage change in the dividend?
b. What was the rate of growth based on beginning and ending dividends?
c. What was the rate of growth using the regression analysis illustrated in the appendix to this chapter?
d. Does each technique give you the same rate of growth?

Suggested Readings

A survey of corporate financial managers suggests that management (1) is concerned with dividend continuity, (2) believes dividends help maintain or increase stock prices, and (3) believes dividend payments indicate the future prospects of the firm. These results are reported in:

Baker, H. Kent, Gail E. Farrelly, and Richard B. Edelman. "A Survey of Management Views on Dividend Policy." *Financial Management* (Autumn 1985): 78–84.

Even though the finance literature attributes no value to stock dividends and stock splits, the following articles identify why some corporate managements still declare them.

Eisemann, Peter C., and Edward A. Moses. "Stock Dividends: Management's View." *Financial Analysts Journal* (July–August 1979): 77–80.
Baker, W. Kent, and Patricia L. Gallagher. "Management's View of Stock Splits." *Financial Management* (Summer 1980): 73–77.
McNichols, M., and A. David. "Stock Dividends, Stock Splits, and Signalling," *Journal of Finance* (July 1990): 857–879.

Reverse stock splits are relatively rare and may be a harbinger of future declines in the stock's price. See:

Woolridge, J. R., and D. R. Chambers. "Reverse Splits and Shareholder Wealth." *Financial Management* (Autumn 1983): 5–15.
Spudeck, R. E., and R. Charles Moyer. "Reverse Splits and Shareholder Wealth: The Impact of Commissions." *Financial Management* (Winter 1985): 52–56.

Stock repurchases have become common. For the characteristics of firms that repurchase their own stock, consult:

Dann, Larry Y. "Common Stock Repurchases: An Analysis of Returns to Bondholders and Stockholders," *Journal of Financial Economics* (June 1981): 113–138.

Finnerty, Joseph E. "Corporate Stock Issue and Repurchase." *Financial Management* (October 1975): 62–66.

Houston, John L. "Common Stock Repurchases: A Bane or Boon to Shareholders," *AAII Journal* (February 1984): 7–10.

INVESTMENT PROJECT

In this chapter a variety of techniques were used to determine a firm's historic growth rate. GTE's annual dividends (adjusted for the two-for-one split distributed during 1990) were as follows:

1982	0.955
1983	0.980
1984	1.005
1985	1.035
1986	1.060
1987	1.230
1988	1.280
1989	1.370
1990	1.520
1991	1.640
1992	1.730

Use these payments to determine the growth rate in the dividend. Calculate the growth rate based on (1) the average percentage change, (2) the terminal values, and (3) regression analysis (illustrated in the chapter appendix). Find the yield on six-month treasury bills and apply the dividend-growth valuation model. You should already have GTE's beta, and you may assume that the return on the market is 5 to 7 percent greater than the yield on treasury bills. If your valuation significantly differs from the current price, you may want to consider the explosion in cellular phones and other technological changes in communications as possible explanations of any divergence in your valuation and the current price of the stock.

Appendix

Use of Regression Analysis to Estimate Growth Rates

In the appendix to Chapter 7, regression analysis was used to estimate beta coefficients. In this appendix, it is used to estimate growth rates. The equation to be estimated is

$$D_0(1 + g)^n = D_n$$

This equation states that the initial dividend (D_0) will grow at some rate (g) for some time period (n) into the future dividend (D_n). This equation may be expressed in the following general form:

$$Y = (a)(b)^x,$$

in which $Y = D_n$, $a = D_0$, $b = (1 + g)$, and $x = n$.

The above equation is exponential, which is difficult to estimate, but it may be restated in log-linear form as:

$$\log Y = \log a + (\log b)X.$$

In this form, least-squares method of regression may be used to estimate a and b. This procedure using Chesapeake Corporation's dividends (Y) and time (X) is as follows:

	Year(X)	Dividend(Y)	Log Y	X^2	X(Log Y)
1981	1	0.33	−0.48184	1	−0.48148
1982	2	0.36	−0.44369	4	−0.88739
1983	3	0.38	−0.42021	9	−1.26064
1984	4	0.39	−0.40893	16	−1.63574
1985	5	0.42	−0.37675	25	−1.88375
1986	6	0.43	−0.36653	36	−2.19918
1987	7	0.46	−0.33724	49	−2.36069
1988	8	0.52	−0.28399	64	−2.27197
1989	9	0.68	−0.16749	81	−1.50741
1990	10	0.72	−0.14266	100	−1.42667
1991	11	0.72	−0.14266	121	−1.56934
	66	5.41	−3.57168	506	−17.4843

$$\log b = \frac{(n)\,\Sigma\,X\,(\log Y) - (\Sigma\,\log Y)(\Sigma X)}{(n)\,\Sigma X^2 - (\Sigma X)^2}$$

$$= \frac{(11)(-17.4843) - (-3.57168)(66)}{(11)(506) - (66)^2}$$

$$= \frac{43.40352}{1210} = 0.035870.$$

$$\log a = \frac{\Sigma\,\log Y}{n} - \frac{(\log b)\Sigma X}{n}$$

$$= \frac{-3.57168}{11} - (0.035870)(66/11)$$

$$= -0.3992.$$

The estimated equation is

$$\log Y = -0.3992 + 0.03587X.$$

Figure 10.2 ✦ DIVIDENDS AND ESTIMATED REGRESSION LINE FOR CHESAPEAKE CORPORATION (1981–1991)

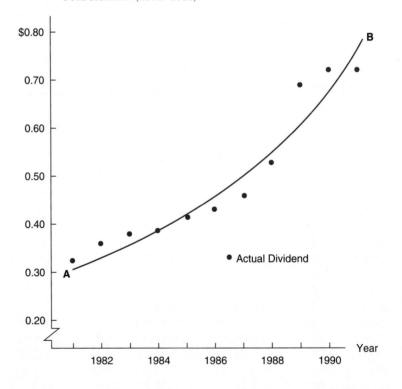

The equation in exponential form is[12]

$$Y = (0.39884)(1.0861)^x,$$

and the growth rate is

$$g = 1.0861 - 1 = 8.6\%.$$

Figure 10.2 plots Chesapeake Corporation's cash dividends over time as well as the estimated equation (line AB). While the observations lie both above and below the estimated line, they tend to follow closely the contour of the line, which suggests that the equation gives a good estimate of the historical rate of growth in the dividend.

---

[12] $10^{-0.3992} = 0.39884$ and $10^{0.03587} = 1.0861$.

11

THE FUNDAMENTAL APPROACH
TO THE SELECTION OF STOCK

*T*wo methods used by investors to select securities other than random choice or "hot tips" are the fundamental approach and the technical approach. The fundamental approach stresses economic conditions, such as the level of employment and economic growth, and financial conditions, such as the level and direction of changes in interest rates. This approach also examines a firm's earning capacity, its growth potential, and its sources of finance. Financial analysts who use this method compare firms within an industry to identify those with the greatest potential and strongest financial position. Emphasis is placed on a firm's economic performance and the potential to improve its relative position within its industry. Ratios, financial data, and astute observation are the primary tools of fundamental analysis.

The technical approach is based on the past market performance of a firm's securities. It attempts to identify superior investments by analyzing the price performance and the volume of transactions in the firm's stock. This type of analysis emphasizes price trends and deviations from these trends. For example, stocks that are rising in price may continue to do so. When the technical analyst perceives that this trend is coming to a halt, it is time to liquidate the position in that security, even if the firm has superior management, excellent growth potential, and a strong balance sheet.

Although both methods attempt to identify superior securities for purchase, the two approaches are significantly different. Fundamental analysis is based on the premise that real factors, such as the firm's productivity and profitability, will ultimately govern the stock's price. Technical analysis, however, stresses market factors and suggests that future stock prices are related to past market behavior.

This and the following chapters will explore these techniques. Chapters 11 and 12 focus on fundamental analysis. The first section in Chapter 11 discusses the general economic environment. The impact of the Federal Reserve's monetary policy on interest rates is explained next. The chapter then considers the federal government's fiscal policy and analysis of a firm in relation to its industry. Chapter 11 ends with a discussion of the expected economic environment and investment strategies. The bulk of the next chapter is devoted to financial analysis of the firm. Particular emphasis is placed on the various ratios used in this type of analysis. Chapter 13 *discusses technical analysis and illustrates several techniques that are used by advocates of this approach. The student should realize that these three chapters cannot cover these important topics in depth; entire books have been written on each topic alone. This text includes only basic methods used in fundamental and technical analysis.*

✦ ✦ ✦

The Logical Progression of Fundamental Analysis

Fundamental analysis has a logical progression from the general to the specific. First, the analyst considers the economic environment, which may give some indication of the future direction of security prices. For example, rising inflation and interest rates argue that security prices should tend to fall. Second, the analyst considers the industry, since industries react differently to changes in the economic environment. The demand for expensive items, such as cars, major appliances, and housing, tends to respond to changes in the level of economic activity while the demand for other products, such as necessities (e.g., food) and some consumer goods, tends to be less responsive to changes in economic activity.

After considering the economy and the industry, the analyst considers the individual firm since what applies to the economy or the industry may not apply to a specific firm. Some firms do poorly even when the general economy prospers. During the 1980s, for example, Pan Am continued to operate at a loss even when many airlines generated record profits. The converse is also true since some firms do well and grow during periods of economic stagnation. These stocks may be good purchases even if it appears that the market as a whole will decline.

It may be difficult to justify purchasing stock when it appears that the economy or an industry is doing poorly. Some analysts, however, believe that this is the best time to purchase stock. If many investors are seeking to liquidate positions, security prices may be driven down, so that the buyer may be purchasing the stock at an undervalued price. These analysts are referred to as **contrarians,** and it should be noted that being a contrarian and going against the general sentiment is not easy.[1] Just think how difficult it would have been to have the courage to buy stock when the Dow Jones industrial average fell over 500 points in one day during October 1987.

Most financial analysts and investors who use fundamental analysis are not contrarians. Instead they follow the general logic of fundamental analysis of considering the economy, the industry, and the firm's performance and position within its industry. They use the analysis to help identify what they believe to be the general direction of the market and undervalued securities.

contrarians
Investors who go against the consensus concerning investment strategy.

---

[1] A similar type of approach is also one of the tools of technical analysis explained in Chapter 13. In technical analysis a contrarian emphasizes doing exactly the opposite of what investment advisory services are recommending.

THE ECONOMIC ENVIRONMENT

All investment decisions are made within the economic environment. This environment varies as the economy goes through stages of prosperity. These stages are often referred to as the business cycle. The name *business cycle* is perhaps a poor choice, since the word *cycle* suggests a regularly repeated sequence of events such as the seasons of the year. The economy does not follow a regularly repeated sequence of events. Instead the term *business cycle* refers to a pattern of changing economic output and growth: an initial period of rapid growth followed by a period of slow growth or even stagnation during which the economy contracts.

The length and amplitude of these periods vary.[2] Prior to the 1930s, expansions averaged 25 months while contractions lasted 22 months. Since World War II the length of the expansionary phase has increased while the periods of contraction have diminished with the average durations of expansions and contractions being 49 and 11 months, respectively. The 1980s produced the longest period of continuous expansion on record starting in late 1982 and continuing to the end of the decade.

While each business cycle differs, there are common characteristics that are illustrated in Figure 11.1. Starting from a point of neutrality (t_1), the economy expands, reaching a peak at t_2. The economy then declines, reaching a trough at t_3, and subsequently starting to rebound to repeat the pattern. The peak may be accompanied by an increased rate of inflation as the economy gets "overheated." Since in the aggregate, prices generally do not fall, there is no deflation (i.e., the opposite of inflation). Instead the levels of employment and output tend to decline. Such a period of economic contraction is called a **recession.**

recession

A period of rising unemployment and declining national output.

One of the major advances within the social sciences is the increased understanding of events that affect the phases of the business cycle and of the causes of economic growth. This understanding has led to the development of tools, such as monetary and fiscal policy, that can alleviate the swings in economic activity. Unfortunately for policymakers, outside events also affect the level of economic activity. The capacity of policymakers to control the economy is constrained by these ever-changing social and political events.

In addition, circumstances that affect the economy during one period may not exist or may have less impact during subsequent time periods. The oil embargo and its sudden and swift change in the price of crude oil severely affected the economy during the 1970s. Since the oil embargo, oil prices have been more stable, and fluctuations in the supply and price of oil ceased to be a disruptive force.

During the 1930s, the failures of many commercial banks had an enormous impact on the economy and contributed to the Great Depression. During the late 1980s, the failure of many savings and loan associations and commercial banks created a financial crisis but had little impact on the aggregate economy. Actions by the federal government to guarantee deposits stopped any run on the savings and loans. Of course, there will be a large cost in the 1990s to taxpayers to finance the bailout of the banks, but that burden will be spread over the population. This cost

---

[2] See, for instance, Jerome B. Cohen, Edward D. Zinbarg, and Arthur Zeikel. *Investment Analysis and Portfolio Management*, 5th ed. (Homewood, Ill.: Irwin, 1987), 229.

Figure 11.1 ✦ PHASES OF THE BUSINESS CYCLE

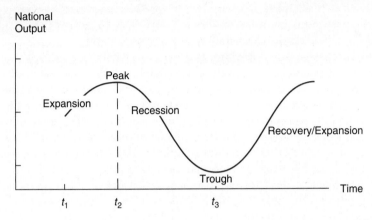

will not have the same impact on the aggregate economy as the 1930s liquidity crisis created when individual investors raced to withdraw funds from commercial banks.

Even the large plunge in the stock market during October 1987 appears in retrospect to have been a nonevent. At that time there were predictions that the large decline in stock prices was a harbinger of another depression. Such a depression did not occur. Instead the economy continued to prosper, and the stock market began 1990 by reaching new historic highs. Of course, some investors did sustain major losses during October 1987, but other individuals who purchased stocks after the decline probably earned profits. Such transfers among investors, however, do not have the same impact on the country that is associated with a decline in the general level of economic activity.

Each of these events was important. The dramatic increase in the price of oil, the collapse in a segment of the banking system, and the severe decline in stock prices did inflict losses on individual investors. It is possible that none of these events will be repeated; the next economic crisis may be perceptibly different from the preceding one. The economy is simply too complex to be characterized as a series of regularly repeated cycles of equal length and magnitude. Even if such repetition were possible, individuals would soon recognize the pattern and adjust accordingly. Such adjustments, of course, would assure that the future will not be a replay of the past. Each economic cycle and each economic crisis differs. Anticipating the differences may lead to superior investment results, which is why emphasis in security analysis is placed on forecasting the future.

Prior to analyzing a firm's financial condition and potential for growth, the financial analyst needs a forecast of the future economy. Firms operate within the economy, and their survival may depend on how the economy as a whole is faring. During periods of economic prosperity, the demand for the goods and services of firms may result in increased sales and higher profits. Even financially weak or incompetently managed firms may experience increased sales and earnings if they are swept up in the general economic prosperity.

Hard times or periods of recession (i.e., periods of rising unemployment) may have the opposite impact. Financially weak firms may fail, and even the financially strong may feel the effects of poor economic conditions. Recession leads to a general decline in economic activity, which in turn results in a lessening of demand for the output of virtually all firms. Sales become sluggish or even decline, and earnings tend to diminish even more rapidly because certain fixed costs (such as interest) must still be met, which may severely reduce profit margins.

During periods of prosperity, security prices as a whole tend to rise. Thus, even poor investment decisions may produce acceptable or even superior results. Conversely, during periods of economic downturn, even excellent security analysis may not protect the investor from declining security prices. For these reasons, the ability to forecast the future economic environment may be even more important than the purchase of specific securities. Unfortunately such forecasting is virtually impossible for the individual investor. Even access to sophisticated techniques, computers, and more complete data does not guarantee accurate forecasts. Certainly, if various economic groups such as the Council of Economic Advisors (to the president) have difficulty predicting the economy, the individual investor cannot expect to do what those trained analysts are unable to do.

The individual investor, however, does have access to the predictions of the various forecasting services, which are reported in the financial press. For example, *Fortune* and *Financial World* publish annual forecasts at the beginning of the calendar year. These predictions include the growth in gross domestic product, which measures the nation's final output of goods and services for the year; the level of unemployment; and the rate of inflation, that is, the rate of increase in the level of prices. Although the various forecasts are different, they vary only in degree, since all analysts are working with essentially the same information.

The importance of these forecasts to individual investors is not so much the actual predicted numbers but the direction and amount of change. Since profits are related to economic activity, forecasts of such activity may be helpful in predicting the level of a firm's earnings. However, the investor should realize that changes in stock prices frequently precede changes in economic activity. Thus, estimates of economic growth may be too late to help investors if stock prices have already risen. The investor should also realize that not all companies benefit from periods of economic growth. Analysis of the financial condition and the growth potential of the individual firm is still warranted.

The Federal Reserve

Federal Reserve
The central bank of the United States.

In addition to forecasts of aggregate economic activity, the investor should be concerned with the monetary policy of the **Federal Reserve** (the "Fed"). The Federal Reserve is the country's central bank. Although in many countries the treasury and the central bank are one and the same, in the United States they are independent of each other. Such independence is an example of the checks and balances of the U.S. political system. However, both the U.S. Treasury and the Federal Reserve have the same general economic goals of full employment, stable prices, and economic growth.

The Federal Reserve pursues these economic goals through the regulation of the supply of credit and money. Monetary policy refers to changes in the supply of money and credit. When the Federal Reserve wants to increase the supply of money and credit to help expand the level of income and employment, it follows an "easy" monetary policy. When it desires to contract the supply of money and credit to help fight inflation, it pursues a "tight" monetary policy.

The Federal Reserve has several tools by which it may affect the supply of money and the availability of credit. These tools work primarily by altering the ability of commercial banks to grant loans, thereby expanding or contracting the money supply. Commercial banks must hold reserves, which are assets held against their deposit liabilities. The amount of the **reserve requirement** is established by the Federal Reserve. Any reserves in excess of those required may be lent. By lowering the reserve requirement, the Fed increases the banks' excess reserves and thus increases their capacity to lend. When the banks do make new loans, they expand the supply of money. By raising the reserve requirement and hence reducing the excess reserves of banks, the Fed decreases the banks' capacity to lend and may cause them to contract their outstanding loans, which reduces the supply of money and credit.

reserve requirement
The percentage that banks must hold in reserve against their deposit liabilities.

In addition to reserve requirements, the other two major tools of monetary policy are the discount rate and open market operations. The **discount rate** is the rate of interest charged by the Fed when banks borrow reserves. If the Fed seeks to expand the money supply, it lowers the discount rate, which encourages the banks to borrow reserves from the Fed. When the banks in turn lend the funds acquired from the Fed, the money supply is expanded. The converse occurs when the Fed seeks to reduce the supply of money. It raises the discount rate, which discourages banks from borrowing reserves from the Federal Reserve.

discount rate
The rate of interest charged by the Federal Reserve when banks borrow reserves.

Of the major tools of monetary policy, by far the most important is **open market operations,** which refers to the purchase or sale of government securities (especially treasury bills) by the Federal Reserve. By buying and selling these securities, the Federal Reserve is able to alter both the supply of money in circulation and the reserves of the commercial banking system. The Federal Reserve may buy and sell securities at any time and in any volume and thus is able to affect the supply of money and credit whenever it chooses to do so.

open market operations
The buying and selling of government securities by the Federal Reserve.

When the Federal Reserve wants to increase the money supply and the reserves of the banking system, it purchases securities. Ownership of the securities is transferred to the Federal Reserve, and the Federal Reserve pays for the securities by writing checks drawn on itself, which the sellers deposit in commercial banks. The banks clear the checks and receive reserves from the Federal Reserve.

The total effect of the transaction is (1) to increase the supply of money by increasing demand deposits and (2) to increase the reserves of the banking system. While the required reserves of the banks rise (because the deposit liabilities of the commercial bank have risen), only a fraction of the increase in reserves will be required reserves. This increase in excess reserves means that the capacity of the commercial banking system to expand the supply of money and to issue more credit has risen. The purchase of government securities by the Federal Reserve from the general public brings about not only an increase in the supply of money but also the potential for additional increases through an increase in the excess reserves of commercial banks.

When the Federal Reserve desires to contract the money supply, it sells government securities. Once again it is the payment for the purchased securities that alters the money supply and the capacity of commercial banks to lend. If the public buys the securities, demand deposits decrease along with the money supply and the reserves of commercial banks.

The total effect of this transaction is (1) to decrease the money supply because demand deposits have decreased and (2) to decrease the total reserves of the banking system because commercial banks have fewer reserves on deposit at the Federal Reserve. Since only a percentage of these reserves is required against deposit liabilities, the banks' excess reserves also decrease. Thus, by selling securities in the open market, the Federal Reserve decreases the supply of money and decreases the excess reserves of commercial banks. The decrease in excess reserves reduces the ability of the commercial banking system to lend and to issue credit.

THE IMPACT OF MONETARY POLICY ON SECURITY PRICES

The importance of open market operations for investment analysis is two-fold. First, the buying and selling of government securities have an immediate impact on interest rates and bond prices. Second, there is an indirect effect on security prices that results from the impact of monetary policy on a firm's earning capacity.

When the Federal Reserve buys treasury securities, it bids up their prices and causes yields to decline. The rate differential between treasury debt and corporate debt widens, and as a result investors purchase corporate securities. This causes their prices to rise and their yields to decline, and the effect on yields of the open market purchases by the Federal Reserve is transferred to other debt instruments.

The converse happens when the Federal Reserve sells government securities. This depresses their prices and increases interest rates. The rate differential between corporate and federal government debt is reduced, and investors move from corporate to government securities. This reduces the price of corporate bonds and increases their yield. Thus, the effect of the sale of government securities by the Federal Reserve is transferred to corporate and all other forms of debt.

The second source of the impact of monetary policy is the effect of changes in monetary conditions on the earning capacity of a firm. Since all assets must be financed, any change in monetary policy affects the cost of a firm's financing. Tightening credit will increase the cost of financing, which by itself will result in lower earnings. The increased cost of credit will be reflected in the prices charged by the firm, which should dampen the demand for the company's output. Its buyers will find their credit more expensive, which may result in individuals, governments, and firms buying fewer goods and services. This reduced demand will reinforce the increased cost of financing and cause earnings to decline.

In addition to the impact on earnings, the tighter monetary policy will result in individuals increasing their required rate of return on equity investments. If investors can earn more on debt instruments than was possible before the increase in interest rates, they will require higher returns on equity investments. Higher returns are possible if stock prices fall. Thus, there is pressure from two sources on stock prices to fall. The higher interest rates will probably result in lower earnings and in higher required rates of return. Both of these will depress stock prices.

This argument can be expressed in more formal terms by using the dividend-growth valuation model that was presented in Chapter 8. That model is

$$V = \frac{D_0(1 + g)}{k - g},$$

where V is the value of the stock, D_0 the dividend that is currently being paid, k the investors' required rate of return on stock, and g the firm's growth rate in earnings and dividends. A tightening of credit by the Federal Reserve may reduce the firm's growth rate and its capacity to pay dividends. Therefore, the value of D or g or both will decline, which will cause the price of the stock to decline. In addition, the required rate of return (k) will rise. This increases the denominator and causes the price of the stock to fall. Thus, tighter credit and higher interest rates generally indicate that the value of stock will decline. In terms of the constant growth valuation model, tight money reduces the numerator and increases the denominator, which puts downward pressure on the value of the stock.

A loosening of credit has the opposite impact. Lower interest rates may increase stock prices by increasing earnings, which leads to higher dividends or increased growth, and by reducing the required rate of return. This suggests that if the investor anticipates lower interest rates, he or she should buy securities and reduce holdings of short-term assets, such as shares of money market mutual funds.

The problem, of course, lies in determining which monetary policy is currently being followed by the Federal Reserve. This is best perceived through changes in the nation's stock of money and the reserves of the banks and through the policy statements of the leaders of the Federal Reserve (i.e., the board of governors). The first two factors are reported weekly in the financial press. Data for several time periods are reported monthly in the *Federal Reserve Bulletin*, which may be readily obtained by subscription or in libraries. Policy statements are published in the financial press but are not neatly collected in one volume or publication for easy access.

Unfortunately, monetary statistics may not clearly indicate the monetary policy of the Federal Reserve. For example, the Federal Reserve's purpose is to control the money supply to stimulate economic growth and to maintain stable prices and full employment, but there is disagreement as to the composition of the money supply. The simplest definition of the supply of money (commonly referred to as **M-1**) is the sum of cash, coin, and checking accounts (including interest-bearing NOW accounts) in the hands of the general public. A broader definition (called **M-2**) adds savings accounts to the above definition. Thus if individuals shift funds from savings accounts to checking accounts, the money supply is increased under the narrow definition (M-1) but is unaffected if the broader definition (M-2) is employed.

M-1
Sum of demand deposits, coins, and currency.

M-2
Sum of demand deposits, coins, currency, and savings accounts at banks.

The growth rate in the money supply will depend on the definition used by the analyst. Figure 11.2 plots M-1 and M-2 for 1986 through March 1992. Over the entire time period, both M-1 and M-2 rose, but there were periods in which the rates of growth differed. For example, during 1988 and 1989, M-2 grew by 4 percent while M-1 was virtually unchanged. An opposite pattern occurred during 1991. There were even periods (such as early 1988) when M-1 declined while M-2 rose.

While M-1 and M-2 may give conflicting signals, there is still a consensus that the Federal Reserve systematically expands the money supply over time to maintain economic growth. While the Federal Reserve cannot exactly control the week-to-week changes in M-1 or M-2, it can maintain growth in the money supply over a period of time within defined targets. These targets are established within the bounds the Fed believes will maintain economic growth without increasing inflationary pressure.

For illustrative purposes, assume that these targets range from a high of 6.0 percent to a low of 4.0 percent annual growth in the money supply. As long as the money supply is expanding within these targets, there may be little reason for the

Figure 11.2 ✦ Money Supply (M-1 and M-2), 1980–1991

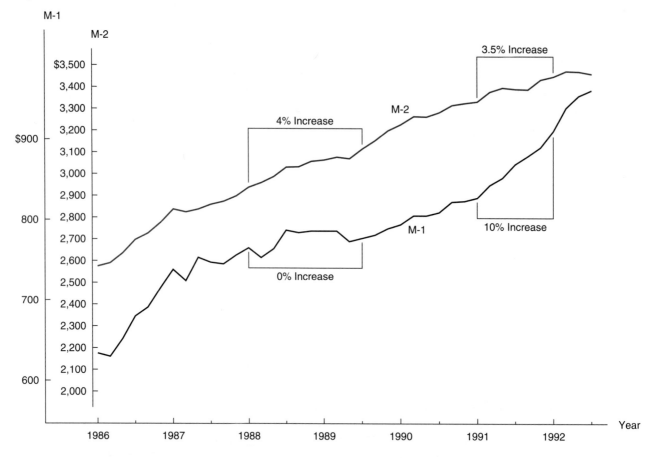

Federal Reserve to change its current monetary policy. However, if the rate of growth begins to exceed the upper limit (e.g., is 7.2 percent), the Fed may then take action to reduce the growth rate in the supply of money. Conversely, if the supply of money is expanding at a slower rate, such as 3.0 percent, the Fed may take action to increase the rate of growth in the money supply.

Such target growth in the money supply is illustrated in Figure 11.3, in which the vertical axis measures the money supply while the horizontal axis measures time. As of the present (t_0), the money supply is some amount X. If this amount grows at the upper limit of 6.0 percent, it will follow line XU. If, however, the growth rate in the supply of money is the lower limit of 4.0 percent, the money supply will follow line XL. The actual money supply may fluctuate between the two targets, as is illustrated during the time period t_0t_1.

If the rate of growth were to increase and exceed the 6.0 percent target growth rate, the money supply would break the upper limit (e.g., t_2 in Figure 11.3). Since this excessive expansion in the money supply is inflationary, the Federal Reserve would probably take steps to reduce the money supply's growth. The financial analyst would then expect monetary policy to tighten, which would cause interest rates

Figure 11.3 ◆ UPPER AND LOWER LIMITS IN THE GROWTH OF THE MONEY SUPPLY

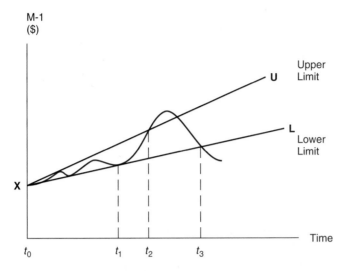

to increase. This then suggests that the investor should liquidate long-term holdings and move into short-term, liquid securities.

Conversely, if the rate of growth in the money supply were to decline below the 4.0 percent target growth rate, the money supply would break the lower limit, t_3 in Figure 11.3. Since this reduction in the money supply would retard economic growth, the Federal Reserve would probably take steps to increase the growth rate in the money supply. The financial analyst would then expect monetary policy to ease credit, which would cause interest rates to fall. Such a scenario suggests that investors should move out of short-term investments into longer-term securities.

It should be noted that the investor is not concerned with the absolute level of the money supply but with the trend (i.e., the rate of growth) and changes in the trend. Emphasis may be placed on anticipating changes in the Federal Reserve's policy. Thus an increase in the money supply might actually be taken as a bearish sign. The current increase in the supply of money may suggest that the Federal Reserve will have to tighten credit and decrease the money supply in the future. Such anticipation of future inflationary monetary policy may imply that interest rates will rise in the future and that now is the time to sell interest-sensitive securities.

FISCAL POLICY

In addition to the monetary policy of the Federal Reserve, the fiscal policy of the federal government can have an important impact on the security markets. **Fiscal policy** is taxation, expenditures, and debt management by the federal government. Like monetary policy, fiscal policy may be used to pursue the economic goals of price stability, full employment, and economic growth.

fiscal policy
Taxation, expenditures, and debt management of the federal government.

Obviously taxation can have an impact on security prices. Corporate income taxes reduce corporate earnings and hence reduce firms' capacity to pay dividends and to retain earnings for growth. Personal income taxes reduce disposable income. This reduces demand for goods and services as well as savings that would be invested in some asset. Federal taxes also affect the demand for specific securities, such as tax-exempt bonds. Thus the tax policies may affect not only the level of security prices but also relative prices, as certain types of assets receive favorable tax treatment.

The potential impact of the federal government's fiscal policy is not limited to taxation. Expenditures can also affect security prices. This should be obvious with regard to the specific products bought by the government. Such purchases may increase a particular firm's earnings and help enhance its stock's price. However, expenditures in general, especially **deficit spending,** can affect the financial markets and security prices.

deficit spending
Government expenditures exceeding government revenues.

When the federal government's expenditures exceed revenues, it runs a deficit. The federal government may obtain funds to finance this deficit from three sources: (1) the general public, (2) banks, and (3) the Federal Reserve. When the federal government sells securities to the general public to finance the deficit, these securities compete directly with all other securities for the funds of savers. This increased supply of federal government securities will tend to decrease security prices and increase their yields.

A similar conclusion applies to sales of treasury securities to banks. If the banks lend money to the federal government, they cannot lend these funds to individuals and businesses. The effect will be to raise the cost of loans as the banks ration their supply of loanable funds. Higher borrowing costs should tend to reduce security prices for several reasons. First, higher costs should reduce corporate earnings, which will have an impact on dividends and growth rates. Second, higher borrowing costs should reduce the attractiveness of buying securities on credit (i.e., margin) and thus reduce the demand for securities. Third, the higher costs of borrowing will probably encourage banks to raise the rates they pay depositors. Especially, the rates on negotiable certificates of deposit should rise as the banks attempt to attract funds. Since all short-term rates are highly correlated, increases in one rate will be transferred to other rates. Once again the higher interest rates in general produce lower security prices.

If the Federal Reserve were to finance the federal government's deficit, the impact would be the same as if the Fed had purchased securities through open market operations. In either case the money supply would be expanded. In effect when the Fed buys the securities issued to finance the federal government's deficit, the Fed is monetizing the debt because new money is created. This new money may initially cause security prices to rise; however, the longer term impact may be to cause security prices to fall. If the public perceives this newly created money as inflationary, required rates of return will rise. Investors will seek higher returns to compensate them for the loss of purchasing power caused by the inflation. The higher required rates of return will drive down security prices.

Thus the security markets are not immune to the fiscal policy of the federal government. As with monetary policy, if the investor could anticipate changes, then he or she could take steps now to profit by the changes in fiscal policy. It is for this reason that investors are so concerned with the policies of both the Federal Reserve and the federal government, since policy actions by either can have a substantial impact on security prices.

Figure 11.4 ◆ LIFE CYCLE OF AN INDUSTRY

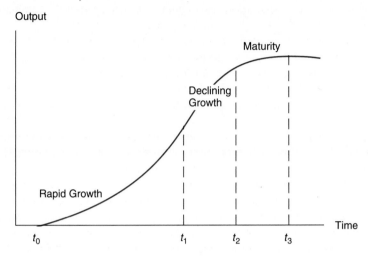

INDUSTRY ANALYSIS

Industries go through a cycle that is analogous to the life cycle experienced by individuals. Initially technology generates a product that spawns an industry. For example, the development of small chips led to the personal computer industry. In other cases change in one area gives rebirth to another. Film studios had many movies that were occasionally shown in re-releases or late-night TV, but the development of home video cameras, video cassettes, and video tape players generated a new market for an old product: the rental and sale of movies on cassettes for home use.

Initially many firms enter a rapidly expanding industry, but as the number of participants increases, the markets become saturated. The rate of growth declines, producing a phase of consolidation. Some firms fail and cease operations while others merge with stronger firms absorbing the weaker firms. The benefits to the surviving firm include a larger market share and increased capacity to survive. A mature industry will tend to have a few remaining participants that share a stable market. Such markets may continue to grow, but the rate of growth is modest.

This life-cycle pattern of growth is illustrated in Figure 11.4, which shows the initial rapid growth in sales (t_0 to t_1), followed by the reduction in the rate of growth (t_1 to t_2), and the inevitable period of maturity (t_2 to t_3). In some cases the industry may even start to decline as total sales diminish (t_3 and on). In a declining industry the competition can be especially fierce as the participants fight for the declining market.

The time period necessary for this life cycle can be long or very short, depending on the rate of technological change, the amount of funds necessary to start operations, and the legal barriers to entry and competition, such as patents. Ease of entry will rapidly saturate the market. In 1990 it may be difficult to realize that McDonald's and Burger King were once two of many rapidly growing fast-food enterprises serving primarily hamburgers. For each of these firms to have survived, Americans would have had to eat hamburgers for breakfast, lunch, and dinner. Only a handful of the initial entrants survived, and today the market is dominated by a few large firms.

In some cases saturated domestic markets have encouraged firms to expand abroad. Deteriorating domestic cigarette sales have driven Reynolds, Phillip Morris, and American Brands to expand foreign markets in an effort to maintain sales and profitability. Thus, firms that had little initial reason to develop foreign operations may develop large foreign operations. Over half of Coca-Cola's revenues are generated by foreign sales.

If management has insight and perceives the decline in its industry, it may alter the firm's core businesses by diversifying into other areas still offering potential growth. For example, increased use of cars and planes led to a decline in the demand for long-distance bus travel. Greyhound, the former leader in city-to-city bus travel, sold its bus operations.[3] While the company continued to manufacture buses for sale to urban and inner city transit systems, it no longer operated a bus system. In addition, Greyhound's management diversified into consumer products (e.g., Dial soaps and Purex laundry products) and services (e.g., Dobbs, which provides catering to airlines) and then changed the firm's name to Dial Corp. to acknowledge the firm's new configuration.

In addition to going through a cycle of growth and decay, industries respond to the level of economic activity. Some industries tend to be very cyclical and move with the economy. Examples of **cyclical industries** include the automobile and building industries. Since consumers can defer such high-priced items from one year to the next, sales in these industries tend to be exaggerated by economic fluctuations. Car sales and housing starts can vary significantly from year to year, and, as would be expected, earnings of firms in these industries also tend to fluctuate.

These fluctuations in the revenues and earnings of a cyclical firm are illustrated in Figure 11.5. The firm, Lennar, builds moderately priced homes in Florida, Texas, and Arizona, and, as noted, its sales and earnings tend to be cyclical. This was evident during the late 1980s when both revenues and earnings rose rapidly, which mirrored economic growth. Sales went from $154 million in 1984 to almost $400 million in 1989, and earnings per share rose from $0.34 to $1.40 during the same time period. The weaker economy in the 1990s had a major impact on Lennar's revenues and earnings as well. In 1991, revenues declined to $262 million while earnings per share somewhat recovered to $1.05 after failing to $0.68 in 1990.

While some industries are cyclical, others are not. Some are quite stable even though the economy may be in a recession. These industries include food processing and some types of retailing. Purchases in these industries are made on a continual basis. People have to eat; such purchases cannot be deferred. Figure 11.6 illustrates a firm that is representative of these industries. As may be seen in this figure, the revenues and earnings per share of Campbell Soups do not fluctuate as much as the sales and earnings of Lennar. Except for a small decline in 1990, the earnings per share of Campbell Soups consistently rise.

The fact that some firms are in cyclical industries while others are in more stable industries does not imply that investors should purchase securities in the latter

cyclical industry
An industry whose sales and profits are sensitive to changes in the level of economic activity.

---

[3]The buyers of the bus operations took the new firm public in 1991, so Greyhound was reborn as a publicly held long-distance bus company.

Figure 11.5 ✦ CYCLICAL SALES AND EARNINGS: LENNAR CORPORATION, 1982–1991

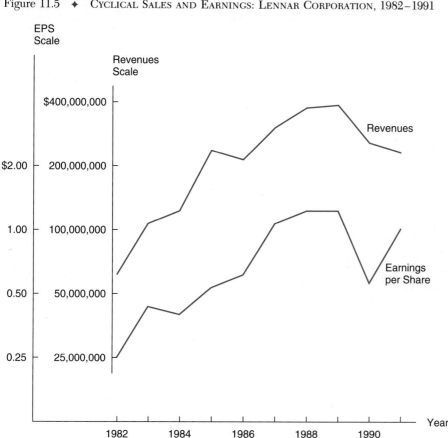

group to the exclusion of those in the former. Security markets tend to smooth out the fluctuations in earnings so the firm's value is related to its performance over a period of time. As the valuation models presented in Chapter 8 indicated, the flow of dividend income and the growth in the firm's earnings over many years (all properly discounted back to the present) ultimately determine the value of the shares. The fact that a firm is in a cyclical industry does not by itself imply that the firm's securities are inferior investments. It indicates that such investments are riskier. Nor does the fact that a firm is in a more stable industry mean that the firm's securities are superior investments. These securities tend to be less risky.

Perhaps the ideal investment is in a firm in a growing industry. Demand for the firm's output can be anticipated to grow, and even if more companies enter the market the expansion of the market itself will permit the firm to maintain its profits in the face of increased competition. Identifying such industries is not easy. Airlines were considered a growth industry in the 1960s but fell on hard times in the 1970s. Other technologically oriented industries, such as those that produce copiers, semiconductors, and computers, have provided excellent examples of past growth. Even industries that were once considered mature may regain their former growth.

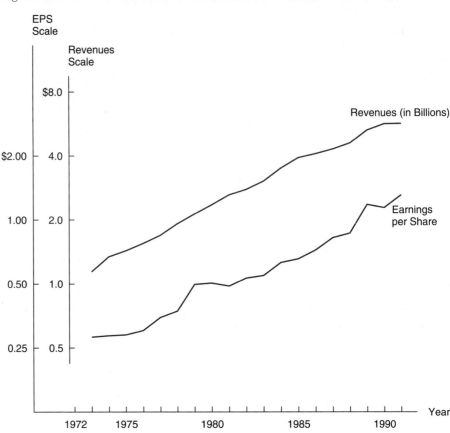

Figure 11.6 ◆ NONCYCLICAL SALES AND EARNINGS: CAMPBELL SOUPS, 1972–1991

While many previous growth industries were based on technological change, future growth need not necessarily be built on technology. Consumer tastes change, and, as incomes increase, consumers may buy different types of products. More income may be spent on services, travel, or fine-quality consumer durable goods, such as crystal instead of glass. Companies in these industries may become the next generation of growth firms. The best investments, then, should prove to be in the securities of firms that are able either to capitalize on technological change or to expand and take advantage of shifts in demand.

In addition to studying the type of industry, the financial analyst will consider such factors as government regulations, labor conditions, and the financing requirements of the industry. While all industries are subject to regulation, some are more heavily regulated than others. For example, utilities such as electric, gas, and tele-communications are subject to a large amount of regulation as to the price firms may charge and the returns they may earn for their stockholders. This regulatory climate varies from state to state. If a utility operates in a state whose utility commission tends to be more stringent, that utility will often experience lower returns on assets and equity. This tends to result in lower dividends and a lower stock price.

Exhibit 11.1   ✦   RATIO OF REVENUES TO TOTAL ASSETS OF SELECTED INDUSTRIAL AND
RETAIL FIRMS

Firm	Revenues	Assets	Sales to Total Assets
Columbia Gas	$ 2.6 billion	$ 6.3 billion	0.41
AT&T	38.8	53.4	0.73
Dial	3.3	3.5	0.94
Allied-Signal	11.8	10.3	1.15
Phillips Petroleum	13.2	11.5	1.15
Premark International (Tupperware)	2.8	2.0	1.40
The Limited	6.1	3.4	1.79
Fluor	6.7	2.4	2.78

Source: 1991 annual reports.

Any improvement in the firm's regulatory climate may increase the stock's price as investors anticipate higher earnings and dividends.

Labor conditions also affect the analysis of an industry. The presence of labor unions or the industry's need for skilled labor can have an impact on earnings. Unions such as those that exist in airlines (e.g., the pilots' union) or mining (e.g., the United Mine Workers) can affect earnings through strikes and expensive contracts. The need for specialized labor such as engineers can also have an impact on earnings as firms pay generous salaries in an effort to bid away skilled workers from other firms. An analysis of the history of strikes and previous labor negotiations or an analysis of the supply of available skilled labor can give the financial analyst considerable insight into the risk associated with the industry as a whole.

Financing requirements also can have an impact on firms' earnings. Industries that are growing or use a large amount of plant and equipment need more funds than more stable and less capital-intensive industries. For example, firms with oil operations need a substantial amount of plant and equipment, since drilling for oil requires investments in rigs, completed wells require transportation systems, and oil refining requires investment in plant and equipment. Differences in the amount of assets used to generate sales are illustrated in Exhibit 11.1, which presents the ratio of revenues to total assets for eight firms with sales and assets in excess of $1 billion. AT&T uses more than $1 in assets to generate $1 in revenues, while Fluor (an engineering firm) generates $2.79 in revenues for every $1 in assets.[4]

---

[4] The Limited's ratio of sales to total assets is probably overstated since The Limited rents (leases) space in malls for its retail stores. These leases do not appear on the balance sheet (i.e., they are not "capitalized"), but the use of the space is comparable to the use of any asset. The financial analyst may wish to recompute the firm's total assets to include the leases; failure to include the leased space as an asset understates The Limited's use of assets (i.e., the ratio of sales to total assets is overstated).

The larger the amount of assets needed to generate sales, the larger is the potential impact on earnings. All assets necessitate a source of funds. Debt financing requires servicing (interest and principal repayment), and additional equity financing spreads earnings over more shares, which may decrease earnings per share. Thus, this need for funds to finance plant and equipment can have an impact on the valuation of an individual firm's stock because such financing can have an impact on the firm's earnings.

THE ANTICIPATED ECONOMIC ENVIRONMENT AND INVESTMENT STRATEGIES

Investing would certainly be easier if there were an identifiable relationship between a specific asset's return and the general economy. Then changes in the economy would lead to predictable changes in the asset's price and its return. In some cases such relationships do exist. For example, real estate values tend to increase with higher prices in general, and bond prices are responsive to changes in interest rates.

However, for many assets, especially common stocks, the linkage between an asset's price (i.e., the return it offers) and the general economy is very complex. An expanding economy may increase the demand for a firm's product, which leads to higher earnings. The higher earnings may permit increased dividends or growth, since the firm has more funds to reinvest. If other factors are held constant, the expanding economy should lead to higher stock prices. Unfortunately, those factors cannot be relied on to remain constant. The expanding economy may result in higher wages and salaries, higher interest rates, increased competition, the deterioration of the value of the dollar in regard to other currencies, higher taxes, and rising prices. All of these factors may have an adverse effect on the firm. The other factors may offset the positive impact of the higher earnings or may even cause the increase in earnings to never materialize.

The relationship between the economy and investment selection is made more difficult when one realizes that security prices are a harbinger of economic activity and not a mirror. Changes in security prices tend to precede changes in economic activity. If an investor waits until the economy has changed before executing a particular strategy based on that economy, the action is often too late. Security prices may have already incorporated the economic change.

While this discussion suggests that it is not simple to link the economy to investing and security selection, there still are strategies the individual investor may follow. For example, changes in interest rates, changes in the rate of inflation or deflation, increased unemployment and recession, and continued economic growth may each suggest a particular strategy that is more desirable and should be followed.

Changes in Interest Rates

Those securities whose return primarily consists of a fixed flow of income, such as long-term bonds, preferred stock, and the common stocks of public utility companies, are particularly sensitive to changes in interest rates. In addition, the common

POINTS OF INTEREST

LEADING ECONOMIC INDICATORS

The direction of the economy might suggest a particular investment strategy. For example, if the economy is heading into a recession, the Federal Reserve might seek to lower interest rates to stimulate it. When the economy is expanding, corporate earnings may rise, leading to increased dividends and capital gains. Lower interest rates and higher earnings and dividends should be bullish. Is it possible to forecast the direction of the economy to help the individual develop an investment strategy? Are there leading economic indicators that can help the individual better time his or her investment decisions?

Leading economic indicators are compiled by the Department of Commerce and are published monthly in its *Business Conditions Digest*. Some of these indicators include:

✦ Average workweek for manufacturing.
✦ New orders for consumer goods and materials.
✦ New orders for plant and equipment.
✦ Changes in inventories.
✦ Number of new businesses started.
✦ Building permits for new homes.

It is easy to understand why these are leading economic indicators. Declines in the average workweek, new orders for goods, materials, plant and equipment, the number of new firms, and building permits suggest that the level of economic activity will fall. An increase in inventories implies that goods are not selling. Retailers will not place orders for future deliveries, so an increase in inventories also suggests that the level of economic activity will decline.

The preceding indicators are re- lated to the level of business activity, but happenings in financial markets are also leading indicators. These include changes in the money supply, changes in total liquid assets, and changes in stock prices. This list has to be disheartening to the investor. Events in the stock and bond markets precede changes in economic activity. If investors forecast lower interest rates or increased earnings and dividends, the buying of securities will drive up prices and decrease yields. Unfortunately, these events occur prior to any changes in the economy.

If changes in the financial markets are harbingers of changes in economic conditions, the investor will be hardpressed to use leading economic indicators to improve investment timing. By the time the leading indicators are available (i.e., are in print), security prices may have already changed. Perhaps the investor will have to develop a system that forecasts the forecasts.

stocks of financial institutions and firms in cyclical industries, such as building supplies, are considered sensitive to interest rate changes.

Most long-term bonds pay a fixed dollar amount of interest each year. As yields rise elsewhere, this fixed flow of income is no longer competitive with other investments whose flow of income is not fixed. Therefore, investors may seek to sell long-term bonds and place the funds in money market mutual funds and other liquid assets whose flow of income will increase with the higher level of interest rates. This selling pressure drives down the prices of long-term, fixed-income securities. Thus, anticipation of higher interest rates certainly implies that the investor should seek to move out of long-term, fixed-income securities. Conversely, anticipation of lower interest rates implies that such securities should be acquired. Purchases of long-term bonds lock in the fixed flow of interest income, and the prices of these bonds will rise when interest rates fall.

The common stock of some firms is also very sensitive to changing interest rates. For example, the prices of public utility stocks, especially those of electric power companies, fluctuate with changes in interest rates. Many of these companies distribute a large proportion of their earnings. Since much of the return the investor can anticipate is the flow of dividend income, the common stocks of public utilities are similar to long-term bonds. Unless the dividends increase to offset rising interest rates, the prices of public utility stocks will decline (the stocks' prices move inversely with changes in interest rates).

The common stocks of financial institutions, such as commercial banks and savings and loan institutions, are also sensitive to changes in interest rates because higher interest rates increase banks' cost of funds. Since their primary sources of funds are the various types of deposit accounts they offer, higher interest rates will require banks to make higher interest payments to depositors. While lending institutions will certainly attempt to pass along their higher interest costs when they make loans, the differential between what they receive and what they pay for deposit funds tends to decline during a period of higher interest rates. This reduces profitability and lowers the prices of their common stock. Thus the anticipation of higher interest rates suggests that investors shift funds from the common stocks of financial institutions into other investments.

Cyclical firms produce goods such as houses, automobiles, and other consumer durables that require a large expenditure by the consumer. The purchase of a new car or durable good may be deferred. The purchase of a house may even be postponed indefinitely if the higher interest rates make mortgage payments more than the individual can afford to service.

The ability of consumers to postpone purchases of durables suggests that the demand for these products will fluctuate with changes in interest rates. Periods of high interest rates reduce demand, which, in turn, leads to lower sales and lower profits for firms in cyclical industries. The lower profits make cyclical firms less attractive to investors, as the capacity to pay dividends and retain earnings to finance future growth is reduced. Anticipation of higher interest rates suggests that the common stocks of cyclical firms should be sold. Conversely, expectations of lower interest rates imply that these stocks should be purchased. Cyclical firms may be among the best performing investments when lower interest rates and economic growth occur.[5]

As the above discussion implies, the anticipation of higher interest rates suggests that investors avoid (1) fixed-income investments, (2) firms, such as utilities or banks, whose cost of funds is sensitive to changes in interest rates and who are unable to pass on the increased cost, and (3) firms in cyclical industries whose product demand is affected by changes in interest rates. Of course, the opposite would hold for expectations of declining interest rates. These investments may prove to be among the most profitable if the investor is correct and interest rates do fall.

While the anticipation of higher interest rates implies that the individual should avoid many assets, that does not answer the question of which assets should be acquired. If the investor anticipates higher interest rates (and correspondingly lower security prices), he or she should acquire more liquid investments and debt instruments with short maturities, such as treasury bills, shares of money market mutual funds, and certificates of deposit. The yields on these assets will tend to increase with any increase in interest rates, and the principal is relatively safe. These short-term debt instruments frequently mature, providing an opportunity to reinvest the funds at the then current rates. Thus if interest rates continue to increase, the investor is in the position to take advantage of the higher rates.

If the investor anticipates that interest rates will fall, a bullish position is estab-

---

[5]While lower interest rates may increase the demand for durable goods, the impact could be lessened by other factors that are simultaneously changing. For example, lower consumer confidence and increased unemployment offset the impact of lower interest rates during 1992. The net effect was that the demand for consumer durables such as automobiles and homes did not rise.

lished by purchasing interest-sensitive securities such as long-term bonds. If the investor wants to follow a more aggressive strategy, that individual may purchase bonds with long terms to maturity or with poorer quality ratings, since such bonds' prices will tend to rise more during periods of declining interest rates.

Inflation

The anticipation of inflation (i.e., expectation of higher prices of goods and services) will also imply an expectation of higher interest rates for several reasons. In an attempt to slow inflation, the Federal Reserve will tighten credit to reduce the supply of money and credit. Monetary policy will also reduce the supply of available credit. In addition, creditors, being aware that inflation reduces the purchasing power of the funds they lend, will protect this purchasing power by demanding a higher return for the use of their funds. All of these actions will also drive up interest rates.

Several of the previously discussed strategies appropriate during periods of higher interest are also appropriate during a period of inflation. In particular, investors should avoid interest-sensitive securities and long-term debt instruments that pay fixed amounts of interest and should acquire short-term instruments (e.g., U.S. Treasury bills) whose yields will increase with the rate of inflation.

However, the anticipation of inflation requires more than a passive strategy of holding short-term liquid assets. The investor should also acquire those assets that will benefit from the inflationary environment. The prices of real estate and other physical assets tend to increase during a period of inflation. Thus, the investor may seek to move out of financial assets into tangible assets.

The common stocks of selected firms may also do well in an inflationary environment. Companies that own substantial amounts of physical resources (e.g., oil, metals, land) tend to prosper during inflation, as their assets' value increases with the general rise in prices. The real value of these assets is usually hidden from investors, as firms carry the assets on their balance sheets at cost rather than at current market value. However, the prices of the common stocks of firms with such "hidden assets" may rise as the replacement cost of these assets increases. In general, any firm with a rich asset base such as metals or real estate may experience rapid growth in earnings that is directly attributable to higher prices (i.e., the inflationary environment).

The expectation of an inflationary environment thus suggests that the investor should stress liquid assets, tangible assets, and the common stocks of firms whose asset base will be enhanced by increased asset values. Correspondingly, the investor should not acquire fixed-income instruments, long-term debt obligations, and the common stocks of firms lacking assets whose prices will rise with inflation. In a sense the strategy is more defensive than offensive, as it is built around retaining and protecting the investor's current purchasing power and the real (deflated) value of assets held.

Deflation

Deflation, the opposite of inflation, is a period of declining prices. Thus, the prices of tangible assets such as real estate, collectibles, and precious metals will fall during a period of deflation. The anticipation of deflation strongly suggests that the investor should acquire those financial assets whose value will appreciate; then the individual can acquire the tangible assets once their prices have fallen.

The safest strategy is to acquire short-term liquid assets such as bank deposits. Since deflation increases the purchasing power of money, the investor will want to hold money (e.g., NOW accounts) and other liquid assets. However, deflation should also be accompanied by declining interest rates and rising bond prices. A deflationary environment should make long-term debt obligations good investments.

If the individual does acquire long-term bonds, he or she should purchase only bonds of excellent quality. Deflation may be accompanied by many bankruptcies as firms become unable to meet their financial obligations. The safest strategy for investors, then, may be to acquire only the bonds issued by the federal government and large industrial firms, major utilities (especially the regulated phone companies), and firms with strong financial statements. The investor should limit purchases to quality fixed-income securities because the bonds' value is primarily related to the ability of the debtor firms to service the debt. If these firms are able to maintain timely interest and principal payments, the value of the bonds will appreciate as falling interest rates accompany the deflation.

The same stress on quality also applies to investments in common stocks. However, since many firms will experience falling demand for their products, difficulty in collecting accounts receivable, and declining profit margins, many firms' stocks may prove to be poor investments during a deflationary period. However, the deflation may create excellent buying opportunities should stock prices be driven down sufficiently.

Recession and Economic Stagnation

Periods of recession and economic stagnation will require different strategies. Recession is a period of rising unemployment (which may or may not be accompanied by deflation). During a recession, the Federal Reserve will put money into circulation and expand the supply of credit. This expansion will at least initially decrease interest rates until the stimulus increases the level of economic activity.

The federal government will adopt an expansionary fiscal policy. Lower taxes and increased government expenditures will increase aggregate demand for goods and services. This increased demand is designed to stimulate economic activity, which, in turn, should reduce the level of unemployment.

To take advantage of the economic stimulus, the investor will seek to move out of short-term money market instruments into financial assets, especially the common stocks of firms that will benefit from the expansionary monetary and fiscal policy. Firms that produce consumer goods or durables such as automobiles and housing may profit from the expansion in the economy. Retailing firms and firms that produce leisure goods or provide services will prosper as the economy moves from the period of economic stagnation and recession toward expansion and economic growth. Increased business activity should also generate increased investment in plant and equipment. Manufacturers of capital goods, machine tools, and other inputs necessary for the production of consumer goods and services will experience increased demand, which may result in increased profits.

The investor, however, should realize that not all firms will perform equally well during a period of induced expansion. Expansionary monetary and fiscal policy does not imply that all firms will prosper. In addition, some forms of stimulatory policy are not general in their effect. The investment tax credit and more generous accelerated depreciation allowances, which have been used to stimulate economic expansion, favor firms that make substantial investments in plant and equipment. Firms that provide services may not require as much of an investment in long-term physical assets to generate sales. Thus these firms will not be helped as much as the firms that are able to take advantage of changes in the tax codes.

Once the investor identifies the firms most likely to benefit from the expansionary monetary and fiscal policy, he or she may adopt any of a number of individual strategies, ranging from conservative to very aggressive. A conservative strategy may include convertible securities (i.e., convertible bonds and preferred stock, discussed in Chapter 18) and common stocks of firms with low beta coefficients. Fixed-income securities may be purchased in anticipation of lower interest rates. But the investor must be willing to rapidly move out of fixed-income securities, because they do not benefit from economic expansion per se and may be hurt if the expansion leads to higher interest rates.

A more aggressive strategy designed to take advantage of expansionary fiscal and monetary policy will stress less current income (i.e., no fixed-income securities) and more potential for capital gains. The investor will then primarily purchase common stocks of firms with low payout ratios that retain earnings to finance expansion. Such common stocks have the best possibility of generating capital appreciation during an expansionary period.[6]

Economic Growth

A period of sustained economic growth differs from a period of expansion generated through the use of stimulatory monetary and fiscal policy. Monetary policy is often designed to thwart a return of inflation and may be only mildly stimulatory. Interest rates may be stable and higher than would be necessary to stimulate the economy. Fiscal policy may also not be designed to generate demand other than for those goods and services that are a necessary component of operating the government. New tax laws designed to stimulate the economy may not be forthcoming.

During such a period, the investor cannot rely on lower interest rates or expansionist government policy to boost security prices, but instead must rely on economic growth to generate returns. Possible investments may include the common stocks of firms with good financial positions and records of sustained earnings and dividend growth. The prospect for continued, sustainable growth is crucial to generate a return during a period of economic growth with neutral expansionary and monetary policy.

Intermediate- and long-term bonds may be acquired during this period by investors seeking current income. There is less need for liquidity to take advantage of anticipated lower prices of tangible assets or securities. Thus investors may be

---

[6]The investor could adopt a very aggressive strategy through the use of options and futures contracts, which are discussed in Chapters 19 and 20. He or she would purchase call options or sell put options for the common stocks that were expected to increase in price. Stock index futures or stock market options could be purchased, since the prices of these contracts will increase if the expansionary fiscal and monetary policy increases security prices in general.

more willing to acquire these long-term investments. However, these individuals must be willing to change such a strategy rapidly should the period of economic growth start to increase the inflation rate.

An aggressive investor may purchase common stocks with an emphasis on growth potential. However, the investor must realize that while a rising stock market will tend to increase the value of most stocks, some will lag behind. Obviously if the investor purchases those laggards, he or she will not participate in the rally.

Portfolio management and asset selection can be designed to meet the investor's expectations of higher or lower interest rates, inflation or deflation, recession or economic growth. Such portfolio construction requires active decision making. If the investor does not want to devote the time and effort to active portfolio management, that individual may buy the shares of investment companies, such as mutual funds. As is discussed in Chapter 23, each mutual fund identifies the strategies and goals (e.g., growth or income) that it follows. The investor then selects the funds whose strategies and goals are consistent with his or her own. For example, if the investor anticipates inflation and wants a position in gold, he or she may purchase shares in a gold fund. Anticipation of lower interest rates suggests purchasing the shares on a bond fund.

Since more than one fund pursues a particular strategy, the individual must choose among the various funds. However, the investor is relieved of the decision as to which individual securities to acquire.

SUMMARY

Fundamental financial analysis selects stocks by identifying the strongest firms within an industry. The analysis starts by considering the direction of the aggregate economy, since security prices respond to economic activity. During periods of prosperity, stock prices tend to rise. Conversely, stock prices will fall when investors anticipate recession and sluggish economic growth.

The aggregate economy is affected by many factors, but the monetary policy of the Federal Reserve and the fiscal policy of the federal government are particularly important. Both the Fed and the federal government pursue the general economic goals of full employment, stable prices, and economic growth. The Federal Reserve affects economic activity through its impact on the supply of money and credit. The federal government affects the economy through taxation, expenditures, and how its deficit is financed. Both monetary and fiscal policy can alter security prices through their impact on interest rates and their impact on firms' earnings (and hence on dividends and growth rates).

Firms exist within an industry. Factors that affect an industry also have an impact on the individual firm. Government regulations, the existence of labor unions, skilled labor requirements, technological changes, and cyclical demand for an industry's output can and do alter the earnings of a firm. The financial analyst thus considers those characteristics of an industry that play an important role in determining the capacity of the individual firm to succeed and grow within its industry.

Investment strategies are affected by the economic environment. During a period of rising interest rates, the investor should seek liquid, short-term invest-

ments and avoid long-term, fixed-income securities. Expectations of increasing inflation also call for avoiding long-term investments, as well as for acquiring those tangible assets whose value will increase with the rate of inflation, such as real estate
and precious metals. Expectation of deflation suggests that these assets should be
avoided.

During a period of recession, the investor should acquire assets such as the
common stocks of firms that will benefit from expansionary monetary and fiscal policy. While in a period of sustained economic growth, the individual may prefer long-
term investments in firms whose position is sufficiently strong to sustain and finance
growth.

None of these economic scenarios has one simple strategy. There are so many
possible investments, ranging from extremely conservative to extremely risky and
volatile, that may be appropriate for a particular investment strategy. Also, some
alternatives may not be appropriate for a particular investor whose willingness to
bear risk differs from the risk exposure generated by the particular asset. However,
these same assets may be combined in ways that will suit another investor's strategy
and willingness to bear risk.

Active management of a portfolio based on moves in the economy requires portfolio shifts before the economy changes. The individual must anticipate when interest rates will rise or fall in order to take advantage of the price changes in fixed-
income securities. The investor must anticipate inflation in order to purchase real
assets before the inflation occurs. To take advantage of sustained economic growth,
the investor must anticipate when that growth will occur and which firms will benefit. Once economic change has occurred, it will be too late, as security prices will
have already changed.

It is not sufficient to base portfolio decisions on today's economy. It is the future
economic environment that is crucial, which helps explain why portfolio decisions
based on the anticipated economy are among the most difficult decisions facing the
individual investor.

Terms to Remember

contrarian	open market operations
recession	M-1, M-2
Federal Reserve	fiscal policy
reserve requirement	deficit spending
discount rate	cyclical industry

Questions

1. What are the phases of a "business cycle"? Have the periods of expansion
   and contraction changed since the Great Depression?
2. What is the Federal Reserve? What are its economic goals? How may the
   Fed pursue its economic goals?
3. What are open market operations? How may they affect security prices?
4. What are M-1 and M-2? How may the Federal Reserve alter M-1 or M-2?
5. What are the differences between monetary policy and fiscal policy?
6. If the federal government runs a deficit, where do the funds come from
   that finance this deficit?

7. What is a "cyclical" industry? Is it undesirable to invest in firms in cyclical industries?

8. Classify the following firms as either cyclical, growth, or stable (based on the nature of their respective industries).
   - ✦ Apple Computer
   - ✦ U.S. Homes
   - ✦ Philadelphia Electric
   - ✦ MCI Communications
   - ✦ Reynolds Metals

9. If an investor expects interest rates and prices to decline, what types of financial assets should be acquired?

10. What are the linkages between higher interest rates and stock prices?

11. Should economic stimulus by the federal government generate higher or lower earnings? What types of industries will benefit from higher depreciation allowances? Why may an expansionary monetary policy encourage investments in long-term financial assets?

12. Which is more important from an investment perspective—current earnings or anticipated earnings?

Suggested Readings

In addition to the readings at the end of Chapter 2, material on the economic and financial environment may be found in:

Board of Governors. *The Federal Reserve System—Purposes and Functions.* Washington, D.C.: Government Printing Office, 1974.
This is a concise introduction to the structure and role of the Federal Reserve.

Federal Reserve Bulletin.
This monthly publication reports financial data including interest rates, employment, gross national product, and the money supply.

U.S. President's Council of Economic Advisors. *Economic Report of the President.*
This annual publication reports the fiscal policy (i.e., taxation and expenditures) of the federal government.

For a discussion of using past money supply data to forecast future stock prices, see:
Rozeff, Michael. "The Money Supply and the Stock Market." *Financial Analysts Journal* (September–October 1975): 18–26.

Evidence from previous business cycles suggests that stock prices lead business activity, which implies that stock purchases should precede economic expansion and that sales should occur while the economy is still expanding (i.e., before recession starts). See:
Pearce, Douglas. "Stock Prices and the Economy." *Economic Review.* Federal Reserve Bank of Kansas City (November 1983): 7–22.
Piccini, Raymond. "Stock Market Behavior Around Business Cycle Peaks." *Financial Analysts Journal* (July–August 1980): 55–57.
Shiller, Robert. "Theories of Aggregate Stock Price Movements." *The Journal of Portfolio Management* (Winter 1984): 28–37.

Several advanced textbooks on investments cover at length the relationships between the aggregate economy and security markets. See, for instance:
Cohen, Jerome B., Edward D. Zinbarg, and Arthur Zeikel. *Investment Analysis and Portfolio Management.* 5th ed. Homewood, Ill.: Richard D. Irwin, 1987, 215–251 and 369–389.

12

SECURITY SELECTION: ANALYSIS OF FINANCIAL STATEMENTS

*T*he preceding chapter considered the aggregate economic picture and how expected changes in the economy may affect investment strategy. However, after deciding on a strategy, the individual still must decide which specific securities to buy. The investor cannot buy every bond or stock but must choose among an almost unlimited number of possibilities. This chapter helps in security selection by focusing on the financial condition of the firm.

Most of the chapter is devoted to ratios that are used to analyze a firm's financial statements. The analysis may cover a period of time to determine trends, or one firm may be compared with similar firms or with industry averages to ascertain the firm's position within its industry.

There are many ratios that the financial analyst may compute, but they all may be classified into one of four groups. These include (1) liquidity ratios, which seek to determine if a firm can meet its financial obligations as they come due; (2) activity ratios, which tell how rapidly assets flow through the firm; (3) profitability ratios, which measure performance; and (4) leverage ratios, which measure the extent to which a firm uses debt financing. Since the data used in this analysis is taken from the firm's financial statements, an understanding of the components of these statements is a prerequisite for understanding ratio analysis.

At the beginning of the chapter, each ratio is defined, explained, and illustrated. This is followed by a discussion of which ratios are the most appropriate for bondholders and which are the most important from the stockholders' perspective. The third section applies ratio analysis to a firm's financial statements to determine the firm's financial condition and if this condition is stable, deteriorating, or improving. This analysis is the backbone of the dividend-growth model presented in Chapter 8, which determined if a stock is under- or overvalued. To answer that question, the financial analyst needs estimates of future earnings and dividends. Ratio analysis helps determine those estimates.

The chapter ends with a discussion of alternative methods used to select common stocks. These include the use of the book value of a stock, P/E ratios, and the firm's cash flow. The difference between these techniques and the analysis of financial statements and the dividend-growth model is more one of degree than of fundamental *differences. In each case, the emphasis is on determining what the stock is worth and comparing that value to its current price. Only through that comparison can the individual determine if the stock is a good investment.*

✦ ✦ ✦

RATIO ANALYSIS

Ratios, which are probably the most frequently used tool to analyze a company, are popular because they are readily understood and can be computed with ease. In addition, the information used in ratio analysis is easy to obtain, for many ratios employ data available in a firm's annual and quarterly reports. Ratios are used not only by investors but also by a firm's management and its creditors. Management may use ratio analysis to plan, to control, and to identify weaknesses within the firm. Creditors use the analysis to establish the ability of the borrower to pay interest and retire debt. Stockholders are primarily concerned with performance and employ ratio analysis to measure profitability.

Although a variety of people use ratio analysis, they should select those ratios that are best suited to their specific purposes. As is illustrated later in this chapter, a bondholder is concerned primarily with the firm's ability to pay interest and repay principal and is less concerned with the rate at which the firm's equipment is used. While the rate at which fixed assets turn over may affect the ability of the company to pay the interest and principal, the typical bondholder is more concerned with the firm's capacity to generate cash.

The investor may find that a specific industry requires additional ratios or more sophisticated versions of a particular ratio. For example, the ratios used to analyze public utilities are considerably different from those used to analyze railroads. Although both are highly regulated and have many similarities, such as large investments in plant and equipment, the natures of the industries are quite different, including factors such as the labor requirements, the element of competition, and the demand for each service. Emphasis, then, is placed on different factors, such as miles traveled per ton of freight for railroads versus the peak load requirements relative to the average demand for electricity for an electric utility.

Ratios may be computed and interpreted from two perspectives. They may be compiled for a number of years to perceive trends, which is called **time-series analysis.** Or they may be compared at a given time for several firms within the same industry, known as **cross-sectional analysis.** Time-series and cross-sectional analysis may be used together, as the analyst will compare the firm to its industry over a period of years.

One ratio by itself means little, but several ratios together may give a clear picture of a firm's strengths and weaknesses. Rarely will all the ratios indicate the same general tendency. However, when they are taken as a group, the ratios often give the investigator an indication of the direction in which the firm is moving and its financial position in comparison to other firms in its industry.

The subsequent sections of this chapter cover a variety of ratios. The illustrations of these ratios employ data taken from the balance sheet and income state-

time-series analysis
An analysis of a firm over a period of time.

cross-sectional analysis
An analysis of several firms in the same industry at a point in time.

ments of Chesapeake Corporation (CSK—the NYSE trading symbol), an integrated paper and forest products company. Its products include paperboard and paper, corrugated containers, commercial and industrial tissue products, and bleached hardwood pulp. Chesapeake's balance sheet and income statement for 1990 and 1991 are given in Exhibits 12.1 and 12.2. The 1991 data is used to illustrate the ratios, and both years plus several additional years' data are employed later in the chapter to illustrate the use of ratios in time-series analysis.

LIQUIDITY RATIOS

Liquidity is the ease with which assets may be quickly converted into cash without the firm's incurring a loss. If a firm has a high degree of liquidity, it will be able to meet its debt obligations as they become due. Therefore, liquidity ratios are a useful tool for the firm's creditors, who are concerned with being paid. Liquidity ratios are so called because they indicate the degree of liquidity or "moneyness" of the company's assets.

The Current Ratio

The **current ratio** is the ratio of current assets to current liabilities.

$$\text{Current ratio} = \frac{\text{Current assets}}{\text{Current liabilities}}.$$

current ratio
Current assets divided by current liabilities; a measure of liquidity.

It indicates the extent to which the current liabilities, which must be paid within a year, are "covered" by current assets. For CSK the current ratio as of December 31, 1991, was

$$\frac{\$196.4}{\$94.7} = 2.07,$$

which indicates that for every $1 that the firm had to pay within the year, there was $2.07 in the form of either cash or an asset that was to be converted into cash within the year. (Dollar amounts are in millions.)

For most industries, it is desirable to have more current assets than current liabilities. It is sometimes asserted that a firm should have at least $2 in current assets for every $1 in current liabilities or a current ratio of at least 2:1. If the current ratio is 2:1, then the firm's current assets could deteriorate in value by 50 percent and the firm would still be able to meet its short-term liabilities.

Although such rules of thumb are convenient, they need not apply to all industries. For example, electric utilities usually have current liabilities that exceed their current assets (i.e., a current ratio of less than 1:1). Does this worry short-term creditors? No, because the short-term assets are primarily accounts receivable from electricity users and are of high quality. Should a customer fail to pay an electricity bill, the company threatens to cut off service, and this threat is usually sufficient to induce payment. The higher the quality of the current assets (i.e., the greater the

Exhibit 12.1 ✦ CHESAPEAKE CORPORATION CONSOLIDATED BALANCE SHEET

	December 31, 1991	1990
Assets	(In millions)	
Current assets:		
Cash	$ 1.0	$ .8
Accounts receivable	84.0	83.0
Inventories	107.2	95.6
Other	4.2	5.6
Total current assets	196.4	185.0
Property, plant, and equipment:		
Plant sites and buildings	126.2	122.7
Machinery and equipment	849.6	828.8
Construction in progress	66.9	19.4
	1,042.7	970.9
Less accumulated depreciation	441.8	394.4
	600.9	576.5
Timber and timberlands	40.7	39.7
Net property, plant, and equipment	641.6	616.2
Other assets	77.5	74.7
	$ 915.5	$875.9
Liabilities and Stockholders' Equity		
Current liabilities:		
Accounts payable and accrued expenses	$ 82.5	$ 80.0
Current maturities of long-term debt	5.1	4.2
Dividends payable	3.7	3.7
Income taxes payable	3.4	4.3
Total current liabilities	94.7	92.2
Long-term debt	415.9	381.0
Deferred income taxes	86.5	88.9
Stockholders' equity:		
Common stock, $1 par value; authorized, 60 million shares; outstanding, 20.6 million and 20.4 million shares	20.6	20.4
Additional paid-in capital	37.5	33.7
Retained earnings	260.3	259.7
	318.4	313.8
	$ 915.5	$875.9

Source: Chesapeake Corporation, *1991 Annual Report.* Reprinted with permission.

Exhibit 12.2 ✦ CHESAPEAKE CORPORATION CONSOLIDATED STATEMENT OF INCOME AND RETAINED EARNINGS

	For the years ended December 31,		
	1991	1990	1989
	(In millions except per share data)		
Income:			
Net sales	$840.5	$841.2	$813.1
Costs and expenses:			
Cost of products sold	616.8	633.2	581.2
Depreciation and cost of timber harvested	62.1	55.8	47.9
Selling, general and administrative expenses	103.1	93.3	81.5
Income from operations	58.5	58.9	102.5
Other income (expense), net	3.0	(.4)	1.9
Interest expense	(35.4)	(29.4)	(25.9)
Income before taxes	26.1	29.1	78.5
Income taxes	10.7	12.4	30.9
Net income	$ 15.4	$ 16.7	$ 47.6
Earnings per share	$ .75	$ .81	$ 2.31
Retained earnings:			
Balance, beginning of year	$259.7	$257.8	$225.0
Net income	15.4	16.7	47.6
Cash dividends declared, $.72 per share each year	(14.8)	(14.8)	(14.8)
Balance, end of year	$260.3	$259.7	$257.8

Source: Chesapeake Corporation, *1991 Annual Report.* Reprinted with permission.

probability that these assets can be converted to cash at their stated value), the less vital it is for the current ratio to exceed 1:1. The reason, then, for selecting a rule of thumb such as a current ratio of at least 2:1 is for the protection of the creditors, who are aware that not all current assets will, in fact, be converted into cash.

Both creditors and investors want to know if the firm has sufficient liquid assets to meet its bills. Obviously, a low current ratio is undesirable because it indicates financial weakness, but a high current ratio may also be undesirable. A high current ratio may imply that the firm is not using its funds to best advantage. For example, the company may have issued long-term debt and used it to finance an excessive amount of inventory or accounts receivable. The high current ratio may also indicate that the firm is not taking advantage of available short-term financing or is mismanaging its current assets, which reduces its profitability. A high or low numerical value for the current ratio may be a signal to creditors and stockholders that the management of short-term assets and liabilities should be revised.

The Acid Test or Quick Ratio

The current ratio gives an indication of the company's ability to meet its current liabilities as they become due, but it has a major weakness. It is an aggregate measure of liquidity that does not differentiate between the degrees of liquidity of the various types of current assets, which may be in the form of cash, accounts receivable, or inventory. Cash is a liquid asset, but it may take many months before inventory is sold and turned into cash. This failure of the current ratio to distinguish between the degrees of liquidity has led to the development of the quick ratio, which omits inventory from the calculation. The **acid test** or **quick ratio** (both names are used) is determined as follows:

quick ratio (acid test)
Current assets excluding inventory divided by current liabilities; a measure of liquidity.

$$\text{Acid test ratio} = \frac{\text{Current assets} - \text{Inventory}}{\text{Current liabilities}}.$$

For CSK the acid test ratio is

$$\frac{\$196.4 - \$107.2}{\$94.7} = 0.94,$$

which is lower than the current ratio of 2.07. The difference lies, of course, in the inventory that the company is carrying, which is excluded from the acid test.

A low acid test ratio implies that the firm may have difficulty meeting its current liabilities as they become due if it must rely on converting inventory into cash. However, a low acid test value does not indicate that the firm will fail to pay its bills. The ability to meet liabilities is influenced by such factors as (1) the rate at which cash flows into the firm, (2) the time at which bills become due, (3) the relationship between the company and its creditors and their willingness to roll over debt, and (4) the firm's ability to raise additional capital. The acid test merely indicates how well the current liabilities are covered by cash and by highly liquid assets that may be converted into cash relatively quickly. Because this test takes into account that not all current assets are equally liquid, it is a more precise measure of liquidity than is the current ratio.

The Components of Current Assets

Another approach to analyzing liquidity is to rank current assets with regard to their degree of liquidity and to determine the proportion of each asset in relation to total current assets. The most liquid current asset is cash, followed by marketable securities (i.e., cash equivalents) such as treasury bills or certificates of deposit, accounts receivable, and finally inventory. For CSK the proportion of each asset to total current assets is

Current Assets	Proportion of Total Current Assets
Cash and cash equivalents	0.5%
Accounts receivable	42.8
Inventory	54.6
Other current assets	2.1
	100.0%

Since this technique ranks current assets from the most liquid to the least liquid, it gives an indication of the degree of liquidity of the firm's current assets. If a large proportion of total current assets is inventory, the company is not very liquid. CSK appears to be reasonably liquid, as 43 percent of its current assets are cash, cash equivalents, and accounts receivable.[1]

This method of separating total current assets into their components and then ranking them according to their degree of liquidity gives management, creditors, and investors a better measure of the firm's ability to meet its current liabilities than does the current ratio. When used with the acid test, these two measures supplement the current ratio and should be used to analyze the liquidity of any firm that carries a significant amount of inventory in its operations.

ACTIVITY RATIOS

Activity ratios indicate at what rate the firm is turning its inventory and accounts receivable into cash. The more rapidly the firm turns over its inventory and receivables, the more quickly it acquires cash. High turnover indicates that the firm is rapidly receiving cash and is in a better position to pay its liabilities as they become due. Such high turnover, however, need not imply that the firm is maximizing profits. For example, high inventory turnover may indicate that the firm is selling items for too low a price in order to induce quicker sales. A high receivables turnover may be an indication that the firm is too stringent in extending credit to buyers, and this may reduce sales and result in lower profits.

Inventory Turnover

Inventory turnover is defined as annual sales divided by average inventory. That is,

$$\text{Inventory turnover} = \frac{\text{Sales}}{\text{Average inventory}}.$$

inventory turnover
The speed with which inventory is sold.

---

[1] The management of some firms seeks to reduce current obligations prior to the end of the fiscal year. Such reductions in current liabilities improve the balance sheet, but they also reduce the firm's cash. If CSK follows this strategy, its cash would constitute a minimal proportion of its current assets.

This ratio uses average inventory throughout the year. Such an average reduces the impact of fluctuations in the level of inventory. If only year-end inventory were used and it was abnormally high at the end of the fiscal year, the turnover would appear to be slower. Conversely, if inventory was lower than normal at the year's end, the turnover would appear faster than in fact it was. Averaging the inventory reduces the impact of these fluctuations. Management may use any number of observations (e.g., monthly or weekly) to determine the average inventory. The information available to investors, however, may be limited to the level of inventory given in the firm's annual reports.

For CSK the level of inventory was $107.2 in 1991 and $95.6 in 1990. The average for the two years was

$$\frac{\$107.2 + \$95.6}{2} = \$101.4.$$

Thus, for CSK inventory turnover was

$$\frac{\text{Sales}}{\text{Average inventory}} = \frac{\$840.5}{\$101.4} = 8.3.$$

This indicates that annual sales are eight times the level of inventory. Inventory thus turns over eight times a year or about once every six weeks.

Inventory turnover may also be defined as the cost of goods sold divided by the inventory. That is,

$$\text{Inventory turnover} = \frac{\text{Cost of goods sold}}{\text{Average inventory}}.$$

If this definition is used, CSK's inventory turnover is

$$\frac{\$616.8}{\$101.4} = 6.1.$$

This definition places more emphasis on recouping the cost of the goods. However, creditors may prefer to use sales, since sales produce the funds to service the debt. Dun and Bradstreet uses sales in its industry averages, and any creditors or bondholders who use Dun and Bradstreet data as a source of comparison must remember to use sales instead of cost of goods sold to be consistent.

Average Collection Period

average collection period
The number of days required to collect accounts receivable.

The **average collection period,** which is also referred to as "days sales outstanding," measures how long it takes a firm to collect its accounts receivable. The faster the company collects its receivables, the more rapidly it receives cash and hence can pay its obligations, such as its interest expense. The average collection period (ACP) is determined as follows:

$$\text{ACP} = \frac{\text{Receivables}}{\text{Sales per day}}.$$

Sales per day are total sales divided by 360 (or 365) days. For CSK the average collection period is

$$\frac{\$84.0}{\$840.5 \div 360} = 35.98.$$

This indicates that the firm takes 36.0 days to convert its receivables into money.

Receivables turnover, which is another way of viewing the average collection period, may be defined as annual credit sales divided by receivables.[2] By this definition,

receivables turnover
The speed with which a firm collects its accounts receivable.

$$\text{Receivables turnover} = \frac{\text{Annual credit sales}}{\text{Accounts receivable}}.$$

An alternative definition of receivables turnover substitutes annual sales for annual credit sales. That is,

$$\text{Receivables turnover} = \frac{\text{Annual sales}}{\text{Accounts receivable}}.$$

Either definition is acceptable as long as it is applied consistently. Although management has access to the information used in both formulas, investors may be limited to the data provided by the firm. If annual credit sales are not reported by the firm, the investor will have no choice but to use annual sales.

Since the CSK income statement does not give annual credit sales, the first definition cannot be used; hence, for CSK,

$$\text{Receivables turnover} = \frac{\$840.5}{\$84.0} = 10.0.$$

This indicates that annual sales are 10.0 times the amount of receivables. The larger the ratio, the more rapidly the firm turns its credit sales into cash. A turnover of 10 times per year indicates that receivables are paid off on the average of every 1.2 months. This is the same information that was derived by computing the average collection period, since 36 days is approximately 1.2 months.

All of the previously mentioned turnover ratios need to be interpreted with much caution. These ratios are static, for they use information derived at a given time (i.e., the year-end figures on the balance sheet). The ratios, however, are dealing with dynamic events; they are concerned with the length of time it takes for an event to occur. Because of this problem with time, these turnover ratios, which are based on year-end figures, may be misleading if the firm has (1) seasonal sales, (2) sporadic sales during the fiscal year, or (3) any growth in inventory and sales during the fiscal year. Creditors and bondholders need to be aware of these potential problems, since they can lead to incorrect conclusions concerning the firm's capacity to service its debt.

---

[2] Some analysts may prefer to average the accounts receivable in the same way that inventory was averaged for the inventory turnover ratio.

Fixed Asset Turnover

Inventory and accounts receivable turnover stress the speed with which current assets flow up the balance sheet. Rapid inventory turnover means inventory is quickly sold and converted into either cash or an account receivable. The average collection period tells how long it takes the firm to collect the account (i.e., how long it takes to receive cash from a credit sale).

Turnover ratios may also be constructed for long-term assets. Such a ratio is the **fixed asset turnover.**

fixed asset turnover
Ratio of sales to fixed assets; tells how many fixed assets are needed to generate sales.

$$\text{Fixed asset turnover} = \frac{\text{Annual sales}}{\text{Fixed assets}}.$$

Fixed assets are the firm's plant and equipment, and this ratio indicates the amount of plant and equipment that were used to generate the firm's sales. For CSK the fixed asset turnover was

$$\text{Fixed asset turnover} = \frac{\$840.5}{\$600.9} = 1.4.$$

This indicates that CSK generated $1.40 in sales for every $1 invested in plant and equipment (i.e., fixed assets).

Many firms (such as utilities) must have substantial investment in plant and equipment to produce the output they sell. Other firms, especially those providing services, need only modest amounts of fixed assets. The more rapidly fixed assets turn over, the smaller the amount of plant and equipment the firm is employing. While the ratio is obviously sensitive to the firm's industry, it does help measure the efficiency with which management is using its long-term assets.

PROFITABILITY RATIOS

The amount that a firm earns is particularly important to investors. Earnings accrue to stockholders and either are distributed to them as dividends or are retained. Retained earnings represent an additional investment in the corporation by stockholders. Obviously a firm's performance is a crucial element in fundamental analysis.

operating profit margin
Percentage earned on sales before deducting interest expense and taxes.

net profit margin
The ratio of earnings after interest and taxes to sales.

Profitability ratios are measures of performance that indicate the amount the firm is earning relative to some base, such as sales, assets, or equity. The **operating profit margin** is operating income (i.e., earnings before interest and taxes) divided by sales, and the **net profit margin** is the ratio of profits after taxes to sales. That is,

$$\text{Operating profit margin} = \frac{\text{Earnings before interest and taxes}}{\text{Sales}};$$

$$\text{Net profit margin} = \frac{\text{Earnings after taxes}}{\text{Sales}}.$$

For CSK, the operating profit margin for 1991 was

$$\text{Operating profit margin} = \frac{\$58.5}{\$840.5} = 7.0\%,$$

and the net profit margin was

$$\text{Net profit margin} = \frac{\$15.4}{\$840.5} = 1.8\%.$$

These ratios indicate that the company earned $0.07 before interest and taxes on every $1 of sales and $0.018 after interest and taxes on every $1 of sales.

The computation of both these ratios may seem unnecessary, but interest (either earned or an expense), extraordinary items, and taxes can have an impact on a firm's profitability. For example, if the investor computes only the net profit margin, an increase in tax rates will decrease the profit margin even though there has been no internal deterioration in the profitability of the company.

Other profitability ratios measure the **return on assets** and the **return on equity.** The return on assets is net earnings divided by assets. That is,

$$\text{Return on assets} = \frac{\text{Earnings after taxes}}{\text{Total assets}}.$$

For CSK, the return on assets was

$$\frac{\$15.4}{\$915.5} = 1.68\%.$$

Thus, CSK earned $0.0168 on every $1 of assets. This ratio measures the return on the firm's resources (i.e., its assets). It is an all-encompassing measure of performance that indicates the total that management is able to achieve on all the firm's assets. This return on assets takes into account the profit margins and the rate at which the assets are turned over (e.g., the rate at which the firm collects its accounts receivable and sells its inventory), as well as taxes and extraordinary items.

Although return on assets gives an aggregate measure of the firm's performance, it does not tell how the management is performing for the stockholders. This is indicated by the return on equity, which is earnings available to common stockholders divided by the equity, or the net worth, of the firm. That is,

$$\text{Return on equity} = \frac{\text{Earnings after taxes}}{\text{Equity}}.$$

Equity is the sum of common stock, additional paid-in capital (if any), and retained earnings (if any). The return on equity measures the amount that the firm is earning on the common stockholders' investment.

Many stockholders may be concerned not with the return on the firm's total equity but with the return earned on the equity attributable to the common stock. To determine this return on common stock, adjustments must be made for any preferred stock the firm has outstanding. First, the dividends that are paid to preferred

return on assets
The ratio of earnings to total assets.

return on equity
The ratio of earnings to stockholders' equity.

stockholders must be subtracted from earnings to obtain earnings available to common stockholders. Second, the contribution of the preferred stock to the firm's equity must be subtracted to obtain the investment in the firm by the common stockholders. Thus, the return to common stockholders is

$$\text{Return on common equity} = \frac{\text{Earnings after taxes} - \text{Preferred stock dividends}}{\text{Equity} - \text{Preferred stock}}.$$

Of course, if the firm has no preferred stock, the return on equity and the return on the common equity are identical.

For CSK, the return on equity for 1991 was

$$\text{Return on equity} = \frac{\$15.4 - 0}{\$318.4 - 0} = 4.84\%.$$

The ratio indicates that CSK earned a return of $0.0484 for every $1 invested by stockholders. Thus, while CSK achieved only 1.68 percent on its total assets, it was able to earn 4.84 percent on the stockholders' investment.

LEVERAGE OR CAPITALIZATION RATIOS

financial leverage
The use of borrowed funds to acquire an asset.

How can a firm magnify the return on its stockholders' investment? One method is the use of **financial leverage.** By successfully using debt financing, management can increase the return to the owners, the common stockholders. For example, if management is able to borrow at 8 percent and earn 10 percent on the funds, the additional 2 percent accrues to the firm's stockholders. The use of financial leverage may be measured by capitalization ratios, which indicate the extent to which the firm finances its assets by debt. These ratios are also referred to as **debt ratios.**

debt ratio
The ratio of debt to total assets; a measure of the use of debt financing.

Since debt financing can have such impact on the firm, each of these ratios is extremely valuable in analyzing the financial position of the firm. The most commonly used capitalization ratios are (1) the debt-to-equity ratio and (2) the debt-to-total assets ratio. These ratios are

$$\frac{\text{Debt}}{\text{Equity}} \quad \text{and} \quad \frac{\text{Debt}}{\text{Total assets}}.$$

For CSK, the values for these ratios for 1991 were as follows.[3]

$$\frac{\text{Debt}}{\text{Equity}} = \frac{\$510.6}{\$318.4} = 1.6.$$

$$\frac{\text{Debt}}{\text{Total assets}} = \frac{\$510.6}{\$915.5} = 55.8.$$

---

[3] Debt = Current liabilities + Long-term debt + Other liabilities =
$94.7 + $415.9 + $0 = $510.6.

WHEN IS AN INCREASE IN EARNINGS A LOSS?

Financial analysis may be more concerned with a firm's operating income than with the bottom line or net income. Analysts will determine how that net income was achieved. Sometimes a firm's income from operations may have declined or the firm may have even operated at a loss, but as the result of other sources of income, such as interest, capital gains, or tax benefits, the firm is able to report an increase in net income.

Consider the following abridged income statements for McDermott International, Inc.

While sales rose during 1986, McDermott operated at a loss. However, the firm was able to report an increase in net income and earnings per share be-cause of interest income, capital gains, and tax benefits. Many of these income-producing items are nonrecurring. For example, the firm may report the benefit of tax credits in the year in which they occur, but such tax savings will not nec-essarily occur every year. Thus the financial analyst may place more emphasis on the operating loss than on the net income as an indicator of the true earning capacity of McDermott.

Years Ended March 31	1986	1985
Revenues (in millions)	$3,257	$3,223
Costs of operations	2,879	2,892
Gross profit	378	331
Depreciation	158	149
Selling and administrative expenses	308	301
Operating income	**(88)**	**(109)**
Other income (interest, capital gains)	88	53
Tax benefits (e.g., investment tax credits)	71	90
Extraordinary items and minority dividends (net)	(12)	(3)
Net income	**$ 59**	**$ 31**
Earnings per share	$1.60	$0.83

For CSK, the debt-to-equity ratio indicates that there was $1.60 in debt for every $1 of stock. The ratio of debt to total assets indicates that debt was used to finance 55.8 percent of the firm's assets.

Since these ratios measure the same thing (i.e., the use of debt financing), the student may wonder which is preferred. Actually, either is acceptable, and preference is a matter of choice. The debt-to-equity ratio expresses debt in terms of equity, while the debt-to-total assets ratio gives the proportion of the firm's total assets that are financed by debt. Financial analysts or students should choose the one they feel most comfortable working with.

These capitalization ratios are aggregate measures. They both use *total* debt and hence do not differentiate between short-term and long-term debt. The debt-to-equity ratio uses total equity and therefore does not differentiate between the financing provided by preferred and common stock. The debt-to-total assets ratio uses total assets and hence does not differentiate between current and long-term assets.

Some definitions of debt ratio use only long-term debt (i.e., long-term debt/total assets). The argument is that short-term debt has to be quickly retired and is not part of the firm's permanent capital structure. There are three possible arguments against this reasoning. First, a firm may always have some current liabilities (e.g., trade accounts payable), and such liabilities are part of its permanent capital structure. Second, during periods of higher interest rates, management may issue short-term debt as a temporary source of funds prior to refinancing once interest rates have declined. Third, there are periods when short-term debt may be used

Exhibit 12.3 ✦ Ratio of Debt to Total Assets for Selected Firms as of December 1991

Firm	Debt Ratio
Georgia-Pacific	66.8%
Exxon	60.1
Fluor	57.9
ARCO	57.6
VF Corp. (Vanity Fair)	55.5
Reynolds Metals	49.6
Hershey Foods	42.7

Source: 1991 annual reports.

prior to issuing long-term debt. For example, when a plant is being constructed, it may be financed with short-term debt prior to more permanent financing once the plant is completed and put into operation. In this text, the term *debt ratio* will always include both short- and long-term debt.

There is also the question of whether to include the deferred taxes as part of the debt structure and hence include them in the calculation of the debt ratio. Since deferred taxes finance 9.4 percent of CSK's assets ($86.5/$915.5), there is a strong argument for including them as part of the firm's debt obligations in which case the ratio of debt to total assets is $597.1/$915.5 = 65.2%. This indicates that over half of the firm's assets were financed by debt and deferred tax obligations. The argument for exclusion of deferred taxes is that they may be deferred indefinitely. Inclusion may ultimately depend upon when the financial analyst believes the taxes will be paid. Changes in tax laws or the firm's operations can accelerate or retard paying these deferred obligations. An acceleration, of course, argues for their inclusion in the calculation.

In spite of the variety of definitions of the debt ratio, all of the ratios measure the extent to which assets are financed by creditors. The smaller the proportion of total assets financed by creditors, the larger the decline in the value of assets that may occur without threatening the creditors' position. Capitalization ratios thus give an indication of risk. Firms that have a small amount of equity capital are considered to involve greater risk because there is less cushion to protect creditors if the value of the assets deteriorates. For example, the ratio of debt to total assets for CSK was 55.8 percent. This indicates that the value of the assets may decline by 44.2 percent (100% − 55.8%) before only enough assets remain to pay off the debt. If the debt ratio had been 80 percent, a decline of only 20 percent in the value of the assets would endanger the creditors' position.

Capitalization ratios indicate risk as much to investors as they do to creditors, because firms with a high degree of financial leverage are riskier investments. If the value of the assets declines or if the firm experiences declining sales and losses, the equity deteriorates more quickly for firms that use financial leverage than for those that do not use debt financing. Hence, the debt ratios are an important measure of risk for both investors and creditors.

That capitalization ratios differ among firms is illustrated in Exhibit 12.3, which presents the debt ratios for seven industrial and manufacturing firms. This exhibit

Exhibit 12.4 ✦ Ratio of Debt to Total Assets for Five Telephone Utilities as of December 1991

Firm	Debt Ratio
Sprint	59.7%
Nynex	55.4
GTE	54.9
Pacific Telesis	49.2
BellSouth	43.1

Source: 1991 annual reports.

is arranged in descending order from the firm that uses the greatest amount of debt financing to the firm that uses the least amount. Georgia-Pacific acquired over 60 percent of its assets through debt financing while Hershey Foods financed less than half of its assets with debt. Some firms use a very conservative financing strategy. American Filtrona, a small manufacturer of filters for felt pens and cigarettes had a debt ratio of 18.5 percent in 1991. Equity accounted for over 80 percent of its financing.

Financing not only varies from industry to industry but within an industry. Exhibit 12.4 presents the debt ratio for five telephone utilities. As in Exhibit 12.3, the proportion of a firm's total assets financed with debt varies, but there is less variation in these debt ratios than those of the selected industrial firms.

Financial theory suggests that in the real world there is an optimal combination of debt and equity financing that maximizes the value of a firm. The optimal use of financial leverage may significantly benefit the common stockholder by increasing the per-share earnings of the company and by permitting faster growth and larger dividends. If, however, the firm uses too much financial leverage or is **undercapitalized,** creditors may require a higher interest rate to compensate them for the increased risk. Investors may also be willing to invest their funds in a corporation with a high usage of financial leverage only if the anticipated return is higher. Thus, the debt ratio, which measures the extent to which a firm uses financial leverage, is one of the most important ratios that managers, creditors, and investors may calculate.

undercapitalized
Having insufficient equity financing.

Coverage Ratios

Leverage ratios also include measures of the firm's ability to service its debt. These ratios indicate to creditors and management how much the firm is earning from operations relative to what is owed. The coverage for interest payments is called **times-interest-earned.** Times-interest-earned is the ratio of earnings that are available to pay the interest (i.e., operating income) divided by the amount of interest. That is,

times-interest-earned
Ratio of earnings before interest and taxes divided by interest expense; a coverage ratio that measures the safety of debt.

$$\text{Times-interest-earned} = \frac{\text{Earnings before interest and taxes}}{\text{Annual interest charges}}.$$

A ratio of 2 indicates that the firm has $2 after meeting other expenses to pay $1 of interest charges. The larger the times-interest-earned ratio, the more likely it is that the firm will be able to meet its interest payments.

For CSK, times-interest-earned is

$$\text{Times-interest-earned} = \frac{\$58.5}{\$35.4} = 1.65,$$

which indicates the firm has operating income of $1.65 for every $1 of interest expense.

The ability to cover the interest expense is important, for failure to meet interest payments as they become due may throw the firm into bankruptcy. A decline in the times-interest-earned ratio indicates declining income relative to debt or stable income but increased use of debt. It serves as an early warning to creditors and investors, as well as to management, of a deteriorating financial position and the increased probability of default on interest payments.

In the previous equation, the times-interest-earned ratio is an aggregate value that lumps together all interest payments. Some debt issues may be subordinated to other debt issues and are paid only after senior debt issues are redeemed. Thus, it is possible to pay the senior debt issues in full and to have no funds left with which to pay the interest on the subordinate debt. When this subordination exists, the times-interest-earned statistic may be altered to acknowledge it. For example, consider a company with $2,000 in earnings before interest and taxes and $10,000 in debt consisting of two issues. Issue A has a principal amount of $8,000 and carries an interest rate of 10 percent. Issue B has a principal amount of $2,000 and carries an interest rate of 14 percent. Issue B is subordinate to issue A. The subordination may explain why the second issue has the higher interest rate, for creditors usually demand higher rates in return for debt issues involving greater risk.

The times-interest-earned ratio for each debt issue is computed as follows. The firm has two debt issues (A and B) and $2,000 in earnings before interest and taxes. The interest on issue A is $800 and on issue B is $280. For issue A there is $2,000 available to pay the $800 in interest expense, and thus the coverage ratio is

$$\frac{\$2,000}{\$800} = 2.50.$$

For issue B there is $2,000 to cover the interest on A and B. Thus, for issue B the coverage ratio is

$$\frac{\$2,000}{\$800 + \$280} = 1.85.$$

It would be misleading to suggest that the coverage for issue B is the amount available after issue A was paid. In such a case that would indicate a coverage of

$$\frac{\$1,200}{\$280} = 4.29,$$

which is incorrect. Issue B would then have the higher coverage ratio and would appear to be safer than the senior debt. The proper way to adjust for subordination is to add the interest charges to the denominator and *not* to subtract the interest paid to the senior debt issue from the numerator. For successive issues of subordinated debt, the interest payments would be added to the denominator. Since the total amount of earnings available before taxes to pay the interest is spread out over ever-increasing interest payments, the coverage ratio declines and hence gives the true indication of the actual coverage of the subordinated debt.

RATIO ANALYSIS FOR SPECIFIC INVESTORS

An investor may not need to compute many ratios; a few selected ratios will probably provide sufficient information concerning the financial condition of the firm. The ratios that should be selected depend on the investor's need, which varies with the type of investment. Bondholders are concerned with the firm's capacity to service its debt (i.e., pay the interest and retire the principal) as well as the extent to which the firm is financially leveraged. Stockholders, however, are more concerned with performance (i.e., earnings, dividends, growth, and valuation). While bondholders and stockholders are both concerned with the financial condition of the firm, their emphasis differs. Hence, they may compute different ratios to determine the firm's financial position as it applies to their specific investments.

Ratio Analysis for Bondholders

Bondholders are concerned with the firm's use of debt and its capacity to pay interest and retire its debt obligations as they come due. Debt financing may increase the return the firm is able to earn for its stockholders but also adds to the financial obligations of the firm, thus increasing the firm's financial risk. Bondholders would prefer that the firm use less debt financing, since equity financing increases the safety of the firm's existing debt obligations.

The extent to which a firm uses debt financing is measured by the debt-to-total assets ratio or debt-to-equity ratio. The greater the proportion of the firm's assets financed with debt, the larger both ratios will be. Bondholders may compute these ratios to ascertain the extent to which the firm uses debt financing and thereby may perceive the financial risk associated with the firm's sources of finance.

While bondholders are concerned with the firm's sources of financing, they are even more concerned with the firm's liquidity position and its ability to generate cash to service the debt. The capacity of the firm to pay current interest obligations is measured by liquidity ratios (e.g., the current ratio and the quick ratio), selected activity ratios (e.g., inventory turnover and the average collection period), and the coverage ratio, times-interest-earned.

The liquidity ratios indicate the extent to which a firm has current assets relative to current liabilities. Since interest owed during the year is a current liability, the more current assets the firm has relative to current liabilities, the greater is the probability that the interest payment will be made. A high current ratio or high quick ratio implies that bondholders will be paid their interest when due.

The current and quick ratios do not indicate the firm's capacity to generate cash. They only indicate current assets relative to current liabilities. For most firms a large percentage of the current assets will be inventory and accounts receivable. Since these assets must be converted into cash before interest can be paid, the bondholder may wish to analyze inventory turnover and the average collection period. These ratios indicate how rapidly inventory and accounts receivable flow up the balance sheet. The more rapidly inventory turns over, the more quickly the firm generates sales. These sales will be either for cash or on credit. The more rapidly the firm collects its accounts receivable, the more rapidly it is receiving cash. Rapid turnover of both inventory and accounts receivable is desirable from the bondholder's viewpoint because it indicates that the firm is generating the funds with which it can make interest payments.

The bondholder should also compute the coverage ratio, times-interest-earned, to determine if the firm is generating sufficient operating income to pay its interest obligations. Individually this is one of the most important ratios, because it measures the extent to which operating income (i.e., earnings before interest and taxes) covers interest expense. Since bondholders are paid after operating expenses are met but before income taxes, they must be concerned with the operating income generated by the firm. Ultimately interest payments must be generated by operations. If the firm's operations cannot generate sufficient income to meet its interest expense, the bondholders' position is tenuous.

The bondholder is not concerned with net earnings, which are earnings after interest and taxes. It is the stockholders who are concerned with the net income that remains after interest and taxes are paid. This net income is the source of cash dividends and retained earnings, which will finance the firm's future growth and generate capital gains for the stockholders.

Any ratio by itself probably does not tell the bondholder very much. A firm could be generating profitable sales but still not have cash. If a firm sells $100 worth of inventory for $120, that is a profitable sale. If the sale is for credit, the firm acquires an account receivable and not cash. Obviously the firm is operating profitably, but until the account receivable is collected, the creditors cannot be paid. It is by combining several ratios (e.g., leverage, liquidity, and the turnover of short-term assets) that bondholders perceive the safety of their current interest payments. The more rapidly the firm turns over inventory and accounts receivable, the more liquid its current position, and the higher the coverage of interest owed, the safer should be the bondholder's interest payment.

In addition to interest payments, bondholders are also concerned with the repayment of their principal, which comes from the capacity of the firm to generate sufficient cash flow. This capacity may not be indicated by the firm's balance sheet or income statement. A firm could be operating at a profit but not be generating cash, and a firm could be reporting an accounting loss but still be generating cash.

Since the income statement does not tell if the firm is generating cash, bondholders should study the firm's consolidated statement of cash flows. This statement enumerates the firm's sources and uses of funds. It adjusts earnings that the firm reports but for which the firm did not receive cash (e.g., equity earnings in another firm's profits from which no cash was received). The consolidated statement of cash flows also adds back to earnings those expenses that did not involve an outlay of cash (e.g., depreciation). A firm with large depreciation expenses could be operating with little profit or even at a loss and still have the funds to retire its bonds as they mature.

The capacity of the firm to meet both the interest and principal repayment may be indicated by the following expanded coverage ratio, which includes interest, principal repayment, operating income, and depreciation expense:

$$\frac{\text{Earnings before interest and taxes} + \text{Depreciation}}{\left(\text{Interest expense} + \dfrac{\text{Principal repayment}}{(1 - \text{Firm's income tax rate})}\right)}$$

For CSK this ratio is

$$\frac{\$58.5 + 62.1}{\left(\$35.4 + \dfrac{5.1}{1 - 0.41}\right)} = 2.74.$$

The current portion of long-term debt due within the year is $5.1, and 0.41 (41 percent) is the firm's average federal and state income tax rate in 1991. The ratio indicates that CSK generates sufficient cash flow to cover not only its interest payments but also the principal repayments.[4]

Depreciation expense is added to earnings before interest and taxes (EBIT) in the numerator to determine cash flow from operations. (Other applicable non-cash expenses such as depletion and amortization should also be added to EBIT.) The principal repayment is added to interest expense in the denominator. Since principal repayment is not a tax deductible expense, the amount of the payment must be expressed before tax. This adjustment is achieved by dividing the principal repayment by 1 minus the firm's tax rate. As with times-interest-earned, the larger the ratio, the safer should be the bondholder's position, because the larger the ratio, the greater is the firm's capacity to pay the interest and repay the principal.

Ratio Analysis for Stockholders

Stockholders, like bondholders, are investors, but stockholders earn their return not through interest payments but through dividends and growth in the value of the shares. Thus stockholders are primarily concerned with performance (i.e., the capacity of the firm to generate earnings). Performance is measured by such ratios as the profit margin on sales, return on assets, and return on equity. Stockholders are also concerned with the source of the return on their individual investments (i.e., dividends and capital gains). Measures of the distribution of earnings, growth in earnings and dividends, and the market's valuation of the stock are also important to the individual stockholder. Thus, in addition to profitability ratios, stockholders are concerned with the payout ratio, measures of growth, and the P/E ratio.

Sales are the firm's source of revenues and profits. Unless the firm earns its revenues from an investment portfolio, the ability to generate profitable sales is ultimately the source of the return earned by the firm for its stockholders. The ability to generate profitable sales is indicated by profitability ratios, especially the net profit margin (i.e., net earnings to sales). Firms with a high net profit margin or whose net profit margins exceed their industry's averages may be attractive investments.

The gross profit margin (i.e., sales minus cost of goods sold quantity divided by

---

[4]The cash outlay associated with timber harvested occurred in the past, so like depreciation it is added back to EBIT.

sales) and the operating profit margin (i.e., earnings before interest and taxes quantity divided by sales) are also important, for they may indicate a specific area in which the firm excels or is having problems. For example, a firm may have a large gross profit margin but its operating and net income may be small if the firm has high operating expenses (e.g., selling and administrative expenses). In this case the operating profit margin will be low. A small change in the firm's administrative cost controls could have a magnified effect on the operating profit margin. Since the analysis indicated an acceptable gross profit margin, the firm may prove to be a good investment if the operating expenses can be reduced.

Computing the gross profit margin, operating profit margin, and net profit margin may isolate why the firm's net profit is low (or high). If the investor believes that such problems may be corrected (or if they are the result of a temporary event such as a strike or an extraordinary item such as a fire), the stock may still be a good investment. While emphasis is often placed on the bottom line (e.g., net profit margin), analysis of gross and operating profit margins may indicate that net profits are artificially under- or overstated.

The return on assets (earnings divided by total assets) indicates what the firm has earned on its resources. The ratio does not indicate what the firm earned on the stockholders' funds. Thus for stockholders the return on equity (earnings divided by equity) is exceedingly important, because it indicates what management has earned on the stockholders' investment in the firm. A high return on equity indicates that the management has achieved high earnings for the stockholders relative to the funds they have invested in the firm.

A high return on equity is by itself not necessarily desirable. Successful use of debt financing (i.e., earning more on the assets acquired through the use of debt financing than must be paid in interest) will magnify the return on equity. If the firm employs a substantial amount of debt financing to acquire assets, this may magnify the return on equity. However, if the firm were to operate at a loss, the use of financial leverage would magnify the loss to the stockholders. Thus stockholders, like bondholders, are concerned with the extent to which the firm uses debt financing. The debt ratios indicate the use of debt financing and hence measure the financial risk associated with the firm.

If a firm has both a high return on equity and a high debt ratio, the return on equity may be the result of successfully using financial leverage to magnify the return on the stockholders' funds. If the firm has a high return on equity but a low debt ratio, that indicates the firm has profitable operations and is not using debt financing as a major source of the return to its stockholders. The latter situation is less risky, as the profits are the result of operating decisions and not financing decisions. Small changes in sales or expenses should not have a large impact on earnings.

Since earnings are either distributed or retained, stockholders are concerned with the payout ratio.

$$\text{Payout ratio} = \frac{\text{Dividends}}{\text{Earnings}}.$$

For CSK the per-share payout ratio in 1991 was

$$\text{Payout ratio} = \frac{\$0.72}{\$0.75} = 96.0\%.$$

This indicates that management distributed almost all of the firm's earnings. The distribution of earnings is a prerogative of the board of directors. Some managements prefer to retain earnings to finance future growth.

If an investor is primarily concerned with the flow of dividend income, a high payout ratio is desirable. Stockholders who seek growth and capital gains will prefer a lower payout ratio, which indicates that a larger proportion of earnings are being retained to finance future operations. Of course, even investors who seek income may not desire a payout ratio of 100 percent, since even modest growth in the dividends will require some retention of earnings.

The capacity of the firm to grow by internally generated funds depends on its return on equity and the distribution of its earnings. For example, consider a firm with $100 in equity that earns $10. The return on equity is 10 percent ($10/$100). If the firm distributes $10, the equity cannot internally grow. If the $100 is retained, the equity grows from $100 to $110, a 10 percent increase. If 40 percent of the earnings are distributed ($0.4 \times \$10 = \$4$), only $6 are retained and the equity grows by 6 percent, from $100 to $106. The firm cannot increase its equity more than 6 percent and maintain the dividend unless it increases its profitability (i.e., increases the return on equity). Thus the larger the return on equity and the smaller the payout ratio, the greater the firm's internal growth will be.

Stockholders who seek capital gains should be particularly interested in the payout ratio. The value of the shares will not appreciate over time unless earnings and dividends grow. The product of 1 minus the payout ratio and the return on equity provides the investor with a measure of internal growth (i.e., $(1 - 0.4)(0.1) = 0.06 = 6\%$ rate of growth in equity). The payout ratio combined with the return on equity indicates the capacity of the firm to grow internally without (1) using additional debt financing, which may increase financial risk, or (2) selling additional shares, which may dilute the existing stockholders' equity and earnings.

Stockholders are concerned not only with the firm's earnings and how they are distributed but also with what the market believes the earnings are worth. In Chapter 8 the price/earnings (P/E) ratio and the dividend-growth model were used to value common stock. Firms with the potential for higher growth in earnings and dividends achieve higher valuations. A higher P/E ratio indicates that the market is currently willing to pay more for $1 worth of the firm's current earnings. Since the P/E ratio is reported daily in the financial press, it is readily available and may be easily used to compare firms.

An alternative valuation ratio that has achieved some prominence is the ratio of the stock's price to sales.[5] The ratio of per-share price to per-share sales offers one particular advantage over the P/E ratio. If a firm has no earnings, the P/E ratio has no meaning, in which case the P/E ratio as a tool for valuation and comparison breaks down. The ratio of price to sales, however, can be computed even if the firm is operating at a loss, thus permitting comparisons of all firms, including those that are unprofitable.

Even if the firm has earnings and thus has a positive P/E ratio, the ratio of price to sales is still a useful tool. Since earnings are ultimately related to sales, the larger the firm's sales per share, the greater is the potential for profit. A low stock price to per-share sales indicates a low market valuation, which may suggest the stock is

---

[5] See, for instance, Lawrence Minard, "The Case Against Price/Earnings Ratios," *Forbes*, February 13, 1984.

undervalued. If the firm is operating at a loss, a low price-to-sales ratio may indicate a potentially profitable investment. If the firm were to return to profitability, it would produce higher earnings per share if sales per share were large. Thus, a low price-to-sales ratio may indicate the unprofitable firm has substantial potential if and when it returns to profitability.

The Need for Comparisons—the Problems with Interpretation

While bondholders and stockholders may emphasize different ratios that analyze a firm's financial statements, both should realize that one ratio by itself can be misleading. The usefulness of ratio analysis is the general picture derived from the ratios. While individual ratios may be contradictory, the total analysis should provide any investor with an indication of the financial position of the firm.

Just as an individual ratio may be meaningless, so may be a set of ratios for a given firm if there is no benchmark with which to compare them. Thus the investor should either (1) compare individual ratios for a firm over a period of time to establish norms for the firm or (2) compare the individual firm's ratios to an industry average. Such comparisons, however, are not easy to interpret. Many firms have a variety of product lines and may not be readily classified into a particular industry. In addition, industry averages may be dated. Material on industry averages published in the current year must be based on financial statements that are at least one year old. There may be inconsistencies comparing this year's financial statements with previous years' industry averages. Such comparisons will have meaning only if the industry averages are stable over time.

The problem of defining the industry may be illustrated by comparing selected ratios in Exhibit 12.5 for CSK with industry averages for pulp and forest products published in the *Almanac of Business and Industrial Financial Ratios—1991 edition* or the *RMA Annual Statement Studies, 1991.* While Chesapeake Corporation may be classified in this industry, it does make products (e.g., tissue paper) that could be classified as consumer products. Hence the financial ratios for CSK may not be comparable to any industry average because the firm does not neatly fit into one industry classification.

Another problem immediately becomes apparent: the sources only publish some of the ratios the individual may wish to use to analyze Chesapeake's financial statements, and even those that are available can have different values. Consider the debt/equity ratios reported in Exhibit 12.5. The industry averages differ, so the individual investor is left with the problem of deciding which industry average to use as the standard. Of course, investors can overcome this problem by computing industry averages for themselves. Such calculations will require access to financial statements that the investors may obtain directly from each firm or through the use of a computer data base.

Problems concerning the use of ratio analysis are not limited to the availability and comparability of industry averages. Differences in accounting practices may also alter a firm's financial statements and thus affect ratio analysis. For example, the use of LIFO (last in, first out) for inventory valuation instead of FIFO (first in, first out) can have an impact on the inventory carried on the balance sheet and on the cost of goods sold. During a period of inflation, many firms will choose to use LIFO instead of FIFO. This choice results in their selling the last (and presumably most

Exhibit 12.5 ✦ Selected Ratios for Chesapeake Corporation and Industry Averages

Ratio	Chesapeake	Almanac of Business Ratios°	RMA Annual Statement Studies[†]
Current ratio	2.1	1.3	1.9
Quick ratio	0.9	0.7	1.1
Return on equity	4.8%	5.8%	Not given
Return on assets	1.7%	6.9%	Not given
Debt/equity	1.6	1.1	0.8
Times-interest-earned	1.7	2.8	7.7

° *Almanac of Business and Industrial Financial Ratios—1991 edition,* 79.
[†] *RMA Annual Statement Studies—1991 edition,* 274.

costly) inventory first. The firm's cost of goods sold is higher, which reduces the firm's earnings and taxes. The cost of the inventory still held is lower, because the more costly inventory was sold first. Any ratio that uses inventory or earnings will be affected by the choice of LIFO instead of FIFO. If a financial analysis is comparing two firms, one of which uses LIFO and the other FIFO, the analysis will be biased. The firm using LIFO will appear to be less profitable. However, since its level of inventory is lower, it will have higher inventory turnover. In actuality there may be little substantive difference between the two firms.

Other accounting choices may also alter the results of ratio analysis. The choice of leasing instead of buying, the expensing of research and development costs instead of capitalizing them, larger allowances for doubtful accounts, or the accounting for pension liabilities may have an impact on a firm's financial statements. While the accounting profession seeks to standardize the construction of financial statements, differences among firms can and do exist, which may raise questions concerning the use of ratio analysis to compare firms.

Even a trend analysis of a firm's financial statements may be suspect. The problems mentioned before also apply to a ratio analysis of one firm over time if it has made accounting changes from one accounting period to the next. While such changes will be noted in the financial statements, they do raise questions concerning the comparability of ratios computed over a number of years.[6]

While there can be weaknesses in the use of ratios to analyze a firm's financial statements, the technique is still an excellent starting point to analyze a firm's financial position. The limitations of the data do not necessarily negate the technique. Instead, the analyst needs to be aware of the weaknesses so that appropriate adjustments can be made in either the construction of the ratios or the interpretation of the results.

---

[6] If possible, the financial analysts should recompute previous years' ratios using the firm's current accounting practices.

Figure 12.1 ✦ Revenues, Earnings per Share, and Dividends of Chesapeake Corporation (1981–1991)

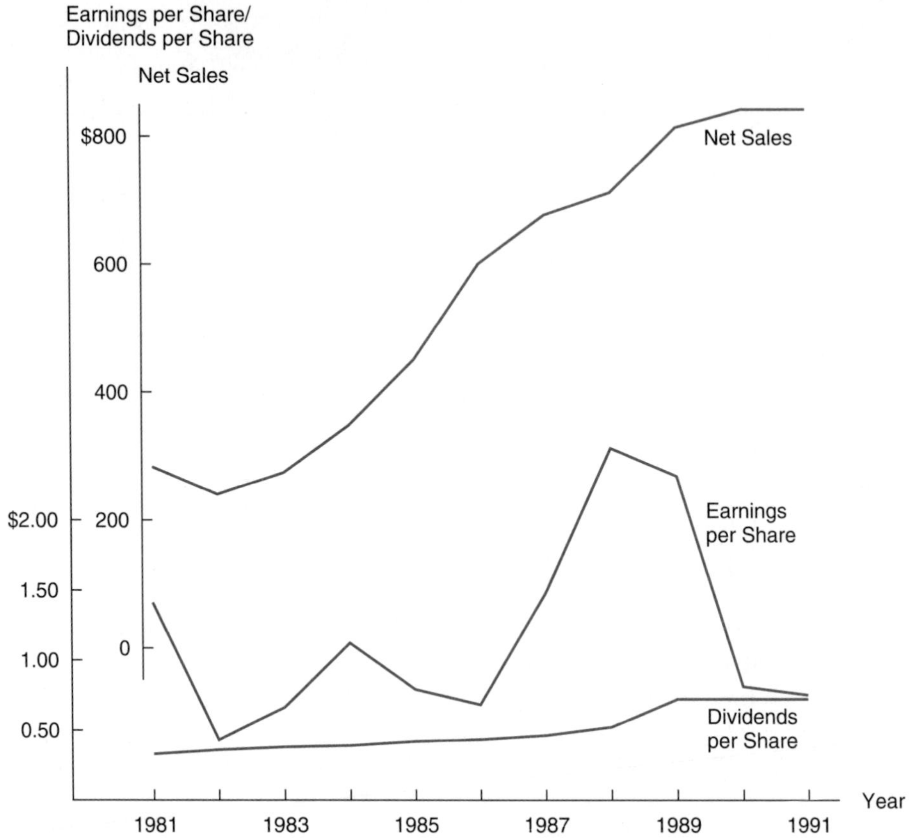

Financial Ratios and Stock Valuation

Many ratios have been presented throughout this chapter. In this section, several ratios are used to analyze the financial position of Chesapeake Corporation. The ratios provide background evidence for the application of the valuation model explained in Chapter 8 and illustrated in Chapter 10 using Chesapeake's common stock.

Figure 12.1 presents Chesapeake's revenues, earnings per share, and per-share dividends for the period 1981 through 1991. As may be seen in the figure, revenues and per-share dividends have grown over time. Earnings per share, however, have been erratic. Many of Chesapeake's products are tied to the business cycle (it may be considered a cyclical firm), so large fluctuations, such as occurred in 1991 (a poor year) or 1988 (a banner year), are to be expected.

Exhibit 12.6 ✦ Ratio Analysis of Chesapeake Corporation, 1980–1991

	1991	1990	1989	1988	1987	1986	1985	1984	1983	1982	1981	1980	Twelve-Year Average
Liquidity Ratios													
Current ratio	2.1	2.0	2.2	2.5	2.2	2.5	2.2	2.6	2.5	2.8	2.6	2.4	2.4
Quick ratio	0.9	1.0	1.1	1.2	1.1	1.0	1.0	1.3	1.6	1.7	1.6	1.7	1.3
Activity Ratios													
Average collection period (days)	36.0	35.5	39.3	38.0	32.6	31.2	35.1	32.3	36.5	34.7	34.5	35.0	35.1
Inventory turnover (sales/average inventory)	8.3	9.0	9.0	9.6	10.2	9.1	9.2	11.2	10.8	9.2	12.0	13.0	10.1
Inventory turnover (cost of goods sold/average inventory)	6.1	6.8	6.4	6.7	7.5	7.0	7.1	8.4	8.6	7.3	9.1	9.3	7.5
Fixed asset turnover	1.4	1.4	1.5	1.6	1.6	1.3	1.0	1.4	1.3	1.1	1.5	1.7	1.4
Profitability Ratios													
Operating profit margin	6.9%	7.0	12.6	14.6	7.4	7.0	7.0	10.0	6.0	5.0	12.0	16.0	9.3
Net profit margin	1.8%	2.0	5.9	7.2	4.5	2.2	3.5	6.3	4.6	2.8	9.3	9.1	4.9
Return on assets	1.7%	1.9	6.0	7.8	5.1	2.2	2.5	6.7	4.2	2.4	10.4	10.4	5.1
Return on equity	4.8%	5.3	17.0	18.5	12.7	6.4	7.6	11.2	6.9	4.1	15.9	16.5	10.6
Leverage Ratios													
Debt/equity	1.6	1.5	1.2	1.1	1.2	1.6	1.8	0.7	0.6	0.7	0.7	0.6	1.1
Debt ratio (debt/total assets)	55.8%	54.0	48.9	44.9	47.8	56.5	59.2	40.8	38.3	41.9	40.8	37.1	47.2
Times-interest-earned	1.7	2.0	4.0	4.7	3.0	1.5	2.2	7.2	2.8	2.1	12.0	13.1	4.3
Other Ratios													
Payout ratio	96%	89	31	21	31	63	53	35	58	84	23	24	50.7
P/E ratio (year-end price)	31.8	16.8	8.6	8.0	11.2	24.7	14.7	12.2	24.8	18.5	7.3	6.1	15.4

Exhibit 12.6 reports a ratio analysis of the firm for the period 1980 through 1991, and Figure 12.2 presents the same material in graphic form, clearly showing the patterns in each of the ratios. As might be expected, there can be considerable variation in the ratios from year to year.

Several of the ratios have been relatively stable. For example, the current ratio only ranged from 2.0 to 2.8 with an average of 2.4 during the twelve-year period. The same conclusion holds for the average collection period. There is no discernible trend, for in any given year the average collection period only modestly deviated from the average 35.1 days. Before 1984, the quick ratio had also been very stable. Starting in 1984, this ratio declined, but it appears to have stabilized, albeit at a lower level than during 1981 to 1984. In 1991, inventory turnover was marginally below its historic average, but fixed asset turnover was equal to the average. In 1985, Chesapeake employed $1 in fixed assets for every $1 in sales, but in 1991, the fixed

Figure 12.2   ✦   RATIO ANALYSIS FOR CHESAPEAKE CORPORATION (1980–1991)

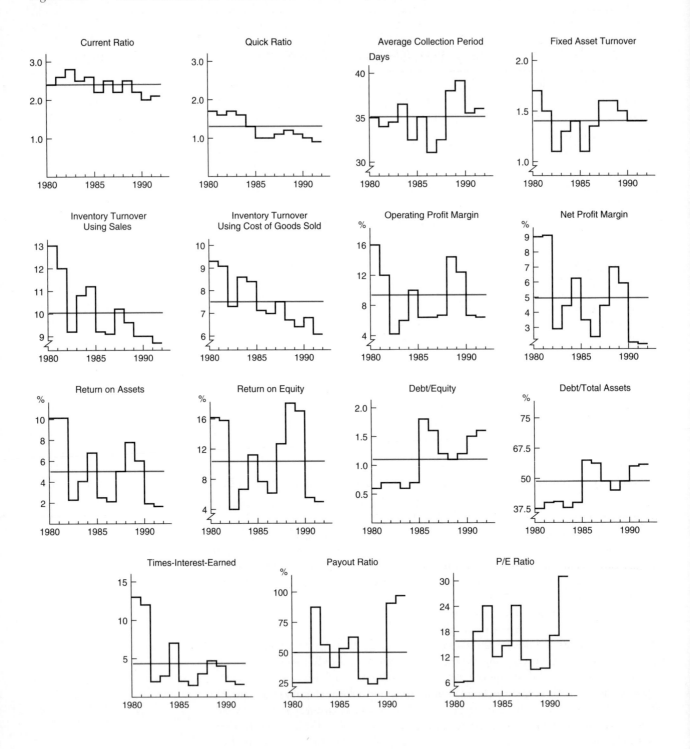

asset turnover was 1.4, which indicates that the firm employed only $0.714 (1/1.4) in fixed assets for every $1 in sales.

Paperboard, corrugated boxes and packaging products, and bleached hardwood pulp tend to be cyclical types of products, so the analyst can anticipate fluctuations in earnings and hence in Chesapeake's profitability ratios. The economic downturn in the early 1990s is clearly shown in the low profitability ratios for 1991 in Figure 12.1. However, the profitability ratios were low in 1985, which was not a period of recession for the general economy. Inventory and fixed asset turnover ratios were also weak during 1985, which when combined with the low profitability ratios should be some cause for concern.

The leverage ratio for 1985 showed dramatic change, as debt to total assets and debt to equity rose. The increased use of debt with its resulting increase in interest expense also produced a large decline in the times-interest-earned ratio. No doubt the large increase in interest expense contributed to the decline in the firm's profitability. This increased use of debt financing must be significant, and in this case Chesapeake made a major acquisition during the year that was financed through the use of long-term debt. (The balance sheet indicated that long-term debt rose from only $60.7 million in 1984 to $308.8 million in 1985.)

This acquisition had to be a major event, since it perceptibly increased the size of the firm as total assets rose from $330.9 million in 1984 to $617.8 million in 1985. The assets acquired were tissue mills to make sanitary paper products. The demand for these products is not cyclical so by acquiring this type of business Chesapeake sought to reduce the cyclical nature of its sales and earnings and to establish itself in a particular market for consumer products. The strategy appears to have worked. 1988 was a banner year with a dramatic increase in earnings.

The strategy, however, did not fare as well during the early 1990s as the prices of many of Chesapeake's products declined. Even though noncyclical divisions of the firm remained profitable, the cyclical products suffered, so that many of the firm's ratios were well below the twelve-year averages. As would be anticipated, profitability declined; the return on assets and on equity reached their lowest levels during the twelve-year period. Since Chesapeake maintained its dividend, the payout ratio also rose dramatically as the firm distributed almost all of its net income.

The poor performance of 1991, however, is not sufficient reason to sell the stock any more than the stellar performance achieved during 1988 is sufficient grounds to purchase the stock, for two reasons. First, past performance may not be repeated in the future. Second, even if past performance is repeated, the investor has to have some concept of what the stock is worth in order to determine if the current price is excessive. That, of course, is the purpose of the valuation model presented in Chapter 8: to determine if the stock is currently under- or overvalued.

ALTERNATE STRATEGIES FOR SELECTING COMMON STOCKS

Besides the valuation model, other techniques may be used to identify possible stocks for purchase. These include the ratio of price to book value, low P/E stocks, small capitalization stocks, and screening techniques. These methods are not necessarily a substitute for analysis of financial statements and valuations but may be used in conjunction with them.

Ratio of Market Price to Book Value

The ratio of market price to book value suggests that the investor should limit purchases to those stocks selling for less than their book value.[7] During 1990 and 1991, the stocks of savings and loan associations sold for less than their book value. For example, the book value of Columbia Savings & Loan exceeded $28, but the stock sold for less than $10. By implication, the stock would be an attractive investment. By the same reasoning, since Chesapeake Corporation's book value was $15.43 and the stock was selling for approximately $25, the stock would not be a good purchase.

The simplicity of this technique is very appealing, but it does not follow that just because a stock is selling below book value that it is a good investment. Unfortunately the ratio does not answer the question "Why is the stock selling below book value?" The answer could be declining earnings or inflated assets. Many savings and loan institutions had problem loans on which no interest was being paid. In effect their book value was overstated. The general negative cloud that hung over the entire savings and loan industry caused the stock prices of virtually all savings and loan institutions to fall. Of course, the problem facing the investor is to determine which firms are truly undervalued and which are in the greatest financial difficulty. The ratio of price to book cannot answer that question, but it can be a good starting point for selecting securities.

Low P/E Stocks

Buying low P/E stocks is a similar strategy in which the investor limits purchases to stocks with low price-earnings multiples or those whose current P/E ratio is near the low end of its historical range. Consider in Exhibit 12.7 the price-earnings ratios over a 16-year period for Bristol-Myers Squibb. On the average the P/E has ranged from 16.7 to 11.8. Unless there has been a change in the composition of the firm (such as AT&T's divestiture), there is little reason for a stock that has traded with a P/E between 16.7 and 11.8 to start selling for a P/E of 30. Instead a P/E of 30 would indicate that the stock is overpriced and should be avoided. A P/E of 5 would indicate the opposite.

While the previous illustration of a P/E = 30 or 5 is an exaggeration, if a stock sells for a P/E near the end of its historic range, that may suggest a specific strategy. If Bristol-Myers Squibb's stock is selling for a P/E of 12 (i.e., near the low end of its historic P/E), that would suggest the stock may be considered for purchase. Conversely, when it sells near its historic high P/E, the stock is not a good purchase and may be a candidate for sale if the investor owns it.

Small Capitalization Stocks

Instead of analyzing the ratio of a firm's stock price to its book value or its per-share earnings, the individual may prefer to invest in firms that are small or that are not

---

[7]A firm's book value may be found readily in the *Value Line Investment Survey*. If the company is not covered by Value Line, the investor may determine the book value per share by dividing the equity available to common stock by the number of shares outstanding. The equity available to common stock is the sum of the common stock, paid-in capital (if any), and retained earnings. These values are found on the firm's balance sheet.

Exhibit 12.7 ✦ PRICE/EARNINGS RATIOS FOR BRISTOL-MYERS SQUIBB

	High	Low
1991	23	15
1990	20	15
1989	21	16
1988	16	13
1987	23	11
1986	21	15
1985	18	13
1984	15	12
1983	16	10
1982	14	10
1981	13	10
1980	13	7
1979	11	9
1978	13	9
1977	13	11
1976	17	13
Average	16.7	11.8

well followed by professional financial analysts. This group of stocks is referred to as small capitalization ("small cap") stocks, which means that the total market value of the company's equity is modest. The total market value of the equity is the number of shares outstanding times the stock's price. Exhibit 12.8 presents the capitalization (i.e., number of shares outstanding, price per share, and total market value) for selected stocks. The exhibit is constructed so the smallest cap stocks are listed first. Obviously AT&T is a large firm whose stock, in the aggregate, is worth much more than the stock of Chesapeake Corporation, which in turn has a market capitalization that is considerably larger than R.G. Barry, manufacturer of Dearfoam slippers.

Small capitalization stocks may lack a following on Wall Street. Analysts often work for large financial institutions such as life insurance companies or the trust departments of banks. These financial institutions tend to avoid investing in the stocks of small companies, so their analysts do not cover them. This lack of coverage by financial analysts suggests that small companies may offer the individual excellent investment opportunities. It should be pointed out that a strategy of investing in small capitalization stocks is based on the belief that the market for large companies is very efficient but the market for small companies is less efficient. It may be possible to identify a specific small company that is currently undervalued and hence is a good investment.

Screening Techniques

Screening techniques are another means designed to identify undervalued securities. The investor identifies specific criteria that must be met (e.g., return on equity of at least 20 percent, dividend yield of at least 5 percent, and a P/E ratio of less

Exhibit 12.8 ✦ MARKET CAPITALIZATION OF SELECTED STOCKS

Firm	Number of Shares Outstanding[*]	Price (2/31/92)	Market Value of Stock
R. G. Barry	3,840,000	$ 4¼	$ 16,320,000
Chesapeake Corporation	20,579,000	28⅛	578,784,375
Georgia-Pacific	87,382,000	65½	5,723,521,000
Apple Computer	118,386,000	64¾	7,665,493,500
AT&T	1,306,187,000	37¼	48,665,465,750

[*]*Source:* Information regarding number of shares is taken from *Standard & Poor's Stock Guide,* February 1992.

than 10). Through the use of a computer and a data base, the investor is able to identify all firms that meet the specified conditions. If the number of firms is large, the criteria may be made more stringent or additional criteria may be added to the screening process. The purpose of the screening technique is to limit the number of possible investments and to select among those stocks that meet the criteria the individual believes to be most important.

ANALYSIS OF CASH FLOW

The bulk of this chapter has been devoted to the analysis of a firm's financial statements with emphasis placed on profitability and net earnings available to the common stockholder. However, increased interest has developed among financial analysts in a firm's operating income and cash flow.[8] Net income may be affected by numerous factors that have little meaning from the perspective of a firm's operations. For example, the use of straight-line depreciation instead of accelerated depreciation will increase earnings (and taxes) but does not affect the firm's operations. Other items, such as the sale of an appreciated asset, an increase in reserves to cover losses on accounts receivable and other loans, or changes in inventory valuation, can have an impact on the firm's net income, but these events need not affect current or future operations.

The previous examples suggest that earnings could be affected without affecting operations. Since these examples may be nonrecurring (e.g., the sale of an asset

---

[8]See, for instance, "Earnings, Schmernings—Look at the Cash," *Business Week* (July 24, 1989): 56–57; James M. Gahlon and Robert L. Vigeland, "Cash Flow Statements," *AAII Journal* (January 1989): 14–18; James A. Gentry, Paul Newbold, and David T. Whiltford, "Predicting Bankruptcy: If Cash Flow's Not the Bottom Line, What Is?," *Financial Analysts Journal* (September–October 1985): 47–58; and Patricia Dreyfus, "Go With the (Cash) Flow," *Institutional Investor* (August 1988): 55–59.

occurs only once), net income from different accounting periods may not be comparable. In addition, the firm could have recurring earnings and still not be generating cash. For example, if Firm A owns stock of Firm B, this investment can affect earnings but not operations. Firm A may report as part of its earnings the earnings of Firm B (i.e., Firm A picks up its proportional share of Firm B's earnings), but that does not necessarily mean that Firm A receives cash. If Firm B retains the earnings, Firm A obviously does not receive any cash for the earnings it is reporting. For a firm like Teledyne, which has substantial equity investments in other firms, a large proportion of its earnings are independent of its own operations and do not represent the receipt of cash.

Since net earnings may be affected by nonrecurring items or need not represent cash, some financial analysts are placing more emphasis on cash flow. The argument is that the cash flow generated by a firm's operations is a better indication of its profitability and value. Instead of isolating income, these analysts seek to determine the capacity of the firm to generate cash flow and use this information for their analysis and valuation of the firm.

Definitions of Cash Flow

One problem using the term *cash flow* is that it is ambiguous. Sometimes cash flow is used to cover the firm's cash cycle: the selling of inventory, the collection of accounts receivable, and the paying of current liabilities. In this context cash flow is concerned with the speed with which cash flows through the firm. The emphasis is placed on selling inventory, speeding up the collection of accounts receivable and retarding the payment of current liabilities. By collecting cash faster and holding it longer, management may increase the firm's profitability.

In other contexts the term **cash flow** is variously defined as (1) net earnings plus depreciation (and any other noncash expense like depletion or amortization), (2) net earnings plus depreciation minus principal repayments and preferred stock dividend payments, (3) net earnings plus depreciation minus principal repayments and required maintenance capital expenditures, or (4) *pre*tax earnings plus depreciation minus principal repayment and maintenance capital expenditures. While the definitions differ, they are similar. In each definition, cash flow is found by adding noncash expenses back to earnings. In the last three definitions, financing and/or investment requirements are subtracted.

cash flow
Net earnings plus noncash expenses minus debt retirement.

The argument for deducting maintenance expense is that these expenditures must be made in order for the firm to retain its productive capacity. Failure to maintain plant and equipment may increase current cash but does so at the expense of the firm's ability to generate future cash.[9] After deducting debt service requirements and investments necessary to maintain plant and equipment, any cash left over may be used as management sees fit. This remainder is sometimes referred to as discretionary or free cash flow. Possible uses for free cash flow include the (1) payment

---

[9] Unfortunately, information on maintenance may not be available for the individual investor. Financial institutions, however, may negotiate for this information as a precondition for granting a loan. Per-share estimates of cash flow are provided by the *Value Line Investment Survey.*

of dividends, (2) additional investments in plant and equipment, (3) acquisitions of other firms (i.e., takeovers), (4) debt retirement, or (5) share repurchases.

Often firms that generate cash become attractive takeover candidates. The acquiring firm can use the acquired firm's free cash flow to repay the debt used to finance the purchase. In effect the acquisition pays for itself. Many of the leveraged buyouts financed with high yield debt (the so-called "junk bonds" to be discussed in Chapter 16) were justified on the basis of the acquired firm's cash flow and not its earnings. The essence of the argument is that if the firm has sufficient free cash flow, the debt issued to finance the takeover will be easily serviced.

Differences in Cash Flow and Earnings

The difference between reported earnings and per-share cash flow can be substantial, especially for firms with physical assets that will appreciate and not depreciate in value. For example, a cable television firm must initially make a substantial investment in the equipment. Once in place, depreciation charges will consume a substantial amount of the operating income generated by the cable. Net income may be small, or the firm may even operate at a loss, but monthly subscriber fees are paid in cash. In addition, the value of the cable and the cable franchise will probably appreciate in value as more subscribers are added. In this case, net income may not be indicative of the firm's capacity to generate cash and may be a poor indicator of the value of the firm's stock.

Some firms have even begun to emphasize some form of cash flow in their communications with stockholders. For example, Chesapeake Corporation reported in its first quarter 1992 "Interim Report to Stockholders" that operating cash flow (defined as earnings before interest, taxes, and depreciation) was $29.7 million, while earnings for the quarter were only $2.5 million. United Dominion Realty Trust started a stockholders' report by emphasizing an increase in *funds from operations* and following that with a discussion of net earnings. This order of presentation is not uncommon, especially for firms with large depreciation charges and hence meager, if any, earnings.

The accounting profession also is placing more emphasis on the sources of cash and how cash is used. Starting with 1988 annual reports, firms have to provide a statement of cash flow, which replaces the previously required statement of changes in financial position. The first part of the new statement identifies cash flow from operations. The statement begins with net income and follows with the adjustments (e.g., depreciation) necessary to determine the net cash provided by operations. Subsequent sections consider cash provided by financing decisions (e.g., the sale of bonds or stock). The statement ends with how the funds were used. The bottom line identifies the increase or decrease in the firm's cash position generated by its operations and financing decisions.

Application of Cash Flow to Valuation

The previous discussion points out the increased emphasis on cash flow and the problems isolating a definition. Once the investor has decided which definition to use and has calculated the estimated cash flow, the next step is to use this information for stock valuation. One method for using cash flow as a valuation tool is to

IS BETA DEAD? LONG LIVE FUNDAMENTAL ANALYSIS!

The capital asset pricing model and its measure of risk, the beta coefficient, are a cornerstone of financial theory. In efficient, competitive financial markets, diversification erases unsystematic risk. This leaves systematic, market risk as the primary factor explaining security returns. Since market risk is measured by a stock's beta coefficient, higher beta coefficients suggest higher returns. While arbitrage pricing theory (APT in Chapter 7) does challenge beta as the sole determinant of returns, it essentially adds additional variables to explain returns.

In 1992, empirical evidence published by University of Chicago professors Eugene F. Fama and Kenneth R. French ("The Cross-Section of Expected Returns," *The Journal of Finance,* June 1992: 427–465) suggested that the relationship between beta and returns did not exist during the period 1963 through 1990. While taking additional risk generates higher returns, variables other than beta coefficients are a better measure of risk. In the Fama-French study, two fundamental variables, market value of equity and the ratio of book value of equity to market value of equity (the reciprocal of the ratio of market to book discussed in the body of this chapter), were used to measure risk. Combined, these two measures of risk better explained stock returns than the traditional beta.

The rational for using these two variables as measures of risk is easy to understand. As the market value of the firm increases (i.e., as the firm's size increases), the firm is less risky. As the ratio of book value of equity to market value of equity decreases, the market views the firm as having better prospects. Such firms are less risky. Fama-French's results supported the anticipated relationships: the stocks of larger companies and those with low ratios of book value to market value generated lower returns. While it is certainly too early to know if this research will be confirmed by additional studies, it is easy to understand why supporters of fundamental analysis will find comfort in this study.

---

multiply the cash flow by the appropriate multiple. This is essentially the same type of technique as employing P/E ratios. In that technique the analyst multiplied the firm's earnings by the appropriate multiple to determine the firm's value. The same method may be used with the firm's cash flow: the cash flow is multiplied by the appropriate multiple to determine the value of the firm. Of course, determining the appropriate multiple, like determining the appropriate P/E ratio, is one of the major problems facing the financial analyst or individual investor.

The use of cash flow, P/E ratios, or the dividend-growth valuation model may appear to be different, but they are fundamentally the same. In each case the analyst is using a type of present value calculation; that is, an amount (e.g., dividends or earnings) is being discounted back to the present. The dividend-growth model uses the required rate of return as the discount factor, while the P/E and cash flow techniques use the appropriate multiple as the discount factor.

FUNDAMENTAL ANALYSIS IN AN EFFICIENT MARKET ENVIRONMENT

This chapter has been devoted to the analysis of the financial statements of an individual firm. The interpretation of the results helps identify under- and overvalued securities. However, the individual must not lose sight of the fact that investment decisions are made in efficient financial markets. Fundamental analysis may improve an individual's understanding and perception of the firm's financial condition, but it does not necessarily produce superior investment decisions.

While it is not necessary to repeat the material on the efficient market hypothesis presented in Chapter 8, it is desirable to remind the reader that there is a considerable body of empirical evidence supporting the hypothesis. There is, however, also evidence that is inconsistent with efficient markets, and these anomalies suggest there may be pockets of inefficiency. Several of the anomalies are built upon fundamental analysis. The small firm effect, low PE ratios, the Value Line ranking system, and unexpected changes in earnings are illustrations of possible anomalies that use fundamental analysis.[10] These inconsistencies give encouragement to investors and financial analysts to pursue fundamental financial analysis.

Of course, without fundamental analysis of accounting statements, financial markets would be less efficient. By performing the analysis and seeking to apply the results to the selection of securities, the investor contributes to the efficiency of the market. But the competition among investors helps assure that a security's price is a fair representation of what the consensus believes the security is worth.

Investors should not bemoan the implications of efficient markets. If the individual does not reach for speculative returns (and hence take excess risk or become vulnerable to investment scams), efficient markets imply that an individual has the opportunity to earn a return consistent with the amount of risk the investor bears. Over a period of time, efficient security markets should reward the patient individual willing to accept the risk associated with investing in stocks and bonds. Participation in financial markets is open to all investors. Any individual may acquire financial assets either directly through the purchase of securities or indirectly through the purchase of shares in investment companies or through participation in pension plans and investment vehicles offered by other financial institutions.

Summary

Ratio analysis is frequently used to analyze a firm's financial position. These ratios are easy to compute and employ data that are readily available on a firm's financial statements. The ratios include those designed to measure liquidity, activity, profitability, and capitalization (leverage). A summary of the ratio definitions follows.

While an investor may compute many ratios, it may be wise to select those ratios pertinent to the analysis. Creditors and investors in bonds are primarily concerned with determining the firm's capacity to meet its debt obligations as they come due, while investors who purchase stock may stress profitability and growth.

Ratios facilitate comparisons. A firm's current financial condition may be compared with previous years, and trends in the financial position may be identified. In

---

[10] It has been suggested that the anomaly associated with the Value Line ranking system (see footnotes 6 and 7 in Chapter 4) can be explained by unexpected changes in firms' earnings. Investing in firms whose earnings differ from analysts' projected earnings may lead to superior returns. Since an unanticipated change in earnings may lead to changes in the Value Line rankings, it is the earnings surprise and not the ranking system that is the anomaly. See John Affleck-Graves and Richard Mendenhall, "The Relationship between the Value Line Enigma and Post-Earnings Announcement Drift," *Journal of Financial Economics*, (February 1992).

addition, the firm may be compared with other firms within its industry. There are different definitions of some ratios, so the analyst must be sure when comparing his or her analysis with industry averages from other sources that the same ratio definitions are employed.

Ratio analysis may be used in conjunction with the dividend-growth model to help identify under- or overvalued stocks. Other selection methods also use financial information to help in the process of security selection. These techniques include (1) the analysis of the ratios of price to book value and price to earnings, (2) the total market value of the firm's stock, and (3) various screening techniques designed to identify superior stocks for possible investments.

Emphasis may also be placed on the determination of a firm's cash flow. This technique seeks to isolate the firm's ability to generate cash. Noncash items, such as depreciation, are added back to earnings and cash requirements, such as principal repayments and maintenance expense, are deducted to determine the firm's free cash. This free cash is used as the basis for determining the value of the firm.

While many investment techniques may be used to help identify individual securities for purchase, such investments are made in efficient financial markets. This suggests that the individual cannot expect to outperform the market consistently on a risk-adjusted basis. Thus fundamental analysis is important for efficient markets to exist, but it does not follow that the use of fundamental analysis by the individual will lead to superior investment decisions.

Summary of Ratio Definitions

1. Liquidity Ratios

   a. Current ratio $= \dfrac{\text{Current assets}}{\text{Current liabilities}}$

   b. Acid test $= \dfrac{\text{Current assets} - \text{Inventory}}{\text{Current liabilities}}$

2. Activity Ratios

   a. Inventory turnover $= \dfrac{\text{Sales}}{\text{Average inventory}}$ or $= \dfrac{\text{Cost of goods sold}}{\text{Average inventory}}$

   b. Average collection period $= \dfrac{\text{Receivables}}{\text{Sales per day}}$

   c. Receivables turnover $= \dfrac{\text{Annual credit sales}}{\text{Accounts receivable}}$ or $= \dfrac{\text{Annual sales}}{\text{Accounts receivable}}$

   d. Fixed asset turnover $= \dfrac{\text{Annual sales}}{\text{Fixed assets}}$

3. Profitability Ratios

   a. Operating profit margin $= \dfrac{\text{Earnings before interest and taxes}}{\text{Sales}}$

   b. Net profit margin $= \dfrac{\text{Earnings after taxes}}{\text{Sales}}$

   c. Return on assets $= \dfrac{\text{Earnings after taxes}}{\text{Total assets}}$

    d. Return on equity $= \dfrac{\text{Earnings after taxes}}{\text{Equity}}$

    e. Return on common equity

$$= \dfrac{\text{Earnings after taxes } - \text{ Preferred dividends}}{\text{Equity } - \text{ Preferred stock}}$$

4. Leverage Ratios

    a. Debt ratios $= \dfrac{\text{Debt}}{\text{Equity}}$ or $= \dfrac{\text{Debt}}{\text{Total assets}}$

    b. Coverage ratio:

$$\text{Times-interest-earned} = \dfrac{\text{Earnings before interest and taxes}}{\text{Annual interest expense}}$$

5. Miscellaneous Ratios

    a. Earnings per common share

$$= \dfrac{\text{Earnings } - \text{ Preferred dividends}}{\text{Number of common shares outstanding}}$$

    b. Payout ratio $= \dfrac{\text{Dividends}}{\text{Earnings}}$

    c. P/E ratio $= \dfrac{\text{Price of stock}}{\text{Earnings per share}}$

    d. Price/Sales ratio $= \dfrac{\text{Price of stock}}{\text{Sales per share}}$

Terms to Remember

time-series analysis	net profit margin
cross-sectional analysis	return on assets
current ratio	return on equity
acid test (quick ratio)	financial leverage
inventory turnover	debt ratio
average collection period	undercapitalized
receivables turnover	times-interest-earned
fixed asset turnover	cash flow
operating profit margin	

Questions

1. What is the difference between the current ratio and the acid test?
2. If accounts receivable increase, what effect will this have on the average collection period?
3. What is the difference between liquidity ratios and activity ratios?
4. What is times-interest-earned and what does it add to the analyst's knowledge of the firm? Would this ratio be of interest to a creditor?
5. What is the difference between the operating and net profit margins?
6. What does the debt ratio measure? Do all firms within an industry use the same proportion of debt financing?
7. Why may the return on equity exceed the return on a firm's total assets?

8. How may a firm's book value or P/E ratio help determine if a stock is undervalued?
9. Should you buy a stock with a high
   a. price to sales ratio;
   b. return on equity;
   c. payout ratio;
   d. debt ratio?
10. What is cash flow and why may it be important for the analysis of a firm's stock?
11. Given the following ratios, has the firm's financial position deteriorated?

	19x6	19x5	19x4	19x3	19x2	19x1	19x0
Current ratio	3.6	3.4	3.0	3.2	3.1	3.1	3.3
Quick ratio	2.2	2.2	2.1	2.2	1.7	1.8	2.0
Average collection period (days)	78	84	83	85	106	105	110
Inventory turnover (sales/average inventory)	4.4	4.5	4.5	4.9	4.6	4.7	4.7
Fixed asset turnover	6.4	6.4	8.6	9.0	9.0	9.6	10.0
Operating profit margin (%)	11.9	13.3	13.2	14.2	14.7	14.9	13.7
Net profit margin (%)	6.1	6.8	6.9	7.3	7.7	7.7	7.9
Return on assets (%)	8.8	10.0	10.4	11.4	11.1	11.1	11.5
Return on equity (%)	13.7	15.2	15.5	16.5	16.7	16.6	16.3
Debt ratio (%) (debt/total assets)	35.5	34.1	32.8	30.1	33.1	33.0	31.5
Times-interest-earned	9.3	14.2	14.5	14.2	11.8	10.7	11.5
Payout ratio (%)	41.4	37.6	35.9	33.5	34.2	34.7	35.3

Problems

1. Using the income statement and balance sheet presented on the next page, compute the following ratios. Compare your results with the industry averages. What strengths and weaknesses are apparent?

Ratio	Industry Average
Current ratio	2:1
Acid test (quick ratio)	1:1
Inventory turnover	
a. Annual sales	4.0×
b. Cost of goods sold	2.3×
Receivables turnover	
a. Annual credit sales	5.0×
b. Annual sales	6.0×
c. Average collection period	2.5 months
Operating profit margin	26%
Net profit margin	19%
Return on assets	10%

Continued on next page

Table—Continued

Ratio	Industry Average
Return on equity	15%
Debt ratio	
a. Debt/equity	33%
b. Debt/total assets	25%
Times-interest-earned	7.1×

Income Statement for XYZ
for the period ending December 31, 19xx

Sales	$100,000
Cost of goods sold	60,000
Gross profit	40,000
Selling and administrative expense	15,000
Operating profit	25,000
Interest expense	5,000
Earnings before taxes	20,000
Taxes	3,200
Earnings available to stockholders	$ 16,800
Number of shares outstanding	10,000
Earnings per share	$1.68

(To compute the inventory turnover, assume
that the prior year's inventory was $40,000.)

Firm XYZ
Balance Sheet as of December 31, 19xx
Assets

Current assets		
Cash and marketable securities		$ 10,000
Accounts receivable	$ 32,000	
Less allowance for doubtful accounts	2,000	30,000
Inventory		
Finished goods	30,000	
Work in progress	5,000	
Raw materials	7,000	42,000
Total current assets		$ 82,000
Investments		$ 10,000
Long-term assets		
Plant and equipment	100,000	
Less accumulated depreciation	30,000	70,000
Land		10,000
Total long-term assets		$ 80,000
Total assets		$172,000

Liabilities & Stockholders' Equity

Current liabilities	
Accounts payable	$ 10,000
Accrued wages	11,000
Bank notes	15,000
Accrued interest payable	4,000
Accrued taxes	1,000
Total current liabilities	$ 41,000
Long-term debt	$ 15,000
Total liabilities	$ 56,000
Stockholders' equity	
Common stock ($1 par value; 20,000 shares authorized;	
10,000 shares outstanding)	$ 10,000
Additional paid-in capital	20,000
Retained earnings	86,000
Total stockholders' equity	$116,000
Total liabilities and equity	$172,000

2. You have taken the following information from a firm's financial statements. As an investor in the firm's debt instruments, you are concerned with its liquidity position and its use of financial leverage. What conclusions can you draw from this information?

	19x0	19x1	19x2
Sales	$1,000,000	$1,500,000	1,700,000
Cash	5,000	7,000	18,000
Accounts receivable	125,000	130,000	152,000
Inventory	200,000	190,000	200,000
Current liabilities	175,000	210,000	225,000
Operating income	90,000	145,000	170,000
Interest expense	20,000	23,000	27,000
Taxes	25,000	45,000	53,000
Net income	45,000	77,000	90,000
Debt	200,000	250,000	260,000
Equity	200,000	300,000	330,000

3. What is the debt/net worth ratio and the debt ratio for a firm with total debt of $700,000 and equity of $300,000?

4. A firm with sales of $500,000 has average inventory of $200,000. The industry average for inventory turnover is four times a year. What would be the reduction in inventory if this firm were to achieve a turnover comparable to the industry average?

5. Company A has three debt issues of $3,000 each. The interest rate of issue A is 4 percent, on B the rate is 6 percent, and on C the rate is 8 percent. Issue B is subordinate to A, and issue C is subordinate to both A and B. The firm's operating income (EBIT) is $500. Compute the times-interest-earned ratio for issue C. What does the answer imply? Does the answer mean that the interest will not be paid?

6. If a firm has sales of $42,791,000 a year, and the average collection period for the industry is 40 days, what should this firm's accounts receivable be if the firm is comparable to the industry?
7. Two firms have sales of $1 million each. Other financial information is as follows:

Firm	A	B
EBIT	$150,000	$150,000
Interest expense	20,000	75,000
Income tax	50,000	30,000
Equity	300,000	100,000

What are the operating profit margins and the net profit margins for these two firms? What is their return on equity? Why are they different? If total assets are the same for each firm, what can you conclude about their respective uses of debt financing?

Suggested Readings

The father of conservative financial analysis is Benjamin Graham. His text is a classic that employs many of the ratios described in this chapter.

Graham, Benjamin, David L. Dodd, Sidney Cottle, and Charles Tatham. *Security Analysis: Principles and Techniques.* 5th ed. New York: McGraw-Hill, 1988. See especially Part 4, "The Valuation of Common Stock," for the conservative financial approach to the analysis of common stock.

Several books that are a cross between traditional texts and publications for the sophisticated investor or the financial analyst are available. These works are a combination of financial analysis and accounting and are particularly useful for fundamental analysis. Titles include:

Bernstein, Leopold A. *Financial Statement Analysis Theory, Applications & Interpretation,* 4th ed. Homewood, Ill.: Dow Jones-Irwin, 1988.
Foster, George. *Financial Statement Analysis.* 2d ed. Englewood Cliffs, N.J.: Prentice-Hall, 1986.
Gibson, Charles H. *Financial Statement Analysis.* 5th ed. Cincinnati, OH.: South-Western Publishing Co., 1992.

A survey of more than 100 firms found that ratio analysis is an important tool used by management and that profitability ratios are the most important for judging performance. See:

Gibson, Charles H. "How Industry Perceives Financial Ratios." *Management Accounting* (April 1982): 13–19.

A survey of 2,000 members of the Financial Analysts Federation found that analysts emphasize expected changes in return on equity, expected changes in earnings per share, prospects for the industry, and the general economic conditions. Importance is also given to qualitative factors such as quality of management and strategic planning, but the former is hard to measure and it is difficult to obtain good information on the latter. See:

Chugh, Lal C., and Joseph W. Meador. "The Stock Valuation Process: The Analyst's View." *Financial Analysts Journal,* (November–December 1984): 41–48.

For a comprehensivve coverage of ratios and financial indicators see:

Renshaw, Edward. *The Practical Forecasters' Almanac.* Homewood, IL: Business One Irwin, 1992.

INVESTMENT PROJECT

In this chapter, ratio analysis was applied to the financial statements of CSK. The following data is drawn from CSK's financial statements for 1992, the year following the analysis in the chapter. Update Exhibit 12.6 to determine if there has been any change in CSK's financial condition during its 1992 fiscal year. If CSK's financial statements are available for subsequent years, continue the analysis to determine if management has maintained CSK's performance.

Balance Sheet Information
as of December 31, 1992

Current assets	
Cash	$ 0.7
Receivables	88.4
Inventory	105.2
Other current assets	17.6
Plant and equipment	626.9
Timberlands	41.4
Other assets	78.7
Total assets	$958.9
Current liabilities	$ 89.7
Long-term debt	402.4
Deferred income taxes	66.4
Equity	370.4
Total liabilities plus equity	$958.9

Income Statement Information
for the Period Ending December 31, 1992

Sales	$888.4
Cost of goods sold	663.0
Depreciation	66.5
Selling and administrative expenses	106.7
Operating income	52.2
Other income	1.7
Interest expense	31.4
Taxes	8.1
Net income	$ 14.4
Earnings per share	$ 0.63
Dividends per share	0.72

In millions, except per share data.

TECHNICAL ANALYSIS

Investing would be much simpler if a trading rule could be found that told the investor when to buy or sell. Then the individual would not have to perform the analysis described in the previous chapters. The technical approach to security selection purports to do just that. By analyzing how the market (or a specific stock) has performed in the past, the investor may forecast how the market (or a specific stock) will perform in the future. Studying historical data concerning prices or the volume of transactions is substituted for analysis of financial statements and forecasts of future dividends and the growth in earnings.

Technical analysis is a very broad topic because there are so many different varieties of this type of analysis. This chapter covers several popular technical approaches to the market and security selection. These include the Dow theory, odd lot purchases and sales, point-and-figure charts, and moving averages. Since these techniques accumulate and summarize data in a variety of charts and graphs, investors who use these techniques are often referred to as chartists.

The discussion in this chapter is primarily descriptive. After presenting several technical approaches, the chapter ends with a consideration of the empirical studies that seek to verify the techniques. The results of these studies strongly suggest that technical analysis does not lead to superior investment results. *However, this lack of empirical support has not stopped the use of technical analysis, and some of its jargon is commonly used by both professional and lay investors.*

◆ ◆ ◆

THE PURPOSE OF THE TECHNICAL APPROACH

The two previous chapters considered fundamental analysis. The investor or portfolio manager studied (1) the firm's financial condition as indicated in the firm's financial statements, (2) the position of the firm in its industry, and (3) the direction of the economy. Such systematic study of the firm's financial condition and potential is the backbone of security analysis. The techniques are the fundamental tools of financial analysis, hence the name "fundamental" analysis. Ultimately the purpose of such analysis is to help identify undervalued assets for possible inclusion in the individual's portfolio.

A different type of analysis uses charts and graphs of price movements, the volume of security transactions, or sales and purchases by selected investors. This approach, especially some of the charts, can appear to be very technical, hence the name "technical" analysis. The use of the name *technical analysis* does not imply that fundamental analysis is simple. The analysis of financial statements can be quite complex; however, in the jargon of investments the term *technical analysis* implies a particular type of analysis that is completely different from the systematic study of a firm's financial statements and its position within its industry. In technical analysis the emphasis is placed on determining when to buy or sell. Such buy or sell signals may be independent of the firm's financial condition. Thus technical analysis may recommend selling a strong firm if the indicators are suggesting that security prices will decline.

THE VARIETY OF TECHNICAL ANALYSIS

Technical analysis attempts to predict future stock prices by analyzing past stock prices. In effect, it asserts that tomorrow's stock price is influenced by today's price. That is a very appealing assertion, because it eliminates the need to perform fundamental analysis. No longer does the investor have to be concerned with ratios, estimating growth, and appropriate discount rates. Instead, he or she keeps a record of specific market factors, such as who is buying and selling the stock, and of specific information on individual stocks, such as the closing price and the volume of transactions. This information is then summarized in a variety of forms, such as charts and graphs, which in turn tell the investor when to buy and sell the securities.

technical analysis
An analysis of past volume and/or price behavior to identify which assets to purchase and the best time to purchase them.

There are many different technical approaches to the selection of securities. Only a few will be discussed in this chapter. These are classified into two groups. The first techniques are designed to indicate the general direction of the market. Since security prices move together, the direction of the market is the overriding factor in the decision to buy and sell securities. In fact, it is the single most important factor in these technical approaches. This first group of techniques includes the Dow theory (which is perhaps the oldest of all the technical approaches to the market), Barron's confidence index, and odd lot purchases versus odd lot sales. These three approaches may be constructed from information reported in the financial press. For practical purposes, the investor may consider these sources of information as virtually free.

The second group of technical approaches discussed in this chapter is designed not only to discern the direction of the market but also to decide when to buy or sell specific securities. These include point-and-figure charts, bar graphs, moving averages of stock prices, and insider transactions. The information necessary to perform this analysis is also readily available in the financial press. Thus, the investor may either perform the analysis or purchase advisory services that perform the analysis.

Before reading further, the student should be forewarned that the presentations of the various approaches make their application appear to be easy. Also, the examples have been constructed to illustrate the techniques. In actual practice the buy and sell signals indicated by technical analysis may frequently be less obvious than the illustrations used in the text. Furthermore, one technical indicator may contradict another. Thus, if the investor follows several technical indicators, they rarely give clear buy or sell signals as a group.

The student should also realize that the efficient market hypothesis suggests that using technical analysis will not lead to superior investment decisions. As was explained in Chapter 8, empirical results are consistent with this hypothesis. Since technical analysis may require frequent buying and selling, which generates commissions for the broker, the little evidence that does support technical analysis suggests that any superior results are marginal at best and do not cover the commission costs. Thus scientific studies suggest that a strategy of buy and hold produces investment results that are equal to or better than those from trading securities using technical analysis.

Even though empirical results do not favor the use of technical analysis, some investors continue to use this type of analysis to help make some investment decisions. While they may not employ technical analysis as the sole criterion for investment decisions, these individuals may employ the analysis to confirm fundamental analysis. In addition the jargon of technical analysis permeates the popular, if not the academic, press on investments. Thus the student of investments needs to be aware of technical analysis even if the individual does not use it as part of his or her investment strategy.

MARKET INDICATORS

Dow theory

A technical approach based on the Dow Jones averages.

The **Dow theory** is one of the oldest technical methods for analyzing security prices. It is an aggregate measure of security prices and hence does not predict the direction of change in individual stock prices. What it purports to show is the direction that the market will take. Thus, it is a method that identifies the top of a bull market and the bottom of a bear market.

The Dow theory developed from the work of Charles Dow, who founded Dow Jones and Company and was the first editor of *The Wall Street Journal*.[1] Dow identified three movements in security prices: primary, secondary, and tertiary. Primary price movements are related to the security's intrinsic value. Such values depend on the earning capacity of the firm and the distribution of dividends. Secondary price movements, or "swings," are governed by current events that temporarily affect value and by the manipulation of stock prices. These price swings may persist for several weeks and even months. Tertiary price movements are daily price fluctuations to which Dow attributed no significance.

Although Charles Dow believed in fundamental analysis, the Dow theory has evolved into a primarily technical approach to the stock market. It asserts that stock prices demonstrate patterns over four to five years and that these patterns are mirrored by indices of stock prices. The Dow theory employs two of the Dow Jones

---

[1] See George W. Bishop, Jr., *Charles H. Dow and the Dow Theory* (New York: Appleton-Century-Crofts, 1960), 225–228.

averages, the industrial average and the transportation average. The utility average is generally ignored.

The Dow theory is built upon the assertion that measures of stock prices tend to move together. If the Dow Jones industrial average is rising, then the transportation average should also be rising. Such simultaneous price movements suggest a strong bull market. Conversely, a decline in both the industrial and transportation averages suggests a strong bear market. However, if the averages are moving in opposite directions, the market is uncertain as to the direction of future stock prices.

If one of the averages starts to decline after a period of rising stock prices, the two are at odds. For example, the industrial average may be rising while the transportation average is falling. This suggests that the industrials may not continue to rise but may soon start to fall. Hence, the smart investor will use this signal to sell securities and convert to cash.

The converse occurs when, after a period of falling security prices, one of the averages starts to rise while the other continues to fall. According to the Dow theory, this divergence suggests that the bear market is over and that security prices in general will soon start to rise. The astute investor will then purchase securities in anticipation of the price increase.

There are several problems with the Dow theory. The first is that it is not a theory but an interpretation of known data. It does not explain why the two averages should be able to forecast future stock prices. In addition, there may be a considerable lag between actual turning points and those indicated by the forecast. It may be months before the two averages confirm each other, during which time individual stocks may show substantial price changes.

The accuracy of the Dow theory and its predictive power have been the subject of much debate. Greiner and Whitcomb assert that "the Dow Theory provides a time-tested method of reading the stock market barometer."[2] However, between 1929 and 1960 the Dow theory made only 9 correct predictions out of 24 buy or sell signals.[3] Such results are less accurate than the investor may obtain by flipping a coin and have considerably diminished support for the technique. These results, however, were not corroborated by another study that concluded that from 1971 to 1980, the technique generated returns in excess of 14 percent.[4]

Barron's Confidence Index

Barron's confidence index is based on the belief that the differential between the returns on quality bonds and bonds of lesser quality will forecast future price movements. During periods of optimism, investors will be more willing to bear risk and thus will move from investments in higher quality debt to more speculative but higher yielding, lower quality debt. This selling of higher quality debt will depress its price and raise its yield. Simultaneously, the purchase of poor-quality debt should

Barron's confidence index
An index designed to identify investors' confidence in the level and direction of security prices.

[2] Perry P. Greiner and Hale C. Whitcomb, *The Dow Theory and the Seventy-Year Record* (Larchmont, N.Y.: Investors Intelligence, Inc., 1969), 130.

[3] See Leonard T. Wright, *Principles of Investments—Text and Cases.* 2d ed. (Columbus, Ohio: Grid, Inc., 1977), 312–317.

[4] David A. Glickstein and Rolf E. Wubbels, "Dow Theory Is Alive and Well," *The Journal of Portfolio Management* (Spring 1983): 28–32.

drive up its price and lower the yield. Thus, the difference between the two yields will diminish.

The opposite occurs when sentiment turns bearish. The investors and especially those who "know" what the market will do in the future will sell poor-quality debt and purchase higher quality debt. This will have the effect of increasing the spread between the yields, as the price of poor-quality debt falls relative to that of the higher quality debt.

Barron's confidence index is constructed by using Barron's index of yields on higher and lower quality bonds. When the yield differential is small (i.e., when the yields on high-quality debt approach those that can be earned on poor-quality debt), the ratio rises. This is interpreted as showing investor confidence. Such confidence means that security prices will tend to rise. Conversely, when the index declines, that is an indication that security prices will fall.

Like the other technical approaches, Barron's confidence index has been subjected to scrutiny. Although it may indicate a tendency, it does not give conclusive signals. Since the signals of the Barron's confidence index are often ambiguous or there is a considerable time lag between the signal and the change forecasted, the index can be of only modest use for investors. Like many technical indicators it may point to the direction that security prices will follow, but it is not a totally reliable predictor of future stock prices.

Purchase and Sale of Odd Lots

odd lot theory
A technical approach to the stock market that purports to predict security prices on the basis of odd lot sales and purchases.

Another technical indicator of the market is the **odd lot theory,** which concerns the purchase and sale of securities by small investors. These investors buy in small quantities (i.e., odd lots or less than 100 shares). The volume of such odd lot purchases and sales is reported in the financial press along with other financial data. The ratio of these odd lot purchases to odd lot sales is taken by some technicians as an indicator of the direction of future prices.

The rationale behind the use of the ratio of odd lot purchases to sales is that small investors are frequently wrong, especially just prior to a change in the direction of the market. Such investors will get caught up in the enthusiasm of a bull market and expand their purchases just as the market is reaching the top. The converse occurs at the market bottom. During declining markets, small investors become depressed about the market. After experiencing losses, they sell out as the market reaches its bottom. Such sales are frequently referred to as the passing of securities from "weak" hands to "strong" hands. The weak hands are, of course, the small investors who are misjudging the market, and the strong hands are the large investors who are more informed and capable of making correct investment decisions.

Generally, the ratio of odd lot purchases to odd lot sales ranges from 1.4 to 0.6.[5] If the ratio approaches 1.25 to 1.30, that means the small investors are increasing their purchases relative to sales, which is a very bearish signal. According to the odd lot theory, such purchases forecast a decline in stock prices. If the ratio approaches

---

[5] See Jerome B. Cohen, Edward D. Zinbarg, and Arthur Zeikel, *Investment Analysis and Portfolio Management,* 5th ed. (Homewood, Ill.: Irwin, 1987), 270–272.

0.6, odd lot sales exceed purchases, indicating that the small investor is bearish. Such bearishness on the part of the small investor is then taken as a bullish sign by believers in the odd lot theory.

Empirical work has not been able to verify that odd lot purchases and sales are a good predictor of future prices.[6] These studies indicate that during rising markets, purchases do tend to exceed sales. Conversely, during periods of declining markets the odd lot sales increase. Like the Dow theory and Barron's confidence index, the odd lot theory illustrates a tendency, but there is also little concrete evidence of its ability to forecast accurately when the market will change. It assumes that purchasers of odd lots make inferior investment decisions, but it should be remembered that many large investors are also sellers at the market bottom and buyers at the market top. Incorrect investment decisions are not the monopoly of small investors!

Investment Advisory Opinions

While the odd lot theory suggests that the small investor is often wrong, the advisory opinion theory suggests that financial advisors are often wrong. This approach is often referred to as a "contrarian" view, since it takes the opposite side of most financial advisors. The theory suggests that when most financial advisors and financial services become bearish and forecast declining security prices, that is the time to purchase securities. When the majority of financial advisors become bullish and forecast rising security prices, the wise investor liquidates (i.e., sells securities). This technical indicator seems perverse, as it suggests that those most likely to know are unable to forecast the direction of security prices accurately.

Advances/Declines

An alternative to the odd lot theory and the opinions of investment advisory services is the advance–decline cumulative series. This indicator is based on the cumulative net difference between the number of stocks that rose in price relative to the number that declined. Consider the following summaries of daily trading on the New York Stock Exchange:

Issues advancing	1,200	820	480	210
Issues declining	400	760	950	1,190
Issues unchanged	200	220	370	400
Net advances (declines)	800	60	(470)	(980)
Cumulative net advances (declines)	800	860	390	(590)

During the first day, 800 more stocks rose than declined. While this pattern continued during the second day, the number of stocks rising was considerably less

---

[6] See Richard A. Brealey, *An Introduction to Risk and Return From Common Stocks* (Cambridge, Mass.: M.I.T. Press, 1969), 129–140. It has even been suggested that today's odd-lotters are the institutional investors and that individual investors may profit by doing the opposite of professional money managers. See Mark Hulbert, "The New Odd-lotters," *Forbes* (December 23, 1991), 183.

than during the previous day, so the cumulative total registered only a small increment. During the third day, the market weakened, and the prices of more stocks fell than rose. However, the cumulative total still remained positive. During the fourth day, the number of stocks that declined rose further, so that the cumulative total now became negative.

According to technical analysis, the cumulative total of net advances gives an indication of the general direction of the market. If the market is rising, the net cumulative total will be positive and expanding; however, when the market changes direction, the cumulative total will start to diminish and will become negative as prices continue to decline. Of course, the converse applies at market bottoms. When the market declines, the net advances fall (i.e., the negative cumulative total increases). Once the bottom in the market has been reached and security prices start to rise, the number of advances will start to exceed the number of declines, which will cause the net advances to increase. Changes in the direction of advances/ declines becomes a barometer of the trend in the market. (This technique is similar to moving averages, which are discussed later in this chapter and which are used to measure both the direction of prices in individual stocks and in the market as a whole.)

SPECIFIC STOCK INDICATORS

The preceding section discussed several technical approaches to the market as a whole. This section considers several techniques that may be applied to either the market or individual securities. When applied to the market, their purpose is to identify the general trend. When applied to individual securities, these techniques attempt to inform the investor when to buy, when to sell, or when to maintain current positions in a specific security.

Point-and-Figure Charts (The X-O Chart)

point-and-figure chart (X-O chart)
A chart composed of Xs and Os that is used in technical analysis to summarize price movements.

Most technical analysis has an underlying basis (or perhaps rationalization) in economics. In effect, these analytical techniques seek to measure supply and demand. Since an increase in demand will lead to higher prices and an increase in supply will lead to lower prices, an analysis that captures shifts in supply and demand will be able to forecast future price movements. **Point-and-figure charts,** which are also called **X-O charts,** seek to identify changes in supply and demand by watching changes in security prices.

If a stock's price goes up, that movement is caused by demand exceeding supply. If a stock's price falls, then supply exceeds demand. If a stock's price is stable and trades within a narrow range, the supply of the stock coming onto the market just offsets the current demand. However, when the stock's price breaks this stable pattern of price movements, there has been a fundamental shift in demand and/or supply. Thus a movement upwards suggests a change in demand relative to supply, while a movement downwards suggests the opposite.

Figure 13.1 ✦ THE CONSTRUCTION OF AN X-O CHART

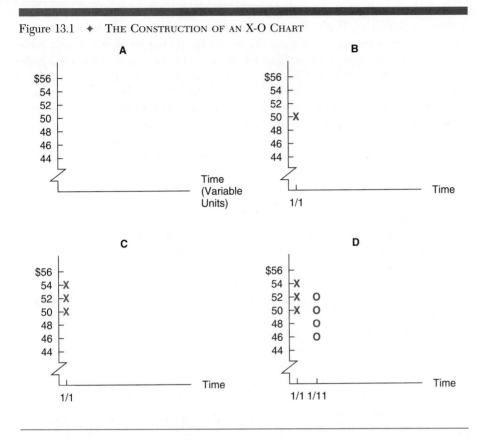

Point-and-figure charts seek to identify these fundamental changes through the construction of graphs employing Xs and Os. Such an X-O chart is constructed by placing an X on the chart when the price of the stock rises by some amount, such as $1 or $2, and an O on the chart when it declines by that amount. Such a chart requires following the stock on a daily basis and noting the price at the end of the day. If the price has changed by the specified amount, an entry is made on the chart.

This procedure is best explained by an illustration. Suppose the price of a stock had the following day-to-day price changes and the investor wanted to construct an X-O chart for price movements of $2. The procedure is illustrated in Figure 13.1.

Daily Closing Prices for January

Date	Prices				
1/1–1/5	$50⅛	$51⅜	$51¾	$52⅛	$54½
1/8–1/12	53½	53⅛	52½	51⅞	51⅛
1/15–1/19	49½	49¾	47⅛	48¾	47⅞
1/22–1/26	49¾	46⅞	46⅛	45⅞	44⅞

Figure 13.1 is divided into four quadrants, which illustrate the four steps necessary to create the chart.

The first quadrant (A) sets up the axes—time on the horizontal axis and dollars on the vertical axis.[7] The dollar unit that is selected depends on the prices of the stock. For lower priced stocks the units should be $1, but for higher priced stocks the units may be larger, such as $2 or $3. Since a movement from $40 to $42 is the same percentage increase as a price movement from $20 to $21, the use of the large increments for higher priced stocks does not reduce the quality of the X-O chart. In addition, the use of larger units will reduce the number of entries necessary to create the chart. Since the price of the stock in question is in the $50 range, a $2 interval is selected, and the vertical axis shows the increments in $2 units.

The second quadrant (B) plots the price of the stock on the first day of observation. Since the price of the stock is rising, the chartist enters an X at $50 on the chart. Additional Xs are entered only after the price of the stock rises by $2 (e.g., $50 to $52). All small movements in price both up and down are ignored, and only after the price has risen by $2 is a second X entered on the chart. Thus, although the price of the stock rose during the first three days, no entry is made. The effect of such omissions is both to reduce the work required to construct the chart and to minimize the effect of small daily price fluctuations.

The third quadrant (C) plots the price increases that occurred on days 4 and 5. The price closed above $52 on day 4, so an X is placed on the chart. The same applies to day 5, when the stock closed above $54.

After reaching a high of $54½, the price of the stock starts to fall. The chartist now uses only Os instead of Xs to indicate the declining price. Once again the price must fall by $2 before an entry is made (i.e., the stock must sell for $52 or less, since $54 was the highest X entry). The date on which Os began to be recorded on the chart is noted on the horizontal axis. The analyst will continue to place Os on the chart until the present downward trend is reversed and the price of the stock rises by the necessary $2. Then the analyst will start a new column and enter an X to indicate an increase in the stock's price.

The fourth quadrant (D) illustrates the decline in the stock's price. After the initial price rise illustrated in quadrant C, the price falls. Once it reaches $52, an O is placed on the chart. This occurs on January 11. The price of the stock now appears to be declining. Should the price fall to $50 or below, another O will be placed on the chart. If, however, the price again reaches $54 an X will be placed in the next column and the date will be recorded to indicate the change in the direction of the price.

In this case the price of the stock continues to decline. Each time the stock breaks the two-point barrier, another O is placed on the chart. If the price continues to decline, the column will fill up with Os. If the stock's price stabilizes, no entries will be made until a two-point movement occurs.

After a period of stable prices, a deviation signals the direction of future price changes. Such signals are illustrated in Figure 13.2. On the left-hand side (A), after a period of trading between $52 and $58, the price of the stock rises to a new high of $60. This suggests that a new upward price trend is being established, which is a buy signal. On the right-hand side (B), the opposite case is illustrated. The price declines below $52, which suggests that a new downward price trend is being established. If the investor owns the stock, the shares should be sold.

---

[7]Time is measured in variable units since a movement along the X axis could occur after a week or a month or a year.

Figure 13.2 ◆ BUY AND SELL SIGNALS

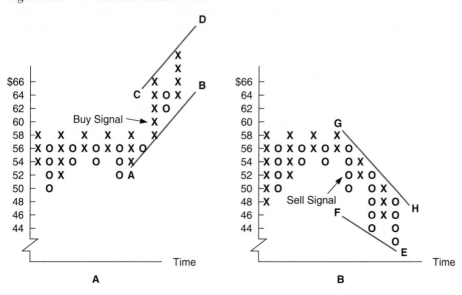

It is interesting to note that in both cases illustrated in Figure 13.2, the purchases and sales appear to be made at the wrong time. In the case of the purchase, it is made after the stock has already increased in price. Conversely, the sale is made after the stock has declined in price. Thus, purchases are not made at the lows, and sales are not made at the highs. Instead, the purchases appear to be made when the stock is reaching new highs, and the sales are made when the stock is reaching new lows. The rationale for this behavior rests primarily on the belief that the charts indicate new trends. Despite the fact that the investor missed the high prices for the sale and the low prices for the purchase, if the price change that is being forecasted proves accurate, then the investor will have made the correct investment decision even though the purchases and sales were not made at the exact turning points.

Besides indicating the buy or sell signals when trends are being established, these charts suggest possible trading strategies during the trends, which are also illustrated in Figure 13.2. While the left-hand side shows a price that is obviously rising, the price is still fluctuating. The right-hand side illustrates a downward trend, but the price is also fluctuating. During the upward trend, which is illustrated in Figure 13.2, part A, each high is higher than the preceding high price, and each low is higher than the preceding low price. Obviously, if an investor buys this stock and holds it, the return will be positive over this period. However, the return may be increased by judiciously buying at each low, selling at each high, and repeating the process when the cycle within the trend is repeated.

In order to isolate these opportunities, a set of lines has been drawn in Figure 13.2 connecting the high and the low prices that the stock is achieving. These lines are believed to have special significance because they indicate when to make the buy and sell decisions. The bottom lines (*AB* and *EF*), which connect the lowest prices, suggest a price level that generates "support" for the stock. Technical analysis asserts that when the price of the stock approaches a support line, the number of purchases will increase, which will stop further price declines. Hence, the approach of a stock's price toward a support line suggests that a buying opportunity is developing. Should the price reach the line and start back up, then the investor should buy the stock.

The opposite occurs at the top line (*CD* and *GH* in Figure 13.2, parts A and B), which represents "resistance." Since the price of the stock has risen to that level, more investors will want to sell their stock, which will thwart further price advances. Accordingly, the investor should sell the stock when the price reaches a line of resistance. After the stock has been sold, the investor then waits for the price to decline to the level of price support.

Bar Graphs

bar graph
A graph indicating the high, low, and closing prices of a security.

Bar graphs are similar to point-and-figure charts. Like the X-O charts, they require a day-to-day compilation of data, and they use essentially the same information. Preference for one over the other is a matter of choice, and while the investor could construct both, such work would seem redundant.

A bar graph is constructed by using three price observations—the high, the low, and the closing price for the day. If the prices were

Price	Monday	Tuesday	Wednesday	Thursday	Friday
High	$10	$9½	$9⅞	$10½	$12
Low	9	9	9¼	9⅞	10⅛
Close	9	9⅜	9⅞	10	11½

the bar graphs for each day would be

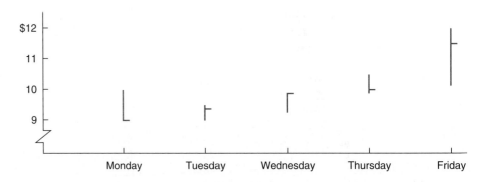

The vertical lines represent the range of the stock's price (i.e., the high and the low prices), and the horizontal lines represent the closing price.

It is obvious that such a chart is easy to construct, but it does require a substantial amount of work to keep several of these charts up to date on a daily basis. Each stock requires 15 price observations per week, which means 150 observations for just ten stocks per week. Since an entry is made on an X-O chart only if the

Figure 13.3 ✦ HEAD-AND-SHOULDER PATTERN

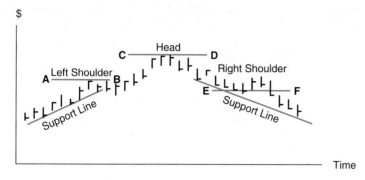

price of the stock has moved to the next interval, less work is required to construct such a chart, and it may be preferred to the bar graph for this reason alone.

As with the X-O chart, the bar graph is supposed to indicate future price movements in the stock by the pattern that emerges. There are several possible patterns. For example, one brief paperback book on charting identifies at least ten patterns, each with a descriptive name such as head and shoulder, wedge, flag, or pennant.[8] Space limits this discussion to only one pattern: the head and shoulder. The student who is interested in the variety of patterns should consult a book that explains the different patterns and how they are used to predict future stock prices.

A **head-and-shoulder pattern** does just what its name implies: The graph forms a pattern that resembles a head and shoulders. Such a pattern is illustrated in Figure 13.3. Initially, the price of the stock rises. Then it levels off before rising to a new high, after which the price declines, levels off, and then starts to fall. To illustrate the head-and-shoulder pattern, several lines have been imposed on the graph. These lines are similar to the lines of resistance and support found on the X-O charts. Line *AB* shows the left shoulder and also represents a line of resistance. However, once it is penetrated, the price of the stock rises to a new high, where it meets new resistance (line *CD*).

When the stock is unable to penetrate this new resistance, the price starts to decline and forms the head. However, after this initial decline in price the stock reaches a new level of support, which forms the right shoulder (line *EF*). When the price falls below line *EF*, the head-and-shoulder pattern is completed. This is interpreted to mean that the stock's price will continue to fall and is taken as a very bearish sign by followers of this type of analysis.

While the head-and-shoulder pattern in Figure 13.3 indicates that the price of the stock will subsequently fall, the same pattern upside down implies the exact opposite. In this case, penetration of the right shoulder indicates that the price of the stock will rise and is taken as a very bullish sign by those who use bar graphs.

head-and-shoulder pattern
A tool of technical analysis; a pattern of security prices that resembles a head and shoulders.

---

[8] See Anthony J. Lerro and Charles B. Swayne, Jr., *Selection of Securities: Technical Analysis of Stock Market Prices* (Morristown, N.J.: General Learning Corporation, 1971).

Moving Averages

A **moving average** is an average computed over time. For example, suppose the closing monthly values for the Dow Jones industrial average were as follows:

January	3287	April	3258	July	3347	October	3374
February	3284	May	3315	August	3334	November	3472
March	3267	June	3335	September	3328	December	3547

A six-month moving average of the Dow Jones industrials would be computed as follows. The average for the first six months is computed first.

$$\frac{3287 + 3284 + 3267 + 3258 + 3315 + 3335}{6}$$

$$= \frac{19746}{6} = 3291.$$

Then the average is computed again, but the entry for July (3347) is added in and the entry for January (3287) is deleted:

$$\frac{3284 + 3267 + 3258 + 3315 + 3335 + 3347}{6}$$

$$= \frac{19806}{6} = 3301.$$

The average is thus 3301, which is greater than the average for the preceding six months (3291).

To obtain the next entry, the average is computed again, with August being added and February being dropped. The average in this case becomes 3309. By continuing this method of adding the most recent entry and dropping the oldest entry, the averages move through time.

Figure 13.4 presents both the Dow Jones industrial average for 1984 through 1991 and the six-month moving average. As may be seen from the figure, the moving average follows the Dow Jones industrials. However, when the Dow Jones industrials are declining, the moving average is greater than the industrial average. The converse is true when the Dow Jones industrial average is rising: the moving average is less than the industrial average. At several points the two lines cross. For example, the Dow Jones industrial average crossed the six-month moving average in early 1988. Technicians place emphasis on such a crossover, for they believe that it is indicative of a change in the direction of the market. (It may also indicate a change in a specific security's price when the moving average is computed for a particular stock.) In this illustration, there appears to be some validity to the claim of the predictive power of the moving average, as the market rose after the buy signals and fell after the sell signals.

The average that is most frequently used is a 200-day moving average. Thus, for a specific stock, the investor must keep a daily tabulation of 200 stock prices and recompute the average daily! Such calculations are obviously tedious if the investor follows a significant number of stocks. A 200-day average may be approximated by

Figure 13.4 ✦ Dᴏᴡ Jᴏɴᴇs Iɴᴅᴜsᴛʀɪᴀʟ Aᴠᴇʀᴀɢᴇ ᴀɴᴅ ᴀ Sɪx-Mᴏɴᴛʜ Mᴏᴠɪɴɢ Aᴠᴇʀᴀɢᴇ

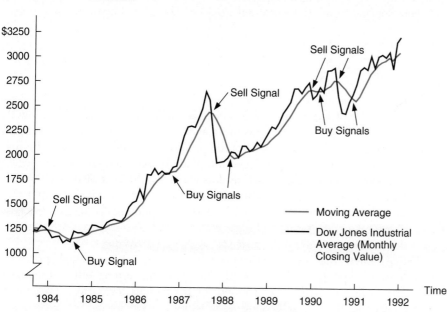

using weekly prices for 35 to 40 weeks. There is little evidence that using moving averages of different durations produces results inferior (or superior) to the 200-day moving average.[9]

Volume

The preceding techniques emphasized price movements as measured by point-and-figure charts, bar graphs, and moving averages. Technical analysts also place emphasis on the volume of transactions and deviations from the normal volume of trading in a specific stock. A large deviation from normal volume is interpreted to mean a change in the demand for or supply of the stock.

Since a price change can occur on small volume or on large volume, the price change itself says nothing concerning the breadth of the change in demand or supply. A price increase on small volume is not as bullish as one accompanied by heavy trading. Conversely, a price decline on small volume is not as bearish as a decline accompanied by a large increase in the number of shares traded. When a price

[9]A study by Van Horne and Parker suggests that the use of moving averages does not increase investment results. See James C. Van Horne and G.G.C. Parker, "The Random Walk Theory: An Empirical Test," *Financial Analysts Journal* (November–December 1967). For an alternative view, see William A. Remaley, "Moving Averages As Market Timing Indicators," *AAII Journal* (October 1987): 11–14.

decline occurs on small volume, that indicates only a modest increase in the supply of the stock was offered for sale relative to the demand. However, if the price decline were to occur on a large increase in volume, that would indicate many investors were seeking to sell the stock and would be considered bearish.

Insider Transactions

In Chapter 4 we learned that insiders, such as officers, directors, and very large stockholders, cannot legally use inside information for personal gain (e.g., buy the stock prior to an important announcement and subsequently sell it after the price has risen). However, they can and often do purchase and sell the stock of the firm in which they have access to privileged information. Such transactions are legal if they are reported to the SEC. Since insiders may have the best picture of how the firm is faring, some devotees of technical analysis feel that these inside transactions offer a clue to future earnings, dividends, and stock price performance. A greater number of purchases than sales is believed to be a bullish indicator, and more sales transactions than purchases imply that the stock's price will fall.

The hypothesis that insider activity may be indicative of future stock prices has received some support in the academic literature concerning efficient markets. While very little support has been found for the various technical approaches to security selection, there is evidence that studying insider activity may indeed lead to superior investment results.[10] Thus, the individual investor would be well advised to keep track of insider purchases and sales of stocks in those firms in which the investor has particular interest.[11]

Short Sales by Specialists

While purchases and sales by insiders may indicate their perception of the firm's future prospects, short sales by specialists may indicate the stock's future price performance. Hence technical analysts may follow both activities. As was explained in Chapter 2, specialists make a market in securities listed on the organized exchanges (i.e., they offer to buy and sell securities for their own accounts).

In order to make a market, specialists must be abreast of the events affecting securities. They continually adjust their portfolios in response to the flow of securities onto and off of the market. It is through this process that they continue to make the market in the individual securities. If they misjudge demand and supply and subsequent price changes, they could suffer large losses.

---

[10]These studies include Jeffrey F. Jaffe, "Special Information and Insider Trading," *Journal of Business* (July 1974); James H. Lorie and Victor Niederhoffer, "Predictive and Statistical Properties of Insider Trading," *Journal of Law and Economics* 11 (April 1968): 35–53; and Dan Givoly and Dan Palmon, "Insider Trading and Exploitation of Inside Information: Some Empirical Evidence," *Journal of Business* (January 1985): 69–87.

[11]The ratio of insider sales to insider purchases may be obtained from Stock Research Corp., 50 Broadway, New York, NY 10004.

If specialists believe that the supply of stock coming to the market will increase and drive down a stock's price, they take short positions in the stock in anticipation of the price decline. Total short sales and specialists' short sales must be reported to the SEC and the NYSE. Generally about half of all short sales are made by the specialists. If, however, the proportion of specialists' short sales to total short sales rises to above 65 percent, technical analysts believe this is a bearish indicator. The high ratio of specialists' short sales indicates that those who may be best able to perceive changes in supply and demand are anticipating price declines. If the ratio of specialists' short sales to total short sales falls to 40 percent, technical analysts interpret that as a bullish sign, indicative of rising future stock prices.[12]

The Verification of Technical Analysis

At first glance technical analysis seems so very appealing. One needs only to construct a set of charts or compute some simple ratios (e.g., insider sales to insider purchases) and then follow the signals given by the analysis. Such simple rules for investing literally beg for verification to ascertain if they are, in fact, good predictors.

Several studies have sought to test the validity of technical analysis. The use of computers has eased calculations and made it possible to test several variations of the technical approach. For example, the investigator may have the computer calculate various moving averages (e.g., 200-day, 100-day, or 50-day averages) to determine if one is the best predictor.

The majority of this research has failed to verify the various technical approaches to investing.[13] This conclusion is the basis for the weak form of the efficient market hypothesis discussed in Chapter 8. The large body of empirical evidence has convinced many investors to believe that the technical approach does not lead to superior investment performance and that the investor would do just as well to buy a randomly selected portfolio and hold it. When commissions are included, the return from following the technical approach may be even less than that earned on a randomly selected portfolio. These conclusions have resulted in a general rejection of technical analysis by many academically trained teachers of finance.

The primary cause for the inability of the technical approach to select securities that outperform the market is that the market is very efficient. Information is readily

---

[12]See Jerome B. Cohen, Edward D. Zinbarg, and Arthur Zeikel, *Investment Analysis and Portfolio Management*, 5th ed. (Homewood, Ill.: Irwin, 1987), 272–273.

[13]For example, see Michael C. Jensen and George A. Bennington, "Random Walks and Technical Theories: Some Additional Evidence," *The Journal of Finance* 25 (May 1970): 469–482; Eugene Fama, "The Behavior of Stock-Market Prices," *Journal of Business* 37 (January 1965): 34–105; F.E. James, Jr., "Monthly Moving Averages—An Effective Investment Tool?" *Journal of Financial and Quantitative Analysis* (September 1968): 315–326; and J.C. Van Horne and G.G.C. Parker, "The Random Walk Theory: An Empirical Test," *Financial Analysts Journal* (November–December 1967): 87–92. (The student should be warned that most of this material may be difficult to comprehend.) Empirical support for technical analysis may be found in Robert A. Levy, "Random Walks: Reality or Myth," *Financial Analysts Journal* (November–December 1967): 69–77.

THE MARKET TECHNICIANS
ASSOCIATION

The Market Technicians Association is an organization for individuals whose "professional efforts are spent practicing financial technical analysis that is either made available to the investing public or becomes a primary input into an active portfolio management process and for whom technical analysis is the basis of their decision-making process." Affiliate memberships are open to individuals who are interested in technical analysis but do not meet the above requirements. The association publishes the *Market Technicians Association Journal* to "promote the investigation and analysis of price and volume activities of the world's financial markets." Information concerning the association and its journal may be obtained by writing the association at 71 Broadway, 2nd Floor, New York, NY 10006.

disseminated among the investors, and prices adjust accordingly.[14] Thus, if an investor were to develop an approach that outperformed the market, it would only be a matter of time before the technique would be learned by others. The method would no longer achieve the initial results as the mass of investors applied it. A system that works (if one can be found) can succeed only if it is not known by many investors. Thus, it is naive for an investor to believe that he or she can use a known technical approach to beat the market. A new and unknown system is needed. However, when one realizes that many investors are looking for and testing various approaches, it is hard to believe that the individual investor will find a technical approach that can beat the market.

Although the technical approach lacks verification, it is still used by some portfolio managers as a supplement to fundamental analysis to help the timing of purchases and sales. The primary users of technical analysis are individuals and advisory services. One frequently sees advertisements in the financial press for advisory services that employ various technical approaches. Perhaps the investor should ask why the service is being sold and not being applied exclusively by those who know the "secret." Certainly if one knows how to beat the market, one should be able to earn a substantial return on investments and should not need to sell the secret for monetary gain.

SUMMARY

Technical analysis seeks to identify superior investments by examining the past behavior of the market and of individual securities. Technical analysts, or "chartists," stress the past as a means to predict the future. This approach is diametrically

---

[14] One study found that the technical approach may be a lagging and not a leading indicator of stock prices. In an efficient market, prices may react before the technical indicator gives a signal of the change. Thus, by the time the signal is observed, prices have already responded, and there is no opportunity for the investor to take advantage of the signal. See Ben Branch and Thomas Schneeweis, "Market Movements and Technical Market Indicators," *The Mid-Atlantic Journal of Business,* (Summer 1986): 31–41.

opposed to the fundamental approach, which stresses future earnings and dividends appropriately discounted back to the present.

Several technical approaches (the Dow theory, Barron's confidence index, and odd lot purchases versus odd lot sales) attempt to identify changes in the direction of the market. Since individual security prices move together, the determination of a change in the direction of the market should identify the future movement of individual security prices.

Other technical approaches (X-O charts, bar graphs, moving averages, and analysis of insider activity) may be applied to individual securities. By constructing various charts and graphs, the technical analyst determines when specific securities should be bought or sold.

Whether or not the technical approach leads to superior investment results is open to debate. However, with the exception of insider activity, little support has been found to verify technical analysis. The results of these studies imply that the investor may achieve similar results by purchasing a random selection of securities.

Terms to Remember

technical analysis	bar graph
Dow theory	head-and-shoulder pattern
Barron's confidence index	moving average
odd lot theory	
point-and-figure chart (X-O chart)	

Questions

1. What is the purpose of technical analysis?
2. Why are those who use technical analysis sometimes referred to as chartists?
3. What changes represent a sell signal in the Dow theory, Barron's confidence index, and the odd lot theory?
4. What is a moving average? What is the significance when a stock's price equals a moving average of that price?
5. Why may technical analysis produce self-fulfilling predictions?
6. Why may the construction of some charts or graphs used in technical analysis be tedious and time consuming?
7. What is the problem with time lags in technical analysis?
8. Why does technical analysis receive little support from academically oriented students of investments?
9. Which technical approach may be the best?

Suggested Readings

Descriptions of various technical approaches may be found in

Bishop, George W., Jr. *Charles Dow and the Dow Theory.* New York: Appleton-Century-Crofts, 1960.

Cohen, A.W. *Point and Figure Stock Market Trading.* Larchmont, N.Y.: Chartcraft, 1968.

Investing in

Fixed

Income

Securities

PART III CONSIDERS INVESTMENTS IN

III

SECURITIES THAT PAY A FIXED ANNUAL

INCOME. THE ANNUAL INTEREST OR

DIVIDEND PAYMENTS ARE THE SAME EACH YEAR. SINCE SUCH INVESTMENTS

CONSIST PRIMARILY OF LONG-TERM BONDS ISSUED BY CORPORATIONS AND

GOVERNMENTS, MOST OF PART III IS DEVOTED TO THESE BONDS. ◆ THESE

SECURITIES PRODUCE A CONSTANT FLOW OF INCOME AND FOR MANY YEARS were considered to be good investments for conservative individuals. However, the wide fluctuations in bond prices and interest rates during the early 1980s and the expansion of the market for junk bonds during the late 1980s have increased the risk associated with investing in bonds. While bonds still offer a flow of interest income and the safety associated with the legal obligation to repay the principal, many individual bond issues can no longer be considered safe investments that are appropriate for conservative investors seeking income and the preservation of capital.

14

THE MARKET FOR DEBT

$\mathcal{M}$any corporations and governments have issued long-term debt to finance long-term investments, such as the expansion of plant and equipment or the construction of roads and schools. Internally generated funds (profits and depreciation for corporations and tax revenues for governments) may be insufficient to finance such investments on a pay-as-you-go basis. Long-term debt, which matures at a specified time longer than one year, permits firms and governments to acquire assets now and pay for them over a period of years. The debt is then retired for corporations by the cash flow that is generated by plant and equipment and for governments by the fees or tax revenues that are collected.

This chapter is concerned with long-term debt and covers (1) the characteristics common to all of these debt instruments, (2) the risks associated with investing in debt, (3) the mechanics of purchasing debt instruments, and (4) the retirement of debt. Chapter 15 covers the valuation of debt. Like stock, debt may be purchased initially either by financial institutions in a private placement or by individuals through a public offering. Once the securities have been issued, secondary markets develop. These debt instruments may be bought and sold on the organized security exchanges or in the over-the-counter markets. These securities are generally very marketable, since there is an active secondary market in many corporate and government bonds.

❖ ❖ ❖

LEARNING OBJECTIVES

After completing this chapter you should be able to

1. Understand the features common to all bonds.

2. Explain the purpose of the indenture and the role of the trustee.

3. Differentiate between bearer bonds and registered bonds.

4. Ascertain the sources of risk to the bondholder.

5. Describe the procedure for buying a bond.

6. Differentiate among the types of corporate bonds.

7. Distinguish between the ways bonds are retired.

GENERAL FEATURES OF DEBT INSTRUMENTS

Interest and Maturity

All **bonds** (i.e., long-term debt instruments) have similar characteristics. They represent the indebtedness (liability) of their issuers in return for a specified sum, which is called the **principal.** Virtually all debt has a **maturity date,** which is the particular date by which it must be paid off. When debt is issued, the length of time

bond
A long-term liability with a specified amount of interest and specified maturity date.

373

principal
The amount owed; the face value of a debt.

maturity date
The time at which a debt issue becomes due and the principal must be repaid.

interest
Payment for the use of money.

to maturity is set, and it may range from one day to 20 or 30 years or more. If the maturity date falls within a year of the date of issuance, the debt is referred to as short-term debt. Long-term debt matures more than a year after it has been issued. (Debt that matures in from one to ten years is sometimes referred to as intermediate debt.) The owners of debt instruments receive a flow of payments, which is called **interest,** in return for the use of their money. Interest should not be confused with other forms of income, such as the cash dividends that are paid by common and preferred stock. Dividends are distributions from earnings, whereas interest is an expense of borrowing.

A bond is illustrated in Exhibit 14.1. This exhibit reproduces the face of a registered 8¼ percent debenture of General Cinema. If this bond were not a sample, the principal amount would have been stated immediately following the words "the principal sum of." This bond matures in 2000. A bond certificate is also individually numbered for identification, and the name of the owner is recorded on the certificate's face. The certificates may be endorsed on the back by the owner, and the

Exhibit 14.1 ✦ EXAMPLE OF THE FACE OF A CORPORATE BOND

Source: Reprinted with permission of General Cinema Corporation.

title may be readily changed from one owner to another by the transfer agent, which is usually the bank that countersigns the security and acts as the trustee for the bond issue.

When a debt instrument such as this bond is issued, the rate of interest to be paid by the borrower is established. This rate is frequently referred to as the bond's **coupon rate** (e.g., the 8¼ percent in Exhibit 14.1). The amount of interest is usually fixed over the lifetime of the bond. (There are exceptions; for example, see the section on variable interest rate bonds later in this chapter.) The return earned by the investor, however, need not be equal to the specified rate of interest because bond prices change. They may be purchased at a discount (a price below the face amount or principal) or at a premium (a price above the face amount of the bond). The return actually earned, then, depends on the interest received, the purchase price, and what the investor receives upon selling the bond or redeeming it.

coupon rate
The specified interest rate or amount of interest paid by a bond.

The potential return offered by a bond is referred to as the yield. Yield is frequently expressed in two ways: the **current yield** and the **yield to maturity.** Current yield refers only to the annual flow of interest or income. The yield to maturity refers to the yield that the investor will earn if the debt instrument is held from the moment of purchase until it is redeemed at par (face value) by the issuer. The difference between the current yield and the yield to maturity is discussed at length in the section on the pricing of bonds in Chapter 15.

current yield
Annual income divided by the current price of the security.

yield to maturity
The yield earned on a bond from the time it is acquired until the maturity date of the bond.

There is a relationship between yield and the length of time to maturity for debt instruments of the same level of risk. Generally, the longer the time to maturity,

Figure 14.1 ✦ Positively Sloped Yield Curve

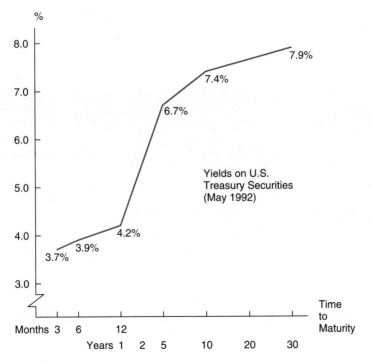

the higher the rate of interest. This relationship is illustrated in Figure 14.1, which plots the yield on various United States government securities as of May 1992. This figure, which is frequently referred to as a **yield curve,** shows that the bonds with the longest time to maturity have the highest interest rates. For example, short-term securities (three months to maturity) had yields of 3.7 percent; one-year bonds paid yields 4.2 percent, and bonds that matured after ten years paid in excess of 7 percent.

One would expect such a relationship because the longer the time to maturity, the longer the investor will have his or her funds tied up. To induce investors to lend their money for lengthier periods, it is usually necessary to pay them more interest. Also, there is more risk involved in purchasing a bond with a longer period to maturity, since the fortunes of the issuer are more difficult to estimate for the longer term. This means that investors will ordinarily require additional compensation to bear the risk associated with long-term debt.

Although such a relationship between time and yield does usually exist, there have been periods when the opposite has occurred (i.e., when short-term interest rates exceeded long-term interest rates). This happened from 1978 to 1979, and again in 1981, when short-term interest rates were higher than long-term rates. The yields on treasury securities (securities issued by the Treasury Department) in June 1981 are illustrated in Figure 14.2. In this case the yield curve has a negative slope, which indicates that as the length of time to maturity increased, the interest rates

Figure 14.2 ✦ Yɪᴇʟᴅ Cᴜʀᴠᴇs (Yɪᴇʟᴅs ᴏɴ Fᴇᴅᴇʀᴀʟ Gᴏᴠᴇʀɴᴍᴇɴᴛ Sᴇᴄᴜʀɪᴛɪᴇs)

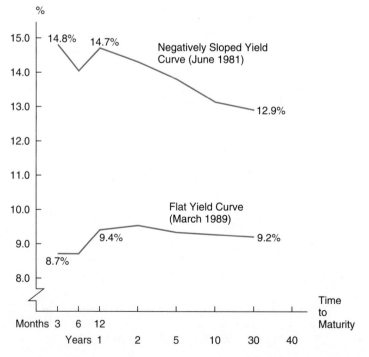

declined. Thus, securities maturing in less than a year had a yield of greater than 14 percent, while the long-term debt that matured after ten years yielded 13 percent.

Such a yield curve can be explained by inflation, which exceeded 10 percent in 1981 to 1982. The board of governors of the Federal Reserve was pursuing a tight monetary policy in order to fight inflation. It sold short-term government securities (i.e., treasury bills) in an effort to reduce the capacity of commercial banks to lend. These sales depressed the prices of all fixed-income securities, which resulted in higher yields. (As is explained in detail in Chapter 15, yields on debt instruments rise as their prices fall.) The yields on short-term securities rose more than those on long-term securities, and this, coupled with other events in the money and capital markets, resulted in the negative-sloped yield curve. When the rate of inflation abated during the mid-1980s, the yield curve returned to the positive slope that it has maintained during most periods.

There have also been periods when the yield curve was relatively flat. Such a yield curve is also illustrated in Figure 14.2 by the yield curve for March 1989. The yield on short-term debt with three to six months to maturity was approximately 8.7 percent, and the rate for thirty-year bonds was 9.2 percent. While the long-term rate did exceed the short-term rate, the small difference produced a gently rising, or flat, yield curve.

Figures 14.1 and 14.2 also illustrate that interest rates do change. (The student should remember that the interest rate is the current rate paid for the use of credit. This should not be confused with the coupon rate, which is fixed when the debt instrument is issued.) Although all interest rates fluctuate, short-term rates are more volatile than long-term interest rates. This is illustrated in Figure 14.3, which plots

Figure 14.3 ✦ YIELD ON TREASURY BILLS AND TREASURY BONDS (1978–JULY 1992)

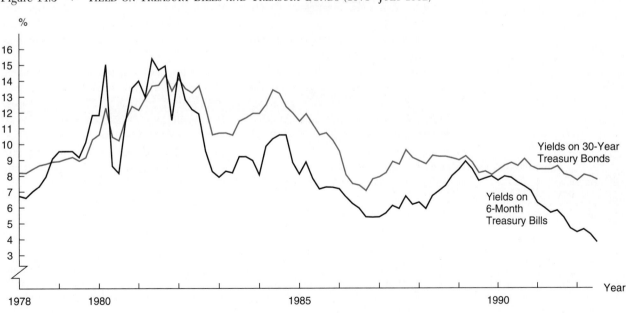

the yields on a six-month treasury bill and on a thirty-year treasury bond. As may be seen from the figure, the fluctuation in yields for the short-term bill is greater than that for the long-term bond. For example, the yield on a six-month treasury bill decreased from 7.0 percent per year in late 1990 to below 4.0 percent in early 1992, while the yield on a thirty-year treasury bond declined from 8.5 to 7.9 percent during the same period. This figure illustrates not only the greater fluctuation in short-term yields but also how quickly changes can occur. For example, the annual short-term rate rose from 10.1 percent to 15 percent in only *three* months in 1979 to 1980 in response to changes in the demand for the supply of short-term credit.[1]

The Indenture

indenture
The document that specifies the terms of a bond issue.

default
The failure of a debtor to meet any term of a debt's indenture.

Each debt agreement has terms that the debtor must meet. These are stated in a legal document called the **indenture.**[2] These terms include the coupon rate, the date of maturity, and any other conditions required of the debtor. One of the more frequent of these requirements is the pledging of collateral, which is property that the borrower must offer to secure the loan. For example, the collateral for a mortgage loan is the building. Any other assets owned by the borrower, such as securities or inventory, may also be pledged to secure a loan. If the borrower defaults on the debt, the creditor may seize the collateral and sell it to recoup the principal. **Default** occurs when the borrower fails to meet not only the payment of interest but *any* of the terms of the indenture. The other conditions of the indenture are just as important as meeting the interest payments on time, and often they may be more difficult for the debtor to satisfy.

Examples of common loan restrictions include (1) limits on paying dividends, (2) limits on issuing additional debt, and (3) restrictions on merging or significantly changing the nature of the business without the prior consent of the creditors. In addition, loan agreements usually specify that if the firm defaults on any other outstanding debt issues, this debt issue is also in default, in which case the creditors may seek immediate repayment. Default on one issue, then, usually puts all outstanding debt in default.

These examples do not exhaust all the possible conditions of a given loan. Since each loan is separately negotiated, there is ample opportunity for differences among loan agreements. During periods of scarce credit, the terms of a loan agreement will be stricter, whereas during periods of lower interest rates and more readily available money, the restrictions will tend to be more lenient. The important point, however, is that if any part of the loan agreement is violated, the creditor may declare that the debt is in default and may seek a court order to enforce the terms of the indenture.

---

[1] For additional discussions of the structure of yields, see the appendices to this chapter and Chapter 17.

[2] For publicly held corporate bond issues, the indenture is filed with the Securities and Exchange Commission.

The Role of the Trustee

Many debt instruments are purchased by individual investors who may be unaware of all of the terms of the indenture. Even if individual investors are aware of the terms, they may be too geographically dispersed to take concerted action in case of default. To protect their interests, a **trustee** is appointed for each publicly held bond issue. It is the trustee's job to see that the terms of the indenture are upheld and to take remedial action if the company defaults on the terms of the loan. For performing these services, the trustee receives compensation from the issuer of the debt.

Trustees are usually commercial banks that serve both the debtor and the bondholders. They act as transfer agents for the bonds when ownership is changed through sales in the secondary markets. The signature of a trustee on the bond is a guarantee of the authenticity of the bond. These banks receive from the debtor the funds to pay the interest, and this money is then distributed to the individual bondholders. It is also the job of the trustee to inform the bondholders if the firm is no longer meeting the terms of the indenture. In case of default, the trustee may take the debtor to court to enforce the terms of the contract. If there is a subsequent reorganization or liquidation of the company, the trustee continues to act on behalf of the individual bondholders to protect their principal.

trustee
A commercial bank that is appointed to uphold the terms of a bond's indenture.

Forms of Debt

Debt instruments are issued in one of two forms: (1) **registered bonds** or (2) **bearer bonds** to which coupons are attached (therefore, they are also called **coupon bonds**). Registered bonds are similar to stock certificates; the bonds are registered in the owner's name. Delivery of the bonds is made to the registered owner who also receives the interest payments from the trustee bank. When the bond is sold, it is registered in the name of the new owner by the transfer agent. The General Cinema bond in Exhibit 14.1 is an example of a registered bond. The names of both the owner (because this is a sample bond, the owner's name has been omitted) and the trustee are stated on the front of the bond.

While many bonds are registered in the name of the owner, a new trend has developed in which registered bonds are issued in "book form." No actual bonds are printed; instead, a computer record of owners is maintained by the issuer or the issuer's agent such as a bank. If a bond is sold only in book form, the investor cannot take delivery, and the bond must be registered in the street name of the investor's brokerage firm or whoever is holding the bond for the investor. Such a system is obviously more efficient than physically issuing the bond, but the brokerage firm may charge custodial fees, which either the issuer or the investor will have to pay.

Bearer bonds are entirely different. Ownership is evidenced by mere possession of the bond and is transferred simply by passing the debt instrument from the seller to the buyer; no new certificates are issued. Thus, securities in this form are extremely easy to transfer. However, if they are lost, they are like currency. Therefore, the possibility of theft is a real concern that requires the owner to be extremely cautious when handling these bonds.

Since the debtor does not know the names of the owners of bearer securities, coupons for interest payments are attached to the bond. The owner must detach

registered bond
A bond whose ownership is registered with the commercial bank that distributes interest payments and principal repayments.

bearer bond
A bond with coupons attached or a bond whose possession denotes ownership.

coupon bond
A bond with coupons attached that are removed and presented for payment of interest when due.

the coupon and send it to the paying agent (the trustee) to collect the interest. In the past, most bonds were of this type. Investors who relied on fixed interest income for their livelihood were frequently called coupon clippers.

Under current law, all newly issued corporate and municipal bonds have to be registered in the owner's name. However, previously issued coupon bonds still exist. An investor who prefers a certain type can consult a bond publication, such as *Standard & Poor's Bond Guide,* to determine which are coupon bonds and which are registered bonds. If the bond issue has both forms, the investor may specify the type desired when the bond is purchased from the broker. The supply of coupon bonds is, however, diminishing, and it is only a matter of time before all corporate and municipal bonds will be in registered form.

An example of a bearer bond with coupons attached is shown in Exhibit 14.2. The bond has 50 coupons (only the first one is illustrated), and each represents a six-month interest payment. This particular bond is an income nonmortgage bond, which means that it is unsecured and among the riskiest of all debt instruments. The bond was never retired, and not one interest payment was ever made!

RISK

An important characteristic of all debt is risk: risk that the interest will not be paid (i.e., risk of default); risk that the principal will not be repaid; risk that the price of the debt instrument may decline; risk that inflation will continue, thereby reducing the purchasing power of the interest payments and of the principal when it is repaid; and risk that the bond will be retired (i.e., called) prior to maturity thereby denying the investor the interest payments for the initial term of the bond; and risk that interest rates will fall resulting in lower interest income when the proceeds are reinvested. These risks vary significantly with different types of debt. For example, there is no risk of default on the interest payments and principal repayments of the debt of the federal government. The reason for this absolute safety is that the federal government has the power to tax and to create money. The government can always issue the money that is necessary to pay the interest and repay the principal.[3]

The procedure is more subtle than just printing new money, however. The federal government issues new debt and sells it to the Federal Reserve Board. With the proceeds of these sales, the federal government retires the old debt. The money supply increases because newly created money is used to pay for the debt. The effect of selling debt to the Federal Reserve Board and then using the proceeds to retire existing debt (or to finance a current deficit) is no different from printing and spending new money. The money supply expands in either case. Thus, the federal government can always pay its interest expense and retire its debt when it becomes due.

Even though the federal government can refund its debt and hence is free of the risk of default, the prices of the federal government's bonds can and do fluctuate.

---

[3]The decline in the value of the dollar in foreign countries may reduce the attractiveness of federal obligations. Fluctuations in the value of the dollar, then, do impose significant risk for foreigners who invest in these securities.

Exhibit 14.2 ✦ A Coupon Bond

In addition, the purchasing power of the dollar may decline as a result of inflation, and, therefore, the purchasing power of funds invested in debt also may decline. Thus, investing in federal government securities is not entirely free of risk, since the investor may suffer losses from price fluctuations of the debt or from inflation.

The debt of firms, individuals, and state and local governments involves even greater risk, for all of these debtors may default on their obligations. To aid buyers of debt instruments, several companies have developed **credit rating systems.** The most important of these services are Moody, Dun and Bradstreet, and Standard & Poor. Although these firms do not rate all debt instruments, they do rate the degree of risk of a significant number.

Exhibit 14.3 gives the risk classifications presented by Moody and Standard & Poor. The rating systems are quite similar, for each classification of debt involving little risk (high-quality debt) receives a rating of triple A, while debt involving greater risk (poorer quality debt) receives progressively lower ratings. Bonds rated triple B or better are considered investment grade, while bonds with lower ratings are often referred to as "junk bonds" or "high-yield securities." The growth in this

credit rating systems
Classification schemes designed to indicate the risk associated with a particular security.

Exhibit 14.3 ✦ BOND RATINGS

Moody's Bond Ratings[*]

Aaa	Bonds of highest quality	B	Bonds that lack characteristics of a desirable investment
Aa	Bonds of high quality		
A	Bonds whose security of principal and interest is considered adequate but may be impaired in the future	Caa	Bonds in poor standing that may be defaulted
		Ca	Speculative bonds that are often in default
		C	Bonds with little probability of any investment value (lowest rating)
Baa	Bonds of medium grade that are neither highly protected nor poorly secured		
Ba	Bonds of speculative quality whose future cannot be considered well assured		

For ratings Aa through B, 1 indicates the high, 2 indicates the middle, and 3 indicates the low end of the rating class.

Standard & Poor's Bond Ratings[†]

AAA	Bonds of highest quality	BB	Bonds of lower medium grade with few desirable investment characteristics
AA	High-quality debt obligations		
A	Bonds that have a strong capacity to pay interest and principal but may be susceptible to adverse effects	B	Primarily speculative bonds with great uncertainties and major risk if exposed to adverse conditions
BBB	Bonds that have an adequate capacity to pay interest and principal but are more valuable to adverse economic conditions or changing circumstances	CCC	
		C	Income bonds on which no interest in being paid
		D	Bonds in default

Plus (+) and minus (−) are used to show relative strength and weakness within a rating category.

[*]*Source:* Adapted from *Moody's Bond Record,* January 1990.
[†]Source: Adapted from *Standard & Poor's Bond Guide,* January 1990.

poor quality debt was one of the phenomena within the financial markets during the 1980s. (The variety of features found in junk bonds is covered in Chapter 16.)

Even within a given rating, both Moody and Standard & Poor fine shade their rankings. Moody adds the numbers 1 through 3 to indicate degrees of quality within a ranking with 1 representing the highest rank and 3 the lowest. Thus a bond rated A1 has a higher rating than a bond rated A3. Standard & Poor uses + and − to indicate shades of quality. Thus a bond rated A+ has a higher rating than an A bond which, in turn, has a better rating than an A− bond.

Since the rating services analyze similar data, their ratings of specific debt issues should be reasonably consistent. This consistency is illustrated in Exhibit 14.4, which gives the ratings for several different bond issues. Generally both Moody and Standard & Poor assigned comparable ratings, such as the Baa2 and BBB, to the Consumers Power bond. When the ratings are different, the discrepancies are small. Moody ranked the AT&T bond Aa3, which is lower than the Standard & Poor's AA rating. (AA− would be the comparable rating.)

These ratings play an important role in the marketing of debt obligations. Since the possibility of default may be substantial for poor-quality debt, some financial institutions and investors will not purchase debt with a low credit rating. Many financial institutions, especially commercial banks, are prohibited by law from purchasing bonds with a rating below Baa. Thus, if the rating of a bond issued by a firm or a municipality is low or declines from the original rating, the issuer may have difficulty selling its debt. Corporations and municipal governments try to maintain good credit ratings, since high ratings reduce the cost of borrowing and increase the marketability of the debt.

While the majority of corporate and municipal bonds are rated, there are exceptions. If a firm or municipality believes it will be able to market the securities without a rating, it may choose not to incur the costs necessary to have the securities rated. Unrated securities tend to be small issues and, since they lack the approval implied by a rating, probably should be viewed as possessing considerable risk.

Besides the risk of default, creditors are also subject to the risk of price fluctuations. Once debt has been issued, the market price of the debt will rise or fall

Exhibit 14.4 ✦ RATINGS FOR SELECTED BONDS (AS OF APRIL 1992)

Firm	Coupon Rate of Interest	Year of Maturity	Moody's Rating	Standard & Poor's Rating
AT&T	7%	2001	Aa3	AA
Consumers Power	7½	2001	Baa2	BBB
Dow Chemical	8⁹⁄₁₀	2000	A1	A
Paramount Communications	7	2003	A3	A−
Mobil	8½	2001	Aa2	AA
Southland	12	1996	B	NR
Xerox	8⅝	1999	A2	A+

Sources: *Moody's Bond Record*, April 1992, and *Standard & Poor's Bond Guide*, April 1992.

depending on market conditions. If interest rates rise, the price of existing debt must fall so that its fixed interest payments relative to its price become competitive with the higher rates. In the event that interest rates decline, the opposite is true. The higher fixed interest payments of the bond make the debt more attractive than comparable newly issued bonds, and buyers will be willing to pay more for the debt issue. Why these fluctuations in the price of debt instruments occur is explained in more detail in Chapter 15, which discusses the valuation of debt instruments.

There is, however, one feature of debt that partially compensates for the risk of price fluctuations. The holder knows that the debt ultimately matures: The principal must be repaid. If the price of the bond decreases and the debt instrument sells for a discount (i.e., less than the face value), the value of the debt must appreciate as it approaches maturity, because on the day of maturity, the full amount of the principal must be repaid.

The final risk that all creditors must endure is inflation, which reduces the purchasing power of money. During periods of inflation the debtor repays the loan in money that purchases less. Creditors must receive a rate of interest that is at least equal to the rate of inflation to maintain their purchasing power. If lenders anticipate inflation, they will demand a higher rate of interest to help protect their purchasing power. For example, if the rate of inflation is 8 percent, the creditors may demand 10 percent, which nets them 2 percent in real terms (before income tax). Although inflation still causes the real value of the capital to decline, the higher interest rate partially offsets the effects of inflation.

If creditors do not anticipate inflation, the rate of interest may be insufficient to compensate for the loss in purchasing power. Inflation, then, hurts the creditors and helps the debtors, who are repaying the loans with money that purchases less.

The supposed inability of creditors to anticipate inflation has led to a belief that during inflation it is better to be a debtor. However, creditors invariably make an effort to protect their position by demanding higher interest rates. There is a transfer of purchasing power from creditors to debtors only if the creditors do not fully anticipate the inflation and do not demand sufficiently high interest rates. A transfer of purchasing power from debtors to creditors will occur in the opposite situation. If inflation is anticipated but does not occur, many debtors may pay artificially high interest rates, which transfers purchasing power from them to their creditors.[4] Hence, the transfer of purchasing power can go either way if one group inaccurately anticipates the future rate of inflation.

THE MECHANICS OF PURCHASING BONDS

Bonds may be purchased in much the same way as stocks. The investor can buy them through a brokerage firm, and some bonds (e.g., federal government securities) can be purchased through commercial banks. The various purchase orders that may be used to buy stock (e.g., the market order or the limit order with a specified price) also apply to the purchase of bonds. Bonds may be bought with cash or through the use of margin.

---

[4] Debtors may seek to protect themselves from the anticipated inflation *not* occurring by having the bond be callable. The call feature is discussed later in this chapter.

The bonds of many companies are listed on the New York and American stock exchanges. In addition, there is a large volume of trading in bonds in the over-the-counter markets. Like listed stocks, transactions in bonds are reported by the financial press. Exhibit 14.5 illustrates *The Wall Street Journal* reporting the trading in the 9 percent IBM bond. The entries are a bit tricky to read. The entry is for a $1,000 bond (though bonds generally trade in units greater than $1,000). Bond prices are reported as a percent of face value, so 106¾ means 106¾% of $1,000, or $1,067.50. The bond has a coupon rate of 9 percent and matures in the year 1998, which is reported as 9s98. The current yield is the annual interest payment divided by the price ($90.000 ÷ $1,067.50 = 8.4%). The number of bonds traded was 35, which means that, according to face value, $35,000 worth of these bonds changed ownership.

After the debt has been purchased, the broker sends a **confirmation statement.** Exhibit 14.6 presents simplified confirmation statements for the purchase and subsequent sale of $10,000 in face value worth of Tesoro Petroleum bonds. In addition to a description of the securities, the confirmation statements include the price, the commission, accrued interest, and net amount due.

Bonds earn interest every day, but the firm distributes the interest payments only twice a year. Thus, when a bond is purchased, the buyer owes the previous owner **accrued interest** for the days that the owner held the bond. In the case of the first transaction, the purchase was made after the last interest payment, so the accrued interest amounted to $54.00. This interest is added to the purchase price that the buyer must pay. When the bond is sold, the seller receives the accrued interest. The second transaction occurred soon after the interest payment, and in this case the accrued interest was only $12.00, which was added to the proceeds of the sale.

The profit or loss from the investment cannot be figured as the difference between the proceeds of the sale and the amount that is due after the purchase (i.e., $8,667.00 minus $7,899.00 in Exhibit 14.7). Instead, an adjustment must be made for the accrued interest. This procedure is illustrated in Exhibit 14.7. First, the accrued interest must be subtracted from the amount due to obtain the cost of the bond. Thus, $7,899.00 minus $54.00 is the cost ($7,845.00) of this purchase. Second, the accrued interest must also be subtracted from the proceeds of the sale. Thus, $8,667.00 minus $12.00 yields the revenues from the sale. To determine the profit or loss, the cost basis is subtracted from the sale value. In this particular instance, that is $8,655.00 (the sale value) minus $7,845.00 (the cost basis), which represents a gain of $810.00.

A few bonds do trade without accrued interest. These bonds are currently in default and are not paying interest. Such bonds are said to trade **flat,** and an *F* is placed next to them in the transactions reported by the financial press. These bonds are of little interest except to speculators. The risk in buying them is substantial, but some do resume interest payments that can result in substantial returns.

confirmation statement
Statement received from a brokerage firm that specifies a purchase or sale of a security.

accrued interest
Interest that has been earned but not received.

flat
A description of a bond that trades without accrued interest.

VARIETY OF CORPORATE BONDS

Corporations issue many types of bonds: mortgage bonds, equipment trust certificates, debenture bonds and subordinated debentures, income bonds, convertible bonds, variable interest rate bonds, and zero coupon bonds. These corporate debt

Exhibit 14.5 ✦ ILLUSTRATION FOR AN ENTRY FOR A $1,000 BOND TRADED ON THE NEW YORK STOCK EXCHANGE

NEW YORK EXCHANGE BONDS

Quotations as of 4 p.m. Eastern Time Monday, January 4, 1993

Volume $35,130,000

	Domestic Mon.	Domestic Thu.	All Issues Mon.	All Issues Thu.
Issues traded	483	432	484	433
Advances	216	217	216	217
Declines	147	114	148	115
Unchanged	120	101	120	101
New highs	24	16	24	16
New lows	1	1	1	2

SALES SINCE JANUARY 1
(000 omitted)

1993	1992	1991
$35,130	$49,560	$33,410

Dow Jones Bond Averages

–1992– High	–1992– Low	–1993– High	–1993– Low		–1993– Close	–1993– Chg.	–1993– %Yld	–1992– Close	–1992– Chg.
103.89	98.41	103.74	103.74	20 Bonds	103.74	– 0.15	7.26	99.20	+ 0.07
103.31	98.45	102.48	102.48	10 Utilities	102.48	– 0.16	7.49	100.85	– 0.04
105.14	97.26	104.99	104.99	10 Industrials	104.99	– 0.15	7.03	97.55	+ 0.18

Bonds	Cur Yld	Vol	Close	Net Chg.
GMA 8¼16	8.8	387	94¼	+ ⅜
GMA 8s930	7.9	25	101¼	– 5/32
GMA 8s94	7.8	55	102⅜	...
GMA 7⅞97	7.9	87	100⅛	...
GMA 8⅜97	8.1	25	103¼	+ ⅜
GTE 9⅜99	9.0	7	104⅜	– 2
GdDyn 5¾11	cv	20	100	...
GHost 8s02	cv	15	109	...
GM 8⅝s05	8.6	20	100½	...
GnSgnl 5¾02	cv	10	99	– 1
Genrad 7¼11	cv	66	67½	+ ½
GaGlf 15s00	13.2	8	113¾	– ¼
GaPw 7½02D	7.5	10	100½	– ½
GaPw 7⅞03	7.9	3	100¼	...
GaPw 10s16J	9.6	6	104⅝	...
GaPw 10¾17	10.4	313	103⅜	– 2½
GaPw 10¾18	10.4	224	103⅜	– ⅞
GaPw 6⅛99	6.4	8	96	...
GdNgF 13¼95	13.1	38	101½	+ ⅜
GrnTr dc8¼95	8.2	135	100¾	– ¼
GreyF zr94	...	25	90⅝	+ ⅛
GrowGp 8½06	cv	30	112½	– 2½
Grumn 9¼09	cv	24	102	– ½
Gulfrd 6s12	cv	16	99¾	+ ¼
GlfUSA 10⅞97	20.3	157	53½	+ 3¼
GlfUSA 12½04	24.0	340	52	+ 4⅝
Hallwd na13½09	...	3	64⅛	...
Hlttrst 10¾02	10.0	25	108	...
HeclMn zr04	...	15	37	– ⅜
Hercul 6½99	cv	7	183	+ 3
Hercul 8s10	cv	12	142	+ ¼
HmGrp 14⅞99	14.3	12	104	...
HomeDp 4½97	cv	22	137	– 6
HudFd 8s06	cv	16	93½	...
HudFd 14s08	cv	69	105½	– 1½
ICN 12⅞98	13.7	141	94⅛	+ ⅜
IMC Fer 6¼01	cv	124	101	+ 1
ITTF 8⅞03	8.1	8	109	+ 2
IllBel 7⅝06	7.5	15	101¼	...
IllPw 8⅝06	8.4	1	103⅛	+ ⅛
IllPw 8¼07	8.1	10	101⅜	...
IllPw 9⅜16	8.9	15	105	+ 1
Inco 7¾16	7.8	24	98¾	...
IndBel 8s14	7.8	11	102¼	+ ½
InldStl 8⅞99	9.3	10	95	+ ¾
InldStl 9½00	9.5	52	99½	+ 1½
Intlgc 11.99s96	18.1	4	66⅛	+ ⅛
IBM 9s98	8.4	35	106¾	– ¼
IBM 8⅜19	8.1	100	103	...
IBM 6⅜97	6.4	498	99½	+ ¼
IBM 7¼02	7.2	145	100⅛	+ ⅜
IntGm dc5½01	cv	5	324	– 10
IPap dc5⅛12	7.0	10	73	– ½
IntTch 9⅜96	10.5	11	89⅝	– ¼
IntJh 7¾11	cv	13	82⅛	– ⅞
Jckpt 8¾14	cv	62	153	+ 8½
Jamswy 8s05	cv	25	66	...
vjJoneL 9⅞95f	...	25	52⅛	...
K mart 8⅛97	7.9	75	102⅜	...
K mart 8⅜17	8.2	36	102½	+ ¼
KerrGp 13s96	12.7	48	102½	...
KerrMc 7¼12	cv	15	107⅛	– 1⅞
Keycrp 7¾02	7.8	2	99⅜	+ ⅜
Kolmrg 8¾09	cv	76	84¼	...
Kroger 9s99	9.0	205	100⅜	+ ⅛
vjLTV 5s88mf	...	19	5	+ ⅛
vjLTV 9¼97f	...	200	10½	– ⅝
vjLTV 11s07f	...	2	4	– ¼
vjLTV 13⅞02f	...	100	10⅛	+ 1
vjLTV 95t f	...	85	3⅞	...
vjLTV 11½97f	...	20	4½	+ ½
vjLTV 15s00f	...	5	10⅛	– ⅛
LaFrg 7s13	cv	100	95½	...
Leucadia 10⅜02	9.7	222	106½	– ⅜
Liberte 10½93f	...	25	57⅞	+ 2⅝
Litton 12⅝05	10.8	1	116¾	– ¾
LoewCp zr04	...	53	49½	+ ¼
LglsLt 8.9s19	8.7	105	102¼	– ¾
vjLykes 7½94f	...	45	3	...
MACOM 9¼06	cv	53	92	...
MGM Grd 12s02	11.5	50	104⅛	– ⅜
MGMUA 12⅝93f	...	189	94⅝	+ ⅛
MGMUA 13s96f	...	250	73¼	+ ¼
MfrH 8⅛04	8.1	117	100	+ ¾
MfrH 8⅛07	8.2	5	98½	– ½
Manvl zr03	...	25	86⅜	+ ⅜
MarO 8.5s06	8.5	7	100½	...
MarO 9½94	9.1	121	103⅞	+ ¼
MarO 9¾99	9.2	30	106¼	+ ⅛
Marriott zr06	...	26	32⅝	– ⅞
Maxus 8½08	9.3	39	91½	– ¾
vjMcCro 7½s94f	...	13	30	...
McDe 10s03	9.8	23	101⅞	– ⅛
McDInv 8s11	cv	16	105	+ ⅛
McDnl zr94	...	15	95 3/16	+ 1/16
McDnl 9¾99	8.7	10	112	+ 2½
McDnlDg 7⅞97	8.4	769	93⅞	– 1⅝
McDnlDg 8⅝97	8.9	358	96⅞	– ⅝
McDnlDg 9¾12	10.2	160	95⅜	+ ¾
MeYk 9.1s02	8.9	15	102	+ 1¼
Mead 6¾12	cv	206	99½	– ½
MesaCap na96	...	83	81	...
MesaCap 13½99	16.3	56	83	...
MichB 7¾11	7.7	17	100⅛	– ⅛
MichB 7s12	7.4	80	94¾	– ⅛
MidlBk 11.35s93	11.3	55	100 7/32	+ 7/32
MPac 4¾20f	...	9	59	+ ½
Mobil 8⅝94	8.2	50	105½	...
Mobil 8s32	7.9	20	101	+ 1½
MoblCda 8⅜93	8.4	25	100 9/32	– 7/32
Monog 10s99	10.6	4	94⅛	...
Monog 11s04	11.5	8	96	...
Moran 8¾08f	cv	20	66	– 1¾
Motrla zr09	...	18	47	– 1⅛
MtSTl 7⅜11	7.6	6	97¼	+ ½
MtSTl 7¾13	7.8	4	99⅛	...
MtSTl 8s17	8.0	30	100	– ¾
MtSTl 8⅝18	8.3	11	103½	+ ⅜
NCNB 8⅜99	8.3	38	100½	...
NJBTl 7¼11	7.5	8	97⅛	+ ¼
NJBTl 7¾13	7.7	9	100¼	+ ⅛
NJBTl 8s16	7.9	19	101¼	...
NJBTl 8¾18	8.4	10	103⅞	+ ⅛
Nabis 7¾s03	7.9	6	98	+ 1
vjNtGyp zr04	...	104	1¼	...
NStl 8⅜06	9.6	20	87	+ 1⅞
NtEdu 6½11	cv	25	72⅞	+ 1⅞
NavFin 7⅝93	7.6	28	99¾	...
NavFin 11.95s95	12.3	234	97	+ ¼
Navstr 8⅝95	9.4	10	92	...
Navstr 6¼98	8.0	15	78	+ 3
Navstr 9s04	11.1	175	81	+ ½
NblAfl 7¼12	cv	5	106	– 2
NwnBl 7⅞11	7.8	7	100¾	+ ¼
OcciP 10⅞96	10.7	75	101⅜	– ⅛
OcciP 11¾11	10.1	44	116¾	+ ¾
OcciP 9⅝99	8.9	305	107¾	+ ½
OcciP 10⅛09	8.8	50	115	+ 2⅝
OcciP 10⅛01	8.8	30	114⅞	+ 2⅜
OceanSh 11⅜02	10.7	65	106	+ ¼
OffDep zr07	...	4	50½	– ½
OhBIT 7½11	7.5	19	99⅜	– ⅜
Orient 10¼98	10.0	10	102	...
Oryx 7½14	cv	55	90½	...
OutbM 7s02	cv	47	116½	+ ½
OwIll 10¼99	10.0	22	103	...
OwIll 11s03	10.1	206	108½	– ⅜
OwIll 10½02	10.1	155	104	– ⅜
OwnIll 10s02	9.9	404	101⅜	+ ⅞
OwnIll 9¾04	9.7	30	100⅛	+ ⅜
OxyOG 9¾00	9.5	35	102⅛	+ 1⅛
PcLumb 12s96	11.8	1	101½	– 1¼
PNwT 8⅝10	8.4	10	102½	+ ⅛
PacTT 8.65s05	8.4	2	102½	...
PacTT 8¾06	8.5	135	102¾	...
PacTT 7¼08	7.4	26	98	+ ⅛
PacTT 9½11	9.1	16	104⅞	...
PacTT 8⅞15	8.5	28	104⅝	...
PacTT 8⅜17	8.2	30	102½	+ ⅛
PacTT 9s18	8.6	44	104¾	...
PGE 8⅞s02	8.5	10	104⅝	+ 1⅛
PGE 7½s03	7.5	20	100⅝	+ ⅞
PGE 7¾05ZZ	7.7	42	100⅜	...
PGE 8¼08	8.1	12	102	...
PacSci 7¾03	cv	50	96	+ 1
ParCm 7s03A	7.4	181	95	+ ¼
ParCm 7s03B	7.3	33	95⅜	+ ⅝
Pennzl 8⅜96	8.2	2	102	– 1
Petrie 8s10	cv	98	118½	– 2½
PhilEl 6⅛97	6.4	5	96	– ⅛
PhilEl 9s95	8.9	10	101½	– ⅛
PhilEl 7¾00	7.7	29	101¼	...
PhilEl 8¼96	8.1	2	102	...
PhilEl 7⅜01	7.4	12	99¾	...
PhilEl 8½04	8.3	5	102½	– ⅛
PierOn dc11½03	11.0	3	104½	– 1½
Pier1 6⅞02	cv	47	123½	+ ⅜
Pittstn 4s97	cv	8	86½	+ ¾
Pittstn 9.2s04	cv	5	101	– 1⅜
PotEl 9¼16	8.8	10	105⅝	+ ⅝
PotEl 7s18	cv	15	102	...
ProcG 7s02	7.0	2	99¾	...
PSCol 8¾00	8.6	2	102	– ⅜
PSEG 7⅝00	cv	10	100¼	...
RJR NbH 17⅜09	9.2	28	189½	+ ⅛
RJR 7⅜01	7.7	90	95⅝	– ⅛
RJRNb 10½98	9.4	387	111½	+ ⅝
RJR Nb 13½01	11.8	82	114⅞	– ⅛
RJR Nb na15s01	...	32	119½	– 1⅛
RJR Nb zr01	...	459	98⅝	...
RalsP 9½16	9.0	23	106	+ ¾
RalsP 9⅜16	8.9	10	104¾	+ 1⅜
vjRapA69 7s94f	...	10	1⅛	...
vjRapA 10¾03f	...	21	1⅛	...
RelGp 9⅞99	10.2	18	97	+ 3

Source: *The Wall Street Journal*, January 5, 1993, C15.

Exhibit 14.6 ◆ SIMPLIFIED CONFIRMATION STATEMENTS FOR THE PURCHASE AND SALE OF A BOND

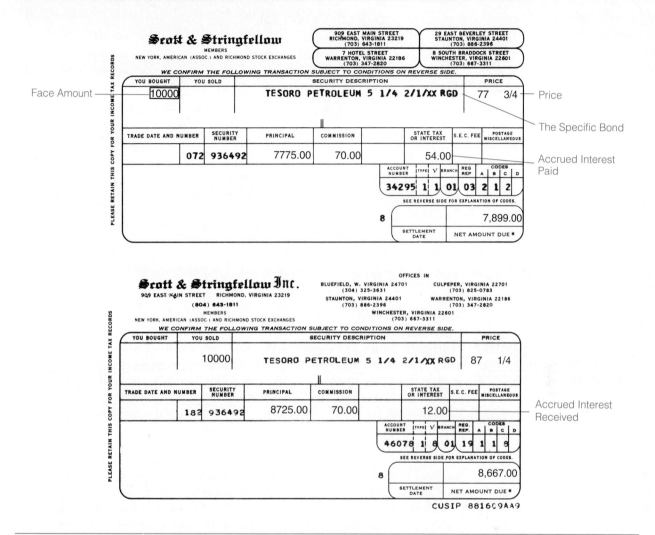

instruments are either secured or unsecured. If a debt instrument is secured, the debtor pledges a specific asset as collateral. In case of default, the creditor may seize this collateral (through a court proceeding). Bonds that are not collateralized by specific assets are unsecured. If the debtor were to default, there would be no specific assets the creditors could seize to satisfy their claims on the borrower. Such unsecured debt instruments are supported by the general capacity of the firm to service its debt (i.e., pay the interest and repay the principal). Thus, the capacity of the borrower to generate operating income (i.e., earnings before interest and taxes) is crucial to the safety of unsecured debt obligations.

Exhibit 14.7 ✦ DETERMINATION OF PROFIT OR LOSS ON THE SALE OF A BOND

Cost basis of the bond:	
Amount due	$7,899.00
Less accrued interest	−54.00
	$7,845.00
Revenue from the sale:	
Proceeds of the sale	$8,667.00
Less accrued interest	−12,00
	$8,655.00
Profit (or loss) on the investment:	
Return from the sale of the bond	$8,655.00
Cost basis of the bond	7,845.00
Profit (or loss) on the investment	$810.00

Mortgage Bonds

mortgage bond
A bond that is secured by property, especially real estate.

Mortgage bonds are issued to purchase specific fixed assets, which are then pledged to secure the debt. This type of bond is frequently issued by utility companies. The proceeds that are raised by selling the debt are used to build power plants, and these plants secure the debt. As the plants generate revenues, the firm earns the cash flow that is necessary to service (pay interest on) and retire the debt. If the firm defaults on the interest or principal repayment, the creditors may take title to the pledged property. They may then choose to hold the asset and earn income from it (to operate the fixed asset) or to sell it. These options should give investors cause for thought: How many creditors could operate a power plant? If the investors choose to sell it, who would buy it?

These two questions illustrate an important point concerning investing in corporate debt. Although property that is pledged to secure the debt may decrease the lender's risk of loss, the creditor is not interested in taking possession of and operating the property. Lenders earn income through interest payments and not through the operation of the fixed assets. Such creditors are rarely qualified to operate the assets should they take possession of them. If they are forced to seize and sell the assets, they may find few buyers and may have to sell at distress prices. Despite the fact that pledging assets to secure debt increases the safety of the principal, the lenders prefer the prompt payment of interest and principal.

Equipment Trust Certificates

equipment trust certificate
A serial bond secured by specific equipment.

Not all collateral has questionable resale potential. Unlike the mortgage bonds that are issued by utility companies, **equipment trust certificates** are secured by assets with substantial resale value. These certificates are issued to finance specific equipment, which is pledged as collateral. Equipment trust certificates are primarily issued by railroads and airlines to finance rolling stock (railroad cars) and airplanes. As the equipment is used to generate cash flow, the certificates are retired. The collateral supporting these certificates is generally considered to be of excellent quality, for, unlike some fixed assets (e.g., the aforementioned utility plants), this equipment may be readily *moved* and sold to other railroads and airlines in the event that the firm defaults on the certificates.

Investors, however, should realize that while equipment may be more readily sold than power plants, these investors could still suffer losses. For example, in 1991 the bankruptcies of Midway and Pan Am dumped a large number of aircraft on the market. The market for used planes was already soft from a worldwide recession, so prices for used aircraft declined. This, of course, meant that even the secured creditors might not receive their principal from the proceeds of the sales of the planes.

Debentures

Debentures are unsecured promissory notes that are supported by the general creditworthiness of the firm. This type of debt involves more risk than bonds that are supported by collateral. In the case of default or bankruptcy, the unsecured debt is redeemed only after all secured debt has been paid off. Some debentures are subordinated, and these involve even more risk, for they are redeemed after the other general debt of the firm has been redeemed. Even unsecured debt has a superior position to the subordinated debenture. These bonds are among the riskiest debt instruments issued by firms and usually have higher interest rates or other attractive features, such as convertibility into the stock of the company, to compensate the lenders for assuming the increased risk.

debenture
An unsecured bond.

Financial institutions, such as commercial banks or insurance companies, prefer a firm to sell debentures to the general public. Since the debentures are general obligations of the company, they do not tie up its specific assets. Then, if the firm needs additional funds from a commercial bank, it can use specific assets as collateral, in which case the bank will be more willing to lend the funds. If the assets had been previously pledged, the firm would lack this flexibility in financing.

Although the use of debentures may not decrease the ability of the firm to issue additional debt, default on the debentures usually means that all senior debt is in default as well. A common indenture clause states that if any of the firm's debt is in default, all debt issues are also in default, and in this case the creditors may declare that all outstanding debt is due. For this reason, a firm should not overextend itself through excessive amounts of unsecured debt.

Income Bonds

Income bonds are the riskiest bonds issued by corporations. Interest is paid only if the firm earns it. If the company is unable to cover its other expenses, it is not legally obligated to pay the interest on these bonds. Owing to the great risk associated with them, income bonds are rarely issued by corporations. One notable exception is a 1992 issue of seven-year Disney bonds that could pay as much as 13.5 percent if a package of twenty Disney movies grosses over $800 million. If, however, the gross is less, the bonds could yield as little as 3 percent.

income bond
A bond whose interest is paid only if it is earned by the firm.

Although income bonds are rarely issued by firms, a similar type of security is often issued by state and municipal governments. These are revenue bonds, which are used to finance a particular capital improvement that is expected to generate revenues (e.g., a toll road or a municipal hospital). If the revenues are insufficient, the interest is not paid.

There is, however, one significant difference between income bonds and revenue bonds. Failure to pay interest does not result in default for an income bond, but it does mean that a revenue bond is in default. Most projects financed by revenue bonds have generated sufficient funds to service the debt, but there have been notable exceptions. Perhaps the most famous default was the multibillion-dollar default by the Washington Public Power Supply System. As of 1993, the defaulted bonds were virtually worthless.

Convertible Bonds

convertible bond
A bond that may be exchanged for (i.e., converted into) common stock.

Convertible bonds are a hybrid type of security. Technically they are debt: The bonds pay interest, which is a fixed obligation of the firm, and have a maturity date. But these bonds have a special feature—the investor has the option to convert the bond into a specified number of shares of common stock. For example, the IBM 7⅞ percent of the year 2004 bond may be converted into 6.51 shares of IBM common stock. The market price of convertible bonds depends on both the value of the stock and the interest that the bonds pay. If the price of the common stock rises, then the value of the bond must rise. The investor thus has the opportunity for capital gain should the price of the common stock rise. If, however, the price of the common stock does not appreciate, the investor still owns a debt obligation of the company and therefore has the security of an investment in a debt instrument.

Convertible bonds have been popular with some investors, and thus firms have issued these bonds as a means to raise funds. However, since convertible bonds are a hybrid type of security, they are difficult to analyze. (They are debt instruments with a built-in option to convert.) For this reason, a detailed discussion is deferred until Chapter 18, which follows the discussion of nonconvertible debt and precedes the discussion of options.

Variable Interest Rate Bonds

variable interest rate bond
A long-term bond with a coupon rate that varies with changes in short-term rates.

Generally, the interest that a bond pays is fixed at the date of issuance; however, some corporations issue **variable interest rate bonds.** Citicorp was the first major American firm to offer bonds with variable interest rates to the general public. Two features of the Citicorp bond were unique at the time it was issued: (1) a variable interest rate that was tied to the interest rate on treasury bills and (2) the right of the holder to redeem the bond at its face value.

The interest rate to be paid by the Citicorp bond was set at 1 percent above the average treasury bill rate during a specified period. This variability of the interest rate means that if short-term interest rates rise, the interest rate paid by the bond must increase. The bond's owner participates in any increase in short-term interest rates. Of course, if the short-term interest rates decline, the bond earns a lower rate of interest.

The second unique feature of the Citicorp bond was that two years after it was issued, the holder had the option to redeem the bond for its face value or principal. This option recurred every six months. If the owner needed the money more quickly, the bond could have been sold in the secondary market, for it was traded on the New York Stock Exchange. An important implication of the variable coupon is that the market price of the bond fluctuates less than the price of a fixed coupon bond. As is explained in the next chapter, the price of a fixed coupon bond fluctuates inversely with interest rates. Such price changes will not occur with a variable rate bond because the interest paid fluctuates with interest rates in general. Hence these bonds avoid one of the major sources of risk associated with investing in bonds—the risk associated with higher interest rates driving down the bond's market value.

Zero Coupon and Discount Bonds

In 1981 a new type of bond was sold to the general public. These bonds pay no interest and are sold at large discounts. The pathbreaking issue was the J.C. Penney **zero coupon bond** of 1989. This bond was initially sold for a discount ($330) but paid $1,000 at maturity in 1989. The investor's funds grew from $330 to $1,000 after eight years. The rate of growth (i.e., the yield on the bond) was 14.86 percent.[5]

After the initial success of this issue, several other firms including IBM Credit Corporation (the financing arm of IBM) and ITT Financial issued similar bonds. In each case the firm pays no interest. The bond sells for a large discount, and the investor's return accrues from the appreciation of the bond's value as it approaches maturity.

Since the return on an investment in a zero coupon bond depends solely on the firm's capacity to retire the debt, the quality of the firm is exceedingly important. Zero coupon bonds issued by firms such as Sears or IBM Credit Corporation are of excellent quality and should be retired at maturity. In these cases the investor will earn the expected return that accrues when the bond approaches maturity. If, however, the investor purchases low-quality zero coupon bonds, these bonds may never be redeemed. If the firm were to go bankrupt, the investor may receive nothing. Thus, it is possible for the individual who buys zero coupon bonds to lose the entire investment and never receive a single interest payment.

zero coupon bond
A bond on which interest accrues and is paid at maturity, and is initially sold at a discount.

---

[5] The yield on a zero coupon bond is calculated using the time value formula (Equation 6.4):

$$P_0(1 + i)^n = P_n,$$

which is solved for i. In this example,

$$\$330(1 + i)^8 = \$1,000$$
$$(1 + i)^8 = \$1,000/\$330 = 3.030$$
$$i = \sqrt[8]{3.030} - 1$$
$$i = 0.1486 = 14.86\%$$

The 14.86 percent was derived by the use of a calculator. If the student does not have access to a calculator with a y^x key, then the future value table is used and that derives an answer of approximately 15 percent.

There is, however, a tax feature that reduces the attractiveness of zero coupon bonds. The IRS taxes the accrued interest as if it were received. Thus the investor must pay federal income tax on the earned interest even though the investor receives the funds only when the bond matures. Thus zero coupon bonds are of little interest to investors except as part of pension plans. Zero coupon bonds may be included in an individual's Keogh account or IRA because the tax on the accrued interest in the account is deferred until the funds are withdrawn. So the primary reason for acquiring a zero coupon bond is to use it in conjunction with a tax-deferred pension plan.

High-Yield Securities—Junk Bonds

High-yield securities (i.e., junk bonds) are not a particular type of bond but a name given to debt of low quality (i.e., bonds rated below triple B). Junk bonds are usually debentures and may be subordinated to the firm's other debt obligations. The poor quality of this debt requires that junk bonds offer high yields, which may be three to four percentage points greater than the yield available on high-quality bonds. Junk bonds are often issued to finance takeovers and mergers, and they may be bought by financial institutions and individuals who are accustomed to investing in poor-quality bonds and who are willing and able to accept the larger risk in order to earn the higher yields.

While some high-yield securities have existed for many years, the volume of new bonds with differing features virtually exploded during the 1980s. Many of these bonds may be treated as if they were equity instruments that will generate their potential return if the firm generates cash flow and survives. For this reason the general discussion of junk bonds will be deferred until Chapter 16, which is devoted to preferred stock and hybrid types of securities.

Euro-bonds

Euro-bonds
Bonds denominated in U.S. dollars but issued abroad.

U.S. firms may also issue bonds in foreign countries to raise funds for foreign investments (e.g., plant and equipment). These bonds fall into two basic types, depending on the currency in which they are denominated. U.S. firms can sell bonds denominated in the local currency (e.g., British pounds or French francs). For example, Exxon reported in its 1992 annual report that $1,309 billion of its $7,273 billion of long-term debt (18 percent) was denominated in foreign currencies. The firm can also sell abroad bonds denominated in U.S. dollars called **Euro-bonds.** This term applies even though the bonds may be issued in, say, Asia instead of Europe.

When a firm issues a Euro-bond, the U.S. firm promises to make payments in dollars. This means that the U.S. investor does not have to convert the payments from the local currency (e.g., British pounds) into dollars. As is explained in detail in Chapter 24, fluctuations in value of one currency relative to another is a major source of risk that every individual who acquires foreign securities must bear. By acquiring Euro-bonds, the U.S. investor avoids this currency risk. However, foreign investors do bear this risk. They have to convert the dollars into their currency, so the yields on Euro-bonds tend to be higher than on comparable domestic securities. The higher yield is a major reason why investors find Euro-bonds attractive.

RETIRING DEBT

Debt issues must ultimately be retired, and this retirement must occur on or before the maturity date of the debt. When the bond is issued, a method for periodic retirement is usually specified, for very few debt issues are retired in one lump payment at the maturity date. Instead, part of the issue is systematically retired each year. This systematic retirement may be achieved by issuing the bond in a series or by having a sinking fund.

Serial Bonds

In an issue of **serial bonds,** some bonds mature each year. This type of bond is usually issued by corporations to finance specific equipment, such as railroad cars, which is pledged as collateral. As the equipment depreciates, the cash flow that is generated by profits and depreciation expense is used to retire the bonds in a series as they mature.

serial bond
An issue of bonds in which specified bonds mature each year.

The advertisement presented in Exhibit 14.8 for equipment trust certificates issued by Union Pacific Railroad Company is an example of a serial bond. This issue of equipment trust certificates is designed so that one-fifteenth of the bonds matures each year. Thus, the firm retires $2,337,000 of the certificates annually as each series within the issue matures. At the end of 2001, the entire issue of certificates will have been retired.

Few corporations, however, issue serial bonds. They are primarily issued by state and local governments to finance capital improvements, such as new school buildings, or by ad hoc government bodies, such as the Port Authority of New York, to finance new facilities or other capital improvements. The bonds are then retired over a period of years by tax receipts or by revenues generated by the investment (e.g., toll roads).

Sinking Funds

Sinking funds are generally employed to ease the retirement of long-term corporate debt. A **sinking fund** is a periodic payment to retire part of the debt issue. One type of sinking fund requires the firm to make payments to a trustee, who invests the money to earn interest. The periodic payments plus the accumulated interest retire the debt when it matures.

sinking fund
A series of periodic payments to retire a bond issue.

Another type of sinking fund requires the firm to set aside a stated sum of money and to randomly select the bonds that are to be retired. The selected bonds are called and redeemed, and the holder surrenders the bond because it ceases to earn interest once it has been called. This type of sinking fund is illustrated in Exhibit 14.9 by an advertisement taken from *The Wall Street Journal.* The specific bonds being retired were selected by a lottery. Once they are chosen, these bonds are called. The owners must surrender the bonds to obtain their principal. If the bonds are not presented for redemption, they are still outstanding and are obligations of the company, but the debtor's obligation is limited to refunding the principal, since interest payments ceased at the call date.

Exhibit 14.8 ✦ EXAMPLE OF A SERIAL BOND ISSUE (EQUIPMENT TRUST CERTIFICATE)

This announcement is under no circumstances to be construed as an offer to sell or as a solicitation of an offer to buy any of these securities. The offering is made only by the Offering Circular Supplement and the Offering Circular to which it relates.

NEW ISSUE   July 17, 1985

$35,055,000

Union Pacific Railroad Company

Equipment Trust No. 1 of 1985

Serial Equipment Trust Certificates
(Non-callable)

Price 100%
(Plus accrued dividends, if any, from the date of original issuance.)

MATURITIES AND DIVIDEND RATES.

(To mature in 15 equal annual installments
of $2,337,000, commencing July 15, 1987.)

1987	6.500%	1992	7.500%	1997	7.800%
1988	7.000	1993	7.600	1998	7.800
1989	7.125	1994	7.700	1999	7.875
1990	7.300	1995	7.700	2000	7.875
1991	7.375	1996	7.750	2001	7.875

These Certificates are offered subject to prior sale, when, as and if issued and received by us, subject to approval of the Interstate Commerce Commission.

Merrill Lynch Capital Markets

Thomson McKinnon Securities Inc.

Source: Reprinted with permission of the Union Pacific Railroad Company.

Since each debt issue is different, there can be wide variations in sinking funds. A strong sinking fund retires a substantial proportion of the debt before the date of maturity. For example, if a bond issue is for $10 million and it matures in ten years, a strong sinking fund may require the firm to retire $1 million, or 10 percent, of

Exhibit 14.9 ◆ EXAMPLE OF A SINKING FUND RETIRING DEBT

NOTICE OF REDEMPTION
To the Holders of

New York State Urban Development Corporation

Project Revenue Bonds (Center for Industrial Innovation)
Series 1982 Bonds 11⅛% Due January 1, 2013
(CUSIP NO. 650033BD4)*

NOTICE IS HEREBY GIVEN THAT, pursuant to the provisions of a resolution adopted by the New York State Urban Development Corporation (the "Corporation"), on November 18, 1982, as amended and restated on December 10, 1982, and entitled "Project Revenue Bond (Center for Industrial Innovation) General Resolution" (the "General Resolution"), as supplemented by a resolution of the Corporation entitled "Series 1982 Project Revenue Bonds (Center for Industrial Innovation) Series Resolution" (the "Series Resolution") authorizing the issuance of the above described Bonds, the Corporation will redeem and the Trustee under the General Resolution has drawn by lot for redemption on January 1, 1993 (the "Sinking Fund Redemption Date"), through the operation of the sinking fund created under the Series Resolution, $465,000 aggregate principal amount of the above described Bonds as set forth below.

Coupon Bonds called for redemption each bearing the
Prefix A and each in the Denomination of $5,000, are as follows:

| 386 | 424 | 854 | 3472 | 3987 | 4417 | 5417 | 5438 | 5513 | 6024 | 6304 | 6746 | 6920 |

Registered Bonds called for redemption, in whole or in part, each bearing the
Prefix AR, are as follows:

Bond Number	Denomination	Amount Called	Bond Number	Denomination	Amount Called
26...	$ 500,000	... $15,000	87...	$2,435,000	... $30,000
39...	50,000	... 5,000	88...	2,460,000	... 30,000
51...	5,000	... 5,000	89...	2,435,000	... 35,000
81...	490,000	... 10,000	90...	2,465,000	... 20,000
82...	95,000	... 5,000	91...	2,405,000	... 40,000
84...	2,430,000	... 40,000	92...	2,450,000	... 35,000
85...	2,420,000	... 35,000	93...	1,945,000	... 30,000
86...	2,480,000	... 20,000	94...	2,415,000	... 45,000

On the Sinking Fund Redemption Date, there shall become due and payable on each of the above mentioned Bonds to be redeemed, the sinking fund redemption price, namely 100% of the principal amount thereof. Interest accrued on such Bonds to said Sinking Fund Redemption Date will be paid in the usual manner. From and after the Sinking Fund Redemption Date, interest on the Bonds described above shall cease to accrue.

IN ADDITION THE CORPORATION HAS ELECTED TO REDEEM ON JANUARY 1, 1993 (THE "REDEMPTION DATE") ALL REMAINING OUTSTANDING BONDS NOT HERETOFORE CALLED FOR SINKING FUND REDEMPTION AT A REDEMPTION PRICE EQUAL TO 103% OF THE PRINCIPAL AMOUNT THEREOF. INTEREST ACCRUED ON SUCH BONDS TO THE REDEMPTION DATE WILL BE PAID IN THE USUAL MANNER. FROM AND AFTER THE REDEMPTION DATE, INTEREST ON THE BONDS SHALL CEASE TO ACCRUE.

The Bonds specified herein to be redeemed shall be redeemed on or after both the Sinking Fund Redemption Date and the Redemption Date upon presentation and surrender thereof, together, in the case of coupon Bonds, with all appurtenant coupons attached, if any, maturing after January 1, 1993, to Bankers Trust Company, as Trustee and Paying Agent, in person or by registered mail (postage prepaid) at the following addresses:

IN PERSON:

Bankers Trust Company
Corporate Trust and Agency Group
First Floor
123 Washington Street
New York, New York

BY MAIL:

Bankers Trust Company
Corporate Trust and Agency Group
P.O. Box 2579
Church Street Station
New York, NY 10008
Attn: Bond Redemption

If any of the Bonds designated for redemption are in registered form, they should be accompanied by duly executed instruments of assignment in blank if payment is to be made to other than the registered holder thereof.

Coupons maturing January 1, 1993 appertaining to the coupon Bonds designated for redemption should be detached and presented for payment in the usual manner. Interest due January 1, 1993 on registered Bonds designated for redemption will be paid to the registered holders of such registered Bonds in the usual manner.

NEW YORK STATE URBAN DEVELOPMENT CORPORATION
By: BANKERS TRUST COMPANY, *as Trustee*

Dated: December 1, 1992

the issue each year. Thus, at maturity only $1 million is still outstanding. With a weak sinking fund, a substantial proportion of the debt is retired at maturity. For example, a sinking fund for a debt issue of $10 million that matures in ten years may require annual payments of $1 million commencing after five years. In this example, only $5 million is retired before maturity. The debtor must then make a lump sum payment to retire the remaining $5 million. Such a large final payment is called a **balloon payment.**

balloon payment
The large final payment necessary to retire a debt issue.

Different sinking funds are illustrated in Exhibit 14.10, which presents the sinking fund requirements for three GT&E bonds. One of the sinking funds is quite strong. The 9⅛ percent bond has a sinking fund that retires 95 percent of the issue prior to maturity. However, there is no sinking fund for the 10¼ percent bond that matures in 2019. Unless GT&E calls the bond and retires it prior to maturity, the entire issue may be outstanding until it matures in 2019.

The strength of a sinking fund affects the element of risk. A strong sinking fund requirement means that a substantial amount of the debt issue is retired during its lifetime, which makes the entire debt issue safer. The sinking fund feature of a debt issue, then, is an important factor in determining the amount of risk associated with investing in a particular debt instrument.

Repurchasing Debt

discount
The sale of anything below its stated value.

If bond prices decline and the debt is selling at a **discount,** the firm may try to retire the debt by purchasing it on the open market.[6] The purchases may be made from time to time, in which case the sellers of the bonds need not know that the company is purchasing and retiring the debt. The company may also announce its intentions and offer to purchase a specified amount of the debt at a certain price within a particular period. Bondholders may then tender their bonds at the offer

Exhibit 14.10 ✦ SELECTED EXAMPLES OF SINKING FUNDS FOR GTE BONDS

GT&E Bonds (General Telephone and Electronics)		Sinking Fund Feature
9⅜%	1999	$3,250,000 face amount retired each year (sinking fund started in 1979) to retire 86⅔% of the issue prior to maturity
9⅛%	2016	$12,500,000 face amount retired each year (sinking fund to start in 1997) to retire 95% of the issue prior to maturity
10¼%	2019	No sinking fund

[6] Some indentures, however, forbid open market repurchases.

price; however, they are not required to sell their bonds and may continue to hold the debt.[7] The firm must then continue to meet the terms of the debt's indenture.

The advantage of repurchasing debt that is selling at a discount is the savings to the firm. If a firm issued $10 million in face value of debt and the bonds are currently selling for $0.60 on the $1, the firm may reduce its debt by $1,000 with a cash outlay of only $600, resulting in a $400 savings for each $1,000 bond that is purchased. This savings is translated into income, because a reduction in debt at a discount is an extraordinary item that is treated in accounting as income. For example, General Cinema reported a gain of $419.6 million in 1992 from the purchase of Harcourt Brace Jovanovich's debt at a discount as part of the acquisition of the publisher.

On the surface, a firm's retiring debt at a discount may appear desirable. However, using money to repurchase debt is an investment decision, just like buying plant and equipment. If the company repurchases debt, it cannot use the funds for other purposes. Management must decide which is the better use of the money: purchasing other income-earning assets or retiring the debt. Unlike a sinking fund requirement (which management must meet), purchasing and retiring debt at a discount is a voluntary act. The lower the price of the debt, the greater the potential benefit from the purchase, but management must still determine if it is the best use of the firm's scarce resource, cash. Many firms do not repurchase their debt, for the discount is not sufficient to justify such a use of funds. These corporations have better uses for their funds.

Call Feature

Some bonds may have a **call feature** that allows for redemption prior to maturity. In most cases after the bond has been outstanding for a period of time (e.g. five years), the issuer has the right to call and retire the bond. The bond is called for redemption as of a specific date. After that date, interest ceases to accrue, which forces the creditor to relinquish the debt instrument.

Such premature retiring of debt through a call feature tends to occur after a period of high interest rates. If a bond has been issued during such a period and interest rates subsequently decline, it may be advantageous for the company to issue new bonds at the lower interest rate. The proceeds can then be used to retire the older bonds with the higher coupon rates. Such **refunding** reduces the firm's interest expense.

Of course, premature retirement of debt hurts the bondholders who lose the higher yield bonds. To protect these creditors, a call feature usually has a **call penalty,** such as the payment of one year's interest. If the initial issue had a 9 percent interest rate, the company would have to pay $1,090 to retire $1,000 worth of debt. This call penalty usually declines over the lifetime of the debt. Exhibit 14.11 illustrates the call penalty associated with the AT&T 8⅝s of 2007. In 1996 the penalty

call feature
The right of an issuer to retire a debt issue prior to maturity.

refunding
The act of issuing new debt and using the proceeds to retire existing debt.

call penalty
A premium paid for exercising a call feature.

---

[7] If more bonds are tendered than the company offered to buy, the firm prorates the amount of money that it had allocated for the purchase among the number of bonds being offered.

Exhibit 14.11 ✦ SCHEDULE FOR THE CALL PENALTY OF THE 8⅝ DEBENTURE OF AT&T MATURING IN 2007

Year	Percentage of Face Value	Amount Required to Retire $1,000 of Debt	Amount of Call Penalty
1995	102.56	$1,025.60	$25.60
1996	102.24	$1,022.40	$22.40
1997	101.92	$1,019.20	$19.20
1998	101.60	$1,016.00	$16.00
1999	101.28	$1,012.80	$12.80
2003	100.00	$1,000.00	0.00

is $22.40 per $1,000, but it declines to nothing in 2003. Such a call penalty does protect bondholders, and the debtor has the right to call the bond and to refinance debt if interest rates fall sufficiently to justify paying the call penalty.[8]

Several such refinancings occurred during the early 1990s when interest rates fell to lows that had not been seen in twenty years. In particular, utility companies that had issued debt when interest rates were higher sold new bonds with lower yields, called the old debt, and paid the call penalty. For example, Illinois Power retired $100 million of bonds with 12.5 percent coupons. The company paid 101.5 per bond (i.e., $1,015 per $1,000) for a penalty of $15 per bond. Non-utility companies also retired debt whose coupons exceeded the current rate of interest. Texas Instruments retired $200 million of its 12.7 percent bonds that were due in 2005. It paid $1,047 to retire $1,000 in face value of debt (i.e., a premium of $47 per bond). The refinancing, however, sufficiently reduced the company's interest expense to justify paying the call premium.

SUMMARY

This chapter discussed the general features of long-term debt. The terms of a debt issue include the coupon rate of interest and the maturity date. A trustee is appointed for each bond issue to protect the rights of the individual investors. The risks associated with investing in debt are attributable to price fluctuations and inflation as well as to the possibility of default on interest and principal repayment. To help investors, several firms have developed rating services that classify debt issues according to risk.

---

[8] How the call feature may affect the price of a bond is discussed in Chapter 15.

The mechanics of purchasing debt are very similar to those of buying stocks. However, while stocks are purchased through brokerage firms, some debt instruments (e.g., federal government securities) may be purchased through banks.

Debt may be retired in several ways. Some bonds are issued in a series, with a specified amount of debt maturing each year. Other debt issues have sinking funds that retire part of the bond issue prior to maturity. For some debt issues, the firm has the right to call the bonds prior to maturity. The debtor can also offer to buy the debt back from investors before it matures. Since creditors are as concerned with the return of their principal as they are with the payment of interest, the ability of the firm or government to retire its liabilities is one of the foremost factors in determining the risks associated with investing in debt.

Security Summary

Corporate Bonds

Source of return: Interest income and possible capital gains if interest rates fall.

Liquidity and marketability: Active secondary market in corporate debt but chance of loss if interest rates rise means that corporate bonds are marketable but not liquid.

Sources of risk: Unsystematic risk from events that affect the firm's capacity to service its debt (i.e., pay the interest and timely retire the bonds). Systematic risk from interest rate risk since bond prices fall when interest rates rise. Possible loss of purchasing power if the rate of inflation exceeds the interest rate.

Taxation: Interest is subject to federal income taxation. Capital gains that occur if interest rates fall are subject to taxation only when the gains are realized.

Terms to Remember

bonds	flat
principal (face amount)	mortgage bond
maturity date	equipment trust certificate
interest	debenture
coupon rate	income bond
current yield	convertible bond
yield to maturity	variable interest rate bond
yield curve	zero coupon bond
indenture	Euro-bonds
default	serial bonds
trustee	sinking fund
registered bond	balloon payment
bearer bond	discount
coupon bond	call feature
credit rating systems	refunding
confirmation statement	call penalty
accrued interest	

Questions

1. What is the difference between bearer bonds and registered bonds? Which type is safer and why?
2. What is the relationship between the yield earned on bonds and the length of time to maturity? Does this relationship always hold?
3. Even though bonds are debt obligations, investing in them involves risk. What are the sources of risk? What service is available to aid the buyers of debt instruments in selecting a particular bond?
4. How may bonds be purchased?
5. What is the difference between a serial issue of bonds and term bonds with a specific maturity date and a sinking fund?
6. A call penalty protects whom from what? Why may firms choose to retire debt early after a period of high interest rates?
7. What advantages and disadvantages do bonds offer to investors?
8. What secures mortgage bonds and equipment trust certificates?
9. Why are many debentures and income bonds considered to be risky investments?

Suggested Readings

For an easy-to-read discussion of the various types of bonds (e.g., the various issues of corporations, municipalities, and the federal government and its agencies), see:
Stigum, Marcia, and Frank Fabozzi. *The Dow Jones-Irwin Guide to Bonds and Money Market Instruments.* Homewood, Ill.: Dow Jones-Irwin, 1987.

For terms of specific bonds, the investor may consult:
Standard & Poor's Corporation. *Bond Guide.* Published monthly. This gives a calendar of new offerings, as well as descriptions of corporate bonds (i.e., coupon, maturity date, amount outstanding, prices, and yields). More detailed information concerning features such as sinking funds and call features may be found in *Standard & Poor's Corporation Records.*

How bonds are rated is obviously important for determining the amount of interest the borrower must pay to obtain the funds. For a discussion of the objective and subjective techniques used by Standard & Poor to rate debt, see:
Sherwood, Hugh C. *How Corporate Debt Is Rated.* New York: John Wiley & Sons, 1976.

For a discussion of bond repurchases, see:
Johnson, Rodney, and Richard Klein. "Corporate Motives in Repurchases of Discounted Bonds." *Financial Management* (Autumn 1974): 44–49. This article suggests that the temporary increase in earnings from retiring debt at a discount is a primary motive for such refundings.

The variety of zero coupon bonds is discussed in:
Rosen, Lawrence R. *Investing in Zero Coupon Bonds.* New York: John Wiley & Sons, 1986.

INVESTMENT PROJECT

Previously the investment project was limited to stocks. In this chapter, we add debt.

Stock	Week	1	2	3	4	5	6	7	8	9	10	11	12	13	14	15
1 S&P 500																
2 CSK																
3 GTE																
4 IBM																
5 MSFT																
6																
7																
8																
9																
10 yield on six-month treasury bills																
11 price of IBM 9% of 1998																

In row 10 record the yield on six-month treasury bills. In row 11 record the price of the IBM 9% of 1998 bond illustrated in Exhibt 14.5. Since the semester has progressed beyond the first week, you will have to go back to previous issues of *The Wall Street Journal* to obtain this information. Remember: if interest rates rise during the semester, the yields on the bills will rise and the price of the IBM bond will fall.

Appendix

The Term Structure of Interest Rates

The relationship between the rate of interest and the length of time to maturity is often referred to as the "term structure of interest rates." During most periods of history, the longer the term to maturity, the higher the rate of interest (for example, see the yields offered by the savings and loan association in Exhibit 2.2 and the yields in Figure 14.1). One possible explanation for this relationship is that investors have a preference for liquidity. To induce these individuals to commit their funds for a longer term, the interest rate has to be higher to compensate them for the loss of liquidity.

This explanation is very plausible, but there have been periods when short-term interest rates have been higher than long-term rates. This has led to the development of an alternative explanation of the structure of yields based on investor expectations concerning future interest rates. This expectations theory suggests that the long-term rate is an average of the current short-term rate and the expected future short-term rate.

Consider an investor faced with the two following investment alternatives:

One-year bond	6%
Two-year bond	8%

If the investor purchases the two-year bond, the yield is locked in for two years. However, if the one-year bond is purchased, the investor will have to reinvest the proceeds when the bond matures. He or she will seek to earn the same return on either alternative: (1) the one-year bond in combination with a second one-year bond or (2) the two-year bond. Thus, the choice between the two alternatives depends on what the expected future rate on the one-year bond will be.

For the yields on the two alternatives to produce the same return over two years, the funds reinvested when the one-year bond matures must earn 10 percent during the second year. The average yield is 8 percent in both cases. The yield on the two-year bond equals the yield on the combination of the 6 percent and 10 percent one-year bonds.

However, suppose the investor anticipates that the one-year rate in the future will be 12 percent. If the current one-year bond is purchased, the individual can reinvest the funds when it matures and earn 12 percent for one year. The average return over the two years is 9 percent and beats the 8 percent annual yield on the two-year bond. Obviously, the two one-year securities will be preferred. However, if the investor anticipates that the future one-year rate will be 9 percent, the average yield over the two years is 7.5 percent annually, which is inferior to the 8 percent earned annually on the two-year bond.

While an individual may move between the one- and two-year bonds, this is not true in the aggregate. Investors as a whole cannot alter their portfolios by selling one security and purchasing another. Such attempts to alter portfolios change the securities' prices and yields. If all investors expected the future one-year rate to be 12 percent, they would seek to sell the two-year bond and purchase the one-year bond. The effect would be to drive up the yield on the two-year bond and drive down the yield on the one-year bond. One possible set of yields that could emerge is

| One-year bond | 8% |
| Two-year bond | 10% |

In this case the average yield on the two one-year bonds is 10 percent (8 percent for one year and 12 percent for the other year). The average yield on the two-year bond is 10 percent. Since the average yield on either investment alternative is the same (for a given risk class), an expectation of higher future interest rates requires a positively sloped yield curve. If investors anticipate that the one-year rate next year will be 12 percent and that two-year bonds are paying 10 percent, the one-year rate today *must be 8 percent*. At 8 percent the average yield on the two alternatives is 10 percent for both. If the current rate on the one-year bond is 8 percent, the term structure is positive. The one-year bond is paying 8 percent and the two-year bond is paying 12 percent, which is a positive relationship between yields and time to maturity.

If, however, investors expect the future one-year rate to be 7 percent while the two-year bond pays 10 percent annually, the current one-year rate must be 13 percent. Only if the current rate is 13 percent will a combination of it and the expected future one-year rate of 10 percent equal the average annual yield offered by the two-year bond. If the current one-year rate is 13 percent, then the current term structure of yields is negative. The one-year bond offers 13 percent and the two-year bond offers 10 percent, which is a negative relationship between yields and time to maturity. Thus, the expectation of lower rates in the future requires a negatively sloped yield curve in the present.

In addition to the liquidity preference and expectations theories of the term structure of yields, a third alternative explanation has been suggested. It is referred to as the "segmentation theory," and it suggests that yields depends on the demand for and supply of credit in various segments of the financial markets. For example, suppose funds were to flow from savings and loan associations to money market mutual funds. Since the S&Ls make mortgage loans but money market mutual funds make only short-term loans and no mortgage loans, there has been a change in the supply of credit in the two markets. The supply of mortgage money has decreased, and the rate charged on these loans should rise. Simultaneously, the supply of short-term credit has increased, which should tend to reduce short-term interest rates. The structure of yields thus depends on the supply and demand for credit from the various segments of the economy. A flow from one segment to another alters the supply of this credit, causing yields (i.e., the term structure of interest rates) to change. A flow of funds from financial institutions that grant short-term loans to those making long-term loans will then result in a negatively sloped yield curve.

There is no consensus as to which of the three theories is correct. Each has appealing elements, but there is insufficient empirical evidence to suggest that the structure of yields is solely explained by only one of the three theories. It is probably safe to assume that all three play some role in the determination of the term structure of interest rates.[9]

---

[9] See J. O. Light and William L. White, *The Financial System,* (Homewood, Ill.: Richard D. Irwin, 1979), especially Chapters 8 and 9. It should be noted that the illustration of the expectation theory in this appendix is limited to two years. However, it may be generalized into more time periods so that the current structure of yields reflects expected short-term rates in three, four, five, or more years in the future. See Light and White, 153–155.

15

The Valuation of Debt

s was learned in the previous chapter, corporations sell a variety of debt instruments to the general public. There is a very active secondary market for these bonds. Since bonds trade daily, what establishes their prices? What yields do they offer investors? If interest rates in general change, what will happen to the prices of existing bonds? Which bonds' prices tend to be more volatile? These are some of the essential questions concerning investing in debt instruments that are addressed in this chapter.

Although there is a variety of debt instruments, each with its specific name and characteristics, for the purpose of this chapter the term bond *will be used to include all types of debt instruments. The price of any bond (for a given risk class) is primarily related to (1) the interest paid by the bond, (2) the interest rate that investors may earn on competitive bonds, and (3) the maturity date of the bond. This chapter will explore the effect of each. Next follows a discussion of the various uses of the word* yield, *including the current yield, the yield to maturity, and yield to call. The chapter concludes with brief discussions of yields and risk, duration, and the management of bond portfolios.*

❖ ❖ ❖

Perpetual Debt

A **perpetual bond** is a bond that never matures. The issuer never has to retire the principal; it has only to meet the interest payments and the other terms of the indenture. Although such a bond may sound absurd, there are some in existence. For example, the British government issued perpetual bonds called consols to refinance the debt that was issued to support the Napoleonic Wars. These bonds will never mature, but they do pay interest, and there is an active secondary market in them.

How much can a perpetual bond be worth? The answer depends on the interest paid by the bond and the return the investor can earn elsewhere. For example, a perpetual bond pays the following stream of interest income annually:

perpetual bond
A debt instrument with no maturity date.

Year 1	Year 2	...	Year 20	...	Year 100	...	Year 1000	...
$100	$100		$100		$100		$100	

How much are these interest payments worth? The question really is, what is the present value of each one of these $100 payments? To answer the question, the investor must know the rate of interest that may be earned on alternative investments. If the investor can earn 15 percent elsewhere, the present value (*PV*) of the perpetual stream of $100 payments is

$$PV = \frac{\$100}{(1 + 0.15)^1} + \frac{\$100}{(1 + 0.15)^2} + \cdots + \frac{\$100}{(1 + 0.15)^{20}}$$

$$+ \cdots + \frac{\$100}{(1 + 0.15)^{100}} + \cdots + \frac{\$100}{(1 + 0.15)^{1.000}}$$

$$= \$100(0.870) + \$100(0.756) + \cdots + \$100(0.037)$$

$$+ \cdots + \$100(0.000) + \cdots + \$100(0.000)$$

$$= \$87 + \$75.60 + \cdots + \$3.70 + \cdots + 0$$

$$= \$667.$$

As may be seen in this example, the $100 interest payments received in the near future contribute most to the present value of the bond. Dollars received in the distant future have little value today. The sum of all of these present values is $667, which means that if alternative investments yield 15 percent, an investor would be willing to pay $667 for a promise to receive $100 annually for the indefinite future.

The preceding may be stated in more formal terms. If *I* is the annual interest payment and *i* is the rate of return that is being earned on comparable investments, then the present value is

$$PV = \frac{I}{(1 + i)^1} + \frac{I}{(1 + i)^2} + \frac{I}{(1 + i)^3} + \cdots.$$

This is a geometric series, and its sum may be expressed as

$$PV = \frac{I}{i}. \tag{15.1}$$

Equation 15.1 gives the current value of an infinite stream of interest payments. If this equation is applied to the previous example in which the annual interest payment is $100 and alternative investments can earn 15 percent, then the present value of the bond is

$$PV = \frac{\$100}{0.15} = \$667.$$

If market interest rates of alternative investments were to increase, say, to 20 percent, the value of this perpetual stream of interest payments would decline; if market interest rates were to fall to, say, 8 percent, the value of the bond would

Exhibit 15.1 ✦ RELATIONSHIP BETWEEN INTEREST RATES AND THE PRICE OF A PERPETUAL BOND

Current Interest Rate (i)	Annual Interest Paid by the Bond (I)	Present Price of the Bond $\left(PV = \dfrac{I}{i}\right)$
4%	$100	$2,500
6	100	1,667
8	100	1,250
10	100	1,000
15	100	667
20	100	500

rise. These changes occur because the bond pays a *fixed flow of income;* that is, the dollar amount of interest paid by the bond is constant. Lower interest rates mean that more money is needed to purchase this fixed stream of interest payments, and with higher interest rates, less money is needed to buy this fixed flow of income.

The inverse relationship between interest rates and bond prices is illustrated in Exhibit 15.1, which presents the value of the preceding perpetual bond at different interest rates. As may be seen from the exhibit, as current market interest rates rise, the present value of the bond declines. Thus, if the present value is $1,000 when interest rates are 10 percent, the value of this bond declines to $500 when interest rates rise to 20 percent.

A simple example may show why this inverse relationship between bond prices and interest rates exists. Suppose two investors offered to sell two different bond issues. The first is the perpetual bond that pays $100 per year in interest. The second is also a perpetual bond, but it pays $120 per year in interest. If the offer price in each case is $1,000, which bond would be preferred? Obviously, if they are equal in every way except in the amount of interest, a buyer would prefer the second bond that pays $120. What could the seller of the first bond do to make the bond more attractive to a buyer? The obvious answer is to lower the asking price so that the yield the buyer receives is identical for both bonds. Thus, if the seller were to ask only $833 for the bond that pays $100 annually, the buyer should be indifferent as to which he or she chooses. Both bonds would then offer a yield of 12 percent (i.e., $100 ÷ $833 for the first bond and $120 ÷ $1000 for the second bond).

BONDS WITH MATURITY DATES

The majority of bonds are not perpetual but have a finite life. They mature, and this fact must affect their valuation. A bond's price is related not only to the interest that it pays but also to its face amount (i.e., the principal). The current price of a bond equals the present value of the interest payments plus the present value of the principal to be received at maturity.

Annual Compounding[1]

The value of a bond is expressed algebraically in Equation 15.2 in terms of the present value formulas discussed in Chapter 6. A bond's value is

$$P_B = \frac{I_1}{(1+i)^1} + \frac{I_2}{(1+i)^2} + \cdots + \frac{I_n}{(1+i)^n} + \frac{P}{(1+i)^n},$$ (15.2)

where P_B indicates the current price of the bond; I, the annual interest payment (with the subscripts indicating the year); n, the number of years to maturity; P, the principal; and i, the current interest rate.

The calculation of a bond's price using Equation 15.2 may be illustrated by a simple example. A firm has a $1,000 bond outstanding that matures in three years with a 10 percent coupon rate ($100 annually). All that is needed to determine the price of the bond is the current interest rate, which is the rate being paid by newly issued, competitive bonds with the same length of time to maturity and the same degree of risk. If the competitive bonds yield 10 percent, the price of this bond will be par ($1,000), for

$$P_B = \frac{\$100}{(1+0.10)^1} + \frac{\$100}{(1+0.10)^2} + \frac{\$100}{(1+0.10)^3} + \frac{\$1,000}{(1+0.10)^3}$$

$$= \$100(0.909) + 100(0.826) + 100(0.751) + 1,000(0.751)$$

$$= \$999.60 \approx \$1,000.$$

If competitive bonds are selling to yield 12 percent, this bond will be unattractive to investors. They will not be willing to pay $1,000 for a bond yielding 10 percent when they could buy competing bonds at the same price that yield 12 percent. For this bond to compete with the others, its price must decline sufficiently to yield 12 percent. In terms of Equation 10.2, the price must be

$$P_B = \frac{\$100}{(1+0.12)^1} + \frac{\$100}{(1+0.12)^2} + \frac{\$100}{(1+0.12)^3} + \frac{\$1,000}{(1+0.12)^3}$$

$$= \$100(0.893) + 100(0.797) + 100(0.712) + 1,000(0.712)$$

$$= \$952.20.$$

discount bond
A bond that is sold for less than its face amount or principal.

The price of the bond must decline to approximately $952; that is, it must sell for a **discount** (a price less than the stated principal) in order to be competitive with comparable bonds. At that price investors will earn $100 per year in interest and approximately $50 in capital gains over the three years, for a total annual return of 12 percent on their investment. The capital gain occurs because the bond is purchased for $952.20, but when it matures, the holder will receive $1,000.

---

[1] While bonds pay interest semiannually, this discussion uses annual compounding to facilitate the explanation.

If comparable debt were to yield 8 percent, the price of the bond in the previous example would have to rise. In this case the price of the bond would be

$$P_B = \frac{\$100}{(1+0.08)^1} + \frac{\$100}{(1+0.08)^2} + \frac{\$100}{(1+0.08)^3} + \frac{\$1,000}{(1+0.08)^3}$$

$$= \$100(0.926) + 100(0.857) + 100(0.794) + 1,000(0.794)$$

$$= \$1,051.70.$$

The bond, therefore, must sell at a **premium** (a price greater than the stated principal). Although it may seem implausible for the bond to sell at a premium, this must occur if the market interest rate falls below the coupon rate of interest stated on the bond.

These price calculations are lengthy, but the number of computations can be reduced when one realizes that the valuation of a bond has two components: a flow of interest payments and a final repayment of principal. Since interest payments are fixed and are paid every year, they may be treated as an annuity. The principal repayment may be treated as a simple lump-sum payment. If a $1,000 bond pays $100 per year in interest and matures after three years, its current value is the present value of the $100 annuity for three years and the present value of the $1,000 that will be received after three years. If the interest rate is 12 percent, the current value of the bond is

$$P_B = \$100(2.402) + \$1,000(0.712) = \$952.20,$$

where 2.402 is the interest factor for the present value of a $1 annuity at 12 percent for three years and 0.712 is the interest factor for the present value of $1 at 12 percent after three years. This is the same answer that was derived earlier (except for the rounding error), but the amount of arithmetic has been reduced.

These examples illustrate the same general conclusion that was reached earlier concerning bond prices and changes in market interest rates: They are inversely related. *When market interest rates rise, bond prices decline. When market interest rates fall, bond prices rise.* This relationship is illustrated in Figure 15.1, which plots the price of the aforementioned $1,000 bond at various interest rates. As may be seen from the figure, higher interest rates depress the bond's current value. Thus, the bond's price declines from $1,000 to $952.20 when interest rates rise from 10 to 12 percent, but the price rises to $1,051.70 when interest rates decline to 8 percent. (Factors that affect the amount of price change are covered later in this chapter.)

The inverse relationship between the price of a bond and the interest rate suggests a means to make profits in the bond market. All that investors need to know is the direction of future changes in the interest rate. If investors anticipate that interest rates will decline, then they are expecting the price of previously issued bonds with a given number of years to maturity and of a certain risk to rise. This price increase must occur in order for previously issued bonds to have the same yield as currently issued bonds. The reverse is also true, for if investors anticipate that interest rates will rise, they are also anticipating that the price of currently available bonds will decline. This decline must occur for previously issued bonds to offer the same yield as currently issued bonds. Therefore, if investors can anticipate the

premium (of a bond)
The extent to which a bond's price exceeds the face amount of the debt.

Figure 15.1 ◆ RELATIONSHIP BETWEEN INTEREST RATES AND A BOND'S PRICE

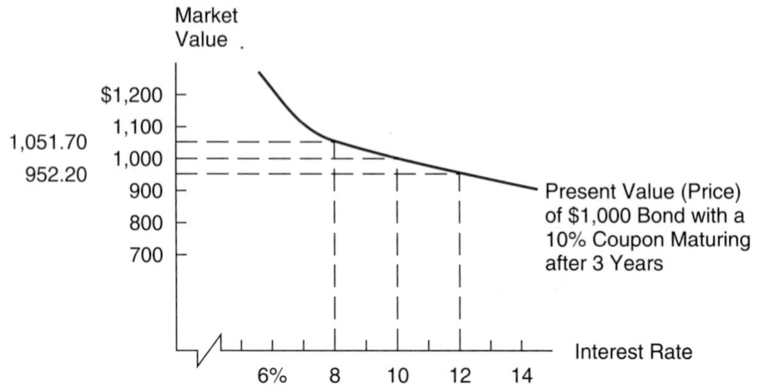

direction of change in interest rates, they can also anticipate the direction of change in the price of bonds.

Investors, however, may anticipate incorrectly and thus suffer losses in the bond market. If they buy bonds and interest rates rise, then the market value of their bonds must decline, and the investors suffer capital losses. These individuals, however, have something in their favor: The bonds must ultimately be retired. Since the principal must be redeemed, an investment error in the bond market may be corrected when the bond's price rises as the bond approaches maturity. The capital losses will eventually be erased. The correction of the error, however, may take years, during which time the investors have lost the higher yields that were available on bonds issued after their initial investments.

Semiannual Compounding

The valuation of a bond with a finite life presented in Equation 15.2 is a bit misleading, because bonds pay interest twice a year (i.e., semiannually), and the equation assumes that the interest payments are made only annually. However, Equation 15.2 may be readily modified to take into consideration semiannual (or even quarterly or weekly) compounding. This is done by adjusting the amount of each payment and the total number of these payments. To adjust the previous example, each interest payment will be $50 if payments are semiannual, and instead of three annual payments, the bond will make a total of six $50 semiannual payments. Hence, the flow of payments that will be made by this bond is

Year 1		Year 2		Year 3		
$50	$50	$50	$50	$50	$50	$1,000

This flow of payments would then be discounted back to the present to determine the bond's current value. The question then becomes, what is the appropriate discount factor?

If comparable debt yields 12 percent, the appropriate discount factor is not 12 percent; it is 6 percent. Six percent interest paid twice a year yields 12 percent interest compounded semiannually. Thus, to determine the present value of this bond, the comparable interest rate is divided in half (just as the annual interest payment is divided in half). However, the number of interest payments to which this 6 percent is applied is doubled (just as the number of payments is doubled). Hence, the current value of this bond, which pays interest twice a year (is compounded semiannually), is

$$P_B = \frac{\$50}{(1+0.06)^1} + \frac{\$50}{(1+0.06)^2} + \frac{\$50}{(1+0.06)^3} + \frac{\$50}{(1+0.06)^4}$$

$$+ \frac{\$50}{(1+0.06)^5} + \frac{\$50}{(1+0.06)^6} + \frac{\$1,000}{(1+0.06)^6}$$

$$= \$50(0.943) + 50(0.889) + 50(0.840)$$

$$+ 50(0.792) + 50(0.747) + 50(0.705) + 1,000(0.705)$$

$$= \$47.15 + 44.45 + 42.00 + 39.60 + 37.35 + 35.25 + 705$$

$$= \$950.85.$$

With semiannual compounding, the current value of the bond is slightly lower (i.e., $950.85 versus $952.20). This is because the bond's price must decline more to compensate for the more frequent compounding. An investor would prefer a bond that pays $50 twice per year to one that pays $100 once per year, because the investor would have use of some of the funds more quickly. Thus, if interest rates rise, causing bond prices to fall, the decline will be greater if the interest on bonds is paid semiannually than if it is paid annually.

Equation 15.2 may be altered to include semiannual compounding. This is done in Equation 15.3. Only one new symbol, c, is added, which represents the frequency of compounding (i.e., the number of times each year that interest payments are made).

$$P_B = \frac{\dfrac{I}{c}}{\left(1 + \dfrac{i}{c}\right)^1} + \frac{\dfrac{I}{c}}{\left(1 + \dfrac{i}{c}\right)^2} + \cdots + \frac{\dfrac{I}{c}}{\left(1 + \dfrac{i}{c}\right)^{n \times c}} + \frac{P}{\left(1 + \dfrac{i}{c}\right)^{n \times c}}. \quad (15.3)$$

When Equation 15.3 is applied to the earlier example, the price of the bond is

$$P_B = \frac{\dfrac{\$100}{2}}{\left(1 + \dfrac{0.12}{2}\right)^1} + \frac{\dfrac{\$100}{2}}{\left(1 + \dfrac{0.12}{2}\right)^2} + \cdots + \frac{\dfrac{\$100}{2}}{\left(1 + \dfrac{0.12}{2}\right)^{3 \times 2}} + \frac{\$1,000}{\left(1 + \dfrac{0.12}{2}\right)^{3 \times 2}}$$

$$= \$50(0.943) + 50(0.890) + \cdots + 50(0.705) + 1,000(0.705)$$

$$= \$950.85,$$

which, of course, is the same answer derived in the immediately preceding example.

Performing such calculations can obviously be tedious and time-consuming. However, the required effort will greatly be reduced if the individual has access to a bond table. A bond table has the following general presentation:

BOND TABLE FOR A BOND WITH AN 8 PERCENT COUPON

Current Interest Rate	Years to Maturity			
	1	3	6	10
6.5%	$101.43	$104.03	$106.32	$110.09
7.0	100.95	102.66	104.16	107.11
7.5	100.47	101.32	102.05	103.47
8.0	100.00	100.00	100.00	100.00
8.5	99.53	98.70	98.00	96.68
9.0	99.06	97.42	96.04	93.50
9.5	98.60	96.16	94.14	90.45

The bond's coupon (i.e., 8 percent) is given in the title. The current rate of interest is read vertically at the left, and the number of years to maturity is read horizontally across the top. If an individual wanted to know the price of an 8 percent bond with a maturity of five years that was priced to yield 7.5 percent to maturity, that investor could consult the bond table and learn that the price would be $102.05 ($1,020.50 for a $1,000 bond).

Not every investor has access to a bond table, but the advent of the pocket calculator has put price calculations at the fingertips of virtually everyone. Sophisticated calculators (some of which are manufactured by Texas Instruments or Hewlett Packard) can be used to determine bond prices, and even the less sophisticated models can perform such computations. As was illustrated previously, all the investor needs to know to determine the bond's price are the interest factors for the present value of an annuity and of a dollar compounded semiannually. Such interest factors may be generated using the less sophisticated pocket calculators. Thus, the individual investor does not need a computer, present value tables, or a bond table to price bonds. Pocket calculators have reduced both the tedium of the calculations and the reliance on sophisticated equipment or mathematical tables.

FLUCTUATIONS IN BOND PRICES

As the preceding examples illustrate, a bond's price depends on the interest paid, the maturity date of the bond, and the yield currently earned on comparable securities. The illustrations also demonstrated that when interest rates rise, bond prices fall, and when interest rates fall, bond prices rise.

The amount of price fluctuation depends on (1) the amount of interest paid by the bond, (2) the length of time to maturity, and (3) risk. The smaller the amount of interest, the larger the relative price fluctuations will tend to be. The longer the term or time to maturity, the greater the price fluctuation will be. Riskier bonds will also experience greater fluctuations in their prices.

This section is concerned with the first two factors that affect price fluctuations, the amount of interest and the term to maturity. The impact of risk is covered in a subsequent section. The effect of the amount of interest and the length of time to maturity may be seen by the following illustrations. In the first case, consider two bonds with equal lives (e.g., ten years to maturity) but unequal coupons. Bond A pays $40 a year (a 4 percent coupon), and Bond B pays $140 annually (a 14 percent coupon). If interest rates are 10 percent, the bonds' prices are

$$P_A = \$40(6.145) + \$1,000(0.386) \approx \$632,$$

$$P_B = \$140(6.145) + \$1,000(0.386) \approx \$1,246.$$

If interest rates rise to 14 percent, the bonds' prices become

$$P_A = \$40(5.216) + \$1,000(0.270) = \$478.64,$$

$$P_B = \$140(5.216) + \$1,000(0.270) = \$1,000.$$

The price of Bond A falls by 25 percent from $632 to $478.64, while the price of Bond B falls 20 percent from $1,246 to $1,000. As may be seen in Figure 15.2, if interest rates continue to rise, the bonds' prices decline further. At 20 percent, the values of the bonds are $330 and $749, respectively. These prices represent declines of approximately 48 and 40 percent from the bonds' initial prices.

The length of time to maturity also affects the fluctuation in a bond's price. Consider the following two bonds. Each pays $100 interest annually (a 10 percent coupon). Bond A matures after ten years, and Bond B matures after one year. If interest rates are 10 percent, the price of each bond is

$$P_A = \$100(6.145) + \$1,000(0.386) = \$1,000,$$

$$P_B = \$100(0.909) + \$1,000(0.909) = \$1,000.$$

If interest rates rise to 12 percent, the price of each bond declines to

$$P_A = \$100(5.650) + \$1,000(0.322) = \$887.00,$$

$$P_B = \$100(0.893) + \$1,000(0.893) = \$982.30.$$

The price of Bond A falls approximately 12 percent from $1,000 to $887, but Bond B suffers only a modest price decline to $982.30.

If interest rates fall, the price of the longer-term bond increases. This price increase (and the price decline caused by higher interest rates) is illustrated in Figure 15.3, which vividly shows the larger price fluctuations in the ten-year bond. Thus Figure 15.3 clearly illustrates that investors in long-term debt bear more risk from changes in bond prices caused by fluctuations in interest rates. For this reason investors who are concerned with the preservation of principal will stress short-term debt instruments. These offer both interest income and safety of principal. However, most investors do not actually buy short-term securities. Instead, they buy shares in money market mutual funds that in turn invest in short-term debt. Money market mutual funds thus offer investors liquidity that cannot be obtained through investments in long-term debt.

Figure 15.2 ✦ RELATIONSHIP BETWEEN PRICES OF BONDS WITH DIFFERENT COUPONS AND VARIOUS INTEREST RATES

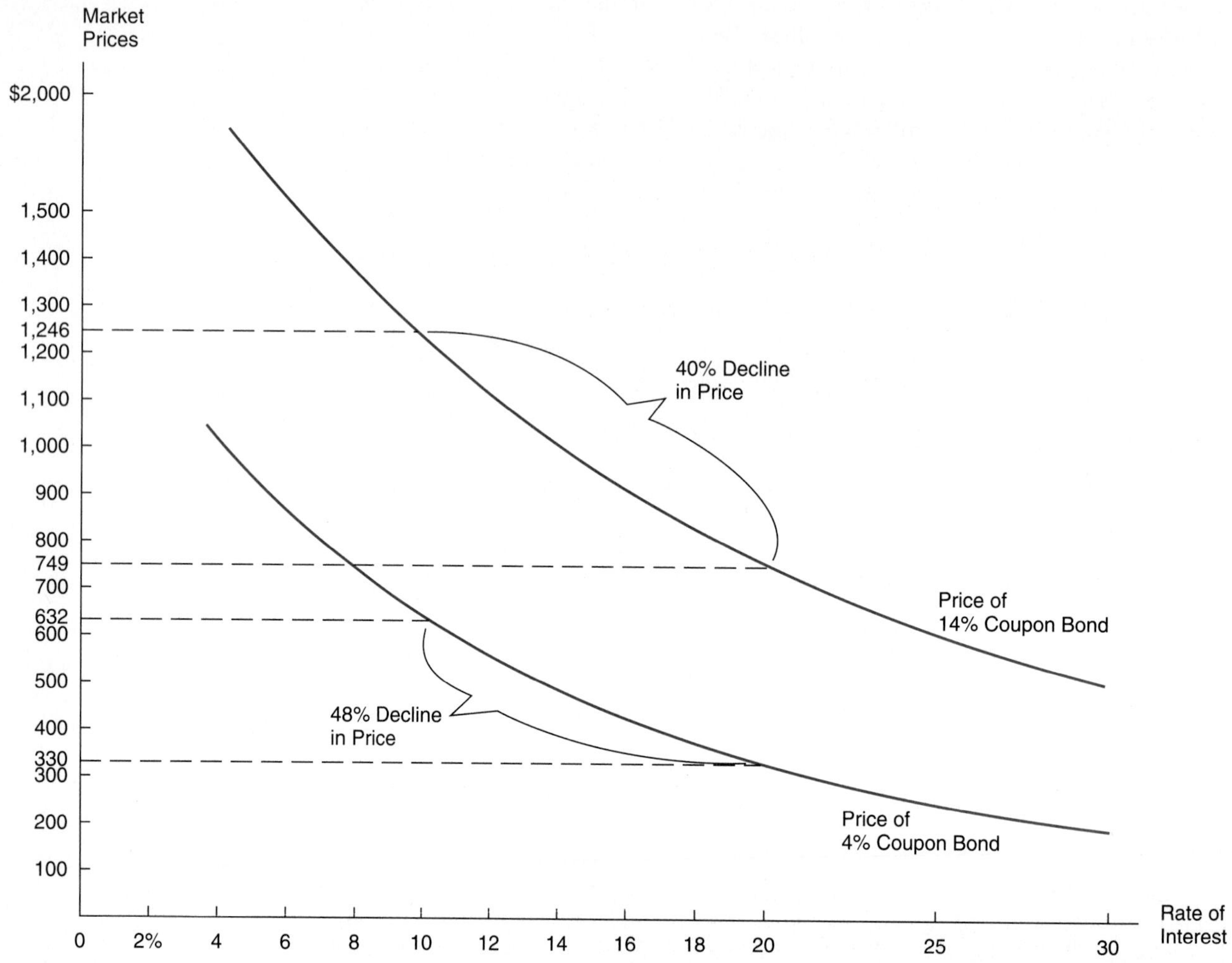

YIELDS

The word *yield* is frequently used with regard to investing in bonds. There are three important types of yields that the investor must be familiar with: the current yield, the yield to maturity, and the yield to call. This section will differentiate among these three yields.

The Current Yield

The current yield is the percentage that the investor earns annually. It is simply

$$\frac{\text{Annual interest payment}}{\text{Price of the bond}} \tag{15.4}$$

Figure 15.3 ✦ RELATIONSHIP BETWEEN BOND PRICES AND TERM TO MATURITY (FOR A GIVEN COUPON)

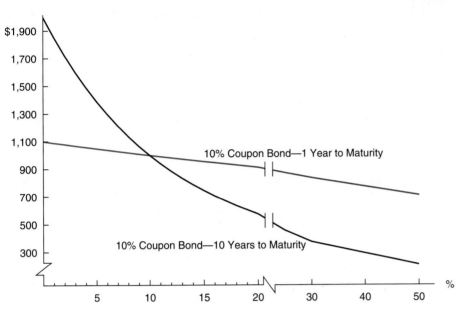

The bond discussed previously in the section on discounted bonds has a coupon rate of 10 percent. Thus, when the price of the bond is $952, the current yield is

$$\frac{\$100}{\$952} = 10.5\%.$$

The current yield is important because it gives the investor an indication of the current return that will be earned on the investment. Investors who seek high current income prefer bonds that offer a high current yield.

However, the current yield can be very misleading, for it fails to consider any change in the price of the bond that may occur if the bond is held to maturity. Obviously, if a bond is bought at a discount, its value must rise as it approaches maturity. The opposite occurs if the bond is purchased for a premium, because its price will decline as maturity approaches. For this reason it is desirable to know the bond's yield to maturity.

The Yield to Maturity

The yield to maturity considers the current income generated by the bond as well as any change in its value when it is held to maturity. If the bond referred to earlier is purchased for $952 and is held to maturity, after three years the investor will receive a return of 12 percent. This is the yield to maturity, because this return considers not only the current interest return of 10.5 percent but also the price appreciation of the bond from $952 at the time of purchase to $1,000 at maturity.

Since the yield to maturity considers both the flow of interest income and the price change, it is a more accurate measure of the return offered to investors by a particular bond issue.

The yield to maturity may be determined by using Equation 15.2.[2] That equation reads

$$P_B = \frac{I_1}{(1+i)^1} + \frac{I_2}{(1+i)^2} + \cdots + \frac{I_n}{(1+i)^n} + \frac{P}{(1+i)^n}.$$

The i is the current rate of interest paid by newly issued bonds with the same term to maturity and the same degree of risk. If the investor buys a bond and holds it to maturity, the yield that is being paid by newly issued bonds (i) will also be the yield to maturity.

Determining the yield to maturity when the coupon rate of interest, the bond's price, and the maturity date are known is not easy, even with the use of an electronic calculator. For example, if the bond were selling for $952 and the investor wanted to know the yield to maturity, the calculation would be

$$\$952 = \frac{\$100}{(1+i)^1} + \frac{\$100}{(1+i)^2} + \frac{\$100}{(1+i)^3} + \frac{\$1,000}{(1+i)^3}.$$

Solving this equation can be a formidable task because there is no simple arithmetical computation to determine the value of i. Instead, the investor selects a value for i and plugs it into the equation. If this value equates the left-hand and right-hand sides of the equation, then that value of i is the yield to maturity.

If the value does not equate the two sides of the equation, another value must be selected. This process is repeated until a value for i is found that equates both sides of the equation. Obviously, that can be a long process. For example, suppose the investor selects 14 percent and substitutes it into the right-hand side of the equation. The result is

$$P_B = \frac{\$100}{(1+0.14)^1} + \frac{\$100}{(1+0.14)^2} + \frac{\$100}{(1+0.14)^3} + \frac{\$1,000}{(1+0.14)^3}$$

$$= \$100(2.321) + 1,000(0.675)$$

$$= \$232.10 + 675$$

$$= \$907.10.$$

$907.10 does not equal $952. That means the selected yield to maturity was too high, so the investor selects another, lower rate. If the investor had selected 12 percent, then

[2] Equation 15.3 is more accurate, since bonds pay interest semiannually. However, Equation 15.2 is less formidable and still illustrates the point.

$$P_B = \$100(2.402) + \$1,000(0.712)$$

$$= \$240.20 + 712$$

$$= \$952.20,$$

and thus 12 percent is the yield to maturity (compounded annually).[3]

The above process to determine the yield to maturity is quite tedious. However, the yield to maturity can be approximated by Equation 15.5.

$$i = \frac{I + \dfrac{\$1,000 - P_B}{n}}{\dfrac{\$1,000 + P_B}{2}}. \tag{15.5}$$

The symbols are the same that were used in Equation 15.2. If the current price of a \$1,000 bond with a 10 percent coupon ($I = \$100$) is \$952 ($P_B = \$952$) and the bond matures in three years ($n = 3$), then the approximate yield to maturity is

$$i = \frac{\$100 + \dfrac{\$1,000 - 952}{3}}{\dfrac{\$1,000 + 952}{2}}$$

$$= \frac{100 + 48/3}{976}$$

$$= 11.88\%.$$

This answer, 11.88 percent, is approximately the 12 percent derived above by the more tedious, but technically correct, method.

A Comparison of the Current Yield and the Yield to Maturity

The current yield and the yield to maturity are equal only if the bond sells for its principal amount or par. If the bond sells at a discount, the yield to maturity exceeds the current yield. This may be illustrated by the bond in the previous example. When it sells at a discount (e.g., \$952), the current yield is only 10.5 percent. However, the yield to maturity is 12 percent. Thus, the yield to maturity exceeds the current yield.

If the bond sells at a premium, the current yield exceeds the yield to maturity. For example, if the bond sells for \$1,052, the current yield is 9.5 percent (\$100 ÷ \$1,052) and the yield to maturity is 8 percent. The yield to maturity is less in this case because the loss that the investor must suffer when the price of the bond declines from \$1,052 to \$1,000 at maturity has been incorporated.

---

[3] If the investor obtains a price greater than the correct price, the yield to maturity is too low, and the investor should select a higher rate.

Exhibit 15.2 ◆ CURRENT YIELDS AND YIELDS TO MATURITY FOR A TEN-YEAR BOND WITH AN 8 PERCENT COUPON

Price of Bond	Current Yield	Yield to Maturity
$1,109.00	7.2%	6.5
1,049.10	7.6	7.3
1,000.00	8.0	8.0
966.80	8.3	8.5
910.50	8.8	9.4
881.50	9.1	9.9
831.30	9.6	10.8
795.10	10.1	11.5
687.28	11.6	14.0

Exhibit 15.2 presents the current yield and the yields to maturity at different prices for a bond with an 8 percent coupon that matures in ten years. As may be seen in the table, the larger the discount (or the smaller the premium), the greater are both the current yield and the yield to maturity. For example, when the bond sells for $881.50, the yield to maturity is 9.9 percent, but it rises to 11.5 percent when the price declines to $795.10.

Discounted bonds offer conservative investors attractive opportunities for financial planning. For example, a person who is currently 60 years old may purchase discounted bonds that mature after ten years to help finance retirement. This investor may purchase several bonds that mature five, six, seven years, and so on, into the future. This portfolio will generate a continuous flow of funds during retirement as the bonds mature. Such a portfolio of AT&T bonds is illustrated in Exhibit 15.3. The first column gives the coupon rate of interest, the second column gives the year of maturity, the third column presents the discounted price for $1,000 in face value worth of debt, and the last column gives the yield to maturity. By purchasing this portfolio for a total cost of $4,633.00 the investor will own $5,000 worth of bonds

Exhibit 15.3 ◆ SELECTED AT&T BONDS SELLING AT A DISCOUNT AS OF JANUARY 1, 1993

Coupon Rate	Maturity Year	Price (per $1000 Face Value)	Yield to Maturity
4⅜	1996	$957.50	5.65%
5½	1997	977.50	6.14
4¾	1998	935.00	6.18
4⅜	1999	888.75	6.55
5⅛	2001	881.25	7.04

Source: Moody's Bond Record, January, 1993.

THE ACCURACY OF THE APPROXIMATE FORMULA

If the student does not have access to a financial function calculator, the approximation formula is a convenient means to estimate the yield to maturity. How accurate is the approximation? To help answer that question, consider two bonds that each have a 10 percent coupon ($100 per $1,000 face amount). Bond A matures in five years, while bond B matures in twenty years. The following table is constructed to show the correct and the approximate yield to maturity at various prices.

As may be seen in this illustration, the approximate yield to maturity is a reasonable estimate of the actual yield to maturity. Only when the bond sells for a large discount does the approximation significantly understate the true yield the bond offers over its lifetime.

| | Bond A | | | Bond B | |
	Price	Correct Yield to Maturity	Approximate Yield to Maturity	Price	Correct Yield to Maturity	Approximate Yield to Maturity
	$1,100	7.56%	7.62%	$1,100	8.90%	9.05%
	1,000	10.00	10.00	1,000	10.00	10.00
	900	12.76	12.63	900	11.26	11.05
	800	15.94	15.55	800	12.78	12.22
	500	29.86	26.67	500	20.42	16.67

that mature between 1996 and 2001. Of course, by purchasing more discounted bonds, the investor will have an even greater flow of income during the particular time period to meet his or her financial goals (e.g., financing retirement or paying for children's college education).

The Yield to Call

Some bonds will never reach maturity but are retired before they become due. In some cases the issuer may call the bonds before maturity and redeem them. In other cases, the sinking fund will randomly call selected bonds from the issue and retire them. For these reasons the **yield to call** may be a more accurate estimate of the return actually earned on an investment in a bond that is held until redemption.

The yield to call is calculated in the same way as the yield to maturity except that (1) the expected call date is substituted for the maturity date and (2) the principal plus the call penalty (if any) is substituted for the principal. Note that the anticipated call date is used. Unlike the maturity date, which is known, the date of a call can only be anticipated.

The following example illustrates how the yield to call is calculated. A bond that matures after ten years and pays 8 percent interest annually is currently selling for $935.00. The yield to maturity is 9 percent. However, if the investor believes that the company or government will call the bond after five years and will pay a penalty of $50 per $1,000 bond to retire the debt permanently, the yield to call (i_c) is approximately

yield to call
The yield earned on a bond from the time it is acquired until the time it is called and retired by the firm.

$$\$935 = \frac{\$80}{(1 + i_c)^1} + \cdots + \frac{\$80}{(1 + i_c)^5} + \frac{\$1,050}{(1 + i_c)^5}$$

$$i_c = 10.5\%.$$

(This answer, like the yield to maturity, may be derived by using the present value tables. To do so, select an interest rate, find the appropriate interest factors, and substitute them for i_c. This process is continued until a value for i_c is found that equates both sides of the equation. This lengthy process may be avoided by the use of computers or calculators that are programmed to determine yields to maturity.)

In this example, the yield to call is higher than the yield to maturity because (1) the investor receives the call penalty and (2) the principal is redeemed early and hence the discount is erased sooner. Thus, in the case of a discounted bond, the actual return the investor earns exceeds the yield to maturity if the bond is called and retired before maturity.

However, if this bond were selling for a premium (e.g., $1,146.80 with a yield to maturity of 6 percent) and the firm were to call the bond after five years, the yield to call would become

$$\$1,146.80 = \frac{\$80}{(1 + i_c)^1} + \cdots + \frac{\$80}{(1 + i_c)^5} + \frac{\$1,050}{(1 + i_c)^5}$$

$$i_c = 5.5\%.$$

This is less than the anticipated yield to maturity of 6 percent. The early redemption produces a lower return for the investor, because the premium is spread out over fewer years, reducing the yield on the investment.

Which case is more likely to occur? If a firm wanted to retire debt that was selling at a discount before maturity, it would probably be to its advantage to purchase the bonds instead of calling them. By doing so, the firm would avoid the call penalty and might even be able to buy the bonds for less than par. If the firm wanted to retire debt that was selling at a premium, it would probably be advantageous to call the bonds and pay the penalty. If the bonds were selling for more than the call penalty, this would obviously be the chosen course of action.

An investor should not expect a firm to call prematurely a bond issue that is selling at a discount. However, if interest rates fall and bond prices rise, the firm may refinance the debt. It will then issue new debt at the lower (current) interest rate and use the proceeds to retire the old and more costly debt. In this case the yield to the anticipated call is probably a better indication of the potential return offered by the bonds than is the yield to maturity.

The preceding example also illustrates the importance of the call penalty. If an investor bought the bond in anticipation that it would yield 6 percent at maturity (i.e., pay $1,146.80) and the bond is redeemed after five years for $1,000, the return on the investment is only 4.6 percent. Although the $50 call penalty does not restore the return to 6 percent, the investor does receive a yield of 5.5 percent, which is considerably better than 4.6 percent.

RISK AND FLUCTUATIONS IN YIELDS

Investors will bear risk only if they anticipate a sufficient return to compensate for the risk, and a higher anticipated return is necessary to induce them to bear additional risk. This principle also applies to investors who purchase bonds. Bonds involving greater risk must offer higher yields to attract investors. Therefore, the lowest yields are paid by bonds with the highest credit ratings, and low credit ratings are associated with high yields.

This relationship is illustrated by Exhibit 15.4, which presents Standard & Poor's ratings and the anticipated yields to maturity for four bonds that will mature in the year 2000. As may be seen in the exhibit, the bonds with the highest credit ratings have the lowest anticipated yield to maturity. An AT&T bond with an AA rating was selling to yield less than the BBB-rated bond of Long Island Lighting (7.64 percent to 8.93 percent). The difference, or "spread," in the yields is partially due to the difference in risk between the two bonds. While the AT&T bond is considered to be relatively safe (as judged by its rating), the Long Island Lighting bond is viewed as involving more risk.

Because interest rates change over time, the anticipated yields on all debts vary. However, the yields on debt involving greater risk tend to fluctuate more. This is illustrated in Figure 15.4, which plots the yields on Moody's Baa-rated bonds in the top line and the yields on its Aaa-rated bonds in the bottom line. In this particular period there was considerable change in the yields to maturity. During periods of higher interest rates, the poorer quality debt offered a higher yield and the spread between the yields was also greater. For example, during 1982 the yields rose to 14.8 and 16.9 percent, and the spread between the bonds also rose to 2.1 percent. When interest rates subsequently declined in the mid-1980s, the spread also declined.

In the late 1980s the spread tended to be larger than it had been during the late 1970s. From 1986 through 1989, triple-A-rated bonds had yields that ranged from 8.6 to 9.6 percent. The yields on triple-B-rated bonds ranged from 10.3 to 11.0 percent and the average spread rose to 1.4 percent. This expansion in the spread may be attributed to an increased use of debt financing, especially the use of poor quality debt. To absorb the additional debt, the differential in yields rose. Not only did the spread between investment grade and the so-called "junk bonds" increase but also the spread between the various investment grade bonds (i.e., the triple-A and triple-B bonds) rose.

As may be expected, all bond prices fall when interest rates rise, but the prices of bonds issued by financially weaker (riskier) firms tend to decline more. As the spread between yields rises, so too does the difference between bond prices. Such price fluctuations are illustrated in Figure 15.5, which plots the annual price range of two bonds with equal length of time to maturity and equal coupons but

---

Exhibit 15.4 ◆ CREDIT RATINGS AND YIELDS TO MATURITY FOR SELECTED BONDS MATURING IN THE YEAR 2000

Bond Issue	Standard & Poor's Bond Rating	Yield to Maturity
AT&T, 6 00	AA	7.64%
Georgia Power Co., 8⅝ 00	A−	8.45
Long Island Lighting, 9⅛ 00	BBB	8.93
Tenneco Corp., 9⅞ 00	BBB−	9.36

Source: Standard & Poor's Bond Guide, April 1992.

Figure 15.4 ✦ Fluctuations in Yield to Maturity for Moody's Aaa- and Baa-Rated Industrial Bonds (1972– June 1992)

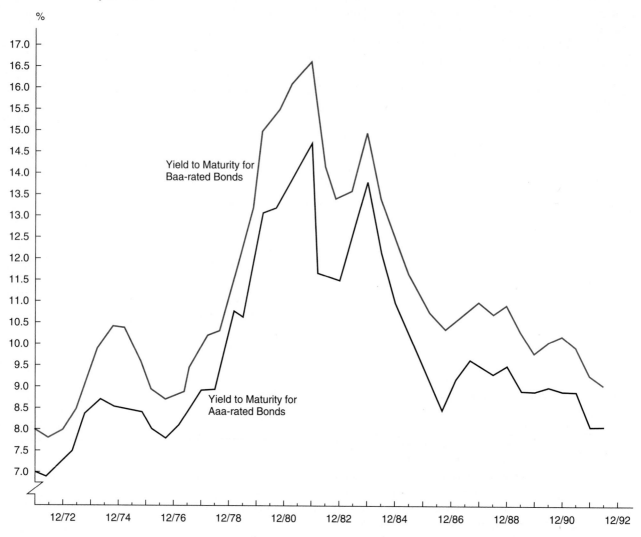

considerable difference in risk. The AT&T 8¾% bond that matures in 2000 was initially rated Aaa while the Jersey Central Power and Light 8¾% bond that also matures in 2000 was rated Baa. As would be expected, the price of the latter bond has experienced greater fluctuations. While the price of the AT&T bond declined from about $1,000 in 1977 to $600 in 1982, the JCP&L bond declined from $1,000 to $435 during the same period.

After the breakup of AT&T, its credit rating was reduced. Simultaneously the credit rating of JCP&L improved, so that by 1990 the two bonds had almost identical credit ratings. Their price fluctuations in 1990 were also virtually identical, ranging from $95 to $100 for the AT&T bond and $94½ to $99½ for the JCP&L

Figure 15.5 ✦ Yearly Price Ranges of an AT&T and a Jersey Central Power and Light Bond (1977–1990)

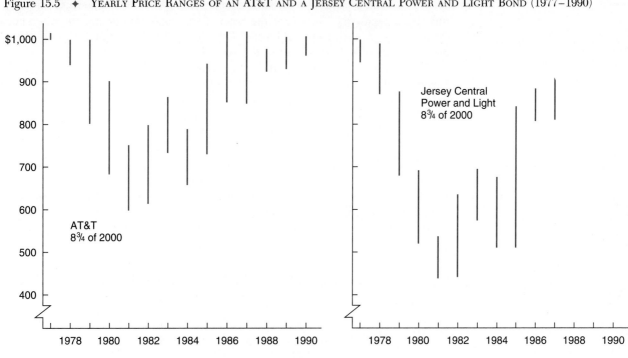

bond. For all intents and purposes, the market was treating the two bonds as identical.

These differences in the fluctuations of bond prices and spreads are the market's way of adjusting for the relative risk of investing in debt instruments of different quality. During periods of high interest rates and relatively scarce credit, weaker firms find it more difficult to finance their assets. Issuing new debt either to finance new assets or to retire old debt is more costly. Lenders must allocate the scarce supply of available credit, meaning that the price of credit (i.e., the interest rate) must rise. In addition, the possibility of default by the borrower is greater when interest rates are higher and the ability to borrow is reduced. The creditor must be compensated for assuming this increased risk of loss. Thus, despite the fact that all yields rise, the yields on the weakest debt instruments rise the most. These bonds, then, sell for the largest discounts and experience greater price volatility than high-quality bonds.

Changes in Risk

Previous sections demonstrated that when interest rates change, bond prices fluctuate in the opposite direction. If interest rates rise after a bond is issued, it will sell for a discount as the price adjusts so that the yield to maturity will be comparable with bonds being currently issued. If interest rates fall after the bond is issued, it will sell for a premium so that once again the yield to maturity is comparable to current interest rates.

The amount of price change depends on the coupon, the term of the bond, and the risk. The smaller the coupon, the greater the price fluctuation for a given maturity and level of risk. The longer the term of the bond, the greater the price fluctuation for a given coupon and level of risk. For given coupons and maturity dates, the prices of riskier bonds tend to fluctuate more.

The coupons and maturity dates of a bond are set when the bond is issued. However, the risk of default on the bond may vary over time as the financial condition of the issuer varies. Firms that were financially sound when their bonds were issued may fall on hard times. Their credit ratings deteriorate. Other firms' financial positions may improve. These changes in risk will, of course, affect the value of outstanding bonds.

This impact of risk was illustrated in Figure 15.5, which presented the price fluctuations in an AT&T bond and a Jersey Central Power and Light bond. The AT&T bond's price fluctuated less because it was the safer bond. However, the creditworthiness of both bonds has changed over time. The Moody's ratings, which were discussed in the previous chapter as indicators of the risk, were as follows:

Year end	AT&T	Jersey Central Power and Light
1977	Aaa	Baa
1978–1979	Aaa	Ba
1980–1981	Aaa	Ba3
1982–1983	Aa1	Ba3
1984	Aa1	Baa2
1985	Aa1	Baa2r
1986	Aa3	Baa1r
1987	A1	Baa1
1988–1990	A1	A2

The threat of and subsequent divestiture of AT&T's phone operation has increased the risk associated with the firm. Its sources of revenue are no longer related to regulated phone service, and the ratings of the AT&T bond have, therefore, been decreased from triple A to A1 to acknowledge the increased risk. Jersey Central Power and Light is part owner of the Three Mile Island nuclear power plant. Obviously the 1979 accident at that power plant changed the risk exposure of JCP&L's bonds. The ratings dropped from Baa, the lowest investment grade rating, to Ba. The price of the bonds declined dramatically, and they sold for a substantial discount. However, the subsequent improvement in the firm's financial condition has resulted in improved credit ratings, so that by the end of 1990, the rating was only one step below the rating given the AT&T bond. The price of the bond has also risen, so that the prices of the two bond issues were approximately equal.

THE REINVESTMENT ASSUMPTION

The yield to maturity makes a very important assumption that answers the following questions: What happens to the interest received in year one, year two, etc. (i.e., does the recipient pocket the money or reinvest the funds)? If the funds are reinvested, what rate do they earn? The yield to maturity calculation assumes that *all interest payments are reinvested at the yield to maturity*. This is an exceedingly important assumption because if the payments are not reinvested at that rate, the yield to maturity will not be realized. This also means that when an investor purchases a bond, the yield to maturity is an expected yield that will not necessarily be the realized yield. The debtor could make all the interest payments and redeem the bond at maturity, but the yield over the lifetime of the bond could be different from the yield to maturity the investor anticipated when the bond was purchased.

The reinvestment rate assumption is the essential difference between compounding and not compounding. If an investor buys a $1,000 bond with an 8 percent coupon at par and spends the interest as received, the investor is earning a simple, noncompounded rate of 8 percent. The yield to maturity, however, assumes that the interest received will be reinvested at 8 percent (i.e., compounded at 8 percent). If the funds are not being reinvested, the compounded yield will be less than the simple 8 percent rate.

The reinvestment rate that the investor does achieve could be greater or less than the anticipated yield to maturity. If interest rates rise (and the price of this bond declines), the individual can reinvest the interest payments at the now higher rate. The yield earned over the lifetime of the bond will exceed the anticipated yield to maturity. If interest rates fall (and the price of this bond rises), the individual can only reinvest the interest payments at the lower rate. The yield earned over the lifetime of the bond will be less than the anticipated yield to maturity.

Perhaps the best way to see the importance of the reinvestment rate assumption is through several illustrations. In each of the following cases, the investor purchases an 8 percent, ten-year $1,000 coupon bond that matures after ten years. The investor wants the funds to accumulate and is curious as to how much will be available at the end of the tenth year. Essentially this question may be restated in the following way: If I invest $80 each year at some rate for ten years and receive $1,000 at the end of the tenth year, how much will I have accumulated? The final amount will depend on the rate earned each year. This is the reinvestment rate.

Case 1: All Interest Payments Are Reinvested at 8 Percent

In this case the terminal value will be $80 times the interest factor for the future sum of an annuity of $1 at 8 percent for ten years. The future value of this annuity is

$$\$80(14.487) = \$1,158.96.$$

This amount is added to the $1,000 principal received at maturity so the investor has a total of $2,158.96 at the end of ten years.

What is the return on this investment that initially cost $1,000 and has grown into $2,158.96? This is a future value of $1 problem:

$$\$1,000(\text{interest factor for 10 years at } X \text{ percent}) = \$2,158.96.$$

$$\$1,000X = \$2,158.96$$

$$X = 2.159$$

An interest factor for the future sum of $1 of 2.159 indicates that $1,000 grows to $2,159 in ten years at 8 percent. The yield on this investment over its lifetime (i.e., the yield to maturity) is the anticipated 8 percent.

Case 2: All Interest Payments Are Reinvested at 12 Percent

Suppose immediately after buying the bond, interest rates rise to 12 percent. Of course, the bond would now sell for a discount and the investor has sustained a loss. But the bond was purchased to receive a flow of interest payments that the individual intended to reinvest at the current rate. So the loss of value is only a paper loss. The bond is not sold, and the loss is not realized. Instead the bond is held and the interest payments are now reinvested at the higher rate. What will be the return on this investment? Will this return be equal to the 8 percent yield to maturity that was anticipated when the bond was purchased?

In this case the terminal value of the interest payments will be $80 times the interest factor for the future sum of an annuity of $1 at 12 percent for ten years. The future value of this annuity is

$$\$80(17.549) = \$1,403.92.$$

This amount is added to the $1,000 principal received at maturity so the investor has a total of $2,403.92 at the end of ten years.

What is the return on this investment that initially cost $1,000 and has grown into $2,403.92? Once again this is a future value of $1 problem:

$$\$1,000(\text{interest factor for 10 years at } X \text{ percent}) = \$2,403.92.$$

$$\$1,000X = \$2,403.92$$

$$X = 2.404$$

The interest table reveals that an interest factor of 2.404 means in ten years $1,000 grows to $2,404 at between 9 and 10 percent (9.17 percent to be more precise). The actual yield on this investment over its lifetime (i.e., the realized yield to maturity) exceeds the anticipated 8 percent. Thus the investor who purchased the bond anticipating a yield to maturity of 8 percent actually earns more. Even though interest rates rose, which caused the market value of the bond to fall, the return over the lifetime of the bond exceeds the expected yield to maturity.

Case 3: All Interest Payments Are Reinvested at 5 Percent

In this case the terminal value of the interest payments will be $80 times the interest factor for the future value of an annuity of $1 at 5 percent for ten years. The future value of this annuity is

$$\$80(12.578) = \$1,006.24$$

This sum of this amount and the $1,000 principal received at maturity is $2,006.24.

What is the return on this investment that initially cost $1,000 and has grown into $2,006.24? The answer is

$$\$1,000(\text{interest factor for 10 years at } X \text{ percent}) = \$2,006.24.$$

$$\$1,000X = \$2,006.24$$

$$X = 2.006$$

An interest factor of 2.006 indicates that $1,000 grows to $2,006 in ten years at less than 8 percent (7.21 to be more precise). Even though interest rates fell and the price of the bond initially rose, the yield on the investment in this bond is only 7.21 percent. The actual return is less than the expected yield to maturity (i.e., the anticipated 8 percent).

These three illustrations are compared in Figure 15.6, which shows the initial $1,000 and the terminal values achieved through the investment of the interest at the different reinvestment rates. Lines *OA*, *OB*, and *OC* represent the growth in each investment at 12 percent, 8 percent, and 5 percent, respectively. The terminal values, $2,403.92, $2,158.96, and $2,006.24, generated through the reinvestment of interest income, are shown on the right-hand side of the figure. Of course, the highest terminal value and consequently the highest realized return occurs at the highest reinvestment rate.

Actually there is little reason to expect the investor will earn the anticipated yield to maturity. To obtain that yield, interest rates must remain unchanged and the bond must be held to maturity. The probability of these conditions being met is very small. Interest rates change virtually every day, and few bonds remain outstanding to

Figure 15.6 ◆ TERMINAL VALUES AT DIFFERENT REINVESTMENT RATES

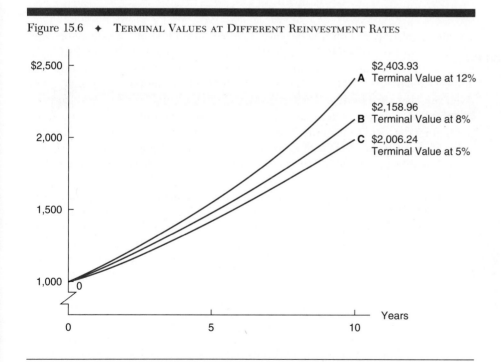

maturity. Most bonds are retired through sinking funds or are called. In either case only a few bonds of the initial issue may remain outstanding at maturity.

Since many bonds are retired prior to maturity, the investor may seek to purchase only those bonds that are noncallable. Some bonds have this feature written into their indentures. They cannot be retired prior to maturity in which case there is no uncertainty concerning when these bonds will be redeemed. Since this uncertainty has been erased, such bonds tend to sell for lower yields. Thus the investor purchases the certainty of when the bond will be retired by forgoing some interest income.

Even if the investor acquires noncallable bonds, there is still the uncertainty associated with changes in interest rates. Thus the realized yield over the lifetime of these noncallable bonds may not equal the yield to maturity that was anticipated when the bonds were purchased. A noncallable feature may reduce one source of risk but cannot erase all the possible sources of risk associated with investing in bonds.

There is only one type of bond that erases both the uncertainty of when the bond will be retired and the reinvestment rate. That bond is the noncallable, zero coupon bond. The entire yield occurs at maturity, and the discounted price considers the compounding of the implicit interest. These bonds offer actual yields to maturity that are equal to the expected yields. As long as the issuer does not default (i.e., repays the principal on the maturity date), the yield to maturity will be the realized return.

DURATION

The price volatility of bonds with equal coupons and different terms may be compared on the basis of time. For a given risk class, the price of the bond with the longer term to maturity should be more volatile. Bonds with equal maturities but different coupons may be compared on the basis of the interest payments. For a given risk class, the price of the bond with the smaller coupon will tend to be more volatile. Bonds, however, may have different coupons and different maturity dates. Computing the yield to maturity is one method for comparing bonds. However, the yields to maturity on bonds with different maturities and different coupons may not be comparable, and the yield to maturity does not indicate which bonds' prices tend to be more volatile.

The previous discussion also indicated that the actual return the investor earns over a bond's lifetime will not equal the yield to maturity if the reinvestment rate differs from the yield to maturity. An alternative calculation that may be used to compare bonds with different coupons and different terms to maturity has been developed. This technique is called the bond's **duration** and seeks to compare bonds with different coupons and different maturity dates by determining each bond's price sensitivity to changes in interest rates.

duration
The average time it takes to collect a bond's interest and principal repayment.

Duration is defined as the average time it takes the bondholder to receive the interest and the principal. It is a weighted average that encompasses the total amount of the bond's payments and their timing, then standardizes for the bond's price. To illustrate how duration is determined, consider a $1,000 bond with three years to maturity and a 9 percent coupon. The annual payments are as follows:

Year	Payment
1	$90
2	90
3	1,090

Currently the rate of interest on comparable bonds is 12 percent, so this bond's price is $928.18. The bond's duration is the sum of the present value of each payment weighted by the time period in which the payment is received, with the resulting quantity divided by the price of the bond.[4] Thus, for this bond, the duration is determined as follows:

Number of payments		Amount of payment		Present value interest factor at 12%		
1	×	$90	×	0.893	=	80.37
2	×	90	×	0.797	=	143.46
3	×	1,090	×	0.712	=	2,328.24
						2,552.07

$$\text{Duration} = \frac{2{,}552.07}{928.18} = 2.75 \text{ years.}$$

A duration of 2.75 years means that the bondholder collects, on the average, all the payments in 2.75 years. Obviously all the payments are not made exactly at 2.75 years into the future. Ninety dollars is received at the end of year one; $90 is received at the end of year two; and $1090 is received at the end of year three. The weighted average of all these payments is 2.75 years.

The above calculation of duration can be tedious. An alternative method simplifies the problem:[5]

$$\text{Duration} = \frac{1+y}{y} - \frac{(1+y) + n(c-y)}{c\left[(1+y)^n - 1\right] + y} \tag{15.6}$$

While this equation is formidable looking, its application is relatively easy. The symbols are

c = the annual coupon (as a percentage)

n = the number of years to maturity

y = the yield to maturity.

---

[4]While the interest factors in this example were derived from the tables in the appendix, they may be easily derived using an electronic calculator with a y^x key. For example, to determine the interest factor for year 3 at an interest rate of 12 percent, enter 1.12 and take the reciprocal (i.e., 1/1.12 = .893). Then use the y^x key to raise .893 to the third power (i.e., $.893^3 = .712$) to obtain the interest for factor.

[5]See Zvi Bodie, Alex Kane, and Alan J. Marcus, *Investments* (Homewood, Ill.: Irwin, 1989), 441–447.

Applying the numbers from the preceding illustration yields:

$$\text{Duration} = \frac{1 + .12}{.12} = \frac{(1 + .12) + 3(.09 - .12)}{.09[(1 + .12)^3 - 1] + .12}$$

$$= 2.75$$

which is the same answer (2.75) derived above.

By making this calculation for bonds with different coupons and different maturities, the investor standardizes for price fluctuations. Bonds with the same duration will experience similar price fluctuations, while the prices of bonds with a longer duration will fluctuate more. For example, consider the following two bonds. Bond A has a 10 percent coupon, matures in twenty years, and currently sells for $1,000. Bond B has a 7 percent coupon and matures after ten years with a current price of $815.66.[6] If interest rates rise, the price of both bonds will fall, but which bond's price will fall more? Since the bonds differ with regard to maturity date and coupon, the investor does not know which bond's price will be more volatile.

In general, the longer the term to maturity, the more volatile the bond's price. By that reasoning, Bond A will be more volatile. However, lower coupons are also associated with greater price volatility, and by that reasoning Bond B's price should be more volatile. Thus, the investor cannot tell on the basis of term and coupon which of these two bonds' prices will be more volatile. However, once their durations have been determined (9.36 and 7.22, respectively), the investor knows that the price of Bond A will decline more in response to an increase in interest rates. For example, if interest rates rose to 12 percent, the prices of the two bonds become $850.61 and $717.49, respectively. Bond A's price declined by 15 percent while Bond B's price fell by 12 percent, so Bond A's price was more volatile.

Since bonds with larger durations are more volatile, investors reduce the risk associated with changes in interest rates by acquiring bonds with shorter durations. This, however, is not synonymous with buying bonds with shorter maturities.[7] If two bonds have the same term to maturity, the bond with the smaller coupon will have the longer duration, since most of the bond's total payment is repayment of principal. If two bonds have the same coupon, the one with the longer maturity will have the longer duration, as the payments are spread over a longer period of time. However, if one bond has a smaller coupon and a shorter term, its duration could be either greater or smaller than the duration of a bond with a higher coupon and longer term to maturity. Thus, it is possible to buy a bond with a longer term to maturity that has a shorter duration. In such a case, the longer term bond will experience smaller price fluctuations than the bond with the shorter maturity but longer duration.

Duration is primarily used by professional portfolio managers, such as managers of pension plans, who know when the funds will be needed and what amount will be needed. These professional investors seek to match the duration of their port-

---

[6] In this illustration it is assumed that the bonds sell for the same yield to maturity. While generally the long-term bond should offer a higher yield, this assumption facilitates comparisons for a given change in interest rates.

[7] The only time when duration equals the term to maturity occurs when the bond makes no interest payments (i.e., it is a zero coupon bond). All the payments then occur at maturity.

folios with the timing of the need for funds. Such matching reduces the interest-rate risk associated with the portfolios. Consider an investor who needs $2,210 at the end of seven years and purchases at par a 12 percent coupon bond that matures at the end of seven years. If interest rates remain at 12 percent, the investor will have $2,211 because the coupons are reinvested at 12 percent. The terminal value is

$$\$1,000 + \$120(10.089) = \$2,211.$$

(The $1,000 is the repayment of the principal and the $120(10.089) is the future value of all the interest payments compounded annually at 12 percent.)

If interest rates rise and the investor reinvests at 14 percent, the terminal value is

$$1,000 + \$120(10.730) = \$2,288,$$

and the investor is even better off. A problem only arises when interest rates fall and the coupons are reinvested at a lower rate. For example, if interest rates decline to 8 percent, the terminal value is

$$\$1,000 + 120(8.923) = \$2,071,$$

and the investor does not have the required $2,210. The lower reinvestment of the interest payments resulted in an insufficient terminal value.

The investor could have avoided the shortage by acquiring a bond whose duration (and not its term) is equal to seven years. For example, if the investor purchases a bond with a 12 percent coupon that matures in twelve instead of seven years, that bond has a duration of 6.9 years which almost matches when the investor needs the $2,210. (The 12 percent seven-year bond has a duration of 5.1 years.) As will be subsequently illustrated, the purchase of the twelve-year bond instead of the seven-year bond eliminates the reinvestment risk.

Since the twelve-year bond will have to be sold at the end of seven years, the obvious question is, "At what price?" The price could rise (if interest rates fall) or decline (if interest rates rise). Must the investor be concerned with interest rate risk (i.e., the fluctuation in the bond's price), which would not apply if the bond matured at the end of seven years? The answer is, "No." The bond's price of course will change, but the impact of the price fluctuation is offset by the change in the reinvestment of the interest payments. The effect, then, of both reinvestment rate risk and interest rate risk is eliminated.

Suppose interest rates immediately rise to 14 percent after the investor buys the bond. The investor holds the bond for seven years and reinvests the interest payments at 14 percent. How much will the investor have at the end of seven years? The answer is the sum of the interest payment reinvested at 14 percent for seven years [$120(10.730) = $1,288] plus the sale price of the bond. Since the bond has five years to maturity, its price is

$$\$120(3.433) + 1,000(.519) = \$931.$$

Thus, the investor has 1,288 + 931 = $2,219, which meets the desired amount ($2,210). The loss on the sale of the bond is offset by the increased interest earned when the annual interest payments are reinvested at the higher rate.

Suppose interest rates immediately decline to 8 percent after the investor buys the bond. The investor holds the bond for seven years and reinvests the interest payments at 8 percent. How much will the investor have at the end of seven years? The answer in this case is the sum of the interest payment reinvested at 8 percent for seven years [$120(8.923) = $1,071] plus the sale price of the bond. Since the bond has five years to maturity, its price is

$$\$120(3.993) + 1,000(.681) = \$1,160.$$

Thus, the investor has $1,071 + 1,160 = $2,231, which once again meets the desired amount ($2,210). The gain on the sale of the bond offsets the reduction in interest earned when the interest payments are reinvested at the lower rate.

Notice that in both cases the individual achieves the investment goal of $2,210 at the end of seven years. Lower reinvestment income from a decline in interest rates is offset by the increase in the price of the bond, while higher reinvestment income from an increase in interest rates is offset by the decline in the price of the bond. Thus, the impact of reinvestment rate risk and interest rate risk is eliminated. Of course, the investor has lost the opportunity to earn a higher return, but the purpose of the strategy is to assure a particular amount in the future.

As the above discussion indicates, the concept of duration is exceedingly important for any investor who knows when funds will be needed and at what amount. For example, pension managers know both when payments must be made and their amount. Mortality tables help establish the same information for life insurance companies. Portfolio managers can use duration to reduce risk exposure and assure that the desired funds are available when needed. (These portfolio managers, of course, still have the risk of default or incorrect forecasts, such as changes in a mortality table.)

Individual investors will probably find duration less useful. For example, even if parents know when their children will attend college, they do not necessarily know the cost and hence the future value is unknown. In addition, the duration of each bond is not readily available and the value changes with each change in the bond's price. Thus, individual investors, who want to apply this concept, will have to perform the calculation themselves and frequently adjust their portfolios as the duration of each bond in the portfolio fluctuates.

MANAGEMENT OF BOND PORTFOLIOS

Since bonds pay a fixed income and mature at a specified date, they are conducive to passive management. The investor may acquire a portfolio of bonds and simply hold them to maturity (i.e., a buy and hold strategy). Each year the interest is received and at maturity the principal is repaid. During the interim, the value of the portfolio could rise (i.e., interest rates fall), or the value of the portfolio could fall (i.e., interest rates rise). Such fluctuations in the value of the portfolio may have little meaning to the investor who is passively holding the portfolio and collecting the interest until the bonds mature. Of course, if the individual had to sell the bonds for any reason, their prices would become crucial since the investor would only receive what the bonds are currently worth.

Bond Swapping

Today not all bondholders are passive investors. Instead they follow an active strategy by selling one type of bond and purchasing another. Since these investors are swapping one debt instrument for another, this type of strategy is often referred to as "bond swapping."[8] Such bond swaps may be used to alter bond holdings to save on taxes, increase yields, change the quality of the portfolio (e.g., reduce risk), or take advantage of any mispricings.

If an investor has bonds whose prices have declined for some reason (i.e., interest rates rose), the investor may sell the bonds for a loss in order to reduce capital gains taxes. The proceeds are then invested in bonds of similar quality and maturity. For example, the investor may sell bonds issued by one utility and acquire bonds issued by another comparable utility. Such a transaction is a "tax swap," and its benefit is the potential tax savings generated by the realized loss.

In a "substitution swap" the investor trades one bond for a different bond with virtually the same characteristics (i.e., same maturity, coupon, credit rating, and call and sinking funds) when their yields differ. If, for example, two virtually identical bonds had different yields, the investor would move out of the bond with the lower yield into the bond with the higher yield. A variation on this strategy is referred to as the "intermarket spread swap" in which the difference in yields between two markets seems excessive. If, for example, the difference between the yields on triple-A-rated bonds rises relative to the yield on federal government bonds, the investor may swap the government bonds for the corporate bonds. In both the substitution swap and the intermarket spread swap, the investor is seeking to take advantage of perceived mispricings of the two bonds.

Figure 14.3 illustrated that generally yields on longer-term bonds exceed yields on short-term debt obligations. The investor may seek to increase interest income by selling short-term bonds and purchasing long-term bonds. Such a strategy is referred to as a "pure yield pickup swap" and is designed to take advantage of the higher yields associated with longer maturities.

All above strategies or swaps are illustrations of actively managed bond portfolios, but they are not concerned with the interest rate risk. "Rate anticipation swaps" seek to take advantage of or avoid the impact of expected changes in interest rates. If the investor anticipates higher rates, bonds with longer terms to maturity are swapped for short-term bonds. Anticipation of lower rates leads to swapping short-term debt obligations for long-term bonds.

Management of Interest Rate Risk

Since interest rates change daily, the value of a bond portfolio fluctuates daily. Of course, the investor could avoid these fluctuations by acquiring only short-term debt obligations. This strategy generates less income since shorter maturities generally

[8] For the development of bond swaps, see Sidney Homer and Martin Liebowitz, *Inside the Yield Book: New Tools for Bond Market Strategy* (Englewood Cliffs, N.J.: Prentice-Hall, 1972).

have lower yields than bonds with longer maturities. The opposite strategy of purchasing only very long-term bonds will increase income but also increases the risk associated with changes in interest rates.

The investor could construct a portfolio of bonds with maturities distributed over a period of time. Such a strategy is sometimes referred to as a "laddered" approach. For example, a $100,000 portfolio could acquire $10,000 worth of bonds that mature for each of the next ten years. If interest rates change, the prices of the bonds with the shorter terms (i.e., the bonds with one to five years to maturity) will fluctuate less than the prices of the bonds with the longer terms (i.e., years six through ten). Hence such a portfolio reduces the impact of changes in interest rates.

In addition to reducing the impact on the value of the portfolio from fluctuating interest rates, a laddered portfolio offers two important advantages. First, since the structure of yields is generally positive, the interest earned on the bonds will tend to be greater than would be earned on a portfolio of short-term debt instruments. (Correspondingly it would be smaller than the interest earned on a portfolio consisting solely of bonds with long terms to maturity.) Second, some of the bonds mature each year. If the individual needs the funds, they are available; if the individual does not need the funds, they may be reinvested. If the funds are reinvested each year in bonds with a ten-year maturity, the original structure of the portfolio is retained.

The primary disadvantage of such a portfolio is that if the investor anticipates a change in interest rates and wants to alter the portfolio, virtually all the bonds have to be liquidated. If the investor anticipates lower interest rates, then a portfolio consisting of only long maturities is desirable. All the bonds with short to intermediate terms would have to be sold and reinvested in bonds with long maturities. The opposite would occur if the individual anticipates higher rates. In that case, the individual wants only short-term securities, so all the bonds with intermediate to long terms would have to be sold.

This lack of flexibility and the need to change a large proportion of the portfolio if the investor seeks to take advantage of anticipated changes in interest rates has led to an entirely different strategy for management of a bond portfolio. In this strategy, which is sometimes referred to as a "dumbbell," the investor may initially acquire a portfolio consisting of very long- and very short-term maturities. If the individual has $100,000 to invest, $50,000 may be used to purchase bonds with short maturities (e.g., six months to a year) and $50,000 to purchase twenty-year bonds. If the investor then anticipates a change in interest rates, only half of the portfolio needs to be changed. Expectation of lower rates would imply selling the short-term bonds and investing the proceeds in the long terms. If the investor anticipates higher interest rates, he or she would do the opposite: sell the long terms and move into the short-term bonds.

A dumbbell strategy will reduce the impact of fluctuating interest rates if the investor anticipates correctly. It will magnify the impact if the investor is incorrect. A movement into long-term bonds just prior to an increase in interest rates could inflict a substantial loss on the value of the portfolio. The strategy also has a second major disadvantage: With the passage of time, the short-term bonds will mature, and the maturities of the long-term bonds will diminish. Thus this bond strategy requires active management, as the proceeds of the maturing bonds will have to be reinvested and some of the longer bonds may have to be sold and the proceeds invested in bonds with even longer maturities. Failure to take these steps means that the investor's cash position will increase and the term of the remaining bonds will decrease.

Matching Strategies

The dumbbell strategy is designed to facilitate swapping bonds of different terms to benefit from anticipated changes in interest rates. Other bond strategies may be designed to match the portfolio with the investor's need for the funds. Two of these strategies are called "immunization" and "dedication." An immunized portfolio seeks to match the duration of the portfolio with the duration of the investor's cash needs. As previously explained, the concept of duration facilitates comparisons of the price volatility of bonds with different coupons and maturity dates. The individual determines the time period over which he or she wants to lock in current yields. Then the individual constructs a portfolio of bonds with different maturities such that the duration of the portfolio is matched with the desired time period. This strategy will require the investor to monitor the portfolio and adjust it should the duration differ from the time when the funds will be needed.

A "dedicated" bond portfolio seeks to match the receipt of cash flows with the need for the funds. Thus interest payments and principal repayments are matched with the investor's anticipated payments. For example, a parent may construct a portfolio of zero coupon bonds, each of which matures when the child's tuition is due. While that is perhaps an exceptionally obvious example, the strategy would also apply to the trustees of a pension plan. In that case, the timing and amount of the payments to the retirees is known. The trustees then acquire bonds such that the interest payments and principal repayments match the required payments.

An individual retiree could seek to construct a similar portfolio with funds in an IRA account or funds received from a distribution from a pension plan or corporate savings plan. While the individual investor will not know exactly when the funds will be needed, he or she can estimate cash requirements. For example, suppose a retiree owns a house with no mortgage, a new car, and supplementary medical insurance. That individual may not know exactly how much each payment will be in the future, but he or she knows when property taxes and insurance payments are due. The retiree may also have an estimate of annual maintenance requirements for the house and the car and when the car would be replaced. Acquiring bonds that pay interest or mature at the same time these payments fall due should facilitate making the payments.

Interest rate risk is irrelevant for both immunized and dedicated bond portfolios. By matching the duration of the portfolio with the duration of the investor's liabilities or by timing the cash received with cash needs, the impact of fluctuations in interest rates is minimized. Such strategies are better than a simple buy and hold strategy because they seek to match the portfolio with the need for funds. Since a simple buy and hold does not consider when the funds will be needed, the investor will be subject to interest rate risk. The possibility exists that the funds will be needed during a period of higher interest rates in which case the investor will not realize the value of the initial investment.

Interest Rate Swaps

Interest rate swaps have emerged as one of the major innovations of the 1980s; they are, however, not to be confused with the swaps discussed above. Individual investors are not concerned with the market for interest rate swaps. Instead these swaps are a means by which financial institutions such as commercial banks or savings and loan institutions manage risk.

Many financial institutions have mismatched assets and liabilities. For example, a savings and loan's primary assets may be long-term mortgages while its primary liabilities are short to intermediate term (i.e., deposits and certificates of deposit). When interest rates rise, a savings and loan institution loses on two counts: the higher interest rate reduces the value of its assets and increases the interest it must pay to attract depositors. To reduce this risk, the savings and loan needs a flow of payments that will vary with changes in interest, so the savings and loan swaps the flow of fixed interest payments it will receive on the mortgages for a series of variable payments.

The swap is made with a corporation that has the need to make fixed payments. For example, suppose a utility has a large number of fixed coupon bonds outstanding. The utility agrees to make variable payments to the savings and loan in exchange for the fixed interest payments. Now the utility will have the funds coming in to make the interest payments. In effect the utility is substituting variable interest payments to the savings and loan for the fixed interest payments that it would have to make to its bondholders while the savings and loan substitutes the receipt of variable interest payments for fixed interest payments from the mortgages. The swap helps both firms better match their assets and liabilities.

The concept of interest rate swaps may also be applied to currency swaps. In either interest rate swaps or currency swaps the participants are primarily pension or corporate financial managers and are not individual investors. These swaps are an involved topic, and the interested reader may wish to pursue them independently.[9] They are briefly mentioned in this text so that the student will not confuse interest rate and currency swaps with the bond swaps discussed previously.

SUMMARY

The price of a bond depends on the interest paid, the maturity date, and the return offered by comparable bonds. If interest rates rise, the price of existing bonds falls. The opposite is also true—if interest rates fall, the price of existing bonds rises.

The current yield considers only the flow of interest income relative to the price of the bond. The yield to maturity considers the flow of interest income as well as any price change that may occur if the bond is held to maturity. The yield to call is similar to the yield to maturity, but it substitutes the call date and the call price for the maturity date and the principal.

Discounted bonds may be attractive to investors seeking current income, some capital appreciation, and the return of the principal at a specified date. Since most bonds mature, the investor knows exactly when the principal is to be received.

All bond prices fluctuate in response to changes in interest rates and changes in risk, but the prices of bonds with longer maturities or poorer credit ratings tend to fluctuate more. These bonds may sell for larger discounts or higher premiums

---

[9] For a discussion of various bond strategies and interest rate swaps, see Zvi Bodie, Alex Kane, and Alan J. Marcus, *Investments* (Homewood, Ill.: Irwin, 1989), 438–463, and John F. Marshall and Kenneth R. Kapner, *The Swaps Market,* 2d ed. (Miami, FL: Kolb Publishing Company, 1993).

than bonds with shorter maturities or better credit ratings. Such bonds may be attractive investments for individuals who seek higher returns and who are willing to bear additional risk.

Investors may determine bonds' duration to ascertain which bonds' prices will fluctuate more. Duration is a weighted average of all of the bond's interest and principal payments standardized by the bond's price. Bonds with smaller durations tend to have smaller price fluctuations in response to changes in interest rates.

The individual may passively or actively manage a bond portfolio. Passive strategies range from buy and hold to a laddered portfolio consisting of bonds with different maturity dates. Active strategies include swapping among different bonds to take advantage of mispricings, expected changes in interest rates, and tax losses and to match the need for funds and the receipt of interest payments and principal repayments.

Summary of Bond Equations

Perpetual Bond

$$PV = \frac{I}{i}. \qquad (15.1)$$

Finite Maturity—Annual Compounding

$$P_B = \frac{I_1}{(1+i)^1} + \frac{I_2}{(1+i)^2} + \cdots + \frac{I_n}{(1+i)^n} + \frac{P}{(1+i)^n}. \qquad (15.2)$$

Finite Maturity—Semiannual Compounding

$$P_B = \frac{\dfrac{I}{2}}{\left(1+\dfrac{i}{2}\right)^1} + \frac{\dfrac{I}{2}}{\left(1+\dfrac{i}{2}\right)^2} + \cdots + \frac{\dfrac{I}{2}}{\left(1+\dfrac{i}{2}\right)^{n\times2}} + \frac{P}{\left(1+\dfrac{i}{2}\right)^{n\times2}}. \qquad (15.3)$$

Current Yield

$$\text{Current yield} = \frac{\text{Annual interest payment}}{\text{Price of the bond}}. \qquad (15.4)$$

Approximate Yield to Maturity

$$i = \frac{I + \dfrac{\$1,000 - P_B}{n}}{\dfrac{\$1,000 + P_B}{2}}. \qquad (15.5)$$

Duration

$$\text{Duration} = \frac{1+y}{y} - \frac{(1+y) + n(c-y)}{c[(1+y)^n - 1] + y}. \qquad (15.6)$$

Terms to Remember

perpetual bond   current yield
fixed flow of income   yield to maturity
discount   yield to call
premium   duration

Questions

1. What causes bond prices to fluctuate?
2. Define the current yield and the yield to maturity. How are they different?
3. When is the yield to maturity greater than the current yield?
4. What advantages do discounted bonds offer to investors?
5. Why may a bond be called if it is selling at a premium?
6. Although all bond prices fluctuate, the price of which bonds tends to fluctuate more?
7. What is the yield to call? How does it differ from the yield to maturity?
8. What differentiates the term of a bond and its duration? If bond A has a 10 percent coupon while bond B has a 5 percent coupon and they both mature after 10 years, which bond has the shorter duration?
9. Why is a dumbbell strategy more flexible than a laddered strategy if an investor anticipates a decline in interest rates?
10. If interest rates rise, bond prices will fall. Given the following pairs of bonds, indicate which bond's price will experience the greater price decline.
    a. Bond A   coupon: 10%
                 maturity: 5 years
        Bond B   coupon: 6%
                 maturity: 5 years
    b. Bond A   coupon: 10%
                 maturity: 7 years
        Bond B   coupon: 10%
                 maturity: 15 years
    c. Bond A   coupon: 10%
                 maturity: 5 years
        Bond B   coupon: 6%
                 maturity: 8 years
    d. Bond A   coupon: 10%
                 maturity: 1 year
        Bond B   coupon: zero percent
                 maturity: 10 years

Problems

1. A $1,000 bond has the following features: a coupon rate of 8 percent, interest that is paid semiannually (i.e., $40 every six months), and a maturity date of ten years.
   a. What is the bond's price if comparable debt yields 8 percent?
   b. What is the bond's price if comparable debt yields 10 percent?

   c. What is the current yield if the bond sells for the prices determined in Questions a and b?

   d. Why are the prices different for Questions a and b?

2. A $1,000 bond has a coupon rate of 10 percent and matures after eight years. Interest rates are currently 7 percent.

   a. What will the price of this bond be if the interest is paid annually?

   b. What will the price be if investors expect that the bond will be called with no call penalty after two years?

   c. What will the price be if investors expect that the bond will be called after two years and there will be a call penalty of one year's interest?

   d. Why are your answers different for the Questions a, b, and c?

3. A company has two bonds outstanding. The first matures after five years and has a coupon rate of 8.25 percent. The second matures after ten years and has a coupon rate of 8.25 percent. Interest rates are currently 10 percent. What is the present price of each bond? Why are these prices different?

4. If a bond with a 9 percent coupon (paid annually) and a maturity date of ten years is selling for $939, what is the current yield and the yield to maturity? (Hint: Try 8 percent or 12 percent and assume the interest payment is made annually.)

5. A zero coupon bond sells for $519 and matures after five years. What is the yield to maturity? (Consult the previous chapter for the discussion of zero coupon bonds, if necessary.)

6. You are offered a $1,000 bond for $850. It pays $75 in interest annually and matures after 12 years. Currently interest rates are 10 percent. Is this bond a good buy?

7. Given the following information:

     XY Inc. 5% bond
     AB Inc. 14% bond
     Both bonds are for $1,000, mature in 20 years, and are rated AAA.

   a. What should be the current market price of each bond if the interest rate on triple A bonds is 10 percent?

   b. Which bond has a current yield that exceeds its yield to maturity?

   c. Which bond would you expect to be called if interest rates are 10 percent?

   d. If CD Inc. had a bond outstanding with a 5 percent coupon and a maturity date of 20 years but it was rated BBB, what would you expect its price to be relative to the XY Inc. bond?

8. Company X has the following bonds outstanding:

Bond A	
Coupon	8%
Maturity	10 years

Bond B	
Coupon	Variable—changes annually
Maturity	10 years

Initially, both bonds sold at $1,000 with yields to maturity of 8 percent.

a. After two years, the interest rate on comparable debt is 10 percent. What should be the price of each bond?

b. After two additional years (i.e., four years after issue date), the interest rate on comparable debt is 7 percent. What should be the price of each bond?

c. What generalization may be drawn from the prices in Questions a and b?

9. A bond has the following features:

principal amount	$1,000
interest rate (the coupon)	11.5%
maturity date	10 years
sinking fund	none
call feature	after two years
call penalty	one year's interest

a. If comparable yields are 12 percent, what should be the price of this bond?

b. Would you expect the firm to call the bond if yields are 12 percent?

c. If comparable yields are 8 percent, what should be the price of the bond?

d. Would the firm call the bond today if yields are 8 percent?

e. If you expected the bond to be called after three years, what is the maximum price you would pay for the bond if the current interest rate is 8 percent?

10. You purchase a 7 percent coupon bond with a term of ten years and reinvest all interest payments. If interest rates rise to 10 percent after you purchase the bond, what is the return on your investment in the bond?

11. The prices of longer term bonds are more volatile than the prices of shorter term bonds with the same coupon. The prices of bonds with smaller coupons are more volatile than bonds with larger coupons for the same term to maturity. However, you cannot compare the relative price changes on bonds with different coupons and maturities unless you consider their durations. Consider the following bonds:

Bond	Coupon (c)	Term (n)
A	8%	8 years
B	14%	10 years

The price of which bond will fall more if interest rates rise from the current yield to maturity of 8 percent? To answer the question, calculate the duration of both bonds.

12. a. What is the price of each of the following bonds ($1,000 principal) if the current interest rate is 9%?

✦ Firm A   coupon 6%
            maturity date 5 years

✦ Firm B   coupon 6%
            maturity date 20 years

✦ Firm C   coupon 15%
            maturity date 5 years

◆ Firm D   coupon 15%
maturity date 20 years
◆ Firm E   coupon 0% (zero coupon bond)
maturity date 5 years
◆ Firm F   coupon 0% (zero coupon bond)
maturity date 10 years

b. What is the duration of each bond?
c. If interest rates rise to 12%, rank the bonds in terms of price fluctuations with the least volatile bond first and the most volatile bond last as judged by each bond's duration.
d. Confirm your volatility rankings by determining the percentage change in the price of each bond.
e. What generalizations can be made from the above exercise concerning (a) low- versus high-coupon bonds, (b) intermediate- versus long-term bonds, and (c) zero coupon bonds?

Suggested Readings

Most of this chapter is devoted to changes in bond prices caused by interest rate fluctuations. Controlling the impact of these fluctuations (called "immunization") has become a major consideration of professional money managers. For discussion of techniques to reduce the sensitivity of a portfolio's value to changes in interest rates and other bond strategies, see:

Bodie, Zvi, Alex Kane, and Alan J. Marcus. *Investments*. Homewood, Ill.: Irwin, 1989, Chapter 16.
Radcliffe, Robert C. *Investment Concepts, Analysis, and Strategy*. 3d ed. Glenview, Ill.: Scott, Foresman, 1990, 398–436.
Kaufman, George G., G.O. Bierwag, and Alden Toevs. *Innovations in Bond Portfolio Management*. Greenwich, Conn.: JAI Press, 1983.

For material on duration, see:
Edwards, Bob. "Bond Analysis: The Concept of Duration," *IIAA Journal* (March 1984): 33–37.

16

PREFERRED STOCK AND HIGH-YIELD SECURITIES

An alternative to investing in long-term debt is preferred stock. Legally, preferred stock represents ownership in a corporation; it is not debt and appears on the balance sheet under equity. As the name implies, it is senior to common stock, as preferred stockholders are paid dividends before common stockholders. In case of liquidation, preferred stock is redeemed before the common stockholders receive any proceeds from the sale of the firm's assets. While there is no legal obligation on the part of the firm to pay a dividend to preferred stockholders, it is generally understood that if the firm has sufficient funds, it will pay the preferred dividends.

Preferred stock is similar to debt in that it pays a fixed dividend just as bonds pay a fixed amount of interest. Thus preferred stock is a hybrid type of security that combines some elements of debt and some of equity. While it is legally equity, the fact that it pays a fixed dividend means that investors should analyze preferred stock as if it were debt.

Some firms have issued preferred stock and debt obligations that are less than investment grade. These high-yield securities or "junk bonds" offer investors large potential returns for bearing substantial risk. The chapter ends with a discussion of high-yield securities. The section covers features such as interest and dividends paid in additional securities in lieu of cash, split-coupon bonds, coupons that may fluctuate, and maturity dates that may be extended. The discussion also covers the returns that have been earned compared to the promised yields. Prior to 1989, the realized returns exceeded the yields on investments in federal government securities and investment grade corporate debt. However, the recession of the early 1990s caused many firms to default, inflicting large losses on investors who held high-yield securities.

◆ ◆ ◆

THE FEATURES OF PREFERRED STOCK

Preferred stock is an equity instrument that usually pays a fixed dividend that is not guaranteed but receives preference over common stock dividends. While most firms have only one issue of common stock, they may have several issues of preferred stock.[1] As may be seen in Exhibit 16.1, Virginia Electric and Power has 21 issues of preferred stock. In 17 cases the dividend is fixed. Thus for the series $8.60 preferred, the annual dividend is $8.60, which is distributed at the rate of $2.15 per quarter. In the four remaining preferred stocks, the dividend is reset every 49 days with changes in money market rates.

The dividend is expressed either as a dollar amount or as a percentage based on the preferred stock's par value. The par value is the stated value of the shares and is also the price at which the shares were initially sold. In the case of the Virginia and Electric $8.60 preferred, the par value is $100 so the dividend rate is 8.6 percent based on the par value.

Preferred stock dividends are paid from the firm's earnings. If the firm does not have the earnings, it may not declare and pay the preferred stock dividends. If the firm should omit the preferred stock's dividend, the dividend is said to be *in arrears*. The firm does not have to remove this **arrearage.** In most cases, however, any omitted dividends have to be paid in the future before dividends may be paid to the holders of the common stock. Such cases in which the preferred stock's dividends accumulate are called **cumulative preferred.** Most preferred stock is cumulative, but there are examples of **noncumulative preferred stocks** whose dividends do not have to be made up if missed (e.g., the Sierra Capital Realty 7 percent preferred stock is noncumulative). For investors holding preferred stock in firms having financial difficulty, the difference between cumulative and noncumulative may be immaterial. Forcing the firm to pay dividends to erase the arrearage may further weaken it and hurt the owners of the preferred stock more than would forgoing the dividends. Once the firm has regained its profitability, erasing the arrearage may become important not only to holders of the stock but also to the company, as a demonstration of its improved financial condition.

Chrysler Corporation provides an example of a firm clearing the arrearage on its preferred stock. In December 1979, Chrysler suspended payments on its $2.75 preferred stock. The dividends accumulated for four years, by which time the arrearage had reached $11 per share. In December 1983, Chrysler paid sufficient dividends to the preferred stockholders to erase the arrearage, and less than a year later (October 31, 1984) it redeemed each share of the preferred stock.

Once the preferred stock is issued, the firm may never have to concern itself with its retirement: It is perpetual. This may be both an advantage and a disadvantage. Since the firm may never have to retire the preferred stock, it does not have to generate the money to retire it but may instead use its funds elsewhere (e.g., to purchase plant and equipment). However, should the firm ever want to change its

preferred stock
A class of stock (i.e., equity) that has a prior claim to common stock on the firm's earnings and assets in case of liquidation.

arrearage
Cumulative preferred dividends that have not been paid.

cumulative preferred stock
A preferred stock whose dividends accumulate if they are not paid.

noncumulative preferred stock
Preferred stock whose dividends do not accumulate if the firm misses a dividend payment.

---

[1] Some corporations have also issued a "preference" stock which is subordinated to preferred stock but has preference over common stock with regard to the payment of dividends. Such stock is another level of preferred stock, and in this text no distinction is made between the two.

Exhibit 16.1 ✦ The Preferred Stocks of Virginia Electric and Power

Preferred Stock Not Subject
to Mandatory Retirement

Annual Dividend per Share		Outstanding Shares
	$4.04	12,926
	4.20	14,797
	4.12	32,534
	4.80	73,206
	5.00	106,677
	7.72	350,000
	7.45	400,000
	7.20	450,000
	7.72	500,000
1987-1	Money market preferred	500,000
1987-2	Money market preferred	750,000
1988	Money market preferred	750,000
1989	Money market preferred	750,000

Preferred Stock Subject to Mandatory
Retirement

Annual Dividend per Share	Outstanding Shares 12/31/81	12/31/91
$7.30	—	500,000
7.325	—	428,419
8.925	280,000	164,500
8.60	**347,000**	**228,764**
8.625	370,000	203,500
8.20	600,000	330,000
7.58	700,000	600,000
8.40	800,000	512,000

Source: 1982 and 1991 Annual Reports.

capital structure and substitute debt financing for the preferred stock, it may have difficulty retiring the preferred stock. The firm may have to purchase the stock on the open market, and, to induce the holders to sell the preferred shares, the firm will probably have to bid up the preferred stock's price.

To maintain some control over the preferred stock, the firm may seek to add a call feature to the preferred issue. This feature gives the firm the option to call and redeem the issue. Such a call is illustrated in Exhibit 16.2, in which Delmarva Power & Light is redeeming an issue of preferred stock. (Such calls were common in the late 1980s after the period of high interest rates in the early 1980s.) While the actual terms of the call feature will vary with each preferred stock issue, the general fea-

Exhibit 16.2 ✦ REDEMPTION OF AN ISSUE OF PREFERRED STOCK

NOTICE OF REDEMPTION
OF
ALL OUTSTANDING SHARES OF
12.56% PREFERRED STOCK
OF
DELMARVA POWER & LIGHT COMPANY

The issue

The company

Notice is hereby given that Delmarva Power & Light Company (the "Company") has called for redemption and will redeem on December 31, 1985 (the "Redemption Date") all outstanding shares of its 12.56% Preferred Stock (the "12.56% Stock"), for the redemption price of $108.38 per share (the "Regular Redemption Price"). Dividends will be paid directly by the Company on December 31, 1985 to stockholders of record on December 10, 1985, and the redemption price will thus not include any dividends. The Company intends to deposit in trust with the Redemption Agent on or before December 31, 1985 moneys sufficient in amount to pay the aggregate Regular Redemption Price of the shares of 12.56% stock to be redeemed. Pursuant to the terms of the Certificate of Incorporation, all rights of the holds of shares of 12.56% stock to be redeemed, as stockholders of the Company, shall thereupon cease and terminate, excepting only the right to receive the Regular Redemption Price upon surrender of the certificates for the 12.56% Stock.

The call price

The rights of stockholder cease

Payment of the Regular Redemption Price will be made on or after the Redemption Date upon surrender of the 12.56% Stock certificates, accompanied by a properly completed and executed Letter of Transmittal, to Manufacturers Hanover Trust Company (the "Redemption Agent") at either of the addresses listed below.

By Mail:

Manufacturers Hanover Trust Company
Reorganization Department
P.O. Box 3083, G.P.O. Station
New York, New York 10116

By Hand:

Manufacturers Hanover Trust Company
Securities Window
130 John Street, Street Level
New York, New York 10038

This redemption is being made pursuant to the Certificates of Incorporation under which the Company has elected to call 12.56% Stock for redemption

DELMARVA POWER & LIGHT COMPANY
Roger D. Campbell
Vice President, Treasurer & CFO

November 27, 1985

Source: Reprinted with permission of the Delmarva Power & Light Company.

tures are similar. First, the call is at the option of the firm. Second, the call price is specified. Third, the firm may pay a call penalty (e.g., a year's dividends). Fourth, after the issue is called, future dividend payments will cease; this, of course, forces any recalcitrant holders to surrender their certificates.

Some preferred stocks also have mandatory sinking funds requiring that the firm periodically retire some of the issue. For example, the $8.60 preferred stock in Exhibit 16.1 has a mandatory sinking fund that started in 1985. It requires Virginia Electric and Power to redeem annually 4 percent of the shares originally issued at $100 per share. Thus, by 2010 all the shares will have been retired. Such issues of preferred stock with mandatory sinking funds are very similar to bonds, which also are not perpetual and must be retired.[2]

---

[2]In 1979 a change in how property and casualty insurance companies account for investments in preferred stock shifted their preference for sinking fund preferred stock vis-a-vis perpetual preferred stock. Utilities, which are the primary issuers of preferred stock, responded to this change by starting to issue preferred stock with mandatory retirement features (sinking funds). See M.J.C. Roth, "New Look at Preferred Stock Financing," *Public Utilities Fortnightly* (March 27, 1980): 26–28.

THE VALUATION OF PREFERRED STOCK

The process of valuing (pricing) preferred stock is essentially the same as that used to price debt. The future payments are brought back to the present at the appropriate discount rate. If the preferred stock does not have a required sinking fund or call feature, it may be viewed as a perpetual debt instrument. The fixed dividend (D) will continue indefinitely. These dividends must be discounted by the yield being earned on newly issued preferred stock (k). This process for determining the present value of the preferred stock (P) is given in Equation 16.1:

$$P = \frac{D}{(1 + k)^1} + \frac{D}{(1 + k)^2} + \frac{D}{(1 + k)^3} + \cdots. \tag{16.1}$$

As in the case of the perpetual bond, this equation is reduced to

$$P = \frac{D}{k}. \tag{16.2}$$

Thus, if a preferred stock pays an annual dividend of $4 and the appropriate discount rate is 12 percent, the present value of the preferred stock is

$$P = \frac{\$4}{(1 + 0.12)^1} + \frac{\$4}{(1 + 0.12)^2} + \frac{\$4}{(1 + 0.12)^3} \cdots$$

$$= \frac{\$4}{0.12} = \$33.33.$$

If an investor buys this preferred stock for $33.33, he or she can expect to earn 12 percent ($33.33 × 0.12 = $4) on the investment. Of course, the realized rate of return on the investment will not be known until the investor sells the stock and adjusts this 12 percent return for any capital gain or loss. However, at the current price, the preferred stock is selling for a 12 percent dividend yield.

If the preferred stock has a finite life, this fact must be considered in determining its value. As with the valuation of long-term debt, the amount that is repaid when the preferred stock is retired must be discounted back to the present value. Thus, when preferred stock has a finite life, the valuation equation becomes

$$P = \frac{D}{(1 + k)^1} + \frac{D}{(1 + k)^2} + \cdots + \frac{D}{(1 + k)^n} + \frac{S}{(1 + k)^n}, \tag{16.3}$$

where S represents the amount that is returned to the stockholder when the preferred stock is retired after n number of years. If the preferred stock in the previous example is retired after 20 years for $100 per share, its current value would be

$$P = \frac{\$4}{(1 + 0.12)^1} + \cdots + \frac{\$4}{(1 + 0.12)^{20}} + \frac{\$100}{(1 + 0.12)^{20}}$$

$$= \$4(7.470) + \$100(0.104)$$

$$= \$40.28,$$

where 7.470 is the interest factor for the present value of an annuity of $1 for 20 years at 12 percent and 0.104 is the present value of $1 to be received after 20 years when yields are 12 percent. Instead of selling the stock for $33.33, the nonperpetual preferred stock would sell for $40.28. The yield is still 12 percent, but the return in this case consists of a current dividend yield of 9.93 percent ($4 ÷ $40.28) and a capital gain as the price of the stock rises from $40.28 to $100 when it is retired 20 years hence.

PREFERRED STOCK AND BONDS CONTRASTED

Since preferred stock pays a fixed dividend, it is purchased primarily by investors seeking a fixed flow of income, and it is analyzed and valued like any other fixed-income security (i.e., long-term bonds). But preferred stock differs from long-term debt, as the subsequent discussion will demonstrate, and these differences are significant.

First, preferred stock is riskier than debt. The terms of a bond are legal obligations of the firm. If the corporation fails to pay the interest or meet any of the terms of the indenture, the bondholders may take the firm to court to force payment of the interest or to seek liquidation of the firm in order to protect their principal. Preferred stockholders do not have that power, for the firm is not legally obligated to pay the preferred stock dividends.

In addition, debt must be retired, while preferred stock is often perpetual. If the security is perpetual, the only means to recoup the amount invested is to sell the preferred stock in the secondary market. The investor cannot expect the firm to redeem the security. Market price fluctuations tend to be greater for preferred stock than for long-term bonds. Figure 15.3 (in Chapter 15) illustrated that price fluctuations for long-term bonds were greater than price fluctuations experienced by short-term debt. This principle holds when comparing long-term bonds and preferred stock. The price of a perpetual preferred stock will fluctuate more than the price of a long-term bond that has a finite life.

This generalization is illustrated in Figure 16.1, which presents the dividend yield, the current yield, and the prices of a Virginia Electric and Power (VEPCO) bond and preferred stock. The bond is the 7.5 percent bond due in 2001, and the stock is the 7.45 percent cumulative preferred. As may be seen in the graph, there is an inverse relationship between the yields and the prices of both the preferred stock and the bond. However, since the bond has a finite life (i.e., it matures in 2001), its price tends to be less volatile. For example, during 1987, the price of the preferred stock fell from $91⅝ to $77 while the price of the bond fell from $87⅜ to $81⅝.

Figure 16.1 also demonstrates that although the yield on the bond and the stock move together, the differential between the two current yields is relatively small. While the differential was 2.0 percent in 1979, there was virtually no difference in the current yields in 1992. This similarity in yields is surprising since from the investor's viewpoint, the bond is less risky than the preferred stock. Presumably the riskier security should offer a higher return.

This small differential between the yields on bonds and preferred stock may be explained by the corporate income tax laws. Dividends paid by one corporation to another receive favorable tax treatment. Only 30 percent of the dividends are taxed

Figure 16.1   ✦   YEAR END PRICES AND YIELDS ON A VEPCO BOND AND A PREFERRED STOCK

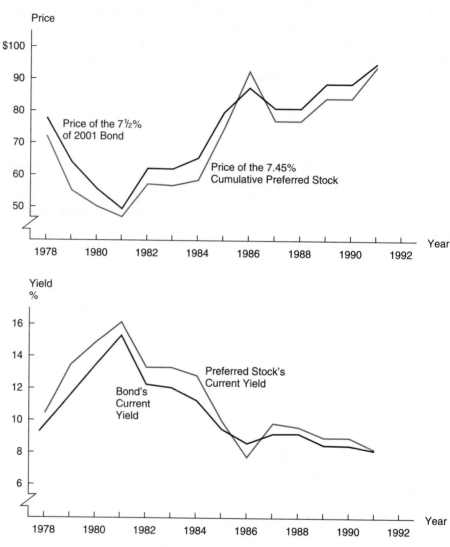

as income of the corporation receiving them. Thus, for a firm such as an insurance company in the 34 percent corporate income tax bracket, this shelter is very important. If the company receives $100 in interest, it nets only $66 as $34 is taxed away. However, if this company were to receive $100 in preferred stock dividends, only $30 would be subject to federal income tax. Thus the firm pays only $10.20 ($30 × 0.34) in taxes and gets to keep the remaining $89.80 of the dividends.

For this reason, a corporation may choose to purchase preferred stocks instead of long-term bonds. This preference drives up the price of preferred stocks, which reduces their yields. Since individual investors do not enjoy the tax break, they may prefer bonds, which offer yields comparable to preferred stock but are less risky.

To induce investors to purchase preferred stock, the firm often offers other features, such as the convertibility of the preferred stock into common stock.

A second important difference between debt and preferred stock (at least from the viewpoint of the firm) is that the interest on debt is a tax-deductible expense while the dividend on preferred stock is not. Preferred dividends are paid out of earnings. This difference in the tax treatment of interest expense and preferred stock dividends affects the earnings available to the firm's common stockholders. Using debt instead of preferred stock as a source of funds will result in higher earnings per common share.

Consider a firm with operating income (earnings before interest and taxes) of $1,000,000. The firm has 100,000 common shares outstanding and is in the 40 percent corporate income tax bracket. If the firm issues $2,000,000 of debt with a 10 percent rate of interest, its earnings per common share are

Earnings before interest and taxes	$1,000,000
Interest	200,000
Earnings before taxes	800,000
Taxes	320,000
Net income	$480,000
Earnings per common share: $480,000/100,000 =	$4.80

If the firm had issued $2,000,000 in preferred stock that also paid 10 percent, the earnings per common share would be

Earnings before interest and taxes	$1,000,000
Interest	00
Earnings before taxes	1,000,000
Taxes	400,000
Earnings before preferred stock dividends	600,000
Preferred stock dividends	200,000
Earnings available to common stock	$400,000
Earnings per common share: $400,000/100,000 =	$4.00

The use of preferred stock has resulted in lower earnings per common share. This reduction in earnings is the result of the different tax treatment of interest, which is a tax-deductible expense, and preferred stock dividends, which are not deductible.

ANALYSIS OF PREFERRED STOCK

Since preferred stock is similar to debt, the tools used to analyze it are similar as well. Because preferred stock is an income-producing investment, the analysis is primarily concerned with the capacity of the firm to meet the dividend payments. Although dividends must ultimately be related to current earnings and the firm's future earning capacity, preferred dividends are paid from cash. Even if the firm is temporarily running a deficit (i.e., experiencing an accounting loss), it may still be able to pay dividends to the preferred stockholders if it has sufficient cash. In fact, cash dividends might be paid despite the deficit to indicate that the losses are expected to be temporary and that the firm is financially strong.

An analysis of the firm's financial statements (such as the ratios used to analyze common stock in Chapter 12) may reveal its liquidity position and profitability. The more liquid and profitable the firm, the safer the dividend payment should be. The investor may also analyze how well the firm covers its preferred dividend. This analysis is achieved by computing the **times-dividend-earned ratio,** which is

times-dividend-earned ratio
Earnings divided by preferred
dividend requirements.

$$\frac{\text{Earnings after taxes}}{\text{Dividends on preferred stock}}.$$

The larger this ratio, the safer the preferred stock's dividend should be. Notice that the numerator consists of *total* earnings. Although the preferred stock dividends are subtracted from the total earnings to derive the earnings available to the common stockholders, all of the firm's earnings are available to pay the preferred stock dividend.

A variation on this ratio is **earnings per preferred share.** This ratio is

earnings per preferred share
The total earnings divided by the
number of preferred shares
outstanding.

$$\frac{\text{Earnings after taxes}}{\text{Number of preferred shares outstanding}}.$$

The larger the earnings per preferred share, the safer the dividend payment. However, neither of these ratios indicates whether the firm has sufficient cash to pay the dividends. They can only indicate the extent to which earnings cover the dividend requirements of the preferred stock.

How each ratio is computed can be illustrated by the following simple example. A firm has earnings of $6 million before income taxes and is in the 40 percent tax bracket. It has 100,000 shares of preferred stock outstanding, and each share pays a dividend of $5. The times-dividend-earned ratio is

$$\frac{\$6,000,000 - \$2,400,000}{\$500,000} = 7.2,$$

and the earnings per preferred share are

$$\frac{\$6,000,000 - \$2,400,000}{100,000} = \$36.$$

Both ratios, in effect, show the same thing. In the first, the preferred dividend is covered by a multiple of 7.2:1. The second ratio shows an earnings per preferred share of $36, which is 7.2 times the $5 dividend paid for each share.

DISADVANTAGES OF PREFERRED STOCK

While most preferred stock offers the investor the advantage of a fixed flow of income, this may be more than offset by several disadvantages. Like any fixed-income security, preferred stock offers no protection from inflation. If the inflation rate were to increase, the real purchasing power of the dividend would be diminished. In addition, increased inflation would probably lead to higher interest rates, which would drive down the market value of the preferred stock. Thus, higher rates of inflation doubly curse preferred stock, as the purchasing power of the dividend and the market value of the stock both will be diminished. This disadvantage, of course, applies to all fixed-income securities.

Preferred stock also tends to be less marketable than other securities. Marketability of a particular preferred stock depends on the size of the issue. However, most preferred stock is bought by insurance companies and pension plans. The market for the remaining shares may be quite thin, so there can be a substantial spread between the bid and ask prices. While this may not be a disadvantage if the investor intends to hold the security, it will reduce the attractiveness of the preferred stock in cases in which marketability is desired.

Several other disadvantages were alluded to earlier in the chapter. The first of these is the inferior position of preferred stock to debt obligations. The investor must realize that preferred stock is perceptibly riskier than bonds. A second disadvantage is that the yields offered by preferred stock are probably insufficient to justify the additional risk. The yields on preferred stock are not necessarily higher than those available on bonds because of the tax advantage preferred stock offers corporate investors and pension managers. As was explained before, only 30 percent of the preferred dividends are subject to corporate income tax, and none of the dividends paid to pension plans are subject to tax. Unfortunately, individual investors are unable to take advantage of these tax breaks except as part of retirement plans. Thus, individual investors may earn inferior yields after adjusting for the risks associated with investing in a security inferior to the firm's bonds.

HIGH-YIELD SECURITIES

High-yield securities is a term used to describe corporate bonds and preferred stock that offer historically high yields. These are the so-called "junk bonds" that have been used to finance takeovers and expansion by firms needing funds but lacking investment grade credit. Generally triple B or better credit ratings are considered to be investment grade. The trust departments of some financial institutions are only allowed to purchase investment grade bonds. Anything with a lower credit rating is not an acceptable risk. Firms with inferior credit ratings have to find alternative sources of funds and issue high-yield securities to induce investors to buy the riskier bonds.

High-yield securities may be divided into two classes. First are the bonds that were initially investment grade, but were lowered as the issuing firms developed financial problems. This type of high-yield bond is often referred to as a **fallen angel.** When RJR Nabisco was purchased and taken private, the surviving firm issued substantial new debt that resulted in the downgrading of outstanding RJR Nabisco bonds. The prices of what were previously high-quality debt declined dramatically, and the issues became high-yield securities. Of course, the high yields were to be earned by new buyers and not by the original investors who suffered losses when the prices of the previously issued bonds declined.

high-yield security
Noninvestment grade security offering a high return.

fallen angel
Investment grade security whose quality has deteriorated.

Some fallen angels ultimately go bankrupt. Manville, Public Service of New Hampshire, and Texaco went bankrupt and defaulted on their debt. However, bonds in default continue to trade, and there is always the possibility that the firm will recover and the price of the bonds will rise. This did occur in the case of Texaco. One of the attractions of the high-yield security market is the possibility that the financial condition of the issuing firm will improve. A higher credit rating should be beneficial to the holders of the firm's debt, because the bonds' prices should increase as the firm's financial condition improves.

The second class of high-yield securities is composed of bonds and preferred stock issued by firms with less than investment grade credit ratings. The maturities of these securities can range from short term (i.e., high-yield commercial paper) to long term (i.e., bonds and preferred stock).

Pay-in-Kind (PIK) Securities

pay-in-kind (PIK) security
Bond or preferred stock whose interest or dividends are paid in additional debt or shares.

Pay-in-kind (PIK) securities are bonds and preferred stock whose interest and dividends may be paid in additional debt or shares. The choice to pay in paper instead of cash rests with the firm. In some cases the option is granted only for the initial years with payment in subsequent years to be made in cash. Since the investor may not receive dividends or interest in cash, PIK bonds and PIK preferred stock are among the riskiest of high-yield securities.

Many firms have issued PIK bonds and preferred stock as parts of leveraged buyouts (LBOs) or in recapitalizations designed to thwart hostile takeovers. How such securities may come into existence and their features can be illustrated by the Joy Technology PIK preferred stock. The company experienced a leveraged buyout in which 94 percent of the outstanding common stock was purchased. The remaining shares were exchanged for the PIK preferred stock. The preferred stock has a stated (i.e., par) value of $20 and pays an annual dividend of $3.25 (i.e., 16.25 percent). While the company may pay the dividend in cash, it has the option to pay the dividend in additional shares of preferred stock. If the annual dividend is distributed in stock instead of cash, the holder of one share receives an additional .1625 shares with a stated value of $20. This is equivalent to $3.25 since the new stock is valued at $20 per share.

The stated yields paid by PIK securities are high even by high-yield security standards. These yields are indicative of the large risk associated with PIK securities. The fact that the firm has the option to pay the interest or dividend in additional securities implies that the bonds and preferred stock are risky since the purpose of this option is to permit the firm to conserve its cash. However, paying the interest or dividend with additional securities has a positive long-term implication. The firm's liquidity position is not hurt by the distribution of the additional securities. Of course, issuing additional debt means that the firm will have to pay more interest and to retire more debt at maturity, but that is some time in the future when the firm's capacity to service the debt may be better.

Many of the PIK bonds and preferred stocks have mandatory sinking funds which require that the securities be retired over a period of time. Such retirements, however, will require the issuer either to generate sufficient cash or be able to refinance the securities. If the company makes the regular repayments on schedule, the potential total return to the investor is substantial, especially if the securities were purchased at a discount. Of course, such returns require the issuer to pay both the dividend or interest and retire the securities. However, if the firm cannot pay the interest and dividend in cash, it is reasonable to assume that the securities will not be redeemed.

While PIK securities may appeal to any investor seeking an extremely risky but very high-yield security, they have a major tax disadvantage. The payments, be they in cash or *in additional securities*, are subject to personal income taxation. The pay-in-kind dividend payments are not the same as stock dividends, which are nontaxable. Securities received by holders of PIK preferred stocks and bonds must pay federal income tax as if the payments had been received in cash.[3]

Split Coupon Bonds

Split coupon bonds combine the features of zero coupon and high coupon bonds. During the first three to five years, the bonds pay no interest. Instead the interest accrues like a zero coupon bond. After this initial period, the bond pays a coupon with a fixed rate. For example, in 1992, Dr. Pepper issued a split coupon bond that pays no interest for the first four years and then must pay a coupon of 11.5 percent until the bond matures in 2002.

split coupon bond
Bond with a low initial coupon followed by a period with a high coupon.

These bonds, which are also referred to as deferred interest bonds, initially sell at a discounted price that is calculated using the coupon rate in effect when the bond starts to pay cash. For the Dr. Pepper bond the flow of payments per $1,000 bond is

Interest:	
years 1–4	$0
years 5–10	$115
Principal Repayment at End of Year 10:	$1,000

The current price of the bond is the present value of these payments. If the yield on comparably risky securities is 15 percent, the price of the bond is

$115 (present value of an annuity for six years at 15 percent) (present value of one dollar for four years at 15 percent) + $1,000 (present value of one dollar at 15 percent for ten years)

= $115(3.785)(.572) + $1,000(.247)

= $496.

The price of a split coupon bond can be very volatile. Suppose the firm's financial condition and credit rating improved, so that the comparable yield is 12 percent.

---

[3] In 1990, Congress changed the tax laws so the interest on PIK bonds paid in additional debt instead of cash is not deductible for corporate income tax purposes. While firms are not excluded from issuing PIK bonds, the tax deduction for the interest no longer exists. This change in the tax regulations suggests that few, if any, new PIK bonds will be issued.

The bond's price would rise to

$$= \$115(4.111)(.636) + \$1,000(.322)$$

$$= \$623$$

for a 20.4 percent increase. Of course, the converse is also true. Higher yields cause the prices of split coupon bonds to decline dramatically.

The advantage to the firm issuing split coupon bonds is that debt service is eliminated during the initial period. As with PIK securities, split coupon bonds conserve cash. Thus these types of securities are often issued in leveraged buyouts and other recapitalizations that result in the firm issuing substantial amounts of debt. (The RJR Nabisco buyout resulted in the surviving firm issuing both PIK and split coupon bonds.)

Split coupon bonds like PIK securities tend to be very costly to the firm issuing them. The high yield to investors means high cost of funds to the issuers. There is an incentive for the firm to retire the securities as soon as possible. Thus most split coupon bond and PIK securities have call features that permit the firm to retire the securities prior to their maturity. For example, Safeway Stores called half of its issue of junior subordinated PIK debentures only eleven months after the bonds were originally issued.

Reset Securities and Increasing Rate Bonds

reset bond
Bond whose coupon is periodically reset.

While the coupons are fixed when most high-yield securities are issued, there are exceptions. With a **reset bond,** the coupon is adjusted at periodic intervals, such as six months or every year. The coupon is usually tagged to a specified rate, such as the six-month treasury bill rate plus 5 percent, and there is often a minimum and a maximum coupon. For example, the coupon of the American Shared Hospital Service reset note can range from 14 to 16.5 percent.

Since the coupon is permitted to change, price fluctuations associated with changes in interest rates are reduced. The minimum coupon, however, means that if interest rates fall on comparably risky securities, the price of the bond will rise since the coupon becomes fixed at the lower bound. And the same applies when interest rates rise. If the coupon reaches the upper limit, further increases in comparable yields will decrease the bond's price. However, within the specified range the changing coupon should stabilize the price of the bond. Of course, if the firm's financial condition changes, the price of the bond will change independently of changes in interest rates.

increasing rate bond
Bond whose coupon rises over time.

Increasing rate bonds are debt securities whose coupons increase over time. For example, in 1989, RJR Holdings issued $5 billion of increasing rate notes. One issue had an initial coupon of 14.5625 percent, but future coupons will be the higher of 13.4375 percent or 4 percent higher than the three-month LIBOR rate. Subsequent coupons will increase by .5 percent quarterly for two years and .25 percent quarterly for years three and four. Unless yields decline dramatically so that 13.4375 percent becomes the coupon, the yield on this bond will rise over time. Obviously, increasing rate securities are an expensive means for any firm to raise funds, so the investor can anticipate that the issuer will seek to retire the debt as rapidly as possible.

Extendible Securities

In the previous discussion, the high-yield securities had differing coupons but fixed maturity dates. PIK securities permit interest and dividends to be paid in additional securities. Split coupon bonds have periods during which interest accrues but is not paid. Reset and increasing rate notes and bonds have coupons that vary. Each of the types of high-yield securities has a fixed maturity date. However, firms may issue **extendible securities** in which the term to maturity may be lengthened by the issuer. For example, Mattel issued a bond with an initial maturity date in 1990, but the company may extend the bond for one-, two-, or three-year periods with a final maturity in 1999. Thus the investor who acquires this bond does not know if the bond will be outstanding for one year or six years or longer. Only the final maturity in 1999 is known.

extendible security
Bond whose maturity date may be extended into the future.

The ability to extend the maturity date is, of course, beneficial to the issuer. If the firm does not have the capacity to retire the debt at the initial maturity date, the date may be extended. This buys time for the firm to find the funds or to refinance the debt. The final date will ultimately come at which time the bonds must be retired. Failure to retire the debt at the final maturity, of course, throws the bond into default.

RETURNS EARNED BY INVESTORS IN HIGH-YIELD SECURITIES

The coupons on high-yield securities are promised or anticipated yields. In some cases the promised return will be the realized return if the firm makes timely payments and retires the securities on schedule. However, security markets and firms are dynamic entities. Change is always occurring, so the returns actually earned by investors will probably differ from the promised yields. The actual returns could be higher, especially if interest rates decline or the firm's financial condition improves. In either case, the price of the high-yield security should rise, so that the investor earns a higher return.

While earning higher returns is possible, the greater concern is usually that something will go wrong and that the investor will earn a lower return. Firms that issue high-yield securities are obviously not financially strong and some will not survive. If the investor is unfortunate enough to select those firms, he or she could lose a substantial amount of money—perhaps all of the funds invested. Avoiding such an outcome is obviously desirable and is the purpose of analyzing the issuer's financial condition and determining the quality of its debt.

Analysis of investment grade debt revolves around the firm's current and future capacity to service the debt. This analysis may start with such ratios as the debt ratio or times-interest-earned. However, for high-yield securities the emphasis is generally placed on cash flow (operating income plus noncash expenses such as depreciation) instead of total debt and earnings before interest and taxes. Many firms that issued high-yield securities used the funds to invest in plant and equipment. While they may currently be operating at a loss, noncash depreciation expense may generate sufficient cash flow to service the debt.[4]

Another important factor in considering the safety of a high-yield security is the issuing firm's position in its industry. Is its market share growing? Does it produce a unique product or have a niche in its market? Is the firm exposed to rapid technological change? Are its sales seasonal or cyclical? Many of the concerns an investor may have when selecting a common stock are applicable to the analysis of a high-yield security. Since high-yield securities are often subordinated to a firm's other liabilities, some financial analysts view them as a type of equity financing with bond covenants.

Spreads in Yields and Realized Returns Prior to 1990

The spread between the yields to maturity on high-yield and investment grade securities can be substantial. From 1982 to 1988, high-yield securities offered returns that exceeded the yields on treasury securities by 3.2 to 5.0 percent.[5] A spread of 5 percent means if the yield to maturity on treasury bonds is 9 percent, the yield to maturity on high-yield bonds is 14 percent. Such a large spread is, of course, the inducement to buy the riskier bonds.

The yield to maturity and the return actually earned are not necessarily the same. Studies of returns actually earned on portfolios of high-yield securities indicate that the returns exceeded the returns on investment grade bonds. One study found the annual return on the high-yield securities from 1977 through 1986 was 11.04 percent while investment grade bonds and federal government bonds earned 9.40 and 9.36 percent, respectively. Only common stock outperformed the high-yield bonds.[6] An alternate study for the period 1978 through 1986 found that high-yield securities returned 12.8 percent compared to 11.1 percent on long-term government securities, a spread of 1.7 percent.[7]

A spread of 1.7 percent seems small, especially since the average spread between the yields to maturity for high-yield securities and treasury bonds often exceeds 4 to 5 percent. It must be remembered that yields to maturity are returns investors except when the bonds are purchased and not necessarily the realized returns. The returns reported above are realized returns. The 12.8 percent return

---

[4] Models have been developed using accounting data that predict corporate bankruptcy. While these models are beyond the scope of this text, any individual who is considering investing in high-yield securities may readily apply the models to analyze specific firms. These models' track records in red-flagging possible defaults have been excellent. See E. Altman and S. Nammacher, *Investing in Junk Bonds: Inside the High Yield Debt Market* (New York: Lipper Analytical Services, Inc., 1986) and E. Altman, *Corporate Financial Distress* (New York: J. Wiley & Sons, 1983).

[5] See Drexel Birnham Lambert's *1989 High Yield Market Report—Financing America's Future*, 112.

[6] Edward I. Altman, "The Anatomy of the High-Yield Bond Market," *Financial Analysts Journal* (July/August 1987): 12–25.

[7] Marshall E. Blume and Donald B. Keim, "Lower-Grade Bonds: Their Risks and Returns," *Financial Analysts Journal* (July/August 1987): 26–33.

included the impact of the defaults that occurred in the high-yield market. If the investor could be more selective and avoid defaults, the spread between the realized return on high-yield securities and other alternative debt instruments would improve.

These studies also indicated that the prices of high-yield securities were less volatile. During periods of changing interest rates, their prices did not fluctuate as much as the prices of investment grade corporate and federal government bonds. This result seems inconsistent with the concept of a risky, high-yield security. However, as discussed in the previous chapter, the prices of bonds with higher coupons tend to fluctuate less than those of bonds with lower coupons. High-yield securities have higher coupons than investment grade bonds, so their prices are less sensitive to fluctuations in interest rates. It is the firm-specific risk (i.e., the unsystematic risk) and not the market or interest rate risk that is the source of risk with which the investor in high-yield securities must contend.

The material in Chapter 7 suggested that unsystematic risk would be reduced through the construction of diversified portfolios. A portfolio of as few as 10 to 12 stocks could erase a substantial amount of the unsystematic risk. The same concept holds for investments in high-yield securities. A diversified portfolio of these securities will significantly reduce firm-specific risk. However, adequate diversification may require 25 to 30 different issues, which is more than twice the number of issues required to diversify a stock portfolio.[8] Since high-yield securities are issued in minimum units of $5,000 and $10,000, diversification may require an investment in excess of $100,000.

This large investment suggests that most individuals who are considering participating in the high-yield security market should select a mutual fund that specializes in high-yield securities. One of the funds' biggest advantages is diversification. Since one default can drastically reduce the realized return on a small portfolio of high-yield securities, diversification is exceedingly important when participating in this market. Unless the individual is willing to commit a substantial amount of money to construct a diversified portfolio of high-yield securities, the best strategy may be to acquire a high-yield mutual fund.

Junk Bonds in the 1990s

Prior to 1989, high-yield securities did generate returns that compensated for the additional risk, but in 1989 the market for junk bonds began to falter. The recession combined with the large amount of debt financing put unbearable strain on the issuers of junk bonds. Some firms were late in making interest payments, and several prominent issues defaulted (for example, Resorts International, Macy's, and Integrated Resources). Campeau put up its prestigious department store, Bloomingdales, for sale in order to raise cash to service its debt. The sale did not go through, and Campeau went bankrupt. Other companies such as Southland, owner of 7-11 stores, Orion Pictures, owner of the Oscar-winning movie *The Silence of the Lambs*, and retailer Carter Hawley Hale defaulted and declared bankruptcy.

---

[8] See Drexel Birnham Lambert's *1989 High Yield Market Report—Financing America's Future,* 51.

The large number of defaults tainted even the high-yield bonds that continued to pay interest, so that the prices of virtually all junk bonds fell. This produced a buying opportunity for the investor able to determine which of the firms would survive. Just as all of the firms that issued high-yield securities could not survive, not every firm whose bonds were selling at significant discounts would fail. During 1991 and 1992, many firms that had previously issued debt now issued equity. Firms that had been taken private in leveraged buyouts were taken public through the issue of stock (e.g., Joy Technologies, Safeway, and Owens Illinois). The prices of their bonds rose as dramatically as they had fallen, and many bonds that had sold for large discounts were redeemed at par after these firms issued new stock and once again become publicly held firms.[9]

Not all investors in high-yield securities fared so well, however. Many of the firms that did default were reorganized and the bondholders were forced to realize large losses. The holders of Southland's debt had to accept bonds with a lower face value and smaller interest payments as part of a court-sanctioned reorganization. The majority of holders of Harcourt Brace Jovanovich bonds accepted about $0.50 on the dollar as part of the HBJ merger agreement with General Cinema. The bondholders of the Trump Taj Mahal accepted equity in the casino and lower interest payments as part of Taj Mahal's reorganization. Why would the bondholders agree to these terms? In short, high-yield bonds are usually unsecured and subordinated to the firm's other debt obligations. Failure to accept the terms of the reorganization would probably result in the bondholders' losing their entire investment. Under the reorganization, there is always the possibility the firm will survive and that the bondholders will recoup some, if not all, of their investment.

High-Yield Foreign Government Securities

Federal governnment securities are considered to be the safest of all securities. Short-term treasury bills offer a risk-free return. While long-term federal government bonds require the investor to bear the risk associated with changes in interest rates and inflation, they are the safest long-term bonds. This safety of government securities, however, is limited to federal government securities. The same does not apply to the debt of other governments whose debts are denominated in the local currency. These obligations could lose their value when converted back into dollars (i.e., exchange rate risk).

To avoid exchange rate risk, loans to foreign governments may be denominated in dollars. The risk associated with fluctuations in exchange rates is transferred to the issuer of the securities. Does this mean that foreign government bonds are as safe as U.S. federal government bonds? The answer is a resounding "No!" Of course, the government obligations of Japan and Great Britain are safe investments compared to corporate securities issued in their countries. There is virtual certainty that these governments are willing and able to service their debt obligations.

---

[9]While junk bonds generated negative returns in 1990, the returns in 1991 exceeded 30 percent. See Edward I. Altman, "Revisiting The High-Yield Bond Market," *Financial Management* (Summer 1992), 79–80.

The same does not apply to the less developed nations of Central and South America. While the face value of their debt exceeds a trillion dollars, the market value has steadily declined. The debt of Brazil and Mexico has sold for a third of its face value and offered possible yields in excess of 30 percent, if paid. Of course, the inability of these nations to service the debt was the reason the bonds sold for substantial discounts.

Servicing and retiring this mountain of debt without bankrupting the countries (and without incurring civil unrest and chaos) is currently one of the major international problems facing lenders and governments. Some governments have borrowed additional funds to pay the interest which, of course, increases the amount they owe. In the late 1980s, many large money center banks, such as the Bank of America and Citibank, wrote down the value of their international loan portfolios and acknowledged the large losses that had been sustained on their investments in foreign debt obligations. Some asset swaps and restructurings have been negotiated, and further restructurings can be expected. However, until the governments become more financially sound, their obligations will have to be considered another type of high-yield security.

SUMMARY

While preferred stock is legally equity, the fact that it pays a fixed dividend makes it similar to debt. Preferred stock's value fluctuates with changes in interest rates. When interest rates rise, the price of preferred stock falls; when interest rates decline, the price of preferred stock rises. Since its price behavior is the same as the price behavior of bonds, preferred stock is valued and analyzed as an alternative to long-term debt.

The prime advantage to the firm of issuing preferred stock is that it is less risky than debt because it does not represent an unconditional obligation to pay dividends. The major disadvantage is that the dividends are not a tax-deductible expense.

The primary purpose for purchasing a preferred stock is the flow of dividend income. However, since preferred stock is riskier than debt (from the viewpoint of the individual investor), it has not been a popular investment with individuals. The majority of preferred stock is purchased by corporations, especially insurance companies, and pension plans, which receive favorable tax treatment on the preferred stock dividends they receive.

High-yield securities are bonds and preferred stocks issued by firms with less than triple B credit ratings. Some high-yield securities were initially investment grade, but the issuers fell on hard times. The market value of their bonds declined in order to offer the high yields associated with the firm's weakened financial position. Other high-yield securities were issued as part of takeovers and recapitalizations and to raise funds for investments in plant and equipment.

The terms of high-yield securities are more varied than traditional investment grade debt. With PIK securities, the issuing firm has the option to pay dividends or interest by issuing new preferred stock or new bonds. Split coupon bonds combine the features of zero coupon and high coupon bonds. The issuing firm does not pay interest during the first years of the security's life and then it pays a high coupon during the remaining years prior to the bond's maturity. Reset and increasing rate bonds have coupons that vary, and extendible bonds have maturity dates that may be extended.

Studies prior to 1989 indicate that realized returns on a diversified portfolio have exceeded the return earned on investment grade and government bonds. While the realized returns were less than the spreads between the yields to maturity on high-yield and investment grade securities, the realized returns took into consideration the defaults that occurred in specific high-yield bonds. During 1990 and 1991, defaults increased inflicting large losses on investors holding the high-yield securities of financially weak firms.

Security Summary

Preferred Stock

Source of return: Dividend income and possible capital gains if interest rates fall.

Liquidity and marketability: Active secondary market in preferred stock of large issues listed on the exchanges. Chance of loss if interest rates rise driving down preferred stock prices.

Sources of risk: Unsystematic risk from events that affect the firm's capacity to service its preferred stock (i.e., pay the dividend and timely retire the stock if required to). Systematic risk from interest rate risk since the price of preferred stock moves inversely with changes in interest rates. Possible loss of purchasing power if the rate of inflation exceeds the preferred stock yield.

Taxation: Dividends are subject to federal income taxation. Capital gains that occur if interest rates fall are subject to taxation only when the gains are realized.

Security Summary

High-Yield Bonds

Source of return: Interest income and possible capital gains if interest rates fall.

Liquidity and marketability: Active secondary market in large issues but with large spreads between the bid and ask prices. The high yield suggests poor quality and virtually no liquidity.

Sources of risk: Unsystematic risk from events that affect the firm's capacity to service its debt (i.e., pay the interest and timely retire the bonds). Systematic risk from interest rate risk since bond prices fall when interest rates rise. The prices of high-yield securities with large coupons may not be very sensitive to changes in interest rates, but the opposite applies to high-yield zero coupon or split coupon bonds.

Taxation: Interest is subject to federal income taxation. Capital gains that occur if interest rates fall or if the bond's ratings improve are subject to taxation only when the gains are realized.

Terms to Remember

preferred stock	fallen angels
arrearage	pay-in-kind securities
cumulative preferred stock	split coupon bonds
noncumulative preferred stock	reset bond
times-dividend-earned ratio	increasing rate bond
earnings per preferred share	extendible security
high-yield securities	

Questions

1. What are the features common to most preferred stock?
2. Must a firm pay preferred stock dividends? What does in arrears mean? What advantage is offered to the investor by a cumulative preferred stock?
3. From the viewpoint of the issuing corporation, preferred stock is less risky than debt. However, from the viewpoint of the investor, the reverse is true: debt is less risky than preferred stock. Why are these statements true?
4. What affects the price of a preferred stock? What will happen to the price of a preferred stock if interest rates rise?
5. What is the earnings per preferred share ratio? Why is it a measure of safety?
6. What types of investors may select preferred stock? What are the advantages and disadvantages associated with investments in preferred stock?
7. What differentiates high-yield securities from investment grade debt?
8. Why would a firm issue a PIK bond? What are the income tax obligations of a PIK preferred stock?
9. Why is there an incentive for firms to rapidly retire split coupon and rising coupon bonds?
10. What is the difference between the spread on yields to maturity and realized returns? Is there any evidence that defaults wipe out the interest advantage associated with high-yield securities?

Problems

1. a. If a preferred stock pays an annual dividend of $6 and investors can earn 10 percent on alternative and comparable investments, what is the maximum price that should be paid for this stock?
   b. If the preferred stock in part a had a call feature and investors expected the stock to be called for $100 after ten years, what is the maximum price that investors should pay for the stock?
   c. If investors can earn 12 percent on comparable investments, what should be the price of the preferred stock in part a? What would be the price if comparable yields are 8 percent? What generalization do these answers imply?
2. What is the times-dividends-earned ratio given the following information?

> 30% corporate income tax rate
> $10,000 EBIT (earnings before interest and taxes)
> $2,000 interest owed
> $2,000 preferred stock dividends

3. A firm with earnings before interest and taxes of $500,000 needs $1 million of additional funds. If it issues debt, the bonds will mature after 20 years and have a coupon of 10 percent. The firm could issue a preferred stock with a dividend rate of 10 percent. The firm has 100,000 shares of common stock outstanding and is in the 30 percent corporate income tax bracket. What are the earnings per common share under the two alternative financings?

4. What should be the prices of the following preferred stocks if comparable securities yield 8 percent, 10 percent, and 14 percent?
   a. MN, Inc. $4 preferred ($100 par).
   b. CH, Inc. $4 preferred ($100 par with the additional requirement that the firm must retire the preferred after 20 years).
   Why should the prices of these securities be different?

5. What is the price of the following split coupon bond if comparable yields are 14 percent?

   > Principal $1,000
   > Maturity   12 years
   > Coupon   0% for years 1–3
   > $120 for years 4–12

   If comparable yields decline to 10 percent, what is the appreciation in the price of the bond?

6. A bond has the following terms:

   > Principal amount $1,000
   > Annual interest paid $140 starting after five years have passed
   >   (i.e., in year 6)
   > Maturity   12 years
   > Callable at $1.14 (i.e., face value + one year's interest)

   a. Why do you believe that the terms were constructed as specified above?
   b. What is the bond's current yield?
   c. What is the bond's price if comparable debt yields 12 percent?
   d. Even though interest rates have fallen, why would you not expect the bond to be called?

7. An extendible bond has the following features:

   > Principal $1,000
   > Coupon   11.5%
   > Maturity   8 years but the issuer may
   >   extend the maturity for 5 years

   a. If comparable yields are 14 percent, what will be the price of the bond if investors anticipate that it will be retired after eight years?

b. What impact will the expectation that the bond will be retired after 13 years have on its current price if comparable yields are 14 percent?

c. If comparable yields remain 14 percent, would you expect the firm to retire the bond after eight years?

8. What is the yield to maturity on a split coupon bond that pays $0 for years one through four, and $115 for years five through ten, if the current price is $57 ($570 per $1,000)?

Suggested Readings

Information on specific preferred stocks may be found in *Standard & Poor's Daily Dividend Record, Standard & Poor's Stock Guide,* and *Moody's Dividend Record,* which report the amount of the dividends and their record and payment dates.

Recent developments in the high-yield security markets has generated a large amount of information on these investments. Initial writings tended to stress the potential yields, and research did indicate that even after adjusting for defaults, high-yield securities offered higher yields than higher quality debt. However, more recent writings have tended to stress the financial difficulty that has beset some of the firms with outstanding high-yield securities. For a sampling of this literature consult:

Altman, Edward I. "The Anatomy of the High-Yield Bond Market." *Financial Analysts Journal* (July-August 1987): 12–25.

Altman, Edward I. "Defaults and Returns on High Yield Bonds: An Update Through the First Half of 1991." *Financial Analysts Journal* (November-December 1991): 67–77. 1991): 67–77.

Block, Stanley. "Are High-Yield Bonds Appropriate?" *AAII Journal* (November 1989): 7–11.

Branch, Ben, and Hugh Ray. *Bankruptcy Investing.* Dearborn Financial Publishing, Inc., 1992.

Frison, Martin S. *High Yield Bonds.* Chicago, Ill.: Probus Publishing Company, 1989.

Howe, Jane Tripp. *Junk Bonds: Analysis & Portfolio Strategies.* Chicago, Ill.: Probus Publishing Company, 1987.

Hradsky, Gregory, and Robert D. Long. "High-Yield Default Losses and the Return of Bankrupt Debt." *Financial Analysts Journal* (July–August 1989): 38–49.

For an extensive bibliography on default rates, returns, and financial distress, consult:

Altman, Edward I. "Revisiting the High-Yield Bond Market," *Financial Management* (Summer 1992): 78–92.

For a varied collection of writings on high-yield securities ranging from academic studies to contributions by investment bankers and congressmen that covers investment performance, credit quality, and public policy issues, obtain:

Altman, Edward I., ed. *The High-Yield Debt Market: Investment Performance and Economic Impact.* Homewood, Ill.: Dow Jones-Irwin, 1990.

17

GOVERNMENT SECURITIES

During the 1980s one of the big political issues in Washington was the size of the federal government's deficit. This deficit is the result of expenditures exceeding revenues. Whenever such a deficit occurs, the general public or various financial institutions must finance the deficit. In order to raise money to cover its expenditures, the federal government issues a variety of securities. This variety helps the government tap the different sources of funds that are available in the money and capital markets.

This chapter is concerned with government securities. The first section discusses the various types of debt issued by the federal government, which range from short-term treasury bills to long-term treasury bonds. The second section briefly considers the debt issued by the various agencies of the federal government, and the last section discusses the debt issued by state and local governments. Special emphasis is placed on the feature that distinguishes state and local government debt from other securities: The interest paid to bondholders is exempt from federal income taxation.

✦ ✦ ✦

THE VARIETY OF FEDERAL GOVERNMENT DEBT

In 1991 the federal government made interest payments of $220.1 billion on its debt. This sum was substantial and amounted to about 16.7 percent of the total expenditures made by the federal government in that year. The debt was financed by a variety of investors, including individuals, corporations, and financial institutions. To induce this diverse group of investors to purchase its debt, the federal government issued different types of debt instruments that appealed to the various potential buyers.

For investors, the unique advantage offered by the federal government's debt is its safety. These debt instruments are the safest of all possible investments, for there is no question that the U.S. Treasury is able to pay the interest and repay the principal. The source of this safety is the federal government's constitutional right to tax and to print money. Because there is no legal limitation on the federal gov-

Exhibit 17.1 ◆ THE VARIETY OF FEDERAL GOVERNMENT DEBT AS OF JANUARY 1, 1992

	Length of Time to Maturity	Value (in Billions of Dollars)	Percentage of Total Debt
Treasury bills	Less than 1 year	$ 618.2	15.5%
Intermediate-term notes	One to 5 years	1517.6	38.1
Long-term bonds	Over 5 years	454.3	11.4
Savings bonds	Various maturities	143.2	3.6
Other debt°	Various maturities	1251.4	31.4

Source: Federal Reserve Bulletin, November 1992.
°Debt held by U.S. government agencies and trust funds and state and local governments.

ernment's capacity to create money, there is no restriction on its ability to pay interest and retire (or at least refinance) its debt.

The various types of federal government debt and the amount outstanding of each are illustrated in Exhibit 17.1. As may be seen in the exhibit, there has been an emphasis on the use of short- and intermediate-term financing by the Treasury. This emphasis is partially explained by interest costs. Interest rates on short-term debt are usually lower than those on long-term debt. Hence, the use of short-term financing reduces the Treasury's interest expense. Furthermore, Congress restricts the interest rate that the Treasury may pay on long-term debt, but it does not restrict the interest rate on short-term securities. Thus, during periods of high interest rates, the Treasury may not be permitted to sell long-term securities even if it desires to do so.

Nonmarketable Federal Government Debt

Perhaps the most widely held federal government debt is the **series E** and **series EE bonds.** The series E bond was designed to encourage saving by people of modest means, as it was sold in small denominations (e.g., $25, $100, $500, and up to $10,000). Although virtually every person should have been able to place modest amounts of savings in these bonds, an individual was allowed to purchase no more than $10,000 worth of series E bonds in a calendar year.

series E and EE bonds
Savings bonds issued in small denominations by the federal government.

Series E bonds paid no interest but were purchased at a discount (i.e., below their face value). For example, if a saver purchased a $25 series E bond for $18.75 and held it until maturity five years and five months later, he or she received $25 and earned 6 percent annually on the investment. If the bonds were cashed in prior to maturity, the holder received less than $25 and earned a yield of less than 6 percent. (The yield started at 4 percent and rose over the lifetime of the bond until it reached 6 percent at the bond's maturity. This ascending structure of yields is an incentive to hold the bonds until maturity.)

Series E bonds were initially issued in 1941 to help finance World War II expenditures. At that time the bonds had a maturity of ten years and a yield of 2.9 percent. As interest rates have risen, the length of time to maturity has been reduced, which has had the effect of increasing the yield on the bonds.

Although series E bonds did mature, the Treasury initially did not require that the bonds be redeemed. Instead, the maturities were extended and interest continued to accrue. The rate earned on these older bonds has been increased, so the yield is comparable to that earned by the series EE bond that is currently being sold. The Treasury, however, will no longer extend the maturity of E bonds. As they reach final maturity, the bonds will cease to earn interest, and holders will have to redeem or exchange them for other bonds.

On January 2, 1980, the Treasury started to issue a new bond, series EE, to replace the series E bonds. Like the E bonds, the new bonds are issued at a discount. The smallest denomination is $50, which costs $25. In November 1982, the Treasury changed the method for computing interest on EE bonds from a fixed rate to a variable rate. The new rate will be 85 percent of the average rate on five-year Treasury securities. This rate will change every six months, and as of early 1993, the annual yield on EE bonds was approximately 5 percent. The variable rate permits the small investor to participate in higher yields if interest rates rise, but the investor earns less if interest rates fall.

There are several major differences between series E and EE bonds and most other investments, such as savings accounts. The interest earned on series E and EE bonds is not subject to federal income taxation until the bonds are redeemed or reach final maturity. The interest earned on other investments, including savings accounts, is subject to federal income taxation during the year in which it is earned. Although the federal income tax on the E or EE series may be deferred until the bonds are redeemed, are disposed of, or mature (whichever comes first), the owner does have the option to have the interest taxed each year. Even though the funds are not received until the bond is redeemed, the owner may report the interest to the Internal Revenue Service on an accrual basis. However, most holders of series E bonds have preferred to defer the tax payment. Presumably owners of series EE bonds will follow the same strategy.

The deferment of interest income until the bonds are redeemed can be advantageous in that the saver can cash in series E and EE bonds in those years when income from other sources is lower. For example, these bonds are potentially good investments to be redeemed during retirement or times of temporary unemployment. It is likely that the individual's taxable income will be lower during these periods, and thus the taxes paid on the accrued interest earned by the bonds will be lower. By allowing investors to determine when the interest will be subject to taxation, series E and now series EE bonds offer the investor an opportunity to reduce the amount of taxes paid on the interest. Since they are sold in small units, these bonds offer a means that is available to virtually every investor to shelter income from taxes. Such tax sheltering of interest income is not available through other savings instruments, such as accounts in commercial banks or savings and loan associations.

Another important difference between series E and EE bonds and other bonds is that there is no secondary market in these bonds. If the owner wants immediate cash, the bonds cannot be sold. Instead, the investor redeems them at a commercial bank. Nor can the bonds be transferred as a gift, although they can be transferred through an estate. The Treasury also forbids the use of series E and EE bonds as collateral. Thus, while corporate debt may be used to secure a personal loan, these bonds cannot.

series H and HH bonds
Income bonds issued by the federal government.

The investor may exchange series E for **series H bonds,** and as of 1980 they may exchange them for **HH bonds.** The HH series (like the EE bonds) is a new series that is designed to replace the series H bonds. Series H and HH bonds are different from E and EE bonds in several ways. They are sold at par in larger denominations, with $500 being the minimum investment. The bonds mature in 20 years and pay 6 percent interest if held to maturity. The interest is paid every year and does not accumulate as it does with the series E and EE bonds. Thus, interest is subject to federal income taxation each year, while taxation on series E and EE bonds may be deferred until the bonds are redeemed. Series HH bonds are more attractive to investors who need safe sources of current income, while series EE bonds are attractive to conservative investors who wish to build up capital but who do not need current income.

Marketable Securities

Treasury Bills   Short-term federal government debt is in the form of **treasury bills.** These bills are sold in denominations of $10,000 to $1,000,000 and mature in 3 to 12 months. Like series EE bonds, they are sold at a discount; however, unlike series EE bonds, the discounted price is not set. Instead, the Treasury continually auctions off the bills, which go to the highest bidders. For example, if an investor bids $9,700 and obtains the bill, he or she will receive $10,000 when the bill matures, which is a yield of 3.1 percent ($300 ÷ $9,700). If it is a three-month bill, the annual rate of interest is 12.4 percent. If the bid price had been higher, the interest cost to the Treasury (and the yield to the buyer) would have been lower.

Once treasury bills have been auctioned, they may be bought and sold in the secondary market. They are issued in bearer form, which makes them highly negotiable and easily marketed. There is an active secondary market in these bills, and they are quoted daily in the financial press and many city newspapers. These quotes and the quotes for other federal government securities are illustrated in Exhibit 17.2. For treasury bills the quotes are given in the following form:

treasury bills
Short-term federal government securities.

Maturity	Days to Maturity	Bid	Asked	Ask Yield
3/4/93	57	3.05	3.01	3.07

These quotes indicate that for a treasury bill maturing on March 4, 1993, buyers were willing to bid a discounted price that produced a discount yield of 3.05 percent. Sellers, however, were willing to sell (offer) the bills at a smaller discount (higher price) that returned a discount yield of 3.01 percent. The annualized yield on the bill based on the asked price is 3.07 percent.

The reason for the difference between the discount yield and the annualized yield is that treasury bills are sold at a discount and are quoted in terms of the discount yield. The discount yield is not the same as (nor is it comparable to) the annualized yield on the bill or the yield to maturity on a bond. It is calculated on the basis of the face amount of the bill and uses a 360-day year. The annualized yield on the bill depends on the price of the bill and uses a 365-day year.[1]

---

[1] The annualized yield is sometimes referred to as the bond-equivalent yield.

The difference between the two calculations may be seen in the following example. Suppose a three-month $10,000 treasury bill sells for $9,800. The discount yield (y_d) is

$$y_d = \frac{\text{Par value} - \text{Price}}{\text{Par value}} \times \frac{360}{\text{Number of days to maturity}}$$

$$\frac{\$10,000 - \$9,800}{\$10,000} \times \frac{360}{90} = 8\%.$$

The annualized yield (y_a) is

$$y_a = \frac{\text{Par value} - \text{Price}}{\text{Price}} \times \frac{365}{\text{Number of days to maturity}}$$

$$\frac{\$10,000 - \$9,800}{\$9,800} \times \frac{365}{90} = 8.277\%.$$

Since the discount yield uses the face amount and a 360-day year, it understates the true yield the investor is earning.[2]

Treasury bills may be purchased through brokerage firms, commercial banks, and any Federal Reserve Bank. These purchases may be new issues or bills that are being traded in the secondary market. Bills with one year to maturity are auctioned once a month. Shorter term bills are auctioned weekly. If the buyer purchases the bills directly through the Federal Reserve Bank, there are no commission fees. Brokers and commercial banks do charge commissions, but the fees are modest compared with those charged for other investment transactions, such as the purchase of stock.

Treasury bills are among the best short-term debt instruments available to investors who desire safety and some interest income (i.e., a liquid asset).[3] The bills mature quickly, and there are many issues from which the investor may choose. Thus, the investor may purchase a bill that matures when the principal is needed. For example, an individual who has ready cash today but who must make a payment after three months may purchase a bill that matures at the appropriate time. In doing so, the investor puts the cash to work for three months.

Perhaps the one feature that differentiates treasury bills from all other investments is risk. These bills are considered the safest of all possible investments. There is no question concerning the safety of principal when investors acquire treasury

---

[2] The discount yield may be converted to the annualized yield by the following equation:

$$y_a = \frac{365 \times Y_d}{360 - (y_d \times \text{Days to maturity})}$$

Thus, if the discount rate on a three-month treasury bill is 8 percent, true yield is

$$y_a = \frac{365 \times 0.08}{360 - (0.08 \times 90)} = 8.277\%.$$

[3] Treasury bills are issued in bearer form and thus are easily transferred if *stolen*. In that sense, they lack some element of safety.

Exhibit 17.2 ✦ PRICES FOR SELECTED GOVERNMENT NOTES AND BONDS, SELECTED GOVERNMENT AGENCY ISSUES, AND YIELDS FOR SELECTED TREASURY BILLS

TREASURY BONDS, NOTES & BILLS

Monday, January 4, 1993

Representative Over-the-Counter quotations based on transactions of $1 million or more.

Treasury bond, note and bill quotes are as of mid-afternoon. Colons in bid-and-asked quotes represent 32nds; 101:01 means 101 1/32. Net changes in 32nds. n-Treasury note. Treasury bill quotes in hundredths, quoted on terms of a rate of discount. Days to maturity calculated from settlement date. All yields are to maturity and based on the asked quote. Latest 13-week and 26-week bills are boldfaced. For bonds callable prior to maturity, yields are computed to the earliest call date for issues quoted above par and to the maturity date for issues below par. *-When issued.

Source: Federal Reserve Bank of New York.

U.S. Treasury strips as of 3 p.m. Eastern time, also based on transactions of $1 million or more. Colons in bid-and-asked quotes represent 32nds; 101:01 means 101 1/32. Net changes in 32nds. Yields calculated on the asked quotation. ci-stripped coupon interest. bp-Treasury bond, stripped principal. np-Treasury, note, stripped principal. For bonds callable prior to maturity, yields are computed to the earliest call date for issues quoted above par and to the maturity date for issues below par.

Source: Bear, Stearns & Co. via Street Software Technology Inc.

GOVT. BONDS & NOTES

Rate	Maturity Mo/Yr	Bid	Asked	Chg.	Ask Yld.
$8\frac{3}{4}$	Jan 93n	100:05	100:07	− 2	0.00
7	Jan 93n	100:08	100:10	− 1	2.32
4	Feb 88-93	98:30	99:14	+ 7	9.08
$6\frac{3}{4}$	Feb 93	100:14	100:16	− 2	2.08
$7\frac{7}{8}$	Feb 93	100:16	100:18	− 2	2.61
$8\frac{1}{4}$	Feb 93n	100:17	100:19	− 2	2.68
$8\frac{3}{8}$	Feb 93n	100:17	100:19	− 2	2.80
$10\frac{7}{8}$	Feb 93n	100:27	100:29	− 2	2.41
$6\frac{3}{4}$	Feb 93n	100:16	100:18	− 1	2.82
$7\frac{1}{8}$	Mar 93n	100:28	100:30	− 1	2.98
$9\frac{5}{8}$	Mar 93n	101:15	101:17	− 1	2.87
$7\frac{3}{8}$	Apr 93n	101:04	101:06	....	2.92
7	Apr 93n	101:05	101:07	− 1	3.05
$7\frac{5}{8}$	May 93n	101:16	101:18	− 1	3.16
$8\frac{5}{8}$	May 93n	101:27	101:29	− 1	3.18
$10\frac{1}{8}$	May 93n	102:12	102:14	− 2	3.16
$6\frac{3}{4}$	May 93n	101:11	101:13	....	3.15
7	Jun 93n	101:24	101:26	− 1	3.19
$8\frac{1}{8}$	Jun 93n	102:09	102:11	− 1	3.20
$7\frac{1}{4}$	Jul 93n	102:00	102:02	− 1	3.25
$6\frac{7}{8}$	Jul 93n	101:29	101:31	− 1	3.35
8	Aug 93n	102:22	102:24	− 1	3.40
$8\frac{5}{8}$	Aug 93	103:03	103:05	− 1	3.35
$8\frac{3}{4}$	Aug 93n	103:04	103:06	− 2	3.42
$11\frac{7}{8}$	Aug 93n	105:01	105:03	− 2	3.36
$6\frac{3}{8}$	Aug 93n	101:27	101:29	....	3.37
$6\frac{1}{8}$	Sep 93n	101:28	101:30	....	3.42
$8\frac{1}{4}$	Sep 93n	103:12	103:14	− 2	3.45
$7\frac{1}{8}$	Oct 93n	102:22	102:24	....	3.49
6	Oct 93n	101:29	101:31	....	3.53
$7\frac{3}{4}$	Nov 93n	103:14	103:16	....	3.57
$8\frac{5}{8}$	Nov 93	104:05	104:07	− 2	3.58
9	Nov 93n	104:16	104:18	− 1	3.55
$11\frac{3}{4}$	Nov 93n	106:26	106:28	....	3.54
$5\frac{1}{2}$	Nov 93n	101:21	101:23	+ 1	3.54
5	Dec 93n	101:09	101:11	....	3.60
$7\frac{5}{8}$	Dec 93n	103:25	103:27	....	3.61
7	Jan 94n	103:09	103:11	+ 2	3.65
$4\frac{7}{8}$	Jan 94n	101:07	101:09	+ 1	3.64
$6\frac{7}{8}$	Feb 94n	103:10	103:12	+ 1	3.74
$8\frac{7}{8}$	Feb 94n	105:15	105:17	....	3.74
9	Feb 94	105:17	105:19	− 3	3.80
$5\frac{3}{8}$	Feb 94n	101:24	101:26	+ 2	3.75
$5\frac{3}{4}$	Mar 94n	102:08	102:10	+ 2	3.81
$8\frac{1}{2}$	Mar 94n	105:16	105:18	....	3.83
7	Apr 94n	103:24	103:26	+ 2	3.90
$11\frac{5}{8}$	Nov 94n	112:24	112:26	+ 4	4.37
$4\frac{5}{8}$	Nov 94n	100:13	100:15	+ 5	4.37
$4\frac{5}{8}$	Dec 94n	100:09	100:11	+ 5	4.44
$7\frac{5}{8}$	Dec 94n	105:29	105:31	+ 1	4.45
$8\frac{5}{8}$	Jan 95n	107:27	107:29	+ 4	4.50
3	Feb 95	98:10	99:10	+21	3.34
$5\frac{1}{2}$	Feb 95n	101:27	101:29	+ 4	4.54
$7\frac{3}{4}$	Feb 95n	106:10	106:12	+ 5	4.55
$10\frac{1}{2}$	Feb 95	111:26	111:28	+ 5	4.53
$11\frac{1}{4}$	Feb 95n	113:07	113:09	+ 2	4.57
$8\frac{3}{8}$	Apr 95n	108:02	108:04	+ 4	4.57
$5\frac{7}{8}$	May 95n	102:15	102:17	+ 4	4.73
$8\frac{1}{2}$	May 95n	108:09	108:11	+ 4	4.72
$10\frac{3}{8}$	May 95	112:15	112:17	+ 6	4.70
$11\frac{1}{4}$	May 95n	114:10	114:12	+ 3	4.73
$12\frac{5}{8}$	May 95	117:12	117:16	+ 2	4.70
$8\frac{7}{8}$	Jul 95n	109:16	109:18	+ 5	4.81
$4\frac{5}{8}$	Aug 95n	99:16	99:18	+ 4	4.81
$8\frac{1}{2}$	Aug 95n	108:25	108:27	+ 7	4.85
$10\frac{1}{2}$	Aug 95n	113:20	113:22	+ 6	4.85
$8\frac{5}{8}$	Oct 95n	109:13	109:15	+ 9	4.93
$5\frac{1}{8}$	Nov 95n	100:14	100:16	+ 8	4.94
$8\frac{1}{2}$	Nov 95n	109:06	109:08	+ 8	4.99
$9\frac{1}{2}$	Nov 95n	111:29	111:31	+ 7	4.96
$11\frac{1}{2}$	Nov 95	117:02	117:06	+ 6	4.97
$9\frac{1}{4}$	Jan 96n	111:12	111:14	+ 8	5.12
$7\frac{1}{2}$	Jan 96n	106:19	106:21	+ 8	5.13
$7\frac{7}{8}$	Feb 96n	107:19	107:21	+ 9	5.18
$8\frac{7}{8}$	Feb 96n	110:13	110:15	+ 7	5.19
$7\frac{1}{2}$	Feb 96n	106:19	106:21	+ 8	5.18
$7\frac{3}{4}$	Mar 96n	107:09	107:11	+10	5.25
$9\frac{3}{8}$	Apr 96n	112:04	112:06	+ 9	5.27
$7\frac{5}{8}$	Apr 96n	106:30	107:00	+ 9	5.30
$7\frac{3}{8}$	May 96n	106:06	106:08	+10	5.32
$7\frac{5}{8}$	May 96n	106:31	107:01	+10	5.34
$7\frac{7}{8}$	Jun 96n	107:24	107:26	+11	5.39
$7\frac{7}{8}$	Jul 96n	107:24	107:26	+ 9	5.41
$7\frac{7}{8}$	Jul 96n	107:25	107:27	+10	5.43
$7\frac{1}{4}$	Aug 96n	105:25	105:27	+ 9	5.46
7	Sep 96n	105:00	105:02	+10	5.50
8	Oct 96n	108:08	108:10	+ 9	5.53
$6\frac{7}{8}$	Oct 96n	104:17	104:19	+12	5.52
$7\frac{1}{4}$	Nov 96n	105:26	105:28	+13	5.54
$6\frac{1}{2}$	Nov 96n	103:08	103:10	+12	5.54
$6\frac{1}{8}$	Dec 96n	102:00	102:02	+14	5.54
8	Jan 97n	108:13	108:15	+15	5.62
$6\frac{1}{4}$	Jan 97n	102:04	102:06	+14	5.64

GOVERNMENT AGENCY & SIMILAR ISSUES

Monday, January 4, 1993

Over-the-Counter mid-afternoon quotations based on large transactions, usually $1 million or more. Colons in bid-and-asked quotes represent 32nds; 101:01 means 101 1/32.

All yields are calculated to maturity, and based on the asked quote. * -- Callable issue, maturity date shown. For issues callable prior to maturity, yields are computed to the earliest call date for issues quoted above par, or 100, and to the maturity date for issues below par.

Source: Bear, Stearns & Co. via Street Software Technology Inc.

FNMA Issues

Rate	Mat.	Bid	Asked	Yld.
10.90	1-93	100:04	100:08	0.00
7.95	2-93	100:14	100:22	0.64
7.90	3-93	100:24	101:00	2.20
10.95	3-93	101:10	101:18	2.06
7.55	4-93	101:04	101:12	2.32
10.88	4-93	101:30	102:06	2.55
10.75	5-93	102:15	102:23	2.74
8.80	6-93	102:08	102:16	2.87
5.10	6-93	100:22	100:26	3.34
8.45	7-93	102:17	102:25	2.96
7.75	11-93	103:10	103:18	3.42
7.38	12-93	103:12	103:20	3.37
7.55	1-94	103:20	103:24	3.73
9.45	1-94	105:16	105:24	3.60
7.65	4-94	104:03	104:11	4.08
9.60	4-94	106:16	106:24	4.05
9.30	5-94	106:08	106:12	4.36
8.60	6-94	105:20	105:28	4.31
7.45	7-94	104:10	104:14	4.39
8.90	8-94	106:19	106:27	4.40
10.10	10-94	109:08	109:16	4.43
9.25	11-94	107:30	108:06	4.56
5.50	12-94	101:20	101:24	4.55
9.00	1-95	108:08	108:16	4.53
11.95	1-95	113:28	114:08	4.46
8.90	2-95*	100:10	100:18	2.83
11.50	2-95	113:02	113:14	4.68
8.85	3-95	108:09	108:17	4.68
11.70	5-95	114:20	115:00	4.85
8.85	6-95*	102:06	102:14	3.13
11.15	6-95	113:25	114:05	4.90
4.75	8-95	99:18	99:22	4.88
10.50	9-95	113:16	113:28	4.91
8.40	11-95*	103:29	104:01	3.50

Federal Home Loan Bank

Rate	Mat.	Bid	Asked	Yld.
8.30	1-93	100:09	100:15	0.00
9.35	1-93	100:10	100:16	0.00
9.50	1-93	100:10	100:16	0.03
10.70	1-93	100:13	100:19	0.00
4.38	2-93	100:05	100:07	2.72
8.05	2-93	100:19	100:25	2.23
4.83	3-93	100:11	100:15	2.65
8.10	3-93	101:00	101:06	2.60
10.80	3-93	101:19	101:25	2.56
7.55	4-93	101:04	101:10	3.17
8.13	5-93	101:24	101:30	3.02
8.90	5-93	102:00	102:06	3.13
9.13	5-93	102:05	102:11	2.95
10.75	5-93	102:24	102:30	3.02
7.08	6-93	101:20	101:24	3.29
7.00	7-93	101:25	101:27	3.60
7.75	7-93	102:11	102:17	3.09
9.00	7-93	103:00	103:06	3.13
11.70	7-93	104:16	104:24	2.96
6.22	8-93	101:22	101:24	3.40
7.45	8-93	102:14	102:20	3.22
8.18	8-93	102:27	103:03	3.20
11.95	8-93	105:09	105:15	3.15
6.21	9-93	101:29	101:31	3.42
7.95	9-93	103:04	103:10	3.27
8.30	9-93	103:12	103:16	3.35
6.09	10-93	101:29	101:31	3.57
7.88	10-93	103:10	103:16	3.40
8.80	10-93	104:00	104:06	3.44
9.13	11-93	104:26	105:00	3.35
7.38	12-93	103:16	103:22	3.49
7.50	12-93	103:20	103:24	3.55
12.15	12-93	108:02	108:08	3.46
5.00	-1-94	101:05	101:09	3.74

TREASURY BILLS

Maturity	Days to Mat.	Bid	Asked	Chg.	Ask Yld.
Jan 07 '93	1	2.17	2.07	+0.36	2.10
Jan 14 '93	8	2.97	2.87	+0.33	2.92
Jan 21 '93	15	3.04	2.94	+0.23	2.98
Jan 28 '93	22	2.92	2.82	+0.15	2.86
Feb 04 '93	29	2.98	2.88	+0.08	2.93
Feb 11 '93	36	3.02	2.98	+0.01	3.04
Feb 18 '93	43	3.04	3.00	+0.05	3.05
Feb 25 '93	50	3.00	2.96	+0.07	3.01
Mar 04 '93	57	3.05	3.01	....	3.07
Mar 11 '93	64	3.06	3.04	−0.01	3.10
Mar 18 '93	71	3.06	3.04	−0.01	3.10
Mar 25 '93	78	3.07	3.05	−0.02	3.11
Apr 01 '93	**85**	**3.08**	**3.06**	....	**3.13**
Apr 08 '93	92	3.12	3.10	+0.01	3.17
Apr 15 '93	99	3.13	3.11	....	3.18
Apr 22 '93	106	3.14	3.12	....	3.19
Apr 29 '93	113	3.16	3.14	....	3.22
May 06 '93	120	3.18	3.16	−0.03	3.24
May 13 '93	127	3.19	3.17	−0.03	3.25
May 20 '93	134	3.19	3.17	−0.04	3.25
May 27 '93	141	3.20	3.18	−0.05	3.26
Jun 03 '93	148	3.19	3.17	−0.05	3.26
Jun 10 '93	155	3.21	3.19	−0.04	3.28
Jun 17 '93	162	3.22	3.20	−0.04	3.29
Jun 24 '93	169	3.23	3.21	−0.04	3.30
Jul 01 '93	**176**	**3.26**	**3.24**	**−0.02**	**3.34**
Jul 29 '93	204	3.28	3.26	−0.03	3.36
Aug 26 '93	232	3.31	3.29	−0.03	3.40
Sep 23 '93	260	3.32	3.30	−0.05	3.41
Oct 21 '93	288	3.35	3.33	−0.05	3.45
Nov 18 '93	316	3.38	3.36	−0.04	3.48
Dec 16 '93	344	`40	3.38	−0.05	3.51

As of Jan. 4, 1993.
Source: The Wall Street Journal, January 5, 1993, C15.

bills. The federal government always has the capacity to refund or retire treasury bills because it has the power to tax and the power to create money.

The primary buyers of treasury bills are corporations with excess short-term cash, commercial banks with unused lending capacity, money market mutual funds, and foreign investors seeking a safe haven for their funds. Individual investors may also purchase them. However, the large minimum denomination of $10,000 excludes many savers. Individual investors who desire such safe short-term investments may purchase shares in mutual funds that specialize in buying short-term securities, including treasury bills. For a discussion of these investments, see the section on money market funds in Chapter 2.

treasury notes
The intermediate-term debt of the federal government.

treasury bonds
The long-term debt of the federal government.

Treasury Notes and Bonds   Intermediate-term federal government debt is in the form of **treasury notes.** These notes are issued in denominations of $1,000 to more than $100,000 and mature in one to ten years. **Treasury bonds,** the government's debt instrument for long-term debt, are issued in denominations of $1,000 to $1,000,000, and these bonds mature in more than ten years from the date of issue. Notes and bonds are issued in both bearer and registered forms. These issues are the safest intermediate- and long-term investments available and are purchased by pension funds, financial institutions, or savers who are primarily concerned with moderate income and safety. Since these debt instruments are so safe, their yields are generally lower than that which may be obtained with high-quality corporate debt, such as AT&T bonds. For example, in 1992, IBM bonds that were rated triple A yielded about 8.5 percent, while treasury bonds with approximately the same time to maturity yielded 8.0 percent. Although the difference is less than a percentage point, the market still placed a higher return on the IBM bonds.

Like treasury bills, new issues of treasury bonds may be purchased through commercial banks and brokerage firms. These firms will charge commissions, but the individual may avoid such fees by purchasing the securities from any of the Federal Reserve banks or their branches. Payment, however, must precede purchase, except when the individual pays cash. Unless the individual investor submits a competitive bid, the purchase price is the average price charged institutions that buy the bonds through competitive bidding. By accepting this noncompetitive bid, the individual assures matching the average yield earned by financial institutions, which try to buy the securities at the lowest price (highest yield) possible.

Once the bonds are purchased, they may be readily resold, as there is an active secondary market in U.S. Treasury bonds. Like corporate stocks and bonds, treasury bonds are quoted in the financial press under the general heading "Treasury Issues." How these bonds are reported was illustrated in Exhibit 17.2, which presented quotes for selected treasury notes and bonds. These price quotes are different from the bid and ask prices for stocks because treasury securities are quoted in 32nds. Thus the 7.25 percent bond due in 1996, which was quoted 105.25–105.27, had a bid price of $105^{25}/_{32}$ and an asking price of $105^{27}/_{32}$ (i.e., $10,578.13 and $10,584.38 per $10,000 face amount).

Treasury bonds are among the safest investments available to investors. As with treasury bills, there is no question that the federal government can pay the interest and refund its debt, but there are ways in which the holder of treasury notes and bonds can suffer losses. These debt instruments pay a fixed amount of interest, which is determined when the notes and bonds are issued. If interest rates subsequently rise, existing issues will not be as attractive, and their market prices will decline. If an investor must sell the debt instrument before it matures, the price will be lower than the principal amount and the investor will suffer a capital loss.

Interest rates paid by treasury debt have varied over time. The extent of this variation was illustrated by Figure 14.3 in Chapter 14, which showed the yields on treasury bills and treasury bonds from 1978 to 1992. Yields also can fluctuate rapidly. For example, yields on three-month treasury bills changed from a high of 15 percent in March 1980 to 8.7 percent only two months later. These fluctuations in yields are due to variations in the supply of and demand for credit in the money and bond markets. As the demand and supply vary, so will the market prices and the yields on all debt instruments, including the debt of the federal government. When demand for bonds becomes strong and exceeds supply at the old prices, bond prices will rise and yields will decline. The reverse occurs when supply exceeds demand: bond prices decline and yields rise.

An investor may also lose through investments in treasury debt when the rate of inflation exceeds the interest rate earned on the bonds. For example, during 1974 the yields on government bonds rose to 7.3 percent, but the rate of inflation for consumer goods exceeded 10 percent. The investor then suffered a loss in purchasing power, for interest payments were insufficient to compensate for the inflation.

These two factors, fluctuating yields and inflation, illustrate that investing in federal government debt, like all types of investing, subjects the investor to interest rate risk and purchasing power risk. Therefore, although federal government debt is among the safest of all investments with regard to the certainty of payment of interest and principal, some element of risk still exists.

Zero Coupon Treasury Securities

With the advent of Individual Retirement Accounts (IRAs), corporations started issuing zero coupon bonds. Because the Treasury did not issue such bonds at that time, selected brokerage firms created their own zero coupon treasury securities. For example, Merrill Lynch created the Treasury Investment Growth Receipt (TIGR, generally referred to as "tigers"). Merrill Lynch bought a block of treasury bonds, removed all the coupons, and offered investors either the interest to be received in a specific year or the principal at the bonds' maturity. Since payment was limited to the single payment at the specified time in the future, these "tigers" were sold at a discount. In effect, they were zero coupon bonds backed by treasury securities originally purchased by Merrill Lynch and held by a trustee.

Other brokerage firms created similar securities by removing coupons from existing treasury bonds. Some of these zero coupon treasury securities were given clever acronyms, such as Salomon Brothers' CATS (Certificates of Accrual on Treasury Securities). In other cases they were just called Treasury Receipts (T.R.s). In each case, however, the brokerage firm owns the underlying treasury securities. The actual security purchased by the investor is an obligation of the brokerage firm and not of the federal government.

In 1985, the Treasury introduced its own zero coupon bonds called STRIPS for Separate Trading of Registered Interest and Principal Securities. Investors who purchase such STRIPS acquire a direct obligation of the federal government. Since these securities are direct obligations, they tend to have slightly lower yields than Tigers, CATS, and the other zero coupon securities created by brokerage firms.

In any case, the primary appeal of these securities is their use in retirement accounts. The interest earned on a zero coupon bond is taxed as it accrues, even though the holder does not receive annual cash interest payments. Thus, there is little reason to acquire these securities in accounts that are not tax sheltered. They are, however, excellent vehicles for retirement accounts, since all the funds (i.e., principal and accrued interest) are paid in one lump sum at maturity. Because any tax on a retirement account is paid when the funds are withdrawn, the tax

POINTS OF INTEREST

FLUCTUATIONS IN THE MARKET PRICES OF ZERO COUPON BONDS

As was discussed in Chapter 15, changing interest rates generate fluctuations in bond prices. The longer the term to maturity, the greater the price fluctuation (see Figure 15.3). For bonds of a given risk class and given term (e.g., ten years or twenty years to maturity), zero coupon bonds are the most volatile. For example, if interest rates currently were 10 percent, a ten-year zero coupon bond would sell for $385.50 while a ten-year 10 per-cent coupon bond would sell for $1,000.* If interest rates rose to 14 percent, the price of the zero coupon bond would fall to $269.70, for a decline of approximately 30 percent. The price of the 10 percent coupon bond would fall to $791.31, for a decline of approximately 21 percent. If the terms of these bonds had been 20 years, their respective prices at 10 percent would be $148.60 and $1,000 but would fall to $72.80 and $735.11 at 14 percent. Such declines are approximately 51 and 26 percent.

The reason for a zero coupon bond's increased price volatility is that the entire return falls on the single payment at maturity. Since the current price of any bond is the present value of the interest and principal payments, the price of a zero coupon bond is the present value of the face amount received at the end of the term. There are no interest payments in the early years of the bond's life that reduce the responsiveness of the bond's price to changes in interest rates.

*The calculations assume annual compounding.

---

disadvantage of zero coupon bonds is circumvented. The investor can purchase issues that mature at a desired date to meet retirement needs. For example, a 40-year-old investor could purchase zero coupon government securities that mature when he or she is age 65, 66, and so on. Such a strategy would assure that the funds were received after retirement, at which time they would replace the individual's earned income that ceases at retirement.

FEDERAL AGENCIES' DEBT

In addition to the debt issued by the federal government, certain agencies of the federal government and federally sponsored corporations issue debt. These debt instruments encompass the entire spectrum of maturities, ranging from short-term securities to long-term bonds. Like many U.S. Treasury debt issues, there is an active secondary market in some of the debt issues of these agencies, and price quotations for many of the bonds are given daily in the financial press (i.e., see Exhibit 17.2).

Several federal agencies have come into existence to fulfill specific financial needs. For example, the Banks for Cooperatives were organized under the Farm Credit Act. These banks provide farm business services and make loans to farm cooperatives to help purchase supplies. The Federal Home Loan Mortgage Corporation was established to strengthen the secondary market in residential mortgages insured by the Federal Housing Administration. This federal corporation buys and sells home mortgages to give them marketability and thus increase their attractiveness to private investors. The Student Loan Marketing Association was created to provide liquidity to the insured student loans made under the Guaranteed Student Loan Program by commercial banks, savings and loan associations, and schools that participate in the program. This liquidity should expand the funds available to students from private sources.

Federal agency bonds are not issued by the federal government and are not the debt of the federal government. Hence, they tend to offer higher yields than those available on U.S. Treasury debt. However, the bonds are extremely safe because they have government backing. In some cases this is only **moral backing,** which means that in case of default the federal government does not have to support the debt (i.e., to pay the interest and meet the terms of the indenture). Some of the debt issues, however, are guaranteed by the U.S. Treasury. Should these issues go into default, the federal government is legally bound to assume the obligations of the debt's indenture.

The matter of whether the bonds have the legal or the moral backing of the federal government is probably academic. All of these debt issues are excellent credit risks, because it is doubtful that the federal government would let the debt of one of its agencies go into default. Since these bonds offer slightly higher yields than those available on U.S. Treasury debt, the bonds of federal agencies have become very attractive investments for conservative investors seeking higher yields. This applies not only to individual investors who wish to protect their capital but also to financial institutions, such as commercial banks, insurance companies, or credit unions, which must be particularly concerned with the safety of the principal in making investment decisions.

Federal agency debt can be purchased by individuals, but few individual investors do own these bonds, except indirectly through pension plans, mutual funds, and other institutions that own the debt. Many individual investors are probably not even aware of the existence of this debt and the potential advantages it offers. Any investor who wants to construct a portfolio with an emphasis on income and the relative safety of the principal should consider these debt instruments.

federal agency bonds
Debt issued by agency of the federal government.

moral backing
Nonobligatory support for a debt issue.

Ginnie Mae Securities

One of the most important and popular debt securities issued by a government agency and supported by the federal government is the **Ginnie Mae,** a debt security issued by the Government National Mortgage Association (GNMA or Ginnie Mae), a division of the Department of Housing and Urban Development (HUD). The funds raised through the sale of Ginnie Mae securities are used to acquire a pool of FHA/VA guaranteed mortgages. (FHA and VA are the Federal Housing Authority and Veteran's Administration, respectively.) The mortgages are originated by private lenders, such as savings and loan associations, and packaged into securities that are sold to the general public and guaranteed by GNMA. The minimum size of each issue is $1 million, and the minimum size of the individual Ginnie Mae securities sold to the public is $25,000.[4]

Ginnie Mae securities serve as a conduit through which interest and principal repayments are made. An investor who buys a Ginnie Mae acquires part of the pool. As interest payments and principal repayments are made to the pool, the funds are

Ginnie Mae
Mortgage pass-through bond issued by the Government National Mortgage Association.

---

[4] Individuals with more modest sums to invest may acquire shares in a mutual fund that invests solely in Ginnie Maes.

channeled to the Ginnie Mae's owners. The investor receives a monthly payment that is his or her share of the principal and interest payment received by the pool. Since such payments may vary from month to month, the amount received by the investor also varies monthly. Thus the Ginnie Mae is one example of a long-term debt security whose periodic payments are not fixed.

Ginnie Mae securities have become particularly popular with individuals financing retirement or accumulating funds in retirement accounts. The reason for their popularity is safety, since the federal government insures the payment of principal and interest. Thus, if a mortgage payer were to default, the federal government would make the required payments. This guarantee virtually assures the timely payment of interest and principal to the holder of the Ginnie Mae.

In addition to safety, Ginnie Maes offer yields that exceed what may be obtained through the purchase of federal government securities. Since the yields are ultimately related to the mortgages acquired by the pool, they depend on mortgage rates rather than on the yields of federal government bills and bonds. This yield differential can be as great as 2 percent (sometimes referred to as 200 basis points, with one basis point equaling 0.01 percent) over the return offered by long-term federal government bonds.

Ginnie Mae securities are exceptionally desirable to investors seeking a monthly flow of payments since interest and principal repayments are distributed monthly. The mortgage repayment schedules define the minimum amount of the anticipated payments. However, if the homeowners speed up payments or pay off their loans before the full term of the mortgage, the additional funds are passed on to the holder of the Ginnie Mae securities.

While these securities are supported by the full faith and credit of the federal government, there are risks associated with Ginnie Maes. One is the loss of purchasing power through inflation. Of course, investors will not purchase Ginnie Maes if the anticipated yield is less than the anticipated rate of inflation.

Even if the anticipated return is sufficient to justify the purchase, investors could still lose if interest rates rise. All the mortgages in a particular pool have the same interest rate, and since Ginnie Maes are fixed-income debt securities, their prices fluctuate with interest rates. Higher interest rates will drive down their prices. Thus, if an investor were to seek to sell the security in the secondary market (and there is an active secondary market in Ginnie Maes), he or she could sustain a capital loss resulting from the rise in interest rates. Of course, the investor could experience a capital gain if interest rates were to decline, thus causing the security's value to rise.

The valuation of Ginnie Mae securities is essentially the same as for other debt instruments described in Chapter 15. The interest payments and principal repayments are discounted back to the present at the current rate of interest. There is, however, one important difference. Individuals owning their homes can (and do) repay their mortgage loans prematurely. This is particularly true when interest rates fall and homeowners refinance at the lower rates and when individuals move and sell their homes (unless the new owners are allowed to assume the old mortgage). Thus, the timing and amount of principal repayments that the holder of the Ginnie Mae will receive is not certain. If a large number of homeowners rapidly pay off their mortgage loans, these payments will quickly retire the Ginnie Mae securities. (This disadvantage associated with Ginnie Maes may be reduced by acquiring collateralized mortgage obligations (CMOs), which are discussed below.)

This uncertainty of future payments can lead to differences in the estimated yields. Consider a Ginnie Mae that has an expected life of 12 years[5] and that is currently selling for a discount (which could result if interest rates rose after this Ginnie Mae pool had been assembled and sold). In such a case the price of the Ginnie Mae would decline so that the anticipated yield is comparable with securities currently being issued. For the Ginnie Mae selling at a discount, the yield would depend on the flow of interest payments and how rapidly the mortgage loans are paid off.

If the mortgages are paid off more rapidly than expected (i.e., if the life of the pool is less than the expected 12 years), the realized return will be higher. However, if the mortgages are retired more slowly, the realized return will be less than the expected return. Thus it is possible that the actual yield may differ from the yield assumed when the security was purchased. This makes it possible for two security dealers to assert different yields for the same Ginnie Mae sold at the same price. If one dealer assumes that the mortgage loans will be retired more quickly, a higher yield is anticipated. However, another security dealer may make a more conservative assumption as to the rate at which the mortgages will be retired.

The speed with which the mortgages are paid off depends in part on the interest rates being paid on mortgage loans. If the Ginnie Mae mortgage loans have relatively high rates, homeowners will seek to refinance these loans when rates decline, so the original mortgages are retired rapidly. The opposite holds when the rates on the Ginnie Maes' mortgage loans are lower than current interest rates. In this case there is less incentive for early retirement, which will tend to extend the life of the mortgage pool. Thus, a Ginnie Mae that sells for a discount because the mortgage loans have lower interest rates will tend to have a longer life than a Ginnie Mae selling at a premium because its mortgage loans have a higher rate of interest.

The investor who purchases a Ginnie Mae security should be aware that the payment received represents both earned interest income and return of invested funds. If the investor spends all the payment, that individual is depleting his or her principal. Thus the investor should be fully aware that the individual payments received are composed of both interest and principal repayment and that the latter should be spent only if there is reason for the investor to consume the principal.

Other Mortgage-backed Securities

While Ginnie Maes were the first mortgage-backed securities, other issues have been created by the Federal Home Loan Mortgage Corporation (FHLMC or "Freddie Mac"), the Federal National Mortgage Association (FNMA or "Fannie Mae"), and other lending institutions. The FHLMC Participation Certificate (PC) is similar to the Ginnie Mae; they are both conduits through which interest and principal payments pass from the homeowner to the certificate holder. There is, however, one important difference—Freddie Mac PCs' payments are not guaranteed by the federal government. The absence of this guarantee means that even though the

---

[5] While the maturity of a Ginnie Mae may be 25 to 30 years, the average life (according to the Government National Mortgage Association) is 12 years.

individual mortgages are insured by private mortgage insurance companies, Freddie Mac PCs offer a higher yield than is available through Ginnie Maes.

Mortgage-backed securities are also issued by the FNMA. Fannie Mae sells both general obligation debentures and mortgage-backed securities. The funds are used to finance mortgages, and, like the Freddie Mac PC, the securities issued by Fannie Mae are secured by mortgage loans. Since the Federal National Mortgage Association is a private corporation (its stock trades on the New York Stock Exchange), its debt obligations are not guaranteed by the federal government; thus, these bonds offer higher yields than Ginnie Maes.

Collateralized Mortgage Obligations (CMOs)

While Ginnie Maes are supported by the federal government so the investor knows that the interest and principal will be paid, the amount of each monthly payment is unknown. Because principal repayments vary as homeowners refinance their homes, the amount of principal repayment received by the investor changes every month. This variation in the monthly cash flow may be a disadvantage to any individual (e.g., a retiree) seeking a reasonably certain flow of monthly cash payments.

collateralized mortgage obligation (CMO)
Debt obligation supported by mortgages and sold in series.

Collateralized mortgage obligations (CMOs) reduce, but do not erase, this uncertainty. Collateralized mortgage obligations are backed by a trust that holds Ginnie Mae and other federal government–supported mortgages. When a CMO is created, it is subdivided into classes (called "tranches"). For example, a $100 million CMO may be divided into four tranches of $25 million each. The principal repayments received by the CMO are initially paid to the first class until that tranche has been entirely retired. Once the first class has been paid off, mortgage principal repayments are directed to the holders of the CMOs in the second class. This process is repeated until all the tranches have been repaid.

Within a tranche, principal repayments may be made on a pro rata basis or by lottery. Whether a pro rata system or a lottery system is used to determine repayment is specified in the CMO's indenture; thus, investors know which system applies to a particular CMO. In either case, no principal repayments are made to the next class until all the funds owed the first class are paid.

When an investor purchases a CMO, an estimated "principal repayment window" is known. This schedule gauges when the investor can expect to receive principal repayments and when a particular tranche will be entirely redeemed. As with Ginnie Mae payments, the CMO payment schedule is based on historical repayment data, but the actual timing of the repayments cannot be known with certainty. Lower interest rates will tend to speed up payments as homeowners refinance while higher interest rates will tend to retard principal repayments.

Since the actual timing of principal repayment is not known, CMOs reduce but do not erase this source of risk. However, less timing risk exists with CMOs than with a Ginnie Mae. When the investor acquires a Ginnie Mae, the repayments are spread over the life of the entire issue. With a CMO, the repayments are spread over each tranche. The investor who acquires a CMO can better match the anticipated need for cash. For example, a 65-year-old retiree may have less immediate need for cash than an 80-year-old. The latter may acquire the first class, while the former acquires the third class within a CMO. The 65-year-old would receive the current interest component but the principal repayment would be deferred until the first and second classes had been entirely retired.

For accepting later repayment of principal, the investor can expect to earn a higher interest return. The interest rate varies with the expected life of the class. The tranche with the smallest expected life earns the lowest interest rate, and the tranche with the longest expected life earns the highest.

STATE AND LOCAL GOVERNMENT DEBT

State and local governments also issue debt to finance capital expenditures, such as schools or roads. The government then retires the debt as the facilities are used. The funds used to retire the debt may be raised through taxes (e.g., property taxes) or through revenues generated by the facilities themselves.

Unlike the federal government, state and local governments do not have the power to create money. These governments must raise the funds necessary to pay the interest and retire the debt, but the ability to do so varies with the financial status of each government. Municipalities with wealthy residents or valuable property within their boundaries are able to issue debt more readily and at lower interest rates because the debt is safer. The tax base in these communities is larger and can support the debt.

The Tax Exemption

The primary factor that differentiates state and local government debt from other forms of debt is the tax advantage that it offers to investors. The interest earned on state and municipal government debt is exempt from federal income taxation. Hence, these bonds are frequently referred to as **tax-exempt bonds** or **municipal bonds.** Although state and local governments may tax the interest, the federal government may not. The rationale for this tax exemption is legal and not financial. The Supreme Court ruled that the federal government does not have the power to tax the interest paid by the debt of state and municipal governments. Since the interest paid by all other debt, including corporate bonds, is subject to federal income taxation, this exemption is advantageous to state and local governments, for they are able to issue debt with substantially lower interest rates.

municipal bond
A tax-exempt bond; a bond issued by a state or one of its political subdivisions.

Investors are willing to accept a lower return on state and local government debt because the after-tax return is equivalent to higher yields on corporate debt. For example, if an investor is in the 28 percent income tax bracket, the return after taxes is the same for a corporate bond that pays 10 percent as for a state or municipal government bond that pays 7.2 percent: The after-tax return is 7.2 percent in either case.

The willingness of investors to purchase state and local government debt instead of corporate and U.S. Treasury debt is related to their income tax bracket. If an investor's federal income tax rate is 28 percent, a 6.5 percent nontaxable municipal bond gives the investor the same yield after taxes as a 9.03 percent corporate bond the interest of which is subject to federal income taxation. The individual investor may determine the equivalent yields on tax-exempt bonds and nonexempt bonds by using the following equation:

$$i_c(1 - t) = i_m, \qquad (17.1)$$

where i_c is the interest rate paid on corporate debt, i_m is the interest rate paid on municipal debt, and t is the individual's tax bracket (i.e., the marginal tax rate). This equation is used as follows. If an investor's tax bracket is 28 percent and tax-exempt bonds offer 6.5 percent, then the equivalent corporate yield is

$$i_c(1 - 0.28) = 0.065$$

$$i_c = \frac{0.065}{0.72} = 9.03\%.$$

Exempting the interest on these bonds from federal income taxation has been frequently criticized because it is an apparent means for the "rich" to avoid federal income taxation.[6] The exemption does, however, reduce the interest cost for the state and municipal governments that issue debt, which in effect is a subsidy to those governments. From an economic point of view, the important question is whether the exemption is the best means to aid or subsidize state and local governments. Other means, such as federal revenue sharing, could be used for this purpose.

The interest exemption is primarily a political question. Changes in the legal structure may alter the tax exemption in the future. Until that time, however, the interest on state and municipal debt remains exempt from federal income taxation, with the effects being that (1) state and local governments can issue debt with interest rates that are lower than individuals and corporations must pay, and (2) these bonds offer the wealthier members of our society a means to obtain tax-sheltered income.

While state and local government interest is tax-exempt at the federal level, it may be taxed at the state level. States do exempt the interest paid by their own local governments but tax the interest paid by other states and their local governments. Thus while interest earned on New York City obligations is not taxed in New York, it is taxed in New Jersey.

It should also be noted that state and local governments cannot tax the interest paid by the federal government. While interest earned on Series EE and HH bonds, treasury bills, notes, and bonds is taxed by the federal government, this interest cannot be taxed by state and local governments. In states with modest or no income taxes, this exemption is meaningless. However, in states with high income taxes such as Massachusetts or New York, this tax exemption may be a major reason for acquiring U.S. Treasury securities. For example, the yield on a treasury bill on an after-tax basis may exceed the yield on a federally insured certificate of deposit or the yield offered by a money market mutual fund. In such cases the tax laws will certainly encourage the investor to acquire the federal security, because that investor has both a higher after-tax yield and less risk (i.e., the support of the full faith and credit of the federal government).

---

[6] Since the minimum denomination for municipal bonds is $5,000 and sometimes $10,000, individuals with modest amounts to invest are excluded from this market except through investing in mutual funds that invest in tax-exempt bonds.

Figure 17.1 ✦ AVERAGE YIELDS AND THE SPREAD BETWEEN AAA- AND BAA-RATED MUNICIPAL BONDS (1970–1992)

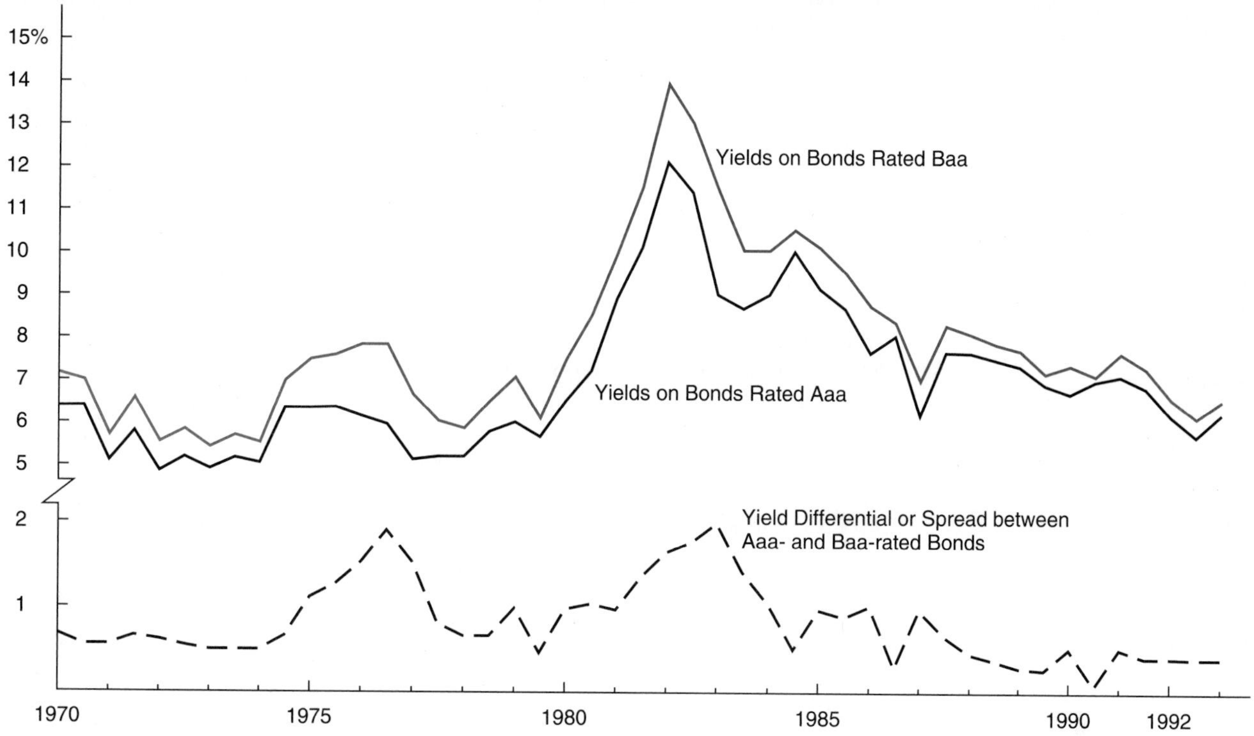

Source: *Moody's Bond Record,* various issues.

Yields and Prices of State and Local Government Bonds

Like yields on other securities, yields on tax-exempt bonds have varied over time. Figure 17.1 shows the average yields on Moody's Aaa- and Baa-rated bonds over several years. During this period there was considerable fluctuation in the interest rates paid by tax-exempt bonds. For example, in 1978 the yields to maturity were 5.5 percent for the Aaa-rated bonds, but these yields rose to 12 percent in 1982. There was a comparable fluctuation in the yields of the Baa-rated bonds, which rose from 6.2 percent to 13.3 percent during the same period. A yield of 12 percent is comparable to a yield of 16.7 percent on a corporate bond for an individual in the 28 percent income tax bracket.

In addition to showing the fluctuations in yields, the figure shows the difference in yields. As would be expected, the yields on Baa-rated bonds exceed those on the Aaa-rated bonds, but the spread in the yields between the Aaa- and Baa-rated bonds varies. During the periods of higher interest rates, the spread widens. For example, the spread rose to 2.0 percent during 1983. However, when interest rates declined, the spread between the yields on the Aaa- and Baa-rated bonds declined to less than 0.5 percent from 1986 to 1988.

Figure 17.2 ✦ Yields on Federal Government Bonds and Aaa-Rated Municipal Bonds

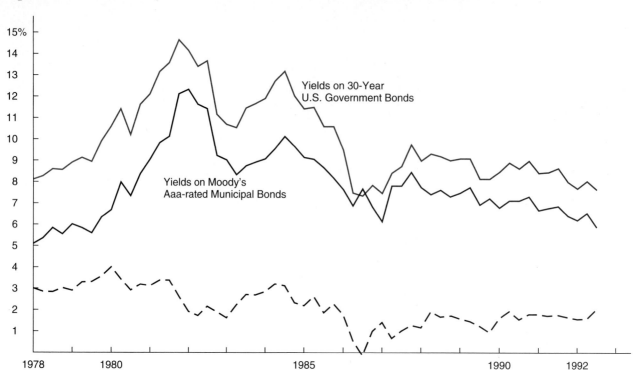

Figure 17.2 presents similar information except it plots the yields on U.S. government bonds and Moody's Aaa-rated municipal bonds. A similar pattern emerges. When interest rates in general rose, the yields on both bonds rose (e.g., 1980 to 1982), and when interest rates fell, the yields on both federal government and municipal bonds fell (e.g., 1987 through 1992). Except briefly during 1986, the yields on the federal government securities exceeded the yields on the municipal bonds throughout the time period. After 1985, the differential between the yields was lower as tax reform and lower federal income tax rates reduced the attractiveness of municipal securities vis-à-vis the bonds of the federal government.

This change in the relative attractiveness of one bond to another points out that the yields (and prices) of municipal bonds, like the prices and yields on corporate and federal government debt, ultimately depend on the demand for and supply of the various types of bonds. When many state and local governments seek credit and desire to issue bonds, the yields on tax exempts will rise. In addition, the conditions in the financial markets will affect yields. As Figures 17.1 and 17.2 illustrate, when interest rates rise in general, the yields on tax-exempt bonds will also rise.

Of course, an increase in yields means that the prices of existing municipal bonds must fall. The equations used to determine the value of a bond that were presented in Chapter 15 also apply to the valuation of municipal and state bonds. The yields on these bonds are inversely related to their prices. When a state or municipality government bond's price rises, its yield declines. When the bond's price falls, the yield rises. Like corporate debt, these bonds can sell at a discount or for a premium, depending on the direction of change in interest rates. Hence investors in tax-exempt bonds bear the risk associated with fluctuations in interest rates.

Types of Tax-exempt Securities

State and local governments issue a variety of debt instruments; these can be classified either according to the means by which the security is supported or according to the length of time to maturity (i.e., short- or long-term). State and municipal debt is supported by either the taxing power of the issuing government or the revenues generated by the facilities that are financed by the debt. If the bonds are secured by the taxing power, the debt is a **general obligation** of the government.

general obligation bond
A bond whose interest does not depend on the revenue of a specific project; government bonds supported by the full faith and credit of the issuer (i.e., authority to tax).

Bonds supported by the revenue generated by the project being financed with the debt are called **revenue bonds.** These are issued to finance particular capital improvements, such as a toll road that generates its own money. As these revenues are collected, they are used to pay the interest and retire the principal.

revenue bond
A bond whose interest is paid only if the debtor earns sufficient revenue.

General obligation bonds are commonly thought to be safer than revenue bonds, since the government is required to use its taxing authority to pay the interest and repay the principal.[7] Revenue bonds are supported only by funds generated by the project financed by the sale of the bonds. If the project does not generate sufficient revenues, the interest cannot be paid, and the bonds go into default. For example, the Chesapeake Bay Bridge and Tunnel did not produce sufficient toll revenues, so its publicly held bonds went into default. The default, of course, caused the price of the bonds to fall. Since the bondholders could not foreclose on the bridge, their only course of action was to wait for a resumption of interest payments. After several years elapsed, toll revenues rose sufficiently so that interest payments to the bondholders were resumed.

Tax-exempt bonds are issued in both registered and coupon form. The minimum denomination is $5,000 in face value. There is an active secondary market in this debt; however, the bonds are traded only in the over-the-counter market, and only a handful are quoted in the financial press. Small denominations (e.g., $5,000) tend to lack marketability, but that does not mean that an investor trying to sell one $5,000 bond issued by a small municipality cannot sell it. It does imply, however, that the market is extremely thin and that the spread between the bid and ask prices may be substantial.

Although most corporate bonds are issued with a particular term to maturity and a sinking fund requirement, many tax-exempt bonds are issued in a series. With a serial issue, a specific amount of the debt falls due each year. Such an issue is illustrated in Exhibit 17.3, which reproduces a tombstone advertisement for bonds sold by the North Carolina Eastern Municipal Power Agency. (These advertisements are placed by the underwriting syndicate to describe a public offering. They are frequently referred to as "tombstones" because they resemble an epitaph on a tombstone.) About half of the $113 million issue is in serial bonds. A portion of the issue

---

[7] General obligation bonds may have to be approved by popular referendum. Such referendums can be costly, and public approval of the bonds may be difficult to obtain. These characteristics associated with issuing the debt reduce the risk of investing in general obligation bonds.

POINTS OF INTEREST

COPs

In addition to general obligation and revenue bonds and notes issued in anticipation of taxes and other revenues, some municipalities have sold *certificates of participation* (COPs). COPs are issued to finance specific projects (e.g., equipment such as police vehicles, correction facilities, or administrative buildings) that are subsequently leased to the municipality. The rental payments cover the debt service payments to the holders of the certificates. The municipal government is not responsible for payments for payments to the investors who purchase the COPs; the municipality only makes the lease or rental payments.

COPs are often issued by governments seeking to circumvent limits on their ability to issue debt or to avoid having to obtain voter approval to sell debt. Since the government makes lease payments and not interest and principal repayments, the debt is not considered an obligation of the government. This exclusion of the debt from the municipality's balance sheet understates its obligations.[*]

The removal also increases the investor's risk. Unlike the required interest and principal repayment of general obligation bonds, there is no assurance the government will allocate the funds to make the lease payments. During 1992, legislative bodies in Brevard County,

Florida, and Florence, South Carolina, considered withholding the lease payments. Without such appropriations, payments to the investors would not be made and the COPs would go into default. While such a default has not occurred, any default on a specific certificate could affect all COPs and lead to their downgrading by the rating services. This increased risk associated with COPs results in their offering higher yields (from 0.1 to 0.5 percent points) than is available through traditional municipal bonds of the same credit rating.

[*]An analogous situation applies to firms that lease plant and equipment. However, corporate accounting may require that the firm "capitalize" the lease. That is, the corporation must determine the present value of the lease obligation and put that amount on its balance sheet as a long-term obligation. In effect, the lease obligation is acknowledged as an alternative to a bond. Both require periodic payments over a period of time, and both increase the financial risk associated with the firm.

Managements that do not want the lease obligation to appear on the firm's balance sheet must be certain that the terms of the lease do not meet the accounting requirements that cause the lease to be capitalized. Even if the lease obligation does not have to be capitalized, it must be disclosed in a footnote to the firm's accounting statements.

matures each year. For example, $2,895,000 worth of the bonds matures on January 1, 2003, and another $5,185,000 matures on January 1, 2013. Serial bonds offer advantages to both the issuer and the buyer. In contrast to corporate debt, in which a random selection of the bonds is retired each year through the sinking fund, the buyer knows when each bond will mature. The investor can then purchase bonds that mature at the desired time, which helps in portfolio planning. Because a portion of the issue is retired periodically with serial bonds, the issuing government does not have to make a large, lump-sum payment. Since these bonds are scheduled to be retired, there is no call penalty. If the government wants to retire additional debt, it can call some of the remaining bonds. For example, if the agency wanted to retire some of these bonds prematurely, it would call the term bonds that are due in 2021. (Most issues like the bonds shown in Exhibit 17.3 require that any debt retired before maturity be called in reverse order. Thus, the term bonds with the longest time to maturity are called and redeemed first.)

Although most of the debt sold to the general public by state and local governments is long-term, there are two notable exceptions: tax or revenue anticipation notes. Tax or revenue **anticipation notes** are what their name implies. The issuing government anticipates certain receipts in the future and issues a debt instrument against these receipts. When the taxes or other revenues are received, the notes are retired. The maturity date is set to coincide with the timing of the anticipated receipts so that the notes may be easily retired.

anticipation note
A short-term liability that is to be retired by specific expected revenues (e.g., expected tax receipts).

Exhibit 17.3 ✦ TOMBSTONE FOR AN ISSUE OF SERIAL AND TERM BONDS

All of these securities have been sold. This announcement appears as a matter of record only.

New Issue

$1,614,620,000

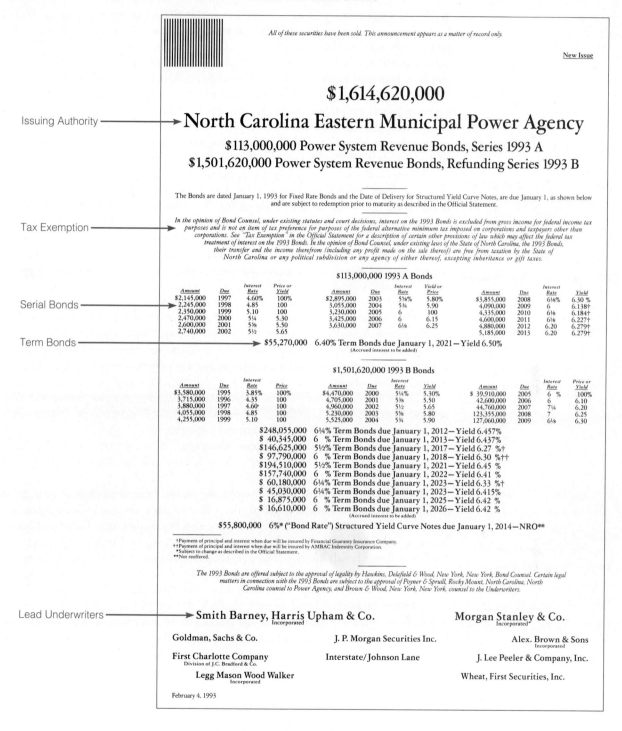

Issuing Authority →

North Carolina Eastern Municipal Power Agency

$113,000,000 Power System Revenue Bonds, Series 1993 A
$1,501,620,000 Power System Revenue Bonds, Refunding Series 1993 B

The Bonds are dated January 1, 1993 for Fixed Rate Bonds and the Date of Delivery for Structured Yield Curve Notes, are due January 1, as shown below and are subject to redemption prior to maturity as described in the Official Statement.

Tax Exemption →

In the opinion of Bond Counsel, under existing statutes and court decisions, interest on the 1993 Bonds is excluded from gross income for federal income tax purposes and is not an item of tax preference for purposes of the federal alternative minimum tax imposed on corporations and taxpayers other than corporations. See "Tax Exemption" in the Official Statement for a description of certain other provisions of law which may affect the federal tax treatment of interest on the 1993 Bonds. In the opinion of Bond Counsel, under existing laws of the State of North Carolina, the 1993 Bonds, their transfer and the income therefrom (including any profit made on the sale thereof) are free from taxation by the State of North Carolina or any political subdivision or any agency of either thereof, excepting inheritance or gift taxes.

$113,000,000 1993 A Bonds

Serial Bonds →

Amount	Due	Interest Rate	Price or Yield	Amount	Due	Interest Rate	Yield or Price	Amount	Due	Interest Rate	Yield
$2,145,000	1997	4.60%	100%	$2,895,000	2003	5⅝%	5.80%	$3,855,000	2008	6⅛%	6.30 %
2,245,000	1998	4.85	100	3,055,000	2004	5¾	5.90	4,090,000	2009	6	6.138†
2,350,000	1999	5.10	100	3,230,000	2005	6	100	4,335,000	2010	6⅛	6.184†
2,470,000	2000	5¼	5.30	3,425,000	2006	6	6.15	4,600,000	2011	6⅛	6.227†
2,600,000	2001	5⅜	5.50	3,630,000	2007	6⅛	6.25	4,880,000	2012	6.20	6.279†
2,740,000	2002	5½	5.65					5,185,000	2013	6.20	6.279†

Term Bonds → $55,270,000 6.40% Term Bonds due January 1, 2021—Yield 6.50%
(Accrued interest to be added)

$1,501,620,000 1993 B Bonds

Amount	Due	Interest Rate	Price	Amount	Due	Interest Rate	Yield	Amount	Due	Interest Rate	Price or Yield
$3,580,000	1995	3.85%	100%	$4,470,000	2000	5¼%	5.30%	$ 39,910,000	2005	6 %	100%
3,715,000	1996	4.35	100	4,705,000	2001	5⅜	5.50	42,600,000	2006	6	6.10
3,880,000	1997	4.60·	100	4,960,000	2002	5½	5.65	44,760,000	2007	7¼	6.20
4,055,000	1998	4.85	100	5.230,000	2003	5⅝	5.80	123,355,000	2008	7	6.25
4,255,000	1999	5.10	100	5,525,000	2004	5¾	5.90	127,060,000	2009	6⅛	6.30

$248,055,000 6¼% Term Bonds due January 1, 2012—Yield 6.457%
$ 40,345,000 6 % Term Bonds due January 1, 2013—Yield 6.437%
$146,625,000 5½% Term Bonds due January 1, 2017—Yield 6.27 %†
$ 97,790,000 6 % Term Bonds due January 1, 2018—Yield 6.30 %††
$194,510,000 5½% Term Bonds due January 1, 2021—Yield 6.45 %
$157,740,000 6 % Term Bonds due January 1, 2022—Yield 6.41 %
$ 60,180,000 6¼% Term Bonds due January 1, 2023—Yield 6.33 %†
$ 45,030,000 6¼% Term Bonds due January 1, 2023—Yield 6.415%
$ 16,875,000 6 % Term Bonds due January 1, 2025—Yield 6.42 %
$ 16,610,000 6 % Term Bonds due January 1, 2026—Yield 6.42 %
(Accrued interest to be added)

$55,800,000 6%* ("Bond Rate") Structured Yield Curve Notes due January 1, 2014—NRO**

†Payment of principal and interest when due will be insured by Financial Guaranty Insurance Company.
††Payment of principal and interest when due will be insured by AMBAC Indemnity Corporation.
*Subject to change as described in the Official Statement.
**Not reoffered.

The 1993 Bonds are offered subject to the approval of legality by Hawkins, Delafield & Wood, New York, New York, Bond Counsel. Certain legal matters in connection with the 1993 Bonds are subject to the approval of Poyner & Spruill, Rocky Mount, North Carolina, North Carolina counsel to Power Agency, and Brown & Wood, New York, New York, counsel to the Underwriters.

Lead Underwriters →

Smith Barney, Harris Upham & Co. Incorporated — **Morgan Stanley & Co.** Incorporated

Goldman, Sachs & Co. — J. P. Morgan Securities Inc. — Alex. Brown & Sons Incorporated

First Charlotte Company (Division of J.C. Bradford & Co.) — Interstate/Johnson Lane — J. Lee Peeler & Company, Inc.

Legg Mason Wood Walker Incorporated — Wheat, First Securities, Inc.

February 4, 1993

Source: Reprinted with permission of North Carolina Eastern Municipal Power Agency.

Tax-exempt Securities and Risk

While the sources of risk associated with investing in tax-exempt bonds were alluded to in the above discussion, it is desirable to summarize them. First, there is the market risk associated with changes in interest rates. Higher interest rates will drive down the prices of existing bonds. This source of risk, of course, applies to all bonds and is not unique to the bonds of state and municipal governments. The investor may reduce this source of risk by purchasing bonds of shorter maturity, because the prices of bonds with longer terms to maturity fluctuate more. If the investor is concerned with price fluctuations and the preservation of capital, then shorter term tax-exempt bonds should be preferred to long-term bonds. The investor, however, should realize that shorter term bonds generally pay less interest.

The second source of risk is the possibility that the government might default on the interest and principal repayment. Unfortunately, finding information on particular bond issues can be fairly difficult for the individual investor. Municipal bonds are not registered with the Securities and Exchange Commission (SEC) prior to their sale to the general public, and many state and local governments do not publish annual reports and send them to bondholders. Instead, investors may consult the latest issues of Moody's *Municipal and Government Manual* or *Standard & Poor's Bond Guide*. Fortunately for investors, both of these firms rate a considerable number of the tax-exempt bonds that are sold to the general public. These ratings are based on a substantial amount of data, for the rating services require the municipal and state governments to provide them with financial and economic information. Since failure of the bond issue to receive a favorable rating will dissuade many potential buyers, the state and local governments supply the rating services with the required information.

The investor can take several steps that will reduce the risk associated with default. The first is to purchase a diversified portfolio of tax-exempt bonds, which spreads the risk associated with any particular government. Second, the investor may limit purchases to debt with high credit ratings.[8] If the investor purchases only bonds with AAA or AA credit ratings, there is little risk (perhaps no real risk) of loss from default.

A third means by which the investor may limit the risk of default is to limit purchases to bonds that are insured. Several insurance companies guarantee the payment of interest and principal of the municipal bonds they insure. Insured bonds almost inevitably have high credit ratings. For example, the Virginia Port Authority Facility revenue bonds are insured by AMBAC and have an AAA rating by Standard & Poor's. AMBAC is the American Municipal Bond Assurance Corporation, which is owned by several financial institutions including Citicorp and Xerox Financial Services. Other municipal bond insurers include MBIA (Municipal Bond Insurance Association), which is composed of a consortium of leading insurance companies, FGIC (Financial Guaranty Insurance Co.), which is owned by several large financial institutions including General Electric Credit and Merrill Lynch, and Industrial Indemnity, a division of Xerox's Crum & Foster insurance subsidiary.

---

[8] Some tax-exempt bonds are secured by lines of credit with commercial banks. If the government defaults, the banks pay the interest and principal.

POINTS OF INTEREST

WPPSS/WHOOPS

In recent years tax-exempt bonds have generally been free from default. Only two municipal governments with investment grade ratings have defaulted on general obligation bonds: New York City in 1975 and Cleveland in 1978. (New York claims that it did not default but had a "moratorium.")

Such safety, however, need not apply to nongeneral obligation tax-exempt bonds. For example, in 1988, Standard & Poor downgraded the debt of Verex Assurance, which insured tax-exempt housing authority bond issues. Lowering the credit rating of the insurance company implies the bonds' risk increased. The insured bonds' prices tumbled, and bonds that were trading at par ($1000) quickly declined to $950 (i.e., $.95 per dollar face amount) for a 5 percent price decrease. The price decline occurred even though the issuers of the bonds had not defaulted.

The most spectacular demonstration of risk through default is the Washington Public Power Supply System (WPPSS and cynically referred to as WHOOPS), which sold $2.25 billion of debt to build two nuclear power plants. The plants, however, were not completed, so the utilities that initially agreed to buy the power refused to make construction payments. In addition, the power authority was not allowed by the courts to raise its rates for electricity generated in the authority's other facilities. Since the plants were not completed and the authority could not recover their costs, the bonds went into default.

The investor who acquires insured bonds should realize that lower yields accompany lower risk. As a result of the insurance guarantees, the yield on the bonds will be lower than the yield available on non-insured bonds. The reduction in risk and yields is also affected by the quality of the company offering the insurance. If the insurance company has a lower credit rating than other insurers, the quality of the insurance may be lower, raising the possibility of default by the insurance company should the municipality default. While such a default has not occurred, its possibility should be considered.

In addition to the risks associated with fluctuations in security prices and the possibility of default, the investor should be aware that tax-exempt bonds may lack marketability. Bonds issued by small governments may be resold, but the secondary markets are thin (i.e., small). Common sense should tell the investor that bonds issued by the Industrial Development Authority of Medium-Town, USA, are not very liquid. If the investor must sell the bonds before maturity, he or she may suffer a loss as the price of the bonds is marked down to induce someone to purchase them. Many investors may not be aware of this lack of marketability until they seek to sell the bonds and receive bids that are below the anticipated price. This is particularly true during periods of high interest rates when the market for existing municipal bonds dries up and prices are significantly marked down.

The existence of these risks does not imply that an investor should avoid tax-exempt bonds. The return offered by these bonds is probably consistent with the amount of risk the investor must bear. If a particular bond were to offer an exceptionally high return, it would be readily purchased and its price driven up so that the return was in line with comparable risky securities. Tax-exempt bonds should be examined by investors with moderate-to-high incomes who are seeking tax-free income and who do not need liquidity. Like any investment, tax-exempt bonds may fit into an individual investor's portfolio and offer a return (after tax) that is in line with the risk the investor must endure.

TAXABLE MUNICIPAL SECURITIES

The previous discussion indicated that the interest on state and local government securities is exempt from federal income taxation. While that is generally true, there are exceptions. There is no requirement that localities issue tax-exempt bonds; they may issue taxable bonds. For example, the Alaska Housing Finance Corporation issued over $2 billion taxable bonds from 1981 to 1986. Few other state and local governments have followed the Alaska Housing Finance Corporation's policy. Instead they have issued nontaxable bonds. Tax reform, however, has limited the ability of local governments to issue tax-exempt bonds as a means to raise funds for financing some projects, such as housing and industrial development.

Prior to tax reform, a local government could create an industrial authority that would issue bonds, build a facility, and then lease it to a firm. Local governments sold these industrial revenue bonds as a means to stimulate economic growth or obtain a desired facility, such as a hospital. Since the local government authority and not the user issued the debt, the interest is tax-exempt. The interest payments are the responsibility of the industrial authority and not the local or state government that created the authority (i.e., the bonds are revenue bonds of the authority and not general obligations of the state or its municipalities). If the firm using the facilities were to fail to make the required payments, the industrial authority would be unable to make the interest payments to the bondholders. While this suggests industrial revenue bonds can be risky investments, many are among the safest tax-exempt bonds because the interest is supported by major corporations. For example, the Waynesboro Virginia Industrial Authority bonds are supported by DuPont.

Tax reform has limited the ability of state and local governments to use this type of financing. In addition, the interest may be subject to the alternative minimum tax that some individuals must pay. This alternative tax is designed to assure that individuals who may not be subject to federal income tax under the regular tax laws will be required to make some federal income tax payments. Hence, interest that is exempt from regular federal income taxation may be subject to the alternative taxation.

An example of tax-exempt debt subject to the alternative minimum tax is the issue of bonds sold by the Richmond Virginia Redevelopment and Housing Authority. The funds raised by the issue will be used to develop and renovate a section of the city referred to as Tobacco Row and will result in the building of condominiums, apartments, and retail space. Part of the financing, which includes both private and public participation, is a $100 million issue of authority bonds. While the interest is exempt from regular federal income taxation, it is subject to the alternative minimum tax.

Bonds that are subject to the alternative tax are not as attractive as other debt instruments, such as bonds issued by the state of Virginia to finance general improvements or the city of Richmond to finance public schools. Bonds subject to the alternative minimum tax tend to have higher yields than bonds not subject to the tax. Individuals who are subject to the regular federal income taxes but are not subject to the alternative minimum tax may find these debt obligations to be attractive investments. They offer higher yields and do not affect these individuals' tax obligations.

SUMMARY

When the federal government spends more than it receives in tax revenues, this deficit must be financed. In order to tap funds from many sources, the federal government issues a variety of debt instruments. These include series EE and HH bonds, which are sold in small denominations, and treasury bills and bonds, which are sold in large denominations.

Federal government debt is the safest of all possible investments, as there is no possibility of default. However, the investor still bears the risk of loss through fluctuations in the price of the marketable debt and through inflation. If the rate of inflation exceeds the yield on the debt instruments, the investor then experiences a loss of purchasing power.

In addition to the debt issued by the federal government itself, bonds are issued by its agencies. These bonds tend to offer slightly higher yields, but they are virtually as safe as the direct debt of the federal government. In some cases the agency's debt is even secured by the full faith and credit of the U.S. Treasury.

Among the most popular securities issued by a federal government agency are the mortgage pass-through bonds issued by the Government National Mortgage Association or "Ginnie Mae." These bonds serve as a conduit through which interest and principal repayments are made from homeowners to the bondholders. Payments are made monthly, so Ginnie Mae bonds are popular with individuals seeking a flow of cash receipts. While these bonds expose investors to some risk of loss from fluctuating interest rates or from inflation, the interest payments and principal repayments are guaranteed by an agency of the federal government. Thus Ginnie Mae bonds are considered to be among the safest of all long-term debt instruments.

An alternative to Ginnie Maes are collateralized mortgage obligations (CMOs), which are issued by a trust that holds mortgages guaranteed by the federal government. CMOs are sold in series, or "tranches," with the obligations in the shortest tranche being retired before any of the CMOs in the next series are retired. Yields tend to increase as the expected life of a CMO is increased.

State and local governments issue long-term debt instruments to finance capital improvements such as schools and roads. The debt is retired over a period of time by tax receipts or revenues. While some of these bonds are supported by the taxing authority of the issuing government, many are supported only by the revenues generated by the facilities financed through the bond issues.

State and municipal debt differs from other investments because the interest is exempt from federal income taxation. These bonds pay lower rates of interest than taxable securities (e.g., corporate bonds), but their after-tax yields may be equal to or even greater than the yields on taxable bonds. The nontaxable bonds are particularly attractive to investors in high income tax brackets, because they provide a means to shelter some income from taxation.

Tax-exempt bonds can be risky investments, since the capacity of state and local governments to service the debt varies. Moody's and Standard & Poor's rating services analyze this debt based on the government's ability to pay the interest and retire the principal. Such ratings indicate the risk associated with investing in a particular debt issue. In addition, investors must bear the risks associated with fluctuations in security prices and the lack of liquidity associated with tax-exempt bonds.

Security Summary

Federal Government Bonds

Source of return: Interest income and possible capital gains if interest rates fall.

Liquidity and marketability: Active secondary market in government debt (except EE and HH bonds that are redeemed) but chance of loss if interest rates rise so federal government bonds are marketable but not liquid.

Sources of risk: The capacity of the federal government to tax and to create money implies no risk of loss of interest or principal repayment. Systematic risk from interest rate risk since bond prices fall when interest rates rise. Possible loss of purchasing power if the rate of inflation exceeds the interest rate.

Taxation: Interest is subject to federal income taxation but is exempt from state and local income taxation. Capital gains that occur if interest rates fall are subject to taxation only when the gains are realized.

Security Summary

Municipal Bonds

Source of return: Interest income and possible capital gains if interest rates fall.

Liquidity and marketability: Active secondary market in municipal debt for large issues but investor may have difficulty selling bonds of smaller government units (i.e., large spread in the bid and ask prices). Chance of loss if interest rates rise means that municipal bonds are not liquid.

Sources of risk: Unsystematic risk from events that affect the government's capacity to service its debt (i.e., pay the interest and timely retire the bonds). Systematic risk from interest rate risk since bond prices fall when interest rates rise. Possible loss of purchasing power if the rate of inflation exceeds the interest rate.

Taxation: Interest is not subject to federal income taxation but may be subject to state and local taxation. Capital gains that occur if interest rates fall are subject to taxation only when the gains are realized.

Terms to Remember

series E and EE bonds	collateralized mortgage obligation (CMO)
series H and HH bonds	tax-exempt bond
treasury bills	municipal bond
treasury notes	general obligation bond
treasury bonds	revenue bond
federal agency bonds	anticipation note
moral backing	
Ginnie Mae	

Questions

1. Why is the debt of the federal government considered to be the safest of all possible investments?
2. What distinguishes series EE bonds from treasury bills?
3. When interest rates rise, what happens to the price of federal government bonds? What happens to the price of state and local government bonds?
4. What is the difference between the following:
    a. a bond secured by a moral obligation and a bond secured by full faith and credit?
    b. a revenue bond and a general obligation bond?

    Are there any similarities between a bond secured by a moral obligation and a revenue bond?
5. What are the sources of risk investing in
    a. federal government debt?
    b. municipal debt?
6. What is the difference between a term bond issue and a serial bond issue? Why are many capital improvements made by state and local governments financed through serial bonds?
7. If an investor or corporation wants to invest in a short-term government security, what alternatives are available? How safe are these securities, and do they offer any tax advantages?
8. What is a mortgage pass-through bond? What risks are associated with investing in Ginnie Mae bonds? What is the composition of the payment received from a mortgage pass-through bond?
9. If interest rates increase, what should happen to
    a. the price of a Ginnie Mae bond and the price of a municipal bond?
    b. the payments received from a Ginnie Mae bond and the payments received from a municipal bond?

    Contrast your answers to parts a and b.
10. What government securities may be appropriate for the following investors?
    a. a retired couple seeking income
    b. an individual in the highest tax bracket seeking a liquid investment
    c. an individual seeking a government bond for inclusion in an individual retirement account (IRA)
    d. a child with no income and a modest amount to invest
    e. a corporation with $100,000,000 to invest for less than three months
    f. a church seeking to invest a modest endowment fund.

Problems

1. If a six-month treasury bill is purchased for $0.9675 on a dollar (i.e., $96,750 for a $100,000 bill), what is the approximate annual rate of interest? What will be the yield if the discount price falls to $0.94 on a dollar (i.e., $94,000 for a $100,000 bill)?
2. An investor is in the 28 percent income tax bracket and can earn 6.3 percent on a nontaxable bond. What is the comparable yield on a taxable bond?

If this same investor can earn 8.9 percent on a taxable bond, what must be the yield on a nontaxable bond so that the after-tax yields are equal?

3. An investor in the 36 percent tax bracket may purchase an AT&T bond that is rated double A and is traded on the New York Stock Exchange (the bond division). This bond yields 9.0 percent. The investor may also buy a double A-rated municipal bond with an 5.76 percent yield. Why may the AT&T bond be preferred? (Assume that the terms of the bonds are the same.)

4. What is the price of the following zero coupon bonds if interest rates are (a) 5%, (b) 10%, and (c) 15%?
   ✦ Bond A: zero coupon; maturity 10 years
   ✦ Bond B: zero coupon; maturity 20 years
   ✦ Bond C: zero coupon; maturity 30 years
   What generalization can be made concerning the term of a zero coupon bond and its price to changes in the level of interest rates?

5. You are in the 28 percent federal income tax bracket. A corporate bond offers you 9.8 percent while a tax-exempt bond with the same credit rating and term to maturity offers 8.1 percent. On the basis of taxation, which bond should be preferred? Explain.

6. A six-month $10,000 treasury bill is selling for $9,844. What is the approximate annual yield according to the discount method? Does this yield understate or overstate the true annual yield? Explain.

Suggested Readings

For information on particular issues or the debt of particular states and municipalities, consult:

Moody's Investors Service. *Moody's Bond Record* or *Moody's Bond Survey.* (These publications are updated continuously and present a wealth of information on particular debt issues.)

Standard & Poor's Corporation. *Bond Guide.* Published monthly. (While primarily limited to corporate debt, these bond guides are a convenient source of S & P's ratings of selected municipal debt.)

For a book of readings on debt securities that includes returns, yield curves, cash management strategies, and options, consult:

Frank J. Fabozzi, ed. *The Handbook of Fixed Income Securities.* 3d. ed. Homewood, Il.: Business One-Irwin, 1991.

For a discussion of mortgage-backed securities, see:

Frank J. Fabozzi. *Mortgage-Backed Securities.* Chicago: Probus Publishing, 1986.
Blume, Marshall E., and Jack P. Friedman, eds. *The Encyclopedia of Investments* 2d ed. Boston: Warren, Gorham & Lamont, 1990. This book devotes chapters to mortgage-backed securities, municipal securities, treasury bonds and agency securities, and treasury bills.

For a general discussion of municipal securities, see:

Feldstein, Sylvan G. *The Dow Jones-Irwin Guide to Municipal Bonds.* Homewood, Ill.: Dow Jones-Irwin, 1986.

Appendix

RIDING THE YIELD CURVE

The positively sloped yield curve suggests a means by which an investor may magnify the return on a short-term investment. Consider an individual with $10,000 to invest in treasury bills. Four investment possibilities are

Term	Price	Annual Yield
3 months	$9,800	8.2%
6 months	9,500	10.5
9 months	9,000	13.2
12 months	8,800	13.6

Notice that in this example the yield curve in Figure 17.3 is positively sloped because as the term of the bill increases, the yields become higher (e.g., 8.2 percent for the three-month bill and 13.6 percent for the twelve-month bill).[9]

The investor may purchase any of the four T-bills. For example, if the individual wants to invest the funds for one year, he or she can buy the twelve-month bill or buy the three-month bill and reinvest the funds for an additional nine months when the three-month bill matures. Even if the individual wants the investment for only six months, any of the T-bills may be purchased, because the three-month bill can be rolled over into another bill and the nine-month or twelve-month bills can be sold after six months. Since there are active secondary markets in T-bills, the investor could buy the twelve-month bill, hold it for six months, and then sell it.

Whether the individual wants to invest for three months, six months, or a year, it may be possible to increase the yield by purchasing the twelve-month bill and selling it after a period of time. This strategy is referred to as "riding the yield curve." To see how the yield may be increased, consider the investor who buys the twelve-month bill with the intention of selling it after six months. What will be the price of the bill when it is sold? There are three general possibilities: (1) the structure of yields will remain the same, (2) yields will rise, and (3) yields will fall.

If after six months the structure of yields has not changed, the twelve-month bill becomes a six-month bill with a price of $9,500 and an annual yield of 10.5 percent. (Remember: T-bills are sold at a discount that declines as the bill approaches maturity.) The bill has moved up two steps in the preceding table of prices and yields and has moved down the yield curve in Figure 17.3. That means the investor may sell the bill for a profit of $700 ($9,500 − $8,800), for a six-month return of 7.95 percent (15.9 percent annually). This profit and yield is greater than the $500 earned (10.5 percent) by purchasing the six-month bill.

---

[9]The student should realize that the exaggerated differences in the yields is designed to illustrate the concept and is not typical of the actual differences in yields.

Figure 17.3 ◆ RIDING THE YIELD CURVE

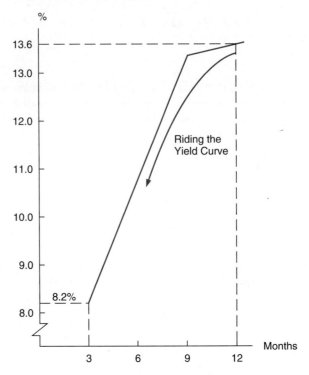

If interest rates have risen, the prices of the bills will not rise as much. For example, suppose after six months the structure of yields is

Term	Price	Annual Yield
3 months	$9,750	10.2%
6 months	9,410	12.5
9 months	9,000	14.8
12 months	8,700	14.9

The original twelve-month bill can now be sold for $9,410, which generates an annual return of 13.8 percent. The investor did not fare as well in this case (13.8 percent versus 15.9 percent) because the bill's price did not rise as much. However, unless interest rates rise precipitously and rapidly, as did occur during 1979 and 1980 (see Figure 14.3), the investor will earn a return that exceeds the yield available through purchasing the six-month bill and holding it to maturity.

If interest rates have fallen, the strategy of buying the twelve-month bill produces an even higher return. Suppose after six months the structure of yields is:

Term	Price	Annual Yield
3 months	$9,850	6.1%
6 months	9,600	8.3
9 months	9,400	8.5
12 months	9,820	8.7

Since interest rates have fallen, the price of the twelve-month bill has risen even more than it would have had there been no change in the yield structure. In this case the investor may now sell the bill for $9,600, generating a profit of $800 and an annual return of 18.2 percent. This is obviously the best scenario since the investor benefits from both riding the yield curve and the declining interest rates.

The opportunity to increase returns by riding the yield curve suggests that a positively sloped yield curve may be unstable. If many investors try to ride the yield curve, they will seek to sell the shorter term bills in order to purchase the longer term bills. This will depress the price of the shorter-term bills and increase their yields while simultaneously increasing the price of the longer term bills and decreasing their yields. These forces will tend to flatten the yield curve. The actual shape of the yield curve at a point in time will depend on the interplay of many factors, including individuals' preference for liquidity and expectations of future interest rates as well as the impact of individuals seeking higher returns by riding the yield curve.

18

CONVERTIBLE BONDS AND CONVERTIBLE PREFERRED STOCK

T *he previous chapters discussed the variety of bonds and preferred stock and the valuation of these securities. This chapter considers bonds and preferred stock with a special feature: the owner may convert the security into the issuing firm's common stock. Generally convertible securities offer more income (higher interest or higher dividends) than may be earned through an investment in the firm's common stock. In addition, convertible securities have some potential for capital gains if the price of the underlying stock rises. Convertibles are issued by a variety of firms generating a range of securities from high quality to extremely risky convertibles.*

This chapter discusses investing in convertible bonds and convertible preferred stocks. Initially the features and terms of convertible bonds are described, followed by a discussion of their pricing. This includes the premiums paid for convertible bonds, and the relationship between their price and the price of the stock into which they may be converted. The third section is devoted to convertible preferred stock. These shares are similar to convertible bonds but lack the safety implied by the debt element of convertible bonds. Next follows the brief histories of two convertible bonds that illustrate the potential profits and risk associated with investing in them. The chapter ends with a description of a new type of bond that permits the holder to sell the security back to the issuer prior to maturity for the bond's face value.

✦ ✦ ✦

LEARNING OBJECTIVES

After completing this chapter you should be able to

1. Describe the features common to all convertible bonds.

2. Determine the "floor" or minimum price of a convertible bond.

3. List the factors that affect the price of a convertible bond.

4. Identify the two premiums paid for a convertible bond.

5. Explain why the two premiums are inversely related.

6. Compare convertible bonds with convertible preferred stock.

7. Explain the advantage offered by a put bond.

FEATURES OF CONVERTIBLE BONDS

convertible bond
A bond that may be exchanged for (i.e., converted into) stock.

Convertible bonds are debentures (i.e., unsecured debt instruments) that may be converted at the holder's option into the stock of the issuing company. As was seen in Chapter 14, firms issue a variety of debt instruments to tap funds in the capital markets. Convertible bonds are one means to do so: The conversion feature is

494

granted to bondholders to induce them to buy the debt. Since the firm has granted the holder the right to convert the bonds, these bonds are usually subordinate to the firm's other debt. They also tend to offer a lower interest rate (i.e., coupon rate) than is available on nonconvertible debt. Thus, the conversion feature means that the firm can issue lower quality debt at a lower interest cost. Investors are willing to accept this reduced quality and interest income because the market value of the bond will appreciate *if* the price of the stock rises. These investors are thus trading quality and interest for possible capital gains.

Convertible bonds have been a popular means for firms to raise funds in the capital markets. A sample of firms and their convertible bonds is presented in Exhibit 18.1. As may be seen in the exhibit, the bonds are not issued just by lower quality firms with poor credit ratings. Some of the country's most prestigious firms, including IBM and Pfizer, have issued convertible bonds.

Since convertible bonds are long-term debt instruments, they have features that are common to all bonds. They are usually issued in $1,000 denominations, pay interest semiannually, and have a fixed maturity date. However, if the bonds are converted into stock, the maturity date is irrelevant because the bonds are retired when they are converted. Convertible bonds frequently have a sinking fund requirement, which, like the maturity date, is meaningless once the bonds are converted.

A noteworthy feature of convertible bonds is that they may be called by the issuing firm. The firm uses the call to force the holders to convert the bonds. Once the bond is called, the owner must convert, or any appreciation in price that has resulted from an increase in the stock's value will be lost. Such forced conversion is extremely important to the issuing firm, because it no longer has to repay the debt.

Convertible bonds are attractive to some investors because they offer the safety features of debt. The firm must meet the terms of the indenture, and the bonds must be retired if they are not converted. The flow of interest income usually exceeds the dividend yield that may be earned on the firm's stock. In addition, since the bonds may be converted into stock, the holder will share in the growth of the company. If the price of the stock rises in response to the firm's growth, the value of the convertible bond must also rise. It is this combination of the safety of debt and the potential for capital gain that makes convertible bonds an attractive investment, particularly to investors who desire income and some capital appreciation.

Exhibit 18.1 ✦ SELECTED CONVERTIBLE BONDS

Corporation	Coupon Rate of Interest	Month and Year in Which Bond Was Issued	Year of Maturity	Moody's Rating
Ashland Oil	6¾%	7/89	2014	Baa1
Control Data	8½	6/86	2011	B3
IBM	7⅞	11/84	2004	Aa3
Kerr-McGee	7¼	7/76	2012	Baa1
Pfizer	4	2/72	1997	Aa1

Source: *Moody's Bond Record*, May 1992.

Like all investments, convertible bonds subject the holder to risk. If the company fails, the holder of a bond stands to lose the funds invested in the debt. This is particularly true with regard to convertible bonds, because they are usually subordinate to the firm's other debt. Thus, convertible bonds are considerably less safe than senior debt or debt that is secured by specific collateral. In case of a default or bankruptcy, holders of convertible bonds may at best realize only a fraction of the principal amount invested. However, their position is still superior to that of the stockholders.

Default is not the only potential source of risk to investors. Convertible bonds are actively traded, and their prices can and do fluctuate. As is explained in detail in the next section, their price is partially related to the value of the stock into which they may be converted. Fluctuations in the value of the stock produce fluctuations in the price of the bond. These price changes are *in addition* to price movements caused by variations in interest rates.

During periods of higher interest rates and lower stock prices, convertible bonds are doubly cursed. Their lower coupon rates of interest cause their prices to decline more than those of nonconvertible debt. This, in addition to the decline in the value of the stock into which they may be converted, results in considerable price declines for convertible bonds. Such declines are illustrated in Exhibit 18.2, which gives the year-end prices of four convertible bonds. Each bond was initially issued for $1,000 but by the end of 1978, each was selling for a discount.

The last three columns of the exhibit illustrate the variety of possible outcomes for convertible bonds. The Ampex and Gulf and Western bonds were called and converted. The price of the underlying stock had risen sufficiently that the bondholders converted the bonds into stock. Seatrain defaulted, declared bankruptcy, and the market for its bonds ceased to exist (i.e., there were no price quotes). The Pan Am bond was redeemed for its face value but was not converted. (Holders of Pan Am convertible bonds that matured in the 1990s were not so lucky since Pan Am, like Seatrain, went bankrupt and ceased to exist.)

Exhibit 18.2 ✦ THE 1978 PRICES OF SELECTED CONVERTIBLE BONDS AND WHAT SUBSEQUENTLY HAPPENED TO EACH BOND

Bond	Prices as of December 31			
	1978	1981	1985	1990
Ampex 5½ 94	61	74½	Called and converted	NA
Gulf and Western 5½ 93	78	Called and converted	NA	NA
Pan American World Airways 4½ 86	59	46¼	96	Redeemed in 1986
Seatrain 6 95	56	16	No price quote	NA

THE VALUATION OF CONVERTIBLE BONDS

This section considers the valuation of convertible bonds. The value of a convertible bond is related to (1) the value of the stock into which it may be converted and (2) the value of the bond as a debt instrument. Although each of these factors affects the market price of the bond, the importance of each element varies with changing conditions in the security markets. In the final analysis, the valuation of a convertible bond is extremely difficult, because it is a hybrid security that combines debt and equity.

This section has three subdivisions. The first considers the value of the bond solely as stock. The second covers the bond's value only as a debt instrument, and the last section combines these values to show the hybrid nature of convertible bonds. To differentiate the value of the bond as stock from its value as debt, subscripts are added to the symbols used. S will represent stock, and D will represent debt. Although this may make the equations appear more complex, it will clearly distinguish the value of the bond as stock from the value as debt.

The Convertible Bond as Stock—The Conversion Value

The value of a convertible bond in terms of the stock, its **conversion value** (C_s), depends on (1) the face or principal amount of the bond (F), (2) the conversion (or exercise) price of the bond (P_e), and (3) the market price of the common stock (P_s). The face value divided by the conversion price of the bond gives the number of shares into which the bond may be converted. For example, if a $1,000 bond may be converted at $20 per share, then the bond may be converted into 50 shares ($1,000 ÷ $20). The number of shares times the market price of a share gives the value of the bond in terms of stock. If the bond is convertible into 50 shares and the stock sells for $15 per share, then the bond is worth $750 in terms of stock ($15 × 50).

This conversion value of the bond as stock is expressed in Equation 18.1,

$$C_s = \frac{F}{P_e} \times P_s,\qquad(18.1)$$

conversion value as stock
Value of the bond in terms of the stock into which the bond may be converted.

and is illustrated in Exhibit 18.3. In this example a $1,000 bond is convertible into 50 shares (i.e., a conversion price of $20 per share). The first column gives various prices of the stock. The second column presents the number of shares into which the bond is convertible (i.e., 50 shares). The third column gives the value of the bond in terms of stock (i.e., the product of the values in the first two columns). As may be seen in the exhibit, the value of the bond in terms of stock rises as the price of the stock increases.

This relationship between the price of the stock and the conversion value of the bond is illustrated in Figure 18.1. The price of the stock (P_s) is given on the horizontal axis, and the conversion value of the bond (C_s) is shown on the vertical axis. As the price of the stock rises, the conversion value of the bond increases. This is shown in the graph by line C_s, which represents the intrinsic value of the bond in terms of stock. Line C_s is a straight line running through the origin. If the stock

Exhibit 18.3 ♦ THE RELATIONSHIP BETWEEN THE PRICE OF A STOCK AND THE VALUE OF A CONVERTIBLE BOND

Price of the Stock	Shares into which the Bond Is Convertible	Value of the Bond in Terms of Stock
$ 0	50	$ 0
5	50	250
10	50	500
15	50	750
20	50	1,000
25	50	1,250
30	50	1,500

has no value, the value of the bond in terms of stock is also worthless. If the exercise price of the bond and the market price of the stock are equal (i.e., $P_s = P_e$, which in this case is $20), the bond's value as stock is equal to the principal amount (i.e., the bond's face value). As the price of the stock rises above the exercise price of the bond, the bond's value in terms of stock increases to more than the principal amount of the debt.

As with speculative options, which are discussed in the next chapter, the market price of a convertible bond cannot be less than the bond's conversion value. If the price of the bond were less than its value as stock, an opportunity to arbitrage would exist. Arbitrageurs would sell the stock short, purchase the convertible bond, exercise the conversion feature, and use the shares acquired through the conversion to cover the short sale. They would then make a profit equal to the difference between the price of the convertible bond and the conversion value of the bond. For example, if in the preceding example the bond were selling for $800 when the stock sold for $20 per share, arbitrageurs would enter the market. At $20 per share, the bond is worth $1,000 in terms of the stock (i.e., $20 × 50). Arbitrageurs would then sell 50 shares short for $1,000. At the same time they would buy the bond for $800 and exercise the option. After the shares had been acquired through the conversion of the bond, the arbitrageurs would cover the short position and earn $200 in profit (before commissions).

As arbitrageurs seek to purchase the bonds, they will drive up their price. The price increase will continue until there is no opportunity for profit. This occurs when the price is equal to or greater than the bond's value as stock. Thus, the conversion value of the bond as stock sets the minimum price of the bond. Because of arbitrage, the market price of a convertible bond will be at least equal to its conversion value.

However, the market price of the convertible bond is rarely equal to the conversion value of the bond. The bond frequently sells for a premium over its conversion value because the convertible bond may also have value as a debt instrument. As a pure (i.e., nonconvertible) bond, it competes with other nonconvertible debt. Like the conversion feature, this element of debt may affect the bond's price. Its impact is important, for it also has the effect of putting a minimum price on the convertible bond. It is this price floor that gives investors in convertible bonds an element of safety that stock lacks.

Figure 18.1 ✦ THE RELATIONSHIP BETWEEN THE PRICE OF THE STOCK
AND THE CONVERSION VALUE OF THE BOND

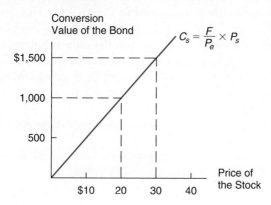

The Convertible Bond as Debt—The Investment Value

The **investment value** of a convertible bond (C_D) is related to (1) the annual interest or coupon rate that the bond pays (I), (2) the current interest rate that is paid
on comparable nonconvertible debt (i), and (3) the requirement that the principal
or face value (F) be retired at maturity (after n number of years) if the bond is not
converted. In terms of present value calculations, the value of a convertible bond
as nonconvertible debt is given in Equation 18.2.

investment value as debt
*The value of a convertible as if it
were nonconvertible debt.*

$$C_D = \frac{I}{(1 + i)^1} + \frac{I}{(1 + i)^2} + \ldots + \frac{I}{(1 + i)^n} + \frac{F}{(1 + i)^n}. \qquad (18.2)$$

Equation 18.2 is simply the current price of any bond. (The derivation of the equation was discussed in Chapter 15.)

Equation 18.2 may be illustrated by the following example. Assume that the
convertible bond in Exhibit 18.3 matures in ten years and pays 5 percent annually.
Nonconvertible debt of the same risk class currently yields 8 percent. When these
values are inserted into Equation 18.2, the investment value of the bond as nonconvertible debt is $798.50.

$$C_D = \frac{\$50}{(1 + 0.08)^1} + \frac{\$50}{(1 + 0.08)^2} + \ldots + \frac{\$50}{(1 + 0.08)^9}$$

$$+ \frac{\$50}{(1 + 0.08)^{10}} + \frac{\$1,000}{(1 + 0.08)^{10}}$$

$$C_D = \$50(6.710) + \$1,000(0.463) = \$798.50.$$

This equation may be solved by the use of present value tables or a bond table.
The 6.710 is the interest factor for the present value of an annuity of $1 for ten
years at 8 percent, and 0.463 is the interest factor for the present value of $1 to be

received ten years in the future when it is discounted at 8 percent. To be competitive with nonconvertible debt, this bond would have to sell for $798.50.

The relationship between the price of the common stock and the value of this bond as nonconvertible debt is illustrated in Figure 18.2. This figure consists of a horizontal line (C_D) that shows what the price ($798.50) of the bond would be if it were not convertible into stock, in which case the price is independent of the value of the stock. The principal amount of the bond is also shown in Figure 18.2 by the broken line F, which is above line C_D. The principal amount exceeds the value of the bond as pure debt because this bond must sell at a discount to be competitive with nonconvertible debt.

The investment value of the convertible bond as debt varies with market interest rates. Since the interest paid by the bond is fixed, the value of the bond as debt varies inversely with interest rates. An increase in interest rates causes this value to fall; a decline in interest rates causes the value to rise.

The relationship between the value of the preceding convertible bond as debt and various interest rates is presented in Exhibit 18.4. The first column gives various interest rates; the second column gives the nominal (i.e., coupon) rate of interest; and the last column gives the value of the bond as nonconvertible debt. The inverse relationship is readily apparent, for as the interest rate rises from 3 percent to 12 percent, the value of the bond declines from $1,170.50 to $631.70.

The value of the bond as nonconvertible debt is important because it sets another minimum value that the bond will command in the market. At that price the convertible bond is competitive with nonconvertible debt of the same maturity and degree of risk. If the bond were to sell below this price, it would offer a more attractive (i.e., higher) yield than that of nonconvertible debt. Investors would seek to buy the bond to attain this higher yield. They would bid up the bond's price until its yield was comparable to that of nonconvertible debt. Thus, the bond's value as nonconvertible debt becomes a floor on the price of the convertible bond. Even if the value of the stock into which the bond may be converted were to fall, this floor would halt the decline in the price of the convertible bond.

The actual minimum price of a convertible bond combines its value as stock

Figure 18.2 ✦ THE RELATIONSHIP BETWEEN THE PRICE OF COMMON STOCK
AND THE VALUE OF THE BOND AS NONCONVERTIBLE DEBT

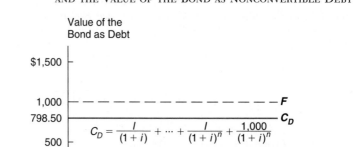

Exhibit 18.4 ✦ THE RELATIONSHIP BETWEEN INTEREST RATES AND THE INVESTMENT VALUE OF A BOND

Interest Rate	Coupon Rate	Investment Value of a Ten-Year Bond (interest paid annually)
3%	5%	$1,170.50
4	5	1,081.55
5	5	1,000.00
6	5	926.00
7	5	864.20
8	5	798.50
10	5	692.25
12	5	631.70

and its value as debt. This is illustrated in Figure 18.3, which combines the preceding figures for the value of the bond both in terms of stock and nonconvertible debt. The bond's price is always greater than or equal to the higher of the two valuations. If the price of the convertible bond were below its value as common stock, arbitrageurs would bid up its price. If the bond sold for a price below its value as debt, investors in debt instruments would bid up the price.

The minimum price of the convertible bond is either its value in terms of stock or its value as nonconvertible debt, but the importance of these determinants varies.

Figure 18.3 ✦ THE ACTUAL MINIMUM PRICE OF A CONVERTIBLE BOND

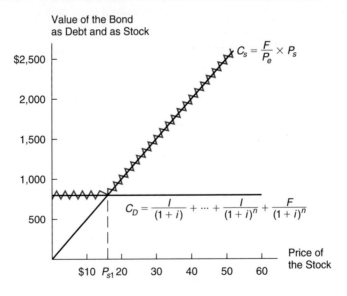

For low stock prices (i.e., stock prices less than P_{s1} in Figure 18.3), the minimum price is set by the bond's value as debt. However, for stock prices greater than P_{s1}, it is the bond's value as stock that determines the minimum price.

The Bond's Value as a Hybrid Security

The market price (P_m) of the convertible bond combines both the conversion value of the bond and its investment value as nonconvertible debt. If the price of the stock were to decline significantly below the exercise price of the bond, the market price of the convertible bond would be influenced primarily by the bond's value as non-convertible debt. In effect, the bond would be priced as if it were a pure debt instrument. As the price of the stock rises, the conversion value of the bond rises and plays an increasingly important role in the determination of the market price of the convertible bond. At sufficiently high stock prices, the market price of the bond is identical with its conversion value.

These relationships are illustrated in Figure 18.4, which reproduces Figure 18.3 and adds to it the market price of the convertible bond (P_m). For prices of the common stock below P_{s1}, the market price is identical to the bond's value as non-convertible debt. For prices of the common stock above P_{s2}, the price of the bond is identical to its value as common stock. At these extreme stock prices, the bond may be analyzed as if it were either pure debt or stock. For all prices between these two extremes, the market price of the convertible bond is influenced by the bond's value both as nonconvertible debt and as stock. This dual influence makes the analysis of convertible bonds difficult, since the investor pays a premium over the bond's value as stock and as debt.

Figure 18.4 ✦ MARKET PRICE OF A CONVERTIBLE BOND

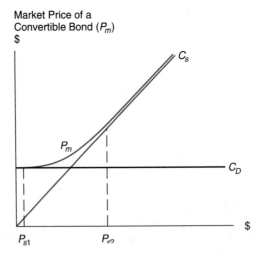

PREMIUMS PAID FOR CONVERTIBLE DEBT

One way to analyze a convertible bond is to measure the premium over the bond's value as debt or as stock. For example, if a particular convertible bond is commanding a higher premium than is paid for similar convertible securities, perhaps this bond should be sold. Conversely, if the premium is relatively low, the bond may be a good investment.

The premiums paid for a convertible bond are illustrated in Exhibit 18.5, which reproduces Exhibit 18.3 and adds the value of the bond as nonconvertible debt (column 4) along with hypothetical market prices for the bond (column 5). The premium that an investor pays for a convertible bond may be viewed in either of two ways: the premium over the bond's value as stock or the premium over the bond's value as debt. Column 6 gives the premium in terms of stock. This is the difference between the bond's market price and its conversion value as stock (i.e., the value in column 5 minus the value in column 3). This premium declines as the price of the stock rises and plays a more important role in the determination of the bond's price. Column 7 gives the premium in terms of nonconvertible debt. This is the difference between the bond's market price and its investment value as debt (i.e., the value in column 5 minus the value in column 4). This premium rises as the price of the stock rises, because the debt element of the bond is less important.

The inverse relationship between the two premiums is also illustrated in Figure 18.5. The premiums are shown by the difference between the line representing the market price (P_m) and the lines representing the value of the bond in terms of stock (C_s) and the value of the bond as nonconvertible debt (C_D).

When the price of the stock is low and the bond is selling close to its value as debt, the premium above the bond's intrinsic value as stock is substantial, but the

---

Exhibit 18.5 ✦ PREMIUMS PAID FOR CONVERTIBLE DEBT

Price of the Stock	Shares into which the Bond May Be Converted	Conversion Value of the Bond in Terms of Stock	Investment Value of the Bond as Non-convertible Debt	Hypothetical Price of the Convertible Bond	Premium in Terms of Stock°	Premium in Terms of Non-convertible Debt[†]
$ 0	50	$ 0	$798.50	$ 798.50	$798.50	$ 0.00
5	50	250	798.50	798.50	548.50	0.00
10	50	500	798.50	798.50	298.50	0.00
15	50	750	798.50	900.00	150.00	101.50
20	50	1,100	798.50	1,100.00	100.00	301.50
25	50	1,250	798.50	1,300.00	50.00	501.50
30	50	1,500	798.50	1,500.00	0.00	701.50

° The premium in terms of stock is equal to the hypothetical price of the convertible bond minus the value of the bond in terms of stock.
[†] The premium in terms of nonconvertible debt is equal to the hypothetical price of the convertible bond minus the value of the bond as nonconvertible debt.

Figure 18.5 ✦ PREMIUMS PAID FOR A CONVERTIBLE BOND

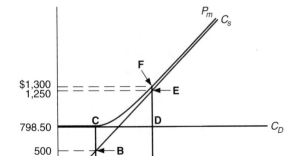

premium above the bond's value as debt is small. For example, at P_{s1} the price of the stock is $10, the bond's value in terms of stock is $500 (Line AB in Figure 18.5), and the premium is $298.50 (Line BC). However, the bond is selling for its value as nonconvertible debt ($798.50), and there is no premium over its value as debt. When the price of the stock is $25 and the bond is selling for $1,300, the premium in terms of stock is only $50 (Line EF). However, the bond's premium over its value as nonconvertible debt is $501.50 (Line DF).

As these examples illustrate, the premium paid for the bond over its value as stock declines as the price of the stock rises. This decline in the premium is the result of the increasing importance of the conversion value on the bond's market price and the decreasing importance of the debt element on the bond's price.

As the price of the stock rises, the safety feature of the debt diminishes. If the price of the common stock ceased to rise and started to fall, the price of the convertible bond could decline considerably before it reached the floor price set by the nonconvertible debt. For example, if the price of the stock declined from $30 to $15 (a 50 percent decline), the price of the convertible bond could fall from $1,500 to $798.50 (a 46.8 percent decline). Such a price decline would indicate that the floor value of $798.50 had little impact on the decline in the price of the bond.

In addition, as the price of the stock (and hence the price of the convertible bond) rises, the probability that the bond will be called rises. When the bond is called, it can be worth only its value as stock. The call forces the holder to convert the bond into stock. For example, when the price of the stock is $30, the bond is worth $1,500 in terms of stock. Should the company call the bond and offer to retire it for its face value ($1,000), no one would accept the offer. Instead they would convert the bond into $1,500 worth of stock. If the investor paid a premium over this conversion value (such as $1,600) and the bond were called, the investor would then suffer a loss. Thus, as the probability of a call increases, the willingness to pay a premium over the bond's value as stock declines, and the price of the convertible bond ultimately converges with its value as stock.

This decline in the premium also means that the price of the stock will rise more rapidly than the price of the bond. While other investments offer potential leverage, convertible bonds do not. As may be seen in both Exhibit 18.5 and Figure 18.5, the market price of the convertible bond rises and falls with the price of the stock, because the conversion value of the bond rises and falls. However, the market price of the convertible bond does not rise as rapidly as the conversion value of the bond. For example, when the stock's price increased from $20 to $25 (a 25 percent increase), the convertible bond's price rose from $1,100 to $1,300 (an 18.2 percent increase). The reason for this difference in the rate of increase is the declining premium paid for the convertible bond. Since the premium declines as the price of the stock rises, the rate of increase in the price of the stock must exceed the rate of increase in the price of the bond. In summary, convertible bonds offer investors the opportunity for some capital growth with less risk.

Because of these advantages, some investors may have the misconception that convertible bonds offer the best of both worlds: high return plus safety. In many cases a convertible bond may prove to be an inferior investment. For example, if the price of the stock rises rapidly, the stock is a superior investment because it will produce a larger capital gain. The stock outperforms the bond because the investor paid a premium for the convertible bond. In the opposite case when the price of the stock does not rise, a nonconvertible bond will outperform the convertible bond because it earns more interest. Thus, the very sources of a convertible bond's attractiveness (i.e., the potential capital growth plus the safety of debt) are also the sources of its lack of appeal (i.e., the inferior growth relative to the stock and the inferior interest income relative to nonconvertible debt).

For investors, the advantages offered by convertible bonds do not include (1) the potential leverage of options, (2) the potential growth of stock, or (3) the safety and interest income of debt. The advantage is some combination of capital gain, interest income, and the safety of debt. As the previous example illustrated, the investor does receive interest income, and if the price of the stock rises, the price of the bond must also rise. If the stock's price does not rise, the convertible bond must eventually be retired because it is a debt obligation of the firm. Hence, the bond does offer some element of safety that is not available through investments in common stocks as well as some growth potential that is not available through nonconvertible debt.

CONVERTIBLE PREFERRED STOCK

In addition to convertible bonds, many firms have issued **convertible preferred stock.** As its name implies, this stock may be converted into the common stock of the issuing corporation. A sampling of convertible preferred stock is presented in Exhibit 18.6. This exhibit illustrates the diversity of companies that have this security outstanding, including defense, steel, computer, and consumer products firms. Thus, while nonconvertible preferred stock is primarily issued by utilities, the entire spectrum of firms issues convertible preferred stock.

Several of these issues of convertible preferred stock came into existence

convertible preferred stock
Preferred stock that may be exchanged for (i.e., converted into) common stock.

Exhibit 18.6 ✦ TERMS OF SELECTED CONVERTIBLE PREFERRED STOCKS AS OF JANUARY 1992

Firm	Dividend Rate	Number of Shares into which Preferred Stock May Be Converted	Price of Common Stock	Value of Preferred Stock	Price of Preferred Stock
American Brands	$2.67	4.08	$45	$183.60	$183⅝
Armco Inc.	2.10	1.27	5	6.35	20
James River	3.375	1.2269	22¾	27.91	42½
Textron	2.08	2.2	36⅜	80.03	80⅛
Unisys	3.75	1.67	7½	12.53	19

Source: Standard & Poor's Corporation Stock Guide, January 1992.

through mergers. The tax laws permit firms to combine through an exchange of stock, which is not taxable (i.e., it is a tax-free exchange). If one firm purchases another firm for cash, the stockholders who sell their shares have an obvious realized sale. Profits and losses from the sale are then subject to capital gains taxation. However, the Internal Revenue Service has ruled that an exchange of "like securities" is not a realized sale and thus is not subject to capital gains taxation until the investor sells the new shares.

This tax ruling has encouraged mergers through the exchange of stock. In many cases the firm that is taking over (the surviving firm) offers to the stockholders of the firm that is being taken over an opportunity to trade their shares for a new convertible preferred stock. Since the stock is convertible into the common stock of the surviving firm, it is a "like security." Thus, the transaction is not subject to capital gains taxation. To encourage the stockholders to tender their shares, the surviving firm may offer a generous dividend yield on the convertible preferred stock. For this reason many convertible preferred stocks have considerably more generous dividend yields than that which is available through investing in the firm's common stock.

Convertible preferred stock is similar to convertible debt; however, there are some important differences. The differences are primarily the same as those between nonconvertible preferred stock and nonconvertible debt. Preferred stock is treated as an equity instrument. Thus, the firm is not under any legal obligation to pay dividends. In addition, the preferred stock may be a perpetual security and may not have to be retired as debt must be. However, many convertible preferred stocks do have a required sinking fund, which forces the firm to retire the preferred stock over a period of years.

The value of convertible preferred stock (like convertible bonds) is related to the price of the stock into which it may be converted and to the value of competitive nonconvertible preferred stock. As with convertible bonds, these values set floors on the price of the convertible preferred stock. It cannot sell for any significant length of time below its value as stock. If it did, investors would enter the market and buy the preferred stock, which would increase its price. Thus, the minimum value of the convertible preferred stock (like the minimum value of the convertible bond) must be equal to the conversion of the stock (P_c). In equation form that is

$$P_c = P_s \times N, \tag{18.3}$$

where P_s is the market price of the stock into which the convertible preferred stock may be converted, and N is the number of shares an investor obtains through conversion. Equation 18.3 is similar to Equation 18.1, which gave the intrinsic value of the convertible bond as stock.

The convertible preferred stock's value as nonconvertible preferred stock (P_{pfd}) is related to the dividend it pays (D_{pfd}) and to the appropriate discount factor (k_{pfd}), which is the yield earned on competitive nonconvertible preferred stock. In equation form that is

$$P_{pfd} = \frac{D_{pfd}}{k_{pfd}}, \tag{18.4}$$

which is essentially the same as the convertible bond's value as debt except that the preferred stock has no definite maturity date. (Equation 18.4 was derived in Chapter 16.) However, this value does set a floor on the price of a convertible preferred stock because at that price it is competitive with nonconvertible preferred stock.

As with convertible bonds, the convertible preferred stock is a hybrid security whose value combines its worth both as stock and as nonconvertible preferred stock. Convertible preferred stock tends to sell for a premium over its value as stock and its value as straight preferred stock. Figures 18.4 and 18.5, which illustrated the value of the convertible bond at various prices of the stock into which it may be converted, also apply to convertible preferred stock. The only difference is the premium that the preferred stock commands over the value as common stock, which tends to be smaller. The reason for this reduced premium is that the preferred stock does not have the element of debt. Its features are more similar to common stock than are the features of the convertible bond. Thus, its price usually commands less of a premium over its value as stock. This smaller premium is illustrated in Exhibit 18.6 as two of these convertible preferreds (American Brands and Textron) are selling near their value as common stock.

Convertible-Exchangeable Preferred Stock

Convertible-exchangeable preferred stock is a security that includes two options. The holder may convert the shares into the firm's common stock, or the company may force the holder to exchange the shares for the firm's bonds. For example, the Federal Paper Board $2.3125 convertible-exchangeable preferred stock may be converted at the holder's option into 2.51 shares of common stock. However, the firm has the option to exchange each share for $25 worth of the firm's 9¼ percent convertible debentures.

The exchange option gives the firm more control over the preferred stock, as it is a means to force retirement of the shares without an outlay of cash if the value of the common stock rises *or* falls. If the value of the common stock were to rise, the investor may voluntarily convert the preferred stock. However, the firm may exercise its option to exchange the bonds for the preferred stock, thus forcing the stockholder to convert or lose the appreciation in the preferred stock's value. In this case the exchange option operates as a call feature—it forces conversion.

If the value of the common stock were to decline, no one would exercise the option to convert the stock. Without the exchange option, there is nothing the firm could do to retire the stock and rid itself of the required dividend payments except repurchase the shares. However, by having the exchange option, the firm can force the preferred stockholder to exchange the shares for debt. The firm will now have to make interest payments, but these are tax-deductible expenses, while preferred dividends are paid from earnings and are not tax deductible.

Preferred Equity Redemption Cumulative Stock (PERCS)

Preferred equity redemption cumulative stock (PERCS) is a preferred stock that will be exchanged in the future for the issuing firm's common stock. Like convertible preferred stock it combines elements of preferred stock with some potential for growth. The cash dividend paid by a PERCS is established when the security is issued and is generally about twice the amount of the dividend being paid by the common stock. Since the stock pays a fixed dividend, the security is similar to preferred stock.

The potential for growth occurs through the redemption feature. This preferred stock may not be converted at the holders option and will not be called by the firm. Instead, the preferred stock is redeemed (i.e., exchanged) at a specified future date into the firm's common stock (usually three years after date of issue). For example, the PERCS issued on February 21, 1992, by Sears will be exchanged for Sears common stock on February 21, 1995. The PERCS pays an annual dividend of $3.75 while the common pays a dividend of $2.00. At the end of three years, the stock will be exchanged for one share of common as long as the price of the common is $59.00 or less. If the price of the common exceeds $59, the number of common shares exchanged is adjusted so that the holder of the PERCS receives common stock worth $59.00. Thus, if Sears is selling for $75, the holder of the PERCS receives 0.7867 ($59/$75) shares.

What advantages to PERCS offer investors? The primary advantage is the higher dividend yield. Suppose the price of Sears stagnates; at the end of the three years, the investor receives one share of common stock whose value has not changed but the investor has received more dividends during the three years than would have been paid to holders of the common stock. If the value of the common stock declines, the additional dividends offset some of the price decline. Thus, if the price of the stock remains stable or declines, the investor ends up better off with the PERCS compared to holding the underlying common stock.

If the price of the common stock rises, the value of the preferred equity cumulative redemption stock also rises up to the specified maximum price, which sets a ceiling on the price increase. If the price of the common continues to rise, the price of the PERCS cannot rise since further price increases are offset by the decline in the number of shares into which the PERCS may be exchanged. Thus, PERCS are of interest to investors who seek additional dividend income and who do not believe that the price of the underlying stock will rise dramatically during the time period.

Of course, the best outcome for the investor in the PERCS would be for the price of the stock to rise to the maximum exchange price. If that were to occur, the investor would receive the higher dividend and realize the highest possible capital gain. The only loss would be an opportunity loss from the price of the common stock rising above the exchange price.

SELECTING CONVERTIBLES

Because convertible bonds are a hybrid security, they are more difficult to select than nonconvertible bonds. These securities are debt instruments and pay a fixed flow of interest income, so they appeal to conservative, income-oriented investors. However, since the bonds sell for a premium over their investment value as debt, investors forgo some of the interest income and safety associated with nonconvertible bonds.

A convertible bond also offers the potential for capital gains if the value of the stock into which the bond may be converted were to rise. Possible capital gains increase the bond's attractiveness to investors seeking capital appreciation. Since the investor pays a premium over the bond's value as stock, the potential price appreciation is less than is available through an investment in the firm's common stock. However, the investor who purchases the bond does collect the interest, which usually exceeds the dividends paid on an equivalent number of shares into which the bond may be converted.

This interest advantage may be seen by considering the 8 percent convertible bond issued by Petrie Stores. Each bond may be converted into 45.2 shares of common stock. The stock paid dividends of $0.20 a share (i.e., the equivalent of $9.04 on 45.2 shares), but the bond paid interest of $80. The bondholder collected $70.96 more in interest income than the stockholder collected on an equivalent number of shares.

This additional flow of income offers one way to analyze the premium paid for a convertible bond. If the bond is held for a sufficient amount of time, the additional income will offset the premium. This time period is sometimes referred to as "years to payback" or the "breakeven time." The following example illustrates how this breakeven time period may be computed.[1] Consider a $1,000 convertible bond with a 7 percent coupon that is convertible into 50 shares of stock. The stock currently sells for $16 a share and pays a dividend of $0.40 a share. In terms of stock the bond is worth $800 (50 × $16), so the premium over the bond's value as stock is $200 ($1,000 − 800). The bondholder receives $70 a year in interest but would receive only $20 ($0.40 × 50) on the stock. Thus purchasing the bond instead of an equivalent number of shares generates $50 in additional income, which offsets the premium over the bond's value as stock in four years ($200/$50 = 4).

---

[1] See Bancroft G. Davis, "Convertible Securities," in *Encyclopedia of Investments*, eds. M.E. Blume and J. P. Friedman, (Boston: Warren, Gorham & Lamont, 1982), 182–184.

This series of calculations may be summarized as follows:

Market value of the bond	$1,000
Minus bond's conversion value	800
Premium over the conversion value	$ 200
Bond's annual income	$ 70
Minus annual income from stock	20
Annual income advantage to bond	$ 50

$$\text{Payback period} = \frac{\text{Premium over the conversion value}}{\text{Annual income advantage}}$$

$$= \frac{\$200}{\$50} = 4 \text{ years.}$$

If the additional income offsets the premium paid over the bond's value as stock in a moderate period of time (e.g., three to four years), the convertible bond may be an attractive alternative to the stock. (This, of course, assumes that the stock is also sufficiently attractive and offers the potential for growth.) If the time period necessary to overcome the premium is many years (e.g., ten years), then the bond should not be purchased as an alternative to the stock but should be viewed solely as a debt instrument and analyzed as such.

The individual should realize that this technique is relatively simple and does not consider (1) differences in commission costs to buy bonds instead of stock, (2) possible growth in the cash dividend, which will increase the time period necessary to recapture the premium, and (3) the time value of money. The premium is paid in the present (i.e., when the bond is purchased), but the flow of interest income occurs in the future. However, the technique does permit comparisons of various convertible bonds. If the individual computes the time period necessary to recapture the premium for several bonds, he or she may identify specific convertible bonds that are more attractive potential investments.

THE HISTORY OF TWO CONVERTIBLE BONDS

Perhaps the best way to understand investing in convertible bonds is to examine the history of two such bonds. The first is a success story, in that the price of the common stock rose and therefore the value of the bond also rose. The second is a not-so-successful story, for the price of the stock declined and so did the value of the bond. However, the story of this bond is not a tragedy, for the bond was still a debt obligation of the company and was retired at maturity even though it was not converted into stock.

The American Quasar Convertible Bond

American Quasar is a firm devoted to exploring and drilling for oil and gas. It not only develops known reserves but also drills wells in search of new discoveries. Such wells (called wildcats) can prove to be highly lucrative; however, the majority of such drilling leads only to dry holes (i.e., no oil or gas is found). Because of the nature of its operations, American Quasar is a speculative firm at best. Speculative firms, however, need funds to operate, so the firm issued $17,500,000 in face value of convertible bonds. The coupon rate was set at 7¼ percent and the exercise price of the bond was $21 (i.e., it was convertible into 47.6 shares), which was a premium of 17 percent over the approximate price of the stock ($18) at the date of issue.

After the bond was issued, American Quasar's stock did particularly well. Perhaps the discovery of some sizable wells in the Midwest helped bolster the firm's stock. Of course, the value of the convertible bond rose as the price of the stock rose. The prices of the bond and the stock moved closely together, and less than two years after being issued the bond was called, which forced conversion of the bond into the stock.

What was the return earned by investors in these securities? Obviously an investment in either the stock or the bond was quite profitable, since the price of the stock rose so rapidly. The bond's price rose from $1,000 to $1,500 during the time it was outstanding. The bond paid $72.50 in interest. The holding period return earned over the 15 months on an investment in the bond was

$$\frac{\text{Price appreciation} + \text{Interest earned}}{\text{Cost}} = \frac{\$1,500 - \$1,000 + \$72.50}{\$1,000}$$

$$= \frac{\$572.50}{\$1,000} = 57.25\%.$$

For the stock the holding period return was

$$\frac{\text{Price appreciation} + \text{Dividends}}{\text{Cost}} = \frac{\$32 - \$18 + \$0}{\$18} = \frac{\$14}{\$18} = 77.7\%.$$

(It should be noted that (1) the bond paid only one year's interest since it was converted prior to the next interest payment and (2) the stock did not pay any cash dividends while the bond was outstanding.) As may be seen by these calculations, the returns are both positive. The stock did better because the bond was initially sold for a premium over its value as stock. However, an investor who purchased this convertible bond certainly would have little cause for complaint.

The Pan American World Airways Convertible Bonds

While the previous example illustrated how the price of convertible bonds may rise as the price of the stock rises, the Pan American World Airways convertible bonds demonstrate the opposite. The 4½ percent convertible bond due in 1986 was issued when Pan Am was riding the crest of popularity. For investors purchasing either the stock or the bond, Pan Am's popularity vanished, and through years of continued deficits, the price of the stock declined drastically. During 1974, both the stock and the bond fell to "bargain basement" prices, as the market expected the firm to default. At that time the bond reached a low of $130 for a $1,000 bond!

Pan Am, however, did not default, and the bond remained an obligation that had to be retired in 1986. Thus, when Pan Am did redeem the bond, investors who purchased it initially for $1,000 received their principal. Holders of the Pan Am convertible bonds due in 2010 and the nonconvertible debt due in 2003 and 2004 were not so lucky because the firm eventually failed and ceased operations in 1991. These bonds thus illustrate that investors who acquire both convertible and nonconvertible bonds of financially weak firms can lose their entire investments if the firm fails.

PUT BONDS

Most of this chapter has been devoted to convertible bonds, which are debt instruments that investors may, at their option, exchange for stock. If the price of the stock rises, the investor profits because the conversion value of the bond rises.

put bond

A bond that the holder may redeem (i.e., sell back to the issuer) at a specified price within a specified time period.

During the 1980s, another type of bond was created with a different type of option. This **put bond** permits the holder to sell the instrument back to the issuer. In effect the firm must redeem the bond at a specified date for its principal amount. These bonds are called "put bonds" because an option to sell stock at a specified price is called a "put option." Since the owner of these bonds has the option to sell the bond back to the firm, this option is analogous to a put option and hence the name "put bond." (Put options to sell stock are explained in the next chapter.) A typical illustration of a put bond is the Industrial Development Authority of Richmond, Virginia, put bond due in 2005, which the investor may redeem in 1995 for the principal amount.[2]

Fear that interest rates would increase and thereby inflict losses on bondholders led to the development of put bonds. Firms and governments need long-term financing, but some investors do not want to commit their funds for extended periods of time, especially if they fear rising interest rates. Put bonds permit firms and governments to sell long-term debt to investors who are reluctant to buy bonds with maturity dates 20 to 30 years into the future.

If, after these put bonds were issued, interest rates were to rise and thereby drive down the price of the bonds, the investor would exercise the put option at the specified redemption date. He or she would receive the principal and could immediately invest it at the current (and higher) rate of interest. Of course, if interest rates were to fall, the individual would not exercise the option. There would be no reason for the investor to seek the early redemption of the principal if interest rates have fallen. Instead the investor may sell the bond on the market for more than the principal amount (i.e., for a premium).

Firms and governments are willing to offer investors this put option for much the same reason that they were willing to offer convertibility: lower interest costs. If an investor acquires an option, he or she must pay a price. For regular puts and calls that price (or "premium" as it is called in the jargon of options) is the amount

---

[2] Governments cannot issue convertible bonds because there is no stock into which the bond may be converted. However, they can issue put bonds, and several municipalities and state agencies have issued them.

paid to purchase the option. With a convertible bond or a put bond, the option's price is more subtle. Its price is the reduction in interest the investor must forgo to acquire the option.[3] Without the option the bond's coupon would have had to be higher to induce investors to purchase the long-term bond.

The put option's potential impact on the value of a bond as interest rates fluctuate may be seen by the following illustration. A firm issues a bond due in twenty years with a 10 percent coupon. It grants the investor the option to redeem the bond at par at the end of five years. If the option is not exercised, the bond will remain outstanding for an additional fifteen years. (This is a simple illustration with only one future date at which the investor may exercise the put option. Some bonds may grant the bondholder the option to redeem the bond more frequently, such as every five years.)

If the current interest rate is 8 percent, the value of the bond is

$$\$100(9.818) + \$1,000(0.215) = \$1,196.80.$$

9.818 and 0.215 are the interest factors for the present value of an annuity and the present value of a dollar at 8 percent for *twenty* years. Twenty years is the appropriate number of years because, since interest rates have fallen, the investor will not redeem the bond. The option thus has no impact on the increase in the price of the bond.

If the current interest rate is 12 percent, the value of the bond is

$$\$100(3.605) + \$1,000(0.567) = \$927.50.$$

3.605 and 0.567 are the interest factors for the present value of an annuity and the present value of a dollar at 12 percent for *five* years. Five years is the appropriate number of years because if the current rate of interest exceeds 10 percent, the investor will exercise the option and redeem the bond.

The impact of the put option on the value of the bond can be seen by comparing the above value and the bond's value *without* the put option. In that case, if the current interest rate were 12 percent, the value of the bond would be

$$\$100(7.469) + \$1,000(0.104) = \$850.90.$$

7.469 and 0.104 are the interest factors for the present value of an annuity and the present value of a dollar at 12 percent for twenty years. Twenty years is the appropriate number of years because the bond lacks the put option. In this illustration the put option increases the value of the bond by $76.60 ($927.50 − 850.90). Thus the put option affects the value of the bond if interest rates increase. Its impact is to reduce the amount by which the bond's price will decline, because the expected life is the redemption date and not the maturity date.

---

[3]This price may be expressed in present value terms—it is the difference between the value of the bond with and the value of the bond without the option.

Since bonds with put options are relatively new securities, one can only speculate as to their future popularity. However, granting the option does alter the interest paid, so one of the participants (i.e., the issuer or the investor) profits from the option. If interest rates remain below the coupon rate, the issuer profits, because the firm (or government) was able to sell a debt instrument with a lower rate than would have been required to sell the bonds without the put option. However, if interest rates rise, investors profit, because they are no longer locked into a debt instrument with an inferior yield. The issuer then will have to pay the higher rates in order to reborrow the funds. Obviously if the investor (1) anticipates rising interest rates or (2) is particularly uncertain as to the direction of future interest rates and wants to hedge against rates increasing, bonds with put options may be attractive alternatives to other types of long-term debt instruments.

SUMMARY

A convertible bond is a debt instrument that may be converted into stock. The value of this bond depends on the value of the stock into which the bond may be converted and on the value of the bond as a debt instrument.

As the value of the stock rises, so does the conversion value of the convertible bond. If the price of the stock declines, the conversion value of the bond will also fall. However, the stock's price will decline faster, because the convertible bond's investment value as debt will halt the fall in the bond's price.

Since a convertible bond's price rises with the price of the stock, the bond offers the investor an opportunity for appreciation as the value of the firm increases. In addition, the bond's value as a debt sets a floor on the bond's price, which reduces the risk of loss to the investor. Should the stock decline in value, the debt element reduces the risk of loss to the bondholder.

Convertible bonds may sell for a premium. For these bonds the premium may be viewed relative to the bond's value as stock or its value as debt. These two premiums are inversely related. When the price of the stock rises, the premium that the bond commands over its value as stock diminishes, but the premium over its value as debt rises. When the price of the stock falls, the premium over the bond's value as stock rises, but the premium relative to the bond's value as debt declines.

Convertible preferred stock is similar to convertible debt, except that it lacks the safety implied by a debt instrument. Its price is related to its conversion value, the flow of dividend income, and the rate that investors may earn on nonconvertible preferred stock.

A recent innovation in the debt instrument market is the put bond that permits the holder to redeem the bond for its principal amount at some specified time in the future. If interest rates increase, the bondholder may exercise the put option. He or she redeems the bond, receives the principal, and thus is able to reinvest the funds at the higher current rate of interest. However, if interest rates fall, the bondholder will not exercise the option, as there is no reason to redeem the bond prior to maturity. Hence, the advantage put bonds offer investors is protection against being locked into an inferior rate of interest if the rates were to increase in the future.

Security Summary

Convertible Bonds

Source of return: Interest income and possible capital gains if interest rates fall or the value of the underlying stock rises.

Liquidity and marketability: Active secondary market in large issues but real chance of loss if interest rates rise or the value of the stock into which the bond may be converted declines implies that convertible bonds are marketable but not liquid.

Sources of risk: Unsystematic risk from events that affect the firm's capacity to service its debt (i.e., pay the interest and timely retire the bonds) or that cause the value of its stock to decline. Systematic risk from increases in interest rates that cause the value of the bond as debt to fall and from declines in the stock market which cause the value of the bond as stock to fall.

Taxation: Interest is subject to federal income taxation. Capital gains that occur if interest rates fall or the value of the underlying stock rises are subject to taxation only when the gains are realized. Conversion of the bond into stock is not considered a realized sale, and the cost basis of the bond is transferred to the stock.

Terms to Remember

convertible bond	convertible preferred stock
conversion value as stock	put bond
investment value as debt	

Questions

1. What differentiates convertible bonds from other bonds?
2. How is the value of a convertible bond in terms of stock determined? What effect does this conversion value have on the price of the bond?
3. How is the value of a convertible bond in terms of debt determined? What effect does this investment value have on the price of the bond?
4. Why may convertible bonds be called by the firm? When are these bonds most likely to be called?
5. Why are convertible bonds less risky than stock but usually more risky than nonconvertible bonds?
6. Why does the premium over the bond's conversion value decline as the value of the stock rises?
7. How are convertible preferred stocks different from convertible bonds?
8. What advantages do convertible securities offer investors? What are the risks associated with these investments?

Problems

1. Given the following information concerning a convertible bond:

Principal	$1,000
Coupon	5%
Maturity	15 years
Call price	$1,050
Conversion price	$37 (i.e., 27 shares)
Market price of the common stock	$32
Market price of the bond	$1,040

    a. What is the current yield of this bond?
    b. What is the value of the bond based on the market price of the common stock?
    c. What is the value of the common stock based on the market price of the bond?
    d. What is the premium in terms of stock that the investor pays when he or she purchases the convertible bond instead of the stock?
    e. Nonconvertible bonds are selling with a yield to maturity of 7 percent. If this bond lacked the conversion feature, what would the approximate price of the bond be?
    f. What is the premium in terms of debt that the investor pays when he or she purchases the convertible bond instead of a nonconvertible bond?
    g. If the price of the common stock should double, would the price of the convertible bond double? Briefly explain your answer.
    h. If the price of the common stock should decline by 50 percent, would the price of the convertible bond decline by the same percentage? Briefly explain your answer.
    i. What is the probability that the corporation will call this bond?
    j. Why are investors willing to pay the premiums mentioned in parts d and f?

2. The following information concerns a convertible bond:
    ✦ Coupon 6% ($60 per $1,000 bond)
    ✦ Exercise price: $25
    ✦ Maturity date: 20 years
    ✦ Call price: $1,040
    The price of the common stock is $30.
    a. If this bond were nonconvertible, what would be its approximate value if comparable interest rates were 12 percent?
    b. How many shares can the bond be converted into?
    c. What is the value of the bond in terms of stock?
    d. What is the current minimum price that the bond will command?
    e. If the current market price of the bond is $976, what should you do?
    f. Is there any reason to anticipate that the firm will call the bond?
    g. What do investors receive if they do not convert the bond when it is called?

   h.   If the bond were called, would it be advantageous to convert?

   i.   If interest rates rise, would that affect the bond's current yield?

   j.   If the price of the stock were $10, would your answer to part i be different?

3.   Given the following information concerning Continental Group $2.00 convertible preferred stock:

   ✦   One share of preferred is convertible into 0.33 share of common stock

   ✦   Price of common stock: $34

   ✦   Price of convertible preferred stock: $17

   a.   What is the value of the preferred stock in terms of common stock?

   b.   What is the premium over the preferred stock's value as common stock?

   c.   If the preferred stock is perpetual and comparable preferred stock offers a dividend yield of 15 percent, what would be the minimum price of this stock if it were not convertible?

   d.   If the price of the common stock rose to $60, what would be the minimum increase in the value of the preferred stock that you would expect?

4.   Two bonds have the following terms:

Bond A

Principal	$1,000
Coupon	8%
Maturity	10 years

Bond B

Principal	$1,000
Coupon	7.6%
Maturity	10 years

Bond B has an additional feature; it may be redeemed at par after five years (i.e., it has a put feature). Both bonds were initially sold for their face amounts (i.e., $1,000).

   a.   If interest rates fall to 7 percent, what will be the price of each bond?

   b.   If interest rates rise to 9 percent, what will be the decline in the price of each bond from its initial price?

   c.   Given your answers to questions a and b, what is the trade-off implied by the put option in Bond B?

   d.   Bond B requires the investor to forgo $4 a year (i.e., $40 if the bond is in existence for ten years). If interest rates are 8 percent, what is the present value of this forgone interest? If the bond had lacked the put feature but had a coupon of 7.6 percent and a term to maturity of ten years, it would sell for $973.16 when interest rates were 8 percent. What, then, is the implied cost of the put option?

5.   Two firms have common stock and convertible bonds outstanding. Information concerning these securities is as follows:

	Firm A	Firm B
Common stock:		
Price of common stock	$46	$30
Cash dividend	none	$1
Convertible bond:		
Principal	$1,000	$1,000
Conversion price	$50	$33⅓
	(20 shares)	(30 shares)
Maturity date	10 years	10 years
Coupon rate	7.5%	7.5%
Market price	$1,100	$1,100

a. What is the value of each bond in terms of stock?
b. What is the premium paid over each bond's value as stock?
c. What is each bond's income advantage over the stock into which the bond may be converted?
d. How long will it take for the income advantage to offset the premium determined in part b?
e. If after four years firm A's stock sells for $65 and the firm calls the bond, what is the rate of return earned on an investment in the stock or in the bond? (You may wish to review the material on calculating rates of return presented in Chapter 9.)

Suggested Readings

For an elementary discussion of convertible bonds, consult:
Noddings, Thomas. *Investor's Guide to Convertible Bonds.* Homewood, Ill.: Dow Jones-Irwin, 1982.

While convertibles have higher default risk than nonconvertible debt, from 1978 to 1987 their returns almost doubled the returns on nonconvertible debt. These returns were highly correlated with returns from common stock, which suggests combining convertibles with common stock does not help achieve diversification. See:
Altman, Edward I. "The Convertible Debt Market: Are Returns Worth the Risk?" *Financial Analysts Journal* (July–August 1989): 23–31.

Techniques used to analyze convertible bonds are discussed in:
Calamos, John P. *Investing in Convertible Securities.* Chicago, Ill.: Longman Financial Services Publishing, 1988.
Gepts, Stefaan J. *Valuation and Selection of Convertible Bonds.* Westport, Conn.: Greenwood Press, 1987.
Calamos is president of a firm that specializes in research and management of portfolios of convertible securities for financial institutions. Both his and Gepts' books are reference guides primarily written for financial professionals and cover risk, returns, and hedging with convertibles. The Gepts' book integrates option valuation theory and the valuation of convertible bonds and includes material on convertible Euro-bonds.

Investing in Options, Futures, and Tangible Assets

IV

PART FOUR IS DEVOTED TO ALTERNATIVES TO STOCKS AND BONDS AND BROADENS THE INVESTOR'S PERSPECTIVE. WHILE SOME OF THESE ALTERNATIVES MAY BE VERY SPECULATIVE, OTHERS, SUCH AS HOME OWNERSHIP, ARE CONSERVATIVE FORMS OF INVESTMENT. ✦ INITIALLY THIS SECTION IS DEVOTED TO OPTIONS. AN OPTION IS A CONTRACT THAT GIVES THE HOLDER THE RIGHT TO BUY OR SELL A SECURITY AT A SPECIFIED PRICE WITHIN a specified time period. An option's value is derived from the underlying stock; hence options are sometimes referred to as derivative securities.

Options can be very speculative investments, and only those individuals who are willing and able to bear the substantial risk should consider buying and selling them. However, options offer the possibility of a large return, so those investors willing to bear the risk for the potential return may find this material to be the most fascinating in the text.

Chapter 20 considers an alternative speculative investment: the futures contract. This contract is for the delivery of a commodity, such as wheat, or a financial asset, such as U.S. Treasury bills. Like options, the value of a futures contract is derived from the value of the underlying commodity. Futures contracts can provide large and sudden profits or losses, and they require that the individual actively participate in the day-to-day management of the investments.

While options and futures are generally speculative investments, they may also be used in risk management. In that context, these speculative assets may be combined with other investments and actually reduce the individual's risk exposure.

The last two chapters of Part Four discuss nonfinancial assets (i.e., tangible assets). These include collectibles, such as works of art; precious metals, such as gold; and real estate, especially home ownership. These investments require specialized knowledge, but may be rewarding to the patient individual who takes the time to learn how these assets may be used as part of a total investment strategy.

19

An Introduction to Options*

*A*n option is the right to do something. In the security markets an option is the right to buy or sell stock at a specified price within a specified time period. Options take various forms, including warrants, calls, and puts. Some securities, such as the convertible bonds discussed in the previous chapter, have options built into them. Owners of options do not receive the benefits of owning the underlying stock. These investors purchase the option because they expect the price of the option to rise (and fall) more rapidly than the underlying stock. Since options offer this potential leverage, they are also riskier investments; the individual could easily lose the entire amount invested in an option.

This chapter is a general introduction to investing in options. After covering the features that are common to all options (their intrinsic value, the leverage they offer, and the time premiums they command), the discussion considers warrants issued by firms to buy their stock. Until the creation of the Chicago Board Options Exchange (CBOE), warrants were the primary option available to investors. With the formation of the CBOE, a secondary market was created for the purchase and sale of put and call options. Put and call options permit investors to take long and short positions and to construct hedged positions to reduce risk. The initial success of the CBOE led to trading of options on other exchanges and to the creation of new types of options such as the stock index option, which is not based on a specific company's securities but on an index of the market as a whole.

◆ ◆ ◆

The Intrinsic Value of an Option

An **option** is the right to buy or sell stock at a specified price within a specified time period. At the end of the time period, the option expires on its **expiration**

* This chapter uses material from Herbert B. Mayo, *Using the Leverage in Warrants and Call to Build a Successful Investment Program* (New Rochelle, N.Y.: Investors Intelligence, 1974). Permission to use this material has been graciously given by the publisher.

LEARNING OBJECTIVES

After completing this chapter you should be able to

1. Define the word *option* as it applies to securities, and differentiate between an option's market value and its intrinsic value.

2. Identify the risks associated with purchasing an option, and the factors affecting an option's time premium.

3. Demonstrate how hedging with warrants or writing covered call options may yield a profit.

4. Differentiate the profit and loss from writing a covered call option versus a naked call option.

5. Explain the relationship between the price of a stock and a put option.

6. Compare buying a put option with selling short.

7. Identify the advantages offered by stock-index options.

option
The right to buy or sell something at a specified price within a specified time period.

expiration date
The date by which an option must be exercised.

intrinsic value
What an option is worth as stock.

exercise price (strike price)
The price at which the investor may buy or sell stock through an option.

premium
The market price of an option.

date. The minimum price that an option will command is its **intrinsic value** as an option. For an option to buy stock, this intrinsic value is the difference between the price of the stock and the per-share **exercise price (strike price)** of the option. The market price of an option is frequently referred to as the **premium.** If an option is the right to buy stock at $30 a share and the stock is selling for $40, then the intrinsic value is $10 ($40 − $30 = $10).

If the stock is selling for a price greater than the per-share exercise price, the option has positive intrinsic value. This may be referred to as the option's being "in the money." If the common stock is selling for a price that equals the strike price, the option is "at the money." And if the price of the stock is less than the strike price, the option has no intrinsic value. The option is "out of the money." No one would purchase and exercise an option to buy stock when the stock could be purchased for a price that is less than the strike price of the option. However, as is explained subsequently, such options may still trade.

The relationships among the price of a stock, the strike price (i.e., the exercise price of an option), and the option's intrinsic value are illustrated in Exhibit 19.1 and Figure 19.1. In this example, the option is the right to buy the stock at $50 per share. The first column of the exhibit (the horizontal axis on the graph) gives various prices of the stock. The second column presents the strike price of the option ($50), and the last column gives the intrinsic value of the option (i.e., the difference between the values in the first and second columns). The values in this third column are illustrated in the figure by line *ABC*, which shows the relationship between the price of the stock and the option's intrinsic value. It is evident from both the exhibit and the figure that as the price of the stock rises, the intrinsic value of the option also rises. However, for all stock prices below $50, the intrinsic value is zero, since security prices are never negative. Only after the stock's price has risen above $50 does the option's intrinsic value become positive.

The intrinsic value is one of the most important aspects of analyzing options. First, the market price of an option must approach its intrinsic value as the option

Exhibit 19.1 ✦ THE PRICE OF A STOCK AND THE INTRINSIC VALUE OF AN OPTION TO BUY THE STOCK AT $50 PER SHARE

Price of the Stock	*minus*	Per-Share Strike Price of the Option	*equals*	Intrinsic Value of the Option
$ 0		$50		$ 0
10		50		0
20		50		0
30		50		0
40		50		0
50		50		0
60		50		10
70		50		20
80		50		30
90		50		40

Figure 19.1 ✦ THE RELATIONSHIP BETWEEN THE PRICE OF A STOCK AND THE INTRINSIC VALUE OF AN OPTION TO BUY THE STOCK AT $50 PER SHARE

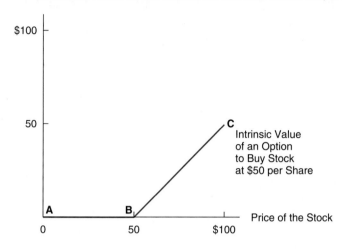

approaches its expiration date. On the day that the option is to expire, the market price can be only what the option is worth as stock. It can be worth only the difference between the market price of the stock and the exercise price of the option. This fact means that the investor may use the intrinsic value of an option as an indication of the option's future price, for the investor knows that the market price of the option must approach its intrinsic value as the option approaches expiration.

Second, because of arbitrage, the intrinsic value of an option sets the minimum price that the security will command. **Arbitrage** is the act of simultaneously buying and selling a commodity or security in two different markets to make a profit from the different prices offered by the markets. In the case of an option, the two markets are the market for the stock and the market for the option. The essence of the arbitrage position is a short sale in the stock and a long position (i.e., a purchase) in the option. After these transactions are effected, the arbitrageur will exercise the option. Then the shares acquired by exercising the option will be used to cover the short position in the stock.

This act of arbitrage may be clarified by using the simple example presented in Exhibit 19.2. If the price of the stock is $60 and the strike price of the option is $50, the option's intrinsic value is $10. If the current market price of the option were $6, an investor could buy the option and exercise it to acquire the stock. By doing so the investor saves $4, for the total cost of the stock is $56 (i.e., $6 for the option and $50 to exercise the option). The investor then would own stock that has a market value of $60.

If the investor continues to hold the stock, the $4 saving could evaporate if the stock's price falls. However, if the investor were to simultaneously buy the option and sell the stock short, the $4 profit would be guaranteed. In other words, the investor uses arbitrage, the required steps for which are presented in Exhibit 19.2. The investor sells the stock short at $60 and purchases the option for $6 (step 1). The stock certificate is borrowed from the broker and delivered to the buyer. Then the investor exercises the option (step 2). After receiving the stock certificate

arbitrage
The simultaneous buying and selling of an asset in two markets to take advantage of price differences.

Exhibit 19.2 ✦ THE STEPS REQUIRED FOR ARBITRAGE

Givens

Price of the stock		$60
Per-share strike price of the option		50
Price of the option		6

Step 1

Buy the option for $6

Sell the stock short for $60

Step 2

Exercise the option, thereby acquiring the stock for $50

Step 3

After acquiring the stock, cover the short position

Determination of profit or loss

Proceeds from the sale of the stock		$60
Cost of the stock		
Cost of the option	$ 6	
Cost to exercise the option	50	
Total cost		56
Net profit		$ 4

---

acquired by exercising the option, the investor covers the short position by giving the certificate to the broker (step 3). This set of transactions locks in the $4 profit, because the investor sells the stock short at $60 per share and simultaneously purchases and exercises the option for a combined cost of $56 per share. By selling the stock short and purchasing the option at the same time, the investor ensures that he or she will gain the difference between the intrinsic value of the option and its price. Through arbitrage the investor guarantees the profit.

Of course, the act of buying the option and selling the stock short will drive up the option's price and put pressure on the price of the stock to fall. Thus, the opportunity to arbitrage will disappear, because arbitrageurs will bid up the price of the option to at least its intrinsic value. Once the price of the option has risen to its intrinsic value, the opportunity for a profitable arbitrage disappears. However, if the price of the option were to fall again below its intrinsic value, the opportunity for arbitrage would reappear, and the process would be repeated. Thus, the intrinsic value of an option becomes the minimum price that the option must command, for arbitrageurs will enter the market as soon as the price of an option falls below its intrinsic value as an option.

If the price of the option were to exceed its intrinsic value, arbitrage would offer no profit, nor would an investor exercise the option. If the option to buy the stock in the previous examples were to sell for $5 when the price of the common stock was $50, no one would exercise the option. The cost of the stock acquired by exercising the option would be $55 (i.e., $50 + $5). The investor would be better off buying the stock outright than purchasing the option and exercising it. The opportunity for arbitrage thus occurs only when the price of the option is less than the option's intrinsic value. The option would not be purchased or exercised when its price exceeded its intrinsic value.

Actually, the opportunity for the typical investor to execute a profitable arbitrage is exceedingly rare. Market makers are cognizant of the possible gains from arbitrage and are in the best possible position to take advantage of any profitable opportunities that may emerge. Hence, if the opportunity to purchase the option for a price less than its intrinsic value existed, the purchases would be made by the market makers, and the opportunity to arbitrage would not become available to the general public. For the general investor the importance of arbitrage is not the opportunity for profit that it offers but the fact that it sets a *floor* on the price of an option, and that floor is the minimum or intrinsic value.

LEVERAGE

Some options offer investors the advantage of **leverage.** The potential return on an investment in an option may exceed the potential return on an investment in the underlying stock (i.e., the stock that the option represents the right to purchase). Like the use of margin, this magnification of the potential gain is an example of leverage. Unless these options offer investors leverage, there is no reason to purchase them in preference to the stock.

leverage
Magnification of the potential return on an investment.

Exhibit 19.3, which illustrates the relationship between the price of a stock and an option's intrinsic value, also demonstrates the potential leverage that options offer. For example, if the price of the stock rose from $60 to $70, the intrinsic value of the option would rise from $10 to $20. The percentage increase in the price of the stock is 16.67 percent ([$70 − $60] ÷ $60), whereas the percentage increase in the intrinsic value of the option is 100 percent ([$20 − $10] ÷ $10).

Exhibit 19.3   ✦   THE RELATIONSHIP BETWEEN THE PRICE OF STOCK, THE VALUE OF AN OPTION, AND THE HYPOTHETICAL MARKET PRICE OF THE OPTION

Price of the Common Stock	Option		
	Per-Share Strike Price	Intrinsic Value	Hypothetical Market Price
$ 10	$50	$ 0	$ 1
20	50	0	5
30	50	0	9
40	50	0	13
50	50	0	18
60	50	10	22
70	50	20	27
80	50	30	34
90	50	40	42
100	50	50	51

The percentage increase in the intrinsic value of the option exceeds the percentage increase in the price of the stock. If the investor purchased the option for its intrinsic value and the price of the stock then rose, the return on the investment in the option would exceed the return on the investment in the stock.

Leverage, however, works in both directions. Although it may increase the investor's potential return, it may also increase the potential loss if the price of the stock declines. For example, if the price of the stock in Exhibit 19.3 fell from $70 to $60 for a 14.2 percent decline, the intrinsic value of the option would fall from $20 to $10 for a 50 percent decline. As with any investment, the investor must decide if the increase in the potential return offered by leverage is worth the increased risk.

THE TIME PREMIUM PAID FOR AN OPTION

time premium

The amount an option's price exceeds the option's intrinsic value.

If an option offers a greater potential return than does the stock, investors may prefer to buy the option. In an effort to purchase the option, investors will bid up its price, so the market price will exceed the option's intrinsic value. Since the market price of an option is frequently referred to as the "premium," the extent to which this price exceeds the option's intrinsic value is referred to as the **time premium** or time value. Investors are willing to pay this time premium for the potential leverage the option offers. This time premium, however, reduces the potential return and increases the potential loss.

The time premium is illustrated in Exhibit 19.3, which adds to Exhibit 19.1 a hypothetical set of option prices in column 4. The hypothetical market prices are greater than the intrinsic values of the option because investors have bid up the prices. To purchase the option, an investor must pay the market price and not the intrinsic value. Thus, in this example when the market price of the stock is $60 and the intrinsic value of the option is $10, the market price of the option is $22. The investor must pay $22 to purchase the option, which is $12 more than the option's intrinsic value.

The relationships in Exhibit 19.3 among the price of the stock, the intrinsic value of the option, and the hypothetical price of the option are illustrated in Figure 19.2. The time premium paid for the option over its intrinsic value is easily seen in the graph, for it is the shaded area that is the difference between the line representing the market price of the option (line *DE*) and the line representing its intrinsic value (line *ABC*). Thus, when the price of the stock and option are $60 and $22 respectively, the time premium is $12 (the price of the option, $22, minus its intrinsic value, $10).

As may be seen in the figure, the amount of the time value varies at the different price levels of the stock. However, the amount of the time premium declines as the price of the stock rises above the option's strike price. Once the price of the stock has risen considerably, the option may command virtually no time premium over its intrinsic value. At $100 per share, the option is selling at approximately its intrinsic value of $50. The primary reason for this decline in the time premium is that as the price of the stock and the intrinsic value of the option rise, the potential leverage is reduced. In addition, at higher prices the potential price decline in the

Figure 19.2 ✦ THE RELATIONSHIPS AMONG THE PRICE OF THE STOCK, THE INTRINSIC VALUE OF THE OPTION, AND THE HYPOTHETICAL PRICE OF THE OPTION

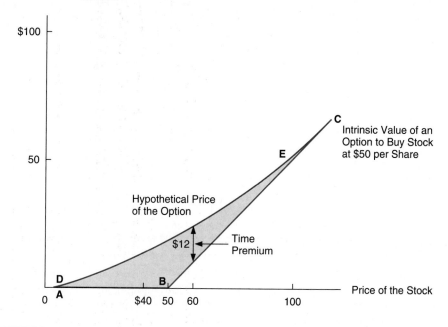

option is greater if the price of the stock falls. For these reasons investors become less willing to bid up the price of the option as the price of the stock rises, and hence the amount of the time premium diminishes.

The time premium decreases the potential leverage and return from investing in options. If, for example, this stock's price rose from $60 to $70 for a 16.7 percent gain, the option's price would rise from $22 to $27 for a 22.7 percent gain. The percentage increase in the price of the option still exceeds the percentage increase in the price of the stock; however, the difference between the two percentage increases is smaller, since the option sells for more than its intrinsic value. The time premium has substantially reduced the potential leverage that the option offers investors.

Investors who are considering purchasing options should ask themselves what price increase they can expect in the option if the price of the underlying stock should rise. For the option to be attractive, its anticipated percentage increase in price must exceed the anticipated percentage increase in the price of the stock. The option must offer the investor leverage to justify the additional risk. Obviously an investor should not purchase the option if the stock's price is expected to appreciate in value more rapidly than the option's price. The previous example illustrates that the time premium paid for an option may substantially decrease the potential leverage. Thus, recognition of the time premium that an option commands over its intrinsic value is one of the most important considerations in the selection of an option for investment.

WARRANTS

The preceding section considered options in general; the remainder of this chapter is devoted to specific options: warrants, calls, and puts. A **warrant** is an option issued by a company to buy its stock at a specified price within a specified time period. This definition includes the essential elements of all warrants, but there can be subtle differences. For example, the specified exercise price may rise at predetermined intervals (e.g., every five years) or the firm may have the right to extend the expiration date of the warrant.

An example of a warrant is the one issued by Global Marine, which offers the right to purchase one share of Global Marine common stock for $3 per share through February 28, 1996. If this option is not exercised by February 28, 1996, it will expire and become worthless. Thus, unlike stock, which is perpetual (i.e., continues in existence until the company is liquidated or merged into another company), warrants have a finite life.

Most warrants are an option, or right, to buy one share of common stock. Some warrants, however, are the option to buy more or less than one share. Such terms may be the result of stock dividends, stock splits, or a merger. For example, a warrant that is the option to buy 0.4 share may have evolved through a merger. The warrant initially represented the option to purchase one share of the company. However, when the company subsequently merged into another firm, the terms of the merger were 0.4 share of the acquiring firm (i.e., the surviving company) for each share of the company being acquired. The warrant then became an option to buy one share that had been converted into 0.4 share of the surviving company.

If a warrant is an option to buy more or less than one share, the strike price and the market price of the warrant can be readily converted to a per-share basis. Such conversion is desirable to facilitate comparisons among warrants. Consider, for example, an option that gives the right to buy 0.4 share at $10 and is currently selling for $4. The warrant's strike price and market price are divided by the number of shares that the warrant is an option to buy. Thus, the per-share strike price is $25 ($10 ÷ 0.4), and the per-share market price is $10 ($4 ÷ 0.4). Stated differently, 2.5 warrants are necessary to buy one share for $25.

Warrants are usually issued by firms in conjunction with other financing. They are attached to other securities, such as debentures or preferred stock, and are a sweetener to induce investors to purchase the securities. For example, AT&T and Chrysler Corporation issued bonds and preferred stock with warrants attached. The warrants were an added inducement to purchase the securities.

When a warrant is exercised, the firm issues new stock and receives the proceeds. For this reason, most warrants usually have a finite life. The expiration date ultimately forces the holder to exercise the option if the strike price is less than the current market price of the stock. However, if the strike price exceeds the stock's price at expiration (i.e., if the warrant has no intrinsic value), the warrant will not be exercised and will expire. After the expiration date, the warrant is worthless. This was the case with the Gulf and Western warrant that expired and was not exercised because it had no intrinsic value as an option. On the expiration day the price of the stock was $11, but the exercise price of the warrant was $19.37. No one would exercise the warrant to buy stock at $19.37 when the stock could be purchased for $11 on the New York Stock Exchange.

Exhibit 19.4 presents selected warrants and their strike price, market price, and intrinsic value, along with the market price of the stock, the expiration date of the warrants, and the time premium paid for each warrant. As may be seen in the exhibit, all of the warrants sell for a time premium (i.e., the market price exceeds the intrinsic value). Two of these warrants have strike prices that exceed the price of the stock. These warrants have no intrinsic value (i.e., they are "out of the money").

As is evident in the last column, there is variation in the time premiums. What accounts for this variation? Obviously as the warrant approaches expiration, its market price will approach the option's intrinsic value. On the expiration date, the warrant cannot command a price greater than its true value. Thus, as the warrant nears expiration, it will sell for a lower time premium. While the time to the expiration date of the option is an important determinant of the observed differences in time premiums, cash dividends and the volatility of the common stock also affect the amount of the time premium.

Warrants of companies that pay cash dividends tend to sell for lower time premiums. There may be two explanations for this relationship. Companies that do not distribute earnings but retain them will have more funds available for investments. By retaining and reinvesting their earnings, the companies may grow more rapidly. This growth may be reflected in the price of their stock, and hence the potential gain in the price of the warrant may be greater if the firm retains its earnings and does not pay a dividend. A second explanation is that if the company pays a cash dividend, the holder of the warrant does not receive the cash payment. The warrant will be less attractive relative to the common stock, for the owner of the warrant must forgo the dividend. Therefore, investors will not be as willing to pay as much for the warrant, and it will sell for a lower time premium.

A third factor that may influence the time premium paid for a warrant is the volatility of the price of the common stock. If the stock's price fluctuates substantially, the warrant may be more attractive and hence may command a higher time premium. Since the price of the warrant follows the price of the common stock, fluctuations in the price of the stock will be reflected in the warrant's price. The more volatile the price of the stock, the more opportunity the warrant offers speculators. Thus, the warrants of volatile common stocks may be more attractive (to

Exhibit 19.4 ✦ THE TERMS AND TIME PREMIUM PAID FOR SELECTED WARRANTS AS OF JUNE 1, 1992

| | | | Warrant | | | |
Company	Price of the Stock	Per-Share Strike Price	Expiration Date	Market Price	Intrinsic Value	Time Premium
Biogen	$25½	$20.00	6/30/94	$14¼	$5.50	$8.75
Manville	9⅛	9.40	6/5/96	2¾	0.00	2.75
Safeway	14	13.51	11/24/96	2¾	0.49	2.26
Veterinary Centers of America	4⅞	7.20	10/10/96	1¼	0.00	1.25

Source: Standard & Poor's Stock Guide, June 1992.

speculators especially), and hence the time premium commanded by these warrants will tend to be greater than that commanded by warrants of less volatile stocks.

HEDGING WITH WARRANTS

hedging
Simultaneous buying and selling to reduce risk.

Although warrants are speculative investments, they can be used in **hedge** positions to reduce risk. A hedge position offers the investor a modest gain in return for this reduction in risk. Before executing a hedge position, the investor must determine whether the reduction in risk is worth the loss in potential profit.

Hedging with warrants means that the investor simultaneously takes a long position and a short position.[1] In the usual hedge position, the investor sells the warrant short and purchases the stock that the warrant is an option to buy. The investor may also reverse this traditional hedge by selling the stock short and purchasing the warrant. The conditions under which such a reverse hedge would be profitable are rarer. Thus, the main concern of this section will be the usual hedge—a short position in the warrant and a long position in the stock.

To determine if a hedge will be profitable, the investor needs an indication of the potential gain or loss from the position. The current market price of the warrant, the current market price of the stock, and the per-share exercise price of the warrant are known. The investor also knows when the warrant will expire and that as the warrant approaches expiration, its market price must approach its intrinsic value. No one will pay more than the intrinsic value of the warrant on the option's expiration date. Thus, on the expiration date the warrant must be worth its value as stock, which is the difference between the market price of the stock and the strike price (i.e., the per-share exercise price of the warrant). This information permits the investor to calculate the possible gain from a hedge position at various prices of the stock.

The possible gain from a hedge position may be seen in Exhibit 19.5. In this example the current market price of the stock and of the warrant are $30 and $20, respectively. The warrant is an option to buy the common stock at $15 per share expiring after one year. Its minimum value is $15 (i.e., $30 − $15), and thus the warrant is selling at a time premium of $5 (i.e., $20 − $15) over its intrinsic value. This time premium must diminish until it is zero on the expiration date of the warrant, for on that day no one would be willing to pay more than the value of the warrant as an option.

Column 1 in Exhibit 19.5 gives various prices of the stock on the expiration date of the warrant. Column 2 gives the profit or loss on the long position in the stock (i.e., the profit or loss from purchasing the stock at $30 now and holding it until the warrant expires a year from now). Column 3 gives the value of the warrant on the expiration date at various stock prices. Since the price of the warrant

---

[1] Hedging with warrants is similar to writing covered call options, which is explained later in this chapter.

Exhibit 19.5 ✦ NET PROFIT ON A HYPOTHETICAL HEDGE POSITION WHEN THE CURRENT PRICE OF STOCK IS $30, THE CURRENT PRICE OF THE WARRANT IS $20, AND THE EXERCISE PRICE OF THE WARRANT IS $15

Price of the Common Stock	Profit or Loss on the Common Stock Bought Long	Value of the Warrant at Expiration	Profit or Loss on the Warrant Sold Short	Net Profit°
$ 5	$−25	$ 0	20	$−5
10	−20	0	20	0
15	−15	0	20	5
20	−10	5	15	5
25	− 5	10	10	5
30	0	15	5	5
35	5	20	0	5
40	10	25	− 5	5
45	15	30	−10	5
50	20	35	−15	5

°The net profit is determined by adding the profit or loss on the common stock bought long and the profit or loss on the warrant sold short.

approaches its intrinsic value as the expiration date nears, this value can be used to estimate the price of the warrant as it approaches expiration.

The profit or loss on a short position in the warrant at different hypothetical prices of the stock is presented in column 4. This is the difference between the purchase and sales prices. The warrant would be sold short today for $20 and would be purchased to cover the short position near its expiration date. The value of the warrant in column 3 indicates the price that the investor will pay when the warrant is purchased in the future to cover the short position.

The net profit or loss on the entire hedge position is presented in column 5. This profit is the sum of the profits (or losses) on the long position in the stock (column 2) and on the short position in the warrant (column 4). The information given in column 5 is plotted in Figure 19.3. As can be seen from either Exhibit 19.5 or Figure 19.3, a hedge position established at a price of $30 for the stock and $20 for the warrant yields a profit for all prices of the stock above $10 per share. The hedge position would be profitable even if the price of the common stock were to *fall* from $30 to $10 a share. Such a hedge position substantially reduces the risk of loss, for the investor earns a profit even if the price of the common stock declines. The investor need not be concerned with the direction of change in the stock's price. A fall in the price of the stock guarantees a profit on the short position in the warrant. A rise in the price of the stock guarantees a profit on the long position in the common stock. As long as the price of the common stock stays within the profitable range (in this case above $10 per share), the investor cannot lose money. However, it should also be noted that the potential profit is modest. In this example, the maximum possible profit before commissions is only $5 for each warrant sold short and each share purchased.

Figure 19.3 ✦ Relationship between the Price of the Common Stock and the Profit on a Hypothetical Hedge Position

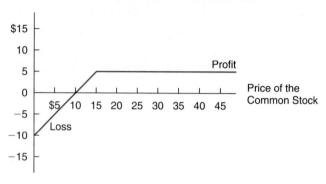

Calls

call option

An option sold by an individual that entitles the buyer to purchase stock at a specified price within a specified time period.

Although warrants were the popular speculative option during the 1960s, they were displaced in popularity in the 1970s by the call. A **call option** is an option to buy a specified number of shares of stock (usually 100) at a specified price (which is frequently referred to as the "strike" price) within a specified time period.[2] The owner of a call has the right *to call forth* the shares of stock and to purchase the shares at the specified price. (There is also the opposite type of option, which is called a put. A put is an option to sell a specified number of shares [usually 100] at a specified price within a specified time period. A put, then, is an option *to place or put* with someone else shares owned by the holder of the option. Puts are discussed later in this chapter.)

Calls are very similar to warrants (their definitions are essentially identical), but they have several distinguishing features. Warrants are issued by companies. Calls are issued by individuals and are sold to other individuals. This ability of the individual investor to write calls is a very important difference between calls and warrants, for the investor may be either a buyer *or* an issuer of call options. By enabling individuals to write options, calls offer investors opportunities for profit that are not available with warrants.

A second distinction between warrants and calls is the duration of the option. When warrants are issued, their expiration date is set. It is generally several years into the future (e.g., five years), and a few warrants are perpetual. Calls are of rel-

---

[2] Actually, call options are not new. They have existed as early as the 1630s, when options on tulip bulbs played a role in the speculative tulip bulb craze that swept Holland. See Burton G. Malkiel, *A Random Walk Down Wall Street* (New York: W. W. Norton, 1973), 28–45, for a fascinating portrait of such speculative periods.

atively short duration: three, six, or nine months. (There are longer-term calls; see the Points of Interest box on LEAPS on page 549.)

The third distinguishing feature of calls becomes evident when they are exercised. When a warrant is exercised, the firm issues new stock and receives the proceeds. The seller of a call, however, cannot issue new stock when the call is exercised but must either purchase the stock on the open market or surrender the stock from personal holdings. When the stock is supplied for the exercised call option, the option writer and not the firm receives the proceeds.

The Chicago Board Options Exchange

Prior to the formation of the **Chicago Board Options Exchange (CBOE),** calls were purchased only in the over-the-counter market. If an investor wanted to buy a call option, it was obtained from an options dealer. Each option sold was different, because the exercise price and the expiration date were negotiated with each sale. Once the option was purchased, the investor who desired to sell it had difficulty, because there was no secondary market in options.

CBOE
Chicago Board Options Exchange; the first organized secondary market in the puts and calls.

With the advent of the CBOE, an organized market in call options on selected securities was created. For the first time investors could buy and sell call options through an organized exchange (i.e., an organized secondary market). An investor purchasing a call on the CBOE knew that there would be a market for that option in the future. This ability to sell options that had been previously purchased gave a degree of marketability to call options that had not existed earlier.

There are several features of the CBOE that are conducive to the development of secondary markets for the calls. First, transactions are continuously reported, and daily summaries of transactions appear in leading newspapers. Exhibit 19.6 presents a clipping of selected calls and puts traded on various exchanges as reported in *The Wall Street Journal*. As may be seen in the exhibit, there are several options traded on each stock. The company, such as Eastman Kodak, is listed first, followed by the expiration date and strike price, such as Jan 40, which is a call option to buy the stock at $40 and which expires in January. (If the option is a put, a small p follows the strike price.) The next entries give the volume of contracts traded (194) and the market on which the option trades (CB for the Chicago Board Options Exchange). The last entries are the closing price (1⅜), the net change in the option's price from the previous day's trading (+¼), the closing price of the underlying stock (41⅛), and the number of contracts in existence, called the **open interest** (4,639).

open interest
Number of option contracts with a specified strike price and expiration date on a particular stock.

Second, a clearinghouse was established for the CBOE that maintains a daily record of options issued in the accounts of its members. The members are required to keep a continuous record of their respective customers' positions in options. No actual options certificates are issued; only the bookkeeping is maintained by the clearinghouse. A centralized clearinghouse greatly facilitates trading in the options, for it serves as the intermediary through which purchases and sales of the calls are recorded.

Third, the CBOE is self-regulated. It has the power to impose requirements that must be met before calls may be traded on the exchange, and options on only a selected number of securities have been accepted for trading on the exchange. Investors must be approved before they can purchase and sell through the CBOE, and there is a limit to the number of options on a single stock that an investor may own. Brokers on the floor of the exchange must have a minimum amount of capital.

Exhibit 19.6 ✦ LISITNG OF SELECTED OPTIONS TRADED ON THE CBOE, JANUARY 3, 1993

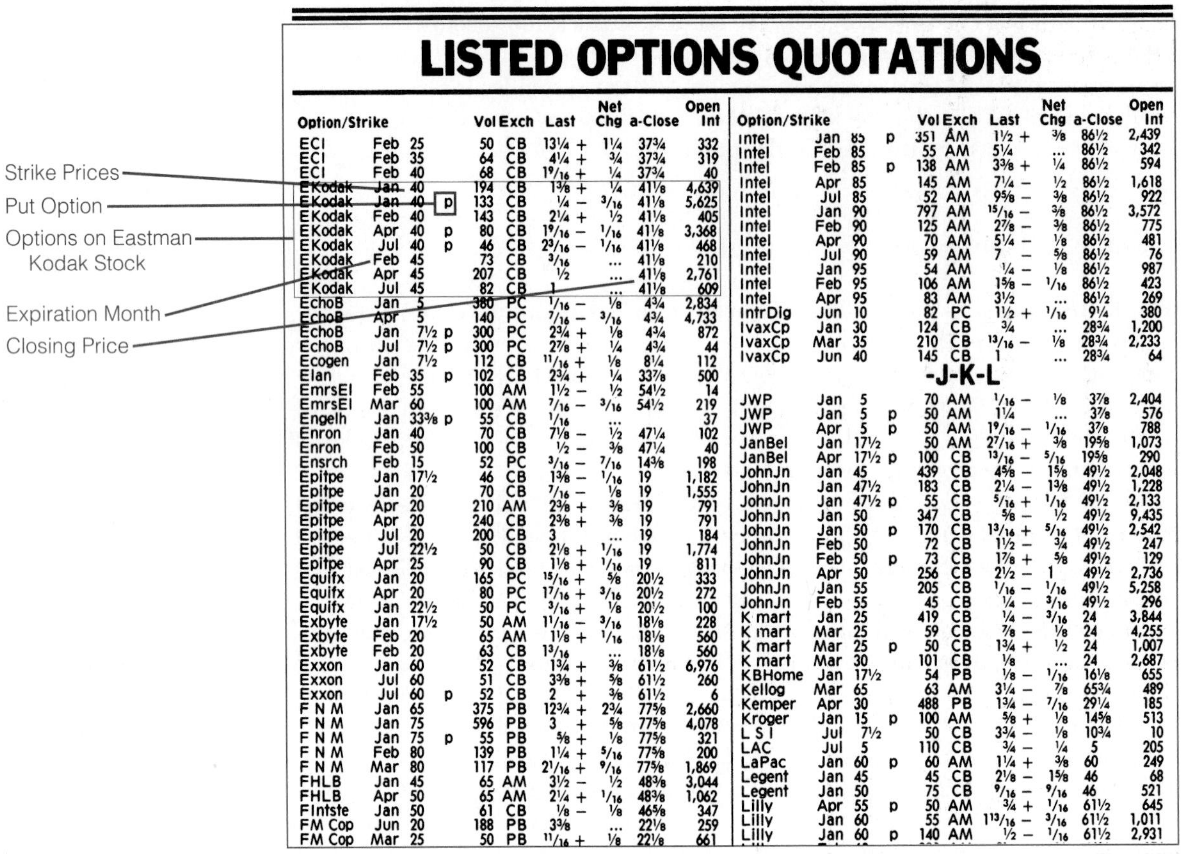
Strike Prices
Put Option
Options on Eastman Kodak Stock
Expiration Month
Closing Price

LISTED OPTIONS QUOTATIONS

Option/Strike				Vol	Exch	Last	Net Chg	a-Close	Open Int
ECI	Feb	25		50	CB	13 1/4	+ 1 1/4	37 3/4	332
ECI	Feb	35		64	CB	4 1/4	+ 3/4	37 3/4	319
ECI	Feb	40		68	CB	1 9/16	+ 1/4	37 3/4	40
EKodak	Jan	40		194	CB	1 3/8	+ 1/4	41 1/8	4,639
EKodak	Jan	40	p	133	CB	1/4	− 3/16	41 1/8	5,625
EKodak	Feb	40		143	CB	2 1/4	+ 1/2	41 1/8	405
EKodak	Apr	40	p	80	CB	1 9/16	− 1/16	41 1/8	3,368
EKodak	Jul	40	p	46	CB	2 3/16	− 1/16	41 1/8	468
EKodak	Feb	45		73	CB	3/16	...	41 1/8	210
EKodak	Apr	45		207	CB	1/2	...	41 1/8	2,761
EKodak	Jul	45		82	CB	1	...	41 1/8	609
EchoB	Jan	5		380	PC	1/16	− 1/8	4 3/4	2,834
EchoB	Apr	5		140	PC	7/16	− 3/16	4 3/4	4,733
EchoB	Jan	7 1/2	p	300	PC	2 3/4	+ 1/8	4 3/4	872
EchoB	Jul	7 1/2	p	300	PC	2 7/8	+ 1/4	4 3/4	44
Ecogen	Jan	7 1/2		112	CB	11/16	+ 1/8	8 1/4	112
Elan	Feb	35	p	102	CB	2 3/4	+ 1/4	33 7/8	500
EmrsEl	Feb	55		100	AM	1 1/2	− 1/2	54 1/2	14
EmrsEl	Mar	60		100	AM	7/16	− 3/16	54 1/2	219
Engelh	Jan	33 3/8	p	55	CB	1/16	...		37
Enron	Jan	40		70	CB	7 1/8	− 1/2	47 1/4	102
Enron	Feb	50		100	CB	1/2	− 3/8	47 1/4	40
Ensrch	Feb	15		52	PC	3/16	− 7/16	14 3/8	198
Epitpe	Jan	17 1/2		46	CB	1 3/8	− 1/16	19	1,182
Epitpe	Jan	20		70	CB	7/16	− 1/8	19	1,555
Epitpe	Apr	20		210	AM	2 3/8	+ 3/8	19	791
Epitpe	Apr	20		240	CB	2 3/8	+ 3/8	19	791
Epitpe	Jul	20		200	CB	3	...	19	184
Epitpe	Jul	22 1/2		50	CB	2 1/8	+ 1/16	19	1,774
Epitpe	Apr	25		90	CB	1 1/8	+ 1/16	19	811
Equifx	Jan	20		165	PC	15/16	+ 5/8	20 1/2	333
Equifx	Apr	20		80	PC	1 7/16	+ 3/16	20 1/2	272
Equifx	Jan	22 1/2		50	PC	3/16	+ 1/8	20 1/2	100
Exbyte	Jan	17 1/2		50	AM	1 1/16	− 3/16	18 1/8	228
Exbyte	Feb	20		65	AM	1 1/8	+ 1/16	18 1/8	560
Exbyte	Feb	20		63	CB	1 3/16	...	18 1/8	560
Exxon	Jan	60		52	CB	1 3/4	+ 3/8	61 1/2	6,976
Exxon	Jul	60		51	CB	3 3/8	+ 5/8	61 1/2	260
Exxon	Jul	60	p	52	CB	2	+ 3/8	61 1/2	6
F N M	Jan	65		375	PB	12 3/4	+ 2 3/4	77 5/8	2,660
F N M	Jan	75		596	PB	3	+ 5/8	77 5/8	4,078
F N M	Jan	75	p	55	PB	5/8	+ 1/8	77 5/8	321
F N M	Feb	80		139	PB	1 1/4	+ 5/16	77 5/8	200
F N M	Mar	80		117	PB	2 1/16	+ 9/16	77 5/8	1,869
FHLB	Jan	45		65	AM	3 1/2	− 1/2	48 3/8	3,044
FHLB	Apr	50		65	AM	2 1/4	+ 1/16	48 3/8	1,062
FIntste	Jan	50		61	CB	1/8	− 1/8	46 5/8	347
FM Cop	Jun	20		188	PB	3 3/8	...	22 1/8	259
FM Cop	Mar	25		50	PB	11/16	+ 1/8	22 1/8	661
Intel	Jan	85	p	351	AM	1 1/2	+ 3/8	86 1/2	2,439
Intel	Feb	85		55	AM	5 1/4	...	86 1/2	342
Intel	Feb	85	p	138	AM	3 3/8	+ 1/4	86 1/2	594
Intel	Apr	85		145	AM	7 1/4	− 1/2	86 1/2	1,618
Intel	Jul	85		52	AM	9 5/8	− 3/8	86 1/2	922
Intel	Jan	90		797	AM	15/16	− 3/8	86 1/2	3,572
Intel	Feb	90		125	AM	2 7/8	− 3/8	86 1/2	775
Intel	Apr	90		70	AM	5 1/4	− 1/8	86 1/2	481
Intel	Jul	90		59	AM	7	− 5/8	86 1/2	76
Intel	Jan	95		54	AM	1/4	− 1/8	86 1/2	987
Intel	Feb	95		106	AM	1 5/8	− 1/16	86 1/2	423
Intel	Apr	95		83	AM	3 1/2	...	86 1/2	269
IntrDig	Jun	10		82	PC	1 1/2	+ 1/16	9 1/4	380
IvaxCp	Jan	30		124	CB	3/4	...	28 3/4	1,200
IvaxCp	Mar	35		210	CB	13/16	− 1/8	28 3/4	2,233
IvaxCp	Jun	40		145	CB	1	...	28 3/4	64
-J-K-L									
JWP	Jan	5		70	AM	1/16	− 1/8	3 7/8	2,404
JWP	Jan	5	p	50	AM	1 1/4	...	3 7/8	576
JWP	Apr	5	p	50	AM	1 9/16	− 1/16	3 7/8	788
JanBel	Jan	17 1/2		50	AM	2 7/16	+ 3/8	19 5/8	1,073
JanBel	Apr	17 1/2	p	100	CB	13/16	− 5/16	19 5/8	290
JohnJn	Jan	45		439	CB	4 5/8	− 1 5/8	49 1/2	2,048
JohnJn	Jan	47 1/2		183	CB	2 1/4	− 1 3/8	49 1/2	1,228
JohnJn	Jan	47 1/2	p	55	CB	5/16	+ 1/16	49 1/2	2,133
JohnJn	Jan	50		347	CB	5/8	− 1/2	49 1/2	9,435
JohnJn	Jan	50	p	170	CB	1 3/16	+ 5/16	49 1/2	2,542
JohnJn	Feb	50		72	CB	1 1/2	− 3/4	49 1/2	247
JohnJn	Feb	50	p	73	CB	1 7/8	+ 5/8	49 1/2	129
JohnJn	Apr	50		256	CB	2 1/2	− 1	49 1/2	2,736
JohnJn	Jan	55		205	CB	1/16	− 1/16	49 1/2	5,258
JohnJn	Feb	55		45	CB	1/4	− 3/16	49 1/2	296
K mart	Jan	25		419	CB	1/4	− 3/16	24	3,844
K mart	Mar	25		59	CB	7/8	− 1/8	24	4,255
K mart	Mar	25	p	50	CB	1 3/4	+ 1/2	24	1,007
K mart	Mar	30		101	CB	1/8	...	24	2,687
KBHome	Jan	17 1/2		54	PB	1/8	− 1/16	16 1/8	655
Kellog	Mar	65		63	AM	3 1/4	− 7/8	65 3/4	489
Kemper	Apr	30		488	PB	1 3/4	− 7/16	29 1/4	185
Kroger	Jan	15	p	100	AM	5/8	+ 1/8	14 5/8	513
L S I	Jul	7 1/2		50	CB	3 3/4	− 1/8	10 3/4	10
LAC	Jul	5		110	CB	3/4	− 1/4	5	205
LaPac	Jan	60	p	60	AM	1 1/4	+ 3/8	60	249
Legent	Jan	45		45	CB	2 1/8	− 1 5/8	46	68
Legent	Jan	50		75	CB	9/16	− 9/16	46	521
Lilly	Apr	55	p	50	AM	3/4	+ 1/16	61 1/2	645
Lilly	Jan	60		55	AM	1 13/16	− 3/16	61 1/2	1,011
Lilly	Jan	60	p	140	AM	1/2	− 1/16	61 1/2	2,931

Source: The Wall Street Journal, January 4, 1993, C11.

Although such self-regulation does not guarantee the absence of illegal transactions, it is conducive to the development of organized security markets.

The initial success of the CBOE exceeded expectations. Soon after its formation, other exchanges started to list call options. Currently, call options are traded not only on the CBOE but also on the New York, American, Pacific, and Philadelphia exchanges. While all companies do not meet the criteria for having options listed, several hundred firms are eligible to have the call options traded on their stock listed.[3]

[3]The criteria for having call options listed on an exchange include the following: The firm must have at least 8,000,000 shares outstanding, 10,000 shareholders, and an annual turnover of 2,000,000 shares for the last two years.

The Pricing of Calls

The price that the investor pays for a call traded on the CBOE or any other exchange is determined by the demand for and the supply of the option. The price of a call is referred to as the *premium*. To some extent this term is a misnomer, for the price may include some intrinsic value as an option.

The minimum price of a call, like the minimum price of any option, is set by the option's intrinsic value. The price of a call cannot fall (for any significant length of time) below the difference between the price of the common stock and the per-share exercise price of the call. If the price of the call were to fall below its true value as an option, arbitrageurs would purchase calls, exercise them, and simultaneously sell the stock. These actions would bid up the price of the call and put downward pressure on the price of the stock until the option's price equaled or exceeded its intrinsic value.

The actual price investors pay for a call traded on the CBOE or other exchanges depends on their willingness to bid for the options and the willingness of other investors to supply the options. Through supply and demand, a single price is determined for each option.[4] Several of the variables that influence the demand for options include (1) the potential leverage the option offers, (2) the duration of the option, and (3) the potential for an increase in the price of the common stock in the immediate future. The long-term potential growth of the company is of little significance in the decision to purchase a CBOE call, for the growth may occur too far in the future. Since the call has a short life span, the emphasis is primarily on short-term increases in the market price of the stock, not on the company's long-term growth potential.

The Advantage of Purchasing Calls: Leverage

Warrants and calls are similar in many ways. Both represent the right to buy stock at a specified price within a specified time period. The reason for purchasing either warrants or calls is the potential leverage that they offer the investor. Calls, however, tend to offer greater leverage than warrants, since they sell for a smaller time premium above their intrinsic value. Because of the short duration of the call option, the time premium paid is less than that paid for a warrant, which is of longer duration.

The considerable potential leverage offered by a call to buy XYZ stock at $60 is shown in Exhibit 19.7. This exhibit presents the price of the XYZ stock (column 1); the strike price of the call (column 2); the intrinsic value of the call, that is, the difference between the price of the common stock and the per-share strike price of the call (column 3); and some hypothetical market prices of the call (column 4). The exhibit also includes the percentage change in the price of the common stock for successive increments of $5 (column 5) and the percentage change in the

---

[4] As with stocks and bonds, option dealers quote bid and ask prices at which they are willing to buy and sell for their own accounts.

Exhibit 19.7 ✦ POTENTIAL LEVERAGE OFFERED BY CBOE CALL TO BUY XYZ STOCK AT $60

Price of XYZ Stock	minus	Strike Price of the Call	equals	Intrinsic Value of the Call	Hypothetical Price of the Call	Percentage Change in the Price of the Stock	Percentage Change in the Price of the Call
$50		$60		$ 0	$ ¼	. . .	. . .
55		60		0	1	10.0%	300%
60		60		0	3	9.1	200
65		60		5	6	8.3	100
70		60		10	10½	7.7	75

hypothetical price of the call (column 6). As may be seen in the exhibit, if the price of XYZ's common stock rose from $60 to $65 (an 8.3 percent increase), the hypothetical price of this call would rise from $3 to $6 (a 100 percent increase). If equal amounts were invested in the common stock and the call, the call would have the potential to yield much more profit.

Although the potential leverage that calls offer is the primary reason for purchasing them, the investor does accept substantial risk.[5] On its expiration date the call can be worth only its intrinsic value. The call will be worthless if the price of XYZ stock is less than the strike price (i.e., below $60). This call will prove to be a profitable investment only if the price of the common stock rises. Thus, for a call to be profitable, the price of the common stock must increase during the call's relatively short life span.

The Advantage of Writing Calls: Income

The preceding section considered the reason for purchasing calls; this section will consider the advantage associated with selling them. (In the jargon of options, the act of issuing and selling a call is referred to as "writing" the option.) While buying calls gives the investor an opportunity to profit from the leverage that call options offer, writing calls produces revenue from their sale. The selling of options may also offer the investor an opportunity to earn a respectable return when the option is used in conjunction with stock already owned. In this case selling call options is similar to hedging with warrants. Both offer modest returns and a reduction in risk.

There are two ways to write options. The first is the more conservative method, which is called **covered option writing.** The investor buys the stock and then sells an option to buy that stock. If the option is exercised, the investor supplies the stock that was previously purchased (i.e., "covers" the option with the stock). The second

covered option writing
Selling an option for which the seller owns the securities.

---

[5]Calls may be combined with other securities such as U.S. Treasury bills so that risk is less than holding only the stock. See problem 11 at the end of this chapter.

method entails selling the call without owning the stock. This is referred to as **naked option writing,** for the investor is exposed to considerable risk. If the price of the stock rises and the call is exercised, the option writer must buy the stock at the higher market price in order to supply it to the buyer. With naked option writing the potential for loss is considerably greater than with covered option writing.

The reason for writing options is the income to be gained from their sale. The potential profit from writing a covered option may be seen in Exhibit 19.8. In this example the investor purchases the common stock of XYZ at the current market price of $50 per share and simultaneously sells for $5 a call to buy the shares at the strike price of $50. Thus, the investor sells the call for $500 (i.e., $5 × 100 shares). The possible future prices for XYZ stock at the expiration of the call are given in column 1. Column 2 presents the net profit to the investor from the purchase of the stock. Column 3 gives the value of the call at expiration, and column 4 presents the profit to the investor from the sale of the call. As may be seen in column 4, the sale of the call is profitable to the investor as long as the price of the common stock remains below $55 per share. The last column gives the net profit on the entire position. As long as the price of the common stock stays above $45 per share, the entire position will yield a profit before commission fees. The maximum amount of this profit, however, is limited to $500. Thus, by selling the call the investor forgoes the possibility of large gains. For example, if the price of the stock were to rise to $70 per share, the holder of the call would exercise it and purchase the 100 shares from the seller at $50 per share. The seller would then make only the $500 that was received from the sale of the call.

If the price of the stock were to fall below $45, the entire position would result in a loss to the seller. For example, if the price of the common stock fell to $40, the investor would lose $1,000 on the purchase of the stock. However, $500 has

naked option writing
The selling (i.e., writing) of an option without owning the underlying security.

Exhibit 19.8 ✦ Profit on a Covered Call Consisting of the Purchase of 100 Shares of XYZ Stock and the Sale of One Call to Buy 100 Shares of XYZ at $50 a Share

Price of XYZ Stock at Expiration of the Call	Net Profit on the Stock	Value of the Call at Expiration	Net Profit on the Sale of the Call	Net Profit on the Position
$42	$−800	$ 0	$500	$−300
44	−600	0	500	−100
46	−400	0	500	100
48	−200	0	500	300
50	0	0	500	500
52	200	200	300	500
54	400	400	100	500
56	600	600	−100	500
58	800	800	−300	500
60	1000	1000	−500	500

POINTS OF INTEREST

BIG PROFITS; BIG LOSSES

Profits and losses can be sustained very rapidly in option trading. Combine options with corporate takeovers and the possible price movements are magnified. Consider the attempted takeover of Cities Service by Gulf Oil. On Wednesday, June 16, 1982, the following options on Cities Service were traded when the stock sold for $37¾.

June Option Exercise Price	Option's Closing Price (6/16/82)
$20	$17⅛
25	12
30	7⅜
35	2
40	⁷⁄₁₆
45	⅛
50	¹⁄₁₆
55	¹⁄₁₆

On Thursday, June 17, 1982, there was no trading in Cities Service stock pending an announcement. The announcement turned out to be that Gulf Oil would buy Cities Service for $63 a share. When trading resumed on Friday, June 18, 1982, Cities Service stock rose to $53⅛. The options' prices rose (and the percentage increases from the previous closing prices) as follows:

June Option Exercise Price	Option's Closing Price (6/18/82)	Percentage Increase In Price
$20	$33¼	94.2%
25	28½	137.5
30	22⅞	210.2
35	18	800.0
40	13⅛	2,900.0
45	9½	7,500.0
50	3½	5,500.0
55	¹⁄₁₆	—

The irony of this incident is that the options were to expire on June 18, 1982. Thus the individual who bought the 40s at ⁷⁄₁₆ ($43.75) with only *two days to expiration* would normally have lost this money. But as a result of the attempted takeover, this speculator earned a return of 2,900 percent in two days!

While few investors earned such a return, the *New York Times* (June 19, 1982, 33) reported that several traders who had sold these options without owning the stock (i.e., had sold the options naked) had sustained heavy losses. If a trader had sold 100 contracts at 40 for ⁷⁄₁₆ ($43.75) per contract on Wednesday, those options were worth $4,375 (100 contracts times $43.75 per contract = $4,375). On Friday those calls were worth $131,250 (100 × $1,312.50 = $131,250). The loss to the naked call writer would be $126,875 ($4,375 − $131,250). Thus naked call writers of Cities Service stock suffered large losses as the unexpected happened and gave value to options that normally would have been worthless at expiration.

been received from the sale of the call. Thus, the net loss is only $500. The investor still owns the stock and may now write another call on that stock. As long as the investor owns the stock, the same 100 shares may be used over and over to cover the writing of options. Thus, even if the price of the stock does fall, the investor may continue to use it to write more options. The more options that can be written, the more profitable the shares become. For individuals who write options, the best possible situation would be for the stock's price to remain stable. In that case the investors would receive the income from writing the options and never suffer a capital loss from a decline in the price of the stock on which the option is being written.

The relationship between the price of the stock and the profit or loss on writing a covered call is illustrated in Figure 19.4, which plots the first and fifth columns of Exhibit 19.8. As may be seen from the figure, the sale of the covered option produces a profit (before commissions) for all prices of the stock above $45. However, the maximum profit (before commissions) is only $500.

Option writers do not have to own the common stock on which they write calls. Although such naked or uncovered option writing exposes the investor to a large amount of risk, the returns may be considerable. If the writer of the XYZ option

Figure 19.4 ✦ PROFIT OR LOSS ON SELLING A COVERED CALL

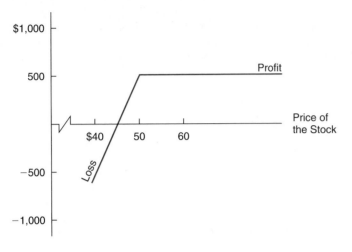

given in Exhibit 19.8 had not owned the stock and had sold the option for $500, the position would have been profitable as long as the price of the common stock remained below $55 per share at the expiration of the call. The potential loss, however, is theoretically infinite, for the naked option loses $100 for every $1 increase in the price of the stock above the call's exercise price. For example, if the price of the stock were to rise to $70 per share, the call would be worth $2,000. The owner of the call would exercise it and purchase the 100 shares for $5,000. The writer of the call would then have to purchase the shares on the open market for $7,000. Since the writer received only $500 when the call was sold and $5,000 when the call was exercised, the loss would be $1,500. Therefore, uncovered option writing exposes the writer to considerable risk if the price of the stock rises.[6]

The relationship between the price of the stock and the profit or loss on writing a naked call option is illustrated in Figure 19.5. In this case the option writer earns a profit (before commissions) as long as the price of the stock does not exceed $55 at the expiration of the call. Notice that the investor earns the entire $500 if the stock's price falls below $50. However, the potential for loss is considerable if the price of the stock increases.

Investors should write naked call options only if they anticipate a decline (or at least no increase in) the price of the stock. These investors may write covered call options if they believe the price of the stock may rise but are not certain of the price increase. And they may purchase the stock (or the option) and not write calls if they believe there is substantial potential for a price increase.

---

[6]This risk may be reduced by a stop–loss order to purchase the stock at $55. If the price of the stock rises, the stop–loss order is executed so that the option writer buys the stock.

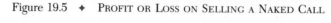

Figure 19.5 ✦ PROFIT OR LOSS ON SELLING A NAKED CALL

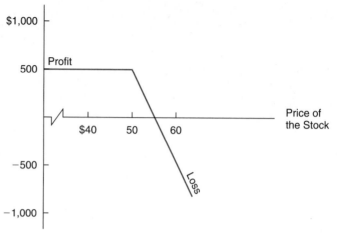

A Comparison of Selling Covered Calls and Hedging with Warrants

Selling covered options and hedging with warrants is very similar. Selling a covered call option is like buying stock and selling the warrant short. In both cases the potential profit from an increase in the price is limited. However, if the price of the stock declines, the sale prices of the call and the warrant protect the investor from loss.

This similarity may be seen by comparing Figures 19.3 and 19.4. In both cases the profit is limited, and in both cases the investor gains even if the price of the stock declines. Thus, there exists potential profit if the price of the stock rises or falls, but the gain is small. This is exactly the reason for hedging—to reduce the risk of loss from price movements. Hedging with warrants or selling covered options does just that. For accepting a smaller return, the investor reduces the risk of loss from fluctuations in the price of the stock. However, since there are many calls traded (in Exhibit 19.6 there were five calls traded on the stock of Eastman Kodak), there are many possible hedging strategies. Several of the problems at the end of this chapter cover these strategies.

PUTS

put option
An option to sell stock at a specified price within a specified time period.

At first, only call options were traded on the CBOE and other exchanges, but as of May 31, 1977, put options were admitted for trading. A **put option** is an option to *sell* stock (usually 100 shares) at a specified price within a specified time period. As with calls, the time period is short—three, six, or nine months. Like all options, a put has an intrinsic value, which is the difference between the strike price of the

Exhibit 19.9   ✦   THE RELATIONSHIP BETWEEN THE PRICE OF A STOCK AND THE
INTRINSIC VALUE OF A PUT

Strike Price	minus	Price of the Stock	equals	Intrinsic Value of the Put
$30		$15		$15
30		20		10
30		25		5
30		30		0
30		35		0
30		40		0

put and the price of the stock.[7] The relationship between the price of a stock and the intrinsic value of a put is illustrated in Exhibit 19.9. This put is an option to sell 100 shares at $30 per share. The first column gives the strike price of the put, the second column presents the hypothetical prices of the stock, and the third column gives the intrinsic value of the put (i.e., the strike price minus the price of the stock).

If the price of the stock is less than the strike price, the put has a positive intrinsic value and is said to be "in the money." If the price of the stock is greater than the strike price, the put has no intrinsic value and is said to be "out of the money." If the price of the stock equals the strike price, the put is "at the money." As with call options, the market price of a put is called "the premium."

As may be seen in Exhibit 19.9, when the price of the stock declines the intrinsic value of the put rises. Since the owner of the put may sell the stock at the price specified in the option agreement, the value of the option rises as the price of the stock falls. Thus, if the price of the stock is $15 and the exercise price of the put is $30, the put's intrinsic value as an option must be $1,500 (for 100 shares). The investor can purchase the 100 shares of stock for $1,500 on the stock market and sell them for $3,000 to the person who issued the put. The put, then, must be worth the $1,500 difference between the purchase and sale prices.

Why should an investor purchase a put? The reason is the same for puts as it is for other speculative options: The put offers potential leverage to the investor. Such leverage may be seen in the example presented in Exhibit 19.9. When the price of the stock declines from $25 to $20 (a 20 percent decrease), the intrinsic value of the put rises from $5 to $10 (a 100 percent increase). In this example a 20 percent decline in the price of the stock produces a larger percentage increase in the intrinsic value of the put. It is this potential leverage that makes put options attractive to investors.

As with other options, investors are willing to pay a price that is greater than the put's intrinsic value: The put commands a time premium above its intrinsic value

---

[7] Note that the intrinsic value of a put is the reverse of the intrinsic value of an option to buy (e.g., a call). Compare Exhibits 19.1 and 19.9.

as an option. As with warrants and calls, the amount of this time premium depends on such factors as the volatility of the stock's price, the duration of the put, and the potential for *decline* in the price of the stock.

The relationships among the price of the stock, the strike price of the put, and the hypothetical prices for the put are illustrated in Exhibit 19.10. The first three columns are identical to those in Exhibit 19.9. The first column gives the strike price of the put, the second column gives the price of the stock, and the third column gives the put's intrinsic value as an option. The fourth column presents hypothetical prices for the put. As may be seen in Exhibit 19.10, the hypothetical price of the put exceeds the intrinsic value, for it commands a time premium over its intrinsic value as an option.

Figure 19.6 illustrates the relationships among the price of the common stock, the intrinsic value of the put, and the hypothetical market value of the put that were presented in Exhibit 19.10. This figure shows the inverse relationship between the price of the stock and the put's intrinsic value. As the price of the stock declines, the intrinsic value of the put increases (e.g., from $5 to $10 when the stock's price declines from $25 to $20). The figure also readily shows the time premium paid for the option, which is the difference between the price of the put and the option's intrinsic value. If the price of the put is $8 and the intrinsic value is $5, the time premium is $3.

As may be seen in both Exhibit 19.10 and Figure 19.6, the hypothetical market price of the put converges with the put's intrinsic value as the price of the stock declines. If the price of the stock is sufficiently high (e.g., $50 in Exhibit 19.10), the put will not have any market value because the price of the stock must decline substantially for the put to have any intrinsic value. At the other extreme, when the price of the stock is low (e.g., $15), the price of the put is equal to the put's intrinsic value as an option. There are two reasons for this convergence. First, if the price of the stock rises, the investor may lose the funds invested in the put. As the price of the stock declines below the strike price of the put, the potential risk to the investor if the price of the stock should start to rise becomes greater. Thus, put buyers are less willing to pay a time premium above the put's intrinsic value. Second, as the intrinsic value of a put rises when the price of the stock declines, the investor

---

Exhibit 19.10 ✦ Relationship between the Price of the Stock, the Strike Price of the Put, and the Hypothetical Price of the Put

Strike Price of the Put	Price of the Stock	Intrinsic Value of the Put	Hypothetical Price of the Put
$30	$15	$15	$15¼
30	20	10	12
30	25	5	8
30	30	0	6
30	35	0	3½
30	40	0	1
30	50	0	—

Figure 19.6 ✦ THE RELATIONSHIPS AMONG THE PRICE OF THE STOCK, THE INTRINSIC VALUE OF A PUT OPTION, AND THE HYPOTHETICAL PRICE OF THE OPTION

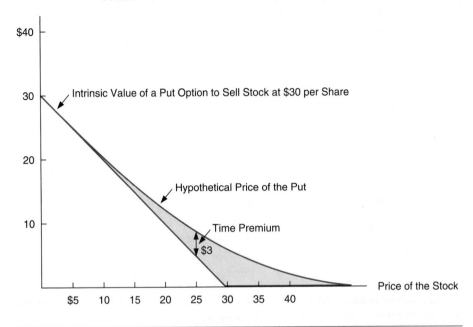

must spend more to buy the put; therefore, the potential return on the investment is less. As the potential return declines, the willingness to pay a time premium diminishes.

Puts Compared with Short Sales

Investors purchase put options when they believe that the price of the stock is going to decline. Purchasing puts, however, is not the only method investors can use to profit from falling security prices. As was explained in Chapter 3, an investor who believes that the price of a stock is going to fall may profit from such a decline by selling short. Buying a put is another form of a short position. However, the put option offers the investor two major advantages over selling short. First, the amount of potential loss is less; second, puts may offer a greater return on the investor's capital because of their leverage.

In order to execute a short position, the investor must sell the stock, deliver the borrowed stock, and later purchase the stock to cover the position. The profit or loss is the difference between the price at which the borrowed stock was sold and the price at which the stock is purchased to repay the loan. If the price of the stock declines, the investor reaps a profit, but if the price of the stock rises, the investor suffers a loss. This loss may be substantial if the stock's price rises significantly. For example, if 100 shares are sold short at $30 and later purchased at $50, the investor loses $2,000 plus commissions on the investment. The higher the price of the stock rises, the greater is the loss that the short position inflicts on the investor.[8]

Purchasing a put option does not subject the investor to a large potential capital loss. If the investor purchases for $300 a put that is the option to sell 100 shares at $30, the maximum amount that the investor can lose is $300. If the price of the common stock rises from $30 to $50, the maximum that can be lost with the put is still only $300. However, the loss on the short position is $2,000 when the price of the stock rises from $30 to $50. Puts reduce the absolute amount that the investor may lose.

Besides subjecting the investor to potentially large losses, the short sale ties up a substantial amount of capital. When the investor sells short, the broker will require that he or she put up funds as collateral. The minimum amount that the investor must remit is the margin requirement set by the Federal Reserve, and individual brokers may require that the investor supply more collateral than this minimum. Selling short thus requires the investor to tie up capital, and the larger the amount that the investor must remit, the smaller the potential return on the short position.

Less capital is required to invest in a put. While the amount of margin varies at different time periods, it certainly will not be as low as the price of the put. Thus, purchasing the put instead of establishing the short position ties up a smaller amount of the investor's funds. The potential return is greater if the price of the stock declines sufficiently to cover the cost of the put, because the amount invested is smaller. Puts thus offer the investor more leverage than does the short position.

Short sales, however, offer one important advantage over puts. Puts expire, but a short position can be maintained indefinitely. If an investor anticipates a price decline, it must occur during the put's short life for the investment to be profitable. With a short sale, the investor does not have this time constraint and may maintain the position indefinitely.

Protective Puts

Purchasing put options may be viewed as a speculative investment strategy. The buyer profits as the value of the underlying stock declines, which causes the value of the put to rise. Since the long-term trend in stock prices is to increase as the economy expands, purchasing a put seems to be betting against the natural trend in a stock's price.

While purchases of puts by themselves may be speculative, they may, when used in conjunction with the purchase of stock, reduce the individual's risk exposure. Such a strategy is referred to as a "protective put," which is the simultaneous purchase of the stock and a put. This strategy is called a protective put because it conserves the investor's initial investment while permitting the investor to maintain a long position in a stock so the profit can grow.

Suppose an individual buys a stock for $40 but does not want to bear the risk associated with a decline in the price of the stock. This investor could purchase a put, whose value would rise if the price of the stock were to decline. Suppose there

---

[8] Once again the investor may limit this potential loss by establishing a stop–loss order to purchase the stock should the price rise to some predetermined level.

Exhibit 19.11 ✦ PROFIT AND LOSS RESULTING FROM A PROTECTIVE PUT

Price of the Stock	Profit on the Stock	Intrinsic Value of the Put	Profit on the Put	Total Profit
$20	($20)	$20	$17½	($2½)
25	(15)	15	12½	(2½)
30	(10)	10	7½	(2½)
35	(5)	5	2½	(2½)
40	0	0	(2½)	(2½)
45	5	0	(2½)	2½
50	10	0	(2½)	7½
55	15	0	(2½)	12½
60	20	0	(2½)	17½

is a six-month put with a strike price of $40 that is currently selling for $2½.[9] Exhibit 19.11 presents the benefit of buying the put in combination with the stock. The first two columns give the price of the stock and the profit (loss) on the position in the stock. The third and fourth columns give the intrinsic value of the put at its expiration and the profit (loss) on the position in the put. The last column gives the net profit (loss), which is the sum of the profits (losses) on the positions in the stock and the put.

As shown in the last column of the exhibit, the worst case scenario is a loss of $2½. No matter how low the price of the stock falls, the maximum loss to the investor is $2½. If the price of the stock rises, the maximum possible profit is unlimited. The only effect, then, is that the potential profit is reduced by $2½, the price of the put. (This reduction in potential profit may be seen by comparing columns 2 and 5.) What the investor has achieved by purchasing the put in conjunction with the purchase of the stock is the assurance that the maximum loss would be $2½.

This protective put strategy may be viewed as an alternative to placing a stop–loss order to sell the stock at $37½. The advantage of the protective put is that the investor is protected from the price of the stock falling, the stock being sold, and the price subsequently rising. Day-to-day fluctuations in the price of the stock have no impact on the protective put strategy. The disadvantage is that the put ultimately expires, while the limit order may be maintained indefinitely. Once the put expires, the investor no longer has the protection and will have to buy another put. Of course, every time the investor purchases an additional put, the cumulative cost of the protection is increased. There are no costs associated with placing the limit order to sell the stock. Thus there is no clear answer as to which strategy is better. The protective put avoids the risk of being sold out by a temporary price decline but requires the investor to pay the cost of the option, which reduces some of the potential profit from the position in the stock.

[9] This strategy requires the existence of a put option on the stock. Obviously it cannot be executed for stocks for which there are no put options.

RETURNS FROM INVESTMENTS IN PUTS AND CALLS

Returns from investments in puts and calls depend on what happens to the price of the underlying stock. This is illustrated in Figures 19.7 and 19.8 for puts and calls on USX (United States Steel) and Teledyne. Figure 19.7 clearly illustrates the impact of the decline in USX's stock price. The stock continuously declined during the time period, causing the price of the call to fall while the price of the put rose. The call, which initially traded for $2½, was worthless at expiration, but during the same time period the price of the put rose from less than $1 to $5.

Figure 19.8 illustrates what happens when the price of the stock does not change. Initially, Teledyne's stock was $34. During the next three and a half months it fell to below $31, then rose to $36, and at the options' expiration was trading for $35, which was the options' strike price. As may be seen in the figure, the price of the put rose rapidly at first (i.e., its price doubled in January); however, the price

Figure 19.7 ✦ PRICES OF USX STOCK AND APRIL PUT AND CALL AT $25

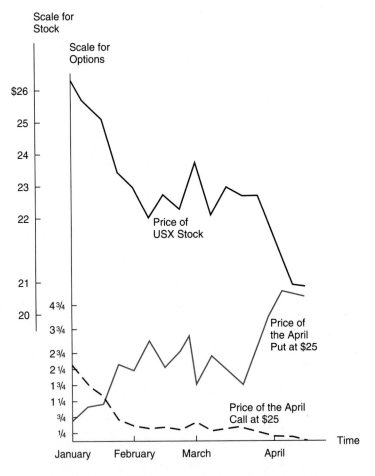

Figure 19.8   ✦   Prices of Teledyne Stock and April Put and Call at $35

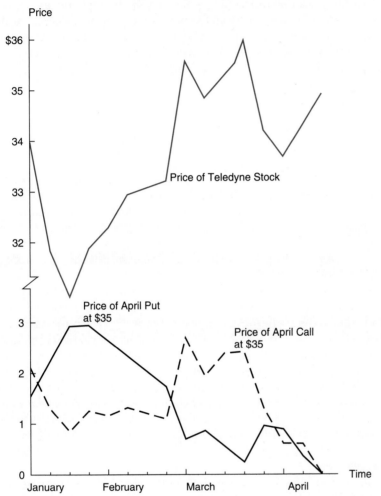

fell almost as rapidly in February, and the option was worthless at expiration. The price of the call initially fell and then rose in late February in response to the increase in the stock's price. However, in late March the price of the call fell and at expiration the call was worthless.

Perhaps what is most striking about Figure 19.8 is the fact that the ending price of Teledyne's stock was only $1 above the starting price. This small percentage increase of less than 3 percent from January to mid-April caused the value of the put to fall from $1⅝ to $0, for a 100 percent decline, and caused the value of the call to fall from $2⅛ to $0 for a 100 percent decline. Even though the price of the stock did rise from $34 to $35, the increase was insufficient to offset the time premium the call initially commanded, so the price of the call fell.

It should be obvious from these illustrations that there can be large variations in the returns from investments in options. Since there are many options for a given stock (Exhibit 19.6 gave the prices for five call options and three put options on Eastman Kodak), the investor has a mind-boggling array of possible strategies.[10] No particular strategy can be expected to yield consistently superior results. If such a strategy existed, many investors would seek to use it, which would reduce the strategy's potential for profit. As with investments in other securities (such as stocks and bonds), profits from investments in options should not tend to exceed the return consistent with the risk borne by the investor.

STOCK INDEX OPTIONS

stock index options
Rights to buy and sell based on an aggregate measure of stock prices.

While put and call options were initially created for individual stocks, **stock index options** have developed. (As is explained in Chapter 20, there are also stock index futures.) These stock index options are similar to options based on individual stocks, but the index option is based on an aggregate measure of the market, such as the Standard & Poor's 500 stock index. In addition to puts and calls based on the aggregate market, there are options based on subsets of the market, such as computer technology stocks or oil stocks. A listing of these index options and where they are traded is given in Exhibit 19.12. Stock index options have proved to be particularly popular and account for a substantial proportion of the daily transactions in options.

These options are popular because they permit the investor to take a position in the market or in a group of companies without having to select specific securities. For example, suppose an investor anticipates that the stock market will rise. What does this individual do? He or she cannot buy every stock but must select individual stocks.[11] Remember from the discussion of risk in Chapter 7 that there are two sources of risk associated with the individual stock: systematic risk and unsystematic risk. Systematic risk refers to the tendency of a stock's price to move with the market. Unsystematic risk refers to price movements generated by the security that are independent of the market (e.g., a take-over announcement, dividend cut, or large increase in earnings).

If the investor buys a particular stock on the expectation of a rising market, it does not necessarily follow that the individual stock's price will increase when the market rises. Investors construct diversified portfolios to reduce the unsystematic risk associated with the individual asset. As the portfolio becomes more diversified, unsystematic risk is reduced further and the return on the portfolio mirrors the return on the market. (Whether or not the return on the portfolio exceeds the market depends on the portfolio's beta. If the individual selects stocks with high betas, the diversified portfolio should tend to outperform the market as a whole in rising markets but underperform the market in declining markets.)

Index options offer the investor an alternative to creating diversified portfolios as a means to earn the return associated with movements in the market. For exam-

---

[10] See the third appendix and the references at the end of this chapter for readings that explore many of the strategies for using options.

[11] As is explained in Chapter 23, the investor could buy an index mutual fund. Such funds construct portfolios that mirror aggregate measures of the stock market.

POINTS OF INTEREST

LEAPS

Initial trading in puts and calls was limited to options of three, six, and nine months. However, in 1990 puts and calls with terms up to two years commenced trading on the CBOE and the AMEX. These options, called LEAPS (Long-Term Equity AnticiPation Securities), work essentially the same as traditional puts and calls, but because the term is longer, LEAPS command a larger time premium. For example, in 1992 a three-month call to buy Ford at $45 sold for $4½ and the eighteen-month call sold for $8½ while the price of the underlying stock was $48⅛. The same price relationship holds for puts. The three-month and eighteen-month puts sold for $1⅜ and $2¾, respectively.

Investors who anticipate that the price of Ford will rise may prefer to acquire the LEAPS instead of the short-term option because LEAPS offer additional time for the price of the stock to rise. Conversely, the writer may prefer to sell the longer-term call because the premium is larger. Of course, for the LEAPS option to be profitable for the buyer, the price of Ford must rise sufficiently to cover the cost of the option. And if that price increase does occur, the writer of the option will sustain a loss.

ple, if the investor anticipates that the market will rise in the near future, he or she may purchase a call option based on an index of the market as a whole (such as the Standard & Poor's 500 stock index). If the market does rise, the value of the call option also increases. The investor has avoided the unsystematic risk associated with the individual stock. In addition, the investor has avoided the large commission costs necessary to construct a diversified portfolio.

If the investor anticipates the market will decline, he or she will purchase a stock index put. If the investor is correct and the market as a whole does fall, the value of the stock index put rises. Of course, if the market does not decline but rises instead, the investor loses the amount invested in the put option. Here, however, is another major advantage offered by stock index options—*the maximum that the*

Exhibit 19.12 ✦ INDEX OPTIONS AND WHERE THEY ARE TRADED

The Option	Where Traded
S&P 100 Index	Chicago Board Options Exchange
S&P 500 Index	Chicago Board Options Exchange
Major Market Index	American Stock Exchange
AMEX Market Value Index	American Stock Exchange
Computer Technology Index	American Stock Exchange
Oil Index	American Stock Exchange
Airline Index	American Stock Exchange
Value Line Index	Philadelphia Exchange
National O-T-C Index	Philadelphia Exchange
Technology Index	Pacific Exchange
NYSE Options Index	New York Stock Exchange

investor can lose is the cost of the option. If the investor had sold stocks short instead of purchasing stock index put options, that individual may have been exposed to a large loss if stocks' prices rose.

Stock index options also give investors a means to hedge their existing portfolios. This is particularly important for portfolio managers with large holdings or individuals who want to improve the tax management of these holdings. Consider a substantial stock portfolio that has appreciated in value. If the investor anticipates declining stock prices and sells the shares, this is a taxable transaction. Instead of selling the stocks, the investor may sell stock index calls or purchase stock index puts. Then if the market declines, profits in these positions will help offset the losses on the individual stocks.

If the investor were to sell stock index call options, the value of these options would decline as the market decreased. The gain on the sale would then offset the loss in the individual stock's value. If the investor were to purchase stock index put options, the value of the options would increase if the market declined. The loss on the portfolio as a whole would be offset by the gain on the put option. (The amount offset would depend on how many put options the investor purchased.) As these two cases illustrate, stock index options offer the investor a means to hedge existing portfolios against a decline in the market without having to liquidate the positions and thus incur the capital gains tax liability. By buying or selling the appropriate stock index option, the investor achieved protection of capital without selling the appreciated securities.[12]

There is one major difference between stock index options and put and call options on specific stocks. With a call option to buy shares of IBM, the owner may exercise the option and buy the stock. With a put option to sell shares of IBM, the owner may exercise the option by delivering shares of IBM stock. Such purchases or deliveries are not possible with a stock index option. The owner of the call cannot exercise it and receive the index. Instead stock index options are settled in cash. For example, suppose the owner of a call based on the Standard & Poor's 500 index does not sell the option prior to expiration (and thereby closes the position). At expiration the intrinsic value of the option is determined and that amount is paid by the seller of the option to the owner. Of course, if the option has no intrinsic value at expiration, it is worthless and expires. The seller of the option then has no further obligation to the option's owner. In that case the premium paid for the option (i.e., its price) becomes profit for the seller.

In addition to stock index options, there are options on debt instruments (e.g., treasury bonds) and foreign currencies. Each of these options permits the investor (1) to take long or short positions on the underlying assets without actually acquiring them or (2) to establish hedge positions that reduce the risk of loss from price fluctuations. For example, if an investor anticipates declining interest rates, he or she will buy a call option to purchase bonds. If interest rates do fall, the value of bonds will rise, increasing the value of the call option. The call option's price will rise more rapidly than the bond's price because the call offers leverage. However, if the investor were to purchase the call option and interest rates rose, the investor's maximum possible loss would be limited to the cost of the option.

---

[12] For additional material on hedging, see the second appendix to this chapter.

Summary

A warrant is an option issued by a firm to buy stock at a specified price within a specified time period. A call is an option written by an individual to buy stock at a specified price within a specified time period. The writer of a call may either own the underlying stock and write covered call options or not own the stock and write naked call options. If the writer does not own the stock, he or she is exposed to a large potential loss should the price of the stock rise dramatically. A put is an option to sell stock at a specified price within a specified time period.

Options permit investors to take long and short positions without owning the stock. If an investor wants to take a long position, that individual may buy a call option or sell a put. Either position may profit if the price of the stock rises. If the investor anticipates that security prices will fall, that individual may establish a short position by selling a call option or buying a put.

The intrinsic value of a warrant or a call is the difference between the price of the stock and the exercise price (i.e., strike price) of the option. As the price of the stock rises, the intrinsic value of the option rises. The intrinsic value of a put is the reverse: the difference between the strike price and the price of the stock. As the price of the stock declines, the value of the put increases.

The intrinsic value of an option is important because it sets the minimum value of the option. If an option were to sell for less than its intrinsic value, a risk-free arbitrage opportunity for profit would exist. Generally options sell for more than their intrinsic value; they command a "time premium." This time premium works against the holder of the option because it reduces the option's potential leverage. On the expiration date, the time premium disappears. The option sells for its intrinsic value, since no individual would be willing to pay a time premium for the option. Unless the stock's price changes sufficiently to increase the option's intrinsic value, the disappearance of the time premium inflicts a loss on the investor who purchased the option.

Since the creation of the Chicago Board Options Exchange, put and call options have been traded on organized exchanges. These secondary markets have increased the popularity of put and call options because investors know there are markets in which they may increase or liquidate their positions in the options. The initial success of option trading has led to the creation of varied types of puts and calls, such as stock index options. These are put and call options based on an aggregate measure of the stock market instead of a specific security. Stock index options offer investors a means to manage their exposure to systematic and unsystematic risk by permitting them to a position in the market as a whole.

Security Summary

Options

    Source of return: Capital gains from the sale of an option for a profit. Income from writing an option.

    Liquidity and marketability: Active secondary market in options but high probability of loss implies no liquidity.

    Sources of risk: Unsystematic risk from events that affect the firm on which the option is written. Systematic risk from tendency of the prices of warrants and calls to move with the underlying stock and from the tendency of puts to move inversely with the underlying option.

Taxation: Capital gains and income generated by the sale of options are subject to capital gains taxation. If an option is exercised and the underlying stock is held, capital gains taxes are deferred until the stock is sold.

Summary of Positions

Long positions:

- ✦ Purchase the stock
- ✦ Purchase the warrant
- ✦ Purchase the call
- ✦ Sell the put naked

Short positions:

- ✦ Sell the stock short
- ✦ Purchase the put
- ✦ Sell the call naked

Hedged positions:

- ✦ Construct a covered call (purchase the stock and sell the call)
- ✦ Construct a covered put (sell the stock short and sell the put—covered in the third appendix in this chapter)
- ✦ Purchase the stock and sell the warrant short

Other positions:

- ✦ Protective put: purchase the stock and purchase the put; additional positions are in the third appendix

Terms to Remember

option	hedge
expiration date	call option
intrinsic value	Chicago Board Options Exchange
exercise (strike) price	(CBOE)
premium	open interest
arbitrage	covered option writing
leverage	naked option writing
time premium	put option
warrant	stock index options

Questions

1. What is an option? How is an option's minimum (or intrinsic value) determined? How does arbitrage assure that the price of an option will not be less than the option's intrinsic value?

2. What is the source of leverage in a call option? Why may an option be considered a speculative investment?

3. If you saw that the selling price of a share of stock was $20, the exercise price of an option to buy the stock was $10, and the price of the option was $5, what would you do?

4. What is the CBOE, and why are secondary markets crucial to the popularity of options?

5. What is the difference between covered and naked call writing? Why do some individuals buy call options while others write calls?

6. If an individual buys a call option and the price of the underlying stock declines, what should happen to the option? What is the maximum amount the investor can lose?

7. In what ways are calls similar to warrants? How do they differ?

8. Why does the intrinsic value of a call rise with the price of the stock, whereas the intrinsic value of a put declines as the stock's price rises?

9. What should happen to an option's time premium as the option approaches expiration? What happens to an "out of the money" option at expiration?

10. If an individual sells a call option, how may that investor close the position?

11. What advantage does purchasing a stock index option offer over buying options on individual securities?

Problems

1. A particular call is the option to buy stock at $25. It expires in six months and currently sells for $4 when the price of the stock sells for $26.
   a. What is the intrinsic value of the call? What is the time premium paid for the call?
   b. What will the value of this call be after six months if the price of the stock is $20? $25? $30? $40?
   c. If the price of the stock rises to $40 at the expiration date of the call, what is the percentage increase in the value of the call? Does this example illustrate favorable leverage?
   d. If an individual buys the stock and sells this call, what will the profit on the position be after six months if the price of the stock is $15? $20? $25? $26? $30? $40?
   e. If an individual sells this call naked, what will the profit or loss be on the position after six months if the price of the stock is $20? $26? $40?

2. What are the intrinsic values and time premiums paid for the following options?

Option	Price of the Option	Price of the Stock
Calls: XYZ, Inc., 30	$7	$34
XYZ, Inc., 35	2½	34
Puts: XYZ, Inc., 30	1¼	34
XYZ, Inc., 35	4¼	34

If the stock sells for $31 at the expiration date of the preceding options, what are the profits or losses for the writers and the buyers of these options?

3. The price of a stock is $51. You can buy a six-month call at $50 for $5 or a six-month put at $50 for $2.
   a. What is the intrinsic value of the call?
   b. What is the intrinsic value of the put?
   c. What is the time premium paid for the call?
   d. What is the time premium paid for the put?
   e. If the price of the stock falls, what happens to the value of the put?
   f. What is the maximum you could lose by selling the call covered?
   g. What is the maximum possible profit if you sell the stock short?
   After six months, the price of the stock is $58.
   h. What is the value of the call?
   i. What is the profit or loss from buying the put?
   j. If you had sold the stock short six months earlier, what would your profit or loss be?
   k. If you sold the call covered, what would your profit or loss be?

4. A particular put is the option to sell stock at $40. It expires after three months and currently sells for $2 when the price of the stock is $42.
   a. If an investor buys this put, what will the profit be after three months if the price of the stock is $45? $40? $35?
   b. What will the profit from selling this put be after three months if the price of the stock is $45? $40? $35?

5. A warrant with an expiration date of two years is an option to buy stock at $24. The current market price of the stock is $35, and the market price of the warrant is $15.
   a. What is the warrant's intrinsic value?
   b. What is the time premium paid for the warrant?
   c. If after two years the stock is selling for $50, what will be the price of the warrant? What is the percentage increase in the value of the stock and in the value of the warrant?
   d. Why does the warrant's time premium disappear?
   e. If after two years the stock is selling for $22, what will be the price of the warrant? What is the percentage decrease in the value of the stock and in the value of the warrant?

6. A warrant is the option to buy stock at $20 per share and expires in one year. Currently the price of the stock is $25, and the price of the warrant is $9. Determine the range of stock prices that will produce a profit for the following hedge positions:
   a. One warrant sold short for every share purchased.
   b. One warrant purchased for every share sold short.

7. Given:

Price of the stock	$26
Price of a six-month call at $25	$4
Price of a six-month call at $30	$2

The investor buys the call with the $25 exercise price and sells the call with the $30 exercise price. What is the profit on the position if at expiration the price of the stock is $15? $20? $25? $26? $30? $40? (Compare these results with your answers to problem 1d.)

If the prices were reversed and the $25 and $30 calls sell for $2 and $4, respectively, an arbitrage opportunity exists. Buy the $25 call and sell the $30 call. What are the profits if the stock's price is $20, $25, $30, and $35? Arbitrage implies what about the price of the call with the higher strike price relative to the call with the lower strike price?

8. A stock that is currently selling for $47 has the following six-month options outstanding:

	Strike Price	Market Price
Call option	$45	$6
Call option	50	1
Put option	45	2

  a. Which option(s) are "in the money?"
  b. What is the time premium paid for each option?
  c. What is the profit (loss) at expiration given the following prices of the stock—$30, $35, $40, $45, $50, $55, and $60—if the investor buys the call with the $45 strike price and the put?
  d. What is the profit (loss) at expiration given the following prices of the stock—$30, $35, $40, $45, $50, $55, and $60—if the investor buys the call with the $50 strike price and the put?
  e. What is the range of stock prices that will generate a profit if the investor sells the stock short and sells the call with the $50 strike price?
  f. What is the range of stock prices that will generate a profit if the investor sells the stock short and sells the put?

9. A straddle occurs when an investor purchases both a call option and a put option. Such a strategy makes sense when the individual expects a major price movement but is uncertain as to the direction. For example, a firm may be a rumored takeover candidate. If the rumor is wrong, the stock's price could decline and make the put profitable. If the rumor is correct and a takeover bid does occur, the price of the stock may rise and the call become profitable. There is also the possibility (probably small, at best) that the price of the stock could rise and subsequently fall, so the investor earns a profit on both the call and the put. The following problem works through a straddle.

    Given the following:

Price of the stock	$50
Price of a six-month call at $50	$5
Price of a six-month put at $50	$3½

the individual establishes a straddle (i.e., buys one of each option).
  a. What is the profit (loss) on the position if, at the expiration date of the options, the price of the stock is $60?
  b. What is the profit (loss) on the position if, at the expiration date of the options, the price of the stock is $40?
  c. What is the profit (loss) on the position if, at the expiration date of the options, the price of the stock is $50?

10. Two hedged positions were considered in the body of the chapter: (1) hedging with warrants and (2) the covered call. Other possible hedges consider buying one call option and selling another. Consider the following:

Price of the stock	$18
Price of a three-month call at $2	$2
Price of a three-month call at $15	$5

   a. What is the profit (loss) at the expiration date of the options if the price of the stock is $14, $20, or $25 and if the investor buys the option with the $20 strike price and sells the other option?
   b. Compare the profit (loss) from this strategy with buying the stock at $18.
   c. What is the profit (loss) at the expiration date of the options if the price of the stock is $14, $20, or $25 and if the investor buys the option with the $15 strike price and sells the other option?
   d. Compare the profit (loss) from this strategy with buying the stock at $18.

11. Options may also be used with other securities to devise various investment strategies. For example, an investor has the following alternative investments and their prices:

Common stock	$50
Six-month call on the stock at $50	$4
Six-month $10,000 U.S. Treasury bill	$9,600

   The investor has $10,000 and thus could buy (a) 200 shares of the stock or (b) one call plus the treasury bill. After six months how much profit or loss will the investor have earned on each alternative (excluding commissions) if the price of the stock is $60, $55, $50, $45, or $40? Which alternative is less risky?

Suggested Readings

The substantial body of literature written on options may be divided into three general classes. First is the material written for the reasonably sophisticated investor. Such material explains how options are traded, the advantages they offer, their risks, and various strategies that use puts and calls. A sampling of this material includes:

Characteristics and Risks of Standardized Options. Chicago, Ill.: The Options Clearing Corporation, 1987.

Fabozzi, Frank J., ed. *Winning the Interest Rate Game: A Guide To Debt Options.* Chicago, Ill.: Probus Publishing Company, 1985.

Gastineau, Gary L. *The Stock Options Manual.* 3d ed. New York: McGraw-Hill, 1988.

McMillan, Lawrence G. *Options as a Strategic Investment.* 3d ed. New York: New York Institute of Finance, 1993.

Nix, William E., and Susan W. Nix. *The Dow Jones-Irwin Guide to Stock Index Futures and Options.* Homewood, Ill.: Dow Jones-Irwin, 1984.

The development of a body of research has led to courses in options, and several textbooks have recently been published directed at this market. These include:

Chance, Don. *An Introduction to Options and Futures.* 2d ed. Hinsdale, Ill.: The Dryden Press, 1992.

Hull, John. *Options, Futures, and Other Derivative Securities.* Englewood Cliffs, N.J.: Prentice-Hall, 1989.

Kolb, Robert W. *Options: An Introduction.* Miami, Fla.: Kolb Publishing, 1990.

Ritchken, Peter. *Options: Theory, Strategy, and Applications.* Glenview, Ill.: Scott, Foresman and Company, 1987.

The third major source of information is the publication of extensive research on options, which covers the theoretical framework for their valuation, empirical evidence of option pricing, and practical applications. For a convenient collection of this material, obtain:

Berry, Michael, and Katrina F. Sherrerd. *CFA Readings in Derivative Securities.* Charlottesville, Va.: The Institute of Chartered Financial Analysts, 1988.

Kolb, Robert W., ed. *The Financial Derivatives Reader.* Miami, Fla.: Kolb Publishing, 1992.

Derivative securities have led to a subfield in finance called "financial engineering," which is the use of innovative processes and financial instruments. For a reference that covers unusual securities and how they are used to manage risk, consult:

Marshall, John F. and Vipul K. Bansal. *Financial Engineering.* Boston: Allyn & Bacon, 1992.

INVESTMENT PROJECT

By now your chart should have a substantial amount of data, and you should be able to see changes in (1) the market as indicated by type S&P 500 stock index, (2) individual stock prices as indicated in rows 2–9, and (3) short-term interest rates asindicated in row 10 and bond prices in row 11. In this part, options on Microsoft's stock are added. Select a call and a put with a strike price that approximates the current market price of the stock and has approximately two months to the option's expiration. If you are in the eleventh week of the semester, record these prices in the column for the eleventh week. Now work your way back to record the same data for prior weeks. Do not be surprised if the option did not trade on a specific day, in which case there is no entry. Also do not be surprised if the data indicate large swings in the prices of the options. During one semester a Teledyne call used in the Investment Project initially cost $10 and sold for over $50 by the end of the semester because of a dramatic increase in the stock price. Of course, during the same time period the put became worthless.

Appendix

PREEMPTIVE RIGHTS AND RIGHTS OFFERINGS

As explained in Chapter 8, some stockholders have **preemptive rights** that enable them to maintain their proportionate ownership in the corporation. If the firm wants to raise additional equity capital by issuing more shares of stock, it must first offer these shares to its current stockholders. The stockholders are not required to buy the new shares, but they do have the privilege of purchasing or refusing them. If the stockholders do purchase the new shares to which they are entitled, they maintain their proportional ownership in the firm.

preemptive rights
The right of current stockholders to maintain their proportionate ownership in the firm.

Firms that have granted preemptive rights present a **rights offering**[13] when they issue new stock. This offering gives the stockholder the option to purchase the additional shares at a predetermined price. Evidence of this option is called a **right,** and one right is issued for every existing share of stock. This right specifies the exercise price of the right, the expiration date, and the number of shares that the right is an option to buy.

rights offering
Sale of new securities to existing stockholders.

rights
An option given to stockholders to buy additional shares at a specified price during a specified time period.

For example, suppose a company has 1,000,000 shares outstanding and wants to raise $12,500,000. The price of its stock is currently $60, and management believes that it can sell additional shares to its current stockholders at $50. The firm then will have to issue 250,000 new shares at $50 each to raise the $12,500,000. These 250,000 new shares will increase the number of shares outstanding by 25 percent. The firm offers its current stockholders the right to buy additional shares. Each existing share receives a right to buy one quarter of a new share at $50 per share. Thus, it takes four rights to buy an additional share. If the stockholder has 100 shares, he or she may purchase 25 additional shares for $1,250 (25 × $50). If the stockholder does buy the new shares, the individual's proportionate ownership in the firm is unaltered. The stockholder then owns 125 shares of the 1,250,000 shares outstanding, whereas before the rights offering that stockholder owned 100 of the 1,000,000 shares outstanding.

The issuing of rights, like the declaration and distribution of dividends, occurs over time. The following series of dates illustrate the time frame of a rights offering. On January 1 stockholders have no knowledge of a rights offering. On January 10 the firm announces that a rights offering will be made and that stockholders owning shares at the close of the business day on January 31 will receive the rights to purchase the new shares. From January 10 through January 31 the stock continues to trade on the open market, and anyone who purchases the stock during that period and holds the stock until February will receive the rights to purchase the new shares.

[13] The number of rights offerings has diminished so that in 1990 only 7 firms listed on the NYSE and 3 listed on the AMEX issued new stock through a rights offering. (See *Moody's Dividend Record,* 1990: 245–247.) This appendix facilitates the coverage of a rights offering but may be omitted without loss of continuity.

During this time the price of the stock includes the value of the right. The stock trades with the *rights on* (i.e., the stock still confers the rights).

On February 1 purchasers of the stock no longer receive the rights, and the stock trades exclusive of the rights, or *ex rights*. Purchasing the stock after January 31 means the purchaser may not participate in the rights offering. However, the price paid for the stock will be lower because the existing shares have been diluted. As with the distribution of cash dividends, stock dividends, or stock splits, the price of the stock must decline on February 1 to account for the dilution of the existing shares.

The stockholders who own the shares on January 31 receive their rights from the company. These stockholders may exercise the rights or sell them in the open market. The rights now trade independently of the common stock. The only constraint on these stockholders is that they act (i.e., exercise or sell the rights) by the expiration date of the right, which is usually about four weeks after the rights are issued (in this case March 1). The market price of the right may rise or fall. If speculators anticipate that the price of the stock will rise, they will seek to buy the right and may even bid up the price so that it sells for a premium over its value as stock. If the stock's price does subsequently rise, these speculators will realize a profit because the value of the rights must also increase.

The value of a right, like the value of any option, is related to the market price of the stock, the exercise (or subscription) price of the right, and the number of rights necessary to purchase a new share. When the firm offers the rights to stockholders it must fix (1) the number of rights necessary to purchase a new share and (2) the exercise price of the rights. The market price of the stock, however, may continue to fluctuate, which will cause the value of the right to fluctuate.

How is the value of a right determined? The answer depends on whether the individual wants the value of the right when it is still affixed to the stock (i.e., when the stock is trading "rights on") or after the right has been issued and is trading independently of the stock. There is a simple formula for determining the value of the right as an option in either case. If the stockholder wants the rights-on value of the option (i.e., the value of the rights before they trade independently of the stock), the simple formula is

$$V = \frac{P_0 - P_e}{n + 1}, \qquad (19A.1)$$

where V indicates the value of the right; P_0, the current market price of the stock including the rights; P_e, the exercise price of the right (which is also referred to as the subscription price); and n, the number of rights necessary to purchase one share. If the investor applies this formula to the example presented previously, the value of the right is

$$V = \frac{\$60 - \$50}{4 + 1}$$

$$= \frac{\$10}{5}$$

$$= \$2.$$

This formula helps to illustrate the dilution that occurs when additional shares are issued. The "$n + 1$" in the denominator adjusts for the dilution that will occur when the stock trades ex rights. The "$+ 1$" represents the new share that will come into existence for every n number of shares the firm currently has. In this case the firm issues one new share for every four shares currently outstanding.

After the stock goes ex rights, its price declines by the value of the right. Thus, in this case the market price of stock declines by $2, from $60 to $58. The rights are now traded independently of the stock (i.e., traded "rights off"). The formula for the value of a right after the stock trades ex rights is

$$V = \frac{P_1 - P_e}{n}. \tag{19A.2}$$

The differences between the two formulas are the price of the stock (P_1), which now excludes the value of the rights, and the "$+ 1$." Since the price of the stock has already been adjusted for the dilution, the "$+ 1$" is no longer necessary. Now the value of the right is

$$V = \frac{\$58 - \$50}{4}$$

$$= \$2.$$

Notice that the market price of the stock is lower as a result of the dilution, but the value of the right is unaltered. The terms of the option have not been changed, but the increase in the total number of shares that will occur when the new shares are issued has caused a dilution of the old shares, and this dilution caused the price of the stock to decline by the value of the right.

These rights are an example of an option and as such may attract speculative interest. Should the price of the stock rise, the value of the right will tend to rise more rapidly because the rights offer potential leverage. If this occurs, speculators may be rewarded for purchasing the right from those stockholders who did not wish to exercise the option. For example, consider the impact of a four-point increase in the price of the preceding stock from $58 to $62. What effect does that have on the value of the right? The answer is

$$V = \frac{\$62 - \$50}{4}$$

$$= \$3.$$

The small increase in the price of the stock causes the value of the right to rise by 50 percent ([$3 − $2] ÷ $2).

Such potential leverage may attract speculators who anticipate an increase in the price of the stock. Of course, if the price of the stock declines, then the value of the right will decline. Leverage works both ways, and speculators who purchase rights for the potential increase in the value of the stock must also bear the risk of loss that will occur if the price of the stock falls.

Appendix

BLACK/SCHOLES OPTION VALUATION AND THE HEDGE RATIO

Valuation is a major theme in finance and investments. The valuation of bonds, preferred stock, and common stock compose a substantial proportion of the chapters devoted to these securities. The valuation of options is also important but is more difficult than most of the material covered in this text. This appendix will briefly cover the model initially developed by Fisher Black and Myron Scholes for the valuation of warrants and subsequently applied to call options. This valuation model, commonly referred to as Black/Scholes, permeates the literature on put and call options. It has also been applied to other areas of finance in which there are options. For example, if a firm has the right to retire a bond issue prior to maturity, the bond has a built-in option. By valuing the option and separating that value from the amount of the debt, the financial analyst determines the cost of the debt.

The following discussion explains and illustrates the Black/Scholes option valuation model. The derivation of the model is not given, so the reader will have to take the model on faith. You may, of course, pursue its development and subsequent option valuation models in the suggested readings at the end of the chapter.

The question of valuation of an option is illustrated in Figure 19.9, which essentially reproduces Figure 19.2. Lines *AB* and *BC* represent the option's intrinsic value, and line *DE* represents all the values of the option to buy for the various prices of the stock. The questions are "Why is line *DE* located where it is? Why isn't line *DE* higher or lower in the plane? What variables cause the line to shift up or down?" The Black/Scholes model determines the value of the option for each price of the stock and thus locates *DE* in the plane.

Figure 19.9 ✦ THE RELATIONSHIP BETWEEN THE VALUE OF AN OPTION TO BUY AND THE UNDERLYING STOCK

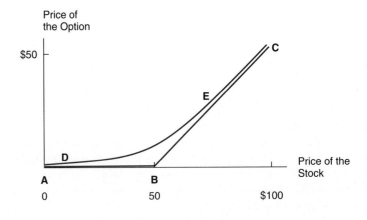

In Black/Scholes, the value of a warrant or call option (V_o) depends on

P_s the current price of the stock

P_e the option's strike price

T the time in years to the option's expiration date (i.e., if expiration is 3 months, $T = .25$)

σ the standard deviation of the stock's annual rate of return

r the annual risk-free rate of interest on an asset (e.g., treasury bill) with a term equal to the time to the option's expiration.

The relationships between the value of the option (the dependent variable) and each of these independent variables (assuming the remaining variables are held constant) are as follows:

◆ An increase in the price of the stock (an increase in P_s) increases the value of the option. This is true since the intrinsic value of the option rises as the price of the stock rises.

◆ An increase in the strike price (an increase in P_e) decreases the value of an option. Higher strike prices reduce the option's intrinsic value for a given price of the stock.

◆ An increase in the time to expiration (an increase in T) increases the value of an option. As time diminishes and the option approaches expiration, its value declines.

◆ An increase in the volatility of the stock (an increase in σ) increases the value of the option. A speculator will find an option on a volatile stock more attractive than an option on a stock whose price tends to be stable. Decreased volatility decreases the value of an option.

◆ An increase in interest rates (an increase in r) increases the value of the option. Higher interest rates are associated with higher option valuations.

Most of the relationships between the independent variables and an option's value seem reasonable with the exception of a change in the interest rate. Throughout this text, an increase in interest rates decreases the value of the asset. Higher interest rates reduce the present value of a bond's interest payments and principal repayment, thus reducing the value of the bond. Higher interest rates increase the required return for a common stock, thus decreasing the valuation of the common stock. This negative relationship between changes in interest rates and a security's value does not hold for options. Higher interest rates increase the value of an option.

The positive relationship between interest rates and the value of an option seems perverse given the previous material in this text, but the relationship makes sense. Remember that the intrinsic value of a call option is the difference between the price of the stock and the strike price. The investor, however, does not have to exercise the option immediately but may wait until its expiration. The funds necessary to exercise the option may be invested elsewhere. Higher interest rates mean these funds earn more. You need invest less at the higher rate to have the funds to exercise the option at expiration. Thus the present value of the strike price (i.e., the funds necessary to exercise the option) declines as interest rates rise. This reduction in the present value of the strike price increases the value of the option.

It should be noted that dividends are excluded from the Black/Scholes model. In its initial formulation, the valuation model was applied to options on stocks that did not pay a dividend. Hence the dividend played no role in the determination of the option's value. The model has been extended to dividend-paying stocks. Since the extension does not significantly change the basic model, this discussion will be limited to the original presentation.

Black/Scholes puts the variables together in the following equation for the value of a call option (V_o)

$$V_o = P_s \times F(d_1) - \frac{P_e}{e^{rT}} \times F(d_2) \qquad (19.B1)$$

The value of a call depends on two pieces: the price of the stock times a function $F(d_1)$, and the strike price, expressed in present value terms, times a function, $F(d_2)$. While the price of the stock (P_s) presents no problem, the strike price (P_e) expressed as a present value (P_e/e^{rT}) needs explanation. The strike price is divided by the number $e = 2.71828$ raised to rT, the product of the risk-free interest rate and the option's time to maturity. The use of $e = 2.71828$ expresses compounding on a continuous basis instead of discrete (e.g., quarterly or monthly) time periods.

The definitions of the functions $F(d_1)$ and $F(d_2)$ are

$$d_1 = \frac{ln\left(\frac{P_s}{P_e}\right) + \left(r + \frac{\sigma^2}{2}\right)T}{\sigma\sqrt{T}} \qquad (19.B2)$$

and

$$d_2 = d_1 - \sigma\sqrt{T} \qquad (19.B3)$$

The ratio of the price of the stock and the strike price (P_s/P_e) is expressed as a natural logarithm (ln). The numerical values of d_1 and d_2 represent the area under the normal probability distribution. Applying Black/Scholes requires a table of the values for the cumulative normal probability distribution. While such a table is readily available in statistics textbooks, one is provided in Exhibit 19.13 for convenience. Once d_1 and d_2 have been determined and the values from the cumulative probability distribution located, it is these values that are used in Black/Scholes model (i.e., substituted for $F(d_1)$ and $F(d_2)$ in Equation 19.B1).

How the model is applied may be seen by the following example. The values of the variables are

Stock price (P_s)	$52
Strike price (P_e)	$50
Time to expiration (T)	.25 (three months)
Standard deviation (σ)	.2
Interest rate (r)	.1 (10 percent annually)

Thus the values of d_1 and d_2 are

$$d_1 = \frac{ln\left(\frac{52}{50}\right) + \left(.1 + \frac{.2^2}{2}\right) \times .25}{.2\sqrt{.25}}$$

$$= \frac{.0392 + (.1 + .02).25}{.1} = 0.692$$

and

$$d_2 = 0.692 - .2\sqrt{.25} = 0.692 - .1 = 0.592$$

The values from the normal distribution are[14]

$$F(0.692) \approx 0.755$$

$$F(0.592) \approx 0.722.$$

These values are represented by d_1 and d_2 in Figure 19.10, which shows the areas under the normal probability distribution for both d_1 and d_2.

The probability distribution seeks to measure the probability of the option being exercised. If there is a large probability that the option will have positive intrinsic value at expiration, the numerical values of d_1 and d_2 approach 1, and the option's value will approach the price of the stock minus the present value of the strike price:

$$V_o = (P_s)(1) - \frac{(P_e)}{e^{rT}}(1) = (P_s) - \frac{P_e}{e^{rT}}.$$

If there is little probability that the option will have positive intrinsic value at expiration, the numerical values of d_1 and d_2 will approach 0, and the option will have little value:

$$V = (P_s)(0) - \frac{(P_e)}{e^{rT}}(0) = 0.$$

Given the values for $F(d_1)$ and $F(d_2)$ determined above from the normal distribution, the value of the call option is

$$V_o = (\$52)(.755) - \left(\frac{50}{2.71828^{(.1)(.25)}}\right)(.722) = \$4.00.$$

If the call is selling for more than $4.00, it is overvalued. If it is selling for less, it is undervalued.

---

[14] $F(0.69) = .7549$ and $F(0.59) = .7224$ which approximates the values given in the text.

Exhibit 19.13 ♦ Cumulative Normal Distribution

d	F(d)	d	F(d)	d	F(d)	d	F(d)	d	F(d)	d	F(d)	d	F(d)	d	F(d)	d	F(d)	d	F(d)	d	F(d)
-3.09	.0010	-2.51	.0060	-1.93	.0268	-1.35	.0885	-0.77	.2207	-0.19	.4247	0.39	.6517	0.94	.8264	1.49	.9319	2.04	.9793	2.59	.9952
-3.08	.0010	-2.50	.0062	-1.92	.0274	-1.34	.0901	-0.76	.2236	-0.18	.4286	0.40	.6554	0.95	.8289	1.50	.9332	2.05	.9798	2.60	.9953
-3.07	.0011	-2.49	.0064	-1.91	.0281	-1.33	.0918	-0.75	.2266	-0.17	.4325	0.41	.6591	.096	.8315	1.51	.9345	2.06	.9803	2.61	.9955
-3.06	.0011	-2.48	.0066	-1.90	.0287	-1.32	.0934	-0.74	.2297	-0.16	.4364	0.42	.6628	0.97	.8340	1.52	.9357	2.07	.9808	2.62	.9956
-3.05	.0011	-2.47	.0068	-1.89	.0294	-1.31	.0951	-0.73	.2327	-0.15	.4404	.043	.6664	.098	.8365	1.53	.9370	2.08	.9812	2.63	.9957
-3.04	.0012	-2.46	.0069	-1.88	.0301	-1.30	.0968	-0.72	.2358	-0.14	.4443	0.44	.6700	0.99	.8389	1.54	.9382	2.09	.9817	2.64	.9959
-3.03	.0012	-2.45	.0071	-1.87	.0307	-1.29	.0985	-0.71	.2389	-0.13	.4483	0.45	.6736	1.00	.8413	1.55	.9394	2.10	.9821	2.65	.9960
-3.02	.0013	-2.44	.0073	-1.86	.0314	-1.28	.1003	-0.70	.2420	-0.12	.4522	0.46	.6772	1.01	.8438	1.56	.9406	2.11	.9826	2.66	.9961
-3.01	.0013	-2.43	.0075	-1.85	.0322	-1.27	.1020	-0.69	.2451	-0.11	.4562	0.47	.6808	1.02	.8461	1.57	.9418	2.12	.9830	2.67	.9962
-3.00	.0013	-2.42	.0078	-1.84	.0329	-1.26	.1038	-0.68	.2483	-0.10	.4602	0.48	.6844	1.03	.8485	1.58	.9429	2.13	.9834	2.68	.9963
-2.99	.0014	-2.41	.0080	-1.83	.0336	-1.25	.1057	-0.67	.2514	-0.09	.4641	.049	.6879	1.04	.8508	1.59	.9441	2.14	.9838	2.69	.9964
-2.98	.0014	-2.40	.0082	-1.82	.0344	-1.24	.1075	-0.66	.2546	-0.08	.4681	.050	.6915	1.05	.8531	1.60	.9452	2.15	.9842	2.70	.9965
-2.97	.0015	-2.39	.0084	-1.81	.0351	-1.23	.1093	-0.65	.2578	-0.07	.4721	0.51	.6950	1.06	.8554	1.61	.9463	2.16	.9846	2.71	.9966
-2.96	.0015	-2.38	.0087	-1.80	.0359	-1.22	.1112	-0.64	.2611	-0.06	.4761	0.52	.6985	1.07	.8577	1.62	.9474	2.17	.9850	2.72	.9967
-2.95	.0016	-2.37	.0089	-1.79	.0367	-1.21	.1131	-0.63	.2643	-0.05	.4801	0.53	.7019	1.08	.8599	1.63	.9484	2.18	.9854	2.73	.9968
-2.94	.0016	-2.36	.0091	-1.78	.0375	-1.20	.1151	-0.62	.2676	-0.04	.4840	0.54	.7054	1.09	.8621	1.64	.9495	2.19	.9857	2.74	.9969
-2.93	.0017	-2.35	.0094	-1.77	.0384	-1.19	.1170	-0.61	.2709	-0.03	.4880	0.55	.7088	1.10	.8643	1.65	.9505	2.20	.9861	2.75	.9970
-2.92	.0018	-2.34	.0096	-1.76	.0392	-1.18	.1190	-0.60	.2743	-0.02	.4920	0.56	.7123	1.11	.8665	1.66	.9515	2.21	.9864	2.76	.9971
-2.91	.0018	-2.33	.0099	-1.75	.0401	-1.17	.1210	-0.59	.2776	-0.01	.4960	0.57	.7157	1.12	.8686	1.67	.9525	2.22	.9868	2.77	.9972
-2.90	.0019	-2.32	.0102	-1.74	.0409	-1.16	.1230	-0.58	.2810	-0.00	.5000	0.58	.7190	1.13	.8708	1.68	.9535	2.23	.9871	2.78	.9973
-2.89	.0019	-2.31	.0104	-1.73	.0418	-1.15	.1251	-0.57	.2843	0.01	.5040	$d_2\rightarrow$ 0.59	.7224	1.14	.8729	1.69	.9545	2.24	.9875	2.79	.9974
-2.88	.0020	-2.30	.0107	-1.72	.0427	-1.14	.1271	-0.56	.2877	0.02	.5080	0.60	.7257	1.15	.8749	1.70	.9554	2.25	.9878	2.80	.9974
-2.87	.0021	-2.29	.0110	-1.71	.0436	-1.13	.1292	-0.55	.2912	0.03	.5120	0.61	.7291	1.16	.8770	1.71	.9564	2.26	.9881	2.81	.9975
-2.86	.0021	-2.28	.0113	-1.70	.0446	-1.12	.1314	-0.54	.2946	0.04	.5160	0.62	.7324	1.17	.8790	1.72	.9573	2.27	.9884	2.82	.9976
-2.85	.0022	-2.27	.0116	-1.69	.0455	-1.11	.1335	-0.53	.2981	0.05	.5199	0.63	.7357	1.18	.8810	1.73	.9582	2.28	.9887	2.83	.9977
-2.84	.0023	-2.26	.0119	-1.68	.0465	-1.10	.1357	-0.52	.3015	0.06	.5239	0.64	.7389	1.19	.8830	1.74	.9591	2.29	.9890	2.84	.9977
-2.83	.0023	-2.25	.0122	-1.67	.0475	-1.09	.1379	-0.51	.3050	0.07	.5279	0.65	.7422	1.20	.8849	1.75	.9599	2.30	.9893	2.85	.9978
-2.82	.0024	-2.24	.0125	-1.66	.0485	-1.08	.1401	-0.50	.3085	0.08	.5319	0.66	.7454	1.21	.8869	1.76	.9608	2.31	.9896	2.86	.9979
-2.81	.0025	-2.23	.0129	-1.65	.0495	-1.07	.1423	-0.49	.3121	0.09	.5359	0.67	.7486	1.22	.8888	1.77	.9616	2.32	.9898	2.87	.9979
-2.80	.0026	-2.22	.0132	-1.64	.0505	-1.06	.1446	-0.48	.3156	0.10	.5398	0.68	.7517	1.23	.8907	1.78	.9625	2.33	.9901	2.88	.9980
-2.79	.0026	-2.21	.0136	-1.63	.0516	-1.05	.1469	-0.47	.3192	0.11	.5438	$d_1\rightarrow$ 0.69	.7549	1.24	.8925	1.79	.9633	2.34	.9904	2.89	.9981
-2.78	.0027	-2.20	.0139	-1.62	.0526	-1.04	.1492	-0.46	.3228	0.12	.5478	0.70	.7580	1.25	.8943	1.80	.9641	2.35	.9906	2.90	.9981

z	P	z	P	z	P	z	P	z	P	z	P	z	P	z	P	z	P	z	P	z	P
−2.77	.0028	−2.19	.0143	−1.61	.0537	−1.03	.1515	−0.45	.3264	0.13	.5517	0.71	.7611	1.26	.8962	1.81	.9649	2.36	.9909	2.91	.9982
−2.76	.0029	−2.18	.0146	−1.60	.0548	−1.02	.1539	−0.44	.3300	0.14	.5557	0.72	.7642	1.27	.8980	1.82	.9656	2.37	.9911	2.92	.9982
−2.75	.0030	−2.17	.0150	−1.59	.0559	−1.01	.1562	−0.43	.3336	0.15	.5596	0.73	.7673	1.28	.8997	1.83	.9664	2.38	.9913	2.93	.9983
−2.74	.0031	−2.16	.0154	−1.58	.0571	−1.00	.1587	−0.42	.3372	0.16	.5636	0.74	.7703	1.29	.9015	1.84	.9671	2.39	.9916	2.94	.9984
−2.73	.0032	−2.15	.0158	−1.57	.0582	−0.99	.1611	−0.41	.3409	0.17	.5675	0.75	.7734	1.30	.9032	1.85	.9678	2.40	.9918	2.95	.9984
−2.72	.0033	−2.14	.0162	−1.56	.0594	−0.98	.1635	−0.40	.3446	0.18	.5714	0.76	.7764	1.31	.9049	1.86	.9686	2.41	.9920	2.96	.9985
−2.71	.0034	−2.13	.0166	−1.55	.0606	−0.97	.1660	−0.39	.3483	0.19	.5753	0.77	.7793	1.32	.9066	1.87	.9693	2.42	.9922	2.97	.9985
−2.70	.0035	−2.12	.0170	−1.54	.0618	−0.96	.1685	−0.38	.3520	0.20	.5793	0.78	.7823	1.33	.9082	1.88	.9699	2.43	.9925	2.98	.9986
−2.69	.0036	−2.11	.0174	−1.53	.0630	−0.95	.1711	−0.37	.3557	0.21	.5832	0.79	.7852	1.34	.9099	1.89	.9706	2.44	.9927	2.99	.9986
−2.68	.0037	−2.10	.0179	−1.52	.0643	−0.94	.1736	−0.36	.3594	0.22	.5871	0.80	.7881	1.35	.9115	1.90	.9713	2.45	.9929	3.00	.9987
−2.67	.0038	−2.09	.0183	−1.51	.0655	−0.93	.1762	−0.35	.3632	0.23	.5910	0.81	.7910	1.36	.9131	1.91	.9719	2.46	.9931	3.01	.9987
−2.66	.0039	−2.08	.0188	−1.50	.0668	−0.92	.1788	−0.34	.3669	0.24	.5948	0.82	.7939	1.37	.9147	1.92	.9726	2.47	.9932	3.02	.9987
−2.65	.0040	−2.07	.0192	−1.49	.0681	−0.91	.1814	−0.33	.3707	0.25	.5987	0.83	.7967	1.38	.9162	1.93	.9732	2.48	.9934	3.03	.9988
−2.64	.0041	−2.06	.0197	−1.48	.0694	−0.90	.1841	−0.32	.3745	0.26	.6026	0.84	.7995	1.39	.9177	1.94	.9738	2.49	.9936	3.04	.9988
−2.63	.0043	−2.05	.0202	−1.47	.0708	−0.89	.1867	−0.31	.3783	0.27	.6064	0.85	.8023	1.40	.9192	1.95	.9744	2.50	.9938	3.05	.9989
−2.62	.0044	−2.04	.0207	−1.46	.0721	−0.88	.1894	−0.30	.3821	0.28	.6103	0.86	.8051	1.41	.9207	1.96	.9750	2.51	.9940	3.06	.9989
−2.61	.0045	−2.03	.0212	−1.45	.0735	−0.87	.1922	−0.29	.3859	0.29	.6141	0.87	.8078	1.42	.9222	1.97	.9756	2.52	.9941	3.07	.9989
−2.60	.0047	−2.02	.0217	−1.44	.0749	−0.86	.1949	−0.28	.3897	0.30	.6179	0.88	.8106	1.43	.9236	1.98	.9761	2.53	.9943	3.08	.9990
−2.59	.0048	−2.01	.0222	−1.43	.0764	−0.85	.1977	−0.27	.3936	0.31	.6217	0.89	.8133	1.44	.9251	1.99	.9767	2.54	.9945	3.09	.9990
−2.58	.0049	−2.00	.0228	−1.42	.0778	−0.84	.2005	−0.26	.3974	0.32	.6255	0.90	.8159	1.45	.9265	2.00	.9772	2.55	.9946		
−2.57	.0051	−1.99	.0233	−1.41	.0793	−0.83	.2033	−0.25	.4013	0.33	.6293	0.91	.8186	1.46	.9279	2.01	.9778	2.56	.9948		
−2.56	.0052	−1.98	.0239	−1.40	.0808	−0.82	.2061	−0.24	.4052	0.34	.6331	0.92	.8212	1.47	.9292	2.02	.9783	2.57	.9949		
−2.55	.0054	−1.97	.0244	−1.39	.0823	−0.81	.2090	−0.23	.4090	0.35	.6368	0.93	.8238	1.48	.9306	2.03	.9788	2.58	.9951		
−2.54	.0055	−1.96	.0250	−1.38	.0838	−0.80	.2119	−0.22	.4129	0.36	.6406										
−2.53	.0057	−1.95	.0256	−1.37	.0853	−0.79	.2148	−0.21	.4168	0.37	.6443										
−2.52	.0059	−1.94	.0262	−1.36	.0869	−0.78	.2177	−0.20	.4207	0.38	.6480										

Critical Values of z for

Significance Level	Two tails	Lower tail	Upper tail
0.10	±1.65	−1.28	+1.28
0.05	±1.96	−1.65	+1.65
0.01	±2.58	−2.33	+2.33

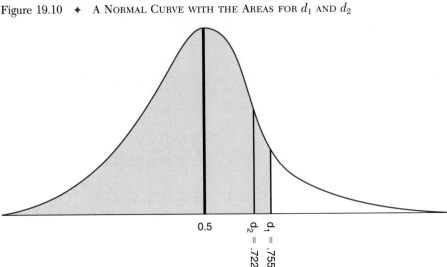

Figure 19.10 ✦ A NORMAL CURVE WITH THE AREAS FOR d_1 AND d_2

If the price of the stock had been $60, the Black/Scholes model determines the value to be $11.25. If the price of the stock were $40, the value of the option is $0.04. By altering the price of the stock, the various values of the option are determined. As shown in Figure 19.11, the different prices of the stock generate the general pattern of option values illustrated by line *DE* in Figure 19.9.

If one of the other variables (i.e., T, σ, P_e, and r) were to change while holding the price of the stock constant, the curve representing the value of the option would

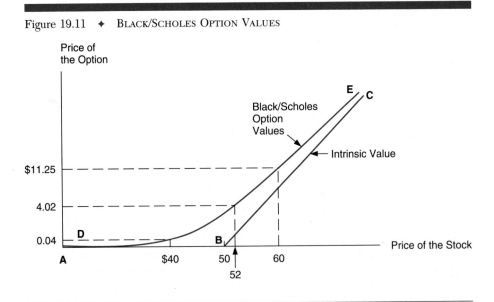

Figure 19.11 ✦ BLACK/SCHOLES OPTION VALUES

shift. If the life of the option had been nine months instead of three months, the curve would shift up. Increased price volatility, a lower strike price, or higher interest rates would also shift the Black/Scholes option valuation curve upwards. A shorter time to expiration, a lower interest rate, a higher strike price, or smaller volatility would shift the curve downward.

Once the option's value has been determined, it is compared with its price to determine if the option is under- or overvalued. Then an investment strategy is developed. Undervaluation suggests the option should be purchased (i.e., the investor takes a long position in the option). Overvaluation suggests the option should be sold. The investor takes a short position and writes the option naked or, if the investor is less willing to accept risk, writes the call covered. Other strategies involving puts or combining the option with treasury bills can also be developed.[15]

The Black/Scholes model is easy to apply, especially since computer programs have been developed to apply the model so the investor does not have to use cumulative probability distribution and do the calculations.[16] All variables, except one, are readily observable. Unfortunately, the standard deviation of the stock's return is not observable, so the individual will have to develop a means to obtain that data to apply the model.[17]

THE HEDGE RATIO

In addition to option valuation, the Black/Scholes model provides useful information to investors seeking to hedge positions. Hedged positions occur when the investor takes one position in the stock and the opposite in the option (e.g., a long in the stock and a short in the option). Unfortunately, the price movement in an option and the underlying stock are not equal. This was illustrated in Exhibit 19.7 in which the price of the call option increased from $3.00 to $6.00 when the price of the stock rose from $60 to $65. The percentage increase in the call exceeded the percentage increase in the price of the stock, and the absolute price changes were not equal. Since absolute price changes are not equal, the investor cannot use one call option to exactly offset price changes in the stock. Thus a hedge position of one call option cannot exactly offset the price movement in 100 shares of the stock.

To exactly offset a stock's price change, the investor must know the "hedge ratio" of the option. This is the ratio of the change in the price of the call option to the change in the price of the stock (i.e., the slope of the line *DE* relating the price of an option to the price of the stock in Figures 19.9 and 19.11). If the ratio

---

[15] This discussion is limited to call options, but, as is explained in more advanced books on options, there is a means to derive put option values from the valuation of call options.

[16] See, for instance, Stuart M. Turnbull. *Option Valuation*, Hinsdale, Ill.: The Dryden Press, 1988, a menu-driven program for determining option values.

[17] Historical option prices may be used to reverse the equation and solve for the standard deviation. This is one means by which the investor may determine the past volatility of the stock's return and then use this historical volatility to determine the present valuation of the option.

is 0.5, this means that the price of the option will rise $0.50 for every $1.00 increase in the price of the stock. Thus, if the investor owns 100 shares of the stock and has written two calls, a $1.00 increase in the stock should generate a $1.00 loss in the options (i.e., a $0.50 increase in the value of each option, which produces a total loss of $1.00 for the individual who has written two options). The gain in one position (e.g., the long position in the stock) is exactly offset by the loss in the other position (e.g., the short position in the option). The entire position is completely hedged.

If an investor or portfolio manager wants to exactly offset price changes by using options, the hedge ratio is crucial information. The reciprocal of the hedge ratio, which is

$$\text{Number of call options for a complete hedge} = \frac{1}{\text{Hedge ratio}},$$

defines the number of call options that should be sold for each 100 shares purchased.[18] Thus, in the previous example, the number of call options sold to construct a complete hedge is

$$\frac{1}{0.5} = 2.$$

The hedger must sell two call options for every 100 shares purchased to have a perfectly hedged position.

The hedge ratio may also be viewed as the number of shares of stock that must be purchased for each option sold. In the above example, the hedge ratio of 0.5 implies that 50 shares purchased for every call option sold is a completely hedged position. Either view of the hedge ratio is essentially the same. One view determines the number of shares to buy per call option, while the other determines the number of call options to sell per 100 shares of stock.

For individuals who wish to hedge their entire stock portfolio, the hedge ratio determines the number of stock index call options to sell. For example, suppose an investor is primarily concerned with collecting dividend income from the stock portfolio and wants to reduce the risk of loss from a movement in security prices. The hedge ratio helps achieve that goal by determining the appropriate number of stock index call options to sell to offset decreases (and increases) in the market as a whole.

Fortunately the hedge ratio is easy to obtain. The numerical value of $F(d_1)$ in the Black/Scholes option valuation model is the hedge ratio. In the preceding illustration of the valuation model, $F(d_1)$ was determined to equal 0.755. Thus at a price of the stock of $52, the number of call options necessary to hedge completely a position in the stock is $1/0.755 = 1.325$ options. Since the investor cannot buy or sell 1.325 call options, the hedge could be expressed as follows: For every call option, the investor takes the opposite position in shares of the stock. Thus one call option completely hedges 76 shares of the stock.

---

[18] For short positions in the stock, the ratio indicates the number of calls the individual must buy for every 100 shares sold short.

The hedge ratio is useful to large portfolio managers who are concerned with the management of risk. Large numbers of stop–loss orders or frequent purchases of puts to execute the protective put strategy may be impractical. The hedge ratio provides these portfolio managers with another tool to reduce the risk exposure of their portfolios.

While the hedge gives the number of call options that must be bought (or sold) for every 100 shares of stock, the numerical value of the ratio frequently changes. This may be seen by observing the curved line DE in Figure 19.9, which represents the value of the option at various prices of the stock. The slope of the line changes from being relatively flat for low prices of the stock to being parallel with the line representing the option's intrinsic value. Since the slope of the line increases with a rise in the stock's price, the numerical value of the hedge ratio also increases. This implies that fewer call options must be sold to construct a perfectly hedged portfolio. To maintain a perfectly hedged position, the individual must frequently adjust the positions in the call options or in the underlying securities. Thus, the use of options to completely erase the risk associated with security price changes may be impractical (if not impossible) to achieve.

Appendix

ADDITIONAL OPTION STRATEGIES

This chapter covered the basics of options and discussed several strategies that employed options such as the covered call and the protective put. This appendix introduces several other strategies involving options. These include the covered put and the protective call, which mirror the covered call and protective put presented in the body of the text. Next follows the "straddle," which combines buying (or selling) both a put and a call. The last strategies are called "spreads," which involve the simultaneous purchase and sale of options with different strike prices on the same stock. While these additional strategies do not exhaust all the possible strategies using options, they do give an indication of the variety of possible alternatives available that employ puts and calls.

The *covered put* is the opposite of the covered call. To construct a covered put, the investor sells the stock short and sells the put. If the put is exercised (forcing the investor to buy the stock), that individual may use the shares to cover the short in the stock. This is, of course, the opposite of the covered call, in which the writer supplies the previously purchased stock, if the call option is exercised.

As with the covered call, the *covered put* limits the potential profit, but it also reduces risk. An investor constructs this position in anticipation of a stable stock price. If the investor anticipates a large change in the price of the stock, an alternative strategy is superior to the covered put. For example, if the investor anticipates a large price decline, selling the stock short or buying the put offers more potential gain if the stock's price were to fall. To see the potential profit and loss from the *covered put,* consider the following example:

Price of the stock (P_s)	$52
Strike price of the put (P_e)	$55
Price of the put	$5½

The put is "in the money," since it has a positive intrinsic value ($P_e - P_s = \$55 - \$52 = \$3$). It is also selling for a time premium ($\$5½ - \$3 = \$2½$). Because the investor expects the price of the stock to remain stable or decline modestly, a covered put is constructed by selling the stock short at $52 and selling the put for $5½. The potential profit and loss at the expiration of the put from this position at various prices of the stock are as follows:

Price of the Stock	Profit (Loss) on the Short	Intrinsic Value of the Put	Profit (Loss) on the Put	Net Profit (Loss)
$40	$12	$15	$(9½)	$2½
45	7	10	(4½)	2½
50	2	5	½	2½
52	0	3	2½	2½
55	(3)	0	5½	2½
57½	(5½)	0	5½	0
60	(8)	0	5½	(2½)
65	(13)	0	5½	(7½)

As long as the price of the stock remains below $57½, the position generates a profit, but the maximum possible net profit is $2.50 (the time premium of the put).

The profit/loss profile is illustrated in Figure 19.12. The horizontal axis presents the price of the stock, and the vertical axis gives the profit and loss on the position. As may be seen in the figure, the maximum possible profit is $2.50 as long as the price of the stock is less than $55, the option's strike price. There is no limit to the possible loss, if the price of the stock rises. The break-even price of the stock is $57½.

Obviously, if the investor anticipates a large decline in the price of the stock, the above strategy is inappropriate because it limits the potential profit from a price decline. Instead, the investor would short the stock (or buy a put). However, there is no limit to the possible loss from a short position if the price of the stock were to rise. The investor could limit the loss by entering a limit order to buy the stock and cover the short if the price of the stock were to rise. A limit order, however, could result in the investor's position being closed by a brief run up in the price of the stock. An alternative strategy would be for the investor to buy a call. Combining a short in the stock with a call is the *protective call* strategy. The protective call is the opposite of the protective put strategy in which the investor buys the stock and a put. In that case, losses on the stock are partially offset by profits on the put. To see how the protective call strategy works, consider the following extension of the previous illustration.

Price of the stock	$52
Strike price of the call	$55
Price of the call	$1½

Figure 19.12 ◆ Profit or Loss from a Covered Put

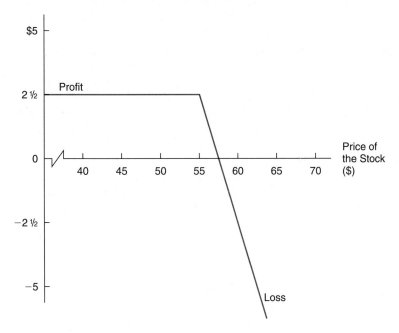

The call is "out of the money" since the strike price exceeds the price of the stock. The option also sells for a time premium of $1½.

To construct a protective call, the investor shorts the stock at $52 and purchases the call for $1½. The possible profits and loss from the position are as follows:

Price of the Stock	Profit (Loss) on the Short	Intrinsic Value of the Call	Profit (Loss) on the Call	Net Profit (Loss)
$40	$12	$0	$(1½)	$10½
45	7	0	(1½)	5½
50	2	0	(1½)	½
52	0	0	(1½)	(1½)
55	(3)	0	(1½)	(4½)
60	(8)	5	3½	(4½)
65	(13)	10	8½	(4½)

In this illustration, the worst case occurs when the price of the stock rises; however, the maximum possible loss is $4.50. Since theoretically there is no limit to the possible loss from a short position, the protective call limits the possible loss from an increase in the price of the stock. To achieve this increased safety, the investor forgoes some possible profit on the short in the stock.

The possible profits and losses at the various prices of the stock are illustrated in Figure 19.13. If the price of the stock rises, the maximum possible loss is limited to $4.50. As long as the price of the stock is less than $50½, the position is profitable. This figure also includes the possible profits and losses from a short in the stock. While the potential profit is larger if the price of the stock declines, there is no limit on the possible loss that is available from the construction of the protective put.

A *straddle* consists of a purchase (or sale) of a put and a call with the same exercise price and the same expiration date. If the investor buys both options, it is possible to earn a profit if the price of the stock rises and subsequently falls or, vice versa, falls and subsequently rises. The price increase may generate a profit on the call, and the price decline may generate a profit on the put. Of course, for this best of all possible worlds to occur, the stock's price must fluctuate sufficiently during the lives of the two options.

Investors may also construct saddles if they expect the stock's price to move but are uncertain as to the direction. Consider a stock that is trading for $50 as the result of takeover rumors. If the takeover does occur, the price of the stock should rise. That argues for a long position in the stock. If the anticipated takeover does not occur and the rumors abate, the price of the stock will probably decline. That argues for a short position.

A long or a short position by itself may inflict losses if the investor selects the wrong position. To avoid this, the investor purchases both a put and a call. A price movement in either direction may generate a profit, and the maximum possible loss is the cost of the two options.

To see these potential profits and losses, consider the stock and the two options used in the previous illustrations. The stock and options were

Price of the stock	$52
Price of a call at $55	$1½
Price of a put at $55	$5½

Figure 19.13 ✦ PROFIT OR LOSS FROM A PROTECTIVE CALL

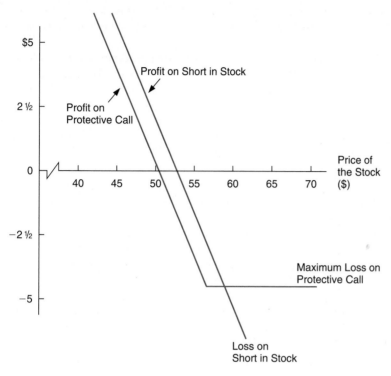

Instead of purchasing or shorting the stock, the investor buys both options. The possible profits and losses at the expiration of the options for various prices of the stock are as follows:

Price of the Stock	Intrinsic Value of the Call	Profit (Loss) on the Call	Intrinsic Value of the Put	Profit (Loss) on the Put	Net Profit (Loss)
$40	$ 0	$(1½)	$15	$9½	$8
45	0	(1½)	10	4½	3
48	0	(1½)	7	1½	0
50	0	(1½)	5	(½)	(2)
52	0	(1½)	3	(2½)	(4)
55	0	(1½)	0	(5½)	(7)
60	5	3½	0	(5½)	(2)
62	7	5½	0	(5½)	0
65	10	8½	0	(5½)	3
70	15	13½	0	(5½)	8

The position generates a profit as long as the stock price exceeds $62 or is less than $48 (i.e., the range of stock prices that generates a loss is $48 < P_s < 62). If the price of the stock moves either above $62 or below $48, the investor is assured of a profit. The maximum possible loss is $7, which occurs when the price of the stock equals the options' strike price at their expiration. At that price, neither option has any intrinsic value and both expire, so the investor loses the entire amount invested in both options.

The profits and losses from purchasing a straddle are illustrated in Figure 19.14. As may be seen in the figure, the position sustains a loss if the price of the stock is greater than $48 or less than $62, with a maximum possible loss of $7. There is no limit to the potential profit if the price of the stock rises, and the position could generate a profit of $48 in the unlikely case that the price of the stock declines to $0.

Why would the investor construct a straddle in which it is possible to sustain a loss, even if the price fluctuates but does not fluctuate sufficiently to cover the cost of the two options? The answer is that the investor anticipates a large movement in the price of the stock but is uncertain as to the direction. This position offers potential profit if such a price change occurs and limits the loss if the anticipated change does not materialize.

If the investor expects the price of the stock to be stable, that individual writes a straddle. The investor sells a put and a call. This strategy is, of course, the opposite of buying a straddle and its profit/loss profile is the exact opposite:

Price of the Stock	Intrinsic Value of the Call	Profit (Loss) on the Call	Intrinsic Value of the Put	Profit (Loss) on the Put	Net Profit (Loss)
$40	$ 0	$1½	$15	$(9½)	$(8)
45	0	1½	10	(4½)	(3)
48	0	1½	7	(1½)	0
50	0	1½	5	½	2
52	0	1½	3	2½	4
55	0	1½	0	5½	7
60	5	(3½)	0	5½	2
62	7	(5½)	0	5½	0
65	10	(8½)	0	5½	(3)
70	15	(13½)	0	5½	(8)

The writer of the straddle profits as long as the price of the stock exceeds $48 but is less than $62. The maximum possible profit is $7, which occurs when the price of the stock is $55 and both options expire worthless. Of course, the writer could sustain a large loss if the price of the stock makes a large movement in either direction.

The profile of profit and loss to the writer of the straddle is illustrated in Figure 19.15. Notice that this figure is the exact opposite of Figure 19.14. The writer accepts a modest possible profit, but there is no limit to the possible loss if the price of the stock were to rise, and there is also the potential for a large loss if the price of the stock falls below $48.

The covered put, the protective call, and the straddle do not exhaust all the possible strategies using puts and calls. The investor can also construct *spreads*, using options with different strike prices and/or expiration dates. In this case, the

Figure 19.14 ◆ PROFIT OR LOSS FROM PURCHASING A STRADDLE

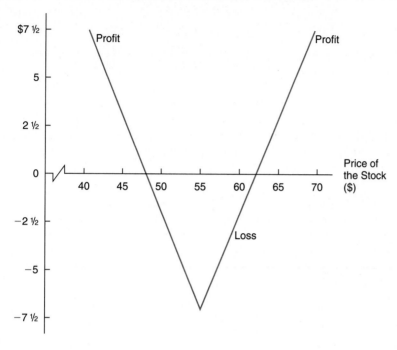

Figure 19.15 ◆ PROFIT OR LOSS FROM SELLING A STRADDLE

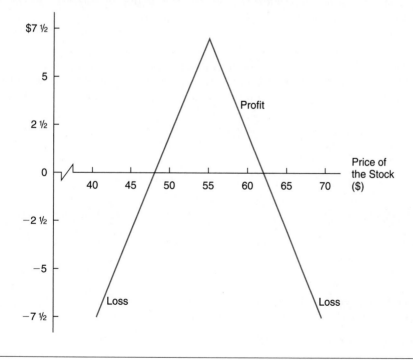

investor takes a long position in one option and a short position in the other. Consider the following:

Price of the stock	$52
Price of a call at $50	$5
Price of a call at $55	$1½

The investor may construct a *bull spread* by purchasing the $50s for $5 and selling (writing) the $55s for $1½. The net cash outlay is $3.50 (the $5 cost of the call at $50 minus the $1.50 received from the sale of the call at $55). The profile of the possible profit and loss at the options' expiration for various prices of the stock are as follows:

Price of the Stock	Intrinsic Value of the Call at $50	Profit (Loss) on the Call at $50	Intrinsic Value of the Call at $55	Profit (Loss) on the Call at $55	Net Profit (Loss)
$40	$ 0	$(5)	$ 0	$1½	$(3½)
45	0	(5)	0	1½	(3½)
50	0	(5)	0	1½	(3½)
53½	0	(1½)	0	1½	0
55	5	0	0	1½	1½
60	10	5	5	(3½)	1½
65	15	10	10	(8½)	1½

The position generates a profit as long as the price of the stock exceeds $53½ with a maximum possible profit of $1.50. The maximum possible loss is $3.50 (the net cash outlay). The amount of the profit may seem trivial, but since only $3.50 was at risk, the percentage return is 42.8 percent ($1.50/$3.50).

The investor could also reverse the above position and construct a *bear spread:* Buy the option at $55 for $1½ and sell the option at $50 for $5. This produces a net cash inflow; however, margin requirements will not permit the individual to remove the entire net proceeds. The possible profits and losses at the options' expiration for various prices of the stock are as follows:

Price of the Stock	Intrinsic Value of the Call at $50	Profit (Loss) on the Call at $50	Intrinsic Value of the Call at $55	Profit (Loss) on the Call at $55	Net Profit (Loss)
$40	$ 0	$ 5	$ 0	$(1½)	$3½
45	0	5	0	(1½)	3½
50	0	5	0	(1½)	3½
53½	3½	1½	0	(1½)	0
55	5	0	0	(1½)	(1½)
60	10	(5)	5	3½	(1½)
65	15	(10)	10	8½	(1½)

As long as the price of the stock is below $50, the investor earns the maximum profit of $3.50 while the maximum possible loss is $1.50 if the price of the stock is $55 or higher.

Figure 19.16 presents the potential profits and losses at various prices of the stock for the bull and bear spreads. Since they are opposite positions, the graphs mirror the two positions. The maximum possible loss is $3.50 in the bull spread if the price of the stock declines, while $3.50 is the maximum possible gain in the bear spread. Conversely, the maximum possible profit in the bear spread is $1.50, and $1.50 is the maximum possible loss in the bull spread.

Both of the above spreads are types of hedge positions because they combine a long position and a short position. The effect in both cases is to limit the possible loss, which has the corresponding effect of limiting the potential profit. Neither may be appropriate if the investor anticipates a large movement in the price of the stock in a particular direction. Instead, these spreads are appropriate when the investor anticipates stable prices or small price movements in a particular direction. If this expected price change is downward, the investor should sell the option with the lower strike price and buy the option with the higher strike price. Conversely, if a modest price increase is anticipated, the investor buys the option with the lower strike price and sells the option with the higher strike price. In either case, if the price of the stock moves in the anticipated direction, the investor earns a modest profit on a small outlay. If the price of the stock moves against the investor, the spread protects the investor from a large loss.

A *butterfly spread* involves three options at different strike prices. The position is established when the investor buys (or writes) two options with the middle strike

Figure 19.16 ✦ PROFIT OR LOSS FROM BULL AND BEAR SPREADS

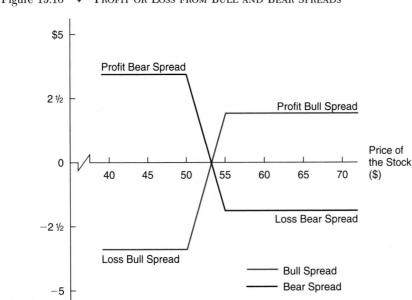

price and takes the opposite position in the two options with the higher and lower strike prices. To see how a butterfly spread is constructed, consider the following options when the price of the underlying stock is $52:

Price of a call at $50	$8
Price of a call at $55	$5
Price of a call at $60	$3

The investor buys two of the options with the $55 strike price and writes one each of the options with the $50 and $60 strike prices. The profile of the possible profits and losses generated by this butterfly spread at the expiration of the options at various prices of the stock are as follows:

Price of the Stock	Intrinsic Value of the Call at $50	Profit (Loss) on the Call at $50	Intrinsic Value of the Call at $55	Profit (Loss) on the Call at $55	Intrinsic Value of the Call at $60	Profit (Loss) of the Call at $60	Net Profit (Loss)
$40	$ 0	$ 8	$ 0	$(10)	$0	$ 3	$ 1
45	0	8	0	(10)	0	3	1
50	0	8	0	(10)	0	3	1
51	1	7	0	(10)	0	3	0
55	5	3	0	(10)	0	3	(4)
59	9	(1)	4	(2)	0	3	0
60	10	(2)	5	0	0	3	1
65	15	(7)	10	10	5	(2)	1

As long as the price of the stock is less than $51 or greater than $59, the spread generates a $1 profit with a maximum possible loss of $4 at a stock price of $55. This short butterfly spread is constructed if the investor expects the butterfly to flap its wings and not hover around the $55 strike price.

The investor could reverse the butterfly spread and write (sell) two options with the $55 strike price and buy one each of the other two options. In this case, the profit (loss) profile at various prices of the stock is as follows:

Price of the Stock	Intrinsic Value of the Call at $50	Profit (Loss) on the Call at $50	Intrinsic Value of the Call at $55	Profit (Loss) on the Call at $55	Intrinsic Value of the Call at $60	Profit (Loss) of the Call at $60	Net Profit (Loss)
$40	$ 0	$(8)	$ 0	$ 10	$0	$(3)	$(1)
45	0	(8)	0	10	0	(3)	(1)
50	0	(8)	0	10	0	(3)	(1)
51	1	(7)	0	10	0	(3)	0
55	5	(3)	0	10	0	(3)	4
59	9	1	4	2	0	(3)	0
60	10	2	5	0	0	(3)	(1)
65	15	7	10	(10)	5	2	(1)

In this butterfly spread the investor earns a modest profit when the price of the stock ranges from above $51 to below $59; however, the maximum possible loss is only $1. Such a butterfly may be attractive if the individual anticipates that the price of the stock will be stable (i.e., the butterfly hovers around the strike price). But if the butterfly does flap its wings (i.e., the price of the stock fluctuates), the maximum possible loss is small.

Figure 19.17 presents the possible profits and losses at various prices of the stock for the butterfly spreads. As in the case of the bull and bear spreads, the two butterflies are in opposite positions. Their profit and loss profiles are exactly opposite. However, in both butterflies, the potential profits and losses are limited because butterfly spreads are types of hedges. The investor has both long and short positions. The purpose of these positions is to take advantage of anticipated price movements in the underlying stock while limiting the investor's potential loss.

As the above discussion illustrates, the introduction of options alters the number of possible strategies the individual may follow in anticipation of changes in stock prices. The above strategies do not exhaust all the possibilities since the illustrations primarily used call options. The investor could, for instance, construct spreads and butterflies using puts, or the investor could alter the number of options in the positions, such as varying a spread by buying two call options at one strike price and selling only one call option at the other strike price.

While the introduction of options increases the number of possible strategies, the investor needs to realize that no one strategy is appropriate for all possible anticipated market price fluctuations. Options permit the individual to speculate, or they may be used to reduce risk through the construction of various hedged positions. Thus, options offer a means to help the investor manage risk as well as to speculate on specific anticipated price movements in the underlying stocks.

Figure 19.17 ✦ Profit or Loss from Butterfly Spreads

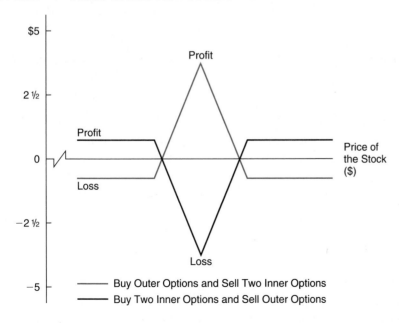

20

COMMODITY AND FINANCIAL FUTURES

*D*o you want excitement and rapid action? Would you prefer to speculate in pork bellies (i.e., bacon) instead of investing in the stock of Swift or Armour? Then investing in commodity futures may satisfy this speculative desire. These futures contracts are among the riskiest investments available, as prices can change rapidly and produce sudden losses or profits.

There are two participants in the futures markets, the speculators who establish positions in anticipation of price changes and the hedgers who seek to employ futures contracts to reduce risk. The hedgers are growers, producers, and other users of commodities. They seek to protect themselves from price fluctuations, and by hedging they pass the risk of loss to the speculators. The price of a futures contract ultimately depends on the demand for and supply of these contracts by the hedgers and speculators.

This chapter is an elementary introduction to investing in contracts for the future delivery of commodities. The chapter describes the mechanics of buying and selling the contracts, the role of margin, the speculators' long and short positions, and how the hedgers use the contracts to reduce risk. Next follows a discussion of financial futures, since commodity contracts are not limited just to physical assets. There are also futures contracts for the purchase and sale of financial assets and foreign currencies. There are even futures based on the Standard & Poor's 500 stock index or the New York Stock Exchange composite index. The chapter ends with a discussion of programmed trading and stock index futures and how changes in the futures markets are transferred to the stock market and vice versa.

◆ ◆ ◆

WHAT IS INVESTING IN COMMODITY FUTURES?

A commodity may be purchased for current delivery or for future delivery. Investing in commodity futures refers to the buying or the selling of a contract to deliver a commodity in the future. For this reason these investments are sometimes referred to as "futures." A **futures contract** is a formal agreement between a buyer or seller and a commodity exchange. In the case of a purchase contract, the buyer agrees to accept a specific commodity that meets a specified quality in a specified month. In the case of a sale, the seller agrees to deliver the specified commodity during the designated month.

futures contract
An agreement for the future delivery of a commodity at a specified date.

Investing in commodity futures is considered to be very speculative. For that reason investors should participate in this market only after their financial obligations and goals have been met. There is a large probability that the investor will suffer a loss on any particular purchase or sale of a commodity contract. Individuals who buy and sell commodity contracts without wanting to deal in the actual commodities are generally referred to as **speculators,** which differentiates them from the growers, processors, warehousers, and other dealers who also buy and sell commodity futures but really wish to buy or sell the actual commodity.

speculator
An individual who is willing to accept substantial risk for the possibility of a large gain.

The primary appeal of commodity contracts to speculators is the potential for a large return on the investment resulting from the leverage inherent in commodity trading. This leverage exists because (1) a commodity contract controls a substantial amount of the commodity and (2) the investor must make only a small payment to buy or sell a contract (i.e., there is a small margin requirement). These two points are discussed in some detail later in this chapter.

THE MECHANICS OF INVESTING IN COMMODITY FUTURES

Like stocks and bonds, commodity futures may be purchased in several markets. One of the most important is the CBT, the Chicago Board of Trade, which executes contracts in agricultural commodities such as wheat, soybeans, and livestock. Other commodities are traded in various cities throughout the country. Over 50 commodities are traded on 10 exchanges in the United States and Canada. As may be expected, the markets for some commodity futures are close to the area where the commodity is produced. Thus, the markets for wheat are located not only in Chicago but also in Kansas City and Minneapolis. The market for several commodity futures is in New York. Cocoa, coffee, sugar, potatoes, and orange juice are bought and sold there. This geographical diversity does not hamper commodity traders, who may buy and sell commodity contracts in any market through their brokers.

Commodity contracts are purchased through brokers just as stocks and bonds are. The broker (or a member of a brokerage firm) owns a seat on the commodity exchange. Membership on each exchange is limited, and only members are allowed to buy and sell the commodity contracts. If the investor's broker lacks a seat, then that broker must have a correspondent relationship with another broker who does own a seat.

The broker acts on behalf of the investor by purchasing and selling contracts through the exchange. Each commodity exchange has a clearinghouse that watches the various buy and sell orders. The investor opens an account by signing an agreement that requires the contracts to be guaranteed. Since trading commodity contracts is considered to be speculative, some brokers will open accounts only after the investor has proved the capacity both to finance the account and to withstand the losses.

Once the account has been opened, the individual may trade commodity contracts. These are bought and sold in much the same way as stocks and bonds; however, the use of the words "buy" and "sell" is misleading. The individual does not buy or sell a contract, but enters a contract to buy or sell. A buy contract specifies that the individual will *accept* delivery and hence "buy" the commodity. A sell contract specifies that the individual will *make* delivery and hence "sell" the commodity.

A commodity order specifies whether the contract is a buy or a sell, the type of commodity and the number of units, and the delivery date (i.e., the month in which the contract is to be executed and the commodity is bought or sold). The investor can request a market order and have the contract executed at the current market price, or he or she may place orders at specified prices. Such orders may be for a day or until the investor cancels them (i.e., the order is good till canceled). Once the order is executed, the broker will provide the speculator with a confirmation statement of the purchase or sale and statements of the investor's positions in the various commodities.

The broker will also charge a fee or commission for executing the orders. This fee tends to be modest. For example, one broker charges $80 per contract, and the fee covers *both the purchase and subsequent sale* of the contract. Perhaps the reduction in paperwork partially explains the modest fees. An investment in commodity futures relieves the broker and the investor of handling dividend checks, the certificates from stock splits and stock dividends, proxies and votes, and other custodial matters associated with an investment in stocks and bonds.

Commodity Positions

The investor may purchase a contract for future delivery. This is the long position, in which the investor will profit if the price of the commodity and hence the value of the contract rise. The investor may also sell a contract for future delivery. This is the short position, in which the seller agrees to make good the contract (i.e., to deliver the goods) sometime in the future. This investor will profit if the price of the commodity and hence the value of the contract decline. These long and short positions are analogous to the long and short positions that the investor takes in the security market. Long positions generate profits when the value of the security rises, whereas short positions result in profits when the value of the security declines.

The way in which each position generates a profit can be seen in a simple example. Assume that the **futures price** of wheat is $3.50 per bushel. If a contract is purchased for delivery in six months at $3.50 per bushel, the buyer will profit from this long position if the price of wheat *rises*. If the price increases to $4.00 per bushel, the buyer can exercise the contract by taking delivery and paying $3.50 per bushel. The speculator then sells the wheat for $4 per bushel, which produces a profit of $0.50 per bushel.

The opposite occurs when the price of wheat declines. If the price of wheat falls to $3.00 per bushel, the individual who bought the contract for delivery at $3.50 suffers a loss. But the speculator who sold the contract for the delivery of wheat (i.e., who took the short position) earns a profit from the price decline. The speculator can then buy wheat at the market price (which is referred to as the **spot price**) of $3.00, deliver it for the contract price of $3.50, and earn a $0.50 profit per bushel.

If the price rises, the short position will produce a loss. If the price increases from $3.50 to $4.00 per bushel, the speculator who sold a contract for delivery suffers a loss of $0.50 per bushel, because he or she must pay $4.00 to obtain the wheat that will be delivered for $3.50 per bushel.

Actually, the preceding losses and profits are generated without the goods being delivered. Of course, when a speculator buys a contract for future delivery, there is always the possibility that this individual will receive the goods. Conversely, if the speculator sells a contract for future delivery, there is the possibility that the goods will have to be supplied. However, such deliveries occur infrequently, because the speculator can offset the contract before the delivery date. This is achieved by buying back a contract that was previously sold or selling a contract that is owned.

This process of *offsetting existing contracts* is illustrated in the following example. Suppose a speculator has a contract to buy wheat in January. If the individual wants to close the position, he or she can sell a contract for the delivery of wheat in January. The two contracts cancel (i.e., offset) each other, as one is a purchase and the other is a sale.[1] If the speculator actually received the wheat by executing the purchase agreement, he or she could pass on the wheat by executing the sell agreement. However, since the two contracts offset each other, the actual delivery and subsequent sale are not necessary. Instead, the speculator's position in wheat is closed, and the actual physical transfers do not occur.

Correspondingly, if the speculator has a contract for the sale of wheat in January, it can be canceled by buying a contract for the purchase of wheat in January. If the speculator were called upon to deliver wheat as the result of the contract to sell, the individual would exercise the contract to purchase wheat. The buy and sell contracts would then cancel each other, and no physical transfers of wheat would occur. Once again the speculator has closed the initial position by taking the opposite position (i.e., the sales contract is canceled by a purchase contract).

Because these contracts are canceled and actual deliveries do not take place, it should not be assumed that profits or losses do not occur. The two contracts need

futures price
The price in a contract for the future delivery of a commodity.

spot price
The current price of a commodity.

---

[1] This process is analogous to the writer of an option buying back the option. In both cases the investor's position is closed.

not be executed at the same price. For example, the speculator may enter a contract for the future purchase of wheat at $3.50 per bushel. Any contract for the future delivery of comparable wheat can cancel the contract for the purchase. But the cost of the wheat for future delivery could be $3.60 or $3.40 (or any conceivable price). If the price of wheat rises (e.g., from $3.50 to $3.60 per bushel), the speculator with a long position earns a profit. However, if the speculator has a short position (i.e., a contract to sell wheat), this individual sustains a loss. If the price declines (e.g., from $3.50 to $3.40 per bushel), the short seller earns a profit, but the long position sustains a loss.

The Units of Commodity Contracts

To facilitate trading, contracts must be uniform. For a particular commodity the contracts must be identical. Besides specifying the delivery month, the contract must specify the grade and type of the commodity (e.g., a particular type of wheat) and the units of the commodity (e.g., 5,000 bushels). Thus, when an individual buys or sells a contract, there can be no doubt as to the nature of the obligation. For example, if the investor buys wheat for January delivery, there can be no confusion with a contract for the purchase of wheat for February delivery. These are two different commodities in the same way that AT&T common stock, AT&T preferred stock, and AT&T bonds are all different securities. Without such standardization of contracts there would be chaos in the commodity (or any) markets.

The units of trading vary with each commodity. For example, if the investor buys a contract for corn, the unit of trading is 5,000 bushels. If the investor buys a contract for eggs, the unit of trading is 22,500 dozen. A list of selected commodities, the markets in which they are traded, and the units of each contract are given in Exhibit 20.1. While the novice investor may not remember the units for a contract, the experienced investor is certainly aware of them. As will be explained later,

Exhibit 20.1   ✦   SELECTED COMMODITIES, THEIR MARKETS, AND THEIR UNITS OF TRADING

Commodity	Market	Unit of One Contract
Corn	Chicago Board of Trade	5,000 bushels
Soybeans	Chicago Board of Trade	5,000 bushels
Barley	Winnipeg Commodity Exchange	20 metric tons
Cattle	Chicago Mercantile Exchange	30,000 pounds
Coffee	New York Coffee and Sugar Exchange	37,500 pounds
Copper	Commodity Exchange, Inc., of New York	25,000 pounds
Platinum	New York Mercantile Exchange	50 troy ounces
Silver	Commodity Exchange, Inc., of New York	5,000 troy ounces
Lumber	Chicago Mercantile Exchange	100,000 board feet
Cotton	New York Cotton Exchange	50,000 pounds

because of the large units of many commodity contracts, a small change in the price of the commodity produces a considerable change in the value of the contract and in the investor's profits or losses.

Reporting of Futures Trading

Commodity futures prices and contracts are reported in the financial press in much the same way as stock and bond transactions are. This is illustrated in Exhibit 20.2, which was taken from *The Wall Street Journal.* As may be seen in the exhibit, wheat is traded on the Chicago Board of Trade (CBT). The unit for trading is 5,000 bushels, and prices are quoted in cents per bushel. The opening price for May delivery

Exhibit 20.2 ✦ SELECTED FUTURES PRICES

FUTURES PRICES

Monday, January 11, 1993

Open Interest Reflects Previous Trading Day.

GRAINS AND OILSEEDS

CORN (CBT) 5,000 bu.; cents per bu.

	Open	High	Low	Settle	Change	Lifetime High	Lifetime Low	Open Interest
Mar	218	218¾	218	218½	....	281¼	214½	111,699
May	225¾	226¼	225½	226	....	284¾	222	51,832
July	231¾	232½	231½	232¼	+ ¼	286	226¼	68,392
Sept	236¼	237¼	236¼	237¼	+ ½	271½	230½	8,062
Dec	241	241½	240¾	241½	+ ¼	268½	233¾	17,190
Mr94	247¼	248¼	247¼	248¼	....	254¾	240½	808

Est vol 20,000; vol Fri 21,790; open int 258,028, +1,842.

OATS (CBT) 5,000 bu.; cents per bu.

	Open	High	Low	Settle	Change	Lifetime High	Lifetime Low	Open Interest
Mar	148	148	146¼	146¾	− 1¼	195¼	122	5,063
May	148½	148½	147	147¼	− 1¼	177¼	126	1,140
July	148¾	148¾	148¾	147¾	− 1¼	163½	129½	579
Dec	152¼	152¼	152	151¾	− 1½	159	146	101

Est vol 500; vol Fri 374; open int 6,930, −77.

SOYBEANS (CBT) 5,000 bu.; cents per bu.

	Open	High	Low	Settle	Change	Lifetime High	Lifetime Low	Open Interest
Jan	574½	577¼	574½	576¾	+ ¼	659	532	5,173
Mar	576½	579¼	576½	578½	− ¾	664	538¾	52,167
May	581½	583	581	582½	− 1¼	668½	546	22,230
July	586½	588¼	586	587¾	− 1½	671	551	25,436
Aug	588½	589¾	588	589¼	− 1¼	655	551	2,428
Sept	588	588¼	588	587¾	− 1¾	630	554	1,224
Nov	591½	592	590¼	592	− 1¾	620	555½	7,516
Ja94	599	599½	598¾	598¾	− 2	608	576½	499

Est vol 23,000; vol Fri 29,672; open int 116,698, +994.

SOYBEAN MEAL (CBT) 100 tons; $ per ton.

	Open	High	Low	Settle	Change	Lifetime High	Lifetime Low	Open Interest
Jan	184.90	185.50	184.40	185.10	− .30	209.00	176.90	6,625
Mar	183.30	183.70	182.60	183.30	− .50	210.00	178.30	28,964
May	183.50	183.50	182.70	182.90	− 1.10	210.00	179.40	13,081
July	184.70	185.10	184.00	184.20	− 1.30	208.00	181.30	11,581
Aug	185.70	185.70	184.80	184.80	− 1.40	193.50	182.20	2,030
Sept	186.80	186.80	185.60	185.60	− 1.70	193.50	183.10	1,313
Oct	187.00	187.20	186.80	186.80	− 1.70	194.50	184.50	556
Dec	189.50	189.50	188.30	188.30	− 1.50	194.00	187.20	381

Est vol 15,000; vol Fri 14,295; open int 64,536, −87.

SOYBEAN OIL (CBT) 60,000 lbs.; cents per lb.

	Open	High	Low	Settle	Change	Lifetime High	Lifetime Low	Open Interest
Jan	21.20	21.38	21.17	21.38	+ .11	23.00	18.28	3,970
Mar	21.40	21.61	21.35	21.59	+ .11	23.20	18.55	39,802
May	21.58	21.79	21.54	21.76	+ .11	23.50	18.85	15,001
July	21.72	21.93	21.70	21.92	+ .10	23.20	19.15	11,346
Aug	21.78	21.95	21.78	21.95	+ .13	23.25	19.29	2,055
Sept	21.77	21.85	21.77	21.85	+ .12	23.25	19.40	1,255
Oct	21.75	21.85	21.75	21.95	+ .15	21.80	19.55	864
Dec	22.00	22.00	22.00	22.00	+ .14	23.45	19.76	1,706

Est vol 19,000; vol Fri 21,477; open int 75,999, −917.

WHEAT (CBT) 5,000 bu.; cents per bu.

	Open	High	Low	Settle	Change	Lifetime High	Lifetime Low	Open Interest
Mar	369½	372¾	369	369½	− 1½	440	319½	28,967
May	348½	350	346¾	348¼	− 1	375	318	6,318
July	321½	323¼	321	321¼	− 1¼	373	302¼	10,678
Sept	327¼	328	325¾	325¾	− 1¾	353	307½	634
Dec	336	337½	335	336	− ½	360	317½	620

Est vol 7,000; vol Fri 9,710; open int 47,244, −534.

WHEAT (KC) 5,000 bu.; cents per bu.

	Open	High	Low	Settle	Change	Lifetime High	Lifetime Low	Open Interest
Mar	359¼	359½	357	358	− 1½	410	309¾	18,874
May	337½	338½	336¾	337	− 1	350	310¾	3,345

	Open	High	Low	Settle	Change	Lifetime High	Lifetime Low	Open Interest
Mr94	8.67	8.80	8.67	8.74	+ .10	9.20	8.50	1,673

Est vol 34,299; vol Fri 54,096; open int 90,121, −6,363.

SUGAR–DOMESTIC (CSCE)–112,000 lbs.; cents per lb.

	Open	High	Low	Settle	Change	Lifetime High	Lifetime Low	Open Interest
Mar	20.85	20.85	20.80	20.80	− .05	22.05	20.80	2,632
May	21.06	21.06	21.01	21.03	− .03	21.88	21.01	2,625
July	21.20	21.23	21.20	21.22	− .01	21.98	21.20	2,734
Sept	21.28	21.30	21.27	21.27	− .03	21.99	21.27	1,835
Nov	21.38	21.39	21.37	21.37	− .02	21.95	21.25	958
Mr94		....	....	21.47	− .02	21.51	21.44	326

Est vol 715; vol Fri 633; open int 11,136, +115.

COTTON (CTN)–50,000 lbs.; cents per lb.

	Open	High	Low	Settle	Change	Lifetime High	Lifetime Low	Open Interest
Mar	60.74	61.60	60.44	60.80	+ .01	67.30	51.32	18,659
May	61.65	62.40	61.30	61.43	− .34	66.25	52.15	9,504
July	62.65	63.25	62.30	62.35	− .30	65.80	53.00	7,929
Oct	61.40	61.40	62.00	61.37	− .13	64.19	54.40	1,154
Dec	60.55	61.20	60.35	60.55	− .31	64.25	54.60	4,681
Mr94	61.43	61.95	61.30	61.30	− .55	62.00	55.62	587

Est vol 6,000; vol Fri 7,066; open int 42,518, +656.

ORANGE JUICE (CTN)–15,000 lbs.; cents per lb.

	Open	High	Low	Settle	Change	Lifetime High	Lifetime Low	Open Interest
Jan	79.90	80.25	78.90	79.25	+ .55	163.00	78.70	1,098
Mar	81.50	82.40	80.75	81.80	+ .75	145.00	80.75	10,504
May	83.85	84.60	83.20	84.25	+ .65	122.75	83.20	3,500
July	85.00	86.25	85.00	85.75	+ .35	130.00	85.00	1,058
Sept	87.10	87.50	86.75	86.70	+ .45	117.25	86.40	542
Nov	89.20	87.25	87.25	86.80	+ .55	116.75	87.25	378
Ja94	89.00	89.00	89.00	88.45	+ .10	117.00	89.00	198

Est vol 1,800; vol Fri 1,964; open int 17,363, +102.

METALS AND PETROLEUM

COPPER-HIGH (CMX)–25,000 lbs.; cents per lb.

	Open	High	Low	Settle	Change	Lifetime High	Lifetime Low	Open Interest
Jan	104.75	104.75	103.10	103.10	− 3.75	115.20	93.30	446
Feb	105.50	105.50	103.65	103.70	− 3.55	114.00	95.50	1,120
Mar	105.20	105.75	103.80	104.05	− 3.55	114.80	92.80	26,274
Apr		....	....	104.05	− 3.45	111.80	96.40	504
May	105.30	105.60	103.80	104.10	− 3.15	112.10	93.70	6,495
June		....	....	104.05	− 3.10	109.60	97.25	327
July	105.00	105.50	103.40	103.95	− 3.05	110.70	95.80	5,208
Aug		....	....	103.90	− 2.95	105.00	98.60	171
Sept	105.00	105.00	103.80	103.85	− 2.85	110.10	95.80	2,434
Oct		....	....	103.75	− 2.70	104.00	99.20	210
Dec	105.00	105.00	103.35	103.50	− 2.60	109.20	97.00	4,410
Mr94	103.25	103.25	103.25	103.15	− 2.35	107.50	99.25	408

Est vol 9,000; vol Fri 10,677; open int 48,140, +1,050.

GOLD (CMX)–100 troy oz.; $ per troy oz.

	Open	High	Low	Settle	Change	Lifetime High	Lifetime Low	Open Interest
Jan		....	....	327.50	− 1.70	332.30	332.30	0
Feb	328.80	328.90	326.90	327.80	− 1.70	404.20	326.50	53,946
Apr	330.00	330.00	328.00	328.90	− 1.70	410.00	327.00	16,210
June	331.10	331.30	329.30	330.20	− 1.70	418.50	328.00	16,392
Aug	332.10	332.10	331.50	331.50	− 1.70	395.50	331.50	8,093
Oct		....	....	333.10	− 1.60	395.00	334.20	2,275
Dec	335.20	335.20	333.80	334.80	− 1.50	402.80	333.80	7,911
Fb94		....	....	336.80	− 1.50	376.80	337.30	1,963
Apr		....	....	338.90	− 1.50	360.00	348.00	1,814
June		....	....	341.00	− 1.50	383.50	342.00	1,992
Aug		....	....	343.40	− 1.50	351.80	350.00	711
Oct		....	....	345.90	− 1.50	....	....	615
Dec	348.00	348.00	348.00	348.50	− 1.50	383.00	348.00	624
Ju95		....	....	357.50	− 1.50	....	....	100
Dec	365.50	365.50	365.50	367.50	− 1.50	403.00	365.50	723

	Open	High	Low	Settle	Change	Lifetime High	Lifetime Low	Open Interest
Dec		....	....	.5328	− .0027	.5490	.5330	184

Est vol 19,040; vol Fri 25,946; open int 76,691, +1,476.

NATURAL GAS, (NYM) 10,000 MMBtu.; $ per MMBtu's

	Open	High	Low	Settle	Change	Lifetime High	Lifetime Low	Open Interest
Feb	1.585	1.620	1.585	1.614	+ .055	2.219	1.520	11,076
Mar	1.555	1.570	1.530	1.539	+ .018	1.915	1.150	7,848
Apr	1.535	1.540	1.515	1.520	+ .005	1.770	1.200	5,887
May	1.545	1.550	1.525	1.537	+ .002	1.770	1.200	5,576
June	1.555	1.560	1.541	1.550	+ .005	1.775	1.215	4,477
July	1.575	1.575	1.555	1.565	+ .005	1.800	1.180	4,461
Aug	1.595	1.595	1.580	1.590	+ .005	1.825	1.250	4,081
Sept	1.610	1.615	1.605	1.610	+ .005	1.855	1.470	3,869
Oct	1.725	1.735	1.725	1.735	+ .010	1.995	1.630	2,851
Nov	1.880	1.885	1.870	1.885	+ .010	2.195	1.765	2,456
Dec	2.040	2.070	2.040	2.065	− .005	2.330	2.000	3,783
Ja94	2.060	2.070	2.050	2.065	− .005	2.310	1.857	8,140
Feb	1.820	1.825	1.820	1.825	+ .005	2.015	1.820	1,145
Mar	1.640	1.645	1.640	1.645	+ .015	1.810	1.627	1,561
Apr	1.620	1.620	1.610	1.605	+ .005	1.760	1.565	1,164
May	1.620	1.620	1.610	1.615	+ .005	1.730	1.540	858
June		....	....	1.630	+ .010	1.730	1.560	833
July	1.630	1.630	1.630	1.630	+ .010	1.630	1.590	175

Est vol 5,748; vol Fri 9,730; open int 70,241, +1,509.

BRENT CRUDE (IPE) 1,000 net bbls.; $ per bbl.

	Open	High	Low	Settle	Change	Lifetime High	Lifetime Low	Open Interest
Feb	17.55	17.70	17.40	17.42	− .06	20.77	17.09	37,646
Mar	17.70	17.84	17.72	17.72	− .08	20.65	17.65	30,138
Apr	17.79	17.94	17.72	17.72	− .04	20.50	17.65	10,257
May	17.97	17.97	17.83	17.84	− .05	19.93	17.72	4,500
June	18.02	18.03	17.91	17.91	− .06	20.08	17.73	10,628
July	18.05	18.05	17.95	17.94	− .10	20.02	17.70	3,863
Aug		....	....	18.00	− .12	19.91	17.97	1,040
Sept		....	....	18.05	− .12	18.37	17.71	760
Oct		....	....	18.08	− .12	18.20	18.20	186

Est vol 36,038; vol Fri 39,382; open int 99,018, +2,917.

GAS OIL (IPE) 100 metric tons; $ per ton

	Open	High	Low	Settle	Change	Lifetime High	Lifetime Low	Open Interest
Jan	167.50	167.75	164.75	165.25	− .75	203.75	167.50	14,789
Feb	167.75	168.25	166.45	167.00	+ .50	207.50	166.00	37,215
Mar	167.00	168.25	166.50	167.25	+ 1.00	194.50	166.25	11,193
Apr	165.75	167.00	165.75	166.25	+ .75	190.50	165.50	7,477
May	164.75	166.25	164.50	165.25	+ .25	187.00	165.00	3,751
June	164.50	166.00	164.50	165.50	+ .50	181.25	164.50	3,711
July	168.00	168.25	168.00	167.75	+ .50	181.25	164.50	1,195
Aug		....	....	169.75	+ 1.00	174.75	168.00	516
Sep		....	....	172.00	+ 1.25	177.00	169.00	509

Est vol 18,333; vol Fri 23,777; open int 80,356, +6,411.

INTEREST RATE

TREASURY BONDS (CBT)–$100,000; pts. 32nds of 100%

	Open	High	Low	Settle	Chg	Yield Settle	Yield Chg	Open Interest
Mar	103-27	104-06	103-23	103-28	− 1	7.619	+ .003	285,967
June	102-19	102-30	102-17	102-20	− 1	7.740	+ .003	16,117
Sept	101-14	101-24	101-14	101-14	− 2	7.856	+ .006	3,630
Dec	100-16	100-21	100-10	100-10	− 3	7.968	+ .009	2,344
Mr94	99-17	99-21	99-09	99-09	− 4	8.073	+ .013	1,144
June	98-16	98-16	98-13	98-13	− 3	8.163	+ .010	126
Sept	....	....	....	97-19	− 2	8.248	+ .007	72

Est vol 220,000; vol Fri 409,684; op int 309,474, −3,621.

TREASURY BONDS (MCE)–$50,000; pts. 32nds of 100%

	Open	High	Low	Settle	Chg	Yield Settle	Yield Chg	Open Interest
Mar	104-01	104-06	103-23	103-29	+ 2	7.616	− .006	10,332

Source: The Wall Street Journal, January 12, 1993, C14.

was 348½¢ ($3.485) per bushel, while the high, low, and closing (i.e., the "settle") prices were 350¢, 346¾¢, and 348¼¢, respectively. This closing price was 1¢ higher than the closing price on the previous day. The high and low prices (prior to the previous day of trading) for the lifetime of the contract were 375¢ and 318¢, respectively. The **open interest,** which is the number of contracts in existence, was 6,318.

open interest
The number of futures contracts in existence for a particular commodity.

This open interest varies over the life of the contract. Initially, the open interest rises as buyers and sellers establish positions. It then declines as the delivery date approaches and the positions are closed. This changing number of contracts is illustrated in Figure 20.1, which plots the spot and futures prices and the open interest for a September contract to buy Kansas City wheat. When the contracts were initially traded in late 19x1, there were only a few contracts in existence. By June 19x2 the open interest had risen to over 10,000 contracts. Then, as the remaining life of the contracts declined, the number of contracts fell as the various participants closed their positions. By late September only a few contracts were still outstanding.

Figure 20.1 ✦ Spot and Futures Prices and Open Interest for a September 19x2 Contract for Kansas City Wheat

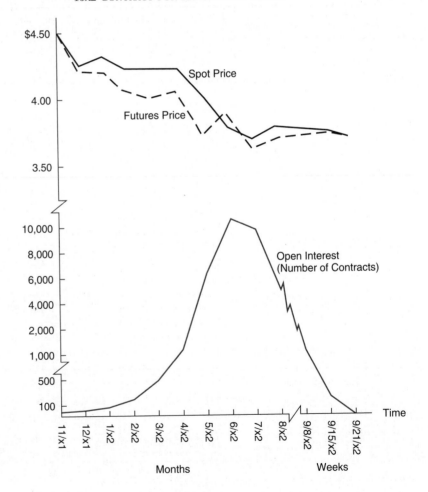

Figure 20.1 also shows the spot price (i.e., the current price) and the futures price for Kansas City wheat. In this case the futures price was generally less than the spot price. Usually the futures price exceeds the spot price, but the reverse may occur if investors believe the price of the commodity will decline in the future. These investors seek to sell contracts now to lock in the higher prices so they may buy back the contracts at a lower price in the future. This selling of the futures contracts drives the futures price down below the spot price.

If investors anticipate higher prices for wheat in the future, they would seek to buy contracts for the future delivery of wheat. The anticipation of inflation and the cost of storing commodities usually drive up the futures price relative to the spot price. The value of the futures contract would then exceed the current price of the commodity.

The futures price must converge with the spot price as the expiration date of the contract approaches. As with options such as puts and calls, the value of the futures contract can be worth only the value of the underlying commodity at the expiration date. This pattern of price behavior is also illustrated in Figure 20.1. In March, April, and May there was a considerable differential between the two prices. However, in late September the futures and spot prices converged and erased the differential.

The Regulation of Commodity Markets

The commodity exchanges, like stock exchanges, are subject to regulation. Federal laws pertaining to commodity exchanges and commodity transaction laws are enforced by the Commodity Exchange Authority, which is a division of the Department of Agriculture. As with the regulation of security transactions, the regulations do not protect investors or speculators from their own folly. Instead, the regulations establish uniform standards for each commodity. The regulatory authority also has control over trading procedures, the hours of trading, and the maximum allowable daily price movements.

LEVERAGE

Commodities are paid for on delivery. Thus, a contract for future delivery means that the goods do not have to be paid for when the individual enters the contract. Instead, the investor (either a buyer or a seller) provides an amount of money, which is called **margin,** to protect the broker and to guarantee the contract. This margin is not to be confused with the margin that is used in the purchase of stocks and bonds. In the trading of stocks and bonds, margin represents the investor's equity in the position, whereas margin for a commodity contract is a deposit to show the investor's good faith and to protect the broker against an adverse change in the price of the commodity.

In the stock market, the amount of margin required varies with the price of the security, but in the commodity markets the amount of margin does not vary with the dollar value of the transaction. Instead, each contract has a fixed minimum margin requirement. These margin requirements for selected commodities are given in

margin
Good faith deposit made when purchasing or selling a commodity contract.

THE PIG AND THE PYRAMID OF GOLD—A FABLE FOR OUR TIMES

Once upon a time, way back at the start of 1979, a pig chanced to meet a wizard, who told him: "The world is going to hell. This means that the price of gold must rise."

"How much will it rise?" the pig asked.

"Before we greet the next new year," the wizard replied, "it shall have doubled."

The pig believed him. Being smart and bold, but a bit short on cash, the pig set out to make his fortune by leveraging and pyramiding in the gold futures market. He could buy a contract for later purchase of 100 ounces of gold with a tiny down payment. As the price of gold rose, so would the value of his contract. With his profits he could buy more contracts without stopping until he was very, very rich. Gold was then $227 an ounce, and the wizard had *assured* him it would double. And so this little pig went off to the gold futures market.

On Jan. 5, the pig bought his first contract—the right to buy 100 ounces of gold in October at $241.50 an ounce. It cost him just $750. At that price, an increase of only $7.50 an ounce would double the pig's money. A decline of $7.50 would wipe him out, of course, but it is not in a pig's nature to think negative thoughts. For a few weeks he was a happy pig, indeed. By Feb. 23, in fact, having pyramided all his paper profits into additional contracts, his $750 was worth nearly $40,000. Alas, on Apr. 12, gold fell and the pig was wiped out.

Undaunted, the pig bided his time. In mid-May, when the U.S. Treasury decided to reduce the amount of gold it sold monthly, he moved again. For a $1,000 deposit, he picked up one contract at $269.60. With scarcely a hitch,

pyramiding again, his equity soared. On July 27, with gold at $311.60, he had 318 contracts worth $373,000 and blessed the day he had run into the wizard. But after some good news on U.S. trade balances, gold fell, and by Aug. 3 the pig was wiped out again.

Still undaunted, and having heard rumors that "the Arabs are buying," the pig anted another $1,000 on Aug. 24 for a contract at $314.40 and was soon off on

another giddy ride. By Oct. 1, pyramiding again, and with gold at $416, his equity had soared to almost $124,000. But he had been richer than that before, on paper, and he held out for more. By Oct. 4, gold had fallen back to $370 and the pig once more was wiped out. Moral: Wizards don't always tell you that in any market, but especially in commodity futures, the shortest distance between two points is almost never a straight line.

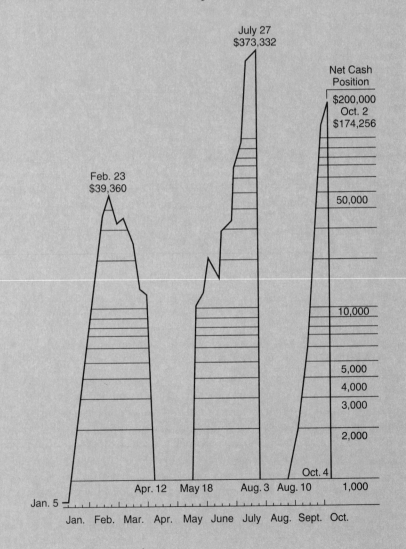

Source: Forbes, October 29, 1979. Reprinted by permission. Copyright 1979, Forbes, Inc.

Exhibit 20.3. Thus, an investor who purchases a futures contract for cocoa must put up $1,000. These margin requirements are established by the commodity exchanges, but individual brokers may require more.

The margin requirements are only a small percentage of the value of the contract. For example, the $1,000 margin requirement for cocoa gives the owner of the contract a claim on 10 metric tons of cocoa. If cocoa is selling for $1,400 a metric ton, the total value of the contract is $14,000. The margin requirement as a percentage of the value of the contract is only 7.14 percent ($1,000/$14,000). This small amount of margin is one reason why a commodity contract offers so much potential leverage.

The potential leverage from speculating in commodity futures may be illustrated in a simple example. Consider a contract to buy wheat at $3.50 per bushel. Such a contract controls 5,000 bushels of wheat worth a total of $17,500 (5,000 × $3.50). If the investor buys this contract and the margin requirement is $1,000, he or she must remit $1,000. An increase of only $0.20 per bushel in the price of the commodity produces an increase of $1,000 in the value of the contract. This $1,000 is simply the product of the price change ($0.20) and the number of units in the contract (5,000). The profit on the contract if sold is $1,000.

What is the percentage return on the investment? With a margin of $1,000 the return is 100 percent, because the investor put up $1,000 and then earned an additional $1,000. An increase of less than 6 percent in the price of wheat produced a return on the speculator's money of 100 percent. Such a return is the result of leverage that comes from the small margin requirement and the large amount of the commodity controlled by the contract.

Leverage, of course, works both ways. In the previous example if the price of the wheat declines by $0.10, the contract will be worth $17,000. A decline of only 2.9 percent in the price reduces the investor's margin from $1,000 to $500. To maintain the position, the investor must deposit additional margin with the broker. The broker's request for additional funds is referred to as a **margin call.** Failure to meet the margin call will result in the broker's closing the position. Since the contract is supported only by the initial margin, further price declines will mean that there is less collateral to support the contract. Should the investor (i.e., the buyer or the

margin call
A request by a broker for an investor to place additional funds or securities in an account as collateral against borrowed funds or as a good faith deposit.

Exhibit 20.3 ♦ Margin Requirements for Selected Commodity Contracts

Commodity	Margin Requirement
Broilers	$ 500
Cocoa	1,000
Cotton	1,000
Hogs	800
Lumber	1,200
Potatoes	500
Soybeans	1,500
Wheat	1,000

seller) default on the contract, the broker becomes responsible for its execution. The margin call thus protects the broker.

Actually, there are two margin requirements. The first is the minimum initial deposit, and the second is the maintenance margin. The **maintenance margin** specifies when the investor must deposit additional funds with the broker to cover a decline in the value of a commodity contract. For example, the margin requirement for wheat is $1,000 and the maintenance margin is $750. If the investor owns a contract for the purchase of wheat and the value of the contract declines by $250 to the level of the maintenance margin ($750), the broker makes a margin call. This requires the investor to deposit an additional $250 into the account, which restores the initial $1,000 margin. This additional deposit protects the broker, since the value of the contract has declined and the investor has sustained a loss.

maintenance margin
The minimum level of funds in a margin account that triggers a margin call.

Maintenance margin applies to both buyers and sellers. If, in the previous example, the price of wheat were to rise by $250, the speculators who had sold short would see their margin decline from the initial deposit of $1,000 to $750. The broker would then make a margin call, which would require the short sellers to restore the $1,000 margin. Once again this protects the broker, since the value of the contract has risen and the short seller has sustained the loss.

These margin adjustments occur daily. After the market closes, the value of each account is totaled. In the jargon of futures trading, each account is *"marked to the market."* If the account does not meet the margin requirement, the broker issues a margin call that the individual must meet or the broker will close the position.

Margin requirements are set by the commodity exchanges, but they cannot be below the minimums established by the Commodity Exchange Authority. These requirements are designed to protect brokers from the losses incurred by speculators. Individual brokers may further protect themselves from price fluctuations by requiring larger amounts of margin for commodity contracts.

daily limit
The maximum daily change permitted in a commodity future's price.

While commodity prices can and do fluctuate, limits are imposed by the markets on the amount of price change permitted each day. The **daily limit** establishes the maximum permissible price increase or decrease from the previous day. The purpose of these limits is to help maintain orderly markets and to reduce the potentially disruptive effects from large daily swings in the price of the futures contract.[2]

Once the price of the futures contract rises by the permissible daily limit, further price increases are not allowed. This does not necessarily mean that trading ceases, because transactions can still occur at the maximum price or below should the price of the commodity weaken. The same applies to declining prices. Once the daily limit has been reached, the price cannot continue to fall, but transactions can still occur at the lowest price or above should the price strengthen. For example, when the 1992 Florida orange crop came in at the higher end of expectations, orange futures prices quickly fell. Contracts for January, February, and March delivery declined the 5 cent daily limit. While trading could have continued at the lowest price, trading ceased because no one was willing to buy at that level and speculators anticipated further price declines.

---

[2]The daily limit applies to many futures prices but not all, especially financial futures based on federal government debt and stock index futures.

HEDGING

One of the major reasons for the development of commodity futures markets was the desire of producers to reduce the risk of loss through price fluctuations. The procedure for this reduction in risk is called **hedging,** which consists of taking opposite positions at the same time.[3] In effect, a hedger simultaneously takes the long and the short position in a particular commodity.

Hedging is best explained by illustrations. In the first example, a wheat farmer expects to harvest a crop at a specified time. Since the costs of production are determined, the farmer knows the price that is necessary to earn a profit. Although the price that will be paid for wheat at harvest time is unknown, the current price of a contract for the future delivery of wheat is known. The farmer can then sell a contract for future delivery. Such a contract is a hedged position, because the farmer takes a long position (the wheat in the ground) and a short position (the contract for future delivery).

Such a position reduces the farmer's risk of loss from a price decline. Suppose the cost to produce the wheat is $2.50 per bushel and September wheat is selling in June for $2.75. If the farmer *sells* wheat for September delivery, a $0.25 per bushel profit is assured, because the buyer of the contract agrees to pay $2.75 per bushel on delivery in September. If the price of wheat declines to $2.50, the farmer is still assured of $2.75. However, if the price of wheat rises to $3.10 in September, the farmer still gets only $2.75. The additional $0.35 gain goes to the owner of the contract who bought the wheat for $2.75 but can now sell it for $3.10.

Is this transaction unfair? Remember that the farmer wanted protection against a decline in the price of wheat. If the price had declined to $2.40 and the farmer had not hedged, the farmer would have suffered a loss of $0.10 (the $2.40 price minus the $2.50 cost) per bushel. To obtain protection from this risk of loss, the farmer accepted the modest profit of $0.25 per bushel and relinquished the possibility of a larger profit. The speculator who bought the contract bore the risk of loss from a price decline and received the reward from a price increase.

Users of wheat hedge in the opposite direction. A flour producer desires to know the future cost of wheat in order to plan production levels and the prices that will be charged to distributors. However, the spot price of wheat need not hold into the future, so this producer *buys* a contract for future delivery and thereby hedges the position. This is hedging because the producer has a long position (the contract for the future delivery of wheat) and a short position (the future production of flour, which requires the future delivery of wheat).

If the producer buys a contract in June for the delivery of wheat in September at $2.75 per bushel, the future cost of the grain becomes known. The producer cannot be hurt by an increase in the price of wheat from $2.75 to $3.10, because

hedging
Taking opposite positions to reduce risk.

---

[3] Hedging cannot erase risk and may even increase it. For a discussion of how such an increase may occur, see Richard J. Teweles, Charles V. Harlow, and Herbert L. Stone, *The Commodity Futures Game—Who Wins? Who Loses? Why?* (New York: McGraw-Hill, 1974), 35–43.

the contract is for delivery at $2.75. However, the producer has forgone the chance of profit from a decline in the price of wheat from $2.75 to $2.40 per bushel.

Instead, the possibility of profit from a decline in the price of wheat rests with the speculator who sold the contract. If the price of wheat were to decline, the speculator could buy the wheat in September at the lower price, deliver it, and collect the $2.75 that is specified in the contract. However, this speculator would suffer a loss if the price of September wheat rose over $2.75. The cost would then exceed the delivery price specified in the contract.

These two examples illustrate why growers and producers hedge. They often take the opposite side of hedge positions. If all growers and producers agree on prices for future delivery, there would be no need for speculators; but this is not the case. Speculators buy or sell contracts when there is an excess or an insufficient supply. If the farmer in the preceding example could not find a producer to buy the contract for the future delivery of wheat, a speculator would buy the contract and accept the risk of a price decline. If the producer could not find a farmer to supply a contract for the future delivery of wheat, the speculator would sell the contract and accept the risk of a price increase.

Of course, farmers, producers, and speculators are simultaneously buying and selling contracts. No one knows who buys and who sells at a specific moment. However, if there is an excess or a shortage of one type of contract, the futures price of the commodity changes, which induces a certain behavior. For example, if September wheat is quoted at $2.75 per bushel, but no one is willing to buy at that price, the price declines. This induces some potential sellers to withdraw from the market and some potential buyers to enter the market. By this process, an imbalance of supply and demand for contracts for a particular delivery date is erased. It is the interaction of the hedgers and the speculators that establishes the price of each contract.

THE SELECTION OF COMMODITY FUTURES CONTRACTS

As with the selection of securities, there are two basic methods for the selection of commodities futures contracts: the technical approach and the fundamental approach. The technical approach uses the same methods that are applied to the selection of securities. Various averages, point-and-figure charts, and bar graphs and their patterns are constructed for various commodities and are used to identify current price movements and to predict future price movements. Since this material was covered previously in Chapter 13, it is not repeated here.[4]

The fundamental approach is primarily concerned with those factors that affect the demand for and the supply of the various commodities. While the approach is

---

[4]The investor who is interested in the application of technical analysis to commodity selection should consult Richard J. Teweles, Charles V. Harlow, and Herbert L. Stone, *The Commodity Futures Game—Who Wins? Who Loses? Why?* (New York: McGraw-Hill, 1974), Chapter 7.

similar to the selection of securities in that it uses economic data, the specifics are different. The price of a commodity depends on the supply of that commodity relative to the demand. Since the commodities are produced (e.g., wheat) or mined (e.g., silver), there are identifiable sources of supply. Correspondingly, there are identifiable sources of demand. However, there is also a variety of exogenous factors that may affect the supply of or the demand for a particular commodity, and these factors can have a powerful impact on the price of a specific commodity.

To illustrate these points, consider a basic commodity such as wheat. It takes several months for wheat to be produced. It has to be planted, grown, and harvested. The amount of wheat that is planted is known because statistics are kept by the Commerce Department of the U.S. government. Such statistics are necessary for government forecasts of the economy, and this information is certainly available to those firms and individuals concerned with the size of the wheat crop.

The size of the crop that is planted and the size that is harvested, however, may be considerably different. The actual harvest depends on other factors. Particularly important is the weather, which can increase or decrease the yield. Good weather at the appropriate time can result in a bountiful harvest. A larger than anticipated supply of wheat should depress its price. On the other hand, bad weather, be it drought or excess rain, will have the opposite effect and will significantly reduce the anticipated supply. A reduction in supply should increase the price of wheat.

Demand, like supply, depends on both predictable and unpredictable forces. The demand for wheat depends on the needs of the firms that use the grain in their products. The producers of flour and cereals are obvious potential customers for wheat. However, the total demand also includes exports. If a foreign government enters the market and buys a substantial amount of wheat, this may cause a significant increase in its price.

Such government intervention in the market is not limited to foreign governments. The U.S. federal government also buys and sells commodities. Sometimes it buys to absorb excess supplies of a commodity and thus supports the commodity's price. In other cases the federal government may sell from its surplus stocks of a given commodity. This, of course, has the opposite impact on the price of the commodity. The increased supply tends to decrease the price or at least to reduce a tendency for the price to rise. These exogenous forces in the commodity markets are just another source of risk with which the speculator must contend.

Obviously the speculator seeks to identify shifts in demand or supply before they occur in order to take the appropriate position. Anticipation of a price increase indicates the purchase of a futures contract, whereas an anticipated price decline indicates the sale of a futures contract. Unfortunately, the ability to consistently predict changes in demand and supply is very rare. This should be obvious! If an individual could predict the future, he or she would certainly make a fortune not just in the commodity futures markets but in any market. Mortals, however, lack such clairvoyance, which leaves them with fundamental and technical analysis as a means to select commodity futures for purchase.

Whether an investor uses technical or fundamental analysis, there is an important strategy for trading futures. The speculator should seek to limit losses and permit profits to run. Successful commodity futures trading requires the speculator's ability to recognize bad positions and to close them before they generate large losses. Many speculators, especially novices, do the exact opposite by taking small profits as they occur but maintaining positions that sustain losses. Then, when price changes produce margin calls, the speculator is forced either to close the position

COMMODITY MUTUAL FUNDS

An alternative to investing directly in futures contracts is acquiring shares in a commodity mutual fund, such as the Commodity Growth Fund, the Commodity Trend Timing Fund, or the Commodity Venture Fund. Purchases of commodity funds are similar to traditional mutual fund investments. The individual buys shares in the fund, and the fund invests in futures contracts and other speculative investments such as options on futures.

Since the fund acquires a variety of futures, the portfolio can be diversified. Diversification requires an individual to maintain positions in many contracts, and few individuals have the resources or time to monitor a diversified portfolio of positions in futures. But without diversification, the individual is subject to large amounts of asset-specific risk (i.e., unsystematic risk). The funds can provide a diversified portfolio, and that is one of the prime advantages they offer.

While diversification may be one reason for considering commodity funds, it is not a sufficient reason to acquire them. Diversification by itself tells the investor nothing about the returns commodity funds have earned. One of the few studies devoted to determination of the returns earned by commodity funds concluded that the returns from investments in these funds were inferior to the returns achieved by stock or bond indices during the same period.* This strongly suggests that commodity funds have been inferior investments, but individu-

als continue to invest in commodity funds in spite of this poor performance.

In a subsequent study the same researchers analyzed why individuals persist in investing in commodity funds and concluded that "this growth continues because of the grossly misleading information on performance presented in prospectuses."† The researchers found that many commodity funds did initially earn positive returns, but these returns were achieved *prior* to the funds' becoming available to the general public. The results of this study imply that the data concerning a fund's return as reported in its prospectus should be viewed with extreme caution. Large returns prior to the sale of the shares to the general public certainly cannot be taken as indicative of future performance.

* Edwin J. Elton, Martin J. Gruber, and Joel C. Rentzler, "The Risks and Returns of Commodity Funds," *AAII Journal* (April 1987): 10–14.
† Edwin J. Elton, Martin J. Gruber, and Joel C. Rentzler, "Commodity Funds: Does the Prospectus Really Tell All?" *AAII Journal* (October 1989): 8–11.

at a loss or to put up additional funds. If the speculator meets the margin call by committing additional funds, that individual is violating the strategy. Instead of taking the small loss, this investor is risking additional funds in the hope that the price will recover.

FINANCIAL AND CURRENCY FUTURES

financial futures
Contract for the future delivery of a financial asset.

currency futures
Contract for the future delivery of foreign exchange.

In the previous discussion commodity contracts meant futures contracts for the delivery of physical goods. However, there are also **financial futures,** which are contracts for the future delivery of securities such as treasury bills, and **currency futures,** which are contracts for the future delivery of currencies (e.g., the British pound or the German mark). The market for financial futures, like the market for commodity futures, has two participants: the speculators and the hedgers. It is the interaction of their demands for and supplies of these contracts that determines the price of a given futures contract.

While any speculator may participate in any of the financial or currency futures markets, the hedgers differ from the speculators because they also deal in the currency itself. The hedgers in currency futures are primarily multinational firms that

POINTS OF INTEREST

THE VARIETY OF FINANCIAL FUTURES

While the text discussion features U.S. Treasury bonds and NYSE Composite Index futures, there are a variety of financial futures available to the investor. These contracts and their respective markets include those in the table below.

In addition to financial futures, there are options available on U.S. Treasury securities. Put and call options on treasury bonds are traded on the Chicago Board of Trade, and put and call options on treasury notes and bills are traded on the American Stock Exchange. And in 1983, put and call options on financial futures were created and commenced trading. The investor may now purchase a put or a call option based on Standard & Poor's 500 futures contracts. For an explanation of these options, see "The New Options on S&P 500 Futures," *The Outlook* (February 23, 1983), 908–909.

Contract	Market
U.S. Treasury bonds	Chicago Board of Trade
U.S. Treasury notes	Chicago Board of Trade
U.S. Treasury bills	International Monetary Market at the Chicago Mercantile Exchange
Bank CDs	International Monetary Market at the Chicago Mercantile Exchange
Standard & Poor's 500 Index futures	Chicago Mercantile Exchange
NYSE Composite futures	New York Futures Exchange
KC Value Line Futures	Kansas City Board of Trade
Major Market Index	Chicago Board of Trade
Muni Bond Index	Chicago Board of Trade
Eurodollar	International Monetary Market at the Chicago Mercantile Exchange
British Pound	International Monetary Market at the Chicago Mercantile Exchange
Canadian Dollar	International Monetary Market at the Chicago Mercantile Exchange
Japanese Yen	International Monetary Market at the Chicago Mercantile Exchange
Swiss Franc	International Monetary Market at the Chicago Mercantile Exchange
German Mark	International Monetary Market at the Chicago Mercantile Exchange

make and receive payments in foreign moneys. Since the value of these currencies can change, the value of payments that the firms must make or receive can change. Firms thus establish hedge positions to lock in the price of the currency and thereby avoid the risk associated with fluctuations in the value of one currency relative to another.

As interest rates and bond prices change, the yields from lending and the cost of borrowing are altered. To reduce the risk of loss from fluctuations in interest rates, borrowers and lenders may establish hedge positions in financial futures to lock in a particular interest rate.

Speculators, of course, are not seeking to reduce risk but reap large returns for taking risks. The speculators are bearing the risk that the hedgers are seeking to avoid. The speculators try to correctly anticipate changes in the value of currencies and the direction of changes in interest rates and to take positions that will yield profits. The return they earn (if successful) is then magnified because of the leverage offered by the small margin requirements necessary to establish the positions.

How financial futures may produce profits for speculators may be illustrated with an example using a futures contract for the delivery of U.S. Treasury bonds. Suppose a speculator expects interest rates to fall and bond prices to rise. This individual would *buy* a contract for the delivery of treasury bonds in the future (i.e., the *long* position). If interest rates do fall and bond prices rise, the value of this contract increases because the speculator has the contract for the delivery of bonds at a lower price (i.e., higher yield). If, however, interest rates rise, bond prices fall and the value of this contract declines. The decline in the value of the contract inflicts a loss on the speculator who bought the contract when yields were lower.

If the speculator expects interest rates to rise, that individual *sells* a contract for the future delivery of treasury bonds (i.e., establishes a *short* position). If interest rates do rise and the value of the bonds decline, the value of this contract must decline, but the speculator earns a profit. This short seller can buy the bonds at a lower price and deliver them at the price specified in the contract. Or the speculator may simply buy a contract at the lower value, thereby closing out the position at a profit. Of course, if this speculator is wrong and interest rates fall, the value of the bonds increases, inflicting a loss on the speculator, who must now pay more to buy the bonds to cover the contract.

The same general principles apply to currency futures. Suppose the price of the British pound is $2. A speculator who is bullish and anticipates that the price of the pound will rise establishes a long position in the pound. This individual buys a contract for the future delivery of pounds. The futures price may be $2.02 or $1.96. It need not necessarily equal the current or spot price. (If many speculators expect the price of the pound to rise, they will bid up the futures price so that it exceeds the current price. If speculators expect the price of the pound to fall, they will then drive down the futures price of the pound.) If this speculator buys the futures contract for $2.02 and is correct (i.e., the price of the pound rises), that individual makes a profit. If, for example, the price of the pound were to rise to $2.20, the value of the contract may rise by $0.18 per pound (i.e., $2.20 − $2.02).[5] Of course, if the speculator who bought the contract is wrong and the price of the pound declines to $1.80, the value of the contract also declines, and the speculator suffers a loss.

If the speculator had been bearish and anticipated a decline in the value of the pound, that individual would establish a short position and sell contracts for the future delivery of pounds. If the speculator is right and the value of the pound declines, the speculator may close the position for a profit. Since pounds are now worth less, the speculator may buy the cheaper pounds and deliver them at the higher price specified in the contract.[6] If the speculator had been wrong and the price of the pound had risen, that individual would have suffered a loss, as it would have cost more to buy the pounds to make the future delivery required by the contract.

Financial and currency futures, like all futures contracts, offer the speculator an opportunity for profit from a change in prices. While such securities are not suitable for the portfolios of most individuals, they do offer more sophisticated investors an opportunity for large returns. Whether the returns justify the large risks is, of course, a decision that each individual investor must make.

While most individuals think of futures contracts as a means to speculate on price changes, financial futures may be used to reduce the risk of loss from an

---

[5] At expiration the futures and spot prices must be equal. Thus, if the pound is $2.20 on the expiration date, the value of the contract must be $2.20 per pound.

[6] Actually the speculator would close the short position by buying an opposite contract (a contract for the future delivery of pounds).

increase in interest rates. Consider an investor who desires a flow of income and has constructed a large portfolio of bonds. The portfolio's market value would decline if interest rates rose. To offset the potential loss, the investor could hedge using financial futures. Since the individual has a long position in the bonds, the investor must take a short position in the futures. Therefore, the investor sells contracts for the future delivery of bonds. If interest rates rise (and therefore cause the value of the bonds to fall), the value of the futures contracts also falls. Since the investor has a short position in the contracts, the individual profits from the rising interest rates. The profits on the futures contracts then offset the decline in the value of the bonds.[7]

STOCK MARKET FUTURES

During 1982, a new type of futures contract based on an index of the stock market (e.g., the Value Line stock index, the Standard & Poor's 500 stock index, or the New York Stock Exchange Composite Index) started trading. These **stock index futures** contracts offer speculators and hedgers opportunities for profit or risk reduction that are not possible through the purchase of individual securities. For example, the NYSE Composite Index futures contracts have a value that is 500 times the value of the NYSE Index. Thus, if the NYSE Index is 140, the contract is worth $70,000. By purchasing this contract (i.e., by establishing a long position), the holder profits if the market rises. If the NYSE Index were to rise to 145, the value of the contract would increase to $72,500. The investor would then earn a profit of $2,500. Of course, if the NYSE Index should decline, the buyer would experience a loss.

    The sellers of these contracts also participate in the fluctuations of the market. However, their positions are the opposite of the buyers (i.e., they are short). If the value of the NYSE Index were to fall from 140 to 135, the value of the contract would decline from $70,000 to $67,500, and the short seller would earn a $2,500 profit. Of course, if the market were to rise, the short seller would suffer a loss. Obviously if the individual anticipates a rising market, that investor should buy the futures contract. Conversely, if the investor expects the market to fall, that individual should sell the contract.

    These contracts may also be bought and sold by professional money managers who are not speculating on price movements but who seek to hedge against adverse price movements. For example, suppose a portfolio manager has a well-diversified portfolio of stocks. If the market rises, the value of this portfolio appreciates. However, there is the risk of loss if the market were to decline. The portfolio manager can reduce this risk by selling a NYSE Composite Index futures contract. If the market declines, the losses experienced by the portfolio will at least be partially offset by the appreciation in the value of the short position in the futures contract.

stock index futures
A contract based on an index of security prices.

---

[7]To determine the exact number of contracts that should be sold to offset the potential loss, see Nancy H. Rothstein, *The Handbook of Financial Futures* (New York: McGraw-Hill, 1984), 262–264.

NYSE Index futures contracts are similar to other futures contracts. The buyers and sellers must make good faith deposits (i.e., margin payments). As with other futures contracts, the amount of this margin is modest, only $3,500 per contract. Thus, these contracts offer considerable leverage. If stock prices move against the investor and his or her equity in the position declines, the individual will have to place additional funds in the account to support the contract. Since there is an active market in the contracts, the investor may close a position at any time by taking the opposite position. Thus, if the investor had purchased a contract, that long position would be closed by selling a contract. If the investor had sold a contract, that short position would be closed by buying a futures contract.

There is one important difference between stock market index futures and other futures contracts. Settlement at the expiration or maturity of the contract occurs in cash. There is no physical delivery of securities as could occur with a futures contract to buy or sell wheat or corn. Instead gains and losses are totaled and are added to or subtracted from the participants' accounts. The long and short positions are then closed.

PROGRAMMED TRADING AND INDEX ARBITRAGE

One of the more controversial developments in the securities market has been the consequence of programmed trading and index arbitrage. Programmed trading arose after the creation of stock index futures and has become a major link between the stock market and the futures market. Through programmed trading and index arbitrage, price changes in one market are transferred to the other and vice versa as the participants move funds between the markets to take advantage of price differentials.

programmed trading
Coordinated buying or selling of portfolios triggered by computers.

The term **programmed trading** refers to the coordinated purchases or sales of an entire portfolio of securities. The managers of mutual funds or financial institutions cannot physically place individual orders to buy and sell large quantities of stocks. Instead large orders are placed through computers that are programmed (hence the name "programmed trading") to enter the trades if certain specifications are met.

As explained earlier in this text, arbitrage refers to the simultaneous establishment of long and short positions to take advantage of price differentials between two markets. If, for example, the price of the British pound were $2.46 in Paris and $2.50 in Bonn, the arbitrageur would buy pounds in Paris and simultaneously sell them in Bonn. The pounds bought in Paris could be delivered in Bonn; hence, the individual is assured of a $0.04 profit on the transaction. This riskless arbitrage position assures that the price of the pound will be approximately the same in Paris and Bonn with minute differentials being explained by transactions costs.

Conceptually, index arbitrage is no different except the arbitrageur is buying or selling index futures and securities instead of pounds. The principle is the same. If prices deviate in different markets, an opportunity for arbitrage is created. Arbitrageurs will seek to take advantage of the price differentials, and through their actions the differentials are erased. This type of arbitrage is frequently done by mutual funds with large holdings of securities that duplicate the various indices of stock prices. These funds shuffle money between stocks and futures to take advantage of price differentials.

Programmed trading-index arbitrage combines the two concepts: Computers are programmed to enter orders to sell or buy blocks of securities designed to take advantage of arbitrage opportunities that exist in the securities and futures markets. If stock index futures prices rise, the arbitrageurs will short the futures and buy the stocks in the index. If futures prices decline, the arbitrageurs do the opposite. They go long in the futures contracts and short the stocks in the index.

Three potential problems arise. (1) There are some transactions costs that must be covered, so the difference between the value of the futures contracts and the underlying securities must be sufficient to cover this cost. (2) There is an obvious problem with buying or shorting all the securities in a broad-based index. Since the Standard & Poor's 500 stock index uses 500 different stocks, positions would have to be taken in all 500. To get around this program, the arbitrageurs have developed smaller portfolios called "baskets" that mirror the larger index. The price performance of these stock baskets then mimics the price movements in the index. (3) For arbitrage to be riskless, both positions must be made simultaneously. If they were not, there would be a period of time when the investor is either long or short (i.e., has only one position) and thus would be at risk. This need for simultaneous executions led to the use of computers that are programmed to coordinate the purchases or sales of the baskets. It is the use of the computers that permits the arbitrageur to enter simultaneously orders to buy or sell large quantities of many individual stocks.

The previous chapter explained why an option's intrinsic value sets a floor on the option's price. If the price were to decline below the intrinsic value, an opportunity for arbitrage would exist. The same concept applies to stock index futures except in this case the option is replaced by the index futures and the individual stock by the stock basket.

The idea may be explained by a simple example. Suppose the S&P 500 stock index stands at 300 and the futures contract is trading for 301.5. Assume that the contract has a value of 500 times the index, so the value of each contract is $150,750. The arbitrageur shorts the futures and buys the $150,000 worth of the stocks in the index (or the shares in the basket). In effect the arbitrageur has paid $150,000 for $150,750 worth of stock, because the arbitrageur has already entered into a contract for the sale of the stock at $150,750 through the short position in the futures.

If, after executing the position, the futures price declines or the prices of the stocks in the index rise, the arbitrageur will close both positions (referred to as "unwinding") and make a profit. For example, suppose the prices of the stocks rise sufficiently that the index is 301.50 and the future contract has only risen to 302. The arbitrageur may now sell the stocks and repurchase the futures contract. The loss on the futures is $250 (301.5 × $500 minus 302 × $500) while the gain on the stocks is $750 (301.5 × $500 minus 300 × $500). Since all the transactions can occur in a matter of minutes, there is negligible cost of carrying the positions. The arbitrageur need only cover the transaction cost associated with the trades.

If the differential between the values of the futures and index are not rapidly erased, the arbitrageur can maintain the positions until the expiration date of the futures contracts. As the expiration date approaches, the futures price must converge with the current (i.e., spot) price. Options can only be worth their intrinsic value at expiration, and futures prices must equal the spot prices when the contracts expire. Thus the arbitrageur knows that the differential between the value of the futures contract and the index must disappear and thus assure the profit. The only difference between this and the previous situation is the cost of carrying the stocks, which may be partially offset by income generated by the securities.

If the prices had been reversed (e.g., the futures were trading at 298.5 when the index was 300), the procedure is reversed. The arbitrageur goes long in the futures and short in the stocks. The simultaneous long and short positions lock in the differential and assure the arbitrageur of the profit. If the price differential rapidly disappears, the positions are unwound and the profit realized. Even if the differential persists, the arbitrageur knows that at expiration the differential must be erased.

This process of index arbitrage is illustrated in Figure 20.2, which presents the differential between the value of the futures contract and the index during a trading day. The line at zero represents no differential, and the lines at +0.1 and −0.1 represent the transaction costs of executing index arbitrage. Once the differential between the futures and the index exceeds +0.1 or −0.1, the opportunity for a profitable arbitrage exists.

Figure 20.2 ✦ Differential between the Value of a Stock Index Futures Contract and the Underlying Stock

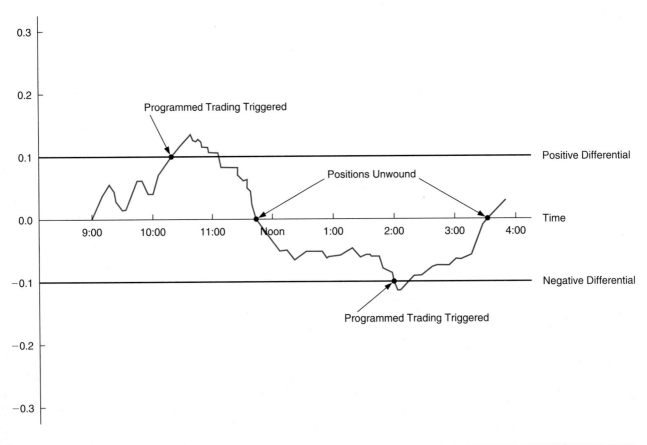

The computers are then programmed to enter the appropriate buy and sell orders when the differential is sufficient to cover the costs associated with the transactions. For example, at 10:15 A.M., the differential is sufficient on the plus side that the arbitrageur would short the futures and buy the stocks. By 11:45 the differential has vanished, so the positions are closed and the profits are realized. At 2:00 P.M. the differential has once again sufficiently increased (on the negative side) that the arbitrageur goes long in the futures and shorts the index. By 3:30, the differential is again erased, and the arbitrageur unwinds the positions.

Of course, as the differentials are erased, the impact is felt in the various markets. Increased demand for futures contracts relative to the underlying stocks generates demand by the arbitrageurs for the stocks and hence their prices rise. In a similar way, an increase in stock prices would be transferred to the futures markets. The converse would also be true. A decline in stock prices would tend to drive down the futures prices.

It is important to realize that index arbitrage-programmed trading does *not* depend on the level of stock prices or the level of futures prices. Instead it depends on (1) spot prices relative to futures prices and (2) synchronized trading. Index arbitrage-programmed trading does not depend on technical analysis, fundamental analysis of a firm's financial statements, changes in information such as an increase in earnings or dividends, or forecasts of the economy.

Programmed trading can distort a stock's price. An individual stock can be fairly valued based on fundamental analysis but experience a large swing in its price if it becomes caught up in programmed trading. As arbitrageurs seek to establish long positions in stocks, the prices of individual securities included in the index or basket can rise rapidly and dramatically. Of course, the converse would be true if arbitrageurs seek to unwind long positions in the stocks or establish short positions. Thus it is possible for the prices of individual securities to be whip-sawed during a trading day in response to the establishing or unwinding of arbitrageurs' positions. Such price volatility can create buying (or shorting) opportunities in individual stocks if their prices deviate from their values as indicated by fundamental analysis.

This price volatility may be particularly noticeable near the expiration dates and especially on the four days during the year that are referred to as the "triple witching hour." On these days the Standard & Poor's 500 stock index futures contract, the Standard & Poor's 100 stock index option contract, and individual option contracts expire. This convergence of expirations can lead to large volatility in the prices and the volume of the securities traded.

On the triple witching day, the time period is so short that even small differentials can create arbitrage opportunities. The various participants in the markets (i.e., the owners and writers of option contracts and the speculators and hedgers with futures contracts) seek to close their positions so price differentials can develop, and computers can spot them. If, for example, the futures price becomes marginally higher than the value of the underlying stocks, the arbitrageurs immediately short the futures and buy the stocks knowing that the differential must disappear in a matter of hours. Conversely, if the values of the stocks rise, the arbitrageurs sell the stocks and buy the futures because any difference between the futures contracts and the underlying stocks must disappear at the expiration of the contracts and the options. The possibility of such arbitrage profits, of course, has the effect of increasing the volume of transactions and driving prices so that any disparity is erased.

The large swings in stock prices may create buying (or shorting) opportunities in individual stocks if they become under- or overvalued. Evidence exists that large price changes in individual stocks on the triple witching day are quickly erased during trading on the day after the expiration date.[8] This is, of course, consistent with efficient markets. If, for some reason, an individual stock were to be mispriced, investors would buy or sell the security so that its price would be indicative of what the market believed the security was worth. The unwinding of stock index arbitrage positions can create, albeit briefly, such opportunities.

The volatility of security prices has raised the question of the desirability of programmed trading. The answer partially revolves around whether programmed trading and index arbitrage are viewed as a cause or as a reaction to other events that are occurring in the security and futures markets. Consider the case in which speculators believe that the Federal Reserve will ease credit and interest rates will fall. These speculators seek to take long positions and purchase stock index call options and futures contracts. The prices of these contracts rise above the value of the underlying stocks, which triggers programmed selling of futures contracts and large purchases of securities. Stock prices rise dramatically.

The converse applies if speculators expect security prices to fall. They sell futures contracts that will be transferred to the security markets. The decline in the futures price would result in programmed trading taking long positions in the futures and short positions in the stocks (i.e., selling stocks). These illustrations, of course, suggest that it is not programmed trading and index arbitrage that are the cause of the changes in stock prices. Instead, it is the speculators who initiated the changes; the programmed trading was only in response to the initial cause.

In any event, programmed trading and index arbitrage are very visible to the investment community, security regulators, and the general public. The increased volatility associated with programmed trading and its use in index arbitrage have led to suggestions that programmed trading be banned or at least curtailed. Some brokerage firms have for periods of time refused to execute programmed trading for customers' or their own accounts. Whether restraints or a total ban on computer-driven strategies will evolve is one of the intriguing questions facing the financial community in the 1990s.

SUMMARY

Investing in commodity futures involves the buying or selling of contracts for future delivery. The speculator may take a long position, which is the purchase of a contract for future delivery, or a short position, which is the sale of a contract for future delivery. The long position generates profits if the commodity's price rises, while the short position results in a gain if the price falls.

Commodity contracts are purchased through brokers who own seats on commodity exchanges. The contracts are supported by deposits, which are called margin, that signify the investor's good faith. The margin requirement is only a small fraction of the value of the contract, and this produces considerable potential for leverage.

---

[8] See, for instance, Hans R. Stoll and Robert E. Whaley, "Program Trading and Expiration-Day Effects," *Financial Analyst Journal* (March–April 1987): 16–28.

A small change in the price of the commodity produces a large profit or loss relative to the small amount of margin. For this reason, commodity contracts are considered very speculative.

Hedging plays an important role in commodity futures markets. Growers, miners, and other users of commodities often wish to reduce their risk of loss from price fluctuations and thus hedge their positions. Growers sell contracts for future delivery, and producers buy contracts for future delivery. Frequently, it is the speculators who are buying and offering the contracts sought by the hedgers. In this way the risks that the hedgers seek to reduce are passed on to the speculators.

The price of a commodity, and thus the value of a futures contract, is related to the supply of and the demand for the commodity. Speculators may use technical or fundamental analysis to help forecast supply, demand, and price movements. Unfortunately, many exogenous factors, such as the weather or government intervention, make accurate forecasting difficult. These forces also contribute to the price fluctuations experienced in the commodity markets and are a major source of the risk associated with investing in commodity futures.

Besides commodity futures there are financial futures, currency futures, and stock market futures. Financial futures are contracts for the delivery of financial assets such as U.S. Treasury bills and bonds. Currency futures are contracts for the future delivery of foreign moneys such as German marks or British pounds. Stock market futures are based on a broad measure of the market (e.g., the New York Stock Exchange Composite Index). Speculators who anticipate movements in interest rates, foreign currencies, or the stock market can speculate on these anticipated price changes by taking appropriate positions in futures contracts. As with all commodity contracts, the potential return may be quite large, but the risk of loss is also large. Speculating in commodity futures is probably best left for those few investors who understand these potential risks and can afford to take them.

The creation of stock index futures and the rise of programmed trading have resulted in stock index arbitrage. When the value of a stock index futures contract deviates from the value of the underlying stocks in the index, an opportunity for arbitrage is created. If the value of the contract exceeds the value of the shares, arbitrageurs will short the contracts and buy the shares. The converse occurs when the value of the contract is less than the value of the shares in which case the arbitrageurs buy the futures and sell the shares. These transactions are done simultaneously through the use of computers that are preprogrammed to enter the buy and sell orders when a divergence between the stock index futures and the stock index develops.

The combining of stock index futures and programmed trading links the securities and futures markets. Changes in one are quickly transferred to the other. This linkage has resulted in significant swings in the prices of individual stocks when the arbitrageurs enter large numbers of buy or sell orders. This increased price volatility has led to the suggestion that programmed trading be banned.

Security Summary

Commodity and Financial Futures

Source of return: Capital gains from price changes.

Liquidity and marketability: Active market in futures contracts but large chance of loss implies no liquidity.

Sources of risk: Unsystematic risk from events that affect the value of the contract, and systematic risk to the extent that the value of the contract responds to changes in interest rates and/or security prices. All sources of risk magnified by the small margin requirements.

Taxation: Profits on futures trades are considered to be capital gains and are taxed. All positions (including open positions) are considered closed as of the end of the calendar year (i.e., taxed at year end).

Terms to Remember

futures contracts	margin call
speculators	maintenance margin
long position	daily limit
short position	hedging
futures price	financial futures
spot price	currency futures
open interest	stock index futures
margin	programmed trading

Questions

1. What is a futures contract? What are the spot price and the futures price of a commodity?
2. Why is investing in commodity futures considered to be speculative?
3. What is the difference between a long and a short position in a commodity future?
4. What is margin and why is it a source of leverage? What is a margin call?
5. Why do farmers and other users of commodity futures hedge their positions?
6. If an investor anticipates a decline in a commodity's price, which futures position should he or she take?
7. How may government intervention affect commodity prices? Are commodity futures markets subject to government regulation?
8. What is a financial futures contract? If you expect interest rates to rise, should you buy a financial futures contract?
9. If you anticipated that the price of the British pound would rise and wanted to speculate on that increase, should you sell or buy a contract for the delivery of pounds?
10. What is the difference between the long and the short positions in a contract for the future delivery of U.S. Treasury bonds?
11. If you expect stock prices to fall, do you buy or sell stock index futures?
12. How do changes in the futures market for stock indices affect the stock market? Why may stock index futures and programmed trading result in dramatic price changes in individual stocks?

Problems

1. You expect the stock market to decline, but instead of selling a stock short, you decide to sell a stock index futures contract based on the New York

Stock Exchange Composite Index. The index is currently 138, and the contract has a value that is 500 times the amount of the index. The margin requirement is $3,500 and the maintenance margin requirement is $1,000.

a. When you *sell* the contract, how much must you put up?
b. What is the value of the contract based on the index?
c. If after one week of trading the index stands at 140, what has happened to your position? How much have you lost or profited?
d. If the index rose to 144, what would you be required to do?
e. If the index declined to 136.6 (approximately 1 percent from the starting value), what is your percentage profit or loss on your position?
f. If you had purchased the contract instead of selling it, how much would you have invested?
g. If you had purchased the contract and the index subsequently rose from 138 to 144, what would be your required investment?
h. Contrast your answers to parts d and g.

2. This problem is designed to illustrate hedging with currency futures. The subsequent questions lead you, the student, through the process of hedging. While this material was not explicitly covered in the text material, your instructor may use this problem to show how hedging may reduce the risk of loss from fluctuations in the price of a foreign currency.

You expect to receive a payment of 1,000,000 British pounds after six months. The pound is currently worth $1.60 (i.e., £1 = $1.60), but the six-month futures price is $1.56 (i.e., £1 = $1.56). You expect the price of the pound to decline (i.e., the value of the dollar to rise). If this expectation is fulfilled, you will suffer a loss when the pounds are converted into dollars when you receive them six months in the future.

a. Given the current price, what is the expected payment in dollars?
b. Given the future price, how much would you receive in dollars?
c. If, after six months, the pound is worth $1.35, what is your loss from the decline in the value of the pound?
d. To avoid this potential loss, you decide to hedge and sell a contract for the future delivery of pounds at the going futures price of $1.56. What is the cost to you of this protection from the possible decline in the value of the pound?
e. If, after hedging, the price of the pound falls to $1.35, what is the maximum amount that you lose? (Why is your answer different than your answer to part c?)
f. If, after hedging, the price of the pound rises to $1.80, how much do you gain from your position?
g. How would your answer be different to part f if you had not hedged and the price of the pound had risen to $1.80?

Suggested Readings

For general but detailed descriptions of commodity futures trading and hedging, consult:
Commodity Trading Manual. Chicago, Ill.: Chicago Board of Trade, 1985.
Kolb, Robert W. *Understanding Futures Markets.* 3d ed. Miami, Fl.: Kolb Publishing Co., 1991.
Teweles, Richard J., Charles V. Harlow, and Herbert L. Stone. *The Commodity Futures Game—Who Wins? Who Loses? Why?* 2d ed. New York: McGraw-Hill, 1986.

Financial futures, currency futures, and stock index futures are covered in:

French, Kenneth. "Pricing Financial Futures." *Journal of Applied Corporate Finance* (Winter 1989): 59–66.

Kriegner, Andrew. *The Money Bazaar.* New York: Random House, 1992.

Loosigian, Allan M. *Foreign Exchange Futures.* Homewood, Ill.: Dow Jones-Irwin, 1981.

Loosigian, Allan M. *Interest Rate Futures.* Homewood, Ill.: Dow Jones-Irwin, 1980.

Smith, Courtney D. *How to Make Money in Stock Index Futures.* New York: McGraw-Hill, 1985.

Weiner, Neil S. *Stock Index Futures.* New York: John Wiley & Sons, 1984.

For a detailed guide to financial futures that includes the mechanics of futures markets, the role of clearinghouses, trading in international currencies, hedging, speculative and hedging strategies, fundamental and technical analysis, and regulation, see:

Rothstein, Nancy H. *The Handbook of Financial Futures.* New York: McGraw-Hill, 1984.

The exchanges also publish a considerable amount of material. For example, see:

Chicago Board of Trade. *Options on U.S. Treasury Bond Futures for Institutional Investors.*

Chicago Board of Trade. *Interest Rate Futures for Institutional Investors.* 1985.

For discussions of programmed trading and index arbitrage, see:

Bodie, Zvi, Alex Kane, and Alan J. Marcus. *Investments.* Homewood, Ill.: Irwin, 1989, 662–668.

Goldman, Ethel R. K. *Computerized Trading Strategies: Programming for the Stock and Futures Markets.* New York: John Wiley & Sons, 1988.

21

INVESTING IN NONFINANCIAL ASSETS: COLLECTIBLES AND GOLD

Some individuals start accumulating objects (e.g., baseball cards, stamps, or dolls) when they are young. While these collections may have only been youthful hobbies, they may stimulate the appetite for collecting. Many individuals who invest in collectibles and other nonfinancial assets have done so for years. However, declining faith in the economy, especially the inflation of the early 1980s, increased the general public's interest in collectibles and other physical assets. In the late 1980s and early 1990s, this interest in collectibles abated as inflation declined, but a collection constructed with thoughtfulness and foresight can still be both satisfying and serve as a store of value.

Investing in collectibles and other nonfinancial assets is essentially no different from investing in financial assets. The investments are made now and the returns are earned in the future. The return comes from possible capital gains. In order to realize capital gains, the asset must be sold. Hence, a market must exist for the asset. Realized gains are subject to capital gains taxation. And, as with any investment, there is the element of risk.

While investing in physical assets is similar to investing in financial assets, there are important differences. Nonfinancial assets have their own markets, and investing in them requires specialized knowledge, which is considerably different from the knowledge used in the selection of financial assets. An entire lifetime may be spent learning the fine points that make an individual an expert in a particular type of asset, such as art or real estate.

This chapter briefly covers investing in two general classes of physical assets: collectibles (including art, Oriental rugs, and antiques), and gold. It can be only a cursory survey of the field. The emphasis will be placed on the elements most similar to those associated with investing in financial assets: the potential returns, an asset's marketability, and the risks involved. Implicit throughout the discussion is the assumption that the individual needs specialized information to know and understand these investments. Such information can best be obtained through careful and extensive study of the particular physical assets of interest to an individual.

While the chapter primarily uses art and gold to illustrate investments in collectibles, these do not exhaust the possibilities. Many physical assets that people accumulate have the characteristics of investments. Old baseball cards, antique fur-niture, bisque dolls, stamps, and autographs can serve as potential stores of value. They may prove to be excellent investments that yield substantial returns for indi-viduals who take the time to learn what differentiates the wheat from the chaff and who judiciously acquire quality representations of these collectibles.

✦ ✦ ✦

RETURNS, MARKETS, AND RISK

Investing in physical assets requires that the investor have a broad definition of mar-kets, returns, and risk. A market brings together buyers and sellers in order to trans-act the exchange of goods and services. When a mutually acceptable price is deter-mined, the goods are transferred from the seller to the buyer. This is obviously what occurs in the organized security markets such as the New York Stock Exchange (NYSE). Sellers and buyers of securities are brought together, and they trade secu-rities for money.

Many securities, however, are bought and sold in that informal market called the over-the-counter market. There is no centralized place where transactions in the over-the-counter market are consummated. It exists wherever a buyer and a seller can trade cash for securities.

The market for art and other collectibles is also an informal market, for there is no organized center such as the NYSE for the transfer of these physical assets. While there may be certain centers, such as the diamond district in New York, the market is geographically dispersed and not formally organized.

Because there is no formal market, there are none of the advantages offered by such formality. For example, price quotations (i.e., bid and ask prices) are not readily available. The volume of transactions is generally not recorded, and when it is, this information is not widely disseminated as are reports of security trades, which are published in the financial press. Specialized publications may report some of this information, but these are frequently not well known to the investor and may not be readily available.

These characteristics mean that the markets for some physical assets (e.g., col-lectibles) may not be efficient. The market for other tangible assets, such as gold, may be very efficient. If the price of gold were $400 in one market and $350 in another, arbitrageurs would quickly pounce on the opportunity for a risk-free profit by buying gold for $350 in one market and simultaneously selling it for $400 in the other. Of course, this would drive the price of gold to some level that was the same in both markets.

The markets for other physical assets are not so efficient. Even if the possibility for arbitrage exists, it would be difficult to execute. If a Dali print were selling for $500 in New York and $400 in San Francisco, an opportunity for arbitrage would exist. But the individual would have to know of the price differences, execute the buy and sell transactions, and ship the print from San Francisco to New York. It is hard to believe that investors in Iowa (or anywhere) will be able to execute such a trade. Compared to the market for financial assets, the markets for many tangible

TANGIBLE ASSETS AND DIVERSIFICATION

Perhaps the strongest rationale for acquiring collectibles and other nonfinancial assets is their possible impact on diversification. The returns on most financial assets tend to be positively correlated. When stock prices rise, the prices of most individual stocks rise in sympathy. The factors that cause stock prices to rise often cause bond prices to rise. Lower interest rates tend to be bullish for both stocks and bonds. Inflation tends to cause the prices of both stocks and bonds to fall as earnings are squeezed and tighter monetary policy raises interest rates.

The returns on some physical assets (e.g., gold and other precious metals, real estate, and art objects) may be negatively correlated with returns on financial assets. The inflation that hurts stocks and bonds may be beneficial for precious metals or real estate. This suggests that these assets can play an important role in the construction of a diversified portfolio. The attractiveness of tangible assets then may not be the returns they offer but the possibility of risk reduction, in which case they are not alternatives to financial assets but complementary to them.

---

assets and collectibles are very inefficient, which certainly increases the risk associated with them.

Furthermore, there is little or no regulation of these markets. While the Securities and Exchange Commission may work to reduce fraud and to assure the timely disclosure of pertinent financial information that may affect the value of a firm's securities, no such government organization exists to protect the buyers of many physical assets. It is a case of "let the buyer beware," and the unsuspecting investor is certainly an easy target for the forger or any other shady dealer who can prey on the individual's desire to find an asset that will offer an exceptional return.

The return offered by an investment in a physical asset such as gold comes from the potential for price appreciation and is taxed as a capital gain when the gain is realized. The return earned through price appreciation is the difference between the net sale price and the purchase price. The net sale price is the realized price minus any commissions or fees necessary to make the sale. While the commissions for buying and selling stock may be 2 or 3 percent of the price, the commissions for buying and selling physical investments may be considerably more. These fees vary with the different types of assets, but they can consume a substantial portion of any profit earned through price appreciation.

In addition to commissions, other expenses may be incurred with an investment in physical assets that are not incurred with financial assets. The investor may take out special insurance to cover insurable risks. For example, insurance may be desirable for investments in art, which are subject to theft and fire. Or the investor may rent space (e.g., a safe deposit box) to store the assets. This certainly would apply to valuable stamps, coins, and gold. These additional expenses reduce the return earned by the investment.

Besides the return earned through price appreciation, the investor may receive a flow of services. Oriental rugs may be functional; works of art are decorative; and housing provides shelter and space. The potential flow of services offered by some physical assets should be the prime reason for buying them.

Investing in art and collectibles subjects the investor to the same basic risks associated with investing in financial assets. These are the elements of risk attributable to the market (i.e., the risk associated with price changes of a class of assets) and the risk associated with a particular company or asset.[1] In addition, the investor must face the risk of loss from inflation and the problems associated with theft and fraud.

The markets for physical assets vary over time. Prices do fluctuate and not always upward. Presumably, if prices in general move in a particular direction, the value of specific assets will move accordingly. Hence, if the price of gold rises, then the value of gold coins will rise. Conversely, if the price of gold declines, the value of gold coins will fall. The investor who buys gold and gold coins cannot avoid this market risk, which applies to all physical assets.

The investor must bear the risk associated with the specific investment. Changes in taste alter the public's demand for specific goods. For example, if the demand for Oriental rugs increases, the value of most Oriental rugs also will appreciate. However, even within this group some will appreciate more than others. The rugs that are popular today will not necessarily be those that are popular tomorrow. Thus, the investor may experience losses on specific investments even though the market as a whole moves upward in price.

A major reason for purchasing physical assets as an investment is that they may help the individual beat inflation. The value of financial assets such as stocks and bonds often decline when the inflation rate increases. This was illustrated earlier in Figure 9.5, which showed the sharp declines in the Dow Jones industrial average during inflationary periods. However, the value of physical assets may keep pace with the rate of inflation, as individuals seek to buy them in preference to financial assets, thus driving up their prices.

The investor should realize that for this above strategy to work, he or she must anticipate inflation in order to purchase physical assets before the price increases. In addition, even if inflation were to occur, it is not necessarily true that the price of all physical assets will rise. Their prices can rise, fall, or remain the same. Inflation inflicts a loss of purchasing power on any investor whose particular portfolio does not keep pace with the rate of inflation. While some physical assets have appreciated in price (e.g., housing during the 1980s), this is not true for all physical assets. For example, the price of gold has stagnated for a decade (1983–1992), but the Consumer Price Index continued to rise. Obviously, the rate of inflation exceeded the rate of return on an investment in gold during that particular period.

The last sources of risk are theft and fraud. Although financial assets such as stocks and bonds can be left with custodians (e.g., brokers), that is not necessarily the case with physical assets. One's house is not left with the real estate broker. The investor in Oriental rugs or art will want to use these items or at least display them in order to enjoy them. The coin and stamp collector probably enjoys looking at the collection and does not leave it with coin and stamp dealers. While coins, gold, stamps, art, and Oriental rugs may be stored with a dealer or in a safe deposit box when the investor cannot care for them, most of the time these items are kept at home, where they are subject to theft and fire. Although the individual may seek to protect these investments with insurance, adequate protection will require detailed records to verify the asset's value.

Finally, the investor must bear the risk of fraud. Fakes and misrepresentations are frequently sold to unsuspecting buyers who lack the knowledge to appraise them

---

[1] In Chapter 7 these sources of risk were called systematic and unsystematic, respectively.

INSURING YOUR COLLECTIBLES

If the investor has a sizable collection of collectibles, it may be desirable to insure it against loss from fire, theft, and other perils. Before purchasing this insurance, the investor should consider the costs and benefits of such coverage. Special insurance may not be necessary since the investor's homeowner's policy generally covers the contents of the house up to one-half the value of the home. There

may, however, be a limit on the coverage of a particular item or class of items.

The investor may remedy this limitation by adding a floater to the policy to cover specific items. This will require that the investor and the insurance company agree on the value of each specific item. Instead of a floater, the investor may buy a specialized policy (e.g., a fine arts policy). This also requires enumeration and valuation of specific items. Such coverage should be updated annually.

Insurance is not free, and for sizable collections (e.g., over $100,000) the insurance company will probably require a security system. The investor should never overinsure, since the companies will pay only the market value of the item. Claim adjusters are not fools and will not accept inflated claims. Overinsurance is a waste of funds that may be used more profitably elsewhere.

properly. This applies not only to novices but also to sophisticated professionals who, on occasion, have been completely deceived. The possibility of fraud, or at least of excessive pricing, truly makes investing in art and collectibles areas in which the novice should move with caution.

This suggests several practical steps for investing in these assets. First, investors should buy only after doing their homework. They should know what they are looking at and what to look for. Second, investors should seek to specialize in those particular physical assets that appeal to them. For example, one should not buy Oriental rugs because they are Oriental rugs but should collect them because they can be enjoyed and are very functional. Third, one should invest in art and collectibles only after sufficient financial assets have been accumulated to meet financial emergencies and contingencies. Physical assets offer little, if any, liquidity. Fourth, the investor should be willing to lose the entire investment in the art object or other collectible. Under these circumstances the investor will not be deluded into thinking that the asset will offer extraordinary gains. Such gains rarely, if ever, accrue to the novice, and investors in art and other collectibles are competing with professionals who have a lifetime of experience on which to base decisions.

ART, ORIENTAL RUGS, AND ANTIQUES[2]

During the 1970s, perhaps no investments performed better than those in art (i.e., paintings, sculpture, and graphics). One art expert, Willi Bongard (who is also an economist), has estimated that the value of the works of leading modern artists

---

[2] The general concepts in this section apply to other collectibles, such as gems or even baseball cards and beer cans.

increased 18 percent compounded annually in the period from 1965 to 1975.[3] That is the equivalent of $1.00 growing to $5.25 after ten years. Such a return compares very favorably with the Dow Jones industrial average or Standard & Poor's 500 stock index. During the same period, the stock market declined according to these two price indices! Such comparisons, however, can be misleading, because stocks are homogeneous and their values are easily measured. Artworks are very difficult to compare (i.e., each is unique), and their values can only be approximated.

The Market for Collectibles

Art objects may be purchased in a variety of ways. The primary means is through dealers, many of whom make a market in the items. Such dealers sell as well as buy. Why do they do both? The art and security markets are very similar in that they are primarily secondhand markets. Since van Gogh and Rembrandt are no longer producing, sales of their work can only be secondary transactions. The same applies to many Oriental rugs and to antiques. Any exchanges after the initial sale are in the secondary markets. In order for dealers to have these items for sale (i.e., inventory), many either acquire them or hold them on consignment. Dealers who purchase art, antiques, and Oriental rugs hold them in inventory for future sale. They may not be able to operate solely on new output, especially since the most valuable works of art and Oriental rugs and all antiques are those already in existence.

Since some dealers make markets, they, in effect, establish bid and ask prices. While such prices may not be readily known to the investor, any dealer who is willing to buy used rugs, antiques, or art is offering a bid. Of course, the offer to sell establishes an asking price.

Since the volume of transactions is low and the number of dealers in these specialized areas is relatively small, the spread between the bid and the ask will be substantial. The buyer may be paying the retail price but only receiving the wholesale price, which will certainly consume a substantial amount of any price appreciation. For example, a dealer in Oriental rugs may be willing to repurchase a rug (in acceptable condition) at the original sale price, in which case the individual has had the use of the rug but has not realized any price appreciation.

Instead of repurchasing the rug, the dealer may offer to hold it on consignment. The title remains with the owner while the dealer tries to sell the rug. If a sale occurs, the dealer receives a set percentage of the price. This commission can be as high as 30 or 40 percent of the sale price. This commission is analogous to the spread between the bid and ask prices for stocks and bonds. If the commission on the sale of a collectible is 30 percent of the sale price, that's like buying a stock at an asking price of $50 and selling it at a bid price of $35. The price of the stock would have to rise above $71 (if the spread remained 30 percent of the sale price) for the investor to start to earn a profit. In effect, many individuals acquiring collectibles are buying at retail prices and selling at wholesale prices. Obviously, the prices must rise substantially for these investors to recoup the initial cost, pay the commissions, and still net a profit.

An alternative market for valuable art, Oriental rugs, and antiques is the auction. While the word *auction* may imply the Saturday afternoon sale of an estate, many major works are sold through auctions. The important auction houses of the world

---

[3] D. McConathy, "Art as Investment," *Artscanada* (Autumn 1975): 46.

(e.g., Sotheby Parke-Bernet or Christie's, both of which have offices in New York and London) hold auctions that handle many valuable art treasures.

Such auction houses permit the owners of valuable art, antiques, and Oriental rugs to offer them for sale, but the sale price that will be realized is unknown in advance. Although the auction house places an estimated value on the item, the realized price can be higher or lower than the estimate. After the sale, the auction house takes its fee or commission from the realized price. This fee can be as high as one-third of the sale price for small dollar amounts. The percentage charged often declines as the realized value increases.

Buyers as well as sellers may have to pay a fee for items bought at an auction. Both Christie's and Sotheby Parke-Bernet add a premium that the buyer must pay of up to 10 percent of the cost of the purchase. This charge is in addition to their fees charged the seller, which range from 2 to 10 percent of the proceeds of the sale.

Although the fees for selling art, antiques, and Oriental rugs are substantial, there is a secondary market for these goods. Although the investor can seek to avoid the costs by directly marketing the items, the dealers and auction houses may be able to realize a better price than the individual could. These specialists have a better idea of the value of a specific item and hence may price it more realistically than, and perhaps more profitably for, the seller.

The Return on Collectibles

The return on investments in art, antiques, or Oriental rugs comes from potential price appreciation. It is obvious how price appreciation generates a return, since it is the difference between the net proceeds of the sale (the sale price minus the commissions) and the purchase price. As has already been discussed, the commissions may consume a substantial portion of any gross profits.

An Oriental rug, antique, or painting may offer a superior total return when both the flow of services and price appreciation are considered. For example, if the investor compares the cost of wall-to-wall carpeting with the cost of an Oriental rug, the return offered by the Oriental rug will probably be superior. The wall-to-wall carpeting depreciates and cannot be readily moved if the investor changes homes. The Oriental rug performs the same service, may not depreciate and may even appreciate in value, and is easily moved. No wonder such rugs are viewed by some individuals as excellent investments, because these rugs generate many years of service and offer the potential for price appreciation.

The same applies to works of art and many antiques. Paintings, lithographs, and sculpture all generate a flow of service. The owner derives pleasure from them, which is part of the reason for making the investment. Of course, quantifying this pleasure is probably impossible, so the true return on an investment in these items cannot be determined.

The Valuation of Collectibles

What gives art, antiques, or Oriental rugs their value? The answer to this question is both simple and complex. The obvious answer is scarcity relative to demand. There are only so many paintings by a master, and certainly this scarcity enhances their value.

Although there is a paucity of works by major artists, there is an abundance of what passes for art. This abundance (or an abundance relative to the demand) has resulted in very low prices for the vast majority of paintings, graphics, and poor quality Oriental rugs. But scarcity alone does not explain value.

The valuation of art objects actually depends on many factors.[4] Value is affected by the reputation of the artist and quality of the work as well as by many other factors, including attributes of the work itself and exogenous factors.

The creator of the work and its quality are the easiest attributes to isolate. The paintings of old and modern masters are readily identified, and the quality of their work is well known. However, the cost of their works frequently exceeds $100,000 and may reach into millions of dollars. Such prices virtually exclude all but a handful of collectors and museums.

Even many lesser-name artists are readily identifiable, and an investor may determine the quality of their work through reading, studying, and viewing the art firsthand. A minor name in art history is usually minor for a reason. Investments in this type of art may appreciate (especially if art prices rise in general), but the probability of a large increase in value is small.

In addition to the artist and the quality of the work, value depends on several factors that are both inherent in and external to the specific piece. Factors indigenous to the work itself include the medium and the subject matter. For example, oil paintings tend to cost more than watercolors by the same artist. Landscapes command higher prices than portraits. Dark or somber scenes may be less valuable than brightly colored and cheerful ones.

Factors affecting value that are independent of the piece itself include the condition of the work, the former owners, the museums or shows in which the work was previously exhibited, and the seller.

Condition obviously affects value. As one would expect, a damaged painting or antique or a badly worn Oriental rug commands a lower price. However, the owner may be able to have damaged works restored (for a price). Such restoration should help increase the value of the work. Just the cleaning of an old painting or an Oriental rug will bring out the colors and perhaps make the piece both more attractive and marketable.

Who has previously owned the work, where it has been exhibited, and who is selling it may also affect the value of an art object. If a painting has passed through the collection of an important museum or major collector, its value is enhanced. In a sense, previous owners and exhibitions are like a pedigree. They establish authenticity and credibility that can enhance the value of a particular art object.

As the preceding discussion suggests, the valuation of art is very subjective. Professionals (e.g., art dealers and museum curators) know this and are capable of making reasonably accurate appraisals. When a piece is offered at an auction, these professionals know approximately how much the work should bring. If it appears that such a price will not be obtained, these professionals may enter the bidding and purchase the piece for their own galleries or collections. For this reason the novice investor should not expect to acquire quality art, antiques, or Oriental rugs at bargain prices. Those in the know will outbid such a naive investor.

---

[4] See Richard H. Rush, "Art as an Investment," in L. Barnes and S. Feldman, *Handbook of Wealth Management* (New York: McGraw-Hill, 1977), 37-1 through 37-16.

POINTS OF INTEREST

WHAT GOES UP MUST COME DOWN

The market for collectibles, like the markets for stocks, options, and commodities, is not immune to speculation fever. As with other speculative binges, the bubble ultimately burst and prices declined dramatically. In 1982, rare stamps and coins declined 40 to 50 percent; diamonds that had sold for over $50,000

sold for $15,000. In 1992, limited edition prints sold for less than half of their 1990 prices. For example, Rauschenberg's *Booster* sold for $20,000 after reaching a high of $165,000 in 1990. In some cases the markets entirely dried up, as there were few buyers, and owners were reluctant to sell at distress prices. The causes of this dramatic price decline included the reduction in the rate of inflation, increased interest in equity investments,

and the recession. These large price declines in stamps, limited edition prints, and other art objects taught investors in collectibles a lesson that investors in securities already know (but must periodically relearn): Speculative excesses ultimately correct themselves and prices fall. Unfortunately the lesson can be expensive for those investors who are sucked in when prices reach their peaks.

The Selection of Collectibles

How does the investor tackle the problem of selecting among the works of art or other collectibles that are available? Essentially the choice is either to buy the works of known artists or to try to identify the artists that will gain acceptance in the future. In a sense, this is similar to buying stock issued by IBM or AT&T, which are known firms in excellent financial condition, versus buying stock in the over-the-counter market that is issued by some small company that offers promise for the future. The works of the known artists, of course, will cost more. However, even the works of minor names in art may command high prices, and the investor, in essence, must decide whether to bite the bullet and pay the price or to select the works of the unknown artists.

The works of an unknown artist will, of course, tend to be inexpensive, and if the artist subsequently acquires a "name," his or her works will appreciate in value. However, the probability of this occurring is small, in which case the investor will probably be lucky to recoup even the meager cost of the investment.

There are, however, several things that the investor can do to help increase the chance of earning a positive return on an investment in a painting or an Oriental rug. First, the investor should buy from reputable dealers. Although prices from dealers will tend to be higher, their reputation verifies the authenticity of the work. Exhibit 21.1 presents the confirmation statement from a dealer for the sale of a painting. In addition to the title of the work and the medium (oil), the statement presents the year of the painting's execution (1974) and the work's identifying number (58). Such a statement is not only proof of purchase but also serves to authenticate the work. Notice also that the purchase may be subject to sales tax. Such taxes do not apply to the purchase of stocks and bonds.

Buying from known dealers or through major auction houses will also aid in any subsequent sale. Dealers often specialize in the work of particular artists and are thus aware of the market for these artists. Should the investor want to sell the piece, the dealer may be a major source of information regarding the market and may even be able to execute the sale.

Second, the investor should avoid buying prints and other objects that masquerade as potential investments. Unsigned prints and reproductions may be an

Exhibit 21.1 ♦ CONFIRMATION FOR THE SALE OF A PAINTING

excellent means to decorate a room and to learn about art, but they are not originals, nor are they unique. Generally, unsigned prints and reproductions are not investments, and the individual should realize this fact and not be deluded into believing that such items will appreciate in value.[5]

Third, the investor should develop a specialty. Just as one cannot learn about all possible firms and their securities, the individual cannot know everything concerning all forms of art. The best strategy, then, is to develop an area of expertise that will permit the investor to learn which factors affect the value of particular art objects. In this way the investor can accumulate a collection that is decorative and that serves as a store of value.

GOLD[6]

Gold has held a specific fascination for centuries. It has been minted into coins and used as a medium of exchange. Its color and durability have made it a popular metal for jewelry. Gold has also been a popular store of value. Some investors, who are frequently referred to as gold bugs, consider it to be among the best investments

---

[5] In the past, print makers (e.g., Dürer) did not sign their works, but these unsigned original prints are potential investments. However, prints and reproductions of these originals should not be considered to be investments.

[6] While this section is devoted to investing in gold, much of the material also applies to investing in silver and other precious metals.

available. A few investment advisory services have even recommend that investors hold a substantial proportion of their portfolios in some form of gold.

The main reason for investing in gold is a belief that it is the best insurance against inflation. The universal acceptability of gold makes it the one commodity to own during a period of rapid inflation. The price of gold tends to mirror fears of inflation. If the rate of inflation rises, purchases of gold will increase along with its price. Conversely, during periods of declining inflation, the price of gold tends to decrease. This is illustrated in Figure 21.1, which plots the price of an ounce of gold and the rate of inflation. As may be seen in the figure, the price of gold does seem to respond to the inflation rate.

Figure 21.1 also points out another fact: Investors can lose money by buying gold. As with any other investment, there is always the risk of loss. Holders of gold not only forgo income, such as dividends and interest, but also have to store the metal and bear the risk of fraud and capital loss from declining prices. Investors who bought gold in the 1970s may have earned a substantial return, as the price of gold rose to over $800 in 1980. Of course, if those investors chose not to realize

Figure 21.1 ✦ YEAR-END PRICE OF GOLD AND THE ANNUAL PERCENTAGE CHANGE IN THE CONSUMER PRICE INDEX (1971–1991)

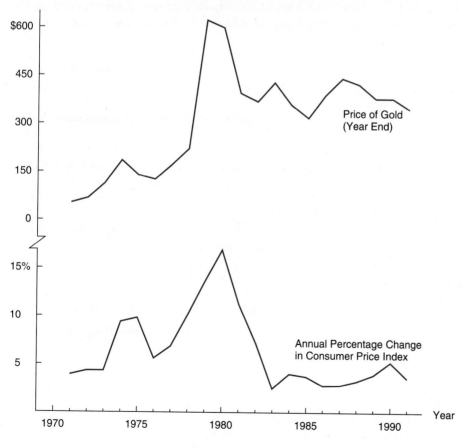

their paper profits, they watched the profits melt away, as the price of gold has steadily declined since it reached those historic highs. A decade later the price still languished well below the historic high.

There are several mediums for investing in gold: jewelry, coins, bullion (which is usually in the form of gold bars), stocks of mining companies, and futures contracts. As an investment gold jewelry is a poor choice, because the cost of the jewelry includes not only the cost of the gold but also the cost of the copper used to strengthen the gold and the wages of the craftspeople who design and construct the jewelry. There may be excellent reasons for buying gold jewelry, but it is not a good choice as an investment. (Jewelry, especially rare gems, may prove to be an acceptable investment. However, the individual is primarily buying the gems instead of the gold, and such investments are very illiquid and produce no monetary income.)

Gold Coins

Gold coins are a better vehicle than jewelry for investing in gold. These coins initially came into existence as currency, but in the United States they no longer serve as a medium of exchange. Many coins still exist from the past and may be purchased through coin dealers and at auctions.

Like jewelry, gold coins have a serious weakness as an investment. Their price is related to two things: the bullion content and the coin's numismatic value. The bullion value of a coin depends on the gold content and the price of gold. This price, in turn, depends on the market's demand for and supply of gold. Gold is used in various products (e.g., jewelry) and is continually being mined. The demand for gold in its various uses (including investments) relative to the supply that is offered determines the market price of gold bullion.

The value of gold coins depends not only on the value of bullion but also on the numismatic value of the coin. Some coins are much scarcer than others and hence are more valuable as collector's items. For example, the value of an uncirculated ten dollar gold piece minted in the United States in 1861 rose from $37.50 in 1946 to $200 in 1974, but an uncirculated three dollar piece minted in 1889 rose in value from $25 to $1,100 during the same period.[7] The difference, of course, is the result of the scarcity of three dollar gold pieces. This gives it great numismatic value in addition to its value as gold.

If the investor is concerned only with accumulating gold, then numismatic rarities may be of little interest because the investor pays more for the same amount of gold. The premium paid over the bullion value can be substantial; the investor, therefore, is really gambling on the coin as a collector's item and not on its gold content.

Investors who wish to acquire both coin collections and gold bullion may prefer such rarities. These will probably increase in value more rapidly than the more common gold coins. In general, it is the rarer items that appreciate the fastest. Collectors

---

[7] See Q. David Bowers, *Collecting Rare Coins for Profit* (New York: Harper & Row, 1975), 303–304.

of gold coins (and stamps, antiques, and other collectibles) may find that the best strategy is to buy a few expensive, high-quality representations instead of trying to amass large collections of less rare and cheaper specimens.

One coin of particular interest to gold collectors is the Canadian Maple Leaf, which is issued by the Canadian government. After the Union of South Africa, Canada is the Western world's main producer of gold. It mints the Canadian Maple Leaf to sell to gold collectors.[8] While the coin may be used as money, it is not circulated, for such use would scar the coins and reduce their value.

The primary attractiveness of the Canadian Maple Leaf is that the coin is issued in exactly one troy ounce of fine gold. This uniformity of metal content increases its marketability in the secondary markets. In addition, the coin sells for a modest premium over the value of the gold bullion in the coin. Other gold coins, especially commemorative coins or limited foreign edition coins, are frequently sold (at least initially) at a considerable premium over their value as bullion. The investor runs a substantial risk in that the price of these commemorative coins may decline relative to the value of the gold bullion in the secondary markets. This potential price decline, however, does not apply to Canadian Maple Leafs.

Gold Bullion

Until January 1, 1975, gold coins and jewelry offered Americans the only legal means to own gold. However, Americans can now own gold bullion in the form of gold bars. These may be bought through gold dealers and brokerage firms. Once the investor purchases the gold, he or she may take possession of it or leave it with the dealer or broker. Leaving the gold with the broker involves storage and insurance costs, which increases the price of the investment.

The investor may take delivery and store the gold in a presumably safe place. The gold ingots should be stamped and numbered by the refiner, who also supplies correspondingly numbered certificates. These must be delivered with the gold should the investor ever sell the ingots. If the certificates are lost, the ingots will have to be assayed to prove their gold content. This expense must be paid by the investor to ensure the marketability of the gold bars. Even if the documentation is not lost, the investor may have to have the gold assayed because taking possession results in a loss of the guarantee of the gold's quality, and this guarantee can only be restored by having the gold assayed.

The need to assay the metal points out a major problem with investing in gold: fraud. Coins and bars can be passed off as gold with fake numbers and fake documentation. By purchasing gold bullion from a reputable dealer or through a brokerage firm, the investor can substantially reduce the possibility of fraud. Certainly, no investor should buy unassayed gold that is offered at a discount from the price of gold bullion. Such a purchase will certainly prove to be a bad investment.

---

[8]The Union of South Africa also mints a coin to sell to collectors, the Krugerrand. Importation of Krugerrands in the United States was banned on October 11, 1985. Investors, however, may still buy and sell Krugerrands that were imported prior to the ban.

Figure 21.2 ✦ PRICE OF GOLD AND YEARLY PRICE-RANGE OF HOMESTAKE MINING STOCK (1981–1992)

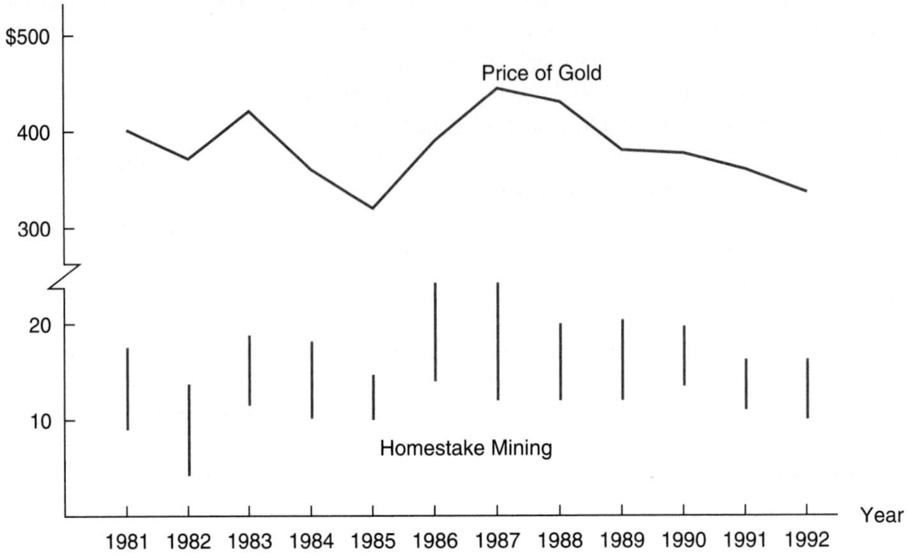

Gold Mining Stocks

The investor may also buy the shares of gold mining companies. This, of course, is not owning gold. Instead, the firm may own gold mines and mining equipment. Presumably, the value of the shares is related to the value of the gold, but it is possible for the price of gold to rise while the price of the mining company's stock declines. Various factors, such as a strike or a fire, can affect the value of the mining firm and its securities, but such events may have no impact on the price of gold.[9]

These exogenous factors (especially political forces) are particularly important in the valuation of gold mining stocks. The Union of South Africa alone accounts for about two-thirds of the world's output of newly mined gold. The political climate in the Union of South Africa is somewhat unstable, and this instability can have an impact on the value of gold mining shares in South African companies.

The investor may avoid these political problems by limiting purchases to shares in gold mining companies in the United States and Canada whose values tend to follow closely the price of bullion. This is illustrated in Figure 21.2, which shows

---

[9] The investor may reduce the impact of such events by purchasing the shares of an investment company that specializes in the securities of gold mining companies. For example, American-South African Investment Company (or ASA) is a closed-end investment company whose shares are traded on the New York Stock Exchange. ASA specializes in the stocks of South African gold mining firms.

the price performance of shares of Homestake Mining (a Canadian firm) and the price of gold. As may be seen in the figure, the price of these shares moved in tandem with the price of gold. Thus, shares of American and Canadian gold mining companies may offer the investor a viable alternative to owning gold bars. Such shares not only avoid the costs of storage, insurance, and assaying but also may pay dividend income, which is not possible from any other form of investment in gold.

While buying gold shares instead of gold does have advantages, this strategy also has disadvantages. Buying shares in gold firms may be more risky than taking a position in the metal. The prices of gold stocks tend to be more volatile than the price of gold. These companies have costs (e.g., wages, interest, depreciation of equipment) that are independent of the price of gold. Once these expenses have been met, further increases in the price of gold tend to increase earnings. Thus a small change in the price of gold can generate a larger change in the earnings of gold mining companies.

The converse is also true since a small decline in the price of gold can cause a profitable mine to operate at a loss. The difference between a profitable and a losing mine can be a matter of a few dollars. For this reason the analysis of gold mining shares tends to stress two considerations: (1) the estimated life of the mine and (2) the cost of recovering the metal. Low-cost, long-lived mines are obviously the most desirable. They will tend to be the most profitable during periods of higher gold prices but may still generate a profit (or smaller loss) during periods when the price of gold declines.

Gold Mutual Funds

While the general discussion of mutual funds is deferred until Chapter 23, these are funds that specialize in gold investments. For example, Franklin Gold and Bull & Bear Gold Investors LTD invest only in gold (i.e., gold mining stocks and bullion) and other precious metals (i.e., silver and platinum). The primary advantage of these funds is the diversification of their portfolios. If the individual expected the price of gold to rise but was uncertain whether to invest in the bullion, gold mining stocks, or other assets that are complementary to gold, then investing in a gold mutual fund gives the investor a diversified mix of gold investments. The individual avoids having to select a specific gold investment or a particular gold stock.

Gold Futures and Options

In addition to gold coins, gold bullion, and gold mining shares, the investor may speculate in gold futures and gold options.[10] Like many other commodities, there exists an active market in contracts for the future delivery of gold. This market is a recent development; it came into existence only after it became legal for Americans

---

[10] Refer to Chapter 20 for a general discussion of investing in commodity futures and Chapter 19 for a discussion of options.

to own gold bullion. The principal markets for these gold futures are the Chicago International Monetary Market and the New York Commodity Exchange (COMEX).

As with other commodity contracts, the appeal of gold futures is in the great leverage that they offer investors. A contract for the future delivery of gold is for 100 troy ounces. At $350 an ounce, the contract has a face value of $35,000. If the margin requirement were $3,500, the speculator would have a claim on $35,000 worth of gold for an outlay of only $3,500. If the price were to rise by only $10 per ounce, the value of the contract would rise by $1,000 to $36,000. The speculator would then make $1,000 on an investment of only $3,500. Of course, if the price of gold were to fall by only $10 per ounce, the speculator would lose $1,000. Since gold prices can and do fluctuate rapidly, there exists considerable potential for large profits and losses, which is a primary reason for the attractiveness of gold futures to speculators.

While all forms of investing in gold involve several sources of risk, gold futures involve a special source of risk. Government and international agencies participate in the market for gold. For example, the U.S. Treasury periodically sells gold, and this additional supply tends to reduce its price. In addition, the International Monetary Fund of the United Nations sells gold to raise currency for its international transactions. This also tends to reduce the price of gold. These sales make investing in gold futures more risky, as they alter the supply and demand of the metal.

The New York Commodity Exchange also offers gold futures options, which are put and call options to sell and buy gold futures contracts. While they are not options to buy and sell gold, their prices move with the price of gold. As with other put and call options, the reason for purchasing them is the potential leverage they offer. Suppose the investor pays $1,000 for a call option to purchase a gold futures contract for 100 ounces at $320. The value of the call option will rise as the price of gold (and the futures price) rises above $320. For example, if the price of gold rose to $350 by the expiration date of the call, the option would be worth $3,000. This $3,000 is the $30 difference between the current price ($350) and the price specified in the call option ($320) times 100, since the option is the right to buy a contract for 100 ounces. Thus, in this illustration the price of gold rose less than 10 percent (from $320 to $350), but the value of the option tripled from $1,000 to $3,000. If the investor had purchased the option for $1,000, this individual would have earned a $2,000 profit on the transaction.

If the price of gold were to decline, the value of the call option would also decline. If the price of gold fell to $300, then the call option to buy the gold futures contract at $320 would become worthless. No one would exercise the option to buy at $320 what could be purchased elsewhere for $300. In that case the investor would lose the $1,000 invested in the call option.

While both futures contracts and put and call options are means to lever one's position when speculating on changes in the price of gold, the gold option offers one major advantage over the futures contract. With a futures contract, the investor could lose a substantial amount if there were a large and sudden change in the price of the commodity. This is because the investor has not purchased anything but has entered into a contract to buy (or sell) gold at a specified price. If the price moved against the investor, that individual could sustain a large loss in order to fulfill the contract. However, with a put or a call option the investor actually owns something (i.e., the option). Thus, the maximum amount that may be lost is the cost of the option. This limit reduces the risk associated with speculating in the movements of the price of gold.

SUMMARY

The poor performance of stocks during the 1970s and the continuation of inflation in the early 1980s increased investor interest in various collectibles and other physical assets. Art objects, Oriental rugs, antiques, stamps, coins, gold, and silver have attracted the attention of some investors as alternatives to the more traditional investments (i.e., stocks and bonds).

These physical assets offer investors potential price appreciation and, in some cases, services. They may be purchased from dealers or at auctions, and while these assets are not purchased on organized exchanges, secondhand markets exist in which the investor can sell the assets.

Investors who acquire physical assets, like investors who acquire financial assets, bear the risk of loss. This risk is due to fluctuations in the prices of the assets in general and of the specific assets, inflation, theft, and fraud. To help overcome these risks, the investor needs to be well informed and to specialize in a particular type of physical asset.

Art and gold were used in this chapter to illustrate two types of possible investments in physical assets. The valuation of art objects is extremely subjective, because it depends not only on the work and its creator but also on several intangibles. However, art objects can be very decorative, and they do suggest to others the taste of the investor.

Gold may be acquired in a variety of forms, including jewelry, coins, and bullion. The investor can also buy the stock of gold mining companies, futures contracts, and gold options. Gold jewelry is the poorest means to invest in gold, and a futures contract is the riskiest. Most investors prefer gold coins and bullion as their vehicles for an investment in gold.

Like any investment, acquiring gold subjects the investor to risk. The price of gold, like the price of other assets, can fall and has done so in the past. This, plus the fact that gold must be stored, insured, and assayed, reduces the potential return on the investment. A positive return on gold, as on all other investments, cannot be assured.

Investment Summary

Collectibles

Source of return: Possible capital gains if the value of the collectible rises.

Liquidity and marketability: No liquidity. Marketability varies with the type of collectible. In general, the marketability is poor, especially if the individual is buying at retail prices and selling at wholesale prices.

Sources of risk: Unsystematic risk from events that affect prices such as fads that can affect the supply and demand for a particular collectible for a period of time. Systematic risk comes from the tendency for the prices of a type of collectible to move together. Since the prices of collectibles may rise with the rate of inflation, they may not have the purchasing power risk associated with financial assets.

Taxation: Realized profits are considered to be capital gains and are subject to taxation.

Questions

1. How are collectibles and gold bought and sold?
2. Why is it important to have specialized knowledge when investing in physical assets such as art or gold?
3. What are the sources of risk from investing in collectibles and gold?
4. Why have the prices of selected art objects risen? Is there a secondary market for art objects? What are the special costs associated with investing in art?
5. What are the sources of return from an investment in art and other collectibles?
6. What are the mediums for investing in gold? What are the special costs associated with these investments?
7. Why may gold bullion have to be assayed? Why may individuals who desire to invest in gold prefer bullion to gold coins?
8. What is the relationship between the rate of inflation and the price of gold?
9. What advantages may gold stocks offer over gold bars?
10. What is the advantage and risk associated with buying a gold option or futures contract?

Suggested Readings

There is a dearth of substantive written material on investing in art and collectibles. Much of what is available falls into one of two categories: (1) how to make a fortune by investing in . . . or (2) a description of past performance, usually of a specific asset. For a sampling of readings, see:

Frey, Bruno S., and Werner W. Pommerehne. "Is Art Such a Good Investment?" *The Public Interest* (Spring 1988): 79–86.

Schonfeld, Robert. "Forum: Investing in Art." *American Artist* (February 1980): 18ff.

Shapiro, Cecile, and Lauris Mason. *Fine Prints: Collecting, Buying, and Selling.* New York: Harper & Row, 1976.

For a general reference on collectibles, consult the following encyclopedia:

Friedman, Jack P., ed. *The Encyclopedia of Investments,* 2d ed. Boston: Warren, Gorham & Lamont, 1990.

This book contains chapters devoted to art nouveau and art deco, books, coins, folk art, gemstones, motion pictures, paintings, furniture, photographs, porcelain, prints, rugs, sculpture, and stamps. Each chapter covers the basic characteristics of the asset, its attractive features and its potential risks, special factors to consider, and custodial care. Each chapter also has a glossary and suggested readings.

Forbes periodically publishes articles on collectibles the themes of which tend to be "let the buyer beware." Examples of these warnings include:

Brown, Christie. "Tides of Prints." *Forbes,* February 17, 1992, 144–145.

Fritz, Michael. "Collectibles Are Not Forever." *Forbes,* August 8, 1988, 100–101.

"Heads They Win, Tails You Lose." *Forbes,* December 12, 1988, 260–262.

O Hanlon, D. "Limited Edition Lithography: Buyer Beware." *Forbes,* July 10, 1978, 65–67.

Schifrin, Matthew. "McArt." *Forbes,* March 7, 1988, 123–125.

One major advantage offered by collectibles is possible diversification of the individual's portfolio. For a discussion of this, including annual price changes in selected collectibles

(e.g., stamps, furniture, baseball cards) and the correlations among these returns, see:
Krause, David. "The Benefits of Diversifying with Collectibles." *AAII Journal* (October 1988): 7–11.

Much of what has been written on gold suggests that gold is the only safe and certain investment. This, of course, is not true as the decline in gold's price during the 1980s proves. Like collectibles, most of the material on investing in gold is descriptive and lacking financial analysis. For a sampling, see:
Dreyfus, Patricia A. "A Gold Buyer's Guide." *Money,* November 1979, 87–88.
Lee, Susan. "Gold: The Ultimate Burglar Alarm." *Forbes,* September 23, 1985, 127–133.

For an explanation of gold futures, read:
Understanding Gold Futures Trading. Chicago: International Monetary Market Division of the Chicago Mercantile Exchange, 1974.

The major producers of gold are primarily located in the Union of South Africa and Russia. For descriptions of North American gold companies and the advantages they offer, consult:
Jackson, Robert S. *North American Gold Stocks.* Chicago: Probus Publishing, 1986.

22

INVESTING IN REAL ESTATE

*H*ome ownership is a very distinctive American characteristic. It is
almost synonymous with the American dream of prosperity. Over
fifty million residential units are owner-occupied. More individuals
own homes than directly own stock.[1] Home ownership, however, is not the only way
to invest in real estate. The individual may also own land, income properties, or
shares in real estate partnerships and real estate investment trusts. This chapter is
an overview of these investments in real estate.

The first section is devoted to home ownership, including the tax advantages of
home ownership and the various types of mortgage loans available to finance the
purchases of homes. Next follows a discussion of investments in both unimproved
and improved land, including limited partnerships that acquire and operate income-
earning properties. Emphasis is placed on the determination of the property's cash
flow and the uncertainties associated with investments in rental properties.

The chapter ends with a discussion of real estate investment trusts (REITs).
REITs are a type of investment company that specializes in real estate. The types of
trusts, their methods of financing, the risks, and the potential returns associated with
this particular investment are covered. The chapter ends with a discussion of how
the dividend-growth valuation model presented in Chapter 8 may be applied to
shares in REITs.

◆ ◆ ◆

HOME OWNERSHIP

Every person must live somewhere. This obvious fact differentiates home ownership
from all other investments. People must secure living space. Their choices are either

---

[1] Many investors may indirectly own stock through pension plans and employee savings
programs.

to rent the property or to own it and, in effect, rent the space to themselves. If they rent, the individuals are consuming space. If they own, they are simultaneously consuming space and making an investment.

Acquiring a home is not the same as purchasing most goods and services. Few individuals can make in one single payment the entire cost of a home. Instead they make an initial payment (i.e., the down payment) and borrow the balance with a loan secured by the property (i.e., the mortgage). The initial down payment may be substantial. For example, a down payment of 20 to 25 percent on a $100,000 home requires the buyer to have between $20,000 and $25,000 in cash. Obviously, the individual will have had to accumulate substantial savings in order to make this required initial payment.

The primary sources of mortgage loans are savings and loans and other financial institutions, such as commercial banks. The potential buyer must apply for these loans, and whether the lending institution grants them will depend on the amount of the down payment and the buyer's capacity to service the debt (i.e., pay the interest and retire the principal). While the loan is secured by the property, the lender is primarily concerned with collecting the mortgage payments and not with seizing the home in case of default. Thus having sufficient income to service the loan is crucial to obtaining a mortgage.

Besides having the down payment and obtaining the mortgage, the buyer must be able to meet other expenses when the home is acquired. Transferring title from the seller to the buyer requires the services of a lawyer. The potential buyer may want the home professionally inspected for possible defects (especially if the home is several years old). Title insurance, which guarantees the title is free and clear of claims, also increases the initial costs associated with the purchase of the home (or any other real estate).

There are many reasons for owning a home instead of renting. These include the psychic income that comes with the pride of owning a place that can be called one's home. However, owning involves considerable costs and possible headaches that the renter may avoid. Suppose your hot water heater breaks. If you rent, you call the manager. You don't have the headache associated with getting the problem fixed. (Your headache may be getting the landlord to fix the problem.) Responsibility for many repairs rests with the owner who also pays expenses, such as property taxes, interest on the mortgage, general maintenance, fire insurance, and supervisory personnel. The owner seeks to recover these expenses through the rents, but failure to cover these costs may result in the investment generating a loss instead of a profit.

Homeowners, of course, have to cover these expenses out of their own pockets. Costs such as general maintenance (e.g., painting and repairs), necessary equipment (e.g., lawn mowers), insurance, property taxes, and interest on the mortgage may consume a substantial proportion of a family's budget. Many of these costs are not recaptured when the home is sold but must be made in order to maintain the property's value. If the individual does not want to perform required tasks or is reluctant to employ others to maintain the property, then renting and passing the expenses (and headaches) to the landlord is a reasonable strategy, especially if the funds invested in the home are not frittered away but are used to obtain some other alternative investments.

Home ownership, however, offers a very pragmatic advantage over renting. It is a means to force saving. Every payment on a mortgage loan represents interest and principal. The amount that the individual has invested in the home increases with each mortgage payment. These payments become a convenient means to force oneself to save. In addition, any repairs and improvements made in the property accrue to the owner and not to the landlord.

There are two major financial reasons for home ownership. The first pertains to the tax benefits, and the second is the potential return on the investment. Of course, this return depends partially on the tax shelters generated by home ownership. These tax breaks are rarely referred to as tax shelters, but they are because they either reduce taxable income or defer tax payments. The tax shelters or tax advantages of home ownership are (1) the deductions from income that the home owner who itemizes is able to take, (2) the possible deferment or even avoidance of capital gains taxes when the property is sold, and (3) the tax-free income generated by the living space.

Income Tax Deductions

The vast majority of homes are purchased through the use of mortgage loans. The interest paid is a tax-deductible expense. If the home owner itemizes deductions, the deduction of interest reduces taxable income and thus results in a tax savings. This savings can be substantial. If the home owner is carrying a $50,000 mortgage at 10 percent, the approximate interest charge is $5,000 in the first year of the mortgage. Itemization of this interest expense reduces taxable income by $5,000.

The effect of this deduction is a reduction in the true or effective cost of a mortgage loan. The individual's true cost of a mortgage is related to (1) the interest rate and (2) the marginal income tax rate. If an investor borrows funds and pays 10 percent, the *before-tax* interest rate is 10 percent, but the true cost of the loan is less.

A simple example illustrates how the deduction reduces the effective cost of the debt. If an investor has a marginal tax rate of 28 percent and borrows funds at 10 percent interest, then the effective cost of the mortgage is 7.20 percent. The effective **cost of debt** is

cost of debt
The interest rate paid adjusted for any tax savings.

Cost of debt = Before-tax interest rate (1 − Marginal tax rate).

For this individual the calculation is

Cost of debt = 0.10(1 − 0.28) = 7.20%.

This effective cost of debt (i_e) is expressed in symbolic form in Equation 22.1:

$$i_e = i(1 - t). \tag{22.1}$$

The effective cost of debt (i_e) is simply the product of the stated interest rate (i) and the tax effect ($1 - t$), where t represents the investor's marginal income bracket. Obviously, the higher the individual's marginal tax rate, the lower is the true cost of borrowing.

The homeowner is also permitted to deduct from taxable income the property taxes that are paid on the home. As with the interest deduction, the home owner must itemize expenses in order to receive the benefit of the deduction. The effect of itemizing property taxes is a reduction in the individual's taxable income and therefore a reduction in the federal income tax liability. Since the property tax charged by some local governments amounts to over $2,000 on even moderately valued homes (e.g., $70,000 to $100,000 homes), the property tax deduction can result in substantial savings on income taxes for middle-income homeowners.

Owing to these deductions, several important expenditures or cash outlays associated with home ownership come from *before-tax* dollars. Most expenditures made by individuals come from *after-tax* dollars. Renters, who cannot take advantage of these deductions, pay rent with after-tax dollars. If an individual is in the 28 percent tax bracket, that person must earn $1,042 to make $750 in rental payments. However, that same individual could reduce taxes by $28 for every $100 paid in interest or property taxes on a house.

Capital Gains Deferment

In addition to the previous deductions, a homeowner may receive a tax break when the home is sold. If the owner sells for a profit and reinvests the funds in another home within 24 months, any realized capital gains may be deferred. Thus, if a home owner bought a house for $20,000 in 1960 and sold it for $100,000 in 1993, the $80,000 capital gain is not realized for federal income tax purposes as long as the home owner buys a new house that costs at least $100,000. Instead of a capital gain, the cost basis of the initial house is transferred to the new home.[2]

If the price of the new house were $105,000, its cost basis would be $25,000, which is the $20,000 cost of the original house plus the $5,000 difference between the purchase price of the new house and the sale price of the old house. If the price of the new house were $95,000, then the cost would be less than the proceeds of the sale by $5,000 ($100,000 − $95,000). This $5,000 must be reported to the Internal Revenue Service as a capital gain. However, the tax on the remaining $75,000 in profit is deferred, and the cost basis of the new house becomes $20,000 (i.e., the cost basis of the original house).

Legislation was passed in 1981 that gives some home owners an even larger tax break. This legislation exempts a capital gain of up to $125,000 from taxation provided the individual is over 55 years old. The investor is allowed this tax break only once. Under this legislation, a home owner who bought a house for $20,000 in 1960 and upon retirement in 1993 at the age of 65 sold it for $145,000 could completely avoid taxation on the capital gain.

Income-in-Kind

Individuals either rent space or own it and "rent" it to themselves. The money that homeowners do not pay to a landlord may be viewed as rent that they pay to themselves. The home owner receives income-in-kind. Such income is not subject to federal income tax. While home ownership generates a tax-free flow of services, renting does not. Tax-free services, like deductions that reduce taxable income, increase the attractiveness of investing in a house or a condominium. While the importance of

---

[2] This tax benefit applies only to a primary residence; it does not apply to a vacation home.

this tax-free income varies with the financial situation and income level of the investor, it generally is more advantageous to own than to rent as the individual's income and tax bracket rise.

In light of these tax advantages, it is not surprising to find that many individuals invest in homes. The ability to reduce taxable income by certain deductions, the capital gains deferment, and tax-free income-in-kind all favor investments in residential homes. In addition, the individual may obtain mortgage money at an effective cost (i.e., after the tax adjustment) that is less than the rate of inflation. Since the tax laws favor the homeowner, investments in houses may offer the individual one of the best possible investments.

Condominiums

condominium
An apartment that is owned instead of rented.

These reasons for home ownership also apply to **condominiums.** A condominium is similar to an apartment, but instead of renting, the individual owns the "apartment." The grounds and general facilities belong to all of the owners of the condominiums, who pay a fee for their maintenance.[3] The portion of the building that the individual owns may be subsequently sold, and the seller may earn a capital gain if the property is sold for a profit. In addition, since the individual owns and does not rent the space, the tax advantages of home ownership apply. Thus, in some ways ownership of a condominium is no different from ownership of a home; a condominium may be treated as an investment just as a home is.

The condominium is particularly attractive to people who have little need or desire for lawns and shrubs. The maintenance of a home and the grounds can be expensive in terms of both time and money. While the condominium owner does not avoid the monetary cost of this maintenance, he or she may not have to expend the effort. If the individual lacks the time or the inclination for home maintenance, the condominium may offer the best of both worlds: the advantages of home ownership and the convenience of renting.

Risks and Returns

Many people believe that residential homes are among the best investments. The appreciation in the value of the home acts as a hedge against inflation, and at the same time the investor receives the services of the home.

The price appreciation in homes is illustrated in Figure 22.1, which presents the median prices of new and existing residential homes for 1973 through 1990.[4] The figure also includes the Dow Jones industrial average for the same period. The top half presents yearly home prices while the bottom half presents annual percentage changes.

---

[3]The investor should read carefully the agreement that specifies what is covered by the maintenance fee. Some managements have defaulted and not fulfilled their part of the contracts, which leaves condominium owners with additional obligations that must be met to comply with local health and fire regulations.

[4]Figure 22.1 uses the median price and not the average price of single-family residential homes since the average is raised by the sales of a few expensive homes. The median price may be more representative of the price of a home to the typical buyer.

Figure 22.1 ✦ Dow Jones Industrial Average and Median Prices of New and Existing Residential Homes, 1973–1990

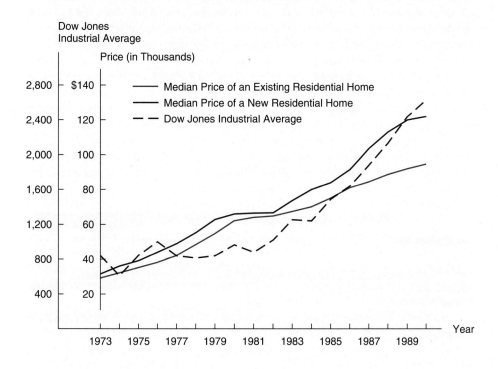

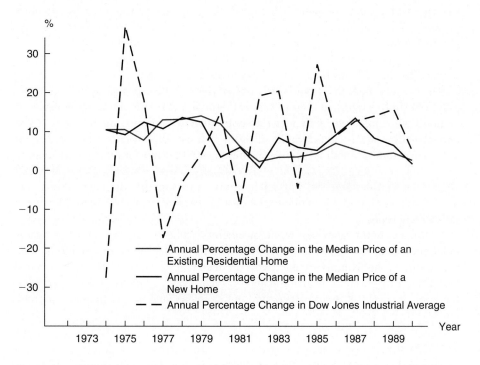

The prices of new and existing homes and the Dow Jones industrial averages rose during this time period. Over the entire time period the annual growth rate in new home prices was 8.1 percent, while the prices of existing homes grew by 7.2 percent. The Dow Jones rose only 6.9 percent. These numbers, however, cannot be considered rates of return, since the growth in the Dow Jones does not consider dividends and hence understates the return the investor would have earned. Correspondingly, the growth in the home prices may overstate returns, since costs (e.g., repairs) associated with home ownership are excluded.

Figure 22.1 also illustrates that there were considerable differences in the year to year price fluctuations. While home prices rose every year, the Dow Jones experienced significant losses in several years (e.g., 1974). There were also periods when stock prices rose dramatically (e.g., 1985), while home prices rose modestly. It is also apparent that the rate of increase in home prices started to decline during the late 1980s. The recession of 1990 and 1991 also took a toll, as home prices in some geographical areas stagnated and even fell. However, prices in the aggregate still tended to rise even if the rate of increase was smaller.

Part of the explanation for the increase in home values is the increased cost of construction. The rising building costs of new homes translate into increased values for old homes. Old and new homes are substitutes for each other. If the cost of one rises relative to the cost of the other, buyers will seek to purchase the cheaper home. As the cost of new homes rises, some individuals will seek to purchase existing homes. This, in turn, will drive up the prices of older homes to keep them in line with the prices of newly constructed homes.

Another explanation for the increased value of homes is the continued increase in demand for them. Conventional wisdom suggests that home ownership is a good investment. This belief encourages individuals to buy homes even though they may have to take on more financial obligations than is prudent for their capacity to service the debt. As is subsequently discussed, the tendency on the part of some home owners to use excessive amounts of debt financing (i.e., excessive financial leverage) is a major source of risk of investing in homes. However, to the extent that these individuals are willing and able to obtain this mortgage money, they increase the demand for homes and hence help to increase their prices.

Is an investment in a home really one of the best hedges against inflation? One pre-1980 study found that *only* private residential real estate offered complete protection against inflation.[5] Other investments, such as debt instruments, were a successful hedge against anticipated inflation, because their yields adjusted for the anticipated rate of inflation. However, these assets did not protect against unanticipated inflation. Only private residential real estate provided a safeguard against both expected and unexpected inflation. This study thus supports the conventional wisdom that home ownership is one of the best investments available, especially during inflationary times.

Although in the aggregate home ownership has been a successful hedge against inflation, it does not follow that there are no risks or that home ownership is desirable for everyone. Home ownership can produce many headaches for the individual. Owners are responsible for maintenance, which (even if the cost is recouped when the home is sold) still requires a current outlay of cash and may require considerable

---

[5] Eugene F. Fama and G. William Schwert, "Asset Returns and Inflation," *Journal of Financial Economics* 5 (November 1978): 115–146.

POINTS OF INTEREST

THE HOUSING AFFORDABILITY INDEX

A measure of the potential demand for housing is the affordability index. This index compares individuals' income to a measure of required debt service. If the index exceeds 1.0, the typical American family has sufficient income to purchase a median-priced house. If the index is less than 1.0, the cost of a median-priced house exceeds the ability of most families to afford it.

Obviously, higher median incomes or lower housing prices increase the index while higher debt service reduces it. Houses are usually purchased through the use of mortgage loans, which require

monthly payments by the homeowner. The mortgage payment depends on the amount of the loan, its term, and the interest rate. Lower interest rates will mean lower debt service, so the value of the index rises. Conversely, higher interest rates reduce the index.

The affordability index changes from month to month with changes in income, house prices, and interest rates. In mid-1989 the index fell below 1.0 for the first time since March 1986. This meant that the typical American family with median income of $32,760 could not afford the median-priced house (i.e., $93,200) using conventional financing (i.e., a 20 percent down payment and a fixed-rate mortgage). Since 1989 was a

period of continuing economic prosperity, it seems almost perverse that the affordability index declined.

Actually the ability to afford a house may rise during periods of economic stagnation since declining interest rates may more than offset declining aggregate incomes. The converse may hold when the economy is expanding and incomes are rising. More economic activity is often accompanied by both higher home prices and higher interest rates because the demand for funds is increased and the Federal Reserve may tighten credit to reduce inflationary pressure. Thus it is possible that during periods of economic expansion, many potential buyers will be unable to afford a single-family home.

effort. In addition, the cost of running a home rises with the rate of inflation. The increased costs of insurance, energy, and various other expenses (which are not deductible from taxable income) may strain the individual's budget if personal income does not rise as rapidly. Even though the resale value of the house may be increasing, that is not cash currently received. But it is current cash that is necessary to meet the expenses associated with running the home.

Another source of risk is the use of debt financing to acquire the home.[6] Carrying the mortgage is a fixed monthly expense that must be met, or the holder of the mortgage may seize the home (through a court proceeding) and sell it to recoup the funds lent to the home owner. Investors thus run considerable risk of loss should they be unable to maintain mortgage payments. Some individuals purchase expensive homes and anticipate that home values and their salaries will rise while mortgage payments remain constant, only to find that the mortgage payment becomes a real burden when adversity strikes (e.g., the loss of a job or an extended illness).

The last source of risk is due to the fact that not all real estate values increase at the same rate. During the 1970s suburban homes appreciated in value more rapidly than city properties. However, pockets within some cities have appreciated more rapidly since 1980. If the individual had the foresight to buy in an area where home values subsequently appreciated, the home has also served as a hedge against inflation. But many individuals do not have this foresight (or are not so lucky), and while their homes may have appreciated in value, the return need not have kept pace with the rate of inflation.

---

[6]Various types of mortgage loans are covered in the next section.

SOURCES OF MORTGAGE MONEY

One problem facing the individual seeking to buy a home is financing. Few individuals have sufficient funds to pay the entire purchase price and hence must borrow to finance the purchase. Prior to the high interest rates experienced during the early 1980s, borrowed funds were obtained through mortgage loans from a financial intermediary such as a commercial bank or a savings and loan association. There were basically two types of mortgage loans: conventional loans and loans backed by an agency of the federal government.

conventional mortgage loan
A standard loan to finance real estate (and secured by the property) in which the loan is periodically retired, and the interest paid is figured on the declining balance owed.

With a **conventional mortgage loan** the individual buys the house with a down payment and borrows the balance. The loan is retired over a period of years by payments (usually monthly) that pay the interest and retire the principal. The amount of the periodic payment is fixed, and the interest is determined on the balance owed. Exhibit 22.1 presents parts of a mortgage schedule for a loan of $70,000 at 10% for 25 years. Each monthly payment is $636.09, which consists of an interest payment and a principal repayment. The first column of the table gives the number of the payment. These range from 1 to 300 because the loan requires 12 monthly payments for 25 years for a total of 300 payments. The second column presents the interest payment, and the third column gives the amount of principal repayment. The balance of the loan is given in the last column. Since the amount of interest is determined on the balance owed, the amount of interest remitted with each payment declines, and the amount of the payment used to retire the principal rises. For example, the amount of interest in the third payment is $582.45, but in payment

Exhibit 22.1 ✦ SELECTED PAYMENTS FROM A REPAYMENT SCHEDULE FOR A $70,000 MORTGAGE LOAN AT 10% FOR 25 YEARS (MONTHLY PAYMENT: $636.09)

Number of Payment	Interest Payment	Principal Repayment	Balance of Loan
1	$583.33	$ 52.76	$69,947.24
2	582.89	53.30	69,894.05
3	582.45	53.64	69,840.41
—	—	—	—
—	—	—	—
—	—	—	—
148	457.41	178.68	54,709.99
149	455.92	180.17	54,529.81
150	454.42	181.68	54,348.14
—	—	—	—
—	—	—	—
—	—	—	—
298	15.64	620.45	1,256.45
299	10.47	625.62	630.83
300	5.26	630.83	0.00

number 148 interest is $457.41. Since the amount of interest declines, the principal repayment increases from $53.64 in payment number 3 to $178.68 in payment number 148. Payments during the early years of the mortgage loan primarily cover the interest owed, but payments near the end of the life of the loan primarily reduce the balance owed.

The periodic payment required to cover the interest and retire the loan is determined through the use of present value calculations presented in Chapter 6. The following simple example illustrates this calculation. An individual borrows $10,000 for ten years and agrees to make annual payments that retire the loan and pay 12 percent interest on the declining balance owed. What is the annual payment? The answer is

$$\$10,000 = \frac{x}{(1 + 0.12)^1} + \cdots + \frac{x}{(1 + 0.12)^{10}}.$$

Since the periodic payments will be equal, this equation may be solved by the use of the present value of an annuity table. The problem collapses to

$$\$10,000 = x \text{ times the interest factor for the present value} \\ \text{of an annuity at 12\% for 10 years}$$

$$\$10,000 = x(5.650)$$

$$x = \frac{\$10,000}{5.650} = \$1,769.91.$$

Annual payments of $1,769.91 for ten years will retire the loan and pay 12 percent on the declining balance owed. This illustration is an oversimplification because payments are made annually only; however, adjustments can be readily made to determine monthly payments.[7] The basic principle remains the same. The given rate of interest and the amount initially borrowed are used in conjunction with the present value of an annuity table to determine the amount of each monthly payment.

––––––––––

[7] To obtain monthly payments (i.e., compounding monthly), divide the interest rate by 12 months and multiply the number of periods by 12. In this case that is

$$\$10,000 = \frac{x}{\left(1 + \dfrac{0.12}{12}\right)} + \cdots + \frac{x}{\left(1 + \dfrac{0.12}{12}\right)^{10 \times 12}}$$

$$\$10,000 = x \text{ times the interest factor for the present value of an annuity} \\ \text{at 1 percent for 120 time periods}$$

$$\$10,000 = x(69.698)$$

$$x = \$143.48.$$

The monthly payment is $143.48. Notice that this amount is less than $1,769.91 divided by 12 months ($147.49 per month). Since the loan is being retired more rapidly (i.e., every month the principal is reduced), the effect is to reduce the total amount of interest paid and thus decrease the total monthly payment.

"POINTS"

"Heads I win; tails you lose." That saying may appropriately describe "points," which many financing institutions charge to grant a mortgage loan. These points are in addition to other costs associated with buying a home such as a mortgage application fee, lawyers' fees to transfer title, surveying, and title insurance.

Points are expressed as a percent of the mortgage loan. Two points means that two percent is added to the amount being borrowed. Thus, if the homeowner requests a loan for $100,000, the cost of the loan is increased by $2,000. This money is paid to the lending institution up front. Thus, if the homeowner does not have the $2,000, he or she will have to borrow an additional $2,000 to cover the points. This effectively increases the cost of the loan, since the individual does not have the use of the entire $102,000 that has been borrowed.

Points charged by lending institutions vary. One lender may offer the loan for 10 percent plus one point while a competing lender may offer the loan for 9.75 percent plus two points. The differences in the interest rates and the points increase the difficulty in comparing the loans. Points may also be tax deductible (if the individual itemizes), which further complicates the analysis.

If the individual does not anticipate living in the home for an extended period before selling, accepting the loan with the higher interest rate and lower points is usually preferable. The anticipation of lower interest rates and the possibility of refinancing also argues for accepting the higher interest and lower points alternative. If, however, the individual expects to be paying the mortgage over many years (i.e., not moving nor refinancing), then accepting the lower interest rate and paying the higher points is a better option. Over the extended number of years, the lower interest costs will tend to more than offset the higher points.

If the borrower defaults and does not make the monthly payment, the lender may seize the property through a legal process called foreclosure. The property then may be sold to recoup the principal and interest owed. Banks and other lenders thus consider the amount of the down payment and the borrower's capacity to service the debt as conditions for granting the mortgage loan.

To broaden the market for homes, the federal government has followed a policy of encouraging mortgage loans. While the government does not originate mortgage loans, it may guarantee them through insurance issued by the **Federal Housing Administration (FHA).** FHA-insured loans started during the 1930s. This insurance reduces the element of risk to the lender because if the borrower defaults, the FHA will make good the loan. The effect of this guarantee has been to make mortgage money available to low- and middle-income individuals who lack the necessary down payment or who may not be able to meet other requirements necessary to obtain conventional mortgage financing.

Federal Housing Administration (FHA) *An agency of the federal government that will insure mortgages granted to qualified recipients.*

A similar program was started in 1944 by the **Veterans Administration (VA)** when the VA began to guarantee mortgage loans made to veterans. As with FHA-insured loans, VA-guaranteed loans reduce the risk of loss to the lender and hence encourage the flow of funds into the mortgage market. The requirements for veterans to obtain the guarantees are less than with conventional, noninsured mortgages, especially the amount of the initial down payment required to obtain mortgage financing.

Veterans Administration (VA) *An agency of the federal government that will guarantee mortgages granted to qualified veterans.*

With the increase in interest rates in general from 1979 to 1981, the market for mortgage loans became very unsettled. Interest rates on mortgage loans rose, as is illustrated in Figure 22.2. This figure shows the sudden and rapid increase during 1980 through 1981 in the interest rate charged for conventional mortgage loans. While the cost of such loans was around 9 percent in 1978, the interest rate rose to about 16 percent in 1981. This increase meant that a $100,000 mortgage at 16

Figure 22.2 ✦ Interest Rates on Conventional Mortgage Loans, 1974–1991

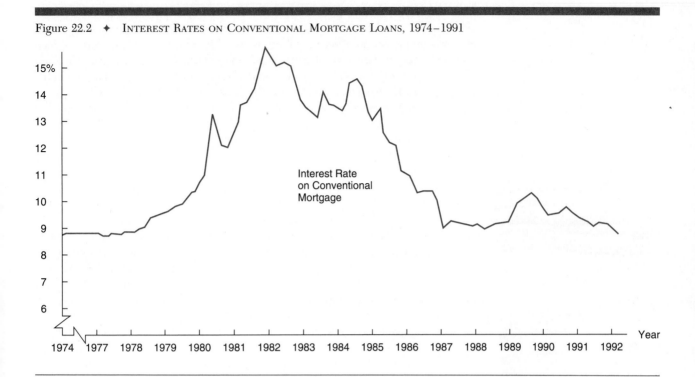

percent for 25 years required annual payments of about $16,400, but the same loan at 9 percent would require annual payments of about $10,000. Obviously the cash payments necessary to service the 16 percent loan are significantly higher, which means fewer people would be able to afford the higher interest rates.

In addition to higher interest rates, lending institutions became increasingly unwilling or unable to make conventional mortgage loans. When a commercial bank or savings and loan institution makes a conventional mortgage loan, it ties up its funds for many years. As with all long-term debt obligations, the value of the mortgage loans is reduced when interest rates rise, inflicting losses on the lenders. This problem is exacerbated when the banks and thrift institutions must pay higher rates of interest to attract deposits. The years 1981 and 1982 were particularly painful for savings and loan associations, since the bulk of their assets were mortgage loans that carried much lower interest rates than they had to pay to obtain deposits. In addition, many depositors withdrew funds and invested them in money market mutual funds, so savings and loan associations had fewer funds to invest in mortgage loans even if they could have earned higher interest rates. The result of the plight of the savings and loans was a reduction in the amount of funds available for mortgage loans, even for individual home buyers who were willing and able to pay the high interest rates.

High interest rates and the shortage of mortgage money led to nontraditional sources of funds and to variations on the conventional mortgage loan. These new loans are frequently referred to as **creative financing,** as buyers and sellers of homes seek to find ways to finance the purchases of houses.

One possible source of creative mortgage financing is the seller of the property. Some sellers are willing to accept the mortgage loan as a means to sell the house.

creative financing
The use of nonconventional mortgages to finance the acquisition of real estate.

The buyer makes a down payment and the seller accepts the mortgage loan for the balance of the purchase price. The seller may even charge several percentage points below the going rate in order to sell the house. The original mortgage may remain outstanding because the seller has not received the cash necessary to retire the original loan. However, the seller may earn more interest than is being paid on the initial mortgage. In effect what occurs is that the buyer pays funds to the seller, who in turn is retiring the initial mortgage on the home. It should be noted, however, that the terms of the original mortgage may preclude such a pass-through. Then the seller will be willing to accept this kind of arrangement only if he or she can retire the original mortgage and does not need the cash to make other payments (such as the down payment on another home).

variable-interest-rate mortgage loan
A mortgage loan in which the interest rate periodically changes to reflect current interest rates.

One variation on the conventional mortgage is the substitution of a **variable interest rate** for a fixed rate. As interest rates vary, the rate of interest on the loan changes. For example, the rate may change ½ percent each year with a limit of 2½ percent over the lifetime of the loan. Thus, if a borrower obtains funds for 10 percent, the rate could rise as high as 12.5 percent. The length of the loan may still be twenty or twenty-five years. If the lender does not correctly anticipate the direction of change in interest rates in the future, the lender would own a mortgage note that offers an inferior yield if interest rates rise above the upper cap.

renegotiable-rate mortgage loan
A mortgage loan in which the parties have the option to renegotiate the interest rate charged on the loan.

Another variation is the **renegotiable mortgage.** In this type of loan the terms may be renegotiated at specified intervals. For example, while the term of the mortgage may be twenty-five years, the lender may renegotiate the interest rate every three to five years. If interest rates rise, the borrower is forced to pay the higher and then current rate of interest.

graduated-payment mortgage loan
A mortgage loan in which the periodic payments rise over time.

A third variation on the conventional mortgage is the **graduated-payment mortgage.** Under this type of mortgage loan the amount of the payment is not fixed (although the rate of interest may be fixed) but rises during the lifetime of the loan. Such loans may be beneficial to home owners who anticipate rising incomes that can service the higher mortgage payments over time. However, such loans could prove to be disastrous if the borrower's income does not rise or if other expenses consume any increase in income. Then the burden of the debt would obviously increase, and since the loan is secured by the home, default could lead to the borrower losing the property.

Besides variable interest rate, renegotiable-rate, and graduated-payment mortgage loans, shorter term mortgage loans have developed. With this type of loan, the borrower has the funds for a short time, such as three years, pays the interest for the term of the loan, but then refinances the loan at the end of the time period. Such an arrangement obviously protects the lender from being locked into a lower rate if interest rates increase. However, these loans place borrowers in a precarious position, because they may not be able to find new financing when the loan becomes due.

Besides showing the higher mortgage rates that existed from 1980 to 1985 and lead to the creative mortgage loan, Figure 22.2 also shows the different mortgage environment from 1987 through 1992. Fluctuations in mortgage rates were smaller and in 1992 mortgage rates fell to their lowest levels in twenty years. While the slow market for homes in 1991 and 1992 and the corresponding smaller demand for new mortgages contributed to these lower rates, the primary cause was the lower level of interest rates in general. The Federal Reserve reduced the discount rate to encourage economic expansion. Declining yields on savings accounts and certificates of deposit reduced the cost of funds to the lending institutions, allowing them to make profitable mortgage loans at lower interest rates.

These lower mortgage rates resulted in many homeowners refinancing existing mortgages. Just as a firm may refinance its high interest rate bonds when rates fall, so homeowners may also refinance by borrowing at the current, lower rate and using the funds to pay off the older, more costly mortgage. A firm, however, will not automatically retire existing debt when interest rates fall because there are costs associated with refinancing. The same applies to individuals who have to pay the costs associated with refinancing. These costs will vary among lending institutions and may include application fees, points, and closing costs (e.g., lawyers' fees as the new loan is recorded). A new survey and new title insurance may also be required. Thus, lower interest rates do not automatically lead to refinancing an existing mortgage since the interest savings over the years of the new loan must cover the upfront costs of refinancing.[8]

LAND AND RENTAL PROPERTIES

An alternative means to invest in real estate is to purchase land and/or rental properties. Land is either unimproved or improved. **Unimproved land** is raw land, whereas **improved land** has curbs and sewers, has buildings constructed on it, or has been cleared for farming or other agricultural uses. Unimproved land is a passive investment that may require little action on the part of the investor. However, improved land may require considerable attention from the investor.

unimproved land
Land that has not been cleared and that lacks improvements, such as curbs and gutters.

improved land
Land that has been cleared or that includes improvements, such as curbs, gutters, or buildings.

Leverage and Tax Write-offs

The primary appeal of investing in real estate is, of course, the potential return on the investment. This return is enhanced by the ability to use substantial amounts of financial leverage and to obtain advantageous tax write-offs, which may be seen in the following simple example. A piece of land costs $100,000. It may be purchased with a 20 percent down payment, with the balance being financed through a mortgage loan at 12 percent annual interest rate. The individual's investment out of pocket is only $20,000.

Land cost	$100,000
Loan	80,000
Equity	20,000

---

[8] Some of these costs (e.g., points required to obtain the new mortgage) are tax-deductible. Others are not tax-deductible but may be recaptured when the home is sold. The tax treatment of the costs of refinancing further complicates the decision to refinance an existing mortgage.

Several of the costs of carrying this investment (e.g., interest and property taxes) are tax-deductible. If the property tax rate is 3 percent, then the deductible expenses are

Interest	$ 9,600
Property tax	+3,000
	$12,600

If the individual is in the 28 percent tax bracket, the effective cost of carrying the land is reduced to

$$\$12,600(1 - 0.28) = \$8,640.$$

There is a tax savings of $3,960 ($12,600 − $8,640). For an initial cash outlay of $20,000 and an annual cash outlay (after adjusting for taxes) of $8,640, the individual has control of over $100,000 worth of land.

The ability to use a large amount of borrowed funds and the capacity to write off certain (and important) expenses against taxable income increase the attractiveness of investing in nonresidential real estate. Although the use of debt financing is not limited to investments in real estate, the ability to apply leverage is greater. The investor's capacity to use leverage in investments in stocks and bonds is subject to the margin requirements set by the Federal Reserve. And these requirements are considerably higher than the down payments required to purchase real estate.

Of course, the use of a substantial amount of leverage does increase the element of risk. However, many investors believe that the continuation of inflation will tend to increase real estate values. The potential for loss is viewed as being smaller than the potential for profits, which justifies bearing the risk that results from the use of a large amount of financial leverage.

Unimproved Land

Unimproved land by itself produces nothing and hence cannot generate a flow of income. Any income generated is the result of using the land for some activity, such as farming or mining. Even cutting down trees for sale as firewood requires expenditures of labor and tools. Since unimproved land cannot by itself generate income, the primary source of the return on such an investment is the potential for price appreciation.

For land to appreciate in value, it must have some potential for use in the future, such as lots for building, acreage for farming, or rights for mining. For the investment to earn a return commensurate with the risk, the investor must acquire land with potential for future value. Such future value may be difficult to foresee, as it depends on location, zoning requirements, road frontage or access to roads, and proximity to population centers. These factors can and do vary. Zoning laws may change, or the owner may be able to obtain a variance. New roads are built and the population moves. All of these factors affect the value of land and in some cases even cause its value to decline.

The potential return on an investment in unimproved land may be reduced by several other factors. First, many state and local governments tax land as well as other real estate investments. Second, land may be difficult to sell. Although the title can be readily transferred, finding a buyer may take several months or even years. Third, real estate commissions on the sale of land may be as high as 10 percent of the sale price. Therefore, the price of the land must appreciate sufficiently to recoup these commissions plus any other fees that may be associated with the sale (e.g., lawyer's fees) and still earn a profit.

To be a good investment, land must have the traits of other investments: marketability, income, and the potential for capital appreciation. Land offers little income, may be very difficult to sell, and has varying potential for future use. The investor should not be swayed by ads claiming "Buy land; they aren't making it any more!" There are still many acres of undeveloped land, but only that land which has the potential for future use will prove to be a desirable investment today. For example, there are undeveloped acres in the middle of Maine that could be very valuable for timber. However, if there is no access to the land and the trees, they are of little value.

The valuation of land, then, is essentially no different than the valuation of any investment. The estimated future cash flow is discounted back to the present at the appropriate discount rate. Therein lies the clue to the problem of investing in unimproved land. The future cash flows are very uncertain, and the discount factor is quite subjective. For most investors, raw, undeveloped land is a poor investment. However, for those knowledgeable individuals who are willing to wait, forgo current income, and even pay out cash to carry the land, the return may be considerable if economic trends alter the unimproved land's potential.

Improved Land

The investor may buy improved land, which includes land on which buildings, such as apartments, are constructed, or land with other improvements, such as curbs and sewers. Such purchases are alternatives to investments in financial assets, but they may also be viewed as business ventures. As with any business venture, the management of improved land requires special knowledge that differs markedly from the knowledge employed in the selection of financial assets. The investor needs to know such things as zoning and other land-use laws, the laws regulating the relationship between landlord and tenant, and the management of accounts receivable (i.e., rent owed).

This does not mean that the individual should avoid purchasing and managing improved land as a viable investment. Obviously the investor must select among options that include both financial assets and business ventures. Investing in improved real estate is a possible alternative, but so are many other business ventures, which may range from becoming a dealer in collectibles to the raising of champion dogs or publishing books. Ultimately, each individual must decide how to allocate his or her savings among the many possible alternatives. These investments may offer superior returns if the investor has the specialized knowledge and capacity to manage them. However, many individuals lack either the knowledge or the inclination to risk their savings on business ventures and thus select financial assets. While business ventures are beyond the scope of this book, the individual should realize that such ventures offer alternatives to investments in financial assets.

For those investors who are willing to invest in rental property, the potential benefits are illustrated in Exhibit 22.2. This exhibit projects the cash flow estimates for an investment in a rental property and illustrates several facets of investing in

Exhibit 22.2 ✦ CASH FLOW PROJECTIONS FOR A REAL ESTATE INVESTMENT

Year (1)	Rents (2)	Depreciation (3)	Cost Basis (4)	Value (5)	Maintenance (6)	Mortgage Payment (7)
1	$12,000.00	$5,000.00	$95,000.00	$105,000.00	$4,000.00	$10,710.30
2	12,600.00	5,000.00	90,000.00	110,250.00	4,200.00	10,710.30
3	13,230.00	5,000.00	85,000.00	115,762.50	4,410.00	10,710.30
4	13,891.50	5,000.00	80,000.00	121,550.63	4,630.50	10,710.30
5	14,586.08	5,000.00	75,000.00	127,628.16	4,862.03	10,710.30
6	15,315.38	5,000.00	70,000.00	134,009.56	5,105.13	10,710.30
7	16,081.15	5,000.00	65,000.00	140,710.04	5,360.38	10,710.30
8	16,885.21	5,000.00	60,000.00	147,745.54	5,628.40	10,710.30
9	17,729.47	5,000.00	55,000.00	155,132.82	5,909.82	10,710.30
10	18,615.94	5,000.00	50,000.00	162,889.46	6,205.31	10,710.30
11	19,546.74	5,000.00	45,000.00	171,033.94	6,515.58	10,710.30
12	20,524.07	5,000.00	40,000.00	179,585.63	6,841.36	10,710.30
13	21,550.28	5,000.00	35,000.00	188,564.91	7,183.43	10,710.30
14	22,627.79	5,000.00	30,000.00	197,993.16	7,542.60	10,710.30
15	23,759.18	5,000.00	25,000.00	207,892.82	7,919.73	10,710.30
16	24,947.14	5,000.00	20,000.00	218,287.46	8,315.71	10,710.30
17	26,194.50	5,000.00	15,000.00	229,201.83	8,731.50	10,710.30
18	27,504.22	5,000.00	10,000.00	240,661.92	9,168.07	10,710.30
19	28,879.43	5,000.00	5,000.00	252,695.02	9,626.48	10,710.30
20	30,323.40	5,000.00	0.00	265,329.77	10,107.80	10,710.30

such properties: the initial tax savings, the reinvestment of the cash flow generated by the property, and the appreciation of the rental property's value. The benefits of such an investment require time. This particular example has a 20-year time horizon. While the investor may sell the property at any time (assuming that a buyer can be found), rental properties should be viewed as long-term investments whose returns are a combination of initial tax advantages, annual flows of cash, and potential long-term growth in property values.

In the example in Exhibit 22.2, the investor purchases a rental property for $100,000. The purchase is financed with a $20,000 down payment and a conventional loan for $80,000 at 12 percent for 20 years. To simplify the analysis, the loan is amortized (i.e., retired) in 20 equal annual installments of $10,710.30 (column 7). The breakdown of this annual payment into interest and principal repayment is given in columns 8 and 9, respectively, in the exhibit.

The first two columns give the year and the annual rental income. Rents are assumed to increase annually by 5 percent. Thus rental income is $12,000 in the first year but grows to $30,323.40 during the twentieth year. The third and fourth columns give the depreciation expense on the property and the resulting cost basis of the property. To simplify the analysis, the property is depreciated by an equal annual amount ($5,000) for 20 years. Thus the cost basis declines annually by

(Exhibit 22.2 CONTINUED)

Year (1)	Interest (8)	Principal Repayment (9)	Earnings before Taxes (10)	Taxes (11)	Net Earnings (12)	Cash Flow (13)	Cumulative Cash Flow (14)
1	$9,600.00	$1,110.30	$−6,600.00	$−1,980.00	$−4,620.00	$−730.30	$−730.30
2	9,466.76	1,243.54	−6,066.76	−1,820.03	−4,246.73	−490.27	−1,308.21
3	9,317.54	1,392.76	−5,497.54	−1,649.26	−3,848.28	−241.04	−1,706.23
4	9,150.41	1,559.89	−4,889.41	−1,466.82	−3,422.59	17.52	−1,893.46
5	8,963.22	1,747.08	−4,239.17	−1,271.75	−2,967.42	285.50	−1,835.17
6	8,753.57	1,956.73	−3,543.32	−1,063.00	−2,480.32	562.95	−1,492.44
7	8,518.76	2,191.54	−2,797.99	−839.40	−1,958.60	849.86	−821.67
8	8,255.78	2,454.52	−1,998.98	−599.69	−1,399.28	1,146.20	225.92
9	7,961.23	2,749.07	−1,141.59	−342.48	−799.11	1,451.82	1,704.85
10	7,631.34	3,078.96	−220.71	−66.21	−154.50	1,766.54	3,675.98
11	7,261.87	3,448.43	769.29	230.79	538.50	2,090.07	6,207.17
12	6,848.06	3,862.24	1,834.65	550.40	1,284.26	2,422.02	9,374.04
13	6,384.59	4,325.71	2,982.26	894.68	2,087.58	2,761.87	13,260.80
14	5,865.50	4,844.80	4,219.69	1,265.91	2,953.78	3,108.98	17,961.08
15	5,284.13	5,426.17	5,555.32	1,666.60	3,088.73	3,462.56	23,578.97
16	4,632.99	6,077.31	6,998.44	2,099.53	4,898.90	3,821.59	30,230.04
17	3,903.71	6,806.59	8,559.29	2,567.79	5,991.50	4,184.91	38,042.55
18	3,086.92	7,623.38	10,249.23	3,074.77	7,174.46	4,551.08	47,158.74
19	2,172.11	8,538.19	12,080.84	3,624.25	8,456.59	4,918.40	57,736.18
20	1,147.53	9,562.77	14,068.87	4,220.42	9,847.65	5,284.88	69,949.40

$5,000, so that at the end of the 20 years, the cost basis has been reduced to $0. (In reality the asset could not be completely depreciated because there would be some residual value, such as the value of the land, that cannot be depreciated. The rate at which the asset may be depreciated and the time period over which it is depreciated is established by the tax laws. Under current tax law residential is depreciated over 27.5 years and other real estate is depreciated over 31.5 years.) While the asset is being depreciated, its market value may increase. In this example the value is assumed to increase by 5 percent annually, so the property that initially cost $100,000 is worth $265,329.77 at the end of 20 years.

To determine the net income generated by the property, all expenses must be deducted from the rental income. These expenses include depreciation (column 3), interest (column 8), and maintenance expenses (column 6). This last expense includes all the operating expenses (e.g., insurance and property taxes) and repair expenses associated with the building. This expense rises by 5 percent annually to adjust for increases in the running expenses that tend to occur over time. The total expenses are subtracted from the rental income to determine taxable income (column 10).

The tax paid on the income is given in column 11. A tax rate of 30 percent is assumed in this example, but the actual tax that would be paid would depend on the rates set by Congress plus any taxes established by state legislatures. After the taxes have been paid, net earnings are determined (column 12). In this illustration the operation generates a loss during the first ten years. The investor uses these losses to offset income from other properties and thus to reduce taxes paid on the other income. These initial losses are an important tax shelter that reduce the investor's total taxes. For example, this tax shelter reduces taxes by $1,980 in year 1 and continues to reduce taxes for the next ten years. However, eventually the property earns income and requires the investor to pay taxes.

The individual who invests in rental property is more concerned with cash flow than with net earnings. Cash flow may be used for reinvestment purposes and is the sum of net earnings plus depreciation minus principal repayment (column 12 plus column 3 minus column 9 = column 13). Depreciation is added back to net income because it is a *non-cash* expense that allocates the cost of the investment over a period of time. Since it is a non-cash expense, it is a source of funds that may be reinvested. Principal repayment is subtracted because it is a cash outlay that has not been previously subtracted. All other cash outlays were tax-deductible expenses (e.g., interest and maintenance) and therefore were deducted from the rental income to determine taxable income. Principal repayment is not a tax-deductible expense; thus, to determine the cash flow generated by the operation, this repayment must be subtracted from the sum of net income plus depreciation.

If the cash being produced exceeds the cash outflow, the property is generating a positive cash flow. If, however, the cash coming in is less than the cash going out, the cash flow is negative. In this illustration, the cash flow is negative for the first three years, so the owner of the property will have to put in more funds to cover this shortage. This causes the negative cumulative cash flow in column 14 initially to rise. However, in year 4 the property starts to generate positive cash flow. The cumulative cash flow becomes positive in year 8 and continues to grow as these funds are reinvested.

In this example, the cash flow is reinvested in other assets that earn 12 percent annually. It is presumed that the investor can earn at least 12 percent because if other alternatives were not available, the mortgage loan could be paid off more rapidly. Since the loan has an interest rate of 12 percent, it is reasonable to assume that the cash flow can be reinvested at that rate. At the end of 20 years, the investor will have accumulated $69,949.11 by reinvesting the cash flow received each year.

The investor should note that in this illustration net earnings start to exceed cash flow in year 15. The principal repayments have risen sufficiently that they exceed depreciation. Thus while the operation now appears profitable, the investor has a large principal repayment that (1) is not tax deductible and (2) consumes cash. Unlike the early years when the cash generated exceeded earnings, earnings now exceed the cash being generated.[9]

If the individual holds the property to the end of the time period, the investor has $69,949.11 through the reinvestment of the cash flow plus property worth $265,329.77. Thus, the original $20,000 investment has grown to $335,278.88. Of course, the individual over time has invested a total of $100,000 in the property as

---

[9] It is possible that the taxes owed on the income will exceed the cash being generated which could occur if principal repayment consumes the cash.

the mortgage is retired. However, while the total investment is $100,000, the final value of the investor's assets (before tax)[10] is $335,278.88—the $100,000 invested in the property, plus the assets acquired through the reinvestment of the cash flow, plus the appreciation in the property's value. Of course, for this result to occur in this example, the value of the property and the rental income must increase annually by 5 percent. Changes in the growth rate of expenses, changes in the tax laws, and the inability to earn 12 percent annually on the accumulated cash flow will also affect the return ultimately earned on the investment in the rental property.

Uncertainties and Investing in Real Estate

While Exhibit 22.2 illustrated the fundamentals to include when determining a real estate investment's cash flow, it also highlights the major factors to consider when acquiring income-earning properties. Forecasting the cash flow is crucial to real estate investments, but this cash flow is very uncertain because so few of the pieces of the analysis are fixed in the present and because the time dimension is so long. The major factors that may be fixed include the cost of the investment, the depreciation schedules, and the cost of financing the mortgage loan.[11] Even the mortgage loan payment could vary if the loan has a variable interest rate.

All the other factors in the analysis are subject to change. For example, rental income could (and probably will) vary with changes in occupancy rates. Rental properties rarely remain 100 percent occupied. Instead, rental income will fluctuate even though the long-term trend in rents is positive (they increase when prices in general rise).

Operating expenses may also fluctuate. Certainly inflationary (and deflationary) pressures will have an impact on expenses. Maintenance and repairs, property taxes, insurance, and management expenses will tend to rise over time. Some expenses (e.g., insurance and especially liability coverage) may rise erratically and perhaps dramatically. Such fluctuations in expenses, along with fluctuations in rental income, make forecasting cash flow many years into the future extremely difficult. Current estimates of future cash flow must be viewed as tentative at best.

In addition to the cash flow generated, the return on an investment in real estate significantly depends upon the appreciation in the value of the asset. In Exhibit 22.2, it was assumed that the value of the property increased annually at 5 percent. If the property had grown at a higher rate, the investment would have been more profitable. Of course, the converse also holds. Unfortunately many individuals act as if property values will only rise, but it is certainly possible for property values to decline.

Appreciation in real estate values critically depends on the local economy. Some geographic areas tend to be more recession-proof than others. For example, the region around Washington, D.C., may prosper during different economic environ-

---

[10] The illustration does not assume that any tax has been paid on the earnings generated by the reinvestment of the cash flow. Nor does it consider any capital gains tax on the property if it were sold.

[11] Even though Congress may change depreciation schedules for new investments, investments made under previous depreciation schedules would not be adversely affected.

ments, but other areas have experienced periods of rapid growth followed by stagnation. During the early 1980s the oil boom produced strong real estate markets in Texas and Colorado. However, the late 1980s were the exact opposite as many properties in Texas and Colorado remained vacant, and prices declined instead of rising.

The individual must also realize that noneconomic factors may affect real estate investments. The political climate may change. For example, rent control or rent stabilization can be imposed. While such laws generally are not applied to commercial properties, they may be applied to residential apartment buildings.

Rental properties are obviously long-term investments and may generate cash flow for many years. They are certainly not liquid assets, and they may also lack marketability. While title to the property may be transferred, such transfers require a buyer. It may take a considerable amount of time and expense (e.g., real estate brokerage commissions, legal fees, and transfer taxes) to sell rental properties. This will be particularly true during periods of high interest rates, low occupancy rates, or political uncertainty. Of course, accepting a lower price will facilitate the sale.

This discussion suggests that real estate investments are fraught with uncertainty. However, they can play an important role in an individual's well-diversified portfolio. While such investments cannot meet financial goals by providing funds for emergencies, real estate may be an excellent means to generate cash flow plus appreciation through growth in the value of the property.

LIMITED PARTNERSHIPS

partnership
An unincorporated business owned by two or more individuals.

Investing in and managing rental property is a business enterprise. It is virtually impossible for the investor to participate passively in such real estate ownership.[12] However, the investor may buy shares, called "units," in limited **partnerships** that own and manage real estate. Like the rental property discussed in the previous illustration, these partnerships offer investors a possible return from cash flows and from appreciation in real estate values.

In a real estate partnership there are two types of partners: the general partners who manage the real estate and the limited partners. The limited partners provide the funds to acquire the properties but are passive owners who do not manage the real estate. Unlike the general partners, the limited partners have limited liability. Since the business is a partnership and not a corporation, the limited partners directly reap the benefits of any profits earned.

In the initial years of the partnership (when the properties are being developed), the partnership generally operates at a loss. After the buildings are completed, the partnership may still generate losses from depreciation expenses. Once again this depreciation expense is a non-cash expense (i.e., it does not require a disbursement of funds) that allocates the cost of investment in the properties over a period of time. While the buildings are being depreciated, these properties may

---

[12]The investor may employ a real estate agent to handle the properties, but this, of course, will consume part of the return earned by the properties.

generate cash that, when distributed to the limited partners, is a return of their capital invested in the project. Such return of capital is *not* income and hence not subject to income taxes. Instead the partners' cost basis in the investment is reduced.

The initial operating losses and the depreciation expense shelter cash payments to the limited partners from income taxation. The losses may also be used to offset income from limited partnerships that are profitable. After a period of years, the cost of the investment will be recouped through the depreciation expenses. When the properties are sold, any appreciation in value of the properties will be treated as capital gains.

The tax laws pertaining to investing in limited partnerships and the tax shelters associated with them are exceedingly complex. These investments are primarily of interest to sophisticated investors. Investors with only modest sums to invest or who are in lower tax brackets should probably choose a home or condominium as a means to invest in real estate.

REAL ESTATE INVESTMENT TRUSTS

One way to invest indirectly in real estate is to buy shares in **real estate investment trusts** (commonly called **REITs**). These real estate trusts are another type of closed-end investment company. They receive the special tax treatment granted other investment companies (e.g., mutual funds). As long as a REIT derives 75 percent of its income from real estate (e.g., interest on mortgage loans and rents) and distributes at least 95 percent of the income as cash dividends, the trust is exempt from federal income tax. Thus, REITs, like mutual funds and other closed-end investment companies, are conduits through which earnings pass to the shareholders.

REIT
Real estate investment trust; a closed-end investment company that specializes in real estate or mortgage investments.

Shares of REITs are bought and sold like the stocks of other companies. Some are traded on the New York Stock Exchange (e.g., HRE Properties), while others are traded on the American Stock Exchange (e.g., Washington REIT) and in the over-the-counter markets (e.g., Price REIT). The existence of these markets means that the shares of REITs may be readily sold. This ease of marketability certainly differentiates shares of REITs from other types of real estate investments.

Real estate investment trusts also differ from some forms of investments in real estate because they offer the potential for monetary income. Most trusts distribute virtually all of their earned income to maintain their tax status. This often results in significant dividend yields on investments in these shares. Selected dividend yields are illustrated in Exhibit 22.3, which presents the prices of the stock of five REITs, their dividends, and the dividend yield (i.e., the dividend divided by the price of the stock).

Whereas other firms may seek to maintain stable dividends and increase them only after there has been an increase in earnings that management anticipates will continue, the dividends of REITs often fluctuate from year to year. This is because tax regulations require the distribution of earnings in order to maintain the trust's tax status. Thus, as earnings fluctuate, so do the dividends that are distributed. This fluctuation in earnings and hence in dividends is illustrated in Figure 22.3, which presents the dividends per quarter for Realty ReFund. As may be seen in the

Exhibit 22.3 ◆ SELECTED REITs AND THEIR DIVIDEND YIELDS

Firm	Price of Stock as of 1/3/93	Annual Dividend	Dividend Yield
HRE Properties	$11⅝	$1.08	9.3%
Pennsylvania REIT	23½	1.80	7.7
Santa Anita REIT	17½	1.36	7.8
United Dominion REIT	25¼	1.32	5.2
Washington REIT	20⅛	0.84	4.2

Source: The Wall Street Journal, January 4, 1993.

exhibit, the dividends varied almost every quarter from 1980 through 1988. Shares of REITs, therefore, may not be desirable investments for individuals who need steady and stable sources of income. These investors may find such fluctuations in dividends undesirable and probably would prefer other stocks that offer high yields, such as those of utilities.

Classification of REITs

equity trust
A real estate investment trust that specializes in acquiring real estate for subsequent rental income.

REITs may be grouped according to either the types of assets they acquire or their capital structure. **Equity trusts** own property and rent it to other firms (i.e., they

Figure 22.3 ◆ QUARTERLY DIVIDENDS FOR REALTY ReFUND, 1980–1992

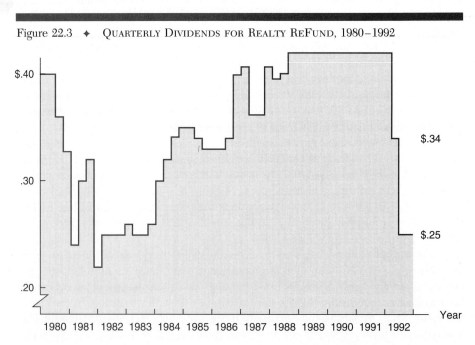

Exhibit 22.4   SELECTED REITS BY TYPES OF ASSETS AND CAPITAL STRUCTURES

Firm	Real Estate Owned as a Percent of Total Assets	Debt Ratio (Debt to Total Assets)
United Dominion Realty Trust	97.1%	59.7%
IRT Properties	82.1	49.3
HRE Properties	94.2	25.3
Washington Real Estate Investment Trust	66.5	11.6

Firm	Mortgages as a Percent of Total Assets	Debt Ratio (Debt to Total Assets)
Realty ReFund	98.9%	76.2%
Lomas & Nettleton Mortgage Investors	61.0	68.7
BRT Realty Trust	92.9	66.8

Source: Annual Reports.

lease their property to others). **Mortgage trusts** make loans to develop property and finance buildings. There is a considerable difference between these two approaches to investing in real estate. Loans to help finance real estate, especially developmental loans, can earn high interest rates, but some of these loans can be very risky. Contractors may be unable to sell or lease the completed buildings, which may consequently cause them to default on their loans. In addition, any inflation in the value of the property cannot be enjoyed by the lender, who owns a fixed obligation.

In an equity trust the REIT owns the property and rents space. This can also be risky because the properties may remain vacant. Unleased property, of course, does not generate any revenue, but the owner still has expenses, such as insurance, maintenance, and depreciation. Like any operation with few variable costs and many fixed expenses, there can be large fluctuations in the earnings of equity trusts. However, should there be an increase in property values, the trust may experience capital appreciation.

The second method for differentiating REITs is according to their capital structure or the extent to which they use debt financing. Some trusts use virtually no debt financing, while others use a large amount of leverage. The latter can be very risky investments, because the trusts borrow from one group either to lend or to invest directly in real estate. If their loans turn sour and the borrowers default or if the properties remain unrented, the trusts that use extensive financial leverage will have difficulty meeting their own debt obligations.

These differences among REITs are illustrated in Exhibit 22.4. The exhibit is constructed in two parts. The top half shows equity trusts whose primary assets are real estate properties. The second half presents trusts whose primary assets are

mortgage trust
A real estate investment trust that specializes in loans secured by real estate.

REAL ESTATE AT A DISCOUNT?

Real estate tends to appreciate in value with inflation; however, for tax purposes the cost of the property may be depreciated. Thus, the value of real estate on a firm's balance sheet (i.e., the book value) may be less than the replacement cost or current market value of the property. In addition, since REITs must distribute their earnings, these stocks may be sensitive to changes in interest rates. If interest rates rise, the value of REIT stocks tends to fall. When this occurs, the price of the stock may sell below its per-share equity value, which in turn may be understated because of the understated book value of the REIT's properties.

Since REIT shares may sell below their equity per share, should investors consider these REITs attractive? The answer is "Not necessarily." If a REIT's shares are selling for less than the equity per share, that alone is insufficient justification to purchase the stock. The investor should determine the cash flow (profits plus depreciation minus principal repayment) generated by the properties. If the properties are generating sufficient cash flow, the REIT may be considered attractive. However, if the cash flow is insufficient, the shares are unattractive even if they sell at a discount from equity per share.

If the REIT is truly undervalued, the stock may be tailor-made for a takeover. The company taking over will be obtaining property at less than current cost. It may then sell the pieces of the REIT's property individually at their current market value. Since the pieces are more valuable than the sum of the parts, this strategy earns profits for the aggressive firm doing the takeover.

mortgages. The entries in each section are listed in descending order according to their debt ratios (column 3). Thus, Washington Real Estate Investment Trust is an equity trust with very little debt, while Realty ReFund uses a great deal of leverage because over 76 percent of its assets are financed by debt.

In addition to equity trusts and mortgage trusts there are finite life REITs (called FREITs). Regular REITs have an indefinite life, but FREITs do not. Their real estate assets will be liquidated within a specified time period, and the funds will be distributed to stockholders. For example, EQK Realty Investors I was sold to the public in 1985 and will be liquidated after 12 years. Of course, such forced sales of the properties could prove to be deleterious to stockholders if the market for real estate is weak when the sales must be made.

Returns Earned by Investments in REITs

Initially REITs were very popular, and several hundred came into existence. Many were financed with substantial amounts of debt. Commercial banks were only too happy to lend them funds because the loans were very profitable for the banks. Not only did the banks lend money to REITs, but they also formed advisory services and received management fees from the trusts.

While interest was being received and properties were leased, the extensive use of financial leverage posed no problems. However, when short-term interest rates rose, many mortgage trusts found that they were unable to collect the interest owed them. Partially completed buildings were left unfinished, as there was virtually no demand for the properties. Those properties that did sell often went for prices that produced losses for the builders, who in turn defaulted on loans from the trusts. The trusts were then unable to meet their own interest payments. A substantial number defaulted on their debt. Some creditors seized properties, and a long period of reorganization for the trusts followed.

The REITs that weathered the storm are much healthier firms today. However, this past experience does suggest that an individual should invest in REITs cautiously. The investor should prefer those trusts with proven records of performance. Obviously the properties must be consistently leased to generate income, so fluctuations in occupancy rates suggest the trust will experience fluctuating revenues and income. The investor should also examine the fees charged to manage the properties, especially to learn if these expenses are related to the properties' performance. In addition, the trust should use only a modest amount of debt financing, and its properties should be diversified with regard to type and/or location. If the trust uses a substantial amount of financial leverage or if it invests in only one type of property (e.g., apartments) or only one location (e.g., California), that will tend to increase the trust's (and the investor's) risk exposure.

The Valuation of Shares in REITs

The valuation of shares in REITs is essentially the same as the valuation of any other security. The valuation model for common stocks that was presented in Chapter 8 also applies to the shares of REITs. According to that model, the value of stock depends on the dividends that the firm will pay in the future brought back to their present value at the appropriate discount rate. However, the application of this model is particularly difficult with regard to the shares of REITs.

First, there is the problem of estimating future earnings and dividends. Although many firms grow and their dividends follow a steady pattern of growth in response to higher earnings, the dividends of REITs fluctuate from quarter to quarter. In many cases the dividend cannot grow because the earnings are not retained but are distributed.

Earnings and dividends may be increased if the firm successfully increases its use of financial leverage. But this may also increase the element of risk, which may offset the value of the increased dividends. This suggests a second important problem in the valuation of the shares of REITs: the determination of the appropriate discount factor. Many REITs are very risky firms. Some have issued a substantial amount of debt, and others own real estate that may lie unrented. Risk is inherent in both sides of a REIT's balance sheet. For many of these firms, the type of assets they own and the sources from which they obtain financing may result in a substantial amount of both business risk and financial risk.

If the investor can account for these risks and estimate future dividends, the valuation of the stock becomes straightforward. This is illustrated in the following example, which uses the security valuation model presented in Chapter 8 and the shares of Washington REIT. Washington REIT is an equity trust so its earnings and dividends can grow as rents increase. From 1972 through 1991 its dividends grew annually by approximately 12 percent.[13] If the current dividend is $1.00 and the

---

[13]The 12 percent growth was taken from Washington REIT's 1991 annual report.

investor seeks a return of 15 percent and expects the *dividend to continue to grow annually at 12 percent,* the value of a share is

$$V = \frac{D_0(1 + g)}{k - g}$$

$$= \frac{1.00(1 + 0.12)}{0.15 - 0.12}$$

$$= \$37.33.$$

Any price below $37.33 produces a yield in excess of 15 percent, and any price above $37.33 produces a yield less than 15 percent.[14]

It must be emphasized that the value that any investor places on the shares through the use of this model is simply the result of the dividends that have been forecast and the application of the appropriate discount rate. This valuation model can only be as good as its inputs. Forecasting the future dividends of a REIT and determining the appropriate discount rate may be extremely difficult. However, the efficient market hypothesis suggests that the current price of a share in a publicly held REIT does appropriately value the future prospects of the firm.

Summary

This chapter has been devoted to three types of real estate investments: home ownership, land and rental properties, and real estate investment trusts (REITs).

Home ownership is a particularly attractive investment, since the individual must live somewhere. It may be more advantageous to own than to rent, especially if the cost of housing continues to rise. The federal income tax laws encourage investments in homes. In addition to untaxed income-in-kind, several expenses (e.g., interest and property taxes) are allowed as deductions in the determination of the individual's taxable income. Under some circumstances, capital gains taxes on the sale of a home may be deferred or even avoided.

Homes may be financed by mortgage loans that are secured by the property. Conventional mortgage loans are retired through monthly payments that include both interest and principal repayment. The federal government has followed a policy of encouraging investments in homes by guaranteeing some mortgage loans. These insurance programs are administered by the Federal Housing Administration and the Veterans Administration. The high interest rates of the early 1980s altered the supply of mortgage money and the terms under which it was obtained. Many mortgage loans use creative financing involving variable interest rates, graduated payments, or renegotiable interest rates. These features are designed to protect lenders

---

[14] A compound growth rate of 12 percent over two decades is exceptional. It is reasonable for the investor to anticipate lower growth, which would reduce the valuation.

and thus encourage them to make loans that they would not make under conventional terms.

Investors may also buy land and rental properties. Unimproved land may appreciate in value if there is potential use for the land in the future. An investment in rental properties is essentially a business venture and may earn a return from the cash flow generated by the properties and the potential for capital appreciation.

Real estate investment trusts (REITs) offer investors an alternative means to invest in real estate. These trusts are a type of investment company, and stockholders enjoy the same tax benefits given to the stockholders of other closed- and open-end investment companies. Real estate investment trusts either make loans to firms that develop and manage real estate or own properties and lease them.

The valuation of the shares of REITs is essentially the same as the valuation of any stock: Future dividend payments are brought back to the present value at the appropriate discount rate. However, estimating future dividends and determining the appropriate discount rate may be extremely difficult.

Security Summary

Real Estate

Source of return: Rental income and possible capital gains when the properties are sold.

Liquidity and marketability: Virtually no liquidity since selling real estate may require a considerable amount of time to find a buyer and transfer title. The secondary markets for real estate vary with the type of property, location, and economic conditions.

Sources of risk: Unsystematic risk from events that affect the property's value, such as occupancy rates, insurance costs, and property taxes. Systematic risk since many of the events affecting the value of one property (e.g., the cost of mortgage money) apply to all properties. Virtually no purchasing power risk since the values of properties tend to rise with the rate of inflation.

Taxation: Rental income is subject to income taxes but only after deducting expenses. The ability to use losses to offset other sources of income has been reduced by tax reform. Realized sales of properties may lead to capital gains taxes.

Terms to Remember

cost of debt
condominium
conventional mortgage loan
Federal Housing Administration (FHA)
Veterans Administration (VA)
creative financing
variable-interest-rate mortgage loan

renegotiable-rate mortgage loan
graduated-payment mortgage loan
unimproved and improved land
partnership
real estate investment trust (REIT)
REIT: equity trust
REIT: mortgage trust

Questions

1. What are the sources of risk and return from investing in a home?
2. What are the special tax advantages associated with home ownership? Do these advantages apply to renters or owners of condominiums?
3. Has an investment in a home been a good hedge against inflation?
4. What are several expenses associated with owning real estate?
5. What is financial leverage and how does it apply to investments in real estate?
6. What are the differences among conventional mortgages, VA-insured mortgages, and variable-interest-rate mortgages?
7. Why may a seller of a home accept a mortgage loan in partial payment?
8. What are real estate investment trusts? How are they both similar but different from corporations such as IBM and AT&T?
9. What differentiates a mortgage REIT from an equity REIT? Which should prove to be the better investment during a period of high interest rates and rising prices?
10. What is the cash flow associated with an investment in real estate? What impact will each of the following have on a rental property's cash flow?
    a. Increase in depreciation expense
    b. Decrease in rental income
    c. Increase in principal repayment
    d. Decrease in interest rates
11. What are the risks associated with investing in real estate? In what ways are they similar to the risks associated with investments in financial assets? Why may an investment in real estate be more risky than an investment in a stock or a bond?

Problems

1. Determine the annual repayment schedule for the first two years (i.e., interest owed, principal repayment, and balance owed) for each of the following. (Assume that only one payment is made annually.)
    a. a $60,000 conventional mortgage for 25 years at 10 percent
    b. a $60,000 conventional mortgage for 20 years at 10 percent
    c. a $60,000 conventional mortgage for 25 years at 8 percent
    d. a $50,000 conventional mortgage for 25 years at 10 percent
    Compare the total annual payment and the amount of interest in the first year of each of the above.
2. What is the expected cash flow and tax liability (or savings) for the first two years for an investment in an apartment building given the following information?

Cost of the building	$800,000
Cost of the land	200,000
Required down payment	25%
Interest on balance owed	10%
Annual principal repayment	20,000

Annual operating expenses	$ 30,000
Rent, year 1	120,000
Rent, year 2	140,000
Annual depreciation expense	40,000
Individual owner's income tax rate	30%

3. In 1978 the average and median prices of a single-family home were approximately $48,700 and $55,100, respectively. Ten years later, these prices had risen to $88,700 and $112,000. During the same time period the Dow Jones industrial average rose from 805 to 2149, and the Standard & Poor's 500 stock index rose from 96 to 271. Compare the annual rate of increase in home prices to the rate of growth in these two popular aggregate measures of the stock market.

4. As a result of lower interest rates, you are considering refinancing your mortgage. The existing mortgage has a 12 percent interest rate. The balance owed is $50,000 and the remaining term is eighteen years, and your annual payment (i.e., interest plus principal) is $6,897. A bank is willing to lend you the money at 10 percent to retire the old loan. The term of the new loan will be eighteen years, so you are not increasing the number of years required to pay off the mortgage. (There is no reason why the number of years should be the same. If there is a reduction in your mortgage payment, you could restore the original payment and retire the loan quicker. Or you may increase the amount of the loan and use the additional funds to improve the property.) Unfortunately the bank will charge you an application fee of $500 and an additional fee equal to 2 percent of the amount of the mortgage. (This fee is referred to as "points.") There will also be additional costs (e.g., court recording costs of the new mortgage) that are estimated to be $500. To help determine if it is profitable to refinance, answer the following questions.

   a. How much will you have to borrow to retire the loan, and what will be the annual payment required by the new loan?
   b. What is the difference between the annual payments under the new and the old mortgage? What is the implied course of action?
   c. What are the total expenses to obtain the new, cheaper loan?
   d. What is the present value (at 10 percent) of the reduction in your annual payment?
   e. If you compare your answers to c and d, what is the implied course of action?

Suggested Readings

General textbooks that cover the area of real estate (e.g., financing, valuation, land use, and development) include:

Floyd, Charles F. *Real Estate Principles.* 3d ed. Chicago: Dearborn Trade, 1992.

Unger, Maurice A., and George R. Karvel. *Real Estate: Principles and Practice,* 9th ed. Cincinnati: South-Western Publishing Co., 1990.

For a guide to the laws governing real estate, consult:

Corley, Robert N., Peter J. Shedd, and Charles F. Floyd. *Real Estate and the Law.* New York: Random House, 1982.

Information concerning investing in REITs may be obtained from the National Association of Real Estate Investment Trusts, 1101 17th Street NW, Suite 700, Washington, DC, 20036. See also:
"A Search for Income through Investments in REITs," *AAII Journal* (January 1993), 3–5.

Investing in undeveloped land is generally more speculative than acquiring rental properties. For a discussion of factors to consider when acquiring land, see:
Sheerin, James J. *The Complete Guide to Buying, Selling and Investing in Undeveloped Land.* Chicago: Probus Publishing, 1986.

The concept of diversification also applies to investing in real estate. A lack of transactions data makes it difficult to estimate the impact on unsystematic risk associated with real estate properties. One study, however, did conclude that the variance of returns declined as the number of office properties in the portfolio increased. See:
Grissom, Terry V., James L. Kuhle, and Carl H. Walther. "Diversification Works in Real Estate, Too," *Journal of Portfolio Management* (Winter 1987): 66–71.

For a general reference book on real estate that covers terminology, real estate forms, practical advice, and other basic source material on purchasing, selling, and investing in real estate, acquire:
Blankenship, Frank J. *The Prentice-Hall Real Estate Investor's Encyclopedia.* Englewood Cliffs, N.J.: Prentice-Hall, 1989.

Constructing

a

Diversified

Portfolio

THE FINAL THREE CHAPTERS IN THIS

V

TEXTBOOK ARE CONCERNED WITH THE

INDIVIDUAL'S PORTFOLIO. MANY INVESTORS

HAVE FOUND THAT MANAGING THEIR OWN PORTFOLIOS IS TIME-CONSUMING

AND EVEN UNREWARDING. THEY PASS THE SUPERVISION OF SPECIFIC ASSETS TO

THE MANAGERS OF INVESTMENT COMPANIES, ESPECIALLY MUTUAL FUNDS, AS

DESCRIBED IN CHAPTER 23.

Chapter 24 adds international investments. While such investments are similar to acquiring specific domestic stocks and bonds, one of the prime advantages of taking a global view of investments is the potential for diversification. Thus risk reduction is a primary reason for considering inclusion of international investments in one's portfolio.

The text ends with a discussion of portfolio planning and construction. This is not an easy task since it requires analytical thought and extensive calculations. There are many assets from which to choose; the economic environment can be very dynamic; the tax code is complex; and individuals' obligations and resources change throughout their lives. But the difficulty is no reason to avoid planning one's financial future and constructing a well-diversified portfolio that offers as high a return as possible consistent with one's willingness to bear risk.

23

INVESTMENT COMPANIES

ecause many investors find managing their own portfolios to be difficult or time-consuming or both, they purchase shares in investment companies. The managements of these companies then invest the funds primarily in a diversified portfolio of stocks and bonds. Since the individual owns shares in the investment company, it owns a claim on the diversified portfolio. Thus the saver can achieve the advantage of diversification while investing only a modest amount. Investment companies have been a popular vehicle for many investors, and they play a significant role in security markets.

There are two general types of investment companies: closed-end and open-end. The open-end investment company is commonly referred to as a mutual fund and is by far the more popular. This chapter discusses both types of investment companies, the mechanics of buying and selling their shares, the costs associated with these investments, and the potential sources of profit. Also included in the discussion are the various specialized investment companies, such as stock index funds or junk bond funds, that have recently developed and that offer investors a broad spectrum of investment alternatives to the direct purchase of stocks and bonds through brokers.

The chapter also discusses factors to consider when investing in mutual funds. These include hidden capital gains and losses, the age and size of the fund, and its previous performance. The chapter ends with a discussion of returns from investments in mutual funds. Special emphasis is given to the difference in the reported returns and the after-tax return the investor realizes, and the impact of fees in addition to sales fees, called loading charges, that the investor pays when the shares are purchased and sold.

❖ ❖ ❖

LEARNING OBJECTIVES

After completing this chapter you should be able to

1. Differentiate between closed-end and open-end investment companies.

2. Define *net asset value*.

3. Identify the costs of investing in mutual funds and closed-end investment companies.

4. List the advantages offered by investment companies.

5. Distinguish among the types of mutual funds.

6. Identify hidden capital gains and losses.

7. Differentiate between a unit trust and an actively managed portfolio.

8. Distinguish between loading fees, exit fees, and 12b-1 plans.

9. Adjust returns for risk.

INVESTMENT COMPANIES: ORIGINS AND TERMINOLOGY

Investment companies are not a recent development but were established in Britain during the 1860s. Initially, these investment companies were referred to as trusts because the securities were held in trust for the firm's stockholders. These firms

**closed-end investment
company**
*An investment company with a
fixed number of shares that are
bought and sold in the secondary
security markets.*

open-end investment company
*A mutual fund; an investment
company from which investors
buy shares and to which they
resell them.*

mutual fund
*An open-end investment
company.*

issued a specified number of shares and used the funds that were obtained through the sale of the stock certificates to acquire shares of other firms. Today the descendants of these companies are referred to as **closed-end investment companies** because the number of shares is fixed.

While the first trusts offered a specified number of shares, the most common type of investment company today does not. Instead, the number of shares varies as investors buy more shares from the trust or sell them back to the trust. This **open-end investment company** is commonly called a **mutual fund.** Such funds started in 1924 when Massachusetts Investor Trust offered new shares and redeemed (i.e., bought) existing shares on demand by stockholders.

The rationale for investment companies is very simple and appealing. The firms receive the funds from many investors, pool them, and purchase securities. The individual investors receive (1) the advantage of professional management of their money, (2) the benefit of ownership in a diversified portfolio, (3) the potential savings in commissions, as the investment company buys and sells in large blocks, and (4) custodial services (e.g., the storing of certificates and the collecting and disbursing of funds).

The advantages and services help to explain why both the number of mutual funds and the dollar value of their shares have grown since the 1940s. This growth is illustrated in Figure 23.1, which presents mutual funds' net sales and total assets from 1965 through 1990.[1] (Net sales are gross sales minus redemptions, which are shares sold back to the mutual fund.) During the 1970s the growth in mutual funds stopped as redemptions exceeded sales for several years. The redemptions, plus the general decline in the market, produced a 23 percent decline in mutual funds' total assets during 1974.

During the mid-1980s sales of mutual fund shares and total assets dramatically increased.[2] In 1986, net sales exceeded $148.8 billion, but the large decline in security prices during 1987 produced a major decline in the sales of mutual funds. In 1988, net sales rose only $2.8 billion. From 1965 to 1982, mutual fund assets grew from $35 billion to $77 billion. During the next eight years assets grew to over $570 billion, an increase of over 500 percent. The bull market of the 1980s obviously contributed to this increase. Rising stock prices plus the high net sales of shares during 1985 to 1987 generated this unprecedented growth in the funds' total assets.

Investment companies receive special tax treatment. Their earnings (i.e., dividend and interest income) and capital gains are exempt from taxation at the corporate level. Instead, these profits are taxed through their stockholders' income tax returns. Dividends, interest income, and capital gains realized (whether they are distributed or not) by the investment companies must be reported by their shareholders, who pay the appropriate income taxes.

For this reason, income that is received by investment companies and capital gains that are realized are usually distributed. The companies, however, offer their stockholders the option of having the firm retain and reinvest these distributions. While such reinvestments do not erase the stockholders' tax liabilities, they are an easy, convenient means to accumulate shares. The advantages offered by the dividend reinvestment plans of individual firms that were discussed in Chapter 10 also

---

[1] The assets of money market mutual funds are excluded.

[2] The value of closed-end investment companies also grew, but the total value of their assets
is less than one-tenth the value of mutual funds' assets.

Figure 23.1 ✦ INCOME MUTUAL FUNDS' NET SALES AND TOTAL ASSETS, 1965–1990

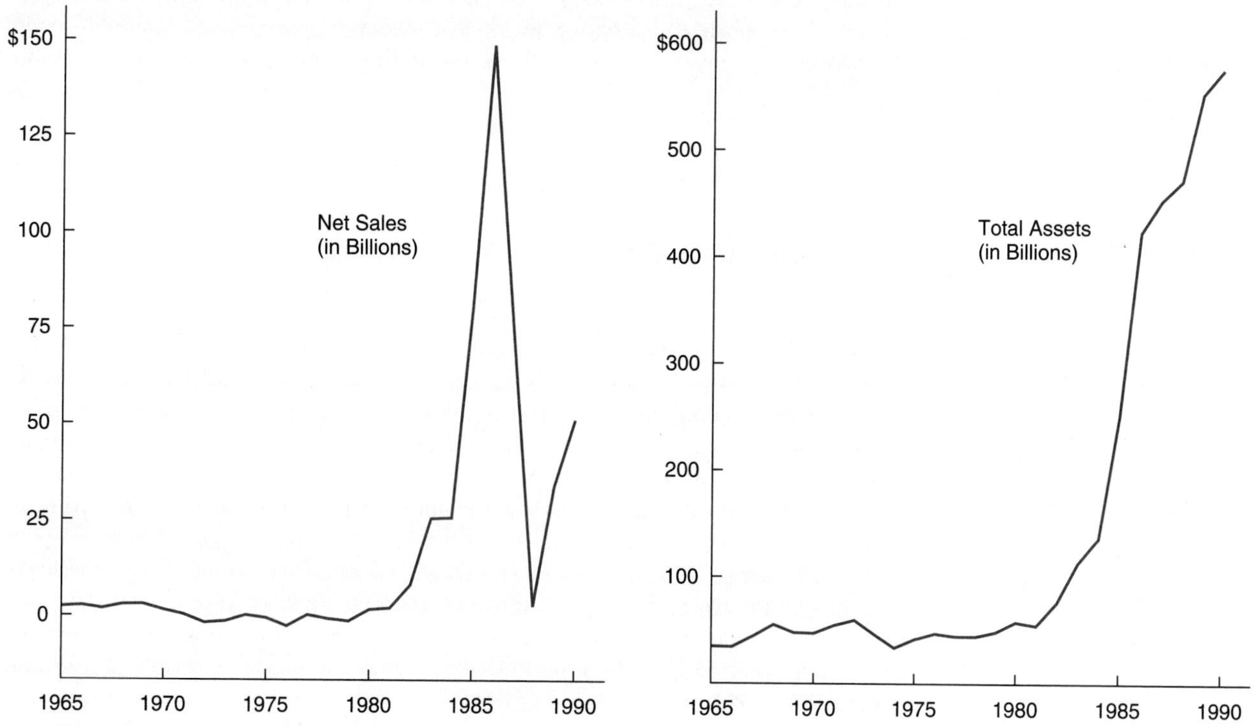

Net Sales
(in Billions)

Total Assets
(in Billions)

Source: 1991 Mutual Fund Fact Book, p. 20.

apply to the dividend reinvestment plans offered by investment companies. Certainly the most important of these advantages is the element of forced savings. Since the stockholder does not receive the money, there is no temptation to spend it. Rather, the funds are immediately channeled back into additional income-earning assets.

One term frequently encountered in a discussion of an investment company is its **net asset value.** The net asset value of an investment company is the total value of its stocks, bonds, cash, and other assets minus any liabilities (e.g., accrued fees). The net value of any share of stock in the investment company is the total net asset value of the fund divided by the number of shares outstanding. Thus, net asset value may be obtained as follows:

net asset value
The asset value of a share in an investment company; total assets minus total liabilities quantity divided by the number of shares outstanding.

Value of stock owned	$ 1,000,000
Value of debt owned	+1,500,000
Value of total assets	$ 2,500,000
Liabilities	− 100,000
Net worth	$ 2,400,000
Number of shares outstanding	1,000,000
Net asset value per share	$2.40

The net asset value is extremely important for the valuation of an investment company, for it gives the value of the shares should the company be liquidated. Changes in the net asset value, then, alter the value of the investment company's shares. Thus, if the value of the firm's assets appreciates, the net asset value will increase, which may also cause the price of the investment company's stock to increase.

CLOSED-END INVESTMENT COMPANIES

As was explained in the previous section, the difference between open-end and closed-end investment companies is the nature of their capital structure. The closed-end investment company has a set capital structure that may be composed of all stock or a combination of stock and debt. The number of shares and the dollar amount of debts that the company may issue are specified. In an open-end investment company (i.e., a mutual fund), the number of shares outstanding varies as investors purchase and redeem them. Since the closed-end investment company has a specified number of shares, an individual who wants to invest in a particular company must purchase existing shares from current stockholders. Conversely, any investor who owns shares and wishes to liquidate the position must sell the shares. Thus, the shares in closed-end investment companies are bought and sold in the open market, just as the stock of IBM is traded. Shares of these companies are traded on the New York Stock Exchange (e.g., Adams Express), on the American Stock Exchange (e.g., First Australia Fund), and in the over-the-counter markets (e.g., United Dominion Realty Trust[3]). Sales and prices of these shares are reported in the financial press along with the shares of other firms.

discount (from net asset value)
The extent to which the price of a closed-end investment company's stock sells below its net asset value.

premium (over net asset value)
The extent to which the price of a closed-end investment company's stock exceeds the share's net asset value.

The market value of these shares is related to the potential return on the investment. The market price of stock in a closed-end company, however, need not be the net asset value per share; it may be above or below this value, depending on the demand and the supply of stock in the secondary market. If the market price is below the net asset value of the shares, the shares are selling for a **discount.** If the market price is above the net asset value, the shares are selling for a **premium.**

These differences between the investment company's net asset value per share and the stock price are illustrated in Exhibit 23.1, which gives the price, the net asset value, and the discount or the premium for five closed-end investment companies. Three of the shares sold for a discount (i.e., below their net asset values) and two sold for a premium. The cause of this discount is not really known, but it is believed to be the result of taxation. The potential impact of capital gains taxation on the price of the shares is illustrated in the following example.

A closed-end investment company initially sells stock for $10 per share and uses the proceeds to buy the stock of other companies. If transaction costs are ignored,

---

[3] Many NYSE, AMEX, and OTC closed-end investment companies are real estate investment trusts.

Exhibit 23.1 ✦ Net Asset Values and Market Prices of Selected Closed-End Investment Companies as of January 1, 1993

Company	Price	Net Asset Value	Discount or (Premium) as a Percentage of Net Asset Value
Adams Express	$20	$20.40	2.0%
General American Investors	30	28.36	(5.5)
Salomon Brothers Fund	13¾	15.13	9.1
Tri-Continental	25½	28.08	9.2
Zweig Total Return	10	9.05	(10.5)

Source: *Standard & Poor's Stock Guide,* January 1993.

the net asset value of a share is $10, and the shares may trade in the secondary market for $10. The value of the firm's portfolio subsequently rises to $16 (i.e., the net asset value is $16). The firm has a potential capital gain of $6 per share. If it is realized and these profits are distributed, the net asset value will return to $10 and each stockholder will receive $6 in capital gains, for which he or she will pay the appropriate capital gains tax.

Suppose, however, that the capital gains are not realized (i.e., the net asset value remains $16). What will the market price of the stock be? This is difficult to determine, but it will probably be below $16. Why? Suppose an investor bought a share for $16 and the firm then realized and distributed the $6 capital gain. After the distribution of the $6, the investor would be responsible for any capital gains tax, but the net asset value of the share would decrease to $10.

Obviously this is not advantageous to the buyer. Individuals may only be willing to purchase the shares at a discount that reduces the potential impact of realized capital gains and the subsequent capital gains taxes. Suppose the share had cost $14 (i.e., it sold for a discount of $2 from the net asset value), and the firm realized and distributed the gain. The buyer who paid $14 now owns a share with a net asset value of $10 and receives a capital gain of $6. Although this investor will have to pay the appropriate capital gains tax, the impact is reduced because the investor paid only $14 to purchase the share whose total value is $16 (the $10 net asset value plus the $6 capital gain).

Since the shares may sell for a discount or a premium relative to their net asset value, it is possible for the market price of a closed-end investment company to fluctuate more or less than the net asset value. For example, during 1985, the net asset value of Adams Express rose from $14.51 to $20.31 (a 40 percent increase), but the stock increased 58 percent (12¼ to 19⅜) as the discount fell from 15.6 to 4.6 percent. Since the market price can change relative to the net asset value, an investor is subject to an additional source of risk. The value of the investment may decline not only because the net asset value may decrease but also because the shares may sell for a larger discount from their net asset value.

Some investors view the market price relative to the net asset value as a guide to buying and selling the shares of a closed-end investment company. If the shares are selling for a sufficient discount, they are considered for purchase. If the shares are selling for a small discount or at a premium, they are considered for sale. Of course, determining the premium that will justify the sale or the discount that will justify the purchase is not simple.

Sources of Profit from Investing in Closed-End Investment Companies

Profits are the difference between costs and revenues. Investing in closed-end investment companies involves several costs. First, since the shares are purchased on the open market, there is the brokerage commission for the purchase and for any subsequent sale. Second, the investment company charges a fee to operate the assets. This fee is subtracted from any income that the firm's assets earn. These management fees range from 1 to 2 percent of the net asset value. Third, when the investment company purchases or sells securities, it also has to pay brokerage fees, which are passed on to the investor.

The purchase of shares in closed-end investment companies thus involves three costs that the investor must bear. Some alternative investments, such as savings accounts in commercial banks, do not involve these costs. Although commission fees are incurred when stock is purchased through a broker, the other expenses associated with a closed-end investment company are avoided. However, the investment company does relieve the individual of some of the cost of storing securities and provides the records necessary for the preparation of tax papers.

Investors in closed-end investment companies may earn profits in a variety of ways. First, if the investment company collects dividends and interest on its portfolio of assets, this income is distributed to the stockholders in the form of dividends. Second, if the value of the firm's assets increases, the company may sell the assets and realize profits. These profits are then distributed as capital gains to the stockholders. Such distributions usually occur in a single payment near the end of the calendar and, for most individuals, the tax year. Third, the net asset value of the portfolio may increase, which will cause the market price of the company's stock to rise. In this case the investor may sell the shares in the market and realize a capital gain. Fourth, the market price of the shares may rise relative to the net asset value (i.e., the premium may increase or the discount may decrease); the investor may then earn a profit through the sale of the shares.

These sources of profit are illustrated in Exhibit 23.2, which presents the distributions and price changes for Salomon Brothers Fund from December 31, 1981, through December 31, 1990. As may be seen in the exhibit, the investment company distributed cash dividends of $0.501 and capital gains of $0.49 in 1988. The net asset value rose from $13.26 to $14.37, and the price of the stock likewise rose (from $11 to $11.63 at 12/31/88). An investor who bought the shares in December 1987 and sold them in December 1988 earned a return of 14.7 percent (before commissions) on the investment.

The potential for loss is also illustrated in Exhibit 23.2. If an investor bought the shares on December 31, 1986, he or she suffered a loss during 1987. While Lehman distributed $0.49 per share in income and $1.88 in capital gains, the net asset value and the price of the stock declined sufficiently to more than offset the income and capital gains distributions.

Exhibit 23.2 ✦ ANNUAL RETURNS ON AN INVESTMENT IN SALOMON BROTHERS FUND, A CLOSED-END INVESTMENT COMPANY

Distributions and Price Changes	1990	1989	1988	1987	1986	1985	1984	1983	1982	1981
Per-share income distributions	$ 0.49	0.59	0.501	0.49	0.515	0.495	0.545	0.625	0.71	0.72
Per-share capital gains distributions	0.71	1.52	0.49	1.88	3.085	1.085	2.44	1.365	2.01	2.04
Year-end net asset value	13.33	15.58	14.37	13.26	15.42	16.78	14.67	18.25	16.64	15.56
Year-end market price	11.00	13.00	11.63	11.00	15.00	16.00	15.00	18.625	17.375	14.875
Annual return based on prior year's market price										
a. Dividend yield	3.8%	6.0	4.6	3.3	3.2	3.3	2.9	3.6	4.8	4.5
b. Capital gains yield	5.5%	11.8	4.4	12.5	19.3	7.2	13.1	7.9	13.5	16.8
c. Change in price	(15.4)%	11.8	5.7	(25.7)	(6.3)	6.7	(19.5)	7.2	16.8	(7.0)
Total return	(6.1)%	29.6	14.7	(10.9)	16.2	17.2	(3.5)	18.7	35.1	10.3

Source: Salomon Brothers Fund, Annual Report, various issues.

UNIT TRUSTS

A variation on the closed-end investment company is the fixed-unit investment trust, commonly referred to as a **unit trust.** These trusts, which are formed by brokerage firms and sold to investors in units of $1,000, hold a fixed portfolio of securities such as federal government or corporate bonds, municipal bonds, or mortgage loans. An example of such a trust is Merrill Lynch's Government Securities Income Fund, which invested solely in U.S. Treasury securities and other obligations backed by the full faith and credit of the federal government.

unit trust
A passive investment company with a fixed portfolio of assets that are self-liquidating.

A unit trust is a passive investment, as its assets are not traded but are frozen. The trust collects income (e.g., interest on its portfolio) and, eventually, the repayment of principal. The trust is self-liquidating because as the funds are received, they are not reinvested but are distributed to stockholders. Since the trust's portfolio is fixed and not altered, operating expenses are low. Such trusts are primarily attractive to investors such as retirees who seek a steady, periodic flow of payments. If the investor needs the funds earlier, the shares may be sold back to the trust at their current net asset value.

More recently the concept of a unit trust has been extended to a broader spectrum of securities. For example, Merrill Lynch developed a trust consisting solely of emerging growth stocks. After a specified period of time, the stocks will be sold and the funds distributed to unit holders. Once again the trust is a passive investment that holds a portfolio for a specified time period and is liquidated. Such a trust may appeal to an investor seeking capital appreciation through a diversified portfolio but who needs the funds at a specific time in the future (e.g., at retirement). Since the liquidation date is specified, that individual knows when the funds will be received.

While the investor knows when the funds will be received, he or she does not know the amount. The prices of the stocks held by the trust could rise or fall. If the value of the stocks were to rise, the investor would earn a profit. However, if the prices of the securities were to decline, the trust's management cannot wait beyond the liquidation date for the stocks to recoup their lost value. Thus the unit holder obtains certainty as to when the funds will be received but cannot be certain of the amount.

This tradeoff is, of course, different from the situation in which the individual has bought an alternative investment such as a bond. If the bond is retired at maturity, the individual knows both when and the amount that will be received. But a bond or unit trust that holds a portfolio of debt instruments does not offer the possible growth associated with the Merrill Lynch trust devoted to emerging growth companies. The trust offers the possibility of a large return if the individual stocks do well by the trust's liquidation date, but there can be no certainty that this growth will be achieved.

MUTUAL FUNDS

Open-end investment companies, which are commonly called mutual funds, are similar to closed-end investment companies. However, there are some important differences. The first concerns their capital structure. Shares in mutual funds are not traded like other stocks and bonds. Instead, an investor who wants a position in a particular mutual fund purchases shares directly from the company. After receiving the money, the mutual fund issues new shares and purchases assets with these newly acquired funds. If an investor owns shares in the fund and wants to liquidate the position, the shares are sold back to the company. The shares are redeemed, and the fund pays the investor from its cash holdings. If the fund lacks sufficient cash, it will sell some of the securities it owns to obtain the money to redeem the shares. The fund cannot suspend this redemption feature except in an emergency, and then it may be done only with the permission of the Securities and Exchange Commission.

A second important difference between open-end and closed-end investment companies pertains to the cost of investing. Mutual funds continuously offer to sell new shares, and these shares are sold at their net asset value plus a sales fee, which is commonly called a *loading charge*. This cost and others, such as the 12b-1 fee covered later in this chapter, are disclosed in the fund's prospectus. When the investor liquidates the position, the shares are redeemed at their net asset value. For most funds no additional fees are charged for the sale.

no-load mutual fund
A mutual fund that does not charge a fee for buying or selling its shares.

load fund
A mutual fund that charges a fee to purchase its shares.

The loading fee may range from zero for **no-load mutual funds** to between 3 and 8 percent for **load funds.** Exhibit 23.3 presents the loading fees for several mutual funds. If the individual makes a substantial investment, the loading fee is usually reduced. For example, the American Balanced Fund offers the following schedule of fees:

Investment	Fee
$0–50,000	5.75%
over 50,000	4.5
over 100,000	3.5
over 250,000	2.5

Exhibit 23.3   ✦   Loading Charges for Selected Mutual Funds

	Net Asset Value	Price	Loading Charge (As a Percentage of Net Asset Value)
American Balanced Fund	$12.29	$13.04	6.1%
American Growth Fund	24.19	25.67	6.1
Dean Witter High-Yield Fund	6.66	7.05	5.8
Franklin Group Gold Fund	9.16	9.54	4.2
Lord Abbott Government Securities	2.99	3.14	5.0
Merrill Lynch Basic Value Fund	20.39	21.81	7.0

Source: The Wall Street Journal, January 6, 1993, C20.

The investor should be warned that mutual funds state the loading charge as a percentage of the *offer* price. The effect of the fee being a percentage of the offer price and not a percentage of the net asset value is an increase in the effective percentage charged. If the loading charge is 8 percent and the offer price is $10, then the loading fee is $0.80. However, the net asset value is $9.20 ($10 minus $0.80). In this example, the loading charge as a percentage of the net asset value is 8.7 percent (8.0%/[1 − 0.08] = 8.0/0.92 = 8.7%), which is higher than the stated 8 percent loading charge.

It is immediately apparent which funds are no-load funds by the way in which mutual fund prices are quoted. Exhibit 23.4, which reproduces a quotation of mutual fund prices from *The Wall Street Journal*, illustrates this difference. The publication reports the net asset value (NAV), the offer price, and any change in the asset value from the previous day. If the offer price and the net asset value are the same (i.e., if the fund has no loading charge), "NL" may be printed in the offer price column. The AHA Balanced Fund has a net asset value of $12.16, and NL appears in the offer column. Thus, these shares may be bought and sold from the company at their net asset value, so the fund is a no-load fund.

The quotation of funds with loading fees includes the net asset value and the offer price. For example, AIM High Yield Fund has a net asset value of $9.43 per share and an offer price of $9.90. It is a load fund. The buyer pays $0.47 ($9.90–9.43) to purchase a share worth $9.43. Such a charge is 4.7 percent of the asking price and 5.0 percent of the net asset value.

In addition to loading charges, investors in mutual funds have to pay management fees, which are deducted from the income earned by the fund's portfolio. The fund also pays brokerage commissions when it buys and sells securities. The total cost of investing in mutual funds may be substantial when all of the costs (the loading charge and management and brokerage fees) are considered. Of course, the cost of investing is substantially reduced when the individual buys shares in no-load funds. The investor, however, must still pay the management fees and commission costs.

The third difference between closed-end and open-end investment companies is the source of profits to the investor. As with closed-end investment companies, individuals may profit from investments in mutual funds from several sources. Any

Exhibit 23.4 ✦ OFFER PRICES AND NET ASSET VALUES (NAV) FOR SELECTED MUTUAL FUNDS

Monday, January 4, 1993
Price ranges for investment companies, as quoted by the National Association of Securities Dealers. The NASD requires a mutual fund to have at least 1,000 shareholders or $25 million in net assets before being listed. NAV stands for net asset value per share; the offering includes net asset value plus maximum sales charge, if any.

	NAV	Offer Price	NAV Chg.		NAV	Offer Price	NAV Chg.
AAL Mutual:				**Benham Group:**			
Bond p	10.35	10.87	+.04	AdiGov	10.06	NL	+.01
CaGr p	14.61	15.34	+.01	CaTFI	10.88	NL	...
MuBd p	10.73	11.27	+.01	CatfIn	9.95	NL	+.01
AARP Invst:				CaTFS	10.18	NL	+.01
CaGr	32.01	NL	−.08	CatfH	9.12	NL	...
GinM	15.99	NL	+.06	CatfL	11.22	NL	+.01
GthInc	29.37	NL	−.04	EqGro	11.63	NL	−.05
HQ Bd	16.14	NL	+.07	EurBd	9.88	NL	−.08
TxFBd	17.64	NL	+.02	GNMA	10.83	NL	+.05
ABT Funds:				Goldin	7.37	NL	−.18
Emrg p	12.61	13.24	−.18	IncGro	14.06	NL	−.05
FL TF x	10.92	11.46	−.02	NITFI	10.67	NL	...
Gthin p	10.72	11.25	−.02	NITFL	11.39	NL	+.01
Utilin p	12.78	13.42	−.02	Tg1995	88.71	NL	+.28
AHA Funds:				Tg2000	62.45	NL	+.50
Balan	12.16	NL	...	Tg2005	42.00	NL	+.40
Full	10.34	NL	+.04	Tg2010	29.83	NL	+.30
Lim	10.41	NL	+.01	Tg2015	21.74	NL	+.24
AIM Funds:				Tg2020	14.78	NL	+.21
AdiGv p	9.86	10.16	...	TNote	10.49	NL	+.03
Chart p	8.53	9.03	−.04	**Berger Group:**			
Const p	14.75	15.61	−.17	100	13.78	NL	−.09
CvYld p	14.10	14.80	−.11	101	9.65	NL	−.07
HiYld p	5.62	5.90	+.01	**Bernstein Fds:**			
IntlE p	8.91	9.43	−.05	GvSh	12.66	NL	+.01
LimM p	....	....		ShtDur	12.74	NL	+.02
Sumit	9.58	...	−.06	IntDur	13.18	NL	+.06
TF Int	10.58	10.91		Ca Mu	13.32	NL	...
Weing p	17.22	18.22	−.11	DivMu	13.30	NL	+.01
AIM Funds C:				NYMu	13.33	NL	+.01
AgrsvC p	18.32	19.39	−.20	IntlVal	11.69	NL	+.01
GoScC p	10.23	10.74	+.04	BerwynFd	14.74	NL	−.11
GrthC p	12.20	12.91	−.08	**Blanchard Funds:**			
HYidC p	9.43	9.90	+.03	GlGr p	9.46	NL	−.01
IncoC p	8.07	8.47	+.04	PrcM p	4.66	NL	−.15
MuBC p	8.28	8.69	+.01	ST GI	1.83	NL	−.01
TeCtC p	10.65	11.18	...	BdEndw	18.71	NL	+.08
UtlIC p	13.27	14.04	−.04	**Boston Co:**			
ValuC p	18.09	19.14	−.15	AAloc p	14.91	NL	−.04
AMF Funds:				AMEF	11.60	11.60	−.02
AdiMtg	9.95	NL	...	CaAp p	25.44	NL	−.02
IntMtg	9.88	NL	+.04	Intl	10.10	NL	−.08
IntlLiq	10.83	NL	+.02	IntGv p	12.82	NL	+.06
MtgSc	11.32	NL	+.05	Mgdl p	11.47	NL	+.02
ASM Fd	9.17	NL	+.02	SpGth p	16.14	NL	−.29
ASO Funds:				TF Bd	12.12	NL	+.02
Balance	11.09	11.61	+.04	BrinsnGl	10.18	NL	−.02
Bond	10.89	11.40	+.05	Brndyw	22.45	NL	−.29
Equity	13.09	13.71	+.04	Bruce	100.14	NL	+.48
LtdMat	10.59	10.86	+.02	BrundgSl	10.59	NL	+.03
Acornin	10.65	10.65	−.04	**Bull & Bear Gp:**			
AcornF	54.89	54.89	−.42	FNCI p	17.55	NL	...
AdsnCa p	20.87	21.52	+.02	GlbInc p	8.62	NL	+.03
Advest Advant:				Gold p	9.77	NL	−.16
Govt p	9.31	9.31	+.09	GovtSc p	14.87	NL	+.07
Gwth p	16.34	16.34	−.02	MuInc p	17.06	NL	...
HY Bd p	9.07	9.07	−.02	SpEq p	24.41	NL	−.47
Inco p	12.05	12.05	...	USOvs p	7.54	NL	−.05
Spcl p	17.35	17.35	−.05	Burnhm x	20.77	21.86	−1.18

Source: The Wall Street Journal, January 5, 1993, C22.

income that is earned from the fund's assets in excess of expenses is distributed as dividends. If the fund's assets appreciate in value and the fund realizes these profits, the gains are distributed as capital gains. If the net asset value of the shares appreciates, the investor may redeem them at the appreciated price. Thus, in general, the open-end mutual fund offers investors the same means of earning profits as the closed-end investment company does, with one exception. In the case of closed-end investment companies, the price of the stock may rise relative to the net asset value of the shares. The possibility of a decreased discount or an increased premium is a potential source of profit that is available only through closed-end investment companies. It does not exist for mutual funds because their shares never sell at a discount.[4] Hence, changes in the discount or premium are a source of profit or loss to investors in closed-end but not in open-end investment companies.

While purchases of shares in investment companies may generate profits, they also subject the investor to risk. In Chapters 1 and 7 several sources of risk were discussed. These included the risk associated with investments in the securities of a particular firm (e.g., the stocks and bonds issued by AT&T). Since investment companies construct diversified portfolios, the impact of a particular investment on the outcome of the portfolio as a whole is reduced. Thus, the risk associated with an individual firm's securities is small (if not nonexistent).[5]

Other sources of risk, however, cannot be eliminated through the purchases of shares of investment companies. If security prices in general rise (or fall), the value of the investment company's portfolio will probably also rise (or fall). The managements of investment companies cannot consistently predict changes in the market and adjust their portfolios accordingly. The value of investment companies' portfolios and the value of their shares tend to move systematically with the market as a whole. Thus the risk associated with movements in the market is not eliminated through the purchase of shares in investment companies.

Inflation is also another source of risk that cannot be eliminated by acquiring shares in investment companies. If the return these firms earn is insufficient (i.e., is below the rate of inflation), their stockholders experience a loss of purchasing power. It is even possible that the value of the investment company's stock may decline while inflation continues, in which case the investors are worse off than if they had held a regular savings account with a commercial bank.

The Portfolios of Mutual Funds

The portfolios of investment companies may be diversified or very specialized, but most may be classified into one of four types: income, growth, special situations, and balanced. Income funds stress assets that produce income; they buy stocks and bonds that pay generous dividends or interest income. The Value Line Income Fund is an example of a fund whose objective is income. Virtually all of its assets are income stocks, such as those of utilities, which pay generous dividends and periodically increase them as their earnings grow.

Growth funds stress appreciation in the value of the assets, and little emphasis is given to current income. The portfolio of the Value Line Fund is an example of a growth fund. The majority of the assets are the common stocks of companies with potential for growth. These **growth stocks** include the shares of very well-known firms as well as those of smaller firms that may offer superior growth potential.

growth stock
The shares of a company whose earnings are expected to grow at an above average rate.

Even within the class of growth funds there can be many differences. Some stress riskier securities in order to achieve larger returns and faster appreciation in their investors' funds. For example, the Janus Venture seeks capital appreciation by investing in smaller companies. Other growth funds, however, are more conservative. The Fidelity Fund is a growth fund emphasizing companies that still are considered to offer capital appreciation, but whose earnings are more stable and reliable.

---

[4] Load funds are actually sold at a premium (i.e., the loading fee).
[5] The investor still must bear the unsystematic risk associated with the individual investment company. This source of risk is reduced by investing in several investment companies.

SOURCES OF INFORMATION ON MUTUAL FUNDS

As you might expect, there is no dearth of information on mutual funds and other investment companies. Two primary sources are the *Mutual Fund Fact Book* published annually by the Investment Company Institute and *Investment Companies*, published annually by Wiesenberger Services, Inc. of New York. The *Fact Book* provides general information on the industry while the Wiesenberger book is devoted to specific funds. It provides a summary of each fund's purpose, price performance, and dividend distribution. This publication also gives addresses so the individual can write to any fund to obtain a copy of its prospectus, which provides such essential information as the fund's portfolio and the costs and expenses associated with the fund.

Similar information for no-load funds is provided by *The Individual Investor's Guide to No-Load Mutual Funds*. Over 300 funds are covered in this guide, which is updated annually by its publisher, the American Association of Individual Investors.

Quarterly data concerning performance of mutual funds is reported in *Barron's* in a section entitled "Barron's/Lipper Gauge—a Quarterly Survey of Mutual Fund Performance." *Forbes* also publishes an annual rating of 1,600 funds that ranks their performance in rising and declining markets. *Forbes* also gives each fund's average annual return for the last 10 years and provides the amount of sales changes and annual expenses.

Business Week publishes the *Mutual Fund Scoreboard*, which is a diskette containing performance data on over 700 mutual funds. The data includes total return and return relative to the S&P 500 stock index for the last three months, one year, five years, and ten years. Other information includes each fund's objectives, portfolio turnover, fees such as sales charges and management expenses, percent in cash, largest held company, and beta coefficients. The data may be converted to Lotus 1-2-3 or ASCII files for ease of analysis and manipulation. The investor may obtain the current diskette or subscribe to quarterly updates. Information may be obtained by writing Business Week Mutual Fund Scoreboard Diskettes, Box 1597, Fort Lee, NJ 07024.

Special situation investment companies specialize in more speculative securities that, given the "special situation," may yield large returns. These investment companies are perhaps the riskiest of all the mutual funds. The portfolio of Value Line Special Situations Fund illustrates this element of risk. The stocks in this portfolio tend to be in small companies or companies that have fallen on bad times but whose course may be changing. Investments in special situation securities can be very rewarding but some do not fulfill their potential return.

Balanced funds own a mixture of securities that sample the attributes of the assets of other mutual funds. A balanced fund, such as the Sentinel Group Balanced Fund, owns a variety of stocks, some of which offer potential growth while others are primarily income producers. A balanced portfolio may include short-term debt (such as U.S. Treasury bills), long-term debt, and preferred stock. Such a portfolio seeks a balance of income from dividends and interest and capital appreciation.

Many investment companies manage a wide spectrum of mutual funds. Each fund has a separate goal and hence has a different portfolio designed to achieve the fund's purpose. As may be seen in Exhibit 23.4, AIM Funds offers investors the opportunity to choose among numerous different mutual funds covering a wide spectrum of investment alternatives. The individual may choose any combination of these funds. For example, an investor who seeks income may acquire shares in the equity income fund, the government securities fund, and the bond fund. Such investments would give that individual a diversified portfolio of income-earning assets.

In addition to offering a variety of funds from which to choose, companies that manage several mutual funds may permit the investor to shift investments from one fund to another fund without paying any fees. For example, an individual who is currently employed may seek capital appreciation and invest in a growth-oriented fund but on retirement may shift the proceeds to a bond fund to collect a flow of interest income. Such a shift could be achieved by converting the shares in the growth fund into shares of the bond fund. In many cases this switch may be made without the investor paying any commissions on the transaction.

The Portfolios of Specialized Mutual Funds

Investment trusts initially sought to pool the funds of many savers and to invest these funds in a diversified portfolio of assets. Such diversification spread the risk of investing and reduced the risk of loss to the individual investor. While a particular investment company had a specified goal, such as growth or income, the portfolio was still sufficiently diversified so that the element of unsystematic risk was reduced.

Today, however, a variety of funds have developed that have moved away from this concept of diversification and the reduction of risk. Instead of offering investors a cross section of American business, many funds have been created to offer investors specialized investments. For example, an investment company may be limited to investments in the securities of a particular sector of the economy or particular industry, such as gold (e.g., ASA, Limited). There are also funds that specialize in a particular type of security, such as bonds (e.g., American General Bond Fund).

During the 1980s the scope of some investment companies became even narrower. For example, the Dreyfus Merger and Acquisition Fund seeks to identify firms that are potential candidates for merger or take-over by other firms. Such mergers and take-overs often result in substantial profits for the stockholders of the target firms. These profits can be even larger if two firms seek to take over a third company and a bidding war erupts. The management of the Dreyfus Merger and Acquisition Fund tries to identify the stocks of companies that appear to be underpriced and that may be bought out at substantial premiums over their current prices. Obviously, this is a very specialized fund, and its investors bear two considerable risks not borne by investors in the traditional mutual fund. These risks involve (1) the ability of the fund's management to identify take-over candidates and (2) the possibility that the mergers and take-overs will not actually occur. If a stock is underpriced but no one seeks to take over the firm, then the stock may remain underpriced for a long period of time![6]

Perhaps the extreme in specialized funds occurred when the shares of Gaming Funds Incorporated were registered with the SEC. This fund specializes in gaming and sports investments. The securities it purchases may even include stocks for which there is no secondary market. Furthermore, the fund employs speculative techniques, such as short selling and the use of financial leverage. Obviously such a fund does not offer the advantages of diversification and risk reduction that are offered by traditional mutual funds.

In addition to these speculative funds, several specialized investment companies have been established that offer real alternatives to the traditional types of mutual funds. For example, money market mutual funds, which were discussed in Chapter 2, provide the individual with a means to invest indirectly in money market instruments such as treasury bills and negotiable certificates of deposit. Funds that acquire foreign securities offer the individual a means to invest in stocks of companies

---

[6]The efficient market hypothesis suggests that such undervaluations will quickly disappear. If a firm were a take-over candidate, its price should already discount that information.

POINTS OF INTEREST

MORNINGSTAR

No, it is not the name of a flower or a celestial body, *Morningstar Mutual Funds* is a comprehensive source of information on mutual funds. An annual publication that is updated every two weeks, Morningstar is for mutual funds what the *Value Line Investment Survey* is for individual stocks. *Morningstar Mutual Funds* begins with a detailed explanation on how to use the guide, which is followed by an alphabetized list of all the mutual funds covered. This summary index includes the fund's objective, total return, dividend information, size of the fund, and Morningstar's rating.

The third section presents detailed information for each fund. Exhibit 23.5 illustrates Morningstar's coverage of Colonial High-Yield Securities, a fund devoted primarily to investing in junk bonds. The information is similar to the data presented by the *Value Line Investment Survey* illustrated in Exhibit 4.5, except the data emphasize the fund's portfolio, expenses, portfolio turnover, and distributions while Value Line data emphasize corporate financial information such as earnings, cash flow, return on equity, and financial structure. However, unlike Value Line, Morningstar does not suggest which funds will be the best performers over the next twelve

months. Individual investors must determine that for themselves.

Morningstar Mutual Funds is also available on computer disks. These combine software, the database, and a graphics package that allows users to compare and track various funds. The individual may search the universe of funds for specific characteristics such as total returns or funds that hold specific stocks. The data then may be transferred into other software programs. Information on the computer package or the survey may be obtained directly from Morningstar, 53 West Jackson Boulevard, Chicago, IL 60604-3608.

located in Europe and Asia. (The discussion of these funds is deferred to Chapter 24.) Other specialized funds include index funds and tax-exempt funds.

index fund

A mutual fund whose portfolio seeks to duplicate an index of stock prices.

The purpose of an **index fund** is almost diametrically opposed to the traditional purpose of a mutual fund. Instead of identifying specific securities for purchase, the managements of these funds seek to duplicate the composition of an index of the market. The Vanguard Index Trust–500 Portfolio is based on the Standard & Poor's 500 stock index. Other funds seek to duplicate different indices. The Vanguard Index Trust–Extended Market Portfolio seeks to duplicate the Wilshire 4500 stock index, which is even more broadly based than the S&P 500 stock index. Some index funds are less broadly based such as the Rushmore Over-the-Counter Index Plus, which is based on the NASDAQ 100 stock index. This index is limited to 100 over-the-counter stocks and obviously is less broadly based than the S&P 500 index.

Index funds should perform in tandem with the market (or at least that part that the fund seeks to duplicate). Although they cannot generally outperform the market, neither should they underperform the market. In a sense, these funds have a defeatist attitude: Because they cannot beat the market, they try to avoid earning a return less than that of the market as a whole. Part of the popularity of such funds has been attributed to the poor performance of mutual funds in general in the past. (The returns earned by mutual funds will be discussed later in this chapter.) While these funds cannot overcome any risk associated with price fluctuations in the market as a whole, they do eliminate the risk associated with the selection of specific securities.

Another recently introduced specialized mutual fund is the investment company whose portfolio is devoted to tax-exempt bonds. Until 1976, open-end mutual funds were legally barred from this market. However, with the passage of enabling legislation, mutual funds were permitted to own tax-exempt bonds, and several funds were immediately started that specialize in tax-exempt securities. These funds offer investors, especially those with modest funds to invest, an opportunity to earn

Exhibit 23.5 ✦ COLONIAL HIGH-YIELD SECURITIES IN *MORNINGSTAR MUTUAL FUNDS*

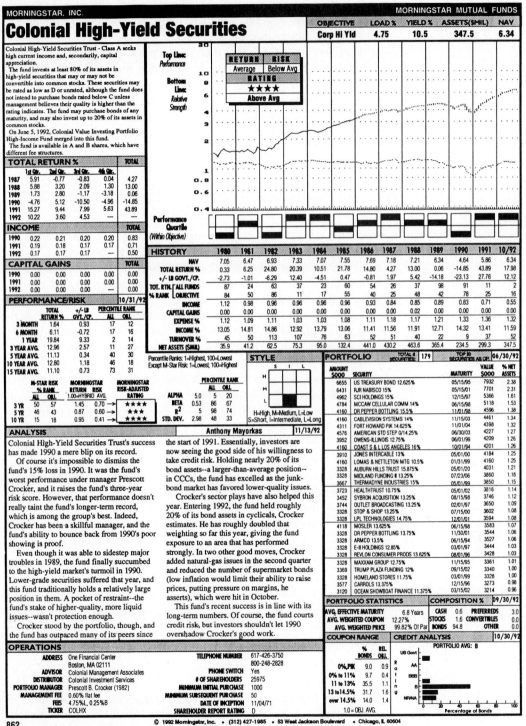

Source: Courtesy of Morningstar, Inc.

tax-free income and maintain a diversified portfolio. Since municipal bonds are sold in minimum units of $5,000, a sizable sum is required for an individual investor to obtain a diversified portfolio. Ten bonds of ten different state and local governments would cost about $50,000.[7] The advantages of tax-free income and a reduction in risk were virtually impossible for many investors.

However, mutual funds that specialize in tax-exempt bonds offer small investors both of these advantages. The funds are sold in smaller denominations. For example, $1,000 may be the minimum initial investment, and additional investments may be made for as little as $100. The ability to buy in small denominations means that modest investors may buy shares in these funds. Since the firms pool the funds of many investors, small investors also obtain the advantage of diversification.

SELECTING MUTUAL FUNDS

Selecting a mutual fund requires matching the goals of the investor and the objectives of the fund. The individual's need for custodial services, diversification, and professional management also affect the selection. In addition, there are several subtle factors that can have an impact on the decision to acquire the shares of a particular mutual fund, including taxation, the maturity of the fund and its management, and rates of return. These considerations may affect not only the decision to purchase mutual funds instead of other investments but also the decision to purchase a particular fund instead of another competing fund.

There are over a thousand mutual funds from which to choose. Obviously the investor cannot buy shares in all of them but must select among the alternatives. Thus, while investment companies may relieve individuals from selecting particular stocks and bonds, they do not relieve investors from having to select among the mutual funds that meet the individual's financial goals (e.g., growth or income).[8]

The choice is not easy. The individual should obtain a fund's prospectus, which states the fund's goals, current portfolio, and recent performance, the services offered, and fees charged. Funds with loading fees also have sales staffs who are a source of information concerning the funds (although the investor will be subjected to a certain degree of sales pressure). No-load funds do not have sales staffs, so information concerning these funds may be obtained by directly writing to the fund.

Hidden Capital Gains

As explained earlier, investment companies receive favorable tax treatment—they pay no federal income tax. They are a conduit through which income and capital gains are passed to stockholders. The investor ultimately has to pay any applicable taxes on the profits earned on the investment or by the fund. If the value of the

---

[7] Like all debt instruments, tax-exempt bonds may sell for a discount, so the investor may be able to acquire $50,000 face amount for less than a $50,000 cash outlay.

[8] There are mutual funds that specialize in acquiring the shares of other funds. Their managements seek to identify which funds will perform best under varying economic conditions. These funds relieve the investor from selecting among the various funds, but he or she in effect pays two management fees for the selection of assets.

POINTS OF INTEREST

DOLLAR COST AVERAGING AND MUTUAL FUNDS

One of the advantages offered investors by mutual funds is dollar cost averaging. As was explained in Chapter 9, an individual may make equal, periodic investments. With such a strategy, the investor acquires fewer shares when prices rise but more shares when prices fall. The larger purchases reduce the average cost of a share, and, if the value of the stock subsequently rises, the low-cost stock generates more capital gains.

While the individual may follow such a strategy by purchasing stock through brokers, transaction fees reduce the attractiveness of dollar cost averaging, especially if the individual is investing a modest amount (e.g., less than $500). Transaction costs may be eliminated or at least reduced through the use of mutual funds. While avoidance of fees is obvious in the case of no-load funds, reduction in costs may also apply to load funds. Consider a load fund that charges 8½ percent. If an individual seeks to invest $300 a month, the load fee will be

$25.50. Many brokers may not execute such a small order. If they do buy $300 worth of stock, brokerage firms (including discount brokerage firms) will charge the minimum commission, which is generally $50 to $60. Thus even with loading fees, mutual funds can still offer investors with modest sums a cheaper means to achieve the advantage associated with dollar cost averaging.

shares increases and the investor sells them for a profit, he or she will have to pay any applicable capital gains taxes. If the mutual fund earns income, the individual stockholder pays the appropriate income tax on those earnings. If the mutual fund realizes capital gains on its portfolio, the investor must pay any capital gains taxes.

Taxes can have an important impact on the individual's selection of a particular fund. Besides creating problems for tax planning, taxation alters the net return the investor earns. As is explained in the section on rates of return, taxation reduces the individual's ability to compare his or her return on money invested in the fund with the performance claimed by the fund's management. Taxation may even offer the investor an opportunity for profit by investing in funds with tax losses. However, the main concern is that even though the fund's objectives are consistent with those of the individual the fund's management still may not follow a policy that is in the best interests of the individual investor's tax strategy.

The individual mutual fund can have built into its portfolio the potential for a considerable tax liability that may not be obvious to the investor. In some cases this liability may fall on investors who do not experience the gains. This potential tax liability is the result of the fund experiencing paper profits on its portfolio (i.e., profits that have not been realized). As long as the gains are not realized, there will be no taxation, which only occurs once the investment company sells the appreciated assets and thus realizes the capital gain.

This potential tax liability is perhaps best seen by a simple illustration. If a mutual fund is started by selling shares for $10, (excluding costs) the net asset value of a share is $10. The fund invests the money in various securities, which appreciate in value during the year. At the end of the year the net asset value of a share is now $14. Since the fund has not sold any of its holdings, its stockholders have no tax liability.

This fund is a going concern and like all mutual funds offers to redeem its shares and sell additional shares to investors. Suppose an original investor redeems shares at the net asset value of $14. This individual has a capital gain because the value of the shares rose from the initial offer price of $10 to $14. Such a capital gain is independent of whether or not the fund realizes the capital gain on its portfolio, because the investor realizes the gain.

Suppose, however, this individual had not redeemed the shares but continued to hold them. The fund then realizes the $4 per share profit and distributes the capital gain. Once again this investor must pay the appropriate capital gains tax. These two cases are exactly what the investor should expect. If the investor redeems the shares and realizes the gain or if the fund realizes the gain, the individual stockholder is responsible for the taxes.

It is, however, possible for an investor to be responsible for the tax without experiencing the capital gain. Suppose the individual purchases shares at the current net asset value of $14 for a cost basis of $14. On the next day the management of the fund realizes the profits on the portfolio (i.e., sells its securities) and distributes the capital gain. The investors who purchased the initial shares at $10 have earned a profit and must pay any appropriate capital gains tax. The individual who has just purchased the shares for $14 also receives a capital gain distribution and thus is also subject to the capital gains tax. Even though this investor paid $14 per share, that individual is the holder of record for the distribution and thus is responsible for the tax.

When the capital gain distribution is made, the value of the stock declines. In this illustration the net asset value of the shares declines by $4 (i.e., the amount of the distribution) to $10. The investor who bought the shares for $14 could offset the $4 distribution by redeeming the shares. Since the shares cost $14 but are now worth only $10, this investor sustains a $4 loss. Such a sale offsets the distribution, and thus the stockholder no longer has any tax obligation. However, the original purchase, the redemption, and any subsequent reinvestment may involve transaction costs that this investor must bear. So the stockholder loses either through having to pay the capital gains tax or having to absorb the fees associated with the redemption designed to offset the tax necessitated by the distribution.

Could the individual have anticipated this potential tax liability? The answer is "Yes" when the investor realizes that the source of the tax is the unrealized capital gains embodied in the mutual fund's net asset value. If a fund's portfolio has risen in value, the fund has unrealized capital gains. When the gains are realized, they accrue to the shareholders to whom they are distributed. These shareholders are not necessarily the stockholders who owned shares when the appreciation occurred. If the individual were to determine the cost basis of the fund's portfolio and the current value of that portfolio, any unrealized capital gains would be apparent. If, for example, the fund has $100,000,000 in assets that cost only $60,000,000, there is $40,000,000 in unrealized gains. If these profits are realized, they will create tax liabilities for current stockholders, not former stockholders.[9]

Hidden Capital Losses

While the existence of unrealized gains implies the potential for future tax liabilities, the existence of unrealized capital losses offers the possibility of tax-free gains. Suppose a mutual fund started with a net asset value of $10 but as the result of a declin-

---

[9]This tax problem could also be avoided by purchasing the shares after the distribution and the decline in the net asset value. Obviously, ascertaining when the shares may be purchased exclusive of the distribution may save the investor considerable tax expense over a period of years.

ing market currently has a net asset value of $6. Any individual who originally bought the shares at $10 and now has redeemed them for $6 has sustained a capital loss, and he or she will use that loss to offset other capital gains or income (up to the limit allowed by the current tax code).

If, however, an individual purchases shares at the current net asset value of $6, the value of the portfolio could rise without necessarily creating a tax liability for that investor. Suppose the portfolio's net asset value rises back to $10, at which time the mutual fund sells the securities. Since the cost basis to the fund of the sold securities is $10, the fund has no capital gain. The shareholder has seen the net asset value rise from $6 to $10 without there being any tax liability created by the mutual fund.

If the net asset value continues to rise to $12 and the fund sells the securities, it realizes a $2 gain ($12 − $10). The investor who bought the shares at $6 will only be subject to capital gains tax on the $2, because the fund's cost basis is $10. The investor has seen his or her investment rise from $6 to $12 but is only subject to tax on the appreciation from $10 to $12. As long as this investor *does not redeem the shares acquired for $6,* the tax on the $4 appreciation from $6 to $10 is deferred even if the mutual fund sells the securities. Thus, if the fund has unrealized losses, this may offer the individual an opportunity for tax savings just as the unrealized capital gains may create future tax liabilities.

The investor should realize that a fund with unrealized losses is not necessarily an attractive investment. The losses may be the result of inept management, and if such performance continues, the fund will generate larger losses. However, if the investor believes that the fund will be acquired or will turn around and perform well so that its net asset value increases, the unrealized tax losses embodied in the fund's portfolio can magnify the after-tax return the investor earns.

Tax Swapping

The ability to take tax losses on an investment in a mutual fund offers another possible strategy to increase the individual's return. Unlike the previous strategy, in which the shares of funds with tax losses were acquired, in this strategy the investor purchases shares in two similar funds (e.g., two modest-sized growth funds). If the shares of one of the funds decline in value, the shares are sold and the proceeds of the sales are then used to acquire additional shares in the fund that has not declined in value. Since the investor continues to hold the original position in the second fund, there is no tax obligation. The loss, however, is used to offset other capital gains or ordinary income.

This strategy is then repeated. The investor always acquires similar pairs of mutual funds and sells the inferior performer. The investor does not sell the shares of the fund that have appreciated in the same year in which the losses are taken, because under current laws capital losses and capital gains are netted out. The object of the strategy is to take losses to offset income from other sources and to increase the investor's position in the better performing mutual fund.[10]

---

[10] Such a strategy is referred to by Gerald Perritt as "semi-active trading." Perritt suggests that for individuals in the higher marginal tax brackets, such a strategy significantly increases the after-tax return earned by portfolios. (See Gerald W. Perritt, "Semi-active Trading:

Mature versus New Funds

All funds had to be created. Those that have been successful have grown as the value of their portfolio has appreciated and as investors have purchased additional shares. Should an investor purchase the shares of new funds or those with the advantage of established track records? *Forbes* annually publishes performance ratings of mutual funds and separates performance into rising and declining markets. Thus, the investor can learn how well a fund has performed when security prices rose and how well the fund protected capital during a period of declining security prices.

A fund's performance record is also a record of its management. While the fund has an indeterminant life, portfolio managers change with the passage of time. The individuals who guided the fund during the period of its initial success and growth may no longer be associated with the fund. A change in a fund's management may reduce continuity and alter investment philosophy. The investor should not assume that new management will be able to match a prior management's record.

Over time mutual funds grow by issuing new shares. As the fund expands, its capacity to perform may decline. It is easier for a small fund to move in and out of the market when it buys or sells in modest-sized blocks. As the fund's portfolio increases, this flexibility decreases. A large fund may be unable to quickly establish a position in an attractive security or to rapidly liquidate a position if the fund is buying or selling large blocks of stock.

Even if the fund is able to establish a position, the market makers may require the fund to pay a higher-than-market price to purchase a large block or to accept a lower-than-market price to sell a large block. The effect is to increase transaction costs. Even if the fund negotiates smaller brokerage commissions on the purchase or sale, the total cost, which includes brokerage commissions, the spread between the bid and ask prices, and any price concessions necessary to execute the transactions, may exceed that which an individual investor pays to buy and sell securities.[11]

Large funds may also have difficulty sustaining growth. It is harder to increase by 20 percent the value of a portfolio worth $2,000,000,000 than a portfolio worth $200,000,000. The base for the former portfolio is so large that a decent performance in the value of one of the fund's holdings may have little impact on the fund's total value.

A smaller and newer fund may not have these problems. The fund's size permits it to readily establish a position in a given security or to liquidate the position. It is small enough that a major move in the market or selected holdings is readily discernible in the fund's net asset value. And the young management may have an aggressiveness (or incentive) that generates more growth and success.

Unfortunately a new fund does not have a track record, and investors do not know how well management will perform under varying conditions in the securities

---

A Strategy for a Taxing Problem," *American Association of Individual Investors Journal,* (November 1984), 24–26.) It should be noted that such a strategy may work for the selection of individual stocks in which the investor purchases the shares of two similar companies, subsequently weeds out the poorer performer, and invests the proceeds in the better performing stock.

[11] See Gerald W. Perritt and L. Kay Shannon, *The Individual Investor's Guide to No-Load Mutual Funds* (Chicago: American Association of Individual Investors, 1984), 2–30.

markets. The fund may have been created during a bull market and thus management would not have been tested during a period of declining prices. There is also the possibility that only funds that perform well are taken public. For example, a fund may be initially sold privately. If the management is unsuccessful, the shares are never offered to the public, but if it succeeds and the value of the portfolio appreciates, the fund is offered publicly. Management has a record of success that will be detailed in the fund's prospectus. Obviously such previous success will help market the shares. Whether management will be able to sustain the growth once the fund is public and its total assets are larger is not known when the initial public offering of the shares is made.

In addition, some funds are created to take advantage of a particular fad or investment opportunity. For example, a fund may be created to invest in high-technology stocks or gambling stocks at the height of speculative fever. The investor who purchases shares in the funds is, in effect, paying top dollar for the underlying securities. When the fad ends or these stocks are unable to sustain their previous growth, the net asset value of the fund declines, inflicting losses on its initial investors.

THE RETURNS EARNED ON INVESTMENTS IN MUTUAL FUNDS

As was previously explained, the securities of investment companies offer individuals several advantages. First, the investor receives the advantages of a diversified portfolio, which reduces risk. Some investors may lack the resources to contruct a diversified portfolio, and the purchase of shares in an investment company permits these investors to own a portion of a diversified portfolio. Second, the portfolio is professionally managed and under continuous supervision. Many investors may not have the time and expertise to manage their own portfolios and, except in the case of large portfolios, may lack the funds to obtain professional management. By purchasing shares in an investment company, individuals buy the services of professional management, which may increase the investor's return. Third, the administrative detail and custodial aspects of the portfolio (e.g., the physical handling of securities) are taken care of by the management of the company.

Although investment companies offer advantages, there are also disadvantages. The services offered by an investment company are not unique but may be obtained elsewhere. For example, the trust department of a commercial bank offers custodial services, and leaving the securities with the broker and registering them in the broker's name relieves the investor of storing the securities and keeping some of the records. In addition, the investor may acquire a diversified portfolio with only a modest amount of capital. Diversification does not require 100 different stocks. If the investor has $10,000, a reasonably diversified portfolio may be produced by investing in the stock of eight to ten companies in different industries. One does not have to purchase shares in an investment company to obtain the advantage of diversification.

Investment companies do offer the advantage of professional management, but this management cannot guarantee to outperform the market. A particular firm may do well in any given year, but it may do very poorly in subsequent years. Several studies have been undertaken to determine if professional management results in superior performance for mutual funds.

Figure 23.2 ✦ ANNUAL PERCENTAGE RETURNS, 1983–1991

A. Aggressive Funds, Growth Funds, and
   S & P 500 Stock Index

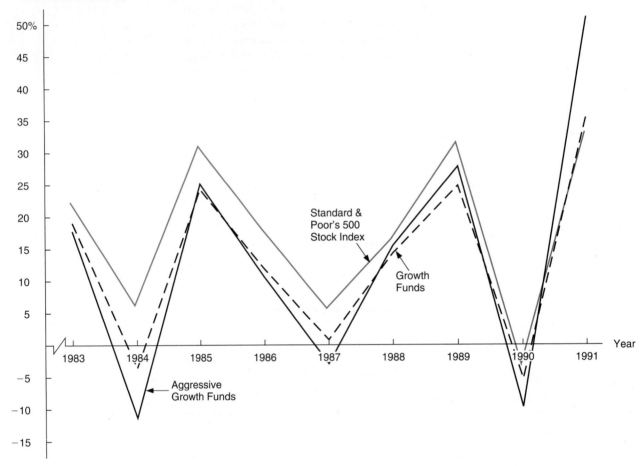

The first study, conducted for the SEC, covered the period from 1952 through 1958.[12] This study found that the performance of mutual funds was not significantly different from that of an unmanaged portfolio of similar assets. About half the funds outperformed Standard & Poor's indices, but the other half underperformed these aggregate measures of the market. In addition, there was no evidence of superior performance by a particular fund over a number of years.

These initial results were confirmed by later studies.[13] When loading charges are included in the analysis, the return earned by investors tends to be less than that which would be achieved through a random selection of securities.

---

[12]See Irwin Friend et al., *A Study of Mutual Funds* (Washington, D.C.: U.S. Government Printing Office, 1962).

[13]See, for instance, William F. Sharpe, "Mutual Fund Performance," *Journal of Business,* special supplement, 39 (January 1966): 119–138; Michael C. Jensen, "The Performance of

(Figure 23.2 CONTINUED)

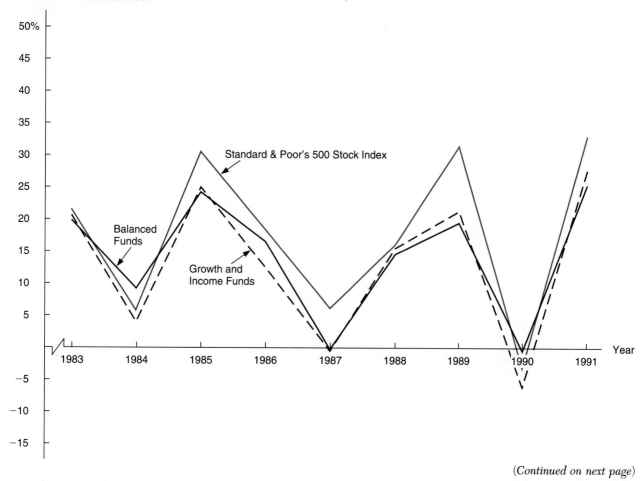

B. Growth and Income Funds, Balanced Funds,
   and S & P 500 Stock Index

(Continued on next page)

These results are mirrored in the graphs presented in Figure 23.2, which plots the annual returns for 1983 through 1991 earned by various types of no-load mutual funds and the Standard & Poor's 500 stock index. Part A gives the annual returns on funds classified as aggressive growth and growth. The primary emphasis of these funds is appreciation of capital and not generation of current income. Aggressive growth funds may take a considerable amount of risk, such as buying and selling options, to obtain their specified investment goal.

Mutual Funds in the Period 1945–64," *Journal of Finance,* 23 (May 1968): 389–416; Patricia Dunn and Rolf D. Theisen, "How Consistently Do Active Managers Win?" *Journal of Portfolio Management,* 9 (Summer 1983): 47–50; and Frank J. Fabozzi, Jack C. Francis, and Cheng F. Lee, "Generalized Functional Form for Mutual Fund Performance," *Journal of Financial and Quantitative Analysis,* 15 (December 1980): 1107–1120.

(Figure 23.2 CONTINUED)

C. International Funds, Precious Metal Funds,
   and S & P 500 Stock Index

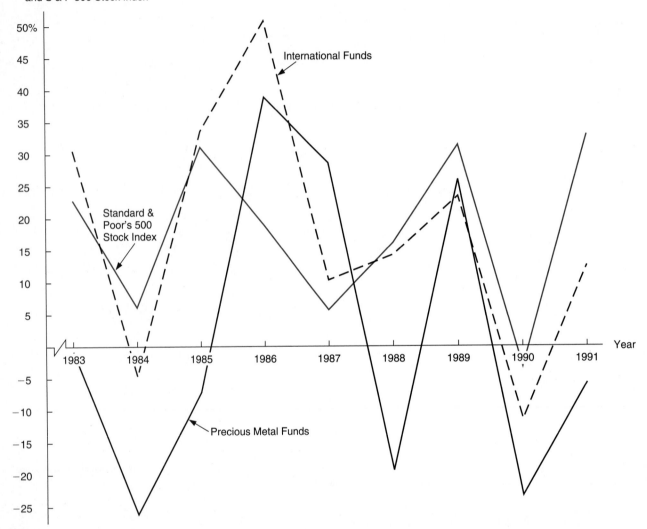

Source: The Individual Investor's Guide to No-Load Mutual Funds, 8th and 11th eds. (Chicago: American Association of Individual Investors, 1989 and 1992).

Part B presents the aggregate annual returns for no-load funds stressing growth and income and funds with balanced portfolios. These funds tend to have more conservative portfolios than those funds seeking capital appreciation. However, the more conservative funds appear to have performed better than the more aggressive funds during this particular time period, especially during 1984 and 1990.

Part C gives the annual returns for two types of specialized funds: the international funds and the precious metal funds. By far the best return was achieved by the international funds whose portfolios are invested solely in foreign securities

Figure 23.3 ✦ Annual Percentage Returns, 1983–1991, Acorn Fund and USAA Growth Fund

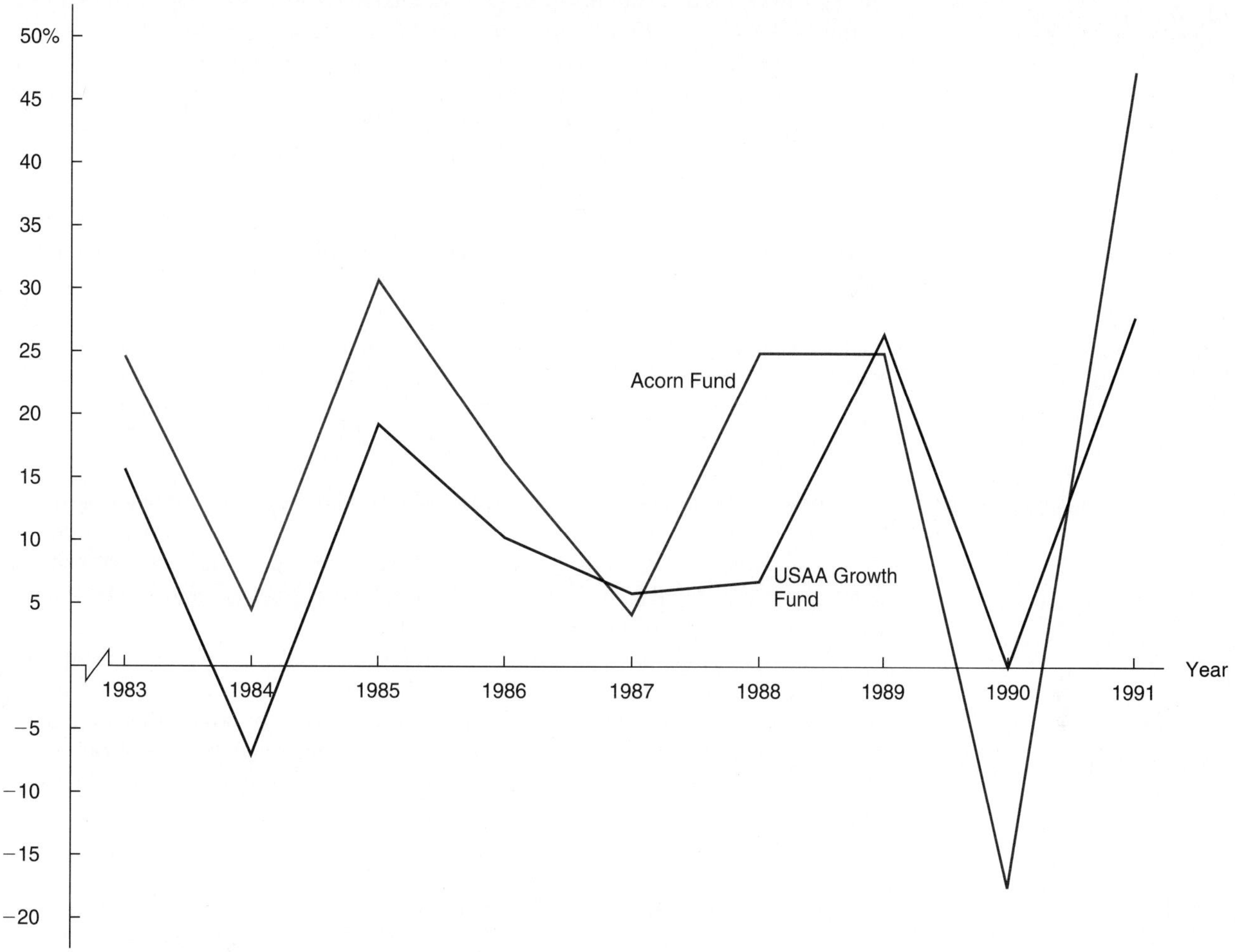

Source: The Individual Investor's Guide to No-Load Mutual Funds, 8th and 11th eds. (Chicago: American Association of Individual Investors, 1989 and 1992).

and include no U.S. securities. As explained in the next chapter on international investments, fluctuations in the value of currencies affect the yields on foreign investments. If the value of the dollar declines relative to other currencies, these moneys are worth more when they are converted into dollars. During the 1980s the dollar declined relative to foreign currencies, which may help explain why the international funds did exceptionally well. However, during the same time period, the price of gold and other precious metals did not rise, which explains why the precious metal funds did the poorest of the no-load funds used to construct Figure 23.2.

Individuals do not earn the return achieved by an aggregation of funds. Individuals choose specific funds; that is, they select among the alternatives. An individual's fund could have done better or worse than the average returns presented in Figure 23.2. This is illustrated in Figure 23.3, which presents the annual returns for the Acorn Fund and the USAA Growth Fund. As may be seen in the figure, the

Acorn Fund did considerably better over the time period than the USAA Growth Fund. Obviously if the investor had selected the Acorn Fund in 1983 and held it through 1991, his investment would have yielded a higher return than an investment in the USAA Growth Fund during the same time period.

Fund performance may also vary during rising and falling markets. A fund that has historically done well during a rising market may be an inferior performer during declining markets. The period used in Figure 23.2 was a time of positive returns, and the *Individual Investor's Guide to No-Load Mutual Funds* ranks Acorn among the best performers during rising markets but below average during declining markets.[14] The USAA Growth Fund, however, has a better ranking during declining markets (e.g., 1990). If the investor could forecast which type of market were going to occur, that individual could switch between the two funds.

Such successful market timing should increase returns earned by individuals or professional investment managers. However, empirical evidence suggests that few managers are able to achieve superior timing.[15] These findings are consistent with the prior studies of investment performance by mutual funds. In the aggregate the returns earned by mutual funds over a period of years do not exceed the return earned by the market as a whole.

These results are easy to misinterpret. They do not imply that the managements of mutual funds are incompetent. The findings give strong support for the efficient market hypothesis discussed in Chapter 8. In an efficient market, only competent managers would be able to match the market over a period of years. The incompetent would be forced out by their inferior results.

What these findings imply is that mutual funds and other investment companies may offer investors a means to match the performance of the market and still obtain the advantages of diversification and custodial services. For some, these are sufficient reasons to invest in the shares of investment companies instead of directly in stocks and bonds. These investors do not have to concern themselves with the selection of individual securities.

Impact of Taxes on Rates of Return

The previous discussion suggested that in the aggregate mutual funds do not outperform the market, and that since the individual investor purchases shares in individual funds, that investor should compare the performance of the various funds in

---

[14] *The Individual Investor's Guide to No-Load Mutual Funds* is published annually by the American Association of Individual Investors, but this publication is limited to no-load funds. *Forbes* in its annual issue devoted to mutual funds ranks both load and no-load funds with regard to their performance in up and down markets. Another means to compare fund performance in rising and declining markets is to ask the question: If $10,000 were invested in the fund, how much would the investor have after five years or ten years, assuming all dividends and capital gains distributions are reinvested? *Barron's* publishes the answer to that question in its periodic reviews of mutual fund performance.

[15] Roy D. Hendriksson, "Market Timing and Mutual Fund Performance: An Empirical Investigation," *Journal of Business*, 57 (January 1984): 73–96, and Stanley J. Kon, "The Market-Timing Performance of Mutual Fund Managers," *Journal of Business*, 56 (July 1983): 323–347.

POINTS OF INTEREST

THE REGULATION OF MUTUAL FUNDS

Mutual funds operate under the Investment Company Act of 1940, which is administered by the Securities and Exchange Commission. The general purpose of this regulation is the same as that which applies to the securities market: the disclosure of information so the individual investor can make an informed decision. Mutual funds must register their shares with the SEC and provide prospective shareholders with a prospectus. The prospectus specifies the fund's investment objectives, the composition of its portfolio, fees and expenses that the investor pays, the composition of the fund's board of directors, and insider transactions.

Regulation does not specify maximum fees nor does it apply to the execution of the fund's objective or its performance. It is assumed that excessive fees or poor performance will lead to the demise of the fund just as the poor management of a firm will lead to its failure. Regulation cannot assure that investors will earn profits nor does it protect them from their own folly or greed.

---

rising and declining markets. Earned returns will help compare the performance among funds, but the individual should realize that the return earned by the fund may not be comparable to the return earned on his or her investment in the fund.

One important problem concerning calculating the individual's realized rate of return pertains to federal income taxation. For example, suppose a fund has a net asset value of $10. During the year it earns $1 per share in income, which it distributes as dividends. For the individual who owns 100 shares and who participates in the dividend reinvestment plan, the $100 in dividends is used to purchase additional shares. The amount invested in the fund now rises to $1,100. The initial investment has appreciated by 10 percent, but the investor must pay income tax on the distribution. The amount of the tax depends on the individual's marginal tax bracket. If the tax rate is 28 percent, the investor must pay $28. There are essentially two choices—liquidate part of the holdings in the fund or pay the taxes with funds from other sources.

If this individual wants to maintain the full investment in the fund, he or she must finance the tax payment from another source. In effect, the investor must commit more funds to maintain the investment, making the net return less than the gross return. The mutual fund, however, cannot be expected to know its stockholders' tax brackets and thus reports returns on a before-tax and not on an after-tax basis.[16]

In the previous illustration, the distribution was income (i.e., dividends). If the fund's net asset value increased by $1 per share through appreciation in its portfolio, the fund could realize and distribute the capital gain. Once again the participant in the dividend reinvestment plan would have these funds plowed back into additional shares. The number of shares obtained would be the same, since $100 of reinvested income and $100 of reinvested capital gains would purchase the same number of additional shares.

---

[16]This problem, of course, applies to all investments subject to income taxation. However, the general existence of the problems does not erase the fact that it reduces the comparability of the individual's realized after-tax return and the before-tax return reported by the mutual fund.

The distribution of the capital gain has the same implication for taxes as the distribution of the income. In either case, the investor must pay federal income tax on the return. If the investor wants to reinvest the full amount of the capital gain distribution, he or she must finance the tax payment from another source. Once again the investor should realize that the return earned is reported by the fund on a before-tax basis, but the investor only has the after-tax return to use.

Calculating the after-tax return earned on an investment in a mutual fund is difficult because of several variables that affect this return. These include (1) the individual's marginal income tax rate, (2) the increase in the fund's net asset value, (3) the fund's distributions, and (4) whether the individual sells some shares to pay the applicable taxes or pays the taxes out of pocket and thus forgoes the alternative uses for that money.[17]

Impact of Fees on Rates of Return

The return earned by the investor is also affected by the fund's fees (e.g., management fees, commissions to brokers, and sales fees called loading charges). Perhaps the most visible are the loading charges, which may be levied when the investor purchases the shares (i.e., the fund is front-loaded) or may be assessed when the shares are redeemed (i.e., the fund is back-end loaded). As with taxes, loading fees make it more difficult to compare the performance reported by the funds and the returns actually realized by the investor.

Consider a front-loaded mutual fund that charges 8.5 percent of the amount invested. If the net asset value of the fund is $10, the investor must remit $10.93 to purchase a share.[18] The fund during the year earns $1, so the net asset value grows to $11. The fund's management reports a return of 10 percent, but the individual investor has certainly not earned 10 percent. Instead the actual amount invested ($10.93) has grown to $11, an increase of less than 1 percent. Over a period of years the loading fee significantly reduces the return. For example, if the fund were to earn 12 percent compounded annually for seven years, its net asset value would grow from $10 to $22.11. However, the investor's return would be only 10.6 percent as the actual amount invested ($10.93) rises to $22.11.

The return is further decreased if the fund has a deferred exit fee (or nuisance fee) that applies if shares are redeemed within a specified time period. For example, the Dean Witter Natural Resources Fund has a redemption fee even though it is considered to be a no-load fund. The fee starts at 5 percent and declines to 1 per-

---

[17] One method has been suggested for the individual to compute after-tax, realized return on an investment in a mutual fund. (See Alan Pope, "Distributions: A Taxing Effect on Mutual Fund Returns," *American Association of Individual Investors Journal* (October 1984): 15–18.) The calculation assumes the investor reinvests all distributions but liquidates sufficient shares to pay the taxes. The technique permits the individual investor to determine the after-tax growth in the value of the holdings after adjusting for (1) the individual's tax bracket, (2) fund's distributions out of income, and (3) capital gain distributions.

[18] This cost of the share is determined as follows:

$$\$10/(1 - 0.085) = \$10/0.915 = \$10.93.$$

The loading fee is $0.93, which is 8.5 percent of the amount invested ($10.93 × 0.085 = $0.93). As was discussed earlier in this chapter, loading fees are figured on the amount invested and not on the net asset value.

cent if the shares are held six years. Several funds have both a loading fee and a redemption fee.[19] Such fees may be designed to reduce switching investments and cover the costs to the funds of handling withdrawals. Such deferred fees reduce the return and make comparisons of the fund's stated return and the individual's realized return more difficult.[20]

This problem of comparisons created by fees is considerably lessened for a no-load mutual fund if (1) the management fees of the no-load fund are no higher than the management fees of the load fund and (2) the no-load fund does not have an exit fee. Some no-load funds assess a sales charge when the investor redeems the shares (i.e., a load fee in reverse). Since the fund lacks a traditional front-end load fee, it may refer to itself as a no-load fund.

The impact of a back-end load fee can be considerable even though the charge may be expressed as a modest 2 or 3 percent. Consider the preceding illustration in which the net asset value grew from $10 to $22.11 in seven years for a 12 percent annual increase. If the fund assesses a 3 percent back-end fee, the investor receives $21.44, so the realized return is reduced from 12 percent annually to 11.5 percent.

If the fund has both a front-end and back-end load, the investor's return is reduced even further. To continue the preceding example, the individual spends $10.93 to acquire a share with a net asset value of $10. The net asset value then compounds at 12 percent for seven years to $22.11, and the fund assesses a 3 percent back-end load. The investor receives $21.44, so that individual has in effect invested $10.93 to receive $21.44 over seven years. This is a return of 10.1 percent annually, which is almost two percentage points below the 12 percent that the fund can report as the growth in the net asset value.

Actually, the impact on the terminal value of an investment in the fund is the same for a back-end and a front-end loading fee as long as the percentages are the same. For example, fund A charges a 3 percent front-end load fee while fund B charges a 3 percent exit fee. The initial net asset value of each is $10, which grows annually at 12 percent for 12 years. The terminal value of fund A is

$$\$10 - 0.30 = \$9.70,$$

$$\$9.70(3.8960) = \$37.79.$$

The terminal value of fund B is

$$\$10(3.8960) = \$38.96,$$

$$\$38.96 - 0.03(\$38.96) = \$37.79.$$

In both cases the terminal value is $37.79.[21]

The impact of these differences in loading fees is substantial when the rate differences are compounded over many years. Consider a $50,000 investment in a fund that is left to compound at 12 percent for 20 years. The $50,000 grows to $482,314. However, if the fund had charged an initial load fee of 8.5%, the investor would have only $45,750 actually invested by the fund. At 12 percent compounded

---

[19] See Gerald W. Perritt, "Playing the Sector Game: Big Wins and Big Losses," *Barron's*, November 11, 1985, 59–63.

[20] The mutual fund quotations in Exhibit 23.4 indicate these fees. The "p" after the AIM funds indicates the fund has a 12b-1 fee. An "f" indicates a redemption charge, and "t" indicates both 12b-1 and redemption fees.

[21] 3.8960 is the interest factor for the future value of $1 at 12 percent for 12 years.

annually for 20 years, the terminal value would be $441,318. This is $40,996 less than would be earned with the no-load fund.

Suppose the investor had purchased shares in a no-load fund with an exit fee of 3 percent. In this case the investor receives $467,845 ($482,314 − $14,469). If the investor had purchased a load mutual fund with an 8½ percent front load and a 3 percent back-end load, this individual would have netted only $424,335, or $57,979 less than the no-load fund with no exit fee. Obviously the loading fees can have a considerable impact on the net return the investor ultimately earns, even though the net asset value increased by the same percentage in each case!

While it should be obvious from the preceding illustrations, the investor should not view the load as a one-time fee whose impact is reduced over time as it is spread over an ever increasing investment. Instead the opposite is true. The longer the investor holds the shares, the greater the absolute differential will be between the terminal values of the load and no-load funds. The funds not lost to the load fee are being compounded over a longer period of time; thus, the terminal value of the no-load fund becomes even larger.

While this discussion suggests that investors should purchase no-load mutual funds in preference to those with load fees, the investor still needs to be aware of an expense some no-load funds charge that may prove over a period of time to be more costly than the loading fees. The purpose of the loading fee is to compensate those individuals who sell the fund's shares. No-load funds do not have a sales force and thus do not have this expense. They may, however, use other marketing devices, such as advertising, that must be paid for.

12b-1 fees
Fees that a no-load mutual fund may charge to cover marketing and advertising expenses.

Some no-load funds have adopted an SEC rule that permits management to use the fund's assets to pay for these marketing expenses. These funds have adopted a **12b-1 fee,** which is named for the number of the SEC rule that enables funds to assess what is, in effect, an on-going charge that stockholders pay. Some load funds also have 12b-1 fees. Since the fund must disclose fees, it behooves the investor to know all the expenses prior to investing. Unlike a front load fee, which is charged when the shares are purchased, this 12b-1 fee can be a continuous annual fee. Thus over a number of years, investors in no-load funds assessing this charge may pay more than they would have paid in loading fees.

Over a period of years 12b-1 fees can significantly reduce the return the investor earns, since the fee is paid not only in good years but also in years when the fund experiences losses and a decline in its net asset value. The investor needs to be aware of 12b-1 fees when selecting a mutual fund, since the growth in the fund's net asset value will be reduced by the fee. Suppose one fund charges a fee that averages 1.0 percent of total assets while another fund does not assess the fee. Both funds earn 12 percent on assets before the fees, so after the fee is paid the returns are 12 percent for the fund without the fee but 11 percent for the fund with the 12b-1 fee. Obviously the stockholder's return is reduced, and over time the impact of this reduction can be surprisingly large. Consider an initial investment of $1,000. After 20 years the $1,000 at 12 percent grows to $9,646 in the fund without the fee but only grows to $8,062 in the fund with the fee. The difference ($1,584) is, of course, the result of the 12b-1 fee. Thus unless the fees lead to higher investment returns, they must reduce the return earned by the investor.[22]

---

[22] See Laura R. Walbert, "Bark Watchdogs," *Forbes,* June 16, 1986, 174, and *The Individual Investor's Guide to No-Load Mutual Funds,* 8th ed. (Chicago: American Association of Individual Investors, 1989), xiv–xv, for a discussion of the impact of 12b-1 fees.

Risk Adjustments for Comparing Rates of Return

Even if the investor is able to determine the rates of return various funds have earned, these rates may still not be comparable. Different funds with the same goal (such as capital appreciation) may not be equally risky. From the investor's viewpoint a return of 15 percent achieved by a low-risk portfolio is preferred to 15 percent earned on a very risky portfolio. If the investor compares absolute rates of return, he or she is implicitly assuming that both funds are equally risky.

While the discussion of portfolio evaluation and risk-adjusted returns is deferred until Chapter 25, the investor in mutual funds needs to realize that absolute returns may not be truly comparable. To compare returns, the investor needs to standardize funds' performance for differences in risk. After making this adjustment, then the individual investor can better determine if the fund's management did outperform the market as a whole.

One way to standardize returns for risk is to use beta coefficients. As was explained in Chapter 7, a beta coefficient is an index of systematic risk that measures the volatility of the fund's returns relative to the market as a whole. A beta of 1.0 indicates that the volatility of the fund's return is the same as that of the market. A beta of greater than 1.0 indicates that the fund is more volatile and a beta of less than 1.0 indicates the fund is less volatile.

To standardize for risk, divide the individual fund's return by its beta coefficient.[23] That is, the risk-adjusted return is

Risk-adjusted return = Return on the fund/beta.

If fund A has a return of 15 percent and a beta of 1.4 while fund B has a return of 15 percent and a beta of 0.8, their risk-adjusted returns are

Risk-adjusted return for A = 0.15/1.4 = 10.7%.

Risk-adjusted return for B = 0.15/0.8 = 18.75%.

Obviously the investor would prefer fund B, whose risk-adjusted return is superior.

If the investor wants to determine whether or not the fund has outperformed the market, the risk-adjusted return is compared to the return on the market. This comparison may be achieved in two ways. The return on the market may be subtracted from the individual fund's risk-adjusted return. For example, if a fund's risk-adjusted return is 13.6 percent and the market return is 12.4 percent, the fund

---

[23]To be technically correct, the risk-free return should be subtracted from the fund's return and the result divided by the beta coefficient. Without this adjustment, it would be possible for a fund consisting of treasury bills and a beta of zero to have the highest risk-adjusted performance. However, after subtracting the risk-free return (i.e., the yield on the treasury bills), the fund's return would be zero and the fund would not have the highest risk-adjusted return. For funds that invest in a portfolio of risky assets, it is not necessary to subtract the risk-free return to compare their performance on a risk-adjusted basis. The risk-free rate is a constant; thus failure to subtract a constant from each return prior to dividing by the beta will not change the ranking of the funds' risk-adjusted returns and hence does not change the interpretation of the results.

outperformed the market by 1.2 percent (13.6 − 12.4). The second method is to divide the risk-adjusted return by the return on the market. Using the numbers of the previous illustration, the calculation is

$$13.6/12.4 = 1.097.$$

Either calculation gives essentially the same information. The latter procedure, however, standardizes each fund's return and may make it easier to compare several funds' risk-adjusted rates of return. All funds with a score of greater than 1.0 outperformed the market while all with a score of less than 1.0 underperformed the market on a risk-adjusted basis.

Whether the investor should purchase individual mutual funds on the basis of management's outperforming the market is open to debate. Previous performance may not be indicative of future performance, and the efficient market hypothesis suggests that it is extremely difficult to outperform the market consistently. The word *consistent* is exceedingly important, since it requires that the fund's management do well in both rising and falling markets. The individual investor may be better off remembering the implications of the efficient market hypothesis than concentrating on the past performance. Even if past performance is repeated, it still may not indicate the return the individual investor earns once the impact of fees, taxes, and risk are considered.

SUMMARY

Instead of directly investing in securities, individuals may buy shares in investment companies. These firms, in turn, invest the funds in various assets, such as stocks and bonds.

There are two types of investment companies. A closed-end investment company has a specified number of shares that are bought and sold in the same manner as the stock of firms such as AT&T. An open-end investment company (i.e., a mutual fund) has a variable number of shares sold directly to investors. Investors who desire to liquidate their holdings sell them back to the company.

Investment companies offer several advantages, including professional management, diversification, and custodial services. Dividends and the interest earned on the firm's assets are distributed to stockholders. In addition, if the value of the company's assets rises, the stockholders profit as capital gains are realized and distributed.

Mutual funds may be classified by the types of assets they own. Some stress income-producing assets, such as bonds, preferred stock, and common stock of firms that distribute a large proportion of their income. Other mutual funds stress growth in their net asset values through investments in firms with the potential to grow and generate capital gains. There are also investment companies that specialize in special situations, particular sectors of the economy, and tax-exempt securities. There are even mutual funds that seek to duplicate an index of the stock market.

Although investment companies are professionally managed, the returns that mutual funds have earned over a period of years have not consistently outperformed the market. This result is consistent with the efficient market hypothesis.

To select a mutual fund, the individual should match his or her objectives with those of the fund. The age and size of the fund, its past performance, and the potential for hidden tax liabilities should also be considered. The investor should realize that it is difficult to compare the returns earned on different mutual funds with the return the individual investor may earn. Differences in the volatility of the funds' returns; differences in loading charges, exit fees, and 12b-1 plan expenses; and differences in taxes on ordinary income and unrealized capital gains further complicate comparing the growth in the fund's net asset value and the individual investor's return on money invested in the mutual fund.

Security Summary

Mutual Funds

Source of return: Interest and/or dividend income and possible capital gains if value of portfolio rises.

Liquidity and marketability: Secondary market in shares of closed-end funds; no market for shares in mutual funds that must be redeemed on demand by the fund. Liquidity varies with the types of fund, which range from very liquid money market funds to risky specialized funds whose shares cannot be considered liquid.

Sources of risk: Diversified portfolio significantly reduces firm-specific risk (i.e., unsystematic risk). Stock funds are subject to systematic risk as the returns on their shares tend to move with the market. The value of bond funds tends to fluctuate with changes in interest rates.

Taxation: Distributions by investment companies of interest, dividends, and capital gains are subject to federal income taxation even if the individual has the funds reinvested. Sales of shares are subject to capital gains taxation.

Terms to Remember

closed-end investment company	unit trust
open-end investment company	no-load fund
mutual fund	load fund
net asset value	growth stock
premium and discount (from net asset value)	index fund
	12b-1 fees

Questions

1. What is the difference between a closed-end and an open-end investment company?
2. Are mutual funds subject to federal income taxation?
3. What custodial services do investment companies provide?
4. What is a loading charge? Do all investment companies charge this fee?
5. Why may the small investor prefer mutual funds to other investments?

6. What is a specialized mutual fund? How is it different from a special situation fund?

7. Should an investor expect a mutual fund to outperform the market? If not, why should the investor buy the shares?

8. What are the differences among loading fees, exit (or nuisance) fees, and 12b-1 plans?

9. How can an investor determine if a mutual fund has hidden capital gains? What impact may these gains have on the return of an investor who currently buys the shares?

10. What advantages may small funds offer over large funds? What advantages may an older fund offer over a new fund? Why may it be important to determine if a mutual fund's management has recently changed?

11. Why may the annual growth in a fund's net asset value not be comparable to the return earned by an individual investor?

12. How may beta coefficients be used to standardize returns for risk to permit comparisons of mutual fund performance?

Problems

1. What is the net asset value of an investment company with $10,000,000 in assets, $790,000 in current liabilities, and 1,200,000 shares outstanding?

2. If a mutual fund's net asset value is $23.40 and the fund sells its shares for $25, what is the load fee as a percentage of the net asset value (i.e., the amount actually invested in the shares)?

3. If an investor buys shares in a no-load mutual fund for $31.40 and the shares appreciate to $44.60 in two years, what would be the rate of return on the investment? If the fund charges an exit fee of 1 percent, what would be the rate of return on the investment?

4. An investor buys shares in a mutual fund for $20. At the end of the year the fund distributes a dividend of $0.58, and after the distribution the net asset value of a share is $23.41. What would be the investor's return on the investment?

5. Fund A experienced a return of 14.5 percent while fund B experienced a return of only 13.2 percent. If their beta coefficients were 1.2 and 0.86, respectively, which fund achieved the superior performance?

6. You purchase a mutual fund for $35 a share. The fund makes the following distributions:

Year	Distribution
1	$1.00
2	3.15
3	2.09
4	1.71

At the end of the fourth year, you redeem the shares for $41. What was the rate of return on your investment? (Refer to Chapter 9, if necessary.)

Suggested Readings

General information on mutual funds may be found in

Investment Company Institute. *Mutual Fund Fact Book.* Published annually.

Dorf, Richard C. *The New Mutual Fund Investment Advisor: Everything You Need to Know about Investing in No-load.* Chicago: Probus Publishing Company, 1991.

Hirsch, Michael D. *The Mutual Fund Wealth Builder.* New York: Harper Business, 1992.

Merriman, Paul. *Investing for a Lifetime: Paul Merriman's Guide to Mutual Fund Strategies.* Homewood, IL: Business One Irwin, 1991.

Perritt, Gerald. *The Mutual Fund Encyclopedia 1992–3 Edition.* Dearborn Finance, 1992.

Rugg, Donald D., and Norman B. Hale. *The Dow Jones–Irwin Guide to Mutual Funds.* 3d ed. Homewood, IL: Dow Jones-Irwin, 1986.

A guide to a mutual fund's prospectus is given in

Perritt, Gerald W. "Fund Literature: A Guide to the Essentials," *AAII Journal* (March 1986): 22–24.

The services rendered by mutual funds is discussed in

Fredman, Albert J. "Investing and Redeeming: A Look at Fund Services," *AAII Journal* (February 1993), 19–23.

Explicit and hidden mutual fund fees are discussed in

Zweig, Jason and Mary Beth Grover. "Fee Madness," *Forbes* (February 15, 1993) 160–164.

The variety of closed-end funds is discussed in

Anderson, Seth C., and Jeffrey A. Born. *Closed-end Investment Companies: Issues and Answers.* Hingham, MA: Kluwer Academic Publishers, 1992.

Fredman and George Cole Scott, "Building and Maintaining a Portfolio of Closed-End Funds," *AAII Journal* (September 1992):14–18.

A discussion of factors that affect the discounts or premiums paid for the shares of closed-end investment companies can be found in

Malkiel, Burton G. "The Valuation of Closed-End Investment Company Shares." *Journal of Finance* (June 1977): 847–859.

Mendelson, Morris. "Closed-End Fund Discounts Revisited." *The Financial Review* (Spring 1978): 48–72.

Weiss, Kathleen. "The Post-Offering Price Performance of Closed-End Funds." *Financial Management* (Autumn 1989): 57–67.

24

INVESTING IN FOREIGN SECURITIES

LEARNING OBJECTIVES

After completing this chapter you should be able to

1. Enumerate the advantages offered by foreign securities.

2. Define foreign exchange rates, foreign exchange markets, and foreign exchange rate risk.

3. Contrast devaluation and revaluation.

4. Identify the special risks associated with foreign investments.

5. Explain how hedging with currency futures is used to reduce the risk associated with fluctuations in exchange rates.

6. Explain how foreign investments help diversify a domestic portfolio.

7. Determine the advantages offered by shares in international investment companies.

F or many individuals living in the United States, investment in stocks or bonds means the purchase of securities issued by American firms. Portfolios are limited to the securities of U.S. companies even though many corporations (e.g., Coca-Cola) have substantial foreign operations. Buying the securities of firms with global operations may not be viewed by U.S. investors as making a foreign investment even though over half of a corporation's revenues may be generated by foreign sales.

Confining investments to the securities of U.S. corporations is a narrow approach to security selection that limits the investor's alternatives. Stocks and bonds are actively traded in many countries. The shares of large, global American firms (e.g., IBM) are traded on several foreign exchanges. Conversely, the shares of large foreign companies (e.g., SONY) trade in the United States. Excluding weekends, securities are being bought and sold somewhere in the world at all times. Trading occurs twenty-four hours a day. While specific markets (e.g., the New York Stock Exchange) have limited trading hours, the shares of many American and foreign firms trade virtually all the time. The effect is to have a continuous market or "around-the-clock trading" in these securities. Events that occur while a particular exchange is closed still have an immediate impact on the value of stocks and bonds traded on international security markets. The trend toward the increased listings of securities on many exchanges and the globalization of financial markets suggest that in the future even more securities will be traded around-the-clock.

Interest in foreign securities by American investors increased during the late 1980s. Today, stock quotes for many foreign companies and major foreign stock indices are reported daily in The Wall Street Journal. *These include the Tokyo Nikkei Average, the London FT 30-share index, the London FT-SE 100-share index, the Frankfurt DAX, the Paris CAC index, and the EAFE index. The EAFE is a general index of non-U.S. stocks, computed by Morgan Stanley, comprising stocks in Europe, Australia, and the Far East, hence the EAFE index. In addition, Salomon Brothers, First Boston, and Goldman Sachs also publish indices of world equity markets. In 1993, Dow Jones launched a comprehensive global index which was initially limited to stocks in ten countries but will be expanded to include every country with stock available to foreign investors.*

This chapter is concerned with foreign investments from the perspective of a U.S. investor. Such investments have been touched upon throughout this text. For example, the creation of American Depositor Receipts (ADRs) for the purchase and sale of foreign stocks was covered in Chapter 3 on security markets. This chapter will stress the special risks associated with foreign investments, the reduction of risk through hedging, the use of foreign securities to diversify the individual's portfolio, and investment companies that offer a means to take a position in foreign securities without having to select specific foreign stocks and bonds.

✦ ✦ ✦

GLOBAL WEALTH AND WORLD FINANCIAL MARKETS

The value of the world's assets is substantial. Exhibit 24.1 presents an estimate of the value of the ten largest equity markets. While the United States is a dominant world economic power, it accounted for less than half of the total value of the world's equity. The growth of a common economic unit in Europe and the development of Far Eastern economies such as Korea suggest that the United States equity market will become a major, but declining, part of the world's total wealth.

The existence and size of global assets argues for foreign assets to be included in the portfolios of American investors. Foreign investments generally imply the acquisition of assets in advanced economies (i.e., developed countries or "DCs"), but emerging economies (i.e., less-developed countries or "LDCs") such as Chile, Korea, or Thailand could offer superior investment opportunities. Emerging economies may grow more rapidly and be less responsive to global economic changes than firms in advanced economies. More rapid economic growth suggests higher potential returns. In addition, less sensitivity to recession experienced by advanced economies suggests more opportunities for diversification.

Exhibit 24.1 ✦ ESTIMATED SIZE OF TEN LARGEST EQUITY MARKETS, 1992

Country	Value of Equity (in billions of U.S. dollars)	Percent of Total
United States	$2,869	44.8%
Japan	1,676	26.2
United Kingdom	777	12.1
Germany	270	4.2
France	254	4.0
Switzerland	119	1.9
Hong Kong	118	1.9
Netherlands	115	1.8
Canada	110	1.7
Australia	91	1.4

Source: Morgan Stanley Capital International Inc. *Business Week,* July 13, 1992, p. 50.

In addition to LDCs, the sudden change in the political environment in eastern Europe and the states of the former Soviet Union may also offer opportunities for the adventuresome investor. While it is premature to determine if security markets will develop in formerly communist countries, certainly American, Japanese, and western European firms will seek to enter these potential markets. It may not be possible for investors to participate directly in these economies through equity investments; however, individuals may purchase the shares of firms seeking to expand operations into eastern Europe and the emerging nations of the former Soviet Union. Of course, for that strategy to generate a positive return, the firm's earnings must increase as a result of these foreign investments. Because most of the firms capable of making these investments will tend to be large, global firms, it may be impossible to isolate the impact that eastern European investments will have on these firm's bottom lines.

THE SPECIAL RISKS ASSOCIATED WITH FOREIGN INVESTMENTS

U.S. residents invest in foreign securities to earn a return through the receipt of income (dividends or interest) and price appreciation. These investments involve special considerations that affect the return the investor earns and the risk that must be borne. These factors include political risks, local taxation, and the fluctuation of the U.S. dollar relative to foreign currencies. The latter is particularly important since any return received in foreign funds must be converted into U.S. dollars before the investor can use the money in the United States. Obviously the investor who receives dividends in British pounds can spend the funds in London, but those pounds must be converted into dollars before they are spent in the United States.

Political Risks

The political climate of a foreign nation creates risks because governments and political systems do change. The potential for this change must be considered by a U.S. business seeking to expand its market through foreign operations. Firms with foreign investments have experienced nationalization and expropriation of assets. These firms are not guaranteed compensation for any seized assets. For example, Cuba did not offer compensation when Fidel Castro came to power and nationalized the facilities of U.S. firms.

Investors also bear this risk. Castro repudiated debts Cuba owed. To this day pre-Castro Cuban bonds are still outstanding. Perhaps even more surprising is that some of these bonds are still traded. The price for an issue of Cuban bonds that was due *in 1977* traded in 1992 from a high of $39⅞ to a low of $26 for $100 face amount of debt. Even though the bond is past maturity and has not paid interest for years, there still exists a market. Presumably, investors who currently purchase these bonds are speculating on an improvement in political relations between the United States and Cuba that might result in repayment of some of the debt. However, the initial investors painfully learned the political risks associated with investing in foreign securities issued in politically unstable countries.

Foreign Taxation

Foreign taxation further complicates foreign investments and reduces the return earned by the individual. Just as the U.S. government taxes dividend income, foreign governments may also tax dividend and interest payments. To facilitate the collection of the funds, these taxes are usually withheld before the U.S. investor receives the money. For example, if the usual withholding rate is 15 percent and a British firm distributes a cash dividend of £100, £15 are withheld and £85 remitted to the U.S. holder, who must convert the pounds to dollars. If the U.S. investor owns ADRs instead of the actual British stock, the bank that is the stock's transfer agent receives the payment, converts the pounds into dollars, and remits the funds to the holder of the ADR. The bank collects a fee for this service. However, since the bank exchanges large amounts of foreign currency, any fee charged will probably be less than the individual investor would have to pay to have the pounds converted into dollars.

The dividends (and interest) received from foreign investments are also subject to income taxation in the United States. If the investor in the previous illustration is in the 28 percent federal income tax bracket, then 28 percent of the £100 is subject to tax. To facilitate the illustration, assume a pound is worth $2, so the dividend is $200 ($2.00 × 100). The federal income tax would be $56 ($200 × .28). This tax is in addition to the £15 ($30) that the British government has already withheld. The U.S. federal government permits the U.S. investor to take a foreign tax credit for the amount of the foreign tax. Thus, the net amount owed to the U.S. federal government is $26 ($56 − $30).

FLUCTUATIONS IN EXCHANGE RATES

In addition to income, investors acquire assets for possible capital gains. In the case of foreign investments, capital gains may occur because the value of the asset rises or because the value of the foreign currency in which the asset is denominated rises. Since capital gains are related to the price of the asset as well as the value of the currency, it is possible for the price of the asset to rise but for this price increase to be offset by a decline in the value of the currency. It is also possible for the price of the asset to decline but for the price decline to be offset by an increase in the value of the currency.

While the previous section considered political risks and foreign taxation, this section covers the risk from fluctuations in the value of the U.S. dollar relative to other currencies. Since fluctuations in the value of currencies can enhance or reduce the return earned on foreign investments, these fluctuations affect the risk associated with investing in foreign assets. This risk is in addition to the usual risks the investor must bear: the diversifiable, unsystematic risk associated with the particular asset and the non-diversifiable, systematic risk from fluctuations in market prices, changes in interest rates, and the loss of purchasing power through inflation.

The value of currencies responds to changes in the demand and supply for the currencies. The demand for foreign investments (as well as foreign goods and services) is also a demand for foreign money. To acquire these funds, buyers must exchange their currency for the foreign currency. For example, if U.S. citizens want

Exhibit 24.2 ✦ SELECTED FOREIGN EXCHANGE RATES, JANUARY 11, 1993

CURRENCY TRADING

EXCHANGE RATES

Monday, January 11, 1993

The New York foreign exchange selling rates below apply to trading among banks in amounts of $1 million and more, as quoted at 3 p.m. Eastern time by Bankers Trust Co., Telerate and other sources. Retail transactions provide fewer units of foreign currency per dollar.

Country	U.S. $ equiv. Mon.	U.S. $ equiv. Fri.	Currency per U.S. $ Mon.	Currency per U.S. $ Fri.
Argentina (Peso)	1.01	1.01	.99	.99
Australia (Dollar)	.6735	.6728	1.4848	1.4863
Austria (Schilling)	.08709	.08640	11.48	11.57
Bahrain (Dinar)	2.6522	2.6522	.3771	.3771
Belgium (Franc)	.02977	.02955	33.59	33.84
Brazil (Cruzeiro)	.0000693	.0000795	14435.01	12584.01
Britain (Pound)	1.5555	1.5325	.6429	.6525
30-Day Forward	1.5495	1.5272	.6454	.6548
90-Day Forward	1.5409	1.5181	.6490	.6587
180-Day Forward	1.5298	1.5075	.6537	.6633
Canada (Dollar)	.7828	.7798	1.2775	1.2823
30-Day Forward	.7803	.7774	1.2816	1.2864
90-Day Forward	.7761	.7729	1.2885	1.2938
180-Day Forward	.7703	.7620	1.2982	1.3123
Czechoslovakia (Koruna)				
Commercial rate	.0349650	.0350754	28.6000	28.5100
Chile (Peso)	.002688	.002689	372.08	371.82
China (Renminbi)	.171233	.171233	5.8400	5.8400
Colombia (Peso)	.001607	.001612	622.20	620.50
Denmark (Krone)	.1586	.1573	6.3054	6.3563
Ecuador (Sucre)				
Floating rate	.000552	.000554	1812.02	1806.00
Finland (Markka)	.18399	.18214	5.4352	5.4902
France (Franc)	.18041	.17873	5.5430	5.5950
30-Day Forward	.17892	.17742	5.5892	5.6365
90-Day Forward	.17667	.17510	5.6602	5.7110
180-Day Forward	.17417	.17279	5.7415	5.7875
Germany (Mark)	.6130	.6079	1.6312	1.6450
30-Day Forward	.6099	.6051	1.6397	1.6526
90-Day Forward	.6054	.6004	1.6518	1.6656
180-Day Forward	.5994	.5948	1.6683	1.6813
Greece (Drachma)	.004579	.004551	218.40	219.75
Hong Kong (Dollar)	.12919	.12916	7.7406	7.7425
Hungary (Forint)	.0120351	.0120700	83.0900	82.8500
India (Rupee)	.03484	.03482	28.70	28.72
Indonesia (Rupiah)	.0004854	.0004843	2060.03	2065.00
Ireland (Punt)	1.6230	1.5970	.6161	.6262
Israel (Shekel)	.3577	.3659	2.7960	2.7328
Italy (Lira)	.0006752	.0006626	1481.13	1509.30
Japan (Yen)	.007993	.007974	125.11	125.40
30-Day Forward	.007989	.007971	125.18	125.46
90-Day Forward	.007987	.007968	125.21	125.49
180-Day Forward	.007990	.007974	125.16	125.41
Jordan (Dinar)	1.4810	1.4789	.6752	.6762
Kuwait (Dinar)	3.2857	3.2927	.3044	.3037
Lebanon (Pound)	.000547	.000544	1828.00	1838.00
Malaysia (Ringgit)	.3855	.3851	2.5937	2.5970

Price of British Pound in Dollars

Price of One Dollar in British Pounds

Price of French Franc in Dollars

Price of One Dollar in French Francs

Source: The Wall Street Journal, January 12, 1993, C15.

to purchase stocks and bonds denominated in British pounds, they must exchange dollars for pounds. The opposite is true when British citizens seek to purchase securities denominated in U.S. dollars. These investors must exchange pounds for dollars.

foreign exchange market
Market for the buying and selling of currencies.

exchange rate
The price of a foreign currency in terms of another currency.

The market for foreign currencies is called the **foreign exchange market.** The price of one currency in terms of another is referred to as the **exchange rate.** Currencies are traded daily, and the prices of major currencies are reported in the financial press. While these prices change daily, such reporting gives the investor a close indication of the currencies' current prices.

Exhibit 24.2, a clipping from *The Wall Street Journal,* gives the exchange rates for selected currencies as of January 11, 1993. At that time the price of a British pound was $1.5555 and the French franc was $0.18041. This exhibit also expresses the value of each currency in terms of a dollar. Thus, $1.00 purchased 0.6429 pounds or 5.5430 francs. (These amounts may be derived by dividing $1 by the dollar price of the foreign currency. For example, $1/1.5555 = 0.6429 units of the British pound.)

An imbalance in the demand for or supply of a currency causes its price to change. Excess demand generates a higher price while excess supply depresses the price. Such price changes are often referred to as devaluations and revaluations. With a **devaluation,** the price of one currency declines relative to all other currencies. A **revaluation** is an increase in the price of one nation's currency relative to all other currencies.

Under the current international monetary system such devaluations and revaluations occur daily, for the prices of currencies are permitted to fluctuate. If the demand for a particular currency rises so that the demand exceeds the supply, the price of that currency rises relative to other currencies. If the supply of the currency exceeds the demand, the price falls. There are continual devaluations of some currencies and revaluations of others as their prices vary daily in accordance with supply and demand.

The demand and supply for a currency is related to the demand and supply of the goods and services the country produces and the flow of investments into and out of the country. If British goods and services are cheaper than in other countries, this will generate an increase in the quantity demanded. If Great Britain offers good investment opportunities, firms and individuals will seek to buy British securities and invest in plant and equipment located in Britain. In both cases, the buying of foreign goods and services and the making of foreign investments created a demand for the British currency and a supply of other currencies. The price of the pound should rise to equate the demand for and supply of each currency. Since demand and supply constantly change, currency prices fluctuate daily in an effort to equate the demand and supply of each currency.

Day-to-day fluctuations in currency values may not be important to the investor, but longer term trends are. Currency values can rise or fall over an extended period of time. Such trends are indicated in Figure 24.1, which plots the price of the British pound from 1975 to 1992. As may be seen in the figure, the pound's dollar price fluctuated from a high of more than $2.40 in 1975 to below $1.10 in 1985. This fluctuation in the value of the British pound (or any currency) is, of course, a major source of risk from investing in securities not denominated in the currency of the investor's country.

devaluation
A decrease in the value of one currency relative to other currencies.

revaluation
The increase in the value of one currency relative to other currencies.

RISK REDUCTION THROUGH HEDGING WITH CURRENCY FUTURES

The U.S. investor who acquires foreign stocks and bonds has to bear the risk associated with fluctuations in exchange rates. If the dollar declines relative to other currencies, those currencies can buy more dollars. As explained previously, the U.S. investor can earn a profit on a foreign investment even if its price declines as long as the decline in the dollar's value more than offsets the decline in the value of the particular asset. The converse is also possible. The value of the particular asset can

Figure 24.1 ✦ DOLLAR VALUE OF THE BRITISH POUND, 1975–1992

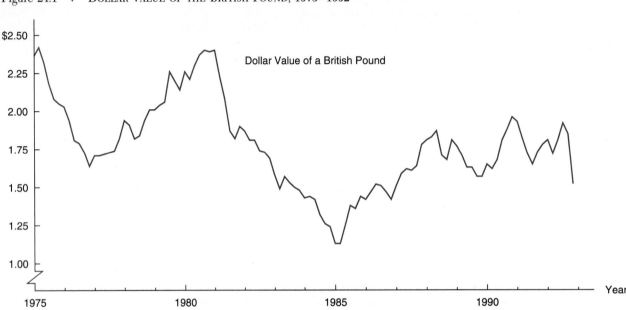

appreciate, but if the value of the currency falls, the U.S. investor can still sustain a loss. And if the value of the dollar rises sufficiently, it can more than offset the gain in the value of the foreign security.

If the prices of currencies were stable, there would be little risk associated with currency price fluctuations. However, this is not the case, as was illustrated in Figure 24.1 (e.g., in 1992 the pound fell from over $1.80 to about $1.50, a decline in excess of 15 percent). The question then arises: Can the investor reduce the risk associated with the variability in the price of foreign exchange? The answer is "Yes," as the investor may reduce the risk of loss by hedging with futures contracts. Of course, for such risk reduction to occur there must be speculators who are willing to accept that risk.

As with all futures contracts, speculators buy and sell foreign exchange futures in order to take advantage of changes in exchange rates. If a speculator anticipates that the value of the British pound will rise relative to the U.S. dollar, he or she enters into a contract to buy pounds (i.e., supply dollars) in the future. The investor has a long position in pounds (which may also be viewed as a short position in dollars). If the speculator is correct and the price of the pound rises, the value of the contract rises, and the speculator earns a profit. As with other futures trading, the margin requirement is so modest relative to the value of the contract that the percentage earned on the margin is substantial.

If the speculator anticipates that the value of the British pound will fall relative to the U.S. dollar, he or she enters into a contract to sell pounds (i.e., buy dollars and deliver pounds) in the future. The investor has a short position in pounds (which may also be viewed as a long position in dollars). If the speculator is correct and the price of the pound falls, the value of the contract declines and the speculator earns a profit. Once again, since the margin requirement is modest relative to the value of the contract, the percentage earned on the margin can be substantial.

Of course, the speculator bears the risk that the currency's value may move in the wrong direction. To a speculator who has a long position in the British pound, a decline in the value of the pound inflicts a substantial loss. (Of course, speculators with short positions profit.) If the speculator has a short position in the British pound and the value of the pound rises, then this individual sustains a loss. (Conversely, speculators with long positions profit.) The willingness of speculators to accept the risk associated with fluctuations in exchange rates means that other investors are able to hedge their positions to reduce the risk of loss from exchange rate fluctuations.

Individuals who acquire foreign securities purchase them for the returns offered by the investments, not for the potential return offered by correctly anticipating changes in exchange rates. For example, a U.S. investor purchases $16,000 worth of stocks and/or bonds denominated in German marks. If the value of the mark is $0.40, the securities are worth 40,000 marks. Should the value of the mark rise, this investor could experience a profit on the price increase. If the value of the mark were to fall, the investor could sustain a loss on the decline in the mark's value. To reduce this risk, the U.S. investor constructs a hedge position. Since the investor has a long position in the German securities, he or she establishes a short position in marks by entering into a contract for the delivery of marks in the future. If the value of the mark declines, the resulting loss on the investment in German securities is offset by the profit on the futures contract.

To see how this works, continue the example started above. Assume that the current price (i.e., the spot price) of the mark is $0.40 ($1.00 = 2.5 marks) and that the futures price of the mark is $0.405. (In this example the futures price of the mark exceeds the spot price. The converse, in which the spot price exceeds the futures price, is also possible.) The investor enters into a contract for the future sale of marks—for example, the delivery of 40,000 marks at $0.405 per mark. The value of this contract is almost the same as the value of the German securities acquired by the investor ($16,200 versus $16,000). Suppose the value of the mark then declines to $0.38. The securities are now worth $15,200 (40,000 marks × $0.38), and the investor has sustained a loss of $800 ($16,000 − 15,200). However, this investor can buy marks at $0.38 and deliver them at the $0.405 specified in the futures contract. The investor thus makes $0.025 per mark on the short position in the currency futures. The total profit is $1,000 (40,000 marks × $0.025), which more than offsets the loss from the decline in the value of the security denominated in marks.

A German investor who acquires U.S. securities would follow an opposite strategy. That individual has a long position in U.S. securities and thus would take a long position in German marks (i.e., a short position in dollars). If this individual acquires $16,000 worth of U.S. stocks for 40,000 marks, he or she would sustain a loss if the value of the mark rises. For example, if the mark's value were to rise to $0.42 (i.e., $1.00 = 2.39 marks), the value of this investment would be 38,240 (16,000 × 2.39) marks. The investor would thus sustain a loss of 1,760 marks (40,000 − 38,200). To protect against this loss, the investor enters into a futures contract for the sale of dollars (purchase of marks). Such a contract would rise in value if the value of the dollar were to decline. If the investor acquired a futures contract for the delivery of 40,000 marks at $0.405 a mark, that investor would gain $0.015 per mark when the price of the mark rose from $0.405 to $0.42. This price increase would generate a profit of $600 (0.015 × 40,000), which would partially offset the loss resulting from the decrease in the value of the dollar relative to the mark.

It should be noted that in both of these examples, the investors did not completely hedge their positions. In the first example the investor profited by the change in the value of the currency, while in the second case there was a net loss. This inability to hedge completely results from (1) differences between futures prices and spot prices and (2) differences between the size of contracts and the amounts invested in the foreign securities. However, the inability to hedge completely and to exactly offset the potential loss does not mean that a substantial amount of the risk associated with exchange rate fluctuations cannot be eliminated through the use of futures contracts in hedge positions.

Advantages Offered by Foreign Securities

Investing in foreign securities offers three possible advantages. The first is the obvious advantage associated with investing in economies and firms experiencing economic growth. The two other advantages, however, may be more important for an individual's portfolio, since economic growth is not unique to foreign firms and foreign economies. (IBM during the 1970s, The Limited during the 1980s, and Microsoft during the early 1990s all exhibited superior growth in earnings.) The remaining advantages, then, are (1) excess returns if foreign markets are less efficient than U.S. security markets and (2) reduction in risk through diversification using foreign instead of domestic investments.

Market Efficiency

As explained in Chapter 8, the rapid dissemination of new information and the intense competition among investors produces efficient U.S. financial markets. If new information becomes available that implies a security is undervalued (or overvalued), its price changes rapidly. The opportunity to profit from incorrect valuations disappears before most investors learn the new information. Unless the investor is able to anticipate new information and to adjust his or her positions before it becomes generally available, the individual cannot expect to outperform the market consistently. Thus, according to the efficient market hypothesis, higher returns can be achieved only by bearing more risk (i.e., by purchasing assets whose returns tend to be more volatile than the market as a whole.)

Foreign markets may not be so efficient. Less analysis may be applied to foreign securities, and the results of the analysis may not be widely disseminated. This suggests that the astute investor may be able to isolate securities that are under- or overvalued. If this is true, the opportunity for an excess return would exist. Foreign investments would offer individuals a means to increase returns on their portfolios that is generally not available with domestic investments.

Of course, obtaining information on which to base foreign investment decisions may be difficult. While foreign firms with securities traded on U.S. exchanges must meet SEC disclosure requirements, this reporting does not apply to non-listed foreign securities. In general, foreign firms do not publish as much information as U.S. firms. For example, many firms do not publish quarterly operating results. Even

obtaining an annual report may be difficult, and there is no reason to assume the
information is available in English.

Even if foreign security markets are not efficient, the individual U.S. investor
may be unable to take advantage of the inefficiencies, especially with regard to the
selection of individual securities. For this reason, foreign investments are often
made through investment companies. (These investment companies are discussed
later in this chapter.) However, even if the individual cannot take advantage of foreign inefficiencies, the possibility of diversification still argues for the inclusion of
foreign securities in a domestic portfolio.

Diversification

Historical average returns and their standard deviations for 1960 through 1980 for
selected countries are presented in Exhibit 24.3. Of the sixteen countries represented, ten generated higher stock returns than the U.S. equity markets. But of
those ten, only two (Austria and Canada) had lower standard deviations, indicating
that only two of the returns were less variable. The higher returns generated by a
specific country's equities are associated with higher risk and thus cannot be taken
as evidence that these markets are less efficient.

More variability by itself is not important from an American investor's perspective if the purpose of including foreign investments is their potential impact on
diversification. The inclusion of foreign investments may reduce the risk associated
with the portfolio even though the individual assets are riskier. As is explained in
Chapter 7, for risk reduction to occur, the returns on the assets included in the
portfolio should not be positively correlated, that is, the returns should not be
related.

The relationship between returns on foreign securities and U.S. securities is
measured by the correlation coefficient.[1] The numerical value of the correlation of

---

[1] In addition to the correlation coefficient, the relationship may be measured by the coefficient
of determination. In statistics, these measures are often referred to as r and r^2. The
coefficient of determination is the square of the correlation coefficient and measures the
proportion of the variation in one variable explained (but not necessarily caused) by
movement in the other. Thus if the correlation coefficient is 0.1, the coefficient of determination is 0.01 (i.e., 0.1^2), which indicates that the movement in one variable explains

Exhibit 24.3 ✦ ANNUAL RATES OF RETURN ON STOCKS, 1960–1980 (ARITHMETIC MEAN PERCENTAGES)

	Rate of Return	Standard Deviation of Returns
Australia	12.2%	22.8%
Austria	10.3	16.9
Belgium	10.1	13.8
Canada	12.1	17.5
Denmark	11.4	24.2
France	8.1	21.4
Germany	10.1	19.9
Italy	5.6	27.2
Japan	19.0	31.4
Netherlands	10.7	17.8
Norway	17.4	49.0
Spain	10.4	19.8
Sweden	9.7	16.7
Switzerland	12.5	22.9
United Kingdom	14.7	33.6
United States	10.2	17.7

Source: Adapted from Roger G. Ibbotson, Richard C. Carr, and Anthony W. Robinson, "International Equity and Bond Returns," *Financial Analysts Journal,* July-August 1982, p. 65.

coefficient ranges from +1.0 to −1.0. If two variables move exactly together (i.e., if there is a perfect positive correlation between the two variables), the numerical value of the correlation coefficient is 1.0. If the two variables move exactly opposite of each other, the correlation coefficient equals −1.0. All other possible values lie between these two extremes. Low numerical values such as −0.12 or +0.19 indicate little relationship between the two variables.

The correlation, or lack of it, between the annual returns on the U.S. stock market and the world stock market is illustrated in Figures 24.2 through 24.5. Figure 24.2 presents the annual return on the S & P 500 stock index and the EAFE, an index comprised of stocks in Europe, Australia, and the Far East. While the two returns tended to move together, there were year to year differences. In particular, the EAFE generated very large returns in 1985 and 1986. The explanation of these abnormally large security returns, however, is not that foreign security markets generated such high returns during those two years but that the value of the dollar perceptibly declined. (See, for instance, Figure 24.1, which illustrated the rise in the dollar cost of the British pound from mid-1985 through mid-1988.)

---

very little of the movement in the other variable. Computation of these two coefficients is part of statistics, and computer programs that generate descriptive statistics or estimate regression equations routinely give the numerical values of the correlation coefficient and the coefficient of determination. See, for instance, George W. Summers, William S. Peters, and Charles P. Amstrong, *Basic Statistics in Business and Economics,* 4th ed. Belmont, Calif.: Wadsworth, 1985, 307–308 and 534–537.

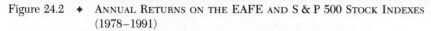

Figure 24.2 ✦ ANNUAL RETURNS ON THE EAFE AND S & P 500 STOCK INDEXES (1978–1991)

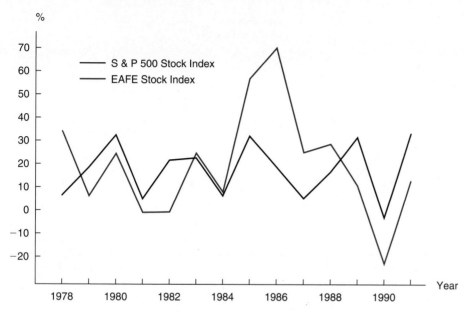

Figure 24.3 presents a scatter diagram of the returns from Figure 24.2. The X-axis gives the annual return in the S & P 500 stock index, and the Y-axis gives the annual return in the EAFE. If the returns on the S & P 500 and the EAFE were perfectly and positively correlated, all dots would lie on the line AB; if the returns were perfectly and negatively correlated, all the dots would lie on line CD. The dots appear to lie closer to line AB than CD. In this case, the correlation coefficient is +0.374, which indicates that there is a positive correlation. The lack of perfect correlation indicates the potential for risk reduction by including foreign stocks in an American equity portfolio and vice versa (i.e., including American equities in a Japanese or other foreign stock portfolio).

Since the EAFE is a weighted aggregate index in which the value of Japanese and British stocks comprise over 75 percent, investors may not purchase securities that are comparable to the composition of this index.[2] These investors may be more concerned with the correlation coefficients relating to the returns on U.S. stocks to stocks in individual foreign countries. Figure 24.4 presents the year-end value of U.S., French, Japanese, and Swiss markets. As may be seen in the figure, there were periods when the markets moved together and periods when they moved in opposite directions. Figure 24.5 presents the annual percentage change in each index. The top half of the figure presents the percentage changes for each market over time,

[2] As of November 1988, Japanese and British equities accounted for 64.6 and 12.3 percent, respectively, of the EAFE index. See Robert C. Radcliffe. *Investment Concepts, Analysis, Strategy.* 3d ed. Glenview, Illinois: Scott, Foresman/Little, Brown Higher Education, 1990.

Figure 24.3 ✦ SCATTER DIAGRAM OF ANNUAL RETURNS ON THE EAFE AND S & P 500
INDEXES (1978–1991)

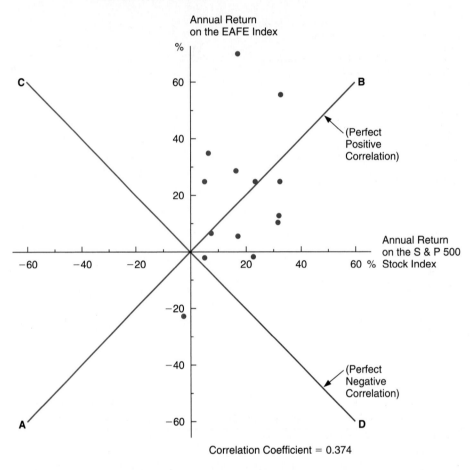

Correlation Coefficient = 0.374

and the volatility of the French market is readily apparent. The bottom half compares the percentage changes in each index for each year. While the percentage
changes tended to move together, especially 1989 and 1990, the direction of change
did differ among the markets for some of the years. For example, the British and
U.S. markets rose during 1992 while the other three declined. Even when the markets moved together, the annual changes differed, indicating that the markets are,
at least partially, independent of each other.

Exhibit 24.4 presents estimates of correlation coefficients for the period 1960
through 1980 and for June 1981 to September 1987 for the United States and twelve
industrialized nations. While the coefficients indicate a high correlation between
U.S. and Canadian stock markets, the correlation is generally less than 0.5 for European markets and even lower for the Japanese stock market.

These results suggest that the advantage of international diversification does
exist. However, during 1987, major U.S. and international security markets rose
together, and when prices dramatically declined during October 1987, 19 of 23

Figure 24.4 ✦ YEAR-END VALUES FOR U.S., JAPANESE, FRENCH, AND SWISS STOCK
MARKETS

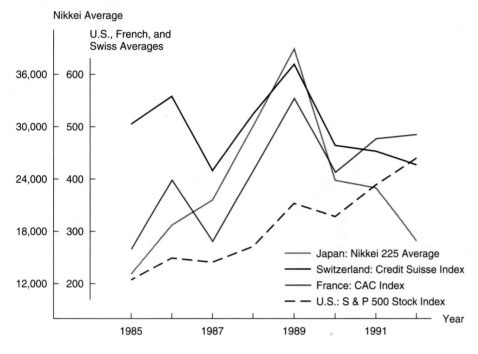

major stock markets fell by more than 20 percent. This suggests that some factor
or variable is common to all markets and during a major price decline, international
diversification may have only marginal benefits.[3]

Diversification with Foreign Bonds

U.S. bond portfolios may also benefit from the inclusion of foreign bonds. Once
again, to receive the benefit of diversification, the returns on the foreign bonds must
not have a high positive correlation with the returns from domestic bonds. Exhibit
24.5 presents the correlation coefficients for returns on U.S. bonds and bonds from
selected countries. With the exception of Canadian bonds, the correlation coefficients are low, indicating that the inclusion of foreign bonds in a domestic debt
portfolio should reduce a risk.

Alternative strategies to increase diversification are the inclusion of foreign
bonds in a U.S. equity portfolio and foreign equities in a U.S. debt portfolio. Exhibit
24.5 also presents the correlation coefficients of returns on U.S. stocks and foreign
bonds and on U.S. bonds and foreign stocks. The low correlation coefficients suggest

---

[3] See Richard Roll, "The International Crash for October 1987," *Financial Analysts Journal,*
September-October 1988, pp. 22–27.

Figure 24.5 ✦ ANNUAL PERCENTAGE CHANGES IN THE JAPANESE, SWISS, FRENCH, BRITISH, AND U.S. STOCK MARKETS (1986–1992)

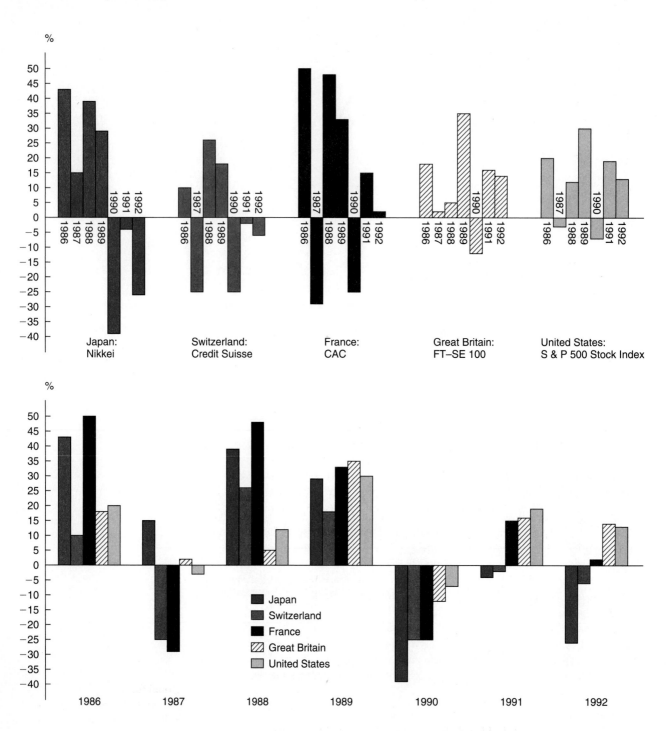

Exhibit 24.4 ✦ CORRELATION COEFFICIENTS BETWEEN U.S. STOCKS AND FOREIGN STOCKS

	1960–1980	June 1981–September 1987
Belgium	.389	.250
Denmark	.243	.351
France	.214	.390
Germany	.210	.209
Italy	.208	.224
Holland	.730	.473
Spain	−.115	.214
Sweden	.398	.279
Switzerland	.454	.500
UK	.617	.513
Japan	.216	.326
Canada	.710	.720

Source: 1960–1980 adapted from Haim Levy and Zvi Lerman, "The Benefits of International Diversification in Bonds," *Financial Analysts Journal,* September-October 1988, p. 64. June 1981–September 1987 adapted from Richard Roll, "The International Crash for October 1987," *Financial Analysts Journal,* September-October 1988, pp. 20–21.

that combining the foreign securities with domestic securities will reduce a portfolio's volatility.

Recent Trends

While historical correlation coefficients are sufficiently low to suggest that combining foreign securities in U.S. portfolios will reduce risk, the trend toward globalization of security markets and the creation of futures and options tied to various stock indices may increase the correlation among global financial markets. This linking of financial markets suggests that factors affecting prices in one market will be rapidly transferred to other markets. As the October 1987 global stock price declines illustrated, major foreign equity markets do respond to a major deterioration in U.S. security prices, and the same conclusion could hold if the Japanese stock market were to initiate a major price decline. Much of the historical record predates these recent developments in the financial markets, so that the past benefits of global diversification may be reduced, if not erased, during the 1990s.

MUTUAL FUNDS WITH FOREIGN INVESTMENTS

global funds
Mutual funds whose portfolio includes securities of firms with international operations that are located throughout the world.

From a U.S. perspective, there are basically three types of mutual funds with international investments. **Global funds** invest in foreign and U.S. securities. Many U.S. mutual funds are global, as they maintain some part of their portfolios in foreign

Exhibit 24.5 ✦ Correlation Coefficients of Returns (1960–1980)

U.S. Bonds and International Bonds

Belgium	.0493
Denmark	.2281
France	.1465
Germany	.0978
Italy	−.1316
Holland	.1656
Spain	.0718
Sweden	.0589
Switzerland	.1040
UK	.0760
Japan	.0959
Canada	.6317

U.S. Stocks and International Bonds

Belgium	−.2406
Denmark	.1252
France	−.0674
Germany	−.3564
Italy	.2496
Holland	−.2746
Spain	.0654
Sweden	−.1688
Switzerland	−.3136
UK	.0258
Japan	.1073
Canada	.0720

U.S. Bonds and International Stocks

Belgium	.1137
Denmark	.1391
France	−.0674
Germany	−.1249
Italy	−.2398
Holland	.0936
Spain	−.3260
Sweden	.0176
Switzerland	.0813
UK	.2153
Japan	.1630
Canada	.0971

Source: Adapted from Haim Levy and Zvi Lerman, "The Benefits of International Diversification in Bonds," *Financial Analysts Journal*, September-October 1988, p. 64.

POINTS OF INTEREST

WHO'S THE LARGEST?

In 1991, Mobil Oil had sales of $62,700,000 and earned $2,589,000. The total value of its stock was $25,900,000,000. Is it the world's largest company? *Business Week* annually ranks the 1,000 largest firms ("The Global 1000"), and Mobil ranked only 33rd in terms of market value (*Business Week*, July 13, 1992, 57–108). Royal Dutch/ Shell had sales of $102,697,000,000, and the market value of its stock was $77,820,000,000—three times the value of Mobil's stock. Right behind Royal Dutch in second place was Japan's Nippon Telegraph & Telephone with stock valued at $77,524,000,000. $77.5 billion is a very large amount, but Nippon Telegraph & Telephone's stock was worth $163.9 billion in 1989, so the value of the stock lost over $86,400,000,000 in value during the large decline experienced by the Japanese stock market during 1990–1992.

While the United States and Japan dominate the Global 1000, European companies are rapidly growing, especially through mergers. Previously, many European firms were willing to be dominant in their own countries, but the elimination of European trade barriers is forcing these firms to combine to form large global corporations. Once these new firms become dominant in Europe, they should also be able to become world powers. Perhaps in the year 2000 the *Business Week* Global 1000 will be dominated by European firms.

---

investments. While these funds do not specialize in foreign securities, they do offer the individual investor the advantages associated with foreign investments: returns through global economic growth, diversification from assets whose returns are not positively correlated, and possible excess returns from inefficient foreign financial markets.

In addition to global funds, there are **international funds,** which invest solely in foreign securities and hold no U.S. securities, and **regional funds,** which specialize in a particular geographic area, such as Asia. (There are also mutual funds that specialize in a particular area within the United States such as the North Star Fund, which invests in firms located in seven upper midwest states.) While the regional funds obviously specialize, the international funds may also specialize during particular time periods. Thus it is not unusual for a fund to invest a quarter or more of its assets in the shares of firms in a particular country.

Many of the regional funds are closed-end investment companies. A list of these funds traded on the New York Stock Exchange is given in Exhibit 24.6. The prices

international funds
American mutual funds whose portfolios are limited to non-American firms.

regional fund
A mutual fund that specializes in a particular geographical area.

POINTS OF INTEREST

EUROPEAN OPTIONS

Put and call options are not unique to American financial markets but are also available in some foreign security markets. However, these put and call options can differ significantly from American options. Specific differences vary from country to country but revolve around the duration of the option and the existence of secondary markets. For example, the duration of the traditional British option is three months. Six-month and nine-month options are not available.

Some secondary markets do exist, but not for all foreign puts and calls. For example, there is no secondary market for the traditional three-month British option. Once purchased, the option cannot be sold. The investor must either exercise the option at a specified time or let it expire. Thus the most important difference between an American option and a so-called European option is the requirement that the investor must exercise the European option to realize any gain achieved through appreciation in the option's value.

Exhibit 24.6 ✦ SPECIALIZED COUNTRY CLOSED-END INVESTMENT COMPANIES
TRADED ON THE NEW YORK STOCK EXCHANGE

Austria Fund	Japan Equity Fund
Brazilian Equity Fund	Korea Fund
Chile Fund	Latin America Equity Fund
China Fund	Malaysia Fund
First Israel Fund	Portugal Fund
First Philippine Fund	Singapore Fund
France Growth Fund	Spain Fund
Germany Fund	Swiss Helvetia Fund
India Growth Fund	Taiwan Fund
Indonesia Fund	Thai Fund
Italy Fund	Turkish Investment Fund
Jakarta Growth Fund	United Kingdom Fund

of these shares can be very volatile since the price depends on both the fund's net asset value and speculative interest in the shares. This volatility is illustrated in Figure 24.6, which plots the price and the premium over net asset value of the Germany Fund during the fall of 1989 when the political climate changed very rapidly. The price of these shares rose dramatically and sold for a large premium over the fund's net asset value, but, by the end of 1991, the premium had declined to 4 percent.

Such a large premium was not limited to the Germany Fund. At the beginning of 1990, the shares of several funds that specialize in particular countries sold above their net asset value. Buying these shares for a large premium over their net asset value may seem illogical. However, these funds may be the only means by which the individual investor may participate in a country's stock markets, since local laws may ban or severely limit foreign ownership of the securities.

American investors may also acquire shares in foreign investment companies, such as the British mutual funds called "unit trusts." Thus, if a U.S. investor cannot find an acceptable domestic fund, the search may be extended to a foreign fund. However, since these securities are not registered with the SEC, some foreign funds will not sell shares directly to U.S. investors, as these funds believe such sales are illegal. In other cases purchases may be made for a fee through foreign banks with branches in the United States. However, the individual should probably ask himself or herself if the potential return is worth the additional expense required to acquire the shares.

SUMMARY

United States investors are beginning to take a global view of investing and to acquire stocks and bonds issued in foreign countries. Foreign investments involve several sources of risk that are in addition to the usual sources of unsystematic and

Figure 24.6   PRICE, NET ASSET VALUE, AND PREMIUM OF THE GERMANY FUND (NOVEMBER 1989–DECEMBER 1991)

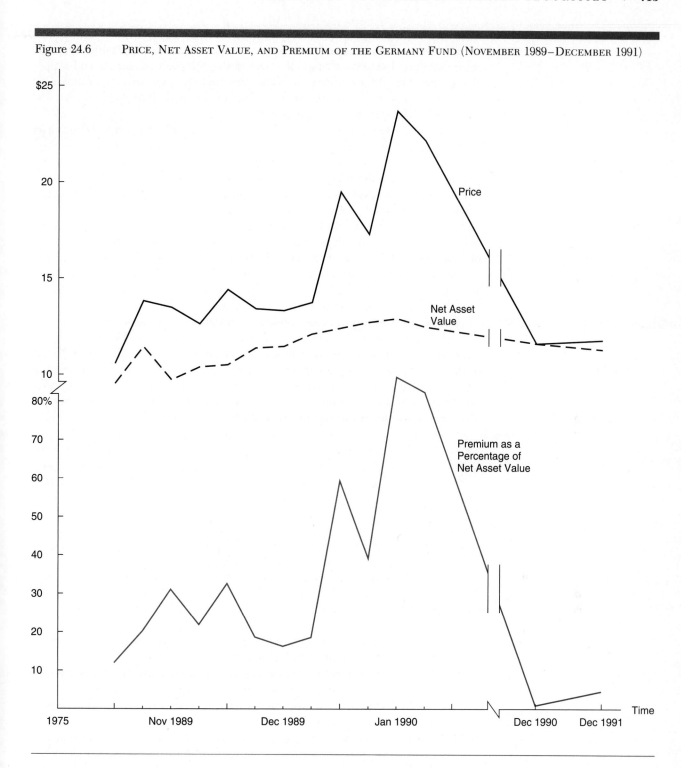

systematic risk. Investors in foreign securities must bear the risk associated with unstable political climates and fluctuations in exchange rates. The values of foreign currencies (i.e., foreign exchange) fluctuate daily with the demand for and supply of each currency. When foreign securities are sold and converted back into U.S. dollars, the value of the dollars may have risen or declined, depending on what has happened in the foreign exchange markets.

The investor may reduce the risk of loss from fluctuations in exchange rates by constructing a hedge position using currency futures. For example, if the individual acquires a long position in foreign securities, he or she can hedge against loss by selling contracts for the future delivery of the currency. The investor thus has a long position in the securities and a short position in the currency, which reduces the risk resulting from fluctuations in the dollar value of the foreign currency.

Foreign investments offer the individual several advantages. Since the returns on foreign securities are not perfectly correlated with returns on domestic securities, such investments are a means to diversify the individual's portfolio. In addition, foreign security markets may not be as efficient as U.S. security markets. Such inefficiencies suggest that foreign investments may offer astute investors an opportunity to increase the return earned on their portfolios.

Instead of selecting specific foreign securities, U.S. investors may prefer to acquire shares in mutual funds that make foreign investments. Many U.S. funds maintain a portion of their assets in foreign securities. Other mutual funds invest exclusively abroad while others specialize in particular countries or geographic regions. Such investment companies relieve the investor of having to select individual foreign securities but still offer the advantages of global diversification and possible increased returns through investments in less efficient markets.

Terms to Remember

foreign exchange market	global funds
exchange rate	international funds
devaluation	regional funds
revaluation	

Questions

1. What is foreign exchange and the foreign exchange market? What causes the prices of currencies to fluctuate?
2. What are the sources of risk associated with foreign investments? What can the individual investor do to manage those risks?
3. Would a U.S. investor who owned foreign securities prefer a devaluation or revaluation of the U.S. dollar?
4. If a British investor who purchased French securities anticipates that the value of the franc may fall but does not wish to sell the securities, what should this investor do?
5. Why may the addition of foreign securities to a U.S. investor's portfolio reduce this individual's risk exposure?

6. Why may investing in mutual funds with foreign investments be preferable to purchasing foreign stocks?

Problems

1. What is the cost of $1.00 in each of the following currencies?

pound	$1.75
franc	0.24
mark	0.46
yen	0.01

2. If you purchase 100,000 lira for $5,000, what is the price of a lira?

3. You purchase 100 ADRs of British Oil for $12 per ADR. What is the value of the shares in dollars given the following information?

Time	Price of the Stock in Pounds	Dollar Price of the Pound
1/1/x0	£ 6.00	$2.00
4/1/x0	7.80	2.10
7/1/x0	9.30	1.85
10/1/x0	10.20	1.70
1/1/x1	14.00	1.65

   Compare the returns earned by a U.S. investor and a British investor.

4. You anticipate buying a German car in six months for $30,000. Currently the spot price of the mark is $0.50 and the six-month futures price is $0.505. You anticipate that the value of the dollar relative to the mark will decline. What course of action should you take and how much will it cost you (excluding brokerage commissions)?

5. A portfolio manager owns a bond worth £2,000,000 that will mature in one year. The pound is currently worth $1.45, while the one-year futures price is $1.40. If the value of the pound were to fall, the portfolio manager would sustain a loss. If the value of the pound were to rise, the portfolio manager would experience a profit.

   a. What is the expected payment based on the current exchange rate?
   b. What is the expected payment based on the futures exchange rate?
   c. If, after a year, the pound is worth $1.33, what is the loss from the decline in the value of the pound?
   d. If, after a year, the pound is worth $1.62, what is the gain from the increase in the value of the pound?
   e. To avoid the potential loss in part c, the portfolio manager hedges by selling futures contracts for the delivery of pounds at $1.40. What is the cost of the protection from a decline in the value of the pound?
   f. If, after hedging, the price of the pound falls to $1.33, what is the maximum amount the portfolio manager can lose? Why is this answer different from the answer to part c above?
   g. If, after hedging, the price of the pound rises to $1.62, what is the maximum amount the portfolio manager can gain? Why is this answer different from the answer to part d above?

Suggested Readings

Descriptions of the major foreign security markets are given in:

Directory of World Stock Exchanges. Compiled by The Economist Publications. Baltimore, Maryland: Johns Hopkins University Press, 1988.

Levine, Sumner, ed. *Global Investing.* New York: Harper Business, 1992.

Nix, William E. *The Dow Jones-Irwin Guide to International Securities, Futures, and Options Markets.* Homewood, Ill.: Dow Jones-Irwin, 1988.

Warfield, Gerald. *How to Buy Foreign Stocks and Bonds.* New York: Harper & Row, 1985.

Books devoted to the Japanese securities markets include:

Matsumoto, Toru. *Japanese Stocks: A Basic Guide for the Intelligent Investor.* Tokyo: Kodansha International, 1989.

Tamashita, Takeji. *Japan's Securities Markets.* Singapore: Butterworths, 1989.

The explosive growth in new foreign security issues, the development of dual-tranche offerings (offering of securities in two countries), and the regulation of foreign securities issued in the United States and domestic securities issued abroad is covered in:

Clements, Jonathan, ed. *Stock Answers—A Guide to the International Equities Market.* New York: Nichols Publishing, 1988.

For a survey of international diversification, including an extensive bibliography, consult:

Madura, Jeff, and Thomas J. O'Brien. "International Diversification for the Individual," *Financial Services Review,* 1991–1992, 159–175.

One of the more successful investors in foreign securities has been John Templeton, who manages several mutual funds with over $4 billion in assets. His methods for selecting foreign securities are covered in:

Berryessa, Norman, and Eric Kirzner. *Global Investing: The Templeton Way.* Homewood, Ill.: Dow Jones-Irwin, 1988.

For a collection of readings on international finance, acquire:

Kolb, Robert W., ed. *The International Finance Reader,* Miami, FL: Kolb Publishing, 1990.

25

PORTFOLIO PLANNING, MANAGEMENT, AND EVALUATION

enjamin Britten in his Young Person's Guide to the Orchestra *describes and illustrates the instruments of the symphony orchestra. Then Britten reconstructs the orchestra one instrument at a time and ends the work with a glorious fugue that combines all the instruments. The preceding chapters of this text have described and illustrated individual investments: bonds, preferred stock, common stock, options, shares in investment companies, commodity futures, physical assets, collectibles, and real estate. In a manner similar to Britten's fugue, the investor combines the individual assets to construct a portfolio. The individual acquires assets one at a time, and they are blended together into a portfolio designed to meet the investor's financial goals.*

Portfolio construction, then, is a process in which the individual specifies financial goals, identifies financial resources and obligations, acquires a diversified portfolio designed to meet the goals within the investor's constraints, and evaluates the portfolio's performance. Of course, this process is affected by the economy (e.g., expectation of inflation), changes in the tax laws, the deregulation of financial markets, and the speed of technological change. In addition, changes in the individual's economic or family environment can have an important impact on financial planning and the resulting portfolio.

The process of financial planning and portfolio construction is not an easy task; it requires considerable analytical thought and extensive calculations. There are so many assets from which to choose; the economic environment can be so dynamic; the tax code is complex; and individuals' obligations and resources change throughout their lives. But the difficulty of the task is no reason to avoid planning one's financial future and constructing a well-diversified portfolio that offers as high a return as possible consistent with the individual investor's willingness to bear risk.

After a well-diversified portfolio has been constructed, there is a need to evaluate results. This chapter ends with a discussion of performance evaluation. This evaluation applies the capital asset model from Chapter 7 and compares the realized return with the return on the market and portfolio's risk. The analysis stresses that a return that is less than the market return is not necessarily inferior if the investor bears less risk. Conversely, a return in excess of the market return is not necessarily superior if the investor bears more risk than the risk associated with the market.

♦ ♦ ♦

After completing this chapter you should be able to

1. Identify financial goals.

2. Enumerate the risk/reward, marketability/liquidity, and tax status of investment alternatives.

3. Match types of assets with individual financial goals.

4. Construct an individual's balance sheet and cash budget.

5. Explain the importance of investment management in an efficient market context.

6. Compare the results of portfolios on a risk-adjusted basis.

THE PROCESS OF FINANCIAL PLANNING

In order to construct a portfolio, the investor should start by defining its purpose. There has to be some goal (or goals) to guide the selection of the assets that should be included. After specifying realistic financial objectives, the next step is determining which assets are appropriate to meet the goals. There are many possible assets, and the individual must choose among these alternatives. This requires knowledge of the assets' features, including the sources of return, sources of risk, and tax implications.

After establishing investment goals and identifying assets that may meet the goals, the investor should analyze his or her environment. Environments obviously vary with individuals and change over an individual's lifetime. The investor needs to be aware of the resources and sources of income with which he or she has to work. The investor then will construct a financial plan designed to fulfill the investment goals within these environmental and financial constraints.

The Specification of Investment Goals

The purpose of investing is to transfer purchasing power from the present to the future. A portfolio is a store of value designed to meet the individual investor's reasons for postponing the consumption of goods and services from the present to the future. Several reasons for saving and investing were offered in the introductory chapter. These goals included

1. the capacity to meet financial emergencies;
2. the desire to finance specific future purchases, such as the down payment for a home;
3. the need for additional future income;
4. the desire to leave a sizable estate to heirs or to charity;
5. the inclination to speculate or the enjoyment derived from accumulating and managing wealth.

These are not all the possible reasons for deferring current consumption, but they indicate several motives for constructing a portfolio. However, not every asset is appropriate for each of the above goals. Matching the goals with the assets requires knowing the features of the specific assets, which are reviewed in the subsequent section.

The Investment Alternatives

The investor has a large variety of assets from which to choose, and within each type of asset there is an almost unlimited number of choices. However, each of the assets have common characteristics: liquidity, marketability, potential income and/or capital gains, risk, and tax implications. Exhibit 25.1 lists the major classes of assets covered in this text and summarizes their characteristics.

The first characteristic reviewed in Columns two and three is the asset's liquidity and marketability. Liquidity is the ease of converting the asset into cash with little risk of loss. NOW accounts, savings accounts, shares in money market mutual funds,

Exhibit 25.1 ✦ A SUMMARY OF INVESTMENT ALTERNATIVES AND THEIR CHARACTERISTICS

Asset	Liquidity	Marketability	Return		Tax Status	Sources of Risk
			Possible Income	Possible Capital Gains		
Money	Complete	Not applicable	No	No	None	Purchasing power risk
NOW and savings accounts	High	None (redeemed at par)	Yes	No	Taxable	Meager purchasing power risk (risk free up to $100,000)[1]
Certificates of deposit	High	None (redeemed at par less any applicable penalty)	Yes	No	Taxable	Meager purchasing power risk (risk free up to $100,000)
Money market mutual funds	High	None (redeemed)	Yes	No	Taxable	Meager purchasing power risk (virtually risk free)[1]
Treasury bills	High	Yes	Yes	No	Taxable[2]	Meager purchasing power risk (virtually risk free)[1]
Treasury bonds	Moderate	Yes	Yes	Yes	Taxable[2]	Purchasing power/ interest rate risk
EE and HH bonds	High	None	Yes	No	Taxable[2]	Purchasing power risk[1]
Federal agency bonds	Moderate	Yes	Yes	Yes[3]	Taxable[2]	Purchasing power/ interest rate risk
Municipal bonds	Moderate to little	Yes	Yes	Yes[3]	Nontaxable[4]	Purchasing power/ interest rate risk
Quality corporate bonds	Moderate	Yes	Yes	Yes[3]	Taxable	Business/financial/ interest rate/ purchasing power risk
Lower-rated corporate bonds	Moderate to little	Moderate	Yes	Yes[3]	Taxable	Business/financial/ interest rate/ purchasing power risk
Preferred stock	Moderate	Moderate (depends on depth of second-ary market)	Yes	Yes	Taxable	Business/financial/ interest rate/ purchasing power risk

[1] Yields may adjust to offset purchasing power risk.
[2] Interest is not taxable at the state and local level.
[3] Capital gains do not apply to zero coupon bonds, bonds sold initially at a discount, or bonds issued after July 18, 1984, and bought at a discount.
[4] Interest on nontaxable bonds may be taxable at the state and local level.

(Continued on next page)

(Exhibit 25.1 CONTINUED)

Asset	Liquidity	Marketability	Return Possible Income	Return Possible Capital Gains	Tax Status	Sources of Risk
Quality common stock	Moderate	Yes	Yes	Yes	Taxable	Business/financial/ market/purchasing power risk
Speculative common stock	Little	Moderate (depends on depth of secondary market)	In selective cases	Yes	Taxable	Business/financial/ market/purchasing power risk
Options: warrants, puts, calls	Low to nil	Moderate (depends on depth of secondary market)	None[5]	Yes	Taxable	Business/financial/ market/purchasing power risk
Closed-end investment companies	Moderate	Moderate (depends on depth of secondary market)	Yes	Yes	Taxable	Market/purchasing power risk
Mutual funds	Moderate	None (shares redeemed)	Yes	Yes	Taxable[6]	Market/purchasing power risk
Futures	Low to nil	Yes	No	Yes	Taxable	Business/market risk
Collectibles	Low to nil	Low	No	Yes	Taxable	Market risk
Gold	Low to moderate	Yes	No	Yes	Taxable	Market risk
Homes	Low	Low to moderate	No	Yes	Tax deferred	Market/interest rate risk
Real estate	Low	Low	Yes	Yes	Tax shelter or tax deferred	Business/financial/ interest rate risk
Foreign investments (bonds, stocks)	Low	Low to moderate (high for listed ADRs)	Yes	Yes	Taxable[7]	Business/financial/ market/purchasing power/political/ exchange rate risk

[5]Writers of options earn income.
[6]Mutual funds that invest in state and local government securities are tax-exempt.
[7]Foreign securities may be taxable both abroad and domestically.

and treasury bills are very liquid assets, since there is virtually no chance of loss of principal. However, only treasury bills are also marketable. There is no secondary market for NOW and savings accounts because the saver simply withdraws the funds on demand, and shares in money market mutual funds are redeemed (i.e., sold back to the fund).

Many assets that are marketable are not truly liquid, as there is the potential for loss. Without the existence of secondary markets, there would be no means by which the investor could convert the asset back to cash. These markets may be very well developed and organized, such as in the case of stock traded on the New York Stock Exchange, or poorly developed and very informal, as in the secondary market for collectibles.

Every asset offers a potential return that comes either through income, such as interest or dividends, or through capital gains. Capital gains offer a modest tax advantage, since the tax is deferred until the gain is realized and the tax rate may be lower than the rate on other sources of income. The sources of an asset's return are reviewed in Columns four and five in Exhibit 25.1. The next column presents the federal income tax status of each asset. The returns earned by most assets are taxable at the federal level, but there are major exceptions, such as the interest earned on municipal bonds. Other assets (such as real estate) also permit the deferral of tax, as the funds generated by the investment are sheltered from income taxes by expenses such as noncash depreciation charges.

The last column reviews the sources of risk. Since the future is uncertain, the investor must bear risk to earn a return. Diversifiable, unsystematic risk applies only to the specific asset, and for firms it covers the nature of the operation (business risk) and how the firm is financed (financial risk). Since unsystematic risk is reduced through the construction of diversified portfolios, non-diversifiable systematic risk is by far the more important source of risk. Sources of systematic risk include market risk, interest rate risk, reinvestment rate risk, exchange rate risk, and purchasing power risk. Those assets whose returns tend to fluctuate with fluctuations in the market as a whole have market risk. Assets whose prices are sensitive to changes in interest rates have interest rate risk, and foreign investments are subject to exchange rate risk. Virtually all investments have reinvestment rate risk. If dividends, interest, and the proceeds of sales and redemptions are reinvested, the individual may realize a lower return than was previously earned.

All assets subject the investor to purchasing power risk, since the realized return may be less than the rate of inflation. For example, when an individual purchases a fixed-income security such as a long-term corporate or municipal bond, the investor locks in a particular return. If inflation increases, the fixed return may be insufficient to compensate for the rate of inflation. Of course, if the rate of inflation declines, the real purchasing power of the fixed return is increased.

An investor seeking to avoid loss of purchasing power should not acquire fixed-income securities but instead should purchase variable-income securities. The return earned on investments in money market mutual funds, money market bank accounts, or any short-term asset that is rapidly retired is not fixed. The rapid turnover of these assets permits yields to quickly adjust, allowing the individual to reinvest the funds at the higher short-term rates. Thus, these assets are among the best means to reduce purchasing power risk.

The diversity of alternative investments available to the individual investor should be immediately apparent from Exhibit 25.1. Obviously not all of these investments are appropriate to meet specific investment goals. Also, some of them would not be appropriate for an individual with modest resources or one who is very risk averse. Since each individual's financial goals, resources, aversion to risk, and tax environment vary, there are many possible portfolios that different individuals can construct. However, each portfolio should seek to obtain the maximum possible return given the investor's resources and willingness to bear risk.

In addition, the individual must decide whether or not he or she wants to manage the portfolio actively or passively. Some individuals have neither the time nor the inclination to oversee their portfolios and thus employ the services of others (e.g., financial planners, stockbrokers, portfolio managers in trust departments, or the managers of mutual funds). However, individual investors must still select who will administer their assets and, of course, suffer any losses that result from poor management of the funds. Ultimately it is the saver who bears the risk and reaps the reward from the portfolio whether the funds are managed by that individual or by others.

The Analysis of the Individual's Environment and Resources

As mentioned before, individuals should be aware of their environment and financial resources. These differ from person to person, and what may be the correct investment strategy for one individual may not be correct for another. While this seems self-evident, many individuals do not recognize their environment and the resources they have.

One's environment includes such factors as age, health, employment, and family. A young bachelor in good health who is securely employed does not need the same portfolio as a young man with a family, even if his health is excellent and his employment is secure. The more current obligations an individual has (be they debt or family), the greater the need for a conservative portfolio of assets. Such assets should stress safety and liquidity so that short-term obligations may be met as they occur. In contrast, the young bachelor could afford to bear more risk in the selection of a portfolio.

In addition to the individual's environment, the investor should take an accurate account of resources. This may be done by constructing two financial statements. The first one enumerates what is owned and owed, and the other enumerates cash receipts and disbursements. The former is, of course, a balance sheet, whereas the latter is a cash budget.

The entries for an individual's balance sheet are given in Exhibit 25.2. It lists all of the individual's assets and liabilities. The difference between these assets and liabilities is the individual's net worth (which would be the estate if the individual were to die at the time the balance sheet is constructed). For clarity, the individual should list short-term assets and then long-term assets, and the same should be done with liabilities. In effect, an individual's balance sheet is no different from a firm's balance sheet.

The entries for the balance sheet given in Exhibit 25.2 consider the individual's financial position as of the present and as of some specified time in the future (e.g., at retirement). For the purpose of financial planning, it is advisable to construct one's current financial position as well as to project what that position will be at some time in the future. Such a projection is often referred to as a **pro forma financial statement.** The construction of a pro forma balance sheet will require that the individual make assumptions concerning (1) his or her ability to accumulate assets and retire liabilities and (2) the rate of growth or rate of return that will be achieved by the assets. While the resulting projections will depend on the assumptions, the projections often bring into sharp focus the individual's future financial needs. Such projects then can prove to be helpful in establishing current investment strategies.

The balance sheets in Exhibit 25.2 are more detailed than is necessary for most individuals. Few individual investors will have entries for each asset or liability enumerated in the exhibit. For example, many investors may not be eligible for Keogh accounts or have deferred compensation owed them. Also, some of the entries may not apply now but may apply in the future. For example, if the individual has not

pro forma financial statement
A projected or forecasted financial statement.

Exhibit 25.2 ✦ An Individual's Balance Sheet and the Determination of Net Worth

	As of Now	In the Future
ASSETS		
1. Bank deposits		
a. Cash, checking accounts	_____	_____
b. Savings accounts	_____	_____
c. Certificates of deposit	_____	_____
d. Money market accounts	_____	_____
e. Credit union accounts	_____	_____
f. Other	_____	_____
Subtotal	_____	_____
2. Liquid financial assets		
a. Money market mutual funds	_____	_____
b. Treasury bills	_____	_____
c. Series EE and HH bonds	_____	_____
d. Amounts owed and payable on demand	_____	_____
e. Tax refunds and other payments owed	_____	_____
f. Cash value of life insurance	_____	_____
Subtotal	_____	_____
3. Retirement and savings plans		
a. IRA accounts	_____	_____
b. Keogh accounts	_____	_____
c. Lump sum distributions and/or IRA rollover accounts	_____	_____
d. Employee savings and investment plan:		
Before tax	_____	_____
After Tax	_____	_____
e. Employee stock ownership plan	_____	_____
f. Deferred compensation due	_____	_____
g. Company options	_____	_____
Subtotal	_____	_____
4. Financial assets		
a. Treasury notes and bonds	_____	_____
b. Corporate bonds	_____	_____
c. Corporate stock	_____	_____
d. Municipal bonds	_____	_____
e. GNMAs and other federal agency debt	_____	_____
f. Mutual funds	_____	_____
Subtotal	_____	_____
5. Tangible assets		
a. Real estate		
1. Home	_____	_____
2. Vacation properties	_____	_____
3. Other	_____	_____
b. Collectibles	_____	_____
c. Cars	_____	_____

(Continued on next page)

(Exhibit 25.2 CONTINUED)

	As of Now	In the Future
d. Personal tangible property (e.g., furs, silver, furniture, jewelry, boats)		
Subtotal	⎯⎯	⎯⎯
Total Assets	⎯⎯	⎯⎯
LIABILITIES		
1. Short-term		
a. Current portion of mortgage owed	⎯⎯	⎯⎯
b. Current portion of car payments	⎯⎯	⎯⎯
c. Personal debts	⎯⎯	⎯⎯
d. Credit card balances	⎯⎯	⎯⎯
e. Miscellaneous	⎯⎯	⎯⎯
Subtotal	⎯⎯	⎯⎯
2. Long-term		
a. Mortgage balance owed	⎯⎯	⎯⎯
b. Balance owed on car or other tangible assets	⎯⎯	⎯⎯
c. Bank loans, amount borrowed on life insurance	⎯⎯	⎯⎯
d. Other long-term debts	⎯⎯	⎯⎯
Subtotal	⎯⎯	⎯⎯
Total Liabilities	⎯⎯	⎯⎯
SUMMARY		
Total assets	⎯⎯	⎯⎯
Total liabilities	⎯⎯	⎯⎯
Net worth (Value of estate) (Assets minus liabilities)	⎯⎯	⎯⎯

started an IRA but intends to, this should be included in the projected balance sheet even though it is not applicable to the current balance sheet.

The mechanics of constructing a balance sheet are relatively easy. The difficult part is enumerating the assets and placing values on them. Such valuation is easy for publicly traded securities such as stocks and bonds. The problem concerns placing values on tangible personal assets such as collectibles or real estate. Since the purpose of constructing a balance sheet is to determine the individual's financial condition, it is advisable to be conservative in estimating the value of these assets. If, for example, the individual had to sell antiques to finance living expenses, it would be better to underestimate than to overestimate the prices for which these assets may be sold. Such underestimation cannot lead to disappointment.

After the individual enumerates what is owned and what is owed and thereby determines his or her net worth, the next step is to analyze the flow of receipts and disbursements. This is done by constructing a **cash budget**. Exhibit 25.3 shows the

cash budget
A financial statement enumerating cash receipts and cash disbursements.

Exhibit 25.3 ✦ An Individual's Cash Budget for One Year

	Present	In the Future
CASH RECEIPTS		
Salary (after deductions)	_____	_____
Social security	_____	_____
Pension	_____	_____
Interest from savings	_____	_____
Dividends on stock	_____	_____
Commissions & bonuses	_____	_____
Royalties, fees	_____	_____
Distributions from businesses	_____	_____
Rental income	_____	_____
Veterans benefit	_____	_____
Annuity payments	_____	_____
Distributions from trusts	_____	_____
Mortgage payments received	_____	_____
Distributions from IRA, Keogh, and IRA rollover accounts	_____	_____
Other receipts	_____	_____
Total Receipts	_____	_____

	Present	In the Future
CASH DISBURSEMENTS		
1. Housing		
a. Mortgage payments	_____	_____
b. Rent	_____	_____
c. Maintenance	_____	_____
d. Utilities	_____	_____
e. Fuel	_____	_____
f. Property taxes	_____	_____
2. Food and personal expenditures		
a. Dining at home	_____	_____
b. Dining out	_____	_____
c. Personal care	_____	_____
d. Clothing	_____	_____
e. Recreation and travel	_____	_____
f. Furniture, appliances	_____	_____
f. Hobbies	_____	_____
3. Transportation		
a. Automobile expense	_____	_____
b. Car replacement	_____	_____
c. Public transportation	_____	_____

(Continued on next page)

(Exhibit 25.3 CONTINUED)

	Present	In the Future
4. Medical		
a. Insurance	————	————
b. Deductibles paid	————	————
c. Miscellaneous expense	————	————
5. Insurance		
a. Life insurance	————	————
b. Homeowner's insurance	————	————
c. Automobile insurance	————	————
d. Other	————	————
6. Estimated taxes	————	————
7. Other disbursements		
a. Gifts	————	————
b. Contributions	————	————
c. Miscellaneous	————	————
Total Disbursements	═══	═══
SUMMARY		
Total receipts	————	————
Total disbursements	————	————
Difference between receipts and disbursements	═══	═══

entries needed for the construction of a cash budget. It lists all of the individual's sources of receipts (e.g., salary, interest, and rental income) and all of the disbursements (e.g., mortgage payments, living expenses, and taxes). As with the balance sheet, the cash budget may be constructed for the present or projected for a specific time in the future (e.g., at retirement). Exhibit 25.3 thus provides for both a current annual cash budget and a pro forma cash budget. While the cash budget illustrated in this exhibit is for one year, cash budgets may be constructed to cover other time periods, such as monthly receipts and disbursements.

As with the balance sheet in Exhibit 25.2, the entries in Exhibit 25.3 are probably too detailed for many individuals. Obviously, not everyone receives veterans' benefits or royalty payments. However, such completeness is desirable, for it brings to the foreground the variety of possible sources and uses of funds. If the individual's receipts exceed disbursements, the excess receipts become a source of funds that should be profitably invested to meet future financial needs. It is quite possible that after constructing such a cash budget, the individual will perceive ways to increase receipts and decrease disbursements and thus generate additional funds for investment.

The Establishment of Financial Plans

After specifying goals and analyzing one's financial position, the investor can establish a **financial plan** or course of action. This plan is the strategy by which the investor will fulfill the financial goals. While plans will vary among individuals, the importance of such a plan applies to all. It is the means to the end—the means to financial success and security.

Plans require the establishment of priorities. Those financial goals that are most important should be fulfilled first. After investments have been made to satisfy these needs, the next most important goals should be attacked. In this way the investor systematically saves and invests to meet the specified goals. For example, an individual may determine the following goals and their priority:

financial plan
The programs designed to meet financial goals.

+ funds to meet financial emergencies
+ funds to finance a child's education
+ funds to finance retirement
+ funds for an estate

The initial goal, then, is sufficient liquid assets to cover emergencies (e.g., unemployment or extended illness). After this goal has been met, the investor proceeds to save and accumulate assets designed to finance the child's college education. The process is continued until all of the goals have been met.

The Capacity to Meet Financial Emergencies   While this financial goal can be well defined, planning to have funds to meet financial emergencies involves considerable uncertainty. The investor does not know when (or even if) the money will be needed. While long-term securities may be used to meet a financial goal that has an identifiable time period, they would probably be inappropriate to meet the goal of having sufficient funds to deal with emergencies. Assets that are very liquid (i.e., that are easily converted into cash without a loss) should be chosen to fulfill this investment goal. These include savings accounts, high-quality short-term debt such as certificates of deposit, and series EE bonds, and money market mutual funds.

Savings accounts, money market accounts, and certificates of deposit with short maturities may be readily converted into cash. While their yields may be lower than would be available from debt with a longer maturity, these liquid assets offer the important advantages of the safety of the principal and the ease of conversion into cash.

Short-term debt instruments, such as treasury bills and commercial paper, are also excellent investments for funds that are being held for emergencies. Although such investments may not maximize the investor's yield, they are more productive than leaving the money in a checking account. If the investor lacks sufficient funds to buy commercial paper or treasury bills, money market mutual funds offer a viable alternative. Of course, the problem of the amount of the minimum unit of purchase does not apply to series EE bonds, and they offer the additional advantage of deferring income taxes until the funds are needed and the bonds redeemed.

The Desire to Finance Identifiable Future Purchases, Such as a Child's Education
By the nature of emergencies, it is impossible to know when the funds will be needed, but this need not apply to other future purchases of goods and services.

The desire to purchase a specified good or service often has a known time dimension. Financing an education and planning for retirement are both examples of expenditures that will occur at a particular time in the future. Individuals know approximately when their children will be in college or when they will retire. While there may be some deviation in the time of the actual occurrence, the investor knows approximately when these events will happen and can plan now to have the funds to finance the purchase.

Consider the financing of a child's college education. If the child is currently eight years old, the funds for a college education will be needed in approximately ten years.[1] What assets are desirable to meet this particular financial goal? The answer to the question is primarily long-term but relatively safe assets. They should be long-term because the funds will not be needed for many years, and such investments tend to offer a superior yield to short-term assets. They should be relatively safe because one should not want to gamble with funds earmarked for this education. What assets are long-term and relatively safe? There are many, including

- ◆ conservative growth stocks
- ◆ high-yielding stocks
- ◆ long-term bonds

Long-term growth stocks offer possible appreciation in the investor's capital. Since the emphasis is on the need for funds many years in the future, steady long-term growth is one means to meet this goal. In effect, this strategy suggests that the investor select known growth stocks, such as IBM, rather than riskier stocks that may offer a higher return but require that the investor bear more risk.

Stocks that offer a high dividend yield may also earn a considerable amount of money over time. Stocks with a 6 percent annual dividend yield may double an investment in twelve years. However, the investor cannot spend the dividends as they are received or the amount of savings will not grow. This forced saving may be achieved by opting for the dividend reinvestment plans that many corporations offer their stockholders. Since the investor never receives the cash dividends, they cannot be spent. Hence, such plans offer a painless means to save for a specified goal.

Long-term bonds are also an excellent means to save for a certain time period. Since the bonds mature at specified times, the investor can purchase an issue that will be redeemed at the desired time in the future. For example, if the funds are needed after ten years, the investor may buy bonds that mature after ten years. If the investor knows when the money will be needed, a portfolio of bonds may be constructed that matches the maturity dates of the bond and the time when the funds will be required.

Each of the aforementioned alternatives requires that the investor choose an individual asset for purchase. The investor may avoid this decision by purchasing shares in a mutual fund that meets the specific investment goal. Investment companies that specialize in growth or in income-producing securities offer another means to accumulate funds designed to finance a specific expenditure in the future, such as a college education. Obviously, investment companies that specialize in risky

---

[1] Although the exact future cost of the education is unknown, the parents can systematically accumulate assets to begin to meet this anticipated expense.

securities or special situations do not meet this investment goal and should be avoided.

Although the preceding discussion used the financing of a college education as the investor's goal, other similar goals could have been used. For example, the accumulation of funds to help finance retirement is a similar goal. Once again, the investor knows approximately when the event (i.e., retirement) will occur. The portfolio should then be constructed with assets that can be converted into cash at a specified time in the future. This general principle actually applies to any portfolio whose purpose is to meet a goal whose time dimension is known with some degree of certainty.

The Need for Additional Future Income and Financial Independence at Retirement
Some investors save and purchase assets so that they may have an increased flow of income in the future. These investors are not particularly concerned with capital appreciation, but they are concerned with the general safety of principal and the flow of income. This is especially true if this investment income is to be a primary source of the individual's total income. Although such investors may receive supplemental income, their investment income is extremely important to their well-being. Such investors should choose assets that offer generous income and assure to some extent the safety of the principal. These include

- ✦ preferred stock
- ✦ bonds
- ✦ federal government securities

All of these assets tend to offer income and the relative safety of the principal. The safest is, of course, the long-term debt of the federal government, but these bonds offer returns that are less than those that may be earned on high-quality corporate debt, such as bonds issued by AT&T. Preferred stocks are the riskiest of the alternatives listed but may offer the highest yield. The bonds and preferred stock are easily sold should the investor need immediate cash.

This investor should also consider common stocks with a history of dividend increments. While the aforementioned securities may be safer than corporate stock, they do not offer the possibility of growth in income. Such growth may be very desirable, especially during periods of inflation, because without an increase in income, the investor's purchasing power would be diminished. Common stocks do offer the possibility of increased dividends, and some companies (e.g., telephone utilities) have a history of annual dividend increments. Such common stocks offer the investor who is primarily concerned with income and the safety of the principal a means to obtain some increment in income for accepting only a modest degree of risk.

The Desire to Accumulate an Estate   The desire to accumulate a substantial estate may be fulfilled by virtually any of the assets discussed in this text. However, there is less emphasis on liquidity and a current flow of income. Instead, the portfolio should stress assets whose values tend to appreciate over time. These may include

- ✦ growth stocks
- ✦ art objects and various collectibles

✦ real estate
✦ convertible bonds

Growth stocks and convertible bonds place emphasis on price appreciation, but they also generate some flow of income. Collectibles and art work produce no income in cash. The yield on such investments is limited to price appreciation. Real estate may be particularly attractive, since it may offer current tax advantages while it appreciates. Although the time of one's death is unknown, an estate portfolio still places emphasis on those assets with potential for long-term growth. Many of these assets would not be appropriate in a portfolio stressing safety and liquidity.

While the above goals are the ones most frequently specified for the purposes for saving, individuals may have other reasons for investing. These may include the enjoyment associated with managing one's own funds or the desire to speculate. The success of casinos or state lottery games suggests that some individuals do enjoy gambling. No doubt others enjoy the game associated with speculating. Of course, prudence dictates that financial goals such as planning for emergencies or retirement should take precedence, but after accumulating sufficient assets to meet emergencies and other financial goals, the individual may seek to increase the return earned by bearing more risk.

Many assets are available that may satisfy an investor's desire to speculate. These include

✦ high-yield securities
✦ stocks of small and risky companies
✦ options
✦ commodities
✦ collectibles

Poor-quality bonds and preferred stocks offer higher potential return as compensation for the additional risk. Debentures, income bonds, even bonds in default may produce speculative gains should the company improve its financial position, which will improve the quality of the bonds. There certainly have been many bonds that at one time fell on bad times, yet returned to respectability and rewarded those willing to bear the risk.

All large companies were small at one time. Although purchasing the shares of small or risky companies may often result in substantial losses (especially if the firm should fail, as many do), the rewards can be substantial if the firm succeeds. Investors who purchased the shares of Coca-Cola, IBM, or Johnson & Johnson when these firms were small and just emerging were well rewarded for bearing this risk. Of course, hindsight is considerably better than foresight; it is extremely difficult to identify which of today's small but growing companies will be the success stories of tomorrow. But it is the possibility of such success that stimulates speculators' willingness to bear the risk and purchase the shares of emerging companies.

Options and futures contracts may offer the speculator the greatest satisfaction. While it may take years for poor-quality debt to improve or for small companies to grow, the action with options and commodity contracts is very rapid. Both are a means to apply leverage to one's position. The potential for large and sudden price changes is substantial. If the price of the underlying stock changes, the resulting change in the price of the option will be magnified. The same applies to the value of commodity contracts. The small margin requirement magnifies the potential return (or loss) on the speculator's funds. This potential for fast action and larger percentage gains increases the appeal of these very risky assets to investors who seek to speculate.

Although not all speculators will invest in collectibles, these assets offer special appeal to some investors who are willing to bear substantial risk. Investing in these assets requires specialized knowledge, and the possibility of buying a collectible at a minimal price and then seeing one's appraisal of the asset's potential value prove to be correct should appeal to some investors who are willing to accept the risk for the possibility of a large return.

Monitoring and Revaluation

While financial planning is the backbone of portfolio construction, the individual must realize that goals and financial conditions do change. Such changes may alter the general financial plan. The birth of a child, the death of a spouse, a promotion, or a new job are just some of the many possible events that shape our lives and alter our financial goals. The individual must be willing to adjust financial plans accordingly. If a financial plan becomes outmoded, the investor should act rapidly to change the portfolio. This requires that investors be continually aware of (1) their financial environment, including their sources and uses of funds, (2) the composition of their portfolios, and (3) conditions in the financial markets.

Firms also change, so their securities may no longer be appropriate for a particular individual's portfolio. For example, AT&T is a different firm today than it was prior to divestiture. While previously it may have been considered a conservative firm that paid stable and slowly growing dividends, such a description may no longer apply now that it is not a regulated utility.

Financial markets are certainly not static. For example, the deregulation of the banking system has had a profound impact on financial markets. Intense competition among financial intermediaries has led to a blurring of distinctions among the various savings institutions. Such was not the case prior to deregulation. Also, new financial products such as stock index futures and bonds with put options have been created. Thus, financial markets are dynamic markets with an expanding array of investment alternatives.

One of the most important facets of investing—taxation—is also subject to change. Taxes alter the environment in which investment decisions are made. Some changes encourage investing or favor specific securities that the individual may acquire. Changes in the tax laws can have a profound impact on the individual's portfolio and thus require the investor to reassess the composition of the portfolio and make appropriate adjustments. It is only possible to conjecture as to what future changes in the tax code may be enacted, but certainly the investor should be aware of current tax laws and the impact that any proposed changes may have on the portfolio.

Finally, the investor must be willing to realize that not all investments will achieve their anticipated return or serve the purpose for which they were acquired. That is the nature of risk; the future is uncertain. If a particular asset is no longer appropriate or the anticipated return has not been realized, the investor should be willing to liquidate that asset and acquire an alternative. This does not mean that the individual should continuously turn over the portfolio. Such a course of action may be counterproductive and perhaps may even reduce the return as the investor pays the fees associated with the sale of one asset and the purchase of another. However, the investor should not become so enamored with particular assets that they are an end unto themselves instead of a means to meet specified financial goals.

Portfolio planning and management are not easy tasks that can be performed casually and infrequently. It is for this reason that many investors employ others who are more versed in the subject to do their financial planning and construct their portfolios. Trust departments of commercial banks, financial planning consultants, and the managers of investment companies partially relieve the individual of making investment decisions. Such professional help is not free. The fees may reduce the return the investor earns, but that is the price the investor must pay for giving up some of the responsibilities of investment decision making.

Selecting a Money Manager or Financial Planner

Since the management of assets requires specialized knowledge and can be time consuming, some individuals prefer to use the services of a money manager or financial planner. Financial planning is an emerging profession, so the terms "money manager" or "financial planner" can be both broad and vague. Many individuals may offer financial counsel. For example, the accountant who completes the investor's income tax forms may be a natural source for financial advice. The same applies to insurance salespeople, bankers, and stockbrokers. Any of these individuals can (and often do) offer financial advice as part of the usual services they provide.

With individuals in a specific area of finance, one must question whether their advice is self-serving. For example, an insurance salesperson or stockbroker may recommend purchasing specific investments. While these investments can be valuable as part of the individual's portfolio, their purchase may not necessarily be in the best interests of the investor.

To avoid this problem, the individual may seek the services of a fee-only financial planner, who develops financial plans for clients. Unlike bankers, brokers, or insurance salespeople who may be compensated through sales commissions, fee-only financial planners are compensated for constructing the financial plan and not for its execution. In effect, there are no sales commissions for the planning service. The individual will, however, have to pay appropriate commissions when the plan is executed. Thus, if a fee-only financial planner suggests the individual sell selected securities and replace them with other assets, the sales will generate brokerage commissions.

The selection of a money manager/financial planner is a highly individual decision. In some cases the choice may have been forced upon the individual. For example, a spouse may have inherited an estate that is managed by the trust department of a commercial bank. Someone, however, had to initially select that trust department to manage the assets. Since financial planning and money management is an emerging field, it may be difficult to identify competent asset managers.

The selection of a money manager/financial planner is not made easier when the individual realizes that financial planning requires access to very personal information. As a medical doctor may require confidential, personal information, so too will a money manager/financial planner require information that many individuals do not care to disclose. One's sources of income, the value of one's assets and outstanding debts, or relationships with one's family are illustrative of the information that a money manager may need. Before an investor seeks the help of a money

POINTS OF INTEREST

WRAP ACCOUNTS

In 1990, E.F. Hutton offered individual investors the first account that included financial planning, custodial services, and professional money management. These "wrap accounts" are available to individuals with a specified minimum amount to invest (e.g., $250,000). Brokers initially work with their clients to determine the individual's financial goals and risk tolerance. After this preliminary financial planning, the broker selects a professional money manager who meets the client's needs. The money manager makes all investment decisions such as purchases and sales of securities designed to meet the investor's goals.

The money manager may work independently of the investor's brokerage firm, but some brokerage firms only use in-house portfolio managers. In either case, the money manager works through the client's brokerage firm. The investor receives periodic account statements, but unless the dollar amount being managed is substantial, the investor does not meet or talk with the money manager. Information on specific assets being included or decisions to buy or sell comes through the broker, thus tieing investors to their brokers and isolating them from the money managers.

The investor pays a fee such as 3 percent of the value of assets being managed, which is split among the broker, the brokerage firm, and the money manager. (Fees may be less for fixed income accounts, which involve less active management.) The fee covers all costs, including commissions on security transactions. However, there may be hidden costs if the money manager does not obtain comparable prices for sales and purchases, a problem that could arise when the money manager works through the client's brokerage firm.°

Wrap accounts' primary advantages to the client are access to professional management and avoidance of having to make specific investment decisions. Of course, these advantages require relinquishing control over timing of transactions and the composition of the portfolio. For individuals who lack the time or inclination to manage their assets, wrap accounts offer a more complete package than investing in specific mutual funds or other investments vehicles.

While wrap accounts have professional money managers, the investor should not assume that the account receives individual attention. The wrap account may only give the impression of individualized professional management. Money managers may have certain predetermined portfolios for certain types of investors. For example, a manager may select the same portfolio for each individual seeking conservative investments with accounts of less than $500,000. In effect, each account has a common position in a portfolio constructed by the money manager.

Perhaps the biggest disadvantage to the wrap account is the reliance on the broker. There is the assumption that the broker correctly identifies the investor's financial objectives and risk tolerance and recommends the appropriate money manager. This assumption could easily be violated when in-house money managers are used. In addition, it is assumed that sufficient information is provided to the investor to evaluate the performance of the money manager. Efficient financial markets suggests that few money managers will consistently outperform the market and that the fee will not be covered by superior results. Of course, the individual would pay other costs (e.g., fees for the services of a financial planner or brokerage commissions) if an alternative to a wrap account is used, but these costs may be less than the cost of the wrap account.

While wrap accounts may not generate superior investment results, they have become popular with investors. In less than three years, the amount managed through these accounts grew to over $40 billion. For individuals who seek to avoid investment decisions or who fear brokers may excessively churn their accounts to generate commissions, wrap accounts offer one-stop investment shopping for a fixed price.

°See Albert J. Golly, Jr. "The Pros and Cons of Brokerage Wrap Accounts," *AAII Journal*, February 1993, 8–11, and Ellen E. Schultz, "Hidden Costs Can Put the Squeeze on Wrap Accounts," *The Wall Street Journal*, January 28, 1993, C1+.

manager or professional financial planner, it is desirable for the individual to determine his or her willingness to reveal personal financial information.

Several considerations should enter the selection of a knowledgeable money manager. Financial planning is a broad area requiring breadth of knowledge in the various investment alternatives as well as risk management through insurance, tax planning, retirement, and estate planning. While it is difficult to measure an individual's breadth and depth of knowledge, credentials such as academic background, previous experience, and professional designations such as CFP (Certified Financial

Planner) or ChFC (Chartered Financial Consultant) help indicate the level of knowledge. References and word of mouth can also be an excellent way to learn about specific individuals. In addition, membership in professional associations such as the International Association for Financial Planning and the Institute of Certified Financial Planners is desirable, as these associations establish codes of ethics to which their members must subscribe.

Finally, the money manager/financial planner and the individual must concur on the individual's financial goals and willingness to bear risk. If the individual believes that he or she can bear more risk than the money manager/financial planner believes is prudent, there may be inherent conflicts. There must be a meeting of the minds between the money manager/financial planner and the client for the process to be successful. Also, without rapport and respect, the individual may not be willing to divulge information necessary for the construction of realistic financial plans.

INVESTMENT MANAGEMENT

After developing a financial plan, the next step is to construct and manage the portfolio. The individual should remember that investment decisions are made in efficient financial markets. From a pragmatic viewpoint, this has several important implications. The investor should not expect to outperform the market over a period of years. Of course, during a particular time period, the portfolio return may be superior but such outstanding performance in one period may not be repeated. Frequent switching from one asset to another in an attempt to beat the market will, in all likelihood, fail to achieve higher returns and may even produce inferior investment performance as the investor must pay the commissions associated with each transaction.

Efficient markets and the large amount of published material on investments suggest that the individual investor need not perform much of the analysis explained and illustrated in this text. For example, the investor may not have to calculate the yield to maturity on a bond or a firm's beta coefficient or to analyze a firm's financial statements. This information is readily available, so there is little reason to reinvent the wheel. The investor, however, does need to understand these concepts and can certainly apply them in portfolio construction and investment management. For example, an investor seeking capital appreciation may limit the portfolio to firms with a return on equity exceeding 15 percent and a payout ratio less than 25 percent. Such firms are currently generating profits and retaining them, which could lead to future growth and capital gains.

A large proportion of the material covered in this text can aid in investment management even if the material cannot produce superior investment results. The material strongly argues for constructing diversified portfolios to reduce the unsystematic risk associated with a specific asset. That is, the individual should accumulate a variety of assets whose returns are not positively correlated. If the investor does not have sufficient funds to create a diversified portfolio, then that individual should acquire shares in an investment company. While such a strategy will help achieve diversification, it should not lead to superior investment results. The mutual funds must buy and sell securities in the same efficient markets in which individual investors participate. In addition, the investor has to pay management expenses and any other fees (e.g., loading, 12b-1, and exit fees) that the fund levies.

In addition to possible diversification, investment companies offer advantages such as custodial services and dividend reinvestment plans. While these services are not unique to investment companies, the latter is exceedingly important for the accumulation of wealth. All dividend reinvestment plans permit the individual to dollar cost average and to compound the return. If the investor consumes dividend and interest income, the advantages of compounding are lost. Investment company and corporate dividend reinvestment plans permit compounding since the funds are used to acquire additional shares. Compounding may also be achieved through investments in retirement plans such as corporate pension plans and individual retirement accounts (IRAs).

If the investor believes that markets are not efficient, that individual may adopt an active portfolio strategy. There is evidence that there are anomalies such as the January effect that may offer opportunities to earn superior returns. There is also the possibility of identifying underpriced and overpriced securities to buy or sell short. This is probably more true for smaller companies than for the large, actively traded stocks, but the possibility of locating such stocks is reason to perform much of the analysis explained in the text.

Even if the markets are very efficient, the possibility of increasing the return only marginally may justify the effort. If the average return turns out to be 10.0 percent and the individual earns 10.2 percent, the difference may not appear to be large. However, over a period of years, the difference can become substantial. For instance, $100,000 at 10 percent grows into $672,500 after 20 years. At 10.2 percent the terminal value is $697,641 for a difference of $25,141. It may be impossible to prove that the additional return is statistically different than a random event. But the investor is probably more interested in the result than verifying or disproving the efficient market hypothesis.

Investors who manage their portfolios actively will also seek to alter their portfolios with anticipated changes in economic conditions. Since higher interest rates are associated with lower earnings and lower bond prices, the investor may seek to liquidate long-term securities and move into short-term securities before the change in interest rates occurs. The anticipation of inflation also suggests a shifting of investment strategy to more tangible assets, such as real estate at the expense of financial assets. Of course, the investor must bear the costs associated with portfolio shifts (i.e., commissions, the spread between the bid and ask prices, and taxes on realized gains) as well as the risk that the anticipated economic scenario may be incorrect.

The investor who does want to shift money among alternative investments should consider acquiring shares in mutual funds that are part of a family of funds. Many professional money management firms offer investors a family of mutual funds and permit investors to shift money among the various funds they manage. In many cases, such swaps are permitted without the investor having to pay any exit fees or sales charges on the subsequent purchase. The investor, however, will be subject to capital gains taxation. The swap is a realized sale.

Shifting among funds permits the investor to alter the portfolio as conditions warrant or as financial goals change. For example, if the investor anticipates rising interest rates, that individual would seek to liquidate positions in bonds and move into a money market fund. This could involve a substantial number of sales if the individual has a large bond portfolio. If, however, the individual had invested in a bond fund that was a member of a family of funds, that individual could easily swap the bond fund for the money market fund and accomplish the desired change. While the swap may not increase the investor's return, it has eased the execution of the desired change in the portfolio.

Investors who follow an active strategy and try to time their security sales to catch changes in market and economic conditions should realize that they run the risk of being wrong. Many investors who raced to sell stock on "Black Monday" in October 1987 may have sold their stocks at some of the lowest prices in years. Individuals who liquidated long positions but who did not reestablish those positions watched security prices (both bonds and stocks) rise during 1988 and 1989. In less than two years, the market had recouped all the losses. While not every stock had regained its prior highs, some were well above their prior highs.

Of course, hindsight always leads to perfect investment decisions, but the essential point remains. Portfolio shifts designed to meet changes in the economic environment such as selecting undervalued securities will produce superior results only when the shifts are proven correct. There is little evidence that professional money managers or individuals will be able to consistently alter their portfolios and achieve superior returns on their investments.

PERFORMANCE EVALUATION

Initially the individual defines his or her investment goals. Individual assets are acquired and portfolios are constructed to meet the specified goals. The security analysis, the valuation techniques, and the portfolio theory discussed in this text play an important role in this process. Even if the individual employs the services of a professional portfolio manager by investing in mutual funds or having funds managed in trust, the techniques in this text are the backbone of portfolio construction and management.

Security selection and portfolio management are obviously important for the individual seeking to invest savings and transfer purchasing power to the future to meet financial goals. Investments are made in anticipation of a positive return, but the realized return may not be the expected return. The investor may do better or worse than anticipated. The question arises as to whether portfolio performance can be evaluated. This is obviously an important question if a professional portfolio manager has been employed to manage the assets. Obviously, the investor would like to be able to measure the performance of one money manager relative to others. However, the question is still important for individuals who manage their own portfolios to give them an indication of their results relative to the performance of professional portfolio managers. If the evaluation indicates inferior performance, the investor may alter his or her investment strategy in order to improve the results.

Three techniques for the measurement of performance, often referred to as "composite performance measures," have been developed. These measures are (1) the Jensen index, (2) the Treynor index, and (3) the Sharpe index, each named after the individual who first used the technique to measure performance.

Any measure for the evaluation of portfolio performance must address two important issues: (1) what benchmark of the aggregate market to use for comparison and (2) how to adjust the realized return for risk associated with the portfolio. Thus, all three composite measures of performance must address these two concerns. That is, each must use a measure of the market return as a standard for comparison and adjust for risk.

The benchmark frequently used to measure the market is the S & P 500 stock index, since it is a comprehensive, value-weighted index. Because many portfolios, especially mutual funds, trust accounts, and pension plans, are comprised of the securities represented in the S & P 500 index, this index is considered to be an appropriate proxy for the market. However, many portfolios include bonds, real estate, collectibles, and numerous types of money market securities, in which case the S & P 500 stock index may be an inappropriate benchmark for evaluating portfolio performance.

The differences among the three composite performance measures rest primarily with the adjustment for risk and the construction of the measure of evaluation. The measurement of risk is particularly important since a lower return is not necessarily indicative of inferior performance. Obviously the return on a money market mutual fund should be less than the return earned by a growth fund during a period of rising security prices. The more relevant question is, "Was the growth fund manager's performance sufficient to justify the additional risk?"

All three composite measures are an outgrowth of the capital asset pricing model (CAPM), which specifies that the required return on an investment (k) depends on (1) the return the individual may earn on a risk-free asset such as a U.S. Treasury bill and (2) a risk premium. This risk-adjusted return (r_s) was expressed in Equation (7.6) in Chapter 7:

$$r_s = r_f + (r_m - r_f)\text{beta} \qquad (7.6)$$

in which r_f represents the risk-free rate and r_m is the expected return on the market. The risk premium depends on the extent to which the market return exceeds the risk-free rate (i.e., $r_m - r_f$) adjusted by the systematic risk associated with the asset (i.e., its beta coefficient). This relationship is shown in Figure 25.1, which

Figure 25.1   CAPM RISK-ADJUSTED RETURNS

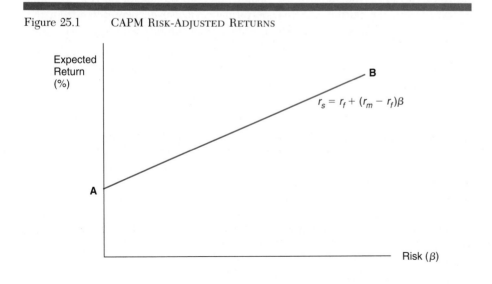

reproduces Figure 7.16. The Y-axis represents the return, and the X-axis represents the risk as measured by beta. Line *AB* gives all the combinations of return at each level of risk. If the investor bears no risk, the return on the Y-axis represents the risk-free rate, and higher returns are associated with bearing increased risk.

The Jensen Performance Index

While the CAPM is used to determine the return that is required to make an investment, it may also be used to evaluate realized performance. The Jensen performance index determines by how much the realized return differs from the return required by the CAPM.[2] The realized return (r_p) on a portfolio (or on a specific investment if applied to the return on an individual asset) is

$$r_p = r_f + (r_m - r_f)\text{beta} + e. \tag{25.1}$$

Equation 25.1 is basically the same as the CAPM equation except that (1) the realized return is substituted for the expected return and (2) a random error term (e) has been added. In this form, the model is used to evaluate performance and not to determine the required return necessary to make an investment.[3]

If the risk-free return is subtracted from both sides, the equation becomes

$$r_p - r_f = (r_m - r_f)\text{beta} + e. \tag{25.2}$$

In this form, Equation 25.2 indicates that the actual risk premium earned on the portfolio equals the market risk premium times the beta plus the error term. Since the errors are assumed to be random, the value of e should be zero.

Figure 25.2 reproduces Figure 25.1 and adds line *CD*, which represents Equation 25.2. The two lines, *AB* and *CD*, are parallel, and since the risk-free rate has been subtracted from both sides of Equation 25.1 to derive Equation 25.2, line *CD* has no positive intercept on the Y-axis. Equation 25.2 indicates that after subtracting the risk-free rate, higher returns are related solely to the additional risk premium associated with the portfolio. Actual performance, however, may differ from the return implied by Equation 25.2. The possibility that the realized return may differ from the expected return is indicated by

$$r_p - r_f = a + (r_m - r_f)\text{beta}, \tag{25.3}$$

---

[2] Jensen's seminal work on portfolio evaluation may be found in Michael C. Jensen, "The Performance of Mutual Funds in the Period 1945–1964," *Journal of Finance,* (May 1968), 389–416.

[3] Application of the Jensen model may require an adjustment in the risk-free rate. Usually a short-term security such as a U.S. Treasury bill is the appropriate proxy for this rate. However, if the time period being covered by the evaluation is greater than a year, it is inappropriate to use a short-term rate, and a different risk-free rate is required for each time interval during the evaluation period. If, for example, the evaluation of the performance of two portfolio managers is being done on an annual basis over five years, a different one-year risk-free rate would have to be used for each of the five years during the evaluation period.

Figure 25.2 ✦ JENSEN PERFORMANCE INDEX—RISK-ADJUSTED RETURNS INCLUDING AND EXCLUDING THE RISK-FREE RATE

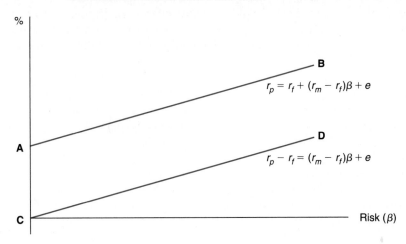

in which a (often referred to as alpha) represents the extent to which the realized return differs from the required return or the return that would be expected for a given amount of risk.

After algebraic manipulation, Equation 25.3 is often presented in the following form:

$$a = r_p - [r_f + (r_m - r_f)\text{beta}] \qquad (25.4)$$

and referred to as the **Jensen performance index.** Since alpha is the difference between the realized return and the risk-adjusted expected return, the numerical value of a indicates superior or inferior performance.

If the portfolio manager consistently does better than the capital asset model projects, the alpha takes on a positive value. If the performance is consistently inferior, the alpha takes on a negative value. For example, if *portfolio manager X* achieved a return of 15.0% with a beta of 1.1 when the market return was 14.6% and the risk-free rate was 7%, the alpha is

$$a = .15 - [.07 + (.146 - .07)1.1] = -0.0036,$$

which indicates inferior performance. If *portfolio manager Y* achieved a 13.5% return with a beta of 0.81, the alpha is

$$a = .135 - [.07 + (.146 - .07)0.81] = 0.0034,$$

which indicates superior performance. Even though portfolio manager Y had the lower realized return, the performance is superior on a risk-adjusted basis.

The Jensen performance index permits the comparison of portfolio managers' performance relative to each other or to the market. The absolute numerical values

Jensen performance index
A measure of performance that compares the realized return with the risk-adjusted expected return.

of alpha permit the ranking of performance with the higher scores indicating the best performance. The sign of the alpha indicates whether the portfolio manager outperformed the market. A positive alpha indicates superior performance relative to the market, and a negative alpha indicates inferior performance. Thus, in the previous example, portfolio manager Y's performance was superior not only to portfolio manager X's performance but also to the market. In other words, portfolio manager Y outperformed the market on a risk-adjusted basis.

The performance of the two portfolio managers is represented in Figure 25.3 by lines *EF* and *GH*. Line *EF* has a positive intercept, which is the distance between *EF* and *CD* for all levels of risk and indicates superior performance. Line *GH* has a negative intercept, indicating inferior performance. If a portfolio manager achieves what would be expected, the intercept is zero. Alpha has no value, and the performance matches the market on a risk-adjusted basis (i.e., lies on line *CD*).

The Jensen performance index measures risk premiums in terms of beta, so the index assumes that the portfolio is well diversified. Since a well-diversified portfolio's total risk is primarily its systematic risk, beta is the appropriate index of that risk. If the portfolio were not sufficiently diversified, portfolio risk would include both unsystematic and systematic risk, and the standard deviation of the portfolio's returns would be a more appropriate measure of risk.

The Treynor and Sharpe Performance Indices

Treynor index
A risk-adjusted measure of performance that standardizes the return in excess of the risk-free rate by the portfolio's systematic risk.

The Treynor and Sharpe indices are alternative measures of portfolio evaluation. **The Treynor index** (T_i) for a given time period is

$$T_i = \frac{r_p - r_f}{\text{beta}}$$

in which r_p is the realized return on the portfolio and r_f is the risk-free rate.[4] The extent to which the realized return exceeds the risk-free rate (i.e., the risk premium that is realized) is divided by the portfolio beta (i.e., the measure of systematic risk). Thus, if portfolio manager X achieved a return of 15% when the risk-free rate was 7% and the portfolio's beta was 1.1, the Treynor index is

$$T_X = \frac{.15 - .07}{1.1} = 0.0727.$$

If portfolio manager Y achieved a return of 12.5% with a beta of 0.81, the Treynor index is

$$T_Y = \frac{.135 - .07}{0.81} = 0.0802.$$

This indicates that portfolio manager Y outperformed portfolio manager X on a risk-adjusted basis, which is the same conclusion regarding the relative performance of

---

[4] Jack L. Treynor, "How to Rate Management Investment Funds," *Harvard Business Review,* January–February 1966, 63–74.

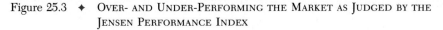

Figure 25.3 ✦ OVER- AND UNDER-PERFORMING THE MARKET AS JUDGED BY THE JENSEN PERFORMANCE INDEX

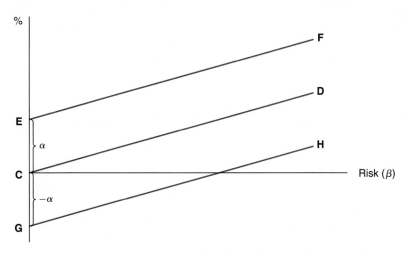

the two portfolio managers derived by the Jensen index of performance. However, it *cannot* be concluded from the Treynor index that either portfolio manager outperformed or underperformed the market. The Treynor performance index must be computed for the market to determine whether the portfolio manager outperformed the market. If during the time period, the market return were 14.6%, then the Treynor index for the market is

$$T_M = \frac{.146 - .07}{1.0} = 0.076.$$

(Notice that the numerical value of the beta for the market is 1.0.) Since the Treynor index for the market is 0.076, portfolio manager X underperformed while portfolio manager Y outperformed the market on a risk-adjusted basis.

This conclusion is illustrated in Figure 25.4. Line AB represents the returns (r_P) that would be expected using the capital asset pricing model for a given risk-free rate, a given return on the market, and different levels of beta. The Y-axis intercept measures the risk-free return, which in the above illustration is 7.0%. The return on the market is 14.6%, and the X-axis gives different levels of beta. Thus, the equation for line AB is

$$r_P = r_f + (r_m - r_f)\text{beta} = .07 + (.146 - .07)\text{beta}.$$

If the portfolio manager outperforms the market on a risk-adjusted basis, the realized combination of risk and return will lie above line AB. Conversely, if the performance is inferior to the market, the realized combination of risk and return will lie below line AB.

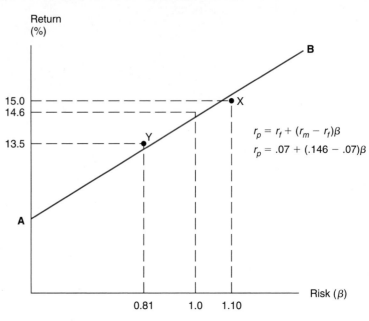

Figure 25.4 ✦ REALIZED VERSUS EXPECTED RETURNS

The beta of portfolio X is 1.1, so the expected return is

$$r_X = .07 + (.146 - .07)1.1 = 15.36\%.$$

The *realized return* is 15.0%, which is less than the expected return of 15.36%, and the portfolio underperformed the market after adjusting for risk. This realized return is represented by point X in Figure 25.4 and the point does lie below line AB.

The beta of portfolio Y is 0.81, so the expected return is

$$r_Y = .07 + (.146 - .07)0.81 = 13.156\%.$$

The realized return is 13.5%, which exceeds the expected return of 13.156%; thus, the portfolio outperformed the market after adjusting for risk. The realized return is represented by point Y in Figure 25.4, and the point does lie above line AB.

Sharpe index
A risk-adjusted measure of performance that standardizes the return in excess of the risk-free rate by the standard deviation of the portfolio's returns.

The third measure of performance, the **Sharpe performance index** (S_i), is

$$S_i = \frac{r_p - r_f}{\sigma_p}.$$

The only new symbol in the index is σ_p, which represents the standard deviation of the portfolio.[5] If the previous examples are continued and portfolio manager X's

[5]William F. Sharpe, "Mutual Fund Performance," *Journal of Business*, January 1966, 1119–1138.

portfolio had a standard deviation of ±.3 while portfolio manager Y's portfolio had a standard deviation of ±.25, their respective indices are

$$S_X = \frac{.15 - .07}{.3} = 0.267$$

and

$$S_Y = \frac{.135 - .07}{.25} = 0.26.$$

Since portfolio manager X has the higher score, the performance is superior to that of portfolio manager Y. The additional return (i.e., 15% versus 13.5%) more than compensates for the additional risk (i.e., the higher standard deviation).

The Sharpe ranking of X over Y is opposite to the ranking determined using the Treynor and Jensen indices of performance. In those measurements, portfolio manager Y had the higher score, which indicated better performance. The reason for the difference in the rankings is the measure of risk. The Sharpe performance index uses the portfolio's standard deviation as the measure of risk. Since the index uses the portfolio's standard deviation, it does not assume the portfolio is well diversified. In effect, the index standardizes the return in excess of the risk-free rate by the variability of the return. The Treynor index uses the portfolio's beta and does assume the portfolio is well diversified. In effect, it standardizes the return in excess of the risk-free rate by the volatility of the return.

It is important to realize that variability and volatility do not mean the same thing. Variability compares one year's return with the portfolio's average return. A variable return implies that from year to year there will be large differences in the annual return. Volatility compares the return relative to something else. A volatile return implies that the return on the portfolio fluctuates more than some base (i.e., the return on the portfolio is more volatile than the return on the market). A portfolio could have a low beta; its return relative to the market would not be volatile (i.e., the return on the market would fluctuate more). However, from year to year there could be a large variation in the portfolio's return, so the returns are variable even though the portfolio is less volatile than the market.

As with the Treynor index, the Sharpe measure of performance does not indicate whether the portfolio manager outperformed the market. No statement can be made concerning performance relative to the market unless the Sharpe performance index also is computed for the market. If the standard deviation of the market return is ±.2, the Sharpe index for the market is

$$S_M = \frac{.146 - .07}{.2} = 0.38.$$

Since this value exceeds the numerical values computed for portfolio managers X and Y (i.e., 0.267 and 0.26), the interference is that both *underperformed* the market on a risk-adjusted basis.

While the Treynor and Sharpe indices yielded different rankings of performance in the example above, this conflict may not occur when the measures are applied to evaluate the performance of most portfolio managers. Since most mutual fund or pension fund managers construct well-diversified portfolios, all three techniques tend to give identical rankings of performance.

Preference for one performance measure over the others depends on the investments being evaluated. If the investments constitute all of an individual's assets, total risk is the more appropriate measure of risk. This argues for the Sharpe performance index since the use of the standard deviation encompasses total risk. However, the portfolio being evaluated could constitute only part of the investor's total assets. Such a situation would occur if the individual has investments in several mutual funds and wants to compare the funds' performance. Each fund does not represent the investor's total risk. Instead the investor is concerned with the non-diversifiable, systematic risk associated with each fund, so beta is the appropriate measure of risk, which argues for the Jensen or Treynor performance indices.

THE BENCHMARK PROBLEM

Since all three techniques require estimates of the market return and beta coefficients, there is a question of the appropriate measure of the market. This is referred to as the "benchmark problem." As was mentioned, aggregate measures of the stock market, such as the S & P 500 stock index or the New York Stock Exchange composite index, encompass only common stocks, which would lead to an incorrect measure of performance. In addition, it has been suggested in a series of articles by Richard Roll that using aggregate indices (such as the S & P 500 stock index or the NYSE composite index) as proxies for the market when computing beta coefficients may produce incorrect or biased betas.[6] This bias is potentially a major problem since estimated betas are used in the capital asset pricing model for the valuation of individual securities and as part of the process for evaluating portfolio performance.

The problem, however, is not one of invalidating modern portfolio theory and the capital asset pricing model. The construction of diversified portfolios in an efficient market environment and the subsequent evaluation of the performance of the portfolios remains a crucial component of the investment process. The obstacle is a measurement problem, not a theoretical problem. It requires researchers to develop a better or more comprehensive aggregate measure of returns on all assets that may be included in the portfolio. This more comprehensive measure of asset returns could then be used as a basis for evaluating individual assets and portfolio evaluation.

---

[6]The seminal works on the benchmark problem include four articles by Richard Roll: "A Critique of the Asset Pricing Theory's Test," *Journal of Financial Economics,* March 1977, 129–176; "Ambiguity When Performance Is Measured by the Securities Market Line," *Journal of Finance,* September 1978, 1051–1069; "Performance Evaluation and Benchmark Errors I," *Journal of Portfolio Management,* Summer 1980, 5–12; and "Performance Evaluation and Benchmark Errors II," *Journal of Portfolio Management,* Winter 1981, 17–22. See the appendix to Chapter 7 for the computation of betas.

SUMMARY

Because investments are made in efficient financial markets, it is very difficult for an individual investor to outperform the market consistently. However, this does not imply that securities or other assets should be acquired randomly. Instead the investor should have a financial plan. First, financial goals are defined and priorities determined. Next, the individual should analyze his or her financial position. This may be achieved through the use of two financial statements—a personal balance sheet that enumerates what the individual owns and owes and his or her net worth, and a cash budget that enumerates the individual's cash receipts and disbursements. These financial statements may be created for the present or may be projected for some time in the future.

After specifying the financial goals and analyzing the financial environment, the investor should construct a diversified portfolio designed to meet these goals. Diversification reduces (and perhaps eliminates) the unsystematic risk associated with each asset; the remaining systematic risk cannot be reduced through diversification. If the individual is willing to bear more systematic risk, he or she may achieve a higher return.

Not all assets are appropriate for every goal, so a diversified portfolio will contain various types of assets, each of which plays a role in the portfolio as a whole through its impact on risk and its capacity to meet specific financial needs.

After the portfolio has been constructed, the individual must continue to make investment decisions. Financial needs change; the individual's resources and environment change; financial markets and the economic environment change; and certainly the performance of individual assets changes. The investor should view the portfolio as a dynamic entity requiring frequent surveillance. When appropriate, adjustments in the composition of the portfolio should be made. Professional financial planners can provide assistance in managing a portfolio, but the individual is ultimately responsible for determining financial goals, managing the portfolio, and bearing the risk associated with investment decisions.

After constructing and managing a portfolio over a period of time, the individual may seek to evaluate the performance. Such evaluation should adjust for risk since a higher return is consistent with more risk taking. It is important to keep in mind that a lower return does not necessarily mean inferior results; instead it may be indicative of less risk taking.

Performance may be judged using the Jensen index by comparing the realized return with the risk-adjusted return that should have been earned. If the realized return exceeds this risk-adjusted return, then there was truly an excess return, and the investor beat the market during that time period. Alternative approaches for portfolio evaluation standardize the realized return by a measure of risk, such as the portfolio's standard deviation (the Sharpe index) or its beta (the Treynor index). The resulting index of performance may be compared with similar standardized indices of performance by mutual funds or the market to determine if the particular portfolio did exceptionally well during the time period.

If the portfolio's performance was exceptional, the investor should realize that repeating such superior returns will be difficult. Efficient financial markets imply that the investor cannot expect to outperform the market consistently, but they do not imply such performance is impossible.

Terms to Remember

Pro forma financial statement   Jensen performance index
cash budget   Treynor index
financial plan   Sharpe index

Questions

1. Why should investors specify financial goals?
2. What types of assets are appropriate to meet financial emergencies? For income?
3. What are the steps for constructing a financial plan? What is a pro forma balance sheet? A cash budget? What role do they play in the construction of financial plans?
4. Which of the following should be part of a balance sheet and which should be part of a cash budget?
    a. mortgage owed
    b. principal payment to be made
    c. dividend payments
    d. Social Security payments
    e. IRA account
    f. gifts to children
    g. mutual fund shares
    h. interest owed
    i. antiques
    j. credit card balances
5. After constructing a financial plan and executing it, does financial planning cease to be important?
6. If the investor follows an active portfolio strategy, what should that individual do if a decrease in interest rates is expected?
7. Is the purpose of diversification to eradicate risk?
8. What is the role of compounding if the investor's goal is the accumulation of capital?
9. If an individual earned 15 percent when the market rose by 12 percent, is this sufficient information that the investor outperformed the market?
10. How may realized returns be adjusted for risk so that investment performance may be judged on a risk-adjusted basis?

Problems

1. You are given the following information concerning several mutual funds:

Funds	Return in Excess of the Treasury Bill Rate	Beta
A	12.4%	1.14
B	13.2	1.22
C	11.4	0.90
D	9.8	0.76
E	12.6	0.95

During the time period the Standard & Poor's stock index exceeded the treasury bill rate by 10.5 percent (i.e., $r_m - r_f = 10.5\%$).

a. Rank the performance of each fund without adjusting for risk and adjusting for risk. Which, if any, outperformed the market? (Remember the beta of the market is 1.0.)

b. The analysis in part (a) assumes each fund is sufficiently diversified that the appropriate measure of risk is the beta coefficient. Suppose, however, this assumption does not hold, and the standard deviation of each fund's return was

Funds	Standard Deviation of Returns
A	±.045 (= 4.5%)
B	.031
C	.010
D	.014
E	.035

Thus Fund A earned a return of 12.4 percent, but approximately 68 percent of the time this return has ranged from 7.9 percent to 16.9 percent. The standard deviation of the market return is .01 (i.e., 10 percent), so 68 percent of the time, the return on the market has ranged from 9.5 to 11.5 percent. Rank the funds using this alternative measure of risk. Which, if any, outperformed the market on a risk-adjusted basis?

2. You are given the following information concerning a 52-year-old male:

Car and consumer loans	$ 14,000
Cash and savings accounts	3,000
Cash value of life insurance	10,000
Education loans	26,000
Home (estimated value of)	175,000
Home mortgage	68,000
Home equity loan	14,000
Pension plan	95,000
Retirement account (IRA)	15,000
Securities (corporate stock)	41,000

a. From this information, construct the individual's current balance sheet.

b. Construct pro forma balance sheets for this individual at ages 62 and 70. To make these projections, assume (1) that the rate of inflation will be 5 percent annually and the value of the house will appreciate at that rate, (2) that no additional contributions will be made to the IRA and the amount of cash and savings will remain $3,000, (3) the IRA and the cash value of the life insurance will grow annually at 6 percent, (4) the annual return on the pension plan and the stock will average 10 percent, (5) $5,000 additional contributions to the pension plan and $3,000 additional stock investments will be made each year, and (6) all liabilities will be retired by age 60. After age 62, contributions to the pension plan will cease.

c. What is the value of the individual's financial assets at ages 62 and 70? Suppose at the age of 70, this individual consolidates all the financial assets into a very safe investment that pays a modest 6 percent annually. How much can the individual spend each year to age 90?

Suggested Readings

Now that you have completed this text, you may expand your knowledge of investments by several approaches. For instance, you could read a more advanced text. Two possibilities are

Bodie, Zvi, Alex Kane, and Alan J. Marcus. *Investments.* Homewood, Ill.: Irwin, 1989.

Radcliff, Robert C. *Investment Concepts, Analysis, and Strategy,* 3d ed. Glenview, Ill.: Scott Foresman, 1990.

Several references on investments have been compiled into books of readings such as

Fabozzi, Frank J. *Readings in Investment Management.* Homewood, Ill.: Richard D. Irwin, 1983.

Kolb, Robert W. *The Investments Reader.* Miami, FL: Kolb Publishing, 1991.

The Institute of Chartered Financial Analysts (Box 3668, Charlottesville, VA 22903) has published a series of readings books that reproduce research done in the various areas of investments. Titles include

Berry, Michael A., and Katrina F. Sherrerd, eds. *CFA Readings in Derivative Securities,* 1988.

White, Gerald I., and Ashwinpaul C. Sondhi, eds. *CFA Readings in Financial Statement Analysis,* 1986.

CFA Readings in Fixed-Income Securities Analysis, 1985.

Financial planning is an integral part of portfolio management and many books have been written for the layman to aid in the process of planning. The following sample of this literature covers financial planning and includes material on budgeting, taxes, estate planning, retirement, and insurance.

Klott, Gary. *The New York Times Complete Guide to Personal Investing.* New York: Times Books, 1987.

Leonetti, Michael E. *Retire Worry-Free.* Chicago, IL: Longman Financial Services Publishing, 1989.

Mittra, Sid. *Practicing Financial Planning: A Complete Guide for Professionals.* Englewood Cliffs, N.J.: Prentice-Hall, 1990.

Vicker, Ray. *The Dow Jones-Irwin Guide to Retirement Planning,* 2d ed. Homewood, Ill.: Dow Jones-Irwin, 1987.

Evaluating performance of professional investment managers is discussed in

Williams III, Arthur. *Managing Your Investment Manager,* 3d ed. Homewood, Ill. Business One Irwin, 1992.

INVESTMENT PROJECT

By now the conclusion of the semester is approaching. Calculate the holding period return for the Standard & Poor 500 and for the individual stocks. (Dividend payments should be included, but since the time period of a semester is relatively short, the exclusion of dividend payments should not significantly affect the returns. Obviously, adjustments should be made for any stock splits or stock dividends.) Sum the individual holding period returns, divide by eight to obtain the holding period return for the portfolio.

Your holding period return assumes that you bought the same number of shares of each stock. You could have invested an equal dollar amount such as $1,000 in each security for a total of $8,000. To determine your portfolio's holding period return under this assumption, first determine the number of shares invested in each stock. Divide $1,000 by each stock's price in Week 1. Multiply the resulting number of shares by the final price to determine the value of each position. Add the individual values, divided by $8,000 and subtract 1 to obtain the holding period of the portfolio.

You may compare the holding period return with the holding period return on the Standard & Poor 500 stock index. If the market rose during the time period and your holding period return is larger, you beat the market (on a risk-*un*adjusted basis). If the market declined and your holding period return is smaller (i.e., a smaller loss), you also beat the market on a risk-unadjusted basis.

Risk Adjustment

Comparing holding period returns with an index of the market may be misleading because the individual returns are not adjusted for risk. A higher return than the market does not necessarily mean that you outperformed the market if you had a riskier portfolio. The returns need to be adjusted for risk. As explained in this chapter, beta coefficients may be used for this adjustment if the portfolio is well-diversified. The eight stocks you have been following will, to some extent, produce some diversification. However, you probably need more than eight stocks to have a well-diversified portfolio.

To give you some indication of the risk adjustment, divide your holding period return for the portfolio by the average beta. (The average beta was calculated in Chapter 7.) Compare this adjusted return with the holding period return for the Standard & Poor 500. Did the portfolio outperform the market on a risk-adjusted basis? If you beat the index, congratulations! Achieve similar results for several years, and you will appear in *Business Week*, *Fortune*, or *Forbes*. If you did not outperform the market, don't fret. You'll probably do much better when you make your first investments because it's difficult to consistently underperform as well as outperform the market on a risk-adjusted basis.

Additional Questions

What happened to interest rates during the semester (as indicated by the yield on the six-month treasury bills and by the price of the IBM bond)? Did stock prices move in the opposite direction? How did the prices of the Microsoft put and call options fare during the semester? Compare the percentage change in the prices of the Microsoft stock, put, and call. Would you have earned a higher return by taking a position in an option than by taking the corresponding position in the Microsoft stock?

Appendix A

MATHEMATICAL TABLES

THE FUTURE SUM OF ONE DOLLAR

THE PRESENT VALUE OF ONE DOLLAR

THE FUTURE SUM OF AN ANNUITY OF ONE DOLLAR

THE PRESENT VALUE OF AN ANNUITY OF ONE DOLLAR

THE FUTURE SUM OF ONE DOLLAR

Period	1%	2%	3%	4%	5%	6%	7%
1	1.010	1.020	1.030	1.040	1.050	1.060	1.070
2	1.020	1.040	1.061	1.082	1.102	1.124	1.145
3	1.030	1.061	1.093	1.125	1.158	1.191	1.225
4	1.041	1.082	1.126	1.170	1.216	1.262	1.311
5	1.051	1.104	1.159	1.217	1.276	1.338	1.403
6	1.062	1.126	1.194	1.265	1.340	1.419	1.501
7	1.072	1.149	1.230	1.316	1.407	1.504	1.606
8	1.083	1.172	1.267	1.369	1.477	1.594	1.718
9	1.094	1.195	1.305	1.423	1.551	1.689	1.838
10	1.105	1.219	1.344	1.480	1.629	1.791	1.967
11	1.116	1.243	1.384	1.539	1.710	1.898	2.105
12	1.127	1.268	1.426	1.601	1.796	2.012	2.252
13	1.138	1.294	1.469	1.665	1.886	2.133	2.410
14	1.149	1.319	1.513	1.732	1.980	2.261	2.579
15	1.161	1.346	1.558	1.801	2.079	2.397	2.759
16	1.173	1.373	1.605	1.873	2.183	2.540	2.952
17	1.184	1.400	1.653	1.948	2.292	2.693	3.159
18	1.196	1.428	1.702	2.026	2.407	2.854	3.380
19	1.208	1.457	1.754	2.107	2.527	3.026	3.617
20	1.220	1.486	1.806	2.191	2.653	3.207	3.870
25	1.282	1.641	2.094	2.666	3.386	4.292	5.427
30	1.348	1.811	2.427	3.243	4.322	5.743	7.612

$P_0(1 + i)^n = P_n$ Interest factor $= (1 + i)^n$

THE FUTURE SUM OF ONE DOLLAR *(continued)*

Period	8%	9%	10%	12%	14%	15%	16%
1	1.080	1.090	1.100	1.120	1.140	1.150	1.160
2	1.166	1.188	1.210	1.254	1.300	1.322	1.346
3	1.260	1.295	1.331	1.405	1.482	1.521	1.561
4	1.360	1.412	1.464	1.574	1.689	1.749	1.811
5	1.469	1.539	1.611	1.762	1.925	2.011	2.100
6	1.587	1.677	1.772	1.974	2.195	2.313	2.436
7	1.714	1.828	1.949	2.211	2.502	2.660	2.826
8	1.851	1.993	2.144	2.476	2.853	3.059	3.278
9	1.999	2.172	2.358	2.773	3.252	3.518	3.803
10	2.159	2.367	2.594	3.106	3.707	4.046	4.411
11	2.332	2.580	2.853	3.479	4.226	4.652	5.117
12	2.518	2.813	3.138	3.896	4.818	5.350	5.936
13	2.720	3.066	3.452	4.363	5.492	6.153	6.886
14	2.937	3.342	3.797	4.887	6.261	7.076	7.988
15	3.172	3.642	4.177	5.474	7.138	8.137	9.266
16	3.426	3.970	4.595	6.130	8.137	9.358	10.748
17	3.700	4.328	5.054	6.866	9.276	10.761	12.468
18	3.996	4.717	5.560	7.690	10.575	12.375	14.463
19	4.316	5.142	6.116	8.613	12.056	14.232	16.777
20	4.661	5.604	6.728	9.646	13.743	16.367	19.461
25	6.848	8.623	10.835	17.000	26.462	32.919	40.874
30	10.063	13.268	17.449	29.960	50.950	66.212	85.850

THE PRESENT VALUE OF ONE DOLLAR

Period	1%	2%	3%	4%	5%	6%	7%	8%	9%	10%	12%	14%	15%
1	0.990	0.980	0.971	0.962	0.952	0.943	0.935	0.926	0.917	0.909	0.893	0.877	0.870
2	0.980	0.961	0.943	0.925	0.907	0.890	0.873	0.857	0.842	0.826	0.797	0.769	0.756
3	0.971	0.942	0.915	0.889	0.864	0.840	0.816	0.794	0.772	0.751	0.712	0.675	0.658
4	0.961	0.924	0.889	0.855	0.823	0.792	0.763	0.735	0.708	0.683	0.636	0.592	0.572
5	0.951	0.906	0.863	0.822	0.784	0.747	0.713	0.681	0.650	0.621	0.567	0.519	0.497
6	0.942	0.888	0.838	0.790	0.746	0.705	0.666	0.630	0.596	0.564	0.507	0.456	0.432
7	0.933	0.871	0.813	0.760	0.711	0.665	0.623	0.583	0.547	0.513	0.452	0.400	0.376
8	0.923	0.853	0.789	0.731	0.677	0.627	0.582	0.540	0.502	0.467	0.404	0.351	0.327
9	0.914	0.837	0.766	0.703	0.645	0.592	0.544	0.500	0.460	0.424	0.361	0.308	0.284
10	0.905	0.820	0.744	0.676	0.614	0.558	0.508	0.463	0.422	0.386	0.322	0.270	0.247
11	0.896	0.804	0.722	0.650	0.585	0.527	0.475	0.429	0.388	0.350	0.287	0.237	0.215
12	0.887	0.788	0.701	0.625	0.557	0.497	0.444	0.397	0.356	0.319	0.257	0.208	0.187
13	0.879	0.773	0.681	0.601	0.530	0.469	0.415	0.368	0.326	0.290	0.229	0.182	0.163
14	0.870	0.758	0.661	0.577	0.505	0.442	0.388	0.340	0.299	0.263	0.205	0.160	0.141
15	0.861	0.743	0.642	0.555	0.481	0.417	0.362	0.315	0.275	0.239	0.183	0.140	0.123
16	0.853	0.728	0.623	0.534	0.458	0.394	0.339	0.292	0.252	0.218	0.163	0.123	0.107
17	0.844	0.714	0.605	0.513	0.436	0.371	0.317	0.270	0.231	0.198	0.146	0.108	0.093
18	0.836	0.700	0.587	0.494	0.416	0.350	0.296	0.250	0.212	0.180	0.130	0.095	0.081
19	0.828	0.686	0.570	0.475	0.396	0.331	0.276	0.232	0.194	0.164	0.116	0.083	0.070
20	0.820	0.673	0.554	0.456	0.377	0.312	0.258	0.215	0.178	0.149	0.104	0.073	0.061
25	0.780	0.610	0.478	0.375	0.295	0.233	0.184	0.146	0.116	0.092	0.059	0.038	0.030
30	0.742	0.552	0.412	0.308	0.231	0.174	0.131	0.099	0.075	0.057	0.033	0.020	0.015

$$P_0 = \frac{P_n}{(1+i)^n} \qquad \text{Interest factor} = \frac{1}{(1+i)^n}$$

THE PRESENT VALUE OF ONE DOLLAR *(continued)*

Period	16%	18%	20%	24%	28%	32%	36%	40%	50%	60%	70%	80%	90%
1	0.862	0.847	0.833	0.806	0.781	0.758	0.735	0.714	0.667	0.625	0.588	0.556	0.526
2	0.743	0.718	0.694	0.650	0.610	0.574	0.541	0.510	0.444	0.391	0.346	0.309	0.277
3	0.641	0.609	0.579	0.524	0.477	0.435	0.398	0.364	0.296	0.244	0.204	0.171	0.146
4	0.552	0.516	0.482	0.423	0.373	0.329	0.292	0.260	0.198	0.153	0.120	0.095	0.077
5	0.476	0.437	0.402	0.341	0.291	0.250	0.215	0.186	0.132	0.095	0.070	0.053	0.040
6	0.410	0.370	0.335	0.275	0.227	0.189	0.158	0.133	0.088	0.060	0.041	0.029	0.021
7	0.354	0.314	0.279	0.222	0.178	0.143	0.116	0.095	0.059	0.037	0.024	0.016	0.011
8	0.305	0.266	0.233	0.179	0.139	0.108	0.085	0.068	0.039	0.023	0.014	0.009	0.006
9	0.263	0.226	0.194	0.144	0.108	0.082	0.063	0.048	0.026	0.015	0.008	0.005	0.003
10	0.227	0.191	0.162	0.116	0.085	0.062	0.046	0.035	0.017	0.009	0.005	0.003	0.002
11	0.195	0.162	0.135	0.094	0.066	0.047	0.034	0.025	0.012	0.006	0.003	0.002	0.001
12	0.168	0.137	0.112	0.076	0.052	0.036	0.025	0.018	0.008	0.004	0.002	0.001	0.001
13	0.145	0.116	0.093	0.061	0.040	0.027	0.018	0.013	0.005	0.002	0.001	0.001	0.000
14	0.125	0.099	0.078	0.049	0.032	0.021	0.014	0.009	0.003	0.001	0.001	0.000	0.000
15	0.108	0.084	0.065	0.040	0.025	0.016	0.010	0.006	0.002	0.001	0.000	0.000	0.000
16	0.093	0.071	0.054	0.032	0.019	0.012	0.007	0.005	0.002	0.001	0.000	0.000	
17	0.080	0.060	0.045	0.026	0.015	0.009	0.005	0.003	0.001	0.000	0.000		
18	0.069	0.051	0.038	0.021	0.012	0.007	0.004	0.002	0.001	0.000	0.000		
19	0.060	0.043	0.031	0.017	0.009	0.005	0.003	0.002	0.000	0.000			
20	0.051	0.037	0.026	0.014	0.007	0.004	0.002	0.001	0.000	0.000			
25	0.024	0.016	0.010	0.005	0.002	0.001	0.000	0.000					
30	0.012	0.007	0.004	0.002	0.001	0.000	0.000						

THE FUTURE SUM OF AN ANNUITY OF ONE DOLLAR

Period	1%	2%	3%	4%	5%	6%
1	1.000	1.000	1.000	1.000	1.000	1.000
2	2.010	2.020	2.030	2.040	2.050	2.060
3	3.030	3.060	3.091	3.122	3.152	3.184
4	4.060	4.122	4.184	4.246	4.310	4.375
5	5.101	5.204	5.309	5.416	5.526	5.637
6	6.152	6.308	6.468	6.633	6.802	6.975
7	7.214	7.434	7.662	7.898	8.142	8.394
8	8.286	8.583	8.892	9.214	9.549	9.897
9	9.369	9.755	10.159	10.583	11.027	11.491
10	10.462	10.950	11.464	12.006	12.578	13.181
11	11.567	12.169	12.808	13.486	14.207	14.972
12	12.683	13.412	14.192	15.026	15.917	16.870
13	13.809	14.680	15.618	16.627	17.713	18.882
14	14.947	15.974	17.086	18.292	19.599	21.051
15	16.097	17.293	18.599	20.024	21.579	23.276
16	17.258	18.639	20.157	21.825	23.657	25.673
17	18.430	20.012	21.762	23.698	25.840	28.213
18	19.615	21.412	23.414	25.645	28.132	30.906
19	20.811	22.841	25.117	27.671	30.539	33.760
20	22.109	24.297	26.870	29.778	33.066	36.786
25	28.243	32.030	36.459	41.646	47.727	54.865
30	34.785	40.568	47.575	56.085	66.439	79.058

$$CS = I(1 + i)^0 + I(1 + i)^1 + \cdots + I(1 + i)^{n-1} \qquad \text{Interest factor} = \frac{(1 + i)^n - 1}{i}$$

THE FUTURE SUM OF AN ANNUITY OF ONE DOLLAR (*continued*)

Period	7%	8%	9%	10%	12%	14%
1	1.000	1.000	1.000	1.000	1.000	1.000
2	2.070	2.080	2.090	2.100	2.120	2.140
3	3.215	3.246	3.278	3.310	3.374	3.440
4	4.440	4.506	4.573	4.641	4.770	4.921
5	5.751	5.867	5.985	6.105	6.353	6.610
6	7.153	7.336	7.523	7.716	8.115	8.536
7	8.654	8.923	9.200	9.487	10.089	10.730
8	10.260	10.637	11.028	11.436	12.300	13.233
9	11.978	12.488	13.021	13.579	14.776	16.085
10	13.816	14.487	15.193	15.937	17.549	19.337
11	15.784	16.645	17.560	18.531	20.655	23.044
12	17.888	18.977	20.141	21.384	24.138	27.271
13	20.141	21.495	22.953	24.523	28.029	32.089
14	22.550	24.215	26.019	27.975	32.393	37.581
15	25.129	27.152	29.361	31.772	37.280	43.842
16	27.888	30.324	33.003	35.950	42.753	50.980
17	30.840	33.750	36.974	40.545	48.884	59.118
18	33.999	37.450	41.301	45.599	55.750	68.394
19	37.379	41.446	46.018	51.159	63.440	78.969
20	40.995	45.762	51.160	57.275	72.052	91.025
25	63.249	73.106	84.701	98.347	133.334	181.871
30	94.461	113.283	136.308	164.494	241.333	356.787

THE PRESENT VALUE OF AN ANNUITY OF ONE DOLLAR

Period	1%	2%	3%	4%	5%	6%	7%	8%	9%	10%
1	0.990	0.980	0.971	0.962	0.952	0.943	0.935	0.926	0.917	0.909
2	1.970	1.942	1.913	1.886	1.859	1.833	1.808	1.783	1.759	1.736
3	2.941	2.884	2.829	2.775	2.723	2.673	2.624	2.577	2.531	2.487
4	3.902	3.808	3.717	3.630	3.546	3.465	3.387	3.312	3.240	3.170
5	4.853	4.713	4.580	4.452	4.329	4.212	4.100	3.993	3.890	3.791
6	5.795	5.601	5.417	5.242	5.076	4.917	4.766	4.623	4.486	4.355
7	6.728	6.472	6.230	6.002	5.786	5.582	5.389	5.206	5.033	4.868
8	7.652	7.325	7.020	6.733	6.463	6.210	5.971	5.747	5.535	5.335
9	8.566	8.162	7.786	7.435	7.108	6.802	6.515	6.247	5.985	5.759
10	9.471	8.983	8.530	8.111	7.722	7.360	7.024	6.710	6.418	6.145
11	10.368	9.787	9.253	8.760	8.306	7.887	7.499	7.139	6.805	6.495
12	11.255	10.575	9.954	9.385	8.863	8.384	7.943	7.536	7.161	6.814
13	12.134	11.348	10.635	9.986	9.394	8.853	8.358	7.904	7.487	7.103
14	13.004	12.106	11.296	10.563	9.899	9.295	8.745	8.244	7.786	7.367
15	13.865	12.849	11.938	11.118	10.380	9.712	9.108	8.559	8.060	7.606
16	14.718	13.578	12.561	11.652	10.838	10.106	9.447	8.851	8.312	7.824
17	15.562	14.292	13.166	12.166	11.274	10.477	9.763	9.122	8.544	8.022
18	16.398	14.992	13.754	12.659	11.690	10.828	10.059	9.372	8.756	8.201
19	17.226	15.678	14.324	13.134	12.085	11.158	10.336	9.604	8.950	8.365
20	18.046	16.351	14.877	13.590	12.462	11.470	10.594	9.818	9.128	8.514
25	22.023	19.523	17.413	15.622	14.094	12.783	11.654	10.675	9.823	9.077
30	25.808	22.397	19.600	17.292	15.373	13.765	12.409	11.258	10.274	9.427

$$PV = \sum_{t=1}^{n} \frac{I}{(1 + i)^t} \qquad \text{Interest factor} = \frac{1 - \dfrac{1}{(1 + i)^n}}{i}$$

THE PRESENT VALUE OF AN ANNUITY OF ONE DOLLAR *(continued)*

Period	12%	14%	16%	18%	20%	24%	28%	32%	36%
1	0.893	0.877	0.862	0.847	0.833	0.806	0.781	0.758	0.735
2	1.690	1.647	1.605	1.566	1.528	1.457	1.392	1.332	1.276
3	2.402	2.322	2.246	2.174	2.106	1.981	1.868	1.766	1.674
4	3.037	2.914	2.798	2.690	2.589	2.404	2.241	2.096	1.966
5	3.605	3.433	3.274	3.127	2.991	2.745	2.532	2.345	2.181
6	4.111	3.889	3.685	3.498	3.326	3.020	2.759	2.534	2.339
7	4.564	4.288	4.039	3.812	3.605	3.242	2.937	2.678	2.455
8	4.968	4.639	4.344	4.078	3.837	3.421	3.076	2.786	2.540
9	5.328	4.946	4.607	4.303	4.031	3.566	3.184	2.868	2.603
10	5.650	5.216	4.833	4.494	4.193	3.682	3.269	2.930	2.650
11	5.988	5.453	5.029	4.656	4.327	3.776	3.335	2.978	2.683
12	6.194	5.660	5.197	4.793	4.439	3.851	3.387	3.013	2.708
13	6.424	5.842	5.342	4.910	4.533	3.912	3.427	3.040	2.727
14	6.628	6.002	5.468	5.008	4.611	3.962	3.459	3.061	2.740
15	6.811	6.142	5.575	5.092	4.675	4.001	3.483	3.076	2.750
16	6.974	6.265	5.669	5.162	4.730	4.033	3.503	3.088	2.758
17	7.120	6.373	5.749	5.222	4.775	4.059	3.518	3.097	2.763
18	7.250	6.467	5.818	5.273	4.812	4.080	3.529	3.104	2.767
19	7.366	6.550	5.877	5.316	4.844	4.097	3.539	3.109	2.770
20	7.469	6.623	5.929	5.353	4.870	4.110	3.546	3.113	2.772
25	7.843	6.873	6.097	5.467	4.948	4.147	3.564	3.122	2.776
30	8.055	7.003	6.177	5.517	4.979	4.160	3.569	3.124	2.778

Appendix B

Answers to Selected Problems

Chapter 3

1. a. 25 percent margin: 300%
   c. 75 percent margin: 100%
2. b. 50 percent margin: −50%
3. At price of the stock = $40 and margin requirement of 60 percent:
       Cash account: −21.2%
       Margin account: −42%
   At price of the stock = $70 and margin requirement of 40 percent:
       Cash account: 31.2%
       Margin account: 63%
4. At price of the stock = $36: 27.8%

Chapter 5

1. The answer depends on the current dividend exclusion. If the exclusion is 70 percent, the taxes owed are
       $2.35 (10,000) (.3) (.34) = $2,397.
2. a. Capital gains: $4,700
       Tax: $1,316
3. Tax on investment income: $6,171
4. b. Net long-term loss after net short-term capital gain: $1,000
       Tax savings: $310
   g. Current year tax savings: $930
       Long-term loss carry forward: $2,000

Chapter 6

Your answers may vary from the following depending on rounding off when using the interest tables. The use of a calculator or the computer program included in Investment Analysis on the Personal Computer (IA/PC) may result in the answer being carried to more places. Differences will also result from interpolating. Use common sense! If your answer is 6.06 percent from IA/PC and approximately 6 percent from the interest table, both answers are "correct."

1. a. $2,207 total interest
   b. $60 annually; $1,200 (The difference, $1,007, is the result of compounding.)
2. Approximately 6 percent (5.8 percent)
3. a. $85,913
   b. $147,521 in the account; $61,608 additional funds
   c. Additional funds: $50,493
4. a. (1) $6,392
       (2) $6,903
   b. (1) $7,572
       (2) $7,951
5. Value: $98,180, which is less than $120,000; don't buy.
6. $54,775; $241,150; purchasing power is maintained but hardly improved.
7. $19,714
8. a. $87,729
   b. $38,276 additional funds
   c. $12,620
9. At 6 percent, select the $900.
   At 14 percent, select the $150 each year.
   (The higher rate stresses receiving the money faster so it may be invested at the higher rate.)
10. a. Annual compounding: $112
        Semiannual compounding: $112.40
        Monthly compounding: $112.70
    b. Annual compounding: $89.30
        Semiannual compounding: $89.00
        Monthly compounding: $88.70
11. Tom: $102,320
    Joan: $111,529
12. a. The $10,000 grows to $21,590; the IRA contributions plus interest total $28,974. The rollover account grows to $118,350. The sum is $168,914.
    b. About 25 years
    c. $19,291
13. The present value of the annuity payments is $62,868. If the annuity costs $75,000, it is overpriced.
14. At 9 percent, the present value of the cash flows is $849, which is more than $800. The yield has to be higher than 9 percent to bring down the present value of the cash flows to $800.
15. $73,212
16. $60,795
17. Budget in year 10: $4,805,550
                    15: $8,607,060
                    20: $15,400,665
18. Bob: $60,247
    Mary: $77,037
    Difference: $16,790

19. Bob contributes $1,500 for ten years and accumulates $23,906. This amount grows for ten years into $62,012. The final sum is drawn down over fifteen years at the rate of $8,153 annually.

    Mike contributes a larger amount ($2,000) for ten years and accumulates $31,874; however, he must start to withdraw the funds after five years, so the final amount grows to $51,349. This final sum is drawn down over twenty years at the rate of $6,031 annually. Even though Mike contributed more than Bob, the fact that he must start withdrawing the funds earlier means that the amount received each year is less. This problem points out the desirability of leaving funds in a tax-deferred account as long as possible in order to take advantage of the growth in tax-deferred interest.

20. Annual payment starting at the end of the year: $5,393
    Annual payment starting at the beginning of the year: $5,041

Supplemental Problems

1. $1,795.23
2. Interest ordinary annuity: $1,827.40
   Interest annuity due: $2,503.06
3. Present value ordinary annuity: $65,848.01
   Present value annuity due: $71,392.41
4. 18.638%
5. Payment at the end of the year: $8,659.91
   Payment at the beginning of the year: $8,075.91

Chapter 7

1. 14 percent in all three cases
2. a. 10.3%
3. a. 12.4%
        standard deviation = 3.12
4. a. 50%A/50%B: return = 16%; standard deviation = 3.14
   c. 25%A/75%C: return = 18%; standard deviation = 4.36
6. Return = 12% when beta = 1.5

Chapter 8

1. $21
2. $21.40, which is less than $25. (Don't buy!)
3. a. $28.53
4. Required return: 18%
5. b. Stock A: $7.78
   d. $12.94
6. Required return for B: 12.6%
8. Present value of dividend payments: $7.66
   Value of stock: $68.91

Chapter 9

1. Approximately 12 percent (11.96%)
2. a. Holding period return: 61%
   b. Annual rate of return: 10%
3. a. 12%
   c. 9%
5. At 12 percent, present value = $35.56, which is less than $40, so return is less than 12 percent.
6. Average price per share: $34.55
7. a. Simple average: $15
      Value-weighted average: $15.60
      Geometric average: $14.50

Chapter 10

1. a. Cash and retained earnings decline by $1,000,000
   b. 100,000 shares issued
      Common stock (1,100,000 shares; $10 par) $11,000,000
      Paid-in capital: $300,000
      Retained earnings: $97,200,000
2. a. Paid-in capital: $1,800,000
      New price of the stock: $20
   b. Paid-in capital: $2,280,000
      New price of the stock: $54.55
3. 162.9 shares

Chapter 12

1. Current ratio: 2:1
   Quick ratio: .967:1
   Inventory turnover: 1.5 (using cost of goods sold)
   Average collection period: 108 days
   Operating profit margin: 25%
   Net profit margin: 16.8%
   Return on assets: 9.8%
   Return on equity: 14.5%
   Debt/Net worth: 48.3%
   Debt/Total assets: 32.6%
   Times-interest-earned: 5.0
2. Average collection period (using a 360-day year)
   19x0: 45 days
   19x1: 31 days
   19x2: 32 days
4. Reduction in inventory: $75,000
5. Issue B: 1.7×
6. $4,754,556

Chapter 15

1. a. $1,000
   b. $875.40
   c. Current yield in b.: 9.1%
(All subsequent answers assume annual compounding.)
2. a. $1,179
   b. $1,054
   c. $1,142
4. Current yield: 9.6%
   Yield to maturity: 10%
5. 14%
8. a. Bond A: $894
   b. Bond A: $1,047
12. b. Bond A: 4.4 years
    Bond E: 5 years

Chapter 16

1. a. $60
   b. $75.48
2. Times-dividend-earned: 2.8
3. EPS with debt financing: $2.40
   EPS with preferred stock financing: $2.00
4. CH, Inc. preferred at 10%: $48.96
5. $712.24
7. b. $853.83

Chapter 17

1. 6.7%
2. Taxable yield: 8.75%
4. Bond B: $377, $149, and $61
6. 3.12% discount yield

Chapter 18

1. a. 4.8%
   b. $864
   c. $38.52
   d. $176
   e. $817
   f. $223
   g. At least $1,728
   h. At least $817
   i. Virtually nil

2. a. $552
   b. 40 shares
   d. $1,200 (value as stock)
   g. $1,040
4. a. Bond A: $1,070 (assuming annual compounding)
   b. Bond B: $946
   d. $4(6.710) = $26.84
5. c. A: $75
   d. A: 2.4 years

Chapter 19

1. a. Intrinsic value: $1; time premium: $3
   b.
Price of the stock	Value of the call
$20	$0
30	5
40	15

   c. 275 percent
   d.
Price of the stock	Profit
$15	($7)
25	3
26	3
40	3

   e. $4, $3, and (11)
2. XYZ calls: $4 and nil
   XYZ puts: nil and $1
   If the price of the stock is $31, the losses to the buyers of the calls are ($6) and ($2½).
   If the price of the stock is $31, the profits to the writers of the puts are $1¼ and $¼.
3. a. $1
   b. $0
   c. $4
   d. $2
   e. rises
   f. $46
   g. $51
   h. $8
   i. $2
   j. ($7)
   k. $4
4. a. ($2), ($2), and $3
   b. $2, $2, and ($3)
5. a. $11
   b. $4
   c. $26 (73.3% increase in the warrant)
   e. $0 (100% decrease in the warrant)
6. a. All prices of the stock greater than $16.
   b. All prices of the stock less than $16.

9. a. Make $5 on the call but lose $3½ on the put; net profit = $1½.
   c. ($8½)
11. If price of the stock is $60, make $2,000 on the position in the stock versus $1,000 in the call and the treasury bill. If the price of the stock is $40, lose $2,000 on the position in the stock versus no loss on the position in the call and the treasury bill.

Chapter 20

1. a. $3,500
   b. $69,000
   c. ($1,000)
   e. 20 percent profit
   f. $3,500
2. a. $1,600,000
   b. $1,560,000
   c. ($40,000)
   d. $40,000
   e. $40,000
   f. $0
   g. $200,000

Chapter 22

1. a. Interest payment: $6,000
       Principal repayment: $610.11
       Balance owed: $59,389.89
2. Earnings year 1: ($3,000)
   Cash flow year 1: $15,000 before principal repayment
3. Home: 6.2%
   S & P 500: 10.9%
4. a. $50,000 + $500 + .02($50,000) + $500 = $53,000

Chapter 23

1. $7.675
2. 6.8%
3. Approximately 19 percent before the exit fee
4. $3.99/$4 = 20%
5. 9.4%

Chapter 24

1. 0.5714 pounds
   2.174 marks
3. At 4/4/x0: $16.38 and 36.5 percent increase

5. a. $2,900,000
   b. $2,800,000
   c. ($240,000)
   e. $100,000

Chapter 25

1. a. The risk-adjusted ranking: E, D, C, A, B
   b. The risk-adjusted ranking: C, D, B, E, A
2. a. Total assets: $339,000
   c. Total assets at age 62: $813,130
      Total assets at age 70: $1,616,527

Appendix C

SELECTED CASES

THE DEMISE OF A SAVINGS ACCOUNT
Chapters 2, 3, and 5: Consider alternatives to the traditional savings account and their tax implications for a conservative investor with modest resources.

BLUE JEANS AND STOCK SELECTION
Chapters 8 and 12: Apply ratios to the analysis of financial statements and the dividend-growth model to determine if a common stock is undervalued.

BONDS, BONDS, AND MORE BONDS
Chapters 14–17: Compare bonds with different coupons, terms to maturity, credit ratings, and tax implications for inclusion in a portfolio designed to generate income.

A SPECULATOR'S CHOICES
Chapters 18 and 19: Select among puts and calls with different strike prices and different expiration dates and a convertible bond issued on the same stock.

COLLECTIBLES ARE NOT COMMODITIES
Chapters 20–22: Differentiate the features and risks associated with tangible assets and futures contracts on tangible assets.

GOALS AND PORTFOLIO SELECTION
Chapter 25: Establish financial goals and develop a strategy to meet the portfolio's objectives.

THE DEMISE OF A SAVINGS ACCOUNT

After completing a degree in education administration, Joseph LaDonne accepted a position with the New Jersey Department of Education. He has worked there for seven years and has experienced annual salary increments and steady promotions. His benefit package includes full medical and dental insurance, pension plan, and life insurance equal to twice his annual salary. A year after graduating from college he married his childhood sweetheart, Mary Klepper, who works as an administrative assistant for the state. Joe and Mary are relatively frugal people and have accumulated $100,000, which is held in a National Bank of New Jersey savings account and which earns a modest 4 percent annually. They also own a three bedroom home with an 8.5 percent mortgage that has 20 years left before it is entirely paid off.

While Mary LaDonne has worked steadily, she is now pregnant with their first child. The LaDonnes are uncertain what changes this addition to the family will make to their economic situation. They doubt that Mary will be able to continue to work for a period of time, and Joe doubts that he will be able to add to their current savings account. He also thinks that this savings account may not be the best vehicle for their savings.

Joe decided that one possible course of action was to explore the various accounts and savings programs offered by the bank. National Bank of New Jersey is a moderate-sized regional bank that offers a variety of savings and checking accounts and a range of certificates of deposit. It also offers IRA and Keogh plans and has a working relationship with Strauss and Strauss Incorporated (S & S), a regional brokerage firm that will buy and sell securities for the bank's customers. Since the brokerage firm offers only minimal research services, it charges discount rates for transactions. However, it will hold securities in street name, and funds may be transferred directly from accounts with the bank to S & S and vice versa. Individuals with IRA and Keogh accounts with National Bank of New Jersey may also buy and sell securities through S & S.

Joe asked a representative of the bank for suggestions and several alternatives to the savings account for the $100,000.

This representative made the following suggestions:

1. Open an IRA and place the maximum permitted by law in the certificate of deposit with the longest term and highest rate. The bank is offering for IRAs a CD that pays 5.25 percent and expires after 18 months. It may be automatically renewed at the then going rate.

2. Open a money market account with the bank. The account currently pays 3.0 percent, but this rate varies weekly with changes in short-term interest rates. The individual may write checks against the account and may deposit or withdraw funds at will. There are no fees unless the amount in the account is less than $2,500.
3. Consider making a modest gift to the child soon after birth and investing the funds in a high-yield certificate of deposit.
4. Complete the paperwork to open a brokerage account with S & S, even if any purchase decisions will be deferred.
5. Close the savings account.

To help make this investment decision, Joe asked the bank's representative the following questions:

1. How safe is each investment and is it insured against loss?
2. How liquid is each investment?
3. What are the tax implications of each suggestion?

Questions for Discussion

1. If you were the bank's representative, how would you respond to each question?
2. What do you think the LaDonnes should do?
3. Why do you think the bank's representative suggested points 4 and 5?

BLUE JEANS AND STOCK
SELECTION

Jeffrey Locko often observed that the clothes worn by his daughters and their friends were made of denim. No matter what the style, blue jeans and other clothes made of denim were popular. While certain styles would remain popular for only brief periods of time, the use of denim continued year after year. Locko reasoned that the manufacturers of denim may be potentially attractive investments, as there appeared to him to be little fluctuation in the demand for denim.

Locko discovered that the primary manufacturer of denim was Dentex, a textile mill in North Carolina. Dentex specializes in denim and produces only a modest amount of other types of cloth. Its sales of denim account for one-third of the total denim market, both domestic and abroad. Dentex's balance sheets and income statements for the last two years are presented in Exhibit 1. Dentex's per-share earnings and dividends are given in Exhibit 2. With the exception of the most recent year, 19x1, and 19y8, per-share earnings have steadily increased, and dividends have risen every year for the last ten years. This pattern of earnings and dividend growth impressed Locko, who tended to think of textiles as a dull industry with little growth potential.

Locko realized that for the firm to be a good investment, it should have strong fundamentals and be financially sound. So he decided to use ratios to analyze the firm's financial statements. From other sources, he found the industry averages given in Exhibit 3.

Currently Dentex's stock sells for $50. Locko could invest in U.S. Treasury bills that yield 3.5 percent, but he believes that the stock market may offer a return over a period of years of 9.5 percent. Should he buy the stock of Dentex? To help answer that question, answer the following questions.

1. What conclusion(s) are indicated by the ratio analysis?
2. What is the annual growth rate in per-share earnings and dividends? Currently what is the dividend yield on Dentex stock? Can the dividend growth be sustained?
3. Is there any reason to conclude that the firm has changed its dividend policy?
4. Risk may be affected by many factors. How may each of the following affect the unsystematic risk associated with Dentex?
   a. The location of the firm
   b. Its use of debt financing
   c. Its product line

Exhibit 1 ✦ Financial Statements of Dentex

Consolidated Statement of Income, Dentex Corporation
(for the years ending)

	19x1	19x0
Sales (in thousands)	$668,000	$730,000
Cost of goods sold	531,000	571,000
Selling and administrative expense	54,000	52,000
Depreciation	24,000	22,000
Interest expense (net)	3,000	3,000
	612,000	648,000
Income before taxes	56,000	82,000
Income taxes	24,000	35,000
Net income	$ 32,000	$ 47,000
Earnings per share	$5.87	$8.82
Dividends per share	2.20	2.00

Consolidated Balance Sheet, Dentex Corporation
(as of December 31)

	19x1	19x0
Assets (in thousands)		
Current assets		
Cash and short-term investments	$ 23,000	$ 5,000
Accounts receivable	80,000	114,000
Inventory	120,000	118,000
Total current assets	223,000	237,000
Property, plant, and equipment		
Land	3,000	3,000
Buildings and equipment	177,000	156,000
Other	20,000	17,000
	200,000	176,000
Total Assets	$423,000	$413,000

Liabilities and Stockholders' Equity

	19x1	19x0
Liabilities		
Current liabilities		
Long-term debt due within a year	$ 6,000	$ 4,000
Accounts payable	22,000	22,000
Accrued expenses	30,000	35,000
Income taxes owed	3,000	10,000
Total current liabilities	61,000	71,000
Long-term debt	20,000	22,000
Stockholders' equity		
Common stock	57,000	57,000
Paid-in capital	5,000	5,000
Retained earnings	280,000	258,000
Total stockholders' equity	342,000	320,000
Total Liabilities and Stockholders'Equity	$423,000	$413,000

Exhibit 2 ✦ EARNINGS PER SHARE AND DIVIDENDS OF DENTEX

	Earnings per share	Dividends
19x1	$5.87	$2.20
19x0	8.82	2.00
19y9	7.49	1.80
19y8	6.21	1.60
19y7	6.75	1.35
19y6	4.90	0.95
19y5	3.97	0.75
19y4	2.51	0.70
19y3	1.58	0.55
19y2	1.33	0.51
19y1	1.00	0.50

Exhibit 3 ✦ INDUSTRY AVERAGES FOR SELECTED RATIOS

Current ratio	3.2:1
Quick ratio	1.6:1
Average collection period	55 days
Inventory turnover (sales/average inventory)	3.7 a year
Fixed asset turnover	4.5 a year
Debt ratio (debt/total assets)	33%
Times-interest-earned	10×
Net profit margin	3.3%
Return on assets	4.5%
Return on equity	7.0%

5. What may the P/E ratio indicate?
6. The current dividend growth rate cannot be maintained indefinitely, but Locko believes that a 6 percent dividend growth rate is sustainable. Is the stock a good purchase if Locko wants a 9.5 percent annual return?
7. If Dentex's beta coefficient was 0.8 and the sustainable growth rate was assumed to be 6 percent, what would be the value of the stock? What should Locko do given this valuation?

BONDS, BONDS, AND
MORE BONDS

Joan Heath is a relatively conservative individual who has just inherited $200,000. She has no immediate needs for the funds but would like to supplement her current income. Thus, Ms. Heath is considering investing these funds in debt instruments, since the interest and repayment of principal are legal obligations of the issuer. While she realizes that the borrower could default on the payments, she thinks this is unlikely, especially if she decides to limit her choices to triple- or double-A rated bonds. Joan does realize that she could earn more interest by purchasing lower rated bonds but is not certain if she is capable of bearing the risk.

Besides risk and expected return, Joan decides that tax considerations must also play a role in this investment decision. She is currently in the 28 percent federal income tax bracket and pays state income tax of 5 percent. She believes that her job is relatively secure and that her salary will increase over time but does not expect it to rise sufficiently so that her income tax brackets will be significantly increased.

Joan quickly learned that there are many bonds to choose among. For example, the PHONE Company has three triple-A bonds outstanding. Their annual interest payments (or coupon rate), term to maturity, and price are

Bond	Interest per $1,000 Bond	Coupon	Term	Price
A	$ 50	5%	1 year	$ 970
B	100	10	5 years	1,000
C	100	10	10 years	1,000

Currently the interest rate of long-term debt is approximately 10 percent, but Joan expects that this rate will fall, as inflation is declining. In addition, the level of unemployment is increasing, so Joan anticipates that the Federal Reserve will take actions to stimulate the economy through reductions in the rate of interest. She believes that interest rates could fall to 8 percent within a year. Of course, she also realizes that this decline may not occur or even if it did, that interest rates could rise again after the initial decline. Joan decided to analyze the three PHONE Company bonds to determine which may be the better investment under various assumptions concerning future interest rate behavior. To do this she sought to answer the following questions:

1. a. What would be the expected price of each bond one year from now if interest rates were 8 percent?
   b. What would be the expected price two years from now if interest rates initially fall but subsequently rise to 12 percent at the end of the second year?
2. If interest rates were expected to fall and not rise back to 12 percent, which alternative is best?
3. If interest rates were expected to decline initially and then rise, which alternative should be selected?
4. If bond A were selected, what would happen after a year elapses? What decision must then be made?

After answering these questions, Ms. Heath realized the importance of expected future interest rates on the selection of a bond. Since she firmly believes that interest rates will fall and remain below current levels for several years, she decided to select bond C, the longest term bond that would lock in the current high yields. However, she also decided to consider other bonds to determine what additional returns she could earn for bearing more risk and what the tax implications of her selections were. She noticed that the following ten-year bonds were available:

Bond	Interest per $1,000	Price	Yield to Maturity	Rating
Besttown USA	$ 80	$1,000	8%	AAA
Besttown USA	60	866	8	AAA
U.S. Treasury	$ 80	$1,000	8%	—
WEAK Inc.	$140	$1,000	14%	B
WEAK Inc.	120	896	14	B

To confuse the selection process further, Joan also learned that the PHONE Company has a preferred stock paying an annual dividend of $4 ($1 each quarter) that is selling for $36 a share.

At this point Joan was sufficiently frustrated to ask the advice of her stockbroker. If you were her stockbroker, which bond(s) would you recommend? In your advice, specifically explain to Joan the tax implications (both in terms of income and capital gains) of each bond. Also consider Joan's willingness to bear risk and the anticipated flow of income both from the bonds and her job. Then construct a portfolio that you believe meets her needs and willingness to bear risk. Assume that the bonds are sold in units of $5,000.

A Speculator's Choices

Rachel Fried is an optimist who likes to speculate. She enjoys watching prices change rapidly and believes that she could make large profits by judiciously taking advantage of price swings. Thus it is easy to see why she is attracted to options whose prices may change rapidly from day to day. She especially likes the securities associated with Fasolt Construction Corporation, a large building and engineering firm that also has considerable holdings of coal and oil reserves.

Currently the economy is in a recession. Fasolt is doubly cursed: the recession has resulted in a significant decline in construction, and commodity prices, including oil and gas, are declining. These two factors have reduced Fasolt's profit margins so that per-share earnings have plummeted from $5.50 to $1.00 during the latest fiscal year. The stock, which at one time had been an outstanding performer, has declined from a high of more than $80 to its current price of $15.

Ms. Fried believes that the stock market has overreacted to the decline in earnings. Furthermore, there are signs that the recession is ending. Retail sales have risen and interest rates are falling. A more robust economy should certainly help Fasolt's sales and earnings, which Ms. Fried believes would result in a higher stock price. Fasolt's fundamentals are sound, as its profit margins have historically been among the highest in the industry. However, the firm has a considerable amount of long-term debt outstanding. Even though the company pays no cash dividends, it has had to issue long-term bonds because retained earnings were insufficient to finance expansion and acquisitions.

Ms. Fried firmly believes that Fasolt Construction offers an excellent opportunity for profit, but she is very uncertain as to the correct strategy to follow. In addition to the stock, the firm has outstanding a convertible debenture with a 7 percent coupon and an exercise price of $30 (33.33 shares per $1,000 bond). The bond is currently selling for $780 per $1,000 face amount and, like the stock, is actively traded. It is rated double B by one rating service but only single B by another service.

Options on Fasolt stock are also actively traded. Currently the following options and their prices are available:

Exercise Price	Three-month Call	Three-month Put	Six-month Call	Six-month Put	Nine-month Call	Nine-month Put
$15	$2	$1½	$3½	$2¼	$5	$3
20	¾	5½	1½	6	2	6¼

To help determine the potential returns from the various alternatives, Ms. Fried decided that answers to the following questions may be useful.

1. What is the current yield offered by the stock, the convertible bond, and the calls and puts?
2. What is the conversion value of the bond in terms of the stock?
3. What is the intrinsic value of each option?
4. What are the premiums paid for the bond and the time premiums paid for each option?
5. What will be the price of each security if after six months the fundamental economic picture is not changed and the price of the stock remains $15?
6. While Ms. Fried considered a further decline in Fasolt's situation to be unlikely, the possibility does exist that after six months the stock would fall to $10. What impact would that have on the prices of the various securities?
7. Ms. Fried believes that the price of the stock will rise to $25 a share within six months. What impact would such a price increase have on the prices of the various securities?

As an outside financial advisor to Rachel Fried, what course of action would you suggest with regard to Fasolt's securities? In formulating your answer, consider the pros and cons of each of the alternatives and which conditions favor each security. There is, of course, no one correct strategy.

COLLECTIBLES ARE NOT COMMODITIES

Mike DeVita is a bachelor who has accumulated a substantial sum, primarily through periodic investments in savings accounts at a commercial bank ($80,000), shares in a mutual fund ($95,000), and a pension plan ($68,000). DeVita has also been a life-long philatelist. Ever since receiving a stamp album for his twelfth birthday, he has been fascinated with collecting stamps. As a child he collected any and all stamps, but for the last 20 years he has devoted his efforts to the stamps of Great Britain and her colonies. DeVita has now obtained a reputation for expertise in this area and has accumulated a sufficiently large collection to have received recognition from a regional stamp organization.

The value of DeVita's stamp collection is unknown, and it has never been insured. DeVita believes that over the years he has spent at least $25,000 on the collection. Unfortunately the exact cost of many of the items is lost in time, as he did not keep records of his early purchases made during the 1960s. Some of these acquisitions have proven to be among the most valuable stamps in the collection.

DeVita has become increasingly concerned with the performance and quality of his financial assets. He realizes the funds in the savings account are insured by the FDIC, but the shares in the mutual fund are not insured. In addition, the fund has not performed well during the preceding year, as it rose less than the Dow Jones industrial average. Except for his pension (which he cannot withdraw until retirement), he believes the portfolio needs changing. DeVita knows very little about stocks and bonds and tends to distrust things he cannot touch. He recently read an advertisement that suggested commodities offered large potential returns. DeVita thought he could buy commodities like silver and hold them for subsequent sale in much the way he has acquired and held the stamps. He has also thought about a purchase of real estate, especially lots slightly out of town since such property may appreciate in value as the town expands.

To finance these purchases, DeVita expects to sell his shares in the mutual fund or some of his stamp collection. His sister Deneen (who is an accountant) was distressed when she learned of Mike's ideas and suggested that they have lunch with her stockbroker, Brian Walmsley. At that time Walmsley could explain some of the features, risks, and potential returns associated with Mike's proposed portfolio changes. Mike agreed to the lunch, which Deneen arranged for the next week. Deneen also privately suggested to Walmsley that he should at a minimum discuss the following:

1. The differences between collecting and investing in stamps and investing in commodities.
2. The risks and liabilities associated with owning the lots.
3. The tax implications (if any) of redeeming the mutual fund shares, closing the bank account, or selling the stamps.
4. The need to insure the stamp collection.
5. Any need to diversify the mutual fund holdings.
6. Alternatives to the savings account with the bank.

If you were Walmsley, how would you respond to each of these considerations? What course(s) of action would you recommend?

GOALS AND PORTFOLIO
SELECTION

William Duffy is a very successful self-employed freelance writer of romantic novels. He has a reputation for writing rapidly and is able to complete at least six books a year, which net after expenses $15,000 to $20,000 per book per year. With this much income, Duffy is concerned with both sheltering income from taxes and planning for retirement. Currently he is 40 years old, he is married, and his only child is entering high school. Duffy anticipates sending the child to a quality college to pursue a degree in computer sciences.

While Duffy is intelligent and well informed, he knows very little about finance and investments other than general background material he has used in his novels. Since he does not plan to write prolifically into the indefinite future, he has decided to obtain help in financial planning from Anthony Patrick, a certified financial planner (CFP). Patrick had served as an accountant and financial advisor before becoming a financial planner. In his present position he specializes in retirement and estate planning.

At their first meeting, Patrick suggested that Duffy establish a tax-sheltered retirement plan and consider making a gift to his child, perhaps in the form of future royalties from a book in progress. Both of these ideas intrigued Duffy, who thought that funds were saved, then invested to accumulate over time, and then transferred to heirs after death. While Duffy wanted to pursue both ideas, he thought approaching one at a time made more sense and decided to work on the retirement plan first. He asked Patrick for several alternative courses of action. Patrick offered the following possibilities:

1. An IRA with a bank with the funds deposited in a variable rate account.
2. A self-directed Keogh account with a major brokerage firm.
3. A Keogh account with a major mutual fund.
4. An account with a brokerage firm to accumulate common stocks with substantial growth potential but little current income.

Duffy could not immediately grasp the implications of these alternatives and asked Patrick to clarify several points:

1. What assets would be owned under each alternative?
2. What are the current and future tax obligations associated with each choice?
3. What amount of control would he have over the assets in the accounts?
4. How much personal supervision would be required?

If you were Patrick, how would you reply to each question? Which course(s) of action would you suggest that Duffy pursue?

How would each of the following alter Patrick's advice?

1. Duffy's wife is not employed and has a record of poor health.
2. Duffy would like to write less and perhaps teach creative writing at a local college.
3. Duffy has expensive tastes and finds saving to be difficult.

INDEX